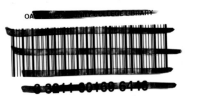

Poetry Criticism

Guide to Gale Literary Criticism Series

For criticism on	Consult these Gale series
Authors now living or who died after December 31, 1999	*CONTEMPORARY LITERARY CRITICISM (CLC)*
Authors who died between 1900 and 1999	*TWENTIETH-CENTURY LITERARY CRITICISM (TCLC)*
Authors who died between 1800 and 1899	*NINETEENTH-CENTURY LITERATURE CRITICISM (NCLC)*
Authors who died between 1400 and 1799	*LITERATURE CRITICISM FROM 1400 TO 1800 (LC)* *SHAKESPEAREAN CRITICISM (SC)*
Authors who died before 1400	*CLASSICAL AND MEDIEVAL LITERATURE CRITICISM (CMLC)*
Authors of books for children and young adults	*CHILDREN'S LITERATURE REVIEW (CLR)*
Dramatists	*DRAMA CRITICISM (DC)*
Poets	*POETRY CRITICISM (PC)*
Short story writers	*SHORT STORY CRITICISM (SSC)*
Literary topics and movements	*HARLEM RENAISSANCE: A GALE CRITICAL COMPANION (HR)* *THE BEAT GENERATION: A GALE CRITICAL COMPANION (BG)* *FEMINISM IN LITERATURE: A GALE CRITICAL COMPANION (FL)* *GOTHIC LITERATURE: A GALE CRITICAL COMPANION (GL)*
Asian American writers of the last two hundred years	*ASIAN AMERICAN LITERATURE (AAL)*
Black writers of the past two hundred years	*BLACK LITERATURE CRITICISM (BLC-1)* *BLACK LITERATURE CRITICISM SUPPLEMENT (BLCS)* *BLACK LITERATURE CRITICISM: CLASSIC AND EMERGING AUTHORS SINCE 1950 (BLC-2)*
Hispanic writers of the late nineteenth and twentieth centuries	*HISPANIC LITERATURE CRITICISM (HLC)* *HISPANIC LITERATURE CRITICISM SUPPLEMENT (HLCS)*
Native North American writers and orators of the eighteenth, nineteenth, and twentieth centuries	*NATIVE NORTH AMERICAN LITERATURE (NNAL)*
Major authors from the Renaissance to the present	*WORLD LITERATURE CRITICISM, 1500 TO THE PRESENT (WLC)* *WORLD LITERATURE CRITICISM SUPPLEMENT (WLCS)*

ISSN 1052-4851

Poetry Criticism

Excerpts from Criticism of the Works of the Most Significant and Widely Studied Poets of World Literature

Volume 110

Michelle Lee
Project Editor

GALE
CENGAGE Learning

Detroit • New York • San Francisco • New Haven, Conn • Waterville, Maine • London

Poetry Criticism, Vol. 110

Project Editor: Michelle Lee

Editorial: Dana Barnes, Sara Constantakis, Kathy D. Darrow, Kristen Dorsch, Dana Ferguson, Jeffrey W. Hunter, Michelle Kazensky, Jelena O. Krstović, Marie Toft, Lawrence J. Trudeau

Content Conversion: Katrina D. Coach, Gwen Tucker

Indexing Services: Factiva, Inc.

Rights and Acquisitions: Beth Beaufore, Sara Crane, and Jhanay Williams

Composition and Electronic Capture: Gary Leach

Manufacturing: Rhonda Dover

Product Manager: Janet Witalec

For product information and technology assistance, contact us at
Gale Customer Support, 1-800-877-4253.
For permission to use material from this text or product,
submit all requests online at **www.cengage.com/permissions.**
Further permissions questions can be emailed to
permissionrequest@cengage.com

Gale
27500 Drake Rd.
Farmington Hills, MI, 48331-3535

LIBRARY OF CONGRESS CATALOG CARD NUMBER 81-640179

ISBN-13: 978-1-4144-5987-5
ISBN-10: 1-4144-5987-4

ISSN 1052-4851

Printed in the United States of America
1 2 3 4 5 6 7 14 13 12 11 10

Contents

Preface vii

Acknowledgments ix

Literary Criticism Series Advisory Board xi

Preface

*P*oetry Criticism (PC) presents significant criticism of the world's greatest poets and provides supplementary biographical and bibliographical material to guide the interested reader to a greater understanding of the genre and its creators. Although major poets and literary movements are covered in such Gale Literary Criticism series as *Contemporary Literary Criticism (CLC)*, *Twentieth-Century Literary Criticism (TCLC)*, *Nineteenth-Century Literature Criticism (NCLC)*, *Literature Criticism from 1400 to 1800 (LC)*, and *Classical and Medieval Literature Criticism (CMLC)*, *PC* offers more focused attention on poetry than is possible in the broader, survey-oriented entries on writers in these Gale series. Students, teachers, librarians, and researchers will find that the generous excerpts and supplementary material provided by *PC* supply them with the vital information needed to write a term paper on poetic technique, to examine a poet's most prominent themes, or to lead a poetry discussion group.

Scope of the Series

PC is designed to serve as an introduction to major poets of all eras and nationalities. Since these authors have inspired a great deal of relevant critical material, *PC* is necessarily selective, and the editors have chosen the most important published criticism to aid readers and students in their research. Each author entry presents a historical survey of the critical response to that author's work. The length of an entry is intended to reflect the amount of critical attention the author has received from critics writing in English and from foreign critics in translation. Every attempt has been made to identify and include the most significant essays on each author's work. In order to provide these important critical pieces, the editors sometimes reprint essays that have appeared elsewhere in Gale's Literary Criticism Series. Such duplication, however, never exceeds twenty percent of a *PC* volume.

Organization of the Book

Each *PC* entry consists of the following elements:

- The **Author Heading** cites the name under which the author most commonly wrote, followed by birth and death dates. Also located here are any name variations under which an author wrote, including transliterated forms for authors whose native languages use nonroman alphabets. If the author wrote consistently under a pseudonym, the pseudonym will be listed in the author heading and the author's actual name given in parenthesis on the first line of the biographical and critical introduction. Uncertain birth or death dates are indicated by question marks. Single-work entries are preceded by the title of the work and its date of publication.

- The **Introduction** contains background information that introduces the reader to the author and the critical debates surrounding his or her work.

- The list of **Principal Works** is ordered chronologically by date of first publication and lists the most important works by the author. The first section comprises poetry collections and book-length poems. The second section gives information on other major works by the author. For foreign authors, the editors have provided original foreign-language publication information and have selected what are considered the best and most complete English-language editions of their works.

- Reprinted **Criticism** is arranged chronologically in each entry to provide a useful perspective on changes in critical evaluation over time. All individual titles of poems and poetry collections by the author featured in the entry are printed in boldface type. The critic's name and the date of composition or publication of the critical work are given at the beginning of each piece of criticism. Unsigned criticism is preceded by the title of the source in which it appeared. Footnotes are reprinted at the end of each essay or excerpt. In the case of excerpted criticism, only those footnotes that pertain to the excerpted texts are included.

- Critical essays are prefaced by brief **Annotations** explicating each piece.

- A complete **Bibliographical Citation** of the original essay or book precedes each piece of criticism.

- An annotated bibliography of **Further Reading** appears at the end of each entry and suggests resources for additional study. In some cases, significant essays for which the editors could not obtain reprint rights are included here. Boxed material following the further reading list provides references to other biographical and critical sources on the author in series published by Gale.

Cumulative Indexes

A **Cumulative Author Index** lists all of the authors that appear in a wide variety of reference sources published by Gale, including *PC*. A complete list of these sources is found facing the first page of the Author Index. The index also includes birth and death dates and cross references between pseudonyms and actual names.

A **Cumulative Nationality Index** lists all authors featured in *PC* by nationality, followed by the number of the *PC* volume in which their entry appears.

A **Cumulative Title Index** lists in alphabetical order all individual poems, book-length poems, and collection titles contained in the *PC* series. Titles of poetry collections and separately published poems are printed in italics, while titles of individual poems are printed in roman type with quotation marks. Each title is followed by the author's last name and corresponding volume and page numbers where commentary on the work is located. English-language translations of original foreign-language titles are cross-referenced to the foreign titles so that all references to discussion of a work are combined in one listing.

Citing *Poetry Criticism*

When citing criticism reprinted in the Literary Criticism Series, students should provide complete bibliographic information so that the cited essay can be located in the original print or electronic source. Students who quote directly from reprinted criticism may use any accepted bibliographic format, such as University of Chicago Press style or Modern Language Association (MLA) style. Both the MLA and the University of Chicago formats are acceptable and recognized as being the current standards for citations. It is important, however, to choose one format for all citations; do not mix the two formats within a list of citations.

The examples below follow recommendations for preparing a bibliography set forth in *The Chicago Manual of Style,* 14th ed. (Chicago: The University of Chicago Press, 1993); the first example pertains to material drawn from periodicals, the second to material reprinted from books:

Linkin, Harriet Kramer. "The Language of Speakers in *Songs of Innocence and of Experience.*" *Romanticism Past and Present* 10, no. 2 (summer 1986): 5-24. Reprinted in *Poetry Criticism.* Vol. 63, edited by Michelle Lee, 79-88. Detroit: Thomson Gale, 2005.

Glen, Heather. "Blake's Criticism of Moral Thinking in *Songs of Innocence and of Experience."* In *Interpreting Blake,* edited by Michael Phillips, 32-69. Cambridge: Cambridge University Press, 1978. Reprinted in *Poetry Criticism.* Vol. 63, edited by Michelle Lee, 34-51. Detroit: Thomson Gale, 2005.

Suggestions are Welcome

Readers who wish to suggest new features, topics, or authors to appear in future volumes, or who have other suggestions or comments are cordially invited to call, write, or fax the Associate Product Manager:

Product Manager, Literary Criticism Series
Gale
27500 Drake Road
Farmington Hills, MI 48331-3535
1-800-347-4253 (GALE)
Fax: 248-699-8054

Acknowledgments

The editors wish to thank the copyright holders of the criticism included in this volume and the permissions managers of many book and magazine publishing companies for assisting us in securing reproduction rights. Following is a list of the copyright holders who have granted us permission to reproduce material in this volume of *PC*. Every effort has been made to trace copyright, but if omissions have been made, please let us know.

COPYRIGHTED MATERIAL IN *PC*, VOLUME 110, WAS REPRODUCED FROM THE FOLLOWING PERIODICALS:

Australian Literary Studies, v. 22, October 2005. Copyright © 2005 University of Queensland. Reproduced by permission.—*Contemporary Literature,* v. 41, spring, 2000. Copyright © 2000 by the Board of Regents of the University of Wisconsin System. Reproduced by permission.—*ELH,* v. 68, 2001. Copyright © 2001 by The Johns Hopkins University Press. Reproduced by permission.—*English Literature in Transition 1880-1920,* v. 45, summer, 2002. Copyright © 2002 *English Literature in Transition: 1880-1920.* Reproduced by permission.—*English Studies,* v. 81, June, 2000 for "Perpetuum Mobile: Reading Wallace Stevens's 'The Man with the Blue Guitar'" by Axel Nissen. Copyright © 2000 Taylor & Francis Group, LLC. Reproduced by permission of Taylor & Francis, Ltd., http//:www.tandf.co.uk/journals, conveyed through Copyright Clearance Center, Inc., and the author.—*European Romantic Review,* v. 13, January, 2002 for "Sainte-Beuve and Wordsworth in Defense of the Sonnet" by Sheila K. Espineli. Copyright © 2002 Taylor & Francis Group, Ltd. Reproduced by permission of Taylor & Francis, Ltd., http//:www.tandf.co.uk/journals, conveyed through Copyright Clearance Center, Inc., and the author.—*Forum for Modern Language Studies,* v. 30, January, 1994 for "Imitation and Individuality: Sainte-Beuve and the Remodeling of the Renaissance Sonnet" by Rachel Killick. Copyright © 1994 Oxford University Press. Reproduced by permission of the publisher and the author.—*Journal of Modern Literature,* v. 27, fall, 2003. Copyright © 2003 Indiana University Press. Reproduced by permission.—*New Literary History,* v. 39, 2008. Copyright © 2008 by *New Literary History.* Reproduced by permission of The Johns Hopkins University Press.—*Nineteenth-Century French Studies,* v. 3, fall-winter, 1974-75. Copyright © 1974-75 by *Nineteenth-Century French Studies.* Reproduced by permission.—*Queensland Review,* v. 15, 2008. Copyright © 2008 University of Queensland Press. Reproduced by permission.—*Proceedings of the British Academy,* v. 111, 2001 for "Wallace Stevens: Hypotheses and Contradictions," by Helen Vendler. Wharton Lecture on English Poetry, 2001. Reproduced by permission of the author.—*Southern Review,* v. 39, winter, 2003 for "Pain Is Human: Wallace Stevens at Ground Zero" by Milton J. Bates. Copyright, 2003, by Milton J. Bates. Reproduced by permission of the author.—*Southwest Review,* v. 85, 2000. Copyright © 2000 Southern Methodist University. All rights reserved. Reproduced by permission.—*Twentieth Century Literature,* v. 50, fall, 2004. Copyright © 2004, Hofstra University Press. Reproduced by permission.

COPYRIGHTED MATERIAL IN *PC*, VOLUME 110, WAS REPRODUCED FROM THE FOLLOWING BOOKS:

Arnold, Matthew. From "Sainte-Beuve," in *Five Uncollected Essays of Matthew Arnold.* Edited by Kenneth Allott. University Press of Liverpool, 1953. Copyright © 1953 Liverpool University Press. Reproduced by permission.—Bird, D. L. From "Wallace Stevens: Appearing in Difference," in *Literary Canons and Religious Identity.* Edited by Erik Borgman, Bart Philipsen and Lea Verstricht. Ashgate, 2004. Copyright © by Erik Borgman, Bart Philipsen and Lea Verstricht, 2004. All rights reserved. Reproduced by permission.—Brogan, Jacqueline Vaught. From *The Violence Within, The Violence Without: Wallace Stevens and the Emergence of a Revolutionary Poetics.* The University of Georgia Press, 2003. Copyright © 2003 by the University of Georgia Press. All rights reserved. Reproduced by permission.—Brogan, Jacqueline Vaught. From "'Sister of the Minotaur': Sexism and Stevens," in *Wallace Stevens and the Feminine.* Edited by Melita Schaum. The University of Alabama Press, 1993. Copyright © 1993 The University of Alabama Press. All rights reserved. Reproduced by permission.—Chadbourne, Richard M. From *Charles-Augustin Sainte-Beuve.* Twayne Publishers, 1977. Copyright © 1977 By G. K. Hall & Co. All rights reserved. Reproduced by permission of the author.—Eeckhout, Bart. From *Wallace Stevens and the Limits of Reading and Writing.* University of Missouri Press, 2002. Copyright © 2002 by The Curators of the University of Missouri. All rights reserved. Reprinted by permission.—Filreis, Alan. From *Wallace Stevens and the Actual World.* Princeton University Press, 1991. Copyright © 1991 by Princeton University Press. All rights reserved. Reprinted by permission of Princeton University Press.—Jones, Jennifer Vaughan. From *Anna Wickham:*

Gale Literature Product Advisory Board

The members of the Gale Literature Product Advisory Board—reference librarians from public and academic library systems—represent a cross-section of our customer base and offer a variety of informed perspectives on both the presentation and content of our literature products. Advisory board members assess and define such quality issues as the relevance, currency, and usefulness of the author coverage, critical content, and literary topics included in our series; evaluate the layout, presentation, and general quality of our printed volumes; provide feedback on the criteria used for selecting authors and topics covered in our series; provide suggestions for potential enhancements to our series; identify any gaps in our coverage of authors or literary topics, recommending authors or topics for inclusion; analyze the appropriateness of our content and presentation for various user audiences, such as high school students, undergraduates, graduate students, librarians, and educators; and offer feedback on any proposed changes/enhancements to our series. We wish to thank the following advisors for their advice throughout the year.

Charles Augustin Sainte-Beuve
1804-1869

(Also wrote under the pseudonym of Joseph Delorme)
French poet, critic, essayist, and novelist.

INTRODUCTION

Known more for his literary criticism than for his poetry, Sainte-Beuve produced five volumes of verse early in his career, the first three under the pseudonym Joseph Delorme. His poetry consists of love poems, odes, and sonnets, most in imitation of the English Romanticists, particularly William Wordsworth, William Collins, and William Lisle Bowles.

BIOGRAPHICAL INFORMATION

Born on December 23, 1804, in Boulogne-sur-Mer, France, Sainte-Beuve was the only child of Augustine Coillot Sainte-Beuve and Charles-François Sainte-Beuve, a customs official who died just before his son's birth. Sainte-Beuve was raised by his mother and his aunt and was taught strict financial discipline at the same time he was encouraged to read from the family's large collection of books. His early education at the Boulogne Institut Blériot earned him recognition as an outstanding Latin scholar, and in 1818 he went on to the Collège Charlemagne in Paris where he added classical Greek to his course of study. From 1821 to 1823, Sainte-Beuve studied the literature of the Romantics—French, English, and German—all the while attending lectures in chemistry and physiology in the evenings. After receiving his bachelor of letters, Sainte-Beuve began studying medicine at the Hôpital Saint-Louis in Paris, but after completing the bachelor of science degree, he returned to literature and began writing for the literary review Le Globe. A favorable review of Victor Hugo's Odes et Ballades in 1827 prompted a friendship between Sainte-Beuve and Hugo, as well as an introduction to the Paris community of writers and artists that included Alphonse de Lamartine and Eugène Delacroix, among others. Sainte-Beuve abandoned his medical career, determined instead to become a poet. He became a frequent visitor to Hugo's home and began writing poetry under the pseudonym Joseph Delorme. In 1832, Sainte-Beuve began an affair with Adèle, Hugo's wife, which quite naturally ended the friendship between the two writers. When the affair ended five years later, Sainte-Beuve turned his attention to writing essays and delivering lectures. He was a very important literary critic and historian—internationally recognized—when he died on October 13, 1869; he is buried in the cemetery of Montparnasse.

MAJOR WORKS

Sainte-Beuve began writing poetry during his friendship with Victor Hugo in 1827. He published his first book of verse, Vie, poesies et pensées de Joseph Delorme, containing autobiographical pieces, a number of love poems inspired by the person he described as his muse, as well as odes and sonnets in the style of William Wordsworth, William Collins, and Thomas Gray. Three years later, inspired by the success of his first efforts, Sainte-Beuve produced Les Consolations, containing sonnets and odes on love and loneliness. This was followed by the poems of Livre d'Amour, inspired by Sainte-Beuve's affair with Madame Hugo, but unpublished until 1843 when it was privately printed. Also inspired by his love for Adèle was the novel, Volupté (1834), which was poorly received by reviewers and critics. In 1837, Sainte-Beuve ended his affair and published Pensées d'août, apparently inspired by the poetry of Wordsworth and William Lisle Bowles, but like his novel, it was very poorly reviewed. Sainte-Beuve all but abandoned poetry in favor of essays and criticism, although he issued all of his poetry in one final volume, Poésies complètes, in 1840.

CRITICAL RECEPTION

Sainte-Beuve has typically been regarded less for his poetry than for his critical works on the poetry of others. Matthew Arnold refers to him as "the most notable critic of our time," but finds his poetry less valuable. Still, according to Arnold, it is not without merit, as it is "readable still" and it provides "greater freedom and variety to the alexandrine." William Sharp acknowledges being in the minority in praising Sainte-Beuve's poetry, but his remarks are tepid at best. For Sharp, Sainte-Beuve was "a true poet—not a great, not even an important, but at least a genuine poet," and the work he produced is "beautiful verse rather than poetry." Elsewhere in his 1901 essay, the criticism is less kind as Sharp contends that Sainte-Beuve's poetry "is often sterile, and is frequently forced, self-conscious, obtrusively sedate in imagery, occasionally even is markedly derivative." However, Sharp assesses Sainte-Beuve's talents as a critic far more positively, claiming that "as the literary critic, as the first who brought into analysis and exposition of literature the methods of exact science, Sainte-Beuve must always have a high place in the literary history of the nineteenth century." A. G. Lehmann, in his study of Sainte-Beuve's first volume of poetry, agrees that the work is derivative, citing Ronsard, Schiller, Hugo, and Lamartine as the sources for the poems in *Vie, poesies et pensées de Joseph Delorme.* Lehmann also finds Sainte-Beuve's poetic persona, Joseph Delorme, to be whiny and full of self-pity, "maudlin, and crude." Marcel Proust, though, departs from the common critical belief that Sainte-Beuve's critical writings were superior to his poetry. Proust's well-known essay, "Against Sainte-Beuve," objects to Sainte-Beuve's insistence that the poet cannot be separated from the poem, and that biographical information is important to achieving an understanding of the writings. Proust finds that Sainte-Beuve's poetry, as opposed to his critical theories, is devoid of "intellectual games" and "endless clevernesses and trickery." "In ceasing to speak in prose he ceases to tell lies," according to Proust, who concludes that he often wonders "whether what is still best in Sainte-Beuve is not his poetry."

Several other critics have attempted to reclaim Sainte-Beuve's poetry from obscurity. Richard M. Chadbourne makes a case for the reevaluation of the much-maligned *Livre d'amour,* the volume of poetry inspired by Sainte-Beuve's affair with Adèle Hugo. Although Chadbourne's praise is not unqualified, the critic contends that the work "possesses an impressive thematic unity" and that it features "many isolated *beaux vers* that would be the envy of much greater poets, many interestingly conceived though not quite successfully executed poems, and a dozen or so excellent if not great ones." Regarding the charge that Sainte-Beuve's poems are poor imitations of the work of others, G. R. Bishop (see Further Reading) acknowledges the Wordsworthian inspiration apparent in Sainte-Beuve's poem "Bonheur champêtre," but insists there are important differences in that in Sainte-Beuve's interpretation "nature penetrates the poet rather than the poet nature" as in Wordsworth's poetry.

Both his admirers and his detractors concede that Sainte-Beuve was not a major poet in his own right, but most agree that he was very influential with respect to other French poets of his own and subsequent generations. Laurent LeSage discusses Sainte-Beuve as an innovator who "introduced the humble and the familiar into French poetry" and who also articulated "a certain psychology that we think of as modern." According to LeSage, Sainte-Beuve "translated the *mal du siècle* into the idiom of his own experience and temperament" the influence of which can be seen clearly in Charles Baudelaire's *Les Fleurs du Mal.* Rachel Killick considers Sainte-Beuve's treatment of the sonnet form as an important influence on later poets, stating that he "passed on to his successors a sonnet whose thematic identity had been radically reorientated, but whose formal identity had for the most part been emphatically reaffirmed." Sheila K. Espineli also credits Sainte-Beuve with the revival of the sonnet form in French literature. "Thanks to Sainte-Beuve, the sonnet form became reborn in France as an experimental tool in which plays on language and the structure of the sonnet itself endured well into the twentieth century with poets such as Paul Valéry," maintains Espineli.

Sainte-Beuve's influence appears to have extended beyond his native France to England as well, although his affiliation with English poets and critics, both as an influence on others and as one who was influenced by English poets, seems to have been limited—chiefly by differences in notions of tolerance, openness, and the use of generalizations, which Sainte-Beuve believed should be avoided. J. Warshaw compares the critical writings of Sainte-Beuve and Arnold and finds a number of parallels, arguing that Arnold profited greatly from his exposure to the thoughts of the elder theorist. Warshaw believes, however, that Arnold would have benefitted even more had he "assimilated his master's beliefs as to tolerance, intellectual flexibility, [and] justness of spirit." In terms of English influence on Sainte-Beuve, Lander MacClintock argues against the common notion that Alexander Pope contributed significantly to Sainte-Beuve's writings, noting that while Sainte-Beuve certainly admired many of Pope's ideas and techniques, there nevertheless was "something irreconcilable between Pope's fastidiousness, preciosity and formalism, and the Frenchman's liberality, tolerance and inclusiveness."

PRINCIPAL WORKS

Poetry

Vie, poesies et pensées de Joseph Delorme [as Joseph Delorme] 1827
Les consolations [as Joseph Delorme] 1830
Pensées d'août [as Joseph Delorme] 1837
Poésies complètes 1840
Livre d'amour 1843

Other Major Works

Tableau historique et critique de la poésie française et du theater français au seizième siècle (criticism) 1828

Volupté [as Joseph Delorme] (novel) 1834
Critiques et portraits littéraires. 5 vols. (essays) 1836-39
Port-Royal. 5 vols. (lectures) 1840-59
Portraits contemporains (essays) 1846
Les causeries du lundi. 15 vols. (essays) 1851-62
Portraits de femmes (essays) 1852; [*Portraits of Celebrated Women* 1868]
Étude sur Virgile (lectures) 1857
Chateaubriand et son groupe littèraire sous l'empire (lectures) 1861
Nouveaux lundis. 13 vols. (essays) 1863-70
Premiers lundis. 3 vols. (essays) 1874-75
English Portraits (essays) 1875
Les cahiers de Sainte-Beuve (notebooks) 1876
Selected Essays from Sainte-Beuve (essays) 1895
The Essays of Sainte-Beuve (essays) 1901
Portraits of the Seventeenth Century, Historic and Literary (essays) 1904
Portraits of the Eighteenth Century, Historic and Literary (essays) 1905
Essays by Sainte-Beuve (essays) 1910
Selections from Sainte-Beuve (essays) 1918
Mes poisons (essays) 1926
La correspondence générale de Sainte-Beuve (letters) 1935-70
Sainte-Beuve: Selected Essays (essays) 1963
Portraits of Men (essays) 1972

CRITICISM

Matthew Arnold (essay date 1886)

SOURCE: Arnold, Matthew. "Sainte-Beuve." In *Five Uncollected Essays of Matthew Arnold,* edited by Kenneth Allott, pp. 66-78. Liverpool: University Press of Liverpool, 1953.

[*In the following essay, originally published in 1886, Arnold presents biographical information on Sainte-Beuve, praises his works of criticism, and judges his poetry flawed, but not without merit.*]

Sainte-Beuve, Charles Augustin (1804-1869), the most notable critic of our time, was born at Boulogne-sur-Mer on 23rd December 1804. He was a posthumous child,—his father, a native of Picardy, and controller of town-dues at Boulogne, having married in this same year, at the age of fifty-two, and died before the birth of his son. The father was a man of literary tastes, and used to read, like his son, pencil in hand; his copy of the Elzevir edition of Virgil, covered with his notes, was in his son's possession, and is mentioned by him in one of his poems. Sainte-Beuve's mother was half English,—her father, a mariner of Boulogne, having married an Englishwoman. The little Charles Augustin was brought up by his mother, who never remarried, and an aunt, his father's sister, who lived with her. They were poor, but the boy, having learnt all he could at his first school at Boulogne, persuaded his mother to send him, when he was near the age of fourteen, to finish his education at Paris. He boarded with a M. Landry, and had for a fellow-boarder and intimate friend Charles Neate, afterwards fellow of Oriel College and member of Parliament for the city of Oxford. From M. Landry's boarding-house he attended the classes, first of the Collège Charlemagne, and then of the Collège Bourbon, winning the head prize for history at the first, and for Latin verse at the second. In 1823 he began to study medicine, and continued the study with diligence and interest for nearly four years, attending lectures on anatomy and physiology and walking the hospitals. But meanwhile a Liberal newspaper, the *Globe,* was founded in 1827 by M. Dubois, one of Sainte-Beuve's old teachers at the Collège Charlemagne. M. Dubois called to his aid his former pupil, who, now quitting the study of medicine, contributed historical and literary articles to the *Globe,* among them two, which attracted the notice of Goethe, on Victor Hugo's *Odes and Ballads.* These articles led to a friendship with Victor Hugo and to Sainte-Beuve's connexion with the romantic school of poets, a school never entirely suited to his nature. In the *Globe* appeared also his interesting articles on the French poetry of the 16th century, which in 1828 were collected and published in a volume, and followed by a second volume containing selections from Ronsard. In 1829 he made his first venture as a poet with the ***Vie, Poèsies, et Pensèes de Joseph Delorme.*** His own name did not appear; but Joseph Delorme, that "Werther in the shape of Jacobin and medical student,"[1] as Guizot called him, was the Sainte-Beuve of those days himself. About the same time was founded the *Revue de Paris,* and Sainte-Beuve contributed the opening article, with Boileau for its subject. In 1830 came his second volume of poems, the ***Consolations,*** a work on which Sainte-Beuve looked back in later life with a special affection. To himself it marked and expressed, he said, that epoch of his life to which he could with most pleasure return, and at which he could like best that others should see him. But the critic in him grew to prevail more and more and pushed out the poet.[2] In 1831 the *Revue des Deux Mondes* was founded in rivalry with the *Revue de Paris,* and from the first Sainte-Beuve was one of the most active and important contributors. He brought out his novel of *Voluptè* in 1834, his third and last volume of poetry, the ***Pensées d'Août,*** in 1837. He himself thought that the activity which he had in the meanwhile exercised as a critic, and the offence which in some quarters his criticism had given, were the cause of the less favourable reception which this volume received.

He had long meditated a book on Port Royal. At the end of 1837 he quitted France, accepting an invitation from the academy of Lausanne, where in a series of lectures his work on Port Royal came into its first form of being. In the summer of the next year he returned to Paris to revise and give the final shape to his work, which, however, was not completed for twenty years. In 1840 M. Cousin, then minister of public instruction, appointed him one of the keepers of the Mazarin Library, an appointment which gave him rooms at the library, and, with the money earned by his pen, made him for the first time in his life easy in his circumstances, so that, as he afterwards used to say, he had to buy rare books in order to spend his income. A more important consequence of his easier circumstances was that he could study freely and largely. He returned to Greek, of which a French schoolboy brings from his *lycée* no great store. With a Greek teacher, M. Pantasides, he read and re-read the poets in the original, and thus acquired, not, perhaps, a philological scholar's knowledge of them, but a genuine and invaluable acquaintance with them as literature. His activity in the *Revue des Deux Mondes* continued, and articles on Homer, Theocritus, Apollonius of Rhodes, and Meleager were fruits of his new Greek studies. He wrote also a very good article in 1844 on the Italian poet Leopardi; but in general his subjects were taken from the great literature which he knew best, that of his own country—its literature both in the past and in the contemporary present. Seven volumes of "Portraits," contributed to the *Revue de Paris* and the *Revue des Deux Mondes,* exhibit his work in the years from 1832 to 1848, a work constantly increasing in range and value. In 1844 he was elected to the French Academy as successor to Casimir Delavigne, and was received there at the beginning of 1845 by Victor Hugo.

From this settled and prosperous condition the revolution of February 1848 dislodged him. In March of that year was published an account of secret-service money distributed in the late reign, and Sainte-Beuve was put down as having received the sum of one hundred francs. The smallness of the sum would hardly seem to suggest corruption; it appears probable that the money was given to cure a smoky chimney in his room at the Mazarin Library,[3] and was wrongly entered as secret-service money. But Sainte-Beuve, who piqued himself on his independence and on a punctilious delicacy in money matters, was indignant at the entry, and thought the proceedings of the minister of public instruction and his officials, when he demanded to have the matter sifted, tardy and equivocal. He resigned his post at the Mazarin and accepted an offer from the Belgian Government of a chair of French Literature in the university of Liége. There he gave the series of lectures on Chateaubriand and his contemporaries which was afterwards (in 1861) published in two volumes. He liked Liége, and the Belgians would have been glad to keep him;

but the attraction of Paris carried him back there in the autumn of 1849. Louis Napoleon was then president. Disturbance was ceasing; a time of settled government, which lasted twenty years and corresponds with the second stage of Sainte-Beuve's literary activity, was beginning. Dr. Véron, the editor of the *Constitutionnel,* proposed to him that he should supply that newspaper with a literary article for every Monday; and thus the *Causeries du Lundi* were started. They at once succeeded, and "gave the signal," as Sainte-Beuve himself says with truth, "for the return of letters." Sainte-Beuve now lived in the small house in the Rue Mont-Parnasse (No. 11) which he occupied for the remainder of his life, and where in 1850 his mother, from whom he seems to have inherited his good sense, tact, and finesse, died at the age of eighty-six. For three years he continued writing every Monday for the *Constitutionnel;* then he passed, with a similar engagement, to the *Moniteur.* In 1857 his Monday articles began to be published in volumes, and by 1862 formed a collection in fifteen volumes; they afterwards were resumed under the title of *Nouveaux Lundis,* which now make a collection of thirteen volumes more. In 1854 M. Fortoul nominated him to the chair of Latin poetry at the College of France. His first lecture there was received with interruptions and marks of disapprobation by many of the students, displeased at his adherence to the empire; at a second lecture the interruption was renewed. Sainte-Beuve had no taste for public speaking and lecturing; his *frontis mollities,* he said, unfitted him for it. He was not going to carry on a war with a party of turbulent students; he proposed to resign, and when the minister would not accept his resignation of his professorship he resigned its emoluments. The *Étude sur Virgile,* a volume published in 1857, contains what he had meant to be his first course of lectures. He was still a titular official of public instruction; and in 1858 his services were called for by M. Rouland, then minister of public instruction, as a lecturer (*maître de conférences*) on French literature at the École Normale Supérieure. This work he discharged with assiduity and success for four years. In 1859 he was made commander of the Legion of Honour, having twice previously to 1848 refused the cross. During the years of his official engagement his Monday contributions to the *Moniteur* had no longer been continuous; but in 1862 an arrangement was proposed by which he was to return to the *Constitutionnel* and again supply an article there every Monday. He consented, at the age of fifty-seven, to try this last pull, as he called it, this "dernier coup de collier";[4] he resigned his office at the École Normale and began the series of his *Nouveaux Lundis.* They show no falling off in vigour and resource from the *Causeries.* But the strain upon him of his weekly labour was great. "I am not a monsieur nor a gentleman," he writes in 1864, "but a workman by the piece and by the hour."[5] "I look upon myself as a player forced to go on acting at an age when he ought to retire, and who can see no term to his engagement."[6] He had reason to hope for relief. Except himself, the foremost literary men in France had stood aloof from the empire and treated it with a hostility more or less bitter. He had not been hostile to it: he had accepted it with satisfaction, and had bestowed on its official journal, the *Moniteur,* the lustre of his literature. The prince Napoleon and the princess Mathilde were his warm friends. A senatorship was mentioned; its income of £1600 a year would give him opulence and freedom. But its coming was delayed, and the strain upon him continued for some time longer. When at last in April 1865 he was made senator, his health was already seriously compromised. The disease of which he died, but of which the doctors did not ascertain the presence until his body was opened after his death—the stone—began to distress and disable him. He could seldom attend the meetings of the senate; the part he took there, however, on two famous occasions, when the nomination of M. Renan to the College of France came under discussion in 1867 and the law on the press in the year following, provoked the indignation of the great majority in that conservative assembly. It delighted, however, all who "belonged," to use his own phrase, "to the diocese of free thought"; and he gave further pleasure in this diocese by leaving at the beginning of 1869 the *Moniteur,* injudiciously managed by the Government and M. Rouher, and contributing to a Liberal journal, the *Temps.* His literary activity suffered little abatement, but the attacks of his malady, though borne with courage and cheerfulness, became more and more severe. Pain made him at last unable to sit to write; he could only stand or lie. He died in his house in the Rue Mont Parnasse on the 13th of October 1869. He had inherited an income of four thousand francs a year from his mother, and he left it six thousand; to the extent of eighty pounds a year and no further had literature and the senatorship enriched him. By his will he left directions that his funeral was to be without religious rites, quite simple, and with no speeches at the grave except a few words of thanks from one of his secretaries to those present. There was a great concourse; the Paris students, who had formerly interrupted him, came now to do honour to him as a Liberal and a champion of free thought—a senator they could not but admit—undeniably, alas, a senator, but *oh, si peu*! Yet his own account of himself is the best and truest,—an account which lays no stress on his Liberalism, no stress on his championship of free thought, but says simply: "Devoted to my profession as critic, I have tried to be more and more a good, and, if possible, an able workman."

The work of Sainte-Beuve divides itself into three portions—his poetry, his criticism before 1848, and his criticism after that year. His novel of *Volupté* may properly go with his poetry.

We have seen his tender feeling for his poetry, and he always maintained that, when the "integrating molecule,"[7] the foundation of him as a man of letters, was reached, it would be found to have a poetic character. and yet he declares, too, that it is never without a sort of surprise and confusion that he sees his verses detached from their context and quoted in public and in open day. They do not seem made for it, he says. This admirable critic knew, indeed, what a Frenchman may be pardoned for not willingly perceiving, and what even some Englishmen try to imagine that they do not perceive, the radical inadequacy of French poetry.[8] For us it is extremely interesting to hear Sainte-Beuve on this point, since it is to English poetry that he resorts in order to find his term of comparison, and to award the praise which to French poetry he refuses. "Since you are fond of the poets," he writes to a friend, "I should like to see you read and look for poets in another language, in English for instance. There you will find the most rich, the most dulcet, and the most new poetical literature. Our French poets are too soon read; they are too slight, too mixed, too corrupted for the most part, too poor in ideas even when they have the talent for strophe and line, to hold and occupy for long a serious mind."[9] And again: "If you knew English you would have treasures to draw upon. They have a poetical literature far superior to ours, and, above all, sounder, more full. Wordsworth is not translated; these things are not to be translated; you must go to the fountainhead for them. Let me give you this advice: learn English."[10]

But, even as French poetry, Sainte-Beuve's poetry had faults of its own. Critics who found much in it to praise yet pronounced it a poetry "narrow, puny, and stifled," and its style "slowly dragging and laborious." Here we touch on a want which must no doubt be recognised in him, which he recognised in himself, and whereby he is separated from the spirits who succeed in uttering their most highly inspired note and in giving their full measure,—some want of flame, of breath, of pinion. Perhaps we may look for the cause in a confession of his own: "I have my weaknesses; they are those which gave to King Solomon his disgust with everything and his satiety with life. I may have regretted sometimes that I was thus extinguishing my fire, but I did not ever pervert my heart." It is enough for us to take his confession that he extinguished or impaired his fire.

Yet his poetry is characterised by merits which make it readable still and readable by foreigners. So far as it exhibits the endeavour of the romantic school in France to enlarge the vocabulary of poetry and to give greater freedom and variety to the alexandrine, it has interest chiefly for readers of his own nation. But it exhibits more than this. It exhibits already the genuine Sainte-Beuve, the author who, as M. Duvergier de Hauranne said in the *Globe* at the time, "sent à sa manière et écrit comme il sent," the man who, even in the forms of an artificial poetry, remains always "un penseur et un homme d'esprit." That his Joseph Delorme was not the Werther of romance, but a Werther in the shape of Jacobin and medical student, the only Werther whom Sainte-Beuve by his own practical experience really knew, was a novelty in French poetical literature, but was entirely characteristic of Sainte-Beuve. All his poetry has this stamp of direct dealing with common things, of plain unpretending reality and sincerity; and this stamp at that time made it, as Béranger said, "a kind of poetry absolutely new in France." It found, therefore, with all its shortcomings, friends in men so diverse as Béranger, Lamartine, Jouffroy, Beyle. Whoever is interested in Sainte-Beuve should turn to it, and will be glad that he has done so.

It has been the fashion to disparage the criticism of the *Critiques et Portraits Littéraires,* the criticism anterior to 1848, and to sacrifice it, in fact, to the criticism posterior to that date. Sainte-Beuve has himself indicated what considerations ought to be present with us in reading the *Critiques et Portraits,* with what reserves we should read them. They are to be considered, he says, "rather as a dependency of the elegiac and romanesque part of my work than as express criticisms." "The *Revue des Deux Mondes,*" he adds, which published them, was young in those days, "mixed a good deal of its wishes and its hopes with its criticism, sought to explain and to stimulate rather than to judge. The portraits there of contemporary poets and romance-writers can in general be considered, whether as respects the painter or as respects the models, as youthful portraits only; *juvenis juvenem pinxit.*" They have the copiousness and enthusiasm of youth; they have also its exuberance. He judged in later life Chateaubriand, Lamartine, Victor Hugo, more coolly, judged them differently. But the *Critiques et Portraits* contain a number of articles on personages, other than contemporary French poets and romance-writers, which have much of the soundness of his later work, and, in addition, an abundance and fervour of their own which are not without their attraction. Many of these are delightful reading. The articles on the Greek poets and on Leopardi have been already mentioned. Those on Boileau, Molière, Daunou, and Fauriel, on Madame de la Fayette and Mademoiselle Aïssé, may be taken as samples of a whole group which will be found to support perfectly the test of reading, even after we have accustomed ourselves to the later work of the master. Nay, his soberness and tact show themselves even in this earlier stage of his criticism, and even in treating the objects of his too fervid youthful enthusiasm. A special object of this was Victor Hugo, and in the first article on him in the *Portraits Contemporains* we have certainly plenty of enthusiasm, plenty of exuberance. We have the epithets "adorable," "sublime," given to Victor Hugo's poetry; we are told of "the majesty of its high and sombre philosophy." All this is in the vein of

Mr George Gilfillan."[11] But the article next following this, and written only four years later, in 1835, is the article of a critic, and takes the points of objection, seizes the weak side of Victor Hugo's poetry, how much it has of what is "creux," "sonore," "artificiel," "voulu," "théâtral," "violent," as distinctly as the author of the *Causeries* could seize it. "The Frank, energetic and subtle, who has mastered to perfection the technical and rhetorical resources of the Latin literature of the decadence," is a description never to be forgotten of Victor Hugo as a poet, and Sainte-Beuve launches it in this article, written when he was but thirty years old, and still a painter of "portraits de jeunesse" only.

He had thus been steadily working and growing; nevertheless, 1848 is an epoch which divides two critics in him of very unequal value. When, after that year of revolution and his stage of seclusion and labour at Liége, he came back to Paris in the autumn of 1849 and commenced in the *Constitutionnel* the *Causeries du Lundi,* he was astonishingly matured. Something of fervour, enthusiasm, poetry, he may have lost, but he had become a perfect critic—a critic of measure, not exuberant; of the centre, not provincial; of keen industry and curiosity, with "Truth" (the word engraved in English on his seal) for his motto; moreover, with gay and amiable temper, his manner as good as his matter,—the "critique souriant," as, in Charles Monselet's dedication to him, he is called.

Merely to say that he was all this is less convincing than to show, if possible, by words of his own, in what fashion he was all this. The root of everything in his criticism is his single-hearted devotion to truth. What he called "fictions" in literature, in politics, in religion, were not allowed to influence him. Someone had talked of his being tenacious of a certain set of literary opinions. "I hold very little," he answers, "to literary opinions; literary opinions occupy very little place in my life and in my thoughts. What does occupy me seriously is life itself and the object of it." "I am accustomed incessantly to call my judgments in question anew, and to re-cast my opinions the moment I suspect them to be without validity." "What I have wished" (in *Port Royal*) "is to say not a word more than I thought, to stop even a little short of what I believed in certain cases, in order that my words might acquire more weight as historical testimony." To all exaggeration and untruth, from whatever side it proceeded, he had an antipathy. "I turn my back upon the Michelets and Quinets, but I cannot hold out my hand to the Veuillots."[12] When he was writing for the *Moniteur* he was asked by the manager of the paper to review a book by an important personage, a contributor; his answer is a lesson for critics and paints him exactly. "I should like to say yes, but I have an insurmountable difficulty as to this author; he appears to me to compromise whatever he touches; he is violent, and has not the tradition of the things he talks about. Thus his article on Condorcet, which the *Moniteur* inserted, is odious and false; one may be severe upon Condorcet, but not in that tone or in that note. The man has no *insight*—a defect which does not prevent him from having a pen with which at a given moment he can flourish marvellously. But, of himself, he is a gladiator and a desperado. I must tell you, my dear sir, that to have once named him with compliment in some article of mine or other is one of my self-reproaches as a man of letters. Let me say that he has not attacked me in any way; it is a case of natural repulsion."[13]

But Sainte-Beuve could not have been the great critic he was had he not had, at the service of this his love of truth and measure, the conscientious industry of a Benedictine. "I never have a holiday. On Monday towards noon I lift up my head, and breathe for about an hour; after that the wicket shuts again and I am in my prison cell for seven days."[14] The *Causeries* were at this price. They came once a week, and to write one of them as he wrote it was indeed a week's work. The "irresponsible indolent reviewer"[15] should read his notes to his friend and provider with books, M. Paul Chéron of the National Library. Here is a note dated the 2nd of January 1853: "Good-day and a happy New Year. To-day I set to work on Grimm. A little dry; but after St. François de Sales" (his Monday article just finished) "one requires a little relief from roses. I have of Grimm the edition of his *Correspondence* by M. Taschereau. I have also the *Memoirs* of Madame d'Épinay, where there are many letters of his. But it is possible that there may be notices of him mentioned in the bibliographical book of that German whose name I have forgotten. I should like, too, to have the first editions of his *Correspondence*; they came out in successive parts."[16] Thus he prepared himself, not for a grand review article once a quarter, but for a newspaper review once a week.

His adhesion to the empire caused him to be habitually represented by the Orleanists and the Republicans as without character and patriotism, and to be charged with baseness and corruption. The Orleanists had, in a great degree, possession of the higher press in France and of English opinion,—of Liberal English opinion more especially. And with English Liberals his indifference to parliamentary government was indeed a grievous fault in him; "you Whigs," as Croker[17] happily says, "are like quack doctors, who have but one specific for all constitutions." To him either the doctrine of English Liberals, or the doctrine of Republicanism, applied absolutely, was what he called a "fiction," one of those fictions which "always end by obscuring the truth." Not even on M. de Tocqueville's authority would he consent to receive "les hypothèses dites les plus honorables,"— "the suppositions which pass for the most respectable." All suppositions he demanded to sift, to see them at work, to know the place and time and men to which

they were to be applied.[18] For the France before his eyes in 1849 he thought that something "solid and stable"—*un mur,* "a wall," as he said—was requisite, and that the government of Louis Napoleon supplied this wall. But no one judged the empire more independently than he did, no one saw and enounced its faults more clearly; he described himself as being, in his own single person, "the *gauche* of the empire,"[19] and the description was just.

To these merits of mental independence, industry, measure, lucidity, his criticism adds the merit of happy temper and disposition. Goethe long ago noticed that, whereas Germans reviewed one another as enemies whom they hated, the critics of the *Globe* reviewed one another as gentlemen. This arose from the higher social development of France and from the closer relations of literature with life there. But Sainte-Beuve has more, as a critic, than the external politeness which once at any rate distinguished his countrymen: he has a personal charm of manner due to a sweet and humane temper. He complained of *un peu de dureté,* "a certain dose of hardness," in the new generation of writers. The personality of an author had a peculiar importance for him; the poetical side of his subjects, however latent it might be, always attracted him and he always sought to extricate it. This was because he had in himself the moderate, gracious, amiably *human* instincts of the true poetic nature. "Let me beg of you," he says in thanking a reviewer who praised him, "to alter one or two expressions at any rate. I cannot bear to have it said that I am the *first* in anything whatever, as a writer least of all; it is not a thing which can be admitted, and these ways of classing people give offence." Literary man and loyal to the French Academy as he was, he can yet write to an old friend after his election: "All these academies, between you and me, are pieces of childishness; at any rate the French Academy is. Our least quarter of an hour of solitary reverie or of serious talk, yours and mine, in our youth, was better employed; but, as one gets old, one falls back into the power of these nothings; only it is well to know that nothings they are."[20]

Perhaps the best way to get a sense of the value and extent of the work done in the last twenty years of his life by the critic thus excellently endowed is to take a single volume of the *Causeries du Lundi,* to look through its list of subjects, and to remember that with the qualities above mentioned all these subjects are treated. Any volume will serve; let us take the fourth. This volume consists of articles on twenty-four subjects. Twenty of these are the following:—Mirabeau and Sophie, Montaigne, Mirabeau and Comte de la Marck, Mademoiselle de Scudéry, André Chénier as politician, Saint-Évremond and Ninon, Joseph de Maistre, Madame de Lambert, Madame Necker, the Abbé Maury, the Duc de Lauzun of Louis XVI's reign, Marie Antoinette, Buffon, Madame de Maintenon, De Bonald, Amyot, Mallet du Pan, Marmontel, Chamfort, Ruhlière. Almost every personage is French, it is true; Sainte-Beuve had a maxim that the critic should prefer subjects which he possesses familiarly. But we should recognise more fully than we do the immense importance and interest of French literature. Certain productions of this literature Mr. Saintsbury[21] may misjudge and over-praise; but he is entirely right in insisting on its immense importance. More than any modern literature it has been in the most intimate correspondence with the social life and development of the nation producing it. Now it so happens that the great place of France in the world is very much due to her eminent gift for social life and development; and this gift French literature has accompanied, fashioned, perfected, and continues to reflect. This gives a special interest to French literature, and an interest independent even of the excellence of individual French writers, high as that often is. And nowhere shall we find such interest more completely and charmingly brought out than in the *Causeries du Lundi* and the *Nouveaux Lundis* of the consummate critic of whom we have been speaking. As a guide to bring us to a knowledge of the French genius and literature he is unrivalled,—perfect, so far as a poor mortal critic can be perfect, in knowledge of his subject, in judgment, in tact, and tone. Certain spirits are of an excellence almost ideal in certain lines; the human race might willingly adopt them as its spokesmen, recognising that on these lines their style and utterance may stand as those, not of bounded individuals, but of the human race. So Homer speaks for the human race, and with an excellence which is ideal, in epic narration; Plato in the treatment at once beautiful and profound of philosophical questions; Shakespeare in the presentation of human character; Voltaire in light verse and ironical discussion. A list of perfect ones, indeed, each in his own line! and we may almost venture to add to their number, in his line of literary criticism, Sainte-Beuve.

Notes

1. See *Correspondance de Sainte-Beuve* (Calmann Lévy, Paris, 1877-8), I, p. 16.

2. Arnold must have felt the parallel between Sainte-Beuve's course and his own. In *The Letters of Matthew Arnold to A. H. Clough* (1932) H. F. Lowry points out (p. 38 fn.) that the essay 'Dix ans après en littérature', in which Sainte-Beuve traces the development of the artist into the critic, is carefully marked throughout in Arnold's copy of *Portraits Contemporains* (Paris, 1847).

3. Sainte-Beuve's own explanation. See the preface to *Chateaubriand et son groupe littéraire sous l'Empire* (1861).

4. Sainte-Beuve's phrase, but not for this occasion. See *Nouvelle Correspondance* (Calmann Lévy, Paris, 1880), p. 225.

5. See *Nouvelle Correspondance*, p. 189.

6. Ibid., p. 189.

7. See *Correspondance*, I, p. 277.

8. Arnold's consistently-held view. Cf. the letter to his mother of 19 May 1863: '. . . except in songs, I do not see that French verse *can* be truly satisfactory' (*Letters*, I, p. 194), and see, among other references, *Essays in Criticism* 1st series (*Works*, [*The Works of Matthew Arnold* in 15 volumes (Macmillan, 1903-4)] III, p. 57) and *Irish Essays* (*Works*, XI, p. 205).

9. See *Nouvelle Correspondance*, pp. 352-3.

10. See *Correspondance*, I, p. 273.

11. Author and editor, 1813-78. His *Gallery of Literary Portraits* (1850) was on Arnold's reading-list for May 1855 (*Notebooks* [*The Notebooks of Matthew Arnold* (Oxford University Press, 1952)], p. 558).

12. See *Nouvelle Correspondance*, p. 98.

13. See *Correspondance*, I, pp. 252-3.

14. Ibid., p. 283.

15. Quoted from Tennyson's untitled hendecasyllabics, one of the 'experiments in quantity' published in the *Cornhill Magazine* (December 1863).

16. See *Correspondance*, I, pp. 179-80.

17. 'Croker's Life' is crossed out as read in Arnold's reading-list for 1885 (*Notebooks*, p. 619). The book referred to is *The Croker Papers: the Correspondence and Diaries . . . of John Wilson Croker*, ed. L. J. Jennings (3 vols., 1884), but I have not found this remark.

18. Cf. 'Sainte-Beuve', *Essays* (Oxford, 1914), pp. 485-6.

19. See *Correspondance*, II, p. 350.

20. See *Nouvelle Correspondance*, p. 98.

21. Arnold's notebook for 1880 has several extracts from Saintsbury's *Primer of French Literature* (1880), including some that give high praise to V. Hugo. See *Notebooks*, pp. 344, 345.

William Sharp (essay date 1901)

SOURCE: Sharp, William. "Critical Memoir." In *The Essays of Sainte-Beuve*, edited by William Sharp, pp. vii-xlviii. London: Gibbings and Company, 1901.

[*In the following essay, Sharp offers an overview of Sainte-Beuve's work, both in verse and in prose, with an emphasis on the wide range of his thoughts and accomplishments.*]

Among the innumerable apt sentences with one of which an essay upon Sainte-Beuve, the sovereign critic, might fittingly be introduced, I doubt if there be any better than this: "I have but one diversion, one pursuit: I analyze, I botanize, I am a naturalist of minds. What I would fain create is Literary Natural History." He was, and is, unquestionably the foremost "naturaliste des esprits:" in literary natural history he is at once the Buffon and Humboldt, the Linnæus and Cuvier, the Darwin even, of scientific criticism. It is conceivable that the future historian of our age will allot to Sainte-Beuve a place higher even than that which he holds by common consent of his cultured countrymen, even than that claimed for him by one or two of our own ablest critics, Matthew Arnold, in particular, and Mr. John Morley. He was not a great inventor, a new creative force, it is true; but he was, so to say, one of the foremost practical engineers in literature,—he altered the course of the alien stream of criticism, compelled its waters to be tributary to the main river, and gave it a new impetus, an irresistible energy, a fresh and vital importance.

I.

During the ten or twelve years in which I have been a systematic reader of Sainte-Beuve, I have often wondered if his literary career would have been a very different one from what we know it, if he had been born ere the parental tides of life were already on the ebb. Students of physiology are well aware of the fact that children born of parents beyond the prime of life are, in the first degree, inferior in physique to those born, say, to a father of thirty years of age and to a mother five-and-twenty years old; and, in the second degree, that the children of parents married after the prime of life, are, as a rule, less emotional than those born of a union in the more ardent and excitable years of youth. The present writer admits that he is one of the seemingly very few who regard the greatest of literary critics as also a true poet,—not a great, not even an important, but at least a genuine poet, whose radical shortcoming was the tendency to produce beautiful verse rather than poetry, but the best of whose metrical writings may confidently be compared with those of any of the notable contemporary lesser poets of France. And it is because in the **"Life, Poems, and Thoughts of Joseph Delorme,"** in **"Les Consolations,"** in the **"Pensées d'Août,"** I for one find so much which is praiseworthy, which is excellent even, that I have often wondered if, his natal circumstances having been other than they were, the author who has become so celebrated for his inimitable *Causeries du Lundi* might have become famous as a poet. That the keen subjectivity of emotion which is at the base of the poetic nature was his may be inferred from a hundred hints throughout his writings: he was very far from being, what some one has called him, a "mere bloodless critic, serenely impartial because of his imperturbable pulse." To cite a single example: in one of his "Notes et Remarques," printed in M. Pierrot's appendical volume (Tome xvime.) to the collected *Causeries du Lundi*, he says, *à propos* of his novel "Volupté," "Why do I not write another novel? To write a romance was for me but another, an indirect way of being in love, and to say so." It was not "a mere bloodless critic" who penned that remark. But, withal, in his poetry, in his essays, in his critiques, in the episodes of his long and intellectually active life, it is obvious to the discerning reader that Sainte-Beuve rarely attained to the white-heat of emotion for any length of time: that a cold wave of serene judgment, of *ennui* often enough, speedily dissipated the intoxication of spiritual ardour. But in those white-heat moments he touches so fine a note, reaches so high a level, that one realizes the poet within him is not buried so deep below his ordinary self as the common judgment would have us believe. Had Mlle. Augustine Coilliot not been past forty when she gave her hand to the cultivated, respected M. de Sainte-Beuve, Commissioner of Taxes at Boulogne-sur-mer, and had he, then in his fifty-second year, been more robust in health (he died a few months after his marriage), their child might have inherited just that impulse of passionate life, to the absence of which perhaps we owe the critic at the expense of the poet. But the century has been rich in poetic literature, while there have been few eminent critics,—till Sainte-Beuve no French critic, great by virtue of the art of criticism alone. It is only since the advent of Sainte-Beuve, indeed, that criticism has come to be accepted as an art, that is in France; for, among us, criticism, as distinct from conventional book-reviewing, can at most be said just to exist.

The Mlle. Augustine Coilliot referred to was the daughter of a Boulogne sailor who had married an Englishwoman, and the writers of biographical articles have been fond of tracing to this Anglo-Saxon strain the great critic's strong predilection for English poetry. It may, however, be doubted if the fact that his grandmother was English had much to do with Sainte-Beuve's love of Wordsworth, Coleridge, Southey, and Cowper. Earnestness, austerity even, always deeply appealed to him; he loved Pascal and Bossuet better than Villon or the Abbé Galiani; and this love would in any case have led him to the British poets who are pre-eminently the exponents of earnest reflection upon human life. Besides this, Sainte-Beuve the elder was a man of culture, of a serious bias of mind, an admirer of Shakespeare in the original, and probably, therefore, of other English authors; and again, Boulogne, even at the beginning of the century, was much frequented by visitors from the other side of the Channel, and its schools contained many young Anglo-Saxons sent thither to learn French. Only once, so far as I can recollect, and that incidentally, does he allude to the strain of English blood in him, though with the non-existence of any serviceable index to his voluminous writings it is impossible to make any such assertion with assurance. The absence of allusion would, with so scrupulous a literary analyst as Sainte-Beuve, indicate that he laid no stress whatever upon the circumstance.

Mlle. Coilliot was of an old bourgeois family which, though it held a reputable position in the lower town, was accustomed to straits of poverty. She had not even the smallest dowry to bring to the man who married her, and this was one reason why M. Sainte-Beuve (*de Sainte-Beuve,* he maintained, though his son discarded the aristocratic prefix, partly from a conviction that the family had no right to it, partly from republican scruple) postponed marriage for a goodly space of time after he had won the already middle-aged Augustine's consent to a betrothal. He himself was also a native of Picardy, having been born at Moreuil: a person, indubitably, of exceptional culture, genial, sympathetic, a student, a man of the world. Sainte-Beuve was convinced that he owed his most distinctive traits not to his mother but to his father, though, as a posthumous child, the sole intellectual communion with the latter which he enjoyed was through the discriminative and suggestive annotations which the "Commissioner" was wont to make upon the margins of many of the books in his well-selected library. A few months (not a few weeks, as sometimes affirmed) after his marriage, M. Sainte-Beuve died suddenly; and within three months from that event, that is on December 23rd, 1804, his wife gave birth to a son, who, in remembrance of both his parents, was christened Charles Augustin. In the invaluable autobiographical fragment which was found among his papers on the morrow of his death, Sainte-Beuve states that he was brought up by his widowed mother, who had been left with sadly straitened means yet not in extreme poverty, and by a sister of his father, who united her slender income to that of Mme. Sainte-Beuve, and so enabled the small family of three to live in comparative comfort. The boy was carefully educated at the lay school of a M. Blériot, and was particularly well grounded in Latin. His intellectual development was rapid. He had scarcely entered upon his teens before he had become a student, and his mother, sympathetic and intelligent if not actively intellectual, gave him every encouragement. It was at this time that he read many of the books which bore his father's marginalia; and no doubt the mere circumstance of annotation impressed him with the importance of the subject-matter. Some ten years or so later he alluded, in one of his poems, to his father and his indirect influence upon him:—

"Mon père ainsi sentait. Si, né dans sa mort même,
Ma mémoire n'eut pas son image suprême,
Il m'a laissé du moins son âme et son esprit,
Et son goût tout entier à chaque marge écrit."

What is even more noteworthy is his consciousness of his educational shortcomings when, in his fourteenth year, he realised that he was not likely to learn anything more at M. Blériot's school. "I felt strongly how much I lacked:" and in this persuasion he urged his mother to take, or send, him to Paris. It was not an easy thing for the widow to do, but she managed to send him to the capital (September 1818), and to arrange for his board with a M. Landry, a man of some note, who had formerly been a professor at the College of Louis-le-Grand, and was a mathematician and philosopher. At the house in the Rue de la Cerisail of this *esprit libre,* this free-thinker, as Sainte-Beuve calls him, the young scholar met several men of high standing in the world of letters, among them certain eminent students of science. He seems to have been noticed by them, though he did not quite relish being treated as a hobbledehoy, "as a big boy, as a little man." He was an instinctive student: to learn was as natural to him as to play is easy for most boys, and yet he does not seem to have been devoid of the gaiety and even *abandon* of youth. At the College of Charlemagne, at the end of the first year of his attendance, he took part in the general competition, and succeeded in carrying off the highest prize for history; and in the following year, at the Bourbon College, he gained the prize for Latin verse, and had the further distinction of a Governmental award, in the form of a medal, as a special recognition of his scholarly achievements. One of his school friends, Charles Potier, the son of the eminent actor, and himself afterwards successful on the stage, has put on record his recollection of how he and Sainte-Beuve acted the familiar old parts of the clever and the stupid boy;—how while he dug or hoed the garden-plot which had been allotted to them, the other Charles sat idly by, obliviously engaged in some book or indolently abstracted; and how, in return, he was helped by his friend in the uncongenial task of class-exercises. Sainte-Beuve was free to spend his evenings as he chose, and he voluntarily studied medical science, at first with the full intention of becoming a physician, later with the idea of making the philosophical study of physiology and chemistry his specialities, and, finally, simply for the value of the training and its bearing upon that new science of literature which he was one of the earliest to apprehend as a complex unity. The lectures of Messieurs Magendie, Robiquet, and Blainville, respectively upon physiology, chemistry, and natural history, interested him profoundly. "I went every evening to these lectures at the *Athénée,* off the Palais Royal, from seven to ten o'clock," he says in his autobiographical fragment, "and also to some literary lectures." It was natural that this preoccupation with strictly scientific study should bias his mind to the materialistic school of thought; and one is not surprised to learn, on the authority of D'Haussonville, his biographer, that in his own judgment he had reached his true ground, "mon fonds véritable," in the most pronounced eighteenth-century materialism. It is, however, interesting and suggestive to note that even at that time Sainte-Beuve was dominated by his exceptional mental receptivity; that he was swayed this way and that by the intellectual duality which has puzzled so many of his readers. Daunou and Lamarck were his prophets; by them he swore, their words contained the authentic gospel; but the same week, perhaps, as that in which he proclaimed his enfranchisement from the most abstract Deism, he would announce his conviction that a Supreme Power controlled the tides of life,—as when he wrote to his friend, afterwards the Abbé Barbe, distinctly asserting his recognition of God as "the source of all things." The mystic in him was always side by side with the physiologist, the unflinching analyst, just as the poet was ever comrade to the critic. It is to this, indeed, that Sainte-Beuve owes his pre-eminence, to this that is to be traced the fundamental secret of his spell. In later life he was fully conscious of his indebtedness to those early medical and scientific studies; and many will call to mind his famous defence of the Faculty, in the Senate of the Second Empire, when an attempt was made to limit the medical professors in Governmental institutions in the free expression of their views. The very least he could do, he declared, was to give his testimony in favour of that Faculty to which he owed the philosophical spirit, the love of exactitude and of physiological reality, and "such good method as may have entered into my writings." As a matter of fact, his early scientific training was of the highest value. It is possible that, with his strong religious bias, if he had been educated at an ecclesiastical seminary he would have become one of the great company led by Pascal and Bossuet, a spiritual comrade of his contemporaries Lamennais and Lacordaire; that, but for his liaison with radical materialism, the Art, the Science of Criticism, would have remained half-formless and indeterminate, and waited long for its first great master.

His several scientific excursions led to his following the regular course in the study of medicine; and, with the goal of a medical career in view, he was an assiduous student till 1827, when he was in his twenty-third year. At that date an event occurred which determined his particular line of energy. But before this he had already begun to write. These tentative efforts, in verse and prose, conventional though they were, encouraged him to believe that he had the literary faculty, though even then his sense of style was so developed that he realized how wide was the gulf between mere facility and a vital dominating impulse. His mother, who had come from Boulogne to watch over her son, saw these literary indications with an annoyance which grew into alarm; for at that time the literary career was rarely a remunerative one, and, moreover, her heart was set upon her son's success as a physician or collegiate professor of medicine. It was not, as a matter of fact, till his election to the Academy, that she admitted the wisdom of his early decision; and even then she complained, and not without justice, of the terrible wear and tear of an unceasingly active literary life. Mme.

Sainte-Beuve, who lived with her son till her death at the goodly age of eighty-six, seems to have been an intelligent and sympathetic rather than an intellectually clever woman; and though her always affectionate Charles loved and admired her, it would not appear that he enjoyed with her any rare mental communion.

The youth who at the College of Charlemagne had gained the History prize attracted the particular attention of his professor, M. Dubois. A friendship, as intimate as practicable in the circumstances, ensued; and when, in 1824, M. Dubois founded the *Globe,* the journal which ere long became so famous and so influential both in politics and literature, he asked Sainte-Beuve to join the staff as an occasional contributor. This was a remarkable compliment, for the young student was quite unknown, and had done nothing to warrant such an honour; so it is clear that M. Dubois must have had a strong opinion as to the young man's capabilities. Sainte-Beuve was all the more gratified because the staff of writers who had promised their practical support comprised men so famous as Guizot and Victor Cousin, Jouffroy, Ampère, Mérimée, De Broglie, and Villemain. It was not long before the *Globe* became a power in Paris, and thereafter throughout France and northern Europe: even the great Goethe read it regularly, and alluded to it in terms of cordial praise. It was regarded as the organ of the principal exponents of that earlier Romantic movement which made the latter years of the Restoration so brilliant, and worked like powerful yeast through contemporary thought and literature. Politically, it was the mouthpiece of those who were characterised as *les Doctrinaires.* Naturally the young medical student, who had scarce unsheathed his virginal literary sword, was not among the first contributors. When M. Dubois did entrust to him several short reviews, he did not allow these to appear without, on his own part, scrupulous revision. They did not attract any particular notice: few were curious as to the personality of the critic whose articles appeared above the initials "S. B." But the editor soon discovered that his youngest contributor was quite able to stand alone so far as literary craftsmanship was concerned. One day he delighted the novice by saying to him, "*Now* you know how to write; henceforth you can go alone." Confidence helped style, and Parisian men of letters read with appreciative interest the new recruit's articles on Thiers' "Histoire de la Révolution" and Mignet's "Tableau" of the same epoch. He may be said to have definitively gained his place as a recognised literary critic by the time that he had published his able and scholarly review of Alfred de Vigny's "Cinq Mars." It was still before he had finally given up a medical career that, by means of a review, he formed a new acquaintanceship which was to prove of great importance to him, and not only as a man of letters. One morning, late in 1826, he chanced to call upon M. Dubois, who was engaged in turning over the pages of two volumes of "Odes and Ballads," which he had just received. The editor of the *Globe* asked Sainte-Beuve to review them, having first explained that they were by an acquaintance of his, "a young barbarian of talent," interesting on account of his forceful character and the incidents of his life—Victor Hugo. The volumes were duly carried off, read, re-read, and reviewed. When the critic took his MS. to his editor he told the latter that this Victor Hugo was not such a barbarian after all, but a man of genius. The review appeared in the issue of the *Globe* for the 2nd of January 1827; and it is interesting to know that among the earliest foreign readers of it was Goethe, who on the 4th expressed to Eckermann his appreciation of Hugo, and his belief that the young poet's fortunes were assured since he had the *Globe* on his side. And of course the author of "Odes et Ballades" was delighted. He called upon M. Dubois, enthusiastically expressed his gratification, maugre the few strictures upon his poetic and metrical extravagances which the article contained, and begged for the address of the writer, which to his surprise he ascertained to be in the same street as that wherein he and his beautiful wife Adèle had their apartments. The latter were at No. 11 Rue Notre Dame des Champs, while Sainte-Beuve and his mother resided in simpler and much smaller rooms on the fourth floor at No. 19. The critic was out when the poet called, but a return visit was speedily made. No doubt Sainte-Beuve was not the man to regret any useful experience, and yet one may question, from knowledge of the man in his later years, if, could he have relived and at the same time refashioned the drift of his life, he would have made that eventful call. From it, indirectly, arose his "one critical crime," that of wilful blindness to short-comings because of the influence of a personal charm; and to it, also, was due the "romantic" prose and poetry of the morbid and supersensitive Joseph Delorme. Poetically, in a word, he would not have had what he calls somewhere his "liaison avec l'école poétique de Victor Hugo." On the other hand, he owed much to his intimacy with the Hugos and their circle, which at that time comprised Alfred de Vigny, Lamartine, Musset, and other ardent representatives of *Jeune France.* The recollection of his critical reception of Alfred de Musset was always, in late years, one of Sainte-Beuve's thorns in the flesh. But the accusation which has been made, that he was chagrined by the poet's manner to him when they first met, and that the critic allowed his personal resentment to bias his judgment, is ridiculous. I was surprised to see something to this effect in some recent critical volume. Surely the writer must, for one thing, have forgotten that passage in "Ma Biographie" (*Nouveaux Lundis,* Tome xiii.) where the author expressly recounts the circumstances.[1]

Sainte-Beuve was impressed by Victor Hugo's genius and captivated by his personal charm; and, at the same time, he was fascinated by Madame Hugo. He became an intimate friend; visited No. 11 whensoever he willed; saw the poet at least twice daily; praised, admired, wrote about the beautiful Adèle—and, indeed, became so enthusiastically friendly that the brilliant group which formed *Le Cénacle* (the Guest-Chamber), a club of kindred spirits in the several arts, must have thought that their latest recruit was qualifying to be the prophet of woman's supremacy in all things. As a matter of fact, the Hugo circle was not fettered by severe social conventionalities; yet even the self-confident Victor made objections when he found his numerous friends, from the polished Alfred de Vigny and the sentimental Lamartine to "Musset l'Ennuyé" and the brilliant light-hearted essayist, whom Monselet afterwards with so much justice called "the smiling critic" (*le critique souriant*), addressing his wife as Adèle, as freely as they called each other Alfred or Victor or Charles, as frequently as they applied one to the other the term "master." In France every writer is called *cher maître* by some other author. As for Sainte-Beuve, his complaint was so severe that, though he laughed at it afterwards as a flirtation with Romanticism, it might best be called *Adelaïsme.* This one-sided passion was no doubt the mainspring of the sufferings, thoughts, and poesies of the melancholy Joseph Delorme, that Gallic counterpart of the much more unendurable Werther. True, something of Sainte-Beuve's deeper melancholy of "seriousness" may have been due to his remote English strain, and his splenetic temperament to the fact that his mother passed several dolorous months between his birth and the death of her husband. It seems strange that so acute a critic of literary physiology should not have seen that his "spleen" was due more to want of outdoor life and to incessant mental preoccupation, and (in the **"Joseph Delorme"** period) to what I have in persiflage called *Adelaïsme,* than to the circumstance of his mother having borne him during months of widowhood, or to that of his grandmother having been an Englishwomen. Although he was never married, Sainte-Beuve was of a susceptible nature. There is absolutely no warrant for the belief that he was so deeply in love with Adèle Hugo that his whole life was affected by the blight of unrequited affection. On the contrary, if he was the *critique souriant* in the world of literature, he was the *critique gai* in the affairs of life.

For a time everything prospered with *Le Cénacle.* Then one member and then another grew lukewarm or directly seceded. Sainte-Beuve slowly diverged from the views he had allowed himself to expound, overborne as he had been by the charm of Victor and the fascination of Madame Hugo. The already famous poet does not seem to have had any particularly high appreciation of his critical friend as a man of letters; indeed, Sainte-Beuve was commonly regarded as nothing more than, at most, a conscientious and able critic, with genuine enough but mediocre original powers. In the first flush of intimacy, however, Hugo was as immoderate in his praise of his new acquaintance as was his wont in the matter of superlatives.[2] But when the "eagle," the "royal meteor," ceased from the making of critical honey, when, in giving a present of a book, he no more inscribed above his signature on the flyleaf such pleasant phrases as, "To the greatest lyrical inventor French poetry has known since Ronsard"—but, instead, uttered such words as "theatricality," "violence," "eccentricity," then there was a cooling of enthusiasm.

But about this time, and indirectly owing to the Hugo connection, two important things happened. A journalistic, a literary career was opened to Sainte-Beuve. He at once availed himself of the chance: so eager was he, indeed, that he left his surgeon's case at St. Louis' Hospital, where he had been a day-pupil, and it is said that he never went back for it. His vocation was in the art of literature, not in the science of medicine. As soon as he realised this, and saw his way to a possibility of living by the pen, he not only busied himself as a journalist, but prepared to undertake an ambitious literary task, a work of real magnitude. Probably if it had not been for Victor Hugo and Sainte-Beuve's ardent if transient romanticism, the admirable studies on "The French Poetry of the Sixteenth Century" would not have been written—then, at any rate, and in the form in which we know them. The critic had been impressed by the enthusiasm of Hugo and his circle for the early poets. He read, studied, and came to the conclusion that these were unworthily neglected. He discerned in them, moreover, the poetic ancestors of the enthusiastic members of *Le Cénacle*: both were unconventional, individual, comparatively simple. The series of studies which, as the result, appeared in the *Globe*, delighted the writer's friends and attracted no little share of literary attention; but it was not till the publication of them collectively in book form that Sainte-Beuve's name became widely known as that of a scholarly and above all an independent critic. It was the prevalent literary vogue to decry the pre-classicists, or, at least, to affirm that there was little of abiding worth prior to Molière, Racine, and Corneille. By insight, critical acumen, felicitous quotation, and a light and graceful while incisive style (not, however, characterised by the limpid delicacy and suppleness of his best manner, as in the *Causeries du Lundi*), he won many admirers and did good service to literature, and particularly to literary criticism.

From this time forward Sainte-Beuve's career was a prosperous one, chequered now and again indeed, but in the main happy and marvellously fruitful. For some years he dreamed of poetic fame; gradually he realized that his well-loved **"Life, Poetry, and Thoughts of Joseph Delorme,"** his **"Consolations,"** and his **"August Thoughts"** would never appeal to a public outside the literary world of Paris, and even there that they were assured of mere respect at most; and finally, he became convinced that it was neither as poet nor as novelist, but as critic, that he was to win the laurels of fame. To the last, however, he had a tender feeling for his poetic performances, and there was no surer way to his good graces than admiration of his poems. The most unsympathetic critic cannot regret Sainte-Beuve's having devoted so much time and so many hopes to those springtide blossoms of a summer that never came. At the least, they helped their author to a wide sympathy, to a deep insight, to that catholicity of taste which enabled him not only to enjoy for himself, but to interpret for others, the essential merits of a great number of poets,—writers so absolutely distinct as Virgil and Victor Hugo, Villon and William Cowper, Dante and Firdausi, Theocritus and Molière, Ronsard and Racine, and so forth.

When Dr. Véron founded in 1829 the *Revue de Paris,* the predecessor of the more famous *Revue des Deux Mondes,* he made haste to enrol Sainte-Beuve among his contributors. He thought it possible that the poet might make a great name, but he was quite convinced that the critic would become a prince of his tribe. The result of his trust was more than satisfactory. Although Sainte-Beuve was only five or six and twenty when he wrote his articles on Boileau, Racine, La Fontaine, Rousseau, André Chenier, and others, how admirable they are, and how well worth perusal even at the present date. In style, it is true, they are graceful and scholarly rather than winsome with individual charm, for the latter does not become a characteristic of his work till he has reached the noon of his maturity; but, even with this qualification, they are unquestionably delightful reading.

In the summer of 1830 Sainte-Beuve was in Normandy, at Honfleur, on a visit to his friend Ulric Guttinguer, when the July Revolution overthrew many institutions besides that of the old monarchy. With the advent of Louis Philippe arose schism among the brilliant staff of the *Globe.* Some maintained that the hour had come in which to cry "Halt" to further innovations; one or two wavered and talked of compromise; the more strenuous affirmed that there was as pressing need of progress as ever. Among the progressists was Sainte-Beuve, who had hurried back to Paris. The *Globe* became the organ of the Saint-Simonians; and though Sainte-Beuve never identified himself with the school of Saint-Simon, he fought valiantly as a free-lance by the side of its exponents. But, before this change in the destiny of the paper (for, after the split, it abruptly lost its place in the van of Parisian journals, and was sold at a loss to a sanguine experimentalist, who in turn speedily disposed of it to the Saint-Simonians), a tragi-comedy, in which Sainte-Beuve and his former good friend M. Dubois were the chief actors, occurred. The clash of opinions at the editorial office begat heated discussions, reproaches, taunts even. Dubois reminded Sainte-Beuve, in not very complimentary terms, of how he had given him a lift into the literary world: the critic made a scathing reply. The blood of all the Dubois boiled in the veins of the worthy editor, and he challenged Sainte-Beuve to mortal combat. So high did feeling run that the matter was really a serious one; though we may hesitate to accept the great critic's after-statement, that he went to the duel with the full intention of killing his adversary. It was the Joseph Delorme lying latent in Charles Augustin Sainte-Beuve who made this affirmation. The preliminaries of the duel were arranged with all circumspection; both antagonists made their wills and felt alternately heroic and despondent; and at last the hour came. It was a chill and wretched morning, for the rain came down in a steady pour. What was the astonishment of M. Dubois and the seconds of both principals to see Sainte-Beuve take up his position with his pistol in his right hand and his unfolded umbrella upheld by his left. To the remonstrances of the seconds, he protested that he was willing to be shot, if need be—but to be drenched, no! (*Je veux bien être tué; mais mouillé, non.*) Four shots were exchanged, and editor and critic remained unhurt. Neither their ill-success nor the rain damped their bloodthirstiness, however, and if it had not been for the firm remonstrances of the seconds, who declared that the demands of honour had been amply satisfied, one or other of the combatants would have suffered for his folly. Happily, this was Sainte-Beuve's sole martial experience. As one of his detractors long afterwards maliciously remarked, thenceforth he confined himself to stabbing with the pen, and to destroying literary reputations by a *causerie*.

Sainte-Beuve's renewed connection with the *Globe* was not of long duration, however. He had no interest but one of curiosity in the doctrines of the St. Simonians: neither more nor less than he, pre-eminently the hedonist of modern literature, felt in those of the enthusiasts who were bent upon reconciling democratic and radical politics with the most conservative Roman Catholicism. Although he knew and admired Lacordaire, Lamennais, and Montalembert, he refused to co-operate with them in the writing of articles for their journalistic organ, *L'Avenir.* These eminent men were not alone in their inability to understand Sainte-Beuve's mental temperament. They thought that because he seemed profoundly interested he was therefore a disciple. But the foremost critic of the day was a man of a passionate intellectual curiosity: his sovereign need was for new mental intellectual impressions. It was his insatiable curiosity into all manifestations of mental activity, as much as his exceptional receptivity, elasticity of sympathy, searching insight, and extraordinary synthetic faculty, that enabled him to become the master-critic. His catholicity of taste was his strength as, with others, it is often a source of weakness. It was not through inability to find anchorage in the sea of truth that his was a restless barque, with sails trimmed for seafaring again as soon as a haven was entered: it

was because he was a literary viking, consumed with a passion for mental voyaging and remote explorations—because he loved the deep sea, and found that even the profoundest inlets, the grandest bays, were too shallow for him to rest content therein.

> "No one," he says, "ever went through more mental vicissitudes than I have done. I began my intellectual life as an uncompromising adherent of the most advanced form of eighteenth-century thought, as exemplified by Tracy, Daunou, Lamarck, and the physiologists: *là est mon fonds véritable.* Then I passed through the psychological and doctrinaire school as represented by my confrères on the *Globe,* but without giving it my unqualified adhesion. For a time thereafter I had my liaison with the school of Victor Hugo, and seemed to lose myself in poetical romanticism. Later, I fared by the margins of St. Simonism, and, soon thereafter, liberal-Catholicism as represented by Lamennais and his group. In 1837, when residing at Lausanne, I glided past Calvinism and Methodism . . . but in all these wanderings I never (save for a moment in the Hugo period, and when under the influence of a charm) forfeited my will or my judgment, never pawned my belief. On the other hand, I understood so well both the world of books and that of men that I gave dubious encouragement to those ardent spirits who wished to convert me to their convictions, and indeed claimed me as one of themselves. But it was all curiosity on my part, a desire to see everything, to examine closely, to analyse, along with the keen pleasure I felt in discovering the relative truth of each new idea and each system, which allured me to my long series of experiments, to me nothing else than a prolonged course of moral physiology."

The short space at my command prevents my enlarging upon the hint conveyed in the last phrase, except to say that it is directly indicative to Sainte-Beuve's fundamental critical principle. To him criticism was literary physiology. With him a series of critiques meant a series of studies of—(1) a writer as one of a group, as the product of the shaping spirit of the time; (2) a writer as an individual, with all his inherited and acquired idiosyncrasies; (3) a writer as seen in his writings, viewed in the light of all ascertainable *personalia*; (4) the writings themselves, intrinsically and comparatively estimated. But, primarily, his essays were as much studies of character, of moral physiology, as of literary values.

After his withdrawal from the too sectarian *Globe,* Sainte-Beuve joined the staff of the *National*. With the ultra-Republican principles of that paper he had but a lukewarm sympathy, but his friend Armand Carrel, the editor, assured him that nothing would be expected from him save purely literary contributions. For about three years (1831-4) he remained on the staff of the *National,* and it was in the last year of the connection that he published his one novel, "Volupté." The book had a gratifying reception so far as wide notice was concerned; but it was generally adjudged to be unwholesome in tone and somewhat too self-conscious in style—though so beautiful a nature and so refined a critic as Eugénie de Guérin affirmed it to be a notable and even a noble book. That the prejudice against the author on account of it must have been strong is evident from the fact that when it was suggested to Guizot, then Minister of Public Instruction, that he should confer upon Sainte-Beuve a professional post at the Normal School, just vacant through the resignation of Ampère, he refused to appoint a man, howsoever brilliantly qualified, who had written such books as **"Joseph Delorme"** and "Volupté." Guizot was conscientiously scrupulous in this matter; and to show that he bore no personal ill-feeling, he appointed Sainte-Beuve to the secretaryship of an historical Commission, a post which the equally conscientious critic resigned in less than a year, on the ground that it was becoming or had become a mere sinecure. Another instance of his conscientiousness is his having declined, about the same date, the Cross of the Legion of Honour—a distinction he would have been proud to accept had he felt assured that it was offered in recognition of his literary merits, but upon which he looked suspiciously because it came when the Ministry of M. Molé and M. Salvandy, both personal friends of his, was in power. Three years after the publication of his novel, he issued the last of his purely imaginative productions, the **"Pensées d'Août."** In the same year (1837) he went to Switzerland, and having been invited by the Academy of Lausanne to deliver a course of lectures, he settled for a time in the pleasant Swiss town. There he delivered in all eighty-one lectures, the foundation of his famous and voluminous work on Port Royal (the story of the religious movement in the seventeenth century known as Jansenism), which occupied him intermittently for twenty years, is a monument of labour, research, and scrupulous historic fairness, and, though the least read, is one of his greatest achievements.

Both before and during his Swiss sojourn, and for about ten years thereafter, Sainte-Beuve was a regular contributor to the most famous magazine in Europe, the *Revue des Deux Mondes,* which had been founded in 1831, heir to the defunct *Revue de Paris.* The first number contains an article by him upon his friend George Farcy, a victim of the July Revolution; and thereafter appeared that long and delightful series of "Portraits Littéraires," studies of contemporary as well as of deceased writers, which not only gave him a European reputation as a leading critic, but ultimately won him his election to the French Academy. This signal good-fortune happened in 1845, on the occasion of the death of Casimir Delavigne; and the irony of circumstances was obvious to many in the fact that the eulogium on the new "immortal" had to be pronounced by the reluctant Victor Hugo, his immediate predecessor. It was a memorable date, that 17th of February; and if among the many "immortals" who have been raised to glory by the Academy there are relatively few whose fame will be imperishable, there are not many with juster claims to remembrance, though in widely different degrees, than the two authors who were then elected to the coveted honour, Prosper Merimée and Sainte-Beuve.

His periodical articles and his books (including five volumes of essays which he had contributed to the *Revue de Paris* and the *Revue des Deux Mondes*) brought him in a very moderate income; and it was not till 1840 that his means were materially improved. In that year he was appointed one of the keepers of the Mazarin Library. The appointment meant not only an increase of income, but a change of residence, for it comprised a suite of residential apartments at the Institute. Up to this time Sainte-Beuve had been living in two small rooms on the fourth floor of a house in a remote street—living extremely moderately, and in a seclusion almost monastic; indeed, he had even adopted the ruse of calling himself Joseph Delorme. In his new abode he was happy as well as comfortable, and thankfully embraced the opportunity of study and leisurely composition which his post afforded him. This pleasant state of affairs came to an end after the Revolution in 1848. A ridiculous charge of corruption was brought up against him by envious and inimical journalists and political adversaries; the ultra-Republicans accused him of having accepted bribes, hush-money, from the late Government. In vain Sainte-Beuve protested, and vainly he demanded a searching inquiry. The hint was taken up: everywhere he was abused, condemned, scathingly ridiculed. Even when, at last, the truth was revealed, and the greedy public learned that the amount of Sainte-Beuve's indebtedness was £4, and that that sum had been expended upon the alteration of a smoking chimney in his department of the Library, and the charge inadvertently entered in the official books simply under the heading "Ste. Beuve,"—even then there were many ungenerous souls who kept up the parrot cry of contumely. It somewhat unfortunately happened that about this time Sainte-Beuve left Paris, and of course there was at once a shout of triumph from his enemies. The real reasons for his departure were primarily financial, though no doubt he was not at all sorry to leave a city which had for the time being become so disagreeable to him—moreover, his distaste for the political issues then in full development was very strong. But after his resignation of his post at the Mazarin Library, which he had given in the heat of his indignation during the bribery controversy, he found that he would have to do something at once for a living. The political turmoil of 1848 was unfavourable for the pursuit of pure literature; and despite his high reputation, the editors whom he knew could not promise him a sufficiency of remunerative work until the times changed for the better. Accordingly, he very willingly accepted the Professorship of French Literature at the

University of Liège, offered to him by M. Rogier, the Belgian Minister of the Interior. Liège he found monotonous and provincial, but he stayed there for some time, and attracted more than local, more even than national attention by his preliminary course of lectures on the chronological history of French literature. There, also, he delivered the famous series on Chateaubriand and his Contemporaries, which amply demonstrated his independence as a critic, though many of his judgments and reservations brought a veritable storm of reproaches and angry recriminations about his ears. For a long time he was called an ingrate, a hypocrite, a resentful critic inspired by pique; but ultimately it was acknowledged that he had written the ablest and justest critique of the celebrated egotist and *poseur*. The fundamental reason of the attacks upon Sainte-Beuve was on account of his so-called inconsistency. True, among his early "Literary Portraits" was a flattering essay on Chateaubriand, but he was then under the magic charm of Madame Recamier, at whose house, Abbaye-aux-Bois, he heard read aloud in solemn state numerous extracts from the famous writer's unpublished "Memoirs." Moreover, Chateaubriand had inspired him with a temporary enthusiasm. When, with fuller knowledge of the man and his writings and with the "Correspondence" to boot, he found that he had been mistaken, he said so. The commonplace mind detests inconsistency with an almost rancorous hatred, oblivious of the fact that, as Emerson has said, only fools never change their views.

"Chateaubriand and his Literary Group under the Empire" is the work which marks the turning-point in Sainte-Beuve's genius. Thenceforth he was, in truth, the foremost critic of his time. In style as well as in matter, his productions from this time are masterpieces; and though there are some essays which could now be dispensed with, either because of the fuller light cast upon their subjects by later students, or on account of certain short-comings in the matter of prejudiced judgment, seven-tenths of them may be read to-day with much the same pleasure as they were perused two, three, or four decades ago.

Late in 1849 Sainte-Beuve, much to the chagrin of his Belgian friends and admirers, left Liège and returned to Paris. He was still hesitating how best to employ his pen, when he received a flattering but to him somewhat startling offer from his friend, Dr. de Véron, editor of *Le Constitutionnel*. This was to the effect that he should write a literary article for that paper every week. The reason of his perturbation was that hitherto he had always composed in leisurely fashion, and for papers or magazines whose readers were cultivated people, much more interested in literature than in politics and local news. Fortunately, M. de Véron overruled his scruples, and so there began that delightful and now famous series of literary critiques which the writer himself entitled *Causeries du Lundi*. He called them "Monday Chats," because each appeared on a Monday. For five days every week he "sported his oak," and occupied himself for twelve hours daily with the study of his subject and the writing of his article; on the sixth he finally revised it; Sunday was his sole holiday from his task. By next morning he was deep in the subject of the *Causerie* for the following week. It was the need to be concise and simple that did so much good to Sainte-Beuve's style. The charm of these *Causeries* can be appreciated alike by the most cultivated and the most casual reader. As two of his most eminent friends said of them, they were all the better insomuch as he had not had time to spoil them. From the end of 1849 to almost exactly twenty years later he wrote weekly, in the *Constitutionnel* or the *Moniteur,* with a single considerable interval, one of those brilliant, scholarly, fascinating articles,—collectively, a mass of extraordinarily varied work now embodied in fifteen goodly volumes.

When the *coup d'état* occurred, Sainte-Beuve gave his approval to the Empire. Thereby he won for himself no little unpopularity. His first materially disagreeable experience of this was when he proceeded to lecture at the Collège de France, to the Professorship of Latin Poetry at which he had been appointed. The students would have none of him. He was an Imperialist, a Government payee, he wrote in the official organ, *Le Moniteur.* He was literally hissed from the lecture-room, whence he retired in high dudgeon. Ultimately the lecture he had tried to deliver, and those which were to have followed, were published in a volume entitled "A Study on Virgil." The single intermission to his regular literary work, already alluded to, was during the four years when he held the post of Maître des Conférences at the Ecole Normale, at a salary of about £240. When he again took up literary journalism, after his resignation of his professional post, it was once more as a contributor to the *Constitutionnel*. He now made a fair income, for his weekly contributions to that journal brought him in, by special arrangement, an annual salary of £624. The *Causeries* were now called *Nouveaux Lundis,* "New Monday-Chats." In the main this series (begun in 1861) is equal to the *Causeries du Lundi,* though there are signs ever and again of lassitude. This might well be. The work was a steady and serious strain, and the great critic's health gradually became undermined. In 1865, when he was in his sixty-first year, he wrote: "I am of the age at which died Horace, Montaigne, and Bayle, my masters: so I am content to die." It was in this very year that good fortune came to him, and greatly relieved the mental strain under which his strength was waning. He was appointed to a Senatorship of the Second Empire, a position which secured him an annual income of £1200. His senatorial career was a dignified though not a brilliant one. He was ever on the side of true freedom, and was so independent in his attitude that he gave offence to those of his fellow-senators who were Imperialists and resented his championship of religious liberty. This muzzled wrath broke into clamorous fury at an incident concerning which an absurd fuss has been made. Sainte-Beuve had arranged to give a dinner to some of his friends, on the occasion of Prince Napoleon's departure from Paris, and, to suit that gentleman, had appointed Friday (which chanced to be Good Friday) as the night. The Prince, Edmond About, Gustave Flaubert, Rénan, Robin, and Taine duly joined their host and spent a pleasant evening. But the jackals were on the trail. A howl arose about a conspiracy to undermine the religious welfare of the nation; the diners were arraigned as impious debauchees; and Sainte-Beuve in particular was upbraided for his "scandalous orgy."

One other and much more serious annoyance troubled the latter years of Sainte-Beuve. This arose from his writing for *Le Temps* (whither he had transferred his *Causeries,* on account of a servile attempt to muzzle him on the part of the temeritous directorate of the *Moniteur*); and as *Le Temps* was hostile to the Government, M. Rouher and his confrères in the Ministry, as well as the whole Senate, thought it shameful that the critic should write for that journal, and did all in their power to force him into conformity with their views. But Sainte-Beuve was firmly independent, and emerged triumphantly from the ordeal.

For some years Sainte-Beuve had been in indifferent health. At last he became ill indeed, and his malady (the stone) caused him such extreme pain that he could only stand or lie when he had writing to do, as to sit was impossible. By the late summer of 1869 his case was desperate. Ultimately a perilous operation was made, but the patient sank under its effects. He died in his house in the Rue Mont Parnasse, on the 13th of October, at the age of sixty-four. Along with the biographical fragment found on his desk on the morrow of his death, which concluded with the celebrated words, "Voué et adonné à mon métier de critique, j'ai tâché d'être de plus en plus un bon et, s'il se peut, habile ouvrier"—"Devoted with all my heart to my profession as critic, I have done my utmost to be more and more a good and, if possible, an able workman;"—along with "Ma Biographie" were found written instructions as to his funeral. He directed that he should be buried in the Cemetery of Mont Parnasse beside his mother; that the ceremony should be as simple as practicable, and without religious rites or even a friendly oration. All due respect was paid to his wishes, and yet seldom has a funeral been attended with greater honour. It was not the Senator of the Second Empire who was carried to the grave, but the greatest of French critics, a writer of European renown. In the immense crowd which formed the voluntary procession—estimated at ten thousand—all political differences were forgotten:

uncompromising Imperialists and equally uncompromising Republicans walked in union for once, in company with nearly all who were distinguished in letters, science, or art. The only words uttered above his grave were more eloquent in their poignant simplicity than the most glowing exordium: "Farewell, Sainte-Beuve; farewell, our friend."

II.

Sainte-Beuve's literary career may be studied in three main phases. The novelist least claims our attention; the poet demands it; while as a critic he appears as of supreme importance.

"Volupté," so far, but, to a much greater extent, the **"Vie, Poésies, et Pensées de Joseph Delorme,"** may be taken as embodying some of the positive and many of the spiritual experiences of Sainte-Beuve's life. We have his own testimony to the fact that **"Joseph Delorme"** was "a pretty faithful representation of himself morally, but not in the biographical details." This alone would give a permanent interest to the book, as it is admittedly in some degree the autopsychical record of the most complex, brilliant, protean spirit of our time. No one indeed has yet limned Sainte-Beuve for us as he, for instance, has revealed the heart, mind, and soul of Pascal. Neither D'Haussonville, his biographer, nor any of his critics, French and English, has done more than introduce us to the author of so many inimitable *Causeries*; none of them has made us intimate with Sainte-Beuve himself, notwithstanding the array of authentic facts and suggestive hints which can now be marshalled. He is easiest to be discerned in his writings: not in this essay nor in that series of essays, not in the grave pages of "Port Royal" nor in the alluring byways of the "Lundis," neither in the sensitive poet of **"The Consolations"** nor in the austere pages of **"Pensées d'Août,"** not in that Gallic Werther, Amaury, the hero of "Volupté," not even in Joseph Delorme, but in all collectively. One is always being surprised in him. There is one man in Amaury, another in Joseph Delorme, a very different one in **"Pensées d'Août,"** a still more distinct one in the "Nouveaux Lundis," and in his single short tale, the charming "Christel," there are hints of a personality whose shadowy features rarely, if ever, haunt the corridors of the "Causeries." As a matter of fact, Sainte-Beuve became more and more reserved as he found himself deceived by the glowing perspectives of youth. Often he was consumed with a nostalgia for a country whence he was half-voluntarily, half-perforce an exile, the country of the Poetic Land where once he spent "six fleeting celestial months,"[3] as a native of which he would fain be regarded even in the remote days when he found himself an alien among those whom he yearned to claim as brothers. Thenceforth the man shrank more and more behind the writer. The real Sainte-Beuve was no doubt less recluse in the days when he was a member of *Le Cénacle,* when he was one of the sprightliest in the Hugo circle, and laughed with de Vigny and sighed with Lamartine, debated with Hugo, and flirted with Adèle. But even then his nature could not have been transparent to all, otherwise Alfred de Musset would not have drawn his picture of him as sitting somewhat apart in the shadow, rhyming a sonnet to a demoiselle's cap, or a lyric to his mistress's eyebrow. Truly, as he himself says, in the preface to his **"Poésies Complètes,"** almost all of us have within ourselves a second self ("nous avons presque tous en nous un homme double").

The **"Vie, Poésies, et Pensées de Joseph Delorme"** has been put forward as an effort on the part of Sainte-Beuve to introduce into France a poetic literature as simple, fresh, and spontaneous as that of the naturalistic poets of England, and of Cowper and Wordsworth in particular. Readers of that notable book will find it difficult to perceive any direct Wordsworthian influence, though the author makes clear his great admiration for the English poet and his school. Joseph Delorme, in fact, is a cousin-german to Don Juan, closely akin to Chateaubriand's René, the French half-brother to Goethe's Werther. He is the most literary of the family, but while he is as sentimental as René, and as melancholy as Werther, he has not the frank debonnaire licentiousness of Don Juan. He is morbid in his thoughts and in his desires. The fellowship of a Tom Jones would have done him good, the laughing Juan, even, would have acted as a tonic. "The road of excess leads to the palace of wisdom," says Blake; but the poet-visionary did not mean the kind of excess in which the too introspective Joseph indulged. He said one good thing, however, for which he will be remembered—when he spoke of his dread of marriage because of its restrictions upon his "rather rude philanthropy" (a euphemism for "free morals"), and defined it as *une egoisme à deux personnes.*

Rousseau and Goethe were the literary godfathers of Joseph Delorme, who was born when the author of his being was only five-and-twenty. The nature of the book is indicated by a passage from Senancour's "Obermann," which exactly strikes the key-note: "I have seen him, I have pitied him; I respected him; he was unhappy and virtuous. He had no transcendent misfortunes; but, on entering life, he found himself in a mesh of distastes and satieties ('il s'est trouvé sur une longue trace de dégoûts et d'ennuis'): there he is still, there he has dwelt, there he has grown old ere age has come upon him, there he has literally buried himself." The Adolphe of "Obermann," indeed, is but a more melancholy and a more austere "double" of Joseph.

The following lines are fairly representative of the dominant sentiment of the book.

"Vœu"

"Tout le jour du loisir; rêver avec des larmes;
Vers midi, me coucher à l'ombre des grands charmes;
Voir la vigne courir sur mon toit ardoisé,
Et mon vallon riant sous le coteau boisé;
Chaque soir m'endormir en ma douce folie,
Comme l'heureux ruisseau qui dans mon pré s'oublie;
Ne rien vouloir de plus, ne pas me souvenir,
Vivre à me sentir vivre! . . . Et la mort peut venir."[4]

But a healthier note is often struck, as in the blithe strain wedded to a pathetic thought, "Ce ciel restera bleu Quand nous ne serons plus;" often, too, one fresh and haunting, as in

"Et dans ses blonds cheveux, ses blanches mains errantes—Tels deux cygnes nageant dans les eaux transparentes." . . .[5]

The **"Life, Poetry, and Thoughts"** are worth reading; the book contains much that is interesting, no little that is suggestive, not infrequently thoughts, lines, and passages of genuine beauty. But it can enthral only those who are enjoying the exquisite sentimentalism of adolescence; ere long it will interest only the student of a certain literary epoch, the epoch begun by Rousseau, that finds its acme in Byron, which knows its autumn in Werther, that has its grave in the René of Chateaubrians, its brief phantasmal second life in Joseph Delorme. The poetry in it is often sterile, and is frequently forced, self-conscious, obtrusively sedate in imagery, occasionally even is markedly derivative. We find Sainte-Beuve the poet much better worth listening to in **"Les Consolations."** In point of style there is not very much difference, though a greater dexterity is manifest, a more delicate metrical tact, perhaps also a more unmistakably natural note. But there is no more kinship between the author of **"Les Consolations"** and Joseph Delorme than between Don Juan and Manfred. The volume was the product of the religious mysticism which underlay Sainte-Beuve's mental robustness—a trait which allured him often by dangerous pitfalls, but also enabled him to understand so well the great religious writers of whom he still remains the most sympathetic as well as the most brilliant exponent. It seemed ultra-saintly to some of those who read it on its appearance. Béranger annoyed the author by some sly disparagement; Prosper Merimée cynically smiled at what he took to be a literary ruse; Gustave Planche and others gleefully whetted their vivisectionary knives. On the other hand, it was for the most part well received by the critics, and no cruel witticism like that of Guizot on its predecessor (that Joseph Delorme was "a Werther turned Jacobin and sawbones") went echoing through Paris. The public remained indifferent, but the poet was gratified when Chateaubriand wrote him a letter of praise, with a characteristic "Écoutez votre génie, Monsieur;" when Hugo and Alfred de Vigny waxed enthusiastic; when Béranger sent an epistle of kindly criticism; and when

Lamartine unbosomed himself as follows:—"Yesterday I re-read the **'Consolations'** . . . they are ravishing. I say it and I repeat it: it is this that I care for in French poetry of this order. What truth, what soul, what grace and poetry! I have wept, I who never weep." (This must have amused Sainte-Beuve, if not then, later. The sentimental Lamartine was always weeping over one thing or another, and the "J'en ai pleure, moi qui oncques ne pleure," is as little apt as though Mr. Pickwick were to say "I have smiled, who never smile."). . . . It was at this time, the period wherein **"The Consolations"** were produced, that Sainte-Beuve dreamed upon Latmos and believed that the goddess whom he loved was going to reward his passion. The "celestial months" passed, but they were ever an oasis to which he delighted to return in memory. He even wished, in later years, that those who desired to know him should seek and find him, a happy Dryad flitting through the shadowy vales and sunlit glades of the woodlands of song. No doubt the real Sainte-Beuve is as much in this book of verse as in any other of his library of volumes, but it is the Sainte-Beuve of a certain period, and even then only one of two selves. **"The Consolations"** always remained his favourite volume. It contains a great deal of gracious and even beautiful verse, in style often clear as a trout-stream, fresh and fragrant as a May-meadow, though even here, as certainly with his other "poésies," one is inclined to say of him, in the words of his own Joseph Delorme, that he had not sufficiently "the ingenuousness of deep faith, the instinctive and spontaneous cry of passionate emotion." Some of the **"Consolations"** are extremely Wordsworthian— how closely, indeed, he could enter into the spirit of the great English poet is evident in the following free translation of that most lovely sonnet beginning, "It is a beauteous Evening, calm and free":—

> "C'est un beau soir, un soir paisible et solennel;
> A la fin du saint jour, la Nature en prière
> Se tait, comme Marie à genoux sur la pierre,
> Qui tremblante et muette écoutait Gabriel:
>
> La mer dort; le soleil descend en paix du ciel;
> Mais dans ce grand silence, au-dessus et derrière,
> On entend l'hymne heureux du triple sanctuaire,
> Et l'orgue immense où gronde un tonnerre éternel.
>
> O blonde jeune fille, à la tête baissée,
> Qui marches près de moi, si ta sainte pensée,
> Semble moins qui la mienne adorer ce moment,
> C'est qu'au sein d'Abraham vivant toute l'année,
> Ton ame est de prière, à chaque heure, baignée;
> C'est que ton cœur recite un divin firmament."

This, of course, is but indifferent verse after the superb original, but it shows both how Sainte-Beuve was inspired by Wordsworth, and how ably he too could write, albeit as a translator, in simple and unaffected strains. Although the second, third, and fourth lines bear no resemblance to

> "The holy time is quiet as a Nun
> Breathless with adoration, . . ."

and the rest of the version is only in a lesser degree unliteral, it must be borne in mind that the full beauty of the original is untranslatable, and that the French poet strove to convey to the French reader the same impression as an English reader would gain from the English sonnet. However, the importance of this and other experiments is not to be overlooked. Many of the younger poets owe much, directly or indirectly, to the lesson taught by Sainte-Beuve in what a hostile critic has called his "Anglo-French metrical essays."

Yet, while it is true that the man is perhaps to be seen most clearly in his poetry,—"it is in following the poet that we find the man," as M. Anatole France says,— even here he is an evasive, an uncertain personality. The strange mixture of a sensuousness that is at times almost sensual, a mysticism which would suit a religious enthusiast, a clarity of thought and an exquisite sense of the beauty of precision and artistic form, a frequent remoteness of shaping emotion, coupled with keen perception of the sovereign value of that resistless formative power which makes the creatures of the imagination more real than the actual beings about us,⁶—all this, along with his complex style, which now is simple, now is heated with fires unlit of the sun, and again is involved, obscure almost, wrought to an excessive finish, *tourmenté,* makes Sainte-Beuve the poet a profoundly puzzling as well as interesting study. In his last volume of verse, particularly, he is, as one of his critics has said, "tourmenté à l'excès, souvent d'une étrangeté qui déconcerte." But it is quite wrong to assert, as has been affirmed more than once, that Sainte-Beuve's poetic melancholy, the undertone of each of his three books, is assumed. One writer in *Le Temps* (or *Le Figaro*) recently found a proof of this literary insincerity in some remarks made by the critic in his old age, remarks treating lightly his former mysticism, with an avowal that "his odours of the sacristy were really meant for the ladies." "I have been guilty of a little Christian mythology in my time," he admitted, "but it all evaporated long ago. It was for me, as the swan to Leda's wooer, merely a means to reach fair readers and to win their tender regard." But this, quite obviously, is mere badinage. If there be any truth in it at all, it is one of those remote filaments of fact which go to the weaving of the web of truth; nothing more. His melancholy was a genuine sentiment, which found expression differently at divers times. Even in his latest essays, when his natural geniality is allowed free play, it is traceable in those occasional bitternesses and abrupt dislikes, those half-weary and yet mordant "asides," which show that the man was by no means wholly absorbed in the critic. He himself, as we have seen, attributed this fundamental strain of sadness in his nature to his mother's early widowhood. "My mother bore me in mourning and grief," he says; "I have been as it were soaked in sorrow and bathed in tears—and, well, I have often attributed to this maternal grief the melancholy of my young years, and my disposition to weariness of mind and spirit."[7] But, as M. France has well said, it was another mother, the Revolution, who inoculated him with the malady of the age—that malady of which M. Taine, the most brilliant of the disciples of Sainte-Beuve, has alluded to so eloquently: "It was then that the malady of the age appeared, the spiritual inquietude typified by Werther and Faust, almost identical with that which, in a somewhat similar time, agitated men at the beginning of the century. I would call it the discontent with present horizons, the vague desire after a higher beauty and an ideal happiness, a pathetically sad aspiration towards the infinite. Man suffers in doubting and yet he doubts: he tries to recapture his lost beliefs, they are really in his hand." (*Hist. de la Lit. Anglaise,* Tome iii.) This melancholy nature, induced by the spirit of the age, derived now from this source and now from that, and occasionally insincere, is most marked in its least genuine aspects in the **"Pensées d'Août."** There is nothing in it so fine, in the poetry of melancholy, as the **"Lines"** in the **"Consolations"** (inscribed to Mme. V. H.; no other, of course, than the immaculate Adéle Hugo) beginning

"Plus fraîche que la vigne au bord d'un antre frais."

The chief poem in the collection, entitled **"Monsieur Jean,"** is an ill-considered attempt at a didactic novelette in verse. The author did not so regard it: he believed that he had wooed and won *Musa Pedestris,* and had given his poetry the tone of serene wisdom. Jean is a natural son of Jean Jacques Rousseau, and is a simple, gentle creature, eager to expiate in his remote village, by piety and endless good deeds, what he cannot but regard as the disastrous glory of his father. But the poet's failure is a signal instance of the folly of metrical didactics. "Jean" bored the reading public, who combined in awarding the **"Pensées d'Août"** what its author called a really savage reception. In this book, more than anywhere else in his poetical writings, is true what Matthew Arnold said of him, that he lacked something of flame, of breath, of pinion: here, more than elsewhere, his poems *côtoient la prose*—coasted perilously near the land of prose. As a matter of fact, the book was a complete failure: it caused the pendulum of his poetic repute to swing back, and to be caught up and never let go again. Moreover, its reception stifled the poet in Sainte-Beuve. It is a poignant personal note that underlies his famous remark, "Every one contains a dead poet in his soul."

But, after all, even the most reluctant reader of Sainte-Beuve as a poet cannot, if he be minded to criticism, afford to overlook this important section of the life-work of the great critic. It is necessary, indeed, not only to an understanding of the man but of the writer. For in these *Poésies Complètes,* to quote the words of a sympathetic critic, "Se peint l'âme la plus curieux, la plus sagace, et la plus compliquée qu'une vieille civilisation ait jamais produite"—"is revealed the most inquiring, the most sagacious, the most complex spirit" to whom the age has given birth.

It is not feasible here, in the limited space at my command, to attempt any analysis of "Volupté," Sainte-Beuve's sole effort in fiction save the short tale "Christel." Some day when a critical historian, curious as to the main-springs of, let us hope, the long since cured *maladie dis siècle,* will occupy himself with the fortunes of Werther and René, Adolphe and Amiel, he will not omit to include in that strange company the amorously sentimental and sentimentally melancholic Amaury. For myself I admit I find that youth quite as entertaining as either of the more famous offspring of Goethe or Chateaubriand.

As a historian Sainte-Beuve showed remarkable aptitude, but it is as an historian of mental phases, episodes, and general events, rather than of the ebb and flow of outer weal, the conflict of kingdoms and the fortunes of internecine warfare, the rise of this house or that dynasty, the ruin of cities and the growth of States. He could have been neither a Gibbon nor a Niebuhr, neither a Guizot nor a Mommsen, not even a Macaulay or an Ampère; but he is in the domain of historical literature what the author of "The History of the Rise of Morals in Europe" and "The History of Rationalism" is in the sphere of ethical research, though, of course, there is a radical distinction between the method of Mr. Lecky and that of the author of "Port Royal." To the accomplishment of this immense undertaking Sainte-Beuve brought his inexhaustible patience, his almost unerring faculty of wise discrimination, his precise and scientific method of analysis and exposition, and a style which gave wings to words yoked to dry and apparently outworn subjects. Still, the work is not one that will be widely read a generation hence. Only exhaustive and definitively accurate detail could save from oblivion so lengthy a history on so remote and secondary a subject; and though in its day "Port Royal" fulfilled the need even of the student, scholars now seek their information in the less ambitious but more thorough "studies" of a score of specialists. It may safely be said, however, that no student of Pascal, or of the religious movement in the seventeenth century, will ever be able to dispense with Sainte-Beuve's masterly work.

As the literary critic, as the first who brought into the analysis and exposition of literature the methods of exact science, Sainte-Beuve must always have a high place in the literary history of the nineteenth century. Ultimately, it may be that his chief glory will lie in his having been the pioneer of a new literary art, in his having been the torch-bearer who gave light and direction to many, not heeding much whether his torch, its service done, should thereafter be seldom seen and rarely sought. His example has been of almost inestimable value, and not among his countrymen only. All of the foremost living critics of France, from the eldest and most brilliant, Henri Taine, to Paul Bourget, the late Émile Hennequin, Ernest Tissot, and Charles Morice, have learned much from him—some a life-long lesson, others guiding hints only. As for our own critics, it is, broadly speaking, scarcely to be gainsaid that with us criticism as an art has no acknowledged existence. There are brilliant exceptions who prove the rule, but they are few and their limitations are so marked as for the most part to deserve the epithet insular.[8] As for the ordinary criticism in our journals and weekly papers, the less said about it the better for our complacency, since little of good as against a great deal of reprobation would have to be uttered. A change must soon come. Personally, I doubt if it will occur till our utterly mistaken and mischievous system of anonymous reviewing—whether in magazines, weekly papers, or journals—is given up in favour of the more just, more valuable, in every way better habit in vogue among our neighbours. It would be ridiculous to urge that there is no sound and honest criticism among us; but it is hypocritical for those who know better to pretend that unsigned critiques are as free from jealousy, spite, and all uncharitableness, as, for the greater part, these would be if it were not for the shield of anonymity. It has come to this pass, that no one occupied in the literary life ever thinks of paying attention to unsigned reviews, be they in the foremost weeklies or in the provincial press, unless the writers be known. Praise and blame, enthusiasm and indifference—each has to be accepted suspiciously. The result is that literary criticism, instead of being an interpreter and a guide, now to warn and now to allure, is a maker of confusion, a will-o'-the-wisp of judgment, and is no longer hearkened to or followed as of yore. The real cure for this lamentable state of affairs is the cultivation of the literary sentiment, of the feeling of the sacredness of literature; and, thereafter, of scrupulous heed, both on the part of the critics and of the cultured public, for the exemplification of criticism *as an art*. Mere book-noticing, of course, like the poor, we shall have always with us: a circumstance not incompatible with the growth and culture of literary criticism. But possibly the best, perhaps the only feasible means to induce this fortunate result, in the first instance, would be the universal adoption of signed and responsible reviews.

In the "Notes et Rémarques" at the end of the sixteenth volume of the *Causeries du Lundi* occurs the following: "I have given no one the right to say—He belongs to us (*Il est des nôtres*)." It is this absolute independence, this many-sidedness of Sainte-Beuve, which is one of the secrets of his success. He can be an intellectual comrade of every poet, from the austere Dante to the gay Villon; of every wit and satirist, from Rabelais to Rivarol; of every builder up of ethical systems and every iconoclast of creeds, of the ancient Latins and Greeks as well as of the modern Germans and English; and, moreover, at all times a comrade with an eye to the exact value of and pleasure derivable from his companion of the hour. Here, it seems to me, is his strength and his weakness. He can be *bon camarade* with every one, but he is never able to forget that he is the observer of the thoughts, speech, action, and principles of those with whom he fares. He has charming ruses for evading detection. He will laugh gaily, he will smile, he will allude to this or that scarcely pertinent matter, he will altogether diverge from his subject, he will reintroduce it casually, and possibly dismiss it lightly, and yet he will have had but one aim in view from the outset,—to analyse and estimate the writings of his author, to discover the shaping circumstances of the latter as an individual, to strip him of what is extraneous, and reveal him as he really is,—in a word, to portray him in one composite photograph, to give us a likeness of the man as well as of the author which shall be none the less true because it resolves into definite features the fleeting and indeterminate traits which we perceive now in the one now in the other. He is no believer in the doctrine of the isolation of an author from his writings; it seems as absurd to him as it would be to assert that no notice of the prism may be taken in a study of the chemic action of light passing therethrough. But, on the other hand, the question arises if Sainte-Beuve is not apt to be misled by his own theory, having to make positive affirmations based on facts necessarily in some degree suppositions. Herein is the hidden reef of literary psychology, and even so great a critic as M. Taine is occasionally missuaded by semblances which he takes for actualities. The elder writer is content to be a careful scientific observer, and delights in artistic demonstration of his newly perceived and otherwise accumulated facts: M. Taine, M. Bourget, and the later literary analysts go further, and wish to reach down through facts to their origins, and to the primary impulsion again of the influences which moulded those origins—and, finally, by cumulative verification to transform hypothesis into demonstrable truth. But, fundamentally, both means are identical; the basis of each is the adoption, for literary research, of the method of exact science. Sainte-Beuve hated fixed judgments; he had none of the arrogances of his critical kindred. He neither said himself, nor cared to hear others saying, that a book was definitively good or definitively bad; he loved the *nuances,* the delicacies and subtleties of criticism, as much as he disliked rigid formulas. Yet his studies in literary psychology, as M. Paul Bourget would call them, are not only acute but are generally profoundly conclusive: it is his suave and winsome manner that makes many think he is too complaisant to be critical, though he has himself said, that in his "Portraits" the praise is conspicuous and the criticism inobtrusive— "dans mes *Portraits,* le plus souvent la louange est extérieure, et la critique intestine." The *man* himself continually evades us, but the *critic* is always trustworthy. He has, to a phenomenal degree, the delicate *flair* which detects the remotest perfume amid a confusion of fragrances; he knows how to isolate it, how to detach it, how to delight us with it—and then when we are just upon the verge of deeper enjoyment he proves that the scent is not so exquisite in itself after all, but owes much to the blending of the exhalations of neighbouring flowers and blossoms and herbs. While we are still wavering between conviction and disenchantment, he explains that it has this peculiarity or that, because of the soil whence it derives its nurture, a thin rocky earth or loam of the valley. Then, finally, lest we should turn aside disappointedly, he tells us something about it which we had but half noticed, praises fragrance and bloom again, and with a charming smile gives us the flower to take with us, perchance to press and put away, like sweet-lavender or wild-thyme, a hostage against oblivion of a certain hour, a certain moment of fresh experience.

What range for one man to cover! Let one but glance at the contents of all these volumes: besides this novel, these three collections of poems, here are seven volumes of "Port Royal" (containing a multitude of vignettes and sketches as well as carefully-drawn pictures and portraits), fifteen volumes of the "Causeries du Lundi," volumes upon volumes of "Nouveaux Lundis," "Portraits Littéraires," "Portraits des Contemporains," "Derniers Portraits" and "Portraits des Femmes," this "Tableau historique et critique de la Poésie Française et du Théâtre Français au xvie Siècle," these miscellaneous essays and studies. Then those richly suggestive "Notes," and "Thoughts," and "Remarks" must be added, and the recent volume edited by M. Jules Troubat, Sainte-Beuve's latest secretary and "good friend with qualifications," and an "Introduction" here and an "Étude" there. Let us take up M. Charles Pierrot's "Table Générale et Analytique" (forming the appendical volume to the *Causeries du Lundi*), and glance through his painstaking analyses. Sainte-Beuve, we find, has written no fewer than nineteen separate studies on celebrities of the sixteenth century, among them personages so distinct as Rabelais and Casaubon, Marie Stuart and Montaigne; seventy-four upon the great spirits of the seventeenth century, including more than one careful essay upon Pascal; forty-three upon the men of the eighteenth century, comprising Le Sage and Voltaire and Vauvenargues, Rousseau and Diderot and Grimm, men of letters, men of science, philosophers, priests, kings, and diplomatists; thirty, again, upon those who flourished in the reign of Louis XVI., with vivid portraits of Malesherbes and Necker, Rivarol and Beaumarchais, Condorcet and Bernardin de St. Pierre; eleven

not less thorough *études* upon the rarest spirits of the Revolution, Mirabeau and La Fayette, André Chenier, Mme. Roland; and, at last, those brilliant essays upon the makers of our own century, from Napoleon and other generals on the one hand, and from Chateaubriand and Joubert on the other, to Gustave Flaubert, and Taine, and Théodore de Banville;—in all, one hundred and five "portraits" of men and women of the most divers genius. To these (close upon three hundred, including the not infrequent two or even three essays upon one individual) must be added the studies upon foreign writers of ancient and modern times,—Theocritus and Firdausi, Virgil and Dante, Frederic the Great, Goethe, Gibbon, Cowper,—not to speak of a score or so of essays on various themes, from "Du Génie Critique" in the "Portraits Littéraires" (Tome i.) to "Du Roman Intime" in the "Portraits des Femmes."

It will readily be understood, therefore, that the essays which succeed these introductory words represent but a fragment of the critical work of Sainte-Beuve. The reader must be generous to the translators, moreover, for the great critic's style does not lend itself to easy reproduction. Yet, though something essential of the charm is lost, enough remains to make a translation from him well worth while; the matter is there, though the charm of manner may escape the ablest interpreter. I cannot honestly say that in these essays Sainte-Beuve is quite as fascinating as in the original; yet they will certainly serve to give the English reader not merely some comprehension of the intellectual range and insight of Sainte-Beuve, but some idea also of his grace of style and individual charm. They have been selected with a view to show his many-sidedness, his genuine sympathies with the most antagonistic types, his delightful method, his guiding principle.

I should like to conclude with a selection from the several hundred detached "Pensées" of Sainte-Beuve which are often so beautiful, so clever, or so witty, which are always so suggestive; but that is impracticable now. Those who would become more intimate with the man as well as with the writer should turn, in particular, to the two hundred and more "Notes et Pensées" in the eleventh volume of the *Causeries du Lundi,* and to the richly suggestive posthumous collection, "Les Cahiers de Sainte-Beuve." For "finis," however, I may select one, peculiarly apt to the great critic himself, as well as to the epoch. It is the cxxvii. of the "Notes et Pensées:" "Great things may be accomplished in our days, great discoveries for example, great enterprises; but these do not give greatness to our epoch. Greatness is shown especially in its point of departure, in its flexibility, in its thought."

Notes

1. "Quelques biographes veulent bien ajouter que c'est alors que je fus *présenté* à Alfred de Musset. Ces messieurs n'ont aucune idée des dates. Mus-

set avait alors à peine dix-huit ans. Je le rencont-rai un soir chez Hugo, car les familles se connais-saient; mais on ignorait chez Hugo que Musset fît des vers. C'est ce lendemain matin, après cette soirée, que Musset vint frapper à ma porte. Il me dit en entrant: 'vous avez hier récité des vers; eh bien, j'en fais et je viens vous les lire.' Il m'en récita de charmants, un peu dans le goût d'André Chénier. Je m'empressai de faire part à Hugo de cette heureuse recrue poétique. On lui demanda désormais des vers à lui-même, et c'est alors que nous lui vîmes faire ses charmantes pièces de *l'Andalouse* et du Départ pour la chasse (*le Lever*)." After this explicit statement that at the Hugo's no one knew that the youthful Musset wrote verse; that the latter sought out the critic, read him some of his poems, which his courteous auditor found charming; and that Sainte-Beuve made haste to announce to Hugo that a promising poetic recruit had come to the fore;—after this, it is absurd to allude to Sainte-Beuve as prejudiced against Musset from the first on account of pique.

2. In Mr. Frank T. Marzials' admirable "Life of Victor Hugo" there is the following allusion to Sainte-Beuve: "There is one of [Hugo's] odes, written in December 1827, and inscribed 'To my friend, S. B.,' in which he addresses that young gentleman as an 'eagle,' a 'giant,' a 'star,' and exhorts him to make the acquaintance of lightning, and to roll through the realms of thought like a 'royal meteor' with trailing locks. We, who chiefly know a later Sainte-Beuve, can scarcely recognise him in the character of a [poetic] comet; and, even then, he himself . . . must sometimes have smiled at these grandiose epithets. Sitting somewhat apart in the shadow, and rhyming a sonnet to a white cap, or an eye of jet—this is how he lives in Alfred de Musset's reminiscences, and I take it the sketch is truer to nature."

3. *Causeries du Lundi,* Tome xvi.

4. A Wish

> "Leisure all the livelong day; to dream, with tears; towards noon, to rest in the shade of great elms; to see the vine-branches trail over my slated roof, and my own little valley smiling under its wooded slope: to fall asleep each evening rapt in my sweet folly, as the happy brook which loses itself in my meadow: to wish for nothing more, to remember nought, in a word, to live as I would fain live! . . . Then death may come!"

5.
> "Through her fair hair her white hands wandering,
> Like two swans swimming in transparent waters." . . .

6. In his own words he sought to arrive "at that particularity and at that precision which causes the creations of our mind to become altogether ours and to be recognised as ours."

7. *Vide* "Correspondance de Sainte-Beuve:" Lettre à M. de Frabière, 25th June 1862.

The "melancholy of my young years" must not be taken too literally. Sainte-Beuve's boyhood seems to have been a happy one. He had love affairs when he was a small child, moreover, if we may take his own word for it. In one of his poems he has the following Boulogne reminiscences:—

> "N'eus-je pas ma Camille,
> Douce blonde au front pur, paisible jeune fille,
> Qu'au jardin je suivais, la dévorant des yeux?
> N'eus-je pas Mathilde, au parler sérieux,
> Qui remplaça Camille, et plus d'une autre encore?"

"Had I not my Camille, sweet white-browed fair maid, calm damsel, whom I followed to the garden, devouring her with my eyes? Had I not Mathilde, who replaced Camille, and many others beside?" "Oh, these nursemaids, these nurse-maids!" the precocious young *roué* may have thought, shaking his curly head, ere he went to play on the sands or upon the old ramparts.

8. I should like to draw attention here to one of the younger and lesser known critics who are working towards a new science of literary criticism: I allude to Mr. John M. Robertson, whose "Essays towards a Critical Method" (*Fisher Unwin*) is one of the few English studies in literary criticism deserving special attention. No one can read this book of Mr. Robertson's, or Émile Hennequin's "La Critique Scientifique," without realising how limitedly apprehended this new art of criticism is in England.

J. Warshaw (essay date March 1910)

SOURCE: Warshaw, J. "Sainte-Beuve's Influence on Matthew Arnold." *Modern Language Notes* 25, no. 3 (March 1910): 77-8.

[*In the following essay, Warshaw discusses the influence of Sainte-Beuve on the English poet and critic Matthew Arnold and argues that Arnold would have benefitted by absorbing more of Sainte-Beuve's sense of tolerance and rejection of overarching generalizations.*]

> "L'art de la critique . . . dans son sens le plus pratique et le plus vulgaire, consiste à savoir lire judicieusement les auteurs, et à apprendre aux autres à les lire de même, en leur épargnant les tâtonnements et en leur dégageant le chemin."

The duty of English criticism is "simply to know the best that is known and thought in the world, and by in its turn making this known, to create a current of true and fresh ideas."

A careful collation of the critical works of Arnold and Sainte-Beuve would show an astonishing number of parallelisms of the kind indicated above. Often, the similarity is not in the thought only, but even in the words. A study of Sainte-Beuve leaves no doubt as to Arnold's parentage in literary criticism.

It sometimes occurred to Arnold to present continental subjects to that dense mass of Philistines in whom he was trying to "inculcate *intelligence,* in a high sense of the word." What more simple than that he should pitch upon Maurice de Guérin, upon Eugénie de Guérin, upon Joubert, because Sainte-Beuve had written illuminating, and above all, handy little articles on them? Also, there was the advantage of maintaining an appearance of recondite wisdom before his benighted people: and Arnold was not above such trivial vanities.

In 1859, Arnold was enjoying the liberating influence of a "certain circle of men, perhaps the most truly cultivated in the world," for whom he had the deepest respect. This circle existed in Paris, and Sainte-Beuve was the center of it. At a dinner given him by the latter, Arnold found him "in full vein of conversation, which, as his conversation is about the best to be heard in France, was charming." Sainte-Beuve's translation of Arnold's poem on Obermann gives our English poet-critic an undeniable thrill of satisfaction. There was, besides, the practical consideration that Sainte-Beuve's praise can carry "one's name through the literary circles of Europe in a way that no English praise can carry it." Arnold, at this time, was thirty-seven years of age; Sainte-Beuve, fifty-five. The broad-shouldered dean of literary criticism, who looked like an Italian prelate, was, to our sturdy Anglo-Saxon lay preacher, a lifelong repository of the traditions and mysteries of the critical faith.

The truth is that Arnold could not have chosen a better master. As a literary critic, Arnold was lacking in ideas: and in Sainte-Beuve, he delved in the richest of mines. It was from him that he drew his notions of curiosity,— the "disinterested love of a free play of the mind on all subjects, for its own sake,"—literary urbanity, charm: it was from him that he learned the value of creating "a current of true and fresh ideas": it was from his teachings that he obtained his definitive opinion as to the critic's rôle, namely, the "communicating fresh knowledge, and letting his own judgment pass along with it,—but insensibly, and in the second place, not the first, as a sort of companion and clue, not as an abstract law-giver": and it was in his works that he found the expression of the critic's highest qualities,—tolerance and justness of spirit.

What Arnold was never able to take to heart was Sainte-Beuve's conviction that generalizations of any kind are both unjust and injurious. For that reason, Arnold spent

himself, fulminating against British Philistinism. If he had really assimilated his master's beliefs as to tolerance, intellectual flexibility, justness of spirit, he could not have spoken of "a wave of more than American vulgarity, moral, intellectual, social, preparing to break over us"; nor could he have passed this crass judgment on Tennyson:

> "I do not think Tennyson a great and powerful spirit in any line,—as Goethe was in the line of modern thought, Wordsworth in that of contemplation, Byron even in that of passion; and unless a poet, especially at this time of day, is that, my interest in him is only slight, and my conviction that he will not finally stand high is firm."

It is not, then, from him that we should expect the following charming and conscientious passage,—which occurs in a letter written by Sainte-Beuve to M. Ratisbonne:

> "I have been told that you have attributed to me a joke about children; 'I love children above all when they cry,—because then they are taken away.' Not only have I never uttered such a jest, but I could not have done so.
>
> "I believe that I have always avoided including in a general blame or aversion whole classes or categories, whether of nations, men, or persons.
>
> "How could I have done so with children?"

Sainte-Beuve singled out the individual. That was the great point of his method. Arnold tried to imitate him in this, but was only partially successful, and then, chiefly, in foreign subjects. Like the preacher in the pulpit, he preferred to deal with masses.

It is a pity that Matthew Arnold was not so situated in life as to come into greater intimacy with the "first of living critics," as he calls Sainte-Beuve. A more frequent contact with him would have changed Arnold's critical method completely. With a style of such ease, fluency, grace, and firmness as Arnold's, it would have required only a little more real flexibility of mind and a more comprehensive groundwork of facts to have left us a body of criticism classical not merely in form, but in substance as well. Arnold wrote to his wife, "I think he (Sainte-Beuve) likes me, and likes my caring so much about his criticisms and appreciating his extraordinary tact and judgment in literature." How that persuasive, insinuating personality of Sainte-Beuve's would have softened the positive style of statement which Arnold inherited from his father, the worthy Arnold of Rugby! How it would have taught Arnold to encourage the literature of his own day; to be sympathetic and helpful to those struggling upward; to regard himself in criticism not as an oracle, but as a workman, with hands to be soiled in the rearing of admirable structures!

Matthew Arnold just missed becoming what Sainte-Beuve has now for a long time been,—an indispensable and lovable guide in literature. Perhaps the English

Channel is to blame. Whatever of Sainte-Beuve's teachings was absorbed by Arnold has enriched English criticism. Both men, as poets, as men of open and inquiring minds, as masters of language, had the same path before them, and the same glory at the end of it. The one became the most pervasive force which has appeared in any literature: the other became a model of style. Less of Jeremiah and more of Sainte-Beuve would have made Arnold a great critic. As it is, we owe to Sainte-Beuve's influence the most charming critical essays in English literature.

Lander MacClintock (essay date June 1926)

SOURCE: MacClintock, Lander. "Sainte-Beuve and Pope." *PMLA* 41, no. 2 (June 1926): 442-51.

[*In the following essay, MacClintock argues that while there are important similarities between the critical thinking of Sainte-Beuve and Alexander Pope, there are also important differences and little evidence for the claim that Pope had a significant direct influence on Sainte-Beuve.*]

It was late in life that Sainte-Beuve wrote to a correspondent:

> Je suis resté, malgré tout, de l'école d'Horace, du
> chantre de la forêt de Windsor, et même en n'y mettant
> plus de tout de passion, je reste obstiné par ce côté de
> mon esprit et dans ce for intérieur de mon sentiment.[1]

This declaration is often cited as a sort of summary and synthesis of his critical theory and experience, witnessing his fixed and final preference for the Classical manner, a preference which he promptly and constantly declared after his conclusive break with the Romantics in 1838. The interest of the scholar is immediately aroused by two things in the passage: the fact that he calls the group or roll of writers whom he indicates a "school"; and more especially by the names he singles out as representing the "school" to which he declares his allegiance—Horace and Pope.

There can be no question of Sainte-Beuve's indebtedness to Horace. He was, of course, deeply grounded in Latin literature and criticism in general, and his approval of Horace in particular is frequently expressed. There was indeed a native kinship between them. But there is a misleading implication in the easy, and as it were, casual linking of Pope with the Latin critic—as if he felt equally indebted to both. More than one student of Sainte-Beuve has been deceived by this association, and has taken it for more than it is worth. The scholar who writes, "He frequently refers to Pope,"[2] or "the frequency with which he refers to Pope,"[3] really overstates the case. As a matter of fact, setting aside the

essay devoted to Pope,[4] in the sixty-odd volumes of Sainte-Beuve's works the name of the Englishman occurs only some thirty-five times; he is quoted but once, and then at no great length;"[5] definite passages are paraphrased seven times;[6] and none of these quotations, direct or indirect, is used in any vital or important connection, being, indeed, in every case incidental or illustrative. These facts would seem to warn us against the term "frequency" as applied to the French critic's use of Pope's name, and to challenge us to ask what is really the nature and amount of Sainte-Beuve's knowledge of Pope.

Sainte-Beuve's reading in English literature began early,[7] yet in Michaut's detailed study of his youth the name of Pope does not occur among the English authors read by the omnivorous young man[8] nor does Léon Séché in his account of the contents of Sainte-Beuve's library include any English books, though he does note the presence of Fontanes' translation of the *Essay on Man*.[9] It may well be that it was through this book that Sainte-Beuve's acquaintance with Pope began, for he was at work on an article on Fontanes in 1838 and would assuredly have had use for the translation.[10] And it is in this article, published in 1844, that his first mention of Pope occurs.[11] Not, however, until the volume of 1848 on Chateaubriand is the name mentioned with what may, by allowance, be termed frequency; and by far the greater number of his references to Pope is to be found in the *Nouveaux Lundis*. It is interesting, though it would be hard to prove it significant, that the beginning of Sainte-Beuve's acquaintance with the English Classicist coincides with his definite revolt from Romanticism, and is usually associated with his acknowledgment of his Classical adherence.

The essay on Pope naturally contains the main body of Sainte-Beuve's opinion of him. This essay is a section of the review of Taine's *Histoire de la littérature anglaise* in volume eight of the *Nouveaux Lundis* and one gathers at once that he felt the English writer was not justly treated by Taine, nor indeed, by the majority of contemporary critics. "Le moment," he writes, "n'est pas bon pour Pope, et il commence à devenir mauvais pour Horace,"[12] and these two represent the Classical school which "on est disposé, si l'on n'y prend garde, à traiter un peu trop sous jambe: une sorte de dédain et de mépris est bien près de les atteindre."[13] Sainte-Beuve tries to redress the balance by discussing Pope sympathetically, for he feels that while we should appreciate "le grand, le fort, le difficile" among the great human forces,[14] we should by no means forget or ignore "ces autres forces, plus contenues, qui, dans leur expression, moins semblable à une explosion, se revêtent d'élégance et de douceur."[15] So he writes appreciatively of Pope, the man, the critic, the philosopher and the stylist, finding him, maybe febrile, possibly sterile, but not ludicrous or contemptible as Taine had portrayed him.

Follow then in the essay, studies of the works of Pope, and from these one may gather what Sainte-Beuve had read with the most interest and approval. First in importance is the *Essay on Criticism,* quoted five times at length and five times in a sentence;[16] it is referred to elsewhere more frequently than any other work of Pope's,[17] from it Sainte-Beuve quotes the defence of the function of the critic,[18] the passage describing the spirit in which the critic should approach a work of art,[19] and the lines which state the genuine Classical creed;[20] in this poem, too, he found a passage which met his profound approval—the portrait or "character" of the ideal critic—verses which he says should be hung above the table of every professional reviewer.[21] Second in importance among Pope's works comes the *Essay on Man,* and from this Sainte-Beuve singles out for extended discussion the passages on the ruling passion[22] and, more briefly discussed, the outline of political theory.[23] In the *First Moral Essay,* "On the Knowledge and Characters of Men," he found the longest and most consistent treatment of the doctrine of the ruling passion—a doctrine on the surface similar to that which Sainte-Beuve incorporated into his own critical-philosophical system—which indeed constituted so important an item in that system. The *First Moral Essay,* discussed at some length in the essay on Pope, is also mentioned in other connections.[24] The *Second Moral Essay,* "On the Characters of Women," is once cited,[25] the preface to the translation of Homer once,[26] the letters of Pope are referred to four times,[27] and Spence's *Anecdotes* thrice.[28]

Notwithstanding, however, his evident acquaintance with Pope, his endorsement of many of the English poet's dicta, and his approval of his technique, it seems unlikely that Sainte-Beuve was in any considerable degree influenced by him—on the very surface of the matter there is something irreconcilable between Pope's fastidiousness, preciosity and formalism, and the Frenchman's liberality, tolerance and inclusiveness. There are, however, unescapable similarities in their critical doctrines and tastes that invite inspection.

The *Essay on Criticism,* Boileau's *Art poétique* and Horace's *Ars poetica* constitute the supreme expression and defense of the "common-sense" school of literary criticism and if we translate, as we may, "common-sense" as "la raison," we at once see the partial correspondence between the views of "the school" and those of Sainte-Beuve. Even during his Romantic period he had constantly made reservations and concessions in the direction of Classicism, and the name of Boileau was ever at his pen's point.[29] And when, after 1838, he came out unreservedly as champion of the school of common-sense, he acknowledged as its typical spokesmen Boileau, Pope and Horace, and was only just and candid in declaring "je suis resté. . . . del'école d'Horace, du chantre de la forêt de Windsor."

The striking similarities of the doctrines of Pope and Sainte-Beuve on the *ruling passion* and *the master passion* might easily mislead a student, suggesting a kind of influence that really does not exist. As a matter of fact, however much they may resemble each other in their final form, the starting point, the germinating center of the doctrines is absolutely different. One has but to read Pope's discussions in their context to see that in his case the idea developed from that historic pseudo-psychology of humours, known to antiquity, prevalent in Elizabethan thought and art, coming down through the analytic studies of the Seventeenth century, surviving into the Eighteenth, and modified and exemplified in Pope's conception of the *ruling passion.*[30] Sainte-Beuve's theory had an entirely different genesis, deriving as it does, from his scientific, deterministic convictions. Of course Sainte-Beuve was keen enough to perceive that his deterministic doctrine pushed to its logical extreme must inevitably prove subversive of the Humanistic point of view—but he hoped, by instinct, training and habit, to avoid extremes, logical or critical. Babbitt suggests that his interest in Pope may possibly be attributed to his ironic satisfaction at finding a Humanistic authority for a conception subversive of both Humanism and religion.[31]

On the whole we must conclude that it was an accident that Sainte-Beuve's first acquaintance with Pope's work coincided with his definite break with Romanticism, and that the increased number of his references to Pope after 1848 indicated that he found in the Englishman corroboration and authority for views that he had developed independently.

Another reason for Sainte-Beuve's interest in Pope, at any rate a sufficient explanation of the number of references to him, has been suggested above, and needs only to be recalled—the fact, as Sainte-Beuve himself says, that the name of Pope is a symbol to him. He writes: "ce nom, qui représente la poésie morale, la poésie correcte et ornée dans tout son fini. . . . est pour moi un prétexte. . . . pour maintenir un certain côté"—that is, precisely, the side of the Classicists, now for some time neglected in favor of the Romantics.[32] The Englishman is thus for him by turn the symbol, by turn the type of the Humanistic appeal, the incarnation of an idea and a theory. "Ce nom représente" is Sainte-Beuve's important phrase,—represents namely that group of writers that he has described in a famous passage as "les écrivains d'un ordre moyen, justes, sensés, élégants, toujours nets, d'une passion noble encore, et d'une force légèrement voilée. . . ."; in short, writers "qui ont gouverné leur inspiration;"[33] or "tous ceux qui, dans l'art, ne sont pas pour la réalité pure."[34]

Pope stands, too, beside Horace, Boileau, and La Harpe,[35] with Montaigne and LaFontaine sometimes added, for Classical criticism,[36] of equal dignity with

Classical creation. In nine out of fifteen passages in which Pope is mentioned he is accompanied by Boileau;[37] "in eight of the fifteen, Horace "leur maître à tous" is also named;"[38] and four times Voltaire is numbered with the goodly company.[39] These four mighty ones, with Montaigne and La Fontaine, "les poètes de la vie civile," dwell together on the slopes of Sainte-Beuve's Parnassus, not far from Virgil.[40] They represent "les seconds âges[41]. . . . les âges véritablement classiques, dans le sens modéré du mot, les seuls qui offrent au talent perfectionné le climat et l'abri."[42]

The constant association of these names in the passages adduced and in others, goes to persuade one that "Pope, Boileau and Horace" is, as it were, a cliché, a mere convention, a stereotyped phrase, constituting a sort of critical counter which Sainte-Beuve used half automatically to stand for the Classical ideal, somewhat as in one's undergraduate days "Keats and Shelley," sometimes enriched by "and those fellows" stood for, and indeed adequately named for everybody but one's professor, the entire English Romantic school.

Sainte-Beuve seems never to have had misgivings as to his classification of Pope and his *confrères,* nor any doubt as to the justice of the rating he gives them. They were, to him, Classicists while they lived, and "le lendemain de leur mort. Aujourd' hui ils sont encore classiques, et ils méritent de l'être, mais ils ne le sont que du second ordre."[43] And this brings us to an apparent contradiction in Sainte-Beuve's attitude toward his chosen models—it is paradoxical, being apologetic in both senses of the word. He proclaims "Je suis resté de l'école d'Horace, du chantre de la forêt de Windsor," and still there is always something patronizing in his commendation of them, his friends, his colleagues, his masters. The Classicists mentioned are less than the great writers, are, indeed, second-rate;"[44] they are "après les plus grands. . . . les plus agréables, peut-être, entre les écrivains et les poètes, et les plus faits pour donner du charme à la vie."[45] He complains that "les poètes modérés" are not popularly put in their rightful place a little *below* the great geniuses,[46] and he is constantly expressing his feeling that both readers and critics are preoccupied with the Romantics to the exclusion of the Classicists. Indeed it would be an interesting and illuminating task to disengage the threads of this psychological and critical tangle in Sainte-Beuve's mind—his deprecatory, often patronizing tone toward certain writers whom he constantly and stoutly declared to be his own favorites. On the one side it clearly has to do with the Romantic cult of genius as seen, for example in Hugo's volume on Shakespeare.[47] Now Sainte-Beuve could not fail to have been moved by this enthusiasm for supreme genius, a religion with the Romantics, so he was forced to recognize the superiority of Homer, Dante, Goethe. On the other size he inherited the classical bent toward classifying, "Order"

(meaning rank), says Pope, "is Heaven's first law." To distinguish a first and a second in the rank of excellence was a primary task with a Classical critic, and so Sainte-Beuve, in spite of his professed and without any doubt sincere veneration for Pope, Boileau and Horace, retained from his Romantic days vestiges of the religion of Genius, just as in these Romantic days he had sensed fully the beauty and measure of the Classicists. Ernest Seillière[48] discovers in his admiration for the new Romantics, Flaubert and Baudelaire, a flaring-up of his youthful zeal, and a return, if momentary, of his early taste. Perhaps Seillière puts too much weight on what may be only an instance of Sainte-Beuve's critical open-mindedness. But it is well to be reminded that Sainte-Beuve may not have been so starkly classical as he often professed.[49]

Whatever apparent contradiction we may find in the large sweep of Sainte-Beuve's critical experiments, we can never believe otherwise than that his admiration for Horace, Pope and Boileau was sincere and permanent. In the individual case of Pope, though we can find little or nothing in his work which derives directly from the Englishman, we can justly say that they had much in common—perhaps they belonged in many essential respects to the same family of minds.

The fact that he assigns the "Classical School" to a second rank may mean only that he regards its members as representatives of normal and typical humanity. Luckily for his office as critic, it was usually the normal and typical, those in whom he found the universally human traits, that particularly interested him. Now Pope and the writers whom he always grouped with Pope represent the normal, the common-sense attitude, and this explains both Sainte-Beuve's fondness for them and the touch of patronage always to be detected in his treatment of them. He recognizes that they are not burning beacons of inspiration, but he feels that they are blood-brothers of his own, apostles of reason and measure, to whom he may confidently turn, if not for enlightenment, at least for sympathy and corroboration as he goes on with his task toward that season in experience when "tous les voyages étant faits, toutes les expériences achevées, on n'a pas de plus vives jouissances que d'étudier et d'approfondir les choses qu'on sait, de savourer ce qu'on sent, comme de voir et de revoir les gens qu'on aime. . . . pures délices du coeur et du goût dans la maturité."[50]

Notes

1. *Nouvelle Correspondance,* p. 235: dated March 29, 1867.

2. Irving Babbitt, *Masters of Modern French Criticism* (Boston, 1912), p. 168.

3. *Ibid.,* p. 169. See also L. MacClintock, *Sainte-Beuve's Critical Theory and Practice after 1849.* (Chicago, 1920), p. 69.

4. *Nouveaux Lundis,* VIII, 104-132.

5. *N. L.* [*Nouveaux Lundis,*], II, 15.

6. *Portraits de Femmes,* p. 99; *Causeries du Lundi,* III, 47; *C. L.* [*Causeries du Lundi*] VII, 327; *C. L.,* IX, 497; *N. L.,* I, 437; *N. L.,* VI, 408; *N. L.,* X, 448.

7. The tradition that Sainte-Beuve knew English well, repeated by most of his critics, has been lately called into question by G. Roth, "Ce que Sainte-Beuve a su d'anglais," *Revue Germanique,* 1920-21, pp. 378-381. He concludes: "En dépit des facilités que son ascendance et son lieu de résidence première auraient pu lui procurer, Sainte-Beuve n'apprit l'anglais qu'assez tard et par des moyens probablement livresques; il ne l'a jamais parlé et il ne l'a su que médiocrement." His admiration for Felicia Hemans (*C. L.,* XI, 118; *C. L.,* XVI, 10) and his bracketing of Kirke White with Keats (*Correspondance,* II, 44) lend weight to Roth's assertion.

8. G. Michaut, *Sainte-Beuve avant les lundis,* (Fribourg, 1903), p. 106.

9. Léon Séché, *Etudes d'histoire romantique: Sainte Beuve,* (Paris, 1904) vol. I. Chapter on "La Bibliothèque de Sainte-Beuve."

10. *Correspondance,* I, 68.

11. *Portraits littéraires,* II, 218: see also *Chateaubriand,* I, 84-85; *N. L.,* VIII, 128.

12. *N. L.,* VIII, 113.

13. *N. L.,* VIII, 115.

14. *Ibid.,* p. 112.

15. *Ibid.,* p. 115.

16. *Ibid.,* pp. 119, 120, 121, 122, 123, 124, 127. Sainte-Beuve never quotes Pope in English.

17. Aiming a shaft at Pontmartin for his bitterness and unbalanced cruelty toward his victims, Sainte-Beuve writes, "Je n'ai jamais lu, sans en chercher l'application autour de moi, ce beau passage de *L'Essai sur la Critique* de Pope; 'but where the man . . . .'" Gustave Planche personified this ideal. *N. L.,* II, 15.

18. *N. L.,* VIII, p. 120.

19. *Ibid.,* p. 121.

20. *Ibid.,* p. 122.

21. *Ibid.,* p. 121.

22. Compare the following: in writing of Benjamin Constant's love of popularity, Sainte-Beuve concludes, "c'était là son rêve, sa passion dirigeante, et, selon la belle remarque de Pope, notre passion maîtresse (*our ruling passion*) persévère, se grave et s'enfonce au coeur en vieillissant." *N. L.* I, 437 (Quoted from Pope, *Essay on Man,* lines 123 ff., and *Moral Essays,* I, *passim.*)

23. Grimm's ideas on politics are contained in Pope's verses, "laissez les fous combattre pour les formes de gouvernement, celui. . . . qui est le mieux administré, est le meilleur." *C. L.,* VII, 327. (Reference to *Essay on Man,* II, lines 303 ff.)

24. *N. L.,* VIII, 128. Sainte-Beuve's ideas on the master passion are studied acutely in Babbitt, *op. cit.,* p. 173.

25. Explaining the penchant of the angel heroine of De Vigny's *Eloa* for Lucifer, he notes that Pope has said that every woman is "plus ou moins friponne dans le coeur et a un faible pour les mauvais sujets." *N. L.,* VI, 408. (Reference to *Moral Essays,* II, lines 216 ff.).

26. Mme. Dacier "ne souffrait pas que Pope. . . . comparât l'*Iliade* à un vaste et fécond verger d'Ionie, ou, si l'on veut, à un jardin anglais." Far from being left wild and crude, it was tamed and cultivated. *C. L.,* IX, 497. (See also *N. L.,* VIII, 116.)

27. Three references to Pope's letters and one to a postscript he wrote to a letter of Bolingbroke. *Portraits de Femmes,* 99; *N. L.,* VIII, 131; *N. L.,* X, 448; *C. L.,* III, 47.

28. The roll of critics of Pope that Sainte-Beuve had read is curious, containing as it does but one or two names of first importance. He mentions Mme. Dacier, Addison, Campbell, Bowles, Bentley, Dowden and Matthew Arnold; he was conversant with the ins and outs of the Byron-Campbell-Bowles controversy; he cites Spence's *Anecdotes* in *C. L.,* XI, 214; *N. L.,* VIII, 107, 111; but the names of Warton, DeQuincey and Johnson are missing from the list.

29. Gustave Michaut, *Études sur Sainte-Beuve,* (Paris, 1905), p. 92.

30. Babbitt, *op. cit.,* 167-169.

31. *Ibid.,* p. 169.

32. *N. L.,* VIII, 112. Note that here, as elsewhere, he uses the term "l'école" to name the tendency, the practice, the appeal which runs through all ages, but has only once or twice crystallized into a formal *school.*

33. *C. L.,* III, 43, 44.

34. *N. L.,* VIII, 122. Here are other passages to confirm this statement: "l'école studieuse et polie des Gray, des Pope, des Despréaux." *Portraits lit-*

téraires, II, 3. The poetic image is, he says, "un peu courte, et un peu juste dans l'école moderne des Pope et des Boileau." *Chateaubriand*, I, 207. He laments the sacrifice of "les poètes que j'appellerai modérés . . . . Autrefois on ne plaid-ait pas pour Virgile, pour Horace, pour Boileau, Racine, Voltaire, Pope, le Tasse, admis et reconnus de tous." *N. L.*, VIII, 115. Pope, Boileau and Fontanes stand together for Classical criticism. *N. L.*, VIII, 116.

35. La Harpe is twice mentioned in connection with Pope, each time in regard to the similarity in their personal appearance, La Harpe being "dans sa chétive personne presque aussi exiguë que Pope." *N. L.*, X, 82. Also *C. L.*, V, 127.

36. *Chateaubriand*, I, 114, note; *C. L.*, V, 129; *C. L.*, VII, 310; *N. L.*, VIII, 123; *N. L.*, XII, 378. In placing Pope as critic Sainte-Beuve notes that the art has gained much ground since the Eighteenth century, so that Lamb, for instance, knew and appreciated Shakespeare far better than Pope, because while the former applied the historical, scientific, philosophical method, the letter, relying on the unaided judgment of taste, failed in full comprehension. *N. L.*, IX, 84.

37. *Portraits littéraires*, II, 3; *Chateaubriand*, I, 207; *C. L.*, III, 44; *C. L.*, V, 129; *C. L.*, VI, 503; *C. L.*, VII, 310; *N. L.*, VIII, 115; *N. L.*, VIII, 116; *ibid.*, 126.

38. *C. L.*, III, 44; *C. L.*, V, 129; *C. L.*, VI, 503; *C. L.*, 310; *N. L.*, VIII, 115; *ibid.*, 123; *N. L.*, XII, 378; *Nouvelle Correspondance*, 235.

39. *Chateaubriand*, I, 114, note; *C. L.*, III, 52; *N. L.*, VIII, 115; *N. L.*, XII, 378.

40. *C. L.*, III, 52.

41. *N. L.*, VIII, 120.

42. *C. L.*, III, 48.

43. *C. L.*, III, 47.

44. *Ibid.*, 47.

45. *Ibid.*, 47.

46. *N. L.*, VIII, 115.

47. *N. L.*, VIII, 123.

48. Ernest Seillière, *Sainte-Beuve, agent, juge et complice de l'évolution romantique*, (Paris, 1921).

49. Seillière does not seem to me to give sufficient weight to Sainte-Beuve's own feeling about his Classicism. A statement like the first quoted in this study cannot be lightly dismissed, when it is, as it seems to be, what the author really felt. His

appreciation of Flaubert and Baudelaire was natural, as he was a critic of catholic tastes and could be trusted to enjoy and praise good work, wherever he found it.

50. *C. L.*, III, 53.

Marcel Proust (essay date 1954)

SOURCE: Proust, Marcel. "The Method of Sainte-Beuve." In *Against Sainte-Beuve and Other Essays*, translated by John Sturrock, pp. 10-23. London: Penguin, 1971.

[*In the following essay, originally published in 1954, Proust takes issue with nearly every aspect of Sainte-Beuve's criticism but judges his poetry to be much more honest and authentic, if sometimes clumsy.*]

I have reached a time or, if you like, I find myself in circumstances such that one may fear that the things one most wanted to say—or, failing those at least, if an enfeebled sensibility and the bankruptcy of talent no longer allow of that, those which came next, which one had been inclined, by comparison with that higher, more secret ideal, not greatly to esteem, but which one has not after all read anywhere, which one may think will not be said if one does not say them oneself, and which one notices stem all the same from an even shallower part of our minds—suddenly one is no longer able to say them. One sees oneself as no more than the trustee, who may depart at any moment, of intellectual secrets which will depart with one, and one would like to counter the force for inertia of an earlier indolence, by obeying Christ's beautiful commandment in St John: 'Work while ye have the light.' Thus it seems to me that I would have things that have their importance perhaps to say about Sainte-Beuve, and presently much more in connection with him than about him, that by showing where he sinned, in my view, both as writer and as critic, I should perhaps come to say some things about which I have often thought as to what criticism should be and what art is. In passing, and in his connection, as he does so often, I shall use him as the excuse for talking about certain forms of life . . . I may say a few words about some of his contemporaries on whom I also have an opinion. And then, having criticized these others and this time letting go of Sainte-Beuve altogether, I shall try to say what art would have been for me if . . .

For the definition and eulogy of Sainte-Beuve's method I have looked to the article by M. Paul Bourget, because the definition was short and the eulogy authoritative. I could have cited twenty other critics. To have written the natural history of minds, to have looked to the biography of the man, to the history of his family, to all his peculiarities, for an understanding of his work and the nature of his genius, that is what everyone recognizes to have been his originality, and what he recognized himself, in which moreover he was right. Taine himself, who dreamt of a more systematic and better codified natural history of men's minds and with whom as it happens Sainte-Beuve did not agree over questions of race, says no differently in his eulogy of Sainte-Beuve: 'M. Sainte-Beuve's method is no less valuable than his work. In this he was a pioneer. He imported into moral history the procedures of natural history. He showed . . .', down to 'positive sciences'.[1] Only he added: 'It has only to be applied . . .' down to '. . . a lasting monument'.

Taine said this because his intellectualist conception of reality allowed of no truth except the scientific. But because he had taste and admired various manifestations of the human mind, he explained their value by looking on them as auxiliaries of science (see the preface to *L'Intelligence*). He looked on Sainte-Beuve as an initiator, as remarkable *for his time,* as having almost discovered his, Taine's own method.

But in art there are no initiators or precursors (at least in the scientific sense). Everything is in the individual, each individual starts the artistic or literary endeavour over again, on his own account; the works of his predecessors do not constitute, unlike in science, an acquired truth from which he who follows after may profit. A writer of genius today has everything to do. He is not much further advanced than Homer.

But those philosophers who have been unable to find what is real and independent of all science in art have been forced to imagine art, criticism, etc., to themselves as sciences in which the predecessor is necessarily less far advanced than whoever follows after him.

But why trouble anyway to name all those who see in this the originality and excellence of Sainte-Beuve's method? One need only let him speak for himself.

'For me,' said Sainte-Beuve, 'literature is not distinct or at any rate separable from the rest of the man and of his organization . . . We cannot go about it in too many different ways or from too many different angles if we are to get to know a man, something more than a pure intelligence, that is. Until such time as one has put to oneself a certain number of questions about an author, and has answered them, be it only to oneself alone and under one's breath, one cannot be sure of having grasped him entire, even though the questions may seem quite foreign to the nature of his writings: What were his religious ideas? How did the spectacle of nature affect him? How did he behave in the matter of women, of money? Was he rich, poor; what was his diet, his daily routine? What was his vice or his weakness? None

of the answers to these questions is irrelevant if we are to judge the author of a book or the book itself, provided that book is not a treatise on pure geometry, if it is a work of literature above all, one, that is, which brings in everything, etc.'[2] This method which he applied instinctively all his life and in which towards the end he saw the first outlines of a sort of literary botany . . .

Sainte-Beuve's is not a profound oeuvre. The famous method which in fact, according to Taine, to M. Paul Bourget and to so many others, made him the peerless master of nineteenth-century criticism—that method which consists of not separating the man from the work, of considering that it is not irrelevant if we are to judge the author of a book, unless the book is 'a treatise on pure geometry', to have first answered questions which seem quite foreign to his work (how did he behave . . .), to surround oneself with all the possible facts about a writer, to collate his correspondence, to question the people who knew him, talking with them if they are still alive, reading what they may have written about him if they are dead—such a method fails to recognize what any more than merely superficial acquaintance with ourselves teaches us: that a book is the product of a self other than that which we display in our habits, in company, in our vices. If we want to try and understand this self, it is deep inside us, by trying to recreate it within us, that we may succeed. This is an effort of the heart from which nothing can absolve us. It is a truth every bit of which we have to create and . . . It is too easy to suppose that it will arrive one fine morning among our mail, in the form of an unpublished letter imparted to us by a librarian friend, or that we shall gather it from the lips of someone who knew the author well. Speaking of the great admiration aroused in several writers of the new generation by the work of Stendhal, Sainte-Beuve says: 'May they permit me to tell them, that if we are clearly to judge that rather complicated mind and not exaggerate at all in any direction, I shall always come back for preference, independently of my own impressions and memories, to what those who knew him in his prime and when he was starting out have to say about him, to M. Mérimée, to M. Ampère, to what Jacquemont would have to tell me about him were he still alive, to those, in short, who saw and savoured much of him in his earlier version.'

Why so? How does the fact of having been a friend of Stendhal make us better able to judge him? On the contrary, it would probably be a serious hindrance. For such intimates the self which produces the works is obscured by the other self, which may be very inferior to the outward self of many other men. The best proof of which moreover is that, having known Stendhal, and having collected up all the facts he could from 'M. Mérimée' and 'M. Ampère', having equipped himself, in short, with everything which, according to him, enables a critic to judge a book more accurately, Sainte-

Beuve judged Stendhal in the following manner: 'I have just reread, or tried to, the novels of Stendhal; they are frankly detestable.' Elsewhere he allows that in *Le Rouge et le noir,* 'so titled no one quite knows why and by an emblem one has to guess at, *at least something happens.* The first volume has some interest, for all its manneredness and improbabilities. *There is an idea in it.* Beyle³ had an exact model, *so I am assured,* for the early part of the novel in someone of his acquaintance and *as long as he kept to it, he managed to seem truthful.* The prompt introduction of the shy young man into a world he has not been brought up for, etc., *all this is well done, or would be at least if the author,* etc. . . . They are not living people but cleverly constructed automata . . . *He did better* in the novellas set in Italy . . . Of all Beyle's novels *La Chartreuse de Parme* is the one which has given some people the highest notion of his talent in this genre. It will be seen that I am far from sharing the enthusiasm of M. de Balzac with regard to *La Chartreuse.* Once you have read it, it seems to me that you quite naturally come back to the French style . . . We ask for an element of reason, etc., such as Manzoni's story of *The Betrothed* offers, or any good novel by Walter Scott or an adorable and truly simple novella by Xavier de Maistre; the rest is the work simply of a wit . . .'

It ends with these two gems: 'Criticize Beyle's novels with some candour though I may, I am far from censuring him for having written them . . . His novels are what they may be, but they are not vulgar. They are like his criticism, for the use chiefly of those who write them . . .' And the concluding words of the article: 'Beyle had a fundamental straightforwardness and reliability in his personal dealings which we must never forget to acknowledge once we have said our piece about him.' A good fellow, Beyle, all things considered. To reach which conclusion it was perhaps scarcely worth the trouble of meeting M. Mérimée so often at dinner or at the Academy, or 'setting M. Ampère talking' so much, and once having read it one is less anxious than Sainte-Beuve was at the thought of the new generations to come. Barrès would have done better than you on one hour's reading and without any 'facts'. I do not say that everything he says about Stendhal is wrong. But when one recalls the enthusiastic tone in which he speaks of the stories of Mme de Gasparin or of Töppfer, it is very clear that, if every nineteenth-century book had been burnt except the *Lundis,*⁴ and that it was from the *Lundis* that we had to get an idea of the *ranking* of nineteenth-century writers, Stendhal would seem inferior to Charles de Bernard, Vinet, Molé, Mme de Verdelin, Ramond, Sénac de Meilhan, Vicq d'Azyr and a good many others, and somewhat indistinct, truth to tell, between d'Alton Shée and Jacquemont. Nor in this case can he have been led astray by the rancour he may have felt against other writers.

'An artist . . .' said Carlyle, and he ends by seeing the world as no more than 'for use in an illusion to be described'.⁵

At no time does Sainte-Beuve seem to have grasped what is peculiar to inspiration or the activity of writing, and what marks it off totally from the occupations of other men and the other occupations of the writer. He drew no dividing line between the occupation of writing, in which, in solitude and suppressing those words which belong as much to others as to ourselves, and with which, even when alone, we judge things without being ourselves, we come face to face once more with our selves, and seek to hear and to render the true sound of our hearts—and conversation! 'Writing . . .'⁶

It is only the deceptive appearance of the image here which lends something vaguer and more external to the trade and something deeper and more contemplative to sociability. In actual fact what one gives to the public is what one has written when alone, for oneself, it is very much the work of one's self . . . What one gives to sociability, that is to conversation (however refined it may be, and the most refined is the worst of all, because it falsifies our spiritual life by associating itself to it: Flaubert's conversations with his niece or with the clockmaker are without risk) or to those productions intended for one's intimates, that is to say reduced so as to appeal to a few and which are barely more than written conversation, is the work of a far more external self, not of the deep self which is only to be found by disregarding other people and the self that knows other people, the self that has been waiting while one was with others, which one feels clearly to be the only real self, for which alone artists end by living, like a god whom they leave less and less and to whom they have sacrificed a life that serves only to do him honour. As from the *Lundis,* of course, Sainte-Beuve was not only to change his life but to rise—not very high!—to the idea that a life of hard labour, such as he led, was basically more productive and necessary to certain wilfully indolent natures which would otherwise not have disgorged their riches. '. . .', he was to say, speaking of Favre, Fauriel, etc., etc.

He was frequently to say that the literary man's life was in his study, despite the extraordinary protest he raised against what Balzac says in *La Cousine Bette.*⁷ But he continued not to understand the unique, enclosed world, incommunicado with the outside, which is the soul of the poet. He believed that others could offer it advice, could excite or repress it: 'No Boileau . . .'⁸

And not having seen the gulf that separates the writer from the society man, not having understood that the writer's self shows itself only in his books, that he only shows society men (even those society men that other writers are, when in society, who only become writers again once on their own) a society man like themselves, he was to launch that famous method which, according to Taine, Bourget and so many others, is his claim to fame, and which consists, in order to understand a poet or writer, in questioning avidly those who knew him, who frequented him, who may be able to tell us how he behaved in the matter of women, etc., that is, on all those very points where the poet's true self is not involved.

At no period of his life does Sainte-Beuve seem to have had a really profound conception of literature. He puts it on the same plane as conversation.

As we shall see, this very superficial conception was not to change, but his factitious ideal was lost for good. Necessity forced him to give up that way of life. Having had to resign as administrator of the Bibliothèque Mazarine, he needed work which would enable him etc., and to accept gladly the offers of . . .

From that moment on, the leisure he had hoped for was replaced by sheer hard grind. 'From first thing', one of his secretaries tells us, etc.

No doubt this industriousness forced him to make public a mass of ideas which, had he stuck to the life of idleness he foresaw to start with, would never have seen the light of day. He seems to have been struck by the advantage certain minds can derive in this way from the need to produce (Favre, Fauriel, Fontanes). For ten years everything that he might have kept back for friends, for himself, for a work long meditated which he would no doubt never have written, had to take on form and come ceaselessly forth from him. Those reserves where we keep precious thoughts, the one around which a novel was to have crystallized, that other which he would work up into a poem, a third whose beauty he had one day sensed, would rise up from the depths of his mind as he was reading the book he had to write about and bravely, so that his offering might be all the finer, he would sacrifice his most cherished Isaac, his supreme Iphigenia. 'I am calling on all my resources,' he would say. 'I am spending my last powder.' It may be said that into the manufacture of those rockets which he loosed off each Monday for ten years with such incomparable brilliance there went the raw material, henceforth lost, for more enduring books. But he knew very well that it was not all lost and that, since something timeless or at the very least enduring had gone into the composition of these ephemera, the ephemera in question would be gathered up, would be collected, that the generations would continue to extract what was enduring from them. Indeed, they became the books that are at times so amusing, at times even truly

agreeable, which enable us to spend moments of such pure entertainment that some people I am sure would apply sincerely to Sainte-Beuve what he says of Horace: '. . .'

Their title of *Lundis* reminds us that for Sainte-Beuve they were the hectic and delightful labour of a single week, his glorious Monday morning reveille-call. In his little house in the rue du Mont-Parnasse, on a Monday morning, at the moment when, in winter, the daylight is still ashen above the drawn curtains, he would open *Le Constitutionnel* in the awareness that at that same moment the words which he had chosen were carrying into many Parisian bedrooms news of the brilliant thoughts he had had, and arousing in many the admiration felt for himself by someone who has seen originate within him an idea better than any he has read in others and who has presented it in all its vigour, in all the detail that he had not himself remarked straight away, in the full light of day, but with shadows too which he has lovingly caressed. No doubt he did not have the emotion of the beginner, who has long had an article with the newspaper but who never finds it when he opens the paper and finally despairs of its appearing. Then one morning, on entering his bedroom, his mother has put the newspaper down beside him with a rather more absent air than usual, as if there were nothing of interest to read in it. Nevertheless she has put it close beside him so that he cannot fail to read it and has quickly withdrawn, and pushed the old servant abruptly back who was about to enter the room. And he smiles, for he has understood that his darling mother wanted him to suspect nothing, wanted him to have the full surprise of his joy and that he should savour it alone and not be irritated by the words of others as he read and be obliged out of pride to conceal his joy from those who had asked indiscreetly to share it with him. Meanwhile, above the ashen daylight the sky is the colour of embers: through the misty streets run thousands of newspapers, still moist from the presses and from the early morning damp, more nourishing and appetizing than the hot brioches that will be crumbled into the *café au lait,* around the still-lit lamps, to carry his thought multiplied a thousandfold into every home. Quickly he sends out to buy more copies of the paper, so as actually to touch with his finger the miracle of this surprising multiplication, to be in spirit a new buyer, to open this other copy with an unsuspecting eye and find there the same thoughts. And just when the sun, having swollen and filled and brightened, has leapt above the purple of the horizon with the brief impulse of its dilation, he sees, at that same moment, triumphing in each mind, his thought rising like a sun to imbue it all through with its colours.

Sainte-Beuve was no longer a beginner, and no longer experienced such joys. Yet, in the first light of a winter's morning, he could see Mme de Boigne in her tall four-poster opening *Le Constitutionnel*; could tell himself that at two o'clock the Chancellor [Pasquier] would pay her a call and discuss it with her, that perhaps, that evening, he would receive word from Mme Allart or Mme d'Arbouville, telling him what was thought of it. So did his articles seem to him like a sort of arch, the beginning of which certainly was in his own mind and in his prose but whose other end plunged into the minds and admiration of his readers, where its curve was completed and received its final colouring. The same holds for an article as for those phrases that we read, with a shudder, in the parliamentary reports in the newspaper: 'M. the President of the Council, Minister for the Interior and for Religious Affairs: "You'll see . . ." (*Lively protests from the right, volleys of applause from the left, prolonged uproar)*', in the composition of which the indication preceding and the signs of emotion that follow are just as integral a part as the words that are uttered. In actual fact, the sentence by no means ends at 'You'll see', it has barely begun, 'lively protests from the right, etc.', is the end, which is better than the middle and worthy of the beginning. So the beauty of journalism does not lie wholly in the article itself; cut off from the minds in which it finds fulfilment, it is no more than a broken Venus. And since it receives its final expression from the crowd (be that crowd an élite), its expression is always somewhat vulgar. It is by the silences of the imagined approval of this reader or that that the journalist weighs his words and balances them against his ideas. Thus his work is written with the unconscious collaboration of others and is less personal.

Just as we find Sainte-Beuve believing that the salon life which he enjoyed was indispensable to literature, and projecting it across the centuries, here to the court of Louis XIV, there to the select circle of the Directory, so . . . In point of fact this seven-days-a-week creator, who often did not rest even on Sundays and who received his wages of fame on Mondays from the pleasure he gave to good judges and the knocks he inflicted on the spiteful ones, saw all of literature as a sort of *Lundis* which may perhaps be reread but which have had to be written in their own time heedful of the opinion of the good judges, in order to please and not relying too much on posterity. He sees literature under the category of time. 'I forecast an interesting season for poetry,' he writes to Béranger. He asks himself whether later on people will like literature, and says to the Goncourts, apropos *Madame Gervaisais*, '. . .'[9] Literature seems to him to be of its period, to be worth what the person was worth. In sum, it is better to play a major role in politics and not to write than to be a political malcontent and write a book on morality . . . etc. He was not like Emerson, therefore, who said that we must hitch our wagon to a star. He tries to hitch his to the most contingent thing of all, to politics. 'I thought it interesting to collaborate in a great social movement,'

he says. Twenty times over he tells of his regrets that Chateaubriand, Lamartine and Hugo should have gone in for politics, but in actual fact politics is more of a stranger in their works than in his own criticism. Why does he say about Lamartine, 'his talent is outside'? About Chateaubriand, 'These *Memoirs* are not very likeable . . . Since as for talent . . .' 'Really I cannot speak about Hugo.'

People had liking for him, and also esteem. 'You must know that if you value the opinions of others, your own too is valued,' wrote Mme d'Arbouville to him, and he tells us that she had given him for a motto: 'Seek to please but keep your freedom.' But so unfree was he in reality that for as long as Mme Récamier was alive he shrank from saying anything hostile about Chateaubriand. For example, as soon as Mme Récamier and Chateaubriand were dead, he made up for it; I do not know whether this in what is his 'Notes and Thoughts' he called: 'Having been the advocate I have a strong desire to become the judge.' The fact is that piece by piece he destroyed his previous opinions. Having had to review the *Mémoires d'outre-tombe* after a reading which had taken place at Mme Récamier's, when he came to the place where Chateaubriand says '. . .',[10] he protested, deciding that such a scruple displayed too great a delicacy: 'No, it is not in you . . .' When he reviewed the *Mémoires d'outre-tombe* after the death of Chateaubriand and of Mme Récamier and came to the same passage, he again breaks in on the august narrator, but not, this time, to say, 'That is only natural.' 'I beg your pardon?' he says to him . . . Even in the case of one of those of whom he said the kindest things, with the greatest brilliance, the best of taste and the greatest regularity, the Chancellor Pasquier, if he did not contradict his enthusiastic praises all that no doubt prevented him, it seems to me, was the endlessly prolonged old age of Mme de Boigne. 'Mme de Boigne complains she does not see you any more,' the Chancellor wrote to him (just as George Sand had written: 'Alfred de Musset . . .'). 'Will you come and take me to the Luxembourg? We can have a chat, etc.' When the Chancellor died Mme de Boigne was still alive. Three articles on the Chancellor, sufficiently laudatory to please this disconsolate friend. But once Mme de Boigne has died we read in the *Lundis*: 'Cousin says . . .' and at the Magny dinner he says to Goncourt,[11] who cannot help saying: 'How ghastly to be mourned by Sainte-Beuve.'

But on the whole his susceptibility, his fickle moods, and his ready distaste for what he had first enthused over, meant that he 'set himself free' even in people's lifetimes. One did not need to be dead, only to have fallen out with him and thus it is that we have the contradictory articles on Hugo, Lamartine, Lamennais, etc., and on Béranger, of whom he says in the . . . This 'recovered freedom' provided the counterweight to his 'wish to please' and was indispensable if he was to be respected. It should be added that, along with a certain inclination to bow before established authority, there went in him a certain inclination to break free from it, a worldly and conservative tendency, with a liberal and free-thinking one. To the first we owe the vast amount of space which all the great political figures of the July Monarchy occupy in his work, where you cannot take one step into the salons where he assembles his illustrious interlocutors, imagining that from their debates will spring enlightenment, without meeting M. Molé and every possible Noailles, whom he reveres to the point of deciding that, after two hundred years, it would be criminal to cite in its entirety, in one of his articles, the portrait of Mme de Noailles in Saint-Simon; yet alongside this, and as if in revenge for it, he inveighs against aristocratic candidacies for the Academy (apropos however the perfectly legitimate election of the Duke de Broglie), saying: these people will end up getting their concierges appointed.

Even towards the Academy his attitude is at once that of a friend of M. Molé, who decides that the candidacy of Baudelaire, albeit his great friend, would be a joke, and who writes that he must feel proud even to have pleased the academicians: 'You created a good impression, is that not something?' and that of a friend of Renan, who decides that Taine demeaned himself by submitting his *Essais* to the judgement of academicians incapable of understanding them, who inveighs against Mgr Dupanloup who prevented Littré from getting into the Academy, and who says to his secretary from the very first day: 'On Thursdays I go to the Academy, my colleagues are men of no significance.' He admits himself that he has written articles on one or other of them out of obligation, but he refuses angrily to say anything good about M. Pongerville, of whom he says: 'He wouldn't get in nowadays.' He had what he called a sense of his own dignity and displayed it in a solemn fashion which at times was a little comic. We can allow it when, foolishly accused of having accepted a sweetener of a hundred francs, he tells us that he wrote a letter to the *Journal des débats,* 'whose tone is unmistakable, such as only an honest man could write'. As we can when, following an accusation by M. de Pontmartin, or believing himself to have been indirectly the target of a speech by M. Villemain, he exclaims: '. . .' But it is comic when, after warning the Goncourts that he was going to say unkind things about *Madame Gervaisais* and having heard through a third party that they had told the Princess: 'Sainte-Beuve is certainly going to . . .' he flew into a furious rage over the word slating, exclaiming, 'I don't slate.' It was one of these Sainte-Beuves who answered . . .

His books, *Chateaubriand et son groupe littéraire* most of all, are like a suite of drawing-rooms into which the author has invited various interlocutors, who are questioned about the people they have known and who provide testimony intended to contradict that of others and hence to prove that there is a great deal more to be said about the man whom it is customary to praise, or else to classify whoever contradicts as of another school of thought.

And the contradiction is not between two visits, but within a single visitor. Sainte-Beuve cannot resist recalling an anecdote, or going to fetch a letter, or calling as a witness a man of wisdom and authority who had been philosophically warming his feet but who asks for nothing better than to add his own little hammer-blow, in order to show that whoever has just given one opinion held a quite different one.

M. Molé, his top hat in his hand, recalls that when Lamartine learnt that Royer-Collard was trying for the Academy he wrote to him spontaneously asking him to vote for him, but when the day of the election came, voted against him, and another time, having voted against Ampère, sent Mme de Lamartine to Mme Récamier's to congratulate him.

I wonder at times whether what is still best in Sainte-Beuve is not his poetry. There the intellectual games have ceased. He no longer comes at things obliquely, with endless clevernesses and trickery. The magic and infernal circle has been broken. In ceasing to speak in prose he ceases to tell lies, as if the constant mendacity of his thought stemmed in his case from his contrived skill in expression. Just as a student, forced to translate his thoughts into Latin, is forced to lay them bare, so Sainte-Beuve finds himself for the first time in the presence of reality and receives a direct sense of it. There is more direct feeling in the ***Rayons jaunes,*** in the ***Larmes de Racine,*** in all of his poetry, than in all of his prose. Only, when mendacity forsakes him, so all its advantages abandon him also. Like a man habituated to alcohol who has been put on to a diet of milk, he loses, along with his contrived vigour, all strength. 'How clumsy, how ugly a creature.' Nothing could be more poignant than this poverty of means in the great illusionist of criticism, practised in all the elegances, the eloquence, the finesse, the waggishness, the sentimentalities, the devices, the caresses of style. Nothing is left. All that remains to him of his immense culture, of his high literary training, is the refusal of anything inflated, anything banal, any loose expression; his images are studied, and chosen with severity: something that is reminiscent of the studious and exquisite poetry of an André Chénier or an Anatole France. But all this is willed, it is not his. He is seeking to do what he had admired in Theocritus, in Cooper, in Racine. Of him, of the deep, unconscious, personal self there is hardly more than the clumsiness. That recurs frequently, as nature will. But the trifling thing, the trifling yet also delightful and sincere thing that is his poetry, that skilful and at times successful attempt to express the purity of love, the sadness of late afternoons in large towns, the magic of memory, the emotion of reading, the melancholy of an unbelieving old age, demonstrates—because one feels that it is the only real thing about him—the lack of significance in his vast, marvellous, ebullient oeuvre as a critic—for all these marvels come down to this. Mere appearance, the *Lundis*. The reality, this handful of poems. The poems of a critic, they it is out of all his writings that tip eternity's scales.

Notes

1. The gist of the words omitted is that Sainte-Beuve practised a kind of 'botanical analysis' on human individuals, thus assimilating criticism with science.

2. These remarks come from one of Sainte-Beuve's *causeries* on Chateaubriand, collected in his *Nouveaux lundis III*. Proust does not quote them continuously.

3. Stendhal's real name was Henri Beyle.

4. The title of Sainte-Beuve's best-known collections of his criticism, *Les Causeries du lundi* and *Nouveaux lundis,* so called from their having first appeared in the press on Mondays.

5. What thought of Carlyle's Proust had in mind is unknown. The second part of the sentence refers not to Carlyle but to one of Proust's favourite quotations from Flaubert, to the effect that with the writer 'the accidents of the world all appear to him transposed as if for use in an illusion to be described'.

6. The passage from Sainte-Beuve Proust proposed to quote here suggests that the writer should not give too much of himself to his 'trade' or 'the public', but should 'cultivate his friends' and not allow his writing to encroach too far on 'what is essential in his soul and his thoughts'.

7. Sainte-Beuve objected to Balzac saying that great artists must work incessantly, and 'took the Muses for their concubines'. Sainte-Beuve thought that the Muses should be visitors, not living-in companions.

8. Sainte-Beuve held the view that in the seventeenth century Boileau had been a strong and good influence on the other writers of his day, and that the contemporary age would benefit from his equivalent.

9. *Madame Gervaisais* was a novel by the Goncourt brothers; Sainte-Beuve's remark to them, recorded in their celebrated *Journal,* questions the likelihood of there being a posterity for contemporary writers.

10. The remark in question by Chateaubriand goes: 'But are these not strange details, and ill-sounding pretensions, in an age when no one was expected to be his father's son? So much vanity in a time of progress, of revolution!'

11. Sainte-Beuve's remarks about Pasquier were contemptuous and their discrepancy with his earlier praise of him led to the comment cited here from Goncourt.

A. G. Lehmann (essay date 1962)

SOURCE: Lehmann, A. G. "Birth of a Poet (1828-1829)." In *Sainte-Beuve: A Portrait of the Critic, 1804-1842,* pp. 59-73. London: Oxford University Press, 1962.

[*In the following essay, Lehmann gives a detailed analysis of Sainte-Beuve's first book of poetry,* Vie, Poésies et Pensées de Joseph Delorme, *focusing on the work's strengths and weaknesses and on its reception by, and influence on, other French writers.*]

> 'Poète, vous avez pu dans le demi-jour découvrir un sentier qui est le vôtre et créer une élégie qui est vous-même.'

(Hugo, Discours Académique, 1845)

ENGLAND: *JOSEPH DELORME*

Since their return to England, Charles and Arthur Neate, at Oxford and Cambridge respectively, had kept open an invitation to their French medical student friend to pay them a visit in the summer. If Sainte-Beuve did not go before 1828 it was because he hesitated to leave his mother or because he was too busy at Hugo's side or because he had not the money. From the *Tableau historique* he had several hundred francs; financial objections removed, the others faded too. David d'Angers and Victor Pavie had been in London in May of this year, trying to introduce themselves to Walter Scott, whom David hoped to model. England was in the air: sentimentally for the Cénacle, politically for the *Globe*. Moreover, Sainte-Beuve still had hopes of developing the vein of 'intimate' poetry which he had glimpsed earlier in Coleridge, Wordsworth, Cowper, Crabbe—something that chimed in with his own distaste for the pretentious and the ornate.[1]

He set off on 16 August; his holiday began at the Neates's home, Tubney Lodge, a few miles from Oxford, where Charles's father was rector, and it ended there in the last week of September: in the middle there was a short tour of the south, followed by ten days alone in London sight-seeing.

Proust noted once, as damning evidence against the romantics with their admiration for the Gothic, that Théophile Gautier when he passed through Chartres did not stop to look at the cathedral.[2] This inconsequential detractor of Sainte-Beuve could hardly have switched the same charge to his *bête noire.* Hugo's conducted tours of the Louvre and Notre-Dame bore fruit in Sainte-Beuve's letters back. Halting at Rouen, he dutifully visited its cathedral and Saint-Ouen and Saint-Maclou—all in two hours—and came out rapturous, though he felt unable to do justice to the portal of Saint-Maclou—'an Epic [. . .]. Why do I know so little of the language of Ogives, spires and pendentives, so as to describe to you what I now hold in memory's eye!'[3] At Southampton the Customs mislaid his trunk; he spent a day going by boat to visit the ruins of Netley Abbey. Staying so near Oxford it was easy to tour the colleges: he admired Christ Church, a little vaguely for Victor's purposes, perhaps; in New College he deplored the eighteenth-century glass. On other occasions, Winchester and Salisbury cathedrals were enthusiastically described. Westminster Abbey, apart from its tombs, was spoilt by an 'over-simple modern Gothic'. He looked at pictures in the Bodleian, went to Blenheim, saw the Earl of Harcourt's collection at Nuneham Courtenay. Hugo expressed himself almost as excited as his friend:

> Your absence leaves a great gap in my life [. . .]. I cannot say with what eager interest I have followed your journey; every detail in your letters is a joy to me; through them I saw each bas-relief stand out, each Gothic stained-glass window in the beautiful churches you visit, lucky man that you are [. . .].[4]

The Neates gave their visitor an introduction to the local M. P., John Ingram Lockhart, with whom he spent a week. It has been conjectured that he also met Abraham Hayward on this occasion;[5] at least he knew him already in 1835, and if the Neates had introduced him, it would be very probably during a stay with Hayward in Wiltshire that he toured Winchester and Salisbury and saw Stonehenge. It could well have been Hayward who told him of the London University project, and the consequent possible post for a Frenchman—a detail he remembered later.[6]

London was a great disappointment. In midsummer all the nobility and gentry were away, most of the public monuments shut; left to his own devices, he fell into 'a fit of wretchedness such as I was pleased to recognize later in a poem of André Chénier'.[7] And there were no men of letters to be found. He whiled away the days, using some of the empty hours to add to the poems in the portfolio he had with him,[8] and adding paragraphs to the prose Introduction and Thoughts[9] of what was eventually to become the very composite ***Joseph Delorme.***[10]

It was a relief to get back to Tubney Lodge and the life of the local squires. 'What a queer life these country squires lead; hunting, fishing, dancing, riding, Church on Sunday.—Most of them are parsons, in fact everyone I see here is a parson, though to be sure one would not notice it: all dancing, married, charming in their way, and though very pious hardly at all *dévots.*'[11] Now for the last part of his stay he saw more of the life which Goldsmith and Gray and Crabbe had conjured up for him. In one respect his view of it was different from theirs—Charles Neate was a disrespectful young radical student, always ready to put his finger on the failings of Church and University and State, and from him his friend got the impression that these 'parsons' were dancing on a volcano—this world was 'very near to breaking up and collapsing in political convulsions which no efforts of human prudence can probably do more than postpone for a little time more'.[12]

Sainte-Beuve is sparing in later allusions to England. Though he could read the language, he never could speak it, and without the aid of a couple of bilingual hosts the voyage of discovery quickly fizzled out. But safely back in France, he had got his line: he was the translator of Coleridge's *Aeolian Harp,* of Wordsworth's *Scorn not the Sonnet, Critic,* of Collins's *Ode to Evening*—the French representative of the 'Lake school', however little he really knew about the men whom he considered to constitute it.

Immediately on his return to Paris, therefore, he collected together the bulk of his poems, added an introduction, and set out in search of a publisher. Ladvocat, Sautelet, Urbain Canel, all progressive publishers of the day, refused him on the mere intimation that a volume of poems was being offered. Eventually Nodier's friend Delangle took pity and offered 400 francs for one year's rights on an edition of a thousand copies (this by the side of Hugo's 3,600 francs for the *Orientales*!). Hugo, given the manuscript, reacted much more encouragingly: 'Words hardly suffice [. . .] grave and beautiful poetry, masculine, simple and melancholy prose [. . .] skilful dissection of a soul [. . .] almost brought tears to my eyes [. . .].'[13] A long letter with much else in the same vein was ample to spur him on to add some finishing touches. Indeed, from that October to the following April when his book came out, he could hardly bring himself to work on anything else, apart from half-a-dozen review notices on the beloved Victor. An insidious habit of life was being formed: 'I prefer to put the last touches to my little book, add a few pieces more if the frost spares them, and enjoy the *dolce far niente* which I am terrified to find myself more and more inclined to than ever.'[14] Going to Guizot's lectures, and Villemain's and Cousin's; spending mornings at home or at the Bibliothèque Royale; discussing with Jouffroy (not too enthusiastically) the latter's scheme to set him up with a Chair of Literature—but at Besançon[15]—chatting contentedly at Hugo's house in the evenings, and occasionally trying his hand at a little inexpensive debauchery with the dashing 18-

year-old Alfred de Musset[16] who confided his (also unpublished) poems to Sainte-Beuve:[17] then at last the proofs were finished, an idle winter was over, and on 4 April 1829 there appeared on sale, anonymously, the 'little book'—*Vie, Poésies et Pensées de Joseph Delorme.*

After four years of brooding, Sainte-Beuve had followed up his conversation with Dubois and written his *Werther.* Only this was *Werther* with a difference—a great many differences. Among the most obvious, *Joseph Delorme* is not a novel but a volume of poems which begins with an imaginary biography (based on what Sainte-Beuve had picked up of the now forgotten Kirke White's untimely death from consumption),[18] and ends with a set of rambling thoughts on topical literary subjects. The formula was not of Sainte-Beuve's invention; but making no great demands on its author's powers of organizing detail into a work of fiction, it served his purposes well enough. It presented a highly original but in parts imprecise poetic ethos; and it created a type, a symbolic figure able to hold its own beside more portentous romantic silhouettes (Childe Harold, Manfred) and even assimilate other less significant figures—Balzac's *Louis Lambert* for example.[19] After the dark and theatrical René, the irrepressible Delphine of Mme de Staël in her revolt of genius against tyranny, or the self-destructive but still socially acceptable Adolphe, Joseph Delorme is not a hero but an *anti*-hero: a pathetic and undistinguished victim of his own ordinary weaknesses. The first of his kind in France, indeed, if one excepts the shadowy *Obermann.*

Joseph's life, told by the 'editor' of his remains, is made up of fragments of Sainte-Beuve's own past, often closely transcribed, though with numerous improvements. Joseph's childhood has been modest but respectable. 'Imbued with moral precepts, brought up to hard work', he starts with golden dreams—a child of the Empire, inwardly participating in its military glory.[20] There are hopeless dumb attachments for flaxen-haired young girls; he wanders through the countryside and by the sea, hearing inner voices, dull and confused elegies, mysterious whisperings of a waking soul; 'and when at meal-times they came to look for him, they found him sitting where he was that morning, with tears on his cheeks'. He goes to Paris. Piety is undermined, and poetry yields before 'scientific curiosity', 'the dark and mystical adoration of Nature', the 'pantheism of a Chénier or a Diderot'. He develops (perhaps significantly, perhaps not) 'a deep love for the suffering portion of humanity, an implacable hatred for the highly-placed'; also a vocation for medicine, whereby he may 'take from some to give to others, be an active link between the most opposed conditions, and repair in some degree the inequality which society countenances and nature disavows'. But to give up poetry is hard:

What he suffered through two or three years of constant trials and daily wrestling with himself—what secret demon grappled with him and undermined his new studies by recalling to him the old—*what tortured shudder he felt at each new triumph of his contemporaries,* and the consciousness of his powers which weighed upon his heart like an eternal rock—what sleepless nights and idle days, his book or pillow drenched in tears—all this he alone could know.

Joseph's medical vocation fails, however; he returns to poetry and listlessly shuts himself off with his books— 'all the novels of the family of *Werther* and of *Delphine, Adolphe, René,* Senancour, Lamartine and Ballanche, Ossian, Cowper and Kirke White'; at last serenity comes. But his lungs are fatally damaged, and life now slips prematurely and silently away.

If plenty here is conventional, Joseph's character as it emerges is not. Sainte-Beuve makes the mistake of forcing the note of revolt, with a touch of nervy suspiciousness from Rousseau; but the central fact about Joseph remains throughout the completely uninteresting character of his life—no great passions, no vast hopes disappointed, no suicide even. His literary gifts are slender—barely a mood, sustained for a moment then extinguished, speaking from the grave to a few kindred souls 'that little band, dispersed in the multitude [. . .] who from an unconquerable taste for *rêverie,* and usually also from a painful uniformity of existence, can feel for the suffering of his heart and his harmonious elegies'.

Rather oddly—but then this part of the story was odd in real life—Joseph Delorme also 'by his taste, his studies and the company he kept, especially towards the end, belonged in mind and heart to that young school of poetry which André Chénier bequeathed from the foot of the scaffold to the nineteenth century, whose glorious heritage Lamartine, A. de Vigny, Victor Hugo, Émile Deschamps, and a dozen others have taken up, embellished and enlarged'. One wonders how this could have been, when it is admitted that bare of colour, short of breath, 'he never attempted anything but pictures of sentimental analysis and landscapes of limited scale'. The monotonous tone, the bent towards humble subjects: this sort of poetic capital is quite out of line with the dazzling *Orientales, Othello,* or *Clara Gazul.* Indeed, Joseph Delorme stands out almost as much for his rejection of the gaudy and the exotic as for his acceptance of anything else.

There is nevertheless plenty of variety in the *Poésies* with which he is credited. Among fifty-five poems which make up the first edition are a dozen sonnets; exercises in metrical virtuosity imitated from Ronsard (*A la rime*); conversation pieces in various moods, even a jocular snatch on book-collectors (*Mes Livres*); near-translations from Schiller (*L'Attente*) and Wordsworth

(*Le Plus Long Jour de l'année*); an Ode in the manner of Hugo (*Le Cénacle*), a *Retour à la poésie* reminiscent of Lamartine. The derivative character of all this has nothing specially to do with Joseph Delorme, unless it draws to our attention what an indefatigable *echo* he is. An impressive list has in fact been assembled of his borrowings:[21] alongside the expected names (Lamartine, Chénier, Horace, the Pléiade, Juvenal) who would expect to find bits of Mackenzie (taken from Bonnet's translations) or Leibnitz? Sainte-Beuve held in later life that his real originality lay partly in just this assimilative power: in his criticism this is taken for granted, but in his poetry one is tempted either to assume an unusually subtle and shaded kind of portraiture of Joseph Delorme's *persona,* or else to write off the whole phenomenon as the gropings of an incompletely formed technique. The truth lies perhaps half-way between.

In *Joseph Delorme* in any case, the derivative pieces do not obscure the firm and unambiguous character of the central poems,[22] which are the **'Elegies'.** Sainte-Beuve calls them that, at least: by the side of Millevoye, or Lamartine, it is hard to see the generic property. Joseph is a *rêveur;* his verse is reflective and 'analytic', but his manner is humdrum; his poems disdain grace in a curiously tortuous way; there is an exasperated search for a tone at once flatly inexpressive and full of unusual half-uttered hints. The result is not easy to convey in translation, with its deliberate infringements of ordinary grammar, neologisms, uncouth obliquities, through to the occasional almost *tangible* felicities of expression. André Bellesort summed up well: 'Chaque fois que Joseph Delorme me parle sentiment je me sens très loin de lui; et dès qu'il me parle sensation, très près.'[23]

It is the 'sentiment', however, which is translatable. Joseph Delorme elegizes after his own manner on his sorrows, his defects, his platitudinous failures, his vain longing for stirring events. Everything is mean, the contrary of worthwhile, *anti-poetic.* His 'Muse' (naturally he has one) is tuberculous and coughs blood (actually *coughs*—a novelty that evoked much antiromantic sarcasm); his dreams are of suicide, but always unobtrusive and unregretted, or of impossible felicity in love. Only one thing is extreme and in a sense heroic: the despondency itself, the *acedia* of Joseph Delorme, his capacity to relish and prolong it. Here Baudelaire found for the first time outside himself an authentic revelation of *spleen*, Laforgue his rainy Sunday afternoons with their endlessness measured out by the jangling of a distant piano. Both of them—and many others—are linear descendants of the author of the **Rayons jaunes,** with his emotional vacuum and arid dissonances:

> In summer, on a Sunday evening,
> At six o'clock, the crowds flock from their homes
>   To wander in the fields;

My shutter closed, I sit before the window,
Look down and watch the cheerful citizens,
  The workmen in their Sunday best

Who pass and disappear, without a care.
A book is open by me on my chair:
  I make pretence to read;
And the sun's setting yellow rays,
Yellower now than on a weekday evening,
  Yellow the curtain's white [. . .].

The characteristic point about this aridity is that it is not, as with Baudelaire, developed through a vivid hallucination or demonic haunting. Beautiful Good is not simply replaced by hideous Evil. To get the full sense of Joseph Delorme's aimless ache, the world itself must be created valueless, void. He achieves his proper note not by plunging into the *fourmillante cité, cité pleine de rêves,* but by going down to the very prosy tea-gardens on the boulevard, jostled by the crowds, and repelled by 'songs, clamours, drunken brawls, open-air love, and unrestrained embraces, and public favours'. Nothing of this drives him out of his senses, there is merely an extinction of energy, of interest, a sort of moral suicide:

> Homewards I turn; around presses the throng;
> All night I hear the drunkards trailing by
> And shouting in the road [. . .].

Vigny was enraptured by the **Rayons jaunes.**[24] More prudent sensibilities reared up at Joseph's nasty yellow mood; what offended most was not the colour theme (daring enough, in terms of rhetoric, and not forgotten by Gautier and Baudelaire and after) but the whine of the *petit bourgeois,* whose self-absorption is so much less excusable than the massive egoism of romantic Lucifers. Also, this young man calls a spade a spade without even taking pleasure in shocking. And that, perhaps, is a subversiveness which can take one far.

Vigny also recognized as outstanding Joseph Delorme's rendering of a theme made illustrious by Lamartine's sumptuous *Vallon*: the title being varied to **Le Creux de la vallée.** Here again we have an exact delineation of the 'elegiac' mood peculiar to Sainte-Beuve. Lamartine's poem was all but a prayer—misty, sugary, idealized. Sainte-Beuve's is duller, less resonant—though for once one comes upon lines here of a thin, sensuous freshness not often matched in French verse.[25] Joseph Delorme had found at last the ideal spot in which to drown himself: a cool backwater in an unfrequented valley. He can slip into the stream and disappear, 'silently, without a crowd of neighbours'. And having savoured the project, he goes on to imagine the discovery of the corpse, the suicide's burial at the hands of men who neither know nor care who he was—the joy of *complete* anonymity. His poem ends at this point; but Sainte-Beuve adds six lines which presumably are addressed by Joseph Delorme *to* himself as an afterthought: 'and what do you suppose the valley and all its beauties has to do with this fine plan?' is about the gist of them. He has caught himself playing at pathetic fallacies. *Where* the annihilation takes place should be a matter of entire indifference:[26] a scenic backcloth is superfluous.

Within this framework of radical dispiritment, Sainte-Beuve develops his hero's poetic moods. Joseph Delorme knows days when inspiration fails and the spirit refuses to blow. He alludes to them in his ***Pensées*** (Sainte-Beuve repeatedly in later years detected like misfortunes in some of his favourite poets); and in the ***Poésies*** there is one unexpected and really very accomplished piece, ***Le Calme,*** which opens a rich vein for Mallarmé with its symbol of the voyage of discovery, the ship becalmed, the breath of inspiration failing.[27] It is clear that Joseph Delorme's Muse must often fail him, from the nature of her gifts; he describes her (***Ma Muse***) 'realistically'—neither odalisque nor peri, virgin nor tearful widow—poor but honest (textually!), tending her blind old father, sometimes singing, but stopping often to cough. The same limitations are set out in another image, in ***Promenade.*** Not for him the savannahs of Chateaubriand, peopled with American lions (*sic*), nor the Jura, symbol of Lamartine's sublime excursions, nor Victor Hugo's Rhine and crumbling Gothic Keeps:

> The eagle to his mountain, the giant to his gulfs,
> Sublime views call for a sublimer vision—

Joseph Delorme is at home in the domestic fields and hedgerows, borrowing contentment from others and mutely complaining he is 'too young, too tender of heart and quick to heal, to be tired of life'. Even *acedia* has its moments of respite.

A number of elegies feature other of Joseph Delorme's chosen fellow sufferers—preferably those who like himself manifest a tendency to reverie or poetic wishful dreaming or to suicide, and with special solicitude for plain young maidens who grow into forlorn spinsters, serious silent girls who (like Natalie Vertel) are sacrificed to duty and pass their days

> Like nameless waves beneath a silent sky,
> Slow-moving, uniform, yet dignified.

The best and most famous of these pieces is of course ***Toujours je la connus,*** where the result for once *is* dignified in a restricted way; a certain austere expressiveness *does* carry the halting verse and rescue a string of anaemic understatements from prosiness, though quite without any verbal charm or resonance. Such success is exceptional, however, because Sainte-Beuve relies unduly on the 'pathetic' character of his situations, and in these situations displays his feelings as thin and tepid.

It is perhaps this fact which caused another 'elegy', ***Rose,*** to offend early readers in precisely the same way that Manet's *Olympia* offended the public in 1865. Rose is the prostitute to whom Joseph Delorme returns for a night. In the choice of subject there is no great originality, but the effect is new; unlike Baudelaire and his *Vénus noire,* Joseph is unmoved by voluptuous memory or remorse: the encounter is not abominable, merely depressing. Rose is not without her attractions; but Joseph is more preoccupied by her character than by her charms, anxious to avoid giving embarrassment, curious how she spends her days, sorry for her.—And more typically, sorry for *himself* because Rose's travesty of love is all he has to put in place of the real thing.

Here one touches on the really glaring defect of the ***Poésies.*** Seeing how much Sainte-Beuve stakes on the sentimental appeal of Joseph Delorme, the self-pity on every page is intolerable: never a grain of irony in these elegies (except in ***Le Creux de la vallée***), nothing to palliate Joseph's endless whine. ***La Veillée,*** where Hugo sitting by the cradle is contrasted with Joseph watching miserably over a dying pauper (an echo of the death of tante Carmier?) or ***En m'en revenant un soir d'été,*** where the poet looks longingly at all the pretty strangers in the street, and wonders whether one of them might not have been able to cure him of his despondency; or ***Premier Amour*** (unreturned adoration), ***Dernier Vœu*** (the same), ***Bonheur Champêtre*** (uselessness of the example of rustic contentment)—an endless whine, maudlin and crude. No doubt it is part of the character, the *persona*; but that does not make it more acceptable. Nerval, Baudelaire, Corbière, Laforgue, Verlaine, all in fact indulge the same self-pity as their ancestor, but in one way or another ironize or distance the theme of Pierrot, the *poète disgracieux*. Only Joseph Delorme tries to deliver his *amours jaunes* direct and ticketed, and the result is frequently disastrous.

As if to vary the tediousness of the sentimental impasse, Sainte-Beuve allows Joseph Delorme to reveal designs and ambitions which are a good deal more jarring than his cries of self-pity. Apart from ***Rose*** there are poems in the collection so crude and sub-adolescent as to be grotesque: in ***Le Rendez-vous*** (dedicated to Musset) Joseph the seducer lies in his victim's arms rehearsing to himself a programme of systematic infidelity—*et que ce soit la vierge ou la veuve ou l'épouse.* He is surprised (but interested) when this *penser odieux* casts a shadow over present satisfactions. In ***À Alfred de Musset*** the dancer indulges in erotic fantasies which his partner is far from surmising. And so on. Experiments in 'psychological analysis'? In the eyes of the Cénacle sincerity and the authentic were an important goal, however unflattering; and the elegies had as much 'realism' as the descriptive ***La Plaine.*** Alfred de Vigny's approbation has been noted: it was typical. The self-pity ('no one has ever loved me') was—to judge from some of his letters—part of Sainte-Beuve's attitude towards his most intimate friends: at the moment of truth with Victor Hugo and Adèle, for example. Significantly, both of them had the most unfeigned sympathy for it, and there is every reason to suppose that they found Joseph Delorme's complaints as moving and pathetic as his author's. Today this whole side of Joseph Delorme is beyond our comprehension. As evidence in the case, it informs us amply about the young poet's chronic sense of insecurity, his unbalanced and uninhibited craving for mother-love, the protracted adolescent sexual fantasies which must have been sufficiently persistent (and common around him) for him to think them important. But they make very nearly the whole of the ***Poésies de Joseph Delorme*** a period piece, a document rather than a book to enjoy. Its surviving merits are there in spite of, rather than because of, any intentions on Sainte-Beuve's part; and these merits had little recognition at the time of publication, or more exactly they were dismissed as part of the same gracelessness of sentiment which set the critics sneering. Worst of all, Sainte-Beuve himself seems to have prized them on autobiographical grounds; and later (he changed little, suppressed nothing) they constituted his last link with the garden of vision, and evidence of a *sans-gêne* which it was gratifying to look back on.[28]

Yet ***Joseph Delorme*** *was* an important volume of poetry in its own time and subsequently.

Its success exceeded the expectations of its author. This is not saying much, at a period when, despite legends to the contrary, poetry was hard to publish. It sold a thousand copies, more than any single subsequent collection of the critic's verse; and this was the direct result of a not altogether desirable kind of publicity. Reviews—apart from Magnin's in the *Globe*—were for the most part hostile, several were virulent.[29] The book was talked about in the salons, which Jouffroy remarks were 'offended by this bourgeois poetry'[30]—offended by its blatant angularity, unpolished metres, mannerless crudity, 'romantic' disregard for established rhetorical patterns, and subversiveness. Joseph Delorme had no business to parade his loss of faith.

> This poor book [Sainte-Beuve wrote to a school-friend] has had all the success I could hope for: it has made honest folk cry out in indignation far more than I thought believable. Mme de Broglie has deigned to judge it *immoral*; M. Guizot pronounces it 'a Jacobin Werther of the medical schools' [*un Werther jacobin et carabin*]. In the *Globe* there have been schisms and arguments: Leroux, Jouffroy, Damiron, Lerminier and Magnin on the one hand, and MM. Vitet, Desclozeaux, Duvergier, Duchâtel, Rémusat on the other. Is not this splendid and diverting? [. . .] I have also seen M. Dubois since his return; [. . .] he seemed a little reserved towards me, though cordial, and perhaps at heart slightly annoyed, more for what is *not* in the book than for what *is*.[31]

A few days later the two men fell out; probably because Dubois published a letter from Duvergier (*un de vos abonnés*) which took Joseph Delorme to task for his critical dogmatism (in reference to the ***Pensées*** with which the volume ends). But in the main Sainte-Beuve endured his public's reactions 'philosophically', and said he was anxious to return to his 'solitude'.

The book went on to enjoy an unobtrusive but in fact durable life, not easy to define. So many of its repercussions are to be traced to bits and pieces, particular features, single lines even, rather than to an overall effect and example. The latter was felt, indeed: by his studied flatness of tone, Sainte-Beuve exercised a strong influence on numbers of his contemporaries and friends—the unjustly forgotten Saint-Valry, for instance, or Antoine Fontaney, Guttinguer too and Jules de Rességuier, mild hangers-on of the Cénacle whose voices are not loud enough to reach across the gap of a century, and whose works, overshadowed by the more considerable *œuvres* of Hugo, Vigny, Musset, have hardly been searched over for the occasional excellence. Joseph Delorme is so fruitful in this direction, indeed, that three years later his creator was being accused of trying to found an 'intimate school'. The thing was in the air, as Professor Praz has shown, all over Europe: it was the reduced scale literature that goes with the reduced scale drawing-rooms of the lower middle classes. Sainte-Beuve is only fully accountable for in this frame of reference; he is—at any rate in ***Joseph Delorme***—the complete representative of unheroic, even anti-heroic thought and feeling; outside conditions gave his verse a wide influence at the start.

Over the longer view, Sainte-Beuve's first volume of poems made the way easier for a galaxy of names to which we should now not instinctively join his. Gautier in early years (*Poésies,* 1830) was an almost blatant imitator, not only of metres but of the domestic prosy touch; he admitted as much, and Sainte-Beuve drew attention quietly to the fact years later.[32] Presently Baudelaire went on record that ***Joseph Delorme*** was the *Fleurs du Mal* of an earlier date;[33] and he was not trying merely to win over an influential critic when he called himself a disciple of 'uncle' Beuve. At 22 he addressed a long poem to him; already he recognized in his bloodless predecessor the same ennui which is celebrated in such high colour in *Spleen et idéal*; in the *Tableaux parisiens* he looked back to the same forerunner for the sordid panorama of suburbia, drab settings for the metaphysical ache. Baudelaire's admiration goes further, of course, than his poems reveal: ***La Veillée*** was 'marvellous', in his view, and ***Rose*** 'charming'. Some poems he thought too baldly rhetorical with their lutes and lyres, but generally speaking Joseph Delorme had brought relief from these things. Verlaine too was more than an ingratiating flatterer: long after the critic's death he declared ***Joseph Delorme*** 'in melancholic intensity and *power* of expression [. . .] infinitely above the jeremiads of Lamartine'.[34] In a dozen corners of *Jadis et naguère* the prosy touch taken from the older poet looks almost like a pastiche. With the coming of Verlaine, as a matter of fact, Sainte-Beuve's example is blended and lost in a wider range of lyrical shades: but until that time **Joseph Delorme** remains an important milestone, a symbol of trust in the allusiveness of plain statement, the natural godfather of any return to thoroughgoing poetic realism.[35]

I have dwelt on what appears to be Joseph Delorme's deliberate readiness to irritate, to grate on sensitive ears, as the price of verse stripped bare of its old connotations in rhetorical moulds and phrases. It is legitimate to wonder what might not have come out of this if the experiment had continued without interruption. Suppose the emollient **Consolations** not written in the following year. Had Sainte-Beuve the natural gift to develop the 'nasty', grating, but original side of his hero without falling into contemporary tricks of frenzy, posturing, or diabolism? One could imagine a Joseph Delorme led up the garden path by the very moral society that has no use for him; a sharper sense of the misfit, perhaps, without the easy way out of wishing for a soul's mate to plaster over the lack of religious conviction (instead of sentimentalism on both counts in the **Consolations**); and a stronger effort to cut out the rhetorical lapses which Baudelaire (and Stendhal) regretted. There might well have been the profile of an exceedingly original and important, disquieting, poet here. But this was not to be. The conditions which helped Sainte-Beuve to finish his book in 1828 acted against his development along the most promising line. The company of a crowd of budding poets, none of whom really shared his imperfectly formed ideal, quickly drew him away from the sour (but evocative) towards the nice (but mawkish). He drifted into conformity. The **Consolations** offered him by friendship with Hugo, Vigny, Guttinguer, were noble—too noble and effective altogether. The edge was lost, never to be recovered. Sainte-Beuve as a poet was—paradoxically—stifled by the Cénacle.[36]

Notes

1. For S.-B.'s knowledge of English poetry, see T. G. S. Combe, *Sainte-Beuve poète et les poètes anglais,* 1937.

2. M. Proust, *Pastiches et mélanges,* 1921, p. 264. The reference is to *Voyage en Espagne,* p. 2.

3. *Corr. gén.* [*La Correspondence générale de Sainte-Beuve*] i. 103, letter to Victor Hugo, 26 Aug. 1828.

4. Hugo, *Correspondance* (Calmann-Lévy), i. 263-4, letter of 17 Sept. 1828.

5. *Bulletin, Mod. Hum. Research Assoc.,* 1927, p. 17, E. M. Phillips, 'English friendships of S.-B.'

6. Cf. *Corr. gén.* i. 174, letter to Villemain of 31 Jan. 1830: 'J'avais pensé, quand j'ai été à Londres, à l'Université de Londres; mais cela n'a pu s'arranger et je préférerais le Continent.' On two occasions therefore S.-B. might with a little luck have settled in England. The second time, in 1848, he wrote to Abraham Hayward to ask whether there was a vacancy at London University; but the matter dropped and he went to Liège instead.

7. Ibid., p. 541, letter to Charles Labitte of 5 Sept. 1835.

8. He had complained to Hugo that life at Tubney Lodge left no time for this (op. cit. 104, letter of 26 Aug. 1828).

9. On the subject of stained glass windows he wrote to Hugo: 'These paintings, constantly interrupted by the leading, remind me of your little ballads, constantly cut across by the rhythm (your Gothic bas-reliefs which I would prefer to call your *Gothic stained glass*). In such compositions there is no great harm in one's seeing the line of the break, provided the total effect, the figure's carriage, his ecclesiastical or monkish or royal gait, is faithfully reproduced. How puerile then, in my view, to try to save all trace of the breaks, like the modern painter in Salisbury Cathedral who makes the edge of his glass coincide exactly with the edge of the draperies, so that one should notice nothing! He is meant to be painting on glass, not on canvas' (*Corr. gén.* i. 106, letter of 12 Sept. 1828). There cannot be much distance of time between this and a similar remark by Joseph Delorme on Hugo's Ballads, added to *Pensée IX* (*Poésies,* i. 160)—a simple variation on Hugo's reiterated theme of *enjambement* and rhythmic liberation or counterpoint.

10. It is almost impossible to date most of the pieces in this collection. An earliest date is all that can be assigned to most, on internal evidence: this has been done competently (see Évrard, 'Les Poésies de Joseph Delorme', *Bulletin de l'Association Guillaume Budé,* Oct. 1952, pp. 13 ff.). Probably the set of Sonnets (*Poésies,* i. 133-7) were begun in England (in particular, *Que de fois près d'Oxford, en ce vallon charmant*). With some obvious exceptions, S.-B. published most of this early verse in the order in which he wrote it. We also know that through the weeks after his return from England he was adding fresh poems for 'as long as the frost spared them' (see p. 62); it is reasonable to suppose that among these are the remaining three 'autumnal' pieces which end the collection, of which one (*La Plaine*) is modelled on Crabbe and another (*Stances*) imitated from Kirke White. Léon Séché is on the right track in conjecturing that S.-B. went to England to steep

himself in 'Lakists' (by which he always meant simply modern English poetry except Byron and Keats); it is not he but M. Billy who is 'hazardous' in advancing the direct contrary on the strength of the assumption that only 'a few weeks after his return' the *Poésies de Joseph Delorme* were ready (*Sainte-Beuve, sa vie et son temps,* i. 70-71). A recent edition of *Joseph Delorme* (G. Antoine, 1957) offers support for these arguments.

11. *Corr. gén.* i. 104, letter to Hugo, 26 Aug. 1828.

12. Ibid., p. 541, letter to Labitte, 5 Sept. 1835.

13. V. Hugo, *Correspondance,* i. 265.

14. *Corr. gén.* i. 111, letter to Loudierre, 6 Dec. 1828.

15. Ibid., p. 112.

16. Ibid., p. 62, 25 Jan. 1829.

17. See *N. L.* [*Nouveaux lundis*] xiii, 'Ma biographie': 'Je le rencontrai un soir chez Hugo, car les familles se connaissent; mais on ignorait chez Hugo que Musset fît des vers. C'est le lendemain matin, après cette soirée, que Musset vint frapper à ma porte. Il me dit en entrant:—Vous avez hier récité des vers; eh bien, j'en fais, et je viens vous les lire. Il m'en récita de charmants, un peu dans le goût d'André Chénier. Je m'empressai de faire part à Hugo de cette heureuse recrue poétique.'

The date of this first meeting is not clear. S.-B. puts it in 1830, which is impossible because three poems in *Joseph Delorme* are addressed to Musset. Summer 1828 is plausible. From the start this precocious boy is associated with shady and disreputable themes in *Joseph Delorme*; he may well have had a decisive part in breaking down certain reticences of outlook in his friend (see P. Josserand, 'Le Fiasco de Joseph Delorme', *Le Divan,* Oct. 1949, p. 193, the text of a revealing letter to Loudierre on a visit to a brothel in Jan. 1829.)

18. Picked up already in 1825 from Pichot's *Voyage littéraire.*

19. G. Antoine, *Vie, Poésies et Pensées de Joseph Delorme,* 1957, p. c, quoting an article of Chaudes-Aigues, *Revue de Paris,* Nov. 1839.

20. Musset, too, in his *Confession d'un enfant du siècle,* of 1835, invents the same memories and inspirations. It is not an exaggeration to say that his *mal de siècle,* born of indolence after the downfall of Napoleon, is directly inspired by Joseph Delorme, who at least was old enough to *remember* the Empire.

21. See Antoine, op. cit., pp. xcvi ff.

22. And it has been shown that in translating or adapting Schiller, Wordsworth, and Kirke White, S.-B. in each case gives his rendering a push in the direction of Joseph Delorme's own manner—flattening the tone, removing traces of 'style noble'. Cf. G. Antoine, op. cit., notes to *Le Plus Long Jour de l'année* and *L'Attente*; also Combe, op. cit., pp. 54-56, on the *Stances imitées de Kirk White.*

23. A. Bellesort, *S.-B. et le 19ᵉ siècle,* 1927, p. 83.

24. Vigny, *Correspondance,* ed. Séché, i. 39-40, 3 Apr. 1829.

25. For example:

> Mais vers le bas surtout, dans le creux, où la source
> Se repose et sommeille un moment dans sa course
> Ou murmure invisible à travers les sureaux,
> Que le vallon est frais! L'alouette y vient boire,
> La sarcelle y baigner sa plume grise et noire,
> La poule d'eau s'y pendre au branchage mouvant
> [. . .].

26. It is hard to accept G. Antoine's view of this epilogue 'où S.-B. se donne tout à fait l'air de plaisanter doucement son double' (op. cit., p. 207, n. 392). Joseph, true to an habitual frame of mind, is stripping off one more illusion, the illusion that natural beauty can comfort, adorn or compensate the wasted life: hence too the derisive echo of the lines which sing the praises of the valley. S.-B. is not 'gently mocking' in his epilogue, but ironical.

27. *Poésies,* i. 90. This is really the first poem in French to link the themes of the voyage, poetic inspiration, and poetic sterility. The hint of Lamartine's *Nouvelles Méditations* (*Les Préludes*) is barely more than a starting-point: his lines

> Sans regrets, sans espoir s'avancer dans la vie
> Comme un vaisseau qui dort sur une onde assoupie

may have caught the fancy of Joseph Delorme in 1823, the rest is very much the latter's own: the flat, *spoken* tone, the material details of the ship's departure—pulleys and hanging sails—the pilot watching for his breeze, and the unrhetorical ending, the day becalmed, the evening mist without a breath of poetry. This remarkable piece deserves much better than oblivion.

28. 'Et je suis encore étonné [. . .] de ce que j'ai osé y dire, y exprimer' (letter to Baudelaire, 20 July 1857, in *C. L.* [*Causeries du Lundi*] x. 82).

29. G. Antoine, op. cit., gives an exhaustive survey of these. The first were two articles in the *Globe*: 26 Mar. 1829, a 'puff', and 11 Apr. 1829, pp. 227-9, Magnin's review.

30. Jouffroy, *Le Cahier vert,* ed. P. Poux, 1923, p. 99, letter to Weiss.

31. *Corr. gén.* i. 128, letter to Loudierre, 23 Apr. 1829. Dubois might have been annoyed at Joseph Delorme's emphatic division between romantics

(pupils of Chénier), and *globistes* (pupils of Mme de Staël). The latter were 'without style or sense of form', diffuse improvisers, confused about poetry. He might also be annoyed *not* to find an ode to the *Globe* alongside one to the Cénacle, or lines to himself alongside the lines to Jouffroy. Unquestionably, there is something rankling still in S.-B.'s relations with his old master: perhaps Dubois's rudeness long ago at the specimen poems?

32. *N. L.* vi. 272. For an exhaustive treatment of J. D.'s influence, see G. Antoine, op. cit., pp. cvi ff.

33. Baudelaire, *Corr. gén.* v. 64-65, dated 15 Mar. 1865.

34. See Antoine, op. cit., pp. civ ff., for details of this admiration.

35. The passionate advocacy of Maurice Barrès puts the accent elsewhere: on the intelligent, voluptuous hyper-sensitivity of Joseph Delorme, hardly to be distinguished here from his author or from the later Amaury (*Le Culte du moi*, 1883, *Un Homme libre*).

36. S.-B. was very sensitive about his own influence, though modest enough on the subject. Once, on the poet Boulay-Paty, he noted that the volume *Élie Mariaker* was a frank imitation of *Joseph Delorme* (*N. L.* x. 181, article of 3 July 1865). In a letter to Baudelaire he harked back to *Joseph Delorme* as an obvious parallel to the *Fleurs du Mal* (*Lundis*, x. 528, letter of 20 July 1857); on another occasion he compares his own creature with Chateaubriand's account of himself in exile (*Lundis*, x. 82). On the other hand, S.-B. shows a certain coquettish interest in tracing affinities between *Joseph Delorme* and trends in painting: in 1857, at the Salon, he was delighted to discern these affinities in canvases of Rousseau and Corot (*Poisons*, p. 120), and later remarked on them in a letter to Théophile Gautier (*Correspondance*, i. 242, letter of 20 July 1859).

Richard M. Chadbourne (essay date fall-winter 1974-75)

SOURCE: Chadbourne, Richard M. "Sainte-Beuve's *Livre d'amour* as Poetry." *Nineteenth-Century French Studies* 3, nos. 1 and 2 (fall-winter 1974-75): 80-96.

[*In the following essay, Chadbourne argues that Sainte-Beuve's most neglected and maligned volume of poetry,* Livre d'amour, *possesses a structural unity not seen in his other volumes and should be accorded equal importance in the canon of Sainte-Beuve's work.*]

J'ai la conscience que je ne suis pas encore jugé comme poète

(*Pensées et maximes*, p. 262)

In the preface to the first edition of his *Pensées d'août* (1837), Sainte-Beuve refers obliquely to an additional volume of verse which he has completed, for which he has a special fondness, but which discretion (*la pudeur*) will not allow him to publish "for a very long time." Continuing the game of hide-and-seek in a postscript added in December 1844 to the original preface, he states: "L'auteur a composé en tout quatre recueils de vers, dans chacun desquels, n'aimant pas trop à se répéter, il aurait voulu avoir fait quelque chose de nouveau et de distinct. On a dans *Joseph Delorme* et *les Consolations* les deux premiers de ces recueils; les *Pensées d'août* sont le quatrième."[1]

The mysterious missing link was, of course, none other than the *Livre d'amour*, inspired by the poet's love affair with Madame Victor (Adèle) Hugo, which lasted approximately from 1830 to the winter of 1836-1837 and which also stimulated two other imaginative works of his, the novel *Volupté* (1834) and the short story *Madame de Pontivy* (1837). By 1844, however, the *Livre d'amour* had already begun to emerge from secrecy. In 1843 Sainte-Beuve had authorized the printing of 500 copies, anonymously; he had given a few to intimate friends and had preserved a few others, before destroying the rest.[2] Vanity had won a concession from *la pudeur*; to some extent the vanity of a man not averse to letting it be known that he had been the successful rival of Victor Hugo; to a greater extent, probably, the vanity of an artist unwilling to leave unpublished any portion of his work that he judged to have merit.

The first true edition of the *Livre d'amour* appeared in 1906, long after the deaths of Adèle Hugo (1868), the author himself (1869), and Victor Hugo (1885). To justify his publication of the complete text, Jules Troubat, Sainte-Beuve's last secretary, quotes from a manuscript dictated to him by the master and designed to serve as a preface for the book: "Ce sont ici des vers d'amour composés autrefois, en ce temps où l'on avait le bonheur de la jeunesse, des vrais plaisirs et des vrais tourments. On s'est décidé à en assurer l'existence, parce qu'ils ont été faits, *de l'aveu des deux êtres intéressés,* pour consacrer le souvenir de leur lien. Ils portent avec eux, d'ailleurs, leur explication plus que suffisante, et n'en souffrent pas d'autre ici."[3] Sainte-Beuve was resolved that in one form or another his book must survive: "Mon intention expresse est que ce livre ne périsse pas" (p. 17).[4] On the annotated copy that he gave to his friend Paul Chéron, who in turn bequeathed it to the Bibliothèque Nationale, he wrote: "Lege atque tace, et fidei tuae commissium secreto in posterum serva" ("Read and be silent and preserve in secret for the future [this work] entrusted to your confidence")—which prompted Troubat to quip, "Il n'y a pas de mystère pour la postérité, qui les évente tous" (p. 19).

Troubat's publication of the *Livre d'amour* set off one of the most violent controversies in the history of French literature, a veritable trial of Sainte-Beuve, pitting the defenders of his veracity against the champions of Adèle Hugo's "honor." In all this furor the book, inevitably, was treated less as a work of poetry, a work of art, than as a document, a "pièce du procès." It was viewed as a kind of verse diary that ought never to have been published, a scandalous account of how its author betrayed his best friend, avenging himself for Hugo's presumed superiority over him and boasting, in all kinds of ungentlemanly detail, of his conquest of a supposedly reluctant Adèle Hugo. A sordid timetable of adultery, in short—as though Sainte-Beuve were the first poet to write of adulterous love! "Rendre ainsi publique une liaison adultère, ce sont jeux de poètes," noted Gustave Michaut, pointing out furthermore that Victor Hugo had published in 1835 his own *Livre d'amour* in the form of the *Chants du crépuscule*, celebrating the joys of loving both his wife and his mistress (the unnamed but easily detectable Juliette Drouet).[5]

The question of adultery aside, the *Livre d'amour* quite simply shares in the ambiguity attached more or less to all love poetry. For whom is such poetry written? To whom does it "belong"? How can the poet reconcile the two beings within him, the lover with his natural desire for secrecy and intimacy, and the artist with his equally natural desire to translate his private experience into universal terms and to receive some degree of public recognition? He must regard his love poetry, as Pablo Neruda has said of *Los Versos del Capitán,* as somehow his and not his, and allow it to "go through the world on its own and grow by itself."[6] "A good love poem," wrote T. S. Eliot in his essay, "The Three Voices of Poetry," "though it may be addressed to one person, is always meant to be overheard by other people. Surely [he adds] the proper language of love—that is, of communication to the beloved and to no one else—is prose."[7] Sainte-Beuve's evasiveness with his public concerning the *Livre d'amour*; the contradictions in such a poem as the one beginning **"Jeune, avide, inconnu, j'ai désiré la gloire"** (XIV), where his love of fame clashes with his sense of *pudeur* ("O Sainte Poésie, intime, et qu'il faut taire"); the self-contradictory nature of such lines as "Poète, fais des vers, non pour qu'on les admire, / Fais-les pour Celle aux bois qui seule les désire, / Pour le silence et l'ombre et tous les dieux cachés" (XXXIV)—all this, rather than being a monstrous aberration on the part of one poet, is inherent in the ambiguous nature of the genre of love poetry itself.

No work of Sainte-Beuve has been so maligned as the *Livre d'amour.* "Méchants vers—méchants aux deux sens du mot," wrote the chief prosecutor in the "trial" of the book, Gustave Simon. Although he found some redeeming features in Sainte-Beuve's letters to Adèle, he approached the discussion of the *Livre d'amour* itself with distaste: "Nous voici arrivé à la partie pénible de notre tâche, à ce qui en est pourtant la conclusion nécessaire; il faut parler du *Livre d'amour.*"[8] Even Gustave Michaut, a friendlier as well as a much more objective and reliable critic of Sainte-Beuve than Simon, in his rebuttal of the latter's charges and elsewhere says little of the poetry itself and concludes that whatever beauty the poems may have is insufficient to absolve their author of the guilt of indiscretion.

Granted that the poet was indiscreet in allowing the 1843 printing, one wonders with Troubat (pp. 19-20) why no hue and cry of scandal went up when over half of the poems appeared in the 1861 edition of the *Poésies.*[9] True, these tend to be what Troubat calls "les [pièces] les moins caractérisées," true also that Adèle's name is withheld; but any alert reader could guess what was going on. There is no evidence, furthermore, that Adèle objected to the publication of any of the poems at any time, or that she was anything but a willing partner in her love affair with Sainte-Beuve. There is, on the contrary, evidence in the text itself to support the theory that the poetic concept of love underlying the work owes as much to Adèle's collaboration as to the invention of the poet.

The *Livre d'amour* is indeed a "journal," as Thibaudet and other critics have claimed, but it is a "journal *poétique,*" and that is the essential difference. What matters in reading it is not the literal accuracy of the account of "what happened," but the internal logic and coherence of the interpretation which it provides of a particular experience. Here Michaut was on the right track when he observed, "Sainte-Beuve a composé le *Livre d'amour* au fur et à mesure des événements . . . Mais le poète n'aura pas seulement noté dans ce journal les paroles et les faits: il y aura noté ses désirs, ses espérances, ses rêves; et ce qu'il envoyait à son amie, ce n'était pas seulement le récit de ce qui s'était passé, c'était encore . . . le récit de ce qui se serait passé si elle avait exaucé ses vœux."[10] But whereas Michaut found Sainte-Beuve's effort "pour rendre le réel poétique et cependant ne s'en écarter point" to be "curieux,"[11] most readers today, I dare say, would assume that this is precisely what poetry is all about.

In an essay on the Abbé Prévost in his *Portraits littéraires,* Sainte-Beuve observed that those who, like the Abbé Prévost, "joignent une âme tendre et une imagination vive à un caractère faible" (he certainly intended to include himself) should be judged by their writings rather than by their lives; for, he reasoned, "si notre vie bien souvent laisse trop voir ce que nous sommes dev-enus, nos écrits nous montrent tels du moins que nous aurions voulu être."[12] His own love affair with Adèle Hugo was fertile ground for imaginative projections of what might have been. The most ambitious and the most ennobling of such fictions was *Volupté*: Amaury's love for Madame de Couaën remains platonic; her virtue becomes an instrument of his return to God and his ordination to the priesthood; her death reconciles him with her husband, a tragic figure of failed political ambi-tion. The **Livre d'amour,** though closer to the actual facts of the *roman vécu,* reshapes and illuminates these in its own manner, providing still another view of its creator, "tel qu'il aurait voulu être."

Heeding Sainte-Beuve's counsel, then, that these poems contain their own "explication plus que suffisante," I turn now to an analysis of the text.

One of the first features to strike the reader about the **Livre d'amour** is that it possesses a unity and a form—an "architecture," one might say today—which were denied to its relatively shapeless companions. It reads, in fact, almost like a novel in verse form. (There are curious allusions in the author's footnotes to the lovers' project of a "roman par lettres" based on their relationship (pp. 38, 58, 199).[13] A kind of "plot" allows us to follow, across the 41 numbered poems and the four unnumbered **"Pièces finales,"** the genesis, growth, fulfillment, and decline of their passion, in more or less chronological order but with occasional use, to good psychological effect, of both anticipation and flashback. The lovers' physical union, although it occurred two years after they first met, is alluded to very early in the work (VI, **"Que vient-elle me dire, aux plus tendres instants"**), as though to express the poet's impatience to reach that moment. On the other hand, the scene *chez les Hugo* in which he was probably first encour-aged by Adèle in his attraction to her is not recorded until **"Récit à Adèle"** (VIII), with its great lines: "J'allais sortir alors, mais tu me dis: *Restez!* / Et, sous tes doigts pleuvant, la chevelure immense / Exhalait jusqu'à moi des senteurs de semence."

The main body of the work ends with an open, one might almost say an infinite, perspective, in the poem beginning "Le long de cette verte et sereine avenue" (**"XLIᵉ et dernière"**). Returning toward Paris from their walk together in the countryside near Saint-Mandé (Seine-et-Marne), the poet expresses the wish that the *barrière* which they are approaching might forever recede, so that their path might become infinite and they might grasp in their embrace "le temps éternisé" (the poem closes with these words). But the end of their affair, already foreshadowed in more than one poem (for example, in **"1ᵉʳ septembre,"** XXXVII), has finally come: the reverie of eternal love is abruptly followed by an epilogue of four poems on the theme of what the

poet calls "le déchirement ou la décroissance [de leur passion]" (p. 209).

As in a novel there are also characters, settings, atmosphere. Basically, as one would expect, the work is a *roman à deux*—the poet and Adèle, "l'Amie," "la Fi-ancée," "Elle," "la pauvre captive"—with "Lui," "le sombre époux," "le jaloux," le dangereux témoin," hovering as a threatening presence in the background. There are significant evocations also of the Hugos' second daughter (**"A la petite Adèle,"** XVI), of whom the poet was the godfather (but probably not the father) and whom he compares, to her advantage, to her older sister: "Cette Léopoldine est fille des Césars: / Elle at-tire, elle impose; elle est fine, elle est belle; / Mais c'est Lui, surtout Lui, que sa lèvre rappelle." Only once, in this same poem, as though moved by his affection for little Adèle, does the poet cast Victor Hugo in a sympathetic light; but what he bestows with one hand in the text—"Mon amitié peu franche eut bien droit aux rigueurs, / Et je plains l'offensé, noble entre les grands cœurs"—he takes away with the other in a typical *re-pentir beuvien* of a footnote: "Non, il n'est pas un noble cœur: artificieux et fastueux, il est vain au fond . . . mais j'ai longtemps été dupe.—J'étais dans l'antre du Cyclope, et je me croyais dans la grotte d'un demi-dieu" (p. 109).

The cast of characters is small not only because the atmosphere is intimate but also because the lovers had almost no intermediaries and because much of their ef-fort consisted of a search for rendezvous where they might be alone. When secondary characters appear—the other guests at the Hugo home, the philosopher Bal-lanche intercepting and detaining the poet on his way to a tryst with Adèle ("Jamais je ne l'ai vu si palingénésique")—it is usually as unwanted presences, as obstacles to communication between the lovers.

The "action" of the work might indeed be summed up as the attempt of two lovers to find suitable meeting places; and these in turn become the characteristic dé-cors of the story: churches, cemeteries, obscure hotels, country lanes, and at least once, a horse-drawn cab (XXX, **"Sonnet. Aux Champs-Élysées"**)—the famous *fiacre* whose erotic possibilities Sainte-Beuve exploited long before Flaubert made use of them in *Madame Bo-vary.*

As for the moral or psychological atmosphere, it is no less well defined and distinctive than the physical. It is marked by frustrations, by separations and long periods of waiting (". . . notre courte joie / Et notre longue attente"—XXIII), by attempts to communicate through glances and gestures ("Le regard du jaloux s'aveugle en quelques jours; / Les amants se font signe et s'entendent toujours"—IV), unobserved by others ("L'invisible courant d'elle à moi répandu, / Le fil éolien entre nous deux tendu"—"Une onde mutuelle en silence établie"— XXXI). What is original about this is not the sense of a frustrated passion that must use all its ingenuity to declare itself, or the sense of secrecy; poets and novelists have traditionally thrived on such handicaps; the new twist which Sainte-Beuve gives to an old theme lies to a great extent in the bourgeois setting of such a poem as XXXII, to which I shall return a bit later.

A veil of sadness, a shadow, hangs over the work; pleasure and joy, though occasionally real, are short-lived. "Notre bonheur n'est qu'un malheur plus ou moins consolé," Sainte-Beuve had already forewarned Adèle in an epigraph from the eighteenth-century dramatist, Jean-François Ducis, affixed to the poem dedicated to her which opens *Les Consolations,* a poem whose first lines even foreshadow the mood of much of the *Livre d'amour*: "Oh! que la vie est longue aux longs jours d'été, / Et que le temps y pèse à mon cœur attristé!" (Had Sainte-Beuve only been able to sustain the beauty of such lines as these, he would have been a great poet indeed.) Unlike Musset, whom he describes in his *cahiers* as belonging to the family of bacchanalian revellers, Sainte-Beuve's group—his "secret group," let it be noted—was that of the "*adultères (moechi) . . . ceux qui sont tristes comme Abbadona, mystérieux et rêveurs jusqu'au sein du plaisir et pâles à jamais sous une volupté attendrie.*"[14] To Adèle, who was disturbed by his lack of hope, he protested that his love for her was real, even though it only rarely wore "cette robe de grâce et d'illusions charmantes" and seldom appeared "étincelant de blancheur." "Il est sombre," he added, "il se confond avec ces nuances tombantes du soir dans ces églises où nous allons; il a été veuf, pour ainsi dire, et un peu découragé dès son berceau; il s'est habitué au deuil, même au sein du bonheur" (p. 7, letter to Adèle quoted by Troubat).

A perfect description of the tone of the *Livre d'amour.* Was not Sainte-Beuve, born to a mother already widowed and himself more than "un peu découragé dès son berceau," predestined to render just this strange nuance in his love-poetry? "J'ai toujours été médiocrement doué de la faculté de l'espérance," he went on to say in the same letter to Adèle, "j'ai toujours senti l'obstacle et l'empêchement en toutes choses: mes sentiments ont toujours un peu manqué de soleil dans la saison propice" (p. 8).

Troubat compared the *Livre d'amour* to "la musique de chambre, concentrée et personnelle" (p. 15). Although Sainte-Beuve is rarely a "musical" poet in the conventional sense, the comparison is not without meaning. "Chaque poète," we read in the *cahiers,* "a les défauts de sa manière"; Hugo, his Vulcan-like hammer strokes, Lamartine his cascades overflowing and scattering watery spray. "Pour moi," noted Sainte-Beuve, "mon rayon de poésie ne m'arrive souvent que dans une petite

chambre bien sombre, à travers une vitre dépolie . . ."[15] In the unpublished preface dictated to Troubat he declared, "Fruit rare et mystérieux de plusieurs années d'étude, de contrainte et de tendresse, [ces vers d'amour] se ressentent par moments de ce manque de grand air et de soleil; ils ont sans doute des parties difficiles et obscures; mais ils y gagnent du moins pour la vérité, pour la sincérité" (pp. 15-16).

This feeling of a life in suspense, of a closed-in, sunless, motionless atmosphere, with its sad kind of happiness, more consolation than real joy or pleasure, is well summed up in the final tercet of the sonnet, **"Octobre. Elle est à Bièvre"** (XVII): "Oh! oui, c'est là ma vie, amoureuse et stagnante, / Calme sous son brouillard, et si peu rayonnante; / Absence de plaisir sur un fond de bonheur!"

Yet despite the relative joylessness of a love which André Maurois accurately described as having been "dès son aube, crépusculaire"[16] (Sainte-Beuve's *Chants du crépuscule*?), strong forces are at work in the *Livre d'amour* which give the concept of love affirmed therein a surprisingly positive quality. These are: the association of love with religion and with the intellectual, quasi-scholarly pursuit which the poet calls "étude" ("notre amour, ma seule et vive étude"—IX); the evocation of various classical and other poetic traditions of love, also a matter of "study"; and above all, the sifting of experience through the poet's (and to some extent his beloved's) imagination and memory. Much the same forces that operate in *Volupté,* they produce a similar ennobling effect, testifying, as in the novel, to the author's determination to extract from the raw material of his experience some spiritual meaning, some ideal worth striving to attain.

The religious aspiration underlying the work, as Sainte-Beuve recognized, is far from pure. In his unpublished preface he refers to "un mélange et comme un conflit de deux inspirations que le poète n'a pas fondues sans doute autant qu'il aurait fallu," and he explains: "L'amour antique, fatal, violent, y perce et revient déjouer par accès l'amour chrétien, mystique, idéal, qui se flattait de régner." It was, he adds, as though "la manière de *Joseph Delorme* revient ici traverser et troubler celle des *Consolations,*" resulting not only in "mélange" but also in some degree of "obscurcissement." If this is a defect in the work he is willing to defend it, once again, on the ground that "la poésie en est sincère, et l'âme a coulé par la blessure" (p. 16).

Adèle Hugo, as the reader of *Les Consolations* knows, attracted Sainte-Beuve in part because her religious faith seemed to promise him support in his own spiritual quest, as well as renewed artistic inspiration after a period of dryness in which it appeared that he might abandon all serious study, all sense of piety and of communication with the Muse. "J'abandonnais l'étude et tant de morts chéris / . . . La Muse, en se voilant, de moi se retirait" (V). Poetry and religious aspiration in this phase of Sainte-Beuve's life are inseparable. If, he wrote to his friend the Abbé Eustache Barbe in July 1829, he seemed to be returning to religion, "ç'a été bien moins par une marche théologique, ou même philosophique, que par le sentier de l'art et de la poésie. Mais peu importe l'échelle, pourvu qu'on s'élève et qu'on arrive."[17] A few years later he might have added (though certainly not to the Abbé Barbe) "le sentier de l'amour . . . même adultère." His *Livre d'amour,* like that other "book of love," *Volupté,* can be understood only as part of a larger whole: his search for a durable faith.

One of his letters to Adèle (it would certainly have found a worthy place in their unrealized *roman par lettres*) provides touching testimony to the sincerity of his association of religion and love. Recalling their rendez-vous the day before in the very chapel where, fourteen years earlier, a lonely homesick adolescent newly arrived in Paris from Boulogne-sur-Mer, he had wept over the Psalm of exile, *Super flumina Babylonis,* he expressed his gratitude to Adèle for re-establishing this link with the past and allowing him to become once again "tendre et pieux de cœur et si tendrement aimé" (pp. 9-10).[18]

The lovers' trysts in churches and graveyards were therefore not simply a matter of accident or expediency, but part of their hope of redeeming their adulterous relationship, somehow even of legitimizing it, through acts of piety toward the dead, through "charité," while at the same time avoiding blasphemy. "Amour et charité n'étaient qu'un dans mon sein / . . . Et nous pouvons ainsi sans blasphème, Elle et moi, / Toucher à ces objets de prière et de foi" (X). The poem from which these lines are quoted concludes as follows:

> La piété funèbre, errant sous les rameaux,
> Donne au bonheur discret le souvenir des maux,
> Le prépare à l'absence; et quand, l'heure écoulée,
> On part,—rentré chacun dans sa foule mêlée,
> On voit longtemps encor la pierre où l'on pria,
> Et la tombe blanchir sous son acacia!

The closing lines of **"L'Enfance d'Adèle"** (IV) read: "Ma vertu vient de toi, j'ai besoin de soutien: / 'Ami, conseillons-nous, m'as-tu dit, dans le bien, / Pour qu'en tous nos soucis et parmi nos orages / La pureté se voie écrite à nos visages." The late Pierre Moreau, in a penetrating analysis of Sainte-Beuve's *tempérament,* wrote: "Hasardons ces définitions de Sainte-Beuve: le célibataire à la recherche de la vertu, le libertin en quête de la pureté."[19]

The linking of love with religion, together with the prospect of aging together and the hope of constancy as time passed, enabled the lovers to cling, even in the midst of adultery, to an ideal of innocence and purity—a paradox that Baudelaire, if not Claudel, would have understood . . . The fine sonnet beginning "Si quelque blâme, hélas, se glisse à l'origine" (XXIV) has as its tercets the following lines:

> Approche, ô ma Délie, approche encor ton front,
> Serrons plus fort nos mains pour les ans qui viendront:
> La faute disparaît dans sa constance même.
> Quand la fidélité, triomphant jusqu'au bout,
> Luit sur des cheveux blancs et des rides qu'on aime,
> Le Temps, vieillard divin, honore et blanchit tout!

As fate would have it, this description, ironically enough, would have applied much better to Victor Hugo's life-long relationship with Juliette Drouet than to the later years of Sainte-Beuve and Adèle, who remained on friendly terms but saw little of each other.

The ennobling effect sought by the poet is also enhanced by frequent allusions to classical mythology and to examples of lovers consecrated by tradition. In the sonnet just quoted, Adèle is cast in the role of Delia, the first love of Tibullus, from whom the epigraph is taken: ". . . Nos, Delia, amoris / Exemplum cana simus uterqua coma" ("We shall be love's exemplar even when our hair is white").[20] Adèle at her *toilette,* at least in the poet's eyes, resembles Hera in the *Iliad* (**"Récit,"** VIII), and the lovers' frustrations are compared with the unhappiness which Penelope, in remarks to Odysseus, attributes to the malevolence of the Gods, "who could not bear to see us share the joys of youth and reach the threshold of old age together" (XVII, in a footnote).[21] Thus does Sainte-Beuve put two of his favorite classical poets to good use—if one is willing to forgive his somewhat pedantic addiction to footnotes—in the shaping of his own myth of love.

A more significant source of this myth, however, is Petrarch, "notre maître à tous en poésie," like Sainte-Beuve a studious and learned poet, "cherchant l'esprit des morts sous la page moisie" (XXXIII, **"Sonnet. L'Amant antiquaire"**). Petrarch had served to bless the concept of friendship celebrated in *Les Consolations* before being called on to render a similar service to love in the *Livre d'amour.*[22] Petrarch's Laura was another model that Sainte-Beuve had in mind for Adèle. But in the final poem of the epilogue on the theme of the decline of love, he suggests that the role of a more passionate heroine than Laura might have suited her better and that his own circumspect preference for something gentler and subtler than ardent passion may have spoiled their relationship: "J'ai voulu, de Didon, ou de Phèdre, ou d'Hélène, / Faire, ô ma Laure aimée, une plus douce Reine, / . . . Je voulais la nuance, et j'ai gâté l'ardeur!"[23]

Of all the forces at work in the *Livre d'amour* to idealize experience none is so strong as the combined power of imagination and memory, assisted by their auxiliaries, *le cœur* and *la rêverie.*

Few women in love poetry have been imagined, anticipated, called forth over such a long period of foreshadowing as Adèle, the object of this "late love" (Propertius' "tardus Amor" of the epigraph introducing **"L'Invocation"**). In 1830 Sainte-Beuve, at twenty-six, felt himself to be prematurely aged—"Adèle, à mon midi, déjà je me sens vieux" (VIII). At first, long before this, his beloved had been but a vague focal point of desire: "Poursuivant dès l'enfance un être inespéré, / Mais sans désir certain, sans objet déclaré" (VIII). In **Joseph Delorme** the details begin to be filled in: "Pourquoi ne pas enfin trouver une âme tendre, / Affligée elle-même et qui saurait m'entendre" (**"Après une lecture d'Adolphe"**). The vision finally assumes substance in **Les Consolations,** dedicated to Victor but meant for Adèle, and already a kind of rehearsal for the **Livre d'amour.** Had Adèle not existed, Sainte-Beuve would have been obliged to invent her.

But even once they met, the very circumstances of their relationship—obstacles in the way of communication, prolonged separations—made it necessary for them to nourish their passion and to keep it alive by musing upon it and recollecting it, by exchanging verbal self-portraits, *récits, histoires de leurs cœurs.* "Seulement rien de nous qui nous vînt par autrui, / . . . Pas un ami commun, et dans nos alentours / Nous seuls à nous connaître, à nous nommer toujours!" (XXXI). All love is a creature of the imagination, but few loves have been so dependent on the imagination as this one.

The poet's knowledge of Adèle is acquired in "the mirror of his heart," and he in turns assumes, as reflected in the mirror of hers, a nobler image than he believed himself to possess in reality. From this point of view, no epigraph in the book is so revealing as the quotation from Ballanche introducing **"L'Enfance d'Adèle"**: "Tout se passe au fond de notre cœur, et c'est notre cœur seul qui donne à tout l'existence et la réalité"— good Romantic doctrine, of which the **Livre d'amour** offers a not unworthy application. In this same poem Adèle, imprisoned by "le sombre époux," dreams of her "Ami," while he in turn assures her, ". . . Au prisme de ma foi, / Au miroir de mon cœur, je te contemple en moi; / Absent, j'ai là ta vie illuminée et peinte; / Là, nuit et jour, j'entends chaque pas, chaque plainte, / Et tu ne peux rien dire, imaginer, sentir, / Qui n'y vienne à l'instant briller ou retentir." He then proceeds, in a kind of *portrait en vers,* to filter through his own imagination the childhood memories she has related to him: "Je te vais reconter ton enfance à toi-même." While waiting for a letter from her, he writes, ". . . D'avance en retour / A mon propre miroir je te peins notre amour; / Je te le peins en moi, tel qu'il fut, tel qu'il aime; / Heureux si mon récit et le tien sont le même!" (VIII). Of

Lamartine's suggestion to Adèle that she have her portrait painted "en peignoir blanc," Sainte-Beuve has her declare: ". . . Je saurai m'y soustraire, / Avec art, s'il le faut, esquiver la prière, / Tenir bon au propos ou flatteur ou moqueur; . . . / Je me veux seulement ressemblante en ton cœur!" (XXVII).

Never given to inflated self-esteem, on the contrary tortured by self-doubts, Sainte-Beuve, in a poem full of apprehension ("Qui suis-je, et qu'ai-je fait pour être aimé de toi"—XV), assumes that Adèle cannot love what he calls "mon peu de prix et ma réalité"—"Elle aime en moi son rêve et non l'être réel"—and he fears that the dream will not last. In a footnote to this poem he proposes a curious epigraph, reading in part: "Je vois que ce n'est pas moi que vous aimez, mais une idée qui vous appartient uniquement et que vous avez rendue digne de vous"—curious, because (as if to suggest an element of "sexlessness" in their love?) the words are those of one woman, Madame de Staal, to another, Madame du Deffand.

Memory is inseparable from imagination in this creation of a poetic ideal of love.[24] The theme of memory— another characteristically Romantic theme—accounts for some of the finest lines in the **Livre d'amour.** Brooding over thoughts that seem to lack the power of inventiveness and wings for flight, the poet writes: "Avant de leur revoir leurs ailes nuancées, / J'ai besoin de couver bien longtemps mes pensées, / De recueillir mes jours en cet unique emploi, / Et de me souvenir, chère Adèle, de toi" (VIII). Rejecting the notion of a rendez-vous with Adèle at Bièvre before Victor arrives (this may, incidentally, be an example of Sainte-Beuve's insufficient *ardeur*), he writes: "Non, non, je n'irai pas; mieux vaut me contenir / Et rester dans l'absence à me ressouvenir" (IX). In still another poem (VII) he invites Adèle not to grieve for love letters that she must destroy but rather to entrust to memory alone the experience which these letters embodied; to memory, described in allegorical terms that are almost *baudelairiens*:

> Abus délicieux! confusion charmante!
> Passé qui s'embellit de lui-même et s'augmente!
> Forêt dont le mystère invite et fait songer,
> Où la Réminiscence, ainsi qu'un faon léger,
> T'attire sur sa trace au milieu d'avenues
> Nouvelles à tes yeux et non pas inconnues!

In one of his *Portraits littéraires,* written only a few years after this poem, Sainte-Beuve notes how Bernardin de Saint-Pierre transposes certain details of his *Voyage à l'Ile-de-France* into his novel, *Paul et Virginie,* and he cites this as an example of how "l'imagination, d'un toucher facile et puissant, transfigure et divinise tout dans le souvenir."[25] Except for the fact that his own imaginative touch is seldom either "facile" or "puissant," he might have been describing the transmutation of experience that occurs in the **Livre d'amour.**

From the point of view of technique, the book offers no radical departure from the theory and practice of its companion volumes. It confirms the author's faithfulness to Joseph Delorme's (i.e. his own) motto, *"L'art dans la rêverie et le rêverie dans l'art,"* and to his goal of developing an "Art poétique moderne."[26] He is careful to vary longer poems of the *récit* type with shorter forms, especially the sonnet, which stimulated some of his finest efforts. Another form he favors, much less "fixed" in nature than the sonnet, is the "élégie d'analyse" (I, 169). As the concluding piece in the *Pensées d'août* he had already published the poem from the **Livre d'amour** beginning **"Elle me dit un jour ou m'écrivit peut-être"** (X), with this comment: "J'ai souvent essayé de l'élégie, et j'en ai fait bien des sortes. En voici une que je crois pouvoir détacher d'une suite où elle était tout à fait à sa place, pour la présenter ici comme échantillon d'un genre assez nouveau: à la fois tendresse et pureté, et réalité toujours" (II, 283). An even better example he might have chosen of this blend is the poem beginning **"D'autres amants ont eu, dans leur marche amoureuse"** (XXXII), contrasting the idyllic spots in nature which served traditionally as lovers' trysting places, with the old hotel in a shabby section of Paris where the poet received his "Châtelaine."

All this is part of Sainte-Beuve's attempt to introduce into the elegy as practiced by André Chénier or Lamartine a greater *modernité,* "la peinture d'un monde moins métaphysique et d'une vie plus réelle" (I, 159). So also are the many touches of *prosaïsme voulu* in vocabulary and syntax—"Moi, vois-tu (ne ris pas, le mot est sérieux)"; "Nonchalamment, hier, la dame que tu sais"; or the Verlaine-like interrogation with which the poem **"Ier Septembre"** concludes: "Est-ce ainsi ton automne, Amour? . . . Oh! . . . pas encore!" But the freedom to use colloquial speech must be compensated for by certain artistic safeguards if "réalité" is not to degenerate into "le prosaïque et le trivial" (I, 159). The often commonplace subjects—"sujets empruntés à la vie privée et rendus avec relief et franchise . . . un incident domestique, une conversation, une promenade, une lecture"—must be heightened somehow if the poet is to meet the challenge he has given himself, the challenge, as he defined it to Victor Hugo, of raising "la réalité la plus vulgaire . . . à une plus haute puissance de poésie" (II, 14). The chief means of redeeming the prosaic is in the use of versification itself, of a more or less regular verse form (though the poet is resolved to make the alexandrine as flexible as possible), of rhyme, of a "strict" form such as the sonnet. Still further means lay in the abundant use of imagery (images of "liquidity" tend to dominate in the **Livre d'amour**), in the classical and other literary allusions we have referred to, and in a kind of *peinture* (as in **"Ier Septembre"**) which, anticipating the *correspondance baudelairienne,* makes a scene or landscape the outward sign of an inner spiritual reality.

To conclude, the passage of time and the death of the figures involved have purified and hallowed the memories evoked in the **Livre d'amour,** exactly as Sainte-Beuve predicted they would, in an 1855 essay on the subject of *Werther.* He was referring to the triangle Goethe-Charlotte-Kestner, but, as so often in his criticism, one may read between the lines an application to his own life and work, in this case (as Pierre Moreau suggested) to the triangle Sainte-Beuve-Adèle-Victor Hugo and to the **Livre d'amour.**[27] Divested of the scandal that once surrounded it, what remains of the book after all these years, again as Sainte-Beuve predicted, is "mêlé à l'affection véritable, un de ces rayons immortels de l'art que le devoir permettait ou disait de dégager."[28]

A pale ray, no doubt; certainly not—nor do I believe that the critic intended to make such a claim—of the same order of magnitude as Goethe's novel; but "un rayon de l'art" nevertheless. The **Livre d'amour,** though far from a neglected masterpiece, should be restored to its rightful place in the canon of Sainte-Beuve's poetry. It is unfortunately not free from the notorious defects of the rest of his verse, so often flat, laborious, clumsy. But it contains many isolated *beaux vers* that would be the envy of much greater poets, many interestingly conceived though not quite successfully executed poems, and a dozen or so excellent if not great ones. It possesses an impressive thematic unity derived from the *roman vécu* which it recreates. A modest but hardly contemptible score for any poet . . .

Notes

1. *Poésies* (Paris: Michel Lévy, 1863), II, 132-133.

2. Jean Bonnerot, *Un Demi-siècle d'études sur Sainte-Beuve, 1904-1954* (Paris: Société d'Édition "Les Belles Lettres," 1957), p. 32.

3. *Livre d'amour,* ed. Jules Troubat (Paris: Mercure de France, 1906), p. 15. Italics added. Page references in the text will be to this edition. All but the last four poems are numbered and will be referred to by their numbers.

4. Quoted from Sainte-Beuve's *testament* of December 19, 1843, the full text of which may be found in *Correspondance générale,* ed. Jean Bonnerot, V, Première partie (Paris: Stock, 1947), 365-367.

5. *Le Livre d'amour de Sainte-Beuve* (Paris: Fontemoing, 1905), p. 162.

6. Quoted in Introduction to *The Captain's Verses,* trans. Donald Walsh (New York: New Directions, 1972).

7. *On Poetry and Poets* (New York: Noonday Press, n. d.), pp. 97-98.

8. *Le Roman de Sainte-Beuve* (Paris: Albin Michel, 1926), pp. vi, 269 (originally published in 1906). The "roman" referred to is Sainte-Beuve's rela-

tions with Victor and Adèle Hugo, which Simon, despite his hostility to the author of the *Livre d'amour,* calls "un des plus beaux et des plus poignants parmi les 'romans vécus' les plus célèbres" (p. vii). Michaut's reply to Simon may be found in his "Le Roman d'amour et le 'Livre d'amour' de Sainte-Beuve," *Pages de critique et d'histoire littéraire (XIXe siècle)* (Paris: Fontemoing, 1910), pp. 156-233.

9. 26 out of the total 45, according to Bonnerot, *Un Demi-siècle d'études sur Sainte-Beuve,* p. 33.

10. *Pages de critique et d'histoire littéraire,* pp. 227-228.

11. *Le Livre d'amour de Sainte-Beuve,* p. 26.

12. *Œuvres,* ed. Maxime Leroy (Paris: Gallimard, 1951), II, 920.

13. For some idea of the content of Adèle's letters to her lover and for an account, which reads like a detective story, of their disposition, see Jean Bonnerot, "Les Lettres de Madame Adèle Victor-Hugo à Sainte-Beuve. Rapport de Henry Havard sur leur destruction en Novembre 1885," *Revue des sciences humaines,* Oct.-Dec. 1957, pp. 353-392.

14. *Pensées et maximes,* ed. Maurice Chapelan (Paris: Grasset, 1955), pp. 177-178. Italics in text. Abbadona was the fallen angel in Friedrich Klopstock's Biblical epic, the *Messias.*

15. *Mes poisons,* ed. Henri Guillemin (Paris: Bibliothèque 10/18, 1965), p. 27, text based on the Victor Giraud edition.

16. *Olympio ou la Vie de Victor Hugo* (Paris: Hachette, 1954), p. 229.

17. *Correspondance générale,* I, 138.

18. For the complete text of this letter, dated by Bonnerot 1831 or 1832, see *Correspondance générale,* I, 281-282.

19. *La Critique selon Sainte-Beuve* (Paris: Société d'Édition d'Enseignement Supérieur, 1964), p. 110.

20. *The Poems of Tibullus,* trans. Constance Carrier (Bloomington and London: Indiana University Press, 1968), p. 51. (Book I, vi).

21. *The Odyssey,* Book XXIII, in E. V. Rieu's translation, Penguin Classics, p. 346.

22. See epigraph from Petrarch's *De Vita solitaria* and Sainte-Beuve's translation of it in the dedicatory preface "A Victor H.," *Poésies,* II, 3, 5.

23. In a note to this poem, Sainte-Beuve refers to his short story, *Madame de Pontivy,* written "pour s'efforcer de *la* ramener." The last of the imagina-

tive works inspired by his love for Adèle, it is a witty *nouvelle historique* set in the Regency period of the early eighteenth century. As befits the less "mystical" Sainte-Beuve of 1837 (when the story first appeared in the *Revue des deux mondes*), it invents a purely worldly dénouement to their affair: M. de Murçay and Mme de Pontivy revive their expiring passion, he by acquiring greater "ardeur," and she, by acquiring greater "subtilité." For the text, see *Le Clou d'or,* ed. Jules Troubat (Paris: Calmann-Lévy, 1921).

24. Compare Amaury: "Quand je goûtais un vif bonheur, j'avais besoin, pour le compléter, de me figurer qu'il était déjà enfui loin de moi, et que je repasserais un jour aux mêmes lieux, et que ce serait alors une délicieuse tristesse que ce bonheur à l'état du souvenir." *Volupté,* ed. Raphaël Molho (Paris: Garnier-Flammarion, 1969), p. 181. (Ch. XIII.)

25. *Œuvres* (ed. Maxime Leroy), II, 112.

26. *Poésies,* I, 172 (italics in text), II, 234. The references in the concluding portion of the text are to this edition, cited above in footnote 1.

27. *La Critique selon Sainte-Beuve,* p. 111.

28. *Causeries du Lundi* (Paris: Garnier, n. d.), XI, 314-315.

Richard M. Chadbourne (essay date 1977)

SOURCE: Chadbourne, Richard M. "Unrequited Love: Poetry." In *Charles-Augustin Sainte-Beuve,* pp. 35-56. Boston: Twayne, 1977.

[*In the following essay, Chadbourne provides an individual analysis of each of Sainte-Beuve's volumes of poetry, as well as a discussion of his overall poetic achievement.*]

In a letter to an unidentified correspondent (it bears no date, but Bonnerot believes it was probably written in 1824), Sainte-Beuve confessed having composed poems for the past two years in an attempt to "define the vague fits of sadness" to which he was subject (B [*Correspondance générale,* ed. Jean Bonnerot and Alain Bonnerot (Paris and Toulouse, 1935-1975)] I, 56). It was not, however, until his momentous meeting with Hugo in 1827, and the beginning of their friendship and exchange of views on poetry, that he acquired enough confidence in himself to think of preparing his first book of verse. The result was the publication two years later of his *Vie, poésies et pensées de Joseph Delorme.* Although still to this day the best known of his poetic works, it was merely the first in a series of four major verse collections that he brought out between the ages of twenty-five and thirty-nine, the others being *Les Consolations* (1830), *Pensées d'Août* (1837), and, in a limited private printing, *Livre d'amour* (1843).

Before attempting to characterize each of these books, I should like to describe the general features that they share in common, so far as content is concerned. I shall return to their stylistic features later.

I THE POETIC WORK AS A WHOLE

What links all four books together is that they are so many fragments of the poet's spiritual autobiography in his late twenties and early thirties, so many chapters of an intimate journal in verse form. The apparently haphazard way in which the poems were arranged was probably as much a matter of plan as of accident. Thomas Hardy, in one of his prefaces, wrote that much of his poetry "comprises a series of feelings and fancies written down in widely differing moods and circumstances, and at various dates." Yet he was not alarmed that this might produce on the reader the effect of "little cohesion of thought or harmony of colouring," because, as he argued, "unadjusted impressions have their value, and the road to a true philosophy of life seems to lie in humbly recording diverse readings of its phenomena as they are forced upon us by chance and change."[1] Sainte-Beuve would, I think, have subscribed to this view. He in fact introduces his *Pensées d'Août* with a very similar concept, in the form of an epigraph from Goethe, who, in his *Conversations with Eckermann*, urged poets to render "all the little subjects that present themselves" from day to day and who described his own poems as "poems of circumstance issuing from everyday reality and finding in it their basis and support."[2]

The recurrence of certain stylistic traits and of certain preferred poetic genres (elegiac, pastoral, narrative, epistolary) contributes much to the unity of the four books, as does the "art poétique" (basically unchanged from first to last) that guided the poet in writing them. But the most powerful unifying force is the spiritual drama underlying them. The poet, consumed with a sense of frustrated ambition and of impending failure, feels himself old before his time, though in calendar years he is still a young man. In the physical effects that accompany his spiritual illness—wrinkling and yellowing of the skin, arching shoulders, thinning hair— there is even the hint of some psychosomatic process at work. Has he ever been young? Is he capable of being young? Lamenting in himself what Senancour's fictional hero, Obermann, a kindred soul, called "le malheur de ne pouvoir être jeune" (epigraph of "Le Dernier voeu"), he nevertheless seeks a way out of his despair, a source of renewal and hope, turning at various times to love, friendship, religion, to poetry itself, but never without

some disillusionment. Tempted by "a great longing for the unknown" ("un grand désir de choses inconnues" ["Le Calme"]), drawn to the terrifying exploration of the "soul's abysses" (**"L'Enfant rêveur"**), yet fearful of shipwreck on the high seas, he returns again and again to the dream of a safe harbor, of the calm lake reflecting his image. Fascinated by the strange beauty of the city (often a paradoxical beauty in ugliness) and by the hidden dramas of its inhabitants' lives, he turns from them frequently to the pastoral motif: the secluded valley, the frugal cottage, an obscure life of study shared with "a beloved spouse" and a few friends (**"Bonheur champêtre"**).

These tensions, with their alternating moods of despair and consolation, are aggravated still further by the conflict between his desire to believe once again as a Christian and his love of the play of a mind inclined to skepticism and unwilling to fix limits to its curiosity. On the one hand, he longs for a resting place, for attachment to some person, to some conviction that might bring him stability; on the other, he delights in savoring various forms of belief without adopting any, in remaining unattached, "mobile," or, as André Gide would have said, *disponible*.

II JOSEPH DELORME

This first collection differs from its successors in two important respects: the fictional disguise by which the poems are presented not as Sainte-Beuve's own but as those of an imaginary poet, and the unusual tripartite form of a prose biography followed first by poems and then by prose "thoughts" supposedly selected from the poet's works.

Sainte-Beuve observed in retrospect that although Delorme's biography was not exactly the same as his own, he represented a "faithful enough moral image" of himself at the time (*NL* ["Ma biographie," in *Nouveaux Lundis* (Paris, 1870)] XIII, 29). Like his creator, Delorme, born in Picardy, an only child orphaned of his father and raised by his mother and a paternal aunt, had come to Paris as an adolescent to complete his studies, had developed an immense curiosity for science and philosophy, had lost his religious faith under the influence of eighteenth century rationalism, had studied medicine, and was given to roaming the *boulevards extérieurs* of Paris as evening fell, to writing poetry into the late hours of the night, and to dreaming of a virtuous and attractive young woman who might be his life's companion. So far the disguise is almost transparent. But Delorme is to some extent a hidden Sainte-Beuve, the depths of whose anguish were little known to his friends at the time, since discretion prevented his "displaying his ulcer" (**Poésies** I, 19).

The main difference between fact and fiction in this case, however, is that Sainte-Beuve projected into the life of his hero (or anti-hero, as it would appear today) an intensified vision of the sufferings that he had experienced, giving these a much more fatalistic, tragic quality than they had in his own existence. He had been poor, but never to the point of extreme poverty—a miserable sixth floor garret in wintertime. He was timid, but never quite so lacking in self-confidence nor quite so convinced that he was being victimized or exploited by others. The darkened coloring of Delorme's fate probably owes more to literary examples—Dr. Johnson, born poor and ugly; the persecuted misfit Jean-Jacques Rousseau; the English poets Chatterton and Kirke White, prototypes of the *poète maudit*—than to Sainte-Beuve's own experience. Thwarted in his attempts to survive honorably, Delorme eventually rejects life, and in a kind of prolonged suicide assisted by a fatal illness (none other than the poetic disease of tuberculosis, which had also carried off "le malheureux Kirke White" [*Poésies* I, 10-11]), dies while still only twenty-eight. His creator, on the other hand, outlived him by almost half a century. Delorme's solution to the anguish of what he felt to be the emptiness of his life was death; Amaury's (I refer to the hero of *Volupté*) will be the Catholic priesthood; Sainte-Beuve's, a vocation as critic.

The invention of a semifictional mask for the expression of intimate feelings was a Romantic tradition already well established by the examples of works admired by Delorme-Sainte-Beuve, such as Goethe's *Werther,* Chateaubriand's *René,* Senancour's *Obermann* (quoted in one of the two epigraphs introducing the life of Delorme), and Constant's *Adolphe.* In this last work, in fact, one finds not only the thinly veiled autobiography but also the story-telling device, dear to eighteenth century novelists and very similar to the one used in *Joseph Delorme,* of the manuscript brought to light by a sympathetic editor. But there is another, less solemn, side of Romanticism with which Sainte-Beuve shows affinity in his strategy of concealment: the love of mystification, of anonymity and pseudonymity, exemplified so well by Mérimée and Stendhal. Although *Joseph Delorme* is hardly a literary hoax of the order of Mérimée's *Théâtre de Clara Gazul* (1825) or *La Guzla* (1827), nor was it ever intended as such, the lengths to which Sainte-Beuve goes, especially in his notes and commentaries, to sustain the illusion that Delorme really existed testify to a sense of humor not unlike Mérimée's or Stendhal's.

Sainte-Beuve's need for *dédoublement,* for taking a critical perspective upon himself as well as upon others, was very keen. The creation of an alter ego permitted him to establish this dialogue with himself. His role as "editor" allowed him to interpret Delorme, to show how he differed from him, even to judge him critically. At one point in the *Life,* for example, he quotes as an illustration of "our poor friend's proneness to exaggerate" (*Poésies* I, 13) a long passage from Delorme's

journal, the emotional style of which contrasts with his own more detached prose.

The idea of casting his work in tripartite form Sainte-Beuve probably derived from Robert Southey's edition of *The Poetical Works and Remains of Henry Kirke White* (1806),[3] adding the original twist of attributing his own verse to a "fictional" character. In a letter to the publisher Ladvocat he insisted, quite correctly, on the relative novelty of a verse collection that also included critical reflections and a kind of brief novel ("de la prose et du Roman" [*B* I, 108]). The imagination that "invented" Delorme was obviously not very high powered; but there is at least some effort at creating suspense, some semblance of a "plot," as we follow Delorme through the *péripéties* of his abandonment of poetry for a more "useful" profession, his return to poetry when his medical career is thwarted, and his final effort to rouse himself from despair by courting a childhood friend who ends up marrying a rival.

Critics who have followed Sainte-Beuve's lead by referring to the *Life* as a "roman" and who have even seen in it a kind of sketch of *Volupté* are thus not too wide of the mark (see Antoine, pp. xliii-xliv). Antoine goes further and suggests that this triptych is a kind of prophetic symbol of the three parts into which Sainte-Beuve's literary production as a whole will fall: fiction, poetry, and criticism.

What may be more original than the form of *Joseph Delorme,* however, is the choice of protagonist and of the milieu in which he moves. When this unhappy poet complains of possessing vital energies deprived of a suitable outlet ("ses facultés sans expansion" *Poésies* I, 11), or of being cursed by fate, he reminds us of René. But René, like his creator, was a nobleman. Joseph Delorme, whose name is deliberately bourgeois, may be a "noble character" (I, 13)—morally noble, that is—but he is condemned nevertheless to middle class status. He is thus closer to Werther than to René. Guizot, quoted by Sainte-Beuve, compared him to a Werther turned partisan of the French Revolution and medical student, "un Werther jacobin et carabin" (I, 299), and the author himself spoke of him as "un Werther ou un René des faubourgs" (*CL* [*Causeries du Lundi* (Paris, n.d.)] X, 82). He is poorer and of lower social status than any Romantic hero who had yet appeared.

Guizot's instinct was sound when he detected in Delorme an enemy of the established order of 1829, the Bourbon monarchy on the eve of the Revolution of 1830. The scarcity of direct political statements or references in the work should not deceive us as to its implied political meaning. Delorme's sympathy with the poor of Paris, his own poverty (even more than his humble social condition), and his distrust of the powerful make him a symbol of failed revolutionary ambitions and of the "liquidation" of revolutionary optimism among his generation—a new kind of Romantic hero, closer to Julien Sorel, whom he anticipates, than to Werther or René.[4] One's very reluctance to call him a "hero" is proof that he is of a different Romantic family than René, Dumas père's Antony, or Hugo's Hernani or Olympio. No grand gestures or noble stances for him, but a seedy, unhandsome appearance; no "illustrious misfortunes" but "a long trail of revulsions and ennuis" (*Poésies* I, 3), lacking in color and bordering on the ordinary.

The setting in which his dull, everyday melancholy and his poor pleasures unfold is also highly unusual in Romantic lyric poetry: the urban landscape of a modern city, in this case the *quartier Montrouge,* in 1829 at the extreme limit of Paris beyond Montparnasse where Sainte-Beuve lived. His "biographer" describes it as follows:

> The long black walls, boring to look at, a sinister belt enclosing the vast cemetery that we call a great city; the hedges with gaps in them revealing, through their openings, the wretched greenery of kitchen gardens; the sad monotonous alleys; the elms gray with dust [*ces ormes gris de poussière*: the name of this tree echoes his very name], and beneath them, an old woman crouching with children at the edge of a ditch; a disabled veteran returning late with drunken step to his barracks; sometimes, across the road, the bursts of joyful laughter from a workingman's wedding party— all this sufficed, during a week, to make up our friend's meager consolations.
>
> (I, 11-12)

Several of the best poems have as their *décor* a comparable urban landscape, among them the most famous piece of the collection, described by Sainte-Beuve as the "most important" (I, 301), **"Les Rayons jaunes,"** an elegy set not in a country churchyard but in a faubourg of Paris. One has only to recall René posturing on the summit of Etna, Lamartine seated atop his mountain commanding the valleys, or Hugo communing with the sea in order to savor the originality of Delorme's visits at nightfall to the outer boulevards of Paris, along which he seems not so much to walk as to prowl (*rôder* is one of his favorite verbs), almost to creep.

III *LES CONSOLATIONS*

All was not gloom in Delorme's life. In addition to his nightly stroll along the boulevard he had other small joys. Despite his "wholly inward life" (I, 20) he was not unsociable; he had literary friends in the Romantic group known as the Cénacle, he conversed and even flirted with women at dances (the *contredanse* or *scène du bal* is the scene of several poems). Poetry itself provided him with even stronger solace. Joachim Merlant observed that Delorme-Sainte-Beuve was an incur-

ably "literary soul," a "craftsman shaping his own image," a "virtuoso," who enjoyed the pursuit of his true self and whose mind, alert in the midst of the worst sorrow, kept real despair at a distance so long as he was writing.[5]

The motif of "consolations," which in *Joseph Delorme* is subordinated to the portrayal of "une certaine naïveté souffrante et douloureuse" (*Poésies* I, 301), becomes the dominant theme of *Les Consolations.*

In the first of the two epigraphs introducing *Joseph Delorme* (the second, from Senancour, I referred to earlier), Sainte-Beuve suggests a comparison of his poet to Saint Augustine before his conversion, as described in the *Confessions*: "Sic ego eram illo tempore, et flebam amarissime et requiescam in amaritudine" ("So I was at the time, and I grieved most bitterly and found my repose in bitterness"). In the end it was Delorme's very lack of hope that became his chief consolation. In a marvelous image foreshadowing Verlaine, Sainte-Beuve compares this refuge in despair to "the sea bird whose wing is broken by the storm [and which] allows itself for a time to be cradled on the brink of the wave that will finally engulf it" (I, 18). But the Sainte-Beuve of *Les Consolations* who succeeds to "that deceased self I call Joseph Delorme" (I, 208) is hardly comparable to Saint Augustine fully converted. He possesses not faith but the desire for faith:

> Pour arriver à toi, c'est assez de vouloir.
> Je voudrais bien, Seigneur; je veux; pourquoi ne puis-je?
>
> ("To reach thee an act of will suffices. I would wish it thus, Lord. I will; why am I not able?"
>
> ["**A M. Viguier**"]).

Sainte-Beuve described the phase of his development during which he wrote *Les Consolations* as "the happiest moment of my youth" (*Poésies* II, 109), "six heavenly months of my life" (II, 127). The far from hostile reception given to *Joseph Delorme* made it appear for the moment at least that he might achieve his ambition to succeed as a poet. Above all, his friendship with the young couple, Victor and Adèle Hugo, promised both renewal of his poetic inspiration and spiritual renewal, perhaps even a way back to the Christian faith.

The passage quoted from Petrarch's *De vita solitaria* as one of the epigraphs of the book shows clearly his intention to draw on a venerable tradition for his concept of the spiritual value of friendship. The major theme of *Les Consolations* is friendship as an instrument of salvation. No less than twenty of the twenty-nine poems bear titles addressing them to friends, but the dominant friendship is by far that of Victor Hugo, to whom the book is dedicated. This relationship is distinct but inseparable from his friendship with Adèle, a form of *amitié* that slowly develops into *amour.* One need not wait for the *Livre d'amour*: the transformation may be observed taking place between the lines by any attentive reader (Hugo, though, seems not to have detected it).

The preface addressed to Hugo, in reality a ten page essay on friendship, is, in its exaggerated language and worshipful tone, an extraordinary document, very uncharacteristic of Sainte-Beuve. It is difficult to believe that such a naive expression of faith in **"L'Ami"** could have come from the critic who, only a few years before, had published his clear-eyed assessment of Hugo in *Le Globe.* But that was before he had met Hugo. Of all Sainte-Beuve's experiments in lending himself momentarily to various forms of doctrine—Romanticism, Saint-Simonianism, Lamennaisianism, Protestantism—only in succumbing to his fascination for Hugo and his world did he admit that he had suspended his will and judgment, and then only for a moment, "as though under a magic spell" (*PM* [*Pensées et Maximes,* ed. Maurice Chapelan (Paris, 1955)] 48).

"This little book," he pointed out to Hugo, "is the faithful image of my soul, for in it a struggle is still taking place between doubts and good intentions" (*Poésies* II, 13-14). It is essentially the record of a failed religious conversion. The poet gives reason after reason for wishing to renounce the world but does not convince us that he has eradicated worldliness from his own heart. Of all the obstacles in the path of his return to God, the most serious, ironically enough, was probably his very concept of Hugo's friendship as a means of salvation. His "friend" becomes a being so much better, purer, happier than himself that one wonders why he needed God when he already had Victor Hugo. How lucky for him that he eventually discovered that Hugo's world had not even been "the grotto of a demigod" but instead "a Cyclops' cave" ("J'étais dans l'antre du Cyclope, et je me croyais dans la grotte d'un demidieu").[6]

Adèle Hugo was a different matter.

IV A BOOK OF LOVE

Les Consolations was followed, in order of publication, by *Pensées d'Août.* However, in the preface to the latter work (1837) Sainte-Beuve alludes to a mysterious third volume of verse that he has already completed, of which he is especially fond, but which "discretion" ("la pudeur") will not allow him to publish "for a very long time" (*Poésies* II, 132). This missing link was *Livre d'amour,* inspired by his love affair with Adèle Hugo, which lasted approximately from 1830 to the winter of 1836-1837 and which stimulated two other imaginative works of his to be discussed in the following chapter: the novel *Volupté* (1834) and the short story "Madame

de Pontivy" (1837). A limited anonymous edition of *Livre d'amour* in fact appeared six years after *Pensées d'Août,* in 1843, and over half the poems also figure in the 1863 edition of his *Poésies.* But it was only in 1906, long after the deaths of the three leading characters in this drama, that Troubat published the first true edition of the work.

No book of Sainte-Beuve's has aroused such controversy or has been so maligned. His enemies, who fancied themselves to be the defenders of Madame Hugo's honor, attacked it as a villainous account of how he had betrayed his best friend, avenging himself for Hugo's superiority over him and boasting of his conquest of a reluctant (so they liked to believe) mistress—if indeed he had not lied to begin with about her infidelity. Vanity undoubtedly played some part in Sainte-Beuve's decision to make these poems for Adèle public—the vanity of letting the world know that he had been the successful rival of Hugo in love if not in poetry. But his indiscretion has been greatly exaggerated. Gustave Michaut reminds us that it is a time-honored custom for poets to publicize their adulterous love affairs, and adds that the deceived husband himself had produced his own *Livre d'amour* only a few years before in *Chants du crépuscule* (1835), in which he had gone so far as to address love poems to both wife and mistress (the unnamed but easily detectable Juliette Drouet) in a single volume.[7] Furthermore, there is no evidence that Adèle objected to the publication of any of Sainte-Beuve's poems, or that she was anything but a willing partner in their affair.

In the heat of this quarrel over the right of *Livre d'amour* to exist, its nature as a work of poetry has been all but completely lost sight of. Although far from a neglected masterpiece (none of Sainte-Beuve's verse collections falls into that category), it contains some of his finest poems and has the advantage over its more shapeless companions of being better constructed. It reads, in fact, almost like a novel in verse form. (There are curious allusions in the author's footnotes to the lovers' project of a "roman par lettres" based on their relationship.) A kind of "plot" enables us to follow, across the forty-five poems, the genesis, growth, fulfillment, and decline of their passion, from their first attraction to each other—

> J'allais sortir alors, mais tu me dis: *Restez!*
> Et, sous tes doigts pleuvant, la chevelure immense
> Exhalait jusqu'à moi des senteurs de semence

("I was about to leave when you told me to remain, and your flowing hair as you undid it gave off a scent as though of seed" [*Livre d'Amour* VIII])—to the acknowledgment in the final sonnet of the reason (at least as he saw it) for their eventual separation: "Je voulais la nuance, et j'ai gâté l'ardeur" ("I sacrificed ardent passion to my need for subtlety of feeling").

As in a novel there are also characters, settings, and atmosphere, both physical and psychological. Basically it is a *roman à deux,* with the husband ("Lui") as a threatening presence in the background. The cast of characters is small not only because the atmosphere is intimate (Troubat compared these poems to a form of "chamber music" [p. 15]), but also because the lovers had almost no intermediaries. The "action" could be summed up as their effort to find suitable places where they might be alone. These in turn become the characteristic *décors* of the poems: churches and cemeteries, obscure hotels, country lanes, and, at least once, (*Livre d'Amour,* XXX), a horse-drawn cab on the Champs-Elysées—the famous *fiacre* whose possibilities for love-making Sainte-Beuve exploited long before Flaubert made use of them in *Madame Bovary.*

The psychological atmosphere is one of frustrations, separations, long periods of waiting, attempts to communicate through glances and gestures in the presence of others. None of this is new to literature of course: poets and novelists have traditionally thrived on such handicaps. Where Sainte-Beuve is original is in the unromantic, bourgeois setting of some of the pieces, as for example in Poem XXXII, contrasting the idyllic rural trysting places of so much love poetry with the old hotel in a shabby section of Paris where he received his "Châtelaine."

A veil of sadness, of shadow, hangs over the work. The pleasures and joys of love, though real, are short-lived. The reader has been prepared beforehand for this melancholy view by the first poem of *Les Consolations,* "A Madame V. H.," with its epigraph from the eighteenth century playwright Jean-François Ducis ("Our happiness is but a form of misfortune more or less consoled") and its opening lines, "Oh! que la vie est longue aux longs jours de l'été, / Et que le temps y pèse à mon coeur attristé!" ("Oh, how long life is on long summer days, and how heavily time weighs on my saddened heart!")—lines which find an echo in such phrases of *Livre d'amour* as "notre courte joie / Et notre longue attente" (XXIII). Born to a mother already widowed, "discouraged from the cradle onward" and "poorly endowed with the faculty of hope" (as he wrote to Adèle in a letter probably of 1836 [*B* II, 114]), Sainte-Beuve seemed almost predestined to render just this strange nuance in his love poetry.

Yet despite the relative joylessness of a love that André Maurois described as having been "like dusk even from the moment it dawned" ("dès son aube, crépusculaire"),[8] several forces are at work in *Livre d'amour* that give the concept of love affirmed therein a surprisingly positive quality. One is the association of love with religion. Part of Adèle's attraction for Sainte-Beuve was her Christian faith, which he counted upon to support him in his own spiritual quest. The lovers hoped to redeem

their adulterous relationship by prayers for the dead and by alms giving; in the midst of adultery they clung to an ideal of innocence and purity—a paradox that Baudelaire, if not Claudel, would have understood. Like that other "book of love," *Volupté,* this one can be understood only on the larger background of Sainte-Beuve's search for a durable faith. Love is also associated with the intellectual, quasi-scholarly pursuit which the poet calls "étude" ("notre amour, ma seule et vive étude" [*Livre d'amour* IX]). Here it is the studious and learned Petrarch who, having served to bless the concept of friendship in *Les Consolations,* is called upon to render a similar service to love (XXXIII). Frequent allusions to classical mythology and to the examples of lovers consecrated by classical and postclassical tradition (Tibullus and Delia, Petrarch and Laura) add further to the ennobling effect, as does the attempt to poeticize the lovers' experience by sifting it through the filter of imagination and memory.

These various forms of the ennobling of reality, similar to the ones that he used in *Volupté,* testify to Sainte-Beuve's determination to extract some beauty, some spiritual meaning from the raw material of a love affair that must at times have appeared to him anything but noble. In this effort to shape his experience into a meaningful fiction or myth, his intention was that of a true poet. The resulting work, unfortunately, is not free from the notorious defects of the rest of his verse, so often flat, laborious, and clumsy in execution.[9]

V THE LATE SUMMER OF LIFE

Because of its great variety of "petits sujets" and "poésies de circonstance," to quote the epigraph from Goethe that Sainte-Beuve uses to describe his *Pensées d'Août,* this last volume of entirely new verse which he published during his lifetime is thematically less unified than the others and consequently more difficult to sum up briefly. Judging from the title, from the original Preface, and from the first poem, also called "**Pensées d'Août,**" he wished to express a certain "moral season of the soul" (*Poésies* II, 131) by establishing an analogy between the month of August, lying just beyond the midpoint of the calendar year, and the late summer of his own life when youthful ardor was beginning to give way to a more disillusioned though perhaps wiser view of things—"l'âge où mon soleil, / Où mon été décline, à la saison pareil" (**"Pensées d'Août"**). He was not a bad prophet: thirty-three when he published this work (1837), he was in fact to live until the age of sixty-five.

Ever since *Joseph Delorme* his ambition had been "not to repeat himself" in successive volumes, to offer "something new and distinct" in each. The poet of *Pensées d'Août,* as he describes him, was "more disinterested, calmer, less given to personal confessions" than his predecessor and could therefore turn his attention to developing two types of verse that were more or less impersonal in nature: the "domestic and moral tale" ("le récit domestique et moral") and criticism in letter form ("l'épître à demi-critique") (II, 133).

It is obvious that each of these genres clearly overlaps with the biographical and critical prose essays of the *Portraits* and with the course on Port-Royal that he was producing during the same period. His Muse, never very robust, appears to be well into her decline. The verse of *Pensées d'Août* resembles more than ever prose in disguise, a fact that critics recognized by giving it the poorest reviews received by any of his books. The poet in him, on the other hand, far from disappearing, was taking refuge in his prose.

There are occasional light-hearted poems in this collection, such as the charming **"Sonnet à Madame P."** with its self-portrait of the poet as a straw-hatted villager strolling near Précy-sur-Oise, "heureux, loin de Paris." The dominant tone, however, is grave. Reminiscing with Franz Liszt in Rome about their younger and presumably happier years, the poet observes, in Pascalian manner, that even happiness contains a void within it reminding man of his "nothingness"—"Je ne sais quel vide / Qui dans le bonheur même avertit du néant" (**"La Villa Adriana"**). Many variations occur on the theme of death, for example, the autumn "death" of leafy trees on a Jura hillside as the evergreens look sadly on (**"De Ballaigues à Orbe, Jura"**), the death of Sainte-Beuve's friendship with Hugo finally recognized as they are obliged to share the same cab on returning from Gabrielle Dorval's funeral (**"En revenant du convoi de Gabrielle"**)—a very different *fiacre* scene this time from *Livre d'amour*!, or the death of the poet himself, to be survived by the man, as described in a poem by Musset included in the collection, with its famous line "Un poète mort jeune, à qui l'homme survit" ("A Sainte-Beuve").

But melancholy, often bordering on despair, is only half the story in *Pensées d'Août*: the other half is that characteristic resilience of spirit with which Sainte-Beuve refused to surrender to despair and continued to seek ways to bypass it. Some of these proved less satisfactory than others. Nature consoled and even appeared to rejuvenate him for a while, especially in the landscape poems inspired by his visit to Lausanne to give his course on Port-Royal; but he confessed that nature meant little to him in itself, without the company of friends (**"Réponse"**). Friendship he still valued highly, but when he treats this theme it is less to celebrate his friends than to compare himself to them unfavorably and to seek strength in their example for overcoming his (supposed) weaknesses. The most persistent of his illusions led him into a final attempt at love—final, that is, at least so far as his recording it in

poetic form is concerned. This time it was indeed an attempt at marriage: his unsuccessful courtship of Frédérique Pelletier (1840), the subject of the pathetic **"Un dernier rêve,"** a kind of short story in verse and prose that serves as an epilogue to *Pensées d'Août* in the 1863 edition of his *Poésies.*

In the end it was his emerging vocation as a critic that seemed to offer him the least illusory form of hope for the future, the least unreliable means of filling the void within him and conferring order and purpose on his existence. Even while expressing envy of the calm, purposeful life of his childhood friend Eustache Barbe (who had become a priest) and comparing it plaintively with his own endless driftings, he seemed not unhappy with his fate as a critic, or with the "metamorphoses" that he underwent as he increased his knowledge of so many different subjects: "C'est mon mal et ma peine, et mon charme aussi bien" (**"A l'Abbé Eustache Barbe"**). For the Christian, prayer and sacrifice were the means of "restoring the dead to life again in ourselves," as Pascal wrote in his essay on the death of his father, quoted in the epigraph to **"Monsieur Jean, Maître d'école."** But could not the biographer-historian, even though an unbeliever, achieve a similar goal through the force of his learning and imagination? Could not a great work of criticism conceived in this generous manner provide him with his own mainstay against the oblivion of death?

VI A MODERN *ART POÉTIQUE*

As a poet-critic Sainte-Beuve, not surprisingly, was a very conscious theorist of poetry. His views, developed mainly in the *pensées* of Joseph Delorme, in several prefaces, and in the manifesto type poem, **"A M. Villemain"** (*Pensées d'Août*), belonged to what he called "l'Art poétique moderne" (*Poésies* II, 234) of the new Romantic school. But within this general movement they represented a kind of rival poetics which, especially in its questioning of certain conventional notions of lyrical poetry, was to have much more impact on succeeding generations of poets than on his associates in the Cénacle. It was a poetics that insisted above all on two concepts, originality and modernity, both of which, as Antoine has observed, were paradoxical in a poet so given to quoting, imitating, even translating other poets, so respectful of tradition and so willing to revive and adapt ancient poetic forms such as the elegiac, the pastoral, the epistolary.

That Sainte-Beuve was acutely aware of his need to stake out his own territory as a poet is very easy to understand. Lamartine, Vigny, and Hugo had already published highly successful and individualized major verse collections when *Joseph Delorme* appeared. He discovered that his originality lay in recognizing his limitations and exploiting a vein that others might consider minor, if not somewhat strange. He even incorporated into his poems this very theme of the latecomer's problem in defining his domain. In the best illustration of this, **"A M. Villemain,"** a long poem built around a central horticultural image, he compares himself to Virgil's farmer in the *Georgics,* reduced to making the best of "a few acres of abandoned countryside"; evoking in rapid succession the revered precursor, André Chénier; Lamartine, "knowing little except his own soul"; the "powerful Hugo"; and Vigny, "withdrawn inside his ivory tower" (like the characterization of Lamartine, this was to become famous), he then goes on to describe the "narrow space" left for him to cultivate, an unpromising little garden confined within melancholy walls and producing flowers of whose names he was not even sure.

The key to both originality and modernity in Sainte-Beuve's poetics was his concept of the "analytical elegy" ("l'élégie d'analyse" [*Pensée* XIX]). It was natural that the man who described himself as prone to "sterile regrets, vague expectant desires, moods of melancholy and languor following upon pleasures" (*PM* 237) should turn to the poetic genre associated more than any other with sadness and reverie. "My imagination is elegiac," he observed, "and my ideal, the picture drawn by Tibullus: *Quam juvat immites*" (*PM* 242)—a reference to the great Roman poet's description of himself by the hearth on a stormy winter's night, holding his mistress in his arms, content not to risk gale and shipwreck in pursuit of fortune and to "savor fully" the "narrow range" of the fire that warms them.[10]

Drawing to some extent on the examples of Chénier and Lamartine as elegists, Sainte-Beuve proposed modernizing the French elegy even further by introducing into it stronger components both of intimacy and of everyday reality. His imagination had also been stimulated by the intimate poems in humble settings of the "Lakistes," the English Lake Poets, but he admitted having recognized them intuitively as "older brothers" rather than having known their work from close study (*NL* IV, 455).[11] In any case he felt that he could surpass them in extracting poetry from nature and the soul observed at close range, "humbly and in bourgeois manner [*bourgeoisement*] . . . calling by their real names the things of private life . . . and attempting to relieve the prosaic quality [*le prosaïsme*] of such domestic details by the description [*la peinture*] of human feelings and natural objects" (*Pensée* XIX). Returning to this concept in his dedicatory preface to *Les Consolations,* he wisely eschewed as beyond his powers Hugo's prophetic aspirations, his "familiar conversations with the Infinite," and claimed, as the hallmark of his own poetry, "the choice of certain subjects taken from private life . . . a domestic incident, a conversation, a stroll, a

piece of reading." His goal, he informed Hugo, was nothing less than to raise this "very commonplace reality" to "a higher power of poetry" (*Poésies* II, 13-14).

Opening up the elegy, and lyric poetry generally, to "la réalité la plus vulgaire" meant not only choosing unconventional subjects but also "nommant les choses de la vie privée par leur nom," and daring to use in verse the rhythms of everyday prose speech. Every reformer of poetry—and Sainte-Beuve was as much a reformer as Du Bellay and Malherbe had been before him or as Rimbaud and André Breton would be after him—is really in search of a new language that alone can express a new thought, a new mode of feeling. This meant for Sainte-Beuve using "lower class words [*de basse bourgeoisie*], for some reason excluded from the language of poetry" (I, 25). Thus in **"La Plaine"** (*Joseph Delorme*)—a serious lyric poem, it must be emphasized, and not a satire, where such words were traditionally acceptable—a shepherd boy, holding a loaf of wholemeal bread (*pain bis*), watches an old woman gleaning in the beetfield (*au champ de betterave*), while in the distance we hear a cart (*la charrette*) creaking along under its load of stinking manure (*le fumier infect*). There are enough objectionable words in these few lines to make the hair—or *perruque*—of any Classical partisan of "noble style" bristle with horror.

Revitalizing the language of poetry meant taking syntactic as well as lexical liberties with accepted practice. The colloquial syntax of many poems is well suited to their nature as "causeries," as for example in **"Italie,"** which begins as though in the middle of a conversation: "Et pourtant le bonheur m'aurait été facile!" ("And yet it would have been so easy for me to be happy!"). The interrogative phrase interjected in the course of a sentence—"Mais dans la plaine, quoi? des jachères pierreuses" (**"La Plaine"**); "Bien des fois, n'est-ce pas? l'enthousiasme amer" (**"A David statuaire"**)—foreshadows the *syntaxe familière* of Verlaine. The noble alexandrine itself is made to serve the purpose of this *prosaïsme voulu,* for Sainte-Beuve, like most of his Romantic colleagues, exacted as the price of remaining within a more or less regular prosody the right to take great liberties with this traditional meter, using it, so to speak, to subvert and humble, if not to democratize, itself. In his hands it becomes what Antoine calls "le vers prosé," an alexandrine without marked rhythm or pause, as in the line "Surtout j'aime ces deux dernières barcarolles," from the highly innovative **"Causerie au bal,"** historically significant as Sainte-Beuve's first "élégie intime" or "causerie domestique" (Antoine, pp. 178-179).

But the problem remained of preventing this "commonplace reality" from becoming merely flat and banal, of transmuting it into true poetry. Here occurs, in Sainte-Beuve's *art poétique,* what might be called Delorme's equation: the more commonplace the material, the stricter the poetic form. "It is exactly in proportion as poetry approaches more closely to real life and lowly things," he cautioned, "that it must check itself with greater rigor," and seek safeguards "against the prosaic and the trivial" (*Pensée* VII). One major safeguard lay in the very use of regular rhymed verse, however numerous the liberties taken with it, for had he been more radical, Sainte-Beuve might have advocated *le vers libre* or *le poème en prose*. Instead, he reaffirmed the need to rhyme, in a virtuoso piece, **"A la rime,"** reviving a difficult six line stanza form rarely used since Ronsard. He also renewed the sonnet, a highly disciplined form neglected (as he pointed out) by the other Romantics, those "swans and eagles" who might have broken their wings attempting to enter its cage, while poets like himself, "birds of less elevated flight and less wide expanse of wing," were at home there (*NL* III, 344).

There were many other means of redeeming the prosaic, advocated in theory though not always successfully practiced by Sainte-Beuve. By juxtaposing modern colloquial speech with archaic or neoclassical "noble" terms, he achieves a mixture of classicism and modernity that anticipates Baudelaire. No scene was too lowly for him not to attempt to ennoble it by alluding to the ancient classical poets. Imagery of course plays an essential role in the desired transfiguration of the commonplace. When an image serves as the outward sign of an inner reality, especially when it is repeated often enough to be associated with that reality—the child-dreamer who disturbs the calm surface of the waters to reveal terrifying depths beneath; the blighted tree; *les rayons jaunes*—it becomes a symbol. The poet is he who gives concrete form to this "inward other world"; it is the poet who has been gifted with "the key to symbols and the understanding of figures" (*Pensée* XX).

This gift in turn is part of the poet's power as a painter in words. Delorme, as we noted earlier, was a *paysagiste* of a new kind, specializing in "small-scale landscapes" (*Poésies* I, 25)—above all, those urban landscapes viewed from his favorite perspective of the *quartier Montrouge*. Many years later Sainte-Beuve claimed that the paintings of Théodore Rousseau and Corot which he saw in the Salon of 1857 had been anticipated in spirit thirty years earlier by his ill-fated poet (*PM* 259); and in a letter to Théophile Gautier of 1859 he called Delorme the "Potterley of poetry," after an obscure young French "peintre-coloriste" (*B* XI, 307). The extensive use of color, the search for *le pittoresque,* characteristic of some of his Romantic colleagues, were not to his taste, however. Instead he favored a technique of allusiveness that both harked back to the Classical *je ne sais quoi* and pointed ahead to the suggestiveness of the Symbolists (*Pensée* XX). "Indefinite, unexplained, vague words" that "hint at the

thought" ("qui laissent deviner la pensée"), he argued, can often be more effective in poetry than precise ones that state it explicitly (*Pensée* XV). Sainte-Beuve had no intention, as he explained in a letter to Hugo, of setting up a "school of intimate literature" opposed to that of visually descriptive poetry, "la poésie visible" (*B* I, 380). But there is no doubt that he was less interested in describing objects, scenes, or landscapes as ends in themselves than in establishing their relationship—their *correspondance,* as Baudelaire would put it—with the invisible world. This emphasis was in keeping with his role as an elegiac poet concerned above all with rendering "the inward truth of feeling" (*Poésies* II, 132).

VII THE REDISCOVERY OF A POET

Joseph Delorme was the object of a mixed critical reception when it first appeared, as we learn from consulting the appendix of critical judgments that Sainte-Beuve added to the 1863 *Poésies* (he used a similar procedure with the revised editions of *Volupté* and *Port-Royal*). Even a friendly critic such as Magnin, in *Le Globe,* though recognizing a poetic talent "full of frankness, vigor, and truth," was uneasy about the harshness and strangeness ("bizarrerie") of so much of the verse (I, 292). As Antoine observed with the benefit of historical perspective, a work so at odds with the rest of Romantic poetry, sacrificing to none of the current fashions, "neither Philhellenic nor Oriental nor Byronic nor Biblical in inspiration, as in Lamartine, Hugo or Vigny" (pp. lxi-lxii), must have seemed too eccentric to be entirely credible. *Les Consolations* fared better; in fact, it alone among Sainte-Beuve's verse collections enjoyed something approaching a real success, perhaps, as Antoine suggests, because (ironically enough) it was less innovative than the others and made more concessions to the continuing public taste for Lamartine. The *Pensées d'Août* met with disaster. Typical was the critic in *Le National* quoted by Bonnerot, who pleaded with the author not to give up writing verse, since he appeared to have a "poet's soul," but simply to refrain from publishing it (*B* II, 342-343).

Yet Sainte-Beuve had faith in all three—in all four, to be exact—of his works of poetry. "I await my judge," he confided to his notebook, "in the belief that I have not yet been judged as a poet." He clung to his dream of a modest "poetic glory," not unlike that enjoyed by Theocritus or Catullus among the ancients, or Goldsmith or Cowper among the moderns (*PM* 262). Without suggesting that his real stature as a poet approaches any of these or, even less, that he is a *grand poète méconnu,* one must recognize that his faith was justified: posterity has indeed shown more esteem than most of his contemporaries for his achievement as a poet.

His influence as a poet upon other poets, as distinct from the rediscovery of his work by critics and the public, a much slower process, began almost with *Jo-*

seph Delorme, which, according to Antoine, launched two fashions in poetry: "la poésie intime" and "la Muse phtisique" or "tubercular Muse" (p. ci). Both Hugo and Lamartine learned much about "la poésie intime" from their less gifted fellow poet, the first in *Feuilles d'automne* (1831) and the second in *Jocelyn* (1836). As the century progressed the younger poets developed almost a kind of underground cult for "l'oncle Beuve," as Gautier affectionately called him. Théodore de Banville dedicated his *Odelettes* (1856) to him in such laudatory terms that Champfleury was provoked to quip that Sainte-Beuve had become "the god of poetry," that *Volupté* had assumed "biblical proportions," and that suddenly "a Sainte-Beuve camp" had been formed (quoted in Antoine, p. cxxii).

Among these younger poets proud to trace their ancestry to Sainte-Beuve were two whose fame would eventually far outstrip his own: Baudelaire and Verlaine. The first remained all his life "an incorrigible admirer of Sainte-Beuve the poet and novelist" (Antoine, p. cxi). In a touching bit of testimony confirming the sincerity and durability of his cult for Sainte-Beuve, Troubat relates how Baudelaire, whom he visited in a nursing home only six months before his death, showed him "everything he loved: the poems of Sainte-Beuve, the works of Edgar Poe in English; a little book on Goya; and, in the garden of the home, a large exotic plant" (Antoine, p. cxi). A deep affinity existed between the two poets which Albert Thibaudet has summarized as consisting of at least four basic elements: an inner feeling for Christianity; critical intelligence; understanding for the secret life of a great capital, in this case Paris; and the desire to make prose an ally of verse.[12] Verlaine's reasons for esteeming Sainte-Beuve the poet were similar to Baudelaire's, with special emphasis on the poeticizing of conversational syntax. In a letter of 1865 to Sainte-Beuve he ranked *Joseph Delorme,* "for its melancholy intensity and power of expression, infinitely above Lamartinian and other kinds of jeremiads [*lamentations*]" (*B* XIV, 448). While pleased to learn this, Sainte-Beuve rose to the defense of Lamartine, reminding his young admirer what a powerful revelation the *Méditations* had been to *his* generation of poets, thirty-five years earlier, on the dreary neo-Classical scene.

The rediscovery of Sainte-Beuve's poetry by the critics took much longer, largely because his own success as a critic overshadowed the rest of his production. In 1861 Charles Asselineau, the friend and first biographer of Baudelaire, pointed the way to the needed reassessment by reminding his contemporaries that Sainte-Beuve was "at once poet, novelist, and critic," and by suggesting that the "real" Sainte-Beuve might in fact be the poet, "the first-born, Joseph Delorme," whom they had lost sight of because the critic's voice had prevailed for so long over the poet's (*B* XII, 126). But rehabilitation

began in earnest only after Sainte-Beuve's death. Anatole France in an essay of 1879 argued that Sainte-Beuve was a poet to reckon with despite his flaws. Ten years later Charles Morice observed that *Joseph Delorme,* jeered at for its eccentricity in the 1830s, was finally ready to be understood in the 1880s, and Paul Bourget, in 1904, went so far as to claim that Sainte-Beuve was "un grand poète," though of a single season only. His reputation received a significant boost between 1910 and 1930 when André Barre and René Lalou showed in how many ways he had been a precursor of the Symbolists, and John Charpentier how "modern" were his use of analysis within the lyric poem and his freedom from the theatrical gestures that often marred the "confessional" poetry of the other Romantics.[13]

From this chapter in literary history, which I have sketched in broadest outline, one might be tempted to draw a moral unflattering to Sainte-Beuve: that his influence was in inverse proportion to his merits as a poet. Ferdinand Brunetière indeed cited his case as proof that the poets "who found a school are those more productive of ideas than of masterpieces, and full of excellent intentions that they are unable to carry out successfully." "The incomplete artist is choice game for more powerful animals," quipped Jacques Vier, citing a long list of poets who "redid" some aspect or other of Sainte-Beuve's poetry. He was certainly "l'artiste incomplet" and probably wrote more bad poetry than any other poet still worth reading. A catalogue of his faults would have to include his frequent lack of ear (few of his lines are musical and some are downright cacophonous), his abuse of neoclassical rhetoric ("Too many *luths, lyres, harpes,* and *Jéhovahs,*" complained Baudelaire, "you were the man to destroy all that"), a syntax that is sometimes confused, and an imagery that is often awkward or labored. Much of his verse gives the painful impression of having been assembled, as a recent critic put it, "drop by drop."[14]

T. S. Eliot once described Samuel Johnson as "a secondary poet at the end of a movement which had been initiated by greater poets than he."[15] Sainte-Beuve was a secondary poet at the beginning of a movement that he helped initiate and that produced greater poets than he. Even secondary poets, however, have their merits. The fairest judgment of Sainte-Beuve's poetry was probably Vigny's: "By applying his mind, he has written some excellent verse without being a poet by instinct."[16] His boldness and originality in both content and form still commend him to our attention. But there is little doubt that his appeal will continue to be to a very narrow circle of readers, perhaps of somewhat perverse taste, who are willing to join Baudelaire in confessing him to be their weakness—"Sainte-Beuve, c'est mon vice" (quoted in Antoine, p. cviii). Patience and good will are needed to do justice to his poetry, as they are needed to discover the strange beauties of that other creation of the "incomplete artist," his novel *Volupté*.

Notes

1. Quoted in *Selected Shorter Poems of Thomas Hardy,* ed. John Wain (London, 1966), p. 115.

2. *Poésies de Sainte-Beuve* (Paris, 1863), II, 129. Poems quoted from this edition will be referred to by title, the *Pensées de Joseph Delorme* by number, and other texts (*Vie de Joseph Delorme,* Prefaces, and Appendices) by volume and page number. I have also made use of Gérald Antoine's edition, *Vie, poésies et pensées de Joseph Delorme* (Paris, 1956), especially for its invaluable Introduction and Notes; further reference in the text to "Antoine" will be to this edition.

3. See George Roth, "Kirke White et 'Joseph Delorme,'" *Revue de littérature comparée,* I (1921): 588.

4. Pierre Barbéris, "Signification de 'Joseph Delorme' en 1830," *Revue des sciences humaines* (July-September 1969): 381.

5. Joachim Merlant, *Le Roman personnel de Rousseau à Fromentin* (Paris, 1905), pp. 332-333.

6. *Livre d'amour,* ed. Jules Troubat (Paris, 1906), p. 109. Poems quoted from this edition will be referred to in the text by their numbers (few have titles), and Troubat's Preface, by page number.

7. Gustave Michaut, *Le Livre d'amour de Sainte-Beuve* (Paris, 1905), p. 162. For the prosecution's case, see Gustave Simon, *Le Roman de Sainte-Beuve* (1906; rpt. Paris, 1926), and for Michaut's reply to Simon, his *Pages de critique et d'histoire littéraire (XIXᵉ siècle)* (Paris, 1910), pp. 156-233.

8. André Maurois, *Olympio ou la Vie de Victor Hugo* (Paris, 1954), p. 229.

9. For a more detailed literary analysis of *Livre d'amour,* see R. M. Chadbourne, "Sainte-Beuve's *Livre d'amour* as Poetry," *Nineteenth-Century French Studies,* III (1974-1975): 80-96. The most objective account of Sainte-Beuve's relations with the Hugos and of his criticism of Hugo the writer is Raphaël Molho's "Critique, amour et poésie: Sainte-Beuve et 'les' Hugo," in Victor Hugo, *Oeuvres complètes,* ed. Jean Massin (Paris, 1967-1969), IV, i-xxvi, and XIII, lxix-lxxxiii.

10. *The Poems of Tibullus,* trans. Constance Carrier (Bloomington and London, 1968), Book I, 1.

11. For further discussion of this question, see Maxwell Smith, *L'Influence des Lakistes sur les romantiques français* (Paris, 1920); Roth; T. G. S.

Combe, *Sainte-Beuve et les poètes anglais* (Bordeaux, 1937); and A. G. Lehmann, "Sainte-Beuve critique de la littérature anglaise, une mise au point," *Revue de littérature comparée,* XXVIII (1954): 419-439.

12. Albert Thibaudet, *Histoire de la littérature française de 1789 à nos jours* (Paris, 1936), p. 324. Unless otherwise indicated, references in the text to "Thibaudet" will be to this work. For further on Sainte-Beuve and Baudelaire, see Antoine, pp. cviii-cxxi; Jacques Vier, *Le Joseph Delorme de Sainte-Beuve,* Archives des Lettres Modernes, No. 29, January-February 1960; and Norman Barlow, *Sainte-Beuve to Baudelaire, a Poetic Legacy* (Durham, N.C., 1964). Antoine and Vier also discuss Sainte-Beuve's influence on other poets.

13. See Anatole France, "Sainte-Beuve poète," in his *Le Génie latin* (Paris, 1913); Morice as quoted in Antoine, p. ci; Paul Bourget, "Sainte-Beuve poète," in his *Sociologie et littérature* (Paris, 1906); André Barre, *Le Symbolisme* (Paris, 1911; reprint ed., New York, n.d.); René Lalou, *Vers une alchimie lyrique* (Paris, 1927); John Charpentier, *L'Evolution de la poésie lyrique de Joseph Delorme à Paul Claudel* (Paris, 1930).

14. Ferdinand Brunetière, *L'Evolution de la poésie lyrique en France au 19ᵉ siècle* (Paris, 1894), I, 254; Vier, p. 53; Charles Baudelaire, *Correspondance générale,* ed. Jacques Crépet (Paris, 1949), V, 218; Roland Derche, *Etudes de textes français,* nouvelle série (Paris, 1966), V, 77.

15. T. S. Eliot, *On Poetry and Poets* (New York, n.d.), p. 184.

16. Alfred de Vigny, *Oeuvres complètes* (Paris, 1965), II, 892. In this same passage from his *Journal d'un poète,* Vigny claimed that Hugo appeared to be the master in poetry, but was really the disciple, of Sainte-Beuve.

Laurent LeSage (essay date 1978)

SOURCE: LeSage, Laurent. "Charles Sainte-Beuve, 1804-1869." In *The Rhumb Line of Symbolism,* pp. 11-15. University Park, Penn.: Pennsylvania State University Press, 1978.

[*In the following essay, LeSage discusses the novelty of Sainte-Beuve's work and its influence on subsequent French poets—Baudelaire in particular.*]

Bereft of his father before he was born, Sainte-Beuve was brought up by his mother and his aunt in Boulogne-sur-Mer. There, in a widowed household, Sainte-Beuve spent a lonely, melancholy childhood given over chiefly to study and religious practice. When he was fourteen, he went to Paris for his schooling.

Sainte-Beuve's interest in poetry dates from 1820. Lamartine's *Méditations* were a revelation for this schoolboy of sixteen. He was fond too of Chateaubriand, whose fame was reaching its zenith about now. He himself began to write verse. At the same time, Sainte-Beuve became interested in science and, under the influence of his new studies, his Christian convictions began to pale. By the time he was ready for medical school in 1823, his agnosticism became complicated by a taste for libertinage, both tendencies being in contradiction to the religiosity and moralism of his poetic inspiration. Here is the source for those conflicts which Sainte-Beuve describes in *Les Poésies de Joseph Delorme.* The havoc wreaked in his views extended to politics, for after being an ardent legitimist like his mother, he became intensely democratic.

Still in medical school but bitten seriously by the literary bug, Sainte-Beuve began to contribute to the *Globe,* a magazine founded by one of his former professors. Eventually he left school and gave himself up entirely to literature. His work on the *Globe* had put him in contract with writers; their company excited and inspired him, particularly that of the young Romantics. In the movement that would triumph in 1830 Sainte-Beuve participated ardently. Lamartine describes him at the time: "C'était en 1829. J'aimais alors beaucoup un jeune homme pâle, blond, frêle, sensible jusqu'à la maladie, poète jusqu'aux larmes . . . il s'appelait Sainte-Beuve. Il vivait à Paris avec une mère âgée, sereine, absorbée en lui, dans une petite maison sur un jardin retiré, dans le quartier du Luxembourg."[1] This is the year of *Vie, Poésies et Pensées de Joseph Delorme,* a collection of poems preceded by a fictitious biography and followed by a miscellany of thoughts on literary matters. In the verses ascribed to this unhappy victim of the *mal du siècle,* Sainte-Beuve strikes chords in a minor key rarely heard in the works of his greater contemporaries. This is his strongest claim to fame as a poet: he introduced the humble and the familiar into French poetry, extolling tranquil pleasures, life with a tender companion, children, a cottage with green shutters. Lamartine describes him as "ayant une grande analogie avec Novalis en Allemagne, avec les poètes intimes qu'on nomme les Lakistes en Angleterre."[2] Sainte-Beuve's modest claim in the territory of poetry is set forth in **"Promenade,"** where he alludes with gentle irony to the grander claims staked out by his peers: "Laissons Chateaubriand, loin des traces profanes, / A vingt ans s'élancer en d'immenses savanes . . ." "Laissons à Lamartine, à Nodier, nobles frères, / Leur Jura bien-aimé . . ." "Qu'aussi Victor Hugo, sous un donjon qui croule, / Et le Rhin à ses pieds . . ." In *Les Consolations,* Sainte-Beuve's second volume of verse,

he works on in the vein struck in the first. His themes are those of ordinary life—a walk, a conversation, a domestic incident. The emotion of friendship (for the Hugos) and of newly recovered Christian piety make it for some critics his best work; for others like Ferdinand Brunetière, humdrum material always remains humdrum.[3] Perhaps Brunetière is right in thinking that Sainte-Beuve lacked the sincerity and moral elevation of Wordsworth and the other Lake poets that he was imitating. He created, nevertheless, something novel in France, and his depiction of the simple life is not altogether without charm. We are tempted to think that the quaint winsomeness that his poetry possesses for us may be in a measure due to the patina that the years have added; yet nineteenth-century readers relished it as well and were just as amused as we are when Sainte-Beuve pushes his Muse too far. "Sur sa table un lait pur, dans son lit un œil noir" was a line widely made sport of in Sainte-Beuve's own day. In the Antoine edition of *Joseph Delorme,* there is a caricatural drawing of Sainte-Beuve before a bowl of milk and a bed which contains a single black eye! Sainte-Beuve's final effort to establish in poetry "un certain genre moyen" is the volume entitled *Pensées d'août,* which appeared in 1837. It is a miscellany of themes and styles, tending perhaps more than his previous works toward the didactic.

Although Sainte-Beuve's place in French literary history is assured by his cultivation of the homely genre, his seminal force is not precisely here. That is to say, no one following him chose to work in this genre as such, but many subsequent French poets found inspiration in certain incidental features of his poetry. In later life Sainte-Beuve uttered these words which were more prophetic than he knew: "Aujourd'hui on me croit seulement un critique; mais je n'ai pas quitté la poésie sans y avoir laissé tout mon aiguillon."[4] This "stinger" has been given various interpretations, pointing in the main to a certain psychology that we think of as modern. Sainte-Beuve translated the *mal du siècle* into the idiom of his own experience and temperament: the result was, as René Lalou calls it, "une poésie intime jusqu'à l'excentricité, originale jusqu'à la création des valeurs paradoxalement neuves."[5] Already in Sainte-Beuve we perceive the accents of Baudelaire, who, in his reference to *Joseph Delorme* as "*Les Fleurs du Mal* de la veille," was not merely currying favor with the important critic. Doubtless he could recognize in Joseph Delorme a kindred spirit, another victim of those inner conflicts which he summarized by the paradox of his own title: "Flowers of Evil." Both *Joseph Delorme* and *Les Fleurs du Mal* set up the opposing poles of the profane and the sublime, between which each poet feels his soul vacillate. The resulting moral and metaphysical suffering made acute by full intellectual awareness of his problem creates the state of mind which Baudelaire recognized as common to himself and his predecessor.

Albert Thibaudet defines the affinities between Baude-laire and Sainte-Beuve as: critical intelligence (analysis of the heart instead of the typical Romantic effusions of the heart); inner Christianity (the theological implication of this analysis, the preoccupation with original sin); and a keen awareness of Paris.[6] This last named point is more important than it sounds because it ties together the theme of the homely and familiar with the spleen theme. The poet projects the Romantic psyche into a depiction of the modern metropolis, making of it a swarming culture of misery and vice. But Sainte-Beuve's realism moved away too soon from city scenes into the purely domestic, leaving the field to Baude-laire. The effect, however, of his "stinger" may be observed not only in the "Tableaux parisiens" of *Les Fleurs du Mal* but also in the "Petits Poèmes en prose," some of which first appeared under the title "Spleen de Paris."

Among the points in common, Thibaudet does not include that of the concept of universal analogies or correspondences. Yet Joseph Delorme heard the harmonies of the "analogie universelle" and saw in material nature the signs of a divine unity. In **"Les Rayons Jaunes,"** the series of associations awakened by the color of the sun's rays is an early exploitation in verse (before Gautier's "Symphonie en blanc majeur" and Banville's "Symphonie de la neige") of the theory of correspondences. Although rudimentary and inexplicit in the poem, it is stated precisely elsewhere in **Joseph Delorme.**[7]

Sainte-Beuve's importance as an initiator is not limited to matters of theme and mood: he left his mark too on poetic techniques. We know about his recovery of the Pléïade poets of the sixteenth century ignored or forgotten by the classical generations that followed them. A great part of his recovery was in metrics and in poetic diction. He promoted sixteenth-century verse forms, pleaded for renewed emphasis on rime, and advocated poetic procedures such as alliteration and assonance proscribed by the arbiters of classical taste.[8] Baudelaire, who would be first admired chiefly as a technician of poetry, was an attentive pupil. An additional feature of Sainte-Beuve's technical innovation is his predilection for the specific and realistic epithet. Here again Sainte-Beuve reaches back to pre-Classical literature to create models for poets to come. In spite of the general impression that he may give us today of being terribly conventional and rhetorical, he does say something new whereas Lamartine and other Romantic poets remained true to the tradition of the colorless generality.

It is to be feared, however, that in spite of its interesting features, the poetry of Sainte-Beuve may be destined to remain in the histories of literature. The homely genre as he practiced it has, as we have asserted, a quaint charm. Yet at bottom if it seemed ridiculous to his generation, it surely seems more so today. What seems even more alien to modern sensibility is Saint-Beuve's *mal du siècle,* although it was once thought to be very moving.

Notes

1. Alphonse Lamartine, *Harmonies poétiques et religieuses* (Hachette, 1879), vol. 14, *Œuvres,* pp. 226-27.

2. Ibid., p. 226.

3. Ferdinand Brunetière, "L'œuvre poétique de Sainte-Beuve," in *Evolution de la poésie lyrique en France au XIXe siècle* (Hachette, 1909).

4. Cited by René Lalou in *Vers une alchimie lyrique,* p. 39.

5. Ibid. See also J. Charpentier, *De Joseph Delorme à Paul Claudel,* pp. 51-52 (Les Œuvres Représentatives, 1930).

6. Albert Thibaudet, *Histoire de la littérature française* (Stock, 1936), pp. 322-23.

7. See *Joseph Delorme,* Texte XVIII (p. 150 of the Antoine edition). Is yellow here "yellow for mourning" of Swedenborgianism? See Anna Balakian, *The Symbolist Movement,* p. 25.

8. "A la Rime." This poem, resuscitating a strophe not used in French poetry since the Pléïade and exhibiting lexigraphical reminiscences of Ronsard and his group, calls for a return to the sixteenth-century emphasis upon rime. Throughout the nineteenth century, it served as a point of reference, a nail from which to hang reaffirmations of the importance of rime or repudiations of rime. See Antoine edition, p. 164, where its importance to Baudelaire is cited.

Rachel Killick (essay date January 1994)

SOURCE: Killick, Rachel. "Imitation and Individuality: Sainte-Beuve and the Remodelling of the Renaissance Sonnet." *Forum for Modern Language Studies* 30, no. 1 (January 1994): 18-36.

[*In the following essay, Killick provides a detailed analysis of Sainte-Beuve's treatment of the sonnet form in both his criticism and his poetry, and discusses his influence on later practitioners of the form.*]

The revival of the sonnet in nineteenth-century France is generally traced to Sainte-Beuve's *Tableau historique et critique de la poésie française et du théâtre français* (1828), an essay undertaken initially for the 1826-7 Académie française competition, "Discours sur l'histoire de la langue et de la littérature françaises depuis le commencement du seizième siècle jusqu'en 1610". The *Tableau*'s rehabilitation of both sixteenth-century poetry in general and of the sonnet in particular is, however, less clear-cut than received wisdom suggests. Reflecting the intentions and sympathies of the competition organisers, Sainte-Beuve seems concerned to establish the sixteenth-century poets as the flawed forerunners of seventeenth-century classicism and it is only at a late stage, after meeting Victor Hugo, that an approving parallel is drawn between Romantic efforts to create a new poetic language and the analogous concern of the Pléiade. The relatively few direct references to the sonnet seem particularly unlikely to attract any poet of the 1820s. Sainte-Beuve declares himself overwhelmed by the sheer mass of similar pieces on which nineteenth-century criteria of individual originality give little purchase:

> Il faut l'avouer à notre honte, sauf un certain nombre de jolies pièces qui frappent au premier coup d'œil, toutes ces centaines d'odes et de sonnets nous semblent d'un caractère assez uniforme: et si l'on n'y revenait à diverses reprises, si surtout l'on n'était soutenu ou redressé par les témoignages qu'ont laissés les contemporains, on aurait peine à départir à chaque auteur avec quelque précision et quelque justesse les traits qui le distinguent entre tous. L'invention, en effet, sur laquelle il est toujours aisé de se prononcer, même à travers la distance du temps et la différence des langues, n'a presque rien d'original chez Ronsard et ses amis; ce n'est d'ordinaire qu'une copie plus ou moins vive ou pâle des Grecs, des Latins, des Italiens. Reste l'élocution, le style. Mais la langue dans laquelle écrivaient ces novateurs est devenue pour nous une espèce de langue morte, et nous ne sommes guère bons juges de ce que pouvaient être, par rapport à elle, l'incorrection ou l'élégance.[2]

The sixteenth-century sonnet, then, for Sainte-Beuve, is remarkable chiefly for its monotony (a point subsequently developed with considerable verve by Gautier in *Les Grotesques*) and its once recherché and now archaic language. He also comments unfavourably on the artistic debasing implicit in its accessibility to the conscientious amateur[3] and, more importantly, in its extensive role in a network of flattery and patronage.[4] He thus gives few sonnet quotations, picking out only those collections or individual poems whose themes most reflect his own nineteenth-century preferences. The single sonnet mentioned with strong approval is Vauquelin de la Fresnaye's "O vent plaisant qui d'haleine odorante", described as "du petit nombre de ceux où le sentiment triomphe du bel esprit, où la forme donne du relief au sentiment, et desquels on serait tenté de dire sans épigramme qu'ils *valent un long poème*" (*THC* [*Tableau historique et critique de la poésie française et du théâtre français*] 115-16), a description prefiguring Sainte-Beuve's own efforts in the form. The same emphasis on personal feeling makes Du Bellay's *Regrets* Sainte-Beuve's preferred collection: "c'est déjà

quelque chose de remarquable que ce sérieux et parfois amer sentiment d'une âme qui s'ennuie et qui souffre." As for Ronsard, both in the *Tableau* and the accompanying volume of *œuvres choisies de Ronsard*, support sometimes seems to go rather less to his work than to the exemplary quality of his long-term fate as a poetic outcast, almost a "poète maudit" *avant la lettre*. Otherwise his best success is seen as lying "dans les genres de moyenne hauteur, dans l'élégie, dans l'ode épicurienne, dans la chanson" (*THC* 71). There is however no specific mention of the sonnet.

It seems initially then both inconsequential and surprising that Sainte-Beuve should have proceeded, almost immediately, to use the sonnet form quite extensively himself: 12 sonnets out of 55 poems in the *Vie, Poésies et Pensées de Joseph Delorme* (1829),[5] 10 sonnets out of 29 poems in *Les Consolations* (1830),[6] 18 sonnets out of 54 poems in *Pensées d'août* (1837).[7] Such figures clearly show that an uncertain academic interest in one of the main forms of sixteenth-century poetry has been translated into new poetic reality, and suggest that it is the combination of Sainte-Beuve's work as a critic and practice as a poet that provides a decisive stimulus for a revival of the sonnet in a way the *Tableau* could never have done alone.[8] Sainte-Beuve's 1862 article on the Lyonnais sonnetist, Joséphin Soulary,[9] reveals a lasting ambivalence towards the genre:

> [. . .] jamais les grands poètes de ce temps-ci n'[ont] fait de sonnets: ceux de Musset sont irréguliers, Lamartine et Hugo[10] n'en ont fait d'aucune sorte, Vigny non plus.[11] Les cygnes et les aigles, à vouloir entrer dans cette cage y auraient cassé leurs ailes. C'était affaire à nous autres, oiseaux de moins haut vol et de moins large envergure. Certes, et je ne l'ai pas oublié, tous les grands poètes de la Renaissance ont fait des sonnets: qui ne connaît ceux de Dante, de Shakespeare, de Milton? C'était alors un genre à la mode, et chacun lui payait tribut en passant, une fois au moins en sa vie. De nos jours le sonnet a été un genre restauré, légèrement artificiel, une gageure ou une gentillesse. Ceux de nos maîtres qui n'y étaient point intéressés par curiosité et par goût s'en sont passés et n'ont que faire de cette prison. Je me flatte d'être le premier chez nous, qui ait renouvelé l'exemple du sonnet en 1828; mais je n'en ai jamais fait que de temps à autre, par-ci par-là, et en entremêlant cette forme aux autres rythmes plus modernes.[12]

This passage is interesting for its shifting and often contradictory argument. Sainte-Beuve emphasises the unsuitability of the sonnet for the large-scale vision of the leading Romantic poets and its association with smaller talents of a less inspired, narrower type. But the negative quality of this assertion is immediately countered by reference to the towering figures of Dante, Shakespeare and Milton. Noteworthy absentees from the list, however, are Petrarch and his emulators, the French sixteenth-century sonnetists. They are instead subliminally present in the next negative twist of the argument where the great tradition of the Renaissance sonnet is promptly undermined by the categorisation of the genre as a fashionable mode, *de rigueur* for everyone at least once, and, by inference, neither particularly personal nor original for anyone. The argument then returns to the nineteenth century to reaffirm the sonnet's character as a lightweight social or virtuoso genre, too limited in scope for the masters of the day. Finally, with a last oscillation between negative and positive, Sainte-Beuve stresses his own innovatory role in the genre he has just criticised, only to retract almost immediately by insisting (quite untruthfully) on his infrequent use of the form.

The carefully worded letter to Baudelaire of 20 June 1857 shows Sainte-Beuve's concern over too close an association of *Joseph Delorme* and *Les Fleurs du Mal*.[13] Perhaps therefore in 1862 he wished to distance himself from the high profile attained by the sonnet as the chief formal vehicle of Baudelaire's notorious collection, newly reissued in 1861. In 1828-9, however, his adoption of the genre despite his comments on the archaic uniformity of its sixteenth-century examples was undoubtedly determined by his complex relationship with his poetic contemporaries and his desire to raise his artistic profile to equal theirs. His late arrival within the Romantic group made a personal niche particularly hard to find. Moreover, as he obsessively indicates in the numerous poems addressed to friends in the Cénacle, the heroic high ground where they had established themselves was not his natural terrain.[14] Emotionally insecure, lacking in self-confidence, painfully self-aware, he was incapable of the grand manner, be it the fluid expansiveness of Lamartine or the imaginative dynamism of Hugo. He did, however, possess one quality which they notably lacked, an intellectual sharpness married to an acute sense of the dangers of excess which even in the heat of his enthusiasm for their achievements was never entirely stilled.[15] This critical self-awareness provided Sainte-Beuve with the strategy and the material for mapping out his own poetic territory. His work would feature a different type of hero more characteristic of the modern age. The reverse of the larger-than-life hero—freedom-fighter, rebel, prophet, lover, tragic victim—of high Romanticism, Delorme, like Sainte-Beuve himself, is politically frustrated and inactive, materially deprived, emotionally isolated, psychologically insecure, artistically limited—and too intelligent for his own good in his clear-sighted vision of these defects in his personality and circumstances. In adopting the "persona" of Delorme, Sainte-Beuve thus makes a calculated decision to foreground limitation, to give inadequacy high profile status, thereby creating a situation where he can simultaneously gain the upper hand over that very limitation and inadequacy and establish vis à vis his colleague-competitors an alternative and more representative modern hero.

In this endeavour the sonnet has a crucial role. Though in the sixteenth century, following the model set by Petrarch, it had figured largely, if not exclusively, in sonnet sequences devoted to the cumulative presentation of the Poet as Lover, there was no reason why, in the nineteenth, it could not stand independently, thus suggesting the isolation and fragmentation inherent in the contemporary stress on the individuality of experience. For Sainte-Beuve's purposes, moreover, the spatial and structural constraints of the genre, so alien to the soaring flight of Lamartine or Hugo, were ideally suited to Delorme's experience of limitation and lack, while simultaneously the principles of control and stability, along with the potential for formal perfection, could restrain and transcend inadequacy and disintegration, producing in compensation a polished artefact capable of holding its own against the more sprawling and exuberant creations of Romantic genius. "Pensée XII" of *Joseph Delorme* with its special mention of the sonnet lays out this possibility with a characteristic mix of self-denigration and awareness of self-worth:

> Tel filet d'idée poétique qui chez André Chénier découlerait en élégie, ou chez Lamartine s'épancherait en méditation et finirait par devenir fleuve ou lac, se congèle aussitôt chez moi, et se cristallise en sonnet; c'est un malheur, et je m'y résigne.
>
> —Une idée dans un sonnet, c'est une goutte d'essence dans une larme de cristal.
>
> (*JD* [*Vie, poésies et pensées de Joseph Delorme*] 145)

The thought pivots on the verb "se cristallise". Initially an equivalent of "se congèle", it functions with it in a dual contrast with the free-flowing expansiveness of the preceding pair "découlerait/s'épancherait".[16] But the negative connotation of "se congèle", absent in "se cristallise", has to be reinstated through the separate indication: "C'est un malheur [. . .]". The qualification, though, is only temporary. In the final aphoristic sentence "cristal" emerges to full, positive significance, the formulaic phrasing echoing and underlining the rarefied intensity and purity of the tiny "goutte d'essence" and supporting its strong implicit challenge to the self-dissipating meandering of Chénier and more especially Lamartine.

The self-abasement and self-assertion surrounding Sainte-Beuve's use of the sonnet gains general formal expression in the overall structure of *Joseph Delorme,* the twelve sonnets, in two groupings towards the beginning and the end, interrelating with adjacent poems in a dialectical pattern which matches modest compression against heroic exuberance. The first two sonnets, a pair, nos. 4 and 5 of the collection, immediately establish the dual suitability of the genre for Delorme's examination of his circumscribed existence, summarising the themes of failure in love and material deprivation, more lengthily developed in nos. 1 and 3, **"Premier Amour"** and

"**Au Loisir**," and simultaneously effecting a formal rescue of the motifs of decline, limitation and death, by applying to them, in the shape of the regular sonnet, the craftsmanship principles of "**A la rime**" (no. 2). The next sonnet, "**Enfant je m'étais dit et souvent répété**" (no. 12), following "**A Mon Ami V. H. . . .**" (no. 11), which characterises Hugo as a powerful eagle soaring up to the sun or away to foreign climes while Sainte-Beuve/Delorme remains miserably earthbound, moves from early dreams of glory to those of obscure study, only to end on conventional protestations of love, phrased in the sixteenth-century mode. One reading would be to see this juxtaposition as a good demonstration of the poverty of Sainte-Beuve/Delorme's imagination. Another reading might rather stress the sixteenth-century reference as a means of investing present inadequacy with the aura of past achievement, thus suggesting alternative poetic strategies to those favoured by Hugo. This reading finds support in the ongoing arrangement of the poems. Thus "**Retour à la poésie**" (no. 13), balancing "**Adieux à la poésie**" (no. 11), is followed by "**Sur un front de quinze ans**" where Sainte-Beuve effects an original transformation of the love sonnet's traditional imagery. After one more poem, "**Bonheur champêtre**", a further sonnet pair, "**Oh! laissez-vous aimer**" and "**Madame, il est donc vrai**" again suggest an original modification for the genre, closely associated this time with the looser syntactic and metrical arrangements of the *rimes plates* poem immediately following, "**Causerie au bal**". "**Le Cénacle**" (no. 19) returns to the elevated struggles of the Romantic heroes, to whom Sainte-Beuve may be assimilated by virtue of the publication of the *Tableau* celebrated in no. 20. The first group of sonnets then concludes with "**A Ronsard**" borrowed from the *Tableau*'s accompanying second volume, Sainte-Beuve's edition of Ronsard, *Œuvres choisies*. The effect is to assert the credentials of the genre and to assimilate Sainte-Beuve's poetic efforts to a long-lived and resilient poetic tradition.

The second set of sonnets occurs in a single group, placed three poems from the end of the collection in general symmetrical balance and with similar organisation to the first group. The poem immediately preceding, "**A David statuaire**", celebrates a monumental genius "puissant dans la pierre féconde" who sets the entire world under the gaze of his heroic figures. Significantly the same stanzaic form of alexandrines extended by hexasyllables (12/12/6/12/12/6) is used as earlier in the equivalently positioned "**A V. H. . . .**". The first sonnet, "**Que de fois près d'Oxford**", offers against the imposing universality of David the inability of the "Pauvre étranger" to identify a true home for his soul but, as in the earlier group of sonnets, sixteenth-century allusion, in this case to the tercets of Du Bellay's "Heureux qui comme Ulysse", elevates his rootless wandering to universal significance, thus balancing

in some degree the adjacent evocation of the mighty creations of the great sculptor. The second sonnet, "**Chacun en sa beauté vante ce qui le touche**", like "**Sur un front de quinze ans**" previously, develops self-assertion more directly with an original modification of love sonnet imagery. The third sonnet, "**En ces heures souvent que le plaisir abrège**", suggests a radically new handling of the broad contrastive structures of the genre for a modern internalising of the conflict between emotion and intellect, while an alternative possibility, the modest "causerie" theme, developed in the earlier sonnet pair "**Oh! laissez-vous aimer**," is re-examined in an imitation of Wordsworth's "Personal Talk", the example of the English poet providing an artistic sanction for a new type of "domestic" sonnet. The group then concludes with a second Wordsworth imitation, "Scorn not the sonnet". Sainte-Beuve follows Wordsworth precisely in his list of great sonnetists but compresses it to leave space in the final tercet for a triumphant assertion of his own ambition: "Moi, je veux rajeunir le doux sonnet en France" (l. 12), followed by somewhat less emphatic mention of the two key sixteenth-century French practitioners, Du Bellay (l. 13) and Ronsard (l. 14).

The *Vie de Joseph Delorme* cites as the characteristic subjects of the protagonist "des peintures d'analyse sentimentale et des paysages de petite dimension" (*JD* 25), the first traditional territory for the sonnet, the second a less familiar enterprise at least in the French context. But even within the love sonnet, similarity with the past is largely superficial. Sainte-Beuve adopts the genre for its historic prestige and formal precision but initiates a redirection of thematic focus away from an externalised and depersonalised debate between "amour" and "esprit" to a subjective analysis of the dilemmas of the individual psyche which can detach itself from the love theme altogether. The first result is a simplification of conventional patterns of metaphor and argument, well illustrated by the first love sonnet of *Joseph Delorme*:

> Enfant, je m'étais dit et souvent répété:
> "Jamais, jamais d'amour; c'est assez de la gloire;
> En des siècles sans nombre étendons ma mémoire
> Et semons ici-bas pour l'immortalité."
>
> Plus tard, je me disais: "Amour et volupté,
> Allez, et gloire aussi! que m'importe l'histoire?
> Fantôme au laurier d'or, vierge au cou d'ivoire,
> Je vous fuis pour l'étude et pour l'obscurité."
>
> Ainsi, jeune orgueilleux, ainsi longtemps disais-je;
> Mais comme après l'hiver, en nos plaines, la neige
> Sous le soleil de mars fond au premier beau jour,
>
> Je te vis, blonde Hélène, et dans ce cœur farouche,
> Aux rayons de tes yeux, au souffle de ta bouche,
> Aux soupirs de ta voix, tout fondit en amour.

(*JD* 51)

The external shape of the sonnet is unchanged from the sixteenth century, following, like the majority of Sainte-Beuve's sonnets, the *abba abba ccd eed* rhyme pattern established by Marot. Unchanged too is the subject, the primacy of love over all other human desires. But this sonnet is schizophrenic. The quatrains are nineteenth-century, discursively articulating the characteristic experience of failed heroic dream (ll. 1-4) and acceptance of modest limits (ll. 5-8) with imagery in the most banal of supporting roles. The tercets in contrast, centred on the theme of love, draw heavily on tighter sixteenth-century practice, developing the metaphors of winter and spring and using the sonnet's structural possibilities of postponement and climax to replicate formally, in line 12 and again in line 14, the *coup de foudre*. Yet, even here, despite the additional emphasis of the Ronsardian name and traditional attribute, "blonde Hélène", the handling of the imagery has been modified. The winter into spring image, used to suggest the softening of the heart to love, runs counter to that other traditional association of youth with spring and age with winter, and there is no attempt to devise, as a sixteenth-century poet might have done, a relationship between the two ideas. Furthermore the analogy seems more loosely applied than is common in Renaissance poetry. The poet refers to the "rayons de tes yeux" and the "souffle de ta bouche", conventional both, but there is little attempt to link the figure of Hélène directly with the "soleil de mars" and the idea of Spring.[17] Similarly "soupirs de ta voix" has no equivalent in the image of the first tercet. Instead, attention is focused on *sensation* with the double use of the verb "fondre" (ll. 11, 14) as the hinge on which the tercets are balanced. Extra emphasis for the verb is provided by *enjambement* (ll. 10-11), by the enumeration, hemistich by hemistich ll. 12-14, which accelerates the chain of events "Je te vis [. . .] tout fondit" and by the symmetrical arrangement of the two events "vis [. . .] fondit" in the first and final position of the tercet. Again, though, in contrast to sixteenth-century practice, there is no play on the paradoxes of heat and cold, ardour and frigidity; the poet concentrates instead on simple notation of emotion.

If **"Enfant, je m'étais dit"** remains a none too successful hybrid, other love sonnets in the collection suggest how the genre might be successfully modified to suit a modern preoccupation with the potentialities and limitations of individual identity. One possibility, the broad structural internalising of the tension between the individual intellect and the individual sensibility, is embryonically visible in the tenth sonnet of *Joseph Delorme*:

> En ces heures souvent que le plaisir abrège,
> Causant d'un livre à lire et des romans nouveaux,
> Ou me parlant déjà des mes prochains travaux,
> Suspendue à mon cou, tu me dis: "Comprendrai-je?"

> Et, ta main se jouant à mon front qu'elle allège,
> Tu vantes longuement nos sublimes cerveaux,
> Et tu feins d'ignorer . . . Sais-tu ce que tu vaux,
> Belle Ignorante, aux blonds cheveux, au cou de neige?

> Qu'est toute la science auprès d'un sein pâmé,
> Et d'une bouche en proie au baiser enflammé,
> Et d'une voix qui pleure et chante à l'agonie?

> Ton frais regard console en un jour nébuleux;
> On lit son avenir au fond de tes yeux bleus,
> Et ton sourire en sait plus long que le génie.

> (*JD* 123)

Here the intricate intellectualising of feeling characteristic of the metaphoric codes of the sixteenth-century sonnet is replaced by a simplified opposition of intellectual activity and physical attraction structured within the individual quatrains and between octave and sestet. Thus, in the first quatrain, literary discussion (ll. 2-3), foreshortened in advance, is further compressed by physical contact and intellectual incomprehension (l. 4). The second quatrain follows a similar pattern, physical contact (l. 5) preceding the mistress' praise of the "sublimes cerveaux" of the poet and his colleagues, and physical attraction asserting itself again, even earlier than in the first quatrain, halfway through line 7. The balance of intellect and emotion, under threat throughout the quatrains, collapses by line 8 and is replaced in the tercets by a one-sided emphasis on emotion alone. Intellectual preoccupations and creative aspirations are engulfed by overwhelming feeling, formally reproduced in the repetitive syntactic patterns of lines 9-11, 12 and 14 and in the cumulative itemisation in successive lines of bosom, mouth, voice, look, eyes and smile.

The portrayal of the subjugation of the individual to his senses and the concomitant reduction of his intellectual and creative ambition is an important new field for the sonnet, entailing substantial changes in formal emphasis. With the stress now firmly on individual emotion, the conventional patterns of tightly intertwined metaphor and argument become irrelevant and disappear. In their place, broad brush emphasis on main stanzaic divisions creates a firm but flexible framework of potential opposition, symmetry and parallel, at once malleable enough to accommodate individual experience and rigid enough to systematise and contain it.

Another new possibility for the modern love sonnet involves the specific question of metaphor. In "Pensée XVI", Sainte-Beuve develops a subjective conception of Beauty founded on the Romantic perception of individual emotional and aesthetic response. The interest and implications of this idea for the sonnet are given preliminary consideration in **"Chacun en sa beauté vante ce qui le touche"**:

> Chacun en sa beauté vante ce qui le touche;
> L'amant voit des attraits où n'en voit point l'époux;

Mais que d'autres, narguant les sarcasmes jaloux,
Vantent un poil follet au-dessus d'une bouche:

D'autres sur des seins blancs un point comme une
    mouche,
D'autres, des cils bien noirs à des yeux bleus bien
    doux,
Ou sur un cou de lait des cheveux d'un blond roux;
Moi, j'aime en deux beaux yeux un sourire un peu
    louche:

C'est un rayon mouillé; c'est un soleil dans l'eau,
Qui nage au gré du vent dont frémit le bouleau;
C'est un reflet de lune aux rebords d'un nuage.

C'est un pilote en mer, par un ciel obscurci,
Qui s'égare, se trouble, et demande merci,
Et voudrait quelque Dieu, protecteur du voyage.

                                              (*JD* 122)

Line 1, boldly contradicting the externally imposed Petrarchan norms of beauty, asserts that individual subjective reaction is all.[18] The fragmentation of opinion
consequent on this view is explored in the remainder of
the quatrains through a list of individual preferences,
odd or otherwise, which culminates with the author's
own predilection (l. 8). In the tercets this is paramount,
the dispersive repetition of "d'autres" superseded by
concentrative insistence ("c'est [. . .] c'est") as the
poet endeavours to define the particular quality of his
own ideal. Within the tercets, though, there is a curious
dichotomy, the image of the final tercet still drawing on
the bank of Renaissance imagery so comprehensively
rejected in line 1. The real interest thus lies in the first
tercet where it becomes apparent that the poet's personal
idea of beauty requires a whole new set of images to
explain it, and imagery moreover that seems to run
counter to all previous concentration of the sonnet on
the clear, sharp lines of an argument or metaphorical
pattern. Mystery, opacity, trembling and indistinct
reflection, ill-defined emotion, these are qualities which
Baudelaire and Verlaine will later incorporate in the
sonnet, using the symmetries of its structure and the
complex interplay of thematic, syntactic, rhythmic and
phonetic patterns within a fixed prosodic form not for
the intellectual elaboration of a rhetorical figure but to
convey a subjective impression or a mood.

These possibilities are limited here to little more than a
statement of intent, but the sonnet **"Sur un front de
quinze ans"** goes further, showing how this inner
modification of the sonnet may be achieved:

Sur un front de quinze ans les cheveux blonds d'Aline
Débordant le bandeau qui les voile à nos yeux,
Baignent des deux côtés ses sourcils gracieux:
Tel un double ruisseau descend de la colline.

Et sa main, soutenant ce beau front qui s'incline,
Aime à jouer autour, et dans les flots soyeux
A noyer un doigt blanc, et l'ongle curieux
Rase en glissant les bords où leur cours se dessine.

Mais au sommet du front où le flot séparé
Découle en deux ruisseaux et montre un lit nacré,
Là, je crois voir Amour voltiger sur la rive;

Nager la Volupté sur deux vagues d'azur;
Ou sur un vert gazon, sur un sable d'or pur,
La Rêverie assise, aux yeux bleus et pensive.

                                              (*JD* 56)

Curiously this sonnet first attracted (adverse) comment
for the expression "ongle curieux".[19] It was also criticised by Magnin in *Le Globe* amongst others for the
sixteenth-century preciosity of its imagery.[20] The
comparison between the girl's hair and the river
dominates and shapes the poem and is further complicated by the introduction in the last tercet of a second
water image, the "deux vagues d'azur" of the eyes.
Sainte-Beuve, however, diverges sharply from traditional sonnet technique in renouncing any attempt to
follow the two analogies to some crowning conceit or
paradox and turns instead from description to suggestion ("je crois voir"). The simile "Tel un double ruisseau" developed as an extended metaphor through lines
5-10, suddenly casts off its precious character and
expands into symbol; the two levels, sentimental and
intellectual, on which the traditional love sonnet was
played, merge in a vision in which the girl is simultaneously herself and something more, a mythical figure
almost, eternally dreaming in an atmosphere of blue,
green and gold.

The allegories of "Amour" and "Volupté" are hardly
new images for the sonnet, but the personification of
"la Rêverie" is, and it receives not only the weight of
the sonnet's closing emphasis but also additional stress
from the tautological balance of "Rêverie" and its
detached adjective "pensive" as the first and last words
of the climactic final line. Furthermore the motif of the
dream (ll. 11-14) is associated with an intensification of
syntactic and phonetic features which create a sense of
fluid musicality that transforms the limited initial commonplace of the flowing hair into a suggestive evocation filled with all the elusive charm of the young girl.
In the second quatrain, Sainte-Beuve attempts, though
rather clumsily, to promote an illusion of movement
through the syntactic overruns of lines 6-7 and 7-8. In
the tercets, this tendency undergoes a considerable
extension. Not only is the technique of the second
quatrain continued in the positioning of the subject and
verb of the subordinate clause over the junction of lines
9-10, but, much more important, both tercets acquire a
quickening tempo, first from the double accusative and
infinitive (ll. 11-12) thrown into additional relief by the
traditional pause at the end of the first tercet, then from
the parallel repetition, this time of adverbial phrases in
line 13, which culminates in the final resolution of the

"je crois voir" construction with the direct object "la Rêverie assise" in line 14. Simultaneously there is an analogous intensification in phonetic patterning. The clumsy reiteration of whole words, "le front", "le flot", "deux (double) ruisseaux" (ll. 1-10) is replaced by a subtle interweaving and positioning of sounds: repetition of [v] (ll. 11-14); of prolonging [ʀ] (ll. 12-3); of [i], [s], [ø] and [] (l. 14). The poet thus creates a gentle obsessive web of sound which parallels on the phonetic level the flowering of the limited simile into a harmonious vision. Suggestion replaces statement as a source of poetic effect. Sainte-Beuve in his unpublished notes indicated "flottant" and "rêve" as key words for *Joseph Delorme*.[21] The introduction of dream into the sonnet and the development of the genre's potential to suggest infinite expansion, an escape from limitation to transcendence, was to be one of the most fruitful nineteenth-century innovations in the form.

The sixteenth-century love sonnet, for all its idealising reference to the eternal time of classical myth or the endless cycle of the changing seasons, in fact presupposes a specific historical and social setting, the privileged aristocratic society of a princely Renaissance court. Sainte-Beuve not only begins the modification of the Renaissance love sonnet towards individual expression of emotion. He also adapts it to a firm setting of individual experience within the limited confines of contemporary time and space. The small domestic interior and the modest social activity of the occasional "bal" are the restricted and specifically nineteenth-century bourgeois settings shaping individual feeling and expectation. Such settings induce not the sophisticated figures of cultured and scholarly utterance but the "causerie" of everyday exchange. The effect on the identity of the sonnet is once again a relaxing of internal structures, this time not only of imagery, but also of rhythm and syntax, even as the genre's predetermined shape continues to impose a modicum of external compression and control. **"En ces heures que souvent le plaisir abrège"** gives a brief glimpse of the "causerie" as thematic motif within the love sonnet, but the sonnet pair **"Oh! laissez-vous aimer"** and **"Madame, il est donc vrai"** provides the fullest demonstration of both its thematic and formal realisation. Despite the epigraph from Dante's *Vita Nuova*,[22] both pieces could take the title of the poem in *rimes plates* that follows them, **"Causerie au bal"**:

> Oh! laissez-vous aimer! . . . ce n'est pas un retour,
> Ce n'est pas un aveu que mon amour réclame;
> Ce n'est pas de verser mon âme dans votre âme,
> Ni de vous enivrer des langueurs de l'amour;
>
> Ce n'est pas d'enlacer en mes bras le contour
> De ces bras, de ce sein; d'embraser de ma flamme
> Ces lèvres de corail si fraîches; non, madame,
> Mon feu pour vous est pur, aussi pur que le jour.

> Mais seulement, le soir, vous parler à la fête,
> Et tout bas, bien longtemps, vers vous penchant la tête,
> Murmurer de ces riens qui vous savent charmer;
>
> Voir vos yeux indulgents plus mollement reluire;
> Puis prendre votre main, et, courant, vous conduire
> A la danse légère . . . oh! laissez-vous aimer!

> Madame, il est donc vrai, vous n'avez pas voulu,
> Vous n'avez pas voulu comprendre mon doux rêve;
> Votre voix m'a glacé d'une parole brève,
> Et vos regards distraits dans mes yeux ont mal lu.
>
> Madame, il est cruel de vous avoir déplu:
> Tout mon espoir s'éteint et mon malheur s'achève;
> Mais vous, qu'en votre cœur nul regret s'élève,
> Ne dites pas: "Peut-être il aurait mieux valu . . ."
>
> Croyez avoir bien fait; et, si pour quelque peine
> Vous pleurez, que ce soit pour un peigne d'ébène,
> Pour un bouquet perdu, pour un ruban gâté!
>
> Ne connaissez jamais de peine plus amère;
> Que votre enfant vermeil joue à votre côté,
> Et pleure seulement de voir pleurer sa mère.

(*JD* 59-60)

The first sonnet, a lover's prevarication reinforcing the initial demand, follows a straightforward scheme, framed within the octave-sestet structure, of denial of any pretension to a reciprocation of love on the lady's part (quatrains) and requests that he merely be allowed to love her from his side (tercets). Imagery is minimal, mere discontinuous cliché on the surface of the purely discursive development of the poem. Syntactical features within the formal framework are similarly relaxed. Non-coincidence of metre and syntax (ll. 5-7, 13-14) echoes the rhythms of ordinary speech. The "circular" repetition of **"Oh! laissez-vous aimer"**, which elsewhere might indicate a densely realised network of formal, thematic and syntactic features, continues the same diffuse approach. In effect, if not in title, this is indeed a "causerie". The second sonnet describes the lady's rejection of her suitor (quatrains) and his magnanimous desire for her happiness nonetheless (tercets). Again no use is made of the structure of the sonnet to underpin a complex argument or to explore an image. There is no elaboration within the possible parallels offered by the form for a contrast between her happiness and his misery; metaphor is confined to such conventional figures as "Votre regard m'a glacé" and "Mon espoir s'éteint". Syntactic structures are again leisurely (notably the repetitions ll. 1-2), and sometimes work against rhythmic patterns (ll. 9-10). The very use of a sonnet *pair* suggests not only the proposition and response of the "causerie" but also its diffuse meandering.

Detached from the love theme, the small-scale evocation of daily concerns in contemporary settings comes increasingly to form the bulk of Sainte-Beuve's sonnet production. This development, already indicated in the second sonnet of **Joseph Delorme** ("Il ne m'aurait fallu, sur un coin de la terre, / Qu'un loisir innocent, un chaume solitaire" [**JD** 35]), is re-examined in the rural description of **"Que de fois près d'Oxford"** and more especially in the provincial social detail of the Wordsworth imitation, "Je ne suis pas de ceux pour qui les causeries" (**JD** 123-4). **Les Consolations** (1830) takes the association further, but largely on the level of illustrative argument, with three sonnets (including an imitation of Wordsworth's "Not love, not War", **PC** [**Poésies complètes**] II: 52) contrasting the noisy demands of public life and the quiet enjoyment of "le foyer domestique et la félicité" (**PC** II: 74) to emphasise the validity of a non-heroic poetry of hearth and home.[23] At the same time Sainte-Beuve remains eager to stress both his artistic originality and his solid literary credentials. **"A Victor Hugo"**, prefacing **Les Consolations,** presents its accounts of "la vie privée" as a domestic relaxation for Hugo, the public hero of theatrical revolution and renewal, but also takes care to place this apparently modest ambition under the aegis of Petrarch. Within the collection in a balancing pattern corresponding to that of **Joseph Delorme,** a poem to Lamartine "grand homme, homme heureux" (**PC** II: 31-4), is followed by a sonnet, **"L'autre nuit je veillais dans mon lit sans lumière"** (**PC** II: 35) which uses the intensifying aspect of octave-sestet structure for a parallel between a grandiose storm scene of lightning and thunder (quatrains) and the corresponding explosion of divine inspiration it calls forth in the poet (tercets). In a converse move, more suited to the prevailing emphasis on the simple life, Victor Hugo, at one moment presented as a Jacob emerging in triumphant exhaustion from his struggle with the Angel, is subsequently "domesticated" within the confines of a sonnet which uses the internal contrastive and progressive potential of quatrains and tercets to highlight, against images of prophetic and warrior-like grandeur, alternative qualities of quiet friendship and quasi-maternal tenderness.[24]

In **Pensées d'août** (1837) the development towards a "domestic" sonnet moves from isolated examples and statements of intent to more consistent practice. On this occasion the promotion of "un certain genre moyen" takes place in reaction to and in competition with Lamartine. Sainte-Beuve's footnote to **"Monsieur Jean"**, echoing his 1836 article on *Jocelyn*,[25] clearly reveals both his sense of resentment at what he sees as Lamartine's invasion of his private territory and a concomitant attempt at damage limitation by a more precise definition of his own individual contribution:

> Dans son admirable et charmant *Jocelyn,* M. de Lamartine, avec sa sublimité facile, a d'un pas envahi tout ce petit domaine de poésie dite intime, privée, domestique, familière, où nous avions essayé d'apporter quelque originalité et quelque nouveauté. Il a fait comme un possesseur puissant qui, apercevant hors du parc quelques petites chaumières, quelques *cottages* qu'il avait jusque-là négligés, étend la main et transporte l'enceinte du parc au-delà, enserrant du coup tous ces petits coins curieux, qui à l'instant s'agrandissent et se fécondent par lui. Or, il m'a semblé qu'il était bon de replacer la poésie domestique, et familière, et réelle, sur son terrain nu, de la transporter plus loin, plus haut, même sur les collines pierreuses et hors d'atteinte de tous les magnifiques ombrages.

> (*PC* II: 150)

The treacherous little phrase "avec sa sublimité facile" goes straight for the jugular of Lamartine, undermining the apparently positive characterisation of Lamartine in the 1836 article as "l'Homère d'un genre domestique, d'une épopée de classe moyenne et de famille". One way of avoiding an inappropriately inflated style is, as in **"Monsieur Jean"**, the adoption of a prosaic type of narrative verse on the model of the English poet George Crabbe. The other, already pioneered in **Joseph Delorme** and in **Les Consolations,** and exemplified in the *"Jocelyn"* article by the translation of three sonnets from Wordsworth's sequence *Yarrow Revisited,*[26] is the use of the sonnet in the manner of the Lake poets to blend meditation and mundane domestic detail in a controlled and harmonious synthesis. Wordsworth, replacing the Petrarchists, thus becomes the model for Sainte-Beuve's adaptation of the genre to the small occasions of private domestic life and the guarantor of the artistic validity of this project. Unfortunately, however, the task of raising "la réalité plus vulgaire [. . .] à une plus haute puissance de poésie" is not automatically achieved by its enshrinement within the highly stylised structures of sonnet form, and this is as true for Wordsworth as it is for Sainte-Beuve. Sainte-Beuve's limited acquaintance with English perhaps prevented his fully appreciating the limitations of many of Wordsworth's sonnets or perhaps, for his imitations, he merely made a quick choice in general line with his own temperamental preference for the unexceptional and ordinary.[27] Be that as it may, of the sonnets imitated, only "It is a beauteous evening, calm and free" shows Wordsworth at anything like his best, transported through the emotional intensity of the individual incident to wider horizons of transcendent feeling. Significantly, however, even in the brief period of religious fervour evoked in **Les Consolations,** Sainte-Beuve's imitation of this sonnet has none of the uplifting grandeur of the original. Where Wordsworth skilfully blends the serenity of the fixed form with internal flexibilities of rhythm to express his vision of the figure of the girl as an integrated part of a universe dynamically filled with divine spirit, Sainte-Beuve relies on the basic octave-sestet structure for a reductive opposition of the beauty of the natural scene to the greater beauty of the girl's heart. The effect is to diminish the vast peace and ecstatic spiritual release that fills the original to a narrow platitudinous conceit.

The attempt to enhance an ordinary incident by building into it a moral reflexion and using the structure of the sonnet as a convenient support for a pattern of illustration and moral comment is increasingly evident in **Pensées d'août.** Cameos of enjoying the garden, of a child in its cradle, of a mother and child on the seashore, of boating on Lake Geneva, of mountain walks (a favourite for a moral message of heavenward ascent) are not creatively interpreted as moments of expanded experience, but are reduced to what is essentially an ancillary function. The ordinary, unredeemed, becomes the typical. The individualising thrust of the early sonnets is subverted into a debased universalising mode, which replaces the intellectual interest of virtuoso variations on a common theme characteristic of the Renaissance with a bland received wisdom. For his "domestic" poetry Sainte-Beuve frequently insisted on the need for strict form to elevate his subject-matter and rescue it from triviality.[28] The elegant rigour of the sonnet clearly seemed to him an excellent vehicle for this salvage operation. Unfortunately the reductive pressure of a short, strongly patterned form served in the end to exaggerate, not retrieve, thematic triviality and to limit moral insights to trite generalisations. The remark offered by Sainte-Beuve as one of his own maxims at the end of his 1840 La Rochefoucauld article: "Dans la jeunesse, les pensées me venaient en sonnets; maintenant, c'est en maximes" provides an excellent gloss on the sonnets of the significantly entitled **Pensées d'août,** indicating the exhaustion of Sainte-Beuve's innovative vision of the poetic potential of individual limitation and revealing his essential character as generalising moral analyst.[29] The combination of stylised form and trivial subject was, however, to be perpetuated by Coppée, who attempts to expand the scope of his domestic poetry by the simple expedient of using the sonnet as a frame to render "poetic" naturalistic description or moral precept.

Though Sainte-Beuve reorientates the sonnet thematically to an analysis of the modern individual in his contemporary setting, his handling of sonnet versification remains unswervingly conservative. The fleeting allusion in the *Tableau historique* to Boileau's celebrated résumé of the genre in *L'Art poétique*[30] establishes a "classical" preoccupation with the rigorous observance of formal rules and a belief in the value *per se* of technically perfect form. Throughout his sonnets Sainte-Beuve adheres to the rule of two rhymes only in the quatrains, arranged in the prescribed enclosed pattern.[31] Similarly, in the potentially more flexible tercets, he sticks with relatively few exceptions to the two main patterns *ccd eed* and *ccd ede.* Structurally, he maintains the octave-sestet division with more vigour than generally shown even in the sixteenth century,[32] and he usually makes a definite break between the two quatrains also.[33] With metre, too, Sainte-Beuve maintains a traditional approach, continuing the association between alexandrine

and sonnet established by Ronsard.[34] However, if the combination of the bipartite/tetrametric line and binary/quadruple pattern of octave-sestet/quatrains-tercets continues to provide mutually reinforcing structures for the development of the logical stages of an argument, Sainte-Beuve clearly sometimes finds it difficult to limit nineteenth-century discursiveness to the fourteen-line framework, hence the significant number of sonnet pairs within his work.[35] More inventively, he does on occasion begin to explore the possibility of an internal discordance between syntactic and metrical structures which would disseminate the overall discrepancy between ordered form and disordered content throughout the entire sonnet, thereby creating a more organic realisation of the themes of individual insufficiency and limitation.

Sainte-Beuve thus passed on to his successors a sonnet whose thematic identity had been radically reorientated, but whose formal identity had for the most part been emphatically reaffirmed. The result was essentially twofold. As the more immediate development, poets such as Nerval, Baudelaire and later Verlaine adapt the sonnet to a more intensive and more sophisticated analysis of the conflicts of individual personality and the limits of personal identity. As a longer-term outcome, the individual is gradually displaced from his central position and the emphasis once again passes to the sonnet form itself. But this is no return to the Renaissance sonnet and its humanist glorification of collective intellectual inventiveness. Instead, moving on from the Parnassian idea of formal control as a sublimation of psychic incapacity, Mallarmé will elevate the formal structure of the sonnet from a role of "technical support" to a central thematic function, proposing it as the microcosmic representation of that transcendence from which modern man seems irrevocably excluded.

Notes

1. For *Joseph Delorme*, reference is to *Vie, poésies et pensées de Joseph Delorme,* ed. Gérald Antoine (Paris, 1957), henceforth *JD.* References to Sainte-Beuve's other collections of poetry are to the *Poésies complètes,* 2 vols. (Paris, 1863), henceforth *PC* I and *PC* II.

2. *Tableau historique et critique de la poésie française et du théâtre français au XVIe siècle* (Paris, 1842), pp. 84-5, henceforth *THC.*

3. *THC* [*Tableau historique et critique de la poésie française et du théâtre français au XVIe siècle*] 38-9: "Durant cette grande renaissance des lettres, les esprits studieux embrassaient tout; la vocation de créer n'était pas distincte du besoin de savoir; et, dans ce vaste champ de conquête, au milieu de cette communauté de connaissances, on ne songeait pas encore à l'apanage du talent. On fai-

sait des vers comme on faisait de la médecine, de la jurisprudence, de la théologie ou de l'histoire, et tout lettré d'alors, pourrait à la rigueur, être rangé parmi les poètes."

4. *THC* 110, n. 1 sketches in the outstanding success of Desportes in the field: "Des Portes avait de bonne heure été attaché au duc d'Anjou, avec lequel il fit, à son grand déplaisir, le voyage de Pologne. Quand ce prince fut devenu roi de France sous le nom de Henri III, Des Portes reçut de lui en bénéfices et abbayes jusqu'à dix mille écus de rente. Cette fortune, prodigieuse alors, était passée en proverbe, et dans les auteurs du temps il n'est question que des trente mille livres de M. l'abbé de Tiron. 'Ce fut un dangereux exemple, dit Balzac, qui fit faire. bien des sonnets, des élégies à faux; un écueil contre lequel dix mille poètes se sont brisés.' Le même écrivain a remarqué que, dans cette cour où le duc de Joyeuse donna à Des Portes une abbaye pour un sonnet, le Tasse eut besoin d'un écu, et le demanda par aumône à une dame de sa connaissance." Sainte-Beuve also cites (p. 133) Mathurin Régnier's satirical figure of the down-at-heel poet: "L'exemple de Ronsard, de Des Portes et de Bertaut, lui revient par la tête, et, tout en méditant un sonnet, il médite un bénéfice ou un évêché." Unfortunately for such dreams, however, "on n'était déjà plus au règne de Henri III, cet âge d'or des sonnets" (p. 130).

5. Another sonnet was added to the *Poésies de Joseph Delorme* in the 1861 Poulet-Malassis edition of the *Poésies complètes.* This was the "Sonnet imité de Keats", "Piquante est la bouffée . . . .".

6. One of these sonnets is a translation of Michelangelo's Sonnet, "Giunto è gia 'l corso della mia", included at the head of the long poem in *rimes plates,* "A mon ami Leroux" (*PC* II: 55-6).

7. In the 1863 Lévy *Poésies complètes,* the *Suite de Joseph Delorme. Poésies du lendemain dans le même ton* which completes Volume I has 17 sonnets out of 75 poems. In Volume II, *Notes et Sonnets, faisant comme suite aux Pensées d'août* has 31 sonnets out of a total of 43 poems, (counting the three sonnets of the sequence "De ces monts tout est beau" as individual pieces). *Un Dernier Rêve,* concluding Volume II, has four sonnets out of nine pieces in verse form.

8. Louis de Veyrières, following his account of the resumption of the sonnet competition at the Jeux Floraux de Toulouse in 1806, the translation of 28 sonnets of Petrarch by Ginguené in 1811 and the use of the form in the early years of the nineteenth century by a few, now long-forgotten writers, comments: "Il est bien évident que des vestales ont entretenu le feu sacré du sonnet jusqu'à notre temps. CH. AUG. SAINTE-BEUVE, mort en solidaire le 13 octobre 1869, n'a donc point ressuscité le sonnet, comme on s'est plu à le dire." However, Veyrières is still forced to agree, "Mais on ne peut en disconvenir il l'a prôné et popularisé" (*Monographie du Sonnet* [Paris, 1869], II, pp. 108-9).

9. *Nouveaux Lundis* (Paris, 1863-70), III, pp. 344-5.

10. In fact Hugo wrote four sonnets, all printed in *Toute la lyre* (1888). "Ave dea; moriturus te salutat", addressed to Judith Gautier, first appeared in the 1874 *Etrennes du Parnasse.* "Roman en trois sonnets", though undated, seems likewise to date from the end of Hugo's life and was almost certainly written after this 1862 article. Hugo's general attitude towards the form is clearly revealed in such lines as: "Dans le parc froid et superbe / Rien de vivant ne venait / On comptait les brins d'une herbe / Comme les mots d'un sonnet" ("Le Chêne du parc détruit", in *Les Chansons des rues et des bois*).

11. Vol. 1 of the Pléiade edition of Vigny's *Œuvres complètes* (Paris, 1986) includes 6 occasional sonnets in the section *Poèmes non recueillis.*

12. A more detailed breakdown of the *Poésies de Joseph Delorme* shows that the twelve sonnets follow *rimes plates* (21 examples) as the most strongly represented form. In *Les Consolations* and *Pensées d'août* also, *rimes plates* and the sonnet persist together as the dominant forms—17 poems in *rimes plates* and 9 sonnets in *Les Consolations* and 17 poems in *rimes plates* and 18 sonnets in *Pensées d'août.* The number of actual *lines* is of course heavily weighted towards the *rimes plates.* The interesting question is whether the predominance of these two forms implies a division of labour or a reorientation of the sonnet towards more descriptive or narrative subject-matter and simpler techniques of presentation.

13. Sainte-Beuve, *Correspondance générale* Vol. 10 (Paris, 1960), pp. 422-5.

14. "A Villemain", *Pensées d'août* (*PC* II: 231-2), retrospectively provides a good summary of the position:

> Lamartine régna; chantre ailé qui soupire,
> Il planait sans effort. Hugo, dur partisan,
> (Comme chez Dante on voit, Florentin ou Pisan,
> Un baron féodal), combattit sous l'armure,
> Et tint haut sa bannière au milieu du murmure:
> Il la maintenait encore; et Vigny, plus secret,
> Comme en sa tour d'ivoire, avant midi, rentrait.
>
> Venu bien tard, déjà quand chacun avait place,
> Que faire? où mettre pied? en quel étroit espace?

> Les vétérans tenaient tout ce champ des esprits.
> Avant qu'il fût à moi l'héritage était pris.

15. Hugo, for example, is criticised not only in the *Globe* article of 1827 on the *Odes et ballades* but also in that on *Les Chants du crépuscule* in 1835 for his lack of a sense of proportion: "En poésie, comme ailleurs, rien de si périlleux que la force: si on la laisse faire, elle abuse de tout; par elle, ce qui n'était qu'original et neuf est bien près de devenir bizarre; un contraste brillant dégénère en antithèse précieuse; l'auteur vise à la grâce et à la simplicité, et il va jusqu'à la mignardise et à la simplesse; il ne cherche que l'héroïque, et il rencontre le gigantesque; s'il tente jamais le gigantesque, il n'évitera pas le puéril." *Premiers Lundis* (Paris, 1886-1894) I, p. 179.

16. A revealing subtext for this "Pensée" is provided by the discussion of the "give-away" words of a range of contemporary authors in Sainte-Beuve's 1832 article on Senancour: "Tel grand poète épanche sans relâche l'*harmonie et les flots*". Hugo, for his part, "à l'étroit dans cette civilisation étouffante, ne peut s'empêcher de remonter à une scène héroïque et au monde des *géants*" (*Portraits contemporains* [Paris, 1870] I, pp. 12-13).

17. For comparison with Sainte-Beuve's sonnet, see Du Bellay, *L'Olive* XXXI, *Œuvres poétiques,* ed. Henri Chamard, Vol. I (Paris, 1908) p. 53, or Ronsard, *Les Amours* CLXV, *Œuvres complètes,* Vol. IV, ed. Paul Laumonnier (Paris, 1939), pp. 156-7. For a mingling of the two images of winter as frigidity and winter as age, see "Puisqu'elle est tout hyver, toute la mesme glace", Ronsard, *Les Amours diverses XXIV, Œuvres complètes,* ed. Laumonnier, Vol. XVII (Paris, 1959), p. 307.

18. This individualised approach differs radically from the sixteenth-century topos of sonnets built on a systematic reversing of Petrarchan attributes.

19. Musset commemorated Sainte-Beuve's fondness for both synecdoche and the sonnet in "Réponse à Charles Nodier", *Poésies complètes* (Paris, 1957), p. 444: "Sainte-Beuve faisait dans l'ombre / Douce et sombre / Pour un œil noir, un blanc bonnet / Un sonnet." The famous "œil noir" of Sainte-Beuve occurs in the dizain "Vœu" (*JD* 77): "Pour trois ans seulement, oh! que je puisse avoir / Sur ma table un lait pur, dans mon lit un œil noir."

20. Magnin lists this amongst the sonnets that Delorme "a eu la fantaisie un peu puérile de calquer sur ceux du XVIᵉ siècle, reproduisant avec une fidélité bien malheureuse l'affectation de cette époque". Quoted *JD* 175, n. 173. Ronsard, for example, opens *Les Amours LXXXVI, Œuvres complètes,* Vol. IV, pp. 77-8, with a similar comparison,

but does not however maintain the same image into the tercets.

21. Coll. Lovenjoul, Armoire D569 f. 198-9. Quoted *JD* LXVI.

22. The epigraph, from Vol. 4 of Dante's *Opera,* reads in E. J. Delecluze's 1847 translation: "La fin de mon Amour a été la salutation de cette Dame [de qui vous voulez peut-être parler] et dans la salutation de laquelle était ma béatitude, but de tous mes honnêtes désirs." Quoted *JD* 178. Characteristically, where Dante idealises, Sainte-Beuve socialises.

23. The two other sonnets are no. XI "Un grand chemin ouvert, une banale route . . ." *PC* II: 47 and no. XXIV "Sonnet à Madame L . . ." *PC* II: 74.

24. The two poems are no. XVI "A V. H . . ." ("Ami, d'où viens-tu, tremblant, pale, effaré") *PC* II: 54-5 and no. XXIII, "Sonnet à V. H . . ." ("Votre génie est grand, Ami, votre penser") *PC* II: 73. Chateaubriand's letter to Sainte-Beuve of 30 March 1830, thanking him for sending *Les Consolations,* includes the encouragement: "Écoutez votre génie, monsieur; chargez votre muse d'en redire les inspirations et pour atteindre la renommée, vous n'aurez besoin d'être porté dans le *casque* de personne." Sainte-Beuve glosses: "Cette lettre, dans son compliment, renfermait le conseil indirect de m'émanciper un peu de Victor Hugo et faisait allusion à un sonnet où j'avais dit, parlant au puissant poète: 'Comme un guerrier de fer, un vaillant homme d'armes / S'il rencontre, gisant, un nourrisson en larmes / Il le met dans son casque et le porte en chemin . . .'" *Portraits contemporains* I, p. 76.

25. "Lamartine 1836 *Jocelyn*", *Portraits contemporains* I, p. 318.

26. These are the "Trois sonnets imités de Wordsworth" which are also included in *Pensées d'août*: "Reposez-vous et remerciez", "La Cabane du highlander" and "Le Château de Bothwell" (*PC* II: 196-8).

27. Sainte-Beuve's limited knowledge of English is effectively demonstrated in a series of articles by E. M. Phillips: "Sainte-Beuve and the Lake Poets", in *French Quarterly* VIII (1926), 215-222; "Sainte-Beuve's criticism of English poetry", in *French Quarterly* IX (1927) 200-209; "Sainte-Beuve et les poètes romantiques anglais", in *Revue anglo-américaine* XII (1935), 493-507. Sainte-Beuve himself admitted his limitations in this area on at least one occasion: "Moi-même [. . .] tout en professant et même en affichant l'imitation des poètes anglais et lakistes, je vous étonnerais si je vous di-

sais combien je les ai devinés comme parents et frères aînés bien plutôt que je ne les ai connus d'abord et étudiés de près. C'était pour moi comme une conversation que j'aurais suivie en me promenant dans un jardin de l'autre côté de la haie ou de la charmille; il ne m'en arrivait que quelques mots qui me suffisaient et qui dans leur incomplet prêtaient d'autant mieux au rêve" (*Nouveaux Lundis* IV, p. 455). He knew of the work of the Lakists through the *Voyage historique et littéraire en Angleterre et en Ecosse* of Amédée Pichot, which he reviewed in *Le Globe* of 17 December 1825. He possessed at his death the 1828 Paris (Galignani) edition, containing all Wordsworth's poems to that date, as well as a life and appreciation of Wordsworth, the "Preface" to the *Lyrical Ballads,* and also the "Preface" to *The Excursion.* However, according to E. M. Phillips (*Revue anglo-americaine* XII [1935], p. 507), the volume does not appear to have been much consulted and, possibly significantly, the sonnets imitated in *Joseph Delorme* and *Les Consolations* all appear on pages 117-20. Similarly the Yarrow imitations are numbers XIII, XIV and XVIII in Wordsworth's sequence.

28. "[. . .] quand Lamartine, exprimant ce qu'il y a de plus rêveur et de plus inexprimable en l'âme humaine, se serait souvent passé avec bonheur d'une forme précise et sévère, en pourrait-on sérieusement conclure qu'il est, à plus forte raison, inutile de s'y asservir dans l'expression de sentiments moins fugitifs, dans la peinture d'un monde moins métaphysique et d'une vie plus réelle? [. . .] Conclusion étrange, en vérité! Disons tout le contraire: c'est précisément à mesure que la poésie se rapproche davantage de la vie réelle et des choses d'ici-bas, qu'elle doit se surveiller avec plus de rigueur, se souvenir plus fermement de ses religieux préceptes, et, tout en abordant le vrai sans scrupule ni fausse honte, se poser à elle-même, aux limites de l'art, une sauvegarde incorruptible contre le prosaïque et le trivial" ("Pensée VII", *JD* 142-3). Or again, *Pensées d'août* (*PC* II: 233): "Plus simple est le vers et côtoyant la prose, / Plus pauvre de belle ombre et d'haleine de rose, / Et plus la forme étroite a lieu de le garder."

29. *Portraits de femmes* (Paris, 1886), p. 312. Sainte-Beuve noted in 1869 that this article on La Rochefoucauld indicated "une date et un *temps,* un retour décisif dans ma vie intellectuelle" (note to p. 321).

30. See pp. 18-19, the comment on Vauquelin de la Fresnaye, *THC* 115-16.

31. In the 1863 *Poésies complètes* there are just three sonnets with an irregular pattern in the quatrains:

"Sonnet à Théophile Gautier", *Suite de Joseph Delorme* (*PC* I: 198-9); "Avignon m'apparaît dans sa charmante enceinte", *Notes et sonnets* (*PC* II: 313-14); "Sonnet à Mlle. Eliza-Wilhelmine", *Un Dernier Rêve* (*PC* II: 341).

32. The one exception is "A Franckfort-sur-le Mein", *Les Consolations* (*PC* II: 72).

33. In the 1863 *Poésies complètes* there are only nine examples of overrun between the quatrains, while overrun between the tercets, a more common occurrence generally, takes place on only seven occasions.

34. Just two sonnets depart from this norm: "Sonnet de Sainte Thérèse à Jésus crucifié" (alternate decasyllables and alexandrines in the quatrains, alexandrines throughout the tercets), *Pensées d'août* (*PC* II: 191-2) and the decasyllabic "Réponse à mon ami F. -Z.", *Notes et sonnets* (*PC* II: 300). The theme of the latter is the deliberate manipulation of rhythm against traditional expectation to achieve an individual modern note.

35. There are two sonnet pairs in *Joseph Delorme* (*JD* 34-5 and 59-60); two pairs in *Pensées d'août* (*PC* II: 181-2 and 244-5); one pair and two trios (one with an additional quatrain repeated at the beginning and the end) in *Notes et sonnets* (*PC* II: 287-9, 294-6, 325-7); one pair in *Un Dernier Rêve* (*PC* II: 340-1).

Sheila K. Espineli (essay date January 2002)

SOURCE: Espineli, Sheila K. "Sainte-Beuve and Wordsworth in Defense of the Sonnet." *European Romantic Review* 13, no. 4 (January 2002): 445-48.

[*In the following essay, Espineli analyzes the differences between Sainte-Beuve's translations of Wordsworth's sonnets and the English originals, and emphasizes Sainte-Beuve's influence on the popularity of the sonnet in subsequent French poetry.*]

> Moi, je veux rajeunir le doux sonnet en France;
> Du Bellay, le premier, l'apporta de Florence,
> Et l'on en sait plus d'un de notre vieux Ronsard.
>
> (Sainte-Beuve 171)[1]

Toward the end of one of his first sonnets, Charles Augustin Sainte-Beuve (1804-1869), best known as one of the first modern literary critics in France, empathetically engages himself in the daunting task of reviving the sonnet, which for almost 150 years virtually had disappeared from French literature. Sainte-Beuve accomplished this remarkable feat largely through his French "imitations" of Wordsworth's sonnets. The epigraph above is from Sainte-Beuve's version of Wordsworth's "Scorn Not the Sonnet," from his first book,

Vie, Poésies, Pensées de Joseph Delorme (**The Life, Poetry, and Thoughts of Joseph Delorme**) (1829), which contains thirteen sonnets. Sainte-Beuve here begins his engagement with Wordsworth's sonnets, marking the return of the form into general use. Sainte-Beuve acknowledges Wordsworth with the subtitle: "Imité de Wordsworth," making it the first of the Wordsworth sonnets to appear in Sainte-Beuve's poetry collections. Why was this English sonnet and this particular English poet the stimulus for Sainte-Beuve's invective to bring the sonnet back to common use? Although his interest in the sonnet form began with his reading of Ronsard's sonnets, Wordsworth's sonnets encouraged and sustained his interest. He found something new and intriguing in Wordsworth because he continued to come back to him, writing several sonnets with the same subtitle, "Imité de Wordsworth," and including them throughout his collections.

Sainte-Beuve's translations of Wordsworth's poems take several departures from the original. Sainte-Beuve adapts the original to the differences of versification between the English sonnet and French sonnet: not only are the line lengths different (hexameters replace pentameters), but also the rhyme scheme is different. Sainte-Beuve's sonnets, however, cannot be categorized solely as translations. He adds other allusions and metaphors, changes passive voice sentences into active ones, and expounds on the concrete detail of some element of a poem that Wordsworth might only have hinted at or suggested originally. Sainte-Beuve's sonnets are imitations of Wordsworth's sonnets, then, only in the sense that they are variations on a theme, rather than being a mimicry or a pastiche of the poet's style.

Like Wordsworth, Sainte-Beuve wanted to continue the poetic legacy that the Renaissance writers had left; he addresses the contemporary negative attitude toward the sonnet form and defends it, asking the reader to consider its history and significance within poetic tradition. In the original, Wordsworth laments the sonnet's present disrepute by recounting its past and wants to enumerate its "just honours" by describing the different ways that the great writers of the past employed the sonnet form. Wordsworth uses seven metaphors for the sonnet: "This key," "the melody," "this pipe," "a gay myrtle leaf," a "glow-worm lamp," and the "Thing" are all metaphors for the sonnet that refer to each poet—Shakespeare, Petrarch, Tasso, Camöens, Dante, Spenser, and Milton respectively. Sainte-Beuve, however, de-emphasizes the metaphorical tradition and transforms this sonnet into a personal statement of purpose:

> Ne ris point des sonnets, ô Critique moqueur!
> Par amour autrefois en fit le grand Shakespeare:
> C'est sur ce luth heureux que Pétrarque soupire,
> Et que le Tasse aux fers soulage un peu son cœur;

> Camoens de son exil abrège la longueur,
> Car il chante en sonnets l'amour et son empire;
> Dante aime cette fleur de myrte, et la respire,
> Et la mêle au cyprès qui ceint son front vainqueur;

> Spencer [sic], s'en revenant de l'île des féeries,
> Exhale en longs sonnets ses tristesses chéries;
> Milton, chantant les siens, ranimait son regard;

> Moi, je veux rajeunir le doux sonnet en France;
> Du Bellay, le premier, l'apporta de Florence,
> Et l'on en sait plus d'un de notre vieux Ronsard.

> (I: 171)[2]

Sainte-Beuve does not employ as many metaphors for the sonnet as Wordsworth does; he retains the metaphors for Petrarch and Dante (the "luth heureux" and the "fleur de myrte," respectively) but otherwise refers to the sonnet directly and alludes to the different subjects of each poet. He also chooses to describe Tasso and Camoens in different terms: he chooses to refer to the moments in these poets' respective lives when they were denied freedom: he describes Tasso in chains and Camoens in exile for a long period of time. While Wordsworth also refers to Camoens' exile, he does so only in one line; Sainte-Beuve uses two lines and emphasizes that Camoens wrote both of love and of empire. Instead of Wordsworth's "glow-worm lamp," Sainte-Beuve reduces his mention of Milton to one line in line eleven, by acknowledging that Milton helped to keep the sonnet tradition strong in England. These variants might only be the result of translating the lines, but it can also signify that Sainte-Beuve chooses to emphasizes the diversity of Camoens' sonnet subjects, but still includes Milton as a significant element in the history of the sonnet. The shift in emphasis from the English tradition to the continental one, moreover, certainly is worth noting.

For the most part, Sainte-Beuve uses the sonnet in the plural to describe it in general (in French, a word can often be made plural to refer to it in a general sense) or as pronouns (*i.e.,* in line 11, Milton sings "les siens," his own sonnets). Rather than addressing the various subjects that Wordsworth mentions in his sonnet, Sainte-Beuve chooses to downplay the pronouns, to shift the emphasis from Wordsworth's nostalgia for earlier sonnets to Sainte-Beuve's personal desire to enter into the sonnet tradition and continue it forward. This change makes sense because, in England, the sonnet revival begun by Charlotte Smith and continued by scores of her imitators had become, to Wordsworth and to many literary critics, cloying—Wordsworth thus must remind the critic of the sonnet's past glory—whereas, in France, it had virtually disappeared.

The familiar tone of Sainte-Beuve's imitation is significant because it gives the sonnet more personal weight, setting it apart from Wordsworth. Sainte-Beuve addresses the "critique moqueur" with a familiar command. He writes in the familiar "tu" form, **"Ne ris point**

des sonnets," instead of the "vous" formal, "Ne riez point des sonnets." Having read Wordsworth's preface to *Lyrical Ballads* and agreeing with many of his new theories on poetry, it is possible that Sainte-Beuve also wanted to avoid artificial formality in poetry, to use more of the familiar address and to use simpler language and subjects. The use of the first person in the twelfth line with the "je," the "I" reinforces the familiar tone of this poem. The "moi," is merely a stress pronoun to emphasize the "je," and is only translatable in English by adding stress to the word "I." While Wordsworth's sonnet avoids familiar language, only using the second person voice in the first line, Sainte-Beuve reinterprets Wordsworth's sonnet as an emphatic personal challenge to the reader and the poet, himself. However, the distinction between the familiar and the formal is something that is particular to the French language and other Romance languages and was simply not an option for Wordsworth to employ. What makes Sainte-Beuve's use of the familiar most striking is that he does so within the formal structure of the sonnet. This helps to emphasize that Sainte-Beuve wants to re-familiarize the public with the sonnet and to bridge the gap of years in which it fell into disuse, in contrast to Wordsworth who implicitly tries to make the critic forget the abuses of his contemporaries.

In his book, *Sonnet Theory and Practice in Nineteenth-century France: Sonnets on the Sonnet,* David H. T. Scott cites **"Ne ris point des sonnets"** as the nineteenth century's first sonnet on the sonnet in France:

> Sainte-Beuve's initial attitude to the sonnet therefore is a guarded one: he does not announce the revival of the sonnet as a panacea for the poet but reintroduces it almost apologetically. . . . This sonnet on the sonnet, the century's first, is not so much about the sonnet as a form as about its great and historic exponents and the kind of *subjects* they tended to develop within the sonnet framework.
>
> (17)

Scott chooses to interpret **"Ne ris point des sonnets"** as a reactionary poem, rather than as a poem that not only acknowledges the past, but anticipates the future in the last tercet. It is possible that Scott interprets the sonnet as such because the personal statement only comes at the end, and because Sainte-Beuve makes his statement but immediately follows it with mentions of Du Bellay and Ronsard to justify his interest in the sonnet. Scott, however, is interpreting Wordsworth's sonnet more than he is Sainte-Beuve's imitation; and he does not acknowledge the difference in tone between the original and the imitation.

Thanks to Sainte-Beuve, the sonnet form became reborn in France as an experimental tool in which plays on language and the structure of the sonnet itself endured well into the twentieth century with poets such as Paul Valéry. Sainte-Beuve latched onto Wordsworth's sonnets more than onto his other poems, finding a connection to Wordsworth in the sonnet—a form that no other English Romantic poet used as frequently as Wordsworth. Sainte-Beuve clearly wanted to appropriate Wordsworth's model and then create his own poetry. Through his imitations of Wordsworth, he was encouraged to help revive the sonnet form in France by evoking its distinguished heritage and the advantages of bringing the form back into common use. Stemming from a common ancestor in Petrarch, the sonnet in English and French, as a result, is essentially the most successful poetic form to return to the continent from across the Channel.

Notes

1. I want to rejuvenate the sweet sonnet in France; Du Bellay, the first, brought it from Florence, Several of which our old Ronsard knows. (All of the following translations from the French are mine.)

2. Never laugh at sonnets, oh mocking Critic! Through love in the past the great Shakespeare wrote them. It is on this happy lute where Petrarch sighed, And where Tasso in chains consoled a little his heart; Camoens shortened the length of his exile, For he sings in sonnets about love and his empire; Dante loves this myrtle flower, and breathes it in (the scent), And the tangle of cypress that wreathes his victorious brow; Spenser, remembering the island of faeries; Expresses in long sonnets his cherished sorrows; Milton, singing his own, revives his [the sonnet's] appearance; *I* want to rejuvenate the sweet sonnet in France; Du Bellay, the first, brought it from Florence, Several of which our old Ronsard knows.

Works Cited

Sainte-Beuve and Charles-Augustin. *Poésies Complètes.* 2 vols. Paris: Librairie Alphonse Lemerre, 1879.

Scott, David H. T. *Sonnet Theory and Practice in Nineteenth-century France: Sonnets On the Sonnet.* London: University of Hull Publications, 1977.

Wordsworth, William. *Poetical Works.* Ed. Thomas Hutchinson, revised by Ernest De Selincourt. New York: Oxford University Press, 1990.

FURTHER READING

Criticism

Bishop, G. R. "The Identity of 'E. T. de la R.' in the Poetry of Sainte-Beuve." *Modern Language Review* 47, no. 3 (July 1952): 378-79.

> Presents the theory that Sainte-Beuve's dedication of the poem "Bonheur champêtre" to E. T. was

meant to express his gratitude to Amédée Pichot, whose *Voyage historique e littéraire en Angleterre et en Ecosse* provided Sainte-Beuve's introduction to several English poets.

Pitwood, Michael. "Sainte-Beuve and Dante." *Modern Language Review* 77, no. 3 (July 1982): 568-76.

Uses the many allusions and references to the poetry of Dante in the work of Sainte-Beuve to argue that the poet possessed a familiarity with Dante's work far beyond that of his French contemporaries.

Switzer, Richard. "French Renaissance Poetry before Sainte-Beuve." *French Review* 26, no. 4 (February 1953): 278-84.

Disputes the notion that Renaissance poetry was virtually forgotten or ignored until Sainte-Beuve revived interest in it with his *Tableau historique et critique de la poésie française et du theater française du XVI ᵉ siècle.*

Additional coverage of Sainte-Beuve's life and career is contained in the following sources published by Gale: *Dictionary of Literary Biography,* **Vol. 217;** *European Writers,* **Vol. 6;** *Guide to French Literature: 1789 to the Present*; *Literature Resource Center*; **and** *Nineteenth-Century Literature Criticism,* **Vol. 5.**

Wallace Stevens
1879-1955

American poet, essayist, and playwright.

For additional information on Stevens's life and career, see *PC,* Volume 6.

INTRODUCTION

An important figure of American Modernism, Stevens was known as a master stylist, lauded for his rigorous attention to detail and his extensive poetic vocabulary. He incorporated such European influences as Imagism, Symbolism, and Romanticism into his uniquely American poetry. Stevens has alternately been considered a poet with an interest in philosophy or a philosopher who happened to write poetry, all the while pursuing a full-time career as an insurance lawyer.

BIOGRAPHICAL INFORMATION

The second of five children, Stevens was born in Reading, Pennsylvania, on October 2, 1879, to Margaretha Catharine Zetter Stevens, a former teacher, and Garrett Barcalow Stevens, a prominent lawyer. He and his two brothers attended an Evangelical Lutheran elementary school; in 1891, Stevens, not yet thirteen years old, entered Reading Boys' High School, studying English, Greek and Latin, as well as history, science, and math. He excelled at writing and oratory, and in September, 1897, he enrolled at Harvard University as a special non-degree student. He was a regular contributor to the Harvard *Advocate* and received a number of writing awards. In 1899, he switched allegiances and became affiliated with the *Advocate*'s rival publication, the *Harvard Monthly,* eventually serving as its editor. Stevens left Cambridge in 1900 for financial reasons and moved to New York City where he worked as a journalist for the *New York Evening Post.* He later attended New York University Law School, graduating in 1903. A year later he met Elsie Kachel and five years later they were married, against the wishes of Stevens's parents, who were thereafter estranged from their son. Stevens and his wife had a daughter, Holly, in 1924. Initially employed by a number of different law firms in New York from 1904 to 1907, Stevens took a position as an insurance lawyer, first in New York, then in Hartford, Connecticut, where he lived for the remainder of his life, working for the Hartford Accident and Indemnity Company. In 1934, he became vice president of the company.

During the 1920s and 30s, Stevens regularly visited the southern United States on business, and was especially attracted to Key West, Florida, a locale that influenced many of his poems, particularly those of his early collections. He continued to work as a full-time insurance lawyer and part-time poet, writing and publishing poetry throughout his lifetime. Stevens died of stomach cancer on August 2, 1955; he is buried in Hartford.

Stevens won numerous awards for his poetry, including the Levinson Prize from *Poetry* magazine (1920); the poetry prize from the *Nation* (1936); the Harriet Monroe Poetry Award (1946); the Bollingen Prize in Poetry (1950); a gold medal from the Poetry Society of America (1951); the National Book Award for *The Auroras of Autumn* (1950); and both the National Book Award and the Pulitzer Prize for *The Collected Poems of Wallace Stevens* (1954). He received honorary degrees from Hartt College of Music (1955); Bard College (1951); Harvard University (1951); Mount Holyoke College (1952); Columbia University (1952); and Yale University (1955).

MAJOR WORKS

The bulk of Stevens's poetry was written during the 1930s and 40s when he was middle-aged. His first collection, *Harmonium,* appeared in 1923, and contains the frequently anthologized individual poems "Le Monocle de Mon Oncle," "Thirteen Ways of Looking at a Blackbird," and "Sunday Morning." He did not produce a second volume of verse until 1935 with the publication of *Ideas of Order,* which includes poetry inspired by his visits to Key West and the well-known "A Postcard from the Volcano." A year later, Stevens issued *Owl's Clover,* featuring poetry far more unstructured than the pieces in his first two volumes; Stevens himself was said to have been unhappy with the book. In 1937, he returned to the structure and unity of his early work with the publication of *The Man with the Blue Guitar, and Other Poems.* The volume is usually considered a turning point in Stevens's poetic career. Other important volumes include *Notes toward a Supreme Fiction* (1942), an exploration into the nature of poetry, first published separately and then as part of *Transport to Summer* (1947). The 1945 single-poem publication *Esthétique du Mal* was also included in the

1947 volume. Steven's final collection of new poems, the prize-winning *Auroras of Autumn,* appeared in 1950 and features the poem "An Ordinary Evening in New Haven."

CRITICAL RECEPTION

While Stevens was at one time considered an apolitical poet, that assessment has largely been reversed in recent years. Mark Schoening explores Stevens's theories on the connection between poetry and politics, and believes that "Stevens implies that poetic practice has come to share with political practice a devotion to resolving 'the conflict between man and organized society,' which threatens in the twentieth century to divide human experience and the world in which it occurs." Justin Quinn refutes the critical belief that Stevens concentrates on natural and pastoral settings in order to avoid contemporary political issues. On the contrary, according to Quinn, "Stevens uses landscape and natural objects in general as the occasions for thinking about politics and ideology," a fact that has gone unrecognized by earlier generations of scholars. Quinn contends that "in Stevens's poetry the pastoral setting is the space in which he meditates most intensely on the way that human societies produce cultural and political meaning, and not a respite from those pressures." Douglas Mao acknowledges the recent change in critical thought about Stevens's involvement in political issues, noting the "recent demonstrations that his insulation from the catastrophes of modernity has been greatly exaggerated." Nonetheless, Mao contends that Stevens is "still a poet who seems intriguingly ill at ease with the transmuting of historical upheaval into poetry, and by the same token one who asks hauntingly what can be made of a life not given substantial color by large events."

Stevens's position regarding gender politics has also been explored recently. Ann Mikkelsen has analyzed his concept of American masculinity and the way he "imagined himself as a male poet and representative lyric voice in early twentieth-century America." Mikkelsen contends that "the specific nature of the masculine ideal has gone unquestioned in Stevens criticism," yet believes that his thoughts on this "must be understood as the product of an American society in which masculinity was an extremely fraught and contested cultural site." Jacqueline Vaught Brogan explores the issue of sexism as it relates to Stevens's poetry, and finds that in his poetry Stevens suppressed what he considered his feminine side. She concludes, however, that "while Stevens would always suffer from a schism within himself, one that was ultimately derived from cultural biases against women, . . . he would also come as close as it was possible for a person in his

time and circumstance to 'curing' himself of the 'infection in the sentence' the dominant, phallocentric structures in our culture inevitably breed."

Stevens also sought to overcome other dominant cultural constraints, including those involving organized religion. According to David Young, the poem "Sunday Morning" represented the poet's attempt to break free from puritanical Protestantism, a break he considered essential for the creation of a "vigorous and original artistic culture," specific to America. Young contends that Stevens's poem, along with similar works by Rilke and Yeats, arrives "at a new definition of the human condition, one that tries to reconcile us with a world of change and flux, arguing for an interaction between humanity and nature that traditional beliefs and practices had managed to obscure." Beverly Maeder (see Further Reading) has studied Stevens's complicated relationship and resistance to "metaphors of transcendental authority," noting that the poem "Delightful Evening" "affirms the centrality of the trope of metaphor in maintaining a life-sustaining concept of a larger order of things, while at the same time it claims that concept to be bankrupt." Maeder concludes that the poet was "implicitly working less against the idea of divinity and its immanence in nature per se than against the hierarchical patterning the idea imposes on human imaginative and linguistic development." Joel Nickels (see Further Reading) also notes Stevens's resistance to "an accretion of dead metaphors and perceptual modes inadequate to the necessities of the present." Nickels believes that Stevens's poem *Owl's Clover* served as a test site for Stevens to try out a wide variety of epistemological positions, some of which would be reformulated for later use. As Nickels puts it, the poem "serves as a vast, originary and somewhat sloppy playbook of all the epistemological attitudes that Stevens will elaborate more carefully in his more canonical work."

PRINCIPAL WORKS

Poetry

Harmonium 1923
Ideas of Order 1935
Owl's Clover 1936
The Man with the Blue Guitar, and Other Poems 1937
Notes toward a Supreme Fiction 1942
Parts of a World 1942
Esthétique du Mal 1945
Transport to Summer 1947
The Auroras of Autumn 1950
The Collected Poems of Wallace Stevens 1954

Opus Posthumous (poetry, dramas, and essays) 1957
The Palm at the End of the Mind (poetry and drama)
1971

Other Major Works

*The Necessary Angel: Essays on Reality and the Imagi-
nation* (essays) 1951
Letters (letters) 1966

CRITICISM

Alan Filreis (essay date 1991)

SOURCE: Filreis, Alan. "Cuba Should Be Full of Cuban
Things." In *Wallace Stevens and the Actual World*, pp.
187-206. Princeton, N.J.: Princeton University Press,
1991.

[*In the following essay, Filreis discusses such issues as
cultural imperialism and the relationship between art
and ideology in the context of Stevens's correspondence
with the Cuban writer Rodríguez Feo.*]

> The fact that [Hemingway] has had such a success
> makes me fear for that hierarchy of values which must
> reign in a nation if its culture is not going to fall into
> the most slappiest of arrangements.
>
> —*José Rodríguez Feo from Havana to Stevens in
> Hartford, February 13, 1945 (SM [Secretaries of The
> Moon: The Letters of Wallace Stevens and José
> Rodríguez Feo] 41)*

> He was provoking me, saying and always insisting
> about me being this Cuban who was too Americanized.
> And I can remember too that we had a political discus-
> sion that day, because when he said this I said, "Well,
> don't forget that we are an American colony." I said,
> "Don't forget that you Americans still regard us as a
> colony. You still have th[e] idea that we Latins are
> inferior." He said, "No, no. How can you say that,
> José? Do you think that I consider you an inferior
> person to me?" I said, "Maybe you don't consider me
> an inferior person because you're a poet. I'm a literary
> critic, so on an intellectual basis that is sort of above
> this idea. But I sometimes wonder, when you're so nice
> to me—you write me here and you write me there—if
> you're not a little patronizing." Then he became very
> sad, [saying,] "Oh, you don't really think that." And I
> said, "Well, I don't know. The Americans are a very
> strange people."
>
> —*José Rodríguez Feo in 1978, in an unpublished
> portion of an interview with Peter Brazeau*

The young Cuban committed his mother to the asylum
several times. At her sanest she deemed herself to be all
intuition. She had not read a book since leaving school,

a nunnery in Pou. Once, when she convinced herself of
the wonderful, preposterous idea that her son's famous
correspondent, Wallace Stevens, raised chickens in his
yard in Connecticut, her son did not try to dissuade her.
One afternoon he brought to the house two friends who
were members of the Cuban Communist party, and the
talk came around to the inevitable subject of Stalin. The
mother, overhearing this, asked if he had finally married
Chencha, the mulatto girl who lived in the neighbor-
hood. While his radical friends gave his mother dirty
looks, José Rodríguez Feo found himself momentarily
taken in by the notion that Stalin was to marry a poor
Cuban girl, until he realized that his mother had thought
he had said "Balin," the name given a young man "who
had been running after Chencha for a long time." Rodríguez Feo discovered his mother's error too late. By
then his radical friends had left the house in disgust. "I
had to give mother a lesson in modern history to avoid
further complications," he wrote. The next day he
decided to locate a single reference to Stalin in an
American newspaper to prove to her that such a man
really existed, and indeed found the Soviet leader
"mentioned rather ungraciously." But his mother, faced
with the evidence in black and white, merely asked her
son why the Americans "called him certain names," and
Rodríguez Feo "had to give up" attempting a serious
explanation. He concluded for Stevens that his mother
knew a great deal about "cows, horses and chickens."
But if one "mention[ed] strange, exotic names in front
of her," he continued, "one never knows where they are
going to pop up again" (*SM* 129-30).

For the charming Cubans who peopled Rodríguez Feo's
letters, "Stalin" was an exotic name. But for Stevens by
this time Stalin was merely the dull daily fare. The
exotic inhered, rather, in the appellations José and his
mother invented for the family colt ("Platon") and the
family cow ("Lucera"). A colt named after Plato! It is
not in the mother's ramblings, however, but rather in
Stevens's poems, at least four of them written directly
in response to Rodríguez Feo's letters, where incidentally mentioned exotic things are more likely to "pop
up again." To Stevens, Balin's possible relation to Stalin was as telling, as delightfully ironic, as the mother's
fool-wise refusal to sanction the taking of sides in political controversies raging everywhere else but in her apparently happy Cuba, even as such partisanship was
beginning to be important to many Cubans of Rodríguez
Feo's generation who would live to see a wholly new
day. Although Rodríguez Feo was genuinely distressed
that his mother's miscues jeopardized his friendships
with young communists and if, in spite of his attempts
to explain to her why Americans were unlikely to refer
to Stalin without calling him "certain names," he really
did hope such scenes would not be repeated, to Stevens,
on the other hand, the political causes or interpretations
of these domestic scenes were not what mattered. Quite
to the contrary, he wanted from these Cuban letters

more of Balin and less of Stalin. In response to this particular charming anecdote, Stevens endorsed the mother's local coloring, admired her unwillingness to comprehend let alone take sides, and thus resisted his young correspondent's anxiety about political correctness. "How much more this mother knows than her son who reads Milosz and Svevo," Stevens wrote Barbara Church, immediately after receiving the letter containing the account of the Stalin-Balin incident. "She is controlled by the force that attaches; he by the force that detaches"—the "force that attaches" being a charitable force. "[A]nd both are puppets on the strings of their relationship to reality. She shrinks from leaving home; he from remaining there" (*L* [*Letters of Wallace Stevens*] 602).

Stevens added, however, as usual, a note of qualification: "The *Stevenses* shrink from everything." Still, he did feel the urge to instruct his Cuban correspondent in the rules of living in an exotic place. Such instruction, often kindly and qualified but sometimes harsh, recurs throughout their ten-year exchange of letters. Stevens's concept of a natural Cuba (at those very times when Rodríguez Feo's letters incited Stevens's poems) kept it from being much more than an ample place of sapodillas, cigars, and sweet drinks. In his harshest criticism Stevens refigured himself as the strong force that attaches, the puppeteer, in his metaphor, controlling the strings of his Cuban's relationship to reality. "Your job is to help to create the spirit of Cuba," he once insisted.

> Every one of your friends who writes a poem, whether or not it is about Cuba which nevertheless is a thing of the place, and every one of your friends who does a painting which in a perfectly natural way is a particular thing as a sapodilla is, or a good fat cigar or a glass of piña fria is, is doing just what you ought to be doing somehow or other.
>
> (*SM* 166-67)

When writing here of Rodríguez Feo's poet and painter "friends," Stevens was referring knowingly to the group associated with *Orígenes: Revista de arte y literatura*, the magazine Rodríguez Feo founded and initially funded after returning to Havana from Harvard in 1943. The life of *Orígenes* and Rodríguez Feo's correspondence with Stevens span exactly the same eventful decade, 1944 to 1954, and their stories are closely connected. Not long after Rodríguez Feo wrote Stevens for the first time (*SM* 33-34), asking for permission to translate **"Esthétique du Mal,"** *Orígenes* contained first appearances of four of Stevens's new poems, in Spanish translations by the *origenista* Oscar Rodríguez Feliú.[1] In total, Rodríguez Feo and his colleagues put out thirty-six handsome outsized numbers of *Orígenes* in Stevens's last decade. More than perhaps any literary journal of its day, *Orígenes* was the organ of a group. The "Orígenes Group" consisted of Rodríguez Feo, the

poets Eliseo Diego, Cintio Vitier, José Lezama Lima, Angel Gaztelu (a priest), Fiña García Marruz, and Lorenzo García Vega, and the painter Mariano Rodríguez. Rodríguez Feo was a competent and energetic editor, with astonishingly extensive contacts. He solicited contributions from F. O. Matthiessen and Harry Levin (both of whom he had known at Harvard), T. S. Eliot, Stephen Spender, and Allen Tate (he met all three), Katherine Anne Porter, Elizabeth Bishop, Alfonso Reyes, W. H. Auden, Albert Camus, Thomas Merton, and Anaïs Nin, and Stevens's friends Walter Pach and James Johnson Sweeney. Rodríguez Feo himself contributed essays on Santayana, Gide, and Melville; a baroque short story called "The Closed Door"; and translations of poetry by Stevens, Williams, Aragon, Spender, and Eliot ("East Coker" and "Burnt Norton," both with Eliot's urging). He also translated James on Balzac, Camus on Nietzsche, Levin on Joyce, Auden on Lawrence, Theodore Spencer on Stephen Hero, Matthiessen on Eliot, and Santayana on himself.

In a statement of purpose introducing the first number of *Orígenes*, the editors explained the name of the journal by defining their goal of soliciting and publishing work that reveals the artist in the act of formulating his ideas, "those moments of creation in which the seed becomes a being and the unknown becomes possessed insofar as is possible and does not engender an unfortunate arrogance."[2] In this sense the *Orígenes* Group *did* dismiss pure poetry right from the start, though they would still soon be accused of loving it. They would also be accused—in a judgment surely made severer by time, given changes in the literary-political climate in Cuba since then—of offering the critical and creative writings printed in *Orígenes* as "universalizations," descriptions without place.[3] "For the first time among us," José Lezama Lima claimed in a retrospective of *Orígenes* in 1952, "the modern is not a provincial nostalgia."[4] Among the *origenistas* Rodríguez Feo was valued for his efforts to bridge the wide waters between national cultures. Lezama Lima singled out for praise Rodríguez Feo's having inspired a poem by the revered Wallace Stevens, **"A Word with José Rodríguez-Feo"** (1945), in which fine details, "the unthought-of groupings," "the far-off poetic imagination," are also "unmistakable signs of *universalization*" (emphasis added),[5] fully in spite of Stevens's deeply seated Americanness and the poem's gross assumptions about Cuba. For his part, Stevens deemed the *origenistas*' notion of universalization naive, and continued to be frustrated in his effort to find something intrinsically Cuban arising from the *Orígenes* project, exactly as he was thwarted when Rodríguez Feo's letters were not full of cows, chickens, and colts, fruit and cigars, resorts and white beaches—descriptions thick with place.

The *origenistas* soon formed their own publishing house, Ediciones Orígenes, and of the seventeen books of poetry they published between 1945 and 1954, no fewer than twelve were by members of the inner circle. The most important of these publications was Cintio Vitier's *Ten Cuban Poets, 1937-1947* (1948), which for the first time clearly identified the group's purposes, not by proclamation but by poetry: an antiregional, international modern art. Because Stevens wanted local color from Rodríguez Feo, he was able to see a contradiction in the *Orígenes* project, and almost immediately he articulated the criticism he would eventually assign to Rodríguez Feo personally. On one hand the group promoted its universalism, and on the other it was utterly sequestered, devoted to self-enclosure. Rodríguez Feo's talented young friends wrote and painted as if untroubled by the very set of conditions that should trouble universalists most, an attitude only reinforced by the fact that they referred to each other and their magazine so often as to be subject still more specifically to the charge of hermeticism. And hermeticism was the very thing they had formed the journal to avoid. The fresh, young Mariano Rodríguez painted oils *about* his friends and his aesthetic, such as one he entitled *Reading Orígenes* and allowed to be reproduced in the magazine.[6] But even this unapologetically programmatic work led Lezama Lima to the naive conclusion that the group was never derivative and never "surrendered to flattery," that Mariano wished only, in Picasso's words, "[t]o express what was within ourselves."[7]

Rodríguez Feo made a similarly innocent claim in writing to Stevens, in part, surely, to test the warmth of the waters between Havana and Hartford. He knew Stevens shared his anxieties about the cultural uses of art, and so he attempted to convince his American friend that the *Orígenes* poets were writing for others and not for themselves—for the postwar literary world and not for Cuba. Nationalism and not aestheticism, he implied often in the first years of the correspondence, was the root of decadence in modern art. Later, when *Ten Cuban Poets* was coming off the press, and obviously with his group's program in mind, he wrote Stevens: "I saw the Mexican show here. I finally came to the conclusion . . . that Rivera, Orozco and Siqueiros are all terribly overrated and are really now embarked upon an academic stage which reveals their decadence. The Cubans are less pretentious, more charming and some have produced works which surpassed the bloody, screaming, *cultural and nationalistic propaganda* of the *mejicanos*" (*SM* 123; emphasis added).

After Rodríguez Feo made him a gift of two Mariano watercolors, both depicting Cuban scenes,[8] Stevens understandably began searching his copies of *Orígenes* for more about this young painter. He not only found Mariano and the others mentioned there, but he also found a myriad of cross-references: *Orígenes* printed Angel Gaztelu's poem to Mariano; Rodríguez Feo and Lezama Lima both wrote essays about Mariano's painting; Lezama Lima's poem "Ronda sin Fanal—Para Mariano" describes one of Mariano's oils in heavily symbolic but still obviously homosexual language.[9] There were also Eliseo Diego's poems dedicated to Lezama Lima, Lezama Lima's to García Vega, García Vega's to Lezama Lima, and Lezama Lima's to Diego. The Winter 1949 number would devote almost all of its pages to poems by *origenistas* about each other or about the magazine itself. Could the *origenistas* long maintain their universalism and yet be so utterly self-involved? At first Stevens was mildly amused to discover how seemingly detached from Cuba these Cubans were. For Church, who knew a good deal about an ambiguous sense of place and had edited the journal of his own coterie, Stevens described how Rodríguez Feo detested "the taste" of his countrymen even though "it is Cuba that has been his own matrix" (*L* 508). When Rodríguez Feo got up the nerve to respond to Stevens on this point, he was engaging an already well-developed strategy. The *origenistas* were prepared for such attacks and held a clearly marked line. In a statement defending his all-*origenista* anthology, Vitier felt he could defend *Orígenes* with the following words: "We are . . . very far from building that exquisite species of escapists that some imagine," he wrote, despising the "accusation of coldness, of obscurity and hermeticism [that] falls, more or less vaguely, over . . . the centrality of our poetic attitude."[10] Vitier, Lezama Lima, and Rodríguez Feo decided together, editorially, on the best line of defense: *Orígenes*, they declared, stood at once for "a poetry of exile and fidelity."[11]

Such a relation between exile and fidelity, however strategically shrewd, was culturally and politically tenuous, its elaboration in *Orígenes* vague. *Orígenes* raised the sort of question Stevens otherwise loved to put to his foreign correspondents: Did these islanders mean exile *from* or *to* the real world? Whereas Stevens craved fidelity, as small but satisfyingly familiar truths, "Cuban things" that were felt to be indigenous because they were inscribed into letters and sent *from* Cuba, José on the other hand believed that what Stevens really wanted was a sense of exile, of foreignness within Cuba itself—Cuba *not* as a home so much as a writer's exotic retreat, a place to come to.[12] If Stevens was not careful and fell into his usual habit of traveling great distances in a single wishful sentence, Rodríguez Feo was likely in his reply to further the imagined tour with a special vengeance. When on March 19, 1945, Stevens whimsically likened Walter Pach's Washington Square studio to Paris, Dresden, and Mexico City (*L* 491), Rodríguez Feo responded explosively four days later by deleting his own Cuba almost entirely from the literary map, energetically inserting into one 614-word letter the non-Cuban names Chesterton, Shaw, Valéry, Mallarmé, Góngora, Pierre Brantôme, J. Malcolm Brinnin, Harry

Levin, Alfonso Reyes (Mexican, of course, not Cuban), Cyril Connolly, Henry Miller, Church's friend Roger Caillois, and Pach. (The letter does mention the Cuban artist George Valdés, but only insofar as his work was filtered through the lens of an observing North American, Elizabeth Bishop.)[13] "My dear Mr. Wallace Stevens," it began (*SM* 47-49),

> I wanted to publish ["**A Word with José Rodríguez-Feo**" and "**Paisant Chronicle**"] in this Spring number, but fear it shall have to be postponed for the Summer. There are already two Americans in this issue—Brinnin and Levin—and there are already accusations of IMPERIALISM in the air.
>
> . . . Chesterton has kept me from [looking out] the window. I find him a most humorous, charming old fellow. . . . I have always disliked however his ultimate defense of the Catholic Faith; although it sustained for a longwhile his famous debates with Shaw and other sceptics. Today came a letter from Elizabeth Bishop, "la poetisa de Cayo Hueso," who has been very kind and offers an article on Valdés. . . . Also, Mr. Pach wrote. . . . By the way, I hope you have received the Caillois book. . . . Yes, Brinnin admires you very much. . . . I think Reyes will bore you. . . . [H]is poetry is only a competent combination of Spanish classical modes and Val[é]ry (with a little Mallarmé to cap it all). His best works are critical like . . . his essay on Góngora, Mallarmé, etc. . . . Reading now a most daring but charming book, *Les Dames Galantes,* by Monsieur Brantôme. This pornographic book tells the inside stories of the great princes and princesses of the age of Francis the First and really puts to shame Mr. Connolly and Mr. Miller's attempts.
>
> I hope you will have interesting remarks sur Monsieur Caillois. . . . I wish you could come across the Channel and stay a while with us.
>
> Yours sincerely,
>
> José

This single exchange is representative of the whole. During ten years of long letters, Stevens's eclecticism was in every case the cause of Rodríguez Feo's. It is clear from the March 23 reply, as from many others, that his name-dropping was an attempt to please and impress. But he was mistaken if he thought Stevens would prefer to discuss *literary* matters as energetically as this.

Stevens's response to such letters could be quite merciless, even while good intentions seemed guaranteed by the nice last touch of self-deprecation: "What I really like to have from you is not your tears on the death of Bernanos, say, but news about chickens raised on red peppers and homesick rhapsodies of the Sienese look of far away Havana and news about people I don't know, who are more fascinating to me than all the characters in all the novels of Spain, which I am unable to read" (*L* 622). Rodríguez Feo understood that this American poet, when he wrote in such a manner, was protesting

too much. He knew full well by then—1948—that Stevens would have loved, actually, to find and buy and read all the books of Spain, and that his notion of the proper description of Havana was itself derivative. Far less physically adventurous than his Cuban friend, Stevens could be assuaged, as Rodríguez Feo eventually learned, by words detailing "the *Sienese* look of far away Havana," despite his knowing even less of Italy than of Cuba. After a certain point, then, Rodríguez Feo began to learn how to respond obligingly. He told another story about his mother's wonderful fears: if her son accepted an offer to live in Paris—he had been offered a job at UNESCO—he would freeze in an unheated hotel, just as another aspiring artist and voracious reader had frozen in Argentina, book in hand. Rodríguez Feo could not really have been surprised, after telling this truly delicious tale, to find it retold in Stevens's poem "**The Novel,**" where Stevens quotes nine lines verbatim from Rodríguez Feo's letter. This was too alluring a story about the mother's provincialism at war with the son's internationalism. Here are the lines from Rodríguez Feo's letter as they appear in Stevens's poem:

> *Mother was afraid I should freeze in the Parisian hotels.*
> *She had heard of the fate of an Argentine writer. At night,*
> *He would go to bed, cover himself with blankets—*
>
> *Protruding from the pile of wool, a hand,*
> *In a black glove, holds a novel by Camus. She begged That I stay away.*[14]

Nor could Rodríguez Feo have been very surprised to receive Stevens's hilarious letter—two full pages of single-spaced elite typewriting—about the farm animals. "I take the greatest pride in knowing Pompilio," Stevens wrote here of the Cuban's mule, "who does not have to divest himself of anything to see things as they are. Do please give him a bunch of carrots with my regards." But Stevens meant to make a point here: "This is much more serious than you are likely to think from the first reading of this letter." What ought to be taken seriously, he went on to explain, was Rodríguez Feo's mostly unmet potential for realizing the primitive element in his surroundings. To push the lesson, Stevens described a fellow who regularly came to The Hartford headquarters, an unskilled man who wandered the polished corridors of that great building, office to office, dispensing with his shoeshine invariably primitive figures of speech Stevens found irresistible. He delighted in the bootblack's homely similes and paratactic constructions, and offered this example: "I was tired and laid down under a tree like a dog." And despite the fact that the image of Rodríguez Feo's family farm in this letter was a bucolic scene of unaffected animals-imagined-as-peasants surrounding a lonely, hyperintellectual, cosmopolitan reader, Stevens expressed his desire to make Rodríguez Feo less like his correspondent, the severe poet-attorney whose language was over-subordinated and whose manner over-civilized—with his own loneliness and devotion to reading—and *much more like* the harmless, semiliterate bootblack. The Hartford bootblack, Stevens urged, "is pretty much the same thing as you, yourself, seated under a tree at the Villa Olga and realizing that the world is as Pompilio sees it, except for you, or that the world is as the Negro sees it because he probably sees it exactly as Pompilio sees it."[15] (The "Negro" mentioned here was a cook who served Rodríguez Feo's family at the Villa Olga, and whom Rodríguez Feo described as continually "silent" [*SM* 69-70].) Thus the image of José reading in his room changed according to the strength of Stevens's wish to maneuver his Cuban friend into the bootblack's supposedly mindless position (lying down under the tree, dog-tired, *like an animal*), as into the cow's animal station (staring in from outside at a reader indoors). "Somehow I do not care much about Lucera," Stevens wrote of the cow outside the window. "I imagine her standing in the bushes at night watching your lamp a little way off and wondering what in the world you are doing."

The long letter, deconstructing the project of reading as an inexplicable, irrelevant act (seen by preconscious beings, it appears to be indistinguishable from the act of eating), became an impressive counternarrative against reading and thinking in the tropics, against "intellectual isolation." The quality of this letter itself as an enchantment, making resistance against its assumptions difficult, served Stevens much as the bootblack's folkloric, monosyllabic incantation ("I was tired and laid down under a tree like a dog") induced an apt linguistic lethargy; that is, the letter was itself meant to transform the insufficiently bucolic scene into a properly primitive state. Stevens's point was first introduced, tellingly, with a reference to van Geyzel as a man aspiring to be the intellectual center who is "actually," essentially, a farmer on the periphery:

> Of yourself you say that you read and write and cultivate your garden. You like to write to people far away and about such unreal things as books. It is a common case. I have a man in Ceylon with whom I have been exchanging letters for some years. He is an Englishman, an Oxford man and a lawyer, I believe, but actually he makes his living and the living of his family by growing coconuts.
>
> (*L* 512-13)

Rodríguez Feo seemed impervious to such pressures against literary discourse and literary reference at first. In 1945 Stevens's arguments against reading—that he had not read Robert Lowell's first book because a writer should not "nourish [himself] on the work of other people" (March 19; *SM* 46), and that he read "less of everything than most people" because "[i]t is more interesting to sit round and look out of the window"

(March 2; *SM* 43)—could not yet bring Rodríguez Feo to throw his Milosz and Svévò away. "I like what you said about reading," the young man replied. "I am getting to prefer looking out of the window, also. *Nevertheless,* Chesterton has kept me from the window" (*SM* 47). So begins the delirious bibliography of March 23. Such imperviousness to Stevens was charming, even the Cuban's willingness to contradict himself in the act of trying to please.[16]

But the pressure from the north would not abate. Stevens made a special point of praising Rodríguez Feo's story of the kidnapping of the family Great Dane, Linda, and the tale of his vengeful neighbor, Consuelo, whom Rodríguez Feo's conspiracy-minded mother suspected to be Linda's kidnapper (*SM* 140). Stevens not only joked wickedly about this incident, once imagining a new "Linda brand" of frankfurters (*SM* 148), but also used the occasion to reiterate his yearning to hear more about Cuba and less about poetry. "Literature nowadays is largely about nothing by nobodies," he wrote. "Is it not so? What kind of book would that dazzling human animal Consuelo sit down to read after she had finished washing the blood off her hands and had hidden once more her machete in the piano?" (*L* 624). The answer to his question is, of course: She reads no book at all.

Finally, all the book-talk flowing from Cuba made Stevens restate the reductive life-literature opposition and repeat his request for tales of the primitive life. "One writes about [life] when it is one's own life provided one is a good barbarian, a true Cuban, or a true Pennsylvania Dutchman, in the linguistics of that soul which propriety, like another Consuelo, has converted into nothingness" (*L* 624-25). Equating the Cuban and himself as barbarians—"barbarians" is a word Stevens probably would not have used had not Rodríguez Feo himself defined the term as a uniquely Cuban form of compliment (*SM* 141)[17]—makes the two men similarly "true" to what they essentially are, gives them a sense of ethnic and national origin that was just then strong in Stevens (at the height of his genealogical interest), even as the equation of a Cuban in impoverished, dependent Cuba and a many-generations-removed Pennsylvania Dutchman in suburban Connecticut may seem disingenuous, even absurd, to us now. Here Stevens was struggling to make a major point about his own poetic writing, which resists being read as the record of a life. When should one write about one's own life? Only when one recognizes the "primitive" in oneself can one create out of one's words a "linguistics of the soul," which social rules eventually diminish to nil. He and the Cuban, he claims, similarly have such a "soul."

In response to Rodríguez Feo's name-dropping letter of March 23, 1945, Stevens wrote again on April 6. He used Rodríguez Feo's request for a comment on Caillois's *Les Impostures de la poesie* as an occasion for criticizing *Orígenes*. Caillois's problem, Stevens decided, was that he attenuated and then ridiculed a taste for pure poetry that no longer existed, setting up a straw dandy, as it were. Caillois misread the trend toward the postwar mode that would deal with people, places, and things. "I think the feeling today very definitely is for an abundant poetry, concerned with everything and everybody" (*L* 495). This assessment gave Stevens the opportunity to measure the extent to which *Orígenes* reproduced the abundance of Cuba. He had just finished looking over the recent number of *Orígenes* containing María Rosa Lida's long article on Chaucer, hardly the sort of regionalism with which to refresh himself after finishing with Caillois's lyric strangeness.

> There is something else that you have spoken of on which I should like to say a word or two, and that is the risk you run in respect to accusations of imperialism. I should say that the risk is not a risk in respect to imperialism but in respect to eclecticism. For instance, that article on Chaucer. The act of editing a review is a creative act and, in general, the power of literature is that in describing the world it creates what it describes. Those things that are not described do not exist, so that in putting together a review like ORIGENES you are really putting together a world. You are describing a world and by describing it you are creating it. Assuming that you have a passion for Cuba, you cannot have, or at least you cannot indulge in, a passion for Brinnin and Levin, and so on, at the same time. This is not a question of nationalism, but it is a question of expressing the genius of your country, disengaging it from the mere mass of things, and doing this by means of every poem, every essay, every short story which you publish—and every drawing by Mariano, or anyone else. The job of the editor of ORIGENES is to disengage the identity of Cuba. I hope you won't mind my saying this. After all, I am not saying it *for your sake, or for the sake of Cuba, but for my own sake.* I agree with Caillois in this, at least, that there should be many things in the world: that Cuba should be full of Cuban things and not of essays on Chaucer.

> (*L* 495; emphasis added)

The rhetorical tradition of imperialism here is quite distinct (though surely unconscious): "We are in Egypt," Arthur Balfour declared to the House of Commons, "not merely for the sake of the Egyptians, though we are there for their sake; we are there also for the sake of Europe."[18] Stevens's letter masterfully substituted eclecticism for imperialism, and thus rationalized an intercultural force as the natural result of reading widely and experimentally. This strategy enabled Stevens to present a criticism that minimized national power. He read "the force that attaches" as "*dis*engagement." He could say directly that by publishing Brinnin's poems and Levin's essays *Orígenes* was being more impressed by American critical values than it ought to be. But to see this as primarily a political matter, Stevens urged,

was to underestimate an editor's capacity for creating a world by including it and denying a world by omitting it. It was within the young Cuban's power to create the world he desired. The irony of inventing a world in this sense was just that shared by Stevens's **"Description without Place"** and Sumner Welles's "Vision of a World at Peace," each promoting postwar reconstruction, or "creating a world," in terms that must mask their necessary association with the cultural desire to—in Joseph Conrad's figure—put one's denoting finger on the still-unnamed part of the map.[19] In drawing attention to this process of imagining a world, Stevens charged Rodríguez Feo with the thankless, unimaginative task of being Cuban for the sake of the writer who wanted to have continuous access to Cuban things—things legitimized *as* Cuban by the native editor who, taking such paternal instruction well, found himself choosing consciously to describe an unfamiliar place in familiar terms. Once Rodríguez Feo understood the irony of Stevens's special wished-for scene of instruction, then Stevens's attempt to maintain the segregation of political from creative forces might be said to have collapsed along with many other false distinctions, such as "This is not a question of *nationalism,* but it is a question of expressing *the genius of your country.*" Stevens's anticipation of an "abundant" poetry, postwar writing that would reproduce the extrinsic plenitude of the real, the "many things in the world" that emerged from the war, paradoxically became a call for restricted access. He had schooled the Cuban in what Cuba should *not* be full of.

How could the Cuban respond? First there was the matter of Stevens's having turned the accusation of imperialism inside out. The *origenistas* were not willingly the friends of cultural imperialists, in fact. On the contrary, Rodríguez Feo and his colleagues decried the influence of the United States. *Orígenes,* wrote Vitier, fortified Cuban art at a time when all Caribbean artists were in danger of being overwhelmed by the most powerful nation in the hemisphere.[20] At times Rodríguez Feo made it clear to Stevens that he abhorred America's proficiency at delivering the cultural goods:

> Amazing how mediocre taste will pervade when the nation who backs it up is powerful enough. The world will in time be inundated by vulgar, detestable American products, because America is all powerful and can deliver the goods. Example: *The Readers' Digest* is the best selling magazine in Latin America, *Red Amber* is a best seller to the South, everybody says Thank you, O.K., never gracias, Muy Bien, and the movies? Well, let's skip that one.

> (*SM* 63-64)

He also told Stevens he deplored North American criticism, by which he meant Yvor Winters in particular (*SM* 36). Winters's "Wallace Stevens, or the Hedonist's Progress" (1943) argued that Stevens's style had degenerated after **"Sunday Morning."** Rodríguez Feo in 1983 recalled that what particularly upset him about Winters's attack was the characteristically American—and, to him, mistaken—notion that a poem is bad if the victim of its irony is small game.[21] No surprise that Rodríguez Feo should think so, as it was not out of character for him to offer himself up as small game if the effect would be to encourage what he considered Stevens's strength as a poet—his irony—and thus to prove to Stevens himself his point about the flaw in American criticism. Such self-sacrifice was never a conscious strategy, but it is clear now to Rodríguez Feo that his letters—disorganized, presumptuous, provocative, irrational at times, and often confessional—created their powerfully disarming effects because they challenged the "hierarchy of values" (*SM* 41) that prevented new American writing from manifesting such qualities. In the letter he wrote that immediately prompted Stevens to compose **"A Word with José Rodríguez-Feo,"** Rodríguez Feo presumed to characterize Stevens's own house as gloomy, asked why Stevens had been called the Whistler of American poetry,[22] related Hemingway's sexual obsession to his being a North American, and asked Stevens to explain the "major man" of the war years, a central concept Stevens had virtually refused to explain to Simons, whose letters full of similarly basic questions were so comparatively methodical. And particularly with Rodríguez Feo's scrawled, nearly indecipherable postscript questioning the grotesque in the Spanish tradition, Stevens's poem-reply found a great deal to respond to. Here is Rodríguez Feo's letter (*SM* 41-42):

My dear Mr. Wallace Stevens:

It was grand to hear from you again and to know that [Mariano's] water-colors are cheering your rather gloomy house. I was surprised to learn that your visit to Cuba was of twenty years ago, for your poetry always has had for me a certain evocation of tropical light and colors which I find quite charming and most unusual. Of course, you know that Hemingway has lived among us for a long time; but I have always maintained that the milieu has not affected him at all. I cannot see how anybody could not be impressed by certain *things* which I find completely absent in his most "Spanishied" works. Of course, I have never quite come to admire Hemingway: I mean that if you are a real blood and bone latino, you find absurd and a bit of an affectation those "virile problems" which seem to bother him so much. I sincerely think him an Illinois Puritan hunting for exotic sensations in the places and things which are naturally empty of all possibilities of adventure. I should not have said PURITAN, because he is really more of a bourgeois and his dislike of certain authors condemns him in my eyes. The fact that he has had such a success makes me fear for that hierarchy of values which must reign in a nation if its culture is not going to fall into the most slappiest of arrangements. You are dead right, as you Americans would put it, about Winters. . . .

You will pardon my stupidity but I don't quite get what you mean by "major men." What do you mean by some "arbitrary object of belief"? I think it was more exact to call them a "source of poetry," but that too is rather ambiguous, eh? Is the intention mythological at all? Why do critics insist in calling you the Whistler of Amer. poetry? What do you think of Brinnin's poetry and Penn Warren?

I am very grateful for the promised volume of poetry. I will have all your poems here with me then. Are you ever returning to our lovely Habana?

Yours modestly,

José

About Hemingway—Picasso's "Guernica" and Dali's mystifying stories are Sp[anish] treatments of the same subject[,] not Romantic but macabre[,] in the tradition of Goya in the case of Guernica—Hemingway has not exploited the grotesque in our lives. Who has?

Stevens wrote **"Paisant Chronicle"** (*CP* [*Collected Poems*] 334-35) to answer one of the questions posed by this tantalizing letter, and with characteristic understatement observed to Rodríguez Feo that in the new poem he "defined major men for you" (*L* 489). Stevens's second poem-reply was equally swift and public, sent to the journal *Voices* within a week of receipt of Rodríguez Feo's letter, along with **"Paisant Chronicle"** and three other poems.[23] He mailed a copy of the typescript to Cuba:

"A Word with José Rodríguez-Feo"

As one of the secretaries of the moon,
The queen of ignorance, you have deplored
How she presides over imbeciles. The night
Makes everything grotesque. Is it because
Night is the nature of man's interior world?
Is lunar Habana the Cuba of the self?

We must enter boldly that interior world
To pick up relaxations of the known.
For example, this old man selling oranges
Sleeps by his basket. He snores. His bloated breath
Bursts back. What not quite realized transit
Of ideas moves wrinkled in a motion like

The cry of an embryo? The spirit tires,
It has, long since, grown tired, of such ideas.
It says there is an absolute grotesque.
There is a nature that is grotesque within
The boulevards of the generals. Why should
We say that it is man's interior world

Or seeing the spent, unconscious shapes of night,
Pretend they are shapes of another consciousness?
The grotesque is not a visitation. It is
Not apparition but appearance, part
Of that simplified geography, in which
The sun comes up like news from Africa.

(*CP* 333-34)

By way of an abashed "Thank you," Rodríguez Feo decided to express his regret that this poem was not for publication in *Orígenes,* rather than fully reveal his excitement over its being a special "Word" for him. Ironically, he had as much trouble understanding it as anyone else, although Stevens did offer a little help to him alone. "The point of the poem," he explained, ". . . is that, although the grotesque has taken possession of the sub-conscious, this is not because there is any particular relationship between the two things" (*L* 489). If we go on this alone, it would seem that Stevens missed entirely the point of Rodríguez Feo's postscript, which had not tried to make a case for the relation between the grotesque and "the subconscious."

The play in the title of this poem of instruction moves Stevens from the idiomatic (*I would like to have a word with José*) to the literal (*I would like to take up the problem of a single word—the "grotesque"—with him*). The poem addresses itself to Rodríguez Feo just as if it were one of Stevens's letters, saluting him as one of the secret-keepers of the moon, one who acknowledges her reign over ignorance but deplores her for not drawing the line at imbeciles. If the Cuban has asked his North American friend why the moon makes everything grotesque, as the poem supposes, he must also wonder if this is because there are special *provinces* for certain experiences. Night, for instance, seems the special province of man's interior world—as is the steamy night of the tropics in particular. Night offers special entrance into that world—that is, into "Cuba," the Roman household goddess who escorts children into the world of sleep. The answer to the North American's rhetorical question—"Is lunar Habana the Cuba of the self?"—apprehends the Cuban as provincial in any case, because it is the same as asking, tautologically, "Are you yourself?" Insofar as you indeed are yourself, you cannot help but reproduce the relaxations of the human, the local color of, "for example," the old man selling oranges. That one can choose "this" old man—*this* man as casually distinguished from *that*—suggests the abundance that the "*particular* José" addressed apparently tries to deny in his own special province.

Once the cultural type seems no more malicious than a random reduction—this point comes as the third stanza begins—the "spirit tires" of the effort to generalize from the regional. Such exhaustion inevitably follows presentations of the real. For even the utterly casual "example" leads us to ask theoretical questions about poetics. Such a spirit, weary of these sorts of questions and craving local fecundities such as things the orange-man sells, proposes the ignorance of indigence as an "absolute grotesque," an untransformed externality. And so this tired spirit finally rejects José's interest in the interior world of places like Havana where the extrinsic life is sufficiently abundant to command every bit of one's attention. The grotesque is actual, visible, "not apparition but appearance"—a part of (the poem admits) "that simplified geography" of the North American imagination thinking *of* and also *for* the Caribbean. In a

simplified geography the weary world is freshened just as the oldest trope (the sun) crosses over from the category of "weather" to that of "news." The sun-trope emerges from anywhere and thus from *nowhere in particular,* from places analogous and interchangeable, from *this* primitive place or *that,* from *Africa,* "for example." So the poem suggests in closing: "The sun comes up like *news* from *Africa.*"

After several years of letters in which he felt he was being urged to be isolated and suitably provincial, to resist Americanization, Rodríguez Feo submitted, significantly if temporarily, in playing the role of Stevens's Cuban primitive, by agreeing to console himself with the task of describing the bougainvillaeas and reproducing the banana vendor's song. **"Attempt to Discover Life"** (*CP* 370), the poem that prompted this confession of limits, thus had an effect quite the opposite of the discovery offered Rodríguez Feo in the title. **"Attempt to Discover Life"** was created out of the Cuban's failed effort to alter the unwritten rules of the relationship. The "Attempt" was made rather suddenly in 1946: Rodríguez Feo invited himself to Hartford for a visit. The letters had become a little more intimate than before, certainly for Rodríguez Feo, who wrote on May 10, 1946, in response to Stevens's gift of *Esthétique du Mal* (*SM* 83-84):

> All the admiration and longing for a more personal friendship could be expressed by my telling you how delighted and grateful I am to you. Reading, caressing (it almost comes to that) your marvelous **"Esthétique"** has been a benediction. . . . It comes to exclaiming that it is the most regaling present I have ever received and from a poet I don't even know personally. What a pity circumstances keep me so far away and prohibit a more intimate colloquy! . . . Do let me know of yourself and what you are doing in Hartford. Are the trees all green and the wild-flowers inciting young men into the woods?
>
> Your fu*rr*iously admiring Antillean,
>
> José

Rodríguez Feo has recalled for Beverly Coyle and me two important functions of this first face-to-face encounter: it would enable him to be explicit about his presumption that he might get to know Stevens's life in Hartford in the same way as Stevens wanted so urgently to know the particulars of his in Cuba; and it might, if planned just so, provide him an occasion to be honest about his homosexuality.[24] Unfortunately, Rodríguez Feo's departure for the United States was ill-timed; he just missed Stevens's response to the idea of the visit, insisting that they meet in Manhattan instead of on Stevens's own ground. What followed was a month-long comedy of errors involving an exchange of four letters, at least one phone call, and no fewer than three near misses.

As planned, Rodríguez Feo proceeded first to Vermont to assist in a summer language program at Middlebury College. From there he wrote to Stevens on August 25 that he would stop briefly in Boston before heading in Stevens's direction. By the time Stevens received this message, there would be no way to head off the young man. Two days later, on the twenty-seventh, Rodríguez Feo wrote again that he planned to visit Stevens at his office in the next week. Despite its pretense of being businesslike and precise, the note captures the spirit of his other letters—playful, inexact (he forgets to name the *day* of the visit), and comically meditative: "[I]t shall be at *exactly* noon so as to trap the poet as he exits from the walled citadel of the insurances. . . . I am motoring; . . . I shall detail *precisely* the route so as not to confirm the old Gothic invention of mañana and retarded overtures. What a triumph; to immortalize with the twelve bells the fame of my timeliness" (*SM* 87-88; emphasis added). This letter would almost certainly have reached the offices of The Hartford by Friday, August 30, and Stevens may or may not have comprehended its message. He and his wife, planning a brief vacation, intended to be away from that Friday until the next Monday (only five workdays away from the desk), and he would have plenty of time to return home and travel back by train to Manhattan to meet up with Rodríguez Feo, which, he had said in a letter sent to Cuba, he very much wanted to do. Later correspondence reveals that he knew Rodríguez Feo would be staying at the Stanhope and would not leave the country until September 23.

Rodríguez Feo tried everything possible when he arrived at "twelve bells" and found the poet gone. His effort included an abortive long-distance call to Stevens's resort in Hershey. Through a bad telephone connection the two men apparently had difficulty sorting out the matter. On this particular visit to Hershey, Stevens became involved in new genealogical research into his mother's family.[25] He extended this rare vacation with Elsie from ten to twenty-five days, arriving in Manhattan on September 24, the day after Rodríguez Feo had left. "I called up the Stanhope, which *confirmed* your departure" (emphasis added). He did seem to regret missing Rodríguez Feo, but wrote to say so a week later in over-apologetic tones. The letter is unnecessarily repetitious, and for the first time Stevens speaks in a protective plural: "[W]e had one of the happiest holidays we have ever had." A paragraph later, he adds: "But, after all, we had one of the happiest times of our lives" (*SM* 88-89).

Rodríguez Feo received Stevens's explanation along with another new poem, **"Attempt to Discover Life,"** which refers to the sulfur-bath resort Rodríguez Feo frequented, San Miguel de los Baños.[26] Here is the first stanza:

> At San Miguel de los Baños,
> The waitress heaped up black Hermosas
> In the magnificence of a volcano.
> Round them she spilled the roses
> Of the place, blue and green, both streaked.
> And white roses shaded emerald on petals
> Out of the deadliest heat.

Whether Stevens meant it as such, Rodríguez Feo accepted the poem as a gift—as the much warmer part of Stevens's apology. As consolation for having missed the poet in his element, here was fresh proof that Stevens could intimately imagine Rodríguez Feo in *his*. The Cuban was humbly and effusively grateful: "How very fine of you, to pay homage to our *little local villages*. . . . How magical the *discovery*!" (*SM* 89-90). Stevens's "discovery" is that the Cuban scene, the resort café, is so thickly abundant—flowers are "heaped," "spilled," colors "streaked," and so on—that it naturally dispels the poor woman who enters and stands by an occupied table, apparently waiting for bits of the patrons' excess wealth to be left behind. In the end, the cadaverousness of the poor is overcome by the natural richness of the place. "The green roses drifted up from the table / In smoke. The blue petals became / The yellowing fomentation of effulgence." And so "The cadaverous persons were dispelled." Next to the table where they had stood "were lying—dos centavos." The poem ends with an inconsequential tip and its obvious message: How easily are such social differences resolved in so natural a retreat.

Yet Rodríguez Feo, interpreting this poem for himself after returning from his trip, did not concentrate on the way in which it suggests the wealthy young Cuban's resort as the site for such a dismissal. He seemed to think the poem carried some message not generally on the differences between their two cultures but on the sentiment shared between them—on their friendship, as a sign of compensation for his failed "Attempt" to know Stevens more intimately. In Rodríguez Feo's view, the final two pennies "were pathetic, not condescending."[27] He wrote, "How come you see from so far-off those touching scenes?" (*SM* 90). Now, then, moved by what he read as tenderness on Stevens's part, Rodríguez Feo translated the poem for *Orígenes* himself (rather than have another *origenista* undertake the job as before).[28] In his letter of November 30 he thanked Stevens and seems to have submitted to the "simplified geography" of the earlier poem by speaking of his new willingness to settle for knowing the "little things" around him. He referred to his loneliness now in such a way as perhaps to suggest his homosexuality, in case Stevens knew how to take such a hint:

> My life flows as usual. I write, read and frequent the company of a few and selected amigos. I am as lonely as ever and yet quite happy in my isolation. All the vines are in bloom now, and looking across its flowery

branches I see the sky remains blue and shining up there. What more can you ask of life? To open one's eyes in the morning and see only flowers and the open spaces blue and white above. And to read kind, friendly messages from our friends below. It doesn't signify that we avert suffering and misery, all that is within us, but we must remain platonic and make the best of the little things the gods so kindly offer us every day: be it the vision of a violet bouganville or the song of a banana vendor. I think that is wisdom, not cowardice. I prefer to be foolish in those little things; not be made a fool reaching for the stars.

(*SM* 90-91)

Stevens's brief reply to these sentiments must have been at least temporarily another disappointment. Answering a direct question about the poem—Rodríguez Feo had asked, "[W]hat are hermosas?" (*SM* 90)—Stevens postponed his response to the more difficult issues raised in the letter concerning the meaning of the poem in the context of their relationship. He simply answered: "Hermosas are a variety of roses," as if it had been Hi Simons, and not José Rodríguez Feo, who had asked for explication. Even in his very generous letter of December 19, he takes up none of the issues Rodríguez Feo raised about his loneliness, his possible consolation offered by his "platonism," the disappointments of his visit to the United States. The image of Rodríguez Feo's resort, San Miguel de los Baños, Stevens now wrote, had not been intended to record his physical response to specific people, to a Cuban as opposed, say, to a Mexican or Argentine. On the contrary, he argued, his poem referred to an entirely unreal place, a description without a necessary sense of place.

From this point in a decade of letters, if Rodríguez Feo was to criticize "that hierarchy of values"—values which, to be sure, he more than once suggested Stevens represented—it had to be embedded, and thus formally qualified, in the letters-of-travel subgenre, a *pensée sauvage* Stevens had desired in the Cuban's letters. Even the politically radical suggestion that the world be "Cubanized" rather than Americanized—that the "civilized" nations ought not prepare for atomic attacks, and thus refuse to acknowledge the survivability of a nuclear exchange—had to be qualified by the idea that Cubanizing the world would actually mean simplifying and primitivizing it:

> [R]eading the paper tonight I felt a little sad. Why don't we "cubanize" a little the world? Then everybody would take it easier, would live for today, leave things for *mañana,* and get along better with their neighbors. I see N.Y. is ready for an atomic attack. From here, my dear friend, everything you read sounds a bit fantastical and absurd. Maybe we are (the Spaniards and Cubans) a race of retarded mortals. We still live by norms of other centuries and will not recognize completely the mechanical urge. Just to prove this point: in Habana

the new *cafetera* (little engine that makes coffee) are called (as advertisement) *La Bomba Atómica.* That sense of humour has saved us from the madness and nonsense that threatens to end your more "civilized" histories.

(*SM* 184)

From "here," from this point in time and place, Rodríguez Feo's Cuba, where cold-war fears of nuclear annihilation seem "fantastical" and "absurd," North American political anxieties are resisted exactly as they are naturalized—Cubanized—in terms powerfully managed by Stevens throughout the correspondence. To resist the anxieties of politics, to go unbothered by what one reads in the newspapers even while still reading them—to make Stalin Balin while remaining well aware of Stalin—was to move the subject to a position where Stevens had wanted to locate it all along: to a place existing not prior to but beyond the mechanical urge, resistant to civilization after having known it utterly.

Notes

1. "Thinking of a Relation Between the Images of Metaphors" (as "Unidad de las imagenes"), "Chaos in Motion and Not in Motion" ("El caos movil e inmovil"), "The House Was Quiet and the World Was Calm" ("La casa y el mundo en calma"), and "Continual Conversation with a Quiet Man" ("Conversación con un hombre silencioso") were first published in the Winter 1945 issue of *Orígenes* (2, 8: 3-6). Their first English publication came as "Four Poems" in *Voices* 127 (Autumn 1946): 4-6.

2. "aquellos momentos de creación en los que el germen se convierte en criatura y lo desconocido va siendo poseído en la medida en que esto es posible y en que no engendra una desdichada arrogancia" (*Orígenes* 1, 1 [Spring 1944]: 5).

3. The "intent to universalize" was most clearly articulated by José Lezama Lima, for instance in "Señales: Alrededores de una Antología" ("Signs: Outlines of an Anthology"), *Orígenes* 9, 31 (1952): 65.

4. "Por primera vez entre nosotros, lo contemporáneo no era una nostalgia provinciana" (ibid., p. 66).

5. "He ahí el detalle, la situación, los impensados agrupamientos, tocando, como arañazo y despertar creadores, la ajena imaginación poética; inequívoco signo de universalización, aparacer en las transmutaciones y misterios imaginativos de otros creadores muy alejados de nuestra latitud y paisaje" (ibid., p. 67).

6. In *Orígenes* 1, 3 (October 1945). The painting is now in the National Museum of Art, Havana.

7. "nada rendida al halago . . . sí de exprimir lo que había en nosotros" (José Lezama Lima, "Notes: Lozano and Mariano," *Orígenes* 1, 4 [December 1944]: 44).

8. For a reading of one of these paintings, a watercolor of pineapples, in relation to Stevens's "Someone Puts a Pineapple Together," see Filreis, "Still Life without Substance," pp. 370-71.

9. I am grateful to Sienah Wold for this characterization. See note 24 below.

10. "Estamos, pues, y a esto quería llegar, los poetas de mi reciente Antología, muy lejos de constituir esa exquisita especie de evadidos que algunos imaginan. Tan lejos, por los menos, como lo estamos de ser los desarragaidos seguidores de las últimas escuelas europeas. Semejante asociación de equívocos no ha de parecer arbitraria si consideramos que una misma acusación de frialdad, de oscuridad y hermetismo recae, más o menos vagamente, sobre aquellas escuelas y sobre lo central de neustra actitud poetica" (Cintio Vitier, "Ten Cuban Poets," *Orígenes* 5, 18 [Summer 1948]: 41).

11. "una poesía del destierro y de la fidelidad" (ibid., p. 43).

12. Indeed, it was a place Stevens had come to—twice. He spent "the greater part of a week" in Havana on business in 1923, staying in a hotel room that "looks out over the Prado, a short boulevard running down to the Malecon or seawall." He took each of his meals at a different restaurant, certain to describe for his wife the luncheon he was served at El Telegrafo, in the following delicious detail: "a big glass of orangeade, a Cuban lobster, banana bread, cocoanut milk ice cream and a pot of Cuban coffee." He found "good cigars" as "cheap as dirt." The whole visit, a digression from business dealings in Miami, made him "feel rather sinful" (*L* 235). His second visit, a briefer and less sinful stop, came later in 1923, when, as he told Rodríguez Feo, "my wife and I stopped there for about a day on the way to California by way of the Canal" (*L* 483-84; see also *L* 241).

13. Bishop's essay about George Valdés appeared in *Orígenes* 2: 6 (July 1945): 27-32.

14. For a full reading of this poem as a response to the Stevens-Rodríguez Feo correspondence, see *SM* 18-21. The letter that found its way into the poem has been reprinted in *SM* 133-34.

15. This reading is supported by Stevens's immediate interest in the bootblacks of Havana. If "everything here," he wrote from Cuba in 1923, "is an object

of interest," that interest could focus on a special kind of subservience—subservience that was somehow proud and lazy both: "the bootblacks *sit down* when they shine your shoes" (*L* 235).

16. The bootblack appeared in Stevens's introduction to Morse's book as follows: "[T]here develops a curiosity about the perceptions of others. . . . The fact is that the saying of new things in new ways is grateful to us. If a bootblack says that he was so tired that he lay down like a dog under a tree, he is saying a new thing about an old thing, in a new way. *His new way is not a literary novelty; it is an unaffected statement of his perception of the thing*" (*OP* [*Opus Posthumous*] 243; emphasis added).

17. Rodríguez Feo also called himself a "savage" (*SM* 69) and once paid Stevens the high compliment of addressing a letter to "My dear Primitive" (*SM* 193).

18. Speech of June 13, 1910, reproduced in *Parliamentary Debates,* 5th series, 17 (1910): 1140-46; quoted by Said in *Orientalism,* p. 33.

19. Joseph Conrad, *Heart of Darkness* (London: Penguin, 1973), p. 33.

20. Vitier, "Ten Cuban Poets," p. 41.

21. José Rodríguez Feo, interview with author and Beverly Coyle, New York City, October 17, 1983. Winters wrote of "The Mechanical Optimist" of 1936 that "the victim of the irony is very small game, and scarcely worthy of the artillery of the author of 'Sunday Morning'" (*In Defense of Reason* [Athens: Swallow Press/Ohio University Press, 1987; first published, 1943], p. 446).

22. The charge that Stevens is "the Whistler of Amer. poetry" was Horace Gregory's, in "An Examination of Wallace Stevens in a Time of War," *Accent* 3 (Autumn 1942): 60.

23. These were published as "New Poems," in *Voices* 21 (Spring 1945): 25-29. With "Paisant Chronicle" were "The Pure Good of Theory," "A Word with José Rodríguez-Feo [*sic*]," and "Flyer's Fall."

24. In an interview on October 18, 1983, Rodríguez Feo speculated on the possibilities of Stevens's perceptiveness in this matter, and he discussed the subtle ways in which he tried to clarify the issue, in 1946 or later, without, so far as he could tell, any success. Rodríguez Feo's homosexuality was not merely a personal matter, of course, but an aesthetic one, as the homosexual thematics of the *origenistas* were central to their development and achievement as a group—as to their political identity. The private poetic language that developed among them, later conjoined with other such

styles under the rubric "neo-Baroque," added to the strength of their manner and identity as well as to the accusations of hermeticism made against them. By coming out to Stevens, in short, Rodríguez Feo would have been contributing to a dialogue already well under way between them, about the problems engendered by the *origenista* aesthetic, problems Stevens knew well from his own struggles with claims made against his apparently secretive language and manner. For more on Lezama Lima's aesthetic, see Severo Sarduy, "The Baroque and Neobaroque," in *Latin America and Its Literature,* ed. César Fernández Moreno (New York: Holmes and Meier Publishers, 1980), pp. 115-32. I am grateful to Marci Sternheim for her suggestions on this point.

25. See Stevens's letter of September 30, 1946, to Charles R. Barker (*L* 534), in which he partially describes his research into the Zeller family history during the previous month. See also *WSR* [*Parts of a World: Wallace Stevens Remembered*] 112.

26. For a reading of Rodríguez Feo's prose poem "The Closed Door" in relation to San Miguel de los Baños, see *SM* 22-23.

27. Interview with Rodríguez Feo, October 18, 1983.

28. Oscar Rodríguez Felíu had translated Stevens for *Orígenes*; so had Eliseo Diego and Cintio Vitier (*SM* 47).

Jacqueline Vaught Brogan (essay date 1993)

SOURCE: Brogan, Jacqueline Vaught. "'Sister of the Minotaur': Sexism and Stevens." In *Wallace Stevens and the Feminine,* edited by Melita Schaum, pp. 3-22. Tuscaloosa, Ala.: University of Alabama Press, 1993.

[*In the following essay, Brogan argues that while Stevens's poetry displays a tendency to suppress what Stevens considered his feminine voice, his attempts to resolve this tension make a feminist study of his work a valuable exercise.*]

It would be easy to oversimplify the subject of sexism and Stevens as sexism *in* Stevens. The various biographies devoted to Wallace Stevens over the last decade have all, individually and collectively, given us information about his private life, especially in relation to his wife, that make it increasingly difficult to think of Stevens as that innocent, cherub-like person that Randall Jarrell once described him as being.[1] I have in mind, for example, Stevens' effective silencing of Elsie (as described by the family chauffeur to Peter Brazeau), or the disturbing way in which he "scripted" her—literally

made her an object of his pen, renaming her according to his needs—as seen in the previously unpublished letters to his wife included in Joan Richardson's biography.[2] In light of these new facts about Stevens' personal life, it is perhaps not surprising to find a recent and almost scathing indictment of Stevens' irresponsibility, if not moral failure, in his relationship with and to women.[3] Yet my subject here is not sexism *in* Stevens, in the sense of Stevens' being a sexist individual, nor am I trying to psychoanalyze what in Stevens' life might or might not have led to a troubled psyche, particularly concerning women. It seems almost too easy to point to Stevens' mother as a figure for the imagination, in continual conflict with his father as a figure for pragmatic action and reason. I think, too, that one could exploit the fact that Elsie Moll Stevens, who was so clearly perceived by Stevens in the early years as his muse, should be at once the girl from the wrong side of the tracks, possibly illegitimate, and the model for the goddess on the liberty coin,[4] the two archetypal—and equally dehumanizing—ways of viewing women in our culture thus both being accidentally inscribed in Elsie's life. Although these various facts may suggest, once again, that the personal *is* political, I want to distinguish as much as possible the subject of sexism *in* Stevens from sexism *and* Stevens, even if finally the two topics prove inseparable. What interests me here, therefore, is what happens to Stevens' poetry as he engages in the (perhaps conscious) suppression of what *he* perceives to be his feminine voice or, more accurately, that part of his poetic voice that is feminine metaphorically in the way the idea of "feminine" itself is metaphorical. My conclusion is, while Stevens would always suffer from a schism within himself, one that was ultimately derived from cultural biases against women (and which would affect his poetry in a number of important ways), he would also come as close as it was possible for a person in his time and circumstance to "curing" himself of the "infection in the sentence" the dominant, phallocentric structures in our culture inevitably breed.[5]

I

The distinction I am making between sexism *in* Stevens and sexism *and* Stevens is not meant to deny the fact that there are sexist innuendoes in Stevens' poetry. Certain sexist assumptions, including the one that denigrating women is humorous, account for a number of his poems, including **"To a High-Toned Old Christian Woman."**[6] It is not merely institutionalized religion Stevens is mocking there. **"To a High-Toned Old Christian Man"** does not seem nearly as funny, and I speculate that trying to make "*widowers*" wince" would not be perceived as being especially witty either. Similar attitudes also inform **"Lulu Gay"** (*OP* [*Opus Posthumous* 1957 edition], 26) and **"Lulu Morose"** (*OP* 27), although the first of these, in which Lulu tells the eunuchs what the barbarians have done to her, is

immediately more problematic. It is probably right to
the point that the males who have been castrated have
lost their "voice" as well—they cannot talk (but only
ululate). Certainly, we find an archetypal expression of
sexism in that poem with the wonderful title, **"Good
Man. Bad Woman"** (*OP* 33). In fact, such basic sexist
attitudes—even if we are charitable and conclude that
Stevens intends to poke fun at such attitudes—govern a
number of his poems. For example, there is no character
in all of Stevens' poetry, for example, with quite the
same sense of grotesque humor as the woman of **"The
Emperor of Ice-Cream"**—dead, lying on a deal dresser
with her "horned feet" protruding (*CP* [*The Collected
Poems of Wallace Stevens*], 184).

When we find instances of such blatant sexism *in*
Stevens, it is useful to remember the cultural context
within which he produced his work. When Stevens
began publishing in earnest, the women's suffrage
movement was well under way and frequently was the
subject of essays in the magazines in which Stevens
was publishing (and which he was presumably reading
himself). Many of these essays are surprisingly
sophisticated. As early as 1914 Edna Kenton was
distinguishing between different kinds of feminisms,
that is, the largely Anglo-American drive for identical
rights versus the German feminists' fight for different
but equal rights for women.[7] Yet even in such magazines
as the *Trend,* which seems far more sympathetic to the
women's movement than most because it kept a running tally on which states were supporting women's
suffrage, we find some rather appallingly sexist essays,
among them "The Land of the Hen-Pecked" or "Rule
the Women or They'll Rule You."[8] The title of this last
one sounds much like Stevens in **"Good Man. Bad
Woman"** when he says, "She can corrode your world,
if never you" (*OP* 33).

In fact, as Joan Kelly and Sandra Gilbert (among others)
have pointed out, the strides women have made in gaining civic and political rights have also historically been
accompanied by periods of increased hostility toward
women.[9] This conflict—the liberation of woman politically and the increased resentment toward, if not repression of her personally—accounts for the overwhelming
number of poems written during Stevens' early period
that expose women's status (or lack of status) in the
early part of this century. For example, we find in
magazines to which Stevens himself was contributing,
H. D.'s "Priapus" and "Acon," Alice Groff's "Herm-
Aphrodite-Us," the five poems about women that Pound
published in a 1915 issue of *Others,* Skipwith Cannell's
"Ikons," published the following year, and Kenneth
Burke's "Adam's Song, and Mine."[10] The overt tension
in this phase of the battle of the sexes toward which all
of these poems point is made explicit in Helen Hoyt's
"Homage,"[11] cited in part below:

Not as a man I felt you in my brooding,
But merely a babe. . . .
　　. . . . .

Sometimes I wished to feed you at my breast.

Not to myself, I knew, belonged your homage;
I but the vessel of your holy drinking,
The channel to you of that olden wonder
Of love and womanhood,—I, but a woman.
　　. . . . .

Do you think I did not kneel when you were kneel-
ing?
Even lowlier bowed my head, and bowed my heart.

What makes this poem particularly interesting is the
difficulty in assessing how much irony may or may not
have been intended, although it is important to note,
both for her own work and for a sense of the times in
which Stevens first began publishing, that Helen Hoyt
would edit a special issue of women poets for *Others*
one year after publishing this poem.[12] Nevertheless,
when we do find sexist assumptions or innuendoes in
Stevens' work, we face a similar dilemma in frequently
being unable to determine precisely how much Stevens
is reflecting cultural biases or just how much he is revising such biases through ironic reflections. Yet despite
this very complicated context, it is possible to see the
ways in which Stevens' perhaps conscious, perhaps
unconscious "phallocentric" perspective manifests itself
in the dynamics, even the problematics of his poetry.
That problematic may not be the conflict between
imagination and reality (as has been traditionally
assumed), nor even the battle between competing
theories of language, but rather a problematic between
feminine and masculine expression—between the male
authorial voice that strives to achieve significance and
the culturally delineated suppression or silencing of
feminine voice that struggles, nonetheless, precisely for
expression in Stevens' works. Put differently, in
Stevens' work we can see the ways in which our culturally inscribed notions of male/author/authority and our
culturally inscribed repression of the rest of our human
voice (even within ourselves, and within Stevens as
well) frustrate the attempt at poetic expression itself,
while informing what expressions are achieved in the
individual poems.

To understand this critical facet of Stevens' work, it is
important first to stress the fact that from the rejection
of the feminine figure in **"Farewell to Florida"** to her
reception in **"Final Soliloquy of the Interior Paramour,"** Stevens' poetry remains highly self-conscious
about the fact that it *is* wrestling with the feminine
figure and, usually in a rather Jungian fashion, specifically with the feminine figure within. As a mere
sampling of this self-conscious struggle, I offer four
texts, taken variously from his essays, letters, *Collected
Poems,* and *Opus Posthumous* over the course of his

career. The first is from **"Farewell without a Guitar,"** written in 1954, just one year before he died:

> Spring's bright paradise has come to this.
> Now the thousand-leaved green falls to the ground.
> Farewell, my days.
>
> . . . . .
>
> The reflections and repetitions,
> The blows and buffets of fresh senses
> Of the rider that was,
>
> Are a final construction,
> Like glass and sun, of male reality
> And of that other and her desire.
>
> (*OP* 98-99)

While the rather poignantly glossed "rider that was" refers to the failure of Stevens' attempt to create—and to become—the "Noble Rider" of 1942 (*NA* [*The Necessary Angel*], 1-36), it is possible to say that from **"To the One of Fictive Music"** (1922) to the end of his life, much of Stevens' corpus is written in response to that significant "other." Yet *this* female figure, so nebulously and delicately evoked, is not the Elsie he largely dominated in his personal life, nor his mother—nor a high-toned old Christian woman for that matter—but precisely a part of himself that he could never fully come to know except as "she" was traced in his poetry.

Significantly, in the second of these texts (section ten of **"Esthétique du Mal"**), Stevens distinguishes between two sets of female figures in his poetry, implicitly suggesting an awareness of a problem in his figurations of women and, even more implicitly, suggesting the possibility of resolution in an androgynous figure:

> He had studied the nostalgias. In these
> He sought the most grossly maternal, the creature
> Who most fecundly assuaged him, the softest
> Woman with a vague moustache and not the mauve
> *Maman*. His anima liked its animal
> And liked it unsubjugated, so that home
> Was a return to birth. . . .
>
> . . . . .
>
> It is true there were other mothers, singular
> In form, lovers of heaven and earth, she-wolves
> And forest tigresses and women mixed
> With the sea. These were fantastic.
>
> (*CP*, 321)

These "other mothers," immediately troped in the text to the monstrous she-wolves and tigresses, are the fantastic manifestations of his own feminine voice, or anima, repressed throughout most of his poetic career. Thus, one effect of his conscious repression of the feminine principle in **"Farewell to Florida"** (though there is ample evidence of unconscious repression before that poem appeared in 1936) manifests itself in the extreme attention to "man number one" in **"The Man with the Blue Guitar"** (1937) with, however, a concurrent monstrous version of his poetic self that he has largely tried to subjugate. It is both culturally and poetically predictable that whereas this "monster" in **"The Man with the Blue Guitar"** *may* be male (the "lion in the lute / Before the lion locked in stone" [*CP*, 175]), in general the uncomposed and, therefore, potentially destructive aspect of his creative energy is perceived or figured by Stevens as a (threatening) woman.

This fact leads to a third text, a passage from "The Figure of the Youth as Virile Poet." After making the rather remarkable statement that "The centuries have a way of being male" (*NA*, 52), and before insisting that the "character of the poet" must be seen as *"virile"* or else "the masculine nature that we propose for one that must be the master of our lives will be lost" (*NA*, 66),[13] Stevens says: "When we look back at the face of the seventeenth century, it is at the rigorous face of the rigorous thinker and, say, the Miltonic image of a poet, severe and determined. In effect, what we are remembering is the rather haggard background of the incredible, the imagination without intelligence, from which a younger figure is emerging, stepping forward in the company of a muse of its own, *still half-beast and somehow more than human, a kind of sister of the Minotaur*. The younger figure is the intelligence that endures. It is the imagination of the son still bearing the antique imagination of the father" (*NA*, 52-53; italics added). The essentially androgynous character of this figure (inasmuch as the "sister" is also the "son"), together with the one cited above, bears further study—particularly in the context of the often frustrated quest for androgynous union traced in much of the romantic poetry preceding (and anticipating) Jungian theory. Nevertheless, as I read this particular essay, Stevens is seriously engaged in a deliberate battle to overcome the kind of schism within himself that would give rise precisely to this kind of distortion in which the feminine aspect is marked and perpetually marred by "monstrous" displacement.[14] Yet at least in 1942 when this essay was written, Stevens' own language inhibits such a cure. Not only does he still think of the poet as someone who must master our lives (and who must be male), he also writes these ironically self-defeating words at the very point the "figure of the youth as the virile poet" supposedly speaks or finds his own voice: "No longer do I believe that there is a mystic muse, sister of the Minotaur. This is another of the monsters I had for nurse, whom I have wasted. I am myself a part of what is real, and it is my own speech and the strength of it, this only, that I hear or ever shall" (*NA*, 60). What is most provocative about this passage, especially because it is in such conflict with the semantic intent, is that even as he rejects the sister of the Minotaur at the supposed moment of self-identification, he reinstates the figure of the monster as a (presumably female) nurse.

The last text is simply the letter that followed Howard Baker's analysis of Wallace Stevens in *Southern Review* ("Wallace Stevens and Other Poets")[15] in which Baker describes Stevens' poetry in Jungian terms. In a letter to Ronald Latimer in 1935, Stevens writes: "There is in the last number of the SOUTHERN REVIEW, or QUARTERLY, an extremely intelligent analysis of my work by Howard Baker. No one before has ever come as close to me as Mr. Baker does in that article" (*L* [*Letters of Wallace Stevens*], 292). This letter shows that, even at an early point, Stevens thought in somewhat Jungian terms about his own poetry, and therefore attention to the male and female figures (and hence to their voices or lack of voices) in Stevens' work is central to our understanding of it.

Stevens engages in the repression of the feminine aspect of his own creativity or creative voice in a variety of ways. It may well be that the culturally encouraged suppression of women—specifically the silencing of women—is internalized in Stevens,[16] so that his psyche feels at once a longing for this displaced self (hence, the omnipresent "she," the "other and her desire") while simultaneously feeling threatened by what might be chaos, uncontrollable, if he abandons his "rage to order" by allowing her to speak. But, whatever the reasons, "a kind of sister of the Minotaur" is the uncanny and uncomfortable figure repressed—ambivalently and ambiguously held—in the white space of Stevens' texts.

II

This repression manifests itself ironically, if not subversively, in Stevens' work throughout his poetic career. Most obviously, Stevens rejects the feminine figures of *Harmonium,* especially the figures of female, fecund nature in the 1936 **"Farewell to Florida"** (the poem he used to open the *second* version of *Ideas of Order*).[17] There he accuses "her" of having bound "him round" and says that he will return to the land of the "violent mind," which is equivalent to the land of the violent men (*CP,* 117-18). Yet repression of the feminine figure occurs in Stevens in more subtle and ultimately more significant ways, although the particular, conscious rejection of the feminine seen in **"Farewell to Florida"** encouraged the more abstract, philosophical poetry of the many years to come.

Ironically, one of the most telling marks of Stevens' repression of the feminine is that in his poetry female figures almost never speak. If any voice is heard at all (and that itself is a subject to take up below), it is that of a male, as in **"Two Figures in Dense Violet Night"**:[18]

Be the voice of night and Florida in my ear.
Use dusky words and dusky images.
Darken your speech.

Speak, even, as if I did not hear you speaking,
But spoke for you perfectly in my thoughts,
Conceiving words,

As the night conceives the sea-sounds in silence,
And out of their droning sibilants makes
A serenade.

(*CP,* 86)

One exception to this generalization is the woman in **"Metropolitan Melancholy,"** the "purple woman" with the "lavender tongue" who "Said hic, said hac, / Said ha" (*OP* 32). Another is the quoted *"Encore un instant de bonheur,"* words that Stevens immediately dismisses: "The words / Are a woman's words, unlikely to satisfy / The taste of even a country connoisseur" (*CP,* 157). Here, it is admittedly difficult to distinguish the repression of the feminine voice from basic sexism. Nevertheless, a glance at the *Concordance* to Stevens' poetry surprisingly reveals that "words" are not Stevens' most popular theme, but "man" or "men" (appearing 507 times) and, especially, man speaking.[19] Women appear in Stevens' poetry about one fifth as frequently—a total of 106 times compared to 507 for men. But in contrast to the men, women almost never have a voice. From the early **"All Over Minnesota,"** where the "voice of the wind is male,"[20] through **"A Thought Revolved"** and *The Necessary Angel,* the idea of "voice" itself is perceived by Stevens as exclusively masculine. But then, I think we can say, he protests too much.

One extension of this verbal repression is the fact that Stevens' female figures not only rarely speak, but they rarely move. Consider the difference between his earliest and most famous male and female characters, **"The Comedian as the Letter C"** and the complacent woman of **"Sunday Morning."** In a very disturbing way, women in his poetry remain too obviously figures— empty ciphers for masculine rumination and scripting, even de-scription.[21] The woman of **"Sunday Morning"** has several sisters, among them **"So-and-So Reclining on Her Couch"** and **"Romance for a Demoiselle Lying in the Grass,"** in which Stevens writes that

The monotony
Is like your port which conceals
All your characters
And their desires.

(*OP* 23)

In the course of the poem this female figure is either troped to or revealed to be a guitar; Stevens closes the poem with "Clasp me, / Delicatest machine." But this revelation, if we can call it that, further "objectifies" the feminine, even if metaphorically, "concealing" her behind a phallocentric and concomitantly erotic perspective that is reminiscent of the elders' view of Susanna in **"Peter Quince at the Clavier"** (*CP,* 89-92).

Nonetheless, precisely because he still retains the idea of a feminine muse (even if she may be figured as a "kind of sister of the Minotaur"), Stevens' attempts to repress or silence the feminine leaves *him* in the position of never being able to speak. Almost without exception, Stevens' greatest attempt at poetic expression, the words of that "virile poet," are instances of failures of speech—words about the words he *would* say, if he could—signs, shall we say, of the failure of both logocentric and phallocentric ordering. For example, Stevens says in **"Notes toward a Supreme Fiction"** that it is "As if the waves at last were never broken, / As if the language suddenly, with ease, / Said things it had laboriously spoken" (*CP*, 387). Again in **"Primitive Like an Orb,"** Stevens writes with an implicit pathos that

> It is
> As if the central poem became the world,
> And the world the central poem, each one the mate
> Of the other, as if summer was a spouse,
> Espoused each morning
>
> (*CP*, 441)

Thus, despite his sustained attempt to evoke—or to become—the "virile" poet, one whose words both master and are a part of what is real, that which he cannot order or master insists upon being heard, however ironically, in the very silence of the gap between "as" and "if," that is, between "order" and the "abyss," as these terms are metaphorically and sexually conceived. The white writing of such texts is perversely and subversively the trace of the repressed voice that refuses to (or cannot) coincide with the phallic and verbal structures Stevens professes to order in his words. Hence Stevens' lifelong frustration about his inability to get "straight to the word, / Straight to the transfixing object" (*CP*, 471)—and hence, also, his desire.

From this perspective, **"The Idea of Order at Key West"** can be seen to reiterate this basic problematic in Stevens' verse, rather than embodying one of his more successful figurations of women as many critics have assumed.[22] In contrast to the other women figures mentioned so far, the celebrated female figure of this poem is, superficially, neither mocked or denigrated; she is also supposedly vocal and dynamic, walking and singing by the shore:

> And when she sang, the sea,
> Whatever self it had, became the self
> That was her song, for she was the maker. Then we,
> As we beheld her striding there alone,
> Knew that there never was a world for her
> Except the one she sang and, singing, made.
>
> (*CP*, 129-30)

However alluring this poem may be, we run the risk of being ruled by rhetoric if we fail to note that ultimately—and even in the narrative development of the text itself—this "woman" is simply a figure for (and thus a sign or empty cipher for) Stevens himself and the way *he* sings. The clearest sign of this is found in the very next line, where he abruptly breaks in with, "Ramon Fernandez, tell me, if you know. . . ." This rupture is the most overt sign in the poem of the nature of the poetic "order" (even "rage for order") that Stevens has in mind. This thematic is inscribed throughout the poem: lights "master" the night, "portion" out the sea, "arrange" and "deepen" night, so that the words, in a kind of phallic "mastering," ironically create the "fragrant portals," essentially create the feminine. But what do we hear from this feminine voice, which is simultaneously created, disclosed in the portals, and repressed—silenced by the "mastering" as well as by Stevens' actual appropriation of the unheard feminine voice? From the opening stanza, that other voice remains literally "beyond" us and ourselves:

> She sang beyond the genius of the sea.
> The water never formed to mind or voice,
> Like a body wholly body, fluttering
> Its empty sleeves; and yet its mimic motion
> Made constant cry, caused constantly a cry,
> That was not ours although we understood,
> Inhuman, of the veritable ocean.
>
> (*CP*, 128)

The need for this control—the imperative to create and to control a world in words—can in part be explained historically and culturally. The Great Depression, the Great War, the threat of a second world war to come, would easily give rise to the need to defend oneself against looming chaos, a fact that is amply demonstrated by the poems of Stevens' middle period.[23] But I think at least part of the explanation for Stevens' apparent need to break into the text—to silence this feminine figure, however lovely we may feel she may be—lies in her uncanny reflection, that "sister of the Minotaur." The lovely, virtually inhuman woman by the sea and the somewhat unsettling half-beast who is "yet more than human" are two faces, as it were, of the same figure that, as figure, also means absence and repression. Instead of the madwoman in the attic, this is a (potentially) mad woman in a maze, specifically a linguistic maze.

The idealized version of the figure, the one who remains beyond speech, desired but controlled, together with her monstrous counterpart account for many of Stevens' more fantastic female characters. The idealized figure is found in **"To the One of Fictive Music,"** where, for example, Stevens creates a feminine trilogy of sister, mother, and diviner love (*CP*, 87-88), in **"Infanta Marina,"** where "She" can make "of the motions of her wrist / The grandiose gestures / Of her thought" (*CP*, 7), as well as in **"Apostrophe to Vincentine"** and **"Bouquet of Belle Scavoir."** Yet her monstrous counterpart is found in **"The Woman Who Blamed**

Life on a Spaniard," where "she never clears / But spreads an evil lustre whose increase / Is evil" (*OP* 34), in the fifth of **"Five Grotesque Pieces"** (entitled **"Outside of Wedlock"**), where she is figured as "an old bitch, an old drunk, / That has been yelling in the dark" (*OP* 77), and even in **"The Common Life,"** where quite significantly, given the title, "women have only one side" (*CP,* 221). In **"The Old Woman and the Statue,"** she has all the attributes of a witch:

> But her he had not foreseen: the bitter mind
> In a flapping cloak. She walked along the paths
> Of the park with chalky brow scratched over black
> And black by thought that could not understand
> Or, if it understood, repressed itself
> Without any pity in a somnolent dream.
>
> (*OP* 44)

Still, it would not be accurate to reduce Stevens' poetry to reiterating endlessly this conflict within himself. If Stevens suffered (and I think he did suffer) from a schism within himself, he also seems not only to have been aware of that but to have tried to "cure" himself. Even as early as **"Last Looks at the Lilacs,"** he is contemptuous of that "rational caliber," that "arrogantly male, / Patron and imager" (*CP,* 48-49). And he also condemns, albeit playfully, that "damned universal cock" in **"Bantams in Pine-Woods"** who, in a quintessentially phallocentric way, thinks that he is the center of the universe (*CP,* 75-76). To this end I see an important development between **"The Idea of Order at Key West"** and his well-known **"Final Soliloquy of the Interior Paramour"** (*CP,* 524).

III

In contrast to the earlier poem of 1934, in Stevens' 1950 lyric, divisiveness in voice and self is recognized rather than being "written over" or suppressed. The divisiveness is even explicitly held within the interior (rather than being described fallaciously as a split between a dominating male poet/author/authority and a submitting, potentially chaotic feminine world). As the word "paramour" suggests, there is a romance, even an intimacy/communion/communication in this poem that is dependent upon "dif-ference" (to use Heidegger's term). The most telling sign of this is the plural pronoun "we" and that most feminine of articles, the "shawl," wrapped tightly round them since they "are poor":

> Light the first light of evening, as in a room
> In which we rest and, for small reason, think
> The world imagined is the ultimate good.
>
> This is, therefore, the intensest rendezvous.
> It is in that thought that we collect ourselves,
> Out of all the indifferences, into one thing:
>
> Within a single thing, a single shawl
> Wrapped tightly round us, since we are poor. . . .
>
> (*CP,* 524)

Even though Stevens' characteristic tone of dominance is absent in this poem, the recognition and recovery of the feminine voice do not undermine the poetic authorship as Stevens obviously feared they would in **"Farewell to Florida."** Instead, the recovery of this voice gives expression to what is beyond control, beyond order, beyond dominance in our actual lives and thereby endows with significance that little which we can order in words: "Out of this same light, out of the central mind, / We make a dwelling in the evening air, / In which being together is enough" (*CP,* 524). In this poem the phallocentric "central mind" is consciously exposed as a fiction—not heralded as the "ideal realm" where the "new bourgeois man feels historically untouchable," as Frank Lentricchia has recently argued.[24] From the opening stanza, there is only "small reason" to "think / The world imagined is the ultimate good," a delicate disclaimer that quietly but continually dismantles the covert assumptions about and equations of reason, thinking, imagination, and essentially all Western (or at least Platonic) idealizations. But in submitting to the realization of the fictionality of our orderings—including the largely phallocentric privileging of the idea of order itself—*this* poem manages finally to be heard as fully human and humane. In essence, the recovery here of the feminine voice, which is so silenced in his early poems, especially after *Harmonium,* opens up the space in Stevens for the magnificent voice of his later years, one heard, for example, in **"The Planet on the Table"** and **"Lebensweisheitspielerei,"** where he admits, in opposition to the "portentous enunciation" (*CP,* 43) of his earlier work, that

> The proud and the strong
> Have departed.
>
> Those that are left are the unaccomplished,
> The finally human,
> Natives of a dwindled sphere

—but a sphere in which "Each person completely touches *us*" (*CP,* 504-5; italics added).

We should note that such a development as I have sketched here is itself reductive in a way. Certainly in **"Madame La Fleurie,"** also a very late poem, we see the monstrous and bearded inversion of mother earth in the "bearded queen" who is devouring him (*CP,* 507). Similarly, the mother in **"World without Peculiarity"** becomes a hating "thing upon his breast" (*CP,* 454). Yet in general, the development I have described is accurate. As he says in **"Artificial Populations,"** a poem written the year he died, "This artificial population [rosy men and women of the rose] is like / A healing-point in the sickness of the mind" (*OP* 112).

How this "cure" was accomplished is itself a topic for another lengthy study, but I would like to offer a brief summary of certain touchstones in this process. After his obvious attempt to gain total voice in "The Figure of the Youth as Virile Poet," Stevens becomes increasingly obsessed with "the sound / of right joining," "The final relation, the marriage of the rest" (*CP*, 464-65). We see this desire thematized in his letters when he, perhaps surprisingly given his personal life, uses the pleasure that "a man and woman find in each other's company" as an illustration of the "pleasure" of "Cross-reflections, modifications, counter-balances, giving and taking" of the "various faculties of the mind" (*L*, 368); and it is repeated two years later in the seventh section of **"Notes toward a Supreme Fiction"**:

> Perhaps there are times of inherent excellence,
>
> As when the cock crows on the left and all
> Is well, incalculable balances . . .
>   . . . . .
>
>   not balances
> That we achieve but balances that happen,
>
> As a man and woman meet and love forthwith.
>
> (CP, 386)

Yet despite his efforts to achieve this balance, Stevens fails to do so in **"Notes"** when, for example, Nanzia Nunzio fails to achieve this promise—her erotic power being so contingent upon her willingness to be scripted or subjugated:

> Speak to me that, which spoken, will array me
> In its own only precious ornament.
>   . . . . .
>
> Clothe me entire in the final filament,
> So that I tremble with such love so known
> And myself am precious for your perfecting.
>
> (CP, 396)

The maiden Bawda and her captain perhaps fare better: at least they are both "love's characters come face to face" (*CP*, 401). Yet the last numbered section of the poem names the "Fat girl" as the "irrational, the more than rational distortion" (*CP*, 406), phrases reminiscent of those used in the same year to describe the "sister of the Minotaur." Certainly Stevens has not achieved communion with his interior paramour at this point, despite his desire to do so.

But in **"Of Modern Poetry,"** written two years before, and later in **"Burghers of Petty Death,"** we find men and women together, more successfully figured as equal representatives of humanity. "Modern Poetry," Stevens says, "has to be living, to learn the speech of the place. / It has to face the men of the time and to meet / The women of the time" (*CP*, 240). In the second poem, written in 1946, Stevens says:

> These are the small townsmen of death,
> A man and a woman, like two leaves

> That keep clinging to a tree,
> Before winter freezes and grows black—
>
> (CP, 362)

This "woman," equal in her humanness to the "man," marks a new moment in Stevens in which "she" is not only validated but recognized both as a presence and as a human being, rather than tracing in either idealized or "monstrous" discourse the path of failed signification and signifiers.[25] If I were to indulge in psychological explanations, I would consider the possibility that the sheer, overwhelming and uncontrollable violence of the Second World War reduced all human beings in Stevens' eyes to the position of "women" in the ironically-realized, metaphorical sense of the word. We are all without power, not just women, in this modern world, unable to control the world and possibly our own lives.

Between **"Of Modern Poetry"** and **"Burghers of Petty Death,"** Stevens dismisses the figure of a "bright red woman" for (presumably) a real one in a poem intriguingly called **"Debris of Life and Mind"**:

> She will think about them not quite able to sing.
> Besides, when the sky is so blue, things sing
>   themselves,
>
> Even for her, already for her. She will listen
> And feel that her color is a meditation,
>
> The most gay and yet not so gay as it was.
> Stay here. Speak of familiar things a while.
>
> (CP, 338)

In the last line the unexpected turn toward domestic intimacy, especially for such a previously "exotic" poet, enacts what is both a personal and poetic passage, a "fall," we might say, into the more fully human. Certainly his request, open to rejection, vulnerable, and wistful, is quite different in tone from the whole panoply of "hero" poems that preceded this poem and the earlier "rage to order."

In **"Auroras of Autumn,"** published in 1947, Stevens implies that he meets his anima in an intense rendezvous that prepares the way for **"Final Soliloquy"**:

> This sense of the activity of fate—
>
> The rendezvous, when she came alone,
> By her coming became a freedom of the two,
> An isolation which only the two could share.
>
> (CP, 419)

As Frank Doggett and Dorothy Emerson have rightly suggested, this "isolation" is an isolation because it is a rendezvous within himself, between his masculine and feminine selves.[26] What is most revealing about this description, however, is that it is specifically a "freedom of the two"—a phrase that claims at least to have achieved finally what Stevens desired as early as **"The Man with the Blue Guitar"**: reduction of the "monster to / Myself" so that he can "be, / Two things, the two together as one" (*CP,* 175). It is also much to the point that the "mother" "who invites humanity to her house" (*CP,* 415) has in this poem "grown old" (*CP,* 413). Ultimately, she too is more vulnerable (and, therefore, human) than mythic—as is the woman in **"Things of August"** (1949), where she is "exhausted and a little old" (*CP,* 496). In addition, as Milton J. Bates has pointed out, it is at this moment in his career that Stevens begins so frequently to characterize himself as a child,[27] but, I would add, usually as a child of both parents, or both sexes, rather than being strictly the son "only of man" (*CP,* 185) as in the earlier **"A Thought Revolved."**

Finally, in **"Angel Surrounded by Paysans"** (1949), we come across a supposedly masculine character, "a man / Of the mind" (*CP,* 497), who finally speaks with what I see as Stevens' previously repressed feminine voice. There is no control, no mastering, no portioning of the night:

> Am I not,
> Myself, only half of a figure of a sort,
>
> A figure half seen, or seen for a moment, a man
> Of the mind, an apparition apparelled in
>
> Apparels of such lightest look that a turn
> Of my shoulder and quickly, too quickly, I am gone?
>
> (*CP,* 497)

The angel is, in fact, a "necessary angel," but one who is questioning rather than "ordering," one who is, admittedly, too easily gone, subject to change—a sign of the mutability of our best linguistic orderings. But he—she—is also finally heard *through* the door (instead of being held off beyond the portals), heard, even if only whispering. This poem, which ends the last volume of poetry that Stevens wrote before *The Rock,* achieves something of a resolution (emphasizing far more the "solution" or mixing than the earlier tone of "resolve") that finds a final plenitude in the great lyrics of his last volume, including **"Final Soliloquy of the Interior Paramour."**

I think, then, that there is real growth in Stevens, and that is why, despite poems like **"O Florida, Venereal Soil"** or **"Good Man. Bad Woman,"** Stevens touches so many women. I have it on good authority, for example, that a leading feminist poet secretly reads Stevens, and Helen Vendler, as we know, has said Stevens has written the poems she would have written if she were a poet.[28] I think this growth also accounts for why, despite what seems to have been a very

unhappy personal life, most of us still feel a certain health—humanity in its fullest sense—in reading Wallace Stevens.

Notes

1. See Randall Jarrell, "The Collected Poems of Wallace Stevens," *The Third Book of Criticism* (New York: Farrar, Straus & Giroux, 1969), 55-73; first published in the *Yale Review* 44 (March 1955): 340-53. There he says of Stevens that "there is about him, under the translucent glazes, a Dutch solidity and weight; he sits surrounded by all the good things of this earth, with rosy cheeks and fresh clear blue eyes, eyes not going out at you but shining in their place, like fixed stars" (p. 67). A similar sense of Stevens' magnanimity is found in Marianne Moore's review of *Harmonium,* "Well Moused, Lion," *Dial* 76 (January 1924): 84-91; and Harriet Monroe's review of the same volume, "A Cavalier of Beauty," *Poetry* 23, no. 6 (March 1924): 322-27.

2. See Peter Brazeau, *Parts of a World: Wallace Stevens Remembered, an Oral Biography* (New York: Random House, 1983), in which Naaman Corn says not only that "Mr. Stevens was very dominating" and that "no one dictated anything else but Mr. Stevens," but that he also caused his wife to "quit talking" by "snapping" at her whenever she spoke (p. 248). With regard to Stevens' "scripting" of Elsie, see Joan Richardson, *Wallace Stevens: The Early Years, 1879-1923* (New York: William Morrow, 1986), especially chapter 5.

3. Mark Halliday, "Stevens and Heterosexual Love," *Essays in Literature* 13 (Spring 1986): 135-55.

4. Milton J. Bates has handled these, and other facts about Stevens' relationship with his wife, with great tact in *Wallace Stevens: A Mythology of Self* (Berkeley: University of California Press, 1985); and "Stevens in Love: The Woman Won, the Woman Lost," *Essays in Literature* 48 (Spring 1981): 231-55.

5. This phrase is taken from Sandra M. Gilbert and Susan Gubar, *Madwoman in the Attic: The Woman Writer and the Nineteenth-Century Imagination* (New Haven: Yale University Press, 1979). See all of chapter 2, "Infection in the Sentence," for a lengthy discussion of the "ill" consequences of our largely phallocentric language (pp. 45-92).

6. With regard to Stevens' attitude toward the "High-Toned Old Christian Woman," see George Lensing's remark that "she is never permitted to present her side in the poem, though the speaker ironically pretends her to represent that side for her" ("'A High-Toned Old Christian Woman':

Wallace Stevens' Parable of the Supreme Fiction," *Notre Dame English Journal* 8 [Fall 1972]: 46).

7. Edna Kenton, "German Women and Feminism," *Trend* 7, no. 2 (May 1914): 147-52. See also "War and the French Working Woman," *New Republic,* June 1, 1918, 145-47; or "War and the Woman's College," *New Republic,* July 6, 1918, 285-87.

8. Louis Sherwin, "The Land of the Hen-Pecked," *Trend* 7, no. 4 (July 1914): 437-41; Cato Major, "Rule the Women or They'll Rule You," *Trend* 1, no. 2 (May 1911): 233-34.

9. Joan Kelly, *Women, History & Theory* (Chicago: University of Chicago Press, 1984), xix; and Sandra Gilbert, "Soldier's Heart: Literary Men, Literary Women, and the Great War," *Signs* 8 (1983): 422-50.

10. The first of these by H. D. is an especially anti-erotic poem; the second seems essentially a poem about rape; both are printed in *Glebe* 1, no. 5 (1914); Groff's poem appears in *Others* 2, no. 1 (1916): 121-22; Pound's are in *Others* 1, no. 5 (1915): 84-85; in Cannell's "Ikons," *Others* 2, no. 2 (1916): 149, woman's sexuality essentially equals man's *value* and *violence*; finally Burke's poem, addressed to a "Virgin," essentially enacts a verbal rape, *Others* 2, no. 3 (1916): 174.

11. Helen Hoyt, *Others* 1, no. 5 (191?): 79.

12. Titled the "Woman's Number," *Others* 3, no. 3 (1916).

13. An interesting point of comparison here is William Carlos Williams' essay, "For a New Magazine," in which he says that new literature should be "the machine of women and men" (thereby not only mentioning women as authors, but putting them first). Nevertheless, he goes on to say, much like Stevens, that "poetry is thus everything that a man of the greatest power could wish to encompass" (*Blues* 1, no. 2 [March 1929]: 30-32). Similarly, George Oppen asserts that Ezra Pound was, at least in the early years, "caught in the idea of being 'macho' though the word didn't exist at that time. He was going to be the pounding poet, the masculine poet" (Burton Hatlen and Tom Mandel, "Poetry and Politics: A Conversation with George and Mary Oppen," in *George Oppen: Man and Poet,* ed. Burton Hatlen [Orono: University of Maine, 1981], 27).

14. In this regard, see Edward Kessler, *Images of Wallace Stevens* (New York: Gordian Press, 1983), who finds that Crispin of "The Comedian as the Letter C" accepts his "masculine and feminine natures" late in the poem (p. 66), and who also argues that the androgynous nature of the "creative imagination" also informs the invocation of "Le Monocle de Mon Oncle" (p. 238 n. 15). In contrast, Frank Lentricchia interprets the possibly androgynous nature of the speaker in "Final Soliloquy of the Interior Paramour" as something much more suspect—"a self-sustaining bisexual unit" that is specifically *not* an "enhanced" individuation (*Ariel and the Police: Michel Foucault, William James, Wallace Stevens* [Madison: University of Wisconsin Press, 1988], 222-23).

15. Howard Baker, "Wallace Stevens and Other Poets," *Southern Review* 1 (Autumn 1935): 373-96. Frank Doggett and Susan Weston have both called attention to the influence of Jung on Stevens. See Doggett, *Stevens' Poetry of Thought* (Baltimore: Johns Hopkins University Press, 1966), 38-45; and Susan B. Weston, *Wallace Stevens: An Introduction to the Poetry* (New York: Columbia University Press, 1977).

16. Although Lentricchia suggests that such disturbing dislocations are largely a modernist malaise (see in particular p. 168), Kelly describes a similar pattern in the poetry of Dante: "She [Beatrice] remains shadowy and remote, for the focus of his poetry has shifted entirely to the subjective pole of love. It is the inner life, *his* inner life, that Dante objectifies" (p. 37). It may well be that such division of masculine identity, in particular the "divestment" of that which is perceived as the feminine, forms part of a larger pattern of poetic experience throughout Western history.

17. The first edition of *Ideas of Order* opened with "Sailing After Lunch," a poem that makes the possible spiritual content and intent of the first edition much more obvious. Just as the first edition (1935) was being published, however, Stevens suffered several well-known critical attacks, most of which condemned his lack of social awareness. (The most famous of these is Stanley Burnshaw's review of *Ideas of Order* in *New Masses* 17 [October 1, 1935]: 41-42.) The second edition, which begins with a new poem written after these reviews—that is, "Farewell to Florida"—might correctly be seen as Stevens' attempt to make his poetry more socially relevant.

18. Although some critics might suggest that the speaker of this poem is a female, I believe a male is much more consistent with the rest of Stevens' verse. As an interesting parallel, consider Lentricchia's (I think) faulty analysis of Stevens' early sketch in which a young man opens a picture of his sweetheart only to find it is an image of himself as an act in which the feminine image is "empathetically assumed," not "trivialized in macho perspective" (p. 222). Despite Lentricchia's dismissal of Sandra Gilbert and Susan Gubar, I do

not think that these critics would interpret this sketch in such a sympathetic way. The replacement of the female with the male image would rightly, I believe, signal an instance of total phallocentric mastery. Similarly, if the speaker of "Two Figures" *were* a female, we would have a poem of extreme empathy rather than of male mastering. Nevertheless, the latter possibility, that the female presence is silenced by masculine ruminations, seems much more consistent with the poetry of Stevens discussed thus far.

19. Thomas Walsh, *Concordance to Wallace Stevens* (University Park, Pa.: Pennsylvania State University Press, 1963). It is also interesting that, combined, forms of speaking and forms of voice appear 285 times in Stevens' corpus. Conversely, and very curiously, words for Stevens are almost never "written"—this term appears a mere 20 times, in fact.

20. "All Over Minnesota" appeared as the first section of "Primordia," published in *Soil* 1, no. 2 (January 1917): 76-78.

21. As a point of comparison for the climate of the times, see *Others: The Spectric School,* a celebrated hoax that contains a number of poems by the actually male "poetess" Elizah Hay, including "Spectrum of Mrs. X," "Of Mrs. Y," "Of Mrs. Z," and "Of Mrs. & So Forth," which intentionally parody the kinds of poems by Stevens I am discussing here. *Others* 3, no. 5 (1917): 10-11.

22. While there are many critics who have discussed "The Idea of Order at Key West" in such positive terms, see in particular, Marie Borroff, "Wallace Stevens: The World and the Poet," in *Wallace Stevens: A Collection of Critical Essays,* ed. M. Borroff (Englewood Cliffs, N.J.: Prentice-Hall, 1963), 9; and Linda Mizejewski, "Images of Woman in Wallace Stevens," *Thoth* 14 (1973-1974): 13-21.

23. I have discussed this aspect of Stevens' poetry at length in "Wallace Stevens: Poems Against His Climate," *Wallace Stevens Journal* 11, no. 2 (1987): 75-92.

24. See Lentricchia, 217.

25. In this regard, see Mary Arensberg, "'Golden Vacancies': Wallace Stevens' Problematics of Place and Presence," *Wallace Stevens Journal* 10, no. 1 (1986): 36-41, in which she discusses the usual figuration of the female in Stevens as an *absence.*

26. I am indebted to Frank Doggett and Dorothy Emerson for this observation. See "A Primer for Possibility for 'The Auroras of Autumn,'" *Wallace Stevens Journal* 13, no. 1 (1989): 53-66.

27. See Bates's *Wallace Stevens,* 277-79.

28. "Though there are poets undeniably greater than Stevens, and poets whom I love as well, he is the poet whose poems I would have written had I been the poet he was" (Helen Vendler, *Wallace Stevens: Words Chosen Out of Desire* [Knoxville: University of Tennessee Press, 1984], 3).

Anca Rosu (essay date 1995)

SOURCE: Rosu, Anca. "Sense, Nonsense, and the Magic Word." In *The Metaphysics of Sound in Wallace Stevens,* pp. 32-51. Tuscaloosa, Ala.: University of Alabama Press, 1995.

[*In the following essay, Rosu discusses the ways in which the sounds and words employed by Stevens can have the effect of an incantation, with the power of divorcing words from their accepted meanings.*]

The earliest comments on Wallace Stevens relate sound to nonsense in arguments that either directly compare him to Lewis Carroll[1] or attempt to demonstrate that nonsense is only an unfulfilled possibility, a matter of flirtation.[2] Some time later, Steven's flirtation with nonsense and his way of associating words on the basis of sound similarity began to be perceived as an unsuccessful effort to make language coincide with reality. Situated in the context of modernism, where imagist theories prevailed, Stevens's poetic performance appeared to some as one more attempt to make language do the impossible. J. Hillis Miller's initial appraisal of the poet's work is characteristic of that trend:

> A poem may start coherently enough, but as it progresses the poet becomes more and more exasperated with the distance between words and things. The language finally dissolves into incoherence and the reader faces words that are nonwords, a thick linguistic paste, like the splotches of paint on an expressionist canvas. By draining all referential meaning out of words Stevens hopes that they will become the thing they represent, or, even more radically, beyond onomatopoeia, that only the sound and appearance of the words will remain.[3]

Hillis Miller's haste to declare the poet's attempt a failure is motivated by his own skepticism about any poet's power to make words stand up as things, which is, in turn, rooted in the idea that language functions primarily as a means of representing reality. But this positivist view of language (Stevens sometimes calls it "realist") is precisely what comes under attack in Stevens's poetic performance, where not language but the conception that it is a reflection of the real is put to such a severe test that it naturally fails.

Yet this apparent failure need not lead to the conclusion that Stevens is inviting us to contemplate a collapse of communication. More recent criticism on Stevens has been probing his own views on language in order to explain the enigmatic character of his writing, the significance of his wordplay, or the sense of his resort to nonsense. J. B. Leggett, for instance, describes the poems in a manner not very different from Hillis Miller's, but he discerns a purpose behind Stevens's notorious obscurity:

> Frequently the poems establish antitheses in which clarity and simplicity are dismissed in favor of obscurity or nonsense. That which has become intellectualized, mastered, explicated is relegated to the junk heap, and the speaker's desire is directed toward that which is beyond the intellect, beyond direct articulation or paraphrase. It is as if the desired world were an obscure poem or song not yet understood, and the familiar world were the stale poem reduced to cliché by the very fact of its accessibility.[4]

Leggett seems to see Stevens's penchant for nonsense and obscurity as the expression of a desire to transcend the normal possibilities of language rather than a failure to exploit its capacity to represent.

The significance of Stevens's inclination to resort to nonsense in his poems is evident to critics who perceive the formal elements as expressive. Alison Rieke, for instance, rejects the idea that communication fails in Stevens: "The position that the poet's recourse to nonsense is symptomatic of a failed and flawed effort to describe the indescribable does not fully account for that which is comic and pleasurable in Stevens' engagement with language."[5] Eleanor Cook, who explores precisely the comic and pleasurable aspects of Stevens's language (without ever overlooking their seriousness), also defends the idea that what appears to be nonsense in his verse is actually a verbal gesture of no small significance. Cook's arguments are the more interesting, as she places Stevens in the context of literary tradition at a juncture between charm and riddle verse: "Personally and historically, he began to write at a time of transition from charm poetry to riddling poetry, from incantatory late-Victorian poetry, to modern, riddling poetry."[6] According to Cook, Stevens never quite decided between riddle and charm and practiced them both with equal success.

The distinction between charm and riddle verse belongs to Northrop Frye, and Eleanor Cook uses it to point out discursive differences: "Riddles tend to be visual and conceptual, charms tend to be aural and hypnotic."[7] This is an important distinction, as it also suggests two different sets of assumptions about the nature and functioning of language. Riddling is reminiscent of the representational function of language, although representation in this case is complicated by the hermetic or enigmatic features of the utterance. Charm, on the other hand, obliges one to perceive totally different qualities of language: its formal design in sound pattern as well as the power resulting from it.

Besides their formal characteristics, charms and incantations are distinguished by their purpose, which goes beyond communication. Charms are supposed to produce practical results, to heal, to make rain, or to rid us of evil spirit. Such a purpose implies a reversal of the relation between language and reality as we normally conceive of it. For instead of representing reality, and therefore being subordinated to it, charms create, and therefore master and control, a reality. This kind of reversal appealed to Stevens on different levels.

Jacqueline Brogan finds that Stevens shares in the medieval belief that language has an essential role in creation: "The medieval conviction that God's thoughts about creation and creation are connected by the Logos (and that our thoughts about the world and the world are connected by our words) is not essentially different from Stevens' suggestion that words not only 'create the world' but approach the 'living ideal.'"[8] In her book *Stanza My Stone*, Leonora Woodman has suggested a more than casual relationship between Stevens and hermeticism, a tradition that also gives a special power to language. Analyzing **"Large Man Reading,"** Woodman states: "Here, too, a similar possibility is entertained, guided equally by the assumption that poetic text prefigures the poetic 'life'—that, indeed, the text is the element from which 'life' springs."[9] Woodman also foregrounds the role of sound in the language of alchemy, hermeticism, and magic.

Sound pattern is in fact the element that operates the reversal of what we consider to be the normal relation between reality and language. It is therefore necessary to approach Stevens's sound-dominated poems bearing in mind that our usual assumptions about language and sense may have to yield to a different conception of what language can and cannot do. What Stevens's poems demand, in my view, is a change of the very assumptions on which meaning itself is understood. For the assumption that language's only function is to reflect "reality" is proved to have weak grounds in the poems that fail not only to represent reality, as it is commonly understood, but also to validate its sense. But not validating sense—the way we usually perceive it—is far from producing nonsense. Assuming forms similar to those of charms and incantations, many of his poems conjure up a reality instead of representing one. The dominance of sound in Stevens's poems operates thus a reversal of what we see as the normal relation between reality and language.

In what follows, I shall look at several poems in which the reversal of the relation reality/language is quite evident and in which the sound dominance achieves the intensity of verbal magic. In the course of my argument, I shall look with something like microscopic attentiveness at the operation of sound in Stevens's verse, and I will simply say at the outset that the method of reading exemplified in my analysis—what might be called a method of "unreading" followed by a *re*reading or reconstitution in terms of underlying sound patterns—is, I think, nothing other than the primary mode of comprehension demanded by the poems themselves. The unreading is the result of the failure to which a certain kind of discourse is brought by Stevens himself, and it is necessary, because it addresses the habits of a reader whom we have to imagine as the one the speakers of the poems address. Such a reader is defined by the very discursive strategies present in the poems, and s/he is therefore reconstructable as a function of discourse conventions. The *re*reading is required by the whole process of understanding, in which the renunciation of certain conventions and the adoption of others is the sole warrant of sense. My argument concerning the "metaphysics of sound" is, in effect, about the outcome of such a process of reading, about the manner in which sound works in Stevens to dissolve certain normative notions or schemes of reality while gesturing, ultimately, toward something that lies beyond them.

Many of Stevens's poems start with an apparently earnest attempt to construct a representation, for they are not explicitly lyrical but rather narrative or even argumentative. The narrative or argumentative setup creates expectations for an intelligible reference, for an accurate account of action, or for coherent argumentation. But most of the time the compliance to such expectations is quite illusory. Some of the poems evoke traditions and conventions that are mocked rather than honored, discredited rather than recognized. Once the convention within which words have a certain value has been compromised, words seem to become empty of meaning and may strike one as pure sound. **"Some Friends from Pascagoula,"** for instance, brings up such conventions in the form of traditional symbols placed in a parodic context:

> Tell me more of the eagle, Cotton,
> And you, black Sly,
> Tell me how he descended
> Out of the morning sky.

[CP [Collected Poems] 126]

Like many other poems by Stevens, **"Some Friends from Pascagoula"** seems to belong to a situational context that is left obscure. The prosodic structure of the stanza is reminiscent of a ballad with its regular rhythm, easy rhyme, and four lines' length. The opening exhortation also reminds one of folkloric narratives: "Tell me" implies the presence of the "singer of tales" and the historical or legendary preexistence of the story's material. The *Iliad* itself starts with a similar formula: "Chant, Goddess." *The Odyssey* comes even closer with "Tell me, Muse."

By virtue of this familiar formula, we are placed in a legendary or mythical realm, but its precise context would be difficult to identify, for this stanza evokes mixed mythologies. The eagle is a traditional heraldic symbol in some European countries, where it represents military or imperial glory, but it is also an element in American Indian mythology, where its rich symbolic value relates to the visionary and the divine. All these associations of symbols from the past first come to mind because of the ancient or medieval flavor of the opening formula, but on second thought, the eagle may stand out as a symbol of contemporary America too, as it gazes at us from mailboxes or the cover of *The American Heritage Dictionary*.

The ambiguity of the image gives rise to a special parodic effect. A more precise context would favor one image and exclude the others, but the possibility of getting all of them, alternately or at once, gives way to comic incongruities. The poem's beginning encourages the assumption that the eagle's image has a symbolic, although uncertain, value, for the speaker takes this image for granted and plans the poem as its extension: "Tell me *more* of the eagle." But this attempt at expanding or enriching the image compromises it as well as its symbolic value. Taken out of its proper context, the verbal image loses its power to signify: whatever the eagle stands for does not seem to be substantial. The significance of the symbol is unstable and dispersed rather than concentrated. The symbol itself has a certain autonomy that may easily be interpreted as mockery either of the reference or of the symbolic function. And the impression that this is a parody is only intensified in the lines that follow:

> Describe with deepened voice
> And noble imagery
> His slowly-falling round
> Down to the fishy sea.
>
> Here was a sovereign sight,
> Fit for a kinky clan.
> Tell me again of the point
> At which the flight began,

[CP 126]

The parodic intent becomes clear here, when the description points ironically to the supposed singer's manner, while ambiguity continues to dominate the poem. Knowledge of geography might disambiguate some lines, but it would create further ambiguities. An awareness of Pascagoula's position on the map, for instance, would make "the sea" a more precise and clear reference, and "fishy" could be read in its literal sense. Geography would also indicate an African-American population in the region and designate "Cotton" and "black Sly" as members of the "kinky clan." Geography is deliberately deemphasized, however, by being hinted at in the title and never mentioned again in the poem. Readers of Stevens are used to titles apparently disconnected from the poems' content. Moreover, "fishy" and "kinky" are placed so close to each other that the suggestion of dubiousness common to both their figurative senses makes the latter more probable than the literal. If nevertheless we accept that the poem is about some African-Americans, we would have to deal with the oddity of the symbolic suggestions of the "eagle" that reminds us first of other races. There would also be the cruel irony of calling African-Americans a "clan"—a word so perfectly echoing Klan—which would be hard to attribute to Stevens.[10]

The sum of such contradictions supports the idea that the poem is essentially parodic. But the target of the parody is less clearly defined than the parodic tone. The beginning would indicate that a story, in which the eagle is a symbol, is being parodied, but the second stanza concentrates more on the manner and the style of the singer. And the ambiguities point to a mockery of the language he uses rather than of his story. Meanwhile, the story itself becomes elusive and immaterial, for while one may suppose that it will be told later in the poem, "Tell me again" suggests that it has already been told, that it is either too well known or too unimportant to deserve our attention. Because the story is thus marginalized, the telling, the manner, and the style are of more consequence, stressing language at the expense of the narrative. The story's immateriality, as well as the direction of the parody toward the language itself, gives language a status equal to (if not higher than) events.

Beyond the obvious mockery, a more important change occurs at this stage. If it pointed to only one symbolic value—eagle as symbol of glory, for instance—the phrase could be considered univocal and semantically clear; but as its meaning is pluralized and thus destabilized, the reader's attention is directed to the materiality of the words. As their sense shifts in an unstable context, as neither the straight story nor its parody comes to a satisfactory ending, the words become present, opaque entities. At first, this transformation may occur as a result of the mocking tone that approaches nonsense. Yet "'Nonsense' is not quite the word for it," as William Pritchard observes, referring to Stevens's work, "but it is a preferable alternative to treating the poem as if it were a statement about or an attitude toward the real world we presumably share."[11] Pritchard here suggests that there is an alternative to sense other than nonsense. The materiality of the words gives them the potential to become meaningful in a different way. Such words seem to function as objects, whose specific properties make it possible for them to be invested with significance, in the way a magical object would. It is quite possible to read the poem as conjuring or incantation.

Because the power of the symbol seems to have been lost in derision, the reader is forced to return to the beginning, to start, perhaps, with the "real" eagle. This new and repeated reading may lead away from the mockery perceived the first time, because, freed from its current meaning, that is, from its depreciated symbolic value, as well as from the ambiguity the context created for it before, the eagle—now recognizable only as a word with symbolic potential—can become a receptacle of new meaning. The traditional usages have been exhausted, and this exhaustion may have liberated the words, for they seem to become clearer:

> Say how his heavy wings,
> Spread on the sun-bronzed air,
> Turned tip and tip away,
> Down to the sand, the glare
>
> Of the pine trees edging the sand,
> Dropping in sovereign rings
> Out of his fiery lair.
> Speak of the dazzling wings.

[*CP* 127]

Although this second part of the poem begins with virtually the same formula, "Say how" and relies on clichéd imagery, the speaker seems to intend to clarify. The slight hesitation of the rhythm gives the impression that this is a fresh start, as if he were having some difficulty fitting his thought into words. The rhythm is accomplished but with some effort. There is even an enjambment—a discordance between rhythm and syntax unusual for the folkloric form the speaker of this poem has adopted. If the first part looked like an imitation carried to the extreme of parody, the second one looks like an original making, a genuine creation.

In this second part of the poem, however, in spite of the expansion of its physical description, the eagle does not become a clearer, more visible image. The reason may be the fact that, within the unity of these two stanzas, the element of expressive effort—giving the impression that a representation is intended—also manifests itself as a return upon the same words. The semantic expansion of the first two lines, "Say how his heavy wings, / Spread on the sun-bronzed air" is restrained in the next line by a repetition, ostensibly meant to clarify the movement: "Turned *tip* and *tip* away." The stanza closes after this, the closure being reinforced by the rhyme of its final line.

At this point, the weakening semantic precision is in climactic conflict with the growing regularity of the sound. Although the rhyme of "glare" closes the stanza, the syntax creates a continuity with the next one, but continuity is not only syntactical here. "Of the pine trees edging the sand" echoes "the sand" from the previous stanza, thus forming another sound pattern, which overrides the previous one. The repetition also changes the semantic stress on the word. At first, "the sand" seems marginal and replaceable: the eagle could be falling on the land, on the grass, or on the sea for that matter. But when it is repeated, "the sand" becomes central, as if it were a special place where the eagle is supposed to land. No precise meaning can be assigned to it, for this suggested centrality offers not only one possibility but many. Placed in the center, the word exercises power, attracts interpretations, yet is ready not to radiate but rather to absorb meaning.

The repetitions of words and sounds, which seemed to mark the difficulty of the semantic expansion, grow into a pattern, which gives an air of aural self-containment and unity to the two stanzas. The last three lines emphasize this self-containment—the rhythm has become regular again; the rhyme is an almost total sound identity; and some words from the first part of the poem, now repeated, create the effect of an echo. The poem ends with its beginning formula, closing upon itself, as if tamed, mastered, and self-contained. The sound pattern of convention, which dominated the first part, was only temporarily lost, and it is now recovered with renewed energy.

What, then, has happened to the meaning of the poem? The semantic expansion of its second part seems to have been confined again by the dominance of the sound. The final impression, however, is that one can "see" the eagle that lacks a precise symbolic value but possesses the undeniable capacity to become a symbol. Its clarity as an image is mainly an illusion created by the self-contained quality of the language, for if we look more closely at this description of the "real" eagle, we notice that the image dissolves with the speaker's effort to make it clearer. As it details the eagle's physical features, the description gets caught in rhetoric: the image of the eagle in light gives rise to an analogy with light, and before long, there is no way to separate the eagle from light. Thus the eagle is literally dissolved in sunlight, and one would not be able to tell whether the "dazzling wings" belong to a real, physical eagle, or to an image made of light and its reflections, or to no image at all. The symbol has been compromised and emptied of meaning, in the first part of the poem, and now the word is free to absorb new significance, for its symbolic potential is regenerated when the power of the word's presence manifests itself as sound. This is no longer the eagle of worn-out heraldry, or the image from the mailboxes, but a new one that is ready to take on the significance of our ideals and aspirations.

In the verbal pattern that has just grown, with the eagle's symbolic potential regenerated, the new description may appear as a real "noble imagery" mainly because it sounds like one. The very play of memory, which permits the language to mock and discredit the symbol in the first part, makes it possible for the word to recover its force in the second. Words live their lives in human memory and are always reminiscent of their previous uses. This remembrance creates the mockery in the first place, for it evokes distant and uncertain contexts and generates incongruities. But the same mechanism of memory helps the word acquire meaningful power in the second part, where, in a recovered sound pattern, sounds echo each other and give a self-contained integrity to the text.

As in a magic formula or charm, the poem's meaning resides in its aural self-containment that can exert power. Reference has failed twice: the reference to the symbol was discredited by mockery, and the reference to the "real" eagle was lost in rhetorical indulgence. There is thus no way to recover the eagle left behind somewhere in a symbolic or sensory reality, but from the words' sound, from their newly found formula, a power is conjured and stands ready to generate reality. **"Some Friends from Pascagoula"** thus achieves a gradual detachment of the words from their accepted meaning.

Such detachment has two main consequences: on the one hand it attracts attention to the words' material presence, and on the other it enlightens us to the illusory nature of "reference" by demonstrating that meaning has actually been attached to words in the process of their use. The process in which words become capable of generating reality starts with a clear detachment from the meaning habitually assigned to them. Meaning appears to be the product of the history of the words' usage, which, in this case, is literary/folkloric convention. Their independence from the habitual usage, their readiness to take on reality, to actually generate it, makes Stevens's words similar to those of charms or incantations, for the eagle of his poem is not spoken about or referred to but rather conjured.

An even more evident verbal conjuring goes on in **"Ploughing on Sunday,"** a poem in which reference to action invites the reader to expect a sequence of events from the outset. Such expectations are encouraged even as they are subverted by the poem's grammar. The two declarative sentences that open the poem may seem, in the first instance, quite straightforward:

> The white cock's tail
> Tosses in the wind.
> The turkey-cock's tail
> Glitters in the sun.
>
> [*CP* 20]

This might well be the description of fowl on a farm, but there is here a grammatical detail that, while luring the reader into the narrative, lends it a kind of mystery, related especially to the context in which the little story is to be read. For instead of the customary indefinite articles, the main agent present on the scene (actually there may be two cocks, but the repetitive structure suggests two descriptions of the same one) is introduced with definite ones, and such introduction creates again the illusion of a context otherwise left obscure. The utterance appears incomplete and fragmentary because it breaks the conventions of a beginning, but its deficiency can alternatively be perceived as an attractive mystery. It is as if we had stumbled into a story whose telling had begun some time before. If the speaker referred to a farm and to its fowl, we wouldn't know it as intimately as he seems to. As readers, we seem to become an uninvited audience, estranged by the fact that nobody bothers to fill us in but at the same time attracted by the power of a verbal utterance that is seemingly constituted on solid grounds. And because the definite articles suggest that the cock is already known, one may think of some traditional symbolic meanings of the word by ascribing to it the value of a sexual pun or that of a biblical allusion or by placing it in some medieval literary context.

The second stanza, however, turns to a description of weather and may give another symbolic value to the cock, which can be interpreted as a magical sign of a storm:

> Water in the fields.
> The wind pours down.
> The feathers flare
> And bluster in the wind.

> [*CP* 20]

In just a few sentences, the context in which the poem's utterance is to be interpreted changes several times, multiplying the possibilities of interpretation. But when we have too many possibilities of interpretation, in effect we have none at all. For this reason the meaning of the poem becomes elusive, and communication seems to fail.

This sense of a failure of communication can only grow stronger with the exhortation that follows: "Remus, blow your horn!" Who is Remus? we may ask, and where did he come from? But like the cock in the opening of the poem, "Remus"—the name thrown in without introduction—may invite symbolic interpretations. Leonard and Wharton, for instance, interpret this stanza in the following way:

> These deceptively simple lines open onto a complex of allusion. The ploughman, like Nietzsche's white bull, ploughs the earth and bellows his exuberance. Celebrating work on the Sabbath, the ploughman is in company with Christ's radically freeing "It is lawful to do well on the sabbath days" (Matthew 12:12). Fittingly, the poem's "Remus" (literally "an oar," ploughlike and propelling) may be both the freed slave invented by Joel Chandler Harris to plough the soil of the rural South with homely fables and another Remus (like Christ, of virgin birth), co-founder of the "eternal" city of Rome.[12]

Planting the poem on firm philosophical ground is, however, only one possible interpretation, based on the conviction that Stevens was a philosophical poet. Yet at the time he wrote this poem, Stevens would never have been suspected of philosophical intentions. Frank Kermode, for instance, considered this poem a proof of Stevens's wild experimentation with rhythms in free verse.[13] And indeed the structure of the stanza suggests nonsense rather than symbolic sense. It ends quite arbitrarily with the same sentence that started it, and its repetitiveness makes it oddly symmetrical. The whole poem arranges itself in the way a dance or a musical piece is arranged, and one may consider this stanza and the two lines that open the next to be the center on which the poem pivots in its symmetry.

The poem loses sense because the form repeats itself, and the repetition threatens to become infinite:

> Tum-ti-tum,
> Ti-tum-tum-tum!
> The turkey-cock's tail
> Spreads to the sun.

> The white cock's tail
> Streams to the moon.
> Water in the fields.
> The wind pours down.

> [*CP* 20]

The "Tum-ti-tums" may go on forever, because there is no reason to stop, and once the speaker seems to have abandoned the rules of reason, the "end" does not look like any definite possibility. The symmetrical arrangement of the words has created a dominance of sound that, together with the repeated misdirection, the suggestion of infinite repetition, and the apparently outrageous references, creates the impression of a loss of sense. "Tum-ti-tum / Ti-tum-tum-tum" seems to confirm that loss, reducing discourse to the imitation of pure rhythm. Even more than in **"Some Friends from Pascagoula,"** the words become so detached from their habitual meaning that the "Tum-ti-tum" sounds do not appear to be very different from the other "meaningful" words present in the poem.

There should be, however, another possible way to make sense out of the poem's apparent incoherence. As shown above, the impression of nonsense is produced mainly by the fact that our expectations for the poem are formed in an unstable context. The poem is hard to read for what it literally says, for its meaning greatly depends on the context of its utterance, a context at which we can only guess. To borrow Wittgenstein's terminology, as the meaning of the words is their "use" in a certain language "game," the trouble here is that we, as readers, are not completely aware of the game we are playing. Meaning depends on a certain frame, on a set of rules according to which sense can constitute itself. We call "sense" that which respects the rules and stays within the game, whereas we consider "non-sense" everything that is left out. But if the rules are suddenly changed, that which looked meaningless within one game may become meaningful in the newly created configuration. There is a strong possibility that the features of the poem that make it seem nonsensical in one "game" might make sense in another and that our difficulty should be caused by the shifting of rules in the middle of the initial game.

Because their precise context is missing, one tends to give the words an extra dimension, to project their significance beyond what they actually say. Attention is, at the same time, drawn to the words' arrangement in a quasi-ritual movement. This movement forms a distinct sound pattern that grows with the symmetrical repetitions of words or phrases. Some of the repetitions seem to be motivated by the desire to make the utterance more precise, as in "I am *ploughing* on Sunday, / *Ploughing* North America," but they soon integrate a pattern, and the semantic precision becomes an indifferent matter. At the "Tum-ti-tum" point, sense seems to have been completely abandoned, but we have to observe that the line, in its context, bears some significance, for it indicates the basic trochaic rhythm— with the final syllable dropped, as is usual—of lines such as "Tosses in the wind," "Water in the fields," or "Remus, blow your horn!" "Ti-tum-tum-tum," on the other hand, gives us the strong anomalous pattern of complete lines such as "The white cock's tail" or "The wind pours down." The nonsense lines actually stand at the center of the poem and rhythmically contain it altogether. It is as if the speaker were trying to teach us to listen to the poem.

After it culminates in pure rhythmic sound, the poem closes with a repetition of elements from its own beginning. The impression that the words have some extra dimension, some significance that grows out of them rather than being left behind somewhere in "reality" is only increased by this sound pattern. For it is not an entirely conventional pattern, something that the poet would have known and decided to follow, but a nascent one, some form that grows. The direction toward a sound pattern seems first to overwhelm the sense, but soon it grows so intense that the poem becomes incantatory. Because of the extra dimension acquired from their contextual indeterminacy, the words seem not to refer to anything but rather to have a material reality of their own. And the feeling of order to which their sound pattern gives rise makes their own "reality" powerfully present.

The grammar that gives the words an extra dimension, the power of the sound pattern, and the impression of sense with which one is left in spite of being unable to decode the meaning of the utterance indicate a change

in the discursive mode. The resulting discourse may be called "poetic" but on different grounds from the conventional, for Stevens departs from the tradition of poetry in many ways. Traditional prosody is here enhanced by additional patterning to achieve an even more powerful effect that is comparable to the effect of an incantation or a magic spell. For the pattern acts upon us, impresses us beyond control, and language becomes significant by virtue of this action. We can no longer be interested in what the words represent, for we must perceive their action, and their "meaning" becomes closer to that of magic:

> Magic is not built up in the narrative style; it does not serve to communicate ideas from one person to another; it does not purport to contain a consecutive, consistent meaning. It is an instrument serving special purposes, intended for the exercise of man's specific power over things, and *its meaning,* giving this word a wider sense, can be understood only in correlation to this aim. It will not be therefore a meaning of logically or topically concatenated ideas, but of expressions fitting into one another and into the whole, according to what could be called a magical order of thinking, or perhaps more correctly, a magical order of expressing, of launching words towards their aim.[14]

Incantation, magic, conjuring—different language games altogether, far beyond common sense and certainly beyond nonsense—give essentially another value to language. According to our commonsense rules, we conceive of language in the following way: things are real, and we perceive them and give them names that refer to them or evoke them. Significance does not go anywhere beyond things, for even the abstractions are derived from things. For this reason, perhaps, we give great attention to things and regard understanding as a sort of unpacking of the thing. But magic discourse is different in that the relation between language and reality changes: the thing is not unveiled but created by the magic word. Malinowski's description of magic discourse may be instrumental in defining Stevens's poetic mode here, for his poems, like verbal magic, privilege sound over sense in a special way. The privilege given to sound changes the role of language from that of a means of representation to that of a generator of reality. The action of conjuring may be the best example and at the same time a metaphor of a discursive mode characterized by a dominance of sound.

Malinowski's description of magic discourse also reveals the differences between magic and commonsense speech, on the one hand, and between magic and nonsense on the other. Unlike commonsense language, magic language does not aim at a usual communication, but it exercises power, and unlike nonsense, it does not break rules programmatically, but it follows its own. Nonsense is a play against sense, a reversal of values,[15] whereas magic operates in a different system altogether. In magic or conjuring, words do not follow things, as we believe they do in our ordinary speech; on the contrary, things gain reality because of the words. The conjuring word is so much more than the referring word: it has the thing at its command rather than serving as its sign. Compared to the magic word, the referring one looks like a debasement. And if such debased words can be reduced to the state of hollow sound, sound without meaning, in magic words such emptiness would be inconceivable. The meaning of magic words is their fulfillment in reality, a fulfillment that is made possible by the power of their sound, which lies at the root of meaning rather than playing its opposite.

Evidently Stevens's poem cannot literally be a magic spell or have the meaning of one, for such meaning would not be possible outside its proper cultural context. In his description of magic, Malinowski stresses the fact that the natives' beliefs about and perception of language play an important role in the "meaning" of the magic utterance. The magic formula would not have the same effect on an audience that does not share such beliefs. For this reason we cannot identify Stevens's poem as a magical spell, although it is technically close to one. The poem relies on our own sense of language, on our rules of inferring representations to change our motivation in reading.

If by some extraordinary chance, the natives whose magic Malinowski describes knew English and came across Stevens's poem, they would certainly take it for a spell, because its form, which we may have identified as "story," is actually closer to that of a magic formula. But because we are not so conversant with magic, or just because we do not expect it here, our involvement in reading goes beyond the recognition of a form. Consciously or unconsciously, we begin to reverse the relation between reality and language. From the secondary, subservient role, the latter takes the lead, and the reality of the things is the one that follows, a mere consequence of the words' power. For while the story stalls, and our expectations remain unsatisfied, our attention must turn to the sound, as we remain compelled to listen, not because we want to find out what happened, for the line of the story is lost, but perhaps because we are under a special kind of spell. And I take this to be the "meaning" of the poem: this event, this change of purpose that, no matter what we expect to begin with, takes place in our reading attitude. The whole process of reading is thus part of the poem's "meaning."

A language of generative power similar to that of verbal magic seems to be the purpose of the poet's endeavor, and Stevens can sometimes declare such purpose explicitly. In **"Certain Phenomena of Sound,"** he "considers speech" and its power to generate rather than reflect reality. Significantly, as the language becomes the origin of things, it manifests itself as sound rather than as sense:

> The Roamer is a voice taller than the redwoods,
>
> Engaged in the most prolific narrative,
> *A sound producing the things that are spoken.*

[CP 287, emphasis added]

In part 3 of the same poem, the human beings themselves are endowed with reality by the language that literally speaks them:

> Then I, Semiramide, dark-syllabled,
> Contrasting our two names, considered speech.
> You were created of your name, the word
> Is that of which you were the personage.
> *There is no life except in the word of it.*

[CP 287, emphasis added]

The power of language to generate rather than reflect reality emerges thus in the very process of reading Stevens's sound-dominated, magiclike poems. As quasi-verbal magic, a poem may take the form of a gesture of domination. An example of such an assertive gesture, of an uninhibited exercise of power through language is the famous **"Anecdote of the Jar."**

> I placed a jar in Tennessee,
> And round it was, upon a hill.
> It made the slovenly wilderness
> Surround that hill.
>
> The wilderness rose up to it,
> And sprawled around, no longer wild.
> The jar was round upon the ground
> And tall and of a port in air.
>
> It took dominion everywhere.
> The jar was grey and bare.
> It did not give of bird or bush,
> Like nothing else in Tennessee.

[CP 76]

It is difficult to look at the **"Anecdote of the Jar,"** "over which an implausible amount of ink has been spilled"[16] with a fresh critical interest. But perhaps the inquisitive, and sometimes exaggerated, attention that critics have devoted to this poem is just a proof of its compelling magic. The **"Anecdote"** is intriguing, as I see it, because it achieves an almost ideal balance between the play against the reader's expectations and the patterning of sound, which makes the poem similar to a charm or magic spell.

Most of the critics consider the jar and the Tennessee landscape in which it is placed as two opposite poles. Either the jar represents imagination and Tennessee is the reality, which it modifies, or the jar represents reason (intellect), which spoils the beauty of the nature symbolized by Tennessee, or the jar is order as opposed to Tennessee, which is the wild, or chaos, and so forth. Yet as some other critics observe, the semantics of the poem does not seem to justify this opposition, for if the wilderness is *slovenly,* the jar, in its turn, is *grey and bare,* qualities that would not exactly recommend it as an aesthetic object.[17] Moreover, the jar does not seem to be in disharmony with the landscape; it just modifies it, nature showing itself willing to comply with the jar's mysterious power.

We may wonder, then, why so many critics, and probably many more readers, remain so keen on this opposition. One reason may be that the two elements may be considered at least potential opposites, even if they integrate so perfectly in the poem. Besides, the jar's oddity in the context is bound to attract attention. For its literary context rejects it as rapidly as the wilderness accepts it, and the reader may find that the easiest way to fit it in is to resort to a symbolic interpretation, which practically changes the meaning of the word. Therefore, critics invoke a quality of the jar that makes it a potential symbol: it is man-made, an artifact, representative of man's creative power or intelligence. As such, it can be set against the forces that oppose man's endeavors, the forces of a nature that resists human activity. Parenthetically, we may notice that critics do not (with the exception, perhaps, of Roy Harvey Pearce, who thinks it is a Mason jar)[18] invoke the jar's capacity to contain pickles, preserves, or cookies, and its utter futility after it had been emptied thereof. Such unpoetic connections would disqualify the jar as symbol, although they might support a parodic interpretation of the poem. The possibility is worth considering that the jar may actually be a very successful spoof of Keats's Grecian urn—another object of the jar kind—which probably fulfilled the same functions in its own time but, given the state of technology, was certainly discarded less often than contemporary jars are. But there may be a more serious reason for any critic to perceive an opposition, the tension of a confrontation, for such tension pervades the whole poem, although it is not explicit in its semantics.

The **"Anecdote of the Jar"** best exemplifies Eleanor Cook's pronouncement that Stevens could never quite commit himself to either riddle or charm poetry but most often combined both.[19] Frank Lentricchia trusts the title of the poem when he places it in the genre of the anecdote, but he also remarks that Stevens's are "cryptically crafted, riddle-like anecdotes."[20] In all its riddling (therefore conceptual) quality, the poem never fails to impress our ear. Lentricchia calls the poem an "aural imperialist."[21] William Bevis is even disposed to hear in the poem the arrangement of a musical piece.[22] But the resemblance to music (of the classical kind) is less intense, I think, than the hint of magic mongering. The relation of this poem to magic has been suggested by Leonora Woodman, who discovered a possible source for Stevens's inspiration in a passage from Jung describing magical practices.[23] Although Woodman's explana-

tion demystifies the poem, which thus contextualized begins to make literal sense, the possibility of perceiving it as a charm remains one of the most attractive ways of reading the **"Anecdote of the Jar."**

As the title says, it is a little story, an "anecdote" that revolves around an event. Like all Stevens's anecdotes, Lentricchia insists,[24] this poem strongly suggests a situational context that it does not reveal. Nevertheless the actual description of the event looks straightforward enough: the wilderness changes its shape in order to accommodate the jar, and the jar, in its turn, transforms itself into some kind of ugly, but dignified object. This clearly depicted event, however, does not make much sense because of the lack of a real cause. One may accept the rather sudden transformation of nature, the unexplained dignity of the jar, but one may not easily give up the question of why the speaker places this jar in Tennessee after all. The motivation of a human action is the primary interest in a narrative or anecdote, so that, by not declaring it, this poem frustrates one's basic expectations. The placing of the jar is a totally arbitrary gesture, as is also the choice of Tennessee over a thousand other places. Yes, we know that Stevens traveled to Tennessee, that he may have seen a jar when he did so, but there is no specific quality of "Tennessee" mentioned in the poem to make it a realistic locale. Lentricchia's speculation that Tennessee may have been chosen because of the echo of an Indian place name, Tanasi, is by his own admission unfounded, for the name remains arbitrary (why not Manhattan?) even as its intriguing presence in the poem invites historical connections. Once again, Stevens faces his reader with a lack of appropriate context, which renders the reference partially obscure and for that reason endows the words with an extra dimension. The mystery of the speaker's motivation is a vacuum of sense that perpetually lures one to guess about it. Consequently, the event described—the transformation of nature in the presence of the jar—although fairly clear in its limited context remains mysterious as it returns us to the unmotivated gesture that started it.

The whole poem is like a circle described around the jar, and it may literally be so, since the action is one of "surrounding," and the repetition of "round" and several of its variants creates a sound dominance that neither critics nor casual readers can fail to notice:

> I placed a jar in Tennessee,
> And *round* it was, upon a hill.
> It made the slovenly wilderness
> *Surround* that hill.
>
> The wilderness rose up to it,
> And sprawled *around,* no longer wild.
> The jar was *round* upon the *ground*
> And tall and of a port in air.
>
> [*CP* 76, emphasis added]

The poem thus constructs itself around the jar, literally surrounding it; and it makes sense only in reference to the jar—the object whose presence there is precisely the element that does not seem to make sense. Like the poems mentioned before, the **"Anecdote"** threatens a loss of its sense, which is kept in a precarious balance only by its curious "surrounding" movement, a movement that is largely the effect of sound.

The poem has a powerful rhythm, although it is far from being a conventional one, and its elegant symmetry strikes one from the beginning. As Samuel French Morse observes, "the neat quatrains and subtly manipulated consonance create an effect of symmetry without actually adhering to any fixed pattern."[25]

This effect of symmetry may result from the textual repetition of the words, for "round," with its variants and its rhyme in "ground," is not the only repeated word. While we try to make sense out of the poem, these repetitions may appear to be a hindrance. It seems that the speaker is not sure that we get his meaning and unnecessarily emphasizes some words. For instance, "upon a hill" in the second line is recalled for us in the fourth, "Surround *that hill,*" as if, afraid we have forgotten, the speaker wanted to remind us of it. The "wilderness" from line 3 reappears in line 5 and is "no longer wild" in line 6. And finally, the poem ends, symmetrically coming back to the initial "Tennessee," and induces us, again, to wonder at the motivation of this choice: why Tennessee? "That hill" could have been anywhere. But in spite of all its tantalizing questions, the poem seems perfect in its symmetry, and given the option, we may not want to change a word of it, simply because it "sounds" all right.

The dominance of the sound, the symmetry, and the repetitions make the poem sound like a magic spell, whose power one may accept without questioning its meaning. And perhaps the most important element of this similarity to magic is the gesture that the opening line describes and at the same time performs: "I placed a jar in Tennessee." Taking the liberty to say it is as arbitrary a gesture as the action that the line describes, a gesture of exerting power just like the lines that sometimes open magic spells and do nothing but "simply describe what the magician is doing."[26] This gesture of exerting power may seem exaggerated, given that, as a magic object, the jar may look ridiculous, if not grotesque. This comic potential, however, as well as the potential for nonsense, is never achieved. Samuel French Morse intuitively feels the extra dimension that the sense of the poem can acquire: "The deliberately 'commonplace guise,' like the comic magnification of a trivial gesture, is a disguise, for in professing or seeming to profess that it is a kind of joke, the poem becomes something more."[27]

Paradoxically, the jar achieves its "magical" purpose precisely because it is an unlikely magical object. All we know about magic is related to stories, fairy tales, that belong to some indeterminate, remote past. We cannot expect that an object from our kitchen might serve magical purposes. And the magic here is not in the object but rather "in the word of it." For this poem, like the others before it, makes sense by appealing to our normal way of inferring meaning in language, by exploiting our expectations. If the speaker had selected a more likely object and made his speech more closely similar to a spell, the effect would have been lost on the audience. The poem may have been *recognized* as the imitation of a spell but would not have exerted any power on us, modern readers liberated from superstition. But the odd jar, which even after the poem is over "would not declare itself" (*CP* 19) as the "song" from another poem by Stevens, performs the role of a magic object to perfection. For every time we read the poem, we are under its spell, and whatever symbolic dimensions we attribute to it, we remain tantalized by its elusive meaning. Ascribing symbolic dimensions may be a sort of defense we put up when faced with such mysteries.

In another "magical" aspect, the poem is an incentive to an action of mastering nature; it opposes the human to the nonhuman just like magic, which "is essentially the assertion of man's intrinsic power over nature."[28] And it is perhaps the tension of this confrontation that we feel as an opposition in the poem when, going by our usual routes of interpretation, we attribute symbolic value to the jar and to the landscape that it comes to dominate. But the actual opposition lies, rather, between the voice that speaks, between the human will that imposes itself to the world, and the reality, or the nature it addresses with the sole purpose of appropriating it.

And although this effect may seem unexpected in a poem, its power lies in its literal sense, the sense that threatens to be lost with the dominance of sound, rather than in the possible symbolic interpretation. For a precisely decoded symbolic value would create the possibility that interpretation could be univocal and thus restrain the energy that words possess. But as the numerous critical appraisals of the poem prove, interpretation is an endless possibility here. The symbolic value would make words transparent, whereas the literal sense allows words to remain opaque and to *mean* through their function rather than through reference.

Meaning is brought to the jar rather than discovered to be there, and this potential tips the balance of power between the "real" and the humanly significant object in favor of the latter. The arbitrariness of the choice plays an important part in this balance of power. For to exert a power equal to that of magic, to perform the appropriation of nature by the human will, and no less to put us readers under its spell, the jar must be no more than a jar, a trivial object whose choice itself can only be an arbitrary gesture, meaningful solely as an exercise of power. Frank Lentricchia suggests that the power exercised in or rather by the poem is part of Stevens's "politics of lyricism" determined by the "necessity of forsaking action and the genre of action—story telling—in favor of aesthetics, praise's ultimate awestruck medium."[29] But aestheticism, the subtle refinement of language, translates for Stevens into another kind of action that, although only verbal, exerts the authority of action proper.

Lentricchia also remarks that the sound of the poem is precisely the element that makes it unsuitable for either formalist or structuralist reading, and without noticing the poem's similarity to verbal magic, he points to its quality as a cultural artifact, which functions both as an expression of the culture and as a formative agent of it. The jar comes to express, in complicated and indirect ways, the spirit of America, and Lentricchia quotes Michael Herr, who alludes to it in a commentary on events taking place during the Vietnam war: "Once it was all locked in place, Khe Sanh became like the planted jar in Wallace Stevens's poem. It took dominion everywhere."[30] In an exemplary way, Lentricchia's connection comes to prove not only the "magic" of the poem but also the capacity of its language to gather meaning and to dominate reality. For the aestheticism that Lentricchia notes in Stevens is not an isolating retreat from reality but an action in its own right, a verbal gesture of unmistakable authority.

The "magic" structure appears in Wallace Stevens's poetry quite frequently, but the poems completely structured in this way are rare. Most often, the verbal magic is only a stage toward achieving a language free of the obligation to maintain its referential function, its conformity to empirical reality. Through the technique of a quasi-verbal magic, the poet demonstrates that language does not have to be representational and liberates the speaker from the task of constructing either stories or arguments, so that he is free to exert his linguistic imagination. After going through the exercise of sound, language proves its dominant role in relation to reality and is able to extend reality's domain beyond the physical. The landscape, unrepresented and undescribed, becomes a landscape of the mind. **"Metaphors of a Magnifico"** is a good example of such transformation, for its initial quasi-philosophical reasoning is soon caught in a pattern of sound that dominates and even displaces its sense, and its refrain comes as a self-critical remark:

> Twenty men crossing a bridge,
> Into a village,
> Are twenty men crossing twenty bridges,

> Into twenty villages,
> Or one man
> Crossing a single bridge into a village.

> This is old song
> That will not declare itself. . . .

> [*CP* 19]

As the poem develops, tautology comes in as an escape from the ambition, frustrated as if by impossibility, to construct an argument. Margaret Peterson demystifies the poem by showing that its line of argumentation was inspired by William James. In her view, it is a parody of philosophical argument in which the ending nonsense—the fact that the song "will not declare itself"—is a way of showing the weakness of this type of reasoning.[31] The sound pattern of the poem cannot be dismissed as pure parody, however, and I must agree with James Guetti that the poem, "'will not declare itself' not merely because as a problem it is too difficult but because . . . it has repeated in the imagination so long that it cannot 'declare': because it is 'song,' and song declares nothing. And so, though it is 'certain as meaning,' it is 'certain' in a very different way from 'meaning.'"[32]

The language of this poem literally closes upon itself and diverts its generative power from the task of arguing to that of achieving a pattern, and tautology appears as the only way to make sense. And only after language has been thus liberated from its representational/argumentative function, an image arises:

> The boots of the men clump
> On the boards of the bridge.
> The first white wall of the village
> Rises through fruit-trees.

> [*CP* 19]

This is a perfectly clear image, the clearer for all the tautological sound pattern that preceded it, but what is its sense? For it is an image that registers some kind of reality, which grows in the imaginative space of the mind without apparent purpose. It is not part of anything, for neither argument nor story can use it, and the reader may share the speaker's confusion: "Of what was I thinking?" But the power of this apparently senseless image is shown by the fact that it persists even after the speaker has noticed that "the meaning escapes": "The first white wall of the village . . . / The fruit-trees" look like a glimpse into the metaphysical, a fragment of a reality beyond the reach of reason.

Such glimpses are made possible by Stevens's verbal magic, a special use of sound effect to enrich language and make it more powerful than reality. Verbal magic is not merely a technique but a different discursive mode based on radically different assumptions about language and about the relation between language and reality.

And the similarity between Stevens's verse and magic is not purely technical either, for it consists, beyond the devices that can be noticed on the surface, in a change of assumptions about the function of language. It is evident that verbal magic is not Stevens's final purpose but a stage toward the discovery of a discourse with a certain specificity, determined by certain epistemological and ontological assumptions. Stevens's explorations into language reach toward a poetic domain that, although based in language, is not exclusively confined to it but expands into the larger area of human existence and cognition.

Notes

1. Randall Jarrell, "Reflections on Wallace Stevens," *Partisan Review* 18 (1952), reprinted in *Wallace Stevens: A Critical Anthology,* ed. Irvin Ehrenpreis (Baltimore: Penguin Books, 1972), 199-210.

2. R. P. Blackmur, "Examples of Wallace Stevens," *Hound and Horn* 5 (1932), reprinted in *Wallace Stevens: A Critical Anthology,* ed. Ehrenpreis, 59-86.

3. J. Hillis Miller, *Poets of Reality: Six Twentieth Century Writers* (Forge Village, Mass.: Harvard University Press, 1965; reprint, New York: Atheneum, 1974), 252.

4. J. B. Leggett, *Wallace Stevens and Poetic Theory: Conceiving the Supreme Fiction* (Chapel Hill: University of North Carolina Press, 1987), 119-20.

5. Alison Rieke, *The Senses of Nonsense* (Iowa City: University of Iowa Press, 1992), 95.

6. Eleanor Cook, *Poetry, Word-Play, and World-War in Wallace Stevens* (Princeton: Princeton University Press, 1988), 17.

7. Ibid., 16-17.

8. Jacqueline Brogan, *Stevens and Simile: A Theory of Language* (Princeton: Princeton University Press, 1986), 60.

9. Leonora Woodman, *Stanza My Stone: Wallace Stevens and the Hermetic Tradition* (West Lafayette, Ind.: Purdue University Press, 1983), 77.

10. Stevens's racism, of which there are proofs both in his poems and in the description of his behavior by contemporaries, is not of an aggressive nature—nothing resembling the attitude of extremists in his time. He does take the derogatory terms that designate African Americans for granted and never questions their effect on other people. Peter Brazeau in *Parts of a World: Wallace Stevens Remembered: An Oral Biography* (New York: Random House, 1983) collected testimony about Stevens's indifference to I. L. Salomon's remark that the title of "Like Decorations in a Nigger Cemetery" was offensive (133) as well as about the casualness with which the poet called Gwendolyn Brooks a "coon" (196). John Rogers (later a professor of black history at the University of Hartford), however, remembered Stevens as having behaved respectfully and deferentially to Rogers, who worked in the same office as a "manservant."

11. William H. Pritchard, *Lives of the Modern Poets* (New York: Oxford University Press, 1980), 216.

12. J. S. Leonard and C. E. Wharton, *The Fluent Mundo: Wallace Stevens and the Structure of Reality* (Athens: University of Georgia Press, 1988), 115.

13. Frank Kermode, "'Harmonium': Wallace Stevens," in *Wallace Stevens: A Critical Anthology,* ed. Ehrenpreis, 235.

14. Bronislaw Malinowski, *Argonauts of the Western Pacific* (New York: E. P. Dutton, 1961), 432.

15. See Susan Stewart, *Nonsense: Aspects of Intertextuality in Folklore and Literature* (Baltimore: Johns Hopkins University Press, 1979).

16. Samuel French Morse, *Wallace Stevens: Life as Poetry* (New York: Western Publishing, 1970), 90.

17. See Yvor Winters's criticism of Stanley P. Chase and Howard Baker in "Wallace Stevens; or, the Hedonist's Progress" (1943), reprinted in *Wallace Stevens: A Critical Anthology,* ed. Ehrenpreis, 120-42.

18. Roy Harvey Pearce, *The Continuity of American Poetry* (Princeton: Princeton University Press, 1961), 381. Pearce's intuition is confirmed by Glen MacLeod in *Wallace Stevens and Modern Art: From the Armory Show to Abstract Expressionism* (New Haven: Yale University Press, 1993), 22-23. MacLeod has traced the real jar and provides a picture of it with the word "Dominion" inscribed on the front.

19. Cook, *Poetry, Word-Play, and Word-War,* 17.

20. Frank Lentricchia, *Ariel and the Police: Michel Foucault, William James, Wallace Stevens* (Madison: University of Wisconsin Press, 1988), 7.

21. Lentricchia, *Ariel and the Police,* 11.

22. William W. Bevis, *Mind of Winter: Wallace Stevens, Meditation, and Literature* (Pittsburgh: University of Pittsburgh Press, 1988), 268.

23. Woodman, *Stanza My Stone,* 131-32.

24. Lentricchia, *Ariel and the Police*, 7.

25. Morse, *Wallace Stevens: Life as Poetry*, 92.

26. Malinowski, *Argonauts of the Western Pacific*, 451.

27. Morse, *Wallace Stevens: Life as Poetry*, 92.

28. Malinowski, *Argonauts of the Western Pacific*, 401.

29. Lentricchia, *Ariel and the Police*, 27.

30. Ibid., 20.

31. Margaret Peterson, *Wallace Stevens and the Idealist Tradition* (Ann Arbor: UMI Research Press, 1983), 102-103.

32. James Guetti, *Word-Music: The Aesthetic Aspect of Narrative Fiction* (New Brunswick, N.J.: Rutgers University Press, 1980), 38.

Douglas Mao (essay date 2000)

SOURCE: Mao, Douglas. "Wallace Stevens for the Millennium: The Spectacle of Enjoyment." *Southwest Review* 85, no. 1 (2000): 10-33.

[*In the following essay, Mao presents his argument that Stevens is a particularly relevant poet for the close of the millennium.*]

The question this essay asks is, "What can Wallace Stevens and the end of the millennium tell us about each other?" Or: "What kind of dialogue might go on between Wallace Stevens, dead more than forty years, and our current historical moment?" Or, transposed into yet a third register: "What are some of the meanings of Wallace Stevens, Cold War poet, for the post-Cold War United States?"

The first and last of these questions are linked by the second more than merely contingently, of course. In asking about the end of the cold war and the end of the millennium in the same breath, I'm doing more than nodding to the fact that the two happen to have occurred at around the same time. I'm also acknowledging that a year numerically magnetic for apocalyptism finds itself following on the heels of another spectacular ending, one that came too far in advance to allow for identification with the millennial turn, but too late not to steal some of the latter's thunder. And I'm also, as it happens, trying to address my own surprise that the end of this millennium hasn't yet seemed more explosively millenarian—even in the United States, a country whose richness in technologies of dissemination and poverty in skepticism would seem to make it especially ripe for this kind of hysteria.

There has been plenty of apocalyptism in some quarters, to be sure. The Heaven's Gate group, whose syncretism of extraterrestrial and Christian mythologies inspired its collective suicide in 1997, was profoundly fascinated by the imminence of 2000, as are numerous NRMs (new religious movements) still in existence—over a thousand, by some estimates. The Association for Research and Enlightenment, founded in 1931 to carry on the work of psychic Edgar Cayce, publishes an online journal called *The New Millennium* in which Cayce's murky predictions on geological upheaval rub elbows with sober reminders that "[a]pocalyptic idealism expressed politically as a simplified 'good' and 'bad' peoples [*sic*] has had devastating consequences (*e.g.*, fascism)." Anyone not already in an underground shelter, meanwhile, has grown weary of hearing about Y2K: a friend in the Boston area reports several of his acquaintances hoarding food and water in anticipation of the fatal click to 00, and subscribers to the website www.Y2KSupply.com (self-proclaimed leader in the online "Y2K preparedness industry") are offered product reviews conducive to doing same, as well as tips on "how to build your own crop-maximizing food growing system." At *Freedom Works*, the home page of House Majority Leader Dick Armey, you can find an online newsletter called *The Year 2000: Are You Ready?*; the microsoft.com search page will return thirty hits if you ask for sites showing not just "millennium bug," "Y2K," or "2000," but all three; and the Metropolitan State College of Denver has jocularly packaged its media guide as a "Y2K Expert Manual," bound in a camouflage cover.

In spite of this commotion, however, I find myself surprised—meaning relieved—that millennial fever has not been bigger, cooler, and weirder (at least not as I write this, in the last months of 1999). By this I mean not only that few people I know personally seem unduly alarmed or even excited by the approach of 2000, but also that millennial craziness as such has infiltrated no official discourse either as an approved mode of thinking or as a high-priority threat. On the contrary: it has been more or less fully peripheralized by the press, the government, Hollywood, the academy, and other traditional loci of authority, which is to say that it has not figured as much more than a human-interest curiosity in the life of the ordinary American constructed by these apparatuses as their imaginary audience and constituency. On the side of religious apocalyptism, this limitableness clearly owes a good deal to larger organizations' recognition that precise dating comports poorly with the need to maintain a membership base: so far, dramatic predictions of radical upheaval have come only from groups small enough to allow for outright journalistic dismissal. Even the dissemination of Y2K anxiety, however, has had a managed quality about it: reassurances of correctability emerged as soon as the problem was announced, and by now the standard line is that most corporate and governmental bodies will be in full "compliance" with bug-defeating guidelines by the date itself. From the point of view of 1999's end, the phenomenon seems a lesson in how levelheadedness is often as profitable a form of hype as hysteria, not to mention a virtual necessity for a press that takes the containment of panic to be one of its responsibilities.

Quite apart from this restabilizing, however, Millennium Bug worry strikes me, as it has struck many others, as low-key, domestic, and—dare one say it?—bourgeois in its very nature. For it's not only that Y2K predicts anarchy loosed by a simple design flaw rather than divine intervention or revolutionary rage; it's also that, at bottom, it's a phenomenon of prudence rather than extravagance. Whatever bug-phobia reveals about beliefs on government control, corporate power, technology, globalization, or numbers themselves, it announces most distinctly that the prevailing American mood is one of secular pragmatism, coupled with a feeling that newness can't mean gain, only amoral and finally accidental loss. That the dematerializing bank account has been the most persistent of Y2K icons does, certainly, speak to fears about an increasing virtualness of resources and even of personal identity, but it also confirms that the dominant image of the United States citizen is that of a person who *has* a bank account—not to say a mutual fund or two—to protect.

Some, of course, would aver that solicitude for the purse has been the presiding fear of ordinary people living in commercial societies since antiquity or the rise of the bourgeoisie or the Great Depression, but this doesn't in itself explain why such an anxiety should become more explicit at some times than at others, and never in a way more charged with mystique than now. Nor would most people who have lived in the American 1990s deny that the presiding impulse (we might say the hegemonic impulse) of the period has been one of consolidation, driven by a belief that prosperity—ever fragile, ever in need of watchful tending, to be sure—has returned. In 1997, NYU Press brought out a collection called *The Year 2000: Essays on the End,* in which most contributors sought evidence of a hyperbolic millenarian impulse shaking society's very roots, but the piece that seemed to me most convincing was one in which Richard Falk took the opposite line:

> With the advent of the new millennium, there exists a strong cultural presumption that the search for terrestrial answers will grow bolder, veering as it did in the 1890s toward radical visions of an imminent apocalypse or else the start of an extraordinary reign on earth of the divine spirit. Yet instead, in the 1990s there exists a pervasive sense of complacency, a turning toward immediate satisfactions, and an imaginative fatigue that is seemingly content with muddling through, barely taking more than ritualistic notice of the millennial shift that awaits us.

In making their case for the intensity of millennial anxieties, several of Falk's fellow contributors assert that apocalyptism has been intensified by the prospect of nuclear destruction, but Falk rightly points out that because the events of 1989 weakened this fear, the 1990s have been marked more authentically by a post-apocalyptic sensibility—not a belief that apocalypse has occurred, but a mistaken and dangerous belief that the nuclear threat has been eliminated. This sense of having passed beyond, Falk also reminds us, is deeply entangled with the neo-bourgeois mindset already mentioned, the departure of the ideological binary of the Cold War having "left the way open for the ascendancy of consumerist preoccupations with economic growth and the expansion of world trade, an essentially materialistic calculus."

If the inhabitants of the United States have proved more resistant to pre-millennial pathology than might have been expected, then, this is so in part because they're still adjusting to the post-Cold War condition, a feeling of freedom from both the nuclear shadow and the only clear historical narrative they have ever known—the one that was supposed to end (in a recedingly distant future, not in anyone's lifetime) with the triumph of democratic good over totalitarian evil, or the reverse. The disappearance of the Evil Empire means, according to a commonly heard (if often disingenuous) lament, that there remains no credible project for the United States; coupled with an economic vitalization that took everyone by surprise, it has led many to wonder whether there's anything left but going ahead and enjoying whatever plenitude has been earned or given. If specialists in the measurement of zeitgeist have found the general malaise of the late 1990s to be one of postness, in other words, a more specific worry has been that life after everything will take the form of an eerie, affectless floating whose best metaphor is continuous circulation through the shopping mall. (Not that actual life at the mall is affectless. Teenage mall rats will tell you how rich its emotional nuances may be, and in December 1998 television news reported that the biological stress levels of men doing Christmas shopping rise to those of on-duty police officers and jet fighter pilots in action. Data on women's stress levels were not given.)

Before proceeding, I should make clear that I don't remotely hold with the claim that the condition of the present is truly one of life after life or emergence into the posthistorical, nor can I quite see why any thinking person should. Even did one find plausible those capacious scenarios wherein the simulacral is to be seen squeezing out the last vestiges of the real (Jean Baudrillard) or free-market ascendancy closes the book on the first and second worlds (Francis Fukuyama), one would be brought up short by these delineations' thorough chauvinism on the matter of what counts as history—whether the chauvinism in question be described best as that of West against East, North against South, the United States against the rest of the world, or affluence against poverty. My point in this essay is absolutely not to endorse the view that "our" task is now to negotiate a predicament of sufficiency, since the "our" in this kind of statement can only point to a wholly phantasmatic unified American populace. This is a "we" roomy enough to include those who can be convinced of their participation in a general prosperity, but far too narrow to encompass those, in this country and elsewhere, whose deprivation proves that we're in fact very far from having entered the age of enough. (On 24 June 1999, network news reported that the number of people calling on food banks in the United States rose 14% in the previous year.)

It would be no less mistaken, however, to believe that because the pain of want and the agony of violence are real, the *feeling* of post-history and sufficiency on the part of many Americans must be purely chimerical—as though sentiments and beliefs have neither a claim on cultural history nor practical effects in the world. And it's here that we find a point of contact with the poet of our opening questions. For if there's one kind of reader who should greet with skepticism the proposition that *belief* in posthistorical sufficiency is irrelevant, it's the reader of Wallace Stevens—not only the poet who returns most relentlessly to the power exercised by fictions upon the real, but also the one who revolves most obsessively the question, "What do we do when we have enough?" Stevens may have died only shortly after the advent of postmodernity, and his last poems fallen closer to the beginning of the Cold War than the end, but he nonetheless remains the premier lyricist of what we might call individual posthistoricalness. In spite of recent demonstrations that his insulation from the catastrophes of modernity has been greatly exaggerated, he's still a poet who seems intriguingly ill at ease with the transmuting of historical upheaval into poetry, and by the same token one who asks hauntingly what can be made of a life not given substantial color by large events. He's a poet who, as some of his most discerning critics have reminded us, generates virtually an entire oeuvre out of the worry that desire might end, a poet who makes the struggle against boredom one of the central human struggles, a poet whose great quest is for change understood as the only possible source of pleasure. And he's the poet to whom we're at last ready to turn.

In Stevens' world, as his devotees know, the changes that satisfy don't have to be large changes. In a letter of 1951, for example, he writes to Barbara Church,

> I like a world in which the passing of the season (or the passing of the seasons) is a matter of some importance; and I have often wondered why newspapers did not contain wires from Italy reporting flights of storks; or from Buenos Aires reporting on the Argentine spring; and most of all I have wanted in winter daily dispatches on the front page of the *Tribune* describing the dazzle over the Florida keys, and so on. However, today General McArthur [*sic*] is more important than the sun.

I first noticed this passage as I was finishing work on a book on modernism and production; since then, it has stuck with me tenaciously, and I've asked myself many times why I can't seem to get it out of my mind. I now think one reason is that it offers, as surprisingly few texts do, a serious response to the question of how we might make something of the quotidian, of how we might learn to value authentically the peaceful daily round that wars are allegedly fought to secure. What might we do if human ingenuity should engineer utopia after all? How would we proceed if, as Stevens himself puts it in the tenth poem of **"It Must Give Pleasure,"** they should "get it straight one day at the Sorbonne"? The implicit answer is that under these circumstances we would need to learn how to revel in the most modest phenomena, how to extract the greatest pleasure from the most minuscule transformations—changes in flora and fauna, say, or the small fluctuations of sea and cloud.

In other letters of the period, Stevens seems to want to show just such extraction in action. If the organizations that produce official news won't report on flights of storks or the dazzle over the keys, he'll at least do his best to make his own Hartford weather a form of news—an innovation that, at least in theory, came to him before the 1950s, as his earlier poem **"The News and Weather"** ("The blue sun in his red cockade / Walked the United States today") attests. To James Powers, he wrote in December 1953 of unusually warm weather bringing "plants of heath in Elizabeth Park in full bloom, notwithstanding the two freezing nights that had covered the pond with ice several inches thick." To Church, he wrote in August 1954 that the days that really seem proper to Hartford are "days of wind and rain, like today," and of how it's "when the wind is blowing from the north-north-east" that one prizes "the destiny of the postman going the rounds and of the bus driver driving the bus." And earlier in the same year, he wrote to Babette Deutsch (whose poetic "Letter to Wallace Stevens" had appeared in the New York *Herald Tribune Book Review*): "A week ago we discovered a snow-drop under the hemlock cover of one of our flower beds. Even in zero weather this has now increased to three. Let that bit of news do you good in return for your *Letter.*"

To be sure, the septuagenarian Stevens was hardly the first letter-writer to take note of local botanical and meteorological occurrences; in this respect, to urge these passages as theoretically or otherwise remarkable is to miss the very essence of their effect, which depends on a certain resistance to grandeur. Further, even if we allow that these reports exceed the common run by dint of the verbal dexterity that made Stevens the poet he was, we may wonder whether thinking of them in the context of major modern poetry doesn't prove them less scintillating in a different sense. In its sweetly miniature way, after all, Stevens' newsmaking seems only to reiterate the great modernist/avant-gardist project of changing the world one experiential instant at a time, the effort to make constant food for wonder out of daily living's smallest details that we find in Woolf and in Williams, in Tzara as in Shklovksy—indeed in any of the writers who hitched their dreams of an artistic renaissance to the project of waking up human perception. Certainly, the theme is always at hand in Stevens' own texts. The poet who in 1915 was insisting that after religion, divinity would be found in "[p]assions of rain, or moods in falling snow" was still in 1950 finding in a "birth of sight" confirmation that life could really be "an incessant being alive" rather than death disguised (**"Sunday Morning," "The Rock"**). But if the passages in question are odd neither as the words of a comfortably settled middle-class executive nor as those of a modern poet, is there any basis for thinking them relevant to the malaise of the posthistorical?

I think there is, and that it arises from the very conjuncture we've just visited, between material comfort and the urge toward newness that really was so important to modernism as a cultural enterprise. Whether or not other modernist writers were comfortably circumstanced—whether their lives are best described as bourgeois, bohemian, or both—few of those not exposed to imminent want reflected on the meaning of their removal therefrom (Woolf's *A Room of One's Own* marks an exception here), or saw their lives as retired enough to make the need for novelty a problem of life as well as art. For Stevens, however, the question of how to find meaning when poverty, scarcity, and vulnerability to material hardship seem things of the past is a treasured question, and it seems to me that in *explicitly* offering new flowers and the pleasure he takes in them as news, he moves to reflect on it in a singularly intimate register. What can anything *matter* after they've gotten it right at the Sorbonne, after one has built a comfortable upper middle-class nest in a Hartford one knows one will never leave, or, for that matter, after the Evil Empire has bitten the dust? The answer gently pressed is that meaningfulness might yet be won if something in this expanse of postness could be called news. And if the snow-drop won't be enough, perhaps the *enjoyment* of it might do the trick. Hadn't I. A. Richards and T. S. Eliot, whatever their other faults or virtues, convinced a younger generation of writers that emotion is the stuff of literature, and perhaps (by extension) of all significance?

The problem with this proposal is that of all species of affect, enjoyment can seem to be the one hardest to reconcile with meaning, and this for reasons having everything to do with the postness of freedom from want. In the midst of a struggle, a project, even a routine chore, one doesn't yet have the capacity to enjoy the product of the effort in question, and indeed can be said to be driven to continued activity by a sense of lack (the lack of the thing being done). It's precisely this sense, however, that guarantees one's significance: as long as the task in question remains uncompleted, one may or may not feel oneself to have meaning in the broadest existential sense, but one does feel oneself to have meaning of a provisional, instrumental kind. The emergence of the possibility of enjoyment, however, seems to coincide with the elimination of the lack that had prevented doubts about meaning from arising. And this is to say that while the felt opposition between enjoyment and meaning may derive from the historically specific phenomenon of a distinctively capitalist work ethic, its plausibility may be rooted in the very structure of productive activity, even in a basic logical incompatibility between having and having not.

It's precisely the intuition that enjoyment and meaning must be at odds that Stevens is at pains to counter, however. Well aware of how the temporality of doing affects the psychology of significance, he devotes some of his most significant poetry to the demonstration that meaning and enjoyment can cohabit, and specifically that the sense of being *in medias res* can be identified with enjoyment as neatly as with anything else—perhaps even *preferentially* allied with an enjoyment of the sensuous world. Consider, for example, the 1940 poem **"Landscape with Boat,"** in which an "anti-master man, floribund ascetic," having jettisoned religion, devotes his life to a quest for the noumenon at the profoundest middle of things, a pure central truth beyond all phenomenal distractions:

> He brushed away the thunder, then the clouds,
> Then the colossal illusion of heaven. Yet still
> The sky was blue. He wanted the eye to see
> And not be touched by blue.
> He wanted imperceptible air.
> He wanted to see. He wanted the eye to see
> And not be touched by blue. He wanted to know,
> A naked man who regarded himself in the glass
> Of air, who looked for the world beneath the blue,
> Without blue, without any turquoise tint or phase,
> Any azure under-side or after-color. Nabob
> Of bones, he rejected, he denied, to arrive
> At the neutral centre, the ominous element,
> The single-colored, colorless primitive.

In other words, the anti-master man doesn't believe that there exists some heaven for which the sky would serve as metaphor, but does believe that the sky stands as a kind of sensuous expression of some "colorless primitive," some non-sensuous ideal or Platonic origin. On this last point, however, he's wrong; or at least so the narrator implies in remarking that the "floribund ascetic"

                                     never supposed
That he might be truth, himself, or part of it,
That the things that he rejected might be part
And the irregular turquoise, part. . . .

              . . . . .

                    He never supposed divine
Things might not look divine, nor that if nothing
Was divine then all things were, the world itself,
And that if nothing was truth, then all
Things were the truth, the world itself was the truth.

Had he been better able to suppose:
He might sit on a sofa on a balcony
Above the Mediterranean, emerald
Becoming emeralds. He might watch the palms
Flap green ears in the heat. He might observe
A yellow wine and follow a steamer's track
And say, "The thing I hum appears to be
The rhythm of this celestial pantomime."

Typically, Stevens resists stating his thesis categorically, limiting himself instead to the walking anaphora of "He might. . . . He might. . . . He might." It's pretty clear, however, that we're to understand the anti-master man as mistaken: if nothing else made this point, the narrator's attribution to him of a failure of imagination, the most crippling of limitations from a Stevensian point of view, would suffice. "Had he been better able to suppose: / He might.": had he possessed a stronger feeling for possibility, he might have ceased trying to find the transparent center of truth and instead noticed that he himself is in the midst of things, in the crucial sense that he resides among phenomena. Even when one observes a scene from its periphery, one isn't peripheral in some absolute sense, the narrator reminds us; wherever one may be looking from, one is still encircled by existence. This point is clinched by the figure of the "balcony / Above the Mediterranean," which represents a perch for the viewer but also constitutes a part of the world surrounding him and, potentially, a phenomenon of interest in its own right. (We might notice also that of all the bodies of water he might have chosen for his poem, Stevens picks the Mediterranean, whose name and mythology both connote utter midstness.)

The significance of the balcony doesn't end here, however, because in combination with the sofa and the yellow wine it also composes a scene of bourgeois comfort, thus reinforcing the point that the better alternative to the protagonist's misguided quest is the kind of enjoyment that's at ease with plenitude. It's not only that this floribund ascetic has missed the truth that meaning is all around, in the sensuous and daily; it's also that the compulsion to asceticism is itself misguided, the product of a mistaken belief that pleasure and significance are always mutually opposed. If there's anything the anti-master man is guilty of, it's guilt itself,

though the tone of the poem is less condemnatory than regretful. Stevens doesn't go so far as to make "Enjoy!" the command of the superego (this is just what modern politics does, in the view of the cultural theorist Slavoj Zizek), but he does more than merely recommend it as the liberation of an anarchic id. Pleasure isn't a responsibility, but it *is* a way of living in harmony with the celestial pantomime.

In taking this line, **"Landscape with Boat"** evokes those Henry James stories ("The Beast in the Jungle," "The Altar of the Dead") in which the hero, who might have been saved by a little timely reading in *William* James, learns too late that meaning lies not in some abstraction or future but in the transient phenomena of the present. The poem's finale, with its balcony, sofa, wine, and nice view, even seems to heighten the resonance: here, we might say, is a setting appropriate to the unfolding of a Jamesian drama. And yet this question of setting shows how Stevens quietly dispenses with a piety that even James usually retains. If in James the tragedy of missed enjoyment typically pivots on a human relationship that just happens to evolve among elegant furnishings and the luxury of time to waste, in Stevens leisure and surroundings are integral to the story, and no intersubjective bond is required. For the writer of poems like **"Landscape with Boat,"** the point isn't to separate the psychology of rich feeling from that of rich surroundings, but to show how the two are linked—or, rather, how a common psychic knot intertwines guilt about worldly comforts with guilt about sensuousness, guilt about enjoyment, guilt about meaninglessness, guilt about irrelevance, guilt about indolence, guilt about failures of spirit. At least for the Stevens of this mood—the Stevens of summer and ampleness—to deplore asceticism in theory while loving all of its concrete manifestations won't do. No wonder, he might complain, so many of James' characters fetishize renunciation after all.

Stevens can be found asserting this position as far back as his first major poetic achievement, 1915's **"Sunday Morning,"** where he had famously insisted that in the modern age Christian austerity must give place not to just any imagination, but to an imagination receptive to all kinds of sensuous pleasures, including unashamedly bourgeois ones. "Passions of rain, or moods in falling snow" may be some of the "measures destined for" the enlightened soul, but the poem begins with the choice of "Complacencies of the peignoir, and late / Coffee and oranges in a sunny chair" over attendance at church. In later poems like **"Landscape with Boat,"** Stevens expands the parameters of his secularism—not only must the "colossal illusion of heaven" be brushed away, so must the colorless primitive of an ideal beyond the phenomenal—but the alternative to a life devoted to the world beyond remains a way of living that relishes the sensuous world we have. "It was when I said, 'There is no such thing as the truth,' / That the grapes seemed fatter," he writes in **"On the Road Home"** of 1938, clearly choosing the fat fruit at hand over some nonexistent truth of truths that one might spend a lifetime pursuing. Even in 1942's ***Notes Toward a Supreme Fiction,*** a work wholly devoted to something that "Must Be Abstract," Stevens is careful to stress that the fiction in question isn't located in some Platonic elsewhere, and to prescribe enjoyment as the praxis of significant existence:

> Whistle aloud, too weedy wren. I can
> Do all that angels can. I enjoy like them,
> Like men besides, like men in light secluded,
>
> Enjoying angels. . . .
>
> Red robin, stop in your preludes, practicing
> Mere repetitions. These things at least comprise
> An occupation, an exercise, a work,
>
> A thing final in itself and, therefore, good:
> One of the vast repetitions final in
> Themselves and, therefore, good, the going round
>
> And round and round, the merely going round,
> Until merely going round is a final good,
> The way wine comes at a table in a wood.

The referent of "[t]hese things" is ambiguous, but the leading candidate is surely enjoyment (or enjoyings), which means that to enjoy is to be occupied, to exercise, to work. Earlier on, we remarked that what makes enjoyment seem so especially incompatible with meaning is its apparent distance from doing, but here Stevens renders pleasure a vigorous activity, even as he locates meaning itself in the merely going round.

In spite of all his injunctions to enjoy the daily goings round of the phenomenal, however, Stevens never completely forgets that the longing for a meaning of meanings, a truth of truths, is a real longing—something that exerts both an ethical claim (because it's a product of the imagination) and a practical one (because we'll never succeed in ridding ourselves of it anyway). Back in **"Sunday Morning,"** the answer to the question, "Shall she not find in comforts of the sun / In pungent fruit and bright, green wings. . . . Things to be cherished like the thought of heaven?" wasn't "She certainly shall," but "Divinity must live within herself," which allows for a certain doubt. It *might* mean "She shall," of course, but it also might mean, "She shall, to the extent that something like divinity is possible, which may be never or only sometimes." While Stevens gives the world of sun, fruit, and birds a moral vocation, in other words, he doesn't promise that it will provide wholly reliable feelings of fulfillment or an unbroken conviction that the good and the true aren't elsewhere. And he deploys similar hedges and qualifications, to similar effect, in his later poetry, where the instruction

to enjoy our midstness among phenomena comes with the reassurance that there's no better way to get a grasp on meaning, but not with a promise that we'll always *feel* utterly easy about our meaning as enjoyment transpires.

The poem in which Stevens makes this point clearest is 1947's **"The Ultimate Poem Is Abstract,"** which seems, in its way, to mock the complacencies of **"Landscape with Boat"**:

> This day writhes with what? The lecturer
> On This Beautiful World of Ours composes himself
> And hems the planet rose and haws it ripe,
>
> And red, and right. The particular question—here
> The particular answer to the particular question
> Is not in point—the question is in point.
>
> If the day writhes, it is not with revelations.
> One goes on asking questions. That, then, is one
> Of the categories. So said, this placid space
>
> Is changed. It is not so blue as we thought. To be
>   blue,
> There must be no questions. It is an intellect
> Of windings round and dodges to and fro,
>
> Writhings in wrong obliques and distances,
> Not an intellect in which we are fleet: present
> Everywhere in space at once, cloud-pole
>
> Of communication.

The writhing phrasing is unusually arcane even for Stevens, but what it seems to do is first to interrogate the consolations of This Beautiful World of Ours and then to endorse them on its own revised terms. It would be wrong to say that the world is simply ripe and right, a best of all possible worlds that always satisfies; but the world *can* be celebrated anyway *because* it's incomplete, meandering, open-ended. The sentiment harks back to ***Notes*** [***Notes Toward a Supreme Fiction,***] and the good of the merely going round, to the pleasures of merely circulating from the poem of that name, and to the famous dictum of **"The Poems of Our Climate,"** "The imperfect is our paradise."

At this point, however, things take a different turn. This is the rest of **"The Ultimate Poem Is Abstract"**:

> It would be enough
> If we were ever, just once, at the middle, fixed
> In This Beautiful World Of Ours and not as now,
>
> Helplessly at the edge, enough to be
> Complete, because at the middle, if only in sense,
> And in that enormous sense, merely enjoy.

Elsewhere, as we've seen, Stevens counters the intuition that there's an antipathy between enjoyment and the feeling of being in the middle of things by reminding us that we're *always* in the middle of things, that we're always among worldly phenomena in whose endless circulation we can take pleasure. In these lines, however, he asks whether such a resolution only meretriciously addresses our sense of peripheralness after all—whether it might not be a mere sleight of hand premised on the punning equation of one kind of "middle of things" with a very different one. We may be immersed physically in the phenomena of This Beautiful World of Ours, but there are frames of mind in which that crudely literal immersion does nothing to counter the feeling of being a mere ghostly observer, eternally relegated to life's edge.

What **"The Ultimate Poem Is Abstract"** doesn't do is to condemn pleasure as eternally corrupt; what it does do, once again, is to depict a mood or point of view complementary to, and no less compelling than, the optimism of **"Landscape with Boat."** At certain times one feels that to enjoy is to be integral to the celestial pantomime; at others, one feels, "helplessly" even, that enjoyment, by its very nature, makes one excessive, parasitic, guilty. And the reason why *enjoyment* should partake of this alienation so acutely is suggested by the first part of **"The Ultimate Poem Is Abstract."** If there's a gap in which questions writhe, in which windings wind round and dodges dodge to and fro, this is a gap of knowledge and identity between the one enjoying and the thing enjoyed. To enjoy this beautiful world—to experience it and to extract pleasure from that experience—is to be prevented from knowing it so faultlessly (as through "revelations") that one would become "in sense" part of its sensuous fullness. Enjoyment can only be a relationship between subject and object in which the two parties remain rigorously distinct. Or so it appears, at least, to the frame of mind delineated here.

For Stevens, then, enjoyment may be the best remedy for crises of meaning, but it's also a highly *unreliable* remedy, because the very intuition of midstness that gives enjoyment its power (at some times) can be precisely what enjoyment forbids (at others). And it's with this insight, I would argue, that Stevens returns us to some of the questions with which we began.

In order to see how this is so, we need to recall, first, one of the morals of Stevens' own meditations, which is that the problem of afterness readily translates into a problem of peripheralness: in both cases, the difficulty lies in a feeling of removal from life, whether that removal is figured temporally as a posthistorical existence, or spatially as a carrying on apart from the real struggles, real politics, and real hardships in which life seems to recognize itself as such. Certainly, Stevens is inclined to write about peripheralness in existential rather than immediately social terms, to speak of helplessness at the edge of a Physically Beautiful World

of Ours rather than removal to some position outside meaningful history. If we think back to **"Landscape with Boat,"** however, we'll recall that one of his premises is that the psychology of economic affluence is inevitably entangled with that of sensuous affluence, that ease among things one might own is never quite separable from aesthetic receptivity toward things in general. In **"Landscape,"** the prognosis following from this entanglement was a happy one: there, removal from anxieties about material necessity went together with removal from anxieties about *one's own* necessity in a cosmic sense, both predicaments dispelled by the play of enjoyment. In **"The Ultimate Poem Is Abstract,"** on the other hand, the same entanglement portends the opposite consequence, Stevens here suggesting how the end of dilemmas of provision might mean the beginning of dilemmas of meaning, how pleasure in things may always be shadowed by estrangement from the world enjoyed.

Taken together, these two texts suggest why the feeling of coming after history might not be enough to induce an immediate search for new narratives and meanings, even with something like the numerical temptation of 2000 to intensify the urge. The sense of afterness coupled with the feeling of prosperity might, it's true, fashion a doubly seductive invitation to fears about loss of direction, lack of purpose, the oppression of routine; but Stevens' explorations suggest that in imagining such fears to be inevitable we mistake the nature of enjoyment, which is not the stable state (and hence not the incitement to restlessness) that it often appears. On the contrary, he proposes, the nature of enjoyment is to oscillate between satisfaction and longing, now presenting itself as fullness, now as dearth, here connoting immersion in life, there pointing to the unbridgeable gap between the taker of pleasure and the world that renders it. Far from antipathetic to temporality, then, enjoyment has an emotional rhythm of its own, creates its own quasi narratives or quasi histories. And this means not only that the restlessness to which it gives rise may ordinarily be too short-lived to allow for dramatic consequences, but also that its own temporality might fulfill some of the psychic needs ordinarily addressed by "real" historical change.

Still, the territory we've traversed so far doesn't quite exhaust Stevens on the topic of meaning and enjoyment. Consider, as a final pronouncement, the skeleton of the very late poem **"Note on Moonlight"**:

> The one moonlight, in the simple-colored night,
> Like a plain poet revolving in his mind
> The sameness of his various universe,
> Shines on the mere objectiveness of things.
>
> It is as if being was to be observed,
> As if, among the possible purposes
> Of what one sees, the purpose that comes first,
> The surface, is the purpose to be seen,

The property of the moon, what it evokes.

So, then, this warm, wide, weatherless quietude
Is active with a power, an inherent life,
In spite of the mere objectiveness of things,

The one moonlight, the various universe, intended
So much just to be seen—a purpose, empty
Perhaps, absurd perhaps, but at least a purpose,
Certain and ever more fresh. Ah! Certain, for sure
  . . .

"Note on Moonlight" is a complicated poem both syntactically and thematically, and my way of abridging it probably forecloses some of the readings it allows. Still, one thing that's clear is that the poem's major question is the founding question of existential crisis: Why should anything exist at all? It also seems fairly clear that the answer proffered here (with that typical Stevensian delicacy in which tentativeness is enlivened by hope) is that in moonlight, at least, we can believe that things exist in order to be perceived, and enjoyed in the perceiving. This may not be much of a statement of final purpose, may be "absurd"; but then what candidate for a final meaning isn't (Stevens tacitly demands) absurd from a rigorously existential point of view?

What makes this poem so instructive for our purposes is that it calls attention to another crucial sense in which we can speak of being *in medias res.* In the scene staged here, being in the middle of things signifies neither carrying out a task nor inhabiting the sensuous world inertly; rather, it signifies standing in the midst of others' fields of vision, existing as a phenomenon among the world's phenomena. Perception, always privileged by high modernism, thus retains its eminence, but Stevens quietly disrupts the usual assumption that it's the heroic perceiver who would be given meaning by this activity. On the contrary, meaning now resides with the perceived, becoming a property of the object rather than the subject.

This proposition may sound counterintuitive, given our habit of associating purpose with productive action, but a little reflection will show why it's apposite both as a moral of Stevens' work in particular and as a general claim about meaning. We might recall, first, that Stevens is a poet singularly—indeed on close inspection stunningly—averse to writing about the accomplishing of tasks, the making of things, the generating of outcomes (by way of contrast, think of all those quests and trials in Eliot, H. D., Auden, Williams, and so on), but singularly happy to celebrate imagining and enjoying. "I can / Do all that angels can. I enjoy like them, / Like men besides. . . . These things at least comprise / An occupation, an exercise, a work. . . . Until merely going round is a final good." Vigorous intervention in reality may be uncongenial as matter for poetry, but the

continuous circulation of pleasure is home; being the object of others' seeing is no less sanctified a condition than that of being in the midst of a project. It makes perfect sense that this poet should find in the purpose to be seen the purpose that comes first, the purpose that comes "ever more fresh."

To lay too much stress on Stevens' distinctive predilections, however, is to risk missing the sense in which **"Note on Moonlight"** also speaks to the question of meaning in general. In thinking about the dilemma of the posthistorical, earlier on, we took absorption in a task as a privileged example of a situation providing meaning (if only of an instrumental and temporary kind). What we didn't remark, though, is that the broader meaning of such absorption would still depend on the completed task's being good for something—and further that if we want to speak of *the task's performer* having meaning, we'll do so much more comfortably if we're sure that the task is good for someone else. If what I've accomplished means something to no one but me, the accomplishment itself may be said to have meaning, but do I? Kant's categorical imperative aside, we violate none of our usual intuitions about meaning if we say that meaning must always, in some sense, be meaning for another. In naming the purpose to be seen the purpose that comes first, then, **"Note on Moonlight"** doesn't so much disrupt our usual understanding of the nature of meaning as clarify it through a temporary estranging.

If it's true that in Stevens the securest purpose is the purpose to be seen, however, a new problem appears to emerge. For if to enjoy is to operate in the mode of a subject, while to have meaning is to function in the mode of an object, it would follow that the possibility of combining one's meaning with one's enjoyment is remote to the point of elimination. From a rigorously theoretical point of view, wouldn't **"Note on Moonlight"** uphold rather than counter the conclusion of **"The Ultimate Poem Is Abstract,"** affirming that to enjoy is to feel oneself excluded from that middle of things where one would be sure of having meaning?

From a rigorously theoretical point of view, the answer is surely yes; and yet even for Stevens, no slouch when it comes to epistemological nuances, such rigor might be beside the point here. This poet's great topic, after all, is less being-in-the-world than the psychology, the feeling, the imagining of being-in-the-world, and he would likely be quick to remark that in actual experience enjoyment can occur in microtemporally close proximity to the feeling of being perceived—such close proximity, indeed, that the two will overlap to all but the fussiest calibration. More to the point, there remains the possibility of bringing enjoyment and meaning into still tighter association by inviting others to enjoy our enjoyment. We sometimes speak of "sharing" pleasure as though it implies dividing some fixed quantity of felicity, but Stevens suggests that we'll be better served by a diction of showing or describing, in which to communicate enjoyment is to disseminate it in a way that allows for its infinite increase. There's a case to be made, in fact, that communicating pleasure is the principal moral action of Stevens' poetry, and this in a double sense: not only the action the oeuvre most values, it often seems the one it most deliberately sets out to perform.

It may be, therefore, that we're most generous to Stevens on his own terms if we conceive of his work not as a mark on reality left for the sake of making a mark, but rather as an effort to put his enjoyment into circulation, and thus to come into his meaning in a world where the purpose that comes first is the purpose to be seen. Nor does the poetry alone make this case. There are also, lest we forget, those letters: ". . . and I have often wondered why newspapers did not contain wires from Italy reporting flights of storks; or from Buenos Aires reporting on the Argentine spring"; "Let that bit of news do you good in return for your *Letter.*" "News," after all, implies not just that the events narrated are important, but that they hold meaning for the particular audience of the narration. Might not Stevens approve if we were to describe his writing as the news of his enjoyment—which is to say, as the venture of his meaning for others?

To consider this possibility is, I think, to see how Stevens and the end of his century speak to each other in yet a different way. Almost every critic attempting sustained engagement with this poet has turned at some point to his 1942 lecture-essay "The Noble Rider and the Sound of Words," which argues that poetry's most important function has become that of assisting the "imagination pressing back against the pressure of reality." As his exemplary vehicle of the latter kind of pressure, Stevens mentions news. "We are close together in every way. We lie in bed and listen to a broadcast from Cairo, and so on. There is no distance. We are intimate with people we have never seen": like so many theorists of media before and since, Stevens stresses how news isn't something one engages or avoids at will, but a force whose very existence transforms experience wholly. What has gone virtually ignored in readings of this essay, however, is the conclusion of the quoted passage's last sentence, which reads in full, "We are intimate with people we have never seen, *and, unhappily, they are intimate with us.*" To be modern (or postmodern) is not only to regard but also to be regarded. If news leaves no corner of experience untouched, this is so partly because it makes us feel that we may at any time be subject to the gaze of others—and indeed always are, as elements of various collectivities if not as individuals.

In "The Noble Rider" itself, the not especially public Stevens finds only cause for dismay in this broadcast-generated proximity, but if we put the essay into dialogue with the **"Note on Moonlight"** and the letters to Deutsch and Church, we can see how the situation it describes has its less purely irritating side. If being (post)modern implies being seen, and if the purpose to be seen is the first purpose, then being (post)modern might also imply a certain (faint, curious, uneven) enhancement of one's confidence that one has meaning. One knows that one is registering on others' consciousnesses, even if only as part of a group and in distorted fashion; one knows that one's drama is unfolding in distant places; one knows that one's enjoyment is somewhere being enjoyed—or envied, or resented, or despised. In the United States of the late 1990s, the mass media have devoted substantial energy to confirming this last possibility for American audiences, relentlessly announcing not only that "we" have more while other economies stagnate or shatter, but also that others regard "our" more with feelings as various as they are intense. (In a *New York Times* article of 18 July 1999 called "America Finds It's Lonely at the Top," Michael Mandelbaum of Johns Hopkins explains the position of the United States this way: "If you are the 800-pound gorilla, you're concentrating on your bananas and everyone else is concentrating on you.")

One of the achievements of Zizek, who may be our most inventive theorist of political psychology at century's end, has been to show extensively how nationalisms and international hostilities are driven by resentments of imputed enjoyment—by envious fantasies, on the part of some "us," respecting the kinds of enjoyments available to some "them." To this we need to add, however, that politics can also be shaped by the ways in which "we" enjoy others' imputed enjoyment or resentment of "our" imputed enjoyment. As a number of observers have suggested, part of what diminishes the anxiety of post-Cold War sufficiency is, precisely, the aforementioned sense that others believe "our" condition to be one of more material comfort, more convenience, more enjoyment, whatever the truth about comparative standards of living. In other words, what helps to render bearable the prospect of a life consisting of shopping, shopping, a little working, some more shopping, and then death is the belief that someone else cares about all this shopping, even if only hostilely. And this is to say that if apocalyptism has been less pervasive, intense, and various than might have been anticipated, one reason may lie in the widely disseminated conviction that "we" are fulfilling the purpose to be seen in an especially compelling way—that is, by enjoying whatever "we" have earned, taken, or been given.

It seems to me that these considerations also bear on what has so far constituted the nearest thing to a coherent nexus for millennial panic: Y2K, once again. We've already noted that the bug connotes prosperity (the condition of having something to lose) and a deeply secular nervousness (loss occurring for no good reason), but a third connotation, which augments signally its power to frighten, is that of invisibility to the naked eye. Y2K is, among other things, the great glitch so apparently minor that it might have gone undetected, the giant flaw so elusive that it slips, even as one thinks about it, from the micromaterial world of the chip to the immaterial world of number. As the invisible truth behind a visibly gigantic prosperity (not to mention a crack in the heart of the product most frequently identified with America's new economic dominance), Y2K fulfills the dramatic requirement that an apocalypse's form be metaphorically appropriate to the human lapse that invited it. We don't need an apocalypse, as it turns out—but if there *were* to be one, something larger and still more appalling than Y2K, tragic irony would demand that it share with the invisible bug some tendency to subvert visibility, to undermine *as spectacle* the spectacular enjoyment through which "we" fulfill the purpose to be seen.

When Stevens describes circuits of pleasure, the merely going round, and the purpose that comes first, his intention is certainly not to provide a glossary for personal resentments, let alone international ones: in his poems, once again, the showing of enjoyment figures as a sharing, not a provocation to violence or (unless by omission) to complacency. Nonetheless, his work bears significantly on what Zizek calls enjoyment as a political factor because it calls our attention so pointedly to enjoyment's mobility, reminding us how easily the subject of enjoyment becomes the object of another's regard. This kind of lesson is especially pertinent to the country of Stevens' birth and life because it has long been taken for granted by Americans that their nation's role is to teach the rest of the world how to enjoy. A being blessed with resources, energy, and a perfect ignorance of the way life thwarts and maims, the American often appeared in early representations as the one who knows or learns precociously how to relish the good life; and this stock figure, though repeatedly bruised by historical failures, continues to reassert itself in periods of perceived ascendancy. There has been ample discussion of the various imaginings of mission used to legitimate American rapacity and imperialism, but relatively little attention has been devoted to what continues to be one of the most effective of them all: the belief that America most exactly fulfills its destiny not in building democracy, promoting freedom, or even raising standards of living, but simply in carrying on the work of enjoying—a belief that would discern in the United States of the late 1990s the United States being most itself. And thus if I were to propose Stevens for the title of essential poet of the American twentieth century, you would understand me to be indicating, by

this, how his engagement with enjoyment makes him perhaps the keenest diagnostician of his country's millennium-closing myths.

Mark Schoening (essay date spring 2000)

SOURCE: Schoening, Mark. "Sacrifice and Sociability in the Modern Imagination: Wallace Stevens and the Cold War." *Contemporary Literature* 41, no. 1 (spring 2000): 138-61.

[*In the following essay, Schoening gives an in-depth account of Stevens's theories concerning the connection between poetry and politics.*]

> A generation ago we should have said that the imagination is an aspect of the conflict between man and nature. Today we are more likely to say that it is an aspect of the conflict between man and organized society.
>
> Wallace Stevens, "Imagination as Value"

In 1949, Arthur Schlesinger Jr. noted that it had become increasingly difficult to articulate a vital center capable of mediating the conflict between autonomy and sociability thought to structure the developing tension between American liberalism and Soviet communism (6-7). Inherent in Schlesinger's remark was the view that the wars of this century had confirmed the failure of "modern culture" to articulate a "new social structure" capable of effecting such a mediation—capable of succeeding "where the ancient jurisdictions of the family, the clan, the guild and the nation-state have failed" (4). Stevens's remarks in "Imagination as Value," quoted above, suggest that he believed modern poetry to have become involved in the conflict that concerned Schlesinger, and that he believed it to have become involved in terms of "the imagination" it privileged.

Eventually this essay will ask how to understand Stevens's sense that poetic practice might bear on and assume some of the functions of political practice.[1] At present, it is important to note the specific terms in which Stevens imagined poetry and politics to be related, since those terms will illuminate at least one landscape in which the two activities have been brought together in this century. In a letter to Leonard van Geyzel, written in May 1945, Stevens reflected on "the place of poetry in society" as follows:

> For a long time, I have felt the most intense interest in defining the place of poetry. It would be current cant to say the place of poetry in society, but I mean the place of poetry in thought and its place in society only in consequence of its place in thought, and certainly I don't mean strict thought, but the special thinking of poetry, or, rather, the special manner of thinking in poetry or expressing thought in poetry.
>
> (*Letters* 500-1)

"The place of poetry in society" is a consequence here of "its place in thought," and the place of poetry in thought is a function of its "special thinking." Here and elsewhere Stevens distinguishes poetry from other forms of cultural activity by referring to the "special manner of thinking" it involves, while implying that poetry shares with other forms of cultural activity certain ends. In "Imagination as Value," Stevens implies that poetic practice has come to share with political practice a devotion to resolving "the conflict between man and organized society," which threatens in the twentieth century to divide human experience and the world in which it occurs. But as the reference to "the imagination" in the epigraph to this essay suggests, Stevens believed that poetry pursued *differently* the ends it shared with other cultural practices; he believed that poetry could be distinguished from other forms of cultural activity by virtue of the means it employed to achieve common ends.

Before addressing the coherency of Stevens's understanding of the relationship between poetry and politics, I will argue that Stevens's view of poetry and its socio-political "place" develops in the context of a distinctly modern reflection on human sociability crystallized in America during the early moments of what has come to be called the cold war. More specifically, this essay will explore the movement by which suspension and speculation came to emerge for Stevens, and others, as values both poetic and social. As an organizational text, the essay will take up an occasional poem called **"Description without Place,"** produced in 1945 for the Phi Beta Kappa services at Harvard. At that event, Stevens would be addressing what he understood to be the future leaders of the nation, in the wake of the second world war in half a century, and he would be sharing the stage with Sumner Welles, former undersecretary of state and sponsor of a political discourse of the kind that would soon be inherited by Schlesinger. To consider **"Description without Place"** is thus to consider the relationship between a certain strain of political discourse in the middle of this century, and a poetic discourse that developed alongside it. And it is also to find oneself considering a powerful dream of human sociability that continues today to govern a good deal of thought about art, society, and sacrifice.

Readers familiar with Stevens's work have rightly perceived that the occasion at Harvard provided the aging poet with an opportunity to revisit earlier positions for public consumption.[2] But from its opening canto, **"Description without Place"** seems not merely to revisit certain positions, but to do so with an eye to situating them in ways that have escaped critical reflection. "It is possible," the poem opens, "that to seem—it is to be, / As the sun is something seeming and it is" (1.1-2). This is the opening gambit characteristic of much of Stevens's verse, the invocation of the "pos-

sible" that Helen Vendler has called the mark of "the pensive style" (13). But it is also the echo of a line that situates the gambit in a particular way. As a Harvard graduate, Stevens would have expected his audience to be familiar with perhaps the most famous line of the young prince of Shakespeare's *Hamlet*: "To be or not to be—that is the question." And Stevens would have expected his audience to hear, in his opening line, the invocation of a way of speaking associated with that prince.

The stakes of Stevens's reference to *Hamlet* can be grasped by nothing that the opening line of **"Description without Place"** recalls another line of Shakespeare's drama more directly. The line in question occurs in the second scene of the first act, when Hamlet has been summoned by Claudius and Gertrude to explain his sulky behavior. "How is it that the clouds still hang on you?" Claudius asks. "Thou know'st 'tis common," Gertrude adds; "all that lives must die, / Passing through nature to eternity." "Ay, madam," replies Hamlet; "it is common." "If it be," says Gertrude, "why seems it so particular with thee?" "Seems, madam?" returns Hamlet; "Nay, it is. I know not 'seems'" (1.2). Hamlet is insisting here that he knows not falsity, that he is not, himself, "seeming," or being false. And he is also revealing a tendency to think of seemings as falsehoods to be eliminated in the pursuit of being.

Another way to put this is to say that Hamlet thinks in terms of a logic that would view the world with an eye to intelligibility and consistency. From the vantage point of this logic, seemings are indeed falsities, since they introduce multiplicity into being and thus challenge the singularity with which truth is identified. And seemings challenge stability as well, for a community divided within itself, like a sentence that contains contradictions, cannot stand, because it makes no sense. As an ambivalent instrument of this authority, Hamlet will pursue, in the course of Shakespeare's play, truth through the elimination of seemings and order through the elimination of contradictions. And the prince will eventually find himself a tragic agent, if by "tragic" we understand the establishment of order by sacrifice. For in the course of Shakespeare's drama, Hamlet will discover that sacrifice is indeed entailed by his commitment to eliminating seemings in the name of being, and contradictions in the name of order.

To the authority of the logic invoked by Hamlet ("I know not 'seems'"), **"Description without Place"** would pose an alternative. Where Hamlet's speech reveals a will that would establish being at the expense of seemings, the opening announcement of **"Description without Place"** projects a will that would relax such impulses ("It is possible that to seem—it is to be"). And that will, as the poem unfolds, is linked to the projection of a principle of order alternative to Hamlet's. The poem continues:

> The sun is an example. What it seems
> It is and in such seeming all things are.
>
> Thus things are like a seeming of the sun
> Or like a seeming of the moon or night
>
> Or sleep.
>
> (1.3-7)

Here speech appears to be informed by thought, since we encounter demonstrative exemplarity ("The sun is an example") and logical entailment ("Thus"). But if there is order it is not the order of logic, since resolutions are stymied by distinctions that slip and repetitions that blur, rather than focus, meaning.

Consider the second line. The sun appears here as something that *is* what it *seems*. And yet the first line has suggested that "the sun is something seeming and it is." *Is* the sun what it *seems*? Or is the sun a thing that both is *and* seems? Is the second thought ("What it seems / It is") a refinement of the first? The sentence that would connect these alternatives ("The sun is an example") merely insists upon the sun's exemplarity without clarifying the possible confusion. And the next sentence continues the tease: the invitation to thought extended by the word "Thus" is frustrated by the proposition that beings are now "like" seemings (the sun is now an example of something that is "like" it seems); and that invitation is further confused by a multiplication of likenesses that bewilders rather than clarifies ("like . . . the sun / Or . . . the moon . . . or night / Or sleep").

Here as elsewhere in **"Description without Place,"** examples and instances of likeness appear and multiply with a rapidity that mystifies rather than clarifies the subject at hand. In this sense, **"Description without Place"** often presents speech that has the appearance of logic without its substance, if with logic we associate clarity and resolution rather than multiplicity and diffusion. Readers familiar with Stevens will recognize this canto as a paradigmatic case of "the unspotted imbecile revery" invoked in **"The Man with the Blue Guitar"** (1937). In that poem, as here, the aim of the "revery" in question is to expand or enlarge rather than to clarify or articulate ("Be content—/ Expansions, diffusions— content to be / The unspotted imbecile revery, / The heraldic center of the world" [13.3-6]). And in both poems the question raised is whether we can make ourselves comfortable in such a place, whether we can "Be content," as **"The Man with the Blue Guitar"** would have it, with such a substitution.

To recall the occasion for which **"Description without Place"** was produced is to begin to address the circumstances in which such a question became relevant. In 1945, in Cambridge and elsewhere, no experience was more pressing than that of the Second World War, and no question was more central than that of how to avoid a recurrence of the tragedy the war seemed to involve. To Sumner Welles and others, this question was made urgent by the fact that postwar tensions between the United States and the Soviet Union seemed already to have escalated to the point where the possibility of "a third world war" seemed real (329). And to Welles and others, this possibility had made more urgent than ever the necessity of recalling to the world's attention the principle of choice on which social life was based.

To Welles, social life depended on choice because the world had proven itself to contain a variety of agents guided by a variety of ends that could not be "reconciled" with one another. The "security" and "stability" of the world depended, for this reason, on sacrificing some of those ends to others (3-5). Tragedy of the kind experienced during the Second World War resulted from the failure to make such choices when they presented themselves, and any hope for peace in the future depended upon deciding now between the available alternatives for the world. In *The Time for Decision* (1944), Welles thus attempted to precipitate in his audience a choice between the developing powers of American liberalism and Soviet communism, for the world, he insisted, could not exist "half Soviet and half American," and the averting of tragedy in the future would depend upon deciding now about "the kind of world in which [we] are to live in the future" (413).

For Stevens, if we judge on the basis of poems like **"Dutch Graves in Bucks County"** and **"Esthétique du Mal"** (1942); the Second World War did raise the question of tragedy and how to avoid it in the future. The speaker of **"Dutch Graves"** intones:

> An end must come in a merciless triumph,
> An end of evil in a profounder logic,
> In a peace that is more than a refuge,
> In the will of what is common to all men,
> Spelled from spent living and spent dying.
>
> (36-40)

And yet, in its reference to "a profounder logic," this passage implies that the "end" in question can only come about by unconventional means. In **"Description without Place,"** a figure soon emerges to embody the means that Stevens had in mind. "It was a queen," we are told in the fourth stanza of the opening canto, "that made it seem / By the illustrious nothing of her name" (1.7-8). This queen is honored because she has introduced seemings into the world, and because she is little more than a seeming herself (she acts by "the illustrious nothing of her name"). She is celebrated for embracing the differences introduced into the world by her perception of it ("This green queen / In the seeming of the summer of her sun / By her own seeming made the summer change"), and for grounding her authority in constant renewal rather than in one state of affairs ("Her time becomes again, as it became, / The crown and week-day coronal of her fame" [1.10-12, 15-16]).

The queen honored in **"Description without Place"** thus emerges as someone who has rejected the singular nature of "being" for the multiple nature of "seeming"; she is someone who has rejected the resolutionary "logic" of both *The Time for Decision* and *Hamlet.* And her rejection of that logic is offered in the poem as a rejection of the terms on which either work would establish sociability. Under the queen of **"Description without Place,"** multiplicity and inconsistency become "the world," rather than its undoing. The link between order and the establishment of sociability that animates Welles is thus rejected by the queen, and along with it goes the atmosphere of sacrifice which that link sustains. Early in **"Description without Place,"** listeners thus find themselves invited to a world united not in the "logic" of *The Time for Decision* but in the "profounder logic" of Stevens's queen, and this invitation evokes a vision of the world released, perhaps finally, from the need for sacrifice that Welles and others understood to be necessary for the establishment of sociability.

In its opening moments, **"Description without Place"** thus casts poetry as a cultural instrument by which to respond to the postwar tensions of 1945, and by which perhaps to move beyond the sacrificial response to those tensions advocated by Welles and other postwar American liberals. The degree to which Stevens understood poetry to be at issue here is confirmed if we recall that the queen of the poem's opening is a familiar personification of the cognitive faculty that Stevens tended to call "the imagination," and that he tended to construe as the sovereign of a distinctly "poetic" practice.[3] To Stevens the imagination often appeared, as the queen appears in the opening canto of **"Description without Place,"** to move the world away from rather than toward any singularity of being (think of **"Thirteen Ways of Looking at a Blackbird"**). And to Stevens the imagination had historically found a home in poetry. In offering his audience in Cambridge a sovereign committed to multiplicity rather than singularity, Stevens thus appears to have been offering not only one power of mind distinct from others, but a poetic practice whose association with that power of mind was intended to give poetry new political relevance.

And yet it would be a mistake to conclude that **"Description without Place"** employs its version of poetry finally, or most seriously, against postwar American liberalism. As an index of the degree to which that conclusion would be premature, consider the fourth

canto of the poem, in which we are invited to see Lenin "on a bench beside a lake," disturbing "swans" (4.15-16). "He was not," we are told, "the man for swans." Lenin's attempt to feed the birds results in their fleeing "to remoter reaches, / As if they knew of distant beaches" (4.23-24). At the center of **"Description without Place,"** Lenin thus appears as a distinctly ominous figure, and given his association in 1945 with the Soviet system, it is clear that while Stevens's poem develops a critique of American liberalism after the Second World War, it also develops a critique of Soviet communism.

The association of Lenin with Soviet communism, and the specific terms of that association, was established for Stevens by Edmund Wilson's *To the Finland Station.* In 1940 Wilson's book had appeared to great fanfare, and in 1941 Stevens mailed it to a friend he knew to be interested in the American left. He explained in a letter that the book was "thought particularly well of in respect to the portraits of the figures with which it deals," and that his own interest lay in the way the work addressed "the personalities of the Marxians, early and late" (*Letters* 381). Chief among the "Marxians" addressed by Wilson was Lenin, who was portrayed as the founder of the Soviet system, and as the paradigm of what one reviewer called "the revolutionary personality" (Schapiro 474). In the framework that Wilson established, Lenin thus came to appear as the originator of the Soviet system, and the nature of that system came to be seen as the function of a certain kind of "personality."

The nature of the personality with which Stevens came to associate Lenin can be grasped by noting the personality to which Lenin's is contrasted in **"Description without Place."** In the fourth canto of his poem, Stevens gives us Lenin in contrast to Nietzsche, who is also observed as he is seated by water, but who responds to the invitations of his environment differently: "Nietzsche in Basel," we are told, "studied the deep pool":

> His revery was the deepness of the pool,
> The very pool, his thoughts the colored forms,
>
> The eccentric souvenirs of human shapes,
> Wrapped in their seemings, crowd on curious
>   crowd. . . .
>
> (4.1, 5-8)

In these lines Nietzsche's "personality" is understood to embrace, rather than resist, variation and fluidity; his mind is understood to accommodate, rather than dominate, the "eccentric souvenirs of human shapes, / Wrapped in their seemings." And in doing so Nietzsche's mind is understood to move the world away from rather than toward the singularity of any being, or to precipitate, as the poem has it, "a kind of total affluence, all first, / All final" (4.9-10).

Where Nietzsche's mind is thus understood to have exchanged the project of establishing being for the project of sustaining the "moving and the moving" of "forms," Lenin's mind is understood to have remained committed to more resolutory activities (4.3). Indifferent to his surroundings ("He was not the man for swans"), Lenin appears in **"Description without Place"** as an abstracted scholar ("The slouch of his body and his look were not / In suavest keeping") consumed with thoughts of "apocalyptic legions" (4.17, 30). His obsession with such "legions" is understood to be a function of his resolutory mind, for this obsession recalls another (not coincidentally Russian) figure from Stevens's late work, Konstantinov in **"Esthétique du Mal."** "One wants," the speaker of **"Esthétique du Mal"** intones, considering the two world wars, "to be able to walk / By the lake at Geneva and consider logic," but "One might meet Konstantinov, who would interrupt / With his lunacy" (14.9-10, 17-18). Konstantinov's "lunacy" consists in what the poem calls his "extreme of logic," the resolutory drive of which is imagined to bring him to the point where he becomes

> the lunatic of one idea
> In a world of ideas, who would have all the people
> Live, work, suffer and die in that idea
> In a world of ideas.
>
> (14.19-20)

The resolutory will by which Lenin is characterized in **"Description without Place"** thus appears in **"Esthétique du Mal"** to have, as its condition, a commitment to "logic." This commitment is understood in **"Description without Place"** to underlie the Soviet system with which Lenin had become associated, and the Soviet system is thus criticized on the grounds that it has remained committed to a "logic" with necessarily "tragic" social entailments. To put the matter this way is to recognize, however, the degree to which the poem's representation of Lenin recalls not merely "Konstantinov" but also Sumner Welles, or at least the disposition associated with *The Time for Decision*. Like Lenin, Welles is the inheritor of a rationalist discourse in which the elimination of contradiction is necessary for order. And like Lenin, Welles is thereby understood to be the practitioner, from Stevens's perspective, of a classically "tragic" principle of union.

The critique that **"Description without Place"** levels at Lenin and the Soviet system thus replays the critique it levels at the liberalism represented by Welles. In the poem's eyes, both systems appear to be inheritors of a tradition of rationalist sociability that is at once sacrificial and tragic. In developing a critique that would apply equally to American liberalism and Soviet communism, Stevens thus seems to have been interested in subverting the framework of choice that presented itself to many Americans in 1945. For to many Americans in

1945, the choice at hand was precisely between American liberalism and Soviet communism. To suggest that American liberalism and Soviet communism were in some sense the same would thus have been to suggest that the choice between them was in some sense false. And it would also, perhaps, have been to suggest that a truer choice might be made.

Or so Stevens appears to have thought. The nature of the choice that **"Description without Place"** offers becomes apparent when we recall that Nietzsche emerges in canto 4 as an embodiment of the disposition or cast of mind associated earlier in the poem with "the queen" and her devotee, the poet. This disposition receives its most focused attention in canto 5, where we find the speaker, in the wake of his consideration of Lenin, returning to the realm of "seeming" with which he has identified poets and poetic practice:

> If seeming is description without place
> The spirit's universe, then a summer's day,
>
> Even the seeming of a summer's day,
> Is description without place.
>
> (5.1-4)

The notion of "description without place" emerges at this point in the poem to summarize the speaker's sense of "seeming" as unconstrained by being; a "description without place" is a "seeming" in that, like a seeming, it is not to be reduced to what *is,* to the "place" in which it is produced. And the realm of "description without place" is "the spirit's universe" in that its freedom from "place" makes it precisely the realm of something other than matter.

That "something other" is unfolded in lines that develop with the looseness to be expected of a discourse of diffusion. In his continuing reflections, the speaker imagines

> a sense
>
> To which we refer experience, a knowledge
> Incognito, the column in the desert,
>
> On which the dove alights
>
> (5.4-7)

At the center of this expansion lies the idea of something that precedes and underwrites "experience," something—"a sense," a "knowledge," a "column"—to which "experience" is *referred.* The interest of **"Description without Place"** in this idea recalls other late poems by Stevens that also concern themselves with "experience" and what we might call its ground. "Was it that," the speaker of **"The Pure Good of Theory"** (1947) asks, considering the base of a particular experience of unhappiness, "a sense and beyond intelligence? / Could the future rest on a sense and be beyond / Intelligence? On what does the present rest?" (2.16-18).

In **"The Pure Good of Theory"** and **"Description without Place,"** a speaker thus considers "experience" and the idea of something on which it "rests." In **"Description without Place,"** the speaker goes on to characterize this resting point as "an expectation, a desire, / A palm that rises up beyond the sea, / A little different from reality" (5.9-11). With these characterizations, the resting point in question comes to have not only a structural priority but a transformational capacity: as an "expectation" or a "desire," this "sense" is not only other than what materially exists, but additive to it. And for this reason the "sense" in question is subsequently characterized as "the categorical predicate, the arc" by which the future, as a state of affairs different from the past and present, is brought into being (5.16).

Practicing a discourse grounded in this "sense"— practicing "description without place"—Stevens's poem would thus celebrate difference in the world and the faculty responsible for it. But **"Description without Place"** would also do something else. For the "sense" with which Stevens's poem is occupied commands attention because it *unifies* the differences for which it is responsible; the "sense" to which **"Description without Place"** continually returns drives the poem because it *gathers* the "seemings" that emanate from it. At the center of canto 5, for example, the speaker affirms that this sense accounts for the "difference that we make in what we see / And our memorials of that difference, / Sprinklings of bright particulars from the sky" (5.12-14). But here and elsewhere the poem is less concerned with any particular "sprinklings" than with the idea that they can all be referred to a particular "sense."

In canto 5, **"Description without Place"** is thus concerned with commonality as well as difference, or with a level of commonality that underlies a field of difference. That level of commonality emerges in the poem in its reflections on difference, so that in the course of the poem's considerations of multiplicity, we are invited to perceive a sense in which, although there are as many "experiences" of the world as there are perspectives from which to experience it, each of these "seemings" can be gathered under the "sense / To which we refer experience." Each of these "experiences," that is, emanates from the "sense" to which "experience" is "referred," and, from this perspective, the "sense" the poem celebrates can be seen to constitute, within a field of differences, a point of unexpected sameness.

Stevens's tendency late in his career to identify poetry with the revelation of such a point of sameness can be confirmed by noting his definition of "the imagination" in "Imagination as Value" (1948): the imagination is "the power of the mind over the possibilities of things," "the source not of a certain single value but of as many values as reside in the possibilities of things" (136).

Identified here with the "source" of all "values," "the imagination" becomes synonymous with something on the order of evaluation, the faculty at work in every structuring of the world by differently situated (and motivated) persons and groups. And as evaluation, "the imagination" becomes, for Stevens, capable of unifying different acts of valuation, for "the imagination" becomes that form of activity under which particular instances of valuing can be gathered, and in this sense becomes capable of both accounting for and unifying difference in the world.

Stevens's attraction to this argument in times of social conflict reveals itself in a letter of 1940. In a time, he wrote, when "ideas of God are in conflict"—by which he meant in a time when the values governing the lives of individuals and nations were everywhere at odds— the practice of "pure poetry" might unify "South, West, North and East" (*Letters* 370) because "pure poetry" is a discourse grounded in "imagination, extended beyond local consciousness," in evaluative power "extended beyond" merely "local" acts of valuing. Grounded in this "power," "pure poetry" is seen to affirm not one particular, and thus contestable, value, but value's ground, the evaluative will. And in affirming this will, "pure poetry" is imagined to obviate disputes about value by referring them to their common origin: though there be as many values in the world as agents, "pure poetry" gathers them under the unity of evaluation.

In performing such a feat, "pure poetry" becomes, for Stevens, an instrument of sociability different from both American liberalism and Soviet communism, and more capable than either of achieving peace in a divisive world. Unlike American liberalism and Soviet communism, "pure poetry" would reconcile persons in the ground of all value rather than in any particular value, in the "sense / To which we refer experience" rather than in any particular "experience." In doing so, "pure poetry" would obviate the need to sacrifice any value to any other, still central to both American liberalism and Soviet communism, since it would secure sociability at a level *prior* to value, and from the perspective of which a multiplicity of values presents, or appears to present, no obstacle to sociability. In this sense, "pure poetry" would inaugurate, Stevens imagined, a new and permanent union in a divided world, no longer predicated on sacrifice.[4]

Does Stevens's position make sense? Before addressing this question, it is worth noting that Stevens's interest in a "profounder logic," and his belief in its political value, extends beyond him. We have become familiar, though under the sign of a postmodernism that typically does not include Stevens, with the idea that the modern world demands a new logic or "economy" of human sociability, and that this economy would distinguish itself not by virtue of the particular structures it would sponsor but by its critical attitude toward structure as such.[5] We have also become familiar with the idea that such an economy would look, for its inspiration, to a discourse other than that of traditional social or political thought.[6] In his belief that the modern world required a "profounder logic" of sociability, and that this counter-logic would be found outside the sphere of traditional political discourse, Stevens thus represents views that have stayed with us, and that continue to govern a good deal of contemporary thought about sociability and the means by which it might be achieved in the modern world.

So what of Stevens's views? Consider the sense in which Stevens's argument for poetry as an emancipatory force—for poetry as the agent of a "profounder" and emancipatory "logic"—contains at least one complicated invitation. Implicit in this argument is the invitation to identify freedom not with the presence of one system or structure rather than another, but with the absence of system or structure generally. In the logic of Stevens's position, freedom is to be found not in this arrangement rather than that, but in the absence of any binding arrangement, in the "pleasure," as one of his poems has it, "of merely circulating" (**Collected Poems** 149). Do human beings, we might ask, find constraining the presence of structure as such and feel most empowered in a world in which nothing extends in space or time? Do they find emancipation in the generalized absence of structure? In an essay on the "superliberalism" of Roberto Unger—a program that also locates freedom in "the structure of no structure"—Martin Stone observes the degree to which this position emerges from a serious reflection on the necessarily limited nature of any particular structure (90). But he also asks whether, in its impatience with limits, this position doesn't overlook the sense in which, for human beings, experiences likely to be identified with freedom necessarily occur within structures, since outside of them there can be no experience of choosing between alternative courses of action, and since for human beings freedom largely *is* that experience (one instance of which may be the experience of opposing the structure in which one finds oneself).

Consider, moreover, the sense in which it may be wrong to speak of Stevens's "profounder logic" as "political" at all. In an essay on the political thought of Drucilla Cornell and Ernesto Laclau—thought that also projects a new politics at the center of which sits a suspension of the structuring impulse—Judith Butler asks whether a position that declines to calculate the advantages and/or disadvantages of particular structures can meaningfully be called "political." Like Stone, Butler observes the sense in which this position seems responsive to a serious reflection on the limits that attach to the establishment of any particular structure in the human world. But Butler also wonders whether this

position hasn't missed something in its commitment to unlimited emancipation, in particular the degree to which a position that would call itself "political" must have an effect on the organization of human life in this world, an effect that depends upon acknowledging the persistence of structure(s) and upon entering into the arena where different structures continue to compete for the authority to organize human affairs differently. Butler's wondering causes her to conclude that in its refusal to offer a way of making choices between alternative ways of organizing the world—a refusal animated by the conviction that any choice will entail limits—this position leads in fact to "a paralyzed or limited sense of political efficacy" (10). If a politics is to be defined by the effect it would have on the organization of human affairs, and if the having of such an effect depends upon affecting the public competition for authority between different ways of organizing the world, then it's not clear that Stevens's "profounder logic" can be called "political" at all.

These concerns suggest that Stevens's poetic program may have had legitimacy as a critical instrument, but not as an "alternative" form of politics. It may have afforded its audience a critique of American liberalism and Soviet communism in the early years of the cold war, at the center of which lay the charge that both doctrines were more sacrificial (and thus less emancipatory) than they let on, but it could not afford an alternative to them, in that its "profounder logic" led finally to an indifference to structure contrary to its acquisition of any "political" force. From this perspective, we might say that the "profounder logic" at the heart of Stevens's poetic program in the forties is limited in ways that Stevens did not understand when he imagined that poetry's "place in society" might turn on its assumption of some of the functions of political practice. But if this is so, an interesting question remains: why has the position that interested Stevens survived?

That the position of interest to Stevens has survived is indicated by the mention of Unger and Cornell and Laclau and their versions of a "new politics" governed by a suspension of the structural impulse. Has this position survived because its limits have gone unrecognized? Or is there something else that accounts for its life? The question might be opened by noting that to Stevens, the appeal of poetry as a political force depended upon a vision of radical difference, and, in the 1940s, specifically upon his sense that it represented a radical break from politics as the world had come to know it. "Poetry must be irrational," Stevens had insisted in his *Adagia*, and when he came to find poetry politically interesting, he did so because he understood politics to have been eminently rational and poetry to stand in relation to the political tradition as radically other (*Opus Posthumous* 162). For Stevens, then, the appeal of poetry as a political force rested in the idea of a radical or absolute break, and from this perspective we might consider the degree to which the appeal of his position rested at some level upon an interest that a number of philosophers and historians have identified with the modern imagination.

Jürgen Habermas perhaps most notably has argued that a central characteristic of the modern imagination is its tendency to embrace the prospect of absolute difference. In *The Philosophical Discourse of Modernity,* Habermas finds this tendency pronounced in the work of Hegel, who wrote in his preface to *The Phenomenology of Spirit*: "our time is a birth and transition to a new period. The spirit has broken with what was hitherto the world of its existence and imagination and is about to submerge all this in the past; it is at work giving itself a new form" (qtd. in Habermas 6). In this passage Habermas contends that we witness a distinctly "modern imagination" entertaining the idea of an absolute difference between itself and everything that has preceded it, and from the perspective of Habermas's work, we might construe the appeal of Stevens's position as a function of the appeal of absolute difference to the modern imagination.

But to understand the appeal of Stevens's position in this way is simply to raise the question of how "the modern imagination" is to be understood. And while that question is too large for what remains of this essay, I do want to suggest that some interesting light can be shed on it by attending another moment to Stevens's thought. In 1937, Stevens remarked that his culture had become "obsessed by the irrational" because "we expect the irrational to liberate us from the rational" (**Opus Posthumous** 225-26). His comment confirms the oppositional movement that Habermas would locate at the center of "the modern imagination," the tendency of that imagination to move in terms of totalized differences, here in terms of the totalized difference between "the rational" and "the irrational." At the same time, his comment links this tendency to the life of something like hope for total emancipation in the face of a history that seems unable to sustain it; "we expect," Stevens says, "the irrational to *liberate us* from the rational" (emphasis added).

In 1937, history seemed unable to sustain emancipatory hopes. It was not merely the case that nineteenth-century liberalism, which had most recently arrogated to itself the rhetoric of general emancipation, had revealed itself to be other than generally emancipatory.[7] It was also the case that the First World War had destroyed much of the emancipatory optimism of the nineteenth century, and that the emergence of various political movements after the war suggested a return to the unavoidability of conflict in social life. In such circumstances, Stevens's comment suggests that the vi-

sion of sheer difference ("the irrational" as opposed to "the rational") emerges to sustain a dream of emancipation that might otherwise die. If the dream of total emancipation can no longer be sustained by reference to "the rational"—if Enlightenment liberalism, as its most recent agent, has revealed itself to be as subject to limitations in its engineering of freedom as previous forms of social organization—then "the irrational" must be solicited. For in its total difference from "the rational," "the irrational" might produce totally different outcomes.

The link that Stevens's remark suggests between the imagination of sheer difference and the dream of total emancipation has been observed by Martin Stone in his essay on Roberto Unger. Readers of Unger's work are invited to consider a community in which "it would be possible to view others as complementary rather than opposing wills," in which "furtherance of their ends would mean the advancement of one's own," in which "[t]he conflict between the demands of individuality and of sociality would disappear" because "[e]ach person, secure in his individuality, would be able to recognize his own humanity in other persons" (Unger, *Knowledge* 220-21). Crucially, the state of affairs envisioned here is offered to readers of political theory insofar as they are willing to consider "a movement beyond the tradition, its overcoming" (Stone 78). A redeemed community of the sort Unger envisions is to be realized, that is, precisely and only insofar as his readers are willing to imagine a "movement beyond" political practice as it has revealed itself in human history, a "movement" that is associated with an "overcoming" of the limitations historically attached to that practice.

The emphasis on "overcoming" or radical difference that Stone detects in Unger, and that this essay has detected in Stevens, can be discovered, moreover, at the outset of "modernity," if modernity can in some ways be said to begin with Enlightenment thought. It is not merely the (obvious) case that Enlightenment thought contains at its center the vision of a principle of social organization ("reason" as distinct from "superstition" or "unthinking custom") imagined to be fundamentally different from those previously guiding human society.[8] It is also the case that at the center of Enlightenment thought exists the representation of human being that would make difference central to the life of emancipatory hope. For at the center of Enlightenment thought, as Stone has observed, we find Kant inviting us "to think of ourselves under a fateful doubling: as something in the world that we experience, known under the same conditions that any part of nature is known, and prescinding from this, as . . . 'autonomous,' 'free'" (Stone 95). In this "fateful doubling" we are invited to see ourselves as known and unknown, and we are invited further to locate our freedom in the unknown rather than the known, in what stands over and against the known world as *other.*

At the center of Enlightenment thought, then, we find a picture of ourselves that occasions emancipatory hope, and that connects its pursuit to the pursuit of difference. To realize a world other than the one(s) we've known will be to realize freedoms other than those we've experienced. This importantly means that limited experiences of freedom can be attributed to failures to overcome fully the world(s) we've known, to realize yet that one difference from the world(s) we've known that would make all the difference. The powerful legacy of this link between emancipatory hope and the pursuit of otherness can be registered by noting that it is found not merely in what Stone calls "all the modernist discourse on personality: in Marx's critique of alienation, in which 'Man . . . is not immediately identical to any of his characterizations'; in Nietzsche's 'as yet undetermined animal'; in Freud's unconscious, 'the true psychical reality . . . as much unknown to us as the reality of the external world,'" but also in a great deal of work often characterized as postmodern (95). Consider, for example, the emancipatory rhetoric that often surrounds Bataille's talk of "the excremental," or Adorno's talk of "parataxis," or Lacan's talk of "jouissance," or Derrida's talk of "differance."[9] In each of these discourses, as in Stevens's discourse of "the imagination," we are invited to the contemplation of something other than what we've known, in the light of which to imagine freedoms less limited than those we've experienced.

From the perspective of this list and the structure it reveals, we might say that the appeal of Stevens's construction of poetry turned upon the appeal of absolute difference to a distinctly "modern imagination," an appeal that depended in turn upon the attachment of that imagination to a vision of emancipation it would not (and perhaps will not? should not?) surrender. We might say, that is, that the appeal of Stevens's construction of poetry turned upon the desire of "the modern imagination" to see (once again) an absolute break between itself and what had come before it, a desire that derived (once again?) from the attachment of that imagination to a vision of emancipation it refused to allow history to qualify. From this perspective, the deepest dream of "the modern imagination" is the dream of total emancipation, once embodied in rationalist liberalism, now more frequently embodied in what we might call irrationalist superliberalism. The latter is related to the former as a further stage in the conflict between "the modern imagination" and history, as a further stage in the tension that continues to exist between the dream of future emancipation and the experience to which that dream is addressed.[10]

It is this dream of future emancipation that underwrites the interesting moment in the 1940s when Wallace Stevens, in the context of the developing cold war between the United States and the Soviet Union, imagines that his poetic work might intervene in the world of contemporary political affairs to emancipatory effect. And it is this dream that characterizes, more broadly, "the modern imagination" at work in Stevens, at the center of which sits a pursuit of freedoms not tied to limits or sacrifices, predicated increasingly on the adoption not of one structure rather than another, but on the adoption of a programmatic skepticism toward structure as such. The idea that Stevens thinks as he does because he embodies "the modern imagination" suggests that the identification of freedom with the absence of structure deserves more attention than it has received as a moment in the continuing evolution of the modern mind. More specifically, it suggests the need to consider further the specific circumstances in which this representation has emerged, as well as the need to consider further the specific cultural instruments by which this representation has been circulated. The identification of freedom with the absence of structure suggests also, and more generally, the need to consider the degree to which the modern imagination has now perhaps arrived at the point where it may be at once ethically profound and ambiguous: ethically profound in its imagination of sociability without sacrifice, ethically ambiguous in its entailment of a skepticism toward structure perhaps less emancipatory than we think. And finally, the identification of the modern imagination with the pursuit of freedoms not tied to limits or sacrifices suggests the possibility of arriving at a better grasp than we now have of the cultural environment in which some of our most cherished contemporary notions—of art, of politics, of sociability and sacrifice—are caught up and repeatedly brought to bear on one another.

Notes

1. Readers of Stevens have long been familiar with the claim that central to his work was the idea that art might assume, in the twentieth century, some of the cultural functions typically associated with religion. They are less familiar with the claim that central to his work was the idea that art might assume some of the cultural functions typically associated with politics (even though his second book is titled *Ideas of Order*). The following discussion of Stevens is intended in part to suggest that our understanding of modernism generally has been crippled by the degree to which we have explored the former idea at the expense of the latter.

2. "Description without Place" is typically read as if it were a transcription of Stevensian philosophy, as developed in other poems. Helen Vendler, for example, describes the poem as "an ode to the adjective" which confirms Stevens's view of real-

ity as a construct of "the self" (218). Harold Bloom reads it as a demonstration of Stevens's view that "the mind's images may be realized, that tropes may be as well as seem" (240). J. Hillis Miller views the poem as an attempt to show that being is a consequence of the merging of "imagination" and "reality" (276), while Michael T. Beehler describes it as a Stevensian assertion that "being is subject to seeming" (241) and Steven Shaviro calls it a demonstration of the degree to which reality is a function of "desire as metamorphosis" (220). Each of these descriptions seems to me apt, and yet none of them addresses the circumstances in which Stevens came to consider such beliefs central to poetic practice, or poetic practice central to the kinds of questions in the air in Cambridge, Massachusetts, in 1945. The only view of the poem that takes account of the circumstances in which Stevens considered and then came to deliver "Description without Place" is that produced by Alan Filreis in *Wallace Stevens and the Actual World* (1991), where Filreis points out that Stevens considered "Description without Place" in the context of the questions raised by the war in 1945 and addressed by his fellow speaker Sumner Welles. But where Filreis finds the poem to be concerned with "trivializing radical thought" through "displacements" and acts of "dehistoricization" (151-60), I find it to be differently engaged with the question of sociability that the war had raised, and that Stevens had long considered central to poetic practice.

3. Other poems in which Stevens figures the imagination as a queen are "Depression before Spring" and "To the One of Fictive Music," both in *Collected Poems.*

4. It is interesting to note here the sense in which the terms of Stevens's critique of both American liberalism and Soviet communism became translated (in the minds of some) into an argument for a "new" American liberalism as different from an older American liberalism as it was from Soviet communism. In *The Liberal Imagination* (1950), Lionel Trilling invited postwar American liberalism to define itself against Soviet communism (and pre-war American liberalism) by its commitment not to one social formation rather than another but to "variousness and possibility" (xv). And he asserted, perhaps thinking of art as Stevens did, that a commitment to those things would be best cultivated by reading and writing imaginative literature, "not merely because so much of modern literature has explicitly directed itself upon politics, but more importantly because literature is the human activity that takes the fullest and most precise account of variousness, possibility, complexity, and difficulty" (xv).

Trilling's sense of a "new" American liberalism is central, moreover, to the argument that Arthur Schlesinger Jr. makes in *The Vital Center* for American liberalism over Soviet communism. The difference between Soviet communism and American liberalism, Schlesinger argued, was not the difference between a system that privileged the rights of the individual and one that privileged the rights of the community. It was not the difference between competing systems grounded in competing values, as earlier liberals like Welles had maintained. The difference was instead one between a system that had come to accept "contradiction" and one that continued to reject it (255), between a (Soviet) system that regarded "the toleration of conflict" as a "weakness," and an (American) system that had come to view conflict as "strength" (255). Schlesinger even insisted that American liberals viewed conflict as strength because they recognized that different values and beliefs were unified by the "creativity" from which they proceeded (255). Unified in this way, different values and beliefs presented no obstacle to sociability, and in promoting the creative will as a basis for sociability, American liberalism was understood by Schlesinger to have finally arrived at a "center" that, in a provocative echo of Yeats, would "hold" in an increasingly pluralistic world (255).

5. For examples of contemporary social thought characterized by such an assertion, see Unger; Laclau and Mouffe; and Laclau.

6. Roberto Unger, Ernesto Laclau, and Chantal Mouffe can all stand as examples of social thinkers committed at some level to this idea; for instances of social thought in which a turn away from political discourse to discourse of another kind is clearly advocated, see Rorty; and Bersani and Dutoit.

7. This story is a long one, but at its center is the development whereby, toward the end of the nineteenth century, the state that had become identified with "liberalism" came under attack for having failed to live up to its ostensible promises. (I choose my language carefully here, since the nature of the promises in question was, and continues to be, in dispute.) In the story that began to circulate, the state in question was said to have grounded itself on the claim that it would be *generally liberating*—on the claim that, unlike previous forms of social organization (most specifically the monarchical and theological ones it would replace), the liberal state would not simply privilege some at the expense of others. By the end of the nineteenth century, if not before, it had become clear that not everyone was equally

liberated. Critiques began to emerge in which the liberal state was credibly portrayed as the expression of a merchant class looking to assert itself at the expense of both an aristocratic and a laboring class. The liberal state thus began to appear, at least on structural grounds, no different from historically prior forms of social organization: like them, it asserted one social ideal at the expense of others; like them, it advantaged some at the expense of others. For one of many works that analyze the liberal state from this angle, see Laski.

8. The language here is very common and forms the basis of a familiar story of new and hopeful beginnings summarized by Larry Seidentop in "The Western Malaise: Attacks on the Enlightenment from Within and Without."

9. I don't mean to run together lines of thought that are importantly different from one another. But I do mean to suggest that despite their differences, these lines of thought have each given birth to emancipatory rhetoric, in large part precisely because they are understood to advocate the pursuit of *real* difference, and to represent thereby the possibility of a genuine (and desirable) movement "beyond" the worlds we know or have known.

10. In attributing this dream to "the modern imagination," I in no way intend to characterize the modern imagination as less ethically problematic than it has been taken to be. I address at least one of the particular complications attached to this dream in the next paragraph, but it is worth noting here that the vision of general emancipation could easily be generated by a frustration at no longer being able to ignore the degree to which the exercise of one's own will conflicts with the exercise of other wills by other (equal) agents. That is, the dream of general emancipation could easily be generated by the desire to imagine conditions in which one could continue to exercise one's own will without having to face the complications that accrue to such exercise in a world in which pluralism and equality are taken for granted. From this perspective, the dream of general emancipation looks less like an advance in ethical thought and more like a retreat into fantasies of autonomy without complication. And though I would insist that this is only part of the story to be told here, it is an important part.

Works Cited

Beehler, Michael T. "Meteoric Poetry: Wallace Stevens's 'Description without Place.'" *Criticism* 19 (1977): 241-59.

Bersani, Leo, and Ulysse Dutoit. *Forms of Violence: Narrative in Assyrian Art and Modern Culture.* New York: Schocken, 1985.

Bloom, Harold. *Wallace Stevens: The Poems of Our Climate.* Ithaca, NY: Cornell UP, 1976.

Butler, Judith. "Poststructuralism and Postmarxism." *Diacritics* 23.4 (1993): 3-11.

Filreis, Alan. *Wallace Stevens and the Actual World.* Princeton, NJ: Princeton UP, 1991.

Habermas, Jürgen. *The Philosophical Discourse of Modernity: Twelve Lectures.* Trans. Frederick G. Lawrence. Cambridge, MA: MIT Press, 1987.

Laclau, Ernesto, and Chantal Mouffe. *Hegemony and Socialist Strategy: Towards a Radical Democratic Politics.* Trans. Winston Moore and Paul Cammack. London: Verso, 1985.

Laclau, Ernesto. "Beyond Emancipation." *Emancipations, Modern and Postmodern.* Ed. Jan Nederveen Pieterse. London: Sage, 1992.

Laski, Harold. *The Rise of Liberalism: The Philosophy of a Business Civilization.* New York: Harper, 1936.

Miller, Hillis J. *Poets of Reality: Six Twentieth-Century Writers.* Cambridge, MA: Belknap-Harvard UP, 1966.

Rorty, Richard. *Contingency, Irony, Solidarity.* Cambridge: Cambridge UP, 1989.

Schapiro, Meyer. "The Revolutionary Personality." Rev. of *To the Finland Station,* by Edmund Wilson. *Partisan Review* 6 (1940): 474.

Schlesinger, Jr., Arthur. *The Vital Center: The Politics of Freedom.* Boston: Houghton, 1949.

Seidentop, Larry. "The Western Malaise: Attacks on the Enlightenment from Within and Without." *Times Literary Supplement* 15 Mar. 1996: 3-4.

Shakespeare, William. *Hamlet. The Complete Works of Shakespeare.* Ed. David Bevington. Glenview, IL: Scott, 1980.

Shaviro Steven. "'That Which Is Always Beginning:' Stevens's Poetry of Affirmation." *PMLA* 100 (1985): 220-33.

Stevens, Wallace. *The Collected Poems of Wallace Stevens.* New York: Knopf, 1954.

———. "Imagination as Value." *The Necessary Angel: Essays on Reality and the Imagination.* New York: Knopf, 1951.

———. *Letters of Wallace Stevens.* Ed. Holly Stevens. New York: Knopf, 1966.

———. *Opus Posthumous: Poems, Plays, Prose.* Ed. Samuel French Morse. 1957. New York: Knopf, 1966.

Stone, Martin. "The Placement of Politics in Robert Unger's *Politics.*" *Representations* 30 (1990): 78-108.

Trilling, Lionel. *The Liberal Imagination: Essays on Literature and Society.* Garden City, NY: Doubleday, 1950.

Unger, Roberto Mangabeira. *Knowledge and Politics.* New York: Free, 1975.

———. *Politics: A Work in Constructive Social Theory in Three Volumes.* New York: Free, 1987.

Vendler, Helen Hennessy. *On Extended Wings: Wallace Stevens' Longer Poems.* Cambridge, MA: Harvard UP, 1969.

Welles, Sumner. *The Time for Decision.* New York: Harper, 1944.

Axel Nissen (essay date June 2000)

SOURCE: Nissen, Axel. "Perpetuum Mobile: Reading Wallace Stevens's 'The Man with the Blue Guitar.'" *English Studies* 81, no. 3 (June 2000): 217-27.

[*In the following essay, Nissen offers a reading of the long poem "The Man with the Blue Guitar," focusing on Stevens's inquiry into the relationship between art (or imagination more generally) and reality.*]

I

Wallace Stevens's **'The Man with the Blue Guitar'** is not one poem, but thirty-three poems tied together by a common concern with the relationship between life and art, reality and the imagination. Any ordering principle one may find has not been given from without, but comes from within. The major connecting elements, apart from formal features such as rhythm, stanzaic form, and voice, are lexical and thematic. Key words keep cropping up in different poems, in different configurations, and all thirty-three poems revolve around the same basic set of questions.[1]

The overarching theme of **'Blue Guitar'** is the relationship between poetry and life, symbolized on the one hand by the blue guitar and on the other by 'things as they are'.[2] This ostensible dichotomy is introduced in the first two poems, where green appears as the color of reality and blue as that of the imagination. The potential conflict, as the first poem portrays it, is that while poetry is bound to represent the world as it is, 'Things as they are / Are changed upon the blue guitar'. In the second poem, the guitarist of the first poem states his case further, explaining that he can only depict patches of the world. His man has 'a hero's head, large eye / And bearded bronze'; he is 'not a man', but through him the

poet hopes to reach 'almost to man'. It is the fault of the imagination if his song fails to convince, if it misses 'things as they are'.

The questions raised by the two first cantos are pursued in a variety of ways in the rest of the poems. Despite the melodrama of the first two cantos, the remainder of **'Blue Guitar'** makes it clear that, though troubled, the relationship between the word and the world is not solely or necessarily antagonistic or unsatisfying. As Robert Fitzgerald noted in an early review: 'blue guitar' rhymes with 'things as they are'.[3]

It is possible to identify six interrelated subthemes in **'Blue Guitar',** aspects of the general theme of the relationship between art and reality: 1) the godless universe and the role of poetry in such a place; 2) an assertion of the truth of the imagination against the claims of science and documentary, social realism; 3) the need for poetry to adhere to reality and the danger of giving too much weight to the imagination; 4) the workaday world's indifference to poetry; 5) the need to see the world anew, to invent a new myth for the age; and 6) poetry's potential to become reality, the blue guitar's ability to play things as they are so convincingly that life begins to imitate art.[4] These six areas of concern will structure my interpretation of Stevens's poetic cycle. In each case I will read and analyze one poem that sets the given theme in motion and briefly discuss other poems that continue to revolve it.

In a letter to Hi Simons, written on August 8, 1940, Stevens said the following apropos of an explication of canto 24 of **'Blue Guitar'**: 'A paraphrase like this is a sort of murder. It makes one say a good many things that are true only when they are not said this way'.[5] Eight years before, R. P. Blackmur had written something similar in his famous essay 'Examples of Wallace Stevens': 'Mr. Stevens' ambiguity is that of a substance so dense with being, that it resists paraphrase and can be truly perceived only in the form of words in which it was given'. 'In its own words it is clear', Blackmur adds, 'and becomes vague in analysis only because the analysis is not the poem'.[6] The extent to which all parts of **'Blue Guitar'** are clear is open to debate, but we may concur with Blackmur when he suggests that 'We use analysis properly in order to discard it and return that much better equipped to the poem'.[7] That is the way in which I will use the analyses of others, including Stevens himself, and that is the spirit in which I hope my own interpretation will be taken, as a classic example of a hermeneutic circle: the text, its various contexts, and the reader produce a new text, an interpretation, through which one hopefully returns to the poem with expanded horizons.

II

Wallace Stevens once observed that 'little of what we have believed has been true'.[8] The difficulty of belief of any kind is suggested by poem XX. Here we find Stevens 'coming upon reality without benefit of clergy'.[9] The problem is not only the loss of religion, but the breakdown of all models that would seek to explain the world as a whole. Ironically, the good air is apostrophied as the speaker's only friend, as he wonders if man is locked in subjectivity, having only his own ideas to depend on. Faith, something transcendent which the poet calls 'believe', would be a friend to make the imagination pale in comparison. Yet the idea that some form of religious faith is not just desirable but possible is undermined by the following canto, where it becomes evident that man has become 'A substitute for all the gods', that he is now lord of his own body and of the land, of nature, and the whole physical world. Gods no longer abide in mountains such as Chocorua, one of the White Mountains in New Hampshire. Religion is dead, the physical world—'The flesh, the bone, the dirt, the stone'—is all we have. This is one of the conditions of modern poetry in general and Stevens's poetry in particular.

Against this background, Stevens makes his famous declaration in the second half of poem V. In a godless universe, where 'There are no shadows anywhere': 'Poetry / Exceeding music must take the place / Of empty heaven and its hymns'. This assertion comes after a rejection of the old mythologies: 'the greatness of poetry / . . . torches wisping in the underground / . . . structures of vaults upon a point of light'. In Ronald Sukenick's reading 'The great poems are no longer meaningful except as poems . . . We need a fiction credible to the present . . . Poems about ourselves must replace hymns to god'.[10] In Stevens's own words in an essay from 1942, it is the poet's role 'to help people to live their lives'; 'he gives to life the supreme fictions without which we are unable to conceive of it'.[11]

Much of **'Blue Guitar'** is taken up with how this grand goal may be attained. Poem XXIV, for example, claims that for the right reader, here pictured as a young man, a poem may become a guide to life and how to live life, like a missal that tells the devout the rituals of worship. A book, a page from a book, or even just a phrase may act as 'A hawk of life', a way of grasping some new aspect of reality. The young man is a critic or scholar, but may represent any 'man of the imagination' who is seeking answers to existential questions.[12]

In poems III, IV, X and XIV, Stevens calls further into question the certainties of the age. Poem III reads:

> Ah, but to play man number one,
> To drive the dagger in his heart,
>
> To lay his brain upon the board
> And pick the acrid colors out,

To nail his thought across the door,
Its wings spread wide to rain and snow,

To strike his living hi and ho,
To tick it, tock it, turn it true,

To bang it from a savage blue,
Jangling the metal of the strings . . .

This canto is clearly linked to the possible conflict between the imagination and 'things as they are' suggested by the first two poems. Poem III seems to oppose an approach to the study of man, be it artistic or scientific, that would murder to dissect, that thinks it can fully and rationally explain or represent man. Rather than the serenade of the hero that ends poem II, we have violent images of discord. The artist who seeks to be a scientist must bang his guitar and jangle the metal of the strings. It is thus difficult to agree with Ronald Sukenick when he claims this section 'asserts the value of dissection, or analysis . . .'[13]

Stevens's scepticism towards science and documentary realism is also the theme of poem IV, where he continues to question the nature of 'things as they are'. He asks whether poetry is duty bound always to depict the representative, the typical, the probable, 'a million people on one string?' In poem XIV, the contrast is again between science and art, this time symbolized by two kinds of light. The brilliant sunrise of science is 'radiant in the sky' and illuminates the day, causing even the mysterious sea to 'append its tattery hues', but is it not possible that 'A candle is enough to light the world?' Stevens's answer is that the candle 'makes it clear. Even at noon / It glistens in essential dark. / At night, it lights the fruit and wine, / The book and bread, things as they are'. In these lines we find an inkling of a different kind of truth, the truth of the imagination.

At least seven of the poems in **'Blue Guitar'** deal with the dangers of an imagination out of touch with reality and remind us of Stevens's adage that 'The real is only the base. But it is the base'.[14] These poems also give a sense of continuity from Stevens's first collection *Harmonium* in their 'awareness of the texture of reality . . . as a factor at once for the enriching and for the limiting of experience'.[15] Poem XIII figures the various possible corruptions of the imagination, symbolized as always by the color blue:

> The pale intrusions into blue
> Are corrupting pallors . . . ay di mi,
>
> Blue buds of pitchy blooms. Be content—
> Expansions, diffusions—content to be
>
> The unspotted imbecile revery,
> The heraldic center of the world

Of blue, blue sleek with a hundred chins,
The amorist Adjective aflame . . .

The poem suggests the danger of the artist succumbing to conventionality, to popularity, to comfort; or of delving so far into subjectivity that expression becomes solipsism, the imagination an 'amorist Adjective aflame'.

In the preceding canto, the speaker had asked where he might find inspiration outside himself when he is all there is: 'Where / Do I begin and end? And where, / As I strum the thing, do I pick up / That which momentously declares / Itself not to be I and yet / Must be. It could be nothing else'. In poem IX, the persona sits waiting for inspiration: 'merely a shadow hunched / Above the arrowy, still strings, / The maker of a thing yet to be made'. Poem XXVII indicates that one need not go far afield for that inspiration. In William Burney's words: 'The refracting, focusing lens of the individual imagination composes the world in terms of the materials immediately at hand'.[16] Poem VII suggests further that the artist requires both the sun and the moon, reality and the imagination. Both have their function. Without reality, the strings would be cold on the blue guitar. In poem XXVI, while the world is 'washed' in the poet's imagination, the world is still the starting point, the ground for poetry. The world is here figured as 'a shore', a 'Rock . . . / To which his imagination returned, / from which it sped, a bar in space'.

That reality may not be so stable an entity as poem XXVI asserts is suggested by poem XV, a long existential query into the nature of reality and how contemporary art might most truly represent it. Is Picasso on the right track when he claims that art must be 'une somme de destructions', a 'hoard / Of destructions'? Have popular songs, such as 'Shine On, Harvest Moon', made it impossible to see both the harvest and the moon? The old truths about the real world have been destroyed, and the speaker asks if he has been destroyed along with them. According to Richard Blessing, poem XV implies that 'All human experience is forever cut off from one who experiences because all of our senses give us information at some distance in time and intensity from the event'. 'This meditation,' says Blessing, 'is on the nature and limitations of the relationship between physical phenomena—the spot on the floor, the food—and the mind of man'.[17] Yet the last couplet of poem XV hints that if we are to discern any hope for man connecting with the physical realities of the world it might be through the imagination, a tool for seeing the similarities and differences between things. As Robert Pack notes: 'It is the discovery and succeeding organization of resemblances and correspondences that for Stevens is the work of poetry'.[18]

Poem XXIII again points up a more troubled relation between reality and the imagination. It is an example of the extent to which **'Blue Guitar'** not only discusses but through its form illustrates the dangerous and delicate balance between originality and solipsism. Poem XXIII, which is one of the most impenetrable cantos in **'Blue Guitar'** and has elicited little commentary, juxtaposes two voices. What may be taken as the voice of the imagination is pictured as 'a voice in the clouds', 'serene and final', while the voice of reality is the voice of an undertaker, earthbound, 'Apostrophizing wreaths'. In a pun that suggests poetry's sublime and anesthetizing qualities, it is said to be the 'voice / Of ether', while the voice of reality smells of drink. The poet has his head in the clouds in a kind of natural high, while the undertaker is dependent on artificial stimulants.

A bleaker scene is presented in poem XXX, where we are confronted with the image of a scarecrow gazing at a power line in a banal suburb. This is the poet's material today. 'From this I shall evolve a man', he triumphantly asserts. From this Oxidia, he will build his Olympia. Oxidia—contemporary reality—is aptly named; as Robert Rehder notes, oxygen is the element in which we live, and oxidisation is a process through which things lose their shine when they come in contact with the oxygen-filled, real word.[19] As is often the case in **'Blue Guitar'**, a similar theme is treated in the poem following, where we find the lines: 'There is no place, / Here, for the lark fixed in the mind, / In the museum of the sky. The cock / Will claw sleep. Morning is not sun, / It is this posture of the nerves, / As if a blunted player clutched / The nuances of the blue guitar'. The lark symbolizes bygone, romantic poetry, which has lost its function in the modern world. The importance of the imagination is once again asserted. As Richard Allen Blessing interprets these lines, they claim that all experience, including the experience of morning, is 'more than external conditions . . . Experience is also a product of the nerves, of the internal alternations which we make in what we see'.[20] The need for balance between the imagination and reality is reasserted in the final couplet: 'It must be this rhapsody or none, / The rhapsody of things as they are'.

Poem XXXI also touches on another recurrent theme in **'Blue Guitar'**, the world's indifference to poetry and the things with which poetry traditionally deals. We have in the poem the image of the employer and employee who 'contend, / Combat, compose their droll affair', as day passes into night and the seasons change. In poem XXV, we have further images of the world's obliviousness to experience and to the imagination. While the poet practices his craft as best he can, life goes on regardless. In Judith Sheridan's view, the artist here is depicted as a juggler, a juggler of words, whose hold on the world is as precarious as a ball balanced on the tip of the nose. That things have been, are, and will be, is the whole extent of certain knowledge.[21]

Poem X, in Harold Bloom's words 'contemplates, with polemical zeal, the reduction of the hero in an unpoetic society'.[22] The modern-day hero is pictured as 'A pagan in a varnished car / . . . whom none believes', yet 'Whom all believe that all believe'. Confetti at the parade is 'the wills / Of the dead, majestic in their seals'. In poem XVI, writing poetry—'to chop the sullen psaltery'—is reduced to just another earthly activity, on a par with going to war, improving sanitation and communications, and worship. The poem begins with a rejection of former ways of symbolizing the world: 'The earth is not earth, but a stone, / Not the mother that held men as they fell / But stone, but like a stone'. Here we see the poet struggling with language, rejecting metaphor only to be forced to employ simile. There is no description without comparison, thus we gather that the only solution is to find better, more telling comparisons.

As I have already mentioned, one major concern of **'Blue Guitar'** in the face of a godless world and the deliquescence of old poetic forms and symbols is the need to see the world afresh, to invent new symbols, in fact, a new myth for the age. This is the subject of one of Stevens's essays, 'The Noble Rider and the Sound of Words', which implicitly throws at least as strong a light on **'Blue Guitar'** as the paraphrases in his letters. Taking as his starting-point Plato's figure from the *Phaedrus* of the soul as a charioteer with winged horses, Stevens tries to explain how it is that symbols lose their impact. In his words: 'The imagination loses vitality as it ceases to adhere to what is real. When it adheres to the unreal and intensifies what is unreal, while its first effect may be extraordinary, the effect is the maximum effect it will ever have.'[23]

The reduction in impact of old symbols and rituals is illustrated by poem XXIX, in which we come upon the speaker seated in a cathedral. Significantly he is reading 'a lean Review' rather than a religious work, as he considers how the past opposes the present, how death opposes life, how the worms feasting on the dead—'the degustations in the vaults'—are in contrast with the marriage ceremony, and create a kind of balance. While poetry may be true in different ways, 'the balance does not quite rest', 'the mask is strange, however like'. The speaker finds no truth in the cathedral's architecture or the music or the bells, but the Franciscan monk depicted in the stained glass window ('this fertile glass') is somehow still true.

The theme of finding a new myth for the age is most vividly illustrated by poem XXXII, which contains an injunction to reject the old, clichéd ways of seeing the world ('the rotted names'). The well-known symbol of

the informing light is inverted and rejected. You must try to face reality head on, says the speaker, without mediation, in conceptual darkness. The imagination will allow you to rediscover yourself as you are.

That reality's sunlight may not be the best illumination for the world is first suggested by canto V. Here the voice of the public speaks, a public that sees the world in black and white, without gradations, without shadows. Things mean what they mean. There is no ambiguity. Yet the canto contains an abrupt change in perspective, marked by an unexpected caesura: 'The earth for us, is flat and bare. / There are no shadows. Poetry / Exceeding music must take the place / Of empty heaven and its hymns, / Ourselves in poetry must take their place, Even in the chattering of your guitar'. Heaven is empty. There is no God. Man is at the center of the world and the public demands that he be placed at the center of art. In Stevens's words from the essay 'Imagination as Value': 'The great poems of heaven and hell have been written and the great poem of the earth remains to be written'.[24]

In poem VIII, we find the poet struggling to portray a traditional subject, a stormy morning, yet his chords are cold, the sound of the guitar is lazy and leaden. He makes order out of chaos, 'brings the storm to bear', but that is all. Poem XI further suggests the danger of clinging to outmoded imagery and writing false poetry. The eternal cycle of life might traditionally be shown as ivy on stone turning to stone, women devolving into cities, children into fields, men into the sea, but this 'is the chord that falsifies', that creates a false sense of harmony. One could say as truly that the 'sea returns upon the men', that 'The fields entrap the children, / brick is a weed and all the flies are caught, / Wingless withered, but living alive'. False art merely makes life harder to live.

We have seen how clusters of poems within **'Blue Guitar'** group themselves around certain questions, themes, or problematics, such as the role of poetry in the godless universe; scepticism towards the truth claims of science and certain types of realistic art; the need for the imagination to stay in touch with reality; the dulling of the senses by quotidian existence; and the concomitant need to refocus our perceptions, to invent new, supreme fictions to live by. In a further group of poems Stevens tries to say something about how poetry can become reality, how the blue guitar becomes the place of things as they are. Preeminent among the poems to approach this question is number VI, which describes a process by which art becomes reality. Things imagined become things as they are. It is not just a question of life influencing art, but also the other way around. Life imitates art. Reality is placed 'beyond the compass of change'; for a moment it seems final, for a moment it seems real. A. Walton Litz calls this poem 'the ideal resolution, a sustaining fiction which embodies "things as they are" while retaining all of the satisfactions of that other reality, the poem', yet as he also points out, 'the process by which this is accomplished remains to be defined'.[25]

Poem XVII, reemphasizes the extent to which the blue guitar may become the moulder of the animal that is the spirit and that, unlike the body, has no given shape. The reliance on the power of the imagination becomes even stronger in poem XVIII, where the speaker searches for a dream in which he can believe, even in the face of reality. Sometimes an artistic creation (the blue guitar) may be so true as to become a thing of the world. On certain nights the artist is inspired and is able to reach beyond the physical: 'the blue guitar / After long strumming on certain nights / Gives the touch of the senses, not of the hand, / But the very senses as they touch / The wind-gloss. Or as daylight comes, / Like light in a mirroring of cliffs, / Rising upward from a sea of ex'. As Ronald Sukenick has written: 'A fiction which is credible in face of reality and through which reality is interpreted, is no longer a fiction. That is to say, a myth which is believed in is not a myth . . . Such a fiction becomes the version of reality as perceived—"things as they are"'.[26] The final poem of the cycle, which, as Litz writes, is 'not so much a conclusion as a reenactment of familiar themes',[27] reemphasizes the importance of the imagination, in daily life and for people other than poets: 'we shall sleep by night. / We shall forget by day, except / The moments when we choose to play / The imagined pine, the imagined jay'.

III

By way of a conclusion I will offer brief readings of three poems in which I feel Stevens tries most actively to forge a synthesis between reality and the imagination, and by doing so, to provide at least a partial answer to the questions he has raised in the rest of the poem.

My first example is poem XIX:

> That I may reduce the monster to
> Myself, then may be myself
>
> In face of the monster, be more than part
> Of it, more than the monstrous player of
>
> One of its monstrous lutes, not be
> Alone, but reduce the monster and be,
>
> Two things, the two things together as one,
> And play of the monster and of myself,
>
> Or better not of myself at all,
> But of that as its intelligence,
>
> Being the lion in the lute
> Before the lion locked in stone.

In this poem, the world is depicted as a monster. Only by delving into the self can one be oneself and face the world. The artist does not seek isolation ('not to be / Alone'), but to be both true to himself and to the world and express himself and the world. To Louis Martz, this canto shows 'man's inner rage for order as the ultimate constructive force in man's universe, and hence the never-ending effort of the mind to control within the mind, that outer monster, the inhuman universe'.[28]

Poem XXVIII reads as follows:

> I am a native in this world
> And think in it as a native thinks,
>
> Gesu, not native of a mind
> Thinking the thoughts I call my own,
>
> Native, a native in the world
> And like a native think in it.
>
> It could not be a mind, the wave
> In which the watery grasses flow
>
> And yet are fixed as a photograph,
> The wind in which the dead leaves blow.
>
> Here I inhale profounder strength
> And as I am, I speak and move
>
> And things are as I think they are
> And say they are on the blue guitar.

It is the world that inspires thought in the speaker. The poet must be part of the world. It will give him strength. One is born into the world not into one's own mind. Poem XXVIII gives a rare sense of harmony between the artist and the world, and bears out Frank Kermode in his observation that reality for Wallace Stevens is 'what you see finely and imagine fully from where you are and as what you are'.[29]

I choose as my final selection poem XXII, the most famous and discussed canto in **'Blue Guitar'**:

> Poetry is the subject of the poem,
> From this the poem issues and
>
> To this returns. Between the two,
> Between issue and return, there is
>
> An absence in reality,
> Things as they are. Or so we say.
>
> But are these separate? Is it
> An absence for the poem, which acquires
>
> Its true appearance there, sun's green,
> Cloud's red, earth feeling, sky that thinks?
>
> From these it takes. Perhaps it gives,
> In the universal intercourse.

Poetry is the subject of the poem: poems are about poetry. This is both the starting point and the end-point of a poem. There is some 'absence in reality' ('things as they are') that lies between the desire to write poetry and the realization of that desire, something is lost on the way, or so it is common to claim. Is this right? Are the issue and return separate? Does the poem necessarily lose something when it tries to represent reality as truthfully as possible? Is not this absence, this difference, necessary? Stevens ends poem XXII by indicating—what he will claim more strongly elsewhere in **'Blue Guitar'**—that while poetry takes from reality, it is also possible that it give something back as well.

Stevens claimed in a letter to Hi Simons that poem XXII stated 'a fundamental principle about the imagination': 'It does not create except as it transforms'.[30] Critics have seen this poem as the climax and resolution of **'Blue Guitar'**, or, what is closer to the truth, as the point where Stevens begins to reconcile the ostensibly opposing forces of the imagination and physical phenomena.[31] To A. Walton Litz poem XXII is a variation on the aphorism from *Adagia* which comes closest to summing up Stevens's poetic: 'Poetry is not the same thing as the imagination taken alone. Nothing is itself taken alone. Things are because of interrelations or interactions'.[32]

Despite all my words and the multitude of other words written about the poem since it entered the world some sixty years ago, the only thing that is certain about **'The Man with the Blue Guitar'** is that any point of rest in the poem is only temporary. For Wallace Stevens, Frank Lentricchia observes, 'To write the long poem . . . is by definition to string together a collocation of moments and to create a book of moments which hangs together by the force of desire for moments, the moving into the moment, the moving out'.[33] The totality of **'The Man with the Blue Guitar'** may be figured as a *perpetuum mobile,* a machine in perpetual motion. As long as there are readers, the poem Wallace Stevens has set in motion will keep on moving.

Notes

1. In emphasizing the unity in disunity of the poem, I am aligning myself with the many critics who have been unwilling to see in it a rigid pattern, overall development, or closure. See J. Hillis Miller, 'Wallace Stevens' Poetry of Being', in *The Act of the Mind: Essays on the Poetry of Wallace Stevens,* eds Roy Harvey Pearce and J. Hillis Miller (Baltimore, 1965), p. 147; Joseph N. Riddel, *The Clairvoyant Eye: The Poetry and Poetics of Wallace Stevens* (Baton Rouge, 1965), pp. 136-37; Helen Hennessy Vendler, *On Extended Wings: Wallace Stevens' Longer Poems* (Cambridge, 1969), p. 141; George S. Lensing, *Wallace*

Stevens: A Poet's Growth (Baton Rouge and London, 1986), pp. 42-43; Robert Rehder, *The Poetry of Wallace Stevens: The Plain Sense of Things* (New York and Oxford, 1991), p. 191. For an opposing view, see William Burney, *Wallace Stevens* (New York, 1968), p. 83; Harold Bloom, *Wallace Stevens* (New York, 1988), p. 152; James Longenbach, *Wallace Stevens: The Poems of Our Climate* (Ithaca and London, 1977), p. 120.

2. All quotations from the poem are taken from Wallace Stevens, *The Collected Poems of Wallace Stevens* (New York, 1957), pp. 165-84.

3. Robert Fitzgerald, 'Thoughts Revolved', in *Wallace Stevens: The Critical Heritage,* ed. Charles Doyle (London, 1985), p. 176.

4. While Stevens treats explicitly of poetry in 'Blue Guitar', it is possible to see that poetry stands in for art in general, just as the poet stands in for 'any man of the imagination'.

5. Wallace Stevens, *Letters of Wallace Stevens,* ed. Holly Stevens (New York, 1966), p. 360-61.

6. R. P. Blackmur, 'Examples of Wallace Stevens', in *Critical Heritage,* p. 97.

7. 'Examples', pp. 98-99.

8. Wallace Stevens, *The Necessary Angel: Essays on Reality and the Imagination* (New York, 1951), p. 21.

9. Riddel, *Clairvoyant Eye,* p. 148.

10. Ronald Sukenick, *Wallace Stevens: Musing the Obscure* (New York, 1967), p. 85.

11. *Necessary Angel,* pp. 29, 31.

12. The quoted expression is taken from Stevens's blurb on the dustjacket of *The Man with the Blue Guitar.* Quoted in A. Walton Litz, *Introspective Voyager: The Poetic Development of Wallace Stevens* (New York, 1972), p. 232.

13. *Musing,* p. 84.

14. Quoted in Sukenick, *Musing,* p. 97.

15. Roy Harvey Pearce, 'Wallace Stevens: The Life of the Imagination', in *Critical Essays,* p. 112. Pearce is describing *Harmonium.*

16. *Wallace Stevens,* p. 89.

17. Richard Allen Blessing, *Wallace Stevens' 'Whole Harmonium'* (Syracuse, 1970), p. 57.

18. Robert Pack, *Wallace Stevens: An Approach to His Poetry and Thought* (New Brunswick, NJ, 1958), p. 56.

19. *Poetry*, p. 169.

20. *'Whole Harmonium'*, p. 60.

21. Judith Rinde Sheridan, 'The Picasso Connection: Wallace Stevens's "The Man with the Blue Guitar"', *Arizona Quarterly*, XXXV (1979), 78.

22. *Poems of Our Climate*, p. 125.

23. *Necessary Angel*, p. 6.

24. *Necessary Angel*, p. 142.

25. *Introspective Voyager*, pp. 240-41.

26. *Wallace Stevens*, p. 93.

27. *Introspective Voyager*, pp. 256-57.

28. Louis Martz, 'Wallace Stevens: The World as Meditation', in *Wallace Stevens: A Collection of Critical Essays*, ed. Marie Borroff (Englewood Cliffs, NJ, 1963), p. 142.

29. Frank Kermode, *Wallace Stevens* (Edinburgh and London, 1960), p. 12.

30. *Letters*, p. 364.

31. See, for example, *Clairvoyant Eye*, p. 144, *'Whole Harmonium'*, p. 57.

32. *Introspective Voyager*, p. 244.

33. Frank Lentricchia, *Ariel and the Police: Michel Foucault, William James, Wallace Stevens* (Brighton, 1988), p. 206.

James Lucas (essay date 2001)

SOURCE: Lucas, James. "Fiction, Politics, and Chocolate Whipped Cream: Wallace Stevens's 'Forces, the Will, and the Weather.'" *ELH* 68 (2001): 745-61.

[*In the following essay, Lucas examines the politics of Stevens's poetry through a close reading of the lesser-known poem "Forces, the Will, and the Weather."*]

I.

In this paper I approach what critics might identify, alternatively, as the political aspects of Wallace Stevens's poetry, or as its lack of an ideological dimension, through **"Forces, the Will, & the Weather."** This poem has been neglected by Stevens's critics ever since its 1942 publication in *Parts of a World*. I intend to show that this particular poem casts much more light on those issues than one might expect, given its marginality to the Stevens canon; indeed, I hope to demonstrate that approaching the ideological through a minor rather than a major text is a course particularly suited to the Stevens case. I would note immediately that the politi-cal significance of Stevens's 1930s and 1940s work has become, increasingly, a matter for debate. While the generalist orthodox critiques of the past three decades have tended to portray Stevens as a more or less culpably right-wing figure, specialist Stevens scholars have often produced a more ideologically palatable, and even a politically responsible, poet.[1] If one finds racist remarks and guarded praise for Mussolini in the poet's private papers and correspondence, one finds also that he voted the Democrat ticket in the presidential elections of 1900, and even, in a letter of October 1935, his expressed hope that he is "headed left."[2] While the Nietzschean affinities of Stevens's "major man" suggest a culpable complicity with fascist mythology and institutional practice, the **"Greenest Continent"** section of **"Owl's Clover"** might be read as an indictment of European imperialism in Africa.[3]

In short, Stevens's politics remain open to debate because he never gave them full, unequivocal, and public articulation. This reticence has itself been read as politically significant. James Longenbach has praised Stevens's equivocalities and figurative modes as a considered and commendable response to the cultural prevalence of more absolutist discourses; Marjorie Perloff has condemned these same tendencies as escapist. I consider both views presently. What is certainly true is that there is no sustained ideological statement in Stevens's published writings comparable to, say, Pound's propagandist tirades against usurers in "A Visiting Card," or Eliot's attempted legitimization of class hierarchy in *Notes towards the Definition of Culture*.[4] Even in William Carlos Williams's 1930s "Proletarian" portraits and his condemnation of "bought courts" of law we find clearly articulated political sympathies, if not systems.[5] We do not find the like in Stevens. His is a case in which questions may be most pertinently asked, not of politics as a recoverable position, but of the general (and I would argue self-conscious) relations between his praxis and the whole ideological sphere. Given this, the points of reference most useful in locating Stevens will be other writers' conceptions, in the 1930s and 40s, of that broad praxis-ideology relation.

"Forces, the Will, & the Weather," as a poem which makes a token reference to politics, only to eschew any serious subject matter, is immediately suggestive *because* it show Stevens at his most ideologically evasive. More, it has a unique interest in Stevens's relentlessly foregrounding this evasion, so much so that he becomes, in this text, fully (if negatively) concerned with ideology, with the uneasy relationship between his own poetic work and a notion of "engagement" which the poem successfully makes abstract. On these counts alone, it takes us quickly to the heart of recent debates about the ideological implications of Stevens's work, and the very latency of those implications. We note, additionally, that it was written during a world political crisis, and at a critical point in Stevens's poetic development; the poem belongs to the final phase of Stevens's poetic prior to the central *Notes toward a Supreme Fiction.* "Forces, the Will, & the Weather" also presents an implicit, subversive gloss on Stevens's most famous lecture, "The Noble Rider and the Sound of Words." It recalls, too, the early **"Anecdote of the Jar,"** and in such a way as to negate that poem and to qualify the aesthetic of *Harmonium.* Finally, **"Forces, the Will, & the Weather,"** in its discovery of a formal maneuver by which certain non-formal difficulties might be indefinitely postponed, strongly prefigures the canonized *Notes* [*Notes toward a Supreme Fiction*]. In this poem Stevens is at a crossroads, conducting a remarkably deep interrogation of his existing repertoire of poetic procedures. Stevens's manner of surmounting the impasse he creates for himself in this text has ramifications for the whole of the later work.

On its surface, **"Forces, the Will, & the Weather"** is so slight as to be provocative:

> At the time of nougats, the peer yellow
> Sighed in the evening that he lived
> Without ideas in a land without ideas,
> The pair yellow, the peer.
>
> It was the time, the place, of nougats.
> There the dogwoods, the white ones and the pink ones,
> Bloomed in sheets, as they bloom, and the girl,
> A pink girl took a white dog walking.
>
> The dog had to walk. He had to be taken.
> The girl had to hold back and lean back to hold him,
> At the time of the dogwoods, handfuls thrown up
> To spread colors. There was not an idea
>
> This side of Moscow. There were anti-ideas
> And counter-ideas. There was nothing one had. There
>   were
> No horses to ride and no one to ride them
> In the woods of the dogwoods,
>
> No large white horses. But there was the fluffy dog.
> There were the sheets high up on older trees,
> Seeming to be liquid as leaves made of cloud,
> Shells under water. These were nougats.
>
> It had to be right: nougats. It was a shift
> Of realities, that, in which it could be wrong.
> The weather was like a waiter with a tray.
> One had come early to a crisp café.[6]

Most strikingly perverse is the poet's inclusion of patently political references even as he pursues a radically apolitical agenda. At the typographical center of this poem positing the world as nougat—a bizarre, a "willful" conceit—Stevens embeds the flat statement, "There was not an idea // This side of Moscow." Because the poem had no journal publication before its inclusion in *Parts of a World,* issued September 1942, it is impossible to determine whether this is a response to the Russian campaign that began in June 1941, or even whether it predates or is subsequent to Pearl Harbor. Its uncertain date resists the attribution of close referential specificity, and yet the mention of "Forces" in the title, of ideas from "Moscow," and of white (Cossack?) horses in the text inevitably alludes to the war, and to war as a confrontation between contesting ideologies, ideas, and "counter-ideas." Having raised them, the text preemptively terminates our consideration of such questions, returning to "the woods of the dogwoods," to the world of nougat.

Crucially, the poem strongly resists all of the standard readings of Stevens's ideology or, as some critics would maintain, his failure to subscribe consciously to one. It resists the practices of critics such as James Longenbach and Alan Filreis who, mining the poems very deeply, attempt to retrieve a Stevens keenly interested in the political and historical circumstances of his United States and responsive to those milieus.[7] In what way might this poem be Stevens's well-considered response, as Longenbach and Filreis would have it, to "what one [read] in the papers"?[8] To find in this text a veiled criticism of ideological torpor in the United States, or of the isolationist policy of its government, would require interpretive extrapolation on a major scale, and an arbitrary assignment of authorial intention. Invoking Longenbach's supplementary argument— that "Stevens felt insecure about his own statements [on politics] precisely because he thought the issues were important"—would seem to ignore the tone and avowed preoccupations of this decadent "nougat" text.[9] Conversely, it would be extremely difficult to assimilate the practices of this poem to those of *Notes toward a Supreme Fiction,* as glossed by Marjorie Perloff; is Stevens's rhetoric really "designed to convince both poet and reader that, despite the daily headlines and radio bulletins, the real action takes place in the country of metaphor"?[10] This poem knowingly exposes, by its minimal reference to ideological and military dimensions, the triviality of its subject matter and of the subject position within it. So far from making any claims for the importance of a "poet's war" (as in the coda to *Notes*), Stevens presents the contesting "forces" here as exerted by a pink girl and a white dog. It is with an admittedly trivial and privatized world that Stevens deals, and in a text composed in the same period as the grandiose pronouncements of "The Noble Rider." Here there are "no ideas"; there are, in Stevens's figure, "no white horses and no one to ride them."

Conceding that ideological forces are operative, but only in some circumscribed elsewhere, while restricting overt meditations to nougat, Stevens indulges in a radical displacement; it is not so much that war becomes "weather" (a euphemism of which he was fond) but that weather becomes nougat. A letter sent by Stevens to Wilson Taylor, dated 13 January 1941, effects similar associations and displacements, providing a supplementary and less labored articulation of the poem's improbable conceits:

> I had no idea that the conquest of Poland was due to the drinking of vermouth-cassis by the Poles. . . . But what a time we live in when one man yowls for vermouth-cassis, another for beer, another for coca-cola, another for rye. Good god, what a mess!
>
> I suppose Denmark was a push-over on account of the pastry they eat there. In any event, I am chock-full of the stuff you sent me. That man in Plainfield is some pastrician! This is not a thing that I say much about, because I feel confident that I am surrounded by people who are based on squash pie and pumpkin pie. In this inimical atmosphere the less one says about chocolate whipped cream the better.[11]

Offering tongue-in-cheek connections between culinary preferences and international power politics, the letter shows affinities with the poem strong enough to suggest that the two texts may be at least approximately contemporaneous. If that were the case, then **"Forces, the Will, & the Weather"** would have been written during exactly that period, from January to March 1941, that Stevens was at work on "The Noble Rider," the lecture he delivered at Princeton in May.[12]

The poem stands to the lecture as ironic counterpoint. At Princeton Stevens spoke of the war and of a "war-like" state in American society in order to argue the urgent need, in such circumstances, of finding in poetry some viable notion of our "nobility," some means of sustaining an idea of "our spiritual height and depth."[13] This strategy, which would make political circumstances tolerable by subsuming them to a redemptive neo-Romanticism, required that the political significations of Stevens's central figure be made secondary to its aesthetic significations. Stevens incarnates his noble rider as General Jackson, and as the *condottiere* Colleoni—as warrior-leader—and dampens the political resonances by a category transition which sees their artistic representations judged according to a putatively apolitical aesthetic. Here is Stevens on Verrocchio's statue of Colleoni:

> It is like the form of an invincible man, who has come, slowly and boldly, through every warlike opposition of the past and who moves in our midst without dropping the bridle of the powerful horse from his hand, without taking off his helmet and without relaxing the attitude of a warrior of noble origin. . . . In this state, the apposition between the imagination and reality is too favorable to the imagination.[14]

Where Pound conjures the historical Sigismundo Malatesta as dramatic hero, Stevens cultivates his audience's nostalgia for an atavistic warrior-hero while suppressing, with an ease we may find disquieting, the *condottiere*'s historical and military actuality.[15] His audience's nostalgia for nobility in the abstract prepares the ground for their acceptance of the "possible poet" offered by Stevens as consolation. No such ascendancy of the aesthetic and private over the political and public is present in **"Forces, the Will, & the Weather."** So far from being subsumed into a less contentious aesthetic ideal, the equestrian figure retains its militaristic potentiality. Unseen, located on some other "side," it resists decisive aesthetic appropriation. Stevens's configuration of *this* noble rider expresses the anxiety of the non-participant, the poet as potential victim. His nougat talk does not make of the world at war an occasion for a great aesthetic project on the part of some elect individual but reframes that world as a private enclave whose terms are defined by epicurean consumption. Here is the Stevens who made private arrangements to receive "the very best tea" direct from Ceylon, whose friends sent him oranges from Florida and pastries from New York.[16]

One might wonder at Frank Lentricchia's not discussing the poem in *Ariel and the Police,* so aptly would it seem to illustrate Lentricchia's theses of class and gender politics in Stevens. Lentricchia regards Stevens's literary aestheticism as a species of commodity fetishism: "The hedonism of bourgeois man bought at the psychic expense of a repression of the economic process which gives rise to commodities . . . is the point of departure for Stevens for an experience that would not be commodity based."[17] Lentricchia, for whom the "issue of Stevens' sexual identity as a writer—his effort to phallicize poetic discourse—is not just related to but just *is* the canonical modernist issue of poetic authority," might have observed further that Stevens's gender anxiety gives rise to his thinly disguised incarnation as "pink girl" walking his lap-dog text.[18] The point I would stress is that the poem is so *consciously* artificial, and so blatantly evasive, that it effectively preempts any reading that Lentricchia, or indeed Perloff, might offer. Stevens concedes the limitations of his lifestyle ("the less one says about chocolate whipped cream the better") and of his poetic world ("There was not an idea. . . . But there was the fluffy dog"). Yet, having done so, he interrogates the trivial construct on its own terms, and to the point of exhaustion. The pink girl and white dog, which become the focus—are they literally intended (even if invented), or does their struggle on either end of a leash represent imagistically the movement of pink and white blossoms as a breeze stirs the dogwoods? Does the dog itself proceed out of, not only a visual association, but the materials of the poem itself as language, out of the *dog*woods? If so, may not "sheets" and "leaves" garnished with blossoms/nougat refer to the poem itself, or to poetry? This play subverts the status of the world presented by problematizing the concreteness or otherwise of its elements, and the stability of the linguistic terms through which the presentation occurs (I will distinguish these strategies from deconstructive practices presently). Stevens works to make his reader party to the dilemma. The change of perspective from that of "the peer" to that of the rhetorically sanctioned "one," in the final line, implicates the reader as participant in this exercise in absurdist pseudo-epistemology. The weather, for this readerly/writerly one in the café, is "like a waiter with a tray." To draw out the buried pun, the waiter is there to take the customer's order. Stevens has been ordering the world by, as it were, ordering "nougat." The reader here is invited to find an order for both this text and, within strict and apolitical parameters, the world.

These compound textual riddles, absorbing the reader's critical energies, imitating and taking the place of more substantive examinations and struggles, give to the word "Moscow" the effect of a reprimand. Paradoxically, they also act as defenses ensuring that the idea of "Moscow," when it comes, is met and parried within a world where the primacy of a trivial question, nougat (or non-nougat), is already established. It is as if Prufrock, having dared to eat his peach, has found its peachiness to be *the* overwhelming question. "Moscow" poses a problem: what is this term doing here at all? As a point of strictly contained rupture, "Moscow" functions antithetically to the "jar" of the famous *Harmonium* anecdote. The inability of "Moscow" to command this world, to make the nougat-world "surround" it, is dramatically and deliberately enacted. The poem implicitly rewrites **"Anecdote of the Jar"** for the early 1940s.

II.

In itself, the jar of Stevens's 1919 **"Anecdote"** is formidably nondescript:

> I placed a jar in Tennessee
> And round it was, upon a hill.
> It made the slovenly wilderness
> Surround that hill.
>
> The wilderness rose up to it,
> And sprawled around, no longer wild.
> The jar was round upon the ground
> And tall and of a port in air.
>
> It took dominion everywhere.
> The jar was gray and bare.
> It did not give of bird or bush,
> Like nothing else in Tennessee.[19]

Or, we might say, like nothing else in Stevens's Tennessee. The jar can of course be read symbolically, as when Helen Vendler nominates it to be the American correspondent to Keats's Grecian urn, or when Michael Herr, discussing the United States military's remapping of Vietnam with a new system of coordinates, cites the poem.[20] Such readings, though tenable enough, remain nominations of meaning, and cannot fully account for

the jar or settle its anecdotal account. The context of the poem is itself too limited to establish within its own lines the jar's symbolic significance. As Lentricchia points out, an anecdote must do what this one, apparently, will not: make its point by appealing to a wider and socially operative narrative.[21] The poem resists explication. The jar itself, though nondescript, is by no means quotidian. So quintessentially bland ("gray and bare"), at once the object of facile rhymes and grand syntactic inversions ("round upon the ground," "round it was"), the jar is made extraordinary, appears "tall and of a port in air." Working as both difficult symbol and difficult image, the jar is doubly and categorically problematic.[22] Its preeminence and uncanniness derive, also, from the general sparsity (linguistic and imagistic) in which it is embedded and from which it provides a measure of relief.

It is this last aspect of the jar, its being placed, that I wish to emphasize here. Approaching the text as production rather than product, the jar's power to command the textual landscape is seen to derive, fundamentally, from the poet's sovereign act of selection and placement. The jar is made the governing center of its world, thereby installing the authority of Stevens, its chooser. Glen MacLeod has astutely compared Stevens's poem to a Duchamp readymade, in which the "choice of an object" may be "seen as a creative act."[23] The jar itself recalls Duchamp's urinal/fountain, I suggest, in being an item which, certainly *not* presacralized by existing cultural associations, is invested, at the very moment it is taken up, with a kind of commanding aura. Its nomination is its (limited) authentication, as the very idea of "aura" is modified, but not extinguished, by the wit involved in its production/placement. Other *Harmonium* poems make analogous use of, for instance, blackbirds and patterned nightgowns, but this jar is the archetype of such items, the most auratically charged, because here Stevens foregrounds the act of placing, the peculiar ritual of nomination: "I placed a jar in Tennessee."

Lentricchia, as we have seen, relates Stevens's *Harmonium* aesthetic to commodity fetishism. It seems to me that, with regard to the specifically ritualistic aspect of this, Walter Benjamin's 1930s critical discussions of the aesthetic "aura" (though they are not, of course, addressed to Stevens) would offer even stronger readings. Throughout history, Benjamin argued in "The Work of Art in the Age of Mechanical Reproduction" (1936), the art institution conferred canonical status on certain artists so that specific works, elevated by this fetish of the master's name, were established as "authentic," auratic objects providing the occasion for a secular ritual. This was art as "ritual function."[24] In these terms we might say that Stevens, as legitimizer of *Stevens*'s jar, *and* as convenor of the ritual of its placement, has assumed the institutional role. Benjamin's further argument, that the mass mechanical reproduction of artworks would eliminate this "aura" by making the idea of authenticity (the unique work) redundant, casts additional light on a characteristic practice of *Harmonium,* and anticipates Lentricchia's analysis. Stevens's aesthetic ritual might be said to resist an economic culture of literary mass production and consumption; the items furnishing his fictive worlds, "jungle feathers," "baboons and periwinkles," are valued and installed as things unavailable to, and even unsought by, the ordinary literary consumer.[25] We might note here that even the left-sympathetic William Carlos Williams elected, given the realities of marketing poetry in the post-Depression era, to publish *An Early Martyr* (1935) in an expensive edition through Latimer's boutique Alcestis Press, and that Benjamin himself was, like Stevens, a self-confessed fetishist when it came to collecting rare books.[26] Certain passages in Benjamin's *Baudelaire* manuscript are more pertinent still; there is no more telling gloss on Stevens's whimsically chosen objects, on his act of selecting and placing them within his idiosyncratic fictive worlds, and on their resistance to explication, than this passage concerning the Paris of the Second Empire, written by Benjamin sometime in the 1930s:

> Since the days of Louis Philippe the bourgeoise has endeavoured to compensate itself for the inconsequential nature of private life in the big city. It seeks such compensation within its four walls. Even if a bourgeois is unable to give his earthly being permanence, it seems to be a matter of honour with him to preserve the traces of his articles and requisites of daily use in perpetuity. The bourgeois cheerfully takes the impression of a host of objects. For slippers and pocket watches, thermometers and egg-cups, cutlery and umbrellas it tries to get covers and cases . . . They are removed from the profane eyes of non-owners, and in particular their outlines are blurred in a characteristic way.[27]

Benjamin's observation on this blurring of outlines is very much to the point; Stevens, full-time insurance lawyer, places a jar in his own textual Tennessee in such a way that it becomes fetishized, difficult to decipher, auratic. In *Harmonium,* items like this jar often provide "compensation" for a surrounding tawdriness, emptiness, or "slovenliness." If the eponymous yokel of **"Gubbinal"** should succeed in banning poetic descriptions, disallowing "animal eye" and "savage of fire" and "seed" as names for the sun, then the world would be uniformly "ugly," the people "sad."[28] In a similar vein, **"The Man on the Dump"** casts the poverty of a hobo as an *aesthetic* deprivation. The late Stevens tends to deny himself the compensations of the aesthetically exotic, as the private textual *interieur* becomes the austere habitat of the ascetic rather than the aesthete, notably in the empty room of **"Professor Eucalyptus."** Lentricchia reads the later poetry as "gourmandizing . . . deliberately teased out. . . . At the poetic, if not at the economic, level of existence, he

found a way to supply the spirit by resisting consumption."[29] On this reading the later poetry becomes a ritual of exquisite foreplay.

The convenor of **"Forces, the Will, & the Weather"** does not preside over either of these kinds of ritual. So conscious of the text as willful production, the articulating voice adopts a register which might more accurately be called theatrical. Here the estranged presence and estranging impact of "Moscow" present a unique case. We note that the text as *interieur* has not yet been emptied out. Instead, its structures have been inverted. The exotic, difficult element—"firecat," "jar," "tuft of jungle feathers"—no longer commands the center; it has been dissipated into the formerly bleak surrounds.[30] What would have been privileged and auratic items in an *Harmonium* text are now omnipresent, trivialized: "blossoms," "pink girl," "fluffy dog." The world is pervaded by a "nougat" atmosphere, an environment that actualizes aesthetic gluttony. Overconsumption is made laughable by its being so conspicuous, and satiation gives way to a kind of psychic indigestion ("had to be right . . . could be wrong"). This text, needing no exotic item at its center, presents us instead with "Moscow," synecdoche for a harsh and politicized reality that the nougat world is unable to accommodate; unlike a deconstructive *aporia,* the term is simply foreign, unable to challenge, let alone dismantle, the informing nougat/not-nougat binary. Beneath this mock challenge, the whimsy, and the elaborate defensiveness of this poem, Stevens seems to own his aesthete self to be, irrevocably and irremediably, the "stuffed goldfinch," and "artificer of his own world of mannerism," that the critic Geoffrey Grigson had identified.[31]

III.

"Forces, the Will, & the Weather" reconsiders, in the early 1940s, a hedonistic strain by then less prominent in Stevens's poetic. *Ideas of Order* (1935) showed, according to Stanley Burnshaw, that the poetry of *Harmonium* was "verse that Stevens [could] no longer write"; it showed, in fact, that as an "acutely conscious" member of "a class menaced by the clashes between capital and labor," Stevens was "in the throes of struggle for philosophical adjustment."[32] Burnshaw's review, the most generous Stevens would receive from an avowed Marxist, acknowledged a new austerity and self-deprecation in the 1935 collection. Burnshaw's Stevens, struggling for philosophical adjustment, seems still to be present in this early 1940s poem, particularly in these extraordinary lines: "It had to be right: nougats. It was a shift / Of realities, that, in which it could be wrong."

I want to suggest that the struggle for adjustment here is tactical rather than philosophical. In this paradoxical statement of self-doubt we have, I believe, Stevens's own review of his post-*Harmonium* work, and a state-ment which is itself the unheroic culmination of his project for a "new romanticism." In a retrospective remark made in January 1940, Stevens described the beginnings of that project in this way: "I began to feel that I was on the edge: that I wanted to get to the center: that I was isolated, and that I wanted to share the com-mon life."[33] In the poems, however, getting to the center (often represented in virtually diagrammatic terms) invariably became an antisocial pursuit. The achieve-ment of a "slight transcendence" required, he found in **"Sailing After Lunch"** (1935), that he "expunge all people and be a pupil / Of the gorgeous wheel" of earth.[34] If he would submit to the world as its student, the world itself would be eye or iris, with the poet as its central and light-admitting "pupil"; this balance between opposing claims for the centrality and for the submis-siveness of the poetic consciousness would become a recurrent motif. In **"Yellow Afternoon"** Stevens says of a fallen soldier, "Everything comes to him / From the middle of his field," a field that is both paddock and field of vision, the synthesis compounded by the paradoxical condition of things coming to him from the point already occupied.[35] Stevens's untheorized pursuit of ideas of order, carried on as it was by a privileged subjectivity in isolation, produced a poetry that, deceptively, appeared to be epistemologically informed. From the mid-1930s, Stevens had evolved linguistic strategies—puns, riddles, grammatical ambiguities—by which different versions or aspects of the mind-world interaction could be accommodated simultaneously within a passage. The "new romantic," as it appeared in the limited apotheoses of *Parts of a World,* had become largely dependent on sleight-of-hand, on linguistically generated paradox.

The principal point of contention when linguistic instabilities were so consistently exploited—and here the apparent epistemological preoccupation again comes into play—was not an "idea," but the content and structure of the poetic world. Producing anomalous but still self-contained worlds, Stevens took to an extreme an approach to poetry common in this period, one that is discussed by Raymond Williams:

> I said to people here at Cambridge; in the thirties you were passing severely limiting judgements on Milton and relatively favourable judgements on the metaphysi-cal poets, which in effect redrew the map of seventeenth-century literature in England. Now you were, of course, making literary judgements—your sup-porting quotations and analysis prove it, but you were also asking about ways of living through a political and cultural crisis of national dimensions. On the one side, you have a man who totally committed himself to a particular side and cause, who temporarily suspended what you call literature, but in fact not writing, in that conflict. On the other, *you have a kind of writing which is highly intelligent and elaborate, that is a way of holding divergent attitudes towards struggle or towards*

experience together in the mind at the same time. These are two possibilities for any highly conscious person in a period of crisis—a kind of commitment which involves certain difficulties, certain naïvetés, certain styles; and *another kind of consciousness, whose complexities are a way of living with the crisis without being openly part of it.* I said that when you were mak-ing your judgements about these poets, you were not only arguing about their literary practice, you were arguing about your own at that time.[36]

We might identify one kind of consciousness with Au-den's "conscious acceptance of guilt in the fact of murder," or Pound's celebration of Italian Fascism.[37] Raymond Williams's delineation of the other kind, "holding divergent attitudes . . . together in the mind at the same time," offers an astute if unsympathetic gloss on the 1930s work of, most obviously, Richards, Emp-son, and Eliot. Explaining the predominance of irony in high modernist poetry, and justifying his own poetic in necessitarian terms, Eliot described (in the last of the 1936 Cambridge Clark Lectures) a post-Christian culture which had severed thought from religious feel-ing, in which the modern writer's twin attempts to ef-fect a new synthesis, by "intellectualising of the feel-ing" on the one hand, and "emotionalising the idea" on the other, must come into conflict, resulting in an irony "employed against himself."[38] Eliot's formula seems to set out definitively the preoccupation with internal textual tensions that would mark the New Criticism.

In practice it is Stevens, whose "highly intelligent and elaborate" linguistic manipulations serve more to hold together divergent options *within* a fictive world ("pupil of the gorgeous wheel," "*dog*woods") than to express divergent attitudes toward experience *outside* fictive parameters, who goes furthest. In **"Forces, the Will, & the Weather"** he bares his own characteristic device. The notion that different, complementary structures might be *resolved* is questioned, as he voices a doubt about the validity and utility of his trivial options. The governing parameter of this fictive world, given in the poem's first phrase as uncontested context ("At the time of nougats") is, in a final turn, isolated, exposed as sup-position: "It had to be right: nougats. . . . It could be wrong." In what amounts to a classic illustration of Raymond Williams's thesis, complex formal riddles concerning "nougat" assume the place of more substan-tive dilemmas. In offering contradictory and elaborately artificial options, in exposing and foregrounding a fecundating though empty riddle (is this poetic world a "nougat" world?), Stevens seems to reveal an acute uneasiness with his whole *Parts of a World* project.

IV.

Foregrounding its own triviality, **"Forces, the Will, & the Weather"** takes Stevens's poetic from *Ideas of Order* to *Parts of a World* to a logical, and apparently untenable, end. Stevens did not place **"Forces"** with a journal, as he did most of his poems. Neither did he go on to investigate the nature of a world constituted by perpetual selection from multiple and always trivial procedural options. It was only a few years after this poem that Samuel Beckett was writing *Watt,* drawing out the absurdist and nihilistic aspects of such a world, in a work at once comic and chilling in its oblique diagnoses of psychological, social, and political processes.[39] Stevens, by contrast, is already in this poem beginning to invest in a new procedural possibility, a new sleight-of-hand, a more sophisticated way of avoiding the ideological contexts which he has putatively acknowledged. And although it seems paradoxical that Stevens could, within so short a period of time, entertain the perspective of a "peer yellow" discoursing on a nougat world and adopt the voice which propounds *Notes toward a Supreme Fiction,* I would argue that the procedures of the two poems are intimately connected.

In **"Forces, the Will & the Weather"** there are certain grammatical keys which prevent the issues of nougatness, or non-nougat-ness, or even Moscow, from being those to which the poem finally reduces itself. The floating noun phrase that concludes the first stanza, "the peer," is not simply redundant, a reminder of the poem's curious persona; it is formally problematic. The "peer" is juxtaposed to that with which it cannot be numerically reconciled, the two things of "the pair yellow," himself and (at this point we assume) a yellow "land." The yellow peer, as gaze, confronts a spectrum restricted to pink and white. As a member of the Peerage, this persona is the embodied antithesis of ideas from Moscow. This "peer" or governing gaze stands in problematic relation to, and outside the ambit of, the contesting concerns of the poem, nougat *and* Moscow. Having signaled this disjunction by opening with a grammatical anomaly, the poem sets up its close with another, even more arresting: "These were nougats. // It had to be right: nougats. It was a shift / Of realities, that, in which it could be wrong." "It had to be right. . . . it could be wrong" *sounds* oxymoronic and derives its effect from that sound. But the case is more complicated. The use of the "in which" construction grammatically subordinates the final "it" ("It could be wrong") to the second ("It was a shift of realities"). The two "it"s cannot have the same referent. The stasis of self-contradiction is avoided. At the same time, there is no evident resolution to the problem of finding distinct referents for the two instances of "it" that will restore the text to seamlessness. We might conjecture that this "shift of realities" refers, self-referentially, to the disruption constituted by the sentence containing that term. Stevens plays off semantics against syntax, sense against structure, so that no position, or structure of sense, will finally gel.

To immerse oneself in complicated riddles about nougat, as this poem seems to do, might test the patience of even the most avid and ideologically disinterested formalist. What is crucial about these riddles, when one begins to consider other less trivial poems, is that the poet's production of grammatical failures serves implicitly to invoke a further and never developed subject position, one which works the grammatical anomalies rather than being governed by them, one for which nougat and Moscow are not the final parameters or concerns. There is a "peer," and there is a "shift of realities," which are alluded to but not encompassed by the text. Once again, Stevens's maneuver here might be called anti-deconstructive, because his *aporia* serves implicitly to establish a paradigmatic context that would itself be immune from self-negating inconsistencies.[40] If Stevens is uneasy about where his poetic has headed even to the point, in this poem, of self-satire, then the partial disjunction between the apparent terms of this poem and the ultimate, implied perspective of its speaker provides Stevens with a last-ditch escape route from *Harmonium* nougat and from 1930s politics.

The poem, which more than any other sets out to expose the artifice that has informed his poetic, also constitutes the point at which Stevens commits himself, irrevocably it seems, to the production of merely formalist solutions. Just beyond the artificiality and artifice, the near contradictions, Stevens produces a further, potentially available subject position, which remains immune to political influence *and* to charges of escapist irrelevance *because* it is never developed. A poem as apparently different as *Notes toward a Supreme Fiction* does essentially the same thing. There, his artificial fictive constructs are legitimized by appeals to a metaperspective which is their ever-potential and ideal telos. Unlike, say, Eliot, who grounds his *Four Quartets* (1944) in a Christian eschatology, Stevens offers no fully conceived end which we might criticize. At the same time, perpetual implication without full realization preserves Stevens from any difficult political commitment. Should we place Stevens's "major" or "central" man in a social context and observe his social operation, we might derive the enigmatic "Mr. Knott" of Beckett's novel—a nihilistic binding principle whose existence dictates, in Beckett's world, not sophisticated hedging between aesthetic options, but the rigorous performance of closely regulated but absurdist duties on the part of "vassals" (Stevens's term).[41] Ultimately, Stevens's "major man" is a less culpable creation than Pound's Colleoni or Mussolini only because Stevens's figure exists in *pre-incarnate* perpetuity. To seem credible, and to avoid political complicity, "shifts of reality" must remain unidentified, just as notes must proceed only toward a supreme fiction.

Notes

1. The "Stevens and Politics" special issue of the *Wallace Stevens Journal* 13.2 (1989) is exemplary of the latter strain.

2. See for instance Stevens's comments in a letter to Ronald Lane Latimer of 21 November 1935 on Mussolini and Ethiopian "coons," in *Letters of Wallace Stevens*, ed. Holly Stevens (1966; London: Faber, 1967), 295; on the election, see *Souvenirs and Prophecies: The Young Wallace Stevens*, ed. Holly Stevens (New York: Alfred A. Knopf, 1977), 89; on "heading left," see Stevens to Latimer, 9 October 1935, Hartford, Conn., in *Letters*, 286-87.

3. Such a reading is offered in Robert Emmett Monroe's "Figuration and Society in 'Owl's Clover,'" *Wallace Stevens Journal* 13.2 (1989): 127-49. For Stevens's "major man" see his *Notes toward a Supreme Fiction* (1942), in *Collected Poems* (1954; London: Faber, 1990), 388.

4. Ezra Pound, "A Visiting Card" (1942), in Pound's *Selected Prose 1909-1965*, ed. with an introduction by William Cookson, trans. Peter Russell (London: Faber, 1973), 306-21; T. S. Eliot, *Notes towards the Definition of Culture* (1948; London: Faber, 1962).

5. William Carlos Williams, "Proletarian Portrait" and "An Early Martyr," from his *An Early Martyr and Other Poems* (1935), in *The Collected Poems of William Carlos Williams*, ed. A. Walton Litz and Christopher MacGowan, 2 vols. (London: Paladin, 1991), 1:385, 377-78.

6. Stevens, "Forces, the Will, & the Weather," in *Collected Poems*, 228-29.

7. Alan Filreis, *Wallace Stevens and the Actual World* (Princeton: Princeton Univ. Press, 1991), and *Modernism from Right to Left: Wallace Stevens, the Thirties, and Literary Radicalism* (Cambridge: Cambridge Univ. Press, 1994); James Longenbach, *Wallace Stevens: The Plain Sense of Things* (New York: Oxford Univ. Press, 1991).

8. Stevens to Latimer, 6 February 1936, Hartford, Conn., in *Letters*, 308.

9. Longenbach, 145.

10. Marjorie Perloff, "Revolving in Crystal: The Supreme Fiction and the Impasse of Modernist Lyric," in *Wallace Stevens: The Poetics of Modernism*, ed. Albert Gelpi (Cambridge: Cambridge Univ. Press, 1985), 42.

11. Stevens to Wilson Taylor, 13 January 1941, Hartford, Conn., in *Letters*, 385.

12. See Stevens to Henry Church, 23 December 1940, 27 December 1940, and 9 January 1941, Hartford Conn., in *Letters*, 382-85. The lecture, reprinted in *The Necessary Angel: Essays on Reality and the Imagination* (1951; London: Faber, 1984), was first published in *The Language of Poetry*, ed. Allen Tate (Princeton: Princeton Univ. Press, 1942), 91-125.

13. Stevens, "Noble Rider," 18, 33-34.

14. Stevens, "Noble Rider," 8.

15. See Pound, Cantos VIII-XI, in *A Draft of XXX Cantos* (1930), collected in *The Cantos of Ezra Pound*, 4th ed. (London: Faber, 1987), 28-52.

16. Stevens to Leonard C. Geyzel, 14 September 1937, Hartford, Conn., in *Letters*, 324. For "possible poet" see "The Noble Rider," 23.

17. Frank Lentricchia, *Ariel and the Police: Michel Foucault, William James, Wallace Stevens* (Madison: Univ. of Wisconsin Press, 1988), 151.

18. Lentricchia, 168.

19. Stevens, "Anecdote of the Jar," first published in "Pecksniffiana," *Poetry* 15.1 (1919), in *Collected Poems*, 76.

20. Helen Vendler, *Wallace Stevens: Words Chosen out of Desire* (Knoxville: Univ. of Tennessee Press, 1984), 45; Michael Herr, *Dispatches* (New York: Avon, 1978), 107.

21. Lentricchia, 3.

22. In this it has much in common with the population of "Earthy Anecdote," of which Stevens disingenuously remarked: "There's no symbolism in the 'Earthy Anecdote.' There's a good deal of theory about it, however" (Stevens to Carl Zigrosser, 20 February 1918, Hartford, Conn., in *Letters*, 204).

23. Glen MacLeod, *Wallace Stevens and Company: The* Harmonium *Years 1913-1923* (Ann Arbor: UMI Research Press, 1981), 38. MacLeod notes that Stevens had a copy of *Blindman* 2 (1917), which carried a full-page photograph of Duchamp's *Fountain by R. Mutt*.

24. Walter Benjamin, "The Work of Art in the Age of Mechanical Reproduction" (1936), in *Illuminations*, ed. Hannah Arendt, trans. Harry Zohn (1968; London: Fontana, 1973), 217.

25. Stevens, "Gubbinal" (1921), in *Collected Poems*, 85 ("jungle feathers"); and "Disillusionment of Ten O'Clock" (1915), in *Collected Poems*, 66 ("baboons and periwinkles").

26. Benjamin writes in "Unpacking My Library" (1931): "The most profound enchantment for the collector is the locking of individual items within a magic circle in which they are fixed as the final thrill, the thrill of aquisition, passes over them" (*Illuminations*, 62).

27. Benjamin, *Charles Baudelaire: A Lyric Poet in the Era of High Capitalism,* trans. Zohn (London: New Left Books, 1973), 46-47.

28. Stevens, "Gubbinal," 85.

29. Lentricchia, 204.

30. Stevens, "Earthy Anecdote" (1918), in *Collected Poems,* 3 ("firecat").

31. Geoffrey Grigson, "A Stuffed Goldfinch," review of *Ideas of Order,* in *New Verse* 19 (1936): 18-19.

32. Stanley Burnshaw, "Turmoil in the Middle Ground," *New Masses* 17 (1935): 41-42.

33. Stevens to Hi Simon, 12 January 1940, Hartford Conn., in *Letters,* 352 ("new romanticism"; "I began to").

34. Stevens, "Sailing After Lunch" (1935), in *Collected Poems,* 120-21.

35. Stevens, "Yellow Afternoon" (1940), in *Collected Poems,* 237.

36. Raymond Williams, *Politics and Letters: Interviews with New Left Review* (London: New Left Books, 1979), 335-36, my emphases.

37. W. H. Auden, "Spain 1937," in *The English Auden: Poems, Essays and Dramatic Writings 1927-1939,* ed. Edward Mendelson (London: Faber, 1977), 212.

38. Eliot, *The Varieties of Metaphysical Poetry,* ed. Ronald Schuchard (London: Faber, 1993), 213. Eliot speaks specifically of Laforgue, but argues that he and his contemporaries "have dealt no better with the problem" (219).

39. So, for instance, Beckett's second chapter opens:

> Mr. Knott was a good master, in his way.
>
> Watt had no direct dealings with Mr. Knott, at this period. Not that Watt was ever to have any direct dealings with Mr. Knott, for he was not. But he thought, at this period, that the time would come when he would have direct dealings with Mr. Knott, on the first-floor. . . .
>
> For the moment all Watt's work was on the ground-floor. Even the first-floor slops that he emptied, it was Erskine who carried them down, every morning, in a pail. The first-floor slops could have been emptied, quite as conveniently, if not more conveniently, and the pail rinsed, on the first-floor, but they never were, for reasons that are not known.
>
> (*Watt* [1953; London: Calder, 1976], 64)

40. Jacques Derrida, discussing the "destructive discourses" of Nietzsche and Heidegger, precludes the possibility of such a decisive metaphysical shift of realities: "We have no language—no syntax and lexicon—which is foreign to this his- tory [of metaphysics]; we can pronounce not a single destructive proposition which has not already had to slip into the form, the logic, and the implicit postulations of precisely what it seeks to contest" ("Structure, Sign and Play in the Discourse of the Human Sciences" [1978], in *Modern Criticism and Theory: A Reader,* ed. David Lodge [London: Longman, 1988], 111).

41. Stevens, "An Ordinary Evening in New Haven" (1949), in *Collected Poems,* 469.

Helen Vendler (essay date 2001)

SOURCE: Vendler, Helen. "Wallace Stevens: Hypotheses and Contradictions." *Proceedings of the British Academy* 111 (2001): 225-44.

[*In the following essay, Vendler employs Stevens's decreasing reliance, over the course of his career, on the words "if," "or," and "but" to indicate "speculation on the one hand, and obstruction of speculation on the other" in support of the argument that Stevens came to view the search for truth in different ways.*]

> The torment of fastidious thought grew slack,
> Another, still more bellicose, came on.
>
> ***The Comedian as the Letter C***[1]

> *The Concept Of The Arrière-Penseur*
> *Reason's Constant Ruin*
>
> (Two of Stevens's titles for poems never written)[2]

> There is no reality; there is the human consciousness ceaselessly forming, reforming, earning, suffering, spiritually stamping worlds from its creative property. . . . In this capacity . . . the uppermost [step] says: there is only the idea, the great, objective idea. It is eternity; it is the world order; it lives by abstraction; it is the formula or art.
>
> (Gottfried Benn, *The Way of an Intellectualist*)[3]

> Your art has deserted the temples and the sacrificial vessels, it has ceased to have anything to do with the painting of pillars, and the painting of chapels is no longer anything for you either. You are using your own skin for wallpaper, and nothing can save you.
>
> (Gottfried Benn, *Artists and Old Age*)[4]

I am happy to continue, by this lecture on an American poet, the literary history of poetry begun in such a memorable way by Thomas Warton. Though my title names hypotheses and contradictions as two aspects of the work of the poet Wallace Stevens, I think of these practices as his *ifs* and *ors* and *buts*. These three words, representing speculation on the one hand, and obstruction of speculation on the other, play a visibly large role in Stevens's poetry. To remark on Stevens's need for these forms of thought, and yet his late resistance to them, is one way to track his evolution—and his idiosyncrasy—as a poet. I hope to show that by using, questioning, and eventually forsaking these rhetorical means, Stevens over time seeks out truth in different ways. First, by dialectical means, he looks for 'the' truth; then, adopting a Nietzschean multiplicity, he argues for 'truths'; but in his late work he aims to approach, by a series of asymptotic figures, 'a' truth plausible to his exacting mind.

Stevens's poems were written during the fifty years between his matriculation at Harvard and his death at seventy-five. His long life was relatively without incident: he was born, in Pennsylvania, of Pennsylvania Dutch—that is to say German—extraction in 1879; his father, Garrett Stevens, was a lawyer who wanted his sons to be lawyers, and all three of them eventually obeyed him. Garrett Stevens was willing to send his brilliant son Wallace to Harvard, but would support him there for only three years, since one could enter law school after three years at the university. On his departure without a degree from Harvard, Stevens, disregarding his father's wishes, did not immediately enter law school, but became a newspaper reporter in New York. Discouraged by both the work and the salary, Stevens capitulated and went to New York University Law School, after which he had various disappointing short-term positions as a lawyer in New York. In 1916 he found a job as a surety lawyer with the Hartford Accident and Indemnity Insurance Company of Connecticut, where he remained till he died in 1955.

In the first years of Stevens's employment at the Hartford his work was arduous, requiring frequent train-travel across the United States to investigate insurance claims, and in those years Stevens wrote little poetry. Eventually, as he rose in the company, his life became less harried, and when he was 44, he published his first book, *Harmonium,* with Knopf. Other volumes followed steadily, and in 1954, some months before Stevens's death from cancer, his *Collected Poems* won the Pulitzer Prize and the National Book Award. Since his death, his fame has grown steadily, but he remains, in the eyes of us all, a difficult poet, the one who wrote, in a collection of pensées to which he gave the Erasmian title *Adagia,* that a poem 'must resist the intelligence almost successfully'.

Although Stevens's life had many ecstatic moments, it was not in the usual sense a happy life. His marriage became increasingly difficult, as his beautiful but uneducated wife Elsie—once the model for the American Liberty dime—retreated into homesickness, estrangement, and suspicion: no friends or acquaintances could be invited to the house, not even by the child of the marriage, Stevens's daughter Holly. Each night,

after dinner, Stevens retreated to his small separate study and bedroom upstairs, where he read, listened to music, wrote letters, and composed poetry. It was an intensely lonely life, relieved by occasional trips to New York museums, and by his eventually good relations with his daughter and her son Peter.

At Harvard, Stevens had abandoned the Protestantism of his parents for the skeptical Lucretian naturalism of his acquaintance George Santayana. This philosophic materialism was buttressed by Stevens's intimate knowledge of the natural world: he was a great walker in his youth, often covering thirty miles in a single day. Spring warmed him into life; winter chilled him into despair. He became the most exquisite poet of seasonal change since Keats, by whom he was permanently influenced. Many of Stevens's early poems became intelligible to readers through their relation to Romantic verse: **Sunday Morning,** for instance, ends in homage to Keats's *To Autumn.* Instead of Keats's agricultural and domestic landscape, populated by lambs, robins, and swallows, Stevens's American scene offers mountains and an uncultivated wilderness, populated by deer, quail, and pigeons. Keats's goddess of the season has vanished, and human beings exist in isolation:

> Deer walk upon our mountains, and the quail
> Whistle about us their spontaneous cries;
> Sweet berries ripen in the wilderness;
> And, in the isolation of the sky,
> At evening, casual flocks of pigeons make
> Ambiguous undulations as they sink
> Downward to darkness, on extended wings.

[70]

As a young reader, I could move easily into such a poem; it was only a step from Keats to the Keatsian elements in Stevens. I had far more trouble in understanding why Stevens would write certain other poems, among them the one that opened **Harmonium** (and which is still the first piece one sees in the **Collected Poems**). I realised that this strategically placed poem, **Earthy Anecdote,** must be some sort of manifesto, but of what was it the proclamation? Like most conceptual art, this 1918 poem[5] offers no elaboration of its stubbornly repeated plot—that of a daily contest between deer (fiercely charging straight ahead) and a mountain lion (named by its folk-appellation, 'firecat') that obtrudes itself in the path of the bucks:

Earthy Anecdote

Every time the bucks went clattering
Over Oklahoma
A firecat bristled in the way.

Wherever they went,
They went clattering,
Until they swerved

In a swift, circular line
To the right,
Because of the firecat.
Or until they swerved
In a swift, circular line
To the left,
Because of the firecat.

The bucks clattered.
The firecat went leaping,
To the right, to the left,
And
Bristled in the way.

Later, the firecat closed his bright eyes
And slept.

[3]

The firecat's only purpose in his waking hours is to make the bucks swerve. The game goes on all day, conceived and prolonged by the bright eyes of the firecat, and it comes to an end only when the firecat sleeps. Had the firecat not 'bristled in the way' the bucks·would have unswervingly clattered over the plain of Oklahoma in an unimpeded straight line.

At least one way of reading this little parable is to see it as an enacting of the response of the mind's original inertia when it encounters new hypotheses and then contradictions of these very hypotheses. Once our thoughts are set on an inertial straight path, they will not become inventive unless blocked: and one can see the bucks as a form of uncreative life forced into creativity by the bright-eyed obstacle of intelligence. In Stevens, the obstacle that forces the swerve is dialectically self-created: *ifs* and *ors* and *buts,* with their bright-eyed queries, force the mind into alternative paths. I believe that this apparently trivial little poem revealed to Stevens, as he wrote it, how much his art depended on obstructions and the consequent swerves provoked by them, and that he therefore gave *Earthy Anecdote* pride of place both in his first volume and in the final collection of his poems.

When in 1922 Stevens comes to organise his long Browningesque autobiography in verse, *The Comedian as the Letter C,* he does so by means of successive geographic hypotheses, each contradicting the former. Should the poet remain in Bordeaux, within the European tradition? or translate himself to the Yucatan, where the new world is the savage landscape discovered by Columbus and the conquistadors? or move to North America's placid and warm English-settled Southern states? Stevens eventually decides for the last of these, and his hero Crispin, treated with comic irony, settles down in the Carolinas, in 'a nice shady home' with a 'prismy blonde' for a wife, and four 'daughters with curls' [40, 42, 43]. Mistakenly, Stevens stops while Crispin is still dwelling in the South: 'Crispin knew / It

was a flourishing tropic he required / For his refreshment' [35]. Later, in 1936, affected by the failure of his marriage and the shock of the Depression, Stevens will write the elegiac *Farewell to Florida,* declaring that he must now seek his fate in the North: 'My North is leafless and lies in a wintry slime' [118]. Because Stevens' speculations in *The Comedian* on the poet's proper geographic home, and the contradiction of Crispin's Romantic aspiration by domestic curtailment, are ensconced within a plot, they are, for this reason, both more visible (because narrated of a protagonist) and less visible (because overgrown by picaresque picturesqueness) than they will be when they appear in more metaphysical form, in those brief parables and anecdotes that Stevens came to prefer, because of their abstraction, to quasi-mimetic, even if allegorical, narrative.

If we turn away from Crispin's narrative to Stevensian lyric, we can see how hypothesis becomes for Stevens a firecat-stimulus to a creative swerve. In a 1923 manifesto, *The Idea of Order at Key West,* Stevens examines, by means of successive hypotheses and contradictions, the relation between lyric language and the element of nature it purports to translate. The speaker, walking with a companion, hears a girl singing on the shore, and asks the relation of her song to the sea:

Whose spirit is this? we said, because we knew
It was the spirit that we sought and knew
That we should ask this often as she sang.

[129]

The question, 'Whose spirit is this?' prompts a set of hypotheses followed, as we might expect, by a contradiction:

If it was only the *dark*   voice
                                  of   the *sea*
That rose
            or even
[if]
                            colored by many waves;
If it was only the *outer*   voice
                                 of *sky* and *cloud,*
                                 of   the sunken *coral*
    water-walled,
                                    however clear,
    it would have been   deep*air;*
          the heaving   speech
                                    of   *air,*
          a summer   sound
                            repeated in a summer with-
out end
                and   sound alone.
But it was more than that,
            more even than
                  her voice
                  and ours,
    among the meaningless plungings

> of   *water* and the *wind,*
> theatrical distances
> bronze shadows heaped on high hori-
>
> zons
>
> mountainous atmospheres
>   of   *sky* and *sea.*

[129]

This sort of elaboration becomes typical of Stevens's opulent middle style. Of what use to him, we ask, are such *if*s, such *but*s? The *if*s here represent temptations towards certain theoretical positions, especially those attributing human art to nothing grander than animal instinct, an evolutionary instinct that prompts us to reflect the various items of our environment, as, say, the mocking-bird does. Perhaps we do nothing but transcribe blindly the example of the sea, and the darkness of our song reproduces its darkness; if our song takes on colors, they have been conferred by the colors of the sea's iridescent waves. Or perhaps if our song by the seashore takes on yet other colors, not of the sea, they are borrowed from the surrounding context—blue sky, white cloud, and red coral. Were blind imitation the case, the girl's song, Stevens argues, would have been sound alone, breath alone, as birdsong is. Her song would have been an imitative vocalise, as meaningless—in its exercise of the animal instinct for melodic expression—as the great physical displays of the natural sublime of sky and sea.

To elaborate, in this way, a possible Darwinian theory of poetry, and to enclose in it a theatrical Wordsworthian mimetic hymn to the 'mountainous atmospheres of sky and sea', sets in relief the alternate poetic Stevens is about to proffer, which is introduced by one of his useful contradictory *but*s—'But it was more than that.' The new poetic is neither instinctual nor mimetic; it is an abstract one of intellectual artifice, of exact measurement, of geometric lines and demarcated spatial zones. At the end of the poem, when the poet and his companion turn away from the shore toward the town, they find that their surroundings have been charted and made intelligible by the words of the singer, in the same invisible way in which the globe has been charted by geographers who create invisible lines of latitude and longitude, marking out the North and South poles and fixing zones above and below the equator. Because of the singer's song,

> The lights in the fishing boats at anchor there,
> As the night descended, tilting in the air,
> Mastered the night and portioned out the sea,
> Fixing emblazoned zones and fiery poles,
> Arranging, deepening, enchanting night.

[129-30]

Stevens's final interpretation of the maker's *furor poeticus*, the 'blessed rage for order', is secure only because it has been arrived at after he has given a full display,

by means of his *if*s and *but*s, of both Darwinian determinism and of the submissive mimetic sublime of Wordsworth's *Elegiac Stanzas,* 'that rueful sky, that pageantry of fear', a phrase akin to 'mountainous atmospheres / Of sky and sea'. Stevens's inching progressions—'If . . . or . . . If . . . But . . . more . . . more'—track a mind at work investigating its first thoughts and rejecting them for a more accurate one—one that announces the spirit's mastery, by the geometrical abstraction afforded by lyric language, of the sublime landscape of the night sky.

How far can the poet carry speculative hypotheses and fertile contradictions? In deciding to write, in 1937, *The Man with the Blue Guitar,* a theoretically interminable sequence in a new populist style, Stevens proposes that one can entertain multiple hypotheses and successive contradictions if they are juxtaposed to one another in a Cubist multiperspectival space:

> Is this picture of Picasso's, this 'hoard
> Of destructions,' a picture of ourselves,
>
> Now, an image of our society?

[173]

In this Nietzschean realm, every description destroys another description, every mouth proclaims a different point of view. We find ourselves in a Mallarméan world in which the supreme ruler is the plural poetic word (of which the 'amorist Adjective aflame' of the sky's unlimited 'blue' is the paradigm). Here, the demands of logical consistency are repudiated as unwelcome 'pale intrusions into blue':

> The pale intrusions into blue
> Are corrupting pallors . . . ay di mi,
>
> Blue buds or pitchy blooms. Be content—
> Expansions, diffusions—content to be
>
> The unspotted imbecile revery,
> The heraldic center of the world
>
> Of blue, blue sleek with a hundred chins,
> The amorist Adjective aflame . . .

[172]

Although we find, in *The Man with the Blue Guitar,* many hypotheses and contradictions, Stevens now experiments with deleting, in various instances, the expected prefacing signals, *if* and *but.* This tactic produces, as in canto XXVII, obdurate sets of implied hypotheses in which parallel statements either mutually contradict one another or else stand in logically oblique relations to each other. Here we find the sea again, but it is far less intelligible than it was when it stood simply for physical nature in *The Idea of Order at Key West.* Many speculative hypotheses about the sea, in no clear relation one to the other, are entertained, but no *ifs, ors,* or *buts* are allowed to appear. The mind's conjecturings, obstructions, and swervings give rise to a series of independent statements, with all logical junctures suppressed as they might be in a succession of objective *prises,* or seizings, of a natural phenomenon:

It is the sea that whitens the roof.
The sea drifts through the winter air.

It is the sea that the north wind makes.
The sea is in the falling snow.

This gloom is the darkness of the sea.
Geographers and philosophers,

Regard. But for that salty cup,
But for the icicles on the eaves—

The sea is a form of ridicule.
The iceberg settings satirize

The demon that cannot be himself,
That tours to shift the shifting scene.

[179-80]

Shifting shifting scenes is now the perplexing task of the poet's 'daimon' that cannot be himself, cannot possess a fixed identity or a fixed truth. Stevens does not want to remain in a masked world of unfixed phenomena, since he still yearns for truth and a stable poetic. Yet, 'There is no place, // Here, for the lark fixed in the mind, / In the museum of the sky' [182]. Where will stability, then, be found? Nowhere, in much of *The Man with the Blue Guitar.*

Stevens's contradictions reappear in a slightly later poem, one despairing of any future stability, the 1942 *Cuisine Bourgeoise,* a piece composed almost entirely of hypotheses, denials, and questions. It begins with a grim scene: 'These days of disinheritance, we feast / On human heads' [227]. After a dismissal of the moribund past ('But that's all done. It is what used to be'), *Cuisine Bourgeoise* launches itself into a frustrating present of betweenness. It does this by means of a series of arid definitions, hypothetical similes, mini-hypotheses in the form of words in apposition, and—in a final alienation in which the governing pronoun changes from 'we' to 'they'—hopeless questions:

It is like the season when, after summer,
It is summer and it is not, it is autumn
And it is not it is day and it is not,
As if last night's lamps continued to burn,
As if yesterday's people continued to watch
The sky, half porcelain, preferring that
To shaking out heavy bodies in the glares
Of this present, this science, this unrecognized,
This outpost, this douce, this dumb, this dead, in
  which
We feast on human heads. . . .

 . . . This bitter meat
Sustains us. . . . Who, then, are they, seated here?
Is the table a mirror in which they sit and look?
Are they men eating reflections of themselves?

[228]

In Stevens's work, a series of words in apposition almost always represents a set of compressed hypotheses. In order to show the rapidity with which Stevens, in his later period, adopts and discards speculative proposals, I stop a moment here on his serial nouns describing the present in *Cuisine Bourgeoise.* This series is remarkable because in it there appears the one distinctly *non-hopeless* word of the poem, the French adjective 'douce,' here transformed into a noun. 'This present' is interestingly first hypothesised to be 'this science'—since science is the dominant modern frame demanding from the poet a fresh description of the universe. This characterisation of the present is dismissed by declaring that we find less unsettling the knowledge purveyed by science than the vast quantity of ignorance ('this unrecognised') it reveals. No longer the Ptolemaic centre of the universe, we have become 'this outpost', a planet knowing nothing of the centre from which it originated. In the middle of such a bleak portrayal of the present we are surprised to find a new, wholly alternative Stevensian hypothesis in the unexpected phrase, 'this douce'. Admitting the melting sweetness of physical experience even in an unintelligible world, Stevens at last has something to write about—but how can he, in 'this dumb'—the next hypothesis, which recognises a failure of speech intensifying the failure of cognition expressed in 'this unrecognised.'

Why does Stevens present some of his appositive hypotheses here as nouns, and some as adjectives-turned-nouns? We can see that the hypotheses about the present embodied in true nouns are focused on *external* reality—this *present* (the twentieth century), this *science* (the new frame), this *outpost* (the marginalised planet). By contrast, the hypotheses that are phrased in nouns derived from adjectives have to do with the poet's *inner* world—what it recognises, what it finds sweet, what it wants to utter in language. This grammatical division of labour makes the hypothesis articulated in the final adjectival noun, the climax of the series, so cutting: 'this *dead*' is, by its adjectival grammar, seen to be an internal quality. Although earlier in the poem death was imagined externally as a quality belonging to the ingested 'human heads' of the past, it now migrates into the subjective world of the poet himself. It is no coincidence that 'head' rhymes with 'dead'.

Stevens attempts to contest his nihilist deadness even as he voices it, and we can see his first efforts toward a recovery of confidence in certain minor poems, such as **'Forces, The Will & the Weather'** [228-9] and **'On**

an Old Horn' [230]. In the second of these, the Darwinian doubts of *The Idea of Order* return in force ('The bird kept saying that birds had once been men, / Or were to be, animals with men's eyes, / Men fat as feathers'), and the poet finds solace only in a precarious set of wavering self-contradictory assertions:

> In the little of his voice, or the like,
> Or less, he found a man, or more, against
> Calamity, proclaimed himself, was proclaimed.

[230]

Yet in spite of such transitory consolations, the dead-ness of *Cuisine Bourgeoise* persists. In *Transport to Summer* (1947), a Darwinian bestiality returns in force as the once-joyous man with the guitar reappears in the poem *Jouga,* its title deformed from the Spanish *jugar,* 'to play.' Both the physical world of *The Idea of Order at Key West* and the human world of *Cuisine Bourgeoise* are now meaningless. The name of the guitar-player, 'Jaime' (Spanish for 'James,' perhaps containing a disillusioned pun on the French 'J'aime') is distorted into a series of meaningless phonemes, Ha-eé-me, just as his notes become unmelodic 'noise', and his guitar is dehumanised to a beast:

Jouga

> The physical world is meaningless tonight
> And there is no other. There is Ha-eé-me, who sits
> And plays his guitar. Ha-eé-me is a beast.
>
> Or perhaps his guitar is a beast or perhaps they are
> Two beasts. But of the same kind—two conjugal
>   beasts.
> Ha-eé-me is the male beast . . . an imbecile,
>
> Who knocks out a noise. The guitar is another beast
> Beneath his tip-tap-tap. It is she that responds.
> Two beasts but two of a kind and then not beasts.
>
> Yet two not quite of a kind. It is like that here.

[337]

The *but*s and *or*s and *perhaps*es and *not*s here reveal the bitterness and self-loathing of the poet confronting an apparently untransformable external world. When Stevens's last resort of joy, the physical world, becomes meaningless it renders the virtual world of language and music meaningless as well. The instability of the physical world had already reached, in the 1939 *Variations on a Summer Day,* as far as Keats's North Star, elegiacally subjected by Stevens to a drifting delineation which thins down further and further:

> Star over Monhegan, Atlantic star,
> Lantern without a bearer, you drift,
> You, too, are drifting, in spite of your course,
> Unless in the darkness, brightly-crowned,
> You are the will, if there is a will,

> Or the portent of a will that was.
> One of the portents of the will that was.

[232-33]

A poet cannot write indefinitely in this oscillating and self-repudiating vein, qualifying his every statement with *unless* and *if* and *or*. How will Stevens escape his uncertainty? Can he arrive at a point of more stable assertion? If steadfast truth does not reside in the North Star, where is it to be found?

Stevens escapes uncertainty at first—and perhaps even at last—by incorporating into his poetic the idea of necessity. This necessity may be moral or aesthetic or historical, or it may be referred to the physical laws of nature. It has already made its appearance, rather theatrically bearing its Greek name, in the 1936 *Owl's Clover*: 'Fatal Ananke is the common god'.[6] Its more common appearance in Stevens is by means of the repeated modal forms *has to* and *must*, visible in the 1940 manifesto *Of Modern Poetry*. Here, philosophical truth is defined not as proposition but as process: the mind's 'act of finding / What will suffice.' And the new poetic of process is prompted by moral obligation; the mind of the modern poet is bound by social and historical duty:

> It has to be living, to learn the speech of the place.
> It has to face the men of the time and to meet
> The women of the time. It has to think about war
> And it has to find what will suffice. It has
> To construct a new stage. It has to be on that
>   stage. . . .
>   It must
> Be the finding of a satisfaction.

[240]

There is much that could be said about this hinge of modal obligation and necessity, which mediates between middle and late Stevens, but I can only remark here the change it represents. There is not an *if* nor an *or* nor a *but* to be seen in this passage; not an *as if* nor a *like*. (I should confess that later in the poem Stevens's signals of qualification—*like, not, but*—do appear briefly, but they are firmly put aside in favour of another *must*.) The Stevens who earlier luxuriated in dialectical speculation now prefers the blind assertions of a desperate necessity. To justify the necessity, Stevens leaves solitude behind, and demands that his work 'face the men of the time' and 'meet the women of the time'. *Of Modern Poetry* voices Stevens's temporary conversion to the colloquial and the social, and to the use of a public rhetoric.

This 'conversion,' prompted by the social convulsions of the Depression and World War II, was not one that Stevens could always maintain; but the poetic of process, of 'finding' that it elicited did spring the poet free from the sterile consumptions and reflections of *Cuisine Bourgeoise,* forcing him to think of a means for looking forward. He begins by analysing his own rebellious disposition, which had always prompted him to contest the received truths of his culture. In the 1940 poem *Landscape with Boat,* Stevens chastises himself for having been hitherto insufficiently fertile in 'supposing', in spite of all the supposing he had done earlier with his *ifs* and *ors.* He was mistaken, he tells us, in supposing that there existed a final propositional 'truth beyond all truths', one that would forever put an end to conjecture. He advances, now, by an inching logic of contradiction and hypothesising, to a final positive assertion. In saying 'The world itself was the truth', Stevens accepts a materialist, rather than a propositional, notion of truth:

> It was his nature to suppose.
> To receive what others had supposed, without
> Accepting. He received what he denied.
> But as truth to be accepted, he supposed
> A truth beyond all truths.
>
>   He never supposed
> That he might be truth, himself, or part of it,
> That the things that he rejected might be part. . . .
>   He never supposed divine
> Things might not look divine, nor that if nothing
> Was divine then all things were, the world itself,
> And that if nothing was the truth, then all
> Things were the truth, the world itself was the truth.
>
>   [242]

This dismissal of '*the* truth' as an intellectual figment— 'Where was it one first heard of the truth? The the.' as Stevens says in the 1940 poem *The Man on the Dump* [201]—and the substitution for it of the laws (and beauties) of the material universe, each of which, in Emersonian fashion, has *a* symbolic truth to tell, liberated Stevens from the constantly undermining of speculation by contradiction, while leaving him open, at least from time to time, to using hypotheses and objections more casually.

In working towards a poetic that is one of process, but also one that can make positive assertions that can resist subversion or contradiction, Stevens reaches increasingly often—as in the 1943 poem *Somnambulisma*— for formulations which will not deny poetry's origin in the animal evolution of language, but which will equally not deny poetry's role in the highest domain of knowledge. Even in that highest domain, the Stevensian poet is not Plato's philosopher king: in a democracy, he is surrounded not by regalia but (winningly) by personalia. The origin of what the poet pours forth in language is in part animal, in part spiritual: but whether we choose to see the poet as evolutionary bird or Emersonian American scholar, he undeniably makes the material world pregnant with reflected human meaning. As *Somnambulisma* returns to the shore of *The Idea of Order at Key West,* we can see how the necessary social relation of the poet to his fellows, declared in *Of*

Modern Poetry, rescues Stevens from materialist solipsism, and enables a triple hybrid refiguring of the poet as the vernacular ocean, an archetypal restless bird, and a solitary scholar:

Somnambulisma

> On an old shore, the vulgar ocean rolls
> Noiselessly, noiselessly, resembling a thin bird,
> That thinks of settling, yet never settles, on a nest.
>
> The wings keep spreading and yet are never wings.
> The claws keep scratching on the shale, the shallow
>   shale,
> The sounding shallow, until by water washed away.
>
> The generations of the bird are all
> By water washed away. They follow after.
> They follow, follow, follow, in water washed away.
>
> Without this bird that never settles, without
> Its generations that follow in their universe,
> The ocean, falling and falling on the hollow shore,
>
> Would be a geography of the dead: not of that land
> To which they may have gone, but of the place in
>   which
> They lived, in which they lacked a pervasive being,
>
> In which no scholar, separately dwelling,
> Poured forth the fine fins, the gawky beaks, the per-
>   sonalia,
> Which, as a man feeling everything, were his.
>
>   [304]

Without the poet, according to *Somnambulisma,* those of his generation would be deprived of a living sense of their own emotional experience, and the world surrounding them, if uncommented-on by the poet, would be 'a geography of the dead'. The Stevensian compulsion to speculate and hypothesise is here imagined first as the restless rolling of the ocean, and next as a bird's inability—represented by intensives of the present progressive tense—to settle on a nest. The 'generations' of the poem are borrowed from Keats's odes to the nightingale and the Grecian urn—from 'No hungry generations tread thee down' and 'When old age shall this generation waste'. The music of *Somnambulisma* comes from Tennyson's song, 'The splendor falls on castle walls . . . Dying, dying, dying', and from *The Passing of Arthur*—'And hollow, hollow, hollow all delight'. What is uniquely Stevensian, here, is the hybrid creation of the ocean-bird-scholar, and the startlingly complex effusion of marine fins, aerial beaks, and human personalia that pour forth from the intensities of the solitary poet's feeling. He feels, after all, 'everything'.

In admitting the function of both animal instinct (in the bird) and emotional intellect (in the scholar feeling everything) in the formation of poetry, Stevens can lay to rest his Darwinian suspicion that poetry might not be a form of knowledge. What he has discovered is the indispensable contribution of the poet's 'invisible geography' to the 'visible geography' of the earth, a 'geography'—as he wrote in an essay—'that would be intolerable except for the non-geography that exists there'.[7]

What becomes of Stevens's speculative *if*s and *or*s and *but*s in his late work? These words cease for the most part to represent obstacles, and become—to put it briefly—accretive, elaborative, and asymptotic instead of alternative and exclusive. In 1949, the 31-canto sequence *An Ordinary Evening in New Haven* begins by announcing its subject—'the eye's plain version . . . , the vulgate of experience'—and adds, 'Of this, / A few words, an and yet, and yet, and yet—/ As part of the never-ending meditation' [465]. The *and yets* are resistant yet additive, like the turning leaves of a book in this 'endlessly elaborating poem' [486]. Elaboration, rather than contradiction, has now become a fundamental principle of composition. And although Stevens begins *An Ordinary Evening* with two rebuttals—saying that the poem is 'part of the res itself and not about it', and that the poet speaks the poem 'as it is, / Not as it was', these merely clear the ground for positive assertion. The space where the poem takes place is increasingly an ever-mobile and yet—because fixed in words—immobile present:

> The poem is the cry of its occasion,
> Part of the res itself and not about it.
> The poet speaks the poem as it is,
>
> Not as it was. . . .
>
>   There is no
> Tomorrow for him.
>
> The mobile and the immobile flickering
> In the area between is and was are leaves,
> Leaves burnished in autumnal burnished trees
>
> And leaves in whirlings in the gutters, whirlings
> Around and away, resembling the presence of thought,
> Resembling the presences of thoughts, as if,
>
> In the end, in the whole psychology, the self,
> The town, the weather, in a casual litter,
> Together, said words of the world are the life of the
> world.
>
>   [473-74]

Multiple truths here coexist additively without strain. The flickering is both mobile and immobile; the leaves exist (in life) in burnished trees and (as pages) in whirlings in the gutters; the leaves (as a single poem-*gestalt*) resemble the presence of thought while (as an evolving sequence of processes) they resemble the presences of thoughts. Just as the life of the world is multiple, so are the words of the world.

But by the end of *An Ordinary Evening in New Haven*—a poem which tends to abandon a materialistic poetry for a virtual one—even the accreting leaves and thoughts seem insufficiently immaterial symbols for the mind's attempt to create a coalescence of outer and inner reality. In canto XXXI, Stevens represents 'the edgings and inchings of final form' as activities by which desire asymptotically approaches its goal. These are

> The swarming activities of the formulae
> Of statement, directly and indirectly getting at,
>
> Like an evening evoking the spectrum of violet,
> A philosopher practicing scales on his piano,
> A woman writing a note and tearing it up.
>
>   [488]

Each of these instantiations of 'getting at' complements the others: we see the evening investigating more and more tints as it tries to evoke the whole spectrum of violet; a philosopher hoping to progress from scales to, say, a Chopin étude; a woman resorting to destruction so as to approach more nearly to perfection. The successive attempts in all these activities lead Stevens to his finest discrimination as he concludes that reality itself need not be conceived of in physical terms:

> It is not in the premise that reality
> Is a solid. It may be a shade that traverses
> A dust, a force that traverses a shade.
>
>   [489]

The first of Stevens's two closing suppositions—'it may be'—calls attention to itself because it is unidiomatic: we do not normally refer to 'a' dust. This traversable dust resembles the Biblical pillar of cloud: it is our physical self imagined as the sum of its mortal collective atoms. This 'dust' is sufficiently permeable to be traversed by a shade—a tint, a hue. Or, in the second of the suppositions, reality may be not a shade but a force—like gravity, like electricity—that traverses the self, which is now not a permeable dust, but a ghostly shade. We scarcely have words for these elusive and delicate traversings, but at least Stevens's language makes us aware that—as the title of a late poem asserts—**'Reality Is an Activity of the Most August Imagination'**:

> There was an insolid billowing of the solid.
> Night's moonlight lake was neither water nor air.
>
>   [136]

In 1948, Stevens wrote that 'central experiment is one of the constants of the spirit which is inherent in a true record of experience'. This statement [*OP* 313] suggests that what we have been following—in tracking the poet's earlier hypotheses and contradictions, his mid-career elaborations and appositions, and his later accretions and asymptotic figures—is his struggle to render first philosophical 'truth', then Cubist perspectival 'truths', then 'a truth', something more personal and intimate. When he is seeking for philosophical 'truth', conceiving of it as an absolute, he relies on a dialectical *either/or* characterised by hypotheses and contradictions. When he is seeking for perspectival 'truths', he relies, as in *The Man with the Blue Guitar,* on endless elaboration, or, as in *Cuisine Bourgeoise,* on appositions. When he is seeking 'a' positive personal truth, he approaches it asymptotically, suggesting various metaphors, each of which comes in some way close to the essence of his desire.

There are many beautiful late poems with which to close my topic, but I want to single out two, both composed in 1954, Stevens's last full year of life. The first of these poems was written in March, the second in November [dated in *OP* 324]. The March poem, *Not Ideas about the Thing But the Thing Itself,* is significant as the piece with which Stevens chose to conclude his *Collected Poems*—the pendant to *Earthy Anecdote,* with which the collection, and this essay, began. *Not Ideas about the Thing but the Thing Itself*—a Kantian title claiming knowledge of the *Ding-an-sich*—harks back to many earlier poems—the desolate winter poem *The Snow Man*; the poem called *The Sun This March* ('The exceeding brightness of this early sun / Makes me conceive how dark I have become' [133]); the many bird-poems; *New Haven*'s assertion that the poem is the cry of its occasion; Stevens' own comic self-naming as the letter C—formerly printed in upper-case, now significantly, with the humility of the old, in lower-case. *Not Ideas* exhibits the familiar counters *but, not, or,* and *like,* but uses them without the uncertainty that used to attend their presence in Stevens's poems.

The plot of *Not Ideas* is a simple one: a speaker who has doubted that he would live to see another spring wakes up uncertain whether the bird-cry he has heard is real or part of a dream. The poem traces his growing conviction that it is real: yes, the sound must be coming from outside because the advancing season is confirmed by the earlier rising of a rejuvenated sun; and though the pale sun and the scrawny cry are merely premonitory heralds of the 'colossal sun' and the 'choir' yet to come, the eventual grandeur of the much-desired spring is implicit in its inception. The leap of the heart as the speaker realises that the axis of the seasons has turned, that spring is miraculously his once again, is like 'a new knowledge of reality'. We can watch, here, how all the early torturing words of uncertainty—*but, not, seem, like, or, part*—are now recruited to play felicitous roles in a drama of the renewal of life:

Not Ideas about the Thing But the Thing Itself,

At the earliest ending of winter,
In March, a scrawny cry from outside
Seemed like a sound in his mind.

He knew that he heard it,
A bird's cry, at daylight or before,
In the early March wind.

The sun was rising at six,
No longer a battered panache above snow . . .
It would have been outside.

It was not from the vast ventriloquism
Of sleep's faded papier-mâché . . .
The sun was coming from outside.

That scrawny cry—it was
A chorister whose c preceded the choir.
It was part of the colossal sun,

Surrounded by its choral rings,
Still far away. It was like
A new knowledge of reality.

[534]

Stevens could not sustain this spring joy. *The Region November,* written only five months before the failing Stevens was finally found to have advanced stomach cancer, reveals that every sign of the mind's lively responses—conjectures, hypotheses, qualifications, comparisons, contradictions—can be abolished by the inertia of age and illness. In *The Region November,* the title suggests that this single winter month has become the space to which living has been reduced. As the poet hears the north wind, he watches it compel the monotonous swaying of the treetops. The trees say only the same thing, over and over, without fluctuation, modulation, correction, apposition, or speculation. They display the melancholy of the contentless, even if effortful, agglutinative inertial repetitions of age, void of any substance, divine, material, or human. The energetic Oklahoma of *Earthy Anecdote,* the rich American wilderness of *Sunday Morning,* has become a waste land of spiritual entropy:

The Region November

It is hard to hear the north wind again,
And to watch the treetops, as they sway.

They sway, deeply and loudly, in an effort,
So much less than feeling, so much less than speech,

Saying and saying, the way things say
On the level of that which is not yet knowledge:

A revelation not yet intended.
It is like a critic of God, the world,

And human nature, pensively seated
On the waste throne of his own wilderness.

Deeplier, deeplier, loudlier, loudlier,
The trees are swaying, swaying, swaying.

[*OP* 140]

It is like the restless Stevens to turn the benign and inclusive poetic process of his late phase, visible in the asymptotic approach to spring of **Not Ideas about the Thing But the Thing Itself,** into its desolate obverse, the agglutinative elaboration of the meaningless into a repetitive swaying and a predicateless saying. Even Ha-eé-me of **Jouga** had his conjugal beast and its meaningful, if minute, sonic oscillation—*tip-tap-tap.* But here tautology rules: deep is deep and loud is loud and the words *deeplier, deeplier, loudlier, loudlier* repeat a single monotonous sound that leads to no crescendo of promised being such as the colossal sun and its surrounding choir. In **The Region November,** the mind is in abeyance, and with it, all its wonderful and stimulating speculative instruments.

Recalling earlier poems, we can say that here the bucks have no firecat, the shore has no measuring singer, the world no cornucopia of parts, the guitar-player no instrument, the poet no responsive audience of men and women, the earth no scholar-bird effusing personalia. It is here, feeling the lack of the exhilarating Stevensian mimesis of the mind's fluctuations, that we realise that in spite of his frequent thematic bleakness, Stevens was above all a poet of fertility of speculative thought and verbal invention. His swerves, hypotheses, contradictions, hybridities, Cubist multiplicities, accretive elaborations, and asymptotic progressions establish in **The Collected Poems** a mental landscape anything but bleak, one that matches the distributed richness of the material world with its own unfailing engendering of emotional, intellectual, and linguistic forms—the fine fins, the gawky beaks, the personalia.

Notes

Read at the Academy 17 May 2000.

1. Wallace Stevens, *Collected Poems* (New York, 1954), 37, henceforth cited as *CP* with parenthetical page references in text.

2. Cited from Wallace Stevens' notebook *From Pieces of Paper,* in George Lensing, *Wallace Stevens: A Poet's Growth* (Baton Rouge, Louisiana, 1986), 183.

3. Gottfried Benn, *Prose, Essays. Poems,* ed. Volkmar Sander (New York, 1987), 33.

4. Ibid., 183.

5. Dates cited for individual poems in this essay follow those given in Holly Stevens ed., *Wallace Stevens: The Palm at the End of the Mind* (New York, 1972), ix-xv.

6. Wallace Stevens, *Opus Posthumous,* ed. Milton Bates (New York, 1989), 89, henceforth cited as *OP* with parenthetical page references in text.

7. 'The Figure of the Youth as Virile Poet', in *The Necessary Angel* (New York, 1951).

Justin Quinn (essay date 2002)

SOURCE: Quinn, Justin. "Wild Flowers." In *Gathered Beneath the Storm: Wallace Stevens, Nature and Community,* pp. 7-34. Dublin: University College Dublin Press,·2002.

[*In the following essay, Quinn argues that the prevalence of natural or pastoral settings in Stevens's poetry does not indicate the poet's disconnection from issues of politics and ideology. Rather, for Stevens, the interface between man and nature serves as the setting for an intense examination of the ways in which political meaning is formed.*]

1

On 20 September 1939, Wallace Stevens wrote a curious letter to Leonard C. van Geyzel in Ceylon (*L* [*Letters of Wallace Stevens*] 342-3). In the first paragraph he thanks van Geyzel for his gift of some translations of poetry from the Sinhalese. The next paragraph abruptly introduces two new subjects to the letter: the first, cursorily, is the outbreak of the war, and the second is peculiar English-influenced architecture of one part of Virginia, where Stevens was staying at the time. He expatiates on the second at length, prompting one to wonder if the apparent apathy with which Stevens refers to the outbreak of World War II perplexed his correspondent in Ceylon. It seems strange that such an important event as this would make no impact on the poet and would serve only as a temporal marker for his distinctions and *aperçus* relating to the houses and landscape of Virginia, where he spent part of the summer. What could the fact that the people there, as Stevens states, 'have some sense of style about living' have to do with the announcement of war? Is Stevens oblivious to the disasters and transformations of international politics, and above all to the fact that large numbers of people will die and many more suffer? The direction of Stevens's thought in this passage seems to confirm the characterisation of him by the New Critics as uninterested in anything beyond aesthetics.

However, the letter continues:

> As the news of the development of the war comes in, I feel a horror of it: a horror of the fact that such a thing could occur. The country is more or less divided between those who think that we should hold aloof and those who think that, at the very least, we ought to help the British and the French. Our sympathies are strongly with the British and the French, but this time there is an immensely strong feeling about staying out.
>
> (*L* 342)

Although the drift is towards US non-involvement, Stevens expresses his 'horror of the fact that such a thing could occur' and also, further on, the hope that the events will not affect his correspondent (for an excellent account of Stevens's changing attitude to World War II see Filreis [*Actual World* 3-28]). Just when it seemed that he was satisfied to wander off into purely aesthetic realms, it turns out that all along he was thinking of the terrible prospect of the impending war. Arguably, there is even a connection made between the landscape of Virginia and his summary of opinions on the war in the US: as James Longenbach points out, that part of the American landscape is clearly English serves as a reminder of America's debts to England, in everything from laws to landscape art (209).

Bracketed as they are by World War II, his descriptions of Virginia present 'a complex of emotions' (*CP* [*The Collected Poems of Wallace Stevens*] 377). There is, on the immediate level, a desire on Stevens's part to convey something of the feel of a particular American place to his distant correspondent (something that he required in turn of van Geyzel, and Stevens's poetry as a result makes occasional reference to Ceylon). But going beyond this, there is also a desire to locate the horrific news in a particular locale, to provide his correspondent with a sense of what the news means in America as opposed to Paris or Ceylon. The fields of Virginia will probably remain oblivious and prosperous whatever happens in Europe; a Londoner's 'complex of emotions' when hearing the news must inevitably be very different, as must an Alsatian's, a Czech's or a Ceylon expatriate's. So, as he continues, we realise that World War II does not provide a backdrop for his consideration of the Virginia landscape, rather the relationship is more complex. What at first seemed like the indulgence of a poet in his ivory tower turns out to be a nuanced account of the different effects the war will have in different parts of the world.

In this book I argue that in his poetry Wallace Stevens uses landscape and natural objects in general as the occasions for thinking about politics and ideology. Previous generations of readers—New Critical, Post-Structuralist, New Historicist—have failed to recognise that in Stevens's poetry the pastoral setting is the space in which he meditates most intensely on the way that human societies produce cultural and political meaning, and not a respite from those pressures. Just as in the letter to Ceylon the reader must often go by indirection to witness Stevens thinking politically, so too in the poetry. A wide open horizon can be the locale for this work of the imagination and equally a flower in a vase, the flower working as synecdoche for landscape and nature in general. In both cases, it is objects shaped by the plastic force of nature that provide Stevens with the means to think about human arrangements of houses and ideologies. It is as though the intricate structures of

nature *interrogate* those of man. After all, humanity only rearranges and recombines materials taken from the land, for the purposes of shelter or nutrition, practical or spiritual. And Stevens's sense of these activities—building a house, constructing a state, painting a landscape, farming a piece of land—as carried out by communities of people is acute. Groups of human beings have to arrange themselves under the huge expanses of the sky if they are not to be physically or spiritually engulfed, as poor Pip in *Moby-Dick*. And in all of these constructions—from the still life to the Capitol building—an ideology is implicit, a set of shared assumptions about the way that society should comport itself: these inform the central matter of style. As he thinks about the space of nature, with its lakes and mountains and flowerings, he is also aware that this is the space of ideology. I shall sketch out this connection later in reading **'The Bouquet'**, but to a large extent it is this particular Stevensian pastoral space that is the subject of the whole book.

For many years, his poetry had the reputation of being about the relation between Reality and the Imagination: the individual's creating mind (Imagination) faces a world of objects (Reality) and meditates on the relations between them. Sometimes the Imagination is in the ascendant, sometimes Reality. Such philosophical arguments couldn't seem further away from the space of political praxis. Nevertheless, in recent years there has been a movement in Stevens criticism to put him back, in Alan Filreis's phrase, in the actual world. Seminal to this movement has been Peter Brazeau's oral biography (1985). Its three-hundred-odd pages of interviews with Stevens's acquaintances, friends and business colleagues presented a view of the poet that helped critics revise old readings of the poems and see how the poetry was informed by the actual world all along.

These revisions have taken various forms. In the same year as Brazeau's biography, Milton J. Bates published his *Wallace Stevens: A Mythology of Self*. Drawing on material that would later appear in his revised edition of **Opus Posthumous** (1989), and with an enviable insight into the connections between Stevens's biography and his poetry, he re-read the poems for us revealing how the imaginative life of the poet was encrypted in them. As a general fact about poetry, this should hardly surprise us: after all, we expect that poetry is, to an extent, the story of a particular imagination's engagement with the world. However, in the case of Stevens, Bates's book was exhilarating news. Alerted to the fact that Stevens's life animated his poetry, that, say, his vacillation over the choice of a career, his personal reactions to World War I, impinged on his imaginative life sent many readers and critics back to the poems. There they encountered a Stevens who, for example, often wrote about war and who was not above addressing part of one long poem to a Marxist critic who had reviewed *Ideas of Order.*

Book after book presented us with yet another revision of Stevens. 1985 also saw the publication of Charles Berger's *Forms of Farewell: The Late Poetry of Wallace Stevens* in which, among other things, he presented a reading of **'The Auroras of Autumn'** that suggested that its scope and ambition were fuelled by the trauma of nuclear war. The same year Albert Gelpi collected a group of essays by critics who had not heretofore written much on Stevens, *Wallace Stevens: The Poetics of Modernism,* including a wide range of approaches and attitudes to his work, from Marjorie Perloff's hostile essay indicting Stevens for ignoring history to Charles Altieri's praise of him as an exemplary poet of the political imagination. This essay adumbrated his magisterial *Painterly Abstraction in Modernist American Poetry* published four years later, a book that read the Romantic tradition in philosophical and ideological terms, and led to a consideration of Stevens at the apex of that tradition. It differed from most ideological critiques in that it was not Leftist and saw in Modernism exemplary political positions that remain important for readers today.

Helen Vendler's study of some of the shorter poems, *Words Chosen Out of Desire* (1986), countered the popular view of Stevens as an impersonal poet. She read the poems for the moments of revelation of personal pain and eros to which so many critics had remained deaf. Yet again we were presented with an 'actual' Stevens, connected on this occasion with the life of the emotions, unafraid to bring matters of personal loss and love into the poems. Frank Lentricchia, drawing on Bates's work, illuminated the poetry with respect to questions of gender-politics and the place of the male in Stevens's society. Underlying his investigations of the work of Michel Foucault and William James, and his readings of Stevens's poems, was the question of the place of the poet in the twentieth century. This was encapsulated in the title of his book, *Ariel and the Police* (1988).

The matter of Stevens's double life also fascinated Lentricchia, but it is perhaps the signal failing of Joan Richardson's two-volume biography of Wallace Stevens (1986, 1988) that there was barely any attention paid to his career in insurance. Richardson exhibited no sensitivity to the way the vicissitudes of this business, like any other, can engross the passions and intelligence of imaginative human beings. The insurance world was considered merely as something solid, a base that allowed Stevens to make his 'real' adventures in the writing of his poetry. Stevens's pre-eminence in the field of legal insurance and his dedication to that career indicate that his work at the Hartford was something more than a day job. Richardson's interest was purely in the literary and family backgrounds to his poetry. Another

biography is waiting to be written that could take account of the daily metamorphosis that took place in Stevens's life, as he moved from poetry to business to poetry again.

And it is to the work of James Longenbach and Alan Filreis that we look for penetrating and exhaustive analyses of the nexus of Stevens's poems with the politics of the day. Without trying to foist political readings on poems that would plainly withstand them, their impressive scholarship placed Stevens's work in the context of contemporaneous politics and their sensitivity to the way that the poems give onto those politics provided a book that was illuminating for its account of the period and Stevens's imaginative involvement with it. The chapters in Longenbach's study, *Wallace Stevens: The Plain Sense of Things* (1991), dealing with **'Owl's Clover'** and *Ideas of Order* are exemplary. Alan Filreis's *Wallace Stevens and the Actual World* came out the same year and concentrated on Stevens during the 1940s; three years later came his *Modernism from Right to Left: Wallace Stevens, the Thirties, and Literary Radicalism* that dealt with the preceding decade. Through extensive and painstaking archival research Filreis reconstructed the ebb and flow of Stevens's mind as he responded to newspapers, letters from friends, and economic and political change. Glen MacLeod's book, *Wallace Stevens and Modern Art* (1993), suggested interesting parallels between Stevens's poetic development and the contemporaneous developments in the New York art world. His scholarly research into the latter produced an interesting array of material that showed not only how Stevens's influenced some of the painters of the time, but also their effect on him from the Armory Show onwards. Stevens chatting in French with Marcel Duchamp at Walter Arensberg's apartment can stand as an image of just how close Stevens was to the revolutionary changes taking place in the art world of the twentieth century.

A healthy loosening of critical approach has occurred, which has served to enrich our sense of Stevens's work as poetry that addresses many issues beyond the purely metaphysical matters of Reality and the Imagination. However, excellent as some of these books are, I began this study out of a dissatisfaction with them. Yes, it's important to know about Stevens's relations with the art world and, yes, it's important to know how his biography informed his poetry, but each time I returned to the poems after reading one of these books I felt that much of the scope and subtlety of Stevens's engagements with that 'actual' world had been missed. The books by Filreis and Longenbach have, perhaps more than any others, changed the face of Stevens criticism in recent years. Exeunt the post-structuralist concerns of the 1970s and early 1980s, as represented by the work of J. Hillis Miller, Joseph Riddel, and Paul Bové; enter the actual world that Stevens lived in. To a great extent, my book quarrels with these critics: they go so far in imbricating Stevens's work in the political and cultural debates of the time that we are left wondering what use the poems can possibly be to us now. I contend that there is a mode of the political in Stevens's work, as revealed through his treatment of nature, and that by recognising this nexus in the poetry our view of Stevens's poems is changed. In a variety of voices and verse-forms, Stevens shows how the dramas and exaltations of the individual imagination abroad in nature or observing an object taken out of nature have a meaning beyond the arena of the transcending consciousness of the individual, that is in a public context: his poems propose that thinking in new ways about a bouquet or the landscape at Oley has a profound impact on the ways in which communities arrange themselves and think about their place in the world, which is, necessarily, the ground for thinking about politics.

The conviction that animates many of his poems is that any separation of these areas of thought is the evasion of a mind incapable of embracing imaginative complexity. Nature and landscape for Stevens are not of the Watteau variety, not sylvan idylls to salve our troubled minds. They are open to politics, to the contingencies of history, and the larger concerns of communities, precisely at the moment when they seem to abscond to pastoral. And although previous critics have discussed his involvement with his times, both in political and cultural terms, they have failed to trace the connections Stevens makes. By following these connections in the pages ahead, I wish to enlarge our ideas of the peculiar tracks Stevens leads us along, tracks that are of great interest to us now when the relations between the categories of the aesthetic and the political are being debated so strenuously. I shall not engage these debates directly in this book, but would nevertheless like to think that by pursuing these particular paths in the poetry, I can show Stevens provided us with an air, a kind of music of the intellect, that is of much value to us when we confront basic questions of culture and politics in the present.

In its devalued state, such pastoral subject matter is considered 'aesthetic', in the pejorative sense of being separated from social and political concerns. The imagination flies the nets of government and country to a realm of aethereal beauty that has its own laws of proportion and balance. However, Stevens brings us back to the ideological valency of pastoral in a new way: it is just when he seems most abstracted in landscape that he is likely to make an abrupt turn and show the reader that there is a world outside the aesthetic object, or, more precisely, that if the aesthetic object is not to become etiolated and ultimately irrelevant it must constantly take cognisance of that world. To make a start at tracing some of these turns in the poetry, I want to go back to an older critical charac-

terisation of Stevens that Frank Lentricchia deftly summarises, and which takes its main terms from Stevens's poetry and prose:

> Reality, as alien being, is a 'violence' which ever pressures us, as he put it in a well-known formulation, and the imagination is the response of our subjective violence which presses back against an inhuman chaos. Imagination makes space between us and chaos and thereby grants momentary release from sure engulfment, madness, and death.
>
> (*After the New Criticism* 33)

And then:

> Against an irrepressible will to identify the projections of desire, those 'longed-for lands,' with reality itself, he sets a critical self-consciousness which incessantly subverts and dismantles his fictions and shows them for what they are: 'intricate evasions of as.'
>
> (*After the New Criticism* 32)

This is the characterisation of the great heroic imagination, a description that engages much of the diction and turns of thought of Western philosophy from the Greeks on. By this account, Stevens's poetry is about the human mind facing an inimical world of objects that it must arrange and interpret, even though these arrangements and interpretations are provisional and will eventually fall apart. Figuring the imagination in terms of the demiurge facing primeval chaos and making something of it, this description of humans' 'fictionalising' takes its lead from Stevens's own statement, 'God and the imagination are one' (*CP* 524). However, it is a description that is more applicable to a work like Book II of *Paradise Lost* than Stevens's poetry: in the former, you have inhuman chaos, interminable voids, etc., whereas Stevens is more likely to have his figure of the capable imagination sitting in a park or looking at a bowl of flowers. And although Lentricchia presents Stevens's poetics in terms of the first-person plural in this passage, the prevailing figuration is that of the individual imagination heroically facing 'inhuman chaos': there is no sense of this imagination being part of a community, or of the invented fictions having a public meaning or of their occurring in public time. If only the inhuman chaos could be conjured up in a living-room, the whole affair could be safely conducted by the agonist from the comfort of his or her armchair.

What this characterisation misses is the way that Stevens is concerned with the public aspect of the imagination's tropes. Taking this further, he is often more interested in how the imagination of a particular community or nation works than in that of the individual. **'Sad Strains of a Gay Waltz'** is about how collective emotion changes and creates new forms of music to answer new social conditions. He is, it is true, interested in how figures of capable imagination (say, the rabbi or the captain—both versions of the major man) can affect transformations in culture and society, but frequently their speech, which situates a community in the world, is part of a dialogue and not merely monologic preaching; moreover, the ultimate significance of their speech has less to do with the satisfactions it affords their own imaginations than with the 'true reconcilings' they provide the community (**CP** 144). Theirs is an art that takes cognisance of public emotion and thought at any particular moment and speaks in reaction to that, as reflection and redirection, and that the community recognise it as such is its ultimate justification for Stevens.

Following from this, we should note that such public figures do not work on the primeval void but more usually on human arrangements of landscapes, gardens or flowers in jars. The given is no inhuman chaos, rather it is a previous human construct that is no longer adequate to the needs of the imagination when trying to make sense of its world. Even when facing the sea—the closest earthly image we have of that 'inhuman chaos'—Stevens's figures encounter an element that has already found a place in human figurations many centuries ago. Observe Crispin crossing the Atlantic from Bordeaux (**CP** 28):

> Could Crispin stem verboseness in the sea,
> The old age of a watery realist,
> Triton, dissolved in shifting diaphanes
> Of blue and green?

As a later Stevens would have it: 'There was a myth before the myth began, / Venerable and articulate and complete' (**CP** 383); indeed, that the previous myth is so venerable, articulate and complete, is its main fault. In the case of this passage in **'The Comedian as the Letter C'** the prior myth is that of Poseidon's son, who makes the roaring sound of the ocean by blowing through his shell, over which is laid the new picaresque myth of Crispin. Elsewhere it is a picturesque view of fields and hills, or the arrangement of a bouquet in a room that is the prior myth to be revised or reappraised; most often it is an object out of nature or nature itself, as, say, in **'The Auroras of Autumn'**.

That landscape and more generally nature provide the most significant occasions for his rethinking of community and imagination raises several interesting points. First and foremost, nature is in so many respects traditionally seen as the fundamental basis for the values of a community, the source of its moral judgements about its members and the world. That an act or a thing is considered 'natural' or 'unnatural' is still used to establish whether it is 'right' or 'wrong'. Thus, when Stevens writes about nature, not as absolute origin that provides us with a moral code, but as the site of herme-

neutic uncertainty and flux, as Bonnie Costello describes it, he is questioning the basis of social value and how it is produced ('Adequacy' 203-18). This he does in various ways, but I give just one example here: nationalist ideology has always moved swiftly to appropriate idealised representations of the landscape of its territory as validation of the national 'spirit'. The very words 'nation' and 'nature' are cognates. Visit any gallery in any country that has undergone a period of national awakening and there the dutiful pictures hang: mountains, sunsets, lakes, trees dramatically positioned against the sky; all scenes that justify a people's ownership of a particular terrain and, above all, its particular spirit. Quite a number of Stevens's poems explore and question these connections between 'nature' and 'nation', as I shall show in Chapter Five.

Nevertheless, Stevens recognises the human need for myths of origin and acknowledges that often nature is seen as the site of those myths, even while rejecting the notion that there can be a return to nature, that an unmediated relationship between a community and its particular landscape can be achieved. (Crispin does not face primeval chaos when crossing the Atlantic, but an ocean that had already been 'storied' by humanity.) This is the dilemma that many of his most important poems face. Nature appears as something that baulks human fictions and makes us aware of their constructedness. By considering a bouquet standing in the middle of the house, we realise that space is shaped in different ways by the flowers and the constructed walls. The phases of this difference are what Stevens often writes about.

Just as in his letter to van Geyzel where he employs the Virginia landscape to help him comprehend the news of the outbreak of war, so too he needs the horizon of nature to understand all of humankind's fictions, be they houses, paintings or nations. Moreover, for all his decreation of romantic correspondences he is acutely aware that it is in the midst of nature that humanity experiences its most exalted moments. A poem like **'The Auroras of Autumn'** has him searching the skies for the forms of nobility that his figure of the 'major man' ultimately couldn't provide. The auroras are a force moving through the heavens, a kind of supreme fiction that changes, gives pleasure, and they are, like the sea, very close to a plastic representation of abstraction; they elicit from him his profoundest meditations on the relations between the individual imagination and the community. A natural phenomenon prompts these thoughts. However, this is so far from our conventional idea of nature poetry that it has never been recognised as such. And yet what are the auroras if not one of nature's grandest performances? Each bidding of farewell is a further decreation, but these cease halfway through the poem as Stevens shifts to wonderment in reaction to the manifestation of the natural world at its most untrammelled and festive moment.

In *Notations of the Wild: Ecology in the Poetry of Wallace Stevens* (1997), Gyorgyi Voros argues that this demonstrates that his poetry can be read as proto-deep-ecological that 'reimagines the Nature / culture dialectic and seeks to reinstate the forgotten term—Nature or, to use Stevens's term, 'reality'—in that dialectic' (11). While Voros makes her case with elegance and inventiveness, she simplifies the poems by seeing in them such a tendency to valorise Nature over humanity. There is no doubt that Stevens is much more occupied with Nature than most of his Modernist peers and in ways that have for many years been overlooked. (One exception to this is Bonnie Costello's 'Wallace Stevens: The Adequacy of Landscape', an article which Voros does not refer to in her book, and which I shall discuss in Chapter Two.) But he shares nothing of the deep ecologist's fear that Nature is near exhaustion. In this respect, his ideas of nature are closer to those of the nineteenth century than our world of global warming and depleted rain forests. Moreover, this approach supposes that Stevens was unaware that things like landscapes and the idea of wilderness itself were cultural constructs (as he so economically points out in **'Anecdote of a Jar'**). Voros's reading is the same as the older characterisation, with the inimical 'inhuman chaos' replaced by a more compliant idea of 'Nature'. Her ecological approach gives a public significance to Stevens's poetry, but is anachronistic in the way it projects our concerns into the past.

His poems argue in different ways and to different ends: they show how our aesthetic thoughts about the landscape and objects from nature extend to the public realm of political praxis, or, in other words, when we are thinking about flowers we are also thinking politically, indeed that the flowers often force us to think in new ways about social configurations. It is this movement between the categories of the 'aesthetic' (that is, natural objects) and the 'political' which constitute the pivot of so many of his poems and makes it difficult for him to be claimed for ecological thought. In **'Prelude to Objects'** (*CP* 195) he intones:

> Poet, patting more nonsense foamed
> From the sea, conceive for the courts
> Of these academies, the diviner health
> Disclosed in common forms.

The 'nonsense foamed / From the sea' belongs to the category of the 'aesthetic', and what the poet must do is give these a wider public meaning. It is Stevens's knowledge that meditations on the landscape or studies of pears, etc., must be brought to court in this way that informs many of his poems.

Even now critics often work on the assumption that if a poet writes about the weather, the timothy grass, etc., and is not ecological as Stevens isn't, then he or she must be an 'aesthete', in the pejorative sense of the word. With such a simplistic opposition it is impossible to comprehend the greater part of Stevens's poetry. In 'Imagination as Value', writing about the relations between the imagination and social contexts he presents us with a set of complex interactions between these two apparent poles:

> Of imaginative life as social form, let me distinguish at once between everyday living and the activity of cultural organization. A theater is a social form but it is also a cultural organization and it is not my purpose to discuss the imagination as an institution. Having in mind the extent to which the imagination pervades life, it seems curious that it does not pervade, or even create, social form more widely. It is an activity like seeing things or hearing things or any other sensory activity. Perhaps, if one collected instances of imaginative life as social form over a period of time, one might amass a prodigious number from among the customs of our lives. Our social attitudes, social distinctions and the insignia of social distinctions are instances. A ceremonious baptism, a ceremonious wedding, a ceremonious funeral are instances. [. . .] Costume is an instance of imaginative life as social form. At the same time it is an instance of the acceptance of something incessantly abnormal by reducing it to the normal. It cannot be said that life as we live it from day to day wears an imaginative aspect. On the other hand, it can be said that the aspect of life as we live it from day to day conceals the imagination as social form.

(*OP* [*Opus Posthumous*] 145-6)

I quote at length to convey how Stevens's thinking is alive to the subtle ways in which the imagination is present in social forms. Beneath this is the Shelleyan conviction that *poesis*, the act of making, is carried out by artists as well as politicians (viz., his statement just a few pages earlier that Communism 'exhibits imagination on its most momentous scale' [*OP* 143]). For Stevens, pastoral is the site for thinking about these ideas. Going back to **'The News and the Weather'** (*CP* 264-65) from *Parts of a World* (1942), we see in the first section how he sets up the world of social forms, invoking the context of the nation with its ceremonies, industry and labour problems, only to show it interpenetrated by natural elements, here the sun. 'The blue sun [. . .] caught the flags and the picket-lines / Of people, round the auto-works: // His manner slickened them. He milled / In the rowdy serpentines'. Poetry like this is very clearly gesturing towards the poetry of the Left with its mentions of the auto-works and picket-lines, but it is equally clear that it is not a Leftist tract. The sun's entrance breaks up the usual dialectic thinking that is associated with workers, and brings ambiguity. Is he for or against? Is he sympathising with the lot of the working class or mocking it?

Conservative or communist? The poem simply won't answer this type of reductive question.

The second part of the poem is almost purely pastoral. For some readers this move might seem escapist (absconding from the picket-lines and auto-workers for the luxurious contemplation of magnolias and the changing seasons); the 'poison' mentioned is more a balm for the mind wracked by the social problems of the first section, '[f]or the spirit left helpless by the intelligence'. But there is a deeper intelligence in Stevens's move, and one that isn't escapist either, a knowledge that the weather, implying the wider horizon of nature and the changing seasons, is necessary to our understanding of the news (the picket-lines, etc.). This is not a rejection of social concerns but the provision of a horizon for them. In the terms of 'Imagination as Value' this poem brings the imagination (the sun, and later the monologue of Section II) into contact with social forms (the colours of the US flag, parades, picket-lines and auto-workers). The greatest moments of vision and emotion for the spirit occur in nature, and we must learn to see the connections between the six distichs of the two sections, just as we must learn to connect those moments with social forms.

Public formations such as the courts and academies in **'Prelude to Objects',** if they are to have any meaning at all, must be capable of comprehending the most ecstatic moments of our being. Emerson abroad in the countryside at the beginning of *Nature* (1836) had to slough off the ties of social responsibility before gaining access to sublime emotions. Whitman followed him, and, borne by expansive feelings of nationalism, discovered how to relate such sublimity to almost everything in the life of the United States in the nineteenth century. For Stevens, as for nearly all the significant writers of Modernism, such nationalism was not an option: it no longer found purchase as an explanation of contemporary life (for a brief but persuasive discussion of this transition period see Pearce 253-6). How, then, can one continue thinking in terms of nations, and communities in general, without losing sight of those private moments of expanded awareness, those spots of time by which we try to steer our lives because they seem a revelation of the central truths of existence? This torsion of transcendence versus a return to the earth (with its courts and academies) is one of the fundamental elements of Stevens's thought.

Moreover, the attitude to nature and the natural object that comes out of all this is fundamentally different from the Coleridgean approach. When discussing the imagination in Chapter XIII of *Biographia Literaria*, Coleridge writes:

> It dissolves, diffuses, dissipates, in order to recreate: or where this process is rendered impossible, yet still at

all events it struggles to idealize and to unify. It is essentially *vital*, even as all objects (as objects) are essentially *fixed and dead*.

[last italics mine] (167)

It is safe to say that sentences like these have conditioned critical views of Stevens for decades as a philosophical poet in this vein. Frank Doggett, discussing Stevens's use of the term 'reality', writes:

> To be real is almost a quality in itself for reality is the truth of existence, a feeling of the verity of things. Since a trust in the reality of things and selves fills out the void that would otherwise exist without a belief in a transcendent ground of being, the word *reality* holds an unconscious store of feeling in Stevens' use of it.

(27)

Doggett's 'void' and Coleridge's expanse of 'fixed and dead' objects, upon both of which the magisterial human imagination works, is at odds at a basic level with the readings of poems that I shall offer in this book. In **'The Rock'** we see that 'things and selves' are not so easily validated, and that 'reality' for Stevens, in one of his most important lyrics, is itself grounded upon the troping force of nature. It is to this agency that he looks in order to find 'a cure of the ground / Or a cure of ourselves, that is equal to a cure // Of the ground' (*CP* 526) and not to some static and featureless Cartesian extension. In a more flippant earlier mood, referring directly to Coleridge's influential coinage, he put it thus:

> He called the hydrangeas purple. And they were.
> Not *fixed and deadly*, (like a curving line
> That merely makes a ring).
> It was a purple changeable to see.
> And so hydrangeas came to be.

(*OP* 43; italics mine)

The outright echo of Coleridge's phrase 'fixed and dead' marks how differently Stevens thinks about nature. For him the latter possesses an agency which challenges that of men, and more generally that of communities whose imaginative constructions work to situate them in the world. Observing the phases of these encounters opens up the poetry in important ways and shows how Stevens was a nature poet of particularly original mark.

2

The erratic trajectory of **'The Bouquet'** (*CP* 448-53) exemplifies that which in other poems remains more oblique. The poem moves between a consideration of the bouquet of flowers, the house and landscape surrounding it, and the larger space of the nation. It demonstrates that, even at this stage in his career, when at least one commentator has said that he had lost most interest in relating matters of the imagination to politics (Longenbach 279), these ideas were still immediate for him. The first part of the poem offers contradictory signals, as Stevens confuses the categories of inside and outside: is the bouquet a part of the genteel world of drawing room and house, or does it stand as synecdoche of the natural world?

> Of medium nature, this farouche extreme
> Is a drop of lightning in an inner world [. . .]

The word 'farouche' itself encapsulates these confusions: French-sounding and recherché, it conjures up a dandyish, effete nineteenth-century atmosphere—the old category of the aesthetic in all its fragility and irrelevance. Above all, that atmosphere is an enclosed space, very much apart from the great outdoors that a poet like Whitman choired. But delving into the word's etymology we see that it comes from the Latin for 'out of doors', with the *OED* [*Oxford English Dictionary*] even noting a connection, albeit obscure, between it and the word 'forest'. This contrast between inside and outside is amplified in the second line which has the lightning of the open sky penetrating 'an inner world'. These are the terms the poem sets for its meditation on the community and the sphere of political, even military action: inner worlds and outer expanses. The lightning penetrating the inner world foreshadows the clumsy officer who will enter the house at the poem's end.

But the poem is also about seeing. It is about the complexities of perceiving a simple human arrangement of flowers in a vase on a table, and the way large intellectual powers can inhere in everyday scenes, the flowers not just being things, but a whole host of 'para-things' that are not the fictive projections of the human imagination, but are a revelation of what lies in experience itself. As Charles Altieri says in his eloquent discussion of this late phase Stevens's career: 'there are not worlds and interpretations, but worlds as interpreted in a variety of ways, each perhaps best articulated, not by descriptions, but by making manifest the energies involved' (*Painterly Abstraction* 347). And, still following Altieri, rather than leaving the door open for a relativism that defers the shared values of a community, such poems establish sites where communities of readers can test the interpretations of the world that structures their lives. To put it differently, how you see the bouquet depends on a whole range of beliefs you hold about the world. In the second part of the poem Stevens makes it clear that the bouquet takes on a different aspect if it is seen 'in a land // Without a god'. The poem then becomes the site in which the arrangement of para-things (with their attendant various interpretations of the world) reveals 'portents of our own powers as readers', to quote Altieri quoting Stevens (*Painterly Abstraction* 340).

To face reality is to face this range of interpretations and this brings an enlargement of our powers:

> One approaches, simply, the reality
> Of the other eye. One enters, entering home,
> The place of meta-men and para-things,
>
> And yet still men though meta-men, still things
> Though para-things; the meta-men for whom
> The world has turned to the several speeds of glass
>   [. . .]

This kind of search for nobility in quotidian experience is what Altieri finds in Stevens's late work, where plain propoundings and straightforward descriptions of objects and events can suddenly taken on great power. For instance, in **'An Ordinary Evening in New Haven'** each canto is not a further abstraction removing us from the reality of the Connecticut town but rather a necessary embellishment that allows us to see it all the more clearly. Those meta-men, Stevens tells us, are those who have a particular nobility. It is the nobility of perceiving well, seeing the bouquet in all its multiplicity and not as belonging to the etiolated category of the aesthetic but as 'para-thing'; the flowers not as 'choses of Provence', but as part of the commonal that calls forth intellectual and more importantly emotional allegiances. The 'emotion' here is not an imaginative projection; it is part of the bouquet, part of the fund of common experience, available for all.

And then the poem turns. The bouquet is an object taken out of nature that precipitates these meditations, not simply another domestic object. Although arranged by human hands and placed in a vase, the flowers have been shaped by the climate and various tropisms, springing up from the earth beneath the open sky. 'Not all objects are equal' (*OP* 188), Stevens states in the Adagia. Thus, since the flowers are special objects, it behoves Stevens to look to that for which they stand as synecdoche: nature itself.

> Through the door one sees on the lake that the white
>   duck swims
> Away—and tells and tells the water tells
> Of the image spreading behind it in idea.
>
> The meta-men behold the idea as part
> Of the image, behold it with exactness through beads
> And dewy bearings of their light-locked beards.
>
> The green bouquet comes from the place of the duck.

The promise hidden in the word 'farouche' is kept: our attention is directed 'out of doors', to the origin of the bouquet itself. The 'inner world' of human arrangements is dependent on an outer expanse, that of the landscape. There the pattern of things and para-things is paralleled by the duck and the ripples that spread out in its wake. It is because the bouquet 'comes from the place of the duck', i.e., the landscape, the horizon of nature, it is able to engender such aggrandisements of the intellect and imagination, like the auroras earlier in the same collection. The bouquet, as 'drop of lightning' from an outer world, might only be, in Emily Dickinson's phrase, 'remotest consulate' of the elemental force of the northern lights (Dickinson 1045), but consulate it is as it forces revisions of the constructed spaces of humanity. To understand the arrangement of the bouquet in the room we need to attend to the landscape stretching out from the house; this dependency of human space and natural space is captured in the enjambment, 'at a window / Of the land'.

The third part of the poem begins by suggesting that such ideas are imaginative investments in the object, not discoveries: the bouquet 'is quirked // And queered by lavishings of [the meta-men's] will to see'; but this is retracted as Stevens proclaimed that it is not a distortion but 'A freedom revealed, a realization touched'. It is only through such 'meta-vision' that the quotidian is experienced; anything else is a distortion, a restriction, an enslavement. The freedom revealed by this 'drop of lightning' from the natural world might lead us to believe that the land and its flowering are some kind of origin. Stevens recognises this need in humanity for such fictions of origin, but he—for want of a better word—disperses them, in the passage beginning 'Perhaps these colours [. . .]'. There is no origin at all except that of the particular arrangement of the bouquet right before our eyes. There is no ultimate apprehension of a nature unmediated by interpretation: there is just this détente between the flowers as shaped by nature and then arranged by human hands.

Beginning this reading of **'The Bouquet'** I mentioned the poem's erratic trajectory. Up to the fourth section, it follows a smooth course as the meditation expanded out from the object, revising and qualifying previous statements at a rather stately pace. The short final section abruptly breaks this rhythm. Now it seems that thoughts that were previously expressed with discrimination and nuance are coarsely bellowed:

> A car drives up. A soldier, an officer,
> Steps out. He rings and knocks. The door is not
>   locked.
> He enters the room and calls. No one is there.
>
> He bumps the table. The bouquet falls on its side.
> He walks through the house, looks round him and
>   then leaves.
> The bouquet has slopped over the edge and lies on the
>   floor.

What preceded was Stevens near his best; what we get now is something like Hemingway near his worst. On the face of it, this passage seems to be awkwardly proclaiming that no matter how subtle our theories and fictions, they can still be obliterated by incursions from the real. The cycle never stops. We had thought, in Section Two, that we had taken cognisance of the real, but

here this is dismissed. This is the kind of dismantling of fictions that Lentricchia talks of.

Or is it? To me, its violence is less clumsy didacticism than a trial and validation of all the preceding thought. In **'Notes Toward a Supreme Fiction'**, Stevens states that the 'final elegance' of thought is not consolation or sanctification 'but plainly to propound' (*CP* 389). That is, if our thought cannot brook such plain speech, cannot take cognisance of a quotidian that includes families, soldiers, war, then it is of no use to us. Rather than an account of the imagination vanquished by reality, this passage is the crucial test of all the meta-seeing in the poem. The reader must be able to perceive objects not only when they are static, enclosed, arranged, but when they become part of larger processes and horizons, part, even, of a different speech. If the poem has not taught us how to continue seeing the bouquet as parathing through the events of the final section, then it has failed.

What is also of note is Stevens's indication that the man is not another visitor from Porlock, but part of a specific social formation: he is an army officer. Stevens reminds us that the space of political praxis, here particularly of martial action, is inextricably connected with all our previous thoughts about the bouquet. In Section Two he reminded us that our perception of the bouquet was dependent on the surrounding 'land', meaning the horizon of nature beyond the house; now it is 'land' as nation, in the figure of the officer, which impinges on our perception of the flowers. To refer again to **'Prelude to Objects'**, the diviner health must be disclosed in common forms. As we ponder the soldier further, we start to wonder why he has called to the house and why it is empty. Have its inhabitants fled before invading troops? Or has he returned from war unexpectedly to find his family absent? In either case, we suddenly become aware of the land in which the bouquet stands as being caught up in a larger international drama, just as in the letter to van Geyzel the Virginia landscape was—in Stevens's idea of it—part, however distant, of the outbreak of World War II.

It might be objected that this reading of the poem does not fit with my thesis about the connections between nature and politics in Stevens's poetry as the bouquet has little to do with the wild, open horizons of nature. It is just a particular arrangement of flowers, an object that could easily be replaced by a guitar, a bottle, a newspaper. This would be a fair comment if Stevens did not repeatedly bring the reader's attention to the fact that the bouquet has been taken out of nature and stands in the room as synecdoche of its wider backdrop. It is worth making this point here as similar situations—in **'The Bouquet'** for example—occur through Stevens's poetry when he juxtaposes natural objects in still lifes with the spacious hinterland of nature beyond the frame of the painting or house. Thinking about the contiguities of nature and human arrangements forces him to think further about political arrangements of the world also. Take for instance **'The Countryman'** (*CP* 429) where Stevens puns on the way a pastoral canto is sung in the political precinct of a canton. He attempts to face the quotidian matters of social structures (cities, polities) through '[a]n understanding beyond journalism' (*OP* 136), in other words without resorting to reductive accounts of life, nurturing the vision in which, as he says in **'The Bouquet',** the world is seen through several speeds of glass. For Stevens, it is the objects of nature that sponsor this vision, a vision that comprehends the panoramas of politics and society as well as the individual imagination's most exalted moments of feeling.

3

I want to turn again to the letter to van Geyzel to draw attention to another aspect that is pertinent to many of his poems about nature and habitations; this is the connection he makes between the people, their houses and the style of the landscape. The connections to which he draws van Geyzel's attention make up the delicate fabric of what we can call 'place'. The English influence differentiates the area in Virginia where he found himself at the time from other places in the state. And while the English elements might be considered by some Americans as foreign, for Stevens the people of this place are natives in it since there is a continuity between the style of their lives, their houses and their land. In Chapter Five I shall look more closely at the idea of the natives and their lands in the poetry, but for now I wish to draw attention to the way in which Stevens, when faced with the idea of global war, needs the support of a particular place and a particular set of arrangements of objects in space to help him think through the looming disaster. Philosophical or political ideas only become sensible for Stevens insofar as he is able to think through them as a set of spatial relationships. In order to think about Nietzsche and Lenin in **'Description Without Place',** rather than polemicising with statements from their writings he figures them in plastic situations: they sit before expanses of water, and their thought is characterised by how they represent that water to themselves. Compare such an approach with a contemporary poet's engagement with the German philosopher:

> [. . .] then we go back to the green-eyed heat, and
>   stare,
> beating on the icy film between each thing, knocking,
>   tapping,
>   to see what's happening,
> 'the wasteland grows; woe to him hiding wastelands
>   within' (*The Portable*
> *Nietzsche*—Viking '54—we look in there) [. . .]

> (Graham, *The Errancy* 55)

Rather than presenting us with the figure of Nietzsche himself Jorie Graham prefers quotation, providing us even with its provenance, which serves to make a physical connection (by giving her particular edition of Nietzsche) between the thought of the philosopher and the poet. Stevens is at once more impersonal and personal: the first because he establishes no autobiographical link as Graham does, the second because he thinks in terms of the philosopher's particular biography (*CP* 342):

> Nietzsche in Basel studied the deep pool
> Of these discolorations, mastering
>
> The moving and the moving of their forms
> In the much-mottled motion of blank time.

When referring to Lenin, the scene-setting is even more specific:

> Lenin on a bench beside a lake disturbed
> The swans. He was not the man for swans.
>
> The slouch of his body and his look were not
> In suavest keeping. The shoes, the clothes, the hat
>
> Suited the decadence of those silences,
> In which he sat. All chariots were drowned. The swans
>
> Moved on the buried water where they lay.
> Lenin took bread from his pocket, scattered it—
>
> The swans fled outward to remoter reaches,
> As if they knew of distant beaches; and were
>
> Dissolved. The distances of space and time
> Were one and swans far off were swans to come.
>
> The eye of Lenin kept the far-off shapes.
> His mind raised up, down-drowned, the chariots.
>
> And reaches, beaches, tomorrow's regions became
> One thinking of apocalyptic legions.

The chariots represent the feudal past that Lenin dispensed with, and the swans are at once the sign of an old aesthetic (they flee him much in the same way that writers like Nabokov, Khodasevich and Bunin did) and a future aesthetic that will reign after Lenin's day has come and gone (one thinks of White Russian writers published once again in their native country contributing to new developments in Russian literature). Arguably Graham's approach has a greater phenomenological purity, bounded as it is by her own experience of Nietzsche, while Stevens must invent these images of political figures facing nature. But what I wish to draw attention to here is Stevens's insistence that ideology and politics are most clearly apprehended in this interview between man and nature. It is worth recalling the conclusion to 'Imagination as Value' in this context:

> [T]o be able to see the portal of literature, that is to
> say: the portal of the imagination, as a scene of normal

love and normal beauty is, of itself, a feat of great imagination. It is the vista a man sees, seated in the public garden of his native town, near by some effigy of a figure celebrated in the normal world, as he considers that the chief problems of any artist, as of any man, are the problems of the normal and that he needs, in order to solve them, everything that the imagination has to give.

(*NA* [*The Necessary Angel*] 155-6)

Randall Jarrell remarked how Stevens was attracted by images of wilderness (138). This is a fair observation, but Stevens was also fascinated by the human boundaries placed on wilderness, thus his jar in Tennessee, and thus nature here arranged into a garden as the primordial site of poetry. The social connections Stevens asserts in the passage are significant: the poet-figure is in his *native* town; also, he cannot abscond from social configurations in his moment of transcendence because his awareness of the statue, which connotes the moral and political values of his community, calls him back to the 'normal' world. This figure rhymes with that in **'Notes Toward a Supreme Fiction'** (*CP* 397):

> A bench was his catalepsy, Theatre
> Of Trope. He sat in the park. The water of
> The lake was full of artificial things,
>
> Like a page of music, like an upper air,
> Like a momentary color, in which swans
> Were seraphs, were saints, were changing essences.

The lakeside scene with swans is not an allegory of the revolutionary transformations that Lenin effected, but rather an example of how political thought changes the way we think about space, that is, changes our descriptions of the world immediately before us. That this is indeed the case is witnessed by the fact that both Nietzsche and Lenin are presented here in suspiciously suburban moments, much like those that Stevens himself spent in Elizabeth Park in Hartford and that appeared in the poems. Rainer Maria Rilke thinks about space, albeit with no reference to politics, in a very similar way as one of his poems shows:

> Raum greift aus uns und übersetzt die Dinge:
> daß dir das Dasein eines Baums gelinge,
> wirf Innenraum um ihn, aus jenem Raum,
> der in dir west.
>
> [Space reaches *from* us and construes the world:
> to know a tree, in its true element,
> throw inner space around it, from that pure
> abundance in you.]

(Rilke 262-3)

Taking this phenomenological tack, we can say that for Stevens the ideas of Nietzsche and Lenin mean nothing unless they mean something first and foremost in this 'Theatre of Trope' (*CP* 397)—our immediate apprehension of space. The French left-wing philosopher, Henri Lefebvre puts it like this:

What is an ideology without a space to which it refers, a space which it describes, whose vocabulary and links it makes use of, and whose code it embodies? [. . .] More generally speaking, what we call ideology only achieves consistency by intervening in social space and in its production, and by thus taking on body therein.

(44)

It might seem at this stage that I am trying to triangulate Stevens by quotation, but that these two passages from such different writers as Rilke and Lefebvre are pertinent to Stevens helps demonstrate the nature of those tracks between the spaces of political praxis and the artwork that I mentioned earlier. Rilke is all aesthetic exaltation of the natural world—trees, skies, fruit; Lefebvre's end is ultimately the transformation of society. Stevens brings these two spheres into collision. Thinking about the transformations of Marxism means thinking about bouquets, lakes and parks, for if those transformations are not apprehensible in such locales—no matter how distant they seem from theatres of action—then they are chimerical and not worth further consideration. Whereas a critic like Alan Filreis considers that **'Description Without Place'** expresses a particular anti-political moment in American society after World War II with its dehistoricisation of the figures of Lenin, Nietzsche and Neruda in this, it is my contention that Stevens, in order to get at the essence of ideologies, reads them against nature (Filreis, *Actual World* 157-8). What Lenin does with the swans characterises accurately what he and his confrères did with those who did not fit into the new political order of Communism.

Stevens's landscapes then are a new version of pastoral by which he tests polities and philosophies against one of the oldest vistas, that of the natural world. To consider new ideas against the city would be fruitless since the city, containing millions and the seat of the latest technologies, is itself a part of the modern. There is no contrast and thus no calibration. Nature, however, provides not a pristine expanse, but a set of terrains that for the most part has remained unchanged by humanity, even while humanity continued to change its interpretation of it. The natural landscape is then 'multi-storied', but plastically constant, thus providing the opportunity to think most clearly about a particular ideology. To examine what Marxism makes of nature, and not how it plans industry or foreign relations, is the most expeditious way of discovering the essence of the ideology.

Here we should remark an important difference between Stevens's representations of nature and those of his Romantic predecessors: that nature is 'storied' (recall the figure of Triton in the waves) means it is historical. In other words, rather than being a source of eternal values (moral, aesthetic), nature is the site of hermeneutic uncertainty, as we are plunged into the awareness that so many people and so many cultures have made so many different things *of* it. This phrasal verb 'make of' is useful in that it captures both the idea of aesthetic interpretation and physical manufacture, both the artworks and industries that look to nature for raw material. When poets like Wordsworth and Emerson leave the gathered dwellings of their fellow human beings to range through the landscape in solitude, they have defined in advance the category into which their perceptions of nature will fall. The nature they see is delimited negatively, in other words it is *not* society, *not* the city, *not* modern, *not* industrial. It is 'wilderness', and as such the site of all the things that Enlightenment society fails to provide: spiritual feeling, moral values, aesthetic awareness. It is eternal in contrast to the contingency of the city. It offers a coliseum for pure private emotion, whereas society imposes the urgency of the newspaper with its mires of political debate and sensational story. Nature is ahistorical, as unchanging as a Platonic Idea, refuge and redoubt for the mind troubled by the modern world. It records the ruins of vanquished empires, thus exhibiting the transience of all human makings against its unchanging truth. There is a double motion in such a romanticisation of nature: while in the process of manufacturing a new meaning for nature, these writers stress its eternal aspect.

These arguments take on special hue when we consider nature and landscape not just as generic categories but as belonging to the space of America. We must take into account the history of the US as a colony, and subsequently nation, that faced the 'wilderness' of the New World, a nature that was very different from that of Europe. Two landscapes by two American writers will serve to outline some of the consequences of this distinction. The first is from James Fenimore Cooper's *The Pioneers* (1823), which takes as its theme the conflicts between the Native American and European societies about the way land is interpreted. Cooper, although he registers the resistance offered by the Native Americans to colonial expansion, is not ultimately their advocate. While he is cognisant of the faults of white civilisation, in his eyes it is ultimately for the best that it will triumph. We see this in the opening chapters of his novel. Natty Bumppo is reluctant to accept that Judge Temple holds a title deed to the huge tracts of land that surround Templeton, the town named after the judge himself, which allows him to control it. It means that Bumppo can no longer hunt that ground without the judge's permission; the fact that this is willingly given is irrelevant to Bumppo. The previous owners of the land were the Native American tribes and they held no deeds to it. The very idea of ownership in the judge's sense of the word is alien to them. This conflict of interpretations of the land provides Cooper with the springboard for his plot. These descriptions do not provide the consolations of a *locus amœnus,* rather they are the overture to the conflicts that will entertain

us for the remainder of the novel. In the following extract we are travelling with Elizabeth, Judge Temple's daughter, in her carriage as she returns to her town after several years away at school:

> Here and there the hills fell away in long, low points, and broke the sameness of the outline; or setting to the long and wide field of snow, which, without house, tree, fence, or any other fixture, resembled so much spotless cloud settled to the earth. A few dark and moving spots were, however, visible on the even surface, which the eye of Elizabeth knew to be so many sleighs going their several ways, to or from the village. On the western border of the plain, the mountains, though equally high, were less precipitous, and as they receded, opened into irregular valleys and glens, or were formed into terraces and hollows that admitted of cultivation. Although the evergreens still held dominion over many of the hills that rose on this side of the valley, yet the undulating outlines of the distant mountains, covered with forests of beech and maple, gave a relief to the eye, and the promise of a kinder soil. Occasionally, spots of white were discoverable amidst the forests of the opposite hills, which announced, by the smoke that curled over the tops of the trees, the habitations of man, and the commencement of agriculture. These spots were, sometimes, by the aid of united labor, enlarged into what were called settlements; but more frequently were small and insulated; though so rapid were the changes, and so persevering the labors of those who had cast their fortunes on the success of the enterprise, that it was not difficult for the imagination of Elizabeth to conceive they were enlarging under her eye, while she was gazing, in mute wonder, at the alterations that a few short years had made in the aspect of the country.

(40)

The landscape that Elizabeth observes from the carriage is not detached from the contingencies of the political and social realities of the time. On the contrary, the fight for 'dominion' between the two civilisations animates it and provides it with a poetic energy. Cooper plays with this idea of dominion as 'wilderness' cedes to 'civilisation'. He is ironic elsewhere in the book about the latter and its careless destruction of the forests and its creatures, but finally is in sympathy with it. However much the book will go on to disparage the wastefulness of the whites, the land here is seen, not through the critical eyes of a Magua, but through those of one of the finest flowers of the conquering race. Elizabeth's is the framing presence: she sets the boundaries of Cooper's sympathy for other races. Without doubt, he feels pity for them as Elizabeth does but he will not look at the landscape through their eyes. The conflicts that swept across the terrain of America in the eighteenth century are the sources of Cooper's fiction, and this contest for the land created his characters, most famously Natty Bumppo. Bumppo is, in so many ways, the frontier itself. He lives between the two cultures. His descriptions of landscape do not occlude its historical aspect as a place contested by different races—they depend on it.

The second landscape I wish to look at is by Cooper's friend and one of the great creators of 'picturesque America', William Cullen Bryant, and is to be found in his poem, 'Thanotopsis':

> When thoughts
> Of the last bitter hour come like a blight
> Over thy spirit, and sad images
> Of the stern agony, and shroud, and pall,
> And breathless darkness, and the narrow house,
> Make thee to shudder, and grow sick at heart;—
> Go forth, under the open sky, and list
> To Nature's teachings, while from all around—
> Earth and her waters, and the depths of air,—
> Comes a still voice [. . .]

> Yet not to thine eternal resting-place
> Shalt thou retire alone,—nor couldst thou wish
> Couch more magnificent. Thou shalt lie down
> With patriarchs of the infant world—with kings,
> The powerful of the earth—the wise, the good,
> Fair forms, and hoary seers of ages past,
> All in one mighty sepulchre. The hills
> Rock-ribbed and ancient as the sun; the vales
> Stretching in pensive quietness between;
> The venerable woods; rivers that move
> In majesty, and the complaining brooks
> That make the meadows green; and, poured round all,
> Old Ocean's grey and melancholy waste—
> Are but the solemn decorations all
> Of the great tomb of man.

> (*Poems* 11-12)

Bryant's consolatory campagna, with its 'Italianate sheen' (*OP* 43), as Stevens called this kind of romanticisation of nature, feels slightly imported. His reference elsewhere in the poem to the Oregon river (now the Columbia) makes it an American landscape, and so it is fair to ask exactly *which* kings and patriarchs are abed in this landscape. Bryant is perhaps gesturing to those of the Old World, thus effortlessly appropriating the American landscape by provisioning it with regal European corpses. This erasure of national difference contributes to the production of the imperial prospect of the poem.

Majesty is easily predicated of the river since the whole poem, with its proprietorial gesture (all nature is but a decoration on the tomb of man) excludes the possibility of any contest for this majesty, and it provides a telling contrast with the dominion of the trees in Cooper's landscape. They 'still hold out' against the settlements. In Bryant, there is no place for this kind of tension and conflict. His river merely *looks* majestic. In the way that it excludes the contingencies of the social world, Bryant's landscape is a deathly one. It is a precinct cordoned off by his mellifluous lines and within them

we are allowed no glimpse of the historical change that humanity's presence in nature brings about. Moreover Bryant's 'deathly locus' seems very un-American since it conveys no sense of this tract of land partaking of the New World. What I mean by this is that there is no sense of contest in the landscape, no feeling that the imagination must work to appropriate it—instead it is waiting there, to hand, as reliable as a chaise longue upon which to flop down and sigh one's last. Bryant's picturesque gaze is a strategy, a kind of dreamwork that refuses to countenance the darker side of the landscape, and this is borne out by his idealisation of Native American populations during the very century when they were being violently extinguished. In Cooper, the landscape metamorphoses before Elizabeth's eyes and she is surprised by it. The contingencies of the time sweep across her field of vision, and landscape becomes the site where we can see the conflicts of character and civilisation being worked out.

My aim here is not an account of the changing representations of nature from the nineteenth to twentieth centuries in the literature of the United States. However, these two landscapes give a brief indication of the historical context of Stevens's poems of landscape and nature. The novelist and the poet were two of the foremost American romantics of the nineteenth century, which means that they made important contributions to the way that the nature of America was represented in literature and the arts in general. This is especially true of Bryant who edited the eight-volume *Picturesque America* (1872-4). And Cooper's landscape is a healthy complication of this historical context since it precludes the inference that nineteenth-century American representations of nature were monolithic Classical scenes left for a Modernist poet like Stevens to decreate.

Pushed to align the poetry of Wallace Stevens with one of these, most readers would choose Bryant's. They might feel that, like Bryant's, Stevens's work excludes social and historical contingencies in order to maintain a sacred site where the humanist imagination can disport itself untroubled by the messier side of life. Of course, Stevens does not replicate Bryant's occlusion of genocide by idealisation of the landscape and its aborigines—his aestheticisation, they would claim, is different. In a century when the United States was rapidly urbanising, Stevens's poetry of skies and mountains, rivers and seas, could seem escapist, an attempt to avoid a field of experience that is industrial and inarguably modern. Unlike his friend Carl Sandburg, Stevens rarely used the city as location for his poems; the closest he came to this was the park. Such a distaste for urban *materia poetica,* when compared to Sandburg or Hart Crane, appears almost cowardly. But such a characterisation of Stevens is wrong: his recourse to landscape as poetic site bespeaks not cowardice in the face of historical contingency but a knowledge that this contingency could be confronted more fruitfully against the horizon of nature. Stevens's landscapes are indeed special precincts of the imagination, but, as I shall show, they are not static and they are not cordoned off from change as Bryant's is: they metamorphose from the actual to the abstract and back again, and interrogate all human fictions.

It was not until the end of the nineteenth century that the United States was fully mapped, and the sense of uncharted land stretching out from the edges of white civilisation could not but affect the sensibility of some American writers. I would go further and say that this sense that the land has yet to be appropriated by the imagination—that 'imaginative' work must be done to perceive it, to live in its midst as an artist—is one of the constitutional elements of American literature. Although created in one of the longest-colonised parts of America, even the Emersonian sublime, with its metaphysical eye abroad in nature, contains within it the knowledge that the transcendental imagination must work to appropriate and perceive the landscape, colonise it for its own ends. This imagination must make something of the nature that surrounds it, construct a landscape, and the freshness of such literature resides in watching this imagination at work, not in the eternal values it promises that nature will provide. Perhaps it is in this context that we can see Jefferson's Declaration of Independence and Emerson's *Nature* sharing a common source of power. The directness and energy of both texts convey the idea of a limitless expanse of nature to be worked upon by the mattocks and dactyls of Americans. Of course, Emerson's attitudes to the society of his day were complex and did not endorse its direction, but nevertheless in his calls, say, for a national poet it is clear that he sees that an American imagination has yet to appropriate and work the land. And even in *Nature* when he and his 'monocle' go promenading, the route he follows capitalises on the collisions of the eyes' circles with the arrangement of nature. As he turns his head, we feel vast radii sweeping the landscape and arranging it into perspectives, tableaux, moral scenes—and the excitement of this writing is not, like Bryant's, generated by some fixed natural scene that the imagination presents, but by the feeling that these transformations are occurring as one reads nature with Emerson.

Stevens's renovations and rearrangements never present nature as some ahistorical transcendental signified and this is clear from **'Botanist on Alp (No. 1)'** (*CP* 134-5) where he remarks:

> Panoramas are not what they used to be.
> Claude has been dead a long time
> And apostrophes are forbidden on the funicular.
> Marx has ruined Nature,
> For the moment.

'Notes Toward a Supreme Fiction' is haunted by the idea of a primordial natural space that is obscured by the myriad fictional spaces man has created within it. Eden could be said to be an earlier version of this. The fictional spaces in which we live and see things through—house, property, state, painting—have created in us an 'ennui' of this first idea. The first idea, the primordial state of nature, the space of the NOT-US is 'Not to be realized because not to / Be seen, not to be loved nor hated because / Not to be realized' (*CP* 385). It is always historical, as are our attempts to reach back to the first idea.

Here we are at the heart of the natural *abîme*, the muddy centre of Stevens's sublime. Instead of weather, we encounter 'Weather by Franz Hals, // Brushed up by brushy winds in brushy clouds, / Wetted by blue, colder for white' (*CP* 385). Here as so often in his work, the signifiers of painting, intervening across the poet's contemplation of nature, serve to indicate the difficulty of such a poetic project, and indeed Stevens himself remarked the difficulty he had in writing this canto (*L* 434). What makes it difficult for us is the tension between the desire to apprehend the first idea, that from which all our ideas and fictions come, and the knowledge that it is unreachable because of the accretions of centuries of mediation (and is indeed a symptom of occupying the moment of the 'late plural'). Negotiating a path between this desire and this knowledge without diminishing the power of either is what this canto (*CP* 385) accomplishes:

> Not to be realized because not to
> Be seen, not to be loved nor hated because
> Not to be realized. Weather by Franz Hals,
>
> Brushed up by brushy winds in brushy clouds,
> Wetted by blue, colder for white. Not to
> Be spoken to, without a roof, without
>
> First fruits, without the virginal of birds,
> The dark-blown ceinture loosened, not relinquished.
> Gay is, gay was, the gay forsythia
>
> And yellow, yellow thins the Northern blue.
> Without a name and nothing to be desired,
> If only imagined but imagined well.
>
> My house has changed a little in the sun.
> The fragrance of the magnolias comes close,
> False flick, false form, but falseness close to kin.
>
> It must be visible or invisible,
> Invisible or visible or both:
> A seeing and unseeing in the eye.
>
> The weather and the giant of the weather,
> Say the weather, the mere weather, the mere air:
> An abstraction blooded, as a man by thought.

The overall rhetorical gesture is a movement from negation ('Not to be realized') to affirmation ('the weather, the mere weather'). The negation—the apprehension of the distance and difficulty of the first idea—is qualified by reference to Hals. Nature here is caught in the seventeenth century, and this is further emphasised by 'the virginal of birds'. A virginal is a keyed musical instrument (common in England in the sixteenth and seventeenth centuries), resembling a spinet, and 'ceinture' is another irredeemably seventeenth-century word. The problem Stevens faces here is that it is not possible to look at a natural panorama and see it with an ignorant eye—the process is more complex than the initial no-nonsense Transcendentalist tone of Canto I would have us believe. The natural object must first be acknowledged as an historical entity. In the third line of the third tercet, Stevens brings together the nature of the past, suspended in our seventeenth-century pictur-esque notion of it, and that of the present: 'Gay is, gay was, the gay forsythia'. This change of tense (which is crucial also in **'The Rock'**) is Stevens's first step towards a 'cure' of nature, and in the next line—as we step across the blank interval between tercets—Stevens characteristically reduces the forsythias to their pure co-lour against the pure colour of the sky. For Stevens such a reduction of objects and scenes to their constitu-ent colours and shapes, far from simplifying issues, signifies a turn of sensibility that marked the modern age. Names are shucked off in this movement and the desire for some kind of access to the first idea is gradu-ally satisfied. The responsibility to 'imagine well' is placed on the human observer facing the natural object.

The tone clearly changes, preparing us for the canto's affirmative end. What the responsibility consists of is 'A seeing and unseeing in the eye'. Stevens, in **'Exami-nation of the Hero in a Time of War'**, remarked 'Sight / Is a museum of things seen' (*CP* 274). In place of Kant's rose-tinted spectacles and complex perceptual schemata, Stevens necessarily wears over his eyes the huge institution of a museum, complete with the mas-sive panoply of columns, curators and display cases. Necessarily, since otherwise he would be avoiding the historicity of nature, evading the modern difficulty of apprehending it. The conclusion affirms that while nature can be seen, it is not seen 'as the observer wills'. The observer must apprehend the historicity of nature as part of his perception, and this apprehension must also become a process of creation and decreation, 'A seeing and unseeing in the eye'.

This dialogue between the poem and Hals's signifiers registers the historicity of nature and also the distance the poet must traverse to apprehend its absence and its lessons: he must immerse himself in dialogue between verbal and pictorial representations to redeem the imagination—and what is this redemption but an empowerment exceeding the limits and divisions of existing knowledge and praxis? But this empowerment is different again from Emerson's: the Transcendentalist

would reduce the natural world to idea. Stevens, on the other hand, privileges the power of nature to change the human observer. Stevens is wary of reducing any part of the natural world to his own conscious mode of be-ing, of offering a final representation of the natural object.

And even though Stevens acknowledges the historicity of landscape in a way that Emerson doesn't, and even though he refuses to abandon the concerns of the com-munity when he wanders out beneath the open skies, he still wishes to leave room for the kind of exaltation that Emerson experienced when walking across the heath at the beginning of *Nature*.[1] It is, to use a favourite col-location of Stevens, a good. A nature poetry of his kind affords the poet a space to inhale the healths of the open air and the wide prospect of nature, while realis-ing that these moments are cathected by a public context. This is no crude politicisation of nature—landscape is still a place of 'diviner health' and ecstatic emotion—but it does suggest a set of complex negotia-tions that the poet must undertake, not in order to sing Nature over humankind, rather to say that on the deep-est level we are always thinking politically and ethi-cally even when we are in its midst. A short poem from ***Ideas of Order*** (*CP* 125-6) has two figures climbing up a mountain to find heroic images. Their expectations of romantic revelation are disappointed:

> Instead there was this tufted rock
> Massively rising high and bare [. . .]
>
> . . . . .
>
> There was the cold wind and the sound
> It made, away from the muck of the land
> That they had left, heroic sound
> Joyous and jubilant and sure.

The title of the poem, which Stevens once said 'so definitely represents my way of thinking' (*L* 293), is of course **'How to Live. What to Do'**.

Note

1. Andrew Zawacki pointed out to me that Emerson is not quite as disengaged from politics as I would have him here, referring me to the following pas-sage from 'Nature': 'The critics who complain of the sickly separation of the beauty of nature from the thing to be done, must consider that our hunt-ing of the picturesque is inseparable from our protest against false society' (395). This quotation makes Emerson look like the Stevens of my argu-ment here. However, Emerson was never really capable of making this connection between the exaltations experienced by viewers of the pictur-esque and the organisation of society; in much of his work he is simply not concerned with such a project. Emerson's failure to think in terms of ideology when mapping out Transcendentalism is

discussed by John Carlos Rowe in the first two chapters of *At Emerson's Tomb: The Politics of Classic American Literature* (1997).

Bart Eeckhout (essay date 2002)

SOURCE: Eeckhout, Bart. "Infuriating Philosophers." In *Wallace Stevens and the Limits of Reading and Writing*, pp. 135-56. Columbia, Mo.: University of Missouri Press, 2002.

[*In the following essay, Eeckhout outlines the philosophical aspects of Stevens's poetry, focusing on issues of the ultimate limitations to perception and to language.*]

Wallace Stevens's reputation, for all the different ways in which his work has been framed, continues to rest largely on the critical possibilities he offers for pondering epistemological, language-philosophical, and literary-theoretical questions. It is no coincidence that his rise on the academic firmament from the sixties onwards ran parallel with that of the interdisciplinary work that went by the awkward and somewhat dubious collective name of "theory." As John Timberman Newcomb notes, "it would hardly be an exaggeration to assert that intellectually and institutionally no single author was more important to the rise of American critical theory than Stevens." Reading Stevens from a theoretical and philosophical angle nevertheless presents unmistakable dangers, and these dangers are both categorial and specific. Frank Kermode's previously quoted warning that it is a "mistake" (literally, a *wrong take* on the subject) to read Stevens seriously as a philosopher rather than as a poet with an impressive "peripheral awareness of the important issues in philosophy" remains as valid as ever. Kermode is right to insist that "[c]ritics who systematize Stevens, work out what, under all his vatic obscurities, his tranced and sometimes impassioned mimesis of thinking, he was really getting at, have occasionally come quite close to making him a bore."[1] It is easy enough, moreover, to find support for this critical verdict from the poet himself. Some passages in the letters echo Kermode's blunt dismissal almost verbatim. This is the case, for instance, when we find Stevens wrapping up a paraphrase of **"Sunday Morning"** in a letter of 1928 to L. W. Payne Jr. by saying: "Now these ideas are not bad in a poem. But they are a frightful bore when converted as above" (*L* [*Letters of Wallace Stevens*] 250).

Repeatedly, Stevens defined his own work in opposition to that of philosophers. "The poet must not adapt his experience to that of the philosopher," he proclaimed in the *Adagia* (*OP* [*Opus Posthumous*] 196), or, even more provocatively: "Perhaps it is of more value to

infuriate philosophers than to go along with them" (*OP* 192). We should realize, however, that both poetic credos were flung in the face of a particular *type* of philosopher: the type who is committed to constructing comprehensive and coherent worldviews, the type who operates under what the pragmatic, skeptical, and elusive Stevens regarded as *Systemszwang*. One of the most telling anecdotes in this respect involves the critic Bernard Heringman, who in 1951 sent Stevens the final chapter of C. Roland Wagner's dissertation—a chapter in which reference was made to Stevens's poetry. Heringman received the following reply:

> Last Sunday I spent several hours and was able to give it careful attention, but it really requires more than that. For me it is a way of synthesizing things that I am never likely to synthesize for myself. It is always somebody else that does this sort of thing. As both you and Mr. Wagner must realize, I have no wish to arrive at a conclusion. Sometimes I believe most in the imagination for a long time and then, without reasoning about it, turn to reality and believe in that and that alone. But both of these things project themselves endlessly and I want them to do just that.
>
> (*L* 710)

Stevens's poetry, it is important to remind ourselves, belongs far less to a philosophical tradition based on logic and rationality than to an Emersonian tradition epitomized by such well-known aphorisms as "A foolish consistency is the hobgoblin of little minds" and vitalistic lines like Walt Whitman's "Do I contradict myself? / Very well then I contradict myself, / (I am large, I contain multitudes.)"[2]

In another letter to Heringman, Stevens went so far as to deny any serious influence from philosophers on his work, protesting in the following terms: "I have never studied systematic philosophy and should be bored to death at the mere thought of doing so. . . . I could never possibly have any serious contact with philosophy because I have not the memory" (*L* 636). The most immediately important word in this dismissal is clearly "systematic," though one should not overlook how the hyperbole of "bored to death" (again that image) is straightaway modified by the admission of an underlying inability: "because I have not the memory." The factual tone in which Stevens declares his memory to be inept, moreover, may be taken as something of a smoke screen: we know that this was a man who had a capacious memory, and we also know that his memory was not merely anecdotally or quixotically structured but proved capable of serving him in fields of systematic knowledge-gathering and knowledge-use—he was, after all, an outstanding and highly disciplined lawyer.[3] His downplaying of philosophy, in other words, may be construed, on one level, as a testimony to his anxiety of influence and his deep-rooted desire for originality. Stevens had always been influenced by philosophers.

By the end of the same letter to Heringman, for example, he refers to his former Harvard mentor, George Santayana, as "the decrepit old philosopher now living in a convent in Rome," hastening to add that of course "Santayana is not a philosopher in any austere sense" (*L* 637). And in Peter A. Brazeau's oral biography, *Parts of a World,* Richard Wilbur recalls that after Stevens's last public reading at Harvard, in 1952, the older poet reminisced at great length about his Harvard days and "that it was all about his teachers in philosophy."[4] It is in the works of these same philosophers also—above all, Santayana, William James, and Josiah Royce—that Frank Lentricchia in *Modernist Quartet* elaborately situates the germs of Stevens's art and ideas. In short, it was not philosophy as such against which Stevens was quick to bristle, but a specific, rigorously and logically organized manner of thinking with which the word could be associated—that of "analytic philosophy," the dominant trend in American universities at midcentury, when the reputation of the humanistic, antiessentialist, and antisystematic pragmatism that was congenial to Stevens happened to be at an all-time low.[5]

American pragmatism is in fact the philosophical tradition within which Stevens's ideas are most easily inscribed, if for no other reason than the intrinsic vagueness and polysemy of the term. "The pages of just one pragmatist work," notes Russell B. Goodman with reference to James's 1907 book *Pragmatism,* "contain at least six accounts of what pragmatism is or contains: a theory of truth, a theory of meaning, a philosophical temperament, an epistemology/metaphysics stressing human interest and action, a method for dissolving philosophical disputes, and a skeptical anti-essentialism." In the same book, James wrote: "The philosophy which is so important in each of us is not a technical matter; it is our more or less dumb sense of what life honestly and deeply means. It is only partly got from books; it is our individual way of just seeing and feeling the total push and pressure of the cosmos. . . . The history of philosophy is to a great extent that of a certain clash of human temperaments." Stevens, the tentative but eager and self-reliant thinker, would have willingly consented with words like these. Indeed, the inspiration for his early antisystematic and pluralistic poetic manifesto, **"Thirteen Ways of Looking at a Blackbird"** (1917), may well have derived in part from a classic paper published by Arthur Lovejoy in *The Journal of Philosophy* one year after James's *Pragmatism* was published, for that paper carried as a title "The Thirteen Pragmatisms."[6] Thirteen, it may be worth recalling, has always been the favorite number for representing uncontainability and irreducible plurality.

We must turn to the 1951 lecture "A Collect of Philosophy" (*OP* 267-80) to find Stevens pondering what were to him the essential divergences between poetry and philosophy, and to observe which intellectual and rhetorical moves he typically deployed to that end. Thanks to Brazeau, we know that the third and final part of this lecture gave him much trouble.[7] Having established, in the first two parts, a degree of similarity and convergence between the disciplines, he proposes to embark on a rundown of fundamental differences. His paintaking attempt is interesting not so much for its results (in terms of clarity and usefulness of its categorial distinctions, that is) as for the illustration it provides of how Stevens's antisystematical, improvisatory mind went to work on the question. The attempt shows, in particular, how his "Emersonian disregard for the syntax of thinking" breaks with the discursive rigor of well-structured argumentations.[8] "The habit of forming concepts unites [poetry and philosophy]," he suggests as a first working hypothesis, quite in tune with one of the more venerable Aristotelian traditions. "The use to which they put their ideas separates them." The difference is developed as follows:

> The philosopher searches for an integration for its own sake, as, for example, Plato's idea that knowledge is recollection or that the soul is a harmony; the poet searches for an integration that shall be not so much sufficient in itself as sufficient for some quality that it possesses, such as its insight, its evocative power or its appearance in the eye of the imagination. The philosopher intends his integration to be fateful; the poet intends his to be effective.

This is immediately slippery. The integrations of philosophy would be autotelic, while those of poetry would live off an external quality—like "insight"? This sounds like turning the tables on philosophy's principal claim for self-legitimation, and so Stevens quickly backtracks:

> And yet these integrations, although different from each other, have something in common, such as, say, a characteristic of the depth or distance at which they have been found, a facture of the level or position of the mind or, if you like, of a level or position of the feelings, because in the excitement of bringing things about it is not always easy to say whether one is thinking or feeling or doing both at the same time.
>
> (*OP* 276-77)

The second half of this sentence takes issue, quite in passing and maybe unintentionally, with Eliot's then-influential "dissociation of sensibility": to Stevens, it does not prove easy at all, either in poetry or in philosophy, to disentangle and sort out thinking and feeling. By dwelling upon this aspect of the creative process shared by both disciplines, however, he is significantly shifting the debate from a cognitive and methodological to a largely psychological one. What is more, he almost immediately manages to modify and qualify his original opposition to the point of collapse.

Maybe, Stevens tries again, the main difference lies in the fact that "the probing of the philosopher is deliberate" and "the probing of the poet is fortuitous." At once he chooses to swerve from the idea of depth and distance just broached:

> In any case, it is misleading to speak of the depth or distance at which their integrations are found, or of the level or position of the mind or feelings, if the fact is that they probe in different spheres and if, in their different spheres, they move about by means of different motions. It may be said that the philosopher probes the sphere or spheres of perception and that he moves about therein like someone intent on making sure of every foot on the way. If the poet moves about in the same sphere or spheres, and occasionally he may, he is light-footed. He is intent on what he sees and hears and the sense of the certainty of the presences about him is as nothing to the presences themselves.
>
> (*OP* 277)

How odd again: the philosopher's sphere appears to be that of "perception" (a world itself a little too ambiguous to bring much clarity to the discussion) rather than that of ideas and abstractions, and the philosopher walks in this sphere only as a rational Cartesian obsessed with "certainty," never apparently as a phenomenologist whose primary interest is in "what he sees and hears" and in the fickle "presences about him." The latter sort of interest is a poet's habit—at least when that same poet enters the sphere of perception, which happens only "occasionally." The drift of Stevens's argument becomes no clearer when next the "philosopher's native sphere"—perception, we have just been told—turns out to be "only a metaphysical one." And when that hypothesis, in turn, is swallowed, we begin to feel caught in the revolving door of what a more impatient reader will be inclined to call prevarication or tergiversation.

The same impatient reader will presumably experience considerable relief to find that Stevens, too, feels it is high time for wrapping up a few things, for finally raising "the question of the final cause of philosophy and the final cause of poetry" (*OP* 278). But the relief is short-lived, since Stevens appears unable to stop putting ideas under erasure. "The answers to this question are as countless as the definitions of philosophy and poetry," he continues. "To define philosophy and to define poetry are parts of the repertory of the mind. They are classic exercises. This could not be true if the definitions were adequate." Lines like these, at the heart of what Stevens's fugitive and wayward lecture tries to enact, have been understandably inviting to both pragmatist and poststructuralist critics, for they seem to express a basic belief in provisionality as well as in a binary thinking that can be neither upheld nor simply dispensed with. Wishing to extract himself from an intellectual stalemate, Stevens flaunts a radical relativ-

ism and fundamental theoretical undecidability, implicitly calling for the endless deferral of intellectual play. Yet this, too, proves to be but one stage in an ongoing exercise. Stevens does not leave off at relativity and undecidability. A less skeptical voice in him takes over, and-yetting one more time:

> And yet for all the different kinds of philosophy it is possible to generalize and to say that the philosopher's world is intended to be a world, which yet remains to be discovered and which, at bottom, the philosophers probably hope will always remain to be discovered and that the poet's world is intended to be a world, which yet remains to be celebrated and which, at bottom, the poets probably hope will always remain to be celebrated.
>
> (*OP* 278)

The elaborate rhetorical flourish of parallelism clearly signals an insistent wish to reach a climax: Stevens *would* arrive at an insight into what separates both intellectual enterprises. Or rather, more recalcitrantly, he would and he would not. He would have his own poetic celebrations, as much as the philosopher's discoveries, be temporary and transient, the finite and provisional products of time, but he would not have the underlying drive that propels all searches for celebration and discovery be diminished thereby and lose its infinitely vital, wholly insatiable character. Desire, as so often, is what ultimately inspires his thinking and writing: both the heuristic and celebratory activities of philosophers and poets are informed by a fundamental sort of human passion whose existence, no matter how aimless and sterile it can at times prove to be, was in the eyes of this poet almost always the one remaining mainstay in life. To be alive, for Stevens, was to desire, and to keep one's desire burning was to stay alive. This was his deep-rooted conviction, and it could never have been the conviction of a melioristic utilitarian or of a socio-politically committed activist—despite all affirmations of a world to be discovered and celebrated—but only of a man whose frustrations and alienations ran so deep as to require a basic vitalizing prop otherwise void of purpose or content.

"A Collect of Philosophy" does not end with this projection of endless desire, and makes a few more surprising sidesteps in its labyrinthine progress, but the point should be taken: even for such a relatively homogeneous unit as a single lecture, Stevens's thought is well-nigh impossible to synthesize or recast in the shape of a narrative that manages to trace the development of a systematic theory. His restive and evasive theoretical quests can only be halted by the illusory dogma of the moment. That dogma of the moment, at the same time, remained what one part of him looked for and even craved, for there is a sort of transcendental power and sincerity to the moment—to the experience of the present in all its possible urgency and with all its possible needs—that cannot be so simply reduced or denied. There is always the serendipitous possibility of happening upon a delimitation of reality that would suffice, for the moment. Without this possibility, we are all condemned to lapse into indifference—a danger that constantly haunted Stevens.

Clearly, it is impossible to pin this poet's work down to a handful of ideas, opinions, and beliefs. We cannot contain his intellectual world in any systematic form and present it as some sort of developed philosophy. Nevertheless, what remains possible, and becomes all the more useful for being possible, is to set up a conceptual *framework* within which to analyze and understand Stevens's poetic experiments. With a poet noted for his remarkable "awareness of the important issues in philosophy," no matter how "peripheral" this awareness may have been, it should be possible to circumscribe a number of these "important issues."

In his own muted and rhetorically deflected way, Stevens was an obsessive man. And his most famous obsessions were with a handful of issues: the workings of desire (in the physical as well as the idealistic senses of the word); the role and theory of poetry in a world fundamentally uprooted by the death of God and the social and political drama of Stevens's own age (including two world wars, a major economic depression, and a cold war); the need for originality (where his obsession could become so compulsive as to border on an originality neurosis); and the aesthetic and performative potential for play in poetry. But no obsession was arguably as striking, as idiomatic and poetically defining, as that with the epistemological nexus of perception, thought, and language—a nexus often parading in the post-Coleridgean guise of a reality-imagination debate. No reader can engage this poetry without a smattering of epistemology, and every literary critic has to take the risk of amateuristic dabbling in this field. More than three decades after the Stevens industry started to boom (and its bias was heavily philosophical to begin with), critical studies still open by claiming that "[t]he essence of a Stevens poem is the continuing dialogue—the ever-changing process—between the mind and the world, and the continuing quest within the mind for the appropriate language—what might be called the semiological quest—to render that dialogue."[9] More particularly, Stevens appears to have been fascinated, time and again, by the *irreducibility* of the three categories of perception, thought, and language, and by the question of their *interaction and (in)separability*. This fascination is itself so intimately linked with the Kantian question of conditions that it would not be too philosophically extraneous to call Stevens a poet obsessed with conditionality.

One illuminating theory of the conditions governing the relations between perception, thought, and language is offered by the French phenomenological philosopher Maurice Merleau-Ponty. It is a theory that is all the more apposite for coming from a phenomenologist, since we have already seen that one of the early philosophical labels to be stuck on Stevens's poetic ideas, however approximative, was precisely that of "phenomenological."[10] Merleau-Ponty expounds the matter as follows:

> The relation . . . of thought to language or of thought to perception is this two-way relationship that phenomenology has called *Fundierung*: the founding term, or originator—. . . language, perception—is primary in the sense that the originated is presented as a determinate or explicit form of the originator, which prevents the latter from reabsorbing the former, and yet the originator is not primary in the empiricist sense and the originated is not simply derived from it, since it is through the originated that the originator is made manifest.[11]

The issue described here has affinities with Derrida's theory of iterability as discussed in Chapter 4. Once again the debate hinges on the difference between "necessary conditions" and "sufficient reasons" and on the complication that results from the fact that the two should be kept apart. Language and perception, argues Merleau-Ponty (and for present purposes we suspend the question of the justifiability of this argument), are both necessary conditions for thought, but they are not sufficient reasons for it: they do not in themselves produce or warrant any concrete thoughts. They precede thought in such a way that thought can never fully encompass perception or language, since thought is determined by these, or developed on the basis of these. But the dependence is mutual and not unidirectional: perception and language themselves derive their foundational status only from thought and are themselves manifested only through thought.

It is not difficult to see how a philosopher originally schooled in phenomenology like Derrida was able to extend this irresolvable ambivalence and interaction into a theory of difference, or even, suspending the notion irresolvably in time and in between activity and passivity, of "differance." From the very first, Derrida emphasized the antitheological and antihomogenizing nature of his philosophical enterprise.[12] Any attempt at inscribing a constitutive difference *within* (the experience of) reality is ultimately antioriginary in that it disallows a single point of origin where necessary condition and sufficient reason are conflated—a conflation that is precisely typical of monotheistic worldviews. (That the word *originary* itself has been popularized in academic jargon almost single-handedly by Derrida only serves to underscore the importance of Kantian questions of conditionality in his work.) Both Merleau-Ponty and Derrida, we could say, have taught us the dangers of privileging any of the entangled, interacting, and even mutually productive categories of perception, thought, and language. The fact that Stevens, in his own poetic way, often highlighted these dangers, entanglements, and interactions helps to explain why critics have moved with remarkable ease from Stevens the phenomenologist to Stevens the deconstructionist.

The middle ground from which Stevens pushed out to the frontiers of the perception-thought-language nexus shares a lot with Kantian, Nietzschean, phenomenological, and pragmatist topoi and perspectives—in particular, the topos of perspectivity itself. Reality to Stevens tended to mean reality *as perceived.* "Things seen are things as seen," he proclaimed in his *Adagia* (*OP* 188), and in **"The Pure Good of Theory"** he insisted: "It is never the thing but the version of the thing" (*CP* 332). In this perspectivist attitude much of his philosophical modernity resides, although it is a modernity that has been nearly defeated by its own success, since we have come to assimilate the idea of perspectivism (and of its descendant, social constructivism) so widely in the humanities as to render it inconspicuous and seemingly "natural." "It is possible," Stevens wrote at the outset of one of his most theoretically sophisticated poems, **"Description without Place,"** "that to seem—it is to be" (*CP* [*The Collected Poems of Wallace Stevens*] 339). And by entertaining this hypothesis he was merely unrolling another stretch of a long intertextual thread that reaches back at least to his own boisterous injunction in **"The Emperor of Ice-Cream"**: "Let be be finale of seem" (*CP* 64). To seem is to be *to a perceiver,* and Stevens, early and late, was fascinated by the freedom (both opportunity and danger) that the human mind is left with in the act of perceiving, as well as by the strictures that operate upon (both limiting and enabling) this freedom. A. Walton Litz describes him as a poetic Ernst Gombrich, who saw the artist "as a creator of *schema* for apprehending the physical."[13] It is part of Stevens's modernist moment that he should have opened **"An Ordinary Evening in New Haven"** by calling houses "difficult objects" (*CP* 465), that he should have talked in that same poem of the "difficulty of the visible" (*CP* 474), and composed what reads like a variation on the famous concluding question to Yeats's "Among School Children" ("How can we know the dancer from the dance?"):

> Suppose these houses are composed of ourselves,
> So much ourselves, we cannot tell apart
> The idea and the bearer-being of the idea.[14]

> (*CP* 466)

Starting out from his perspectivist middle ground, Stevens was nevertheless given to exploring the various limit situations of the perception-thought-language nexus—limit situations that are, not coincidentally, crucial to the act of writing. And since that nexus is triadic, those limit situations are themselves of three kinds. Each one of the three interacting terms offers the possibility for autonomization or hypostatization, to the point where they may try to swallow the other two whole. Stevens liked to experiment with such situations—instances where limits come close to being lifted up or falling away, thus paradoxically announcing themselves:

> One of the limits of reality
> Presents itself in Oley when the hay,
> Baked through long days, is piled in mows. It is
> A land too ripe for enigmas, too serene.

> (*CP* 374)

The first manifestation of a limit situation, illustrated by these lines from **"Credences of Summer,"** has to do with what we have earlier touched upon in the context of **"The Snow Man."** It occurs whenever Stevens falls back on the irreducibility of the real and seeks to express a sense of full presence and satisfaction in immediate reality or, as his color symbolism would have it, in "green's green apogee" (*CP* 373). At such times, he tends to be impressed by, or attracted to, the possibility of an unmediated perception of the world. He then seeks to cancel the conflict between perception and thought (which in this case includes language) by deactivating one side, that of thought (and language). But inevitably this also means that he moves, in Jerry Fodor's terms, "very close to the edge of what we know how to talk about at all sensibly," since "perception is a hybrid of what the senses are given and what the mind infers. . . . Granting something unconceptualised that is simply *given* to the mind in experience has generally been supposed to be the epistemological price one has to pay for an ontology that takes the world to be not itself mind-dependent."[15] Analogously with how the category of the "real" functions in Lacanian psychoanalysis—as something that falls outside the symbolic order and whose existence can only be affirmed, not further discussed—Stevens's rock-bottom reality tends to show itself in its irreducible alterity as that residual other of thought and language which cannot ultimately be incorporated in terms of knowing or describing. In "On Poetic Truth," a text by H. D. Lewis which Stevens considered so fascinating that he transcribed it for his own use (thereby misleading Samuel French Morse into including it in the first edition of *Opus Posthumous*), this otherness of reality is precisely central to the argument. What we want from art, argues Lewis, is to be brought into contact with "reality as it impinges on us from the outside, the sense that we can touch and feel a solid reality which does not wholly dissolve itself into the conceptions of our own minds. . . . And the wonder and mystery of art . . . is the revelation of something 'wholly other' by which the inexpressible loneliness of thinking is broken and enriched" (*OP* 1957, 236-37).

The attachment to "the wonder and mystery of art" that consists in breaking the shell of the self and striking out to something "wholly other" (like nature, or in George

S. Lensing's most recent book, the four seasons) was undoubtedly great in Stevens. But it was not a naive attachment. For all his longing to invoke the real, material world in its untainted alterity, Stevens simultaneously showed himself to be exceptionally sensitive to the fact that we ultimately cannot have unmediated access to that something other which exists in excess of all intentionality and interpretation. And so the earnestness and eagerness of his representations of an immediately, transparently perceived reality treacherously fluctuate from poem to poem. The fact that the (re)presentation of the *fondant* (perception) can happen only by way of the *fondé* (thought, here again including language) produced an irresolvable irony that left Stevens in a predicament he sometimes tried to efface and suppress, but more often allowed to be inscribed in his rhetorically self-conscious texts. To what extent these textual forms of self-consciousness were intentional is frequently hard to tell and often depends on the way we are willing to color the tone of the poems. But on the whole, Stevens was only too aware that if language and thought could be deactivated experientially, they could not therefore be deactivated performatively: they are the indispensable tools for the communication of this deactivation; they are the means for the simple attestation of unmediated perception. The furthest a poet can go is to use suspension points (and Stevens, as I have argued elsewhere, was one of the two prominent high modernist poets in English, the other being Hart Crane, to have made repeated and astonishingly rich use of that typographical device).[16] Falling back on the stop-stand-and-listen sign of suspension points and the concomitant rhetorical ploy of aposiopesis was the most extreme maneuver he had at his disposal for conjuring up moments when the senses tried to take over entirely from the perceiving subject, as in the following instances:

> Look, Master,
> See the river, the railroad, the cathedral . . .
>
> (*CP* 227)

> Here, being visible is being white,
> Is being of the solid of white, the accomplishment
> Of an extremist in an exercise . . .
>
> (*CP* 412)

> The leaves cry . . . One holds off and merely hears
>   the cry.
>
> (*OP* 123)

William W. Bevis's case for seeing Stevens as somebody who meticulously tried to represent a meditative state of consciousness works as an important reminder of the insufficiency of epistemological readings on those occasions when Stevens's poems seem to be deactivating

thought and language. The poet recollecting his meditative tranquilities in writing was a variously divided person, alternately contented and calm, restive and skeptical, or more playful and ironical. Yet Bevis's de-epistemologizing argument should not be pushed to such an extreme as to blind ourselves to the many ways in which Stevens's self-conscious rhetoric—perhaps at a different level from that of the attempt to report meditative experience—is replete with self-undercutting scenes.

In sharp contrast with the deactivation of thought (which may be interpreted as the deactivation of all cortical activity), we find in Stevens's work several forms of extreme idealism in which the thinking mind appears to encompass or envelop the entire world. Writing in his usual paternal tone to José Rodríguez Feo in 1945, Stevens insisted that "there is no passion like the passion of thinking which grows stronger as one grows older, even though one never thinks anything of any particular interest to anyone else. Spend an hour or two a day even if in the beginning you are staggered by the confusion and aimlessness of your thoughts" (*L* 513). It was precisely the strength of this passion for thinking that called forth countermoments of complete surrender to perception, for Stevens knew only too well how dangerous the aimless and fruitless confusions of a spinning mind could be. "The mind is the most terrible force in the world," he wrote in his *Adagia,* "principally in this that it is the only force that can defend us against itself" (*OP* 199). One of the most arresting manifestations of Stevens's inclination to autonomize, or even ontologize, thought (or the inventions of the mind; we are not, here, in a cognitive-scientific realm where we may always rigorously distinguish between categories) was his long-standing interest in fiction and the possible fictionality of the world.

The word *fiction*—a "terribly equivocal word," according to Derrida[17]—appears for the first time in Stevens's poetry in the opening line of **Harmonium**'s **"A High-Toned Old Christian Woman,"** with its resounding prolepsis: "Poetry is the supreme fiction, madame" (*CP* 59). The Christian addressee of that poem reminds us of the soil from which Stevens's further theorizations sprang: a concern with the death of the gods, associated with Nietzsche's famous proclamation. Significantly, it was Nietzsche who provided Frank Kermode with the first epigraph to his chapter on "Fictions" in *The Sense of an Ending,* where the philosopher is quoted as saying: "What can be thought must certainly be a fiction." The epigraph immediately following Nietzsche's was borrowed, just as significantly, from Stevens, to whom Kermode's whole book was a disguised "love-letter." This second epigraph concerns "the nicer knowledge of / Belief, that what it believes in is not true." The link between Stevens and Nietzsche has often been made, and B. J. Leggett has gone to great lengths in comparing the two writers' respective views of fiction. But Nietzsche stands in a longer Kantian tradition, which he radicalized and polemicized and which in Stevens's own day was continued by phenomenology. Paul Kenneth Naylor, for example, quotes Husserl as saying that "the element which makes up the life of phenomenology as of all eidetic science is 'fiction.'" In this perspectivist and subjectivist tradition, it became possible to construct fiction as a "transcendental" illusion—a necessary illusion, that is, not a delusion, or, as Rudolf Boehm explains the concept, an appearance that does not disappear when seen through.[18]

Stevens can be situated in that tradition, if perhaps only on the margins of it, in that eccentric, nonphilosophical realm where less systematically conceptualized, more improvisatory and intrinsically poetic concerns contaminate the notion of fiction. The following lines from *Adagia,* for example, which are among the most-quoted of his many obiter dicta, must be read as a post-Coleridgean defense of the imagination mixed in with a wider philosophical claim about the necessarily fictional structure of reality: "The final belief is to believe in a fiction, which you know to be a fiction, there being nothing else. The exquisite truth is to know that it is a fiction and that you believe in it willingly" (*OP* 189). Having made this claim, Stevens was able to write his best-known long poem, **"Notes toward a Supreme Fiction,"** providing for it the following instructively confusing explanation:

> One evening, a week or so ago, a student at Trinity College came to the office and walked home with me. We talked about this book [**"Notes"**]. I said that I thought that we had reached a point at which we could no longer really believe in anything unless we recognized that it was a fiction. The student said that that was an impossibility, that there was no such thing as believing in something that one knew was not true. It is obvious, however, that we are doing that all the time. There are things with respect to which we willingly suspend disbelief; if there is instinctive in us a will to believe, or if there is a will to believe, whether or not it is instinctive, it seems to me that we can suspend disbelief with reference to a fiction as easily as we can suspend it with reference to anything else. There are fictions that are extensions of reality. There are plenty of people who believe in Heaven as definitely as your New England ancestors and my Dutch ancestors believed in it. But Heaven is an extension of reality.
>
> (*L* 430)

In this excerpt from a letter to Henry Church (which finds Stevens proceeding to dismiss Nietzsche in ambiguous terms well analyzed by Leggett),[19] Stevens typically vacillates between broader and narrower conceptions of fiction. This leads him to contradict his provocative opening proposition that we can really believe in something only if we recognize it to be a fiction—a proposition we might gloss as: only if we

recognize it to be a construction and structuration by the mind, an experience of the world that is always, necessarily, mentally and subjectively shaped, not simply imprinted from the outside on a blank slate. Stevens immediately undercuts the universalizing sweep of this idea by moving on to the particularity of "things with respect to which we willingly suspend disbelief" and by winding up with the classic opposition between reality and narrowly defined fictions, of which there are some that can be seen as "extensions of reality."

To realize the full range of Stevens's poetic exploitations of the concept of fiction, we should in fact turn to etymology. Stevens was an addict of the Lewis and Short *Latin Dictionary,*[20] and so would have known that *fiction* derives from *fingo* (infinitive *fingere*) and that this verb in general means "to form, shape, fashion, frame, make," as well as "to form mentally or in speech, to represent in thought, to imagine, conceive, think, suppose" and "to contrive, devise, invent, feign," and is additionally able to take more specific meanings like "to make into something or in a certain manner" or "to form by instruction, to instruct, teach, train." All of these meanings went into his use of the word as it moved from context to context. He conceived of *fiction* as an umbrella term for the entertaining of hypotheses that explored the inescapability, primacy, even self-sufficiency of the mind (or consciousness, or thought) in our human experience of the world—the only experience available to us.

Stevens's concern with fictionality runs deep in his work, and one of the most pervasive lexical indices signaling its constancy is that of the conjunctive cluster "as if."[21] In the concordance to his work, the cluster figures no less than 113 times. It is, we might quip, as if Stevens possessed a special feeling of *as if*—a feeling that accorded well with William James's remark from his epoch-making chapter on "The Stream of Thought": "We ought to say a feeling of *and,* a feeling of *if,* a feeling of *but,* and a feeling of *by,* quite as readily as we say a feeling of *blue* or a feeling of *cold.* Yet we do not: so inveterate has our habit become of recognizing the existence of the substantive parts alone, that language almost refuses to lend itself to any other use."[22] As a poet, Stevens was ceaselessly out to undercut the priority that our linguistically molded minds tend to attribute to the substantive (the material, the solidified, the static, or, in one of his preferred shapes, the statuesque) by foregrounding the role of grammatical connectives and shifters (the immaterial, the fluid, the dynamic, the relational, the provisional, the hypothetical, the transitory).

Yet the phrase "as if" does more in Stevens than function as a token of the skeptically qualifying and dynamic mind: it tends to open up the world to observability as well. As Wolfgang Iser argues: "Self-disclosure of fictionality puts the world represented in brackets, thereby indicating the presence of a purpose which turns out to be observability of the world represented." Stevens's insistent as-ifness is part of his modernity, situating us at the heart of a dynamic and open-ended heuristic process that conditions and shapes our human self-consciousness. We cannot even begin to understand the world unless we fall back on as-if reasonings and approach nature by way of what Daniel C. Dennett calls "approximating confabulation." For Stevens, as Lee Edelman wittily points out, "'is' is only made available to us as 'as.'"[23] Or in the language of **"An Ordinary Evening in New Haven"**: the world is only available to us "in the intricate evasions of as" (*CP* 486).

Although today's scientific cognitive and neurolinguistic evidence suggests that thought and language are clearly divided from each other and thinking is far less a matter of words and sentences than writers and academics in text-oriented disciplines are inclined to believe,[24] in Stevens's case the extremes of idealizing and hypostatizing thought, on one hand, and language, on the other, are often difficult to disentangle. What is clear, though, and what has been noted over and over again, is that Stevens's texts are more than usually self-referential and that the question of the limits of language was often at some level involved in his writing. With the possible exception of Gertrude Stein, he is the most "textual" and (meta)linguistic of high modernist poets in English (and for that reason, he stands as a father figure to many postmodernist poets and critical theorists).

Language, as the sometime popularity of deconstruction has shown, has an extraordinary potential for being idealized and hypostatized. Its "invention," after all, is the great watershed in the evolution of the human species. As Steven Pinker notes: "People can be forgiven for overrating language. Words make noise, or sit on a page, for all to hear and see. Thoughts are trapped inside the head of the thinker."[25] During the past century, when modernist artists started focusing their attention on the formal aspects of art-making and, no less important, Saussurian linguistic theory began to foreground the arbitrariness of the sign, the inclination to let language fall back on itself became stronger than ever. Stevens did not know the structuralist jargon we use to talk of the radical alienability of signifiers from signifieds and of signifieds from referents, but that did not prevent him from having his own sense of these things: a similar insight, for instance, underlies the polysemous title of one of his most crucial language-philosophical poems, **"Description without Place."** His work offers multiple illustrations of the heavily idealistic notion that things not described do not exist (or that describing the world actually creates it), as well as of the Hegelian idea that no concrete empirical experience or phenomenon can be communicated, since language is essentially general

and abstract. The related notion that we are captives of language (the strongest possible form of limitation) can also be found upon occasion. Such language-philosophical ideas frequently underlie his alternatively exasperating and exhilarating moments of blatant, laconic circularity in formulation and imagery.

What is more, the philosophical limits of language were not the only ones with which Stevens was preoccupied. Margaret Dickie calls him a poet who was more than usually given "to arrest attention at the letter itself, both as a character of the alphabet and as a material token." The limits of the materiality of language, too, were repeatedly tested by him. This could take the moderate form of a search for exotic and foreign scraps of diction or of an at times outré sesquipedalophilia—two stylistic habits that signaled a high verbal and linguistic self-consciousness and were meant to be in large part self-sufficient. But occasionally, Stevens went further and struck out for the most distant frontiers of verbal sense—to those regions where sense passes into nonsense and only acoustical materiality seems to remain. Alison Rieke, in *The Senses of Nonsense*, studies this aspect most extensively, following the poet into the Joycean realm of "ithy oonts," "tunk-a-tunk-tunk," "ti-rill-a-roo," and "hoobla-hoobla-hoobla-how," where he was "purposefully manipulating language at its limits to confound his readers." For strategical reasons, Eleanor Cook avoids the word "nonsense" in her own *Poetry, Word-Play, and Word-War in Wallace Stevens*, but she does an even more convincing job of showing the many ways in which this poet sprang the bounds and straitjacket of hackneyed denotation. "More even than Joyce," she provocatively claims, "[Stevens] can make us hear the words we have inherited in a new way." His "sophistication in etymological word-play and word-war is extraordinary. So is his multilingual punning."[26] We would be much amiss, in other words, to restrict Stevens's exploration of the limits of language to a metapoetic realm of philosophical ideas only: it is just as diversely and richly worked into his handling of words at the most immediately poetic level.

These are, in a nutshell, the limits of perception, thought, and language that constitute the core dynamic out of which Stevens's poems are generated and to which they continually return. A critical framework of the kind just elaborated contributes to our understanding and appreciation of the work even if, and precisely because, such a systematized overview was constantly resisted by Stevens himself. Indeed, we should not forget this element of tactical resistance. It was above all by resisting the limitations of limits at the same time that he established them—by problematizing identities, if you like, in the very process of defining them—that Stevens betrayed his obsession with our human finitude. When pressured, for instance, to elucidate the notion of "supreme fiction," he typically preferred to be evasive by coming up with his own version of Joyce's notorious (though probably apocryphal) claim that *Ulysses* is so filled with "enigmas and puzzles that it will keep the professors busy for centuries arguing over what I meant."[27] Stevens merely substituted a different brand of scholar for the Joycean professor: "The next thing for me to do will be to try to be a little more precise about this enigma. I hold off from even attempting that because, as soon as I start to rationalize, I lose the poetry of the idea. . . . As I see the subject, it could occupy a school of rabbis for the next few generations" (*L* 435). And almost twelve years later, pressed by another critic, Stevens was still adamant: "That a man's work should remain indefinite is often intentional. For instance, in projecting a supreme fiction, I cannot imagine anything more fatal than to state it definitely and incautiously. . . . I don't mean to try to exercise the slightest restraint on what you say. Say what you will. But we are dealing with poetry, not with philosophy. The last thing in the world that I should want to do would be to formulate a system" (*L* 863-64).

Poetry, Stevens was convinced, is not meant to offer an awkwardly elaborate and circumstantial, somewhat frivolously attired, repetition of philosophical tenets and reasonings. It is not a literally misplaced illustration of philosophical ideas. Although it can contain such ideas—and even does so lavishly in his case—it assimilates them to its own imaginative purposes and sets them to work on a poetic level. As early as his Harvard years, Stevens protested (in the margin of his copy of James Russell Lowell's letters) against the idea that poetry should "in some way convey a truth of philosophy" when he observed: "I like my philosophy smothered in beauty and not the opposite."[28] The critical longing for a minimal systematicity in coming to terms with Stevens's explorations of the limit situations of perception, thought, and language can never escape a tension with Stevens's own poetic project, rightly inscribed in the native tradition of Emersonian pragmatism by critics like Richard Poirier. That tradition "depends on certain key, repeated terms," says Poirier. "But to a wholly unusual degree it never allows any of these terms to arrive at a precise or static definition. Their use is conducive less to clarification than to vagueness." As readers who want to get a purchase on these repeated terms in Stevens's poetry, we are forced to negotiate between pleasure, doubt, and irritation as we shuttle back and forth between positions, cross boundaries, slide from perspective to perspective, watch the dance of the signifiers, and enjoy the aesthetic play of the text. A certain cognitive dissonance, after all, is one of the major motivations for appropriating cultural artifacts, and the act of shifting and shuttling is simply inherent in dealing with the question of limits: the condition of liminality, as Angus Fletcher emphasizes, is precisely a condition of betweenness.[29]

The following chapters are organized so as to deepen our understanding of that condition of betweenness in Stevens's poetry. From a methodological point of view, they are even subject to that condition themselves, for they try both to credit the specific performativity of Stevens's irreducibly concrete extemporizations and to take into account the powerful human need for binding specific readings together under larger, synthetic rubrics. My strongest emphasis, admittedly, will be on the detailed reading of a handful of shorter lyrics that are particularly well-suited for showing the knottedness and contaminations of the perception-thought-language nexus that we so hastily cut up for the sake of analysis. To study individual poems is, I would argue, crucial for appreciating the different, complex ways in which Stevens's poetic efforts at limitation not only succeed in clarifying boundaries but also require our constant attention to the necessity of traversing these boundaries. This bifurcation means that the conceptual dividing lines among the ensuing chapters are necessarily porous. My particular clustering of poems cannot escape the largely associative, unrigorous principle expressed in the poet's motto "Thought tends to collect in pools" (*OP* 196). Yet if the metaphor used by Stevens is a treacherously organic one, it nonetheless offers an image of delineation. Each of the following four chapters is thus intended to test what is limited by limitation in his poetry and then folded over again: in the effort to separate the painterly gaze from various domains of immediacy; in the effort to sort out our "sense" of reality from what the senses convey as well as from the translations of these impressions by our sense-making brain; in the effort to disentangle mimesis from music and description from elucidation and artifice; and in the effort, finally, to trace the "other" that is implicitly circumscribed by the identifications of metaphor.

Notes

1. For the term "theory," see esp. Jonathan Culler, *On Deconstruction: Theory and Criticism after Structuralism*, 8, and *Framing the Sign: Criticism and Its Institutions*, 15. Newcomb, *Literary Canons*, 207; Kermode, interview, 115; Kermode, preface, xvii.

2. Ralph Waldo Emerson, "Self-Reliance," 265; Walt Whitman, *Song of Myself*, 246.

3. See esp. Grey, *The Wallace Stevens Case*, 10-21, for an authoritative assessment. We might note here Stevens's insistence to one correspondent: "I don't have a separate mind for legal work and another for writing poetry. I do each with my whole mind" (*L* [*Letters of Wallace Stevens*] 414).

4. Quoted in Brazeau, *Parts of a World*, 169.

5. See Russell B. Goodman, introduction to *Pragmatism: A Contemporary Reader*, 1, corroborated by

Stevens's confession in a letter of November 1944: "I think that most modern philosophers are purely academic" (*L* 476).

6. Goodman, introduction, 3; James quoted in ibid., 10; for Lovejoy, see ibid.

7. Peter A. Brazeau, "'A Collect of Philosophy': The Difficulty of Finding What Would Suffice"; Wallace Stevens, "Three Manuscript Endings for 'A Collect of Philosophy.'"

8. Sharpe, *Wallace Stevens,* 179.

9. Schwarz, *Narrative and Representation,* 1.

10. The most prominent instances of this link with phenomenology are J. Hillis Miller, *Poets of Reality*; Hines, *Later Poetry of Wallace Stevens*; Jeanne Ruppert, "Nature, Feeling, and Disclosure in the Poetry of Wallace Stevens"; Bevis, *Mind of Winter,* 110-11; Leonard and Wharton, *Fluent Mundo,* 83-102; and Paul Kenneth Naylor, "'The Idea of It': Wallace Stevens and Edmund Husserl." As recently as 1997, critics were still describing Stevens as a poet who moved from the romantic to the phenomenological (Voros, *Notations of the Wild,* 11).

11. Maurice Merleau-Ponty, *Phenomenology of Perception,* 394.

12. Derrida, *Positions,* 63-64.

13. Litz, "'Compass and Curriculum,'" 239.

14. Allusions to Yeats's "Among School Children" can arguably also be heard in lines like "He is the heroic / Actor and act but not divided" from "Examination of the Hero in a Time of War" (*CP* [*The Collected Poems of Wallace Stevens*] 279) and in the scene with the "negresses" brought in "to dance, / Among the children" in "The Auroras of Autumn" (*CP* 415). Surprisingly, not even Harold Bloom has recognized the intertextual possibilities of this link, though we know Yeats to have been one of the few writers from whom Stevens explicitly borrowed lines (in "Page from a Tale" [*CP* 421-23]; see Lensing, *Poet's Growth,* 224, and Jenkins, *Rage for Order,* 123-24).

15. Jerry Fodor, "Encounters with Trees," 10-11.

16. Bart Eeckhout, "When Language Stops . . . Suspension Points in the Poetry of Hart Crane and Wallace Stevens."

17. Derrida, "'Strange Institution,'" 49.

18. Epigraphs: Frank Kermode, *The Sense of an Ending: Studies in the Theory of Fiction,* 34; "love-letter": Kermode, interview, 113; Leggett, *Early Stevens,* 213-52; Naylor, "'Idea of it,'" 47; Rudolf

Boehm, *Aan het einde van een tijdperk: Filosofisch-economische aantekeningen,* 20. Freud, in *The Future of an Illusion,* likewise drew a distinction between illusions, on one hand, and factual errors and delusions about reality, on the other (30-31). Stevens, unsurprisingly, took a strong interest in the notion of illusion as well. He picked up Freud's question of whether there could possibly be a science of illusions in his own essay "Imagination as Value" (*NA* [*The Necessary Angel: Essays on Reality and the Imagination*] 139) and wrote in a 1942 letter to Hi Simons: "The use of the word illusion suggests the simplest way to define the difference between escapism in a pejorative sense and in a non-pejorative sense: that is to say: it is the difference between elusion and illusion, or benign illusion. Of course, I believe in benign illusion" (*L* 402).

19. Leggett, *Early Stevens,* 47ff.

20. Cook, *Poetry, Word-Play, and Word-War,* 40.

21. The recurrent "as ifs" in Stevens, increasing in frequency over time, are at the heart of Jacqueline Vaught Brogan's study *Stevens and Simile: A Theory of Language.* The conjunction has inevitably spurred critics into establishing intertextual extensions, the most eye-catching of which is with Hans Vaihinger's *Die Philosophie des "Als Ob"* (The philosophy of "as if"), a turn-of-the-century classic dug up by, among others, Frank Kermode (see esp. *Sense of an Ending,* 39-41, and preface, xvii; also Frank Doggett, "This Invented World: Stevens' 'Notes toward a Supreme Fiction,'" 20, and *Stevens' Poetry of Thought,* 105-6, 185). Vaihinger himself feeds into a longer tradition that runs from Kant through Nietzsche, though he appears to have written independently of the latter. Freud, in *The Future of an Illusion,* dismissed Vaihinger as patent nonsense (28-29), and both Joan Richardson (*Wallace Stevens: The Later Years, 1923-1955,* 58-62) and James Longenbach (*Plain Sense,* 287-88) have analyzed Stevens's familiarity with, and response to, the Vaihinger-fiction-Freud connection.

22. William James, *The Principles of Psychology,* 159.

23. Iser, "Feigning in Fiction," 220; Dennett, *Kinds of Minds,* 127; Edelman, *Homographesis,* 141.

24. Steven Pinker, *The Language Instinct: The New Science of Language and Mind,* 55-82.

25. Ibid., 67.

26. Dickie, *Lyric Contingencies,* 11; Alison Rieke, *The Senses of Nonsense,* 96; Cook, *Poetry, Word-Play, and Word-War,* xii, 7.

27. Quoted in Don Gifford, *Ulysses Annotated,* v.

28. Quoted and reproduced in Milton J. Bates, "Stevens' Books at the Huntington," 49, 50.

29. Poirier, *Poetry and Pragmatism,* 129; Fletcher, foreword, xvii.

Works Cited

WORKS BY WALLACE STEVENS

The Collected Poems of Wallace Stevens. New York: Alfred A. Knopf, 1954.

Letters of Wallace Stevens. Ed. Holly Stevens. New York: Alfred A. Knopf, 1966.

The Necessary Angel: Essays on Reality and the Imagination. New York: Vintage Books, 1951.

OTHER WORKS CITED

Bates, Milton J. "Stevens' Books at the Huntington: An Annotated Checklist." *Wallace Stevens Journal* 2:3/4 (fall 1978): 45-61; 3:1/2 (spring 1979): 15-33; 3:3/4 (fall 1979): 70.

Bevis, William W. *Mind of Winter: Wallace Stevens, Meditation, and Literature.* Pittsburgh: University of Pittsburgh Press, 1988.

Boehm, Rudolf. *Aan het einde van een tijdperk: Filosofisch-economische aantekeningen.* Weesp, Netherlands: Het Wereldvenster; Berchem, Belgium: EPO, 1984.

Brazeau, Peter A. "'A Collect of Philosophy': The Difficulty of Finding What Would Suffice." In *Wallace Stevens: A Celebration,* ed. Frank Doggett and Robert Buttel, 46-49. Princeton: Princeton University Press, 1980.

———. *Parts of a World: Wallace Stevens Remembered.* New York: Random House, 1983.

Brogan, Jacqueline Vaught. *Stevens and Simile: A Theory of Language.* Princeton: Princeton University Press, 1986.

Cook, Eleanor. *Poetry, Word-Play, and Word-War in Wallace Stevens.* Princeton: Princeton University Press, 1988.

Culler, Jonathan. *Framing the Sign: Criticism and Its Institutions.* Oxford: Blackwell, 1988.

———. *On Deconstruction: Theory and Criticism after Structuralism.* 1982. Reprint, London: Routledge & Kegan Paul, 1985.

Derrida, Jacques. *Positions.* Trans. Alan Bass. 1981. Reprint, London: Athlone Press, 1987.

———. "'This Strange Institution Called Literature': An Interview with Jacques Derrida." By Derek Attridge. In *Acts of Literature,* by Jacques Derrida, ed. Derek Attridge, 33-75. New York: Routledge, 1992.

Dickie, Margaret. *Lyric Contingencies: Emily Dickinson and Wallace Stevens.* Philadelphia: University of Pennsylvania Press, 1991.

Doggett, Frank. *Stevens' Poetry of Thought.* Baltimore: Johns Hopkins Press, 1966.

———. "This Invented World: Stevens' 'Notes toward a Supreme Fiction.'" In *The Act of the Mind: Essays on the Poetry of Wallace Stevens,* ed. Roy Harvey Pearce and J. Hillis Miller, 13-28. Baltimore: Johns Hopkins Press, 1965.

Eeckhout, Bart. "When Language Stops . . . Suspension Points in the Poetry of Hart Crane and Wallace Stevens." In *Semantics of Silences in Linguistics and Literature,* ed. Gudrun M. Grabher and Ulrike Jessner, 257-70. Heidelberg: Universitätsverlag C. Winter, 1996.

Emerson, Ralph Waldo. "Self-Reliance." In *Ralph Waldo Emerson: Essays and Lectures,* ed. Joel Porte, 257-82. New York: Library of America, 1983.

Fodor, Jerry. "Encounters with Trees." *London Review of Books* 17:8 (April 20, 1995): 10-11.

Freud, Sigmund. *The Future of an Illusion.* In vol. 21 of *The Standard Edition of the Complete Psychological Works of Sigmund Freud,* trans. under the general editorship of James Strachey et al., 3-56. 1961. Reprint, London: Hogarth Press, 1968.

Gifford, Don, with Robert J. Seidman. Ulysses *Annotated.* 2d rev. ed. 1988. Reprint, Berkeley and Los Angeles: University of California Press, 1989.

Goodman, Russell B. Introduction to *Pragmatism: A Contemporary Reader,* ed. Russell B. Goodman, 1-20. New York: Routledge, 1995.

Grey, Thomas C. *The Wallace Stevens Case: Law and the Practice of Poetry.* Cambridge: Harvard University Press, 1991.

Hines, Thomas J. *The Later Poetry of Wallace Stevens: Phenomenological Parallels with Husserl and Heidegger.* Lewisburg, Pa.: Bucknell University Press, 1976.

Iser, Wolfgang. "Feigning in Fiction." In *Identity of the Literary Text,* ed. Mario J. Valdés and Owen Miller, 204-28. Toronto: University of Toronto Press, 1985.

James, William. *The Principles of Psychology.* Great Books of the Western World, vol. 53. Chicago: Encyclopaedia Britannica, 1952.

Jenkins, Lee Margaret. *Wallace Stevens: Rage for Order.* Brighton, U.K.: Sussex Academic Press, 2000.

Kermode, Frank. Interview by Imre Salusinszky. In *Criticism in Society: Interviews with Jacques Derrida, Northrop Frye, Harold Bloom, Geoffrey Hartman, Frank Kermode, Edward Said, Barbara Johnson, Frank Lentricchia, and J. Hillis Miller,* by Imre Salusinszky, 98-121. New York: Methuen, 1987.

————. Preface to 1989 edition of *Wallace Stevens,* by Frank Kermode, xi-xix. 1960. Reprint, London: Faber & Faber, 1989.

————. *The Sense of an Ending: Studies in the Theory of Fiction.* New York: Oxford University Press, 1967.

Leggett, B. J. *Early Stevens: The Nietzschean Intertext.* Durham: Duke University Press, 1992.

Lensing, George S. *Wallace Stevens: A Poet's Growth.* 1986. Reprint, Baton Rouge: Louisiana State University Press, 1991.

Leonard, James S., and Christine E. Wharton. *The Fluent Mundo: Wallace Stevens and the Structure of Reality.* Athens: University of Georgia Press, 1988.

Litz, A. Walton. "'Compass and Curriculum': Teaching Stevens among the Moderns." In *Teaching Wallace Stevens: Practical Essays,* ed. John N. Serio and B. J. Leggett, 235-41. Knoxville: University of Tennessee Press, 1994.

Longenbach, James. *Wallace Stevens: The Plain Sense of Things.* New York: Oxford University Press, 1991.

Merleau-Ponty, Maurice. *Phenomenology of Perception.* Trans. Colin Smith. 1962. Reprint, Atlantic Highlands, N.J.: Humanities Press; London: Routledge, 1989.

————. *Poets of Reality: Six Twentieth-Century Writers.* Cambridge: Harvard University Press, Belknap Press, 1965.

Naylor, Paul Kenneth. "'The Idea of It': Wallace Stevens and Edmund Husserl." *Wallace Stevens Journal* 12:1 (spring 1988): 44-55.

Newcomb, John Timberman. *Wallace Stevens and Literary Canons.* Jackson: University Press of Mississippi, 1992.

Pinker, Steven. *The Language Instinct: The New Science of Language and Mind.* 1994. Reprint, London: Penguin Books, 1995.

Poirier, Richard. *Poetry and Pragmatism.* London: Faber & Faber, 1992.

Richardson, Joan. *Wallace Stevens: The Later Years, 1923-1955.* New York: William Morrow, Beech Tree Books, 1988.

Rieke, Alison. *The Senses of Nonsense.* Iowa City: University of Iowa Press, 1992.

Ruppert, Jeanne. "Nature, Feeling, and Disclosure in the Poetry of Wallace Stevens." *Analecta Husserliana* 18 (1984): 75-88.

Schwarz, Daniel R. *Narrative and Representation in the Poetry of Wallace Stevens.* New York: St. Martin's Press, 1993.

Sharpe, Tony. *Wallace Stevens: A Literary Life.* London: Macmillan, 2000.

Whitman, Walt. *Song of Myself.* In *Leaves of Grass,* by Walt Whitman, 188-247. New York: Library of America, Vintage Books, 1992.

Milton J. Bates (essay date winter 2003)

SOURCE: Bates, Milton J. "Pain Is Human: Wallace Stevens at Ground Zero." *Southern Review* 39, no. 1 (winter 2003): 168-80.

[*In the following essay, Bates disputes the idea that Stevens's poetry lacks emotional sympathy, and argues that Stevens's treatment of pain (and of politics) is cerebral and aesthetic rather than visceral.*]

Like many professors on college campuses throughout the country, I found it impossible to conduct business as usual during the first class after the events of September 11, 2001. But neither did I know exactly how to proceed. How does one speak of the unspeakable? I was not up to the challenge, and I could hardly ask my students to do what I could not. Fortunately, I teach English and American literature, and so could turn to masters of the language to speak for us. I settled finally on a passage in the last of T. S. Eliot's *Four Quartets,* for which I happened to have an audiotape recording in the poet's own voice.

In the section of "Little Gidding" that I played in class, Eliot recounts an imaginary meeting with a "familiar compound ghost" in the early dawn of a day during the London Blitz of 1940-1941. The ghost, a composite of Dante and Yeats, apprises him of the personal pain and regret that he will have to suffer in old age, when even his accomplishments as a poet will not matter. I chose the passage not so much for the nature of the poet's distress, which differed from ours, as for the purgatorial setting and atmosphere. Eliot's ghost hovers, as he says, "between two worlds become much like each other," the worlds of the Inferno and of London after a night of German bombing. The air is murky with the smoke of burning buildings.

Whether Eliot expressed the students' feelings I can't say for sure. We listened to the poet's uncannily prescient words, allowed them to sink in, and moved on to the day's assigned material. The passage worked for me, at least, and in the days that followed I was not surprised to learn that several colleagues, including a political science professor, had done likewise, generally choosing poems by Yeats ("The Second Coming" being a favorite) or Auden ("September 1, 1939"). In the ensuing weeks student groups organized poetry readings on campus to memorialize September 11, performing works that they had composed themselves or found apt. The *New York Times,* meanwhile, ran articles entitled "Poetry's Insights on Pain and Joy" and "The Eerily Intimate Power of Poetry to Console" as well as pieces about the solace to be found in family, friends, religion, and even food. To the lengthening list of consolatory poems the *Times* added works by (to mention only those who wrote in English) Shakespeare, Shelley, Edwin Arlington Robinson, Marianne Moore, and Seamus Heaney.

Lately I have wondered why I gravitated to "Little Gidding" rather than a poem by Wallace Stevens, whose work I know better and prefer to Eliot's. September 11 posed a similar challenge to other Stevens devotees, to judge from postings on a Stevens listserv. Contributors mentioned the relevance of Stevens's **"In a Bad Time," "A Fading of the Sun," "Chaos in Motion and Not in Motion," "Repetitions of a Young Captain,"** and Canto IV of **"Esthétique du Mal,"** but seemed more inclined to look elsewhere for comfort—to Auden, for example, and Larkin ("The Explosion").

The sad fact is that Stevens's poetry, though intellectually demanding and esthetically satisfying, has long seemed emotionally unsympathetic even to sympathetic readers. Mark Halliday has argued this case most forcefully, in *Stevens and the Interpersonal.* Halliday opens his study with an oft-quoted Stevens adage: "Life is an affair of people not of places. But for me life is an affair of places and that is the trouble." Though astute in self-diagnosis, Stevens was apparently unable to remedy his "trouble." On the contrary, as Halliday demonstrates, he—or, to be more precise, the implied poet of his poems—resorts repeatedly to strategies that avoid confronting the suffering of others. Even **"Esthétique du Mal,"** his most direct and ambitious attempt to engage human suffering, leaves us feeling, says Halliday, that Stevens "would be the wrong person to turn to if we were particularly in pain."

Halliday is by no means alone in his judgment of the poem. Even Helen Vendler, who is arguably Stevens's most ardent proponent, famously dismisses **"Esthétique"** in *On Extended Wings* as "at once the most random and the most pretentious of Stevens' long poems." Her "random" signals another problem with the poem besides its tone. What is it ultimately *about*? **"Esthétique"** is like the elephant in the fable: what it is about seems to depend on where the blind man touches it. The poem concerns pain and evil, to be sure, but also war, esthetics, the sublime, politics, and religion.

Eleanor Cook has developed perhaps the most satisfying synthesis of these themes in *Poetry, Word-Play, and Word-War in Wallace Stevens.* She contends that **"Esthétique,"** which began as a response to a soldier's letter, cultivates a "psychological sublime"—Stevens

called it "nobility"—to counter the pain and evil of modern reality. "It takes some time," Cook remarks at the end of her chapter on the poem, "to see the strength of Stevens' title and the scope of his answer to the soldier of 1944. I hope that soldier also saw it." Though Cook goes a long way toward salvaging the poem, her parting hope sounds like wishful thinking, a hope against hope. For her as for Halliday, **"Esthétique"** is probably the wrong poem to turn to when we are in pain.

I propose to turn to it anyway in this essay, while moving discussion of the poem to somewhat different ground. I consider **"Esthétique du Mal"** as primarily a meditation on the claims and consolations of nature and culture. The latter terms are variations on reality and imagination, words worn smooth by their constant handling in Stevens criticism. They serve, however, to relocate the poem in a less anthropocentric universe. With this shift in perspective we can begin to appreciate Stevens's strengths as a poet of consolation as well as the shortcomings identified by Halliday and Vendler. We can also reassess the role of poetry—indeed of the arts in general—following events like those of September 11.

As Cook and others have pointed out, Stevens wrote **"Esthétique"** in response to two events, one cultural and the other natural. The first was World War II, which was already much on Stevens's mind when he encountered a soldier's letter in the spring 1944 issue of the *Kenyon Review.* I will turn to that letter in a moment. The second event was a spectacular eruption of Mount Vesuvius, which had been quiescent for decades. Beginning on March 18, 1944, and continuing for several days, the volcano spewed smoke, ash, and finally a river of lava that engulfed half of the village of San Sebastiano as villagers tried to halt its advance with crucifixes and images of the saints.

Nature seemed to be mimicking upheavals in the human world. Fifty-five miles northwest of Vesuvius, Allied troops were engaging the German army in the mountains around Cassino. British and American soldiers had occupied Naples and established a beachhead further up the coast at Anzio, but were unable to advance on Rome. Norman Lewis, a British soldier stationed in Naples, witnessed the eruption of Vesuvius across the bay and describes it as follows in *Naples '44*:

> Today Vesuvius erupted. It was the most majestic and terrible sight I have ever seen, or ever expect to see. The smoke from the crater slowly built up into a great bulging shape having all the appearance of solidity. It swelled and expanded so slowly that there was no sign of movement in the cloud which, by evening, must have risen thirty or forty thousand feet into the sky, and measured many miles across. . . . At night the

lava streams began to trickle down the mountain's slopes. By day the spectacle was calm but now the eruption showed a terrible vivacity. Fiery symbols were scrawled across the water of the bay, and periodically the crater discharged mines of serpents into a sky which was the deepest of blood reds and pulsating everywhere with lightning reflections.

The scene has an apocalyptic quality as reported by Lewis, especially against the backdrop of artillery fire and Luftwaffe raids. It also partakes of the sublime, as this literate soldier well knew, though he never invokes Longinus or Edmund Burke. Volcanic eruptions are among the preferred subjects of writers and artists who strive for sublimity, because they combine beauty and danger on a vast scale. Burke speaks to the latter component in his *Philosophical Enquiry into the Origin of Our Ideas of the Sublime and Beautiful.* "Whatever is fitted in any sort to excite the ideas of pain and danger . . . ," he writes, "is a source of the *sublime*; that is, it is productive of the strongest emotion which the mind is capable of feeling." Danger does not preclude esthetic pleasure, provided the observer maintains a proper distance. "When danger or pain press too nearly," Burke allows, "they are incapable of giving any delight, and are simply terrible; but at certain distances, and with certain modifications, they may be, and they are, delightful, as we every day experience."

The eruption of Vesuvius was front-page news in the weeks before Stevens began to compose **"Esthétique du Mal,"** often juxtaposed with dispatches from the Italian front. It is not surprising, therefore, that he chose to open his poem with a reference to the volcano. The surprise lies in what he leaves out—namely, the war—and the way he represents the eruption:

> He was at Naples writing letters home
> And, between his letters, reading paragraphs
> On the sublime. Vesuvius had groaned
> For a month. It was pleasant to be sitting there,
> While the sultriest fulgurations, flickering,
> Cast corners in the glass. He could describe
> The terror of the sound because the sound
> Was ancient. He tried to remember the phrases: pain
> Audible at noon, pain torturing itself,
> Pain killing pain on the very point of pain.
> The volcano trembled in another ether,
> As the body trembles at the end of life.
>
> It was almost time for lunch. Pain is human.
> There were roses in the cool café. His book
> Made sure of the most correct catastrophe.

It would be hard to imagine a scene more remote from those in Lewis's account. Whereas Lewis describes ragged and starving Neapolitans, children reduced to begging, and women driven to prostitution in order to survive, Stevens gives us a writer, apparently a noncombatant, at ease in a chic café. Though the writer's medium is the lowly genre of the letter home,

he forgoes realism for sublimity, laboring self-consciously in the tradition formulated by Burke and Longinus. That would be an appropriate tradition if he were close enough to Vesuvius to experience any danger. But he is distant from the volcano both geographically and epistemologically. Seated pleasantly indoors, he can hear the eruption but not observe it directly. Its flickering fulgurations, glimpsed as reflections in the café window, are no more threatening than the ornamental roses. They belong to the picturesque rather than the sublime. Though the writer borrows freely from the lexicon of pain—using words such as "terror," "torturing," "killing," and "catastrophe"—he experiences only the mild discomfort of appetite: "It was almost time for lunch. Pain is human."

Pain is human: in context, the line is a glib joke, meaning something like "People who are in pain have to eat too, even when the pain is mostly imaginary." Why would Stevens risk beginning a poem about human suffering on this flippant note? His strategy appears all the more inexplicable when we consider the poem's genesis. In June 1944 Stevens told John Crowe Ransom, the editor of the *Kenyon Review,* that he decided to write "an esthetique du mal" after reading excerpts from an unidentified soldier's letter in Ransom's essay "Artists, Soldiers, Positivists," which appeared in the spring issue of the magazine. A few weeks later he sent the complete **"Esthétique"** to Ransom, who placed it at the front of the fall issue.

The soldier, who was then serving overseas, had objected to the *Review*'s preoccupation with Eliot and "even poets of charming distemper like Wallace Stevens (for whom we all developed considerable passion)." Contrasting these eminent esthetes with those whom he called the "commandos of contemporary literature," poets such as Karl Shapiro, John Berryman, and Delmore Schwartz, the soldier argued that in time of war the world needs more commandos and fewer esthetes: "The question of poetry as in life (and in the Army) is one of survival, simply. . . . I find the poetry in *Kenyon Review* lamentable in many ways because it is cut off from pain. It is intellectual and it is fine, but it never reveals muscle and nerve."

There is no way of knowing whether the soldier had read Eliot's "Little Gidding" or Stevens's **"Notes toward a Supreme Fiction."** Eliot published his poem separately in 1942, rather than save it for the complete *Four Quartets* (1943), because friends persuaded him that it would assist the war effort. John Hayward, for instance, wrote to Frank Morley that "in these times the less delay the better in bringing into the world the kind of work that consolidates one's faith in the continuity of thought and sensibility when heaven is falling and earth's foundations fail."

The same year in which Eliot published "Little Gidding," Stevens published *Notes* as a separate book. In its epilogue he compares the poet's battle with reality, using words as his weapons, to the soldier's more mundane mode of warfare. Critics disagree as to whether the epilogue is the poem's culmination or a lame attempt at relevance. Few people saw the poem anyway, in the small-press editions of 1942 and 1943; and the war was over by the time it appeared in the trade edition of *Transport to Summer* (1946). **"Notes toward a Supreme Fiction"** suggests nonetheless that Stevens, though he might not pass muster as a commando, wanted to contribute in his own way to the war effort.

Which brings us back to the first canto of **"Esthétique du Mal."** Considering the poem's inception, we might regard the opening skit as self-parody. It is as though Stevens were saying to Ransom's soldier: "You consider me a literary mandarin who remains above the fray? Fair enough. But let me show you how the consummate esthete would behave in a war zone, and watch how I take it from there." Stevens takes it from there by kneading his throwaway line, "Pain is human," into a serious proposition about the relationship between nature (including such physiological phenomena as pain and death) and culture (all that human beings have added to nature). The last half-dozen lines of Canto I announce the thesis to be developed in the rest of **"Esthétique"**:

> Except for us, Vesuvius might consume
> In solid fire the utmost earth and know
> No pain (ignoring the cocks that crow us up
> To die). This is a part of the sublime
> From which we shrink. And yet, except for us,
> The total past felt nothing when destroyed.

Here Stevens (to use his name as shorthand for the poem's presiding consciousness) reproves the writer in the café by reminding him of the inhuman Vesuvius, the volcano that knows, feels, and thinks nothing whatsoever. Its groaning, trembling, and even sublimity are so much anthropomorphism. Like the phrases in Burke and Longinus, these personifications belong to culture rather than nature. The same is true, by analogy, of physiological phenomena such as death and pain, which are in themselves morally and esthetically neutral. By mythologizing these natural events, culture gives them an additional negative valence. They not only hurt, but are also bad and ugly. For those who hear intimations of immortality in the rooster's *aubade,* the finality of death is a cruel joke. As for pain, it was never the same once it became a literary trope, the *mal* of the French Symbolists.

To say that pain is human is to say that it is cultural as well as natural, fictional as well as factual. It is an imaginary as well as a neurological and emotional event. In the ensuing cantos of **"Esthétique du Mal,"** Stevens brackets this insight by examining the varieties of cultural experience that shape our experience of pain. He also gauges the effect of mistaking—or deliberately substituting—culture for nature.

For Stevens our chief cultural artifact, our supreme fiction, is the idea of God. He devotes Cantos III, IV, V, and part of VIII to this idea and its corollary, the idea of Satan. Moral symmetry requires pure evil to balance pure good. Much as Eliot uses terza rima to narrate his meeting with the "familiar compound ghost"— preeminently Dante—in "Little Gidding," Stevens adopts the prosody of the *Divina Commedia* in Canto III. In contrast to Eliot, however, he nods only briefly to the Tuscan poet whose "firm stanzas hang like hives in hell." In the second stanza he turns to Dante's antithesis, the German philosopher who declared that God is dead. If pain is human, then God is human to a superlative degree. He is, in Nietzsche's familiar words, too, too human. God originated, the canto suggests, in the natural human impulse to create imaginary friends and parental figures. In the theological scheme of things, pain is "satanic mimicry," an evil to be abolished by divine goodness. Paradoxically, pain becomes more painful when mythologized in this way, for then its "fault / Falls out on everything" (Canto IV). If heaven requires a hell, Canto III proposes, we would be better off without heaven, free to enjoy the "health of the world" in its natural state.

After religion, the cultural form that most affects our lives is government. In Canto XIV Stevens suggests that politics, like religion, begins as inchoate feeling but is soon rationalized into ideology. Here the Dante-Nietzsche confrontation is recast as a meeting between Konstantinov, a magistrate for the Russian secret police, and Victor Serge, a partisan of the Left Opposition to Lenin. Shortly before writing this canto, Stevens read Serge's memoir of the Russian Revolution in the June 1944 issue of *Politics* magazine and copied an excerpt in his commonplace book. He opens Canto XIV with the same quotation, pushing Serge's specific (and, in context, qualified) judgment of Konstantinov to a higher level of generalization: political revolution is always logical lunacy because it ignores so much of human experience. Like the religious martyr, the canto implies, the political martyr cannot embrace nature—all that people experience as they "Live, work, suffer and die"—due to a cultural obsession.

From politics it is an easy step to war, which Clausewitz famously described as politics by other means. Why, one wonders, does it take Stevens so long to get around to the subject of war in a poem that was prompted by a soldier's letter, especially when that letter virtually dared him to enter the fray? Did this poet of "charming distemper" feel that he lacked the authority to hold forth on the subject? He was neither a soldier nor, like air-raid warden Eliot, a civilian engaged directly in the war effort. Still, he had managed to overcome this scruple not only in **"Notes toward a Supreme Fiction"** but also in a sequence of World War I poems inspired by a French soldier's letters from the front. In the best known of these **"Lettres d'un Soldat"** (1918), Stevens compares the soldier's death to the passing of a season:

> Life contracts and death is expected,
> As in a season of autumn.
> The soldier falls.

It was a sentence in one of Eugène Lemercier's letters that inspired Stevens's analogy, and he uses it as the epigraph to the poem: "La mort du soldat est près des choses naturelles." Almost (*près des*), but not quite: for if the soldier's death is a natural event, its occasion is cultural. War is among the most artificial of our cultural creations, notwithstanding its raw violence. Cultural factors determine why people fight, how they arm and dress for battle, how they perceive and engage the enemy, and when they decide that the war is won or lost. Perhaps this is why Stevens initially omits any reference to the contemporary military and political situation in **"Esthétique."** Though war was as conspicuous a feature of the Neapolitan landscape as Vesuvius, it straddled the line between nature and culture. By restricting our attention to the volcano and the writer in the café, Stevens maintains a clear distinction between the two. Once we understand the principle, illustrated satirically in Canto I, we are prepared for its application to other spheres of experience.

Stevens finally gets around to the war in Cantos VII and XI. The latter envisions the military equivalent of the sublime rhetoric in Canto I, as paratroopers "select adieux" before plunging into battle. Though their gesture makes good theater, it is rejected by the "man of bitter appetite" whose hunger feeds on hungriness. From his perspective, we flatter ourselves that we reside "at the centre of a diamond," in a realm of egocentric luxury. We actually live, he believes, in a gelatin of "bitter aspic," where soldiers behave absurdly rather than heroically. As Alan Filreis informs us in *Wallace Stevens and the Actual World,* the poet lifted the image of lawn-mowing paratroopers from phantasmagoria. His friend Barbara Church, exiled from her home in France, had dreamed of a military invasion in which little men descended from the sky with lawn mowers. Canto XI acknowledges the power and appeal of poetry in this surreal, impoverished landscape. But "gaiety of language" remains at best compensatory, at worst delusional.

If Canto XI preceded Canto VII, it would be hard to take Canto VII seriously. As it is, the satire of Canto I prepares some readers either to deplore the sentimental-

ity of the lines beginning "How red the rose that is the soldier's wound" or to regard them as a crafty bit of satire. Harold Bloom, in contrast, treats the canto in *Wallace Stevens: The Poems of Our Climate* as a poignant and moving elegy in the Whitman tradition. Whether its tone is ironic or elegiac may not matter. Either way the point of the canto remains the same, namely, that our cultural constructions of martial valor—and for some readers these include the conventional imagery and Parnassian diction of the canto itself—take their value from the natural, organic facts of human life and death. Much as the actual Vesuvius precedes the volcanic sublime, a flesh-and-blood soldier precedes the funeral rhetoric. To recall a passage in Canto I: "The volcano trembled in another ether, / As the body trembles at the end of life." Whatever cultural capital may accrue to either kind of trembling is secondary.

I regard Canto XI, the second and more austere of the two war cantos in **"Esthétique,"** as the poem's "ground zero." So closely has this phrase become associated with the wreckage of the World Trade Center that we may forget its pre-September 11 currency. A couple of decades ago, in *Words Chosen Out of Desire,* Helen Vendler applied the phrase not to Canto XI of **"Esthétique"** but to Canto X, which represents nature as home, a place that is relatively free of mythology's "sleek ensolacings." In nature so conceived, pain is innocent rather than Satanic. It remains human, however, for the canto's persona clings to a vestigial fiction of nature when he installs a sympathetic mother figure in the home. Earth is thereby humanized, indeed maternalized. Besides protecting us from "impersonal pain," earth-as-mother renders the world explicable: "It was the last nostalgia: that he / Should understand."

Insofar as Canto X accommodates culture, it represents not "ground zero" but "ground zero plus." Does the relentlessly reductive Canto XI cancel the cultural surplus of Canto X? Not entirely, for reasons that become clearer when we examine the "esthétique" of Stevens's title. For him the word meant not a systematic theory of the beautiful but, as he told Ransom, "the equivalent of aperçus," which he believed to be its original meaning. He was probably thinking of the word's derivation from the Greek *aisthanesthai,* "to perceive," in which case he could just as well have called the poem "Fifteen Ways of Looking at Pain." The cantos complement rather than cancel one another.

Another understanding of "esthetic" seems germane to the poem. Neil Evernden, an ecologist who has written extensively on epistemological questions in natural science, proposes in his essay "Beyond Ecology" (in *The Ecocriticism Reader,* edited by Cheryll Glotfelty and Harold Fromm) that we adopt the term "esthetic" to describe our relationship to nature. In esthetic experience so conceived, the traditional subject-object division gives way to a more intimate association, one akin to the animal's sense of territory. "There appears to be a human phenomenon," Evernden writes, "similar in some ways to the experience of territoriality, that is described as aesthetic and which is, in effect, a 'sense of place,' a sense of knowing and being part of a particular place. There's nothing very mysterious about this—it's just what it feels like to be home, to experience a sense of light or smell that is inexplicably 'right.'" When we try to express that esthetic in words, Evernden observes, we turn instinctively to metaphor. The pathetic fallacy is a fallacy only for those who insist on an absolute Cartesian division between the self and its surroundings.

Canto X corresponds closely to this ecological esthetic, with its description of nature as home and mother. **"Esthétique du Mal"** endorses other moments of cultural construction, such as the fable of the sun and the "big bird," the latter being possibly a metaphor for everything that depends on the sun for sustenance (Canto VI). According to Canto VIII, the "mortal no" that obliterates culture cannot be the final word because "under every no / Lay a passion for yes that had never been broken." That passion for yes need not eventuate in another theory of the sublime, a divine comedy, or a communist millennium. At its best it promotes the "territorial" esthetic conjured up in the final canto of **"Esthétique."**

Canto XV opens by comparing the purely cultural experience of "non-physical people" unfavorably with the sensations of people who are "completely physical in a physical world." As the canto builds to a conclusion, however, it gradually encompasses what we make as well as what we feel, the metaphysical as well as the physical. The canto, and **"Esthétique"** as a whole, concludes with a rhetorical question:

> . . . out of what one sees and hears and out
> Of what one feels, who could have thought to make
> So many selves, so many sensuous worlds,
> As if the air, the mid-day air, was swarming
> With the metaphysical changes that occur,
> Merely in living as and where we live.

Stevens realized that the poem should end with a question mark, but he could not bring himself to compromise his affirmation even typographically. Thus his passion for yes causes him to veer away from the prospect of a purely natural world and inhuman pain. Stevens would doubtless insist that his metaphysic differs fundamentally from that of Longinus, Dante, Marx, and Eliot. It nonetheless reopens the door to culture. Metaphor, as a cultural strategy, may very well express our sense of being at home in the world, as Evernden argues. But it also anthropomorphizes pain in ways that may make it more painful. The poet who imagines "mother earth" in Canto X will in a subsequent poem, **"Madame La Fleurie"** (1951), recoil from the image of earth as devouring mother. Though apparently antithetical, these images are merely two sides of the same cultural coin. Insofar as pain induces "hallucination," Stevens reflects in Canto II, it cannot see "How that which rejects it saves it in the end." That is, nature—typified in Canto II by the moon—provides abiding solace only if we allow it to remain indifferent to our pain.

Herein lies another paradox: a world completely devoid of our fictions exists only in our dreams. As the biologist Edward O. Wilson remarks in *Consilience*, it was culture, not disobedience of a god's command, that drove humankind from the paradise of unreflecting nature. With thought and self-consciousness came psychological exile. Precisely in the way that **"Esthétique"** wobbles at the end, it epitomizes the dilemma posed by an event like the terrorist attacks of September 11. On the one hand, we turn instinctively to the cultural forms of religion, poetry, music, art, philosophy, and politics when trying to make sense of the slaughter. The attacks were culturally motivated, after all, and took culturally calculated forms. On the other hand, we recoil from the additional suffering in which this process involves us and look for solace in unthinking nature. Why was the sky so blue that Tuesday morning, the air so clear and temperate for miles in every direction from the World Trade Center and the Pentagon? Can we find comfort in these natural phenomena, or are we destined to remain, in the words of another Stevens poem, "unhappy people in a happy world"?

What we require, besides more finely calibrated cultural expressions of pain and grief, are more sophisticated and satisfying versions of pastoral. The ecocritic Glen Love points out in "Revaluing Nature" (also in *The Ecocriticism Reader*) that literature as a medium of expression and a field of academic study is largely anthropomorphic and egocentric in its values and assumptions. Like Stevens's jar in Tennessee, these take dominion everywhere. Consequently, nature, when it figures at all in literature and literary criticism, is a place of ideal simplicity to which people retreat from the complexities of civilization. Love advocates a version of pastoral more in keeping with what we currently know about the complex relationships within an ecosystem. Aldo Leopold, the Wisconsin pioneer in the field of ecology, provides one model for the new pastoral in essays such as "Thinking Like a Mountain," from *A Sand County Almanac*. His version of pastoral is still thinking, to be sure, and therefore still a cultural form. But it offers a nearer approach to nature, hence a less anthropocentric pastoral.

Intimations of the new pastoral can be found in the poems of Robert Frost, William Stafford, and Robinson Jeffers—and also, I believe, in the work of Wallace Stevens. The "Stevens" of Stevens's poetry will never be the person to whom we turn first when we are in pain. As Helen Vendler observes in *Words Chosen Out of Desire,* his poems "are often second-order reflections on the stormings of first-order sensation." He typically engages religion, politics, and pain not at the visceral level of primary feeling (esthetic in its root sense) but at the more cerebral level of *esthétique.* He is our foremost "meta-" poet, the poet who transforms religion into metareligion, politics into metapolitics, and pain into metapain.

So who needs second-order poetry? We do, all of us, in season, for it plays an essential if unsettling role in the economy of suffering and consolation. Without its austere but salutary critique of our visceral responses, those responses are apt to become self-indulgent, derivative, or even dishonest. Given another chance at choosing a poem for my literature class to ponder in the days immediately after the attacks of September 11, I would still pass over **"Esthétique du Mal"** for Eliot's "Little Gidding" or a poem by Yeats or Auden. With every day that passes, however, I believe that we are better disposed to benefit from Stevens's insights into human pain.

Ann Mikkelsen (essay date fall 2003)

SOURCE: Mikkelsen, Ann. "'Fat! Fat! Fat! Fat!'— Wallace Stevens's Figurations of Masculinity." *Journal of Modern Literature* 27, nos. 1/2 (fall 2003): 105-21.

[*In the following essay, Mikkelsen extensively analyzes references to body type and body image in Stevens's work and relates these to Stevens's image of the model poet and his overall poetic aesthetic.*]

In his seminal essay, "The Figure of the Youth as Virile Poet" (1943), Wallace Stevens concludes by affirming the necessity of a model man and writer who retains the essential "masculine nature that we propose for one that must be the master of our lives."[1] This "virile" poet conforms largely to early twentieth-century male physical ideals: disciplined, capable of extraordinary self-restraint and feats of strength, he is not unlike turn-of-the-century bodybuilder Eugene Sandow or dietician Horace Fletcher in his capacity to forge a trim, muscular "figure." His unique understanding of the laws and limitations of real and imagined worlds are the direct result of his embodiment of pure, American masculinity as well as the pragmatic sensibility he inherited from intellectual fathers such as William James.[2] The image of this assertive, "virile" young man dominates our understanding of how Stevens, once a young "rowdy" and football player, imagined himself as a male poet and representative lyric voice in early twentieth-century America. However, while a great deal of ink has been

spilled over Stevens's investment in conceptual figures such as the "dandy," "man number one," the "hero," the "major man," "medium man," the "subman," and the "giant," little attention has been paid to the physical aspects of these figures or the rare but revealing images of male bodies in Stevens's work.[3] The specific nature of the masculine ideal has gone unquestioned in Stevens criticism: it is taken for granted that a real man must be muscular and physically masterful, and that Stevens himself must have admired such a physique exclusively. Yet Stevens and his interest in poets "virile" and otherwise must be understood as the product of an American society in which masculinity was an extremely fraught and contested cultural site.[4]

By the turn of the century, the concept of a firm, character-driven manliness was replaced by the more amorphous, anxiety-laden category of masculinity that was dependent upon its opposition to women and those racial and ethnic groups perceived as cultural, social, and political threats.[5] Stevens, while from a middle-class family, a product of Harvard and a lawyer, nonetheless was keenly aware of his proximity to the feminine practice of poetry as well as the working-class world of his Dutch and German-American ancestors. For example, writing in his journal shortly after college, Stevens defended poetry from "effeminate" ideas, inextricably linking "Poetry and Manhood."[6] His attitude towards ethnicity and class, however, is more complex, suggesting both a pride (and snobbery) rooted in his family's Colonial origins as well as a sense of himself as an [American man whose white ethnic background marked him as relatively ordinary]. In letters to his fiancée, Elsie, he declared himself "German to the uttermost . . . Peasants are glorious" (*Letters,* 120). Later genealogical work reaffirmed his probable descent from individuals he described as comfortingly "real people": "a decent sort of carpenter, or a really robust blacksmith, or a woman capable of having eleven sons and of weaving their clothes" (*Letters,* 499).

While Stevens's interest in his background could be attributed to a typical desire on behalf of middle-class men to recapture their more "masculine" and "primitive" essence from working-class counterparts, it must also be considered in the context of Stevens's consistent interest in his own body as a manifestation of this working class, ethnic background. Rather than predictably muscular, however, Stevens perceived his Germanic body to be "fat" and even freakish, disruptive yet oddly ordinary in its tendency towards overweight and even possibly acromegaly.[7] The result of this self-perception, combined with his fascination with his ancestry, is that Stevens, the poet perhaps most frequently associated with aesthetic abstractions and "ideas of order," often ends up writing paeans to "man's passionate disorder" (*Letters,* 300). Frequently embodied in distinctly fat characters that serve as tropes for a fertile yet potentially stifling everydayness, Stevens's interest in disorder ultimately affirms the necessity of flesh, appetite, and desire for life in a world that provides too frequent opportunities for a facile nihilism. Rejecting this and other popular ironic and even so-called anorexic Modernist postures, Stevens instead creates a poetics pragmatically rooted in what William James described as the "tangled, muddy, painful, and perplexed" bodily and physical worlds, in the process shaping an implicit portrait of the poet that undermines Stevens's overt celebration of the ideally virile and masculine individual.[8] A response to overly aggressive and threatening trim and muscular masculine bodies, the fat body is evoked as a sign of the common man, albeit in a limited sense: Stevens considers that common man to be kin to the poet's own country cousins, white "natives" in their proper, often rural, environments. Where the presence of fat conjures racial and ethnic associations for the poet and reader, such bodies emerge largely as caricatures in Stevens's work. His acceptance of the "fat girl" as a possible poetic heir, however, signals an acceptance of a selfhood and poetic vocation that may at least be open to the feminine and all that it represents in terms of an expanding public sphere and consumer culture. Stevens's ambivalence concerning the multiple valences of fat suggests the contradictions inherent in constructing a putatively white national body for the Modernist poet to represent. As such, Stevens's poems suggest a poet whose sense of earth's possibilities is not confined by artificial distinctions between the self, the other, and world. Rather, Stevens's gestures towards the human manifestations of a universal fat or excess ground him in society in which aesthetic continuity and ethical persistence contrast sharply with the hollowness of ostensibly purer physical ideals.

Read against this backdrop, **"Bantams in Pine-Woods,"** published in 1922 but the product of many of the same intellectual currents that shaped the later essay, suggests a vision of masculine rivalry and aggression that is both a spoof of contemporary standards of manliness and a curious re-enactment of the same. As such, the poem is representative of an important but overlooked tendency in Stevens's work to invoke and then disrupt and exceed mainstream images of masculinity. Although the poem traditionally has been read rather literally, as a light-hearted, parodic approach to the young Wallace Stevens's anxiety as a younger poet (a "virile" "inchling" and small "bantam" bird) confronting a larger "cock" and "ten-foot poet," critics such as Eleanor Cook have emphasized the "phallic subtext" in Stevens's play upon the word "cock," and Rachel Blau DuPlessis makes a compelling argument for reading the poem as a Stevens's response to the threat of Vachel Lindsey's potentially emasculating "colored" power.[9] Yet these readings all maintain the fiction that the "cocks" in question represent Stevens and some other individual. These "cocks," however, can also be understood as pragmatic variations upon the male poet's multiple possible physiques and experiences. Within the text of the poem the protagonists quickly become indistinguishable, their aggressive posing dispelled by the persistence of a fat body that undermines the contemporary masculine ideal in surprising ways. In order to dispel what he later characterized as the "hero" and "virile poet's" "masterful" body, however, Stevens first playfully invokes it by referencing a very specific kind of physical, famously manly art: the highly popular sport of boxing and prizefighting.

As boxing emerged as a middle-class activity and entertainment during the late nineteenth and early twentieth centuries, the term bantam was coined to refer to the lightweight class of fighter. Amidst fears of effeminacy in the growing ranks of white-collar workers and middle-managers, boxing emerged as a key component of the fitness craze that swept the nation and elite institutions such as Harvard during the late nineteenth century and well into the twentieth (at Stevens's alma mater Teddy Roosevelt boxed and Dudley A. Sargent, director of the Hemenway Gymnasium, actively promoted physical activity). A repudiation of early nineteenth-century ideologies that prized slimmer male physiques as proof of higher social status while tolerating mild obesity as proof of one's enjoyment of the good life, the new emphasis upon the muscular male body focused fears of race suicide and class instability upon a discreet, seemingly controllable entity. Boxing allowed for the popular adulation of the "Heroic Artisan," a working-class, often ethnic figure, while allowing middle and upper-class men the opportunity to prove their mettle and reassert the virility of the Anglo-Saxon.[10] While Stevens does not directly mention boxing or sports at Harvard in his letters, it can be assumed that the large and hearty former athlete at least would have been familiar with such campus activities.[11]

Within the context of boxing, the poem can be understood as a kind of public challenge or even the kind of trash-talk common among practitioners of the original manly art (as well, at times, among writers: witness Stevens's provocation of a fistfight with Hemingway in Key West in 1936).[12] The speaker inaugurates his address with a series of taunts:

> Chieftain Iffucan of Azcan in caftan
> Of tan with henna hackles, halt!
>
> Damned universal cock, as if the sun
> Was blackamoor to bear your blazing tail.[13]

The mocking diction and tone ostensibly serve to differentiate two "bantams" that the poem's title, curiously enough, indicates are indistinguishable (in an equally vague if somewhat pastoral "pine-woods"). As readers, we are encouraged to imagine a dialectical, pastoral, and distinctly masculine tension between large and small, simple and complex, strong and quick-witted characters, although other features of the poem belie this narrative cliché.[14] According to this fiction as suggested in the opening lines, the speaker's bravado is addressed to a figure in a "caftan," similar to the dressing robe adopted by boxers. The figure's absurd moniker, however, designates him as the "Chieftain" of an unreal, highly rhetorical world. The odd chiasmus of phonemes in the first line (the "tain"/"tan" and "can"/"can" "Chieftain" and "Iffucan" mirrored by "Azcan" and "caftan") accentuate his hypothetical, conditional properties ("if you can," "as [I] can") as well as his status as a self-reflective, self-regarding figure whose power and masculinity are as stylized as the "can-can" of French dancing girls, or as outdated as the supposedly extinct and certainly exotic Native Americans "chiefs" whose iconic photographs gained cultural currency even as their bodies were quickly disappearing from the continent.

An additional sound at play here also affirms this curious confluence of sport, art, and the performance of manhood: while commentators have noted the links between "Iffucan of Azcan" and the artists designated the Ashcan school, none has pointed out the further connection between Ashcan painters such as Bellow and his favorite subject, boxing, or the exoticism and carnivalesque atmosphere that came to dominate fights as they moved towards the mainstream. As Bellows's paintings so vividly illustrate, however, these grandiose and glamorized scenes of working-class triumph were small compensation for the grimmer realities of political and social losses the ethnic poor experienced during these years. That Stevens begins the poem with such an elaborate invocation suggests his investment in exposing the illusory features (or feathers) of such contests of strength, while concurrently exploring the ways in which masculinity was itself a figure with varyingly real correlates. For example, in the next stanza this "[d]amned universal cock," as arrogant "as if the sun / Was blackamoor to bear your blazing tail" may seem "universal" and apparently "representative," but his world is clearly not the real world, with its fanciful slave or "blackamoor" and the impressive "blazing tail." Here, the rhetoric of medieval chivalry, closely aligned with the cultural anxieties that spawned the rise of boxing, is invoked to depict a pauper turned prince, the working-class body elevated to a knightly, masculine, yet specularized (and hence also implicitly feminine) cultural ideal.

All of this talk climaxes with an attempt to deflate the proposed antagonist in favor of the speaker's own brand of masculinity, which he attempts to assert in the next stanza. "Fat! Fat! Fat! Fat! I am the personal. / Your world is you. I am my world," the "bantam-weight" snarls in a fit of inarticulate indignation. Once again the

contrast between Jack and the Giant, small and large, quick and dull is suggested, but the antipathy never seems to materialize convincingly, in part because the speaker's diction here is stilted and abrupt, his formerly rich vocabulary impoverished as it approaches the true nature of the "bantams." In fact, the patent illogic of the poem overtakes its diction in the magical third stanza: both figures are in their own "world[s]" in a chiasmus that has each mirror the other ("Your world is you. I am my world."); each is a version or reflection of the other, just as the Chieftain originally appeared to be a comical doubling or exaggeration of himself. The now abjectly "fat" "other" emerges as a version of the "bantam's" own self, a monstrous and very "personal" (for Stevens) "ten-foot poet among inchlings" whom Carl Van Vechten described in 1914 as a "rogue elephant in porcelain" and who by 1926 wrote that "[a]ll [his] attention [was] devoted to reducing." (*Letters*, 247)[15] At this point in the poem, it is the "fat" male body that must now be dealt with rather than the formerly (it was implied) muscular fighter and performer.

Over the next two stanzas, it becomes clear that the "fat" presence is a curiously and often humorously productive one. In his attempt to exorcize this possible physical self and nemesis, the speaker appears to succeed only in reasserting its presence, the "fat," an archaic term for a large jar or vat, remaining its "portly" self much as its namesake in Tennessee ("Anecdote of the Jar"). "Bantams" continues with the following lines:

> You ten-foot poet among inchings. Fat!
> Begone! An inchling bristles in these pines,
>
> Bristles, and points their Appalachian tangs,
> And fears not portly Azcan nor his hoos.

Indeed, the "bristling," newly bearded bantam has a rural, Appalachian tongue or "tang" that can take shape only around the figure of this "cock;" the Pennsylvania Dutch poet apparently given voice when presented with something appropriately substantial to address in himself. The other "bantam" or "bantams" seem inconsequential in contrast with this figure, not to mention textually indeterminate in number (why *their* Appalachian tangs"?), as the speaker collapses with his putative subject. This ambiguity regarding the speaking self and his elusive fellow "cocks" reinforces the implication that these displays of masculinity are themselves a charade, an elaborate "cock-fight" with rhetoric, rituals, and regalia that are borrowed and anachronistic. Absent these distractions, it is the "fat" male body that continues to resonate as the focal point of concerns as to the true substance of masculinity (is it muscle or fat?) and Stevens's ability to work creatively with such cultural tropes.

The fat body itself was newly perceived to be a disfigured body by the turn of the century, a disruptive presence that reflects a kind of social disorder with its overactive orifices and lack of self-control—yet it also was (and is) alarmingly ordinary.[16] And perhaps, at one level, it is precisely this disruptive ordinariness, this capacity to assert reality and bodily experience over theoretical norms, that made the trope of the fat man an attractive one for Stevens. A fat man is a man who understands the simple pleasures of life, a poet who admires "a photograph of a lot of fat men and women in the woods, drinking beer and singing Hi-li Hi-lo," an image that convinces him "that there is a normal that I ought to try to achieve" (*Letters,* p. 352). Yet the "portly" body also suggests a port, or place of shelter and civility, in a more disturbing sense: in a world where the rules of sport must compensate for a lack of rules in the marketplace, the powerful fat man oversees the continuance of traditions intended to regulate and control his fellow men. After all the imposing President Taft, unlike the athletic Roosevelt, abetted the trusts and corporate monopolies, and Stevens worked for the very insurance companies whose standard body charts denied him coverage. The fat man with his mysteriously breathy, joyful, or jeering "hoos" may inspire affection or a respectful "fear," but it is unclear that he is a vision of the masculine self that Stevens truly intended to exorcise ("Begone!"). Rather, the puffed up "bantams" in their rural "pine-woods" can be understood as reflecting the poet's insights into the amorphous nature of masculinity and the uneasy peace that he continually made with a world whose physical, ethical, and aesthetic standards were ever-shifting and often not in accord with his own experience.

What **"Bantams in Pine-Woods"** most aptly illustrates is the ultimately unsatisfactory nature of the "hero" or ideally masculine body, which Stevens constantly invokes and then deflates in his poetry in favor of the "large" or "fat" man. At the other end of the spectrum from both the weakling and strongman, the fat man is the man whose bulk is decidedly not muscle, his size alone inspiring both respect and ridicule. While the "large" man may at first seem a version of the "masculine" "hero" so many Stevens critics have invoked, his cultural history is quite different from that of his more studied, self-absorbed, and later vaguely fascist, cousin. By the early twentieth century, the national focus upon the ideal, or what Emerson might term the "representative," individual turned towards bodies deemed abnormal by virtue of their undisciplined size. While fat men early in the nineteenth century could be prominent and admired, "protective and reassuring" members of society, their days as representative citizens were numbered.[17] The popular Fat Men's Club of Connecticut, for example, was founded in 1866 and long maintained a distinguished membership, but by the 1903 the club had folded and the public perception of fat had altered. "Fat men and women were increasingly self-conscious," as were those who observed them. The very term "fat" began to take on negative connotations during this time,

and additional epithets were coined rapidly, among them "dumpy," "tubby," and "porky."[18] The young Wallace Stevens, upon seeing the notoriously large President Taft in a 1910 New York parade, had a characteristically ambivalent reaction: "His Excellency looked stupid to me. His eyes are very small—his hair is white with a yellow tinge. He is very heavy but not in a flabby way, specially. I say he looked stupid; but at the same time, we all know him to be a man of much wisdom, patience and courtesy" (*Letters,* p. 167). While an individual such as Taft would have attracted no censure for his size in the nineteenth century, the President became a touchstone for national jokes concerning weight by the end of his administration, his bulk contrasted with the younger and more fit Theodore Roosevelt. "Fat implied not the assertion of power but its false promise," a point brought home by the athletic former Rough Rider's crusades against corrupt trusts and the large monopolists (or "Fat Cats") who controlled them.[19]

By the 1910s and 1920s, attitudes toward overweight bodies stressed their inefficiency, their deviancy from "Yankee" frugality in a period of wartime conservation, and overall irregularity in an era of mass production and postwar ideological conformity. Insurance companies promulgated weight charts to be used to assess the health of potential clients. Americans began to diet in large numbers by the 1920s, closely following new fads as they attempted to stem a tide of consumption, constipation, and heart disease: "Reducing has become a national pastime . . . a craze, a national fanaticism, a frenzy," a journalist observed in 1925.[20] In 1905 Henry James took up Horace Fletcher's practice of systematically chewing one's food in order to avoid constipation and weight gain, soon declaring himself a fanatic of the technique (although by 1911 he disavowed it, claiming that he "starved" under the regimen). Edith Wharton even linked his literary practice to his diet, indicating that in his prose he "chewed a good deal more than he bit off."[21] Stevens, too, was caught up in the phenomenon, writing to Philip May in 1936, "At the moment, I am on a diet and shall have to be rather fussy about the diet for some time to come" (*Letters,* p. 307). This observation was likely the result of Stevens's meetings with a Dr. Herrick, whose dieting recommendations Stevens followed on and off for much of the rest of his life. While the six-foot poet was told to lose about twenty of his 229 pounds at this point, by the mid-1930s he weighed 234 and acquaintances estimated his weight at 250 and even 300 pounds by the late 1930s and early 1940s (when he wore a size 48 jacket).[22] From the mid-1920s on, Stevens struggled to maintain good eating habits in public and implemented a strict regimen within the household.[23]

Stevens's weight obviously dominated several aspects of his domestic life in addition to affecting his work and social life as a lawyer and poet. Several of Stevens's co-workers in Hartford and Washington D.C. mentioned not only his extreme weight but also his tendency to turn irritable when on a diet.[24] Stevens was extremely self-conscious about his size, refusing to do a reading at one point due to "the mingled problems of obesity and minstrelsy," recalling in 1948 that he "felt more like an elephant at every step" while walking down the aisle to the lectern at a previous engagement (*Letters*, p. 583). When taking family pictures during a visit to Reading, he demurred on the grounds that he was "so obese," a word he apparently invoked frequently to describe himself.[25] This self-consciousness did not extend to every aspect of his life and personality, however. Stevens seems to have gone on regular eating binges in Key West while vacationing with friends, and later in life seemed to take special pleasure in indulging in treats where his wife Elsie could not see him. In 1934 Stevens greeted a friend while staying at a hotel in New York with the announcement that he had just eaten "several pounds of Pennsylvania Dutch sausages," and in 1953 wrote to a relative, "if my wife knew I had two apples for breakfast she would get up early in order to prevent it" (*Letters*, p. 807).[26] Stevens's early journals and letters are filled with detailed descriptions of meals, and his youthful enthusiasm for gourmet treats continued throughout his life. He was known to have a sweet tooth, and frequently took special trips to New York City to markets such as "Dean's" to find his preferred plum cakes and Viennese chocolates. When a French bakery opened in Hartford in 1947, Stevens observed with delight and chagrin that "to start the day so full of these [brioches] that every time one breathes one whistles does not help to get things done" (*Letters*, p. 561). Other letters regale his correspondents with the delights of corn-on-the-cob, blueberries, Turkish figs, Spanish melons, oysters, Parmesan cheese with soft-boiled eggs, wines, and other foods both rare and commonplace.

It should come as no surprise, then, that obesity or fat was a trope with a special resonance for Stevens, who associated his own girth with his Pennsylvania Dutch ancestry, and all that it suggested of the "normal" life of "fat men and women in the woods" that he aspired to capture in his poetry.[27] Indeed, the use of "fat" as a poetic trope enabled Stevens to finesse class and other distinctions between himself and his more ordinary counterparts, facilitating his representation of them. For, despite the traditional association of "fat" with monstrosity—Stevens already referred to his body as "that monster" quite early in his career (*Letters*, p. 176)—and gluttony, as well as with mid-twentieth-century consumerism and overproduction, Stevens dispensed with such cultural truisms and substituted a curiously positive valence for the fat or large man. While Stevens may have been what was termed by the 1910s an "exogenous" body type, vulnerable to its own overstimulated

appetites in a world of plenty, his poetry does not contain predominantly negative images of the obese.[28] Nor does Stevens's later work incorporate the psychological theories linked to fatness popular in the 1930s and 1940s.[29] While numerous theories of the overweight individual stressed his inner emptiness, and Stevens himself attempted to conform to the new social norms to an extent, it is highly significant that Stevens's poetics encoded a highly nuanced and ambivalent, yet often positive, perspective upon the fat male body. Figures such as "Chief Iffucan," "Fat Jocundus," the "human globe," **"Jumbo,"** and **"Large Red Man Reading,"** as well as the "fat roseate" people of **"Credences of Summer"** and even the "fat girl" of **"Notes toward a Supreme Fiction"** all suggest attitudes both rooted in and transcending Stevens's fluctuating body image and appetites.

Stevens's use of the fat man as a trope also must be understood in the context of a literary movement that valorized the opposite physical ideal: the anorexic. Critics have asserted that "for white, male modernism a dominant aesthetic was anorexic," stressing the disgust of poets such as Eliot and Pound with the presence of a feminized waste associated with fat, overproduction, and consumption.[30] Many modernist poets imbibed Byron's bizarre stipulations that the poet be wraithlike, with the hope that self-starvation would produce an inversely bloated book.[31] Yeats imagined all poets as "old as well as thin, because their poetry consumes their youth and potency."[32] Marginalized social groups such as women, the working class, and ethnicities and races associated with weight problems are all implicitly excised from the purer national, poetic dialect that would be the result of such self-purgations. Stevens seems to have absorbed these body images to a degree, insisting in a letter to Peter Lee that Eastern poets must have been thin—"it is unnatural to think of men who have grown venerable in asceticism and meditation as plump babies"—yet in the same letter he insists that these Eastern poets were unlike the "rollicking characters" who were "the poets of antiquity in the West" (*Letters*, p. 873). For Stevens, thinness is associated with poetic and intellectual power only in exotic locales, but not in the West or, implicitly, a United States whose cultural heritage is overwhelmingly Western. In sharp contrast to colleagues such as Eliot and Pound (whose work he disliked), and oddly more like William Carlos Williams (towards whose work Stevens was ambivalent), Stevens produces a representative poetic self that, pragmatically rooted in his personal experience, suggests a more expansive approach to the numerous and supposedly irregular bodies of the national population.[33]

* * *

In **"Owl's Clover"** (1936), written in the midst of the Depression, Stevens addresses directly the question of the chaotic, excessive modern masses and their relation to the poet as the ideal man, citizen, and speaker. In the first sections of the poem, Stevens offers an almost bewildering variety of model men, none of whom is ultimately a satisfactory poetic subject. At first, the speaker acknowledges that the national ideal can no longer be the "buckskin" pioneer, but suggests the "sculptor," whose work speaks to the masses on "summer Sundays in the park," as a possible substitute.[34] By the section entitled **"Sombre Figuration,"** however, this alternative has already faded, and the speaker presents the "subman" as a possible re-creator of a despoiled world depicted in **"Mr. Burnshaw and the Statue"** as largely "waste," albeit both a "hopeless waste of the past" and a "hopeful waste to come," its light revealing "faint, portentous, lustres . . . of what will once more to rise rose."[35] The "subman" "dwells below," "in less / Than body and in less than mind, ogre, / Inhabitant, in less than shape, of shapes / That are dissembled in vague memory / Yet still retain resemblances, remain / Remembrances." The "subman," while not quite human, is the original "native" of the imagination, but it is unclear to what extent he is a "native" of the earth itself. Even the true "native," "The man . . . for whom / The pheasant in a field was pheasant, field," "Lives in a fluid, not on solid rock," like all men in a pragmatic, modern age. Only in a distant, mythic past might the "man and the man below" have been "reconciled," and even now neither model is quite adequate for the poetic task to which the speaker would set them. The subman dispensed with, the "sculptor" reappears, his vision potentially manifested in a grotesque statue all muscular marble ("a ring of heads and haunches, torn / From size, backs larger than the eye, not flesh / In marble, but marble massive as the thrust / Of that which is not seen and cannot be"). A parody of classical representations of youthful, virile male bodies, this statue "scaled to space" is a monument to an idea that never should be given a physical form. Set in a "true perspective," the statue is proper only to "hum-drum space;" this stone embodiment of the people's hero is a ghastly failure.

In place of these would-be artists and creators, a relatively familiar, comforting presence emerges, but he is initially presented in terms that have caused many critics to question his efficacy. In the final lines of the last stanza of **"Sombre Figurations,"** Stevens imagines "Jocundus," the opposite of the "black-blooded scholar," a "medium man among other medium men," an apparently wasteful creature who lives "for the gaudium of being," "indifferent to the poet's hum." He exists in a time that at first seems distopic, "Without imagination, without past / And without future," yet in this state "Night and the imagination [are] one" (**OP [Opus Posthumous]**, p. 101). The speaker's tone is a nuanced manifestation of the alternatives presented, at once speculative and passionate, precise and rhetorically

elusive as the speaker evaluates the attraction of this merry, comedic figure who is both suggestively ordinary and the namesake of an obscure Roman-era martyr. Reappearing in the **"The Glass of Water"** (1942), "fat Jocundus" is a central, rather than a marginal figure in Stevens's texts, but his status with respect to the poet's cultural and ideological project is far from agreed upon. While Milton Bates suggests that Jocundus is the anti-poet, wholly "indifferent to the poet's hum," Joseph Riddel describes Jocundus as an antiquated poet, a "seeker after the center, not the surface" unlike **"The Glass of Water"**'s more successful maker of forms, the "lion" of light.[36] What "fat Jocundus" represents most suggestively in the latter poem, however, is the poet as metaphysician himself, now given shape in a decidedly "portly" body rather than a muscular one. He appears in the midst of a poem about abstraction, a Falstaffian anchor to a discourse upon the nature of true being:

> The *metaphysica,* the plastic parts of poems
> Crash in the mind—But, fat Jocundus, worrying
> About what stands here in the center, not the glass,
> But in the centre of our lives, this time, this day,
> It is a state, this spring among the politicians
> Playing cards. In a village of the indigenes,
> One would have still to discover. Among the dogs
>   And dung,
> One would continue to contend with one's ideas.
>
>   (***Poems,*** p. 198)

While others are interested in forms for their own sake, Jocundus is caught up in "worrying / About what stands here in the center, not the glass," the particular, "plastic," object or state (***Poems,*** p. 197-8). He seeks ideas about objects rather than the objects themselves, yet he is also Stevens's figure for the common man, the ordinary made manifest. Odder still, within the logic of the sentence, Jocundus himself is curiously frozen in time, without a verb to mobilize him, or else turned into an "it," modified by the phrase: "It is a state, this spring among the politicians / Playing cards." He seems at once classical, as his Latinate name suggests, and aboriginal, one of the "indigenes" of a village not unlike that of "Chieftain Iffucan." As such, Jocundus is transformed into a joker, a trickster face card in Stevens's rhetorical gaming, an elastic idea signifying the eternally true (the classical) and the native (the "indigene"). At the same time, however, he is suggestive of contemporary—and rather unsavory—"politicians" not unlike Taft, those who profess to be natives but are only outsiders to their constituencies. In a last sleight of hand, Jocundus's association with a "village of the indigenes" also suggests the value of a site in which "dogs and dung" would necessarily co-exist "with one's ideas." In this most natural and original of locations, the true poet examines both the ordinary and the realm beyond, sifting through his experiences in search of those fragile truths and fictions that provide temporary solace. Jocundus as the poet heartily embodies the elusive and disorderly fat figure, a trope for the comedic, role-playing imaginer and source of poetic language. This elaboration upon the Jocundus of **"Sombre Figurations"** allows the reader to see the connections between a figure for whom "night and imagination" are "one" and the poet who seeks a deep, if domestic order in dreams and "[his] ideas," whether at home in the "village" or among "politicians."

In a series of shorter poems such as **"Asides on the Oboe"** (1940), **"Jumbo"** (1942), and **"Large Red Man Reading"** (1950), successive versions of "fat Jocundus" emerge with a certain regularity. Like Jocundus, these figures absorb and incorporate into themselves elements of the mass culture that surrounds them, whether in the form of a feminized spectacle or a quasi-racial caricatures. In **"Asides on the Oboe,"** the speaker proposes a man who is at once fiction and the originator of fictions: "the impossible possible philosopher's man" (**Poems,** p. 250). He is "the man who has had the time to think enough, / The central man, the human globe, responsive / As a mirror with a voice, the man of glass, / Who in million diamonds sums us up." He is a being who reflects the self, is one's reflection, and is also a "globe" that absorbs and contains the world, including the self. He is both exceedingly ordinary and "impossible," the imagined "rational man" of the economist, or the ideal "pragmatist" and citizen who sees, reflects upon, and responds to his world. Also like the spectacular, exotic Iffucan, he is the quintessential object of the subject, a "mirror" and a "million diamonds," deceptively reportorial or dazzlingly distortive. In a world of fictions, his vaguely feminine artifice is nearly indistinguishable from reality and even an improvement upon it: "in his poems we find peace." Even in wartime, he persists in his task, he "suffer[s]" as do "we," and in the wake of tragedy "we and the diamond globe at last were one." He is a "glass man" not unlike Emerson's "transparent eyeball," the medium by which the world becomes the poem of its possibilities. Not "impossible" at all, he is the necessary transmitter and mediator of our "mythologies of self."

In **"Jumbo,"** Stevens explicitly invokes a comic term for "fat" that contrasts decidedly with the fragile but enduring "globe" of the "philosopher's man." A relatively recent coinage for "fat," derived from the Gullah for "elephant" and evocative of the "hooing" Iffucan, **"Jumbo"** opens up a world of rhetorical possibilities for the poet. More specifically, in adopting an implicitly African-American version of the "fat" man, Stevens is able to appropriate a racialized rhetorical and physical power for himself, while obscuring the distinctions between self and other that such racialized caricatures putatively reinforce. The overall effect of this gesture is to acknowledge the presence of racial otherness as desirable only insofar as it is colonizable, the speaker replacing its presence with his buffoonish

impersonation. At the same time, **"Jumbo"** also indicates the extent to which a critical perspective upon white masculinity entails reference to a racial other. The first stanza suggests an almost animalistic creature breaking out of a contained space that seems simultaneously authentic and artificial, a natural environment and a cage: "the trees were plucked like iron bars / And jumbo, the loud general-large / Singsonged and singsonged, wildly free." The tone is gleeful and playful, as Stevens explicitly links exotic, animalistic **"Jumbo"** to his former poetic self, Crispin, mock-inquiring: "Who was the musician, fatly soft / And wildly free, whose clawing thumb / Clawed on the ear these consonants?" (**Poems,** p. 269). The distinctive 'C' sounds of **"The Comedian as the Letter 'C'"** hint that the true presence here is Stevens himself, the "transformer" himself, "himself transformed," whose "single being, single form / Were their resemblances to ours." Self-reflective and transforming, a capacious mirror for the audience he resembles and reassembles, he is also our comforting "companion in nothingness." "Loud, general, large, fat, soft," from certain perspectives he might seem unattractive, ordinary, but this "secondary man" is "wild and free." A Picasso-esque "blue painter," a Lincoln-esque "hill scholar," he is the ideal combination of artist, intellectual, and politician. At the same time, he is the "bad-bespoken lacker, / Ancestor of Narcissus," one who cannot communicate with others, who craves only his own beauty as reflected in the natural world. He senses an internal "lack" that drives him to love these natural mirrors—and it may be precisely this porous sense of self that is the root of his powers. As an amalgamation of men both black and white, he is the forger of an almost corporate composite self, and as such is both master of and subject to his fluctuating environment. Less ominously, he is also "prince of the secondary men" and hence like the "subman," a sort of collective unconscious for humanity. But he is also more than that, an "imager" who is resolutely embodied, he is a creature of this world as well as the imagination.

As such, he is not unlike the **"Large Red Man Reading,"** or, the "large red man" of "Reading," Pennsylvania (**Poems,** p. 423). This oddly colored and more uniformly affirming presence is evoked in terms both intellectually abstract and emotionally precise, drawing upon the pragmatic potential of the "human globe" while suggestive of **"Jumbo"**'s racialized subjectivity. It is he who "sat there reading, aloud" the "poem of life" that draws the "ghosts" back to earth, longing for their solid bodies. The speaker recounts: "They were those that would have wept to step barefoot into reality," and "cried out to feel it again, have run fingers over leaves / And against the most coiled thorn, have seized on what was ugly / And laughed." Listening to the "vatic lines," "the literal characters" of "poesis," they take on the reality of which the large man reads. "In those thin, those spended hearts" and in "those ears" the lines "took on color, took on shape and the size of things as they are / And spoke the feeling for them, which was what they had lacked." Here the "imager" grants these ghosts what they had "lacked"; now well bespoken, he grants and gives, creating a fiction of a reality they are unable to experience directly. In the world of the poem, the "night" and "imagination" are again "one," the ghosts gain back their human forms, and "lack" is replaced by "what will suffice." The poet grants sustenance, offering bodies, emotions, and implicitly the ability to articulate desire. His "largeness" and "red" flush, moreover, are not incidental to these gifts. His expanded human capacity as both the complex "reader" and the simpler resident of "Reading," as both the urbanite acquainted with other colors of men as well as the rural white insider, enables him to recall these presences—perhaps the ancestors he so carefully inscribed into his genealogy. The "red" people who his predecessors displaced are not thus implicitly enfranchised, however, but serve instead as mystical mediums for their colonizers. This exclusive gesture, while not terribly surprising from a man of Stevens's background, should not go unnoted as the poet offers a virtual Thanksgiving to his extended family: in place of their "spended" hearts, he offers a cornucopia of experience, a feast for the family of man.

A similarly evocative, albeit more socially limited aspect of "fat" returns in the poem **"Credences of Summer"** (1947), a homage to Reading and the poet's at times ambivalent memories of his childhood there. Read in the context of poems in which fat and experiences of the bodily are celebrated, it can be better understood as a definitive statement upon the significance of the poet's native land and all that it entails. While some critics have suggested that **"Credences"** is a meditation upon the limitations of this world, and as such inferior to its counterpart, **"The Auroras of Autumn,"** such readings neglect the poem's tendency to re-evaluate and re-imagine the parameters of the poet's creative locus.[37] Regarded in the context of similarly oriented poems, however, the various pleasures of the poem are more apparent, and Stevens's own preference for it elucidated.[38] This poem in turn illuminates one of Stevens's most memorable poems, **"Notes Toward a Supreme Fiction,"** and the "fat girl" around which it coalesces. The daughter of "fat Jocundus" and his bride from Reading, both a product of their worldview and her own person, she remains one of Stevens's most poignant creations and in some sense most fully embodies the radical potential of "fat" to cautiously re-center and creatively undermine inherited orders.

"Credences" begins with the speaker describing a world of "midsummer" that is at once the very essence of the real and the point from which imagination springs: "This is the last day of a certain year / Beyond which there is nothing left of time. It comes to this and the imagination's life." The speaker breathes life into an intimate, loving scene of "fathers standing round, / These mothers touching, speaking, being near, / These lovers waiting in the soft dry grass" (*Poems,* p. 372). Immersed in the world he once was native to, the speaker forestalls its examination and his inevitable shift into an outsider: "Postpone the anatomy of summer, as / The physical pine, the metaphysical pine." The parodic "pine-woods" of *Harmonium* have turned back into themselves, the rhetorical figures of "cocks" and "bantams" exchanged for their simpler, less aggressive forefathers. Such a world has limits, however, as "the fertile thing that can attain no more," it may also forestall the production of modern poetry itself. Trapped in a world of reminiscence, the speaker struggles half-heartedly to move from "green's green apogee" to a site more suited to the poet's "clairvoyant eye." Here the "secondary sounds" that the "secondary man" might pick up on are absent, present only are the "last sounds," and a "good" that is accepted simply because it is "what is." This is a universe in which a "rock" appears as "truth," and a "youth, the vital son, the heroic power" may emerge in tandem with the villagers who unthinkingly believe in him.

This world with its healthy, if thoughtless, inhabitants is a world stripped of desire: "They sang desiring an object that was near, / In face of which desire no longer moved." In succeeding lines, however, the fruitfulness of this world is suddenly heralded, as the tone shifts again and the uses of such sites are affirmed. Trumpets, those triumphal noisemakers, joyfully proclaim "what is possible," "the visible announced." This trumpet "supposes that / A mind exists, aware of division," presumably the complete mind of the poet, "grown venerable in the unreal." The poet is figured as a "cock bright," which is exhorted to "[f]ly low . . . and stop on a bean pole" (*Poems,* p. 377). Suddenly, the natural world he hovers over takes on a new vitality as this "soft, civil bird" witnesses the "decay" of one "complex," a process that in turn that gives rise to "another complex of emotions, not / So soft, so civil." The "cock" then will "make a sound, / Which is not part of the listener's own sense," and perhaps not even a word yet, but it is something new and, like the poem of impossible possible philosopher's man, "responsive." Sharing a key consonant with "Crispin" and echoing previous Stevensian figures for the expansive and expanding poet, the "cock" signals the return of the poet to this landscape as both native son and lofty, if slightly absurd (perched on his "bean-pole") observer.

The poem is careful to assure readers, however, that the poet as odd, if virile, bird cannot exist outside of the environment that nurtured him. The sounds and creative gestures surrounding the "cock" immediately prefigure the poem's conclusion in section X, in which the whole world of "midsummer" is evoked in terms that reinforce our collective need for such seasons and their celebrants.

Rather than a return to the beginning of the poem, though, here the scene shifts to an artificial "summer play," its people "characters / Of an inhuman author." The world of the ordinary and everyday, what has seemed a self-enclosed world without room for rhetoric or desires, gives way to its mirror opposite, the imagined and surreal. Within the economy of the poem this seemingly fixed and suffocating realm has become the impetus for poetry after all. By this point, the poem itself has come to serve as a container for the real and imagined in one, as the colorful "mottled mood of summer's whole" is dreamed up before the reader's eyes. This emphasis upon sight and passive observance then gives way to an even more auspicious emphasis on "speaking" in the final stanza, as the "characters" take on a life of their own, artifice suddenly turning back into the real as if both were part of a plastic, liquid continuum. "[T]he characters speak because they want / To speak, the fat roseate characters," but their world is not the stifled "midsummer" of the early sections of the poem. Rather than blissful, they are only "free, for a moment, from malice and sudden cry," the "complete-[ness]" of their scene a temporary state. Although they "speak," they give voice to "their parts *as in* a youthful happiness" [italics mine]: happiness and youth, it is suggested, are things of the past. As autumn approaches, loss and desire take the place of surfeit, but imagination could not have been reborn without its temporary idyll. Despite the speaker's ambivalence regarding the world these "fat" "roseate characters" inhabit, he figures it here as a necessary landscape to which the poet—as "soft" or "not / so soft civil bird"—may return in the appropriate season.

* * *

Even before **"Credences of Summer," "Notes toward a Supreme Fiction"** (1942) permitted Stevens to re-order and imagine the poet's role in the world, prefiguring the ultimate and necessary emergence of a complementary "disorder"—his truest "angel." Just as in **"Credences,"** late summer, with its intimations of autumn, is the talismanic site of poetic production, so is fatness in this poem a sign of stasis shifting towards alteration. Even more radically, however, in **"Notes"** Stevens allows the "portly" male physicality to transform into a womanly, anxiety-provoking embodiment of alterations both inevitable and bittersweet. While pre-dating **"Credences," "Notes"** contains Stevens's most memorable attempt to resolve his own anxieties about the "fat girl" and her counterpart in the "hero," both of whom are imagined as the poet's heirs—but only one of whom emerges as his true child. Stevens's resolution of this dilemma is startling and rarely discussed by critics, who all too often take at face value Stevens's equation of the "fat girl" with the "earth."

Within the context of Stevens's larger poetics of fat, however, her wider poetic, ethical, and aesthetic integrity become more fully manifest.

The poem begins with a series of deceptively programmatic descriptions of the poet and the origins of poetry. He first instructs a young "ephebe" to "become an ignorant man again," to approach the "difficulty of what it is to be" without the too-bright rhetoric of the "sun" that often obscures rather than illuminating experience (*Poems,* p. 380). He celebrates the poet who "refreshes life so that we share, / For a moment, the first idea," the poet who hears the "hoobla-hoobla-hoobla-how," of the exotic "Arabian" or the curiously foreign "hoobla-hoo" of the more common "wood-dove." These voices of the "first idea," suggestive of pure "otherness" and Romantic attempts to resolve the self's relation to the "other" in transcendental "chant[ing]," are part of the same essence as the "howls" and "hoo" of what Stevens termed elsewhere the "obese machine" of the ocean, its fluidity a reminder of life's "strange relation" to art (*Poems,* p. 383). The interconnection of these elements is reinforced in the person of "major man" as "MacCullough," an apparently ordinary individual who, influenced by the movements of the sea, may absorb its tendency to break down forms, setting "language" itself at "ease." The speaker is careful to note that the poet is not a divine or transcendent figure, however, but a human seeker, who "goes from the poet's gibberish to / The gibberish of the vulgate and back again." "He tried by peculiar speech to speak / The peculiar potency of the general, / To compound the imagination's Latin with / The lingua franca et jocundissima" (*Poems,* p. 397). Not surprisingly, in his plays upon language both common and refined, the poet ends up alluding to "fat Jocundus" and his ilk, shortly to be embodied in the poem's culminating image.

The "fat girl" spins into the orbit of the poem as it concludes, constituting, with the "soldier" of the last section, one of the speaker's two most important poetic and possibly real legacies.[39] One of the few definitively fat female entities in Stevens's poetics, this girl is obviously the child of her father—"Chief Iffucan," "fat Jocundus," the "transformer" himself. Stevens, the father of an only girl, could hardly have separated the "feeling" here from the "fiction that results from feeling": which is precisely the point of this section. Like the previous "fat" figures, she is full of promise: "my summer, my night" (*Poems,* p. 406). Yet she is also immature, on the brink of alteration: found "in difference," "a change not quite completed." The speaker addresses her lovingly, recognizing her as both self and not self: "you are familiar yet an aberration." He attempts to remain merely "civil" in his speech towards her, but at the same time he is anxious to "name you flatly, waste no words." The futility of this gesture, however, is implied in the rush of words that follow, as the speaker admits to the rounded, feminine, almost foreign nature of this new self. She is radically real and present. The poet cannot help but dwell upon her domestic, everyday forms, how she appears when "strong or tired, / Bent over work, anxious, content, alone." While obviously fond of her the poet is also bemused by her effect upon him: she is "the irrational / Distortion, however fragrant, however dear."

The puzzle of her powers, though, turns out to be the key to his—and possibly one day her—poetics: "That's it," he realizes, "the fiction that results from feeling" is proof that "the irrational is rational," the world and imagination, female and male, are one. He imagines how "we" will one day hear this at the Sorbonne, father and daughter returning home from the "lecture" at "twilight." The moment as imagined is tender and surreal. In that impossible possible moment, the poet and father, "flicked by feeling," will "call [her] by name, my green, my fluent mundo." But in the very moment of naming, of attempting to immortalize the moment and the person in the poem, the idyll turns cold and unreal. The girl suddenly transmogrifies into another realm entirely, perhaps into the workings of a pocket watch, or the translucence of a lyric: "You will have stopped revolving except in crystal," she is told. The poem ends suddenly on a note of overt beauty and suppressed anguish, as the poet anticipates not only the loss of his child and his own body to time, but also the evaporation of an imagined Paris in which love is unchanging and poetry radically alive.

Written during World War II, the poem is an elegy both for a Europe Stevens was never to know and for the passing childhood of his daughter. Moving out of the direct sphere of his influence and resisting his requests that she return to college, Holly was asserting a selfhood that could not be congruent with Stevens's own. The experience must have been at once painful and illuminating for this distant yet generous father. In response, the poet attempts once more, if not wholly convincingly, to affirm his legacy to his spiritual "sons," those soldier boys who, during the same time period, were enduring an equally decisive coming of age. But the shift to these final exhortations, in a section that reads as if tacked on, is incomplete and unconvincing. The speaker affirms that his "war" "depends on yours," the violence and ethical demands of the war infusing his poetry, which in turn helps to form the soldier: "The soldier is poor without the poet's lines." He imagines how "simply the fictive hero becomes the real," transformed by the "proper words" and "faithful speech" that see him through death or on to the next battle. The poet figures himself as a healthful, giving presence, in love with a world that needs what he can offer it, eager to share the poetry that has been the stuff of life for him. But his turn to the soldier, his half-hearted exhortation of heroic poetry and death, rings false, a hollow

counterpart to images of femininity, otherness, and living transformation.

Unlike his Modernist brethren Eliot and Pound, so virulent in their disgust with a world awash in goods and people, chaotic and odorous, Stevens consistently prefers a universe of plenty and abundance, or at least adequate sustenance. While at times he doubts the efficacy of the "fat" world of "midsummer," he constantly returns to it as the site in which the "possible" has its roots. "Fat Jocundus" embodies both the end of desire and its eternal generation, bringing together "night" and the "imagination" in a fluid state of "one[ness]" that reflects a truer, underlying order that is also a kind of disorder. The contradiction of Stevens's fascination with order and what he once called "man's passionate disorder" is ultimately this: that they themselves are one, the universe simply the fluidity of experience itself, subject to shaping and transformation as the poet speaks (*Letters*, p. 300). The "gibberish of the poet" and of the "vulgate" are not opposed but variations on a tune to be piped on the "Arcadian flute" that is also a "metropolitan corn-pipe" (*Letters*, p. 58). Over the course of his career, Stevens constantly called upon these fat presences, these variations on the self, to belie the starved poetics of his peers, nourishing instead what he found most exasperating and pleasing in his own experiences of the physical world. Bodies both muscular and fat make manifest a certain potency in Stevens's work, although neither is a completely stable form. Disruptive to the end, fat progresses from a trope for comic selves to a metaphor for the self's limited but fertile origins to a sign for the body of the poet's physical and aesthetic heir. Expressing both satisfaction and dissatisfaction with the self, these tropes for the fat body also allow Stevens to protest the predominance of an aggressive and highly performative masculinity that often had little to do with an individual's intellectual or moral fiber. A reminder of his own ethnic roots and an idealized American society, as well as an at times clumsy harbinger of a nation that might be more accepting of difference, Stevens's own fat body served as a metaphor for a sensibility both traditional and pragmatic. Emblematic of the "hopeful waste" Stevens once saw in the world, his aesthetic of "fat" serves as a comedic yet wise response to a world that could be both banal and unbearably tragic.

Notes

1. Wallace Stevens, *The Necessary Angel* (New York: Vintage Books, 1951) p. 66.

2. While I do not discuss William James's influence upon Stevens in any detail in this article, my understanding of Stevens as a pragmatic thinker is based upon the numerous and useful readings of the poet in this regard. These sources include: Frank Lentricchia's *Ariel and the Police: Michel Foucault, William James, Wallace Stevens*

(Madison: University of Wisconsin Press, 1988); Richard Poirier's *Poetry and Pragmatism* (Cambridge: Harvard University Press, 1992); and Jonathan Levin's *The Poetics of Transition: Emerson, Pragmatism, and American Literary Modernism* (Durham: Duke University Press, 1999).

3. For example, see Joseph Riddel's chapter "The Hero's Head" in *The Clairvoyant Eye: The Poetry and Poetics of Wallace Stevens,* (Baton Rouge: Louisiana State University Press, 1965); also Milton J. Bates, "Supreme Fiction and Medium Man" and "Major Man," in *Wallace Stevens: A Mythology of Self* (Berkeley: University of California Press, 1985); and James Longenbach, "The Fellowship of Men that Perish," and "It Must Be Masculine," in *Wallace Stevens: The Plain Sense of Things* (New York: Oxford University Press, 1991).

4. Such figures and the cultural anxieties that gave rise to the national fascination with muscular masculinity are discussed in E. Anthony Rotundo's *American Manhood: Transformations in Masculinity from the Revolution to the Modern Era* (New York: Basic Books, 1993), Michael Kimmel's *Manhood in America: A Cultural History* (New York: The Free Press, 1996), and Harvey Green's *Fit for America: Fitness, Sport and American Society* (New York: Pantheon Books, 1986).

5. See Gail Bederman's *Manliness and Civilization* (Chicago: University of Chicago Press, 1995) p. 16-19 for an account of this distinction.

6. Wallace Stevens, *The Letters of Wallace Stevens* (1966; Berkeley: University of California Press, 1996) p. 26. Further citations will be parenthetical.

7. It is significant to keep in mind that Stevens himself was diagnosed as an "acromegalic type," a condition "in which the thorax, head, and extremities continued to grow long after normal development has stopped." Such a disease probably heightened Stevens's sense of his body as grotesquely, even freakishly large. See Joan Richardson, *Wallace Stevens, A Biography: The Later Years, 1923-55* (New York: William Morrow, 1988) 45.

8. William James, *Pragmatism,* 1907 (Indianapolis: Hackett Publishing Company, 1981) 14. I understand Stevens as a pragmatist insofar as he bases his poetics upon experiences in the real world, in the process destabilizing accepted "truths," such as the definition of "masculinity."

9. Helen Vendler suggests the former reading, stressing that Stevens "identifies with the bantam," a smaller lyric animal approaching a grander epic tradition. See "Wallace Stevens," in *The Columbia History of American Poetry,* ed. Jay Parini (New York: Columbia University Press, 1993) pp. 379-380. See also Eleanor Cook, *Poetry, Word-Play, and Word-War in Wallace Stevens,* (Princeton: Princeton University Press, 1988) p. 70; and Rachel Blau DuPlessis, "'Hoo, Hoo, Hoo': Some Episodes in the Construction of Modern Whiteness," *American Literature* 67 (Dec. 1995) pp. 678-680.

10. See Kimmel, *Manhood in America,* p. 138 for a discussion of this phenomenon.

11. Certainly Stevens worried about his body's physical condition, writing to his father during college that he longed for summer activities that would enable "muscular development" (*Letters,* p. 19).

12. See Elliot Gorn, *The Manly Art: Bare-Knuckle Prize Fighting in America* (Ithaca: Cornell University Press, 1986) for a history of the sport and the ways in which it reflected contemporary anxieties regarding class, race, and gender.

13. Wallace Stevens, *The Collected Poems of Wallace Stevens,* 1954 (New York: Vintage Books, 1990) pp. 75-6. Further references will be cited parenthetically.

14. My understanding of pastoral is based upon William Empson's discussions of pastoral's political and class-based inflections in *Some Versions of Pastoral* (1935; London: The Hogarth Press, 1986).

15. See also Carl Van Vechten, "Rogue Elephant in Porcelain," *The Yale University Library Gazette,* 138 (Oct. 1963) p. 42.

16. See Rosemarie Thomson's "Introduction" to *Extraordinary Bodies: Figuring Physical Disability in American Culture and Literature* (New York: Garland Press, 1997), especially pages 33-36 and 41-44, for a discussion of physical disability as a kind of "dirt" and creative disorder as well as its relation to the kind of normative subjectivity and citizenship proposed by Emerson.

17. See Hillel Schwartz, *Never Satisfied: A Cultural History of Diets, Fantasies and Fat* (New York: The Free Press, 1986) p. 89. Further citations will be parenthetical.

18. Schwartz, p. 88-89.

19. Schwartz, p. 90.

20. Schwartz, p. 173.

21. Maud Ellmann relays this remark in *The Hunger Artists: Starving, Writing, and Imprisonment* (Cambridge: Harvard University Press, 1993) 8. Further citations will be parenthetical.

22. See Joan Richardson, p. 45, 118; *Letters,* p. 749. Further references to Richardson's biography will be parenthetical.

23. The domestic sphere for Stevens, as for all Americans, soon became key to the control of appetite and waist size: "the muscle of domestic science was flexed in the kitchen . . . here one fought off the fear of abundance and the golem of waste" (Schwartz, p. 82). In 1931 he even sent Elsie and Holly to a special Vassar conference on "Euthenics," a series of courses designed to help housewives improve their childrearing and domestic skills by applying the "naturalist" conclusions of philosophers such as John Dewey. In addition to courses on the psychology of the child, Elsie likely attended courses on "Physiology and Nutrition," with a strong emphasis on "maintenance of weight," as well as "Food Selection, Preparation, and Service." [See *Bulletin of Vassar College,* 21 (Jun.-Aug. 1931), Subject File 26.5, VC Vassar Summer Inst. 1931, courtesy of Vassar College Library, Archives and Special Collections.] Although Elsie was universally acknowledged to be an excellent cook of the elaborate dishes typical of the era and their social class, she evidently was quite involved in Stevens's efforts to reduce and maintain his weight. Stevens mentions at one point "the value of my wife's interest in calories and things of that kind," and one of the family's few intimates in the 1930s remarked upon the special dinners Elsie served: everything was "very healthful but very simple," there were "no rich sauces or anything like that" (*Letters,* 619). Joseph M. Holly's nanny from 1933-1935, recalled these meals. See Peter Brazeau, *Parts of a World: Wallace Stevens Remembered* (New York: Random House, 1983) p. 233.

24. Richardson, p. 49.

25. Brazeau, p. 276.

26. Brazeau, p. 76.

27. Stevens clearly saw his weight problem as hereditary, writing to his cousin Emma Jobbins: "although I am perhaps overweight, I am not nearly as much overweight as a Stevens usually is at my age" (*Letters,* p. 807).

28. Schwartz, p. 136.

29. Such theories included the now familiar idea that "fat people were paradoxically incomplete people, fearful of sex, adulthood, independence;" or the Freudian chestnut that "fat people ate to satisfy a devouring mother now inside them" (Schwartz, p. 195; p. 202).

30. See Leslie Heywood, *Dedication to Hunger: The Anorexic Aesthetic in Modern Culture* (Berkeley: University of California Press, 1996) p. 56. See also Maud Ellmann's *The Hunger Artists,* and Tim Armstrong's *Modernism, Technology and the Body* (New York: Cambridge University Press, 1998), especially "Chapter Two: Waste Products."

31. Ellmann, p. 22.

32. Ellmann, p. 27. For such writers, while "eating . . . is identified with knowing from the early months of life," and "eating" with "the origin of subjectivity," it also exposes the "'nothing' at the core of subjectivity" (Ellmann, p. 30). The abjecting forces of the smothering "other" enable one to establish the parameters of one's being only while revealing their fragility—as well as the fragility of the language predicated upon an individual self.

33. While I do not agree with Alan Filreis that Stevens's vision of the "hero" becomes decisively "more democratic" over time, I do agree that Stevens's sense of what was physically "normal" made him more sympathetic to the general, and increasingly overweight, American population. See Filreis, *Wallace Stevens and the Actual World* (Princeton: Princeton University Press, 1991) p. 34.

34. Wallace Stevens, *Opus Posthumous,* ed. Milton J. Bates (New York: Vintage Books, 1990) 75-101. Further citations will be cited parenthetically as *OP.* Helen Vendler discusses "Owl's Clover" and the inadequacy of the "pioneer" figure in *On Extended Wings: Wallace Stevens' Longer Poems* (Cambridge: Harvard University Press, 1969) p. 92-3. Vendler's discussion of the "subman" is also useful (p. 85).

35. James Longenbach quotes Stevens paraphrasing his discussion of waste in these lines: "it is a process of passing from hopeless waste to hopeful waste. This is not pessimism. The world is completely waste, but it is a waste always full of portentous lustres. We live constantly in the commingling of two reflections, that of the past and that of the future, whirling apart and wide away." See *Wallace Stevens: The Plain Sense of Things,* p. 180.

36. Bates, p. 214; Riddel, p. 155.

37. My reading here stands in direct contrast to Helen Vendler's dismissal of these lines as sentimental (*On Extended Wings,* p. 244).

38. When recommending favorite poems to be included in an Italian edition of his work, to be edited by Renato Poggioli, Stevens listed: "A Rabbit as King of the Ghosts," "Credences of Summer," and "Large Red Man Reading." (*Letters,* p. 778).

39. In a letter to Henry Church, Stevens writes: "The fat girl is the earth: what the politicians now-a-days are calling the globe, which somehow, as it

revolves in their minds, does, I suppose, resemble some great object in a particularly blue area" (*Letters*, p. 426).

Jacqueline Vaught Brogan (essay date 2003)

SOURCE: Brogan, Jacqueline Vaught. "Poems against His Climate." In *The Violence Within, The Violence Without: Wallace Stevens and the Emergence of a Revolutionary Poetics*, pp. 9-23. Athens, Ga.: University of Georgia Press, 2003.

[*In the following essay, Brogan posits that during the middle portion of his career, Stevens became more engaged with respect to socio-political issues and came to practice a form of poetic resistant to the dominant political rhetoric of his time.*]

Wallace Stevens's response to the climate that surrounded his middle years became, at its best, a technique for subverting the social, even political, descriptions of his world through an act of sustained though also changing poetic "resistance."[1] It was an evolving technique initially prompted, however ironically, by his artistic resistance to contemporary "objective" or "descriptive" poetry, especially that of William Carlos Williams. This response, and the ensuing poetic strategies he developed as well, inevitably pushed Stevens during the last half of his middle period more deeply into poetic theory, including the "theory of description" (*CP* [*Collected Poems*], 345). It is not surprising that the great poems of these years (roughly 1938-45), as well as much of the prose of this period, are consistently preoccupied with poetic theory, as **"The Poems of Our Climate," "Poetry Is a Destructive Force," "Notes toward a Supreme Fiction," "The Pure Good of Theory,"** and the earlier essays of *The Necessary Angel* all testify.

Nevertheless, just what Stevens's "theory" is has continued to be a major point of controversy among Stevens's critics, a controversy fueled by conflicting ideas expressed not only in different poems of Stevens's canon but within single poems as well.[2] For example, in **"Description without Place,"** the evocation of the

> Book of a concept only possible
> In description, canon central in itself,
> The thesis of the plentifullest John
>
> (*CP*, 345)

celebrates what could be accurately called a "logocentric theory" of poetry,[3] that is, that words are ultimately grounded in *being*. Yet only a few lines earlier in the poem Stevens counters the possibility that language could be "central in itself" by defining description as

> a desire,
>
> . . . . .
>
> A little different from reality:
> The difference that we make in what we see
>
> And our memorials of that difference.

This "alternative theory," which anticipates poststructuralist theories of signification, reminds us that the word is never equivalent to *being* but consistently evades the "thing itself."[4]

That these two conflicting theories should appear side by side in one poem, particularly one so obviously devoted to an exploration of poetic "description," is symptomatic of Stevens's interest in both the creative capacity and the inherent liability of the linguistic medium with which he worked. Yet, however much they preoccupied both his imagination and his poetry, it is useful to remember that what critics abstract as competing theories of poetry within his verse had a greater urgency, even immediacy, for the poet himself than our criticism sometimes suggests. Although a growing number of critics have begun to show that Stevens's poetry was deeply responsive to his own contemporary climate, it seems to me that at least until the advent of World War II, the majority of Stevens's responses to his actual times remained aesthetically and cognitively at a far remove from what he would come to call the "pressure of reality." In fact, despite the title of one of his better-known poems, during his middle years Stevens's overwhelming reaction was not finally "of" but pointedly "against" the climate of his time as his poetry became increasingly engaged with the actual or political world. Put differently, during his middle period, Stevens's poetics changed from one committed to the aesthetic consolations of poetry as an enduring artifice to one countering and perhaps correcting the increasingly violent rhetoric of his actual times.

The poem entitled **"The Poems of Our Climate,"** written in 1938, offers a useful point of departure for exploring this response. The context for this poem is quite complicated, both aesthetically and historically. As Joseph N. Riddel argued years ago, the opening lines of **"The Poems of Our Climate"** recall the "dix-huitième quality of Imagist exercises," although he also suggests that its main purpose is to place the imagination in a modern climate—one of "chaos and change"—as opposed to a lost, earlier climate of "orderly and fixed laws, a still life."[5] But, as Harold Bloom later pointed out, its "cold porcelain" is also the modern American substitution for Keats's "cold pastoral," an observation that allows him to conclude that the "opening irony, or alternation of imagistic presence and absence" of this "Keatsian mediation" is "perhaps Stevens's most ineluctable swerve away from poetic origins."[6] (Actually, a more overt "swerve away" from this particular "poetic origin" is to be found in a poem written one year later in which Stevens explicitly writes, "It is cold to be forever young" [**"Variations on a Summer Day,"** *CP*, 233].) Although imagism and Keats and even the more generalized "chaos and change" that began to accompany the late 1930s are undoubtedly part of the larger climate that informs this poem, the self-reflective irony of the title suggests that **"The Poems of Our Climate"** is primarily an ironic critique of the particular *poetic* climate at the time, one dominated to a large degree in 1938 by the "objective" poetry of his well-known contemporary, William Carlos Williams, far removed from what would subsequently become Stevens's critique of the *political* climate of his time.[7]

Even this particular context of Stevens's poem is quite complicated: Stevens's and Williams's friendship, though nearly lifelong, was alternately bullying, playful, respectful, and somewhat "uneasy."[8] For example, although he once criticized Williams for being "more interested in the way of saying things than in what he has to say" (*L* [*Letters of Wallace Stevens*], 544), Stevens also said, quite simply, "I love his stuff" (*L*, 286). But, however positive or competitive their relationship may have been, there was on Stevens's part a real misunderstanding of Williams's poetic enterprise. Stevens's conclusion, for example, that Williams "rejects the idea that meaning has the slightest value" and that he "describes a poem as a structure of little blocks" (*L*, 803) may be an unfair assessment, but it is one that nonetheless informed Stevens's various critiques and reviews of Williams's poetry that, in turn, broadened the misunderstanding between the poets.

Of these various critiques, the preface Stevens wrote for Williams's 1934 *Collected Poems* is of particular interest here, for it tells us quite specifically how Stevens read, or even "misread," his contemporary during this period.[9] After the opening remark that the "slightly tobaccoy odor of autumn is perceptible in these pages. Williams is past fifty," Stevens describes Williams as a "romantic poet," albeit a unique kind of romantic poet, who has a "passion for the anti-poetic." He then expresses his admiration for Williams's "sentimentality," which, he says, "cures" Williams's otherwise excessively "anti-poetic" poetry: "Something of the sentimental is necessary to fecundate the anti-poetic. Williams, by nature, is more of a realist than is commonly true in the case of a poet." Toward the end of the preface, Stevens notably praises Williams for the "ambiguity produced by bareness" and the "addition to imagism" achieved in "Young Sycamore": "The implied image, as in YOUNG SYCAMORE, the serpent that leaps up in one's imagination at his prompting, is an addition to imagism, a phase of realism which Williams has always found congenial." He then says, "In respect to manner he is a virtuoso. He writes of flowers exquisitely" (*WCP*

[William Carlos Williams, *Collected Poems: 1921-1931*], 1-4). Although Kurt Heinzelman has argued that this preface is "honorific," such praise as is given appears clearly backhanded, and it certainly "nettled" Williams.[10]

More important, the preface cues us to the ways in which **"The Poems of Our Climate,"** written four years later, uses poems in that collection as a background, even a "con-text," for its own artistic production (within which Stevens elaborates a very different "theory of description"). For example, in addition to describing "exquisite flowers," the opening lines of the poem are noticeably "bare" and "sentimental," imitating Williams's particular form of imagism far more than "dix-huitième exercises":

> Clear water in a brilliant bowl,
> Pink and white carnations. The light
> In the room more like a snowy air,
> Reflecting snow. A newly-fallen snow
> At the end of winter when afternoons return.
> Pink and white carnations.
>
> (*CP*, 193)

There are a number of precursors to this passage in Williams's 1934 *Collected Poems*. Williams's "The Lily," for example, begins with a description of flowers and air in much the same way that **"The Poems of Our Climate"** does:

> The Branching head of
> tiger-lilies through the window
> in the air.
>
> (*WCP*, 37)

Again like Stevens's poem, "Birds and Flowers" focuses on flowers, enhancing their color with white:

> the white
> shellwhite
> glassy, linenwhite, crystalwhite
> crocuses with orange centers.
>
> (*WCP*, 53)

However, "Nantucket," possibly the best-known poem in that collection, offers the most striking "pre-text" for Stevens's poem:

> Flowers through the window
> lavender and yellow
>
> changed by white curtains—
> Smell of cleanliness—
>
> Sunshine of late afternoon—
> On the glass tray
>
> a glass pitcher, the tumbler
> turned down, by which

a key is lying—And the
immaculate white bed.

(*WCP,* 42)

The exquisite flowers, glass pitcher, and "immaculate white" are the most immediate precursors to Stevens's "pink carnations," "brilliant bowl," and "snowy air," constituting a "source" that stands in an intensely ironic relation to Stevens's text.

It is important to clarify that although "Nantucket" sustains the illusion of accurate, objective description throughout the poem, in its strategy it moves from "pure" description (if that is possible) to something quite close to phenomenological transformation as the interior is revised by the larger context of the external world. As such, the poem is precisely what David Walker calls a "transparent lyric," in which the "dramatic center" of the poem has been shifted from a "lyric speaker to the reading experience itself."[11] Yet Stevens's preface to the 1934 *Collected Poems,* in which this poem was included, in no way acknowledges that facet of Williams's poetry, and **"The Poems of Our Climate,"** as allusion to Williams, certainly does not.

However, as a notable critic has argued in a different context, "The etiology of the allusion, like the etiology of the word, originates in ignorance, in the inevitable slippage of understanding that divides us from our past."[12] Such slippage, it seems to me, is also inevitable (and perhaps intentional) in contemporary allusions. From this perspective, **"The Poems of Our Climate"** may be said to demonstrate Stevens's "ignorance" of Williams's poetry or, more specifically, of Williams's poetic strategy. However much we may find that Williams ultimately succeeds in evoking the "act of the mind" (*CP,* 240) that Stevens desires of modern poetry, such "objective" poetry remains for Stevens far too "anti-poetic." Against what he describes in "Rubbings of Reality" as Williams's desire to present an "exact definition" of his subject (*OP* [*Opus Posthumous*], 245), Stevens attempts to demonstrate that the subject is "not seen / As the observer wills" (*CP,* 197)—and most certainly not if it is willed to be seen "objectively."

As he will continue to do so, with increasing sophistication throughout the poems of these middle years, Stevens counters the notion of objective, descriptive poetry in **"The Poems of Our Climate"** by subverting the notion of description itself—in this case by exploiting the latent, if not inherent, irony of textual allusion in order to debase both Williams's subjects and his style of writing. Thus, immediately after the opening lines (cited above), he clarifies his somewhat contemptuous attitude toward such poetry, saying, "[O]ne desires / So much more than that" (a statement reiterated again in the second stanza: "Still one would want more, one would need more, / More than a world of white and snowy scents"). This self-reflective intrusion clearly describes the critical distance between itself and its pretext, intentionally divorcing the poem from the poetry inscribed in its own first lines.

The crucial rupturing of text and pre-text. occurs, however, before that intrusion and can be described through the difference between Stevens's poetic strategy and that of Williams. In contrast to the "objective" descriptions sustained throughout "Nantucket," **"The Poems of Our Climate"** immediately violates the possibility of objective description, primarily through the similes of its second sentence:

> The light
> In the room more like a snowy air,
> Reflecting snow.

These similes ensure that the descriptions are not merely objective. Quite subtly but irrevocably, the words "like" and "reflecting" disrupt the illusion of verisimilitude in language itself, debasing, in consequence, the very kind of poetry they pretend to imitate. The opening passage is not, finally, a "Williams's exercise" but a deliberate act of "sub-version." Such subversions continue throughout the poem. The "vital I" of the second stanza (recalling Williams's "eye") is "evilly compounded" here. Even if it were possible to attain some "complete simplicity," a "world of white, / A World of clear water, brilliant-edged," says Stevens,

> There would still remain the never-resting mind,
> So that one would want to escape, come back
> To what had been so long composed.

The irony here is devastating. Against the presumption of stasis in artistic "composition"—elaborated in Williams's "A Sort of a Song" as "Compose. (No ideas / but in things)"—Stevens's poem reminds us that what has really been "composed" is this "compounded" world and an "evilly compounded" (and thus "vital") "I" that continually confronts the radical drift between the world and the words through which we describe the world. The "perfect" world of Williams's sharp-edged delineations is not, at least according to Stevens, possible, either in life or in poetry, and this constitutes part of a "theory" that he reiterates from **"Sunday Morning"** to **"Notes toward a Supreme Fiction."** Pushed to its extreme, then, **"The Poems of Our Climate"** discloses "description" as "de-scription."

As sophisticated as this strategy may seem to contemporary critics, it must be stressed that in 1938 Stevens did not intend to "deconstruct" poetry, either Williams's or his own. Despite his acute awareness that language may be a **"Destructive Force"** (*CP,* 192), Stevens still insists upon the creative capacity of the medium in which he works. Thus, after disrupting the "still life" of Williams's "objective" poetry, Stevens concludes **"The Poems of Our Climate"** by validating language as the only (however ironic) source of meaning:

> The imperfect is our paradise.
> Note that, in this bitterness, delight,
> Since the imperfect is so hot in us,
> Lies in flawed words and stubborn sounds.
>
> (*CP*, 194)

On the one hand, Stevens's affirmation of the "imperfect" is made at the expense of Williams's "perfectionisms."[13] On the other, this affirmative play is a serious confirmation of the very "reflective" nature of both language and the "never-resting mind." As many modern critics have shown, and as Stevens seems to have fully realized, both language and the mind depend upon "original" rupture.[14] The poem, then, succeeds as a tour de force in which the "original" parody of Williams's descriptive poetry ironically comes to describe the elusive, even allusive, relation of world, mind, and word. Thus, although it may be a poem more "against" than "of" its climate, it is one that transcends its climate through the not-so-casual litter of its words.

The intertextual play of **"The Poems of Our Climate"** is obviously complicated by Stevens's ongoing, personal relationship with Williams as well as by its interaction with other poems written at approximately the same time.[15] Significantly, in both its original publication as part of **"Canonica"** and later as part of *Parts of a World*, Stevens chose to precede **"The Poems of Our Climate"** with **"Poetry Is a Destructive Force"** and to follow it with **"Prelude to Objects,"** the title of which is an obvious gesture toward Williams.[16] In the latter poem Stevens once again undermines "objective" poetry even as he affirms the creative power of poetic "conceits." For example, after seeming to "grant" the hypothesis of accurate reflection ("Granted each picture is a glass"), Stevens fractures the possibility of accurate reflection with the assertion that "the walls are mirrors multiplied." Stevens then "de-scribes" both the power of conception and the lewdness of deception inherent in poetic "conceits" by telling the "Poet" to

> Fix quiet. Take the place
> Of parents, lewdest of ancestors.
> We are conceived in your conceits.
>
> (*CP*, 195)

Stevens used this **"Canonica"** of 1938, in its entirety, as the first twelve poems of *Parts of a World*, first published in 1942. It is a group of poems that clearly, if somewhat playfully at times, is intended to summarize Stevens's maturing sense of aesthetics. Williams, again, is not the only "context" for this **"Canonica."** The first poem of the group, **"Parochial Theme,"** challenges the most traditional of poetry and themes. In addition, as

Glen MacLeod has convincingly argued, **"Canonica"** in particular bears a relation to surrealism and Dutch painting, as well as serving as a specific rejection of the kind of "strict rationalism" associated with the "geometric-abstract tradition" in the visual arts.[17] However, the majority of the poems, such as **"Study of Two Pears," "The Glass of Water," "Add This to Rhetoric"** (perhaps a specific "revision" of Williams's "To a Solitary Disciple"), and **"Dry Loaf,"** are rather obviously pitted against "objective" poetry. In all of these poems Stevens exposes descriptive "delineations" (*OP* 245) of reality, which Stevens says Williams tries to create, as mere "rubbings of a glass in which we peer" (an ironic phrase taken from **"Notes toward a Supreme Fiction"** [*CP*, 398], anticipating Stevens's critique of Williams in **"Rubbings of Reality"** [*OP* 244-45]).

As intricately related to Williams's poetry as these poems are, it is appropriately the last of the **"Canonica," "The Latest Freed Man,"** that most clearly anticipates the "canon" developed in the later poems of this middle period:

> Tired of the old descriptions of the world,
> The latest freed man rose at six and sat
> On the edge of his bed. He said,
>   "I suppose there is
> A doctrine to this landscape. Yet, having just
> Escaped from the truth, the morning is color and mist,
> Which is enough. . . ."
>
>   . . . . .
>
> It was how the sun came shining into his room:
> To be without a description of to be,
> For a moment on rising, at the edge of the bed, to be,
> To have the ant of the self changed to an ox
> With its organic boomings, to be changed
> From a doctor into an ox.
>
> (*CP*, 204-5)

Here Stevens suggests both that the "old descriptions" can be an imprisoning "doctrine" that denies *being* and that description is not only inevitable but also inescapable. With a playful gesture toward the poet he elsewhere calls "old Dr. Williams" (*L*, 286), **"The Latest Freed Man"** describes the possible freedom from "doctrinal" descriptions through subversive poetic descriptions.

Stevens, it would appear then, is almost obsessed during this period with demonstrating that the word has the power to create, that "[i]n the way you speak / You arrange, the thing is posed" (*CP*, 198), and that for this very reason it is all the more crucial that language not be taken naively for the "thing itself," that the most exquisite images be recognized as an "evading metaphor" (*CP*, 199). The increased urgency for this recognition, at least on the part of Stevens, is implied by the degree to which he reiterated this point in the many poems of this period, such as **"Illustrations of the Poetic as a Sense," "The Sense of the Sleight-of-Hand Man,"** and **"A Dish of Peaches in Russia"** (a poem that rather ferociously counters Williams's "This Is Just to Say" and its well-known plums). But this urgent recognition is made quite explicit in one of the later poems of this period, **"Description without Place"** (1945), a poem that proves pivotal to Stevens's developing poetics not only in relation to this "aesthetic" stage but to other stages in his evolving poetics to be discussed in the following chapters:

> Things are as they seemed to Calvin or to Anne
> Of England, to Pablo Neruda in Ceylon,
>
> To Nietzsche in Basel, to Lenin by a lake.
> . . . . .
>
> The eye of Lenin kept the far-off shapes.
> His mind raised up, down-drowned, the chariots.
> And reaches, beaches, tomorrow's regions became
> One thinking of apocalyptic legions.
>
> (*CP*, 341-43)

The possible "apocalyptic" extension of the "eye," that is, the potential consequence of our interpretations of reality made precisely through descriptions of reality, leads Stevens to conclude in another poem written in the same year that "the nicer knowledge of / Belief" is that "what it believes in is not true" (*CP*, 332). This, as the title tells us, is **"The Pure Good of Theory."**

Stevens rehearses similar themes in many of the poems written during this period. In **"Certain Phenomena of Sound"** (1942), to choose just one example, the "vital I" is potentially reduced to a linguistic sign inscribed in the word *Semiramide*:

> There is no life except in the word of it.
> I write *Semiramide* and in the script
> I am and have a being and play a part.
> You are that white Eulalia of the name.
>
> (*CP*, 287)

Yet as the poem demonstrates, the "I" is present, ironically but necessarily, in its description—in this case, through *intratextual* allusions (such as the "I am" that also appears "in the script"). As Stevens explains, with a certain clarity and urgency, "the power of literature is that in describing the world it creates what it describes. Those things that are not described do not exist, so that in putting together a review like ORIGENES you are really putting together a world. You are describing a world and by describing it you are creating it" (*L*, 495). In this letter, written in 1945, there is an implied responsibility, perhaps even an implicit moral imperative, in choosing our descriptions that is not found in **"The Poems of Our Climate."** That imperative is, strictly speaking, phenomenological, for in 1939 the world went to war again.

The poems written between the **"Canonica"** (1938) and the "canon central in itself" of **"Description without Place"** (1945) mark the rapid maturing of a poet into one of the greatest poets of the twentieth century. In part, this development may be accounted for by Stevens's working through his own "theory of poetry," which meant, among other things, that it "must not be fixed" (*NA* [*The Necessary Angel: Essays on Reality and the Imagination*], 34). For Stevens, the subject of poetry is the "act of the mind," with its implicit movement and ambiguity, rather than "'a collection of solid, static objects extended in space'" (*NA*, 25), with its implicit stasis and flat objectivity. As he says with great force in **"Extracts from Addresses to the Academy of Fine Ideas"** (1940), the "mind is the end and must be satisfied" (*CP*, 257), and seemingly flat descriptions, like those in "Nantucket," would never do.

Yet despite his persistent inquiries into the nature and theory of poetry, and despite his rather personal response to Williams, Stevens's nearly explosive poetic growth during these few years must finally be accounted for by the most significant element in his climate after 1939, the Second World War. In **"Forces, the Will & the Weather"** (possibly with a pun on Williams and his essay "Against the Weather" of the same year),[18] Stevens suggests, with humor in this case, one of the potential catastrophes of the war:

> There was not an idea
>
> This side of Moscow. There were anti-ideas
> And counter-ideas. There was nothing one had.
> . . . . .
>
>   It was a shift
> Of realities, that, in which it could be wrong.
>
> (*CP*, 229)

The "latest freed man" of the **"Canonica"** is no longer free in this poem, having become imprisoned by the times and its overpowering ideas. The "shift / Of realities," Stevens warns, with both aesthetic and ethical consequences, "could be wrong."

Part of this shift included the new kind of poetry that began to enter the climate, that is, antiwar poems such as those of Karl Shapiro and Randall Jarrell that, following the new tradition of war poetry established in the Great War, were meant to be "objective" (albeit in a way entirely different from that of Williams's poetry) and specifically antiheroic.[19] Thus, despite the ongoing criticism of Williams's kind of "objectivist" poetry that may have influenced **"Forces, the Will & the Weather,"** the most critical "shift / Of realities" appears, at least for Stevens, to have been created precisely by the more generalized and violent "descriptions" of his time rather than by any particular poetics. As he had eloquently, though painfully, explained in the

1936 essay "The Irrational Element in Poetry," even before the Second World War had begun

> [t]he pressure of the contemporaneous from the time of the beginning of the World War to the present time has been constant and extreme. No one can have lived apart in a happy oblivion. For a long time before the war nothing was more common. In those days the sea was full of yachts and the yachts were full of millionaires. It was a time when only maniacs had disturbing things to say. . . . People said that if the war continued it would end civilization, just as they say now that another such war will end civilization. It is one thing to talk about the end of civilization and another to feel that the thing is not merely possible but measurably probable.
>
> (*OP* 229)

There may be a possible reference here to Williams's 1935 poem, "The Yachts," a reference that, given the "horror of the race" described in that poem, is once again highly ambiguous. Nevertheless, Stevens's reaction to modern war is quite clear, as it is in many of his poems written during the actual war years.

After the **"Canonica"** of 1938, most of the poems of Stevens's middle period are explicitly concerned with this pressure and with finding what will "suffice" to resist its suffocating power, as is the essay "The Noble Rider and the Sound of Words," first read at Princeton in 1941. The third section of that essay is devoted to explaining how "an extraordinary pressure of news—let us say, *news incomparably more pretentious than any description of it*"—is threatening the "consciousness to the exclusion of any power of contemplation" (*NA*, 20, my emphasis). He goes on to explain, more suggestively, that "[l]ittle of what we have believed has been true. Only the prophecies are true" (*NA*, 21).[20] It is for these reasons—both the pressure that necessitates resistance and the implied responsibility of what we choose to prophesy—that Stevens insists that the measure of the poet is, "in spite of all the passions of all the lovers of the truth," a "measure of his power to abstract himself, and to withdraw with him into his abstraction the reality on which the lovers of truth insist" (*NA*, 23), that is, quite specifically during this period, the "violence from within that protects us from a violence without" (*NA*, 36).

Similarly, **"Extracts from Addresses to the Academy of Fine Ideas,"** written in 1940, also insists on both the liability of language as well as its necessity. It concludes with an especially harsh section that asks, specifically in relation to the war, whether we "live in evil and afterward / Lie harshly buried there." Yet the same section of the poem begins by saying that although "[w]e live in a camp," "[s]tanzas of final peace / Lie in the heart's residuum" (*CP*, 258), stanzas presumably of the "new" world in which "all men are priests":

> They preach and they are preaching in a land
> To be described. They are preaching in a time
> To be described.
>
> (*CP*, 254)

This new world, however, as Stevens well knows, has not yet been described; the final lines of the poem say, "Behold the men in helmets borne on steel, / Discolored, how they are going to defeat" (*CP*, 259). Yet the possibility of a land and a time yet "[t]o be described" (or "prophesized," to use the vocabulary of "The Noble Rider and the Sound of Words") is the ironically nostalgic center of the poem:

> He . . . wanted to think his way to life,
> To be happy because people were thinking to be.
> They had to think it to be. He wanted that,
> To face the weather and be unable to tell
> How much of it was light and how much thought,
> In these Elysia, these origins.
>
> (*CP*, 257)

This "he" who "think[s] his way to life" is placed in direct opposition in this poem to "Ercole," whose way of thinking is the "way to death" (*CP*, 256).

Stevens's resistance to that "violence without" is readily seen in a poem entitled, appropriately enough, **"Examination of the Hero in a Time of War"** (1942), the poem with which he chose to conclude *Parts of a World* (and to which I will return in chapter 2). In contrast to "realistic," antiheroic war poems, this one is intentionally abstract and, to some degree, idealistic: "Unless we believe in the hero," Stevens asks, "what is there / To believe?" (*CP*, 275). Yet as he clarifies later in the poem, the hero he has "in mind" cannot be reduced to a particular image:

> It is not an image. It is a feeling.
> There is no image of the hero.
> There is a feeling as definition.
>
> . . . . .
>
> The hero is a feeling, a man seen
> As if the eye was an emotion,
> As if in seeing we saw our feeling
> In the object seen and saved that mystic
> Against the sight, the penetrating,
> Pure eye.
>
> (*CP*, 278-79)

In contrast to any attempt to arrive at a precise description of this "hero," Stevens insists upon trying to capture the "feeling, / In the object," the emotion that ironically "describes" and "saves" the human from the "penetrating, / Pure eye," perhaps even an "objective" eye. At the very least, this feeling is pitted elsewhere in the poem against the *"dry descriptions"* of images and allegory upon which, Stevens says, we cannot live (my emphasis).

Although the "con-text" for this poem of his middle years is no longer strictly Williams, we see in **"Examination of the Hero in a Time of War"** a certain resistance to his climate—again, in the interest of mental freedom—that was learned, at least in part, from his resistance to the earlier "objective" poetry. This rather odd conjunction of Stevens's preoccupation with the limitations of objective poetry and with the pressure of the Second World War suggested by **"Examination"** does not mean, of course, that Stevens felt that the forces behind the poems of his climate equaled the forces behind the war. Rather, this conjunction suggests the degree to which Stevens recognized that words taken naively as fact are dangerous—even as he insists that without words people are not only not heroes but less than human. Believing in the "hero" becomes metonymically equivalent to believing in poetry and in its ability to "truly bear" (*CP*, 281) and bare our truer selves. **"Examination of the Hero in a Time of War"** thus provides a specific marker for the number or "parts" of a world to which Stevens responds in a book that begins with **"Canonica"** (and his aesthetic resistance to Williams), only to end with poetic resistance to war. However, looking forward to the following chapters, I should also clarify here that this poem proves important in demonstrating yet another stage of Stevens's evolving poetics—essentially a stage in which Stevens went through a difficult change from the felt need for aesthetic disagreement, through political "resistance," to a more torturous necessity to "witness" to the horrors of his time. This critical change explains why much of his poetic production during this period can be seen as a subversion of and resistance to the political descriptions of his world that had increasingly come to dominate it in escalating violence. "Resistance," he had already clarified in "The Irrational Element in Poetry," "is the opposite of escape" (*OP* 230). Not "revolving in crystal" at all.[21] The following chapters take up Stevens's growing insistence that both poetically and politically, "resistance" (which, etymologically, means "stand") is the necessary response to a violent (and increasingly violent) reality.

Notes

1. This particular word is taken from "The Irrational Element in Poetry," reprinted in *OP*, 230.

2. The earliest parameters of this debate were first summarized in Riddel's "The Climate of Our Poems," discussed at length in my *Stevens and Simile* and traced in great detail in Schaum's *Wallace Stevens and the Critical Schools*.

3. See Mills, "Wallace Stevens: The Image of the Rock," in which he discusses the "transfer of the generative power from the divine Logos" to "the human spirit" achieved in these lines (100).

4. Though deconstructive approaches to language have been a commonplace for over three decades, it is still useful to see Derrida, "Structure, Sign, and Play," perhaps the earliest and clearest statement of this position (first given as a paper in 1966).

5. Riddel, *The Clairvoyant Eye,* 154, 65.

6. Bloom, *Wallace Stevens: The Poems of Our Climate,* 150, 140-41.

7. For example, William Carlos Williams had published his *Collected Poems: 1921-1931* as well as *An Early Martyr and Other Poems* immediately prior to the period we are examining here—in 1934 and 1935, respectively.

8. See MacLeod, *Wallace Stevens and Company,* esp. chap. 6; Heinzelman, "Williams and Stevens," 85-113; and Strom, "The Uneasy Friendship," 291-98.

9. Reprinted in *OP,* 254-57.

10. Heinzelman, "Williams and Stevens," 95; Williams cited in MacLeod, *Wallace Stevens and Company,* 90.

11. Walker, *The Transparent Lyric,* xii. Walker convincingly demonstrates that Stevens and Williams cannot be critically distinguished as "polar opposites" (ix). Yet despite the similarities that we may be able to perceive in the lyrics of each poet, Stevens still placed himself in opposition to Williams's poetry. It is this ironic "source" with which I am concerned here.

12. Greene, *The Light in Troy,* 18.

13. As Albert Cook points out in *Figural Choice in Poetry and Art,* "perfection" is one of Williams's favorite words (137).

14. With regard to the inherently ironic "reflective" nature of consciousness and language, see DeMan's discussion of the "conscious dialectic" of "reflective poetic consciousness" in "Intentional Structure of the Romantic Image," 65-77. It is worth noting that Stevens challenges the idea of "perfection" in a number of poems during this period, including "Of Bright & Blue Birds & the Gala Sun" (1940):

> It is there, being imperfect, and with these things
> And erudite in happiness, with nothing learned
> That we are joyously ourselves.

> (*CP,* 248)

15. Among the more amusing of the "sub-texts" to Stevens's poems is the relation of Williams's 1937 review of *The Man with the Blue Guitar and Other Poems* to Stevens's preface for Williams. In each, the one accuses the other of having aged. For a

lively discussion of the lengthy "dialogue" between these two poets, see Heinzelman, "Williams and Stevens."

16. "Canonica," *Southern Review* 4 (1938): 382-95.

17. See MacLeod, *Wallace Stevens and Modern Art,* 95, as well as the larger discussion of this group of poems (79-102).

18. See Williams, "Against the Weather," 196-218. Interestingly, Williams notes that "Dante was the agent of art facing a time and place and enforcement which were his 'weather.' Taking this weather as his starting point, as an artist, he had to deal with it to affirm that which to him was greater than it. By his structure he shows his struggle" (205).

19. In this regard we might also consider *For Whom the Bell Tolls,* a novel published immediately after the actual onset of a war that, like Wallace Stevens, Ernest Hemingway did not want us to join. Although Robert Jordan of Hemingway's novel may be highly romanticized, both as the hero and as a lover, the overall tone of the novel is finally quite grim, almost passionately antiwar, as Hemingway ruthlessly exposes the absurdities and atrocities of both political camps (Fascists and Communists) that not only occurred in reality in Spain but also would be enacted (as Hemingway prophesied) in the atrocious powers and alignments of World War II. See, in particular, Hemingway, "A Program for U.S. Realism," written from Spain. Put in this context, the lines cited above from the 1939 "Forces, the Will & the Weather" virtually summarize the moral quandary of Hemingway's novel.

20. Perhaps Stevens is even referring to those stinging prophecies Hemingway had written for and published in *Esquire* in the late 1930s, not only of the next world war, which he saw as the next stage of Spain's "civil" war, but also of Japan's involvement to come, of the civil war looming on the horizon in China, and of continued European expansion and concomitant warfare in Africa. See "Notes on the Next War," 205-12.

21. I am, of course, alluding to Perloff's well-known essay "Revolving in Crystal," 41-63.

Jon Kertzer (essay date fall 2004)

SOURCE: Kertzer, Jon. "The Course of a Particular: On the Ethics of Literary Singularity." *Twentieth Century Literature* 50, no. 3 (fall 2004): 207-38.

[In the following essay, Kertzer examines the similarities between the aesthetics of Stevens's poetry and the ethics of philosopher Emmanuel Levinas.]

In Wallace Stevens's poem **"The Course of a Particular,"** the cry of wintry leaves provokes a shift in mood from robust assurance that "one is part of everything" to a depleted sense of the world drained of meaning:

> The leaves cry.
>
> . . . . .
>
> In the absence of fantasia, without meaning more
> Than they are in the final finding of the ear, in the thing
> Itself, until, at last, the cry concerns no one at all.
>
> (*Palm* [*The Palm at the End of the Mind*] 367)

These two dispositions—one expansive and gregarious, the other contracting to the vanishing point of consciousness—suggest two complementary responses to literature. I will be concerned with the latter, which tries to acknowledge the uniqueness of a literary work; but it must first be set against the "fantasia" whose absence it announces in order to trace a path of diminishing returns. My purpose is to explore the rhetoric of singularity in order to detect its "final finding," that is, its aesthetic and ethical limit. My hope is that artistry and ethics will converge: the course of a literary particular leads to ethical discovery.

According to Stevens, however, such a discovery "concerns no one at all." This hardly sounds like a strong moral position,[1] and defining that position in relation to the artistry that exposes it will be my subject. My own path, which runs from the numerous to the singular, requires some signposts. I intend, first, to mark the path's two limits by contrasting a criticism of plenitude with a criticism of austerity; then to inspect some rhetorical devices through which singularity is indicated; then to show how this rhetoric isolates the here-and-now in the instant of its inception and deception, its birth and death; and finally to examine how an aesthetic of singularity raises a comparable ethical challenge that sets moral generality against the dignity of the unique. Stevens will serve as one of my guides.

THE SHIPWRECK OF THE SINGULAR

When studying any literary work, we customarily nudge it in two directions, though not in equal measure. Usually we relate it to other texts in an expanding pattern of interdependence within larger contexts and communities. Whether the terms of explication are historical, cultural, biographical, national, generic, or religious, a work gains significance within a wider field to which it contributes, however modestly. No artist or artifact has its meaning alone, T. S. Eliot advises in a famous dictum, because it participates in an "ideal order," a totality that is temporarily complete yet continually altered as new works are added to it (38). A text is intelligible through its relation to other texts: as one elegy in an elegiac tradition, or as an American lyric, or as a novel by Virginia Woolf, or as an example of women's writing, and so on. At the imagined limit of this expansive view lies a glimpse of all literature conceived as one ongoing discourse—a grand intertextual poem, myth, or conversation forever in progress. Northrop Frye provides one of the most daring modern attempts to see literature steadily and to see it whole by fitting every work into a vast network of modes, myths, and genres,[2] all combining in a sublime vision of cultural totality corresponding to what Eliot calls "the mind of Europe" (39). A poem is like a single thought within that mind.

As the critic's field of vision expands, however, individual works become more and more significant, yet less and less discernible as they are engulfed by the whole. Ideal readers catch every allusion and influence, but at the cost of losing the shock of first discovery. As a countermeasure, they try to savor a literary work not in relation to other writing but in and for itself. It may be another eighteenth-century, middle-class novel written by a Protestant man for women readers, but it is this particular text and not another one, read here and now, not elsewhere. How are we to account for its specificity? Even an ardent advocate of intertextuality like Harold Bloom admits, "There can be no poem in itself, and yet something irreducible does abide in the aesthetic" (*Western* 23).

Although the specificity of a literary work may strike us forcefully on first reading, it is difficult to define because all the modes of definition at our disposal have the perverse effect of depriving a work of its particularity. Explanations inevitably generalize. Whether we explain a text by means of categorization, analogy, paradigm, function, influence, or genealogy, the process of understanding in each case is contextual and systematic. It is relational, whereas specificity is what precedes any relation and then enters into it. Do the primary units have any identifiable standing before they contribute to a larger structure of meaning, or are they created only by the act of being differentiated within it, just as left has no meaning until paired with right? Even analyzing a poem into its constituent parts fails to disclose its particularity, because analysis is possible only if we are already able to recognize those parts and their functions. To do so requires that we rely on general structural principles, which specify the parts as parts in the first place. In this case, to specify does not mean to isolate what is unique in a poem but to draw from a repertoire of established practices. To analyze a sonnet into quatrains and tercets is to recognize it as a sonnet, and so to relate it to a conventional lyrical category.

If the imagined limit of the expansive critical view is a total literary universe where "one is part of everything," the limit of the contracting view is irreducible singularity—"the thing / Itself" apart from all else. Neither extreme is attainable, but the path to the first is more inviting than the path to the second. The first promises glory, the second threatens ruin. The first is accommodating, because it finds room for everything, whereas the latter founders on what George Oppen calls the "shipwreck / Of the singular":

> Obsessed, bewildered
>
> By the shipwreck
> Of the singular
>
> We have chosen the meaning
> Of being numerous.
>
>   (151)

Meaning is never really a matter of choice, since we cannot live without it, and it is always "numerous" in the sense that it is relational and participatory. To understand is to relate, and relations always proliferate. The challenge, therefore, is to renounce the numerous with its fantasy of totality in order to focus on singularity, even if it invites disaster.

Indeed, we seem to be offered a choice between too much or too little—either the disaster of unassimilable multiplicity or the shipwreck of singularity. Stevens succinctly calls the former a fecund "principle," the latter a chaste "particle" (*Palm* 215). Principle pushes the imagination to "a point / Beyond which thought could not progress as thought"; particle pulls it to "a point / Beyond which fact could not progress as fact" (229). Because each extreme leads Stevens's character, Canon Aspirin, to "nothingness," it is tempting to seek a common ground accommodating both. But accommodation is itself an activity of expansive critical intelligence, as it aspires to "the whole, / The complicate, the amassing harmony" (229). The challenge to imagine the singular remains.

According to Bloom, we treasure "something irreducible" in each poem, which is all the more precious for the enigmatic immediacy of its appeal. Even Frye, the great systematizer, agrees that criticism can only give knowledge *about* literature, which is quite different from actual literary experience felt on the pulse. The original pulsation has no voice of its own, because critical understanding

> is founded on a direct experience which is central to criticism yet forever excluded from it. Criticism can account for it only in critical terminology, and that terminology can never recapture or include the original experience. The original experience is like the direct vision of color, or the direct sensation of heat or cold, that physics "explains" in what, from the point of view of the experience itself, is a quite irrelevant way. However disciplined by taste and skill, the experience of literature is, like literature itself, unable to speak.
>
>   (*Anatomy* 27)

The dilemma of critical knowledge is captured in the oxymoron "aesthetic distance." Sensory or aesthetic experience is direct, not distanced. Criticism makes the immediate experience of art intelligible only by rendering it less and less immediate. It speaks about art by preventing it from speaking for itself. Theory establishes the general principles and preconditions from which literature arises, yet theory itself is belated, always trailing after "the direct experience of literature, where uniqueness is everything" (*Anatomy* 361). Generalizing on this dilemma, Jean-François Lyotard argues that philosophy can never comprehend the instantaneous "gesture" made enigmatically by art. Aesthetic presence is punctual, whereas philosophical understanding is postponed:

> The artist asks of us philosophers that we think the perceptible singularity that is presented here and now: a work or works that are here, now, in the singularity of their occurrence. But we should bear in mind that this possessive of occurrence is only reconstituted by memory after the fact.
>
> (75)

Because understanding lags behind the experience that it interprets retrospectively, it will always miss the singularity of its object. It will be baffled by a unique gesture that "no mode of thought is capable of thinking" directly, only of reconstituting in a displaced form:

> the fact that there is a gesture in space-time-matter, the fact that it *is* there and is a gesture—constitutes the impenetrability of the work for thought. It is precisely to the level of this enigma that the artist obligates the philosopher to place or displace his thought, and this is so whether the artist is aware of it or not. It is up to the philosopher, in the awareness of his debt, to know this for both himself and the artist.
>
> (75-76; Lyotard's emphasis)

How are we to acknowledge literary uniqueness, when any systematic explanation of it must rely on generalities?

In opposition to a critic like Frye, who enlarges his theoretical gaze to accommodate everything, is Paul de Man, who renounces such grandiose presumption by forcing poetic thought back toward particularity, knowing very well that it can never achieve its goal. Both critics undertake pilgrimages to the limit of thought, though in different directions, and both find their efforts thwarted by the very nature of literature, whose vitality springs from a uniqueness that theory can only dissipate. But whereas Frye patiently constructs a baroque system culminating in a glorious "anagogic" vision that compensates us for the original loss, de Man follows the opposite course. He devises an ascetic path leading to the expiry of meaning in singularity—the final finding that concerns no one at all. He agrees that literature

itself is unable to speak, but he respects its muteness by resisting the appeal of comprehension—the inclusiveness of critical thought. According to Tobin Siebers, "Generality is the hallmark of the kind of theory that de Man most opposes" (100) because he believes that "[p]hilosophical generality is the death of genuine self-knowledge" (120). He renounces comprehension because it is driven by a will to power through violent totalization. As a corrective, he stubbornly resists theory's philosophical tendency to convert the unique into the general by summoning the arsenal of rhetorical disfiguration and erasure associated with deconstruction. By these means he retraces the course of the particular almost to the point of nullification. Insofar as something is truly unique, it is unknowable and unsayable, because knowing and saying both rely on signification, which operates through equivalences: this for that, signifier for signified. The unique eludes the web of signification because it is not comparable or equivalent to anything else. It is solely itself; as soon as equivalence is found, uniqueness is lost. To propose any analogy or relationship, even contrast, which requires some commonality on which to distinguish the contrast, would be to forfeit "something irreducible" abiding in the aesthetic.

I begin, therefore, by offering Frye and de Man as opposing responses, each daring in its own way, to the need for criticism to respect aesthetic singularity even as it relies on theoretical generality. The word *accommodate* suggests what Frye welcomes and de Man repudiates: the spaciousness of thought. In the comprehensiveness of literary appreciation, Frye finds a sublimity that restores to literature the splendor of the innumerable, discrete poetic moments on which his grand system rests. For de Man, on the other hand, literature's value lies in its uncanny ability to dismantle all equivalences and renounce all compensations until we can almost imagine the uniqueness of being. Where Frye's critical vision culminates in the timeless copresence of all literature, de Man's confines itself to a random instant. The cost of this austere revelation is devastating, for we must accept, de Man concludes bleakly,

> that nothing, whether deed, word, thought or text, ever happens in relation, positive or negative, to anything that precedes, follows or exists elsewhere, but only as a random event whose power, like the power of death, is due to the randomness of its occurrence.
>
> (*Rhetoric* 122)

To Frye, this inchoate world of dislocated singularities would look like hell.

Its Single Emptiness

Given a choice between an all-encompassing totality and an all-excluding singularity, most literary theorists nowadays would probably choose neither. The present climate of opinion welcomes pluralities of all kinds—multicultural, heteroglossal, polysemic, interdisciplinary—but under two competing conditions. First, these pluralities must never be subsumed within a single overarching system; and second, they must never pretend to be autonomous. In exploring the rhetoric of singularity, then, I might seem to be backing the wrong horse. I am not eager to follow de Man's example, only to show that whether we grasp the specificity of a literary work by emulating his critical self-martyrdom, as Siebers calls it (117), or by thinking austerely with "a mind of winter," as Stevens advises in **"The Snow Man"** (*Palm* 54), we require some analogy to express a poetic individuality that precedes any analogy and will be falsified by it. Ironically, we require a double strategy to contemplate singularity. Because analogy invites us into a "fantasia" of correspondences that entice us to become "part of everything," we must first consider but then decline the invitation through a policy of denial, isolation, or annulment. In Stevens's terms, we must reject a principle in order to isolate a particle. Here are a few rhetorical tactics that allow us to particularize.

A simple but intriguing way of evoking singularity is through insistence, as in Gertrude Stein's refrain: "A rose is a rose is a rose." Each repetition narrows the focus, as one flower belonging to the large class of roses is finally distinguished as *this* rose and no other. In her lecture "Composition as Explanation," Stein explains (repeatedly) that repetition is her way of "groping for a continuous present" small yet capacious enough to include everything: "I naturally made a continuous present an including everything and a beginning again and again within a very small thing" (518-19). As her novel *The Making of Americans* mushroomed to a thousand pages, however, she realized that she could only cherish a thing's particularity by marking its difference from all other small things. Her singular style had to show not only that we always live in a present stuffed with innumerable details, but that the present is forever changing—"if it is all so alike it must be simply different and everything simply different was the natural way of creating it then" (519). At the limit of this contracting process she finds an enigma. As a single object like a rose is progressively isolated from everything else, it loses the commonality it shares, first with other flowers, then with other roses, until it stands solitary but indefinable even as a rose. It is not this flower or this rose but merely *this.*

The deictic *this* recalls the insistent gesture concluding Stevens's poem **"The Man on the Dump"**: "Where was it one first heard of the truth? The the" (*Palm* 164). This poem drastically shrinks its focus until it points not at the thing itself but at the verbal function (the definite article) through which things are specified. Here is an act of specifying without content. Another, less esoteric example of definition through insistence appears in Martin Amis's enthusiastic praise for Philip Roth: "There aren't supposed to be degrees or intensities of uniqueness, and yet Roth is somehow inordinately unique. He is bloodymindedly himself, himself, himself" (290). Amis makes a show of defying logic by placing Roth in a class by himself. If his peculiar style pervades his writing, then it is recognizable for being repeated, but that repetition is traced back to a unique source—presumably Roth's creative personality—which cannot be named, only circled relentlessly and marked out by that circling. These examples suggest that the rhetoric of singularity is positional and indicative; that is, it seeks ways of pointing from a distance at an untouchable source—the rose itself, the unique personality, the the.

Another gestural tactic is the hapaxlegomenon, a word that appears only once in a document or corpus, such as a neologism or unrecognizable word. Whereas Stevens resorts to the definite article, a word so common that it has no meaning of its own, other writers imagine words that can be used only once. In practice, a word that is truly unrepeated or unrepeatable would be incomprehensible. Iterability makes words both intelligible and ambiguous, because they can only be understood when they are used and shared, yet reiteration also makes them constantly change their meaning in new contexts. If they were never repeated, they might seem frozen at the moment of utterance, pure but without resonance. A. M. Klein uses the Hebrew form *millot bodedot* ("words alone," corresponding to "hapax legomena") to evoke this magical insularity:

> Isolated words. Lonesome words. They occur but once in the whole Torah, and are related to no other word. In English, or rather in Greek, they are called hapaxlegomena, words of single occurrence. Once, only once, do they appear in the Bible, and then are not heard from again.
>
> (*Notebooks* 131)

Even to cite a hapaxlegomenon is, perversely, to destroy it by using it a second time, thus converting it into common currency. Instead, Klein accords exclusive value to the word of single occurrence by identifying it with God's divine fiat—"let there be light"—a genesis that occurs only once. The poet imitates this creative moment by "uttering" a fictional world, and Klein's eloquent example from "A Portrait of the Poet as Landscape" illustrates how quickly the single utterance proliferates into a fantasia of correspondences:

> Look, he is
> the nth Adam taking a green inventory
> in world by scarcely uttered, naming praising,
> the flowering fiats in the meadow, the
> syllabled fur, stars aspirate, the pollen
> whose sweet collision sounds eternally.
>
> (*Poems* 638-39)

The hapaxlegomenon is performative—a self-creating word—but as Zailig Pollock shows in his commentary on Klein, it must also be self-destructive if it can be performed only once. There is a demonic parody of the hapaxlegomenon in the death sentence: the irrevocable word that hangs over us all and that, for Klein, finds its worst exclamation as a nuclear explosion or the Holocaust (Pollock 207-08).

Both genesis and death decree, the singular word is ascribed an uncanny power exerted at either the very beginning or the very end of things. Or more correctly, it offers a way of imagining how beginnings begin and where endings end. Because of its proximity to creation and destruction, it is too dangerous to touch. Anne Carson asks why neologisms should be so disturbing, and answers:

> If we cannot construe them at all, we call them mad. If we can construe them, they raise troubling questions about our own linguistic mastery. We say "coinages" because they disrupt the economic equilibrium of words and things that we had prided ourselves on maintaining. A new compound word in [Paul] Celan, for example, evokes something that now suddenly seems real, although it didn't exist before and is attainable through this word alone. It comes to us free, like a piece of new air. And (like praise) it has to prepare for itself an ear to hear it, just slightly before it arrives—has to invent its own necessity.

> (134)

A neologism has to prepare for its own coming; otherwise it cannot be received intelligibly at all. "Coinage" suggests a fresh minting of meaning, but the image is wonderfully inappropriate, since singularities are not commensurate with other things and therefore cannot be exchanged for them. Their value is not economic but inspirational, as Klein shows, Perhaps that is why both poets immediately associate the creative burst of language with praise, but also with irrationality.

The same is true of my third example, catachresis, which is the other side of the coin. If neologisms upset the equilibrium of words and things, and the hapaxlegomenon is a word without a thing, then catachresis is a thing without a word. Also known as *abusio,* it is a strained metaphor ("take up arms against a sea of troubles") but is also used to point at something with no proper name of its own. Common examples are *table leg, book leaf,* and *mother tongue.* Here again, the verbal economy is disrupted by an odd performance. In most metaphors one term is substituted for another, but there can be no substitution of a figurative word for a literal one if the literal one does not exist. Instead, we have what the witches in *Macbeth* ominously call "A deed without a name" (4.1.49). In the heyday of deconstruction, catachresis was regarded as the abusive rhetorical deed *par excellence.* Jacques Derrida treats it

as the way language strains between sense and reference (59-60); J. Hillis Miller sees it as a primal misnaming that lurks in all words (19-20); de Man calls it "[t]he trope which coins a name for the still-unnamed entity, which gives face to the faceless" ("Lyrical Voice" 57), and he warns:

> Something monstrous lurks in the most innocent of catachreses: when one speaks of the legs of the table or the face of the mountain, catachresis is already turning into prosopopeia [personification, literally "to give a face"], and one begins to perceive a world of potential ghosts and monsters.

> ("Epistemology" 19)

As Klein's Adamic poet illustrates, these metamorphoses quickly proliferate into a hallucinatory fantasia, but only after they have been invoked by an unnameable singularity that remains faceless and wordless. It is the power of speech that has not yet been spoken, the inhuman substratum of humanity to which de Man's analysis constantly leads him. In his wintry mood, Stevens annuls the creative fiat invoked by Klein by abjuring personification and relinquishing metaphor (even if he must do so metaphorically) in order to return to the instant before light emerges from the first sound:

> In this bleak air the broken stalks
> Have arms without hands. They have trunks
>
> Without legs or, for that, without heads.
> They have heads in which a captive cry
>
> Is merely the moving of a tongue.
> Snow sparkles like eyesight falling to earth,
>
> . . . . .
>
> It is in this solitude, a syllable,
> Out of these gawky flitterings,
>
> Intones its single emptiness,
> The savagest hollow of winter-sound
>
> (*Palm* 247-48)

Here is a deed without a name, a form without a shape, a word without a meaning. The poem's imagery pinpoints singularity at the convergence of light, sight, and sound by evoking a temporality in which the present is isolated in the precision of its immediacy. It focuses not on a rich, contemplative moment as in Marvell's "The Garden" or Milton's "Il Penseroso," and not on Stein's bulky continuous present, but on the here-and-now, which is always singular, always transient, and always different.

THE LAST ONSET

Right here, right now, Stevens says in **"Man Carrying Thing,"** "The bright obvious stand motionless in cold" (*Palm* 281), but the reality so brilliantly revealed stands only for an instant. In the rhetoric of the instantaneous, the bare present, which vanishes as we touch it, is more elusive than the past, which can be exhibited by memory, and more elusive than the future, which can be anticipated. Past and future join in the comfortable continuity of a "major reality"—an explanatory myth like Frye's—that poets entice us to enjoy but also warn us to resist whenever we retreat to the cold, solitary present. These rival dispositions again offer a rhythm of elevation and relapse in **"As You Leave the Room"**:

> Now, here, the snow I had forgotten becomes
>
> Part of a major reality, part of
> An appreciation of a reality
>
> And thus an elevation, as if I left
> With something I could touch, touch every way.
>
> And yet nothing has been changed except what is
> Unreal, as if nothing had been changed at all.
>
> (396)

A "major reality" seems fully tactile yet proves to be specious or "unreal." It is a lofty fantasy that appreciates in value under the aegis of imagination, but then must be depreciated imaginatively in its turn. In **"The Sail of Ulysses"** the "particular thought" is a "difficult inch," which is easily coaxed into "Plantagenet abstractions" and "stellar largenesses"; but Stevens warns that the poet must also resist the "law / that bends the particulars to the abstract" (392) in order to face the present in its strange momentariness. It is the barely imaginable reality that first provokes sensation and cognition. Time, sight, and thought converge in the image of light—one of Stevens's favorites—as in the common expression "to see things in a flash."

Singularity, sensed fleetingly as the brilliant intersection of time, being, and thought, finds more familiar expression in the modern fascination with photography, for instance in Roland Barthes's *Camera Lucida*. The click of a shutter and the illuminating flash mark the beginning of another double strategy whose goal is to reclaim the present:

> What the Photograph reproduces to infinity has occurred only once: the Photograph mechanically repeats what could never be repeated existentially. In the Photograph, the event is never transcended for the sake of something else: the Photograph always leads the corpus I need back to the body I see; it is the absolute Particular . . . the *This* . . . the Real, in its indefatigable expression.
>
> (4; Barthes's emphasis)

Here again is a preoccupation with first and last moments, with cognition and recognition, with first utterance and last breath. Barthes, too, imagines singularity as a mere "This," which he can only point to from a distance measured by the lapse between taking the

photograph and viewing it later. The creative instant is characterized by "contingency, singularity, risk" (20), which Barthes sums up nicely in the figure of "surprise" (32), a jolting discovery that lies "outside of meaning" (34) yet is the precondition for any subsequent understanding. The second, recuperative moment is characterized in various moods as interpretation, objectification (13), nostalgia, and justice (70), but also, since the past is gone forever, as melancholy, mourning (79), and catastrophe (96).

Modernist poetics, especially in its early formulation as imagism, also stresses the singularity of visual or tactile stimulus in conjunction with intuitive thought and spontaneous language. The best-known examples are Ezra Pound's definition of the poetic image as an emotional and intellectual complex released instantaneously (4) and T. E. Hulme's equating of meaning with sight and touch, in contrast to the tardiness of sound (77-78). A better example for my purposes is D. H. Lawrence's attempt to cast off tradition and aspiration (past and future) in order to formulate a poetry of the immediate present:

> But there is another kind of poetry: the poetry of that which is at hand: the immediate present. In the immediate present there is no perfection, no consummation, nothing finished. The strands are all flying, quivering, intermingling into the web, the waters are shaking the moon. . . . We look at the very white quick of nascent creation. A water-lily heaves herself from the flood, looks around, gleams, and is gone. We have seen the incarnation, the quick of the ever-swirling flood. We have seen the invisible. We have seen, we have touched, we have partaken of the very substance of creative change, creative mutation. . . . Give me the still, white seething, the incandescence and the coldness of the incarnate moment: the moment, the quick of all change and haste and opposition: the moment, the immediate present, the Now.
>
> (85-86)

For Lawrence, the present is at once the most palpable and the most intangible of states. He associates it with the quick of life, which he pictures as a creative spark that ignites change but cannot share in it, since it lives only in the instant of its passing. He condenses this paradox in the word "still," which ambiguously suggests both quietude and continuance, stasis and motion: "the still, white seething." Most revealing is the way his imagery links vitality to death (here the trope is as much romantic as it is modernist), because life is felt most intensely at the instant of its loss. Similarly Barthes identifies the ageless photograph with mourning, and de Man in a quotation above associates particularity with both random energy and "the power of death."

These examples suggest that the course of a particular comes into focus if we imagine it situated in a present that expires as soon as it occurs, and is only known when it haunts us afterwards. Dylan Thomas evokes such a moment in "A Refusal to Mourn the Death, by Fire, of a Child in London," a Second World War elegy that steadfastly refuses to lament a child's death in the Blitz and then concludes: "After the first death, there is no other" (192). Because we die only once, contemplating the instant when life ceases—a traditional, devotional exercise—can give ecstatic assurance of the uniqueness of our being, which is most precious at the moment of loss. Following his own double strategy, Thomas draws on religious imagery (Zion, synagogue, sackcloth, "stations of the breath") which he renounces in order to lament all the more strongly. He, too, evokes a comforting fantasia—the ceremonies of mourning, the solace of religion and the afterlife—only to reject their comforts through a series of oratorical denials stretching from the first word ("Never") to the last ("no other"). Some readers may interpret this poem as subtly (or not so subtly) reaffirming the religious faith that it makes a show of denying, as it mourns for the dead child by pretending not to. But we might also hold Thomas to his word: after the first death, there is no other.[3] De Man identifies lyric poetry with two mutually exclusive kinds of mourning. The more familiar is expressed in the lyrical impulse to establish a temporal harmony that humanizes death through a "pathos of terror": to mourn is to cling to the past and so to preserve it, however painfully, as ongoing testimony to the value of one's grief. The more stringent form of mourning offers no such comfort. It insists on looking death in the face by refusing even to personify a face:

> True "mourning" is less deluded. The most *it* can do is to allow for non-comprehension and enumerate non-anthropomorphic, non-elegiac, non-celebratory, non-lyrical, non-poetic, that is to say, prosaic, or, better, *historical* modes of language power.
>
> (*Rhetoric* 262; de Man's emphasis)[4]

As the parade of negations indicates, we are back in de Man's world of random events, which precede any historical continuity and resist being assimilated into it. Viewed in this way, Thomas's refusal to mourn is not a way of defying death or of triumphing over it but of submitting to its power by relinquishing past and future and renouncing even the pathetic continuity of bereavement. The death of a child thus portrays most poignantly what must be true of all people at any moment: all are unique, mortal, and therefore irreplaceable.

Dying may take a lifetime, but death is instantaneous. The desire to isolate the final second of life by filling it with all the significance that is about to vanish appears in proverbial notions such as prophesying with one's dying gasp, like John of Gaunt in Shakespeare's *Richard II*; or having one's life flash before one's eyes, as in Ambrose Bierce's story "An Occurrence at Owl Creek Bridge" and in A. M. Klein's poem "And in that drown-

ing instant," which condenses not only an individual life but the Jewish diaspora into its glimpse of a "preterite eternity" (*Poems* 609). Literature is full of fine death-bed scenes, and none more poignant than Bottom's theatrical death throes in *A Midsummer Night's Dream*:

> Thus die I, thus, thus, thus.
>   Now am I dead,
>   Now am I fled;
> My soul is in the sky.
>   Tongue, lose thy light;
>   Moon, take thy flight.
> Now die, die, die, die, die.
>
> (5.1.295-302)

The joke is that the last moment goes on and on and on, yet when the noblemen scoff,

> Demetrius: No die, but an ace, for him; for he is but one.
>
> Lysander: Less than an ace, man; for he is dead, he is nothing.
>
> (5.1.303-304)

they illustrate how death is painful proof of a uniqueness that language strains to express. Through their wordplay, dying becomes gambling—a bet that we all lose—and singularity (the ace, or single spot on the die) is proclaimed only as it is nullified.

Compare this bombastic display of mortal singularity with three other examples. The first concludes Tolstoy's "The Death of Ivan Ilych," when Ivan's prolonged suffering grants a charitable insight that ultimately redeems him from the futility of his life. As he feels his son kissing his hand, he is surprised by a joyful intuition, which is expressed as falling, as light, as release from pain, and as the euphoric temporality of dying:

> There was light instead of death.
>
> "So that is it!" he suddenly said out loud. "What happiness!"
>
> All of this took place in an instant, but the significance of that instant was lasting. For those present his agony continued for another two hours. Something rattled in his throat, his emaciated body twitched. But gradually the wheezing and the rattling ceased.
>
> (283)

A similar pattern appears more ironically in Yuri Olesha's story "Lyompa," which again entices the reader toward the unimaginable, in this case by inventing the odd word that serves as the title. Critically ill, Ponomarev turns away from all the bubbling, snorting sounds that animate his house. In contrast to a young child, whose world is expanding explosively as he discovers a bewildering fertility of things that he cannot name, Ponomarev feels reality contracting:

First, the number of things on the periphery, far away from him, decreased; then this depletion drew closer to the center, reaching deeper and deeper, toward the courtyard, the house, the corridor, the room, his heart. . . . Death was destroying things on its way to him. Death had left him only a few things, from an infinite number. . . . The vanishing things left the dying man nothing but their names.

(142, 144)

Fading into abstraction, he is left with a lone, absurd hapaxlegomenon, which he associates with a noisy rat in the kitchen:

He knew that at any cost he must stop thinking about the rat's name. But he kept searching for it, knowing that as soon as he found that meaningless, horrifying name, he would die.

"Lyompa!" he suddenly shouted in a terrifying voice.

(145)

The word is all the more frightening for naming the unnameable. My third example is Emily Dickinson's poem "I heard a Fly buzz—when I died" (223-24), in which light, sight, and sound again converge at the moment of death. The speaker patiently awaits "the last Onset" (death as oxymoron), wills her "Keepsakes," and finally concentrates on the "uncertain stumbling Buzz" of a fly. Like Olesha's rat, it becomes the focal point of her expiring life, its tiny furious energy revealing all that she is about to lose. Instead of wordplay or neologism, Dickinson ingeniously contrives a reflexive doubling that turns insight into blindness, as if a word could be in oxymoronic relation to itself:

And then the Windows failed—and then
I could not see to see—

I noted that the rhetoric of singularity is positional: it points from a distance at an untouchable source. In these last examples, the configuration fixes on a contracting point—the dead center—where the powers of speech and vision are confounded at the moment of revelation. This pattern is familiar in mysticism, but it is also a formation that Elaine Scarry ascribes to the perception of pain. Although aesthetic experience is usually associated with pleasure—or with the vicarious pleasures of tragic, pathetic, or sentimental pain—pain demonstrates even more forcefully the severe concentration of particularity. Pain concentrates the present moment with the severity of its command; or as Pascal said with epigrammatic polish: "The present usually hurts. . . . it afflicts us" (39, my translation). In Scarry's account, as the world contracts for the torture victim (32-33), the self is first isolated and then dissolved (47), until the "absolute privacy" of its suffering becomes confused with utter self-exposure (53). An experience of pure interiority deepens until it is suddenly externalized. Pain, she argues, is the one somatic state that has no object in the external world:

desire is desire of x, fear is fear of y, hunger is hunger for z; but pain is not "of" or "for" anything—it is itself alone. This objectlessness, the complete absence of referential content, almost prevents it from being rendered in language.

(162)

For this very reason, however, it incites an imaginative fantasia—a "dense sea of artefacts and symbols" (162)—that never suffices to render the uniqueness of the experience, and therefore circles it restlessly. The name Lyompa is such a symbol-without-reference, while Dickinson's self-nullifying phrase, "I could not see to see" evokes such an experience-without-object. Scarry's analysis of this phenomenological pattern explains why intense physicality so readily finds expression as intense spirituality. It also illuminates Stevens's oracular decree that the course of a particular gradually excludes all others until it "concerns no one at all." The absolute privacy of pain obliterates everything but the self, suffering here and now; then the strange singularity of death obliterates even the self. We experience the pain of dying, but how do we experience our death?

The Supreme Dignity of the Unique

A religious response to the above discussion would see the course of a particular as a moral path leading to God. "One is one and all alone and ever more shall be so," sings the refrain of an English folksong celebrating the original singularity, and the singular originality, of the divine source of life.[5] Alexis de Tocqueville speculates that God alone does not require general ideas because "[a]t a single glance he sees separately all of the beings of which humanity is composed" (411). Because the human mind cannot encompass such bewildering variety, it must reduce "the immensity of detail" to inexact generalities:

General ideas do not attest to the strength of human intelligence, but rather to its insufficiency, because there are no beings in nature exactly alike: no identical facts, no rules indiscriminately applicable in the same manner to several objects at once.

General ideas . . . never provide it with anything but incomplete notions, and they always make it lose in exactness what they give it in extent.

(411)

A religious sensibility must acknowledge the precious uniqueness of each soul, a uniqueness expressed, for instance, in Egyptian mythology where the god Anubis weighs souls after death but never finds two with exactly the same weight.[6] At the beginning of this essay I wondered what moral footing might be offered by an aesthetic insight that, in Stevens's words, grows "less and less human" (**Palm** 264) until it "concerns no one at all." Through its very exclusiveness the rhetoric of singularity poses an ethical challenge, since in each of my examples the unique moment of sensory impact, of illumination, of the here-and-now, of pain and death, is simultaneously a moment of moral awakening and its frustration. Ethical conduct depends on the *duality* arising from a practical, principled confrontation between oneself and another person for whom one is responsible or to whom one is answerable. Each example discloses personal responsibility—what one owes to others (Tolstoy, Thomas, Klein), to the social and physical world (Olesha, Stein, Lawrence), or even to oneself (Dickinson)—but it does so just as one's power to exercise that responsibility is lost. The unique moment vanishes just as its demand is felt, its loss only heightening the perplexity of the obligation. In Kant's famous formulation, "ought implies can": we can be morally obligated to perform only actions that are within our power. To be obliged to perform an impossible or unknowable act is meaningless, because "duty commands nothing but what we can do" (Kant qtd. in Stern).[7]

The paradox of literary singularity, which is impenetrable to the critical understanding that explicates it, thus corresponds to a comparable ethical dilemma. Ethical insights, like aesthetic ones, become intelligible only within a larger system framed by general principles and rules, but that very generality dispels the uniqueness of the insight and the urgency of its call. Individually what we encounter is not duty as an abstract principle but *my* need to act here and now. The ethical imperative occurs instantaneously; only later can we assess its wider implications. Zygmunt Bauman explains the dilemma as a contrast between duty and responsibility:

> Only rules can be universal. One may legislate universal rule-dictated *duties,* but moral *responsibility* exists solely in interpellating the individual and being carried individually. Duties tend to make humans alike; responsibility is what makes them into individuals. Humanity is not captured in common denominators—it sinks and vanishes there. The morality of the moral subject does not, therefore, have the character of a rule. One may say that the moral is what *resists* codification, formalization, socialization, universalization.
>
> (54; Bauman's emphasis)

Like de Tocqueville, Bauman sees generality as an enabling limitation of human thought that conflicts with the particularizing imperative of ethical being. What I called the expansive critical view, which sees literature as one vast system, finds a partner in the Kantian ethical tradition, with its categorical imperative that submits every personal decision to the stringent test of universality: "What we call good must be an object of desire in the judgment of every rational man, and evil an object of aversion in the eyes of everyone" (Kant, *Practical* 80). Far from concerning "no one at all," desire for the good requires that "one is part of everything."[8] For

Kant, the test of both aesthetic and moral judgments is universality. The paradox of aesthetic experience is summed up in the notion of taste, understood as a subjective universal. As the metaphor of sensory taste implies, aesthetic experience is purely subjective, a pleasurable feeling, yet it is also disinterested, without ulterior purpose, and universal—a "necessary delight" enjoyed by all who share the same "common sense" (Boos 20).[9] We can distinguish "good" and "bad" taste concerning the beautiful only within a community of shared responses, a community whose standards Kant treats as universal. Similarly, ethics is rooted in our "sensible nature" (Kant, *Practical* 80) with its urgent demands of the moment. The good, like the beautiful, is commanding: it imposes itself directly; it is thrilling. Nevertheless, morality is intelligible only as a social discipline based on general rules impartially applied. Ethical encounters transpire through the interplay between personal will and social law (81), between discrete experience and universal rule. However, their interplay is asymmetrical rather than harmonious. Slavish conformity to the rule obscures the justice of individual cases; excessive insistence on peculiarity (the exception to the rule) threatens the law's authority. There is always a tug-of-war between generality and specificity.

In this contest, Kant ensures that the general always commands the specific: rational law must be the a priori determination of the particular will. However, maintaining this deductive pattern requires what he calls a "paradox of method": *"The concept of good and evil must not be determined before the moral law (of which it seems as if it must be the foundation), but only after it and by means of it"* (82; Kant's emphasis). Rules are not framed in accordance with what is good; rather, the general law precedes the discrete experiences from which it seems to arise: "it is the moral law that first determines the concept of good, and makes it possible, so far as it deserves the name of good absolutely" (83). Modern theory tends to twist this paradox in the other direction by asserting the priority of the particular over the general, as is illustrated by a comment from Ludwig Wittgenstein's notebook: "ethics presupposes the *uniqueness* of life" (qtd. in Greisch 74). "Presupposes" suggests that the uniqueness of the moral agent comes first as the precondition of moral generalities, which then follow inductively. Responsibility precedes duty; or in Fabio Ciaramelli's words,

> Ethical obligation arises not from the logical and ontological universality of reason which discloses to knowledge criteria for freely determined action, but rather immediately from the uniqueness of the moral situation itself. . . . moral obligation takes hold immediately, before understanding or decision on the part of the subject.
>
> (85)

The philosopher who argues most passionately and enigmatically on behalf of ethical singularity is Emmanuel Levinas.

From Levinas's richly opaque writing, I wish to stress only how he offers the novelty of the self as an enigmatic point of departure for all ethical encounters—as a radical singularity that permits duality yet remains aloof from it. He begins with a customary clearing of the rhetorical ground. The singular self ("ipseity") is not displayed in essential qualities: it is not a "distinguishing characteristic, a *unicum* or a *hapax,* like fingerprints"; it is not an ego, agent, consciousness, or "individuated quiddity resulting from any incomparable quality inherent in the body or character, or the unicity of a natural or historical conjuncture" (*Basic* 84). Ethics begins before any of these have been formulated with the summoning of "an indefeasible unity." The precious uniqueness of each soul is marked not just when it expires at death, but when it is startled into moral being. This is the first onset: the instant when "the essential, primary and fundamental structure of subjectivity" (*Ethics* 95) is constituted through an "assignation" between two solitary selves who realize themselves only through that encounter. "The ego is an incomparable unicity" (*Basic* 114) that must be "troubled" from its passivity into moral, intellectual, and social consciousness. This occurs when the "uniqueness of the I" (55) confronts the "nameless singularity" (85) of the "face" of the Other:

> Before the neighbor I am summoned and do not just appear; from the first I am answering to an assignation. Already the stony core of my substance is dislodged. But the responsibility to which I am exposed in such a passivity does not apprehend me as an interchangeable thing, for here no one can be substituted for me; in calling upon me as someone accused who cannot reject the accusation, it obliges me as someone unreplaceable and unique, someone chosen. Inasmuch as it calls upon my responsibility it forbids me any replacement.
>
> (143)

"[T]he I qua I is absolutely unique" (28), but it only asserts its uniqueness when summoned to responsibility by another "pure individual" (7).

Like de Man, Levinas wants to imagine the disconnected particularities of being before they are rendered intelligible by "the labor of thinking" (*Basic* 153), which then disposes them into general categories. The moral moment precedes thought and therefore cannot be thought ("thematized"). Its irreducible specificity is prior to all the systems of definition that I listed earlier (analogy, category, causality, etc.), and according to Levinas, it even precedes the fundamental structure of symbolic exchange that makes linguistic signification possible. It is therefore unspeakable and unknowable (85), although it provides the primary unit from which

speech and knowledge will arise. Happily, where this anarchic state made de Man think only of death, it makes Levinas think of life:

> This is the bursting forth of incessant novelty. The absolute novelty of the new. This is the spirituality of transcendence, which does not amount to an assimilating act of consciousness. The uninterrupted bursting forth of novelties would make sense, precisely beyond knowledge, through its absolute and unforeseeable novelty.
>
> (155)

Stevens imagines the original cry of life as a wintry genesis: a syllable that intones its single emptiness. For Levinas, however, it is "a cry of ethical revolt, bearing witness to responsibility" (147) as it sounds the first moral injunction: "The first word of the face is the 'Thou shalt not kill.' It is an order. There is a commandment in the appearance of the face, as if a master spoke to me" (*Ethics* 89).[10] The moment when moral power is summoned is also the moment when it is restrained in view of "the supreme dignity of the unique" (101).

In this dramatic account, genesis (emergence of selfhood), mortality (awareness that one could kill the Other) and responsibility (altruism) are all revealed instantaneously. What poet could achieve more? Ethics and aesthetics again exhibit the same structure, but now a specific obligation or artistic response is not subsumed within general rules or aesthetic forms; instead, the particular stubbornly resists the generality to which it contributes. This asymmetrical relationship appears in one of Levinas's phrases, "Nous n'est pas le pluriel de Je" (qtd. in Bauman 48)—the solitary I is not absorbed by a collective we. And he expresses this paradox not as poverty but as excess. In contrast to de Man's ascetic withdrawal is Levinas's prophetic affirmation of responsibility as startling, commanding, overwhelming, transcendent. Precisely because the atomic I precedes any rational, social, or psychological articulation of its character, when summoned into proximity with the Other it is awed by the transcendence of limitless responsibility: "I am responsible for a total responsibility, which answers for all the others and for all in the others, even for their responsibility. The I always has one responsibility more than all the others" (*Ethics* 99). In defiance of fairness, adequation, harmony—of any rational judgment—he invokes "[t]his surplus of being, this existential exaggeration that is called *being me*" (*Basic* 17).

"For Levinas, the ethical shows itself as the prophetical" (Ciaramelli 92). If we look to literature for prophetic moments when singularity encounters its own excess, we find them most readily in romance and in the sublime. We are back in Northrop Frye's territory.

Frye treats romance as a transgressive genre that foresees not a return to the stability of family, duty, and political order but revolutionary transformation. It exhibits not the circularity of comic restoration but a spiral of creative revelations. Comedy offers restitution; romance promises deliverance. Comedy offers justice by granting characters what they deserve; romance grants more than they deserve. Frye finds a remarkable expression of redemptive singularity in the romantic motif of the threat to virginity, often accompanied by risk of torture or sacrifice (*Secular* 80). While these threats obviously express patriarchal conventions of male dominance and female modesty, for Frye they also point to "a vision of human integrity" menaced by

> the one fate which really is worse than death, the annihilation of one's identity. . . . What is symbolized as a virgin is actually a human conviction, however expressed, that there is something at the core of one's infinitely fragile being which is not only immortal but has discovered the secret of invulnerability that eludes the tragic hero.
>
> (86)

Romances are about the loss and recovery of identity, but that unique core of being cannot really be described. Identity feels all the more fragile when it is threatened, yet it is "a state of existence in which there is nothing to write about," a state that romances gesture at from a distance by invoking an earlier ("once upon a time") and a later ("they lived happily every after") time beyond record (*Secular* 54). In the meantime, where all stories occur, what protects the "beleaguered virgin" or faithful wife (or heals her if she is sacrificed) is not so much the intrepid male hero as "a certain redemptive quality" (87) inherent in her patient, untouchable singularity." Virginity cannot be touched or "known" either conceptually or physically, since what is touched is not virginity but only its apparent loss. "[W]hat is objectively untouched symbolizes what is subjectively contained," Frye states quaintly of a wonderfully fertile purity, a virginity that is "perpetually renewed . . . in a world where every experience is fresh and unique" (153). This, too, may be a male fantasy, but it also expresses an energy that perpetually animates the novelty of an innocent world. Working within the conventions of romance, it "emphasizes the uniqueness, the once-for-all quality, in the creative act" (184). Or in Stevens's words, it marks "an immaculate beginning" (*Palm* 209).

The final scene in Shakespeare's *The Winter's Tale*, where the faithful wife Hermione apparently is resurrected, can be seen as an example of aesthetic and ethical creativity corresponding to Levinas's notion of ethical awakening. After the first death—Hermione's patient 16 years in hiding, which enacts a kind of chastity—there is a magical rebirth through the recreation of life

through art: the statue comes to life to the sound of music. Her resurrection is a gift in excess of the occasion. Just as the earlier sacrifice of Leontes's innocent son Mamillius is far worse than justice demands, his wife's return to life is far better than any reward commensurate with his expiation of his sins. Remorse cannot reanimate the dead. Nor does the found daughter Perdita replace the lost Mamillius, since no unique self is equivalent to any other self. When Levinas speaks of the self as "hostage," he is not referring to a fair substitution of one for the other but to an "involuntary election" (*Basic* 121-22). Similarly, the final moment in *The Winter's Tale* points to a power beyond moral calculation—a blessing. With startling simplicity Leontes's words, "O, she's warm" (5.3.109), evoke the shock of aesthetic and moral insight, the sudden gesture whereby a scene that in realistic terms would be absurd becomes enchanting.

Finding moments of transcendent particularity in Stevens's poetry is tricky, because for all his love of "transport"—the triumph of delight over bare fact—he expresses his triumphs ambiguously or achieves only a "satisfaction" of reason or imagination (*Necessary Angel* 42). To be satisfied is to find enough (Latin: *satis*), not to pursue excess. Whereas Levinas prophetically announces "[t]his growing surplus of the infinite that we have ventured to call *glory*" (*Basic* 144), Stevens is more diffident. In **"Sailing After Lunch"** he foresees only a "slight transcendence to the dirty sail" (*Palm* 112) of his craft; in **"Extracts from Addresses to the Academy of Fine Ideas"** he proposes that the world's familiar climate is enough:

> There is nothing more and that it is enough
> To believe in the weather and in the things and men
> Of the weather and in one's self, as part of that
> And nothing more.
>
> (183)

And in **"Final Soliloquy of the Interior Paramour"** he concludes modestly:

> Out of this same light, out of the central mind,
> We make a dwelling in the evening air,
> In which being there together is enough.
>
> (368)

Only "together" hints that the unique self is not self-sufficient but must probe beyond limits. The same hesitancy appears in section 7 of **"The Man with the Blue Guitar,"** which first proclaims, "The blue guitar / And I are one," but later asks if one can ever remain all alone:

> I know that timid breathing. Where
> Do I begin and end? And where,
>
> As I strum the thing, do I pick up
> That which momentously declares

Itself not to be I and yet
Must be. It could be nothing else.

(139)

The haunting phrase "that timid breathing" recalls the first hint (and last gasp) of life in *The Winter's Tale,* but as it leads to a "momentous" (momentary, crucial, imperative) assignation with an Other, Stevens seems wary of venturing too far, as if the glory might fade if affirmed too romantically.

One can twist Stevens into any convenient shape—Emersonian, Nietzschean, Santayanian, Derridean, etc.[12]—and I would like to avoid contriving a clumsy application of Levinas's ideas to the poetry. Instead, we should hope for a coincidence of mood, image, or situation, since Levinas delineates his drama of solitude, summons, and transcendence in such lyrical terms. The two dispositions with which I began this essay can lead Stevens, on the one hand, to an omnivorous imagination that consumes whatever it surveys; and on the other hand, to a dense solipsism that recognizes the Other only as a stunted expression of oneself. The former appears in **"Anecdote of the Jar"** (*Palm* 46), where the artifact placed on a hill in Tennessee composes the landscape (just as "Tennessee" and the "anecdote" are themselves compositions) by taking dominion over it.[13] The latter appears in images of confinement or monotony. His provocative question, "Where / Do I begin and end?" is often posed in such a way as to leave the reader uncertain how to proceed. Nevertheless, in his essay "The Figure of the Poet as Virile Youth," when Stevens asks only for "satisfaction" of reason or imagination, he promptly suggests that "an idea of God" just might satisfy both and so would provide "a sanction for life" (*Necessary Angel* 42-43). His coy understatement ("This is an illustration") cannot disguise the enormity of his intimation: such a sanction (blessing) would "momentously" exceed any egotism. Similarly, **"Academic Discourse at Havana"** begins skeptically by restraining the lusty imagination with its promise of glory ("perfect plenitude," "ornatest prophecy"), but through the chastening of thought it raises a hope that poetry still might achieve "An infinite incantation of our selves" (*Palm* 87-89).

"Credences of Summer" (287-92) offers a final illustration of how aesthetic particularity can be troubled into opening an avenue to ethical insight. Here is a modest example of Klein's Adamic poet discovering the world, but its peaceful evocation of summer is upset by anxieties expressed in oxymorons and paradoxes. Instead of being frozen in a wintry present, the poem is poised at "the axis of everything" between "spring's infuriations" and "the first autumnal inhalations." Its celebration of ripeness ("green's green apogee") is an odd occasion to look for the virginity of the particular, yet the season is so fruitful that it reveals an "essential

barrenness": "This is the barrenness / Of the fertile thing that can attain no more." If the instant of death marks the summation of life, then this moment of completion "[b]eyond which there is nothing left of time" is the summation of the year. Stevens stresses the uniqueness of the present and of the perspective that it affords by isolating the here and now. "Now" the poem begins, here at "[o]ne of the limits of reality," the landscape's festival of light, sight, and sound pinpoints attention on "the very thing and nothing else . . . [w]ithout evasion by a single metaphor." (Levinas notes that the "oneself" lives "without metaphor, which palpitates" [*Basic* 84]). Here and now "[i]t comes to this"—the unassigned demonstrative pronoun marking a particularity without defining it—"and we accept what is / As good. The utmost must be good and is."

To find sensory and contemplative joy in a summer day is necessarily to appeal beyond oneself to the earth and its vital gifts. "Dear life redeems you," proclaims Paulina in *The Winter's Tale* (5.3.103), and Stevens's speaker claims more modestly to be "appeased" by the generous scene. While Frank Kermode feels that the subject of **"Credences"** is "total satisfaction" (106), most readers have been less convinced (Jarraway 225). The limit of reality should be a place where belief (credence) is justified and desire is fulfilled ("Exile desire / For what is not"), but by section 5 the rhythm grows restless as the speaker wonders about the goodness that he has just argued himself into affirming. Some dissatisfaction turns his meditation into what Charles Berger calls the "dark countersong" of a "countersublime" (83, 86), as it questions the relation between "concentred self" and Other, between particular and general. Does the valiant particular dominate generality ("One day enriches a year") as the jar claimed—both heroically and absurdly—to dominate Tennessee; or does a defining generality ennoble all its particulars ("Or do the other days enrich the one")? Where do I begin and end?

The beginning is the "rock" (section 6)—unique, "extreme," elemental, conveying no secret meaning ("hermit's truth") beyond its bare existence "on this present ground." The end is more difficult to foresee, because Stevens persists in renouncing the traditional solaces of romance or the egotistical sublime (section 7). As he explains of a similar situation in **"Angel Surrounded by Paysans"**: "the point of the poem is that there must be in the world about us things that solace us quite as fully as any heavenly visitations could" (*Letters* 661). The visitations in **"Credences"** arrive with the awakening call of the trumpet (section 8) and cock (section 9), which can be compared to Levinas's "cry of ethical revolt, bearing witness to responsibility" (*Basic* 147), at least in the sense that they herald a challenge from the world beyond the self that forever implicates the self. For Levinas, too, ethics is an "awakening" that "designates the improbable field where the Infinite is in relationship with the finite without contradicting itself by this relationship. . . . The Infinite transcends itself in the finite" (*Basic* 146). Stevens would agree with the last sentence. His trumpet does not herald the resurrection of the dead, only of the summer with its virginal fertility. The "resounding cry" urges us to "share the day." It not only startles the mind into awareness of its own precious existence, but makes it "aware of division . . . [a]s that of a personage in a multitude." Commenting on these lines, Justin Quinn argues that Stevens's specific landscape in Olney, Pennsylvania, is "already woven through with social meaning by the generations of the people who have lived here" (119), and therefore the "multitude" refers not to abstract humanity but to a local community "with its ceremonies, family ties, and transmission of cultural and ethical values" (118). The scene draws the speaker into its intimacy. The cock, too, is a "civil bird" that momentously makes "a sound / Which is not part of the listener's own sense," and which urges him to speak his part in "[t]he huge decorum, the manner of the time, / Part of the mottled mood of summer's whole." What the self earns here is not dominance but dignity.

Notes

1. There is little moral advantage in Joseph Carroll's summation of "The Course of a Particular":

   In the absence of fantasia, these two aspects of particularity, the self and the world, are equivalent in their meaninglessness. Stevens repudiates essential unity, but he does not then revert to a celebration of the parts of the world. The failure of transcendental effect leaves him at the nadir of the cycle from Romanticism to indifferentism.

   (306)

2. This is the effort of Frye's whole career as a critic, not just of a single work, but *Anatomy of Criticism* presents his widest view of literature.

3. Other readings of this poem note allusions to Revelations 2.11: "He that hath an ear, let him hear what the Spirit saith unto the churches; He that overcometh shall not be hurt of the second death" and to Revelations 20.6: "Blessed and holy is he that hath part in the first resurrection: on such the second death hath no power, but they shall be priests of God and of Christ, and shall reign with him a thousand years."

4. De Man's use of *"historical"* is deliberately provocative, since he is not appealing to a historical explanation but to the rhetorical ground of historical narratives: "One would then have to conceive of a rhetoric of history prior to attempting a history of rhetoric or of literature or of literary criticism. Rhetoric, however, is not in itself an historical but an epistemological discipline" ("Epistemology" 28)

5. "Green Grow the Rushes O" is a song with a pagan version (http://www.paganlibrary.com/music_poetry/green_grow_rushes.php) and a Christian version (http://www.know-britain.com/songs/green_grow_the_rushes-o.html), both celebrating the divine source of life and revealing in its multiplying power.

6. I owe this point to Philippe Beaussant: "c'est Anubis qui pèse les âmes de l'autre côté de la mort et n'en trouve pas deux qui aient le même poids" (259-60).

7. Stern collects and analyzes 11 instances where Kant expresses this principle.

8. Ciaramelli explains:

   The ethical project, then, is to submit freedom of will to the rule of rationality in the attempt to find criteria for human action that are universally intelligible and valid for everyone. In this way, particular human situations are subsumed under a general and universal order from which they receive their meaning.

   (84)

9. Kant writes:

   Consequently the judgment of taste, accompanied with the consciousness of separation from all interest, must claim validity for every man, without this universality depending on objects. That is, there must be bound up with it a title to subjective universality.

   (*Judgment* 46)

   Stephen Boos explains subjective universality as follows:

   A judgment of taste is . . . not a logical judgment but an aesthetic one, by which Kant means a judgment whose basis is subjective. On the other hand, an aesthetic judgment is not simply a matter of the agreeable, since it makes a claim to universality. When I claim that x is beautiful, I am not simply claiming that *I* feel that it is beautiful but making a claim that is valid for others as well. . . . When we judge an object as beautiful rather than merely pleasant, one judges not only for oneself but for everyone else, that is, one judges with a universal voice, yet one does so without a concept, that is, without a category of the Understanding. To make this demand is to presuppose that the taste and feeling by which we make the judgment is common to everyone and hence implies a *sensus communis,* a "common sense."

   (19-20)

10. Leonard Grob explains the first moral cry as follows:

    Before the totality is rent by the manifestation of the face, there can be no will to act *immorally,* as there can be no will to act *morally,* in any ultimate sense of that word. . . . Morality makes its first appearance when I confront the Other who is truly Other.

    Although the Other appears to me now, on principle, as someone I could wish to kill, he or she *in fact* summons me to respond with nonviolence: I am called to willingly renounce my power to act immorally. What I hear from the Other, Levinas claims, are the words "Thou shalt not kill." Harkening to this injunction constitutes my inaugural act as an ethical being.

(8-9; Grob's emphasis)

11. Frye briefly extends his discussion of virginity to include men in *Words with Power,* p. 195.

12. An Emersonian Stevens: Harold Bloom's *Wallace Stevens*; Nietzschean: B. J. Leggett's *Early Stevens*; Santayanian: Joseph N. Riddel's *The Clairvoyant Eye*; Derridean: J. Hillis Miller's "Stevens's Rock and Criticism as Cure," parts 1 and 2.

13. Even here Joseph N. Riddel finds ambiguity and excess as "the imagination's forms invariably leave something out of account" (44).

Works Cited

Amis, Martin. *The War Against Cliché: Essays and Reviews 1971-2000.* New York: Vintage, 2001.

Barthes, Roland. *Camera Lucida: Reflections on Photography.* Trans. Richard Howard. New York: Hill, 1981.

Bauman, Zygmunt. *Postmodern Ethics.* Oxford: Polity, 1993.

Beaussant, Philippe. *Stradella.* Paris, Gallimard, 1999.

Berger, Charles. *Forms of Farewell: The Late Poetry of Wallace Stevens.* Madison: U of Wisconsin P, 1985.

Bloom, Harold. *Wallace Stevens: The Poems of Our Climate.* Ithaca: Cornell UP, 1976.

———. *The Western Canon.* New York: Riverhead, 1995.

Boos, Stephen. "Rethinking the Aesthetic: Kant, Schiller, and Hegel." *Between Ethics and Aesthetics: Crossing the Boundaries.* Ed. Dorota Blowacka and Stephen Boos. Albany: State U of New York P, 2002. 15-27.

Carroll, Joseph. *Wallace Stevens's Supreme Fiction: A New Romanticism.* Baton Rouge: Louisiana State UP, 1987.

Carson, Anne. *Economy of the Unlost (Reading Simonides of Keos with Paul Celan).* Princeton: Princeton UP, 1999.

Ciaramelli, Fabio. "Levinas's Ethical Discourse between Individuation and Universality." *Re-Reading Levinas.* Trans. Simon Critchley. Ed. Robert Bernasconi and Simon Critchley. Bloomington: Indiana UP, 1991. 84-105.

De Man, Paul. "The Epistemology of Metaphor." *On Metaphor.* Ed. Sheldon Sacks. Chicago: U of Chicago P, 1979. 11-28.

———. "Lyrical Voice in Contemporary Theory: Riffaterre and Jauss." *Lyric Poetry: Beyond New Criticism.* Ed. Chaviva Hosek and Patricia Parker. Ithaca: Cornell UP, 1985. 55-72.

———. *The Rhetoric of Romanticism.* New York: Columbia UP, 1984.

Derrida, Jacques. "White Mythology." Trans. F. C. T. Moore. *New Literary History* 6 (Autumn 1974): 5-74.

Dickinson, Emily. *The Complete Poems of Emily Dickinson.* Ed. Thomas H. Johnson. Boston: Little, 1961.

Eliot. T. S. *Selected Prose of T. S. Eliot.* Ed. Frank Kermode. London: Faber, 1975.

Frye, Northrop. *Anatomy of Criticism.* New York: Atheneum, 1966.

———. *The Secular Scripture: A Study of the Structure of Romance.* Cambridge: Harvard UP, 1976.

———. *Words with Power: Being a Second Study of the Bible and Literature.* Toronto: Penguin, 1990.

Greisch, Jean. "The Face and Reading: Immediacy and Mediation." *Re-Reading Levinas.* Trans. Simon Critchley. Ed. Robert Bernasconi and Simon Critchley. Bloomington: Indiana UP, 1991. 67-82.

Grob, Leonard. "Emmanuel Levinas and the Primacy of Ethics in Post-Holocaust Philosophy." *Ethics After the Holocaust: Perspectives, Critiques, and Reponses.* Ed. John K. Roth. St. Paul: Paragon, 1999. 1-14.

Hulme, T. E. *Further Speculations.* Ed. Sam Hynes. Minneapolis: U of Minnesota P, 1955.

Jarraway, David R. *Wallace Stevens and the Question of Belief: Metaphysician in the Dark.* Baton Rouge: Louisiana State UP, 1993.

Kant, Immanuel. *Critique of Judgment.* Trans J. H. Bernard. New York: Hafner, 1951.

———. *Critique of Practical Reason.* Trans. T. K. Abbott. Amherst: Prometheus, 1996.

Kermode, Frank. *Wallace Stevens.* New York: Chip's, 1960.

Klein, A. M. *Complete Poems: Part 2.* Ed. Zailig Pollock. Toronto: U of Toronto P, 1990.

———. *Notebooks: Selections from the A. M. Klein Papers.* Ed. Zailig Pollock and Usher Caplan. Toronto: U of Toronto P, 1994.

Lawrence, D. H. "Introduction to *New Poems.*" *D. H. Lawrence: Selected Literary Criticism.* Ed. Anthony Beal. New York: Viking, 1966. 84-89.

Leggett, B. J. *Early Stevens: The Nietzschean Intertext.* Durham: Duke UP, 1992.

Levinas, Emmanuel. *Emmanuel Levinas: Basic Philosophical Writings*. Ed. Adriaan T. Peperzak, Simon Critchley, and Robert Bernasconi. Bloomington: Indiana UP, 1996.

———. *Ethics and Infinity: Conversations with Philippe Nemo*. Trans. Richard A. Cohen. Pittsburgh: Duquesne UP, 1985.

Lyotard, Jean-François. "Gesture and Commentary." *Between Ethics and Aesthetics: Crossing the Boundaries*. Ed. Dorota Blowacka and Stephen Boos. Albany: State U of New York P, 2002. 73-82.

Miller, J. Hillis. "Stevens's Rock and Criticism as Cure." Part 1, *Georgia Review* 30.1 (Spring 1976): 5-31. Part 2, *Georgia Review* 30.2 (Summer 1976): 330-48.

Olesha, Yuri. *Envy and Other Works*. Trans. Andrew R. MacAndrew. Garden City: Anchor, 1967.

Oppen, George. *Of Being Numerous. George Oppen: New Collected Poems*. New York: New Directions, 2002.

Pascal, Blaise. *Pensées et Opuscules*. Paris: Larousse, 1934.

Pollock, Zailig. *A. M. Klein: The Story of the Poet*. Toronto: U of Toronto P, 1994.

Pound, Ezra. *Literary Essays of Ezra Pound*. New York: New Directions, 1968.

Quinn, Justin. *Gathered beneath the Storm: Wallace Stevens, Nature, and Community*. Dublin: U College Dublin P, 2002.

Riddel, Joseph N. *The Clairvoyant Eye*. Baton Rouge: Louisiana State UP, 1965.

Scarry, Elaine. *The Body in Pain: The Making and Unmaking of the World*. Oxford: Oxford UP, 1985.

Shakespeare, William. *The Complete Works of Shakespeare*. Ed. David Bevington. New York: Harper, 1992.

Siebers, Tobin. *The Ethics of Criticism*. Ithaca: Cornell UP, 1988.

Stein, Gertrude. *Selected Writings of Gertrude Stein*. Ed. Carl Van Vechten. New York: Vintage, 1962.

Stern, Robert. "Does 'Ought' Imply 'Can'? And Did Kant Think It Does?" Online posting. 12 May 2004. <http://www.utilitas.org.uk/pdfs/stern.pdf>

Stevens, Wallace. *Letters of Wallace Stevens*. Ed. Holly Stevens. New York: Knopf, 1966.

———. *The Necessary Angel: Essays on Reality and the Imagination*. New York: Vintage, 1951.

———. *The Palm at the End of the Mind*. Ed. Holly Stevens. New York: Vintage, 1972.

Thomas, Dylan. *The Poems of Dylan Thomas*. Ed. Daniel Jones. New York: New Directions, 1971.

Tolstoy, Leo. *Six Masterpieces by Tolstoy*. Trans. Margaret Wettlin. New York: Laurel, 1963.

Tocqueville, Alexis de. *Democracy in America*. Trans. Harvey C. Mansfield and Delba Winthrop. Chicago: U of Chicago P, 2000.

D. L. Bird (essay date 2004)

SOURCE: Bird, D. L. "Wallace Stevens: Appearing in Difference." In *Literary Canons and Religious Identity*, edited by Erik Borgman, Bart Philipsen and Lea Verstricht, pp. 189-200. Aldershot, England: Ashgate, 2004.

[*In the following essay, Bird characterizes Stevens's central project and struggle as an attempt to use language to bridge an apparent—but not actual—divide between the mind and the outside world.*]

'Life is an affair of people not of places', said Wallace Stevens. 'But for me life is an affair of places and that is the trouble.'[1] For a man who spent so much time in the nowhere of the mind, place is a problem. Stevens's troublesome affair with places is the inspiration for his poetry and it is here, within the space of his poems, that he attempts to find a home for an otherwise homeless, thinking ego. Poetry is a 'visibility of thought', the general turned particular in its movement from the nowhere of the mind to the somewhere of language. This manifestation of thought through poetry answers the thinking ego's urge to make an appearance, an urge that takes on particular importance in the perceived absence or otherness of the body. Thus poetry for Stevens may be said to be a struggle for embodiment through the medium of speech.

Place and appearance are pervasive themes in the work of Stevens, specifically the possibility of appearances in spite of a (perceived) lack of 'local habitation'. By this I mean that Stevens's poems are concerned with the 'appearing-ness' of the inner life of the mind, that no-place where he felt most at home, and the desire to arrest, albeit momentarily, the activity of thinking by *placing* it in words. Just as immaterial thoughts become things through poetry, so the thinking ego makes an appearance in the poem. This urge to make an appearance stems from the very human desire to be 'seen', to be on display in the physical world.

In *The life of the mind* Hannah Arendt argues that 'to be alive means to be possessed by an urge toward self-display', and this yearning to make an appearance comes from the need for living things to 'fit themselves into a world of appearances'. She says:

[A]ll sense-endowed creatures have appearance as such in common, first, an appearing world, and second, and perhaps even more important, the fact that they themselves are appearing and disappearing creatures, that there always was a world before their arrival and there always will be a world after their departure.[2]

To say that the world is an appearing world, located on the surface, seems obvious—that is, until we think about the life of the mind and the activity of thinking. Arendt posits an unanswerable question. Where are we when we think?[3] If the world is ultimately an appearing world, then where are we when we withdraw—or feel ourselves to withdraw—from the world into the invisible place of the mind? This is a question that seems to have plagued Stevens, as evidenced by his comment about his troublesome affair with places. For one cannot assign 'place' to mind; it exists nowhere. The *activity* of thinking can be *experienced* but it can never be located. Thus, the thinking ego 'is homeless in an emphatic sense'[4] and this sense of homelessness, a source of despair, is intensified for a modern poet like Stevens who experienced fully that profound crisis, the death of God.[5] For when there is no longer that divine receptacle for thought and memory as expounded by Augustine in Book X of his *Confessions*, the abyss that takes its place—that nowhere of the mind—becomes a mere warehouse for storing 'the debris of life and mind'. Stevens writes of this experience of the death of God:

> To see the gods dispelled in mid-air and dissolve like clouds is one of the great human experiences. it is not as if they had gone over the horizon to disappear for a time; nor as if they had been overcome by other gods of greater power and profounder knowledge. It is simply that they came to nothing. Since we have always shared all things with them and have always had a part of their strength and, certainly, all their knowledge, we shared likewise this experience of annihilation.[6]

The dissolution of the gods marks the annihilation of the self, an experience that brings both the despair of loss and the freedom of possibility. Says J. Hillis Miller:

> In the impoverishing of the world when the gods disappear man discovers himself, orphaned and dispossessed, a solitary consciousness. Then are men truly 'natives of poverty, children of malheur'.[7] The moment of self-awareness coincides with the moment of the death of the gods. God is dead, therefore I am. But I am nothing. I am nothing because I have nothing, nothing but awareness of the barrenness within and without.[8]

Without the comfort of the gods, who have hitherto provided a home or a ground for human consciousness, it remains for the thinking ego to relocate itself in the appearing world where it may be made manifest through language. The poet's task is to provide the thinking ego with another dwelling, by placing it in the appearing and participatory world through the medium of speech. For without language human consciousness is nowhere and nothing.

It must be noted that Stevens is fully aware of the metaphysical fallacy of the two-world theory—that 'most plausible delusion with which the experience of thought is plagued'.[9] In fact, it is the awareness of this delusion that necessitates his poetry. For the poet's urge to bring the invisible objects of the mind into the world of appearances through language is precipitated by the knowledge that the appearing world is the only actual world. Furthermore, this effort to bring to appearance what is hidden in the mind is the effort to bring to appearance the thinking ego, the thinking self. Stevens longs to participate in the appearing world, to self-display.

Considering this invisible world of the thinking ego, Arendt writes:

> Mental activities, invisible themselves and occupied with the invisible, become manifest only through speech. Just as appearing beings living in a world of appearances have an urge to show themselves, so thinking beings, which still belong to the world of appearances even after they have mentally withdrawn from it, have an *urge to speak* and thus make manifest what would otherwise not be a part of the appearing world at all.[10]

Stevens *speaks* through poetry in order to make the invisible and familiar world of his mind visible so that he might feel himself to be a part of that other not-so-familiar, embodied world. This longing to 'in-place' or embody the world of the thinking ego is not surprising for a man who 'knew that he was a spirit without a foyer':

> And that, in this knowledge, local objects become
> More precious than the most precious objects of home:
>
> The local objects of a world without a foyer,
> Without a remembered past, a present past,
> Or a present future, hoped for in present hope,
>
> Objects not present as a matter of course
> On the dark side of the heavens or the bright,
> In that sphere with so few objects of its own.
>
> Little existed for him but the few things
> For which a fresh name always occurred, as if
> He wanted to make them, keep them from perishing,
>
> The few things, the objects of insight, the integrations
> Of feeling, the things that came of their own accord,
> Because he desired without quite knowing what,
>
> That were the moments of the classic, the beautiful.
> These were that serene he had always been approaching
> As toward an absolute foyer beyond romance.[11]

The local objects of the mind, 'objects not present as a matter of course . . . for which a fresh name always occurred', are what the poet longs to bring into existence, 'to make them, keep them from perishing'. These objects of the mind make their arrival in the appearing world as the poet succeeds in calling them by name.[12]

Through the particularity of speech the abstract objects of the mind make an appearance. Their arrival is made possible by the *seeming* difference between the visible, appearing world and the invisible world of the mind. Not that there *is* a difference, but there *seems* to be a difference. Words are 'located' between these two points, between the this and that of a perceived duality.

> . . . Description is
> Composed of a sight indifferent to the eye.
> It is an expectation, a desire,
> A palm that rises up beyond the sea,
>
> A little different from reality:
> The difference that we make in what we see
>
> And our memorials of that difference,
> Sprinklings of bright particulars from the sky.[13]

In its particularity, the poem stands as a memorial to the poet's desire to bridge the perceived gap between the mind and the appearing world. It is the poet's effort to overcome the difference and make an appearance through speech.

Engaging in an appearing world is problematic for someone like Stevens who feels himself so utterly cut off from that primary place for appearances, the body. Indeed, 'the greatest poverty', says Stevens, 'is not to live / In a physical world',[14] knowing at first hand the deep despair connected with the poverty of living in the non-physical world of the mind. In **'Notes toward a supreme fiction',** Stevens writes of this feeling of alienation from the body:

> From this the poem springs: that we live in a place
> That is not our own and, much more, not ourselves
> And hard it is in spite of blazoned days.[15]

Commenting on these verses, Peter Brooks says:

> If the 'place that is not our own' and 'not ourselves' is the world, it can often seem that the body, our body, belongs to the world and not to our ideally constructed selves. If the motive of poetry is an attempted recuperation of an otherness, often that otherness is our own body.[16]

This attempt to recover the body in language reflects the poet's desire to participate in what Stevens calls the peopled world. It is the urge to self-display through the 'gesture' of speech, which reaches out from the invisible world of thought to make contact with the visible. In poetry words become flesh, providing the poet with a kind of dwelling, a locale, making it possible to connect with others in the appearing world. 'Poetry is what really lets us dwell', asserts Heidegger.[17] And this poetic dwelling comes through 'building', through *poiesis,* the creative act of naming and appropriating both the visible, appearing world and the non-visible world of the mind.

It is ironic, however, that words should be the vehicle for appearances, because the metaphysical fallacy of the two-world split has its origin in language. As Arendt notes, it was 'precisely the discovery of a discrepancy between words, the medium in which we think, and the world of appearances, the medium in which we live, that led to philosophy and metaphysics in the first place'.[18] Thus words give rise to the two-world theory; and yet it is through words that the poet seeks to build a bridge between these worlds. *Therefore language is understood to be both the source of, and the solution to, the problem of a perceived duality.*

In recognition of this, Stevens seeks to overcome the problem by asserting the thing-ly quality of words. Words do not merely point to ideas located in the nowhere of the mind; they are not *mere* appearances: they are things themselves, located on the surface and a part of the appearing world. They actually provide a habitation, a locale for otherwise homeless thoughts. This is closely aligned to what Heidegger is saying when he states that the 'poetic is the basic capacity for human dwelling' and 'poetically man dwells'.[19] Language provides a dwelling place for the thinking ego, and as such is essential for embodiment.

Words as things take on depth; they have texture and shape and cast a metaphorical shadow whenever spoken or read. Just as the body existing in space can be seen in endless perspective, so words can be the source of endless meaning. Words, like the body, are a part of the appearing world, a world which is never finally present but which continues to unfold in changing perspective.

Although he realises that it is not possible, Stevens longs to capture the world in words, to call it by name, to know it in a final knowing:

> Fat girl, terrestrial, my summer, my night,
> How is it I find you in difference, see you there
> In a moving contour, a change not quite completed?
>
> You are familiar yet an aberration.
> Civil, madam, I am, but underneath
> A tree, this unprovoked sensation requires
>
> That I should name you flatly, waste no words,
> Check your evasions, hold you to yourself.[20]

The 'civil' poet's desire is unleashed. He is stirred; he must have her, this evasive world, this elusive body. And yet he cannot, for she exists in difference, 'in the intricate evasions of as'. The 'fluent mundo' resists his embrace: she cannot be fully known nor finally named.

This inability to name the world flatly is what ensures the future of Stevens's poems: it is 'from this the poem springs'. The poem springs from *difference* and *desire,* the desire to overcome the difference between the appearing world of particularity and the invisible world of generalities. In **'Extracts from addresses to the academy of fine ideas',** Stevens writes of the poetic process that melts the frozen generalities of static being and turns them into the fluid river of becoming. On an early Sunday in April, a feeble day,

> He felt curious about the winter hills
> And wondered about the water in the lake.
> It had been cold since December. Snow fell, first,
> At New Year and, from then until April, lay
> On everything. Now it had melted, leaving
> The gray grass like a pallet, closely pressed;
> And dirt. The wind blew in the empty place.
> The winter wind blew in an empty place—
> There was that difference between the and an,
> The difference between himself and no man,
> No man that heard a wind in an empty place.
> It was time to be himself again, to see
> If the place, in spite of its witheredness, was still
> Within the difference. He felt curious
> Whether the water was black and lashed about
> Or whether the ice still covered the lake. There was
>   still
> Snow under the trees and on the northern rocks,
> The dead rocks not the green rocks, the live rocks. If,
> When he looked, the water ran up the air or grew
>   white
> Against the edge of the ice, the abstraction would
> Be broken and winter would be broken and done,
> And being would be being himself again,
> Being, becoming seeing and feeling and self,
> Black water breaking into reality.[21]

Desire—here curiosity, wonder—calls upon the poet to look again and see. It marks the return of the question after a long winter of unquestioning satisfaction, living among the frozen abstractions of the mind. The question of the 'difference between the and an' dislodges the generality of 'an' and breaks it down into the particularity of 'the'. This difference between 'the' and 'an' is the 'difference between himself and no man'. And the no man, here, is 'The snow man', 'who listens in the snow / And, nothing himself, beholds / Nothing that is not there and the nothing that is'.[22] But the question of difference, which comes about through looking and seeing—through perspective—breaks through the icy abstraction that the poet feels he has become and frees him to be himself again, to be a part of the appearing world of particularity.

In the extract above, Stevens writes about the return of desire and the subsequent freedom it brings in its power to dissolve an abstraction. In another poem, **'The dwarf',** the poet conveys the feeling of despair as this freedom of the self comes to a halt in the crystallisation of thought:

> Now it is September and the web is woven.
> The web is woven and you have to wear it.
>
> The winter is made and you have to bear it,
> The winter web, the winter woven, wind and wind.
>
> For all the thoughts of summer that go with it
> In the mind, pupa of straw, moppet of rags.
>
> It is the mind that is woven, the mind that was jerked
> And tufted in straggling thunder and shattered sun.
>
> It is all that you are, the final dwarf of you,
> That is woven and woven and waiting to be worn,
>
> Neither as mask nor as garment but as a being,
> Torn from insipid summer, for the mirror of cold,
>
> Sitting beside your lamp, there citron to nibble
> And coffee dribble . . . Frost is in the stubble.[23]

Without the question of difference the self that was large in possibility is reduced to a single idea: 'It is all that you are, the final dwarf of you . . .' And what was once a garment or mask, allowing the self to play and display in the physical world, now becomes 'a being' located not on the surface of things but in the nowhere of the mind. In this way, *seeming* and all the possibilities it affords in the world of appearances is replaced by the burden of *being* which has no home in the peopled world.

The self suffocates and is silenced under the weight of being, which is the weight of dead language. When metaphor—which operates within the (seeming) difference—loses its power, the connection between the two worlds is lost and the thinking ego is homeless once again. For without the unifying power of metaphor the mind has no vehicle through which it can display itself. Only words that stay on the surface, that maintain their buoyancy, their vitality, can provide a home for the thinking ego; only through metaphor is the mind able to engage in the visible world and locate itself there. 'All human discovery is by metaphor', says Sallie McFague TeSelle. She continues:

> To see connections, to unite this with that, is the distinctive nature of human thought; only human beings, it appears, can make novel connections within their familiar worlds in order to move beyond where they are . . . Metaphor is, for human beings, what instinctual groping is for the rest of the universe—the power of getting from here to there.[24]

Metaphor affords self-discovery as it allows for that migratory movement of the thinking ego from the nowhere of the mind to the somewhere of language. It has the power to connect the two worlds and to provide a dwelling place for the thinking ego. But metaphor does not come of its own accord. Stevens knows that human desire is the motive for metaphor, the desire to move outward and beyond the invisible world of the mind and into the 'difference', that place where 'nothing solid is its solid self'.[25] You like it under the trees in autumn,

Because everything is half dead.
The wind moves like a cripple among the leaves
And repeats words without meaning.

In the same way, you were happy in spring,
With the half colors of quarter-things,
The slightly brighter sky, the melting clouds,
The single bird, the obscure moon—

The obscure moon lighting an obscure world
Of things that would never be quite expressed,
Where you yourself were never quite yourself
And did not want nor have to be,

Desiring the exhilarations of changes:
The motive for metaphor, shrinking from
The weight of primary noon,
The A B C of being,
The ruddy temper, the hammer
Of red and blue, the hard sound—
Steel against intimation—the sharp flash,
The vital, arrogant, fatal, dominant X.[26]

Stevens feels most alive in the difference. He likes it 'under the trees in autumn, / Because everything is half dead' and is equally happy in spring with its 'half colors'. In this place of in-betweens, this obscure world where things are never quite expressed, Stevens enjoys the freedom of the self in possibility. It is the freedom of existing in metaphor with its exhilarations of changes.

Desire and its craving for change saves us from the despair of the 'arrogant, fatal, dominant X', 'the A B C of being'. Desire seeks the exhilarations of changing perspective that are only possible in the plurality of a peopled world. Here on the surface of the appearing world nothing is ever certain or final as long as it is on display for people to look at and, in seeing, to speak. The appearing world, of which speech is a part, is the place of never-ending surprises. We are surprised as we encounter, through the gesture of speech, ourselves and others and the difference that lay between us. We are surprised by the differences in our experience of the shared world of appearances and *how we express* those differences. For although we are the inhabitants of a single, appearing world which existed before our arrival and will continue to exist after our departure, it is only our home inasmuch as it provides a place for a plurality of perspectives and endless appearances:

And out of what one sees and hears and out
Of what one feels, who could have thought to make
So many selves, so many sensuous worlds,
As if the air, the mid-day air, was swarming
With the metaphysical changes that occur,
Merely in living as and where we live.[27]

The world must be experienced *as if*. It must always be *on the way* without ever actually arriving. Always being *on the way* holds off the arrogant, fatal, dominant X of being.

To be at home in the world is to be forever on the way, as the title of this next poem suggests. In **'On the road home'**, Stevens demonstrates the power of plurality to bring about a sense of wonder through changing perspective. His use of dialogue here is significant.

It was when I said,
'There is no such thing as the truth',
That the grapes seemed fatter.
The fox ran out of his hole.

You . . . You said,
'There are many truths,
But they are not parts of a truth'.
Then the tree, at night, began to change,

Smoking through green and smoking blue.
We were two figures in a wood.
We said we were alone.[28]

Dialogue contains the question of difference, the difference in perspective between 'I' and 'You'. Stevens knows that truth in the singular is impossible when there are two people, even between these two figures who, standing together, say that they are alone. The irony of the lines, 'We were two figures in a wood. / We said we were alone', serves to emphasise further the impossibility of the existence of *a* truth, as irony itself operates within the difference. Irony is elusive; it is always open to more than one meaning and, in this way, remains buoyant on the surface of the appearing world.

It was when I said,
'Words are not forms of a single word.
In the sum of the parts, there are only the parts.
The world must be measured by eye';

It was when you said,
'The idols have seen lots of poverty,
Snakes and gold and lice,
But not the truth';

It was at that time, that the silence was largest
And longest, the night was roundest,
The fragrance of the autumn warmest,
Closest and strongest.[29]

In this second half of the poem Stevens continues using dialogue between 'I' and 'you', and through the exchange that takes place the world begins to undergo change. 'It was *when* I said' and 'It was *when* you said' 'that the silence was largest / And longest, the night was roundest, / The fragrance of the autumn warmest, / Closest and strongest'. It was when they spoke in one another's company that the world in its possibilities was revealed anew. It was at this time that they were filled with wonder and responded with silence.

The peopled world with its multiplicities of perspectives and endless surprises provides a home for Stevens and the local objects of his mind. But this home is not always a comfortable place. Living in this embodied world presents Stevens with a problem, for to live here requires taking a risk and making a sacrifice. It is risky because in order to display in the appearing world one must be seen by others, one must entrust oneself to the gaze of others. And it involves sacrifice, because for the thinking ego to make an appearance through speech it is necessary to say *something* at the expense of saying *everything*. Maurice Merleau-Ponty calls this 'the sorrow of language'—'the necessity of not saying everything if one is to say something'.[30]

It seems that at times Stevens longs to gather himself up in language, to make a full appearance and be finally present. But such an epiphany is not possible in the appearing world of particularity. The presence of other people makes it impossible, as Stevens considers in **'Wild ducks, people and distances'**:

> The life of the world depends on that he is
> Alive, on that people are alive, on that
> There is village and village of them, without regard
> To that be-misted one and apart from her.
>
> Did we expect to live in other lives?
> We grew used so soon, too soon, to earth itself,
> As an element; to the sky, as an element.
> People might share but were never an element,
>
> Like earth and sky. Then he became nothing else
> And they were nothing else. It was late in the year.
> The wild ducks were enveloped. The weather was
>   cold.
> Yet, under the migrations to solitude,
>
> There remained the smoke of the villages. Their fire
> Was central in distances the wild ducks could
> Not span, without any weather at all, except
> The weather of other lives, from which there could
>
> Be no migrating. It was that they were there
> That held the distances off: the villages
> Held off the final, fatal distances,
> Between us and the place in which we stood.[31]

The life of the world, the possibility of appearances, depends on people to provide the necessary plurality of perspectives to hold off 'the final, fatal distances / Between us and the place in which we stood'. People de-centre us with their gaze; they call us out of the nowhere of the mind and back into the difference—into the appearing world of particularity. In spite of Stevens's fear of the gaze, he knows that it is this that saves him from being merely the 'snow man' who makes his home among icy abstractions.

Notes

1. Stevens, Wallace (1990), *Opus posthumous*, ed. J. Bates Milton, New York: Vintage Books, p. 185.

2. Arendt, Hannah (1978), *The life of the mind: Vol. one/Thinking*, New York: Harcourt Brace and Company, pp. 20-34.

3. Ibid., p. 197.

4. Ibid., p. 199.

5. Helen Vendler says that 'Stevens is one of the last of our writers to experience fully the nineteenth century crisis of the death of God'. See Vendler, Helen (1984), *Wallace Stevens: words chosen out of desire*, Knoxville: University of Tennessee Press, p. 30.

6. *Opus posthumous*, p. 260.

7. Stevens, Wallace (1990), *The collected poems of Wallace Stevens*, New York: Vintage Books, p. 322.

8. Miller, J. Hillis (1966), *Poets of reality*, London: Oxford University Press, p. 219.

9. Arendt, p. 110.

10. Ibid., p. 98; emphasis original.

11. 'Local objects', in *Opus posthumous*, pp. 137-8.

12. See Vendler, p. 5.

13. 'Description without place', *Collected Poems*, pp. 343-4.

14. 'Esthétique du mal', *Collected Poems*, p. 325.

15. 'Notes toward a supreme fiction', *Collected Poems*, p. 383.

16. Brooks, Peter (1993), *Body work: objects of desire in modern narrative*, Cambridge, MA: Harvard University Press, p. 2.

17. Heidegger, Martin (1971), *Poetry, language, thought*, trans. Albert Hofstadter, New York: Harper & Row, p. 215.

18. Arendt, p. 8.

19. Heidegger, pp. 227-8.

20. 'Notes toward a supreme fiction', *Collected Poems*, p. 406.

21. 'Extracts from addresses to the academy of fine ideas', *Collected Poems*, p. 255.

22. 'The snow man', *Collected Poems*, p. 10.

23. 'The dwarf', *Collected Poems*, p. 208.

24. McFague TeSelle, Sallie (1975), *Speaking in parables: A study in metaphor and theology*, Philadelphia: Fortress Press, pp. 56-7.

25. 'Description without place', *Collected Poems*, p. 345.

26. 'The motive for metaphor', *Collected Poems*, p. 288.

27. 'Esthétique du mal', *Collected Poems*, p. 326; emphasis added.

28. 'On the road home', *Collected Poems*, p. 203.

29. Ibid., pp. 203-4.

30. Merleau-Ponty, Maurice (1973), *The prose of the world*, trans. John O'Neill, Evanston, IL: Northwestern University Press, p. 145.

31. 'Wild ducks, people and distances', *Collected Poems*, pp. 328-9.

B. J. Leggett (essay date 2005)

SOURCE: Leggett, B. J. "Stevens' Final Fiction." In *Late Stevens: The Final Fiction*, pp. 1-21. Baton Rouge, La.: Louisiana State University Press, 2005.

[*In the following essay, Leggett suggests the possibility that Stevens's late work, in particular* The Rock, *enacts Stevens's vision of a supreme fiction in a way that the earlier "Notes to a Supreme Fiction" failed to do.*]

> The exquisite truth is to know that it is a fiction and that you believe in it willingly.
>
> —Stevens, "Adagia," **Opus Posthumous**

When, in the year before his death, Wallace Stevens was asked to supply a statement of the major ideas in his work, his response was in one regard surprising. A reader who had followed his career to that point might have anticipated an account centered on what he termed his "imagination-reality complex" (*Letters* [*Letters of Wallace Stevens*] 792), since his collection of theoretical papers, *The Necessary Angel*, published three years earlier, had been subtitled *Essays on Reality and the Imagination.* Yet in the statement written to accompany the reprinting of **"The Auroras of Autumn"** Stevens marginalizes the imagination-reality theme in deference to another concept he now regards as more central: "There are many poems relating to the interactions between reality and imagination, which are to be regarded as marginal to this central theme," which is "the possibility of a supreme fiction, recognized as a fiction, in which men could propose to themselves a fulfilment" (*Letters* 820).

Stevens is careful not to say that his work embodies such a fiction, only that it suggests the possibility of one. As in his most ambitious treatment of the concept, **"Notes toward a Supreme Fiction,"** his construction here appears to place it in the future, although the phrasing is ambiguous: "In the creation of any such fiction, poetry would have a vital significance" (*Letters* 820). More than a decade earlier, after the publication of **"Notes,"** Stevens had made a number of similarly guarded statements with the same implications. "I have no idea of the form that a supreme fiction would take," he had told Henry Church, to whom the poem was dedicated (*Letters* 430); he also had told Hi Simons that **"Notes"** had not in fact adequately characterized the supreme fiction: "I ought to say that I have not defined a supreme fiction. . . . In principle there appear to be certain characteristics of a supreme fiction *and the Notes is confined to a statement of a few of those characteristics*" (*Letters* 435; Stevens' underlining).

The supreme fiction is an old and complicated story in Stevens criticism that, as he noted, "could occupy a school of rabbis for the next few generations" (*Letters* 435), and I don't intend to reopen the whole issue. I want to pursue initially a collateral issue, which can be stated as a set of questions. Does Stevens' 1954 statement, in which the possible supreme fiction has become the "central theme" of his work, reflect a change in his thinking about the concept from the earlier **"Notes"**? Is the statement related to the poetry Stevens was writing in the last years of his life, that is, primarily the poems that became **The Rock,** the final section of the **Collected Poems**? Does Stevens' poetry embody or realize a version of the supreme fiction or does his work merely suggest some of the characteristics such an unrealizable concept might take?

It is this last option that Stevens' critics have generally chosen, following the drift of what appears to be his own view. William York Tindall calls **"Notes toward a Supreme Fiction"** "a preliminary draft of the great poem [Stevens] will never write." Joseph Riddel concludes that "Stevens' search for the ultimate or central or supreme speaks always in terms of possibility, of the potential of the mind and not of actuality." Robert Rehder notes that the supreme fiction "is something that 'is going to be.'" For Daniel Schwarz, it "exists always as possibility, as ideal," and for Rafeev Patke, **"Notes"** "concedes not a necessary arrival but only the recession of a theoretical possibility, always toward, toward, but never finally there."[1]

The most recent version of the view that the poetry can only gesture *toward* the supreme fiction, never arriving at it, is articulated in David Jarraway's study of the question of belief in Stevens. Jarraway rechristens the supreme fiction the "Supreme Absence" and writes, "It would become the fiction (or the abstract) that one approached asymptotically, so to speak, the 'Limitless' for which the more one compiled one's 'notes,' the more one sensed its retreat further away into the abyss of distance." **"Notes toward a Supreme Fiction"** is "a discourse directed toward metaphysical absence" that turns the question of belief into "an infinitely renewable problematic." To read the later poems in the light of **"Notes,"** he finds, is to see them as "a discontinuous series of attempts or random wagers at moments more or less fraught with spiritual insight . . . without the expectation of some kind of apodictic payoff lying in store at the close of a seamless, epiphanic theodicy or of any other such conventionally homogeneous master narrative."[2]

I want to suggest that there *is* a kind of master narrative in Stevens' last poems, especially those that comprise *The Rock*—or more properly, perhaps, a master intertext, since it is not always explicitly present in the poems—and that this intertext is based on the supreme fiction. I want to argue that Stevens' concept of the supreme fiction has mutated by the time of his last poems, since he comes more and more to give form to what was formless in **"Notes,"** and that his 1954 statement is colored by the fact that the supreme fiction has become the central preoccupation of the poetry he is writing at the time. My argument, in other words, is that Stevens' late poetry, unlike **"Notes,"** does in fact embody a version of the supreme fiction, not merely as description or illustration but as a belief given concrete form, realized.

I am not the first of Stevens' readers to interpret his late poems in the context of the supreme fiction. In a recent study, Janet McCann notes correctly that Stevens' "late poems show an attempt to represent the supreme fiction as something beyond poetry, something to which poetry is an approach." She points to the "transcendent vision" of the last poems and places great significance on Stevens' apparent deathbed conversion, which she calls "a final leap of faith" that adds the "never-written fourth criterion for his supreme fiction: 'It must be human.'"[3]

Joseph Carroll's excellent *Wallace Stevens' Supreme Fiction* makes the most extensive and detailed argument for the presence of the supreme fiction in the later poems. Against the grain of Stevens criticism, Carroll argues that Stevens finally arrives at his supreme fiction in three late poems, **"The Owl in the Sarcophagus,"** **"The Auroras of Autumn,"** and **"A Primitive Like an Orb."** In these poems Stevens "gathers together the ideas and images of a poetic lifetime, and he fashions these materials into a comprehensive mythology of life, death, and the imagination." After the visionary poems of *The Auroras of Autumn* Carroll finds, however, that Stevens enters a new phase of experience, a confrontation with "the poverty of old age," which carries with it a decline of visionary power. With the exception of a few poems in *The Rock,* such as the title poem, **"Final Soliloquy of the Interior Paramour,"** and **"To an Old Philosopher in Rome,"** "he can no longer look forward to a culminating moment of visionary realization," and "he redefines the visionary goal as an ever-receding ideal." According to Carroll, **"The Plain Sense of Things"** reveals that "Stevens' 'fantastic effort' to cre-

ate a supreme fiction has failed to fix itself in a permanent realization," and **"The Rock"** gives evidence "that Stevens' visionary power 'is exhausted and a little old.'"[4]

Although Carroll's reading of the three visionary poems of *The Auroras of Autumn* is persuasive, I want to make the case that it is in the poems whose visionary powers he most deprecates—those that follow in *The Rock*—that Stevens is finally able to embody his fiction. While **"The Auroras of Autumn"** is a speculation on the possibility of such a fiction, and **"A Primitive Like an Orb"** is, as Carroll terms it, "a definition with several illustrations,"[5] poems such as **"The Rock"** and **"The Plain Sense of Things"** depend on the supreme fiction as intertext for their full significance, although this has not been generally recognized. My distinction is between the earlier poems' specifications, definitions, or speculations in regard to a supreme fiction and the later poems' assumption of its actual presence, a fiction now functioning paradoxically as the belief or "reality" that lies behind the poems.

Stevens' fiction, of course, depends on such a paradox. In a memorandum of 1940 concerning a chair of poetry, he wrote, "The major poetic idea in the world is and always has been the idea of God" (*Letters* 378). A few months earlier he had written to Hi Simons that the "extreme poet will produce a poem equivalent to the idea of God." In explicating a section of **"Owl's Clover,"** he states further,

> If one no longer believes in God (as truth), it is not possible merely to disbelieve; it becomes necessary to believe in something else. Logically, I ought to believe in essential imagination, but that has its difficulties. It is easier to believe in a thing created by the imagination. . . . In one of the short poems that I have just sent to the *Harvard Advocate* [**"Asides on the Oboe"**], I say that one's final belief must be in a fiction. I think that the history of belief will show that it has always been in a fiction. Yet the statement seems a negation, or, rather, a paradox.
>
> (*Letters* 370)

More than a decade later Stevens modeled his supreme fiction on the idea of God—not as a heavenly god, but as a god of reality might be. The fiction is not the human imagination itself but something created by it and modeled on it. Stevens' final fiction is a fusion of the idea of God and the idea of the imagination, or the idea of God as a purely aesthetic principle, the supreme imagination, although that is to put it somewhat too simply, since it is neither God nor imagination as these are normally conceived.

Stevens toyed with the idea of God (softened to "the gods") as a purely aesthetic figure in "Two or Three Ideas," a paper he read at a meeting of the College

English Association in 1951. Here he conceives of the gods not as objects of belief but as "aesthetic projections" (*OP* [*Opus Posthumous*] 260). And when their time was over, "it was a time when their aesthetic had become invalid in the presence not of a greater aesthetic of the same kind, but of a different aesthetic" (*OP* 264). "A poem is a restricted creation of the imagination," he states. "The gods are the creation of the imagination at its utmost." And he notes finally that "we use the same faculties when we write poetry that we use when we create gods" (*OP* 266). At the time Stevens delivered these pronouncements he had already written in **"Final Soliloquy of the Interior Paramour,"** "We say God and the imagination are one"—a line, however, sufficiently ambiguous to veil its more fanciful implications.

The merging of God and the imagination is treated playfully in **"Credences of Summer,"** from the 1947 volume *Transport to Summer*. In 1942, **"Notes"** had spoken enigmatically of the existence of a "muddy centre before we breathed," "a myth before the myth began, / Venerable and articulate and complete" (383), suggesting that Stevens had earlier confronted the idea of a non-human mythic reality of some order. There are fainter and more debatable examples in even earlier poems—the "nothing that is" of **"The Snow Man,"** for example. But as Stevens himself recognized, **"Credences of Summer"** signals the most obvious shift from the privileging of the human imagination in the early poems (and in **"Notes"**) toward an attempt to articulate a reality independent of the observer's mind. "From the imaginative period of the *Notes* I turned to the ideas of **Credences of Summer**," Stevens said (*Letters* 636), and this tendency persisted though the remainder of his later poetry. Speaking of **"An Ordinary Evening in New Haven"** (from *The Auroras of Autumn*), he said, "This is not in any sense a turning away from the ideas of **Credences of Summer**: it is a development of those ideas" (*Letters* 637). To the poet Charles Tomlinson, Stevens wrote of **"Credences,"** "At the time when that poem was written my feeling for the necessity of a final accord with reality was at its strongest: reality was the summer of the title of the book in which the poem appeared" (*Letters* 719). One of the many paradoxes of Stevens' later use of the supreme fiction is that it appears almost always in conjunction with attempts to posit a reality independent of the poet's imagination.

This is indeed the case in **"Credences of Summer"** (*CP* [*Collected Poems*] 372), which depicts a reality so entirely self-contained, "Complete in a completed scene," that the individual imagination is inoperative in the face of it, in "exile" in the poem's language. The singers of canto VII are forced to turn away from such a reality to sing "their unreal songs": "It was difficult to sing in face / Of the object. The singers had to avert

themselves / Or else avert the object." It is a reality beyond the mind, beyond analysis, of which the speaker says, "Let's see the very thing and nothing else. / Let's see it with the hottest fire of sight," a seeing "Without evasion by a single metaphor." In **"Credences"** Stevens posits a summer world in which the sound of a morning bird "is not part of the listener's own sense."

It is in this context that he introduces his fiction of reality as a cosmic imagination. Throughout the poem Stevens has found ways of calling attention to the physical presence of the objects of summer. They are things to be seen, the gold sun, the tower, the rock that "cannot be broken," a mountain, "the visible announced" that is "the successor of the invisible." Yet at the poem's conclusion these solid objects become the fiction of an "inhuman author." They are "personae," costumed "characters," who are merely "speaking their parts" in a "completed scene":

> The personae of summer play the characters
> Of an inhuman author, who meditates
> With the gold bugs, in blue meadows, late at night.
> He does not hear his characters talk. He sees
> Them mottled, in the moodiest costumes,
>
> Of blue and yellow, sky and sun, belted
> And knotted, sashed and seamed, half pales of red,
> Half pales of green, appropriate habit for
> The huge decorum, the manner of the time,
> Part of the mottled mood of summer's whole,
>
> In which the characters speak because they want
> To speak, the fat, the roseate characters,
> Free, for a moment, from malice and sudden cry,
> Complete in a completed scene, speaking
> Their parts as in a youthful happiness.

Readers of the poem have had difficulty with this concluding canto, in large part because they ignore the implications of its fiction of the inhuman author. Harold Bloom believes it is "the poem's most problematic canto," but that is because he mistakenly determines that Stevens sees *himself* as the inhuman author and is thus forced to offer an explanation for "inhuman": "Stevens means something like 'not yet wholly human,' that is, not yet knowing himself wholly, beyond illusion." Joseph Riddel and Helen Vendler also mistake Stevens' reference to the inhuman author as a reference to himself, producing distorted readings. For Riddel, this means that in the end, the "physical [is] re-posed in the order of mind"; that is, the reality of summer is dissolved into the poet's imagination. Vendler's exemplary and influential reading goes wrong only with the final canto, which she believes begins "with the poet as a deliberate and distant manipulator of marionettes." Such a move is "Stevens' desperate, if truthful, expedient with which to end the poem."[6]

Stevens' inhuman author is perhaps an expedient, but it is relatively easy to show that he is not to be identified with the poet; the true difficulty of the final canto is to fathom why this author only *sees* his characters and does not hear them talk. David Jarraway confuses the issue by assuming that it is the "speeches" of the personae of summer that the inhuman author meditates, and that this undermines the poem's conclusion: the "'inhuman author' . . . is somewhat absurdly given to meditate their speeches 'late at night' even though he cannot hear them, much less see them."[7] But the poem says something more fanciful—that it is the objects of summer themselves that comprise the inhuman author's thought. They are what he thinks *with* (he "meditates / With the gold bugs"). He sees his characters and does not hear them talk because the poem has identified reality with the visible and the unreal with language, which is once removed from reality, as are the "unreal songs" of the singers of canto VII. In the fiction of the poem, reality is the *visible* meditation of a cosmic mind, and the objects of reality are the means by which this mind meditates. In the trope within this fiction, reality is also like a text, in that material objects are in fact playing roles dictated by the author who produced them. They are free to speak because their speech is not seen as a part of the reality meditated by their inhuman author, whose imagination operates with the visible, the blue and yellow and green of sky and sun and earth. Their speech is a sign of their sense of being "for a moment" free from "malice," freed from the exigencies of their "parts," in the same way that summer has been seen throughout the poem as a momentary sense of complete satisfaction, a moment of freedom from time in which "the mind lays by its trouble."

But does such a conception not undermine the entire poem, in which reality is not to be evaded by a single metaphor, not to mention the elaborate fiction of an inhuman author who meditates with gold bugs? To understand the place of the final canto in the poem as a whole, it is useful to read it against other passages in Stevens that adopt similar strategies. In all these instances the fiction of the supreme imagination addresses one difficulty while creating others. What it addresses is Stevens' attempt, toward the end of his career, to discover a way of representing poetically a separate and independent reality that is something more than the "muddy centre" of **"Notes."** The difficulties that it creates are perhaps obvious even from the example of **"Credences of Summer,"** but chief among them are the contradictions it appears to engender and the misreadings it has produced. The *concept* of the supreme fiction in Stevens has been much better understood than his attempts to realize it.

The principal contradiction, which Stevens recognized and labeled a mere "paradox" (*Letters* 370), is a variation on his concept of a fiction "recognized as a fiction, in which men could propose to themselves a fulfillment" (*Letters* 820). In other words, the recognition of one's belief as a fiction does not impede its sufficiency as a fulfillment or sanction. Similarly, in **"Credences of Summer"** and throughout the late poems Stevens the poet imagines reality as the imagination of a mind independent of the poet. It could not in fact be independent of the poet who imagines it (any more than the poet's fiction could be real), but this difficulty does not apparently curb the efficacy of Stevens' fiction. His personae find satisfaction and ultimately fulfillment in a fiction "recognized as a fiction," in which, in his ambiguous phrasing, "the absence of the imagination had / Itself to be imagined." One of the several meanings of this paradox from **"The Plain Sense of Things"** (although not its primary meaning, as we will see) is that Stevens' fiction of an independent imagination is not simply a playful expedient. It is a necessity; it *has* to be imagined. Any attempt by the poet to depict a reality independent of his depiction would encounter the same paradox. Portraying that reality as itself an imagination, however, sharpens the sense of paradox, recognizes it as a fiction.

"Credences of Summer" and **"The Auroras of Autumn"** (*CP* 411) have frequently been read as companion poems—"the same day seen from two perspectives," Vendler says[8]—and one of the components they share is the fiction of the cosmic imagination. In **"The Auroras of Autumn,"** as in the earlier poem, it makes its appearance near the end, and its primary function is to offer a fictional solution to the problem the poem has formulated. In **"Credences"** the problem was to imagine a pure and luminous reality independent of the human imagination; the solution, necessarily paradoxical, was to create the fiction of reality as the contents of a pure and brilliant *external* imagination, independent of the human, the imagination of an "inhuman author." The problem in **"Auroras"** is much more difficult to resolve, since the poem is not about the realization of such moments of complete luminosity and satisfaction but the breaking down of such moments and the dissolution of the fictions or ideas that produced them.

If **"Credences"** is about stasis, a moment "Beyond which there is nothing left of time," **"Auroras"** is about flux, a reality in which one is continually saying "Farewell to an idea"—the phrase that begins cantos II, III, and IV. In each of these cantos a point of order is dissolved: the ancestral house in II, the domestic comforts of the mother in III, and the fictions of the father in IV. These three motifs are brought together in canto V, when the mother "invites humanity to her house / And table" and the father "fetches tellers of tales and musicians." But this attempt to impose order degenerates into a "loud, disordered mooch," and by the end of canto VI it would appear that all ideas of order, all sustaining fictions, have been obliterated. The source of these fictions, the human imagination seen as a single candle, is ludicrously ineffectual against a destructive universe in flux, seen as the aurora borealis. The antithesis of the complete happiness of **"Credences"** is the total fear of **"Auroras,"** the speaker's sense of an overwhelming and destructive universe: "He opens the door of his house / On flames."

> The scholar of one candle sees
> An Arctic effulgence flaring on the frame
> Of everything he is. And he feels afraid.

The poem cannot go further in this direction, and it is here that the supreme imagination of its companion poem makes its appearance.

The aurora borealis of the title is, interestingly, both the problem to be addressed and its solution. It represents a relentlessly destructive universe that, Dylan Thomas-like, kills everything it brings into being:

> It leaps through us, through all our heavens leaps,
> Extinguishing our planets, one by one,
> Leaving, of where we were and looked, of where
>
> We knew each other and of each other thought,
> A shivering residue. . . .

But in another version of **"Death is the mother of beauty"** (in **"Sunday Morning"**), it also represents what Stevens calls "An innocence of the earth and no false sign / Or symbol of malice." The auroras of autumn, that is, represent the universe as a cosmic genius who "meditates" things into and out of existence not maliciously but innocently, on a purely aesthetic basis, because he wants to experience vicariously all the lives that he imagines,

> The vital, the never-failing genius,
> Fulfilling his meditations, great and small.
>
> In these unhappy he meditates a whole,
> The full of fortune and the full of fate,
> As if he lived all lives, that he might know. . . .

Unlike the more elusive inhuman author of **"Credences of Summer,"** the cosmic imagination of **"The Auroras of Autumn"** is depicted too unambiguously to be confused with the imagination of the poet. The fiction is, however, first introduced tentatively, as if the poet refused to take full responsibility for such an outrageous notion. Later, in the poems of *The Rock,* he will find other devices to soften its impact, such as his ploy in **"Looking across the Fields and Watching the Birds Fly"** of attributing the theory to the Emerson-like Mr. Homburg of Concord. Here, he cushions its introduction by presenting it as a series of questions:

> Is there an imagination that sits enthroned
> As grim as it is benevolent, the just
> And the unjust, which in the midst of summer stops
>
> To imagine winter? When the leaves are dead,
> Does it take its place in the north and enfold itself,
> Goat-leaper, crystalled and luminous, sitting

> In highest night? And do these heavens adorn
> And proclaim it, the white creator of black, jetted
> By extinguishings, even of planets as may be,
>
> Even of earth, even of sight, in snow,
> Except as needed by way of majesty,
> In the sky, as crown and diamond cabala?

By the end of the canto, however, the questions have reverted to statements, and the fiction of the universe as a cosmic imagination that creates seasons by stopping in the midst of summer to imagine winter is firmly established in the poem and in the remainder of Stevens' later poetry.[9]

Stevens plays with variations on the cosmic imagination in other poems of *The Auroras of Autumn.* In **"The Ultimate Poem Is Abstract"** (*CP* 429), a day about which the speaker cannot make up his mind is itself seen as mind, "an intellect / Of windings round and dodges to and fro, / Writhings in wrong obliques and distances." It is not, the speaker adds, "an intellect in which we are fleet"; rather, like the imagination of **"The Auroras of Autumn,"** it is "present / Everywhere in space at once, cloud-pole / Of communication." In **"Large Red Man Reading"** (*CP* 423) ghosts from heaven return to earth to hear the mythical figure of the title read from "the poem of life," which, we are led to understand, is the ordinary reality—"the pans above the stove, the pots on the table"—that they have lacked. As he reads, the words become the physical objects themselves: "the literal characters, the vatic lines, / . . . Took on color, took on shape and size of things as they are." In **"Puella Parvula"** (*CP* 456), autumn is the triumph of "the mighty imagination," and the speaker asks his own mind to "Hear what he says, / The dauntless master, as he starts the human tale." In canto XXX of **"An Ordinary Evening in New Haven"** (*CP* 465), autumn is "a visibility of thought, / In which hundreds of eyes, in one mind, see at once." The poem concludes, "It is not in the premise that reality / Is a solid. It may be a shade that traverses / A dust, a force that traverses a shade." In the penultimate poem of the volume, **"Things of August"** (*CP* 489), the concept of reality as mind is again introduced as a series of questions: "The world? The inhuman as human? That which thinks not, / Feels not, resembling thought, resembling feeling?"

Joseph Carroll, as I have noted, finds the supreme fiction present in two other poems of the volume, **"The Owl in the Sarcophagus"** and **"A Primitive like an Orb,"** but these, although clearly visionary poems, present very different fictions from the one I am tracing here. **"The Owl in the Sarcophagus"** (*CP* 431) is a deeply-felt but failed attempt to create what it calls "the mythology of modern death" by inventing (somewhat crudely) human figures for sleep, peace after death, and the memory of the dead. **"A Primitive like an Orb"** (*CP* 440) tackles an issue related to the cosmic imagination, an abstraction that Stevens calls the "essential poem" or the "central poem," whose existence cannot be proven: "It is something seen and known in lesser poems."

The concept that informs **"A Primitive like an Orb"** is much less daring than the fiction of reality as inhuman imagination. Although at some points in the poem Stevens mythologizes the concept by picturing it as a giant ("an abstraction given head / . . . given arms, / A massive body and long legs"), at other points it appears to be no more than a version of Eliot's notion in "Tradition and the Individual Talent" that all existing works of art together form an ideal order, an abstraction complete in itself but changed slightly by the addition of each new work. In the final stanza of the poem Stevens suggests that each artist, of whatever art, is a "part" of "the total of letters, prophecies, perceptions, clods of color." And earlier he had defined the central poem as "the poem of the whole, / the poem of the composition of the whole." It is

> the miraculous multiplex of lesser poems,
> Not merely into a whole, but the poem of
> The whole, the essential compact of the parts,
> The roundness that pulls tight the final ring. . . .

The concept of art contained in **"A Primitive like an Orb"** is not unlike the idea introduced in Stevens' 1951 paper, "The Relations between Poetry and Painting," and attributed to Baudelaire—"that there exists an unascertained and fundamental aesthetic, or order, of which poetry and painting are manifestations, but of which, for that matter, sculpture or music or any other aesthetic realization would equally be a manifestation" (*NA* [*The Necessary Angel*] 160). Such a notion—that "One poem proves another and the whole," as Stevens puts it in **"A Primitive"**—is at best a minor fiction or simply a way of conceiving of the relation of each work of art to the totality of art. Although it bears some relation to the more fantastic fiction Stevens was elaborating at the same time, it is this latter fiction, reality as cosmic imagination, that serves as one of the essential intertexts for the final collection, *The Rock.*

By the time of *The Rock* this fiction has become pervasive. The great majority of the poems of *The Rock* and a number of other poems written at about the same time (and collected in *Opus Posthumous*) depend on it in various ways. In the latter group are poems written in 1954 and 1955—**"Presence of an External Master of Knowledge," "Reality Is an Activity of the Most August Imagination," "Artificial Populations," "A Clear Day and No Memories"**—whose titles are sufficient to suggest its presence. This is true as well of

one of the key poems of *The Rock,* **"The World as Meditation"** (*CP* 520), whose epigraph (from the composer Georges Enesco) states in part, "Je vis un rêve permanent, qui ne s'arrête ni nuit ni jour."

An uncollected poem of 1950, **"Nuns Painting Water-Lilies"** (*OP* 120), concludes, "We are part of a fraîcheur, inaccessible / Or accessible only in the most furtive fiction." Stevens' fiction is indeed furtive in many of the poems of *The Rock,* accessible only in the figures and images of poems such as **"A Quiet Normal Life," "Long and Sluggish Lines,"** and **"One of the Inhabitants of the West."** It is, however, overtly described in others—**"The Rock," "The World as Meditation,"** and **"Looking across the Fields and Watching the Birds Fly,"** to take the three most obvious examples. In the first section of **"The Rock"** (*CP* 525), the speaker conceives of the events of his life as the "invention" of a "fantastic consciousness"; in **"Looking across the Fields"** (*CP* 517), an afternoon is "Too much like thinking to be less than thought"; in **"The World as Meditation"** Penelope senses "an inhuman meditation, larger than her own."

In the following chapters I will examine these poems and others as specimens of Stevens' final fiction of the world as inhuman meditation, but for the moment I want to suggest some of the implications of its presence in *The Rock* by reading it as the intertext of one of the least likely candidates of the volume, **"The Plain Sense of Things"** (*CP* 502). It is the poem that Joseph Carroll reads as "an end of the visionary process," an indication that "Stevens' 'fantastic effort' to create a supreme fiction has failed to fix itself in a permanent realization."[10] I want to demonstrate the way in which the poem, to the contrary, depends for its significance on the presence of the supreme fiction, or at least a version of it. And since one of the qualities of the supreme fiction is that it must change, no formulation could be more than a "version."

Carroll's negative reading of the poem depends on his assumption (the general assumption of readers of the poem) that the third stanza's failed "fantastic effort" is Stevens' own. He assumes, moreover, that the plain sense of things is Stevens' own sense, "and that it discloses itself as a sense of imaginative inanition." The poem thus becomes an account of Stevens' "imaginative impotence," and the "inevitable knowledge" of the final stanza is the poet's knowledge of the emptiness to which his earlier Romantic vision has been reduced.[11] But such a reading ignores the central insight of the poem—that "the absence of the imagination had / Itself to be imagined"—and it ignores as well Stevens' characterization of the imaginative effort the poem describes as "fantastic." Most crucially, it ignores the poem's ambiguity of agency.

Like many of the poems of *The Rock,* **"The Plain Sense of Things"** is careful not to ascribe the plain sense or the failed imagination to the speaker or to any specific agent. It begins,

> After the leaves have fallen, we return
> To a plain sense of things. It is as if
> We had come to an end of the imagination,
> Inanimate in an inert savoir.

Whose plain sense of things is it to which we return? And whose lack of imagination and inert savoir do we come to, or come upon? Although the second sentence has been read as a statement about the condition of the poet's imagination, the "as if" of the second line indicates the presence of a poetic figure. It appears to be a variation of the central figure of **"Note on Moonlight"** (*CP* 531), also from *The Rock,* in which moonlight in a "simple-colored night" is seen as "a plain poet revolving in his mind / The sameness of his various universe." If reality is conceived of as the thought of such a poet, or as the "inhuman meditation" of **"The World as Meditation"** or the "pensive nature" of **"Looking across the Fields and Watching the Birds Fly,"** then winter can be thought of as a particular state of mind of that consciousness. It is as if winter is such a mind's plain sense of things, its lack of imagination. Winter necessarily represents such a mind's knowledge, even imagination, as we learn later in the poem, but now it appears inanimate, inert. The first two lines of the poem, in which the "plain sense of things" is associated with the fallen leaves, also appear to contain as intertext the description of the cosmic imagination in **"The Auroras of Autumn,"** which conceives its winter world "When the leaves are dead."[12]

If we read the poem as responding to its intertext of Stevens' fiction of the inhuman imagination, many of its figures begin to take on a new sense. The second stanza begins, "It is difficult even to choose the adjective / For this blank cold, this sadness without cause." Here, "this sadness without cause" is clearly in apposition to "this blank cold"; it is not the speaker's sadness but the weather's. Moreover, to think of winter's cold as "blank" is to suggest that the inhuman author who created it did not supply its adjective or description. And it is important to note that the speaker, unlike the cosmic imagination, *is* able to fill in the blank with a succession of imaginative figures:

> The great structure has become a minor house.
> No turban walks across the lessened floors.
>
> The greenhouse never so badly needed paint.
> The chimney is fifty years old and slants to one side.
> A fantastic effort has failed, a repetition
> In a repetitiousness of men and flies.

There is apparently nothing wrong with the poet-speaker's own imagination, as is testified to by the poem as a whole. The "fantastic effort" that has failed belongs not to the poet, as has been assumed, but to the imagination that, in the poem's fiction, creates summer, its yearly "repetition / In a repetitiousness of men and flies." Neither the repetition nor the flies make sense in reference to the poet's own imagination; the "fantastic effort" was the creation of summer, which now appears to have failed. It is "fantastic" in the same sense as the "fantastic consciousness" of **"The Rock,"** conceived by unrestrained fancy, so outrageous as to challenge belief.[13] The poem, in short, plays a variation on the enthroned imagination of **"The Auroras of Autumn,"** which "in the midst of summer stops / To imagine winter." This imagination, however, initially gives the impression not so much of imagining winter as of failing to imagine it, although the speaker later corrects himself when he recognizes that "the absence of the imagination had / Itself to be imagined."

These lines, which begin the penultimate stanza, have naturally been read as referring to the poet's own imagination, to suggest, as Anthony Whiting puts it, that "the imagining of the absence of the imagination is itself a powerful expression of the creative activity of the imagination."[14] This sense of the paradox is certainly present, as I suggested earlier. It is in part Stevens' recognition of the quandary into which his late conception of an external imagination has led him. Yet to read the lines in the context of the poem's conclusion as a whole suggests another reading, which was implicit from the beginning—that is, even what appears initially to be an absence must necessarily be a presence, at least in terms of the poem's fiction. If the speaker is true to this fiction, then even the pond "without reflections," the leaves, mud, and water, and "the waste of the lilies" must themselves have been thought into being by the inhuman meditation to which everything in the winter scene is attributed:

> Yet the absence of the imagination had
> Itself to be imagined. The great pond,
> The plain sense of it, without reflections, leaves,
> Mud, water like dirty glass, expressing silence
> Of a sort, silence of a rat come out to see,
> The great pond and its waste of the lilies, all this
> Had to be imagined as an inevitable knowledge,
> Required, as a necessity requires.

The ambiguity of agency is maintained ingeniously through the two stanzas' use of the infinitive "to be"; the speaker avoids a construction that attributes the imagination or the knowledge to himself. His discovery is their inevitability, their necessity. Why does the imagination *have to be* an "inevitable knowledge," and why is it required "as a necessity"? It would appear that Stevens wants to suggest (although not too clearly) that the mood of winter is a mental act, an external knowledge, operating according to some necessary principle. Winter is not the absence of the imagination that created summer, as it first appeared, but a different imaginative act, one required by the necessity through which the inhuman imagination operates in Stevens' larger fiction.[15]

"The Plain Sense of Things" is in part a reworking of canto XXX of **"An Ordinary Evening in New Haven,"** and reading the two together throws some light on both poems.

> The wind has blown the silence of summer away.
> It buzzes beyond the horizon or in the ground:
> In mud under ponds, where the sky used to be
>   reflected.
>
> The barrenness that appears is an exposing.
> It is not part of what is absent, a halt
> For farewells, a sad hanging on for remembrances.
>
> It is a coming on and a coming forth.
> The pines that were fans and fragrances emerge,
> Staked solidly in a gusty grappling with rocks.
>
> The glass of the air becomes an element—
> It was something imagined that has been washed away.
> A clearness has returned. It stands restored.
>
> It is not an empty clearness, a bottomless sight.
> It is a visibility of thought,
> In which hundreds of eyes, in one mind, see at once.

Expression such as "something imagined" and "a visibility of thought" in **"An Ordinary Evening"** preserve the same kind of ambiguity as in the later **"Plain Sense of Things."** The insight here is also that of the later poem—that what appears as an absence, a lack, is in fact "a coming forth," a clarity of mind, "a visibility of thought," although a mind and a visibility not a part of the speaker's own sense. The canto's conclusion again evokes Stevens' fiction of reality as the visualization of inhuman thought, "In which hundreds of eyes, in one mind, see at once."

In "Some Reflections on Intertextuality," Barbara Johnson notes that when a work is read intertextually it "becomes differently energized, traversed by forces and desires that are invisible or unreadable to those who see it as an independent homogeneous message unit."[16] Among the consequences of reading Stevens' late poems as having absorbed his fiction of the supreme imagination is the recognition both of the extent to which they are intratextual commentaries on each other and the whole, and of the extent to which they are traversed by forces otherwise unreadable.[17] The last line of **"Not Ideas about the Thing but the Thing Itself"** (*CP* 534) provides an interesting illustration, especially because of its position as the last line and thus the last word of the *Collected Poems.*

The poem is set "At the earliest ending of winter," and it begins with "a scrawny cry from outside," a bird's song "at daylight or before," which initially seems to be a sound in the speaker's mind. The struggle of the poem is to push it outside: "It would have been outside. / . . . / The sun was coming from outside." Like many of Stevens' late poems, it is an attempt to grant external reality—here only the faintest of sounds—an independent existence, free from his own mind: "It was not from the vast ventriloquism / Of sleep's faded papier-mâché." The poem ends,

> That scrawny cry—it was
> A chorister whose c preceded the choir.
> It was part of the colossal sun,
>
> Surrounded by its choral rings,
> Still far away. It was like
> A new knowledge of reality.

If the poem is read independently, outside its context in *The Rock,* it is a poem about the speaker's new knowledge of reality. Read intertextually, it is a poem about the coming of spring as itself a new knowledge of reality. The trope is appropriately bold; it is not the speaker's knowledge but a new season as a new knowledge, not ideas *about* the thing but the thing itself. The *it,* which occurs three times in the passage and six times in the poem, always refers to the bird's cry, as it does in the final sentence. It is the bird's scrawny cry, from *outside,* evoking the sound of a newborn baby, that is like a new knowledge of reality. It is Stevens' final version of the final fiction, a supreme imagination that awakens at the end of winter to imagine spring.

Notes

1. William York Tindall, *Wallace Stevens* (Minneapolis, 1961), 32; Joseph Riddel, *The Clairvoyant Eye: The Poetry and Poetics of Wallace Stevens* (Baton Rouge, 1965), 275; Robert Rehder, *The Poetry of Wallace Stevens* (London, 1988), 219; Daniel R. Schwarz, *Narrative and Representation in the Poetry of Wallace Stevens* (New York, 1993), 149; Rajeev S. Patke, *The Long Poems of Wallace Stevens: An Interpretative Study* (Cambridge, 1985), 117. I must admit to having once held the same view. See *Wallace Stevens and Poetic Theory* (Chapel Hill, 1987), 55.

2. David R. Jarraway, *Wallace Stevens and the Question of Belief: Metaphysician in the Dark* (Baton Rouge, 1993), 141, 142, 174.

3. Janet McCann, *Wallace Stevens Revisited: "The Celestial Possible"* (New York, 1995), 101, 120, 137.

4. Joseph Carroll, *Wallace Stevens' Supreme Fiction: A New Romanticism* (Baton Rouge, 1987), 9, 303, 309, 313.

5. Ibid., 260.

6. Bloom, *Poems of Our Climate,* 251-52; Riddel, *Clairvoyant Eye,* 221; Helen Vendler, *On Extended*

Wings: Wallace Stevens' Longer Poems (Cambridge, Mass., 1969), 243, 245.

7. Jarraway, *Wallace Stevens and the Question of Belief*, 232.

8. Vendler, *On Extended Wings*, 231.

9. This fiction should not be confused with one of the master tropes of the early poetry, which Dorothy Emerson calls "the sky as mind," the use of natural objects as "symbolic replications of the mind in action." For a discussion of this figure see Emerson's "Wallace Stevens' Sky That Thinks," *Wallace Stevens Journal* 9 (1985): 71-84.

10. Carroll, *Wallace Stevens' Supreme Fiction*, 309.

11. Ibid., 309-10.

12. In a recent discussion of the poem, David Humphries also notes that it echoes the enthroned imagination passage in "The Auroras of Autumn." He does not, however, recognize the presence of this inhuman imagination in "The Plain Sense of Things." His argument is that the poem exhibits a "new kind of meditation" on Stevens' part that leads, in turn, to "a new sense of perception and a new sense of identity, one more in harmony with our modern understanding of nature." See his "A New Kind of Meditation: Wallace Stevens' 'The Plain Sense of Things,'" *Wallace Stevens Journal* 23 (1999): 38, 47.

13. Humphries argues, to the contrary, that the "fantastic" imagination is the poet's former imagination: "the old, 'fantastic' imagination has dissolved, and a new imagination and a new reality are in the process of being conceived." Ibid., 44.

14. Anthony Whiting, *The Never-Resting Mind: Wallace Stevens' Romantic Irony* (Ann Arbor, 1996), 168.

15. In "The Auroras of Autumn" the cosmic imagination is not free to act "by chance" but must follow some necessary law that is not clearly specified. In the parodic "Looking across the Fields and Watching the Birds Fly," the "pensive nature" is described as "a mechanical / And slightly detestable *operandum*." Stevens also associates necessity with the "angel of reality" of "Angel Surrounded by Paysans" (*CP* 496), a variant of the godlike imagination of the later poems.

16. Barbara Johnson, "*Les Fleurs du mal armé*: Some Reflections on Intertextuality," in *Lyric Poetry: Beyond the New Criticism*, ed. Chaviva Hosek and Patricia Parker (Ithaca, 1985), 265.

17. In the fifth chapter I attempt to show how Miller's weak misreading of "The Rock" can be traced in

part to his inability to read the poem's intertext of reality as the invention of a "fantastic consciousness."

David Young (essay date 2006)

SOURCE: Young, David. "Wallace Stevens Writes 'Sunday Morning.'" In *Six Modernist Moments in Poetry*, pp. 46-67. Iowa City, Iowa: University of Iowa Press, 2006.

[*In the following essay, Young depicts "Sunday Morning" as an attempt by Stevens to formulate a specifically American form of modernism by means of overcoming the strictures of puritanical Protestantism.*]

I

Complacencies of the peignoir, and late
Coffee and oranges in a sunny chair
And the green freedom of a cockatoo
Upon a rug mingle to dissipate
The holy hush of ancient sacrifice.
She dreams a little and she feels the dark
Encroachment of the old catastrophe,
As a calm darkens among water lights.
The pungent oranges and bright, green wings
Seem things in some procession of the dead,
Winding across wide water, without sound.
The day is like wide water, without sound,
Stilled for the passing of her dreaming feet
Over the seas, to silent Palestine,
Dominion of the blood and sepulchre.

II

Why should she give her bounty to the dead?
What is divinity if it can come
Only in silent shadows and in dreams?
Shall she not find in comforts of the sun,
In pungent fruit and bright, green wings, or else
In any balm or beauty of the earth,
Things to be cherished like the thought of heaven?
Divinity must live within herself:
Passions of rain, or moods in falling snow;
Grievings in loneliness, or unsubdued
Elations when the forest blooms; gusty
Emotions on wet roads on autumn nights;
All pleasures and all pains, remembering
The bough of summer and the winter branch.
These are the measures destined for her soul.

III

Jove in the clouds had his inhuman birth.
No mother suckled him, no sweet land gave
Large-mannered motions to his mythy mind.
He moved among us, as a muttering king,
Magnificent, would move among his hinds,
Until our blood, commingling, virginal,
With heaven, brought such requital to desire
The very hinds discerned it, in a star.
Shall our blood fail? Or shall it come to be
The blood of paradise? And shall the earth
Seem all of paradise that we shall know?

The sky will be much friendlier then than now,
A part of labor and a part of pain,
And next in glory to enduring love,
Not this dividing and indifferent blue.

IV

She says, "I am content when wakened birds,
Before they fly, test the reality
Of misty fields, by their sweet questionings;
But when the birds are gone, and their warm fields
Return no more, where, then, is paradise?"
There is not any haunt of prophecy,
Nor any old chimera of the grave,
Neither the golden underground, nor isle
Melodious, where spirits gat them home,
Nor visionary south, nor cloudy palm
Remote on heaven's hill, that has endured
As April's green endures; or will endure
Like her remembrance of awakened birds,
Or her desire for June and evening, tipped
By the consummation of the swallow's wings.

V

She says, "But in contentment I still feel
The need of some imperishable bliss."
Death is the mother of beauty; hence from her,
Alone, shall come fulfillment to our dreams
And our desires. Although she strews the leaves
Of sure obliteration on our paths,
The path sick sorrow took, the many paths
Where triumph rang its brassy phrase, or love
Whispered a little out of tenderness,
She makes the willow shiver in the sun
For maidens who were wont to sit and gaze
Upon the grass, relinquished to their feet.
She causes boys to pile new plums and pears
On disregarded plate. The maidens taste
And stray impassioned in the littering leaves.

VI

Is there no change of death in paradise?
Does ripe fruit never fall? Or do the boughs
Hang always heavy in that perfect sky,
Unchanging, yet so like our perishing earth,
With rivers like our own that seek for seas
They never find, the same receding shores
That never touch with inarticulate pang?
Why set the pear upon those river-banks
Or spice the shores with odors of the plum?
Alas, that they should wear our colors there,
The silken weavings of our afternoons,
And pick the strings of our insipid lutes!
Death is the mother of beauty, mystical,
Within whose burning bosom we devise
Our earthly mothers waiting, sleeplessly.

VII

Supple and turbulent, a ring of men
Shall chant in orgy on a summer morn
Their boisterous devotion to the sun,
Not as a god, but as a god might be,
Naked among them, like a savage source.
Their chant shall be a chant of paradise,
Out of their blood, returning to the sky;
And in their chant shall enter, voice by voice,
The windy lake wherein their lord delights,

The trees, like serafin, and echoing hills,
That choir among themselves long afterward.
They shall know well the heavenly fellowship
Of men that perish and of summer morn.
And whence they came and whither they shall go
The dew upon their feet shall manifest.

VIII

She hears, upon that water without sound,
A voice that cries, "The tomb in Palestine
Is not the porch of spirits lingering.
It is the grave of Jesus, where he lay."
We live in an old chaos of the sun,
Or old dependency of day and night,
Or island solitude, unsponsored, free,
Of that wide water, inescapable.
Deer walk upon our mountains, and the quail
Whistle about us their spontaneous cries;
Sweet berries ripen in the wilderness;
And, in the isolation of the sky,
At evening, casual flocks of pigeons make
Ambiguous undulations as they sink,
Downward to darkness, on extended wings.

(Collected Poems)

The rich and sensuous language of this poem lays immediate claims upon us. The diction is a curious mix of plain and fancy. The rhythms feel confident, and, along with the sonorities, they draw us forward, fascinated. Yet the poem's progression, which is never quite narrative, never quite drama, never quite an oration or measured argument, is difficult to grasp. Does **"Sunday Morning"** possess an overall unity, or is it a group of poems around a common subject, somewhat arbitrarily associated? And if its unity consists of its repeated challenges to the authority of Christianity, exactly why is religion such a dominant concern?

Reading **"Sunday Morning"** has been likened to entering a picture gallery and coming upon one colorful canvas after another.[1] The first "painting" we see is informal and domestic, touched with exotic hues and details. The final one is a great panoramic landscape. In between, we discover a considerable variety of picturesque styles and tonalities. At the time Stevens wrote the poem, he was experiencing enthusiasm for new developments in the visual arts. The people he knew in New York, who included collectors of modern art like Walter Arensberg and modern artists like Marcel Duchamp, had given him "permission," we might say, to break out of a certain decadent preciousness in his own poetic style and to experiment with language and form in startling and exciting ways. The New York Armory Show of 1913 had jump-started American modernism in all the arts. One task of a poet was to figure out how the innovations in sculpture and painting could be translated into language to help lay the foundation of a new poetics.

Becoming a modernist while remaining American was the task that confronted the next three poets in this study. Stevens, Williams, and Moore can all be differentiated from poets like Pound, Stein, H. D., and Eliot, who threw in their lot with modernism while living in Europe. This is not to say that those writers weren't profoundly American, too, in various ways; it is simply to acknowledge that those who stayed at home were pressed to think about how to formulate their modernism in distinctly local terms. Place and landscape play a significant role in their experiments, and direct responses to certain facts of American culture characterize their poetry.[2] In Stevens's case that response was to the limitations, as he saw them, of traditional Protestant Christianity. For him, it formed an obstacle to art and to modernism, one that he felt he must address directly. Thus his first great modern poem is, among other things, a concerted attack on organized religion. The criticism of religion, in his understanding, opens the door to innovation and achievement in the realm of art.

While tradition in the form of religion may be rejected in **"Sunday Morning,"** traditional poetry is by no means unwelcome there. As we respond to the poem's images, we are also responding to Stevens's command of traditional verse-paragraphs, a use of blank verse that draws on Shakespeare, Milton, Wordsworth, and Browning, shaping a steady but highly flexible iambic pentameter. The regular fifteen-line stanzas feel rather like unrhymed sonnets.

Given this use of blank verse and picturesque images, might not the poem be called romantic? In its concern for the human relation to the natural world and to questions of the supernatural, it certainly displays something of a romantic sensibility. Moreover, its kinship with the great romantic odes of Keats, Coleridge, and Wordsworth has been much noticed. At the same time, we sense how American this poem is. Whatever it owes to the English romantics, it would never be confused with their poetry.

How about transcendentalist, then, that American version of the romantic? That is closer, but it will not suffice as an identifying tag either, because there is something distinctly modern about this poem's approach and atmosphere. The attitude toward Christianity is harsher and more explicit. The poem's tones are elusive and complicated, from line to line and stanza to stanza. Ironic reflections abound. The sonorities often slide sideways, reaching a parodic pitch, as in the passage about Jove in stanza III. And romantic sensibility is clearly being mocked in the passage about the boys, the maidens, and the fruit that closes stanza V, just as a tone of burlesque tends to dominate stanza VI.

Something about this poem's way of looking at the world, its manner of posing issues, its spirited voice, and its notions of beauty locates it in the early part of the twentieth century.[3] Separating its European elements from its American ones and its transcendentalist ele-

ments from its modern ones is part of our challenge here as readers. Having experimented with modernism in several shorter poems, Stevens apparently felt ready to formulate a kind of artistic Declaration of Independence. **"Sunday Morning"** stakes a claim to a new aesthetic, distinctly modern and distinctly American, and it is both the articulation of a thesis and the most impressive demonstration of that thesis.

The poem emerged rather suddenly. Stevens had written very promising poetry while an undergraduate at Harvard, but he had then given it up while he explored careers, first in journalism and then in the law. All the while living in New York City, he was reading widely and keeping a journal, as well as writing love letters to his future wife, Elsie. He wrote some poems for her as a part of this courtship in 1906 and 1907 but made no attempt to publish or show them to other readers at that time. His own Sunday mornings during this period tended to be given over to long walks in the country. His adventures in exploring the natural world had culminated, in a way, during a hunting trip to British Columbia with his employer. There, at the age of twenty-two, he seems to have had a full realization of what the natural world meant to him, especially in its character as wilderness, and some commentators have seen this vacation as a kind of spiritual and intellectual turning point for the young Stevens.[4]

Ten years later, established as a lawyer and settled in his marriage, still living in New York, Stevens found himself responding enthusiastically to new developments in the arts. He experienced the 1913 Armory Show and the growing collection of modern art that belonged to the collector and connoisseur Walter Arensberg. Gatherings at Arensberg's apartment included like-minded people who were founding little magazines and writing experimental poems. Stevens now began writing again and showing poems to friends in the Arensberg circle like Carl Van Vechten and William Carlos Williams.[5] The next ten years were quite productive, producing most of the poems in his first collection, *Harmonium* (1923).

Most of what he wrote in these beginning years was quite different from **"Sunday Morning."** The poems tended to be sketchy and imagist, playful and experimental, clearly responding to the developments in cubism and the dada movement. The poem that opens *Harmonium* is typical of this period:

"Earthy Anecdote"

Every time the bucks went clattering
Over Oklahoma
A firecat bristled in the way.

Wherever they went,
They went clattering,

Until they swerved
In a swift, circular line
To the right,
Because of the firecat.

Or until they swerved
In a swift, circular line
To the left,
Because of the firecat.

The bucks clattered.
The firecat went leaping,
To the right, to the left,
And
Bristled in the way.

Later, the firecat closed his bright eyes
And slept.

(Collected Poems)

The celebration of energy here, along with the severe and precise use of geometrical representation and the free verse, eschewing rhyme and meter, evokes the paintings of the futurists and cubists. The addition of Oklahoma, bucks, and firecat introduces American details to a manner that would otherwise be associated with European modernism. The deliberately flat ending, along with the resistance to obvious beauty and ready metaphorical decoding would have shocked and outraged traditionalists, while delighting those who were taken by the newness and the confrontational manner of modernist painting, music, and poetry. Knowing that Stevens was associating with Marcel Duchamp at the time, one can imagine that artist's appreciation for the poem, reciprocating the poet's fascination with Duchamp's experiments in sculpture and painting. Stevens's desire to create an American version of modernism is easy to identify and understand in such a case.

Nevertheless, **"Sunday Morning"** is trickier. Written in 1915, in the midst of a series of more obviously modernist experiments, it seems to stand out as an articulation of an American and modernist aesthetic. It looms up above the smaller experiments like a mountain among foothills. We need to ask how this grand set of statements helped both to define and to extend the more obvious modernist experiments that surround them.

One clear answer lies in the issue of religion and the sacrilegious. A redefinition of the sacred, in terms of the human and natural realms, lies at the heart of the poem. For Stevens, no true modern art could be created, especially in America, before the issue of religion was settled. There was a significant tension around the subject in his own mind, given his religious upbringing and his wife's steadfast piety. Resolving the question of the quarrel between religion and art as comparable manifestations of human spiritual need was therefore paramount to him.

To address it, he turned back to the writings of George Santayana, his teacher at Harvard, using them to help inform this extended consideration of the role of religion and art in human life.[6] Santayana had argued that poetry and religion were essentially the same thing, with the advantage going to poetry because it does not require or perpetuate dogma. Subscribing to this, Stevens wanted, as part of his artistic declaration, to announce the ways in which he felt that poetry could replace organized religion. He wished to resolve, both in and for himself, an issue he saw manifesting itself everywhere in his culture. When Sunday morning came around, you were supposed to be in church or in Sunday school. If you were raised that way and chose not to be in church, you then had to deal with a sense of guilt, an uneasiness, and a depression that could make the free and open time of Sunday oppressive. The week seemed to organize itself around the question of your obedience or apostasy.[7]

Rightly or wrongly, Stevens felt that Americans could not create their own vigorous and original artistic culture until they freed themselves from their puritanical Protestant heritage. The tomb in Palestine needed to be acknowledged as a foreign place where a historical figure named Jesus had died—just that and nothing more. It was in exploring and trying to resolve such issues that Stevens suddenly found he could write in a particularly eloquent and extended style, turning away from the playful and opaque experimentation of his concurrent poems and drawing on the romantic and Miltonic tradition that seemed to be reserved for larger issues. His explicitness about the drawbacks of organized religion shocked Harriet Monroe, the editor of *Poetry,* to whom he sent **"Sunday Morning."**[8]

Stressing both the foreignness and the historical remoteness of Christianity thus becomes one strategy by which Stevens reinforces his views. The here and now is an America, sunny, capacious, and newly modern, where one might enjoy oneself on a Sunday morning. The encroachment upon this pleasure comes from a far-away time and place, a distant oppressiveness that stifles the spirit, darkening and silencing the world. Stevens fought that oppression in himself, and of course he wished his wife and neighbors could fight it, too. Whether or not they could and whatever their sentiments and pieties, he meant to stake out his antitheological and proaesthetic position. He needed to clear his own artistic ground for a new start in a new world, a place where Sunday and morning could acquire an entirely new meaning.

So we begin with a domestic interior. The emphasis is on sensuous pleasure: a bathrobe elegant enough to be called a peignoir and some imported tropical pleasures, including bright fruit, stimulating coffee, and a pet bird from the rainforest, being given what is perhaps its weekly moment of freedom from its cage. Even the rug will feel exotic in this context since the bird takes its leisure there.[9] Even though it is simply called "rug," more than one commentator has decided it must be oriental, evidence of the lively imaginative response we bring to this scene.

While we may be disposed to think of this domestic scene as a painting, we are not able to identify it in terms of any one painter, school, or period. Domestic interiors had been a subject for paintings ever since the seventeenth-century Dutch began to cultivate them. Women at leisure, in what was known as deshabille,[10] a subgenre falling between the formal portrait and the nude study, had been a frequent subject for French painters in the nineteenth century. More recently, artists such as Whistler, Sargent, and Manet had shown elegant women in exotic robes and dressing gowns, sometimes with pets nearby. Meanwhile, the emphatic use of colors, orange and green, naturally evokes postimpressionist and Fauvist painters like Matisse, Bonnard, Van Gogh, and Gauguin. The painterly associations, in other words, are rich and complex, and they aid the reader's imagination without specifying a particular period or style.[11]

For a moment the sensuous and exotic pleasures seem to dominate; they "mingle to dissipate"—the verb is probably chosen for its innate ambiguity—the Protestant Sunday morning preoccupation with biblical matters. But their dominion, attractive though it may be, is not enough to overcome the woman's upbringing and psychology. We move inward to discover that as she "dreams a little," a natural extension of her relaxed "complacencies," there comes a "dark encroachment" of an "old catastrophe," presumably the Crucifixion. The domestic interior is displaced by a rather spooky seascape, calm and silent, with water lights and a procession of ghosts heading for Palestine. It is as though the living and dead alike are compelled to join this ghastly Easter parade. The progression of the entire stanza is from sunny "complacencies" to gloomy "sepulchre," and the pungent fruit and cockatoo wings are swept along, as is the woman's sunnier mood, by the tremendous force of religious preoccupation.

The drama, combining inner and outer, may recall the drama in Yeats, but the differences are instructive. It is not an "I" but a "she." The meditative space is subjective but not personal. It does not express the situation of the speaker and, through that, connect to the author. And the resort to darker imaginative landscapes is involuntary and unwelcome, not a refuge from contemporary reality but rather a sinister invasion by tradition. The stanza's repeated words and phrases, especially "wide water, without sound," in successive lines, underline its portrayal of obsession and a sort of spiritual kidnapping.

We should not be surprised, then, that the woman's experience provokes the speaker/narrator's direct protest: "Why should she give her bounty to the dead? / What is divinity if it can come / Only in silent shadows and in dreams?" Having presented her and delighted in her, just as a painter might in his model, he now wants to protect her from the "dark encroachment" that disrupts her sensuous enjoyment and spoils her Sunday. He wants to assume that her sensibility matches his, but the reader senses his urge rather than his success. He may or may not understand her mind and emotions. This problematizing of their situation opens a creative space in which the reader faces choices and entertains speculations that may undermine the speaker's authority.

In any case, the speaker is sure of his ground: He wants to counterbalance "the thought of heaven" with the beauty of the earth:

> Shall she not find in comforts of the sun,
> In pungent fruit and bright, green wings, or else
> In any balm or beauty of the earth,
> Things to be cherished like the thought of heaven?

The speaker is stacking his argument by making religion a "thought," located in a mental realm of silent shadows and dreams, a "dominion" of something long gone—bloody, lugubrious, and preferably forgotten—while the humanist side gets the real and material things that can be touched, smelled, tasted, and listened to. The world of the senses is firmly associated with pleasure, both physical and aesthetic, while the world of dogma is presented as a threat that turns sense experience vague and dark, silencing and obscuring it.[12] For the woman in deshabille, it is a matter of her reconciling her inner world with the outer one:

> Divinity must live within herself:
> Passions of rain, or moods in falling snow;
> Grievings in loneliness, or unsubdued
> Elations when the forest blooms; gusty
> Emotions on wet roads on autumn nights;
> All pleasures and all pains

Sadness is more acceptable on these terms, a cool companion to pleasure. The mix of weathers and seasons with interior events, both painful and pleasurable, feels quite persuasive. It is also recognizable—we may invoke Rilke and Yeats by now, as colleagues—in terms of the modernist attack on the discontinuities of inner and outer, spirit and matter. One thing that is crucial to the argument is the imagination's ability, aided by the senses and sense-memory, to mix and match experiences, acting not only in the present but also retrospectively. The ability to remember "the bough of summer and the winter branch" gives one the ability to balance and compare, relishing sense experience and offsetting the painful with the pleasurable. That is the kind of spiritual activity the poem endorses, as against religious activities involving guilt, fear, and the anticipation of heavenly reward. By the time the speaker closes this section with "These are the measures destined for her soul," the main issues of the poem have been fully set out. The rest will be variations on this theme.[13]

The first variation, in stanza III, is a sort of potted history of religion. Its tongue-in-cheek tone is signaled in part by the excessive alliterations:

> Jove in the clouds had his inhuman birth.
> No mother suckled him, no sweet land gave
> Large-mannered motions to his mythy mind.
> He moved among us, as a muttering king,
> Magnificent, would move among his hinds.

This is the first phase of human religion, in which the deity's otherness is stressed. It will do for Zeus, for Jupiter, and for the Jehovah of the Old Testament. The stories of these deities' relations with their human subjects emphasize their inequality and the sense of subjection to their arbitrary behavior (Zeus and Europa, etc.). The absence of any interdependence between the human and the divine is next replaced by the idea of the Incarnation: "Until our blood, commingling, virginal, / With heaven, brought such requital to desire / The very hinds discerned it, in a star." This brings us to the Christian Nativity and to a mingling of the divine and the human. Now it is not a matter of arbitrary exercise of power, but rather, as in Rilke, human desire ascending and aspiring to the condition of godhead. The next step, Stevens's speaker is happy to suggest, might be to let the human take over the divine altogether: "Shall our blood fail? Or shall it come to be / The blood of paradise? And shall the earth / Seem all of paradise that we shall know?" It's clear how the speaker, from the attitudes expressed in stanza II, thinks these questions should be answered: no, yes, and yes. He sees a natural evolution of spiritual belief from the positing of gods as others, through the incarnation of divinity in human form, to a final human acknowledgment of independence from supernatural beliefs. The prospect is welcomed:

> The sky will be much friendlier then than now,
> A part of labor and a part of pain,
> And next in glory to enduring love,
> Not this dividing and indifferent blue.

The tone has moved from burlesque treatment of religious mythology to humanist declaration of kinship with nature. Divinity is humanized now as part of the activity of the imagination.[14]

As stanza IV opens, the woman speaks. The situation becomes more fully dramatized, a dialogue or debate in which we realize that she has perhaps been listening to the speaker's arguments and wishes to respond:

> She says, "I am content when wakened birds,
> Before they fly, test the reality
> Of misty fields, by their sweet questionings;
> But when the birds are gone, and their warm fields
> Return no more, where, then, is paradise?"

This question, which echoes Keats's great odes, is a lyrical expression of two contrary things: the human response to nature and the human resistance to natural change. It is cast in terms of morning, a summer dawn with birdcalls beginning and a preliminary mist. It also provokes an emphatic response from the speaker, who once again rehearses the history of religion, this time in terms of versions of the supposedly perfect world from which humanity fell and/or the perfect world to which it aspires to return. He lists a string of phony oracles and paradises, sometimes using archaic terminology ("chimera," "golden underground," "isle / Melodious, where spirits gat them home"), in order to dismiss them. None of them

> has endured
> As April's green endures; or will endure
> Like her remembrance of awakened birds,
> Or her desire for June and evening, tipped
> By the consummation of the swallow's wings.

His response takes her language and imagery into account, matching her misty morning with a protracted summer evening and birds that are active at dusk and adding a kind of superword, "consummation," to clinch his argument. Green endures, we learn, and so do sensations of memory and desire; ideal constructs, meanwhile, come to seem ephemeral.

We should note in passing that their "dialogue" is not very direct. He does not say "your remembrance." He still discusses her as though she occupied a different space or time, such as a picture, and he stood commenting on her. Yet her responses, as stanzas IV and V both demonstrate, suggest that she can listen to him as well as object. The implications of this point again to the complications of modernist art, where the destabilizing of the speaker's authority and singularity opens the text and furnishes a more creative role for the reader.

When stanza V opens as IV did, we realize that his mockery of various human inventions of paradise has not settled her objections: "She says, 'But in contentment I still feel / The need of some imperishable bliss.'" Fair enough, we might say, taking her point. If he talks of "desire" for June and evening, why not also acknowledge her desire, "feel[ing] the need," for lasting bliss? Why must pleasure be ephemeral? Who says we can't have a paradise where beauty and happiness are prolonged indefinitely? Her contention turns out to be precisely the provocation the speaker needs to spring his most direct and powerful argument, couched as an aphorism that echoes Plato's "Necessity is the mother of invention": "Death is the mother of beauty; hence from her, / Alone, shall come fulfillment to our dreams / And our desires." The sentiment matches those that Rilke and Yeats have expressed less directly. It can also be traced back to the romantics, particularly to Keats and especially to his "Ode on Melancholy."[15]

The logic of this is tricky: If our dreams and desires include paradise, how can death bring any kind of fulfillment for them? The implied answer is that desire for false beauty (i.e., permanent beauty) is illegitimate. If the beauty is genuine, it will be bound up with change and death. That insight is further addressed in stanza VI.

The dramatized confrontation has somehow made the unusual directness possible. Moreover, Stevens now borrows from religion the habit of positing deities; his is admittedly constructed for the occasion, but a goddess of death is an especially convenient personification to summon at this point.[16] We learn that she "strews the leaves / Of sure obliteration in our paths," paths associated variously with sorrow, triumph, and tender love, and that she "makes the willow shiver in the sun" and "causes boys" to proffer fruit. As the maidens taste the fruit "and stray impassioned in the littering leaves," the poem slides into a burlesque manner again. These boys and maidens sound rather like the silly lovers in *A Midsummer Night's Dream*. However, the central phrase and concept, "Death is the mother of beauty," continues to resonate, spreading out from the poem's center to dominate its aesthetic and outlook.

We do not know whether the woman is convinced or simply silenced. Whichever is the case, the speaker takes over for the final three stanzas. He presents her as hearing a voice in stanza VIII, but she utters no further objections to his viewpoint. She has served her purpose, provoking his eloquent outbursts and opening new space in which readers may speculate on the complications of the questions the speaker is trying to settle authoritatively. Her implied presence continues to trouble both the surface and the depths of the poem, allowing us to see the speaker as a version of Stevens who, like the "Yeats" who wanders through "Among School Children," is less capable or comprehending than the author. His emphatic declarations are deliberately undermined by a whisper of objection that suggests, for example, that he has not managed to persuade his target audience. We may admire his sentiments, framing them in terms of his rejection of religion and celebration of a humanist aesthetic, but we do so with an awareness that they can isolate him—from the woman, from his neighbors, and from the potential audience for his art. He is not a ludicrous comic hero like Crispin, whom Stevens made the protagonist of his uneven long poem, **"The Comedian as the Letter C,"** but he has in common with Crispin a mixture of success and failure that complicates our perspective.

Stanza VI is a series of rhetorical questions, over nine lines, followed by an exclamation and then a reiteration of the key phrase from stanza V, "Death is the mother of beauty." In the questions, paradise is mocked for being made up of natural beauties that in their essence necessarily imply change and loss: ripe fruit, unchanging sky, rivers that never make it to the ocean or even touch their own banks. The absurdity is summarized: "Why set the pear upon those river-banks / Or spice the shores with odors of the plum?" And the absurdity provokes a kind of crocodile tear, feigning sympathy: "Alas, that they should wear our colors there, / The silken weavings of our afternoons, / And pick the strings of our insipid lutes!" Alas, indeed. The denizens of paradise (which means for Stevens, I think, both the Eden from which Adam and Eve presumably fell and the heaven to which humankind is supposed to aspire in the afterlife) sound like pallid imitators of life, emulating its sensations but unable to make them effective because of their prolongation. To "spice the shores with odors of the plum" is necessarily to admit that fruit ripens and falls and that sensations like smell are ephemeral. The mockery of heavenly phoniness is swept aside in favor of a ringing and mysterious close: "Death is the mother of beauty, mystical, / Within whose burning bosom we devise / Our earthly mothers waiting, sleeplessly." The final image captures the human paradox triumphantly. We see Death and acknowledge her creation of beauty, but we also resist, positing mothers who are waiting up for us, as if we were tardy children. This "devising" disrupts the truth of Death and the vision of her "burning bosom." It is an understandable nostalgia—who does not want his or her mother back, want a reunion and a life after death?—but, in the speaker's view, it needs to be looked at skeptically. Of course we do this, he suggests, but we also need to step back from it. No mothers wait sleeplessly for us, in Stevens's view of the matter; we need to let them rest and accept the fact of their sleep, their death.

If we trace the presence of the feminine through the poem, we can say it has been both troublesome and enriching to the arguments the speaker is pursuing. The woman raises objections to his dismissal of the supernatural and the eternal. Motherhood is problematic to the gods and to humans; no mother suckled Jove, but Jesus attained his incarnation through Mary, whose traditional color blue has become "dividing and indifferent," as the sky in stanza III. Maidens and mothers are displaced somehow by the mother who turns out to be Death, the mother in whom we devise our mothers waiting sleeplessly for us.[17] But through her mothering authority. Death brings labor and generation and the consequent desire for more permanence back into the poem's foreground.[18] Small wonder, then, that the pagan celebration envisioned in stanza VII turns out to be male, a religious ritual of nature worship performed exclusively by men:

> Supple and turbulent, a ring of men
> Shall chant in orgy on a summer morn
> Their boisterous devotion to the sun,
> Not as a god, but as a god might be,
> Naked among them, like a savage source.

They may or may not be clothed. The speaker doesn't specify, although the nakedness of the sun, the sunlight "as a god," along with their dew-covered feet (instead of shoes or sandals) has led many commentators to reasonably infer nakedness in the men. As for summer and morning and sunlight, it begins to be clear how their recurrence in the poem establishes an emerging foundation for a natural religion.

Again, we are apt to think of paintings. Matisse's famous ring of naked dancers was not all male, but it certainly comes to mind.[19] So do the naked male bathers of painters like Eakins and Cézanne. For Stevens's readers, moreover, in 1915, the image might well have summoned up not a painting but a recent and famous modernist performance, Stravinsky's *Rite of Spring* as produced by Diaghilev and choreographed and danced by Nijinsky.[20] The orgiastic music and the frankness of the dancing constituted a landmark of modernist primitivism that achieved a rapid notoriety. A ring of dancing men could also be said to call up Native American practices that were beginning to be discussed by Stevens's generation in their search for alternatives to mainstream European culture. In many tribes it was primarily the men's business to dance, while the women served as spectators and commentators.

These men, however, do not literally take the sun to be a god. They are post-Christian, representing a reborn paganism, and their praise does not mistake the sun for something else. Rather, it acknowledges how divinity can be personified metaphorically, "as a god might be." There's no question about the human origin of their practice: "Their chant shall be a chant of paradise, / Out of their blood, returning to the sky." There's also no question but that it replaces traditional religion in its eloquence and praise:

> And in their chant shall enter, voice by voice,
> The windy lake wherein their lord delights,
> The trees, like serafin, and echoing hills,
> That choir among themselves long afterward.

This is not a muttering king moving among his hinds, but a celebration of the holiness and beauty of the natural world, reinforced by biblical language and traditional associations of worship. The result is a "heavenly fellowship":

> They shall know well the heavenly fellowship
> Of men that perish and of summer morn.

> And whence they came and whither they shall go
> The dew upon their feet shall manifest.

In other words, their bond is partly in the recognition of their common mortality.[21] The dew speaks of it eloquently by standing, as is usual in Stevens, for the ephemeral nature of all life in this world. Words like "perish," "whence," "whither," and "manifest" continue the heavy borrowing from traditional religious discourse, and they make the tone of this stanza almost impossible to capture. It can seem profoundly serious in its vision of an earth-oriented and humanist religion of the future, and it can simultaneously register as slightly parodic and tongue-in-cheek, a send-up of the whole idea of communal worship and religious ritual. This simultaneity, which characterizes so much of the poem, has always intrigued readers and, insofar as they could stand to leave matters unresolved, made them acknowledge its elusiveness.

Does this all-male ritual signal a final gulf between men and women, especially on the subject of worship? Hardly. But it certainly continues the poem's framing of questions about belief in terms of gender. Stevens brings his female opposite back one more time in the next stanza, to hear what he considers a truth, but then he turns his face to the American wilderness. The implication seems to be that men are in advance of women—as represented primarily by the poet's mother and by Elsie, although Harriet Monroe can be included, given her insistence on censoring the poem—in questioning traditional religion's relevance to modern American life. The men forge on ahead in this area, and the women are free to follow if they choose. That it should be cast in terms of gender may seem unfair to later readers, but it is scarcely surprising in its reflection of Stevens's own life and circumstances.[22] And the ways in which it enhances the interest and drama of the poem are not altogether a disadvantage.

The final section of the poem has two distinct parts, a report of the woman's hearing a voice, followed by a summary of humanity's position with relation to the natural world. The implicit relation between the two parts seems to reflect the kind of interaction found elsewhere in the poem: hearing about the death of the historical Jesus and dismissing the idea of resurrection and paradise seems to release the poem into some of its most eloquent speech and imagery. In that sense we can say that the engagement of Christian and pagan viewpoints, with the pagan displacing the Christian, happens one final time, achieving an emphasis that is particularly memorable.

Bringing the woman back at least raises the possibility that the entire poem has been a drama in her mind. It also undermines, once again, the full authority of the speaker, which in turn, as I have suggested, opens new speculative (modernist) space for the reader. She "hears" a "voice that cries": "The tomb in Palestine / Is not the porch of spirits lingering. / It is the grave of Jesus, where he lay." The voice is "upon that water without sound," where her dreaming feet were passing in stanza I. It sounds disembodied and authoritative, as if it were a supernatural utterance. Who is speaking? History? Common sense? Reason? We are left to speculate.

We are also left to speculate on her response. One critic assumes that the lines that follow represent her insight.[23] In that reading all of the different positions of belief expressed in the poem become her territory, part of her mental theater, with this the final one. It's an intriguing suggestion. However, since we have been acutely aware of a difference between her viewpoint, drawn away from her pleasures toward her sense of duty to Christian belief and ritual, and that of a speaker who comments on her and argues against her distraction, I think most readers will feel that she is more or less dismissed here, left to ponder what she has heard. One can liken her to a passive Mary, hearing a kind of anti-Annunciation. Turning away from her, in effect, the speaker moves stage front to chant the final lines, representative once more of the position of atheism and paganism he has been championing. She may hear his voice, and she may or may not assent. The question is left open.

The final unit can be broken into two subsections. The first is extremely generalized:

> We live in an old chaos of the sun,
> Or old dependency of day and night,
> Or island solitude, unsponsored, free,
> Of that wide water, inescapable.

"We" is all humanity. The "old chaos," which replaces the "old catastrophe" of stanza I, is both the literal origin of the solar system and the sentiment that we cannot look to the disorder of nature for signs of a purposeful creator. The sun is the sun, not a god and not a mirror of a deity practicing "intelligent design." It confers a "dependency" on us because, no matter how ingenious our technology and civilization, the basic facts of day and night continue to rule our lives. This dependence upon the fact of the earth circling the sun and rotating as it goes can also be expressed as an "island solitude," like Robinson Crusoe's. There is no deity to share our island/planet with us, no "sponsor" of our activities. This leaves us "free," but it also maroons us. The reappearance of the "wide water," which invokes the size and majesty of the oceans as well as the vastness of outer space, reinforces the sense of being marooned in an immensity. Some readers will find this negative and forbidding, though I do not think that Stevens found it so. For him, "unsponsored" and "free" outweigh "dependency," "inescapable," and "chaos."

The reason I do not think Stevens found the insight depressing is contained in the lovely description and invocation of the natural that follows.[24] Generalizations are now replaced by images of considerable beauty and power:

> Deer walk upon our mountains, and the quail
> Whistle about us their spontaneous cries;
> Sweet berries ripen in the wilderness;
> And, in the isolation of the sky,
> At evening, casual flocks of pigeons make
> Ambiguous undulations as they sink,
> Downward to darkness, on extended wings.

It turns out that our "island solitude" is shared, in fact, by creatures and plants whose existence is relatively independent of ours. We may think of mountains as "our mountains," and we may hear the whistling and spontaneous cries of the quail "about us," locating them in relation to where we are. Nonetheless, the deer walk whether we see them or not—they usually make sure that we don't—and the quail are well hidden, while the berries ripen whether or not we eat them. Since they ripen "in the wilderness," it's much more likely that the bears and birds get them.

The flocks of pigeons, too, come home to roost whether we witness or ignore them.[25] Their undulations are ambiguous partly because it is hard to tell whether they intend to fly more or cease flying. In addition, undulations, as the whole poem has taught us, are always likely to be ambiguous, to mean flux and chaos on the one hand and to mean beauty on the other, in this case the beauty of birds: cockatoos, swallows, and pigeons. They are birds of paradise—of the real paradise, that is, this earth we share with them.

The American wilderness, the great biosphere that the American settlers found waiting to explore, to fear, to conquer, and to conjure, is a fact that finally outweighs the tomb of Jesus and any of the old mythologies of death and resurrection. Voros quotes from a journal that Stevens was keeping shortly after his trip to British Columbia:

> I thought, on the train, how utterly we have forsaken the Earth, in the sense of excluding it from our thoughts. There are but few who consider its physical hugeness, its rough enormity. It is still a disparate monstrosity, full of solitudes + barrens + wilds. It still dwarfs + terrifies + crushes. The rivers still roar, the mountains still crash, the winds still shatter. Man is an affair of cities. His gardens + orchards + fields are mere scrapings. Somehow, however, he has managed to shut out the face of the giant from his windows. But the giant is there, nevertheless.[26]

This sounds more like the romantic version of the sublime than the quiet wilderness depicted in the final stanza. However, its more general sentiment, that we separate ourselves from nature at great risk to our psychic health, is a particularly American sentiment, framed in terms of a direct response to the size and majesty of the continent. Having had it, Stevens had been waiting to put it in a poem; it bursts forth in **"Sunday Morning"** as a long-delayed and deeply cherished insight, and it helps identify the poem as both modern and American—modern because it rejects an important part of tradition and asks for new insights and a new beginning, sponsored by a new aesthetic, and American because it finally frames the issues of newness in relation to the landscapes and wildlife of the New World.

The poem ends with evening and darkness, as it began with morning and sun, acknowledging in this arc the "dependency of day and night." But the image of enveloping darkness, which is also a rest and homing for the pigeons, is reassuring and different from the "dark encroachment" of catastrophe. This time it is not a disruption of the sunny Sunday but a natural complement to it. It is evening. There's likely to be a vivid sunset of the kind that Hudson River and American Luminist painters loved to depict. The birds are casual, performing a familiar and daily act. The darkness is night, but it is also some of the other things darkness has come to mean. The darkness is death, and, in Stevens's understanding of the matter, that involves a frank acceptance of human mortality and its interpenetration with beauty, the central insight of the poem.

This is not to say that the ending does not also carry an elegiac edge; earth's presences become absences all too readily, always, as the woman has clearly felt; her consciousness of loss qualifies and shadows the narrator's more optimistic affirmations, enriching and deepening the poem enormously.

This splendid and memorable ending makes it hard to understand Harriet Monroe's pressuring Stevens in a way that made him both cut the poem and scramble the order, putting this closing stanza second. She certainly does not seem to have grasped the poem in its entirety. Furthermore, Stevens's cooperation with her, presumably a compromise bred of the temptation to appear in her magazine, was purely temporary. When he put *Harmonium* together, he "rehung" his exhibition in its original order, fully understanding that, while the stanzas/sections can be viewed, read, and studied separately, there is a crucial order of arrangement that takes us from the woman in the peignoir, among her coffee and oranges and cockatoo, to the vast American landscape at the end.

The reader will perhaps think of some points of comparison between this poem's close and the memorable closures of "The Bowl of Roses" and "Among School Children." All three arrive at a new definition of the human condition, one that tries to reconcile us with a world of change and flux, arguing for an interaction between humanity and nature that traditional beliefs and practices had managed to obscure. A common purpose among the modernist poets seems to have been emerging in the years in which these poems were written. Rilke, Yeats, and Stevens, on very different terms, can be said to mount a double attack: on transcendentalist philosophies on the one hand and materialist philosophies on the other. They feel their way forward to a third alternative, in which body and spirit are interdependent aspects of each other, inseparable in their activities and meanings.[27] This is nothing less than an attempt to redefine the human, for it locates the understanding of what it means to be human in this world, in this life, and it does so in order that readers may participate in it and feel their humanity more fully and more truly in the music and candor of the poems.

Notes

1. Several commentators remark on this, most notably Michel Benamou: "The best example of Stevens' pictorial method of composition is to be found in the structure of 'Sunday Morning,' his most celebrated long poem" (12). MacLeod discusses this as well. See also Buttel, who is almost persuaded that Stevens had set out "to abolish the distinctions between poetry and painting" (148).

2. Robert Frost and Hart Crane, while not treated in this study, present further examples of the way that American modernism, on the ground, developed around a more specific response to place and local culture.

3. I find myself connecting it with American painters like Marsden Hartley, Stuart Davis, Georgia O'Keeffe, and Charles Burchfield, as well as with those nature writers who can be seen as descendents of the transcendentalists—John Muir, John Burroughs, and Henry Beston.

4. See especially Voros's study and her second chapter, "'The Westwardness of Everything': Stevens's Ktaadn." Excerpts from the journal Stevens kept in British Columbia during August 1903, are to be found in L [*Letters of Wallace Stevens*] (64-67).

5. For accounts of this period see Richardson and MacLeod.

6. Sidney Feshbach argues for the close correspondence between "Sunday Morning" and Santayana's *Interpretations of Poetry and Religion* in "A Pretext for Wallace Stevens' 'Sunday Morning.'" I stress Santayana's importance to Stevens's thought in "A Skeptical Music."

7. Emily Dickinson had struggled with similar issues in her life and poems: "Some keep the Sabbath

going to church—/ I keep it, staying at Home—/ With a Bobolink for a Chorister / And an Orchard, for a Dome." The poem concludes with a phenomenological insight: "So instead of getting to Heaven, at last—/ I'm going, all along."

8. Her uneasiness led to a shortened and reorganized version, dropping stanzas II, III, and VI and reordering the poem I-VIII-IV-V-VII. Richardson notes: "In excluding Sections II, III, and VI from the poem as it was published in *Poetry,* Harriet Monroe . . . heard in her mind the censorious comments of the commonsense society were the excised stanzas to appear" (436). On June 6, 1915, Stevens had written Monroe: "Provided your selection of the numbers of *Sunday Morning* is printed in the following order: I, VIII, IV, V, I see no objection to cutting down. The order is necessary to the idea" (*L* 183). On June 23 he agreed to add stanza VII as an ending and to a change of the phrase "on disregarded plate," even though his explanation had clarified its meaning.

9. Readers have wondered whether the bird might be an image woven into the rug rather than a real pet, but that does not really account for "green freedom" satisfactorily.

10. Or dishabille: "A loose negligee; also the state of being dressed in a loose or careless style; undress" (*Webster's Second Unabridged*).

11. Ezra Pound had written a poem with a peignoir in it the year before, in 1914, "Albatre":

> The lady in the white bath-robe which she calls a peignoir,
> Is, for the time being, the mistress of my friend,
> And the delicate white feet of her little white dog
> Are not more delicate than she is,
> Nor would Gautier himself have despised their contrasts in whiteness
> As she sits in the great chair
> Between two indolent candles.

This is both painterly and aesthetic enough to have given Stevens a precedent. Its whiteness recalls Whistler's aesthetics and suggests that Stevens is deliberately invoking the newer painting styles (e.g., Fauve) by means of his bright and contrasting colors. Stevens's poem can be seen in part, then, as a vigorous rewriting of the indolence and decadence Pound was borrowing from Whistler and Gautier.

12. The choice of "measures" of course reinforces the preference for art over theology. It invokes poetic measure as well as the idea of music and dancing. The emphasis on pleasure led Yvor Winters to accuse Stevens of hedonism, along with dandyism, but as numerous commentators have demonstrated,

the poem is Epicurean rather than hedonist, and the dandyism, a kind of verbal clowning that Stevens was prone to use as a protective mask, is put aside for the most part.

13. Feshbach, in "Elegy Rebuffed by Pastoral Eclogue," summarizes the position nicely: "The doctrinal implication of his argument is that if she will rid herself of a desire to escape this, the only world and her desire to cling to moments essentially and necessarily subject to natural change, his Epicurean philosophy allows her to retain her pursuit of pleasure and, most importantly, to perceive beauty in nature and in the laws of nature. She should sacrifice sacrifice" (245).

14. Stevens had written to Elsie in 1907: "I am not in the least religious. The sun clears my spirit, if I may say that, and thinking of blue valleys, and the odor of the earth, and many things. Such things make a god of a man; but a chapel makes a man of him. Churches are human" (*L* 96). An earlier letter is similarly explicit: "An old argument with me is that the true religious force in the world is not the church but the world itself; the mysterious callings of Nature and our responses" (*L* 58).

15. I have in mind especially the lines "She dwells with Beauty—Beauty that must die; / And Joy, whose hand is ever at his lips / Bidding adieu."

16. Death is often masculine (e.g., the Grim Reaper), but in Italian, for example in Petrarch, death is feminine, partly by virtue of the language itself.

17. This may be what leads Helen Vendler to remark that "The exquisite cadences of *Sunday Morning* are in fact corpse-like, existing around the woman's desires in a waxy perfection of resignation" (57).

18. Shades of Yeats, who of course had not yet written "Among School Children."

19. *Le Danse,* painted in 1909, was already justly famous. Its ring of naked women seems to be an enlargement of a group Matisse had put at the center of *Le bonheur de vivre* (1905-1906, owned by Gertrude and Leo Stein), probably after a composition by Ingres called *L'age d'or.* If Stevens knew of this, the transformation from "Golden Age" to "the happiness of life" would have both amused him and reinforced his views.

20. It was Anne Tashjian who first suggested this to me. The Stravinsky had premiered on May 29, 1913, in Paris, and the performance had an instant notoriety. The Arensberg circle would no doubt have been discussing it, perhaps from eyewitness accounts by some of its members, right around the time Stevens wrote "Sunday Morning." The

coincidence of primitive dancing and modern art, along with the date, make the event and music, as a source for Stevens, too great to ignore. (This doesn't mean that Stevens had actually heard the music; the U.S. premiere wasn't until 1922 in Philadelphia, by Stokowski.) For a useful account of Stravinsky's piece and its place in the modernist preoccupation with spring, primitivism, and renewal, see the "Spring, Sacred and Profane" chapter in Conrad, *Modern Times, Modern Places* (381-99).

21. Longenbach (1991, 65-66) feels that the death of so many young men in World War I contributed to the feeling of the fellowship among men that perish. The historical circumstance makes that plausible, but it is important to recognize that for Stevens the democracy of mortality is universal, not dependent on wars, plagues, or any other special forms of loss.

22. Jacqueline Vaught Brogan feels that Stevens often suppresses "what *he* perceives to be his feminine voice, or, more accurately, that part of his poetic voice that is feminine metaphorically in the way the idea of 'feminine' itself is metaphorical" (4). She adds that "while Stevens would always suffer from a schism within himself, one that ultimately derived from cultural biases against women (and which would affect his poetry in a number of important ways), he would also come as close as it was possible for a person in his time and circumstance to 'curing' himself."

23. Bates (112): "[S]he concludes that we live on a physical and temporal island, at once free of divine despotism and shackled to a world of flux and death." In 1928 Stevens answered a query about the poem as follows: "This is not essentially a woman's meditation on religion and the meaning of life. It is anybody's meditation" (*L* 250). This surely confirms the wish to lessen the speaker's authority and open the poem to speculation and creativity from the reader.

24. Vendler feels that the particulars that follow the generalizations "are allegorical instances of the abstract formulation. . . . The scene, in short, is being used largely as an instance of a thesis, not surrendered to in and for itself" (49). While I see her point, I can only propose that that is not how the lines feel to me when I read them. For me, the particulars *balance* the generalizations.

25. Our hunting them will affect them adversely, however. The last passenger pigeon, one symbol of the American wilderness and the human

depredations on it, had died in the Cincinnati zoo the year before Stevens wrote his poem. The event was widely reported in the press.

26. *L* (73), quoted in Voros (44-45).

27. Bethea stresses this in a discussion of "Peter Quince at the Clavier": "For Stevens blurs the historical distinction between soul and body, noumenon and phenomenon; in his view spirituality is composite with, not separate from, corporeality, and it is *through* sensuality that we augment the soul. . . . Real *existence* constitutes a composite of the imaginary and the actual, the spiritual and the material, the ideal and the real" (215-16).

Works Cited

Bates, Milton J. *Wallace Stevens: A Mythology of Self.* Berkeley: University of California Press, 1985.

Benamou, Michel. *Wallace Stevens and the Symbolist Imagination.* Princeton, N.J.: Princeton University Press, 1972.

Bethea, Dean Wentworth. "'Sunday Morning' at the Clavier: A Comparative Approach to Teaching Sevens." In *Teaching Wallace Stevens: Practical Essays,* edited by John N. Serio and B. J. Leggett. Knoxville: University of Tennessee Press, 1994.

Brogan, Jacqueline Vaught. "Sexism and Stevens." In *Wallace Stevens and the Feminine,* edited by Melita Schaum. Tuscaloosa: University of Alabama Press, 1993.

Buttel, Robert. *Wallace Stevens: The Making of* Harmonium. Princeton, N.J.: Princeton University Press, 1967.

Conrad, Peter. *Modern Times, Modern Places.* New York: Knopf, 1999.

Feshbach, Sidney. "Elegy Rebuffed by Pastoral Eclogue in Wallace Stevens' 'Sunday Morning.'" *Analecta Husserliana* 62: 231-46.

———. "A Pretext for Wallace Stevens' 'Sunday Morning.'" *Journal of Modern Literature* 23 (1999): 59-78.

Longenbach, James. *Wallace Stevens: The Plain Sense of Things.* New York: Oxford University Press, 1991.

MacLeod, Glen. *Wallace Stevens and Modern Art: From the Armory Show to Abstract Expressionism.* New Haven, Conn.: Yale University Press, 1993.

Richardson, Joan. *Wallace Stevens: The Early Years.* New York: William Morrow, 1986.

Stevens, Wallace. *Letters of Wallace Stevens,* edited by Holly Stevens. New York: Knopf, 1966.

Vendler, Helen. *On Extended Wings: Wallace Stevens's Longer Poems.* Cambridge: Harvard University Press, 1969.

Voros, Gyorgyi. *Nations of the Wild: Ecology in the Poetry of Wallace Stevens.* Iowa City: University of Iowa Press, 1997.

Yeats, W. B. *The Poems: A New Edition,* edited by Richard J. Finneran. New York: Macmillan, 1983.

Young, David. "A Skeptical Music: Stevens and Santayana." *Criticism* 7 (1965): 263-77.

Alfred Guzzetti (essay date 2008)

SOURCE: Guzzetti, Alfred. "A Few Things for Themselves." *New Literary History* 39 (2008): 251-58.

[*In the following essay, Guzzetti, drawing on the film theory of André Bazin, compares Stevens's poetic technique to that of a camera—"a machine for turning the real into the imagined."*]

> A few things for themselves,
>   Convolvulus and coral,
>   Buzzards and live-moss,
>   Tiestas from the keys,
> A few things for themselves,
>   Florida, venereal soil,
>   Disclose to the lover.[1]

I

In a documentary called *Tupamaros,* a shot of a bird in flight briefly interrupts the testimony of a former political prisoner.[2] At first I am puzzled, then realize that the bird must represent the freedom that the man once longed for and now may—or may not—have won.

As a figure of film rhetoric, the shot is hardly unusual, illustrating as it does what the interviewee is saying. Professionals even have a name for material of this kind, material which affords relief from the supposed monotony of the talking head; they call it the "B-roll."

Neither is the metaphor itself uncommon. In Yeats's "On a Political Prisoner," a bird flies down to a woman's cell and eats from her hand, recalling her lost wildness and youth. In the poem, the bird is "a grey gull," a category. In the film, it is, inevitably, a particular bird. In making the metaphor, the filmmaker profits from our lack of facility in identifying individual birds as we do dogs or people; for us a bird in flight is close to the generic.

Despite this, the shot cannot be but of an individual bird, unless it were to depart from the photographic for an animated or still drawing (not a promising idea). The attributes that the image records may even be sufficient to support the fantasy that, if we could mobilize the needed resources and act quickly, we might locate and identify this individual. We could put its mug shot on a "wanted" poster and see what turned up.

In fact, being good viewers, we have no interest in the bird as an individual, since it is, we understand, only a term of comparison. It is the interviewee whose individuality is of interest. But the image, given its photographic nature, does not entirely cooperate. Wedded as it is to the particularity of things, it resists and subverts our good intentions. It awakens an interest of its own.

"A few things for themselves," Wallace Stevens writes, "Convolvulus and coral, / Buzzards and live-moss, / Tiestas from the keys." How do things get to be on such a list? Are these things for themselves because they possess a special power or because they are the object of a certain regard? Does this regard, I ask myself, resemble that of the camera?

II

André Bazin didn't like metaphors in film. He thought of them as the baggage of montage, atavisms, and remarked on how old-fashioned they seemed even by the early 1930s. They are the filmmaker's inventions and rest on his authority. Against them Bazin set the authority of the real, by which he meant, more often than not, the spatial. We can more easily accept the bird as metaphor if it is in the same shot as the Tupamaro or even in a separate one, providing we are convinced that the shot shows a contiguous space. In this case the meaning originates not from the filmmaker but from either the mind of the viewer or the order of the real, depending on whether or not one's view of things, like Bazin's, has religious overtones.

Stevens may not be so far from this himself, though in speaking of his poem one would have to use the word "physical" rather than "spatial." It is the physicality of things that he is celebrating, and the destination of his celebration is, this time at least, the erotic. Of course we need not go there too every time we take an interest in things for themselves. Nor is every thing equally capable of awakening such an interest, erotic or otherwise. The bird can hardly compete with "convolvulus," a word that I have to look up and that, even as a sound, has a commanding allure.

III

My glance falls upon a bird in flight. What I see provokes a reflection, a thought, an interpretation. I could not claim that the sight has a meaning but I could say that I give it one. I have ways of attempting to convey this meaning if I thought it worth the trouble—for instance by making a moving picture.

In fact, this is not a good model of what happens in *Tupamaros*. As far as the viewer is concerned, whether the viewer be myself or someone else, the glance and the bird are gone, out of play; the point of origin is the moving picture. In the presence of the bird in flight, I might have thought about freedom, and, viewing the moving picture, I might think about the same thing, but the picture adds to my contemplation elements that belong only to the photographic—for instance, the boundaries of time and of a flattened space, the relation of figure to ground, perhaps even the attributes of the animal as an individual and of the space surrounding it.

Looking to recruit Stevens as an ally, I am tempted to say that the picture by its nature cannot do otherwise than number the object, the bird, among the few—or, for all I know, the many—things for themselves. Bazin says something of the sort when, in celebrating the impersonal, physical link of the photograph to its object, he claims that the photograph alone, as opposed to the painting or drawing, presents the object "in all its virginal purity to my attention and consequently to my love."[3] Though his account may rehearse a common experience, it is more than a bit puzzling. Words may be able to invoke visible objects—the convolvulus, the buzzard—without bringing along what is around them, but the camera ordinarily does the opposite. It embeds the object, or one aspect of it, in a daunting tangle of surrounding elements. In this respect, I may have been careless in describing the shot as "of a bird." I should have said, "a shot that includes a bird" or something even more lengthy and awkward. But here I am on the verge of being overwhelmed by the problem of using words to think about pictures—a problem, by the way, that is oddly asymmetrical: do we ever use pictures to think about words?

I may also be misreading Bazin. When he says "object," he may not mean the equivalent of the bird in the image. He may mean the totality of what, before the lens, gave rise to the image, rather than the elements of that totality which his phrases specify: "here a reflection on a damp sidewalk, there the gesture of a child." Theorists sometimes name this totality, this object, the profilmic. It becomes such an object, of course, only after it has been filmed. It is defined, even constructed, by the picture made from it. For until the picture comes into my sight, I ordinarily have no occasion to experience or imagine its object.

IV

Since our firsthand experience of the profilmic is only occasional, our comparison of it to the picture consti-tutes something of a special case. We are disappointed that the motel room is smaller than it looks in the brochure and pleased that the Grand Canyon is bigger. For the most part, we see images of objects to which we have no other access. We know the objects only through their images. We seldom doubt that the objects exist, and, in seeing their pictures, we imagine them: that is, we imagine the real. One might even describe the camera as a machine for turning the real into the imagined.

What happens to the real when it is imagined in this way? Is it significantly transformed? Certainly, it cannot rid itself entirely of the attributes of the pictorial—the frame limits, flatness, or the privilege given to a particular spatial viewpoint. It acquires the trace of an author, a figure who shaped our access to it, selected the viewpoint and the limits of the frame, and who meant something by these choices, even if that something is vague or ephemeral. The ghost of this figure haunts us. We do not so much imagine the scene as re-imagine it, repeat an act whose vestiges constitute the image.

But the real, as imagined, is commanding in its own right. As viewers we cannot entirely stifle the temptation to slip the author's leash and conjure up, whether in a rigorous or casual way, the profilmic in all its depth, continuousness, and opportunity. Is this impulse perverse and pointless, interfering with our comprehension in the same way as mnemonic irrelevancies such as the possible resemblance of the bird to a pet I may once have had? It might seem so, yet if we do not make the effort to imagine the spaces beyond the frame-limits of the interviewee and bird, spaces to which we have no independent access, how can we ask what relation the two might have? The relationship of metaphor, that is, of the nonspatial, depends, as a structuralist might say, on a signifying opposition with the spatial, which, though it here turns out to be absent, is nonetheless a lurking and indispensable possibility.

V

Unschooled in botany, I search for a photograph of convolvulus on the Internet. Less tropical and erotic than I envisioned, neither the flowering plant nor the photograph that portrays it conceivably belongs among the few things "for themselves." Rather, what I have before me is an illustration of a botanical category. I might sever the photograph from this function by printing it out and putting it on my wall, where I could regard it more in the way Stevens recommends. The intention of the photographer, and of the Web page editor, to present a paradigm useful for the identification of living examples, will have receded. But the thing in itself, or rather, for itself, will not be quite in evidence either.

The author of the photograph leaves upon it a trace that is irreducible, one that has been described by semiologists as indexical, a gesture of pointing, and by Roland Barthes as signifying "look" or "there it is."[4] My act of viewing has no alternative but to reproduce this gesture imaginatively.

Of course films are not photographs. Neither are they concatenations of photographs. My possible contemplation of the flowering plant is unbounded, or, to misappropriate another term from Stevens, "unsponsored."[5] No one has pointed at it or inscribed the gesture of pointing in a medium; or if someone had, I would know something of the person and the reason. The photograph allows me to imagine but not experience unboundedness in my contemplation.

A motion picture erects further obstacles. However long a motion picture might present the plant to my gaze, I cannot escape the awareness that this time will end—and, more to the point, that I will not be the one who ends it. A hand falls between the thing and the invitation to regard it for itself.

I am tempted to say that there is a radical difference between this case and the one I earlier called "metaphor." While the elements of the metaphor derive from the spatial, the metaphoric relationship itself does not. In contemplating a lengthy shot where there is no such relation, I may have the impression that the thing is presented for itself. But the passive voice of the previous phrase masks something important—namely, the agency of the filmmaker, the one who points and who, by pointing, disappointingly reduces the difference between this case and the case of metaphor to one of degree.

VI

Wallace Stevens traffics in categories, too. He invents one, "things for themselves," then places convolvulus in it. We soon realize that this is a rhetorical gesture, for in the poem the plant illustrates something as unmistakably as it does on the botanical Web site. Photographers or filmmakers might indulge in the same rhetoric, collecting images under the title "A Few Things for Themselves." But each of their things will be situated in space and shown in relation to other elements, however vague, such as the background. Like the maker of *Tupamaros*, they can present us only with things that are parts of fields.

Is this difference consequential? Might we simply say that these irreducible fields, along with the attribute of particularity, are constituents of the medium and that the filmmaker can do with them what the poet may do with nouns or the botanist with photographs? As viewers of the film called "A Few Things for Themselves," we will in one way or another be directed to regard an element in each shot—a convolvulus plant or buzzard, say—and to disregard the rest.

The injunction to disregard, so characteristic of the cinema, has no counterpart in the poem. Wallace Stevens need not entreat the reader to overlook certain elements of what his words express. His turns of phrase, his vocabulary, his diction evoke a speaking voice, just as the words on the page, though printed, evoke the writing hand. He, or his persona, is not hopelessly remote. The same is not true of the author of the image. When I speak of that author's hand, I am conscious of using a metaphor, for I need not envision the hand—or the body of which it is part—unless the author chooses to reveal it to me; it is distant from the phenomenological facts before my senses. At the same time, the filmmaker, remote as he or she may be, is more aggressive, directing my attention not only toward but away. It is this doubleness that colors the experience of watching film—the things for themselves in contest with the agenda the director must pursue in fashioning a discourse from them or even simply presenting them to my gaze.

VII

At a screening of a videotape I've made, I sit next to a friend who in a whisper asks where this or that shot was taken. I am annoyed, thinking that my friend should understand that what I most wish is for attention to be directed fully to the sounds and pictures.

Watching Abbas Kiarostami's *Five Dedicated to Ozu*, I find myself preoccupied with the unidentified locale. In the first take, surf is seen from above and I wonder if the cinematographer is on a cliff or a dune. In another, I scrutinize the passing people to see if they are Japanese, or if not, what their nationality might be. The sun is low behind the camera, and the camera looks out beyond a boardwalk to the sea. If the time is near evening, I calculate that we must be looking east and try to figure out where one may see such large breakers while facing in that direction. Japan, in homage to Ozu? France, where I know Kiarostami has been living? The answer is probably to be found on one of the DVD's extras.

I am aware that Kiarostami has an agenda, akin to Stevens's, which leaves no room for such questions. It is not easily put into words but has to do with the contemplation of the real, the accidental, beyond the customary limits set by the cinema. He, after all, is the director who for an unforgettable minute in *Close-Up* turns away from the narrative to follow an aerosol can, an incidental element in the frame, erratically rolling down a hilly street.

Like my friend, I am remiss as a viewer. Distracted by details outside the frame, I am not entirely available to accept Kiarostami's invitation to attend to the rich details of ordinary life within it. My imagination wanders into the spaces the image portrays and seeks out the hidden filmmaker.

Are these divagations inevitable? Might there be a wholly commanding cinematic poet of things for themselves? Might that filmmaker find a better viewer than I?

VIII

Watching another film with a numerical title, *66 Scenes from America,* I have no need to identify locations. At the conclusion of each scene, the director, Jørgen Leth, obligingly includes a brief spoken phrase naming the subject and place. As the film progresses, I am aware that I miss certain words, then realize that the dialogue is in Danish, which contains enough cognates and place names to have given me the illusion that the language is mine. I become absorbed in what this foreigner chooses to film, what he finds remarkable, and I speculate about who he is, the routes he has chosen, why the scenes he includes strike him as significant. My mind is on all this as much as on the things for themselves.

Leth's film, like *Five Dedicated to Ozu,* stakes out a territory at the other end of cinema from the metaphoric cutaway to the bird. Its posture is to point at the real, at the tissue of visible things woven into space. Yet the purity of the gesture is subverted by the seductive, even ineluctable, path from what we see on the screen, the possible instances of things for themselves, to the real spaces we imagine, and to the authors, however retiring and self-effacing they may be. The obstacle in the end is not intention or rhetoric. It is not the failure of the spectator's attention. It is the medium itself.

What is cinema after all? Contemporary theorists have reached a consensus that this question—Bazin's question, Eisenstein's question, Arnheim's question—makes little sense, that the quest for the medium's essence is quixotic. Yet there does appear to be some irreducible, energizing, obstructing character to cinema. Inscribed in the image is the exhortation to regard. Inscribed in the flow of images and sounds is the concomitant injunction to disregard, without which the discourse risks opacity, even meaninglessness. In the end, the thing that must be at least partially disregarded is the continuum the image forms with the spatial world, which is, paradoxically, the spring of cinema's power and seductiveness. It is only in that world that things offer the entire promise of being for themselves. As the processes of optics, chemistry, and electronics allow

them to pass into the realm of the moving image, they acquire the attributes from which the mind makes metaphor and all its ancillary mechanisms of meaning. Of these attributes they can never be fully divested.

Notes

1. Wallace Stevens, "O Florida, Venereal Soil," in *The Collected Poems of Wallace Stevens* (Vintage: New York, 1982), 47.

2. *Tupamaros,* directed by Heidi Specogna and Rainer Hoffman (Berlin: Specogna Film, 1996).

3. André Bazin, "The Ontology of the Photographic Image," in *What is Cinema?,* trans. Hugh Gray (Berkeley and Los Angeles: Univ. of California Press, 1971), 1:15.

4. Roland Barthes, *Camera Lucida: Reflections on Photography,* trans. Richard Howard (New York: Hill and Wang, 1981), 5.

5. Stevens, "Sunday Morning" in *The Collected Poems,* 70.

FURTHER READING

Criticism

Estrin, Barbara L. "'Form Gulping After Formlessness': Petrarch's Resistant Lauras in Stevens's 'Auroras of Autumn.'" In *The American Love Lyric after Auschwitz and Hiroshima,* pp. 49-72. New York: Palgrave, 2001.
> Posits that Stevens's "Auroras" suggests the poet's belief that World War II, the Holocaust, and Hiroshima were consequences of the cultural values of Western society.

Maeder, Beverly. "Wormy Metaphors and Poems of Againstness." In *Wallace Stevens' Experimental Language: The Lion in the Lute,* pp. 11-43. New York: St. Martin's Press, 1999.
> Presents the struggle against stifling "metaphors of transcendental authority" as central to Stevens's body of work, with success measured in terms of reinvention rather than outright overcoming.

Nickels, Joel. "Wallace Stevens' *Owl's Clover* and the Dialectic of Deceit." In *Arizona Quarterly* 64, no. 4 (winter 2008): 103-28.
> Presents Stevens's long poem *Owl's Clover* as a proving ground of sorts in which Stevens articulates a wide variety of epistemological positions that appear, reformulated and refined, in his later work.

Renza, Louis A. "Wallace Stevens: Parts of an Autobiography, by Anonymous." *Journal of Modern Literature* 31, no. 3 (2008): 1-21.

Discusses the self-referential and autobiographical elements in certain of Steven's poems, noting that some of his later works "edge toward the disappearance of self altogether."

Additional coverage of Stevens's life and career is contained in the following sources published by Gale: *American Writers*; *American Writers Retrospective Supplement,* Vol. 1; *Concise Dictionary of American Literary Biography, 1929-1941*; *Contemporary Authors,* Vol. 124; *Contemporary Authors—Brief Entry,* Vol. 104; *Contemporary Authors New Revision Series,* Vol. 181; *Contextual Encyclopedia of American Literature*; *Dictionary of Literary Biography,* Vols. 54, 342; *Discovering Authors*; *Discovering Authors 3.0*; *Discovering Authors: British*; *Discovering Authors: Canadian Edition*; *Discovering Authors Modules: Most-studied Authors* and *Poets*; *Encyclopedia of World Literature in the 20th Century,* Ed. 3; *Exploring Poetry*; *Literature Resource Center*; *Major 20th-Century Writers,* Eds. 1, 2;*Modern American Literature,* Ed. 5; *Poetry Criticism,* Vol. 6; *Poetry for Students,* Vols. 13, 16; *Poets: American and British*; *Reference Guide to American Literature,* Ed. 4; *Twayne's United States Authors*; *Twentieth-Century Literary Criticism,* Vols. 3, 12, 45; *World Literature Criticism,* Ed. 5; and *World Poets.*

Anna Wickham
1884-1947

(Pseudonym of Edith Alice Mary Harper; also wrote under the pseudonym John Oland) English poet and playwright.

INTRODUCTION

A feminist poet who resented giving up her artistic aspirations to become a wife and mother, Wickham was amazingly outspoken about the frustrations associated with the prescribed role for women in the early years of the twentieth century. Her poetry encompasses both free verse as well as more traditional rhymed forms. Her work was virtually ignored after her death in 1947, but has been attracting renewed attention in recent years.

BIOGRAPHICAL INFORMATION

Born in Wimbledon, England, in 1884, Wickham was the only surviving child of Alice Whelan and Geoffrey Harper, a piano repairman. The family emigrated to Australia when Wickham was five years old and settled in Maryborough, Queensland, where her father managed a music shop and her mother gave elocution lessons. A few years later, the family moved to Brisbane. At her father's urging, Wickham began writing poetry at a very early age; she was also a talented singer, encouraged in that pursuit by the nuns at the convent school she attended.

In 1904, Wickham returned to London to study drama and singing, then went to Paris a year later to continue her studies. In 1906, she gave up her ambition to become an opera singer, returned to London, and married Patrick Hepburn, a solicitor and amateur astronomist. Wickham lost her first child when a boating accident caused her to go into premature labor; this was followed by a miscarriage. The Hepburns went on to have four sons: James (1908), John (1909), Richard (1917), and George (1919). Wickham had difficulty adjusting to the conventional role of wife and mother and felt stifled intellectually—particularly since her husband and his family disapproved of her ambitions. After the publication of her first book of poetry, *Songs* (1911), Patrick had Wickham committed to an asylum since in his view, her desire to write and publish poetry proved that she was mentally ill. Her husband's plan to force her to give up poetry backfired, however, since

the hospitalization resulted in a period of great creativity during which Wickham produced approximately eighty new poems. In 1921, Wickham's son Richard died of scarlet fever and she was consumed with guilt, convinced that her failure to give her undivided attention to her children caused the boy's death—despite the fact that the disease was nearly always fatal. Early in 1922, she went to Paris with her oldest boy James; they stayed for five months and when she returned Wickham once again tried, without success, to adjust to domestic life. She met with other artists and writers on a regular basis and corresponded with a number of others. In 1926, she and Patrick separated, but reunited two years later, just before his accidental death in 1929. Wickham spent the 1930s in London as a well-known member of the literary community and continued to write poetry, although she was finding it difficult to get her work published. When World War II began, Wickham's three sons left home to serve in the military, leaving her alone in her London home. During the war some of her manuscripts and correspondence were destroyed when her house was bombed. In a state of depression after the war, Wickham took her own life on April 30, 1947, leaving behind several hundred unpublished poems.

MAJOR WORKS

Wickham's first volume of poems, privately printed in 1911 under the pseudonym of John Oland, was entitled *Songs*. It contains such poems as "The Town Dirge" and "Song of the Young John," as well as a number of pieces that speak of imprisonment and suffocation within middle class married life. Wickham then published nine poems, including the often anthologized "The Tired Man," in the journal *Poetry and Drama*. Those poems were included in *The Contemplative Quarry*, her second collection, which was published in 1915 under the name Anna Wickham. Her poetry was becoming more overtly feminist, as she increasingly rejected societal restrictions associated with gender. A year later, Wickham published *The Man with a Hammer*, one of her more strident works. This was followed by *The Little Old House* in 1921, her last publication during her lifetime. Some of her work was lost in the bombing of her house during the war, and many others were unpublished. A volume of selected poems appeared in 1971, and an additional volume of her writings in 1984.

CRITICAL RECEPTION

Wickham's poetry was acknowledged during her lifetime, but virtually ignored for many years following her death. Celeste M. Schenck reports that the poet was well known internationally by 1932 and that "anthologies of the day printed more of her poems than those of de la Mare, Graves, and, in some volumes, even Yeats." Yet afterwards, she seems to have disappeared and much of the recent scholarship on her poetry attempts to account for this critical neglect. Myra Stark (see Further Reading) contends that her work was ignored for the same reason that it has now been rediscovered, that is, because of the feminist subject matter of her poetry. Contemporary critics "didn't know what to make of her," according to Stark. Today's readers, however, find Wickham's themes familiar: "the breaking of the cultural myths concerning women's nature and role; the rebellion against the restraints placed on women in a rigidly sex-role segregated society; the search for the free, authentic self." Wickham's position as a feminist has been lauded by many critics, including Margaret Newlin (see Further Reading) who contends that Wickham went "a step beyond many recent feminists" since she "was intent on laying bare the harassed and unadjusted spirit—lonely, sexless, hungry for communion—not only of one woman in her proudly female body but of all incarnate creatures." R. D. Smith praises her as a "bonnie fetcher for freedom—especially freedom for women—for children's future, against cant hypocrisy, and, more significantly, within herself against her fierce, contradictory nature." Schenck also comments on Wickham as "a mass of contradictions" contending that her Australian upbringing apparently gave her "a robust sense of sexual entitlement, a view of social inequality, and an authentic personal voice, all of which set her apart from other women poets of that period."

Several critics today—among them Anne Pender, Schenck, and Nelljean McConeghey Rice—believe that Wickham should have been included in the modernist canon. Pender notes her "distinctive modernist poetic voice," and Schenck contends that "Wickham's poems of class consciousness are a salutary addition to a modernist canon insufficiently concerned with the differentials of class and ethnicity." Rice attempts to account for the fact that she was ignored by scholars formulating the modernist canon, again suggesting that her exclusion was based on "woman-centered subject matter" which "was not considered to be as important as the themes of . . . male colleagues." Additionally, her poetry came from her life because "she had no academic background to provide a codified philosophy to progress from, or to react against," which Rice believes also played a part in her exclusion.

The formal features of Wickham's poetry have been considered a weakness by some critics and a strength by others. Pender suggests that "some of her chosen poetic forms and techniques do not illuminate her experiments in thought"; they are, in fact "at odds with the radical sensibility and questioning incisiveness of their author." Schenck acknowledges that Wickham's poetic forms were "unfashionable" and that her poetry has "escaped notice for its failure to adhere to the experimentalist demands of a masculinest modernism." She insists, though, that Wickham's "formal conventionality is often the very vehicle of her politics," as it is meant to be taken ironically and "should not be read as merely unsophisticated concessions to the popular conventions of the day."

PRINCIPAL WORKS

Poetry

Songs [as John Oland] 1911
The Contemplative Quarry 1915
The Man with a Hammer: Verses 1916
The Little Old House 1921
Selected Poems by Anna Wickham 1971
The Writings of Anna Wickham: Free Woman and Poet 1984

Other Major Works

The Seasons: A Speaking Tableaux for Girls (play) 1902
Wonder Eyes: A Journey to Slumbertown (play) 1903

CRITICISM

R. D. Smith (essay date 1984)

SOURCE: Smith, R. D. "Anna Wickham: A Memoir." In *The Writing of Anna Wickham, Free Woman and Poet*, edited and introduced by R. D. Smith, pp. 1-48. London: Virago, 1984.

[*In the following essay, Smith provides an overview of Wickham's poetry and an evaluation of several individual poems.*]

ANNA WICKHAM (BORN EDITH ALICE MARY HARPER) 1884-1947

Here is no sacrificial I,
Here are more I's than yet were in one human,
Here I reveal our common mystery:
I give you *woman*.

Anna Wickham said that these lines must preface all her books. In this, as in many things, she was frustrated; her thousand and more poems, most of them dashed off in pain, for fun, in anger, with glee, for cash or in desperation, are largely a record of her frustrations and her triumph over them. W. B. Yeats said that out of the quarrel with others we make rhetoric (or in our modern sense, propaganda); that out of the quarrel with ourselves we make poetry. He might have had Anna in mind. She was a bonnie fechter for freedom—especially freedom for women—for children's futures, against cant hypocrisy, and, more significantly, within herself against her fierce, contradictory nature. Lust, love, duty, will, restraint, passivity, ambition and a mistrust of ambition warred within her. So did a social rebelliousness with a need to conform. Since poetry with her came out of living, out of her immediate uncensored experience, and since her experience was simultaneously felt, thought about and analysed, it is not surprising that (as with all major artists) early experiences of parental conflict resulting in a crippling tension and areas of insecurity were lived out in both later relationships and her poetry.

Some of these deep contradictions were apparent in her own person. She was a woman with a strong, sensitive face and a sturdy body, who appears in photographs both observant and withdrawn. She gives an impression of being sunk in reflection while tensed for action. The poets, Louis Untermeyer, Oswell Blakeston and Paul Dehn, and the novelist David Garnett, who all fell in love with her at first sight, over a long span of years have described her appearance and manner. They agree to a remarkable extent, which indicates the consistent naturalism of her manner, and her 'star' quality, the breath-taking effect she had on people: even Harold Acton, whose aesthetic preciosity found her not *comme il faut,* and American celebrity-hunters were taken by the force of her personality.

She is remembered as handsome, big, and dark, of nectarine colouring, with flushed cheeks, and very humorous eyes. 'A magnificent gypsy of a woman, who always entered a room as if she had just stamped across the moors', she was careless of her appearance. Although she loved magnificent clothes, she had, as she indicates often in her writings, a touch of the slattern, which her more doting friends called 'a gypsy carelessness'. Garnett, though fascinated, was uneasy with her 'rag-bag' coterie. Acton was snooty about her performance at an upper-class lesbian poetry soirée in Paris, and an American culture snob called her 'a burly lady fortified in advance with garlic and wine'.

In England, 'struggling between dreams and domesticity', she enjoyed café and pub life as natural extensions of her curiosity about and care for all manner of people from Hampstead tramps to Lord Northcliffe eating a meat pie off the kitchen table; from obstreperous Betty May and Silvia Gough and Nancy Cunard at the Fitzroy, to the diligent social works of the School for Mothers; from the cramped economy of Harold Monro's Poetry Bookshop to the aristocratic, plutocratic and indeed artistic splendour of Natalie Barney's Temple of Sappho. These inner contradictions gave thought to her poems: like MacNeice she felt 'the drunkenness of things being various'. But in life they often made difficulties: 'Her personality was tremendous: she could build up or she could destroy.' As in an old Shropshire saying, 'She was like a cow who gave a good pail of milk, and then kicked it over.'

Anna was a worker for peace, but supported the Great War effort. She quarrelled bitterly with her husband, but stayed faithful to her marriage till her husband's death. In her children she found her only unspoiled happiness, in her vocation of poet her unshakeable centre, and in her passion for freedom and intellectual clarity, strength to endure long years of sexual, artistic and economic privation. But not without paying a heavy price. Her mother's manic and histrionic energy, overacted emotional scenes, rages, physical violence and her effusively demonstrated love for the infant Edith, had imposed on her child a too heavy load of emotional responsibility. All through her life a letter from her mother would cause Anna to retire to bed. She drained herself in support of other people: she had no means of conserving her energy, deeply as she wished to, both for her family, and for her art.

The inner contradictions expressed themselves in her social and political activities. Paul Dehn, as good a journalist as he was a poet, brings her before us in her energy and charm. He met her at Muriel Dean Paul's. 'Much of her verse is delicate as the wind on a saucer of milk,' he wrote. But Anna herself was beetle-browed, leonine, shaggy and unashamed, with a heavy hunch in her bearing like that of a peasant bowed down after centuries of toil. And, in an earthy way, beautiful at that.

She read her poems in a voice deep as the bittern, interrupting herself constantly with odd conversational asides and explanatory phrases: '"Twenty nine years of Hell are dying in me"—can I have a drink? Thanks. Now here's an intelligent bit . . .'

This habit of instant self-criticism, of on-the-spot rejection of what had just flowed from her pen persists in her letters, and in her manuscript poems, of which there are over eleven hundred. 'Bunk'; 'Rubbish, but there it is'; 'Not much sense but some rhythm.' Written of herself, these remarks justify her often savage criticisms of her friends' unsuccessful poems. Her incisive analytic intellect complemented her tumultuous feelings.

She told Dehn, 'Young man, all men are theorists and all women are practical'. (She thought this, in a Shavian way, about G. B. Shaw.) 'If you wanted to feed the nation, you'd do nothing but scribble figures on your blotting-pad at an office desk. But a woman would be thinking in terms of beans and broccoli, Ribstone pippins and potatoes. *She'd* get it *done*!' After twenty minutes she wrote him a poem:

> Paul Dehn
> Must not refrain—
> But conjure doves:
> He must defy
> Such menace of the sky
> As shall control his loves.
> He shall be faun
> On Leonora's lawn—
> God grant me gratitude for slaves.

'Not so hot that last bit,' said Anna. 'Bit obscure, what?'

It's clear that she had a strong dramatic sense. 'The bittern voice' reminds us that had she not married she would certainly have triumphed as a singer; the leading London and Paris voice-coaches, including Randaegger and De Reszke, had the highest opinion of her future. Her voice was matched by an electrifying stage presence. She wrote of her mother, 'you could imagine a ray coming out of her!' So it was with Anna. Indeed, the novelist, Eliot Bliss, in her frightfully titled *A First Meeting with God* speaks of 'her genius a kind of major star' and of the 'tremendous electric force which emanated from her. At night I felt through the walls what I can only describe as powerful magnetic rays, disturbing and exciting even terrifying.'

Certainly Anna owed these gifts of a magnificent natural voice with a star's magnetism and a talent for performance to her mother; from her father, she was blessed with an artist's sensitivity, intelligence and integrity. From both parents she inherited a facility for charming, encouraging and teaching others.

GEOFFREY HARPER 1860-1929

As her autobiography tells, Anna was brought up to pity, and later, despise her father, Geoffrey, as an ineffective failure. Alice, her mother, was a dazzler in public: 'She looked marvellous, big and impressive in a very beautiful evening dress, and with a lot of golden hair piled in a crown on her head.' She ran her home efficiently: with guests she reserved her energies for the evening's entertainment. A child remembers with fascination how she would, just for the two of them, put on an evening of Shakespeare or *The Ingoldsby Legends* (adapted for dramatic presentation). 'She was really wonderful . . . her complexion was like a beautiful rose.' From this enchanting mother she learned that her father had failed as a businessman, and, evidently,

as a husband and father. By the time she was fifteen her parents slept separately. As Anna grew older Alice became more hostile to Geoffrey, and increasingly independent as a bread-winner. This Geoffrey admired, saying that if she were dropped into the middle of the Sahara she would quickly be making a good living by teaching the Arabs something or selling them something. She was a goer, if not quite a bolter. Her energy, beauty, tumultuous love for the child, her remarkable talent for reciting, teaching, fortune-telling, managing and money-making, above all, her energetic eccentricity and inventiveness fascinated young Anna. Her love was not shaken by Alice's often farouche behaviour, or by her sometimes savage discipline, which included use of stick and later a strap. All this left an unhealed unconscious wound that expressed itself in the poems, and probably in some aspects of her life, in various sado-masochism symptoms that showed in episodes of depression, and in extravagant outbreaks, and from time to time, in her emotional sex life. The hammer and the whip recur as images in her poems and so do extremes of abasement, domination, and exaltation through suffering. 'As she beat me, I cried to her "Beat me, mother, but love me—O love me."' (p. 80).

When Anna was ten, the Queensland poet Brunton Stephens told her anxious father: 'She will be a poet on a condition you can hardly wish her since you are her father: she will be a poet if she has pain enough.'

Her education at the Roman Catholic convent also gave her a precocious preoccupation with Christ's wounds and the virtues of suffering, as well as a heightened, if repressed, sensuality. It also provided a substitute for her often withdrawn mother-love.

Her father she loved for his tenderness, care, and passionate will for her to be successful. She may have been influenced by his encouraging her 'boyishness'. Anna, no doubt taking entirely her mother's point of view, shows a true but pitying affection for Geoffrey, and always felt an obligation to make an acknowledged success of her writings in order to gratify his ambitions for her, and no doubt to assuage the guilt she must have felt for her own ambivalence to him whom she both loved and in some respects despised.

Certainly the leaving of Sydney incident is embarrassingly funny. As the boat begins to pull away from the wharf taking the daughter off, on a £4 weekly allowance, to conquer Europe with her art, father shouts, '*Punch,* Anne, *Punch*!' Twenty years later, one of her best-known poems was parodied in *Punch,* and she was written up by Humbert Wolfe in the 14th edition of the *Encyclopaedia Britannica,* so Geoffrey had some gratification at least.

But this picture of her father as an ineffectual salesman hawking in the Queensland bush his grand pianos in vain always seemed contradicted by other facts that existed independent of her mother's impatient complaining and dismissals.

He never aspired to be a musician: he would have liked to have been a writer. In this certainly he failed. So do most aspirants, after all. But he was a sensitive intellectual, respected as an independent mind, an amateur philosopher and a Rationalist, a crony of men of intellectual repute, and a close friend and adviser, in the early stages of his rise to fame or notoriety, of George Riddell, later Editor of the *News of the World,* and Lord Riddell. (He saw Geoffrey off on the boat to Australia with a present of a copy of the *Origin of Species*.)

Evidently there was much more to Anna's father than her mother put about. Moreover, whether or not the music shops in Haverstock Hill and in Wimbledon did provide a decent living for the family, the job he obtained when he decided (no doubt with some reluctance) to move on led to growing success. It was to manage a music shop in Maryborough, South Queensland, with two branches in nearby sugar towns, Bundaberg and Gympie. (See p. 92 for their way of life and the marital quarrels, in their house on stilts on the Mary River.) Floods wrecked the branches and piano selling in Maryborough was supplemented by piano-tuning.

Life in Queensland was tough, and primitive, but the settlers were beginning to 'civilise' themselves. A piano (or pianola) was becoming a necessary pleasure, an educational tool, and a symbol of respectability.

After a year or two, Geoffrey moved to Brisbane as tuner and repairer in the leading music shop there. No doubt the ruinous floods of that time meant there was a deal of repairing to do. Alice set up as Mme Reprah, Physiognomist and character-reader-by-the-face, 2/6 for spoken reading, 5/- if written down.

Typhoid brought him close to death, and he gave up his job while he convalesced. He then moved to a firm in Sydney and went on the road selling pianos. He proved an able salesman and made a good thing of it. He earned enough to buy a house and to send Anna to England with an allowance of £4 a week—no doubt partly provided by Alice's thriving elocution practice (see p. 118).

Geoffrey was handsome, well-turned-out, and generally thought of, outside the family, as a live-wire, charming and kind. This is, of course, in flat contradiction of the contemptuous cracks put about by Alice and repeated in three written memoirs by David Garnett, in a good deal of pub gossip, and, to a considerable extent, by Anna in the Autobiography. An Australian friend who first met him when she was ten years old is much distressed by what she feels is a wrong and slanderous picture. She writes that he was a brilliant conversationalist, with a wonderful sense of humour, witty, an intellectual inspiration to all her family, and a fascinating promoter of new movements in the arts and new ideas generally. Her father, a prominent newspaper editor, used to say, 'he should have a Boswell'. 'It was always a real treat when he came to dinner . . . It wasn't that he held the floor, but . . . in fact he opened the door on a new world for us.'

So he did for Anna. She adopted her professional name Wickham because of an evening of passionate rapport with him, when at the age of ten she stood with him in Wickham Terrace, Brisbane, half-way between an Anglican Church and a Presbyterian Church from both of which sprayed showers of emotional hymn singing, and he urged her to promise him that she would be a poet. (Her first, immediately-to-be-ditched pen name was John Oland, chosen because of a visit to the Jenolan Caves with her feminist friend May Mukle, the cellist.) The return to a close family association was characteristic of Anna's behaviour: she took all vows and commitments as binding, even when they were not formalised. (W. H. Auden was blessed with the same quality.)

As we see later, Anna makes clear the social antagonisms that divided her mother's family, the Whelans, and her father's family, the Harpers, and takes great stock of each side's ancestors as far as she knew them, which she did mainly from family tradition and gossip. The rival traditions became part of her poetic apparatus, and their complex antagonisms often settled the direction of her political values and activities. She wrote at great length about all this in her autobiography, but told the Harper tale with more impact and precision in a poem at different times entitled **'Descent of Dorelia,** and **'Eugenics'**.

'Descent of Dorelia'

My great-grandfather was a pious man,
He lived carefully and well as a Methodist can.
He was thrifty and laborious, he made no waste,
He closed his house at nine at night, was faithful and
  chaste.

He was just to all men according to degree,
He went to class meetings, and had the minister to
  tea.
From birth to death he rose two grades in rank,
Born a labourer, he died a farmer with savings in the
  bank,
But all the calculations of his life-time were undone
By my grandfather, who was his only son.

My grandfather was naturally addicted to sin,
At the age of eight he bought a violin.
Alone he learned to play that instrument of evil,
Though well he knew that music was the language of
  the devil.

Sweet sounds and sin were wedded joy
To the perverted sense of that farm-boy.
He practised waltzes in a barn, using a mute,
When he had fiddled long in secret, bought a flute.

One day his Father found his fiddle and in ire
Broke the vile thing, and threw it on the fire.
Savage and unpersuaded, the mad fellow
Begged, stole and starved, until he bought a cello.

The rogue, my grandfather would never stop
On any farm, or patient in a shop;
He wished the spade and yard-stick both to Hades,
And took the road with a tragedian, and two light
   ladies.

The minister never knew, all his poor life,
Whether one or both of these women was my grandfa-
   ther's wife.
I, a Conservative, am descended from their com-
   munion;
And I am married to the Squire.
My Grandfather died in the Union.

'The Little Old House' is a variation on this subject.

The Harpers had been tenant farmers in Shropshire at least since the sixteenth century. Some broke away and succeeded in the professions or even in commerce. One, Andrew, married the daughter of a Knight and Alderman of the City of London. She treated him ostentatiously as her social inferior, a piece of history that (like the Boyne in Ulster) stayed naggingly alive in Anna's head. When this lady died in the last of her many confinements, Andrew busied himself with the scientific improvement of wheat. He left most of the fortune he had inherited to found the Harper Adams Agricultural College, which exists to this day.

When Anna married into a family of aristocratic lineage, now settled in the upper-reaches of the professional middle class, she found its conventionality oppressive in every aspect, and especially in its 'Victorian' attitude to women. The themes of Them against Us—the Villa-dwellers against the struggling poor; Men against Women; and the Artist against the Philistine—are central in much of her writing, and, therefore, in much of her best work. Sometimes, though, as in the poem **'Nervous Prostration',** she conforms to Yeats' 'rhetoric' in the way Betjeman does in *Come Friendly Bombs*: she makes good propaganda, but it feels strident, and at the last, unfair.

The events of her father's family history became part of her poetic equipment, so that she could unselfconsciously use the effect of genes *and* the effect of past environments to create poems and explain present situations.

ALICE WHELAN

The picture Anna gives of her mother, Alice Whelan, needs little comment from me. Her influence dominated every aspect of the poet's life, not least in the painful ambivalence she felt for her father.

Anna's great-grandmother, Joanna, used the name Burnell, but this was an Anglicisation of the Italian Bournelli. Illiterate, in youth a lady's maid at the Belgian Court, she died at a great age in a workhouse, leaving only some beautiful needlework pieces. Her husband had been a courier: when her daughter, Martha, was born she had the King of the Belgians for godfather. Inevitably, in the common romantic habit, the family hinted at royal bastardy. The courier died two months after Martha's birth: Joanna then came to England and married a shoe-maker. Martha stayed in Belgium for fifteen years before coming to England. There she married Michael Whelan, a poor but decent plumber, and by the age of twenty she had three children: Helen, George, and Anna's mother, Alice. When her husband died of T. B., Martha was helped by George Cruikshank who paid for the funeral, and made it possible for her to become an artist's model. She was beautiful and 'middle-Victorian pictures seem full of [her] head and hands and feet'. Charring, home-working on chenille hair nets, and letting rooms, saved the family (now augmented by an illegitimate girl) from destitution.

The School Board for London was established in 1870 and Martha seized this chance of giving her daughters a future. Helen and Alice became teachers, two of the first lot of working-class people to escape economic insecurity and to enter the uncertain status of the Board School teacher. (If many doctors, clergymen and ushers were not fully socially acceptable, what could one make of a Board School teacher? Anna, with her experience of Board Schools, and D. H. Lawrence, who had been a Board School teacher, found common ground here when they first met.)

The ruling classes used the new Board School-educated and declassed teachers and bureaucrats as cadets for maintaining the status quo, just as the products of the minor public schools founded two generations before had produced a new class of 'acceptable gentry' to keep the Empire going. Anna saw this stage in maintaining upper-class hegemony as operating 'by penalising imagination and putting genius under restraint. They have allowed no heroes to rise to save the citadel of democracy, for no hero after his contact with popular education has ever been wholly himself. The Board School castrated the mind of my father, as it did later that of D. H. Lawrence.'

The painter, Frank Potter, became engaged to Helen and his *The Music Lesson* in the Tate shows Alice teaching a young girl. Aveling, to whom Alice became secretary, made his usual pass at Helen, and being refused went off to wreck the life of Eleanor Marx.

Her mother's family took only a minor place in Anna's ancestral mythology: nevertheless their (and her own) class position influenced crucially her social and political reactions, and the Irish/Italian and artistic connections played their roles too. Alice, her mother, courter of disasters and diseases and deaths, seemed to transcend all class barriers, being more a force of nature than a social being.

PARENTS' COURTING AND MARRIAGE

Alice was already a stunning performer; although an amateur she had been praised in the *Illustrated London News*. An improbable and modest stage-door Johnny became her Boy in the Gallery. He was Geoffrey Harper, who had met her at a dance in the Holborn Town Hall. Her family tried to prevent their wedding, but Geoffrey, in direct contradiction of his later family reputation of being 'ineffectual', persisted, and they got married on a shoestring, the loan of a few pianos to sell if possible, and practically no cash at all. He was twenty-one. They went to live over the Wimbledon music shop.

In what Anna liked to call 'domestic economy' they were Jack Sprat and his wife in reverse. Geoffrey was for spending, laying out for the future: Alice for lean living, and building up a cash reserve. The best room over the shop was let to a curate. Geoffrey adored books; Alice needed people, or at least an audience.

A stillborn son led to increased help from grandfather William: he also caused Geoffrey to use Anna, born a year later, as a substitute son, and so established a longing for Anna to stay 'boyish'. 'My strong impression was that it was Geoffrey who felt the grief and Alice who manifested it,' writes Anna with antenatal confidence.

Quarrels between her parents became more violent, and, when Anna was eighteen months old, Alice quit— first to a furnished room, then on to a sailing ship for Australia. She worked her passage, possibly as the skipper's mistress.

In Australia Alice caught pneumonia and Anna was put into an institution. The authorities got in touch with Geoffrey, who had not a clue about where they were. His family offered help with fares, and a year later Alice sailed back with the now two-and-a-half-year-old Anna. At the age of four she wrote her first poems for her father. Her parents' quarrels became more vicious and when she was five, they took separate rooms, her father the attic.

An imposing new piano shop opened near Wimbledon Station, and Geoffrey realised he would have to get out. Two of Geoffrey's sisters, May and Beatrice and an Uncle Charles had gone to Australia. Geoffrey followed, leaving Alice teaching at a school near Primrose Hill. She soon made up her mind to follow him, arranged to travel as mother's help for a well-off family, rowed with them en route, and swapped her servant status for passenger. From Sydney they set off to join Geoffrey in Maryborough, Queensland. The autobiography gives details of the rest of their married life, though not of Alice's later escapades and exploits that took in the U.S.A., Mrs Annie Besant, a new 'religion' to whose 'community' she invited Geoffrey as a disciple. All of this followed logically from her fortune-telling as Mme Reprah and her own gargantuan appetite for drama and domination.

Nor does it tell of Geoffrey's remarriage. Heather Sherrie writes, 'We were not told whether they were divorced or if Mrs Harper had died, or if he was committing bigamy. When he brought his new wife to see us, we were amazed. Mother and I were very shocked, and felt she wasn't worthy of him, but Mother said wisely, "I expect Geoffrey is tired of living in hotels, and wants someone to look after him".' I wonder if it was not more a case of 'some shy gazelle, some gentle dove, something to love, something to love', for Geoffrey's married life seems to have been an eternity of being denied love, and being deprived for most of the time of his adored Anna. From the series of economic ups-and-downs and the bruised feeling of not having his considerable talents decently recognised, I imagine his good nature and his brains provided him with shelter and healing.

ANNA IN LONDON AND PARIS 1905-1906

Of this period Anna gives a lively account. The determination to succeed shown by her pertinacity at the various stage and music auditions did not fade as she grew older. Nor did the need she had taken from her mother for performing. In London, in addition to her efforts to get on, she had to renew family contacts, and in Paris she was busy with her music, quite apart from the exciting enchantments of that capital, and no doubt as on the boat from Australia a growing urge to enlarge her experience with men-friends.

Her astute observation of the feuds and jealously preserved social distinctions between the Harpers and the Whelans was undimmed. Harper Aunt Matilda, or Tid, as she was known, thought Anna too self-possessed and bossy for so young a lady. The Harper grandparents, Alicia and Edwin, seemed old, but he played Mozart beautifully. The Aunts Matilda and Muriel sang a duet in cracked voices that had never recovered from their training (Anna was relentlessly hostile to uninspired routine teaching).

She renewed her old friendship with the cellist May Mukle and, through her, met the Goossens. She felt some envy of their technical efficiency, which she knew she lacked: 'I could never work at an art: I could either do it, or refrain from doing it'.

Next she won a scholarship at the Tree Academy of Acting, and soon, while on a trip to His Majesty's Theatre to hear G. B. Shaw talk on 'The Economics of Art', she was picked up by, or got off with, a freelance reporter called William Ray. At that time she felt lonely, rejected by both sides of her family and slighted by her old friend May, and by the Goossen girls. He chatted her up with a conventional line in lying about his posh connections, but once she had got this out of the way, they became engaged. (So she acquired a second engagement ring, having had a brief fling in Australia.) Her fiancé's work took her to Wonderland, the Whitechapel boxing ring—not for a fight, but for a Russian Exiles' protest meeting about St Petersburg's Black Friday.

Soon William introduced her to Patrick Hepburn, a thirty-two-year-old solicitor with a passion for Romanesque churches, for marathon rides on his push-bike, and for star-watching. His obsessional devotion, devoid of ambition, to architectural photographs, the absorbed pleasure he took in making them into lantern slides to be used for modest lecture engagements touched her, for it reminded her of her father's pure passion for his books. Also Patrick was of a superior class, and much as Anna despised the villa-dwellers, she felt that they had in most ways greater possibilities for independence, neglected or stifled though these were by the blanket of conformity. 'He was high bred, and beautiful, though prematurely bald'.

However, encouraged by the highest praise from her singing tutor Randaegger, she decided to chance her luck in Paris. William followed her and they became lovers. (This was the first time Anna records going to bed with anyone: for a woman who had had so many adventures and such a rackety life she was rather innocent sexually.)

Patrick now asked Anna if his sister Ellen could come over and stay with her. Anna agreed: 'It was the most disastrous decision of my life'. To her, Ellen was the archetype Croydon villa-dweller, though the worst crime she seems to have actually committed was to take Anna 'to the Bon Marché to buy woollen combinations'. Whatever the rights and wrongs of this heavily dramatised antagonism, Ellen went deep into those inner springs from which Anna's poems sprang, while reinforcing her already formed views on the class struggle.

Anna was by now in Jean de Reszke's Master Class. The public success which was her father's life-long ambition would not be delayed too long!

Ellen and Anna left Paris to spend Christmas in England. William was still around, but happy to 'lend' Anna to Patrick for a visit to Oxford where Patrick

kissed her and they decided to chuck William. They left immediately for Paris, and Patrick, after one night in a different hotel, asked her to marry him: 'You'll never leave me, will you? It would be such a shock to my family.' Later, on a visit to some cousins in Watford, he said, 'You won't show me too much affection before Eleanor, will you?'

Anna ignored these danger signals (they were both much in love) but continued her relentless recording of class habits and conventions. 'I was struck by the narrow range of the Hepburn family. Their habits were set and their circle limited. They would have as soon asked the baker to dinner as get to know the peerage.' It did not occur to her that the insecure, that is most people, are on the make: security generally brings with it complacency and self-satisfaction.

Marriage 1906-1929

Anna and Patrick were married at St Margaret's Church opposite the Bank of England, a fitting place for Patrick, a Freeman of the City of London. The marriage was almost private: no best man, Ellen as bridesmaid, and a congregation of a one-eyed man and the pew opener. They took twenty-two books with them on their honeymoon, during which they were to visit and photograph twenty-two Romanesque churches.

For the first few months they were happy—'not a single crumpled rose-leaf'. Anna became pregnant. Then Alice announced that she was coming home to see her dear daughter and Anna cried all through the night: her brief peace of six months she felt had now gone. She was right. Her child, a girl, died in premature birth. Alice rampaged, until deciding on a return to Australia. Before she left, Anna had a miscarriage. Patrick had taken her on several strenuous holidays, and she determined the third time was to be lucky: to make sure she insisted on rest. She went to full term, and James, an eleven-pound boy, was safely born: it was the happiest day of her life. James always 'sustained my imagination and my craving for tenderness and beauty, and I had always my preoccupation of my dream for him'.

She took up baby-training with scholarly passion: 'For a year no other subject entered my mind'. With her mother's energy and bossiness she broke nurses into her ways. She joined the St Pancras School For Mothers, though not so much to instruct the poor, as to learn what she could from them, for she remembered how well her own grandmother had coped. She began, against the wishes of the Committee, to give away new saucepans so that milk could be clean and boiled: she took sick babies into her own nursery.

The school was one of a number of similar organisations, set up to fight the evils of infant mortality by instructing and training mothers in better methods of hygiene and diet. (The first National Conference for the Prevention of Infant Mortality took place in 1906.) It was a move to promote self-help in place of the Victorian doctrine of institutional philanthropy and benevolent guidance of the poor or 'slumdwellers' by the well-to-do. The Medical Officer for Health for St Pancras, Dr J. P. T. Sykes, enlightened, energetic, able and articulate, was also a friend of many influential middle-class and aristocratic liberals and socialists. He promoted the principle of the mother as 'the centre round which all the agencies revolved for the protection and preservation of the health of both mother and child'. All this Anna later realised she had plunged into with far too much hysterical commitment: 'I overtaxed [James] and induced a nervous stammer that will inconvenience him all his life.'

What she was doing without being aware of it was running away from the cloud over her marriage that began to loom with her mother's arrival. It was now swelling and darkening as the incompatibility of Anna's and Patrick's natures led to suspicion, aloofness, and soon to open hostility. Anna was passionate, impulsive, intensely fixed on motherhood: Patrick was guarded, controlled, and disliked the way babies stole Anna's attention which he needed for himself. Both were inhibited by different senses of duty, she by the duty that coition should be without pleasure, he by the duty that coition should be frequent. She thought fucking was to make the babies she loved, and who fulfilled her; he thought fucking was part of a husband's obligations, and what a man was expected to do. She lived for the present and the future: he lived in, and by, and off the past.

There were other, some less serious, points of conflict. Their ideas on holidays and housekeeping were different; she was ambitious for him to be publicly successful as a lecturer while he thought that kind of success ostentatious; she loved to shine in company, he thought that bad form; she basically lacked confidence and he was brought up with too much of it. Their bitterest clash was caused by Anna's need to write and publish her poems, and Patrick's insanely furious reaction to her insistence on this—unjustifiable in a man who was himself a loner, rejecting success in the law for his private passion of astronomy.

Despite this, however, a tether of regard, at least, and probably of passion, was twisted tightly. Anna defended him against all outside criticism, and much of her best poetry celebrates the violent struggles of their relationship which, after all, despite outrageous affronts and vengeful separations, lasted until his death twenty-two years after James' birth.

Early in her next pregnancy, they decided they needed a garden for the children, and moved to a beautiful house, 49 Downshire Hill, Hampstead, where John was born in

1909. Here she established a kind of salon, with music and entertainments in the garden and lectures on women's suffrage. Patrick resented this further diversion of her attention from him. Anna replied that he should enlarge the range and scope of his lectures, which she thought too piffling. They continued to grow apart.

In five years of marriage, Anna had suffered two disastrous accouchments and given birth to two children. She poured out her energies in looking after her babies and in her enthusiastic work with the School for Mothers. From her preoccupation with this came in 1909 and 1910 two interesting lectures: 'The School for Mothers' and 'Notes for a Lecture'.

All this, and her unresolved conflict with her husband, made her run-down and nervously exhausted. Her doctor recommended a sea voyage. She decided to meet her father in Ceylon, and they toured that island, and parts of South India. They returned together: Geoffrey and Patrick got on well enough. Soon after Geoffrey's return to Australia, Alice arrived, but was not put up in the home. Then burst out an insanely violent battle over Patrick's forbidding Anna to publish poems which she had had printed for her father (see *Songs by John Oland*). James Hepburn writes: 'Patrick and Anna quarrelled, Patrick showed violence, Anna, in resisting, accidentally pushed her hand through a glass panel and cut her wrist. Patrick called in a doctor to attend to the injury, and Anna soon found herself certified and confined to a private asylum near Epping, where she spent about six weeks. She was discharged a few days before an inspection by visiting doctors, discharged subject to a "probationary month". Anna and Patrick shared their marriage bed that night, "It is good to have you back," he remarked. When recalling this time, Anna thought it odd that Patrick should risk her conceiving if he considered her to be mad.' If any proof is needed of their passion, this surely is it.

The 'probationary month' had barely passed before Anna made her way to the Poetry Bookshop, which Harold Monro and his wife, Alida Klementaski, were running in Red Lion Square, Bloomsbury. She asked, "'Have you any free rhythms?" He looked at me, interested, realising I meant Free Verse. He said, "We've all been trying to write them". I gave him my *Songs*.' In the next months Anna also widened her acquaintance with distinguished writers, and artists in the studios of Chelsea and the Hampstead Road. She met Augustus John, Jacob Epstein, T. E. Hume, Ezra Pound, Hannen Swaffer, Nina Hamnett, David Garnett and a chirrup of young poets.

Anna's forays to the watering holes of the intelligentsia were not rejections of her husband and children: she always put them first in her practical and moral priorities. She was trying to assuage the complicated anguish she felt as her husband (whom she loved, as he, in his somewhat immature way, loved her) tried to force her to give up her writing and social activities because he felt they were diverting her energy from himself. He would have been proud of her success if only it could have been complementary to his own life but he felt that her poetry, like her children, was depriving him of the total attention he needed.

Meanwhile Harold Monro printed nine of her poems in *Poetry and Drama* (summer 1914) for which he paid her the not bad sum of £9. She wanted to buy Patrick a sextant with the money, but he would not have it. This rebuff did not dampen her pleasure that this success of hers would delight and fulfil her father's lifetime longing for her to make a 'meritorious' public triumph. (Maurice Hewlett, then a name to conjure with, was a fellow-contributor.) 'Here I was, from the pit of obloquy to the pinnacle of pride.' Anna was only twenty-five and already had had two fruitless and two successful pregnancies as well as a triumphant period as an aspirant professional singer. Yet she told Oswell Blakeston, 'Harold Monro ruined my life by encouraging me to be a poet. I should have been a maker of popular mottoes!'

Her work to this point had been privately printed. *The Seasons—A Speaking Tableaux for Girls (100 Performers),* and *Wonder Eyes—A Journey to Slumbertown (For 80 Little People),* written when she was 17, were printed by W. A. Pepperday and Son, Sydney, under her real name, Edith Harper. And, 1911, **Songs** by the Women's Printing Society Ltd, Brick Street, Piccadilly, under the pseudonym John Oland.

War-Time 1914-1919

Patrick was in Siberia, observing an eclipse of the sun with a scientific expedition, when the Great War was declared on 4 August 1914. It took him some months to get back to England for they had to travel via Japan. Although over forty, he volunteered as a Kite balloon observer in the Royal Naval Air Service, and later became an original member of the Royal Air Force.

Civilians did not have such a bad time in the Kaiser's War as they did under Hitler's buzz-bombs. I mean, materially, for they suffered infinitely more from the mass killings on the Western Front, and, of course, wives and mothers suffered most. Anna, who gave birth to a third son, Richard in 1917, had a busy war. In her house in Hampstead she continued to meet artists of all kinds, and made friendships that lasted till her death in 1947.

Her reputation grew with the publication in 1915 of **The Contemplative Quarry** (Poetry Bookshop) and a year later of **The Man with a Hammer** (Grant Richards).

Louis Untermeyer, the American man-of-letters and busy anthologist, caused both volumes to be printed as one by Harcourt Brace & Company, New York, though the volume did not appear till 1921.

Early in the war she became closer friends with Frieda and D. H. Lawrence. In 1915 she worked on the production of *Princess Marie-José's Children's Book* brought into this by a friend, Carmel Haden Guest, mother of David Guest who was killed in the Spanish Civil War. She contributed two poems, **'Baby Marigold'** and **'The Bad Host'**, written to provide captions for a series of drawings by W. K. Haselden of the *Daily Mirror*:

'The Bad Host'

When Archibald Percival Minns turned three
His mother invited his friends to tea;
She bought chocolate and cakes and cook made toast,
And they all told the boy he must be a good host.

The artist has drawn his behaviour. Just look!
While his nice friends are dancing he's reading a book;
When they have 'Hunt the Slipper' he won't play at
  all,
But goes off and stands on his head near the wall.

Then his kind cousin Maud starts a fine tug of war,
But Archibald Minns just behaves as before:
The queerest of hosts, and the rudest of boys,
He's under the table alone with his toys.

So his mother sent up for the naughty boy's nurse,
Which makes a sad end to the tale and this verse;
For they put him to bed with no tea for his sins
Which serves him well right—wicked Archibald
  Minns.

As the war went on, her husband being away, Anna became more 'Bohemian'. One night at the Café Royal she heard some news about Russia which seemed to connect with the revolutionary contacts she had made when she first came to London. She rushed off to her aunt Gertrude Chester's house to pour out the story in a histrionic style worthy of her mother. Gertrude's daughter, Peggy, a child at the time, writes: 'She was sure she was going to be shot . . . we had to lock ourselves in the bathroom while it was being related. My mother let me go and sleep the night with her. I was years younger and small, and she was six foot. It was moral support that was required.' The next day Anna went down to Fleet Street and persuaded Lord Northcliffe to see her. He took the story seriously. That night he drove Anna home. On the way they bought a meat pie which they ate together at the kitchen table.

At the end of the war, Anna, not worried about what would have been a sharp fall in income, suggested that Patrick give up the law to join the Meteorological Service. But Patrick's partner, George Cutcliffe, who had carried on the practice alone throughout the war, wanted to retire, so Patrick had to return to an occupation that now bored him. He and Anna were often at loggerheads, but agreed on finding a new house. They left the decaying Downshire Hill residence for a fine and larger house with a garden and a view, in Parliament Hill, Hampstead, where the family still lives.

In December 1919, the youngest son, George, was born, and together with the two-year-old Richard, gave Anna the happiness she had enjoyed ten years earlier with the infants, James and John.

DEATH AND PARIS 1921-1922

In 1921 the Poetry Bookshop brought out **The Little Old House,** and Harcourt Brace & Company published in one volume **The Contemplative Quarry** and **The Man with a Hammer.** The feminist drive in her verse was now much praised. In an introduction, Untermeyer wrote, 'But already a small and widely-scattered group of women are taking stock of themselves—appraising their limitations, inventions and energies without a thought of man's contempt or condescension. Searchers like May Sinclair, Virginia Woolf, Rebecca West, Willa Cather and Dorothy Richardson are working in a prose that illuminates their experiments. In poetry, a regiment of young women are recording an even more vigorous self-examination. The most typical, and in many ways the best of these seekers and singers is Anna Wickham.'

Then came disaster. The four-year-old Richard caught septic scarlet-fever. After removal to the Fever Hospital in Lawn Road, Hampstead, he rallied but six days later he was dead. In agony and despair Anna decided to get away to Paris to sort out her problems, which, apart from the death, were mainly concerned with the war inside her between her irreconcilable and unassuaged obsession to be an artist and her duty to devote all her energy to her family. She had happy associations with Paris, from the days, now seventeen years past, when she had been a student there. She used this time to restore her vigour, to 'get the smell of the sickroom from her nostrils', and to make new acquaintances in the arts, including a talented, wealthy lesbian, Natalie C. Barney, who was soon to become the emotional centre of her life outside the family. Outside it had to be, for Anna was adamant about the sanctity of the family, as her poetry clearly shows.

HOME, AND PATRICK'S DEATH 1922-1929

Back from Paris, Anna determined to become a model housewife. She had a cook and living-in housemaid, and an aspiring ballet dancer to look after George. Patrick had even blacker moods, and Anna felt he was suffering from melancholia. However, his fame as an astronomer increased. At various times Jeans and Eddington came to dinner; Patrick made important

discoveries connected with the Rings of Saturn and became treasurer of the Royal Astronomical Society, and President of the British Astronomical Association.

Anna kept up her literary contacts, indeed, she increased them. Through Mrs Dawson-Scott she had joined P. E. N. which gave her a dinner shared with Edith Sitwell. 'Anna thought Edith would turn up in brocade so she wore a woollen jumper out of devilment.' She began to use Kleinfelt's, as the Fitzroy Tavern was generally known, to keep up her pre-war acquaintance with Nina Hamnett and Augustus John. Betty May was also about at this time, singing at the Crabtree Club. Though into cocaine and booze, she was still strikingly beautiful and worthy of her soubriquet 'Tiger Woman'.

Apart from these Bohemian forays, Anna gave poetry readings, and had a wide 'respectable' circle of friends through her social, charitable and political activities. Also she had great compassion for down-and-outs, often employing them to give them a 'fresh start'. 'If she saw an old tramp on Hampstead Heath looking at the sky, she would talk to him and tell him to go to her husband's lectures on astronomy at the Observatory. Where he did go—for a nice warm—but was not popular with the rest of the class or her husband.'

Preparing to go off to Hull for a poetry reading she could not find her silk stockings and fine blouse. 'The cook was wearing them in the kitchen—incidentally we had to hunt everywhere for her good velour hat, and eventually found it in the waste-paper basket. She rang up from the station to say she had missed the train, but found a machine which told fortunes.'

The rows with Patrick became more frequent and more violent. In 1926 Patrick engineered a judicial separation, and the family moved to a little house in Hampstead. After a few months the family moved to stay in Alida Monro's house in Bloomsbury, while Patrick lived alone at Parliament Hill. This form of solitude was too much even for Patrick, and it was agreed that the adolescent James and John should keep him company, while Anna and the eight-year-old George should lodge in High Street, Hampstead. Next year, 1928, the judicial separation lapsed, and the family reunited itself in Parliament Hill. Relations were more peaceful, though Patrick became difficult about money. He had no partner in the practice, and was running it with the help of an aged managing clerk.

Just before Christmas 1929 he went (as he had done before) on a solitary walking holiday in the Lake District. On Christmas Day he fell off a mountainside and died of exposure. Anna's poem of 1921, **'The Homecoming'.** now became deadly fact, and suggests that she may have inherited something of her mother's clairvoyant powers.

WIDOWHOOD, NATALIE C. BARNEY, AND THE
GREAT SPRING CLEAN 1926-1935

It took the next two years for Anna and James to wind up Patrick's law practice. By 1932 she found herself a widow with two sons able to start earning their own living, and a boy of school age. There was little cash. What was she to do with her life now that she was, in a way, free to choose?

She had an international reputation as a poet: improbable as it seems today, anthologies printed more of her poems than they did of such greater poets as de la Mare, Graves, and even in some volumes, W. B. Yeats. She was in *International Who's Who* and Humbert Wolfe had written of her in the great 14th Edition of the *Encyclopaedia Britannica*. She was proud of their recognition, but sensible enough to realise that it was not enough to ensure her a living as a professional poet. She had long realised that her talent was special, intensely personal, slapdash and essential to her sanity. Though the odds were against proper financial reward, what else could she do but try to promote her career as a poet? As almost all of her correspondence, and goodness knows how much verse and prose of her own, were destroyed by a fire-bomb that burnt out the attic in Parliament Hill in 1943, it is impossible to know what she may have intended to put out if she had found a willing publisher. There is evidence that in 1919 she had projected a volume entitled *The Disorderly Shepherdess* and that around 1928 she had planned a dramatic poem, 'The Boy and the Daffodil'. We know too that she did try, or said she tried, to write a novel, at the request of Horace Shipp, talent scouting for Sampson Low, Marston & Co.

But the centre of her hopes and the place to which she directed her energies, while not failing to keep up her U. S. A. connections, was Paris, and Paris meant Natalie C. Barney, and the Temple of Sappho.

After meeting Natalie Barney in 1922, she had made fairly frequent trips to Paris and increasingly they centred on Natalie's house and salon in the rue Jacob. The attraction was emotional, sexual and artistic, three areas in which Anna had been parched for years by her fidelity to her husband and devotion to domesticity. Her love for her children was always unclouded, but naturally could not fulfil these other needs, although her children always gave her perfect happiness.

She maintained from 1926 to 1937 a correspondence of passionate love-letters (which was also a passionate discussion of the problems of being a woman and an artist).

Natalie Barney was a cosmopolitan personality, very American, and very French. Born in Ohio in 1877 she was bilingual, a patron, hostess, propagandist for lesbianism, and later for peace, poet (in French) and writer, mainly of aphorisms. Not as discriminating as Sylvia Beach or as rich and pushing as Peggy Guggenheim, but more talented than either, she gathered round her in her Temple à l'Amitié, leading scholars, academicians, intellectuals, artists, and socialites with sapphic and aesthetic enthusiasms. 'She represented the *Mercure de France* as Gertrude Stein represented *transition*.' Remy de Gourmont was a close friend and collaborator. Great figures included Anatole France, Rilke, Paul Valery, Rodin, d'Annunzio, Colette, Ezra Pound, Sinclair Lewis, Proust; and lesser personalities were Alan Seeger, Paul Geraldy, Sherwood Anderson, Richard Aldington, Gertrude Stein and Janet Flanner (for so long Gênet of the *New Yorker*). Her immediate circle of friends and lovers included the painter Romaine Brooks, the poets Lucie Delarue Mardrus and Elizabeth de Gramont, who concealed her aristocratic family under the by no means plebeian *nom de plume* of Lily de Clermont-Tonnerre.

Natalie in her *Pensées d'une Amazone* (Emile-Paul, 1920), refers to '*Cette catastrophe; être femme*', a sentiment that Anna shared, and that led her to attempt translations of some of the poems written by Natalie's friends. She also read her own poems at the Temple, as Natalie translated spontaneously with a running commentary. 'She is only a *demi-revoltée*—has four sons but no daughter—reared a family of males of which she is both pelican and nightingale [loud applause]. Feminist leagues have inscribed her poems on their banners. One of them has been used by the Women's Movement against corsets.' (Anna herself wore old-fashioned whale-bone stays. In the gallery of the Holborn Empire she once wrestled them off herself and enjoyed the show in relaxed comfort. They were pink.) Lucie Delarue Mardrus brilliantly translated some of Anna's poetry, which appeared in 1935 in *Edition des Poèmes Choisis de Lucie Delarue Mardrus* which gave Anna great pleasure. Another saying of Natalie's evidently impressed Anna as she struggled to order her life:

> *Si mes études furent nulles c'est que*
>   'My only books
>   Were woman's looks'
> *Mes amours? Multiples,*
> *Mes amitiés? Fidèles et loyales,*
> *Ma jeunesse? Elle dure encore, comme pour le vieux*
>   *Goethe:*
> *que de premières amours vont à la rencontre de nos*
>   *dernières*
> *amours. Et que défuntes élections s'y retrouvent!*

Anna was fascinated by Natalie, though never subdued by her. Natalie, even after Anna's death, continued her admiration for her poems, but their correspondence reveals that Anna's mainly long-distance passion for Natalie was not reciprocated. More satisfactory was their artistic rapport. Anna was looking for a collaborator in various literary ventures, and, insofar as the activities at the Temple made her personally and artistically known, she found one. But the lover-soulmate-fellow worker in the arts she hoped for was not there, despite Natalie's true affection, admiration for the poems and, in times of crisis, financial help.

The letters they exchanged were equally concerned with love and art. Anna enclosed hundreds of what she called Post-card Poems (***Des Cartes à l'Amazone***). Having noticed an old spelling of the philosopher's name as Des Cartes, Anna thought she might make something out of playing off Descartes' thought against her own problems, but nothing came of it.

In America, Untermeyer remained a faithful promoter, and she found in London an effective admirer and impressario, the poet, John Gawsworth, pseudonym of Fytton Armstrong, later to succeed M. P. Shiel as King of Redonda. He included her work first in *Edwardian Poetry* (1937) and then in *Neo-Georgian Poetry* (1937). The adjectives in the title refer to the change in monarchs, not to poetic styles. In 1936 Gawsworth also edited ***Thirty-Six New Poems*** (Richards' Shilling Selections): there were thirty new poems actually; six came from an earlier volume.

The year before, 1935, was the year of *The Great Spring Clean,* a year in which Anna struggled to exorcise her complicated guilt feelings over having done those things she might not have done, and having left undone those things she ought to have done for so many years in all matters concerned with domesticity. She longed for a clean slate on which she could, without inhibition, write her poetry. But the quarrel with herself was 'never quiet': she 'found no discharge' in the war between her two opposites, family and art, nor in the war between her 'biting lust' and her essential fastidiousness, nor in the war between her indifference to social forms and her sense of what was permissible and decent.

La Tour Bourgeoise and the Last Years
1935-1947

Anna continued to watch over her sons, to play the generous hostess, and to make occasional forays to Fitzrovia. In these years her interest in theatre and the ballet intensified. Her friends ranged from Anton Dolin to Bud Flanagan, who enjoyed and admired her poems. The 'gypsy' or, as she referred to it, the 'slattern' part of her became more prominent. She had always suffered from bouts of nervous exhaustion, bronchitis, and other, possibly psychosomatic, upsets, and from time to time had drunk a good deal, but always in company. In these years café-pub anecdotes began to accumulate, mostly very much to her credit.

In the Fitzroy she knocked down a silly poet to prove that "'I am more immortal then he is". Then she picked him up, saying, "'tonight I'm not a witch but a

warlock'". She could be frighteningly dismissive if she took against anyone. One gushing admirer begged, 'Anna, dear, do ring me up soon. We're on the'phone now.' Anna replied, 'Oh yes—any particular number?' At an art show where she had been scornful in too loud a voice, the art dealer whispered to Oswell Blakeston to take her away: she stood up to her full height and muttered, 'You'd better retract, my good man. I may be a minor poet, but I'm a major woman!'

She knew that war was approaching. She had been a pacifist, but when it came, she expected her sons to do their bit and was unmoved by the Phoney War arguments. She knew evil when she smelt it.

After a period of professional eclipse, which was not surprising given the violent change in poetic fashion brought about by Auden, and given her unbiddable originality, which was rooted in Victorian values, Edwardian social aspirations and Fabian politics, she was beginning to have a revival.

On 18 April 1938, Friends of the Library of Chicago wrote to her as one of a select group of poets asking for a message celebrating the memory of the editor of *Poetry, a Magazine of Verse,* Harriet Monroe, who had died the year before, climbing in the Andes. She collected signatures including those of Beatrice Kean Seymour and Carmel Haden Guest, and sent a cable 'Honouring a valiant woman, celebrating a courteous spirit, and remembering Harriet Monroe'. (The slightly old-fashioned use of 'courteous' here is typical of Anna and, I think, derives from her youth in Australia.)

She also busied herself gathering the support of seven feminists who signed, on 16 June 1938, a manifesto she had drawn up *The League for The Protection of The Imagination of Women. Slogan: World's Management by Entertainment.* Professor J. B. S. Haldane lent his considerable weight to the project. Anna was beginning to buzz again.

The BBC contracted her to take part in a television programme (probably through Royston Morley). She almost certainly would have been a tremendous performer in this infant medium, but the date was 3 September 1939. War was declared and the programme cancelled.

I went to work for the British Council in Bucharest soon after Munich in 1938. Anna's elder sons, James and John, had for some years been a successful dance-act as the Hepburn Brothers, and played Bucharest at this time. My first wife, Olivia Manning, wrote *The Spoilt City,* which vividly recreates the exotic, if seedy, background to their engagement. Now they were to travel wider, James as an R. A. F. navigator, John as an artillery officer. The youngest, George, now nineteen, soon went off to the Middle East.

Anna stayed at the house in Parliament Hill for the duration of the war, unshaken by a fire-bomb that destroyed some of her manuscripts and almost all the letters she had kept, including what would have been of great interest to us, most of the Natalie Barney half of their long correspondence. She had always rated courage as the central virtue: she thought it her duty to help maintain morale. She was lonely, for she missed her sons badly.

On 27 April 1946 *Picture Post* did a feature on her, 'The Poet Landlady'. This recalled the time after Patrick's death in 1929 when she had let off parts of her house, and hung in the hall this notice:

> Tour Bourgeoise68 Parliament Hill, N.W.3
> ANNA WICKHAM'S
> Stabling for Poets Painters and their Executives
> Saddle your Pegasus here
> Creative Moods respected Meals at all Hours.

Dylan Thomas slept there from time to time, once with Caitlin. Then, in a not uncharacteristic way, he later bit the hand that had fed and watered him. Different in his generous thanks was Malcolm Lowry, a frequent visitor in the early thirties.

The sons were demobilised, but James was still flying and John preoccupied with learning Chinese. In April 1947, Anna hanged herself. George found the body, and was amazed that she, so clumsy with her hands, had succeeded in tying an efficient knot. This came to him at the first moment of shock: later he ran into the street howling wordlessly like a dog.

WOMAN AND POET: NO DISCHARGE IN THE WAR

Like many poets Anna was a just and ruthless critic. Unlike some she was so with her own work:

> The tumult of my fretted mind
> Gives me expression of a kind;
> But it is faulty, harsh, not plain—
> My work has the incompetence of pain.

> **'Self Analysis'**

And also of haste, impatience with working on, or working up, her material. Direct expression, spontaneous speech, instant form were what she wanted: 'a poet rediscovers all creation; this instinct gives her beauty, which is sensed relation.' **'The Egoist'.** Sometimes, rather wistfully, or in rage because she could, with some justification, blame her husband for her lack of time and peace of mind she would dream of what might be, if:

> If I had peace to sit and sing,
> Then I could make a lovely thing;

> **'The Singer'**

but she knows most of her work is botched, fine lines, vivid images, original themes, a personal voice, are not brought to completion in the finished poem; so

> Let it be something for my song
> If it is sometimes swift and strong.

> **'The Singer'**

She both envied and despised professional technique: 'I could never learn to study technique: with me it has to come spontaneously, or not at all'. There are many reasons for this reluctance to work to make perfect. First is her loathing of all dull conventional teaching that inhibited creative shoots: then her contempt for personal showing off, for displays of virtuosity that falsified the truth of what was being expressed: most important perhaps her passionate intellectual commitment to immediate feeling, from which all truth is inseparable.

Her remark about writing mottoes for Christmas crackers is apt. She had considerable dexterity in versifying, and could readily and easily do parodies and, like Louis MacNeice, 'Knew and could write in all the classical metres'.

> Of the dead poets I can make a synthesis,
> And learn poetic form that in them is;
> But I will use the figure that is real
> For me, the figure that I feel.

> **'The Egoist'**

And:

> I first wrote poetry to please my Dad
> Who wanted to write novels and was sad;
> He never could write more than the first pages,
> And then he wrote so slowly that it took him ages
>
> But I wrote easily
> Although in poetry;
> And when I was a girl at school,
> When I learned grammar and was taught a rule
> Or I was taught the meaning of a word such as
>   inanimate,
> I'd write a poem out upon my slate,
> With all I knew of words and grammar to that date.

> **'Letter to a Boy at School'**

Her vocation as poet came rather late: music, or rather singing, was her first vehicle, and the detailed work she put into her singing training, influence her poetic values.

> Tone
> Is utterly my own.
> For less exterior than skill,
> It comes from the deep centre of the will;
> For nobler qualities of Song
> Not singing, but the singer must be strong.

> **'Comment'**

And:

> If my work is to be good,
> I must transcend skill, I must master mood.
> For the expression of the rare thing in me
> Is not in *do,* but deeper in *to be.*
>
> **'Examination'**

It is not surprising that her first professional poet venturings (to the Poetry Bookshop) started with a discussion of **'Free Rhythms'**.

> A varying energy and lethargy
> Sets contrast in the speech . . .
> When the creative depths are stirred,
> There are new rhythms, like a primal word.

At this time she was suspicious of the constraining and distorting effect of rhyme, which she saw as something arbitrary and mechanical:

> Likeness of sound,
> With just enough of difference
> To make a change of sense:
> So we have contrast,
> A piquancy,
> And a certain victory of contrivance:
> But Heaven keep us from an inevitable rhyme
> Or from a rhyme prepared!
> Rhymed verse is a wide net
> Through which many subtleties escape.
> Nor would I take it to capture a strong thing,
> Such as a whale.
>
> **'Note on Rhyme'**

She hammered away at this problem:

> And now of this matter of ear-perfect rhyme,
> My clerk can list all language in his leisure time;
> A faulty rhyme may be a well-placed microtone,
> And hold a perfect imperfection of its own.
>
> **'The Egoist'**

Knowledge of G. M. Hopkins, Wilfred Owen and Louis MacNeice, and the widespread use of assonance and half-rhyme, made her original formulation seem dated and over-anxious. But in 1915 she was pioneering in this field, which probably contributed to the high regard she gained, especially in the U. S. A., in the years after the First World War.

Another of her characteristics now so commonplace it needs an act of imagination to realise that she was considered to be pioneering, is her quickness to use images from industrial progress. This, of course, is all of a piece with her practice of giving tongue whenever she saw or felt, or heard, or smelled anything that fired her mind or her curiosity, or her emotions.

> It was as fit for one man's thoughts to trot in iambs as
>   it is for me,

> Who live not in the horse-age but in the day of
>   aeroplanes, to write my rhythms free.
>
> **'The Egoist'**

More important, though, was what was then considered her daring in writing of a woman's passion, and in doing so in the way of frank autobiography. She describes war in marriage, her own marriage to a man of decency, intellect and principle, indeed of courageous unconventionality and daring originality except in his attitude to his wife, where he was crushingly, obliteratingly conventional. Anna's poems on this war are of two distinct types: those that generalise, or even mythologise the middle-class, convention-bound bourgeois husband as the killing opposite of the working-class and imaginative wife, and those that transcend social categories and feminist appeals, to achieve a depth and completeness she only rarely brings off, even when writing of sexual frustration or fulfilment, or of her children.

Both types were essential to, indeed means to, her sanity. The struggle in her writing for freedom, for immediate expression, was the kind of self-cure against despair, annihilation, and the dark-night of the soul so vividly described by Ionesco when speaking of his own art. Anna called this **'Mad Song'**.

> Sometimes I think my head is a spider
> Built with a little loom inside her
> She spins a web so thin and long
> That is my simple song
> Alas! Alas! at the full of the moon
> I think in tune.

Fear of defeat, of total breakdown, recurred throughout her life. She was aware of the strain that had driven other women poets—Sappho, Lawrence Hope, and Charlotte Mew—to suicide, and of course, in the end, she took her own life, a generation before Sylvia Plath.

Like Ionesco, Anna relieved the choking fear of annihilation with a humour that ranged from black to gay: 'she could improvise a verse that cut the air into witty packs of cards'. Witty but not frivolous: truth was the core of her. Her work was generally unfinished, unworked on, rough notes and sketches for poems, like D. H. Lawrence's 'Pansies' only without his preaching and self-pity. She dashed them off as the image, or rhythm, or thought or joke or aperçu came to her. Some like **'Inelegant Evangelist'** came out as knockabout:

> For you can't keep a good man down . . .
> Paul—Paul, think of old St Paul,
> He had hardly any clothes at all,
> Yet he was a gentleman by birth
> And managed the best advertised
> Syndicate on earth.

> He walked into Nazareth
> In his only coat,

Left it by the railings
It was eaten by a goat,
He bivouacked a moment
To rebuke the goat for sin,
Then walked right on to Galilee
And preached there in his skin
      For you can't keep a good man down . . .

Others, like **'Concerning the Conversation of Mr H—',** were satiric:

This gentleman will only talk to us of *dogs*
Because he wishes to disguise that he's a poet,
If he should mention lions, dolphins, frogs,
He thinks by misadventure, we should know it!

He tells us things of white dogs, and of brown,
Of curious breed with one distinctive spot,
Of all the dogs that ever walked this town,
Of dogs of his acquaintance that have not.

I cite a dog I once set eyes upon
Which, lacking doggy lore, I say looked like a swan;
He takes me, says, 'That hound was bred in Russia,
Three such are owned by Henry, Prince of Prussia.'

O, modest violet! cowering in your green
Your scent betrays you though you are not seen!
Only unveterinary wights, like you and me,
Would see in dogs a swanny quality!

Many were polemical, like **'Biology for Breakfast'** (Nine hundred and ninety-nine types of domestic argument):

Why does the peacock spread his jewelled tail,
And walk so proud a prince of gentlemen?
Has he not hopes his beauty will prevail
With that small critical brown hen? . . .

Why does the throstle clear his mellow throat,
Till all the wood a magic draught receives?
Has he not faith some individual note
May yet convince Herself among the leaves?

Think of the tiger and his fiery zest,
Of all hot fights the wilds among,
If she who waits approves not of the test
She'll brook the lover, but devour his young.

Good scientist, review all things alive,
And for male strength and beauty you will find
If not a cause a fixed co-relative
Within the female mind.

Some, though comparatively few, were of their time, trailing an echo of de la Mare, or, as in **'Direct Interpretation',** of W. B. Yeats:

I heard two splendid simple sounds today,
The singing of some little ribald boys at play.
These songs were not good songs and not well sung,
But they were frank and faithful, and the boys were
   young.

Then, when the evening kissed the sun-loved land,
A poor man took fiddle in his hand
And flung the honest joy of his poor tune
To the high night, and to his friend the moon.

I heard two splendid simple sounds today,
A madman's music and young boys at play.

Others are fantasies, at times recalling fairy or folk tales, as does **'A Wizard Considers a Lady'**:

This woman is an apple-tree,
And a small yellow cat.
Her gracious genius is dear to me,
And I thank God for that.
But the indolent cat, with the prey in its mouth
Is a spirit of sloth, and death, and drouth,
And the sight of that beast is so loathed by me,
I go from the orchard, and run from the tree,
And yet if I tarried a Queen would be free.
But the beast sits up in the gracious boughs,
Mouthing its prey in a sullen carouse.
Till I hate the tree its sap and its root,
And I will not stretch my hand for fruit.
Yet could I eat, for my hunger's sake,
A beast would perish, a Queen would wake.

Anna's children inspired a number of charming yet perceptive and accurate anecdotes. As in the many poems about her husband and their marriage, **'The Impressionist'** is straight autobiography: James is Roman, John, Greek.

I have two sons,
One is born of my content,
The other born of sorrow.
Though they are still quite little sons,
I know that one is Roman and the other Greek.
I know this from the boys' looks.

When these two children play with clay
Rome will build bridges, but the little Greek
Will form a pixie.
The first will fill the garden
With real boys with sticks.
The second has made my garden quite untidy with his
  fairies;
These throw early apples down from the trees
And so are proved for my sake.

Lately my Greek son, being turned three,
Found his true medium:
He happened on a piece of brown chalk
And scored his first interpretation on the garden wall.
With gold hair ruffled like fire at a shrine, he called
'Brother come and see,
I have made this very beautiful picture of the black
  night'.

Rome came, muddy-handed from an aqueduct,
'It is a splodge,' he said, 'there are no differences in
  your picture.
Where are the houses? Where are the trees? And where
  is the blue sky?'

Greece drew himself up in infinite contempt,
'There is no blue sky in a black night,' he said.

Years later, for her youngest son, she wrote **'Letter to a Boy at School'**:

George and me
We'll sing to one another
Like two birds upon a tree.
And that has seldom happened
With a boy and his own Mother.

That George and me
Both write poetry
Shows there's a sympathy
More than in every family
Between George and me.

I first wrote poetry to please my Dad
Who wanted to write novels and was sad;
He never could write more than the first pages,
And then he wrote so slowly that it took him ages.

But I wrote easily
Although in poetry;
And when I was a girl at school,
When I learned grammar and was taught a rule
Or I was taught the meaning of a word such as
  inanimate,
I'd write a poem out upon my slate,
With all I knew of words and grammar to that date.

But when I wrote for my dear father,
I always used to worry rather
And think that for a girl it might be waste of time
To spend her life and love in making rhyme;
And I thought, maybe
I should be better knitting for my baby.

And now my dear and youngest son
Has brains enough to find my verses fun;
And so my head's no longer in a whirl
Wondering if I ought to write them, being born a girl.

And so I'll make,
For George's sake,
As soon as I have time,
The very finest thing I can in rhyme;
And everything I know
And dream and hope will go
Into this book,
Which will be a good pie,
Since I write better than I cook.

And George and me
Will sit and sing to one another
Like two birds upon a tree.
And in our pie
I'll not write 'George and I',
Though both are in the nominative case;
Our poetry will be a pleasant place,
Where grammar is most right when it is wrong,
In ways that sound well, in a song.

From time to time Anna has a quirky, cheeky, wry truthfulness that recalls Stevie Smith, as do the many poems she wrote to be sung, and as does this cautionary tale **'The Tigress'**:

There was a man who kept a young, tame tigress.
He loved her because she was beautiful;
It pleased him to stroke her neck.
He said to her, 'Tigress, my time is much occupied
But, because you are lovely,
I will see you on the last Thursday of every month,
And, because you are tame,
I will bring you a biscuit'.

With the passing of time the tigress grew strong,
More lithe and full of courteous love.
One morning she rose early and came to the man's
  house.
He was in bed. By his bedside
Was shaving water and a safety razor.
The tigress said to him, 'My Lord,
This is the first Friday of the month
And I am come because I want meat'.

The man said to her, 'I am a vegetarian'.
The tigress blinked at him
Like a complacent, slightly squinting woman.
Puzzled by the word 'vegetarian' she took to kissing
  the man's feet.
She kissed with the concentration of a strong thing
  that has been idle,
She was also irritated,
A dilettante offended by a word.
In the end she broke a vein in the skin of the man's
  instep,
Then, quick as fire, she ate the man.

She left nothing of him
But the smallest of his vertebrae.

Stevie Smith had no voice at all, and fitted her lyrics to hymn tunes, but Anna wrote her own melodies. I can hear Stevie creakcrooning these lines from **'Anne's First Exercise in Adverbs'**.

Maiden where is the Mayor
Is he gone to shoot the swan
Her who held our Lord in thrall
Not at all and not at all
Mayor was seen with Maggie Mean
Herding turkeys on the green
Oh the poor Queen! Woe the poor Queen.

A surprising number of verses celebrate her domestics, whom for the most part she loved, and nurses whom she execrated, as in **'Conflicting Occupation'**:

If the baby playing typewriter would only let me write,
I might compose him something on the spirit of
  delight,
Something as accurate and rhythmical as Shelley's.
But if I turn my back, my young fill their small bellies
With ink and sealing-wax and tacks,
So I forget my emotions and my facts.
I've even lost my sense of rhyme
By this time.
As for sustaining couplets on things Greek,

I cannot chant, I've scarcely strength to speak
After I've chased this pair of bandits up the stairs,
Lassoed them into bed, or bullied them to prayers.
Nurses? An ugly noxious race,
Soft in the head, and hard in heart and face.

Not so Emily in **'The Housemaid'**:

A natural satirist was Emily,
She saw the weakness of our life, and had her fun
  with it!
And when she left me for the munition factory
I asked, 'You don't like service?' 'No', said she
'I find the work so chronic slow', said she
'I might as well be married and have done with it'.

And some, like **'The Little Love'** are lyrics such as a
poet might have written in any period:

At the height of the May
Your excellence thrilled me,
For a night and a day,
The love of you filled me;
But when the sweet weather
Resolved to the rain,
Like a colt on the tether
My heart felt a strain;
And back to the pasture
That God had ordained me
I lept, with the pleasure
My straying had gained me.

Unique to her seems the compulsion to set down in
verse each passing thought and sensation. The poems
on the kitchen wall, and in what she called her Butcher
Book, the ones she called Post-card Poems, and
enclosed in letters to her friends, Natalie Barney and
John Gawsworth (leaving aside many failures, fragments and botched exercises in various forms of metre),
are often more interesting than some of the more
finished and more predictable published poems.

Because she attracted so many different kinds and
classes of people, and because of her music activities
she had a myriad continuing impressions to write about.
As shown above, although her voice was always her
own, in manner she sometimes echoes other poets. An
uncharacteristically bad poem, **'A Love Letter'**, catches
D. H. Lawrence's hectoring sententiousness; these lines
show why I find it the least pleasing of all her writings.

It is well I cannot eat with you all my days,
I would not take my soup from a consecrated cup.
I have before me a wealth of happy moments when I
  shall see you.
They are like holy wafers, which I will eat
For stimulation, for absolution, and for my eternal
  hope.

This is untypical too of her general acute appraisal of
D. H. Lawrence. She expressed her affection for him in
'Multiplication' (For D. H. L)', while pulling his leg
about his monstrously absurd machoism:

Had I married you, dear, when I was nineteen
I had been little since but a printing machine
For before my fortieth year had run
I well had produced you a twenty-first son.

'Multiplication' (For D. H. L)'

Along with her delight in her children went a kind of
fearful joy in the possibility of their growing up to be
artists. The heavy load she felt such a vocation had
imposed on her would fall with all its painful pleasure
on them. **'The Boy and the Doom'** records a fine image as well as an anxious recognition.

He looked out over the sunset
And said, 'It is a fire sea'.
Should I most treasure or regret
This charming phantasy?
I see him with my burden on his back,
The love of beauty, the inevitable lack,
And him—just three!

She was not so besotted by her love and ambition for
them as to lose her sense of humour and response to
facts, as the charming **'The Boy and the Dream'**
shows.

I thought of the delicate things he had said,
And, ruthless marauder, I went to his bed:
'You'll be a poet one day, maybe,
I'm hoping a far better poet than me.'
With a catch in the throat the thing was done,
I had thrown my load to my slip of a son.
He thrilled, and sat bolt up in his bed,
'Will you *really* buy me those soldiers?' he said.

Her interest in the theatre, ballet and music hall was
intensified by her two elder sons' tap-dancing success
and by her friendship with C. B. Cochran, Anton Dolin
and Bud Flanagan:

Oi! Flanagan:
Joy! Flanagan:
Not a goy! Flanagan.

When Dolin was fighting to keep ballet alive in Britain
in the mid-thirties, he and Markova (as Pavlova had
done earlier) played the halls from time to time. She
wrote **'For Anton Dolin in Carnival (Golders Green
Hippodrome 1936)'**:

Poor lily in a turnip field
Don't yield!
Stand out for Beauty,
Do not succumb to duty.
Feed middling things to cattle.
Now, join the battle
Spirits of British dead
With Shakespeare at their head
To stir your bitter skies
To winds worthy of your enterprise,
Rains of inventions new,
Fit for a flower like you.

'Middling', as used here, suggests Irish associations, which, of course, could have been acquired only through her maternal family, or picked up in Queensland or New South Wales. Her outback life and later education in Australia (after all, it lasted for years from the age of six to twenty), in my view imprinted in her some of the old-fashioned Empire patriotism, which her more intellectual friends found surprising in a poet of feminist rebellion, and an opponent of the old, class, bureaucratic establishment. These years also strengthened her certainty that courage and will were the two essential virtues, and this the passion of her poetry abundantly illustrates.

From her mother's violent physical punishments and her Roman Catholic schooling with its emphasis on Christ's suffering, His wounds, self-humiliation, redemption through pain and so on, she developed and retained a strong sado-masochistic streak. The images of whips, hammers, 'gay love with rods' and battles to death recur throughout her long life as a writer. Most significantly, they are central, though sublimated, in some of her few completely achieved poems, such as **'The Man with a Hammer'**:

> My dear was a mason
> And I was his stone.
> And quick did he fashion
> A house of his own.
>
> As fish in the waters,
> As birds in a tree,
> So natural and blithe lives
> His spirit in me.

And they show more obviously in many of the lesser poems, such as **'The Cruel Lover'**:

> I ask your pardon that your pain
> Should be so quick your lover's gain.
> But when I know your love's distress,
> My heart leaps high with happiness.
> It sends kind tincture to my lips,
> I walk with a new rhythm . . . from the hips.

They also appear with odd ambiguity in **'The Cherry-Blossom Wand (to be sung)'**, which was very popular when published in 1915:

> I will pluck from my tree a cherry-blossom wand,
> And carry it in my merciless hand,
> So I will drive you, so bewitch your eyes,
> With a beautiful thing that can never grow wise.
>
> Light are the petals that fall from the bough,
> And lighter the love that I offer you know;
> In a spring day shall the tale be told
> Of the beautiful things that will never grow old.
>
> The blossoms shall fall in the night wind,
> And I will leave you so, to be kind:
> Eternal in beauty are short-lived flowers,
> Eternal in beauty, these exquisite hours.

> I will pluck from my tree a cherry-blossom wand,
> And carry it in my merciless hand,
> So I will drive you, so bewitch your eyes,
> With a beautiful thing that shall never grow wise.

Sometimes the infliction of pain is a scourge to stiffen the sinews and summon up the will to intolerable effort: sometimes it is naturally part of pleasure, as in **'The Marriage'**:

> What a great battle you and I have fought!
> A fight of sticks and whips and swords,
> A one-armed combat,
> For each held the left hand pressed close to the heart,
> To save the caskets from assault.

The reverse of this fierce joy in marriage is expressed in poems about the stifling mediocrity of bourgeois values and routine. They tend to be rather journalistic, but when Anna is touched personally by unexpected contacts she produces odd, lively verses, such as **'Meditation At Kew'**:

> Alas! for all the pretty women who marry dull men,
> Go into the suburbs and never come out again,
> Who lose their pretty faces and dim their pretty eyes,
> Because no one has skill or courage to organize.
>
> What do these pretty women suffer when they marry?
> They bear a boy who is like Uncle Harry,
> A girl who is like Aunt Eliza, and not new,
> These old dull races must breed true.
>
> I would enclose a common in the sun,
> And let the young wives out to laugh and run;
> I would steal their dull clothes and go away,
> And leave the pretty naked things to play.
>
> Then I would make a contract with hard Fate
> That they see all the men in the world and choose a
>   mate,
> And I would summon all the pipers in the town
> That they dance with Love at a feast, and dance him
>   down.
>
> From the gay unions of choice
> We'd have a race of splendid beauty and of thrilling
>   voice.
> The World whips frank, gay love with rods,
> But frankly, gaily shall we get the gods.

When she transcends her faults of hastiness and carelessness of finish, there is a metaphysical quality of her work, the thinking, analysis and feeling being fused in the poem. Although her own opinions, prejudices and principles were strongly, indeed aggressively, maintained in her social life, she showed a sympathy and understanding that made her loved by a wide range of people. In her work she had the true poet's gift of empathy: she picked with the sparrow in the gravel. Freedom is the dominant theme in her work, a freedom that abhorred licence and recognised necessity. She was preoccupied with the tension between the exact, though 'free', form she worked for, and the spontaneous flow of inspiration. (Her singing training had focused her mind on the problem of freedom of rhythm, of intonation within strict musical limits: she did not write seriously till marriage had terminated her singing career.)

She desperately wanted 'to achieve one perfect thing'. There are poems where she came nearer to it than we might, after all this criticism, have expected.

'Envoi'

> God, thou great symmetry
> Who put a biting lust in me
> From whence my sorrows spring,
> For all the frittered days
> That I have spent in shapeless ways,
> Give me one perfect thing.

There is a Brechtian tone about **'Domestic Economy'**:

> I will have few cooking-pots,
> They shall be bright,
> They shall reflect to blinding
> God's straight light.
> I will have four garments,
> They shall be clean,
> My service shall be good,
> Though my diet be mean.
> Then I shall have excess to give the poor,
> And right to counsel beggars at my door.

'Tribute to the Nursing Staff' seems to me a summing up of her character, and of her personal style:

> Let me die unafraid
> Beyond the reach of aid.
> Let me lie proudly dead
> Where no efficient smooths my bed—
> A lion in the wilderness
> In all my lovely loneliness,
> Unsoiled by science or the least
> Contamination of the priest.

'The Fired Pot', too, could not have been written by anyone but Anna:

> In our town, people live in rows.
> The only irregular thing in a street is the steeple;
> And where that points to, God only knows,
> And not the poor disciplined people!
>
> And I have watched the women growing old,
> Passionate about pins, and pence, and soap,
> Till the heart within my wedded breast grew cold,
> And I lost hope.
>
> But a young soldier came to our down,
> He spoke his mind most candidly.
> He asked me quickly to lie down,
> And that was very good for me.
> For though I gave him no embrace—

> Remembering my duty—
> He altered the expression of my face,
> And gave me back my beauty.

To end this section, here is a poem that can stand with the best love lyrics in the language, **'The Mill'**:

> I hid beneath the covers of the bed,
> And dreamed my eyes were lovers,
> On a hill that was my head.
> They looked down over the loveliest country I have
>   seen,
> Great fields of red-brown earth hedged round with
>   green.
> In these enclosures I could see
> The high perfection of fertility,
> I knew there were sweet waters near to feed the land,
> I heard the churning of a mill on my right hand,
> I woke to breathlessness with a quick start,
> And found my mill the beating of your heart.

Celeste M. Schenck (essay date 1990)

SOURCE: Schenck, Celeste M. "Anna Wickham (1884-1947)." In *The Gender of Modernism: A Critical Anthology,* edited by Bonnie Kime Scott, pp. 613-21. Bloomington, Ind.: Indiana University Press, 1990.

[*In the following essay, Schenck argues that Wickham has been improperly excluded from the canon of poetic modernism and that her formal conventionality heightens, rather than detracts from, the sociopolitical impact of her poems.*]

Anna Wickham, like her exact contemporary Charlotte Mew, has lapsed into obscurity for reasons that have everything to do with the form of her verse and the manner of her dress—Harold Acton, for example, found her poetry as unfashionable as her person (Smith, in Wickham 2). Unlike Mina Loy, whose elegance after four babies was continually remarked, Wickham was large and haphazard in appearance. She once deliberately wore a wool jumper to an affair where Edith Sitwell was sure to show up in gold brocade. Wickham was prolific (nearly 1,400 poems in twenty years) where Mew was spare, yet both wrote overtly feminist poetry that has escaped notice for its failure to adhere to the experimentalist demands of a masculinist modernism. Thomas Hardy called Mew "far and away the best living woman poet—who will be read when others are forgotten" (Fitzgerald 174), and Anna Wickham had by 1932 an international reputation. Anthologies of the day printed more of her poems than those of de la Mare, Graves, and, in some volumes, even Yeats (Smith, in **Wickham** [*The Writings of Anna Wickham*] 23).

Neither Wickham nor Mew came from literary families or had anything like a formal education, and neither studied poetry formally, although Wickham's father apparently made her promise to become a poet. Mew destroyed everything that might constitute a record of her life except for the few pieces that make up her *Collected Poems* and some stories, and most of Wickham's papers and letters were lost in the 1943 bombing of her Hampstead home. Both Wickham and Mew questioned the Catholic church, but whereas Wickham's revisionary supplication of the feminized deity poignantly redresses banishment—"In nameless, shapeless God found I my rest, / Though for my solace I built God a breast"—Mew's resignation, in "Madeleine in Church," is complete—"I do not envy Him His victories, His arms are full of broken things" (Mew 26). Finally, both Wickham and Mew committed suicide. The indignity of Mew's death by the ingestion of disinfectant was matched only by the carelessness of her obituary: "Charlotte New [sic], said to be a writer" (Monro, in Mew xii). Wickham's fate is as banal: The *London Picture Post* did a feature on her in 1946 called "The Poet Landlady" (Smith, in Wickham 28).

A closer look at the life's work of the colorful Wickham, a free-spirited, half working-class Australian emigrée who began her career as an opera singer, then divided her life between London and Paris, might cause us to agree with Stanley Kunitz that the neglect of Anna Wickham is "one of the great mysteries of contemporary literature."[1] A pacifist who nonetheless supported the Great War effort, a deprived and unhappy wife who remained faithful to her husband during the entire course of their tumultuous relationship until his death, an acquaintance of Ezra Pound, Djuna Barnes, Natalie Barney, D. H. Lawrence, and Dylan Thomas who was as comfortable in a London pub as she was on the fashionable Left Bank, a staunch feminist and supporter of women's rights who harbored a masochistic sexuality founded in mother-lack and Catholic education, Wickham was an exciting mass of contradictions of which her poetry is the record. Her Australian childhood offered freedoms unavailable to Englishwomen, and it seems to have stamped Wickham as well with a robust sense of sexual entitlement, a view of social inequality, and an authentic personal voice, all of which set her apart from other women poets of that period. For all the exhilaration of her Australian exile, however, the return to England and her sensitivity to inequalities of class heightened her sense of herself as an outsider. The social rivalry between her mother's and father's families finds its way into poems such as **"Descent of Dorelia"** and **"The Little Old House."** And her own marriage into a family of aristocratic origins initiated her into the oppression of Victorian femininity.

Like Charlotte Mew's, Wickham's formal conventionality is often the very vehicle of her politics: her forced rhymes are meant to be funny and irreverent and to set off the political conflicts of which her poetry is made; they should not be read as merely unsophisticated

concessions to the popular conventions of the day. **"Meditation at Kew,"** outlining a poignant but humorous utopian program for marital reform, is the poetic version of her 1938 feminist manifesto, *The League for the Protection of the Imagination of Women. Slogan: World's Management by Entertainment.*

> Alas! for all the pretty women who marry dull men,
> Go into the suburbs and never come out again,
> Who lose their pretty faces and dim their pretty eyes,
> Because no one has skill or courage to organize.
>
> What do pretty women suffer when they marry?
> They bear a boy who is like Uncle Harry,
> A girl who is like Aunt Eliza, and not new,
> Those old dull races much breed true.
>
> I would enclose a common in the sun,
> And let the young wives out to laugh and run;
> I would steal their dull clothes and go away,
> And leave the pretty naked things to play.
>
> (*Wickham* 45)

In **"Nervous Prostration,"** a poem analyzing the politics of marriage into the upper class, the rhyme scheme and alternating meter sets off rather than contains the rage driving the poem.

> I married a man of the Croydon class
> When I was twenty-two.
> And I vex him, and he bores me
> Till we don't know what to do!
> And as I sit in his ordered house,
> I feel I must sob or shriek,
> To force a man of the Croydon class
> To live, or to love, or to speak!
>
> (210)

There is defiance in the emphasis of the rhyme scheme, and in its metrical regularity not a little irony. In fact the poem is closer to folk balladry than to the genteel metrics of the Croydon class; we might even term it deliberately low-bred, even doggerel, a formal as well as political spoof on bourgeois values. This poem and **"Dedication of the Cook," "The Angry Woman," "Definition," "The Wife," "All Men to Women," "Divorce,"** and **"The Song of the Low-Caste Wife"** criticize prevailing domestic politics, especially in their analysis of sexual difference within the culture that Wickham, marginalized by caste and country as well as gender, could see clearly as triple outsider.

When Wickham writes at the head of her extraordinary autobiography, "I am a woman artist and the story of my failure should be known" (52), she compels the kind of rereading the inclusion within this anthology guarantees, one which accounts not only for her disappearance from modernism's archives but also for the politics of feminist collusion in that exile.[2] Wickham's poems of class consciousness are a salutary addition to a modernist canon insufficiently concerned with the differentials of class and ethnicity. Her poems range from feminist pieces on marital relations and on the conflict between mothering and writing to analyses of the domination of one class by another, as in **"Laura Gray," "Comments of Kate the Cook," "The Butler and the Gentleman," "Daughter of the Horse-Leech,"** and **"Woman to a Philosopher." "Song of the Low-Caste Wife,"** unlike **"Meditation at Kew,"** is rhythmically uneven and unrhymed, but it is no less than revolutionary in its dramatization of the rift between herself and the women of her husband's family and class, its claim for "new myths" conceived by the "new men" mothered by underclass women, its valorization of lust and energy, change and growth, over "old glories" and "dead beauty" (165). **"The Angry Wife"** is similarly unremarkable in its formal aspects, but trenchant in its analysis of motherhood as both experience and institution. The poem first describes marriage in political terms—"If sex is a criterion for power, and never strength / What do we gain by union?" (202)—and then protests the institutional version of parenting which issues from that sexual politics, necessitating the male child's revolt against the mother.

Finally, in a love poem called **"The Mill,"** the concord of heart at one with specific, palpably felt environment is expressed by means of a regularized rhyme scheme, the purposive flowing of alternating rhyme into matched concluding couplets.

> I hid beneath the covers of the bed,
> And dreamed my eyes were lovers,
> On a hill that was my head.
> They looked down over the loveliest country I have
>   seen,
> Great fields of red-brown earth hedged round with
>   green.
> In these enclosures I could see
> The high perfection of fertility,
> I knew there were sweet waters near to feed the land,
> I heard the churning of a mill on my right hand,
> I woke to breathlessness with a quick start,
> And found my mill the beating of your heart.
>
>   (48)

I do not mean to suggest that the enormously uneven Wickham corpus remains undiscovered as a pre-text of literary Modernism. Mew must be admitted to the canon as an undiscovered treasure, while Wickham remains important for reasons other than either experimentalism or formalism in verse. Still, the personal and material specificity of **"The Mill"** should have its history among our modernisms, reflecting—alongside Eliot's phlegmatic portrayals of deceptive lovers, Joyce's spoofs on the magazine romanticism of the day, Loy's send-ups of the masculine sexual principle, and Barnes's decadent New Women poems—its own particular vision, neither ironized nor sentimental, of the way we loved then.

APPENDIX

"Song of the Low-Caste Wife"

What have you given me for my strong sons?
O scion of kings!
In new veins the blood of old kings runs cold.
Your people thinking of old victories, lose the lust of
    conquest,
Your men guard what they have,
Your women nurse their silver pots,
Dead beauty mocks hot blood!
What shall these women conceive of their chill loves
But still more pots?

But I have conceived of you new men;
Boys brave from the breast,
Running and striving like no children of your house
And with their brave new brains
Making new myths.

My people were without while yours were kings,
They sang the song of exile in low places
And in the stress of growth knew pain.
The unprepared world pressed hard upon them,
Women bent beneath burdens, while cold struck babes,
But they arose strong from the fight,
Hungry from their oppression.

And I am full of lust,
Which is not stayed with your old glories.
Give me for all old things that greatest glory,
A little growth.

Am I your mate because I share your bed?
Go then, find each day a new mate outside your house.
I am your mate if I can share your vision.
Have you no vision king-descended?
Come share mine!
Will you give me this, for your sons?
O scion of kings!

The Writings of Anna Wickham. Ed. R. D. Smith. London:
                                            Virago, 1984. 165-166.

"Divorce"

A voice from the dark is calling me.
In the close house I nurse a fire.
Out in the dark cold winds rush free
To the rock heights of my desire.
I smother in the house in the valley below,
Let me out to the night, let me go, let me go.

Spirits that ride the sweeping blast,
Frozen in rigid tenderness,
Wait! for I leave the fire at last
My little-love's warm loneliness.
I smother in the house in the valley below,
Let me out to the night, let me go, let me go.

High on the hills are beating drums.
Clear from a line of marching men
To the rock's edge the hero comes
He calls me and he calls again.
On the hill there is fighting, victory or quick death,

In the house is the fire, which I fan with sick breath.
I smother in the house in the valley below,
Let me out to the dark, let me go, let me go.

Writings. 166-167.

"The Angry Woman

I am a woman, with a woman's parts,
And of love I bear children.
In the days of bearing is my body weak,
But why because I do you service, should you call me
    slave?

I am a woman in my speech and gait,
I have no beard, (I'll take no blame for that!)
In many things are you and I apart,
But there are regions where we coincide,
Where law for one is law for both.

There is the sexless part of me that is my mind.

You calculate the distance of a star,
I, thanks to this free age can count as well,
And by the very processes you use.
When we think differently of two times two,
I'll own a universal mastery in you!—

Now of marriage,—
In marriage there are many mansions,
(This has been said of Heaven).
Shall you rule all the houses of your choice
Because of manhood or because of strength?
If I must own your manhood synonym for every
    strength,
Then must I lie.
If sex is a criterion for power, and never strength,
What do we gain by union?
I lose all, while nothing worthy is so gained by you,
O most blessed bond!

Because of marriage, I have motherhood.
That is much, and yet not all!

By the same miracle that makes me mother
Are you a father.

It is a double honour!
Are you content to be from henceforth only father,
And in no other way a man?
A fantastic creature like a thing of dreams
That has so great an eye it has no head.
I am not mother to abstract Childhood, but to my son,
And how can I serve my son, but to be much myself.

My motherhood must boast some qualities,
For as motherhood is diverse
So shall men be many charactered
And show variety, as this world needs.

Shall I for ever brush my infant's hair?
Cumber his body in conceited needle-work?
Or shall I save some pains till he is grown?
Show him the consolation of mathematics
And let him laugh with me when I am old?

If he is my true son,
He will find more joy in number and in laughter
Than in all these other things.

Why should dull custom make my son my enemy
So that the privilege of his manhood is to leave my
    house?
You would hold knowledge from me because I am a
    mother,
Rather for this reason let me be wise, and very
    strong,—
Power should be added to power.—

And now of love!—
There are many loves.
There is love, which is physiology,
And love, which has no more matter in it than is in
    the mind.
There is spiritual love, and there is good affection.
All these loves women need and most of all the last.

Kiss me sometimes in the light,
Women have body's pain of body's love.
Let me have flowers sometimes, and always joy.
And sometimes let me take your hand and kiss you
    honestly
Losing nothing in dignity by frank love.
If I must fly in love and follow in life,
Doing both things falsely,
Then am I a *mime,*
I have no free soul.

Man! For your sake and for mine, and for the sake of
    future men,
Let me speak my mind in life and love.
Be strong for love of a strong mate,
Do not ask my weakness as a sacrifice to power.
When you deny me justice
I feel as if my body were in grip of a cold octopus,
While my heart is crushed to stone.

This rapture have I of pretence!

Writings. 202-204.

Notes

1. There is at present disappointingly little critical bibliography on Wickham. The notable exception is the excellent centenary volume published by Virago and edited and introduced by R. D. Smith, *The Writings of Anna Wickham: Free Woman and Poet.* The collection includes poetry, prose, her "Fragment of an Autobiography," and Smith's comprehensive memoir and introduction.

2. I do not mean to imply, by asking that we review the work of less experimental poets of the period, that radical critiques of power and status remained the exclusive province of nonexperimenters, but rather to include, within feminist rewriting of periodization, poets who were not compelled, stylistically speaking, to "make it new." My concern for the way in which an alternative canon—Barnes, Loy, H. D., Stein, Moore—might

be positioned and coopted does not displace my recognition of the difficulty feminist critics faced in getting these poets into the canon in the first place. Restriction of feminist critical interest to the sentence-breaking, experimentalist women authors of this period may inadvertently work to reify Modernism as a term.

Works Cited

Fitzgerald, Penelope. *Charlotte Mew and Her Friends.* London: Collins, 1984.

Mew, Charlotte. *Charlotte Mew: Collected Poems and Prose.* Ed. and intro. Val Warner. Manchester: Carcanet (Virago), 1981.

Wickham, Anna. *The Writings of Anna Wickham.* Ed. and intro. R. D. Smith. London: Virago, 1984.

Jennifer Vaughan Jones (essay date summer 2002)

SOURCE: Jones, Jennifer Vaughan. "An Intriguing Mystery: How Did Editor Harold Monro Come to Know Poet Anna Wickham?" *English Literature in Transition 1880-1920* 45, no. 3 (summer 2002): 306-21.

[*In the following essay, Jones discusses the relationship between Wickham and Harold Monro—her publisher and the owner of London's Poetry Bookshop—focusing on the question of how they might have initially met.*]

The story of Anna Wickham (1883-1947) and Harold Monro (1879-1932) is a long and complicated one. Within a year after Monro opened his one-of-a-kind Poetry Bookshop inaugurating a time of "poetry intoxication,"[1] he became Wickham's publisher. Ultimately the two survived not only the growing pains of Wickham's publication in the U.S. and the planning of a joint visit to the heiress Natalie Barney's Paris salon, but also irritation, perturbation, denunciation and embrace. Nevertheless Wickham remained one of Monro's most important poets, and Monro was Wickham's steadfast champion.[2] But the tale starts with a mystery: just how did the two come to find each other?

When the Poetry Bookshop, just five minutes away from the British Museum in a rough area of Bloomsbury London, was officially opened for Monro by Henry Newbolt on 8 January 1913, poets, writers and others who loved literature quickly became familiar with the narrow Georgian-era house at 35 Devonshire Street (now Boswell Street). Upstairs in the attics, poets could rent cheap lodgings. On the ground floor, the small selling room of 12' by 12' was lined floor to ceiling with oak shelves that carried poetry: poetry in periodicals, pamphlets, chapbooks; fat volumes of poetry bound in

leather and gilt-stamped; thin volumes of poetry in cloth covers; lives of the poets, literary criticism and, on a large table of oak (the massive furniture all built by Arthur Romney Green, who shared his friend Monro's ideals), the latest publications issued by the Bookshop. For it was as a publisher and bookseller that Monro made his mark during the 'teens. Though a poet, he did not find his own strongest voice until toward the end of his career.

There was of course normally little mystery involved in a writer's coming to Harold Monro's shop. Almost from its beginnings in late 1912, the little haven was advertised, written about, much discussed, and frequented by those who quickly came to appreciate the warmth, atmosphere and dedication to poetry that they found there. The mystery here lies in how much each of the main players in one particular drama, thirty-four-year-old owner Harold Monro and Anna Wickham, wife of a City of London solicitor, mother of two sons, thirty years old and recently released from an asylum for supposed nervous disorders, may have known about each other. Had Monro learned of Wickham before she showed up? Had Wickham learned of Monro in a way much differently from others of their generation? There are no conclusive answers to these questions, but in asking them we delve a little beneath the surface of the literary terrain to find some intriguing possibilities.

Anna Wickham was the pen name of Edith Alice Mary Hepburn, who in 1913 lived in the leafy London suburb of Hampstead only a few blocks from the Heath, and who had recently begun writing poetry again after primarily devoting the years since her marriage in 1906 to her husband, their two young sons and her philanthropic and charitable activities such as The School for Mothers. Her husband Patrick Hepburn (1873-1929), a man proud of his family connections, was well-regarded both as a lawyer and as an amateur astronomer. Terribly possessive of his much younger wife and already impatient with her singing (she had trained as a singer in London and Paris and infrequently sang in London and Hampstead), he smoldered in fury when he discovered that his wife had, under the pseudonym John Oland, published at her own expense a book of modernist poetry called *Songs*; not only this, but she had captured the interest of one of his new friends in astronomical circles.[3] During a fierce argument, Anna resisted his attempts to drag her from the garden, where she was singing loudly, into the house and she cut her wrist on a glass doorpane. Her injury, her attitude, even her belief in herself as a poet, were cited as symptoms requiring attention. Mr. Hepburn accused her of being insane and in May 1913, with the help of two doctors, arranged for her to be transported to what was then referred to either in crude terms as a lunatic asylum or, in gentrified parlance, a private hospital:

I keep a bird in my heart,
He lives on sorrow.
His name is Faith.
He is so quick a conjurer that he can borrow
Flesh from a wraith.

He swallows the harsh weeds of pain
And gives me scope,
To tend my little garden-plot again
And wait for Hope.[4]

So later wrote Anna Wickham. During her stay of some eleven weeks in the "private hospital," Wickham had experiences which inspired her to write poetry.[5] For instance, among the patients important to Anna, first and foremost was "George Morris," formerly a medal-winning student at the Slade School, who won Anna's affection and interest by introducing himself with the words, "Your husband must be a great fool to let you come here."[6] Anna considered his hearing of voices and his "spirit companions" no more disturbing than were, say, Martin Luther's. Though she did not act on what she calls the "crude desire" that often assailed her in the asylum, the interactions with Morris and others sparked her poetic imagination. But that she was able to write at all in the asylum came about from the intervention of one of the doctors, a Scotsman who was attracted to Anna and fond of poetry. When he heard that she wrote he supplied her with paper and pencil. It may have been this doctor's act that truly encouraged Mrs. Patrick Hepburn to emerge from the asylum's walls as Anna Wickham, poet, for within the asylum was every reason to write out pain and suffering, and the time to do it. Anna first pretended to be uninterested in the doctor's gift, but his act was probably a catalyst for Anna's life-changing transformation in the year ahead. And it may have led her to the man who first published her work, Harold Monro.

This doctor had asked Anna to repeat to him the poem, **"Nervous Prostration,"** which, he had been told, she had once shouted at Patrick before the hospital commitment:

I married a man of the Croydon class
When I was twenty-two,
And I vex him, and he bores me
Till we don't know what to do!
It isn't good form in the Croydon class
To say you love your wife,
So I spend my days with the tradesmen's books
And pray for the end of life. . . .[7]

The poem, which the doctor copied down, is explicit about Anna's dilemma—she was married to a man whose character was so unlike her own that she felt she was slowly dying inside. A later poem says not only that but makes clear she felt Patrick's psychological domination of the family was harming the children as well:

I had two lively children in my youth. . . .
[the man's] "solemn constancy" [or "solemn will"]
Prisoned us round—until the
boys
were mechanised past any
natural joys
And I was maddened—impotent & ill.[8]

Though Patrick had sought to control Anna by putting her in the asylum, being in the asylum had paradoxically put her out of the range of Patrick's control. Once Anna stamped down her fears enough to take the paper and pencil out of her bedside drawer, the verse poured from her, "just as a rush of oil."[9] The asylum doctor, by giving Anna the means to write out her pain without trying to obtain the poems as evidence one way or another, essentially gave Anna not only confirmation and recognition of her talent but also freedom to use it. Given Patrick's extremely negative reaction to Anna's poetry, the behavior of this doctor showed courage, or perhaps there was something unusual about this asylum. And in fact, as we shall see, the asylum did have a connection, how strong or how tenuous we do not know, with someone who was making poetry his life-work.

By the time Anna Wickham was released she had written eighty poems which she secretly carried out with her. In the asylum she had a lot of time to think about the previous few years. How did things turn out the way they did? In her attempt to be a perfect wife and mother, in her attempt to please Patrick, obligation and responsibility had ruled and the impetuous and creative (and free) Anna had had to fight for air. The asylum had shown her the extremes of human behavior—wild, frenetic activity, on the one hand; a blasted uncomprehending inactivity on the other. Dealing with those extremes and with her own fears and shudderings had actually deepened her. Her asylum stay had reacquainted her with the artistic world and with behavior outside the iron template of "the villa dweller." In addition, she had come full-face with sexual desire—her own and others. Mrs. Patrick Hepburn had gone to the asylum; Anna Wickham, poet, had come home. And according to a son, James Hepburn, she surrounded herself with people so that never again would she be defenseless against her husband's decrees.

First she caught up with the rest of the world. A new spirit had been building in Edwardian England and she had kept apart from it. While 5,000 suffragettes had marched through London's summer streets to protest the jailing of women working for the vote, Anna's big event had been the Hepburn's staid garden party. Worker strikes, modern art, the great Liberal victory in General Elections—challenges to society had been proceeding apace.[10] Meanwhile Anna had done volunteer work that Patrick approved of, borne and taken care of their two children, run the household and made the choices "betwixt the baked and boiled," and tried to be a supportive wife to a man with the makings of a scientist.[11] But her own singing had been discouraged and her first poetry had been published to her husband's irritation and distaste.

A new era began at 49 Downshire Hill. By her own assessment, Anna's energy "had been stimulated by . . . incarceration." She gave her own garden party, invited the politician and writer Israel Zangwill, and dressed up her boys and one of their friends so that the tussah blouses spelled out VOTES-FOR-WOMEN.[12] She became friends with artists and writers, and drank beer in the Café Royal. This necessitated a strong front against Patrick and a change similar to that in her poem, **"Gift to a Jade"**:

> For love he offered me his perfect world.
> This world was so constricted, and so small,
> It had no sort of loveliness at all,
> And I flung back the little silly ball.
> At that cold moralist I hotly hurled,
> His perfect pure symmetrical small world.[13]

She took a new look at the house and "painted out" the Victorian Liberty wallpapers and bought paintings for the walls.[14] In an earlier time, seeking to keep track of the sheer number of things in their household, Anna had filled page after meticulous page in a standard Victorian "Where is it?" book. Now she tossed aside this desire for orderly perfection and her youthful admiration for such Hepburn concerns as neatly compartmentalized sewing boxes, special champagne, signature dinner gongs, and immaculate white paint. She began singing again at home, "raising my invincible voice in free and self-invented song."[15] She took over the main care of the boys and resumed "our games and our readings . . . and our happy treks abroad."

Most important of all, Anna went to Harold Monro's Poetry Bookshop. Halfway up a dingy Bloomsbury street, off the clamor of Theobalds Road, Anna found, a few days after her release from the asylum, the center of poetry in London. Harold Monro was, by the fall of 1913, known as the only man bold or stupid enough to think that poetry deserved and could support a home of its own. He had spent several years of wandering and thinking in Europe and had come back determined to "do something" about what he saw as the abysmal state of poetry in England.[16] Shortly after his return, he agreed to assume financial risk and editorship for a revamped journal, the *Poetry Review,* under the auspices of the Poetry Society. When his nature (sown with the seeds of radicalism, according to Ezra Pound) conflicted with their conservative expectations, the Society firmly cleared the way for him to leave. Monro, undaunted, decided not only to found his own journal, which he christened *Poetry and Drama,* but to spread the gospel of poetry-is-necessary by providing a meeting place. There, he hoped, poet would meet poet; book would

face book across the shelves; and the public, the great public which needed verse, would be able to buy poetry and hear poetry read in a way that would move the hearer to appreciate it, not merely the reader of it.

"Have you any free rhythms?" Anna asked Monro. Black-browed and grave, Monro looked up at the sound of her resonant voice and responded with interest, "We've all been trying to write them."[17] Anna passed him the modest pamphlet of poems written by her friend, "John Oland," but Monro quickly guessed that the real author was standing directly in front of him in an attractive hat.

Harold Monro liked Anna Wickham's poetry. Her concerns and his often mirrored one another's, although Anna did have a respect for machines that Monro did not share, and she sometimes, though not always, downgraded the domesticity that some of Monro's works featured. He took an amazing fifteen of her most recent poems for his quarterly literary magazine though he generally did not print that many at one time from one contributor. As time went on, he enlisted her often-praised voice for the Poetry Bookshop's twice-weekly readings, for not only reading her own poetry and that of other poets, but at least once for reading, behind a curtain, a play by Gordon Bottomley.[18] Monro eventually published two of her books (**The Contemplative Quarry,** 1915; **The Little Old House,** 1921) and he included her in his anthologies and his rhyme sheet series. Other writers, editors and publishers such as Grant Richards and John Gawsworth in London, Natalie C. Barney in Paris, and Harriet Monroe and Louis Untermeyer in the U.S. later enthusiastically would bring Anna Wickham's work before the public, but it was Harold Monro who got her career off to a rousing start.

Monro's quarterly, which ran until the beginning of World War One, focused on poetry, criticism and reviews but included art (often woodcuts), dramas and writing on theatre.[19] Anna's poetry debuted June 1914 and made a very favorable impression. *The Morning Post* of 25 June 1914 singled out "Miss Anna Wickham" as seeking after new truth and beauty. The reviewer praised her "strangely-enhancing poems" and favorably cited her **"Cherry-Blossom Wand."**

Why Harold Monro, whose own poetry had by that time been published by Elkin Matthews (*Poems,* 1906), Constable (*Before Dawn: Poems and Impressions,* 1911) and his own joint-venture Samurai Press, would have been attracted to Anna's poetry is easy to see. When she presented her thin pamphlet of poems, he probably was shocked by the way her poetry spoke to his own concerns. In the poems he had written or would write were the longing, love of freedom, anti-clericalism, loss of religious faith, love and passion, which he would find also in Wickham's poetry. But those initial moments must have been freighted with tension—Monro's head bent over the book perhaps, Anna uncomfortably picking up books from the table or scanning the shelves—"nervous and shy, like you" as she would once write to Monro.[20]

Monro may have been nervous and shy, but he was a man fighting for a vision. He opened the annual poetry reading series by always reading the same poem, Percy Bysshe Shelley's "Hymn to Intellectual Beauty." He had earlier spent years trying to achieve discipline, either through short-lived group work such as the Samurai or the various "crank settlements" in Europe which he investigated. Though he was now making headway with his shop, he often felt alone, having to be responsive to the dictates of commerce, the demands of family, and even the aching unresolved issues of his own desires. When Anna walked in, a woman who seemed to many people larger than life and possessed of a clear, decisive wit, a way of mocking that seemed to give her a higher moral ground (yet at the same time truly lamenting her own inadequacies), she must have struck a deep chord in Harold Monro.

A year or so before, in a lecture at Cambridge, Monro had defined the contemporary poet as one that "caught the spirit of Darwin, that spirit which had so altered our attitude, and rendered obsolete so many ways of talking about life."[21] Anna, of course, had been schooled in Darwinian thought by her progressive father almost from the time she was able to take in words. But since as a small child she had also attended church school in her birthplace, Wimbledon, with the family housekeeper and in Australia had attended convent schools for several years, her view of the state of religious faith in a scientific world was quite panoramic. In this way, among others, the poems Anna had written worked for Monro. And though they were fascinating to listen to, they did not have entertainment as their aim, a goal Monro would have despised.[22] It is possible that Monro might have seen the possibility of a friendship with a woman his equal as he turned the pages of **Songs** of John Oland.

A look at several poems by each poet shows how similar are their concerns. Both feel a lack in their lives. For Monro, in "The One, Faithful. . . . ," it is a painful longing for the solace and understanding of friendship, and as we see in poems such as "Officer's Mess," friendship that is not either of the bottle, or fickle and shortlived. For Anna, on the last page of **Songs,** it is a desire for wholeness and perfection:

> God, thou great symmetry,
> Who put a biting lust in me,
> > From whence my sorrows spring,
> For all the frittered days

> That I have spent in shapeless ways
> > Give me one perfect thing.[23]

Anna's tone in this poem is more demanding than the tone Monro generally uses. And she also feels free to address a God which Monro has, as early as 1908, as a diary entry shows, given up on, though he felt the loss of his faith profoundly.[24] But as other poems show, Anna is with Monro in despising any religion calcified and empty. In her **"Call for Faith,"** a poem which ultimately seeks solace in the evolutionary principle which she calls "Good Chance," she says,

> Where in this wildness shall I find my path?
> When in this whirling night, know one thing true?
> From the ruins of temples shall I take a dead saint,
> Prop him in some new shrine,
> And cry that God still lives?
> This is the faith of fools.[25]

Monro surely would have responded to the argument Anna presents—and this type of engagement with an issue is exactly what Monro, according both to his own admission, and to conclusions by scholars who have studied him, looked for again and again in his interactions with people, and only too rarely found.

Monro had had homosexual loves and encounters since his school days. It had not stopped him from marriage, however, first to Dorothy Browne, the sister of one of his best friends, Maurice. During that marriage, which lasted, at least in name, from 1903 to 1916 and produced a son, Nigel, he and Dorothy lived part of the time in Ireland, where rain, isolation, and the married state drove him nearly to suicide. It was at this juncture that Monro, stuck in his painful present and remembering the long walks and intense conversations of his school days, confided to his journal, "Why did I surrender my dear, dear freedom?"[26] Among the poems Anna showed him that day in 1913 was **"Divorce,"** lines of which might have been written expressly for Monro:

> A voice from the dark is calling me.
> In the close house I nurse a fire.
> Out in the dark cold winds rush free,
> To the rock heights of my desire.
> I smother in the house in the valley below,
> Let me out to the night, let me go, let me go.[27]

Whatever their problems with marriage, however, both poets had a deep need for love. In the poem, "Unto Her," Monro spoke of "Peace and eventual Heaven in your mind; / And in your body, that one place I have sought, / A tranquil lodging for my stormy thought," while Anna wrote in **"The Wife's Song"**:

> I would carry you in my arms,
> > My strong one,
> As if you were a child;

Over the long grass plains by the sea,
Where dunes are piled.[28]

Of course by the time that Harold Monro met Anna she had been in the asylum. There she had written many more poems than those he saw in her John Oland *Songs,* an undated volume which is thought to have been published in 1911 or 1912. Since Harold was always after fresh work, it was from Anna's newer poems that he chose the fifteen to print in *Poetry and Drama.* Of these **"The Cherry Blossom Wand"** became an immediate and lasting favorite of poetry readers. Flirtatious, confident, mysterious, the poem was to be sung to a tune that Anna composed and that many people eventually heard her sing. If one poem could be said to have made her name in the 'teens, it was this one which Monro, a music-lover and concert-goer himself, chose and published. Monro also selected one narrative poem, **"The Slighted Lady,"** from Anna's work, but in general he was after a different sort of poem for this *Poetry and Drama* issue. **"Singer"** ("If I had peace to sit and sing"), **"Gift to a Jade," "Song"** ("I was so chill, and overworn, and sad"), **"The Tired Man,"** and **"Self Analysis,"** are all poems whose style, so in harmony with their sense, makes them emotionally immediate in their impact.[29]

True to the paradigm Anna established for her best poetry, each of these poems reads almost like a position paper, containing assertion and reasons. Words are not wasted; intensity is carefully gauged. She distills a question to its essence and her word choices are pointed and deliberate. The length of her lines and the rhythm she chooses often intensify[30] the effect of the sense of the lines. This compositional self-control, in poems about self-control and its ambiguous results, acts as a flying carpet—supporting the sense, delivering the goods, effortless in effect, magical for its seeming lack of machinery.

In the Wickham poems that Monro published, the theme of balance often recurs. On one side of Anna Wickham's self-control are balanced the qualities of chasteness and goodness, orderliness and duty. These, however, are often scattered like so many feathers by the heavy emotions weighing in on the other side: longing, passionate love, lust and desire. In the poetry of Anna Wickham self-control is heroic, for example, when a woman is trying to control an illicit desire which might overwhelm her, or when a would-be conqueror prepares himself for battle. But in other poems self-control is nearly physiologically maddening when its overuse in ordinary life results in a predictable, suffocating sameness.[31]

By the time Anna met him, Monro may have already taken on, as his shop assistant, Alida Klementaski, seventeen years his junior. She seems to have loved Monro almost from the day they met and when Monro's first shop assistant left to marry poet Wilfrid Gibson, Alida began to make herself indispensable in the shop. She had ambitions of her own and could teach herself almost anything, from bookkeeping to hand-coloring of book covers and rhyme sheets. Harold came to love her idealism, her innocence and her tender ministrations, but most authorities agree that she didn't understand Monro's sexuality. This made Monro evasive and guilt-ridden, while Alida compensated for her lack of understanding by abhorring anyone who dwelt on sexual matters. Mrs. Hepburn, she wrote to Monro, was one.[32]

Klementaski's letters, expressing a love of Monro almost smothering in its intensity, reveal a vitriolic antagonism toward those people or things which she perceived as a threat to Monro's stability and to their combined happiness (they married, at the urging of one of Monro's friends, in 1920): hence the antagonism toward Anna Wickham. But since Monro always maintained an existence apart from Klementaski—including lunching and dining almost daily with writers and artists and going to the continent without her—Anna's friendship with Monro flourished to the extent her husband and family life left her time to be with others, and to the extent that Klementaski's objections were brushed aside. Anna was well-respected by Monro for what he called her "rare power of condensing a troublesome problem of social psychology into the form of a lyric."[33] He liked her "chiefly conversational" style, and the variety in the moods of her work. He noted with satisfaction that "there is plenty here to shock those mild beings who delight in the thrill of a good shock," but felt that she was certainly more than "a brilliant writer of psychological gossip." Finally, he admired her "frank sensuality," and advised men, in particular, to read her poems in order to appreciate "a woman whose intellect controls her senses, and whose love-poems are as natural as daylight or snow."

Just as it was no secret that Alida Klementaski "loathed" Anna (as one of Wickham's sons has said), it was no secret that Harold Monro had "a great feeling for Anna both as a poet and as a person."[34] She could match his sadness and bitterness, she could jolly him along in letters, excuse his dourness to others, even "drink level with him and understand, what was more, why he drank himself."[35] Nevertheless, toward the end of their publishing relationship she grew more and more irritated with him, complaining that in his fear of the censors (a force to be reckoned with in those days of the ordered destruction of D. H. Lawrence's *The Rainbow* and James Joyce's *Ulysses*) Monro was printing her so "innocently" that her reputation would "die forever."[36] In the poem **"To Harold Monro,"** she even accused the bookshop of "filching" the fees due to her (though some account slips showing that her royalties did not at times cover the books she ordered from the shop complicate the question).[37]

But Monro was always sympathetic to Anna and attracted to her as well. At a time when Anna was in personal despair, it was Monro who consoled her in bed—and unfortunately Anna's son Jim who found them together in one of the sleeping rooms above the bookshop.[38] It is not known if Alida ever learned of this incident.

But how Anna Wickham and Harold Monro first learned of each other is the intriguing issue. Not just anybody could open a bookshop—even in the great city of London—devote it solely to the sale and cosseting of poetry, and expect it to be and stay a going financial concern. This the Poetry Bookshop did (with ups and serious downs) until 1935, when it closed under Alida's ownership three years after Monro's death. It could not possibly have been done without the almost tireless energy of Alida, of course, who kept the place going during the First World War and after. But even with her assistance, it is fair to say, and based on record, that it could not possibly have been done unless the owner was lucky enough to have a private income. This was exactly the case with Harold Monro. Five generations of his family (his father, an engineer, was an exception) had nourished a business which was stable enough to provide Monro with an income sufficient for a modest, but decent living.[39] This business was none other than Brooke House, the private asylum belonging to the Monros since the late seventeen hundreds—and where Anna, just before coming into Harold Monro's shop, had spent a long and horrific summer.

A few caveats should be mentioned. Works about Harold Edward Monro which detail his publishing and poetic career only touch on his connection with Brooke House. Joy Grant calls the asylum by name; Ruth Tomalin gives an idea of how much income Monro derived from the business.[40] Dominic Hibberd, Harold Monro's biographer, notes that when Monro ordered his affairs before his World War One service began he made a visit to Brooke House as part of that planning. By 1928, Hibberd's biography states, Harold was a trustee and had regular meetings with the trustees and with Dr. Johnson, the Brooke House physician in charge.[41] But in 1913, when the License for the private asylum was held by Mr. H. T. Monro and two others, Harold may not have had as much to do with the business, though even then a Dr. Gerald Johnston was resident physician and co-holder of the License.[42]

If Monro had a close relationship with the doctor at the asylum that doctor surely knew that Monro had opened a bookshop devoted to poetry, and he may have thought that Monro would be interested to hear of this most unusual woman hospitalized, at least in part, for the egregious sin of writing her heart out in poetry. The doctor, after giving Anna the means to write, may have mentioned the publications of The Bookshop. Then again, at that time, Monro may have simply collected his share of proceeds from an asylum trust, had no communication with the doctors running the business, and no interest in the place other than as a producer of his yearly income.

So did the doctor tell Anna of this bookshop—happy that his fascinating patient might find a supportive and interesting society there? Did Monro tell her of his interest in Brooke House?[43] If the doctor never told Monro of the new patient, would Anna herself have told Monro where she had just spent her summer? As a matter of fact, how many people knew that Anna had been hospitalized?[44] Perhaps there was a general agreement to keep such information quiet.

Does it really matter? First, for example, does it weaken or strengthen Anna's poetry to know where or why it was written? No, for the poems on the page stand on their merits, not on the fact that they were composed because of or in spite of circumstances. The information added makes them more biographically interesting, but it does not make a bad poem good or vice-versa. Secondly, would it matter that Harold Monro chose Anna's poetry knowing that some of it was composed in his family's asylum? Yes.

Harold Monro has taken some criticism, including self-criticism, for rejecting early poetry of T. S. Eliot and Edward Thomas.[45] (John Drinkwater, poet, playwright, actor and friend of Monro sheds light on this by explaining, "although he was often unaffected by good work he never liked bad. . . .")[46] Some have faulted him (he gets praised for the same reason) for attempting to walk some sort of middle line in poetry—always scanning the horizon for the poet who will speak to the people without offending too many of them.[47] If Harold Monro took Anna's poems without knowing where she had written them, he risked no more criticism than was usual in the press. If Harold Monro, however, knew that Anna had recently been released from his asylum, and if he thought her stay was widely known, he opened himself up to further scrutiny. Was he irresponsible in publishing the work of an asylum patient? Was he generous in promoting such work? There was already interest in the intersection of art and madness; for example, the psychiatric clinic doctors at the University of Heidelberg had begun assembling drawings and paintings by patients in German. Swiss and Austrian asylums.[48] Was the venerable Monro asylum, often in the forefront of developments, part of this trend?

From their early meetings ("tea with Mrs. Hepburn," reads one Monro diary entry), the relationship between Monro and the modern-thinking Hampstead poet grew less formal and more direct. "Mrs. Hepburn" came to insist that he address his letters to "Anna Wickham." She felt free to harangue him about small matters (the deportment of his clerk, for example). She sometimes regretted his reserve and felt he should publish bolder, riskier works. She shrewdly assessed and disapproved of Alida's attempts to restrict his freedoms. Monro, who over the years probably heard, read and edited well over a hundred of Wickham's poems, probably came to know her as well as anyone did. It seems almost certain that the asylum, Brooke House, would have come up in their conversations eventually. The question of how much Harold Monro and Anna Wickham knew about each other when they met is still a literary mystery. The Hepburn sons were told it this way: Harold Monro saw her poetry, liked it, and encouraged her to write.[49] Anna just says that after her release, ". . . I heard of the Poetry Bookshop."[50]

Notes

Acknowledgement: I am indebted to Professor Emeritus James G. Nelson for reading an earlier draft of this essay and making valuable suggestions, and to the librarians and archivists of The British Library for their kindness and courtesy.

1. Rose Macaulay's term "poetry intoxication" is quoted by Penelope Fitzgerald on p. xxv of her intro. to J. Howard Woolmer's *The Poetry Bookshop 1912-1935* (Revere, Pennsylvania: Woolmer/ Brotherson Ltd., 1988).

2. Anne Born, "Harold Monro & The Poetry Bookshop." *Antiquarian Book Monthly Review,* 7:4 (April 1980), 184-95. The others were poet F. S. Flint, chronicler of French imagism, and Charlotte Mew, poet and short-story writer Monro published two collections each of the work of Wickham, Flint and Mew.

3. The latter explanation is given in an autobiographical fragment (n.d.) collection of the author and courtesy of the Hepburn family.

4. Anna Wickham. *The Writings of Anna Wickham, Free Woman and Poet.* Preface, James Hepburn. Ed. and with biographical "Memoir" and critical analysis by R. D. Smith (London: Virago Press, 1984), 227. Hereafter referred to as *WAW*. The research and thorough inventory of Anna Wickham's poetry by Smith and Hepburn family members James, George and Margaret Hepburn is here gratefully acknowledged.

5. Anna Wickham, "I & My Genius," *Women's Review.* March 1986, 18 Any otherwise unidentified quotations having to do with Anna Wickham's asylum experience are from this article, 16-20.

6. Many of Anna Wickham's autobiographical writings use pseudonyms; therefore "George Morris" should not automatically be taken to be the man's true name.

7. *WAW* 210. The entire poem has four stanzas.

8. In manuscript, the poem contains "solemn will" as a variation. Addt'l Mss 71879. British Library, London.

9. Addt'l Mss 71879. British Library, London.

10. Marina Warner, *The Crack in the Teacup: Britain in the 20th Century* (New York: Houghton Mifflin/ Clarion Books, 1979), 38.

11. "betwixt the baked and boiled," from "Dedication of the Cook," most recently published in *The Norton Anthology, Literature by Women. The Traditions in English,* Sandra M. Gilbert and Susan Gubar, eds. (2nd ed., New York: W. W. Norton, 1996), 1382. Contains an introduction. For a fuller introduction, see Celeste Schenck's Anna Wickham entry in *The Gender of Modernism,* Bonnie Kime Scott, ed. (Bloomington: Indiana University Press, 1990), 613-21.

12. James Hepburn interview (5-25-92) with the author.

13. *WAW,* 189.

14. Mark Gertler and Nina Hamnett were only two of her painter-friends.

15. "I & My Genius," 20.

16. Joy Grant, author of *Harold Monro and the Poetry Bookshop* (Berkeley: University of California Press, 1967), 24, is somewhat suspicious about the neatness of the "do something" exhortation supposedly made by Maurice Hewlett, already a famous author, to Monro, but the words do capture the zeal and spirit with which Monro began his work in England.

17. "I & My Genius." We now use the term "free verse," but at the time Monro's friend F. S. Flint favored the term "unrhymed cadence." See Joy Grant, 118.

18. Laura Severin, author of *Stevie Smith's Resistant Antics* (Madison. University of Wisconsin Press, 1997), is writing on Anna Wickham in relation to the performance aspects of poetry.

19. *Poetry and Drama* was first issued in March 1913. Anna Wickham's first appearance in any little magazine was in volume 2, number 6, an issue which contained criticism and reviews by Ford Madox Hueffer (later, Ford), Edward Thomas, T. E. Hulme and F. S. Flint, as well as poetry by

Maurice Hewlett and John Gould Fletcher. The June 1914 issue of Monro's *Poetry and Drama* contained fifteen poems by Wickham: "Bad Little Song," "The Cherry-blossom Wand," "The Comment," "Gift to a Jade," "Sehnsucht," "Self-Analysis," "The Singer," "The Slighted Lady," "Song" ('I was so chill. . . .' "A Song of Morning," "Susannah in the Morning," "The Tired Man," "To D. M.," "To a Young Boy," and "The Woman of the Hill."

20. n.d. letter Anna Wickham to Harold Monro. Special Collections, University Research Library, University of California, Los Angeles.

21. Harold Monro, *Collected Poems*, Alida Monro, ed., with a Preface by Ruth Tomalin (1933, London: Duckworth, 1970), xxv.

22. Ruth Tomalin, xxiii.

23. In *The Writings of Anna Wickham*, 46, this poem appears with the title "Envoi."

24. Ibid., xxv.

25. *Songs* of John Oland (London: Women's Printing Society, n.d.), 3.

26. Ruth Tomalin, Preface to Harold Monro's *Collected Poems* (1933; London: Duckworth, 1970).

27. Ibid., 18.

28. For Monro, "Unto Her." *Collected Poems*, 6. For Wickham's "The Wife's Song," *Songs*, 13.

29. These can be found in *WAW*.

30. For more on Anna Wickham's poetry and her place in literary modernism, see unpublished dissertations by Jennifer Vaughan Jones, "The Poetry and Place of Anna Wickham 1910-1930." University of Wisconsin-Madison (1994), and by Nelljean McConeghey Rice, "A New Matrix for Modernism: A Study of the Lives and Poetry of Charlotte Mew and Anna Wickham," University of South Carolina (1997).

31. Celeste M. Schenck, who along with Myra Stark, Margaret Newlin and Andrew Field champions Anna Wickham's work, writes: "Wickham was an exciting mass of contradictions of which her poetry is the record," See *The Gender of Modernism,* 614.

32. Alida Klementaski letter to Harold Monro, 8 February 1916. Addt'l Mss 57748. British Library.

33. Harold Monro, *Some Contemporary Poets* (London: Leonard Parsons, 1920), 196-99.

34. James Hepburn interview (5-30-92) with the author.

35. Penelope Fitzgerald, *Charlotte Mew and Her Friends, with a selection of her poems.* Foreword by Brad Leithauser. (Reading, MA: Addison-Wesley Publishing [Radcliffe Biography Series], 1988), 156. First published in 1984 by London: William Collins Sons.

36. Inscription to "G. 3" and "my beloved Uncle," in the frontispiece of the *Chapbook,* Number 39 (1924), Hepburn private collection.

37. This seems a bit cruel of Anna, and perhaps it was a judgement she changed, since in the mid 1920s during a marital separation Klementaski did rent a house on Heathcote Street off Mecklenburgh Square to Anna and her sons.

38. Margaret Hepburn interview (11-14-96) with the author.

39. Fitzgerald, 43.

40. Grant, 6. Tomalin, xviii.

41. Dominic Hibberd, *Harold Monro, Poet of the New Age* (Houndmills, Basingstoke, Hampshire, Palgrave, 2001), 177, 240.

42. *The Medical Directory 1913* (London: J. & A. Churchill, 1917), 2068.

43. Brooke House was damaged by bombing in 1940, demolished in 1955.

44. Anna's granddaughter Tom Price had never been told this by her father John Hepburn. Toni Price interview (1-22-2000) with the author.

45. In both cases, Monro came to regret his decision and later publicly praised the work of both Eliot and Thomas. See Ann Born, "Harold Monro & The Poetry Bookshop," 184-95.

46. John Drinkwater. *Discovery; being the second book of an autobiography, 1897-1913* (Boston: Houghton, 1933), 224.

47. This attitude explained, though disagreed with in Marvin Magalaner's "Harold Monro. Literary Midwife," *Arizona Quarterly* (Winter 1949), 328-38.

48. Roberta Smith, "Where Insanity and Modernism Intersect," *New York Times,* 21 April 2000, B34.

49. George Hepburn interview (11-25-96) with the author.

50. "I & My Genius," 16-20.

Jennifer Vaughan Jones (essay date 2003)

SOURCE: Jones, Jennifer Vaughan. "Writing Her Life (1934-1939)." In *Anna Wickham: A Poet's Daring Life,* pp. 231-52. Lanham, Md.: Madison Books, 2003.

[In the following essay, Jones details the events of Wickham's life in the period leading up to the writing of her

"most bitter and probably most honest" autobiographical poem, "Life Story."]

At age fifty-one, Anna was a lively mother, an excellent friend to the arts, a highly original poet whose lines ranged from sledgehammer-strong to ethereally delicate, and at times a woman in the grip of despair. The next years would be spent in writing her story, over and over again. But one of the first things she had to do was release herself from the hold that Natalie Barney had on her imagination.

"Song" and Natalie had not seen each other since around 1931, but letters and poems had continued. Anna hoped to see Natalie in a proposed visit to London around the end of 1933, promising dancing herons for Natalie and "all the taxi-men to adore you," but then Anna turned "ill and liable to die like Descartes of my lungs" and the meeting never took place.[1]

In April 1934 Natalie wrote fondly, "I'm always glad to see your writing because it has conveyed so much to me that is new and inspired."[2] One day in May of 1934 Anna retrieved her mail to find a letter inviting her to Paris. The paintings of Natalie's mother, Alice Pike Barney, were going to be displayed in Paris and Natalie wanted Anna to be present. Anna, busy with Tour Bourgeoise, did not go. But the letter that she wrote to Natalie on Sunday, May 27, though signed, "Your affec. Anna," has a cold clarity that sets it apart both from some of the raving letters she had written and certainly from the passionate ones.

> You will forgive me for speaking to you emotionally for the last time. Without your O.K. I shall not write to you again—& for this reason—When I met you eight years ago I had so much pleasure from contact with your mind, from your society & from the observation of your spirit—that I feared to drown of happiness. Fear tinged my behavior to you with protective eccentricity—In presenting to you who are so good a judge of truth something that was spurious, there was a shade of impertinence. I don't think this impertinence harmed you—for you are immune from it—But it hurt & lessened & strumpeted me—I had always been afraid of happiness. . . . Even in my silences there will be Truth—(a little arrogance perhaps in my speech!)—I no longer fear to drown. I will therefore write for you—if you tell me to [crossed out] ask me [penned in above].[3]

The last lines of another Wickham poem, **"P. P. C.,"** also show her freeing herself artistically and emotionally from Barney: "Now my aspiration's new / I'll not dream again from you."[4]

Another letter, undated, shows part of the process of Anna coming to her senses in regard to Natalie. In this case a somber epiphany during an encounter in a café. She met there

a fat blonde illiterate whore I have known by sight for years. She was amusing . . . & she began to be professionally inviting & brush her great breasts along my back & I liked her too much to repulse her—& I sat and cowered with repulsion & suddenly I thought of you! I remembered that I have been writing love-poetry to you for years—& that you have been nice about it / & I thought that your imagination—was to my imagination as was I to the large blonde whore—& I was sorry for you.[5]

Anna had closed that letter by saying that "as this part of my spirit dies" she asks for forgiveness, "& a beginning in good sense."

Natalie wrote again later in 1934, but this was to ask a favor. Dolly Wilde, Anna's irritant in the late 1920s, had been going through tough times and even tried to commit suicide in September. Natalie, who remained loyal to Dolly in her excesses, had written hoping that Anna would release Dolly from a curse made by Anna years before. Fearing that perhaps Anna's "malific [sic] light-hearted power. . . . may have brought about this unhappy chain of events," Natalie writes, "May I beg that you will exert your more serious power, in which I've unlimited faith, to bring about a change for the better?"[6] In gratitude (or bribery) Natalie bought Anna a much appreciated coat and skirt. Anna had an ornate certificate drawn up, taxing Natalie the sum of £9.4.6. (perhaps the cost of the clothing) "for mentioning a mistress to her true lover."[7]

Still, a bond survived. Natalie and Anna continue to send each other their newly published books, a few gifts, and tokens. During her various readings around the city Anna included poetry written to Barney. In November 1935 a "packet of poems" reached Natalie Barney then visiting in New York, and Anna still professes a desire "to beat Rémy [de Gourmont in] letters to you."[8] In 1936 there is a flurry of letters, a few undated letters discuss hopelessness in Anna's situation (Delarue-Mardrus unsympathetically said that no one could help Anna, while Anna, chillingly, responds that anyone who could send her a ladder could help her). Sometimes long-distance lust reappears, sometimes the love is likened to mother-love. But Anna never relinquishes her pleasure in Natalie's "exquisite" and "sustaining" appreciation.[9] And Barney continued to give that admiration to the verse of "Anna, dear and incorrigible Anna."[10]

The years from 1930 to 1934, in which Anna directed her attention outward, seem to give way to somewhat more of an inward focus in the years from 1935 to 1939, a woman trying to come to terms with herself, interpreting and reinterpreting her life over and over again in works that gradually become more and more truthful. And more bleak.

Anyone who wants to learn more about the poet behind Anna's poetry should read "Prelude to a Spring Clean," her partial autobiography in prose. A work funny, candid (but not too candid), emotional, she meant to explain the life of a "failure," but succeeded in telling a lively story. Never published until 1984, a British journalist and teacher, R. D. (Reggie) Smith, together with the Hepburn family, pored over stacks of material to bring out the largest-ever selection of Anna Wickham material. Included in that selection are portions of the autobiography covering her childhood, youth, marriage, and the first two years of their first son, James.[11] She wrote it beginning in March, 1935, as a survival technique during an extremely low and unstable point in her life, saying that "self-knowledge and self-expression are the only techniques of my continuance."[12] "For the whole twenty-nine years [since marriage] my resources have been decreasing," she writes.[13]

Her financial situation is as poor as ever. Her first publisher, Harold Monro, is dead, her new work has not been picked up by other book publishers (if she even offered it), her last volume was published in 1921, and most of the Americans who liked her work in Paris had gone home when the franc's hospitality diminished. She is older, getting shabby, and has no viable love interest. The gains of the last few years begin to seem inadequate and Tour Bourgeoise is proving to be a lot of work with little return. She loses a briefcase with a large notebook of poems.[14] New poets are taking over the field. She suffered toothaches and poor health in 1933. Then in June of 1934 her stepfather, William Henry Geake, committed suicide by drowning, leaving seventy-seven-year-old Alice a widow. By 1935 Alice was living in Russell, Bay of Islands, New Zealand, but she moved on from there, probably leaving New Zealand.[15]

Besides all the worries, Anna seems to be standing still while others are not: Natalie Barney is spending the winter in the U. S.; Anna's older sons, well-reviewed in *The Evening Standard,* are touring (with the famous "Crazy Gang" on the bill) and honing their act for the continent. John is soon to marry.[16] Within a year the Hampstead Scientific Society will build an observatory on the Heath "to the memory of Patrick Hepburn." With all this in mind, Anna begins to order the house.

Anna's house by this time was almost famously filthy, at least the kitchen. Disorder ruled. Now she cleaned and sorted, energy from those ongoing tasks providing energy for the task of writing. Her gruesome intent she depicts with a mordant twist—that one cannot commit suicide using a dirty oven:

> This year I shall conquer the sets of drawers; my self-discipline is complete enough. I shall have every pin, rag, tot and tittle in the villa in its place, and everything will be splendidly clean. But I am finished: I am utterly defeated: there is nothing before me but suicide. I order the villa for my death. When the stove is clean enough I shall turn on the gas.[17]

In many ways, Anna had been writing her life ever since she picked up pen and put it to paper. The poems often sprang out of incidents in her life, her speeches for the School for Mothers from the self-sufficiency she saw in her Whelan foremothers, her short stories by the raw material of her courtship and marriage to Patrick. Now for the first time Anna was ready, or forced herself to be ready, to write her life story in a more straightforward fashion. She began the work of revealing herself, perhaps the hardest, most original work an artist can do.

She wants to understand the roots of things: why she is antagonistic toward the more privileged, why she strives toward self-expression and self-knowledge, why she gave of herself to the extent that in trying "to serve three generations of men . . . I seem to have ruined them all," why she never felt completely at ease with her friends and was never really *sure* of another's affection.[18] It is a self-analysis to try to answer those and other questions.

About two-thirds of the autobiography, begun when she was fifty-two years old, is devoted to her ancestors and to her own youth and childhood. Much analysis of family dynamics is from a psychological point of view, not surprising since she had read Sigmund Freud (a Hampstead resident for a time) and probably Adler and Jung. She rejected Freud's conclusions about sons and mothers, but believed in the interpretation of dreams. She also conjectures about inferiority and superiority and analyzes the family romance with faint brush strokes. She uses a feminist interpretation of her mother's woes, ascribing much of the trouble to the limited stage available for her mother's talents (theatrical and in a larger sense), while her own troubles stemmed from, she thought, her father's and mother's own neuroses and displaced desires. She felt that in trying to please both parents she lost herself, while in choosing Patrick, another one she sought to please, she made both of them miserable and affected their sons as well.

This work is the first we have that shows Anna lengthening her stride, a writing style in a way cinematic, with strong visual appeal and a strong appeal to incident. In fact the story is so dramatic that the biographer tends to distrust it. Several extant versions of parts of the autobiography show that she did take a writer's license to exaggerate to create more drama when she felt it necessary, giving partial accounts of complicated matters and complicated accounts of simple matters.[19] But research reveals that though her style obfuscates at times (especially birth and marriage dates), events usually happened roughly how and when she says they did, though (distinct from editing cuts) there are tantalizing gaps.[20] Most of what initially makes the biographer uneasy turns out to be Anna Wickham's skillful crafting of the work, a selection of details, for example, which serves as a shorthand to character traits, or a picking and choosing of incidents, to give another example, for the way that they reinforce and comment on each other.

Anna, for example, gives us insight into each of the "characters" in the autobiography by their books. Alice Harper, the elocution specialist, teaches her children from "The Women of Mumbles Head." Her father's touchstone book is Darwin's *On the Origin of Species by Means of Natural Selection*. Patrick Hepburn reads aloud to Anna from Stevenson's "Wrecker." Anna the child reclines on a sofa with *Alice in Wonderland* and for her first grown-up novel reads Olive Schreiner's *Story of an African Farm*. When Anna's mother becomes extremely irritated at Geoffrey, what else does she throw at him but a book! Anna's selection of the titles, chosen from the many, many books that passed through the Harper household, lends humor to her autobiography *and* reveals the intellectual preoccupations of Victorian society moving toward modernism.

An example of the second aspect of Anna's craft in writing (how she connects events to each other) can be seen in her account of herself as an awkward, needy, and unbeautiful child. A Harper uncle offers a coin in return for eating what turned out to be a dreadful tasting pill; Anna is richer, but dismayed and betrayed. Her autobiography gives many instances of being dismayed by her own clumsiness, ineptness, and inaccuracy. The cumulative effect is to make plausible that Anna, too often feeling a failure, would be vulnerable to the rewards and the criticisms of the Alices and Patricks of the world.

Shifting judgments in the autobiography lend the work a kind of staggering gait that is hard to track at times. Sometimes she seems to be blaming one person, sometimes another, sometimes herself. This seems, however, the traditional progress of an analysis. As a person examines a memory or a dream, he or she begins to think deeper and differently about each person involved, and each person from the past may be seen in a new perspective.

Anna is trying to understand her adult character. Why am I disorderly? she is asking. Why am I lonely? Why do I write? Why did my parents act the way they did? Where did they come from? What effect did it all have on me? Why am I a failure? For in spite of Anna's past successes, this is how she felt:

> In spite of my long endurance and impotent courage, I have made some profound mistakes. I feel that I am myself a profound mistake and that I was doomed from my conception by being myself: I feel that women of my kind are a profound mistake. There have been few women poets of distinction, and, if we count only the suicides of Sappho, Lawrence Hope [Violet Nicolson] and Charlotte Mew, their despair rate has been very high.[21]

But at the end of writing her autobiographical work in or around 1935, Anna did not try to commit suicide. There is no evidence that she finished cleaning the house either. Instead life had other things in store for her: new friends and new books.

Wickham, both according to her sons and judging from her letters, was a somewhat casual promoter of her own work. The coupling of her first efforts to publish with the volcanic scene with Patrick may have induced in her a detached attitude to publication efforts. At any rate, later books evidenced always the presence of such shepherds as Harold Monro, Anita Brackenbury, or Louis Untermeyer, who served as prod and guide through to print. This is not to say that Anna Wickham refused to deal with the publishing world directly. She had been tireless in trying to find an English publisher for Natalie Barney and could be very persistent in following up on a book's progress. It is also not to say that Wickham was one of those who wrote not caring if the poems would be read or heard, for as she wrote to Louis Untermeyer,

> I am sending you a few fragments that I have written during the last weeks—I am the vulgarian who must have a public.[22]

On February 2, 1935, Anna sent a young man frequently to be seen in the environs of Charlotte Street a postcard poem. **"Little Shakespeare in a bonnet,"** the first line ran, for John Gawsworth claimed to be descended from Shakespeare's Dark Lady.[23] George Hepburn grew used to seeing this slightly fox-faced new visitor at the dining room table, which had a very pleasing view of the walled garden, as he quizzed Anna on her work while together they went through the hundreds of poems she had written in her lifetime so far. Time after time George found the pair laughing, for Gawsworth had a quick wit to match Anna's and a deep impulse to "resurrect" her poetic career.[24] "A rogue," Anna always said, "but a likeable rogue."[25] He collected her poems, a lock of her hair, and drew her likeness, all the while trying to convince Anna that the time was ripe for her poetry to be printed again. She was, as always, stimulated to write by the active interest of another person.

Born in 1912, Terence Ian Fytton Armstrong, or John Gawsworth, as he was known, was slightly younger than Anna's eldest sons. But there seems not to have been any sort of mother-figure yearning in Gawsworth's attentions. Friendship with Anna at Tour Bourgeoise would further his reputation as a Bohemian. And a connection with her works was part of his signature "warm-hearted concern" with those whose work he felt had met "unjustifiable neglect."[26]

Anna, writing to Natalie to request old poems be sent over to England for examination, describes him as a bibliographer who "likes to have all the verses."[27] He ingratiated himself as "This courtly boy who brings me books / Is agate in my childhood's brooks."[28] She calls him "very young & industrious" with a "very sincere & charming interest in poetry."

He was a writer himself, before age twenty publishing seven volumes of poetry, mostly with Twyn Barlwm Press of which he was director. His *A Study and Bibliography of P. Wyndham Lewis* came out in 1932, he wrote about Ernest Dowson and T. E. Lawrence, was a coauthor with the science fiction and detective novelist M. P. Shiel, and had also edited books of horror stories. His press connections included E. H. Samuel, Scholartis, and Richards (and by the late thirties included Secker and Oxford University Press).[29]

Gawsworth was entertaining. In October 1936 he and Shiel made a blood brother pact naming Gawsworth future "King of Redonda" (a real island in the Caribbean Sea, which was and still is a mythical and real international society). Anna chided him saying, "Proper kings / Wear better rings."[30] He enjoyed alcohol. On June 27, 1938, Audrey Beecham wrote to Lawrence Durrell, "Gawsworth is drinking himself into D.T.s. He'll be dead before he has time to sue you over your new novel [The Black Book]."[31] ("King Juan" Gawsworth lived until 1970.) He was a born mimic, a trader, and a scholar rolled into one. His friend Lawrence Durrell had known Gawsworth to purchase breakfast by buying low and selling high along the bookshops on the Charing Cross Road.[32]

A picture comes through of Anna being swept off her feet by Gawsworth's attentions and attentive reading and desire for collaborative efforts. Gawsworth becomes her editor and sometime amanuensis. From 1938 on he keeps a linen-bound book called "Poems by Anna Wickham" in which he records her poems. He seemed to take special pride in her bawdy ones such as the untitled quatrain, "I keep my cunt / In front / But you'll be kind / And see to me behind." He copies down some of her correspondence, jots down snippets of their conversations and, in a separate section called "Obiter Dicta," records Anna's conversational wit. "That's a nice kind of a bloke to meet on the underground" (upon seeing a photograph of the esteemed critic Walter Pater). Or "Beauty is truth in a net." Or on Henry Miller: "Miller represents the deep black hunger of America. He wanted publicity the way America wants bread. And it is a disgraceful thing that our men recognize him." Even years later in a bar around Notting Hill Gate he would repeat Anna's words to a young newcomer, Barry Humphries, now the illustrious Dame Edna Everage.[33]

As much as Anna liked Gawsworth, she was also deeply suspicious of her visitor. He had a habit of asking Anna to autograph her poems and then paying her a small sum for them. Anna was leery of Gawsworth's reputa-

tion as someone "making money out of my signatures."[34] He may have helped her to sell first editions when she needed money. He purchased "a great many" of her old broadsides for £10. He irritated her by proffering a pen with red ink for her to sign his second-hand "birthday book." When he criticized her phrasing Anna called it "savage" and battled until she convinced him of the rightness of her criticized punctuation. The two must have had many comma wars; Anna said he was too "economical" with them.

For his part, Gawsworth sometimes had to tiptoe around Anna's moods to avoid having any "injustice" he might do raise "obscenity" in Anna, arousing her "wicked" imagination.[35]

But Gawsworth seemed to have a special dispensation for avoiding Anna's real wrath. "Back to civilization," he would tell her, on leaving. He had figured out the right combination of flippancy and concern and, especially the ability to keep a certain distance when necessary. He adopted the attitude, according to Anna, that he was "wasting" his time in her house, and gave no encouragement to Anna when she talked of her "project to be a journalist."

She mused that she might find someone more "congenial" to work with, but ended up viewing him as "part of my destiny." But awful for Anna was the feeling that Gawsworth would prefer for her "a posthumous reputation" (made by him) and that she was a poet of the past.

There is little in Gawsworth's promotion of Anna to suggest this. He made sure her work was published: in her book, *Thirty-Six New Poems* and in two anthologies within a year and a half. Not coincidentally and not without effort, he thus gained another notch in his editor belt. Amanuensis, taskmaster, he also probably provided Anna with a notebook in which to record new work and then checked on her at intervals.[36] And the presence of the Anna Wickham collection at the University of Reading seems to bear out Gawsworth's good and honest intentions and support his notation: "The records of Richards Press & my cheque book will correct her 'impressions' if anyone is interested."[37]

Gawsworth had an acute awareness of the past and he relied on past successful models, hoping to be catapulted into like prominence. Edward Marsh, editor and force behind the *Georgian Poetry* anthologies issued before during and after World War I, was one of his models. Marsh's anthologies had provided some income for the poets lucky enough to be included (Anna and most other women were not). Gawsworth put together *Edwardian Poetry* hoping to imitate the success of Marsh's anthologies. His prefatory note quotes the earlier anthologies' disclaimer ("no pretension to cover the field") and also states a clear preference for formal, lyrical verse.

With *Edwardian Poetry,* issued sometime in the spring of 1936, Gawsworth expected to capitalize on the immense popularity of the attractive bachelor monarch, crowned Edward VIII in January of that year. The second poem of the volume was laureate material: "Prince, knight, pilot, king, guider / Captain, defender, adviser," an "Ode Royal Addressed to His Majesty King Edward VIII" by Herbert Palmer.[38]

This book was published by Richards, which had come down in the world. (Grant Richards, who had published Anna and was the founder of the company, had distanced himself from the firm as both bankruptcy and an uncongenial management team had soured him on involvement. Without Grant Richards's eye for quality the bulk of the business involved backlists and reprint rights.)[39] Forty-seven poems written by seventeen living poets, among them Ruth Pitter, Hugh MacDiarmid, and Roy Campbell, made up the anthology. It was attacked on several fronts. Following Marsh's example, Gawsworth had not identified himself as editor (though this may have been a politic move since he had included six poems of his own). Some reviewers were affronted that the editor was not named, others mulled over what they saw as the odd focus of the book. It purported to represent the new era, but excluded such famous names as W. H. Auden and Louis MacNeice. Other reviewers disputed the amount of talent displayed. Through this inky brouhaha Anna emerged almost shining, especially for her powerful **"Mare Bred from Pegasus."** She and Ruth Pitter were praised, even by reviewers who found the book otherwise lacking.[40]

Gawsworth almost immediately began a series (never completed) of inexpensive small books with yellow paper covers called, "Shilling Selections from Edwardian Poets." Three came out about the same time, one by E. H. Visiak, one by M. P. Shiel, and one by Anna Wickham (***Thirty-Six New Poems,*** dedicated "to George Hepburn"). All three books were well reviewed, but mostly by obscure newspapers and journals. For Gawsworth's plan to capitalize on the new king's reign had backfired. The king decided to leave the throne for Wallis Simpson, the divorced woman he loved. He abdicated the throne in December 1936, giving a sad farewell broadcast to the nation. Just in time for the all-important Christmas market, the "Edwardian" poets had lost their reason for being collected together. As one reviewer stated, the series "will now presumably have to find another title."[41]

Not defeated, John Gawsworth charted a new course and adjusted his sails. His next anthology, issued in April, 1937, with Maurice Wollman's help "in selection and arrangement" carried a safe "Neo-Georgian" label; no kowtowing preface to the Royal Family, only a Latin quotation from Tacitus, a Roman historian. In this forty-two-page anthology (which could not seem to decide if it was a book or a periodical) issued in April of 1937, Anna had six poems. By this time Anna's opinion that poetry was not going to be her financial salvation was confirmed, and she could not, as she said, "pawn eloquence."[42] But she had made a friend for life, one of the most irrepressible and original drinkers of Fitzrovia and, as he would often say, a king.

As a result of John Gawsworth's hard work, Anna's name came up again before a new generation of poetry readers. A few new requests came in for use of her poems in anthologies.[43] Anna gave several readings and new faces came by Tour Bourgeoise.

By the time young Dylan Thomas met and married Caitlin Macnamara in July 1937, he had been a frequent visitor at Anna Wickham's house, usually arguing long and hard about something.

He had been introduced to Tour Bourgeoise by John Davenport and it fit his hopes to meet writers in London.[44] There he saw Malcolm Lowry and, later, Lawrence Durrell. Dylan Thomas's description of a bathroom in *Adventures in the Skin Trade* comes straight from no. 68, and perhaps the engaging title, too, from the Hepburn family's old commercial connection in the leather business.

Thomas hated Anna's method of producing a poem from the stimulus of reading. He felt this produced a bad poem and was unnecessary, since "with a little constriction of the muscles," [it] "could have been voided anyway."[45] Dylan himself had not, at that time, read widely, at least in the opinion of Lawrence Durrell.[46] But he was an extraordinary craftsman and this business of taking years to work over a poem as Thomas sometimes did must have seemed bewildering, if not downright obstructionist, to someone like Anna who said, "take time and think / and *then* spend ink."[47] Not that Anna didn't work over her poems—she did, and when she gave a reading she would often (at least in the later years) editorialize herself on the spot "with odd conversational asides and explanatory phrases," or write comments about her own work: "'Rubbish, but there it is,'" or "'Not much sense but some rhythm.'"[48] Thomas's agonizing method of revision would not have been something that Anna wanted to spend a lot of time doing.

Through Thomas, Anna met friends of his such as Rayner Heppenstall. Anna, Thomas, and Caitlin came together on the number twenty-four bus to visit Heppenstall, then living on Lisburne Road. Heppenstall, who had known of Anna because his friend George Orwell once lived across the road from no. 68, was quite intimidated by the poet. He found her "big" and "ferocious-looking" with a complexion "blackhead-pitted" and brown.[49] Her apparel too he found unusual:

"rugger stockings" (undoubtedly hand-knit). Heppenstall was, by his own admission, frequently pugnacious and it might have been a sizing up of a potential adversary that made him so observant. She was, when drunk, Heppenstall said, "reputed to bite people's heads and try to pull other women's breasts off."

Twenty-five-year-old Lawrence Durrell, on the other hand, wrote back to Henry Miller in Paris saying Anna Wickham was "the most amazing woman I have yet met in England."[50] Durrell was impressed by Anna, "who in order to escape the brutality of men had to become first woman and then Lesbian," copying into his own notebook her comments about female artists and "submission" ("a leg that must be broken and re-set"). He, too, found her "rather formidable . . . of intimidating size and forthrightness" but relations between them were cordial and easy.[51] She probably respected his interest in psychology (he was there in late 1937 to talk with a London psychologist), and she responded to his personality, which Henry Miller called "always merry and bright . . . countenance a-gleam . . . youth incarnate. Plus brains. . . . Above all, he could laugh. . . ."[52] On returning to Paris, Durrell arranged to send Henry Miller's books to Anna via Anaïs Nin (who was "very keen" to meet Anna after hearing so much about her from Durrell). And Henry Miller sent Durrell to London hoping to obtain from Anna "a large private diary for publication, parts of which might be regarded as actionable if produced in England itself."[53] But the juicy diary "was a myth," is what Durrell reported back to Miller.

Anna certainly knew enough people to fill one hundred diaries. If she recorded even half the trouble she saw, and sometimes participated in, the reading world would be a livelier place. Such a diary might explain just why she forbade the Thomases their bed on the dining room floor after a disagreement and threw them out "in a pantomime snow."[54] She might have related some of the dangerous antics of Napper Dean Paul, a friend she knew from the Kleinfeldts' tavern.[55] She might have explained why she lifted books from Anthony Thorne's orderly bookshelves and broke his china.[56] Or tormented poor Susan Miles.[57] Or scratched Wyn Henderson, another woman who had helped Dylan Thomas.[58] She might have explained her exchanges of wit with performer Bud Flanagan.[59] She might have recorded just what hymns she played when a wild party at Belsize Park was raided by police and Anna played church music to successfully give the appearance of decorum.[60] She might say just who were all those men in women's clothing at another Hampstead party or just what sort of conversations she and cape-wearing Count Potocki of Montalk enjoyed. And what she thought of friends like Nina Hamnett, who seemed ever less likely to work at their art and more and more likely to cadge drinks.

As the years went on she was much less likely to allow herself to be "muted." At the Green Curtain Club, a small Hampstead venue where one-act plays were staged during the hours the pubs were closed, she interrupted the drama to tell the actors to speak up.[61] She and son George once attended a West End performance, before World War II, at which Anna clapped so often in all the "wrong places" that the audience rose, turned, and said, "shut up!" to quiet her. At some parties she was the life and soul of the fun. At others she took over and raised havoc that was hard to put down. She bought a new hat and went with George to a party on Guy Fawkes Day where Hitler hung in effigy; Stephen Spender was there, and the master of Westminster school. Anna made such a continuous racket that people went from room to room saying, "Who is this dreadful woman?" Spender and the Westminster man stuck up for her and she stayed.[62] Probably there were champions for Anna even on the night of a Hampstead party when she was infuriated past endurance by some woman in a diamond necklace and proceeded to rip the necklace off the woman and toss it out the window. Anthony Thorne remembers, though, watching Anna being thrown out of one Hampstead party and, raging alone in the street, smash a storefront weighing machine with her fist. Once she knocked her son John to the floor with a blow that shot straight out and caught him before he knew what was happening. Oswell Blakeston, another writing and good pub friend, admitted that he was "petrified at the thought of her straight left."[63]

Of course, Anna was not the only person swinging her fists at that time; Malcolm Lowry, John Davenport, Roy Campbell, and many others were too. But she was one of the few women, and it gave her a reputation that she capitalized on. At an art show where she had criticized the works too loudly,

> the art dealer whispered to Oswell Blakeston to take her away: she stood up to her full height and muttered, "You'd better retract, my good man. I may be a minor poet, but I'm a major woman."[64]

She had her friends and enemies and a few in either camp might have actually sickened someone like Virginia Woolf who could not mix milieus the way Anna did.

In May, 1938, Anna suffered her second bout of pneumonia, at that time often fatal. She was hospitalized at New End hospital for over a week, visited by son Jim daily before he went on to sit for a portrait that Cedric Morris was doing of him. Perhaps, thought Jim later, Anna was "chatted up by some visiting clergy." Certainly she must have been upset by the sterile routine, and the disturbing visions it all conjured up for her, for she put her feelings into **"Tribute to the Nursing Staff,"** a poem that like **"The Homecoming"** would foreshadow tragedy yet to come.[65]

Actually, it was Anna's illness and subsequent forced recovery time that gave her the opportunity "to be ambitious again."[66] When she got out of the hospital she concentrated her reading: "eight books on Marxism" and "four books on money." With the weak peace of the World War I agreements collapsing into murderous and land-grabbing chaos, Anna wanted to get to the root of the problem. Integrating the new information with her past reading and political thinking she devised a curious, poetic manifesto for an organization she titled "The League for the Protection of the Imagination of Women." Of course, her Manifesto had its roots in a very personal issue, a hatred of men correcting women's expression. When Eric Partridge made changes to Natalie Barney's book Anna was extremely irritated by what she saw as his high-handedness. When her stepfather William Geake had "corrected" some of Alice's letters to her, she was aghast. And, of course, what she had suffered from Patrick's frequent "editing" of her speech and behavior, she said, "leaves my brain bleeding."[67] Now she married the issue of men editing women to the larger issue of tyrannical governments in Italy, Germany, and Russia:

> We do not like the way Mussolini has organised his
>   colonial empire.
> We do not like the way Hitler has managed his Jews.
> And we don't like Stalin's effect on Russian poetry.[68]

Anna subscribed to what her eldest son has described as a "leadership principle." She had a belief that a strong leader "could . . . effect the development of, as it were, the nation's business. And she found such people attractive. . . . at one time she thought that, for instance, Mussolini, was effecting a necessary change in the arrangements that guided the forces of Italy." In fact, Anna had nicknamed her briefcase (presumably for organization reasons) Mussolini. But her admiration for Mussolini and an even shorter-lived interest in Hitler had given way quickly.[69]

Jim and John had come back from their dance engagement in Bucharest in 1938 with a clear understanding that the Nazis posed a great threat and that appeasement played right into their hands.[70] Her sons' firsthand knowledge, combined with Anna's old conversations with Israel Zangwill, who had called for safe haven for the persecuted Jews of Europe, convinced Anna to write the Manifesto.

The Manifesto, on first reading, is an incoherent, rambling connecting of all the big ideas of Anna's autodidactic programs, with a "slogan": "World's Management by Entertainment." Anna's aims for her league, however, are clearly stated in the last paragraph: "to stimulate original work from women in the fields of economics, psychology and political theory."

"Peace and Plenty," Anna explains in the first part of the Manifesto, is the modern problem for government and has been ever since society moved from matriarchy. "The machine," theorized and then materialized by man, actually liberates the spirit of woman who has all along been creative in the family, she continues. The stumbling block is the state of the world, and "we, the committee, have gathered ourselves together because the state of the world does not amuse us."

Anna's Manifesto, June 16, 1938, was signed by seven feminists, among them Charlotte Haldane, who had paid a lot of attention to Malcolm Lowry when he attended her Cambridge salon and who now went to the same Communist suppers that Anna did; Carmel Haden Guest, one of Anna's earliest friends in London; and Kate O'Brien. Anna's political thinking at this time brought her close to O'Brien, a writer, and to Pat Dooley, a fiery speaker on political issues. With O'Brien she fell in love. With Dooley she felt loved. Both of these people were important to Anna in the late 1930s.

Although Anna had lesbian affairs after Natalie Barney, there are no letters so far, with the exception of these to Kate O'Brien, that give hints to the nature of the relationships. In the case of O'Brien, Anna may have been the disappointed party in a love triangle. But before that happened she did write a few letters, parts of which show Anna at her most tender.

O'Brien started out her career in the 1920s as a playwright, but became best known for her novels. Born in Dublin and familiar with cultured middle-class Irish families, she plumbed this familiarity in her prize-winning 1931 first novel, *Without My Cloak*. O'Brien understood how Catholic puritanism could cripple the emotions and this must have struck a chord with Anna, who in Australia had seen the Catholicism of young women from inside the fort while remaining outside the practicing faith. By 1938 O'Brien had written three more novels, and *Farewell Spain*, a travel book.

She lived in Hampstead for a time and breezed in and out of no. 68 Parliament Hill. Then when O'Brien, and a friend who was recovering from pneumonia, stayed at an inn outside London, Anna was inspired to send several letters and poems.

"I feel very bitter and my soul in the corner like a sick bat," writes Anna on June 17, 1938, in mock agony, "because you are in the country with a routine breakfast, fresh air and friendly conversation . . . and no one supplies me with any routine whatever."[71] Anna mentions her own recent recovery from a severe case of pneumonia ("a fortnight" on the danger list as opposed to the friend's "not very poignant" two days), and describes her posthospitalization trials with a light touch. Her apt word choices, quotations, and helpless hands-in-the-air resignation at the loss of house "decorum" make high farce:

. . . me tottering out of hospital to find daffodils in my room and . . . to retire with a book rest to read . . . the first week with everybody watching me to see when I will become normal and take up my bag of crosses. Then the charming young man on the top floor who sings madly to start reforming a whore, and to sleep in the same bed with her and his hag of a mistress. Innocently doubtless but so taking all the validity out of my decorum. And him also letting the girl wash off her whoreishness in the fine white bath upstairs, which is the delight of old Mr. Ames whose brother was the tallest major in the Life Guards, and the girl leaving her whoreishness visible in the Bath. Never was there so dirty a bath. And after Mr. Ames with his Sultana flouncing on me—For retribution and the cleaning of the Bath. And from me—what a hero—"I will in person clean that Bath." And me tottering to the scum refusing all rags but my own. Anointing all with Vim, afterwards with eau de cologne thus restoring order.

After this crisis as landlady, another crisis (mother of dancing sons) arises:

Whereat Jim "Can you bear a little worry." From me: "Let us try." "Someone has stolen our stage clothes and on Monday we perform." Then I must sell first editions and dress them in white face cloth. Never any peace— never any love—never any easy conversation, no organised sunshine.

After an Eeyore-like pause Anna adds the wry lament, "Never any comrade but Almighty God who is not visibly a domestic executive" and then calmly launches into an update of the league.

Anna sought to amuse O'Brien because, "I begin to want to have phrases between us," which for Anna was a code for intimacy. "I love you and no one may know—what we say." She wrote to O'Brien, whom she called "the heart of Schubert's 'Young Nun,'" saying, "I put a kiss also on the heart and inside the left hand and I summon five thousand holy bees to wax up the ears—so that nothing at all boring is heard by my [brave] baby for a fortnight." Anna paid O'Brien the same high compliment that she gave Natalie and others who moved her only in the highest way: "For I can imagine / From you."[72]

The second friend Anna saw a lot of around the time of the league and after was Lawrence Dooley, who on Sundays during the 1930s and 1940s would speak to the crowds who brought their chairs and sat down to listen to his rousing speeches at the top of Parliament Hill only a short distance from Anna's house. Pat, as he was called, an antifascist who spoke movingly in favor of communism, was someone with whom Anna could feel completely at ease. In her poem to him, **"Home for the Imagination,"** it is evident that she felt comfortable with the Dooley family in the same way that she had once felt with a few select others. Most likely it was partly Dooley's free and welcoming spirit, but not

just that. Anna responded most fully to those who knew what she was getting at in her work and life, and Dooley did. A former miner himself, he became a skilled orator and debater by virtue of his passion for labor issues and his devotion to the intellectual life. According to his sister Kitty, he read a page of the dictionary each day while still a miner, and built up a wonderful library of books. For Anna, "in this frozen hour" he was "a tower," his wife was "a kind field," and their home a "summer landscape" and "refuge for starved birds, / Lamed rabbits, tortured kings, / And Words."[73]

For despite Anna's many interests, she had come to see herself as "at a frozen hour." And again she began to rewrite her life, this time in poetry. But where the 1935 autobiography's prose had considerable wit and charm, this new autobiographical writing is harsh. The types of images she was capable of in the past, those lines that poet Paul Dehn had described as "delicate as the wind on a saucer of milk" are missing.[74]

It was probably sometime in February or March, 1939, when Anna sat down to write this most bitter and probably most honest account she called, **"Life Story."**[75] For forty-nine pages she wrote, ending the poem

With this narration I
    could cloy myself /.
But I've had fury to
    destroy myself—

I've suffered these
    fool trials—
Because of endless
    self-denials /
So much I'll yield
I'm always some
    [?] sadist field—

Anna the boxing fan pulls no punches here. She lays out the narrative of her life in such bald terms that the lines have a brute force. The rhyming couplets and the inexorable iambs double the strike value of the lines. In this work she doesn't hide behind pseudonyms—it is "Hepburn," "my father," "my mother," "my first son," etc. She is more honest than ever before about events that have happened, and is increasingly forthcoming about her own speculations, too, for example, saying Patrick committed suicide to "dodge gaol."[76]

The work answers unstated questions. Who was the first "sadist" in Anna's life? Who gave her "lust for sympathy?" Her beautiful mother. How did she feel about her father? Ashamed of his tuning forks and convinced that "he told Hepburn I was mad." Why, "revengefully," did she "whore" during the war years? To pay back Patrick for coming to her bed when she was still under threat of the asylum. Why did she sleep with Harold Monro? "I was maddened / by the tragedy."

Why did she hang herself after Patrick's death? Her nerve broke. How did she feel about Jim's cutting her down from the rope? "Why did you cut me down I knew I'd had enough." How did she feel about some of her lovers? They were "bits and pieces . . . And later I'd burlesque—Love with fool women—how I was then / grotesque." Why was she writing **"Life Story"**? To "rage out my grief—/ For my sick soul's relief / Then stutter to inanity." What is her life like at this point? Teeth knocked out by her last lover, poor, "snowing again and no coal," no prospects. Yet, and this is a pretty big yet, there could be possibility. "Life could be sweet," she writes, "Had I a conduit for my energy / And just one hand to succor me," for she still has her ability to converse.

> O I am brilliant—brilliant
> How splendidly I talk
> when I'm abroad—
>   . . . . .
> . . . some public place
> Where there is interest & space
> And show my quality
> And earn its subsidy.

Anna's supreme frustration is with the state of her life at age fifty-five, a time when some people may be starting to enjoy rewards from their efforts, an age where the years left to achieve all the great things dreamed of may seem perilously few. She regrets her powerlessness, she crows over her powers and she lays them both out for inspection of the reader, or perhaps for herself, since this work was never published, or perhaps for John Gawsworth, who may have given her the notebook.

In this poem, as a confessional poet in a continuum from George Meredith's "Modern Love" to Robert Lowell's later works and beyond, she is concisely trying to lay out the impossible: a map of herself, with alliances broken and unbroken, hopes, anger, fears, and passions. She has too often been a burden or carried a burden, she writes: her husband "woke & found / himself an ass / That he had married far / beneath his class"; her third son, "has no start." She freely admits that she is struggling against the self-destructive urge. She doesn't *want* to commit suicide because it's "not new / with woman poets;" it would be almost the expected thing for a troubled woman poet and to Anna, doing the expected is anathema. She also remembers the "scant pity" that a suicide attempt elicits. Finally, Anna wants to live, simply because she has already survived so much. "I have come whole / from so much strife—/ I have desire of life."

It is impossible not to be moved by her confession, and by her conclusion that in the important relationships with adults she'd too often been the "sadist field" for other people to work their pain upon.

How could a woman who positively terrorized some people paint herself as such a powerless figure? She answers this question toward the end of the poem: "I've suffered these / fool trials—/ Because of endless / self-denials." Despite her constant criticism, found in other of her poems, of a sacrifice-based religion, in her life she kept throwing herself into the pit, onto the cross. This tendency for all-or-nothing led her affairs and her friendships into storms and difficulties, for many of the people she was attracted to were not the kind to reciprocate with her level of intensity. Patrick Hepburn wanted love, but would not or could not love back in a way that would satisfy her. Natalie Barney could easily shrug off any serious threats curtailing her freedom to love whomever and whenever she chose. Lately Kate O'Brien, John Gawsworth, her many pub friends, and theatre friends, were not interested in Anna's need to be devoted. Her devotion fell onto the one person who seems never to have disappointed her or quarreled with her, her son George. As youngest son, who still commanded her complete loyalty and returned it, she felt, correctly or not, that she owed him something that she could not deliver, especially protection, as war and conscription loomed ahead.

By the end of May, 1939, however, when Anna writes to Natalie Barney to thank her for a book, she's feeling good. Natalie has used one of Anna's poems in *Nouvelles Pensées de l'Amazone.*[77] Anna has been, independently of Natalie's interest, getting her manuscripts in order, "designing to devote the next seven years of my life almost exclusively to poetry."[78] Then too, a new venture has come her way: a swan song on television.

On at least a few occasions after he finished school at Bushey, George Hepburn had joined his brothers on the road, or helped out on the sets when John did some filming in London. Anna continued to be proud of her sons' interesting acting and dancing careers, but music hall performances, once so important to communities, had come into competition from radio and the cinema, making the Hepburn brothers rising stars in a falling universe. A new medium was about to change the world of entertainment, and Anna was getting in first.

The British Broadcasting Corporation had in 1936 purchased part of the North London Alexandra Palace complex for television studios, putting up the world's first television transmitter, making the first-ever transmission and by November 1936 broadcasting regularly.

Anna's longtime friend and neighbor, Poppy Vanda, had conceived the idea of a program on swans. The "presentation" was by Philip Bate. The music was "The Swan of Tuonela," which Finnish composer Jean Sibelius originally intended to be the overture for an opera. The BBC Orchestra, conducted by Hyam Greenbaum, was to play the score to "an original ballet for television."[79] Wendy Toye and Keith Lester were to appear and dancing the headliner on the program was Anna's friend from the 1920s and the Ballets Russes de Monte Carlo, Anton Dolin. Anna, famous for her voice, was to be the offstage narrator.

"The Swan," one of Sibelius's most striking and foreboding works, musically describes the dismal and melancholy setting along the banks of the River of Death (the river Tuonela) where a dwarf searches for the swan he must kill. Given that the dwarf had earlier been hacked into bits by a foe and then been pieced together (though resurrected by his mother's magical energy), the prognosis is naturally dim for the dwarf. The television program was, oddly enough, to be entitled "To the Praise of the Swan."[80] Anna must have enjoyed the prospect of narrating, for it brought out her sense of humor in some extra lines beginning, "Swan, I like thee not / nor any quality you've got."[81]

On August 25, 1939 she signed a contract with the BBC to be at the Alexandra Palace at 7:00 p.m. on September 8 to rehearse. At 10:05 p.m. the show would be broadcast, live, of course, and those people lucky enough to own televisions would see Dolin dance and hear Anna's voice reading extracts, off camera, for the half-hour show. And her eloquence would finally be earning funds—"five guineas, to include copyright in respect of this occasion of own original poem."[82] But the date was ill-fated; the broadcast never took place, though the guineas were paid in full. At Christmastime.

Notes

1. AW [Anna Wickham] to NCB [Natalie Clifford Brown]. Letter, 11-16-1933. JD [Fonds Littéraire Jacques Doucet, Bibliotheque Ste. Genevieve, Paris].

2. NCB to AW. Letter, 4-24-1934. Addt'l Manuscript 78194. BL [British Library and Manuscript Room, London, England].

3. AW to NCB. Letter, 5-27-1994. JD.

4. Dated 6-24-1930. Hepburn Collection.

5. AW to NCB. Letter, "Monday." NCB C2 2908 276. JD.

6. NCB to AW. Letter, "November 4, 1934." Addt'l Manuscript 71894. BL.

7. "Item" dated "towards the end of 1934." NCB C2 2908 223. JD.

8. AW to NCB. Letter, 10-26-1935, copied into John Gawsworth's "Poems by Anna Wickham. Taken Down from the Author by John Gawsworth, 1938-1947." References in this chapter not otherwise described have come from this notebook. Wickham MS 523. Reading University Library archives, Reading, England.

9. AW to NCB. Letter, 5-22-1939. JD. Barney has sent Wickham her book, to which Anna responds: "so much pleasure to read & so much pride to have a poem in it."

10. Typed copy of letter in Hepburn collection. Dated "November," n.d.

11. Additional autobiographical material now under a twenty-five year seal of privacy will be available after the year 2020. Perhaps Eliot Bliss's papers or other material in the Natalie Clifford Barney Collection in JD will also provide material not researched for this biography. BL.

12. *WAW* [*The Writings of Anna Wickham, Free Woman and Poet*], p. 53.

13. *WAW*, p. 53.

14. In 1933. James Hepburn. Letter, 8-2-1993.

15. Delyth Sunley, Dunedin (NZ) Public Library. Letter 6-21-2000.

16. On 1-7-1936, John, aged twenty-six, married Victorine (Vicky) Buesst, age twenty-five, daughter of Vanda and London music conductor Aylmer Buesst. Despite Buesst's caring family and her good education, capped by Swiss finishing school, Anna felt that her son had chosen wrongly. John planned a secret wedding but reporters called Anna for a statement. She did then attend the wedding, and when baby Antonia Patricia Hepburn arrived later that year Anna is said to have welcomed the child and never lost the feeling of pride in her granddaughter.

17. *WAW*, p. 52.

18. *WAW*,, p. 52.

19. For *WAW* the Hepburn family and R. D. Smith identified most of the real names behind the pseudonyms. BL AW manuscripts will of course show the pseudonyms.

20. Nelljean McConeghey Rice, "A New Matrix for Modernism: A Study of the Lives and Poetry of Charlotte Mew and Anna Wickham," an unpublished 1997 dissertation, uses the *WAW* version of the autobiography to make several speculations on "the pattern of freedom in . . . dealings with men" among Whelan women. According to McConeghey's speculations, Alice Whelan was probably the child of the artist George Cruikshank, a family friend and sometimes her mother's employer (*WAW*, p. 74). Rice surmises that Alice's son (William Harper, lived only eighteen hours) was probably the son of Edward Aveling. In her writings Anna does often make allusions to "premature" births and uncertain parentage. For

example, a letter to Natalie Clifford Barney dated 5-27-1934, [JD] references "the royal bastard blood of my mother" [a reference to a connection between Emma Alice Whelan nee Burnell and the Belgian Court]. Anna deliberately makes the chronology of her relationship to Patrick misleading—she intimates a long courtship when actually it was short, and states "we were married in the autumn" [*WAW,* p. 140] when they were actually married in February, probably only a little over a month after Geoffrey proposed. As far as her mother is concerned, however, Anna has written that Aveling seemed to have preferred Alice's elder sister.

Rice goes on to make a strong case for Anna as a leading Modernist poet in a vein different from male modernist poets such as Ezra Pound and T. S. Eliot.

21. *WAW,* p. 53.

22. 9-21-1921. Untermeyer mss., Manuscripts Department. Courtesy Lilly Library. Indiana University, Bloomington, Indiana.

23. Anna Wickham, "Apostrophe X." Reading [The Library, University of Reading, Reading, England].

24. George Hepburn. Interview, 4-14-2000.

25. George Hepburn. Interview, 1-17-1995.

26. Hugh MacDiarmid, *When the Rat-Race is Over: An Essay in Honour of the Fiftieth Birthday of John Gawsworth* (London: n.p., 1962).

27. AW to NCB. Letter, "Tuesday." [1936] n.d. NCB C2 2908 272-3. JD.

28. Addt'l Manuscript 71879. BL.

29. *Contemporary Authors.* Entry for Armstrong, Terence Ian Fytton. Gale Research, 1997. Available from http:galenet.gale.com/m/mcp/neta.

30. 2-9-1935. Reading.

31. Poetry Notebook, 1938. SIU [Special Collections Morris Library, Southern Illinois University, Carbondale, Illinois].

32. Lawrence Durrell, "My Friend John Gawsworth," *The Kingdom of Redonda 1865-1990,* ed. Paul de Fortis (Wirral: Aylesford Press, 1991), p. 56.

33. Barry Humphries. Telephone conversation, 11-3-1999.

34. "August 22, From Book Ten." Reading.

35. This is how she characterized herself to Natalie Barney. AW to NCB. "Saturday," 5-4-1929. JD.

36. "Life Story." Addt'l Manuscript 71879. BL.

37. "Aug 24, From Book Ten." Reading.

38. *Edwardian Poetry Book One* (London: Richards, 1936).

39. William S. Brockman, "Grant Richards," *British Literary Publishing Houses, 1881-1965,* Dictionary of Literary Biography, Vol. 112 (Detroit: Gale Research Inc., 1991), pp. 272-79.

40. Publishers Archives, Grant Richards, 1897-1948, Reel 49 Review Scrapbooks, Vol. 2, 1929-1937.

41. *Cornish Guardian,* January 28, 1937.

42. "Life Story." Addt'l Manuscript 71879. BL.

43. A. S. Cairncross, scholar of Thomas Kyd and Shakespeare, requested "The Fresh Start" for his *More Poems Old and New,* of the "Scholar's Library Series." The publisher J. M. Dent requested "The Mummer" and "Sehnsucht" for *Selection of English Poetry* planned for 1938.

44. Gordon Bowker, *Pursued by Furies: A Life of Malcolm Lowry* (London: HarperCollins Publishers, 1993), p. 163.

45. Dylan Thomas, *The Collected Letters of Dylan Thomas,* ed. Paul Ferris (London: JM Dent & Sons, Ltd., 1985), p. 266.

46. Lawrence Durrell, "The Shades of Dylan Thomas," *Encounter,* IX (December, 1957), p. 57.

47. In Gawsworth's "Poems by Anna Wickham," notebook. Reading.

48. *WAW.* p. 3.

49. Rayner Heppenstall, *Four Absentees* (London: Barrie and Rockliff, 1960), pp. 142-43.

50. Durrell, "The Shades of Dylan Thomas," pp. 56-59.

51. Ibid.

52. Henry Miller, "The Durrell of the Black Book Days," *The World of Lawrence Durrell,* ed. Harry T. Moore (Carbondale: Southern Illinois University Press, 1962), p. 95.

53. Ibid.

54. Dylan Thomas to Lawrence Durrell. Letter [?Dec. 1937]. "Morals are her cup of tea," said Thomas. *The Collected Letters,* pp. 265-66.

55. His unpublished autobiography mentions AW. Huntington.

56. Anthony Thorne, "Anna Wickham," unpublished memoir, n.d. [March 1955]. Courtesy Kershaw family. Thorne found Anna "alarming" and "intensely feminine" and was present once when she and Dylan Thomas were arguing at 68 Parliament Hill.

57. Susan Miles to James Hepburn. Letter, 10-28-1972. Addt'l Manuscript 71894. BL.

58. Susan Watson (Wyn Henderson's daughter). Interview, 1-17-1995. Susan Watson was cheerful when she talked about Anna: "I liked her bizarre behavior."

59. Flanagan told the crowd, "You know who's in the audience tonight." James Hepburn notebook, n.d. Collection of the author. Peggy Chesters' unpublished manuscript retells the same anecdote but with impresario C. B. Cochrane recognizing Anna. Addt'l Manuscript 71896. BL.

60. George Hepburn. Interview, 10-16-1998.

61. John Rowland to John Kershaw. Letter, 3-4-1955. Courtesy Kershaw family.

62. George Hepburn. Interview, 1-17-1995.

63. Oswell Blakeston, "Anna Wickham," unpublished memoir, 1972. Addt'l Manuscript 71896. BL.

64. *WAW*, p. 27.

65. *WAW*, p. 47.

66. AW to Kate O'Brien. Letter, "Friday, 17 June [1938]." Reading.

67. AW to NCB. Letter, n.d. [1930] headed "Tour Bourgeoise." NCB C2 2908 301. JD.

68. *WAW*, pp. 390-91.

69. George Hepburn. Interview, 6-14-1992.

70. *WAW*, p. 27.

71. All AW to O'Brien. Letters are at Reading.

72. AW poem "Curve on the Category." Sent to Kate O'Brien on 5-23-19[38?]. Reading.

73. Kathleen Gibbons. Interview 12-10-1996. The poem is also in Addt'l Manuscript 71889.

74. Paul Dehn, "Mustard and Cress," *Sunday Referee,* June 12, 1938.

75. Addt'l Manuscript 71879. BL.

76. James Hepburn, who knew his father well, rejected this opinion completely. John, who presumably knew him just as well, thought he did commit suicide by jumping deliberately.

77. "For now I am a clear passivity. . . ." The other poets Natalie Barney used on the same page are Renée Vivien and W. B. Yeats. (Paris: Mercure de France, 1939), p. 14.

78. AW to NCB. Letter, 5-22-1939. JD. The poem is a shortened version of "Technician." The beginning lines are omitted in *WAW,* p. 323.

79. George Hepburn. Interview, 1-17-1995. George had a copy of p. 19 of a BBC magazine giving the details.

80. George Hepburn. Interview, 5-23-1992.

81. George Hepburn. Interview, 5-23-1994.

82. BBC Contract. Addt'l Manuscript 71894. BL.

Nelljean McConeghey Rice (essay date 2003)

SOURCE: Rice, Nelljean McConeghey. "Anna Wickham 1911-1947: 'I am a raw uneasy parvenue.'" In *A New Matrix for Modernism: A Study of the Lives and Poetry of Charlotte Mew and Anna Wickham,* pp. 111-34. New York: Routledge, 2003.

[*In the following essay, Rice argues that Wickham deserves a much more prominent role in the modernist canon and discusses the aspects of Wickham's poetic style and biography that, in Rice's opinion, have led to the lack of attention to Wickham's poetry.*]

> Formalist
> As men whose bones are wind-blown dust have sung,
> Let me sing now!
> I'll sing of gourds, and goads, of honey, and the
>   plough.
> I am a raw uneasy parvenu,
> I am uncertain of my time.
> How can I pour the liquor of new days
> In the old pipes of Rhyme?

(*WAW* [*The Writings of Anna Wickham, Free Woman and Poet*] 195)

In spite of her self-designation as a parvenue, Edith Alice Mary Harper, as Anna Wickham, wrote poetry all her adult life, and published in periodicals such as *Poetry and Drama, The New Republic,* and *Poetry* between the years 1914 and 1947. She wrote over 1,400 poems, about one fifth of which were published during her lifetime in five books of poetry. She was also widely anthologized from the 1920s to the 1940s, then forgotten until the late 1970s when a brief flurry of interest in her poems arose in connection with feminist gynocriticism. However, these rediscovery articles focus primarily on Wickham's themes as they relate to feminism and freedom for women, and neglect the wide range of subject matter and styles that Wickham employs to sing her song.[2] A more thorough discussion of Anna Wickham's *oeuvre* must begin with the works that she read and acknowledges as germinal. The only clues she leaves to the development of her poetic self are contained in the autobiographical "Fragment." These clues are concealed in her accounts of family history, and at first glance appear contradictory. Oblique and ambiguous, the clues can be read several ways, just as the clues in Charlotte Mew's work leave themselves open to multiple explanations and interpretations. Wick-ham makes an honest assessment of herself in the poem **"Formalist."** She believed herself to be a literary as well as a social *parvenue*. An examination of her upstart mentality and style will reveal the motivations behind her inconsistencies.

In the academic and critical endeavor to develop a modernist canon, poets such as Charlotte Mew and Anna Wickham were disregarded because their work did not fit neatly into the whole and because their woman-centered subject matter was not considered to be as important as the themes of their male colleagues. As I have argued in my discussion of Mew's poetry, she deserves to be included in our re-vision of modern-ism. So does Anna Wickham. Although neither of these poets belonged to a particular school or group of poets, and although both "poured the liquor of new days / into the pipes of Rhyme," they did pioneer a voice for women "degraded and alienated by family structures" (Scott "Introduction," *Gender* 15). Schenck reminds readers that both Mew and Wickham were simulta-neously exiled both from and to poetic form. Today's reader, freed from the constrictions of the formalist critical mode, might see their flexibility as strength, not flaw. Experimentation with form, even an ironic flirting with the clichés of previous poetic dogmas or the speech of contemporary life, is a modernist given. However, when women poets produce these kinds of freewheeling or ironic pastiches, they are often misconstrued as naive or slavish imitations. Until very recently, few critics acknowledged that either Mew or Wickham were forerunners in the development of a feminine poetic aesthetic.

A case could be made for Wickham as a pioneer of *post*modernism because her poetic impulses were often spur-of-the-moment reactions to contemporary phenom-ena; they were dashed off in haste and thrown in a drawer or scrawled on the wall of her kitchen in response to a comment made by a child or a visitor. Wickham's barrage of poem-making could happen anywhere. In a July 20, 1922 letter to Edmund Wilson, Edna St. Vincent Millay says, "She writes ten thousand poems a day, writes them on the café tables, on the backs of menus, on the waiter's apron [. . .]" (154). Wickham brought home the habit from the Fitzroy Tavern crowd, who wrote couplets or quatrains as asides to each other, or as ironic commentary on the general conversation, while they were drinking. Garnett com-ments, "Anna often pulled pieces of paper out of her bag and passed them over to me. [. . .] Sometimes something I said struck her and instead of replying she would reach for a pencil, scrawl a few lines and push them across the table. Her answer to my remark was a poem" ("Introduction" *Selected* [*Selected Poems*] 9). Wickham was always more interested in *what* her poetry presented as her immediate *now,* rather than in *how* it

said she was a woman. In **"Examination"** she states, "If my work is to be good, / I must transcend skill, I must master mood" (*Selected* 15). Epistemologically, stance is more important than style. Her stance is that she will, moment by moment, tell us "*woman.*"

In Wickham's aesthetic, poetry must be a daily activity written in response to life. If we realize that this at-titude colored all Wickham's work, then her kitchen and pub table scribbles should be recognized as a link in the chain that joins American Indian ritual songs to the poems pasted on the Democracy wall in Beijing during the student-led protests. The idea of the poet as high priest(ess) or philosopher-king(queen) would only have appealed to Wickham if she were using it as a spoof of another writer. Wickham's poetry is down-to-earth and domestic on the one hand, and yet it harks back to the university wits on the other. She could be categorized as a magazine poet, a groundbreaking feminist, a non-Georgian, a writer of doggerel, and an early advocate of free verse. Wherever she is placed in the history of modernism by scholars, they must begin their reassessment remembering that Wickham's aesthetic grew out of her lived life, through her contact and conflicts with family, other writers and artists, her incidental reading, and the society she inhabited. Although this truism could be applied to most writers, it is especially important for an understanding of Wick-ham's style because, like Mew, she had no academic background to provide a codified philosophy to progress from, or to react against.

In the family tradition of her grandmother and mother, Anna Wickham insisted on her right to constant re-vision. Family stories could be told in multiple ver-sions, from antithetical stances, in warring tones. However, this kind of polyglossia, which Wickham employs in tone and style, in both her prose and poetry, makes her poetry hard to categorize, hard to attach to a school and, therefore, easier to dismiss, using the most current critical clichés of each succeeding era. Hers is defiant poetry from the margins. She also creates a problem for herself by siding with the forces that believe amateurs to be truer writers than professionals. Whether she professed this view out of misguided loyalty to her ineffectual father's ambitions for himself, or out of her embarrassment regarding some of her mother's so-called "professional" artistic ventures is hard to judge. It is also possible that her later friendship with Natalie Barney influenced her thinking on this matter, placing Wickham's stance as a poet on the side of the private, coterie writer as opposed to the public, professional, and even academic type best exemplified by T. S. Eliot.

Eliot's influence on the later twentieth-century assess-ment of modernist poetics has been thoroughly discussed by many scholars and critics. His attitude toward women writers, reviewers, and editors has been analyzed in many books and essays, including Gilbert and Gubar's three volumes of *No Man's Land: The Place of the Woman Writer in the Twentieth Century.* Eliot's own letters to his parents and Ezra Pound, among others, reveal his negative response to women in the literary arts. On May 13, 1917, in a letter to his mother announcing his new position as a contributing editor of *The Egoist,* Eliot remarks, "At present it is mostly run by old maids"; in September he writes to Pound about a reading series at the Poetry Bookshop, "I thought too many women—it lowers the tone: [. . .] perhaps there should be a special evening for males only, as well as this. Eeldrop on the feminisation of modern society" (*Letters* 179, 198). To his father he writes that he distrusts the "Feminine" in literature and that he tries to keep *The Egoist*'s writing as much as possible in male hands. On July 11, 1922, he reiterates this position to Pound, commenting that he feels there are only a "half a dozen men of letters (and no women) worth printing" (*Letters* 204, 593).

Perhaps Eliot was trying to distance himself from the anxiety of influence caused by his mother's poetic aspirations. Peter Ackroyd discusses the complex emotional and literary relationship between Eliot and his mother. Much as is the case with Wickham and her parents, Eliot was "the late son of two parents who were thwarted artists," and Charlotte Eliot was very much like Alice Harper in her frustrated ambitions and dedication to the "militant mould of her generation." Ackroyd continues, "a fleeting image of the mother can be glimpsed in much of Eliot's own work" (21-22). Veiling themselves from the parental gaze entailed a physical distancing for both Eliot and Wickham. Both only began their artistic careers in London, after escaping the antipodes, the landscapes of their youth. Both were also shaped by their connection to another escape artist, Ezra Pound.

Critics and scholars have variously described Ezra Pound's contributions to modernism. Hugh Kenner calls the whole enterprise the Pound era while Shari Benstock in *Women of the Left Bank,* and other feminists, remind readers that Pound's agenda for modernism included isolating and then dropping the women who contributed to this movement because he felt they had no talent (21-23). If the development of modernism is viewed in terms of mastery and control, then Pound first and Eliot later could be called the masters of the fate of many other writers' places in the era's history. Recently, the evaluation of modernism has expanded to include both female and male writers who were previously thought to have little, if any, significance in the shaping of the modernist aesthetic. Scholars such as Bonnie Kime Scott have embarked on a project to refigure modernism. Scott states that "Modernism becomes a much more variable text when we consider

the versionings of it by women helping to direct one another as writers" (*Refiguring* 230). The place of the Brontës, Alice Meynell, Olive Schreiner, May Sinclair, and other women writers and editors as influences on both male and female writers of the period is opening new vistas. In terms of poetry, what these new views show is that there was much activity in circles that were known to Pound and Eliot, but disparaged by them.

The most important circle for both Mew and Wickham is centered in the Poetry Bookshop. But because both of these women viewed their poetic lives as separate from their domestic lives, even the supportive and benign culture of the Poetry Bookshop circle was problematic. For Wickham, the problems associated with her connections to it arose from her perceptions of how her class and sexual politics might be perceived. Jones mentions James Hepburn's comments that Alida Monro loathed Anna because of Anna's overt sexuality. He also describes one poem, **"The Indictment,"** which is wickedly cruel about Alida's devotion to her dogs (105-06). James Hepburn says of his mother's relationships: "To anyone who offended her code she could be devastatingly rude. [. . .] Any attack, real or imaginary, would be emphatically resisted" (*Preface xx*). While the Monros were the most important early supporters of Wickham's work in England, by the end of their relationship Wickham felt neglected and betrayed, as is evidenced in the following diatribe:

"To Harold Monro"

You bloody Deaconess in rhyme,
You told me not to waste your time—
And that from you to me!

Now let Eternity be told
Your slut has left my books unsold—
 And you have filched my fee.

(*WAW* 332)

As always with Wickham, an untangling of her motivations has to begin with a close examination of her family life. The constant war between her father's sisters' Royal Academy belief that true art is the province of the professional, only achieved through the pain of hard work, and the legacy of her mother, Alice Whelan Harper, who believed that art was a product of the artist's charisma and overpowering emotion, created the poetic persona, Anna Wickham. Her artistic self-searching layered every word that she wrote. She never saw herself as a model in the rapidly changing fashions of modern poetry. As she said on one occasion, "'Harold Monro ruined my life by encouraging me to be a poet. I should have been a maker of popular mottoes!'" (R. D. Smith 18). Monro believed that the successful modern poet had a vast instinct for self-aggrandizement, which is the opposite of Wickham's instinct for self-disparagement.

Add to her poor artistic self-image the reality of her parents' lives, in which her father, whose family privileged the professional, became the eternal amateur. His great novel never made it from the mind to the page. Alice Whelan Harper, whose spirit-induced art seemed spontaneous, became the major financial contributor for the family through her professional artistic endeavors. Her parents' conflict, between the professional amateur, Geoffrey Harper, and the amateur professional, Alice Whelan Harper, never resolved itself. Therefore, the only way to understand Anna Wickham's work is to read it both ironically and sincerely, because that kind of schizophrenic pose was bred into her by heredity and circumstance.

One reason Harold Monro backed Wickham's efforts to publish her verse is that he could see its worth. As he said about the poems of another woman, Emilia Stuart Lorimer, they are "'the raw and inevitable product of personality, or nothing. Sometimes [they] may seem almost ingenious through the sheer force of [their] sincerity'" (qtd. in Grant: 50). Harold Monro looked for poets who could sincerely express a unique personality, and, even though Anna Wickham might play down her stylistic facility, she would not dispute that she had a unique personality, which she tried to express sincerely. In fact, the majority of her poems try to do just this.

Wickham's peculiar literary schizophrenia is also evident in her choice of mentors. Along with the artistic attachment she formed for the wealthy expatriot American lesbian Natalie Barney, Wickham confessed to Louis Untermeyer that her favorite American poet was Ella Wheeler Wilcox (340). As muses, these two women stand for antithetical aesthetics. Barney's emphasis on coterie production, lesbian aesthetics, and salon performance was completely different from the domestic, magazine verse style favored by Wilcox. Where the two merge is in their love of rhymed verse, aphorisms, and the belief that poetry is not diminished when it is used to commemorate an occasion. As well, both Barney and Wilcox celebrate women's sexual natures and romantic feelings. They did this through the veil of classical and literary allusion, distancing their personal selves from the passionate personae of their poetry. In forming her mature poetic voice, Wickham learned a great deal from both Barney and Wilcox. However, what Wickham learned from Wilcox and Barney came to fruition when she was an adult. Wickham's earliest poetic and philosophical models, the Reverend Richard Harris Barham, author of *The Ingoldsby Legends*, Charles Stuart Calverley, a nineteenth-century translator and minor poet of light verse, and Olive Schreiner, whose *Story of an African Farm* is the only novel mentioned by Wickham in "Fragment," all contribute significantly to aspects of Wickham's style and subject matter.

Various critics trying to describe Wickham's work have called it "New Elizabethan," metaphysical, "poet's poetry," wildly mystic on the order of Blake or Emily Brontë, "pebbles of fine prose," and extreme feminism. In an omnibus review in *The Nation*, Mark Van Doren writes of Wickham, Marianne Moore, and Edna St. Vincent Millay that they would be prized more highly in seventeenth-century England than they are in their own times and countries. He continues, "It [*The Contemplative Quarry and the Man with a Hammer* (1921)] is the work of an inspired metaphysician [. . .] a very contemporary John Donne" (484). A description of Wickham's poetry as metaphysical would place her as a modernist. T. S. Eliot's influential essay, "The Metaphysical Poets" appeared in the *Times Literary Supplement* in 1921. In it he draws a line from the poets of the seventeenth-century to the late nineteenth-century symbolists and on to the moderns, praising these poets' ability to translate idea into sensation (Menand 146-47). Most of her contemporaries who mention her work do classify her as a modern poet, but when the New Critics codified the modernist poetic canon, she was not included, although Marianne Moore was. The neglect of Wickham's contributions to modernism is understandable only when both her lifestyle and her poetic style are considered together.

Wickham's style, subject matter, philosophy, and her overt feminism all contribute to this neglect. Aside from the most obvious observations about her feminist stance, no critic has ever seriously discussed Wickham's ontology. Wickham's association with the important modernist philosopher and poet, T. E. Hulme, has not been explored. Because Wickham never completely eschewed rhyme and because her subject matter is domestic for the most part, her affinities with Hulme's ideas have been overlooked. Her work is undeniably modern when readers realize that one of the driving impulses behind it is Hulme's view that modern poetry expresses momentary mental phases, vague moods, and the maximum individual and personal expression. For Hulme, the modern poet remains tentative and half-shy (Levenson 43-44); or in Wickham's words, a parvenue. On the other hand, the modern poet is constantly struggling against the seductions of metaphysics, a seduction to which Wickham frequently succumbed because she needed a metaphysical brace for her *outre* feminism. Unfortunately for Wickham's reputation, the interest in *fin de siècle* philosophies that she inherited from her parents stuck her in this early phase of Hulme's ideas. If we accept Nietzsche's remark that philosophy is autobiography, we can understand why Wickham could not follow Hulme when he modified his Bergsonian romanticism to embrace classicism and anti-humanist and geometric art (Levenson 80-98). Because Wickham was so intent on merging the desires of her parents into her art, she remains a poetic impressionist "rooted in Victorian values, Edwardian social aspirations and Fabian politics" (R. D. Smith 27).

While her father attended Fabian and Positivist Society lectures, read Aristotle, and preached Walter Pater and the joys of amateur enthusiasms, her mother orchestrated the four-year-old Wickham's performances of "whole passages from *The Ingoldsby Legends*." As Wickham ruefully confesses, "there is no school of facile composition better than these verses" ("Fragment" 86). *The Ingoldsby Legends*³ contains stanzas such as the following from the poem "The Babes in the Wood":

Moral

> Ponder well now dear Parents, each word
>   That I've wrote, and when Sirius rages
> In the dog-days, don't be so absurd
>   As to blow yourself out with Green-gages!
> Of stone fruits in general be shy,
>   And reflect it's a fact beyond question
> That Grapes, when they're spelt with an *i*,
>   Promote anything else but digestion.

(338)

Actually, it is amazing that Wickham's own poetry survived this early infusion of doggerel. Perhaps some readers would say it did not.

Yet today's scholars forget that an explosion of doggerel, designed to shatter the mannered, genteel verse of the later nineteenth and early twentieth century, was hailed as a modern breakthrough. The question of the place of doggerel in modernism and its influence on other modern poets has not been thoroughly explored. At the time that Wickham was placing herself among the group of poets considered modern, Harold Monro says that interest had been awakened in a style that Wickham adopts. In *Some Contemporary Poets* Monro writes, "the rapid free doggerel of 'The Everlasting Mercy' [by John Masefield], its modernity, its bald colloquialism, and its narrative interest" (23) revived an interest in contemporary poetry in 1911. As Masefield (and Wickham) use it, doggerel critiques class structure and bourgeois tradition. Celeste Schenck points out that Wickham's use of it in **"Nervous Prostration"** is both closer to folk balladry than the genteel verse favored by the suburbanites Wickham is excoriating, and is a "formal as well as a political spoof on bourgeois values" ("Anna Wickham" 615). Wickham learned this kind of rollicking irreverence from the Reverend Barham.

The Ingoldsby Legends also directed Wickham's subject matter. The book is full of fairy tales and a spurious medievalism; "As I Laye A-Thynkynge" is the final poem. These poems and tales influenced Wickham to the extent that she writes in **"The Mummer"**:

> Strict I walk my ordered way
> Through the strait and duteous day;

> The hours are nuns that summon me
> To offices of huswifery.
> Cups and cupboards, flagons, food
> Are things of my solicitude.
> No elfin Folly haply strays
> Down my precise and well-swept ways.

> When that compassionate lady Night
> Shuts out a prison from my sight,
> With other thrift I turn a key
> Of the old chest of Memory.
> And in my spacious dreams unfold
> A flimsy stuff of green and gold,
> And walk and wander in the dress
> Of old delights, and tenderness.

(*WAW* 178)

This poem has a medieval gloss; in fact, this poem might be categorized as the poetic equivalent of Charlotte Mew's Kendall ancestor's Neo-Gothicism. The most interesting aspect of Wickham's use of outmoded poetic device and diction is that she employs it in the service of a very contemporary feminism. Here the formal, and some would say anti-modern, versification is being used to structure a rage of dis-order. It is apparent from the title that the persona of this poem is acting in an ancient performance (marriage), the religious meaning of which has been obliterated by the modern disjunction of the ritual act from its original intent. Mourning the loss of pagan "elfin Folly," the speaker feels imprisoned by the convent(ional) nuns/no-ones into the hollow "offices" and "well-swept" (empty) rounds of housework supposed to satisfy the female half of a marriage. Not only are the hours nuns and no-ones (not one's own), they are also the time of *nones*, the mid-afternoon prayer and contemplation for those dedicated to a religious order. For (superior) mothers, it is the time when the children are down for their naps and the woman can turn her mind to other affairs. A codified religious ritual is compared to a no less codified domestic ritual. Domesticity, in this sense, is ironically equated with prayer, and pagan folly with whatever the speaker is giving up for the nonce (nuns).

The second stanza, just as the first turns on the multiple puns on the word "nun," and the whole line, "The hours are nuns that summon me" is leveraged by line three, "With other thrift I turn a key" and the weight of the word "thrift." Of course, thrift means economy in the household sense, but readers can only understand the import of this line when they remember that thrift comes originally from the Norse word *thrifask* meaning to thrive. In Middle English thrift meant prosperity, a flourishing, profit, or savings. The spurious medievalism then becomes a necessary setting, revealing the persona's hatred of the prison of the daily grind, the religious domestic's delight, and setting this hatred against the continuous joy of dreams and desire, fueled by memory, "the dress of old delights." All domestic economy, presented in this poem as a remnant of the dark ages, turns to ash if it does not rekindle tenderness in the night. Certainly desire, struck against "Cups and cupboards," is "flimsy stuff." It can vanish altogether, except in dreams. In the **"The Mummer,"** published in 1915 in *The Contemplative Quarry,* Wickham has provided us with a hollow woman to set before Eliot's hollow men. But instead of "Lips that would kiss / form[ing] prayers to broken stone" (Eliot *Collected* 58), the mummer's lips pray at/to *nones* (no ones). The effect is the same. Society's hypocritical expectations for the individual crush the persona's ability to love. Certainly the complicated wit of the central images of **"The Mummer"** justifies Van Doren's "inspired metaphysician" label.

Besides *The Ingoldsby Legends,* one other poetic influence that Wickham mentions in "Fragment" is the poet, Charles Stuart Calverley.[4] A Judge Paul, an Australian high court judge whom she met when she traveled alone, aged eleven, to meet her parents during the school holidays, gave a volume of his poems to her. The journey included an overnight boat trip and a long ride on the steps of a "corridor coach." During this trip the judge also gave her a copy of Laing's *Modern Science and Modern Thought,* and she also read a copy of a children's annual. Her reading on this epiphanic journey reflects the liminal state in which one experiences intellectual and emotional *stimulae* that profoundly affect the future. Recalling this betwixt and between time, Wickham states: "The poems by Calverley I have always remembered" ("Fragment" 107-08). A. A. Milne, a devotee of the writer since childhood, believed that Calverley was the best at a form he thought both lovely and difficult—light verse. Milne declared light verse the hardest type to write because it is the most severely technical of forms. Still, he acknowledges that most writers are ashamed of writing it. Yet Milne was still recommending Calverley to aspiring writers as late as 1945 (Thwaite 70, 270, 464). What Wickham remembered were parodies and pastiche such as his poem "The Arab," which tricks the unwary reader into thinking that it is about an Arabian horse when it is really a description of a magazine-selling street urchin. The poem begins "On, on my brown Arab, away, away! / Thou hast trotted o'er many a mile today" and ends "And the bit in thy mouth, I regret to see, / Is a bit of tobacco-pipe—Flee, child, flee!" (Spear 62). Spear also points out that this poem echoes a line from *The Ingoldsby Legend*'s "The Witches' Frolic" which Wickham would have known (62 n.).

Wickham turns the horse/person metaphor to her own ends in one of her most powerful poems, **"Mare Bred from Pegasus,"** which appeared in *Richard's Shilling Selections*. In it, rather than gently pulling the reader's leg as Calverley does, Wickham rails against a male writer's condescending comment to her. When he says, "Make Beauty for me!" she replies:

> For God's sake, stand off from me;
> There's a brood mare here going to kick like hell
> With a mad up-rising energy;
> And where the wreck will end who'll tell?
> She'll splinter the stable and eat a groom.
> For God's sake, give me room;
> Give my will room.

Later in the poem, she sneers, "My pretty jockey, you've the weight / To be a rider, but not my mate," and ends several stanzas later with "Run, run, and hide you in some woman's heart, / In a retreat I cannot kick apart!" (*WAW* 283). Rather than amuse the reader, as does Calverley with his pun on arab as a name for one of the best breeds of horse and as the slang term for homeless urchins (street arab), Wickham throws her metaphor into an unnamed male poet's face. Her point is that a woman poet, the mare bred from Pegasus, would stand beside male poets to fashion a contemporary poetry only if male poets accept her as an equal. If these male writers choose to view women as sex-objects and mother-figures only, then the stable of their art will be kicked to pieces.

Of the many poems Wickham has written about the plight of the woman poet, this one is the most passionate and direct. It chronicles the "fierce hope and more fierce distrust" of the woman writer who is asked by a fellow artist to "make beauty." The Victorian social assumptions that this demand reflects demean the intellect of the woman writer and limit her to a subject not highly prized by the avant-garde. Instead of being encouraged to use "all my wit, all imagination, / And every subtle beauty of creation"; the woman poet is mocked by the condescension of the command to the point where "Desire rose up [. . .] to strike you dead, / With that mad mare my will / To lash and smash her fill" (283). The "masterless hard state" kicked against by Wickham's mare is the location of the exiled woman poet, "the quintessential stranger in the paradise of male letters" (Marcus 270). In the mare's rage to bring the whole stable down is also the energy to create her own poetics so she will no longer have to laconically "cower [. . .] at your dying fire" nor "blow [. . .] at your chill desire"; Wickham is predicting a time in the future when male writers will retreat to the comfort of non-writing women's hearts to hide from the wrecked male aesthetic stable that the women writers and critics have smashed. She was furious that she would not be alive to see the day. In letters to Natalie Barney Wickham's anger flares at Harold Monro and John Middleton Murry. She castigates them for giving women writers, and herself in particular "little stimulus" and rails against the "subtle and dangerous sexual assault" of male editors' corrections of her phrasing (qtd. in Jones:

71). Contemporary critical theory has wrecked the stable canon of modernism, and a reevaluation of women writing in the modernist era is part of that wrecking.

It is significant that the two poets that Wickham cites as early influences are high Victorian light-verse writers. Both Barham and Calverley's poems were most often published as occasional verses in popular weeklies and monthly magazines, including *Punch*. Yet no contemporary of Wickham's approached her verse as parodic writing, and neither have later critics. An exiled voice often becomes a mocking voice. Discarding the weighty concerns of the eminent Victorian writers, Barham and Calverley make fun of many aspects of British life. A case can be made for a primary parodic impulse in many of Wickham's poems. And as Milne asserts, light verse should be taken as seriously as serious verse because "'in modern light verse the author does all the hard work, and in modern serious verse he leaves it all to the reader [. . .]'" (qtd. in Thwaite: 271). In his later career, even T. S. Eliot might have agreed with this sentiment. *Old Possum's Book of Practical Cats* qualifies as serious light verse. Wickham's small imagist poem written after a session at the Cafe du Dome with Ezra Pound parodies "the better maker." Perhaps her poem, **"Imperatrix,"** written to commemorate a bit of gossip about Frieda Lawrence and a younger lover (told to Wickham by David Garnett), might also qualify. The point that Spears is careful to make about Calverley—that his poetic style is like a mockingbird—is also a point to explore as a way into the poems of Wickham. If many of her poems are mockeries, parodies in other voices, then the inconsistencies of style and subject matter that critics have stumbled over in their efforts to categorize Wickham's place in the modernist experiment are understandable. These different voices also ally Wickham's work to Mew's, whose dramatic monologues capture a more serious side of the woman poet's attempt to find a voice. The misreadings that critics have fostered about both Mew's and Wickham's work could explain why their verse has not received a more sympathetic hearing.

From these tutors, Anna Wickham's aesthetic was formed. What they taught her has more of the wit of the late seventeenth and early eighteenth centuries than characteristics of the nineteenth century's high Victorian seriousness. Berham and Calverley are certainly minor writers, but both write poems full of *jeux d'esprit* perhaps not as apparent in the major writers' poems. Mark Van Doren calls Wickham "a very contemporary John Donne," and he continues his praise by saying she is "one of England's most honest and inviting minds today" (484). What she may be is a twentieth-century Aphra Behn, Katherine Philips (the Matchless Orinda), Anne Finch, Countess of Winchilsea, or even a Lady Mary Wortley Montagu.[5] Van Doren's impulse is correct, though he may not have known the work of these women poets. Wickham's yoking of the metaphysical, or even sometimes the magazine-Victorian, style to her feminist and bohemian critique of the villa-dwellers, places her as a modernist because it is proof that she willingly takes from a variety of styles and impulses to fashion her own form.

Wickham's brief against the society in which she found herself after her marriage to Patrick Hepburn has also been categorized as the attitude of the colonized to the colonizer. Both Jane Dowson and Celeste Schenck believe that Wickham's years in Australia stamped her with an outsider's skeptical view of the establishment. Even further, Schenck postulates that Wickham's Australian childhood endowed her with a sense of "robust [. . .] sexual entitlement" and "freedoms unavailable to Englishwomen" ("Anna Wickham" 614). These gross generalizations, about both Wickham and the social conditions of late Victorian Australian life, try to slip Wickham's case into a current critical theory. There is no evidence that either of these statements holds true. Rather, Wickham's Australian experience seems to have left a negligible impression on her. She never uses images of Australian flora or fauna or Australian language patterns. R. D. Smith concurs. He believes that the sojourn in Australia made Wickham more aware and proud of her Englishness, not less. "Her outback life [. . .] imprinted in her some of the old-fashioned Empire patriotism, which her more intellectual friends found surprising in a poet of feminist rebellion, and an opponent of the old class, bureaucratic establishment" (43). Even the latest critical response from Australia concurs. It was only at the peak of her writing career that she felt comfortable enough to publish in *The London Aphrodite*, a short-lived, irreverent journal designed to outrage modernists, reactionaries, academicians and sentimentalists. This journal, edited by two Australians, Jack Lindsay and P. R. Stephensen, poked fun at everything pompous and British; its brief existence allowed Wickham one time to "pronounce her affinities with the Australian larrikin" (Jones 76, Vickery 33-34).

If Wickham exhibits the traits of an exile in her writing, she received her perceptions of colonialism not from her own experience in Australia, but from her reading of the third of her earliest influences, Olive Schreiner. Books, along with "kippered herrings and Cross and Blackwell's pickles" were a way for the Harpers to "keep in touch with the old life" ("Fragment" 92-93). In this context, while the young Wickham felt she "belonged to a civilised family: the bushwacker who lived in the bush in a log hut seemed to be immeasurably distant from us," she read *The Story of an African Farm* ("Fragment" 92-93). While her family adopted the role of lonely exiles from the politics, culture, and art of the continent, stuck unwillingly in a colony of philistines, Wickham read about another girl who considered herself an exile. Lyndall Gordon, the heroine of Schreiner's novel, is both an intellectual and a sexual exile, even while she is still living amid the *kopjes, kraals,* and *Kaffirs* at the Boer farmhouse of her Tant' Sannie. In this novel, those who seek and strive for social, intellectual, and sexual freedom, Lyndall and her soulmate, the farm-boy, Waldo, rebel and die. While the reader's first impulse would be to see the clear reasons that Wickham could equate her own young self to both Waldo and Lyndall, in the sense that "The barb in the arrow of childhood's suffering is this: its intense loneliness, its intense ignorance" (Schreiner 43), the more accurate reading of the importance of this text to Wickham's life and work looks at the parallels that it provides to her parents' situation and the stylistic choices it opens. Schreiner's style, which Showalter characterizes as "a genuine accent of womanhood, one of the chorus of secret voices speaking out of our bones, dreadful and irritating but instantly recognizable," taught Wickham how to say her themes (*A Literature* 198).

The connection between Olive Schreiner and Alice Harper is through Eleanor Marx. Schreiner was Marx's best friend; she told their mutual friend, the author of *The Psychology of Sex,* Havelock Ellis, that she had a horror of Edward Aveling. Aveling's reputation as a sexual predator is well documented. He might have been the father of Alice and Geoffrey Harper's first child. Around the same time that the Harpers married, Aveling began living with Eleanor Marx; they posed as husband and wife, although he was legally married to yet a third woman (W. S. Smith 73-83). In Schreiner's novel, Lyndall Gordon has a child with a man she will not marry. Another man, Geoffrey Rose, is compelled by his love for her to dress as a woman and nurse her during her decline into death, after the death of her child. Intellectual, emotional, and physical freedom mean more to Lyndall Gordon than life. She wants neither a master nor a slave; neither a he-man nor a she-male. In *The Story of an African Farm,* Schreiner delineates the issues that obsessed the New Woman. New Women like Alice Harper, Olive Schreiner, and Eleanor Marx wanted Lyndall Gordon's freedoms and more. They wanted the sexual freedom that some men possessed. They wanted to be considered equals in all ways. Most importantly, they wanted their work to be considered of equal value.

For Alice Harper at least, freedom seemed most possible in a less civilized locale. She responded romantically to the lure of the antipodes. She sailed off, without her husband, but with the young Anna, when the child was only eighteen months old, and returned for a much longer stay, when Wickham was about six or seven ("Fragment" 79, 90). Post-colonial criticism can help the scholar explain Alice Harper's response and how it affected her daughter's art. The question posed by Alan

Lawson, "'Who am I when I am transported?' is an inevitable colonial question" (168). A completely new linguistic, social, cultural, historical, and metaphorical self can be created. Lawson continues, saying that the discrepancies between a different place and the old language we use to describe that place pose a problem for a people who feel culturally disadvantaged; therefore, the language undergoes great strain (168-69). What Lawson does not factor into his cultural equation are the metaphorical implications of his use of the word "transported." Alice Harper and Olive Schreiner possess this linguistic site, and it is the birthplace of Anna Wickham's poetry. Literally, Anna Wickham, free-woman and poet, was born on Wickham Terrace, Brisbane, Queensland, while she was standing with her father listening to great gusts of hymns roll out of two opposite churches. Figuratively, Anna Wickham, free-woman and poet, was born out of her mother's struggles with the question, "Who am I when I am transported?"

Although she did not know it, Wickham received the answer to her mother's always unspoken question, "Who am I when I am transported?" as she was reading *The Story of an African Farm.* Lyndall Gordon is most comfortable and truthful with herself when she is talking with Waldo about the life of the mind/spirit, and what it means to be a woman. Lyndall explains to him the pitfalls of sexual allure and the opposite pull of the New Woman's needs:

> A little weeping, a little wheedling, a little self-degradation, a little careful use of our advantages, and then some man will say—'Come, be my wife!' with good looks and youth marriage is easy to attain. There are men enough; but a woman who has sold herself, ever for a ring and a new name, need hold her skirt aside for no creature in the street. They both earn their bread in one way. Marriage for love is the beautifullest external symbol of the union of souls; marriage without it is the uncleanliest traffic that defiles the world. [. . .] When we ask to be doctors, lawyers, law-makers, anything but ill-paid drudges, they say—No; but you have men's chivalrous attention; now think of that and be satisfied!
>
> (190)

This statement serves as both an indictment and a defense of Alice Harper's actions as they are detailed in earlier chapters. What Wickham learned from *The Story of an African Farm* is contempt for her mother's solutions to her problems, but she also learned to justify a woman's need for complete freedom. She learned this without understanding its significance as an explanation of her parents' behavior toward each other. Wickham also never directly articulated how her reading of *The Story of an African Farm* influenced her poetry, but a perusal of any of her poems reveals it. **"Gift to a Jade"** expresses Lyndall's diatribe more succinctly:

> For love he offered me his perfect world.
> This world was so constricted and so small

It had no sort of loveliness at all,
And I flung back the little silly ball.
At that cold moralist I hotly hurled
His perfect, pure, symmetrical, small world.

(Selected 21)

And again in **"The Resource"** Wickham rephrases Lyndall's complaint:

When I gave you honest speech
You were annoyed,
When I gave you honest love
Your taste was cloyed.
And now I give you silence,
And a smile you take for chaste.
In these things I am less worthy than a harlot.
And your pride has worked this waste.

(Selected 27)

To completely answer Alice Harper's question, "Who am I when I am transported?" and to understand its implications for her daughter's work, the critic must first examine the negative meaning that "transport" has for the Australian.

Convicts were the first Europeans who were transported to a land so barren that it was considered useless for any purpose other than a gigantic jail. These outlaws included paupers, prostitutes, and political dissidents.[6] In the mid-to-late nineteenth century, when more people from England began immigrating, they felt a cut above the "natives" whose ancestors were law-breakers. However, if we view Alice Harper's escape to Australia in the light of New Womanhood, we can begin to see just why she transported herself. In Lyndall Gordon's eyes, Alice Harper would have been no better than a prostitute. Seduced by Edward Aveling, she in turn seduced Geoffrey Harper, knowing she was pregnant. She became a "woman who had sold herself, ever for a ring and a new name" (Schreiner 190). She could easily have become a fallen Magdalen.

For the sale of her freedom, she wanted an equal share in the marriage. When she saw that she would not get it from Geoffrey, she convicted herself for her weakness in failing to live up to her convictions. Alice Harper acted as judge, jury, and accused, sentencing herself to penal servitude both in and out of her marriage. In the life and times of Alice Harper the perceptive reader can see in microcosm not only the dilemmas posed to society by the tenets of New Womanhood, but also the problems of a paternal imperialism which was at its height at the turn of the century. Why not go to Australia? And why not work her passage as the ship captain's mistress? If she was already outside of the law (pregnant with an illegitimate child) before her marriage, did not that marriage merely further her "transportation" as a moral exile? If the New Woman's search for freedom often led to the same old imprison-ment in conventional society, then could that woman perhaps find her freedom in prison, or, as her daughter found it, in "the regime of the private asylum" which she characterizes as "an invaluable discipline for the woman artist" ("Genius" 19)?

The second transportation practiced by Alice Harper can provide an answer. If the New Woman still could not have ascendancy in sex or work, she ironically could fall back on the position where Victorian women had already been given moral superiority—spirituality. In this instance, Alice Harper's, and to some extent Anna Wickham's, attitudes about the spirit of women mirror Charlotte Mew's. Patmore's ideas about the redirection of sexual energy toward religious ecstasy, and T. H. Green's beliefs about renunciation and sublimation elevating human life, worked to free Alice Harper from her wifely duties. However, from her exiled, colonized stance, the fathers' religion that had made a convict (without convictions) of her would not do. The second sojourn in Australia was marked by Alice Harper's success in transportation of another kind. As Madame Reprah, she practiced Physiognomy, and hypnotism, functioning as an early psychoanalyst and as a medium and contact healer ("Fragment" 103-04). From this position, Alice Harper could retain her distance from the bush-whackers, using her charisma to make money and become a celebrity. Calling her mother a pioneer, Wickham acknowledges the strain Alice's activities put on her parents' marriage. Geoffrey Harper "had a strong sense of *comme il faut* towards the objects of his serious intention and eliminated all subjects not included in[. . .] the *Synthetic Series* of Herbert Spenser, which neglected hypnotism" ("Fragment" 104). Geoffrey's rational, imperialist position was threatened by (yet in their daughter it blended with) his wife's successful primitivism. Alice's position allowed her to become more aboriginal, to convict and convince the gullible ex-convicts. The Harpers' marriage exemplifies the imperial/colonial paradigm. Poor Alice Harper had to finally remove herself to America, the colony that successfully revolted, before she could enter a community that suited her code of New Womanhood. Because Alice Harper started early to arouse Anna Wickham's emotional response and because of both parents' need to "make [her] all over again and develop [her] into a child worthy of their aspiration," her poetry bears the marks of their parental imperialism. Just as the brightest students from the colonies were sent to England for finishing, so was Wickham. She was sent for the same reason—to serve as living proof that the imperialist agenda could benignly produce heirs worthy of the system.

The kinds of subtle subversions, layering colonized/colonizing/colonizer, practiced by Alice Harper, shape the texts of her daughter. Wickham's feminist themes are imprisoned in the forms of the past just as Olive

Schreiner's narrative of feminist inspiration and prophesy is couched in the language and doctrines of Romanticism, because there is no colony where the mind can express itself outside the language of the patriarchy (Colby 69). The endless philosophical musings of Waldo and Lyndall served as an Ur-text for Wickham because reading them was like reading the minds of her parents. That is why echoes of Schreiner's diction and *dicta* can be heard in Wickham's poems.

As well as sharing an interest in spiritualism and Theosophy, Schreiner shared with Alice Harper a delight in celebrity. This pairing also figured in the success of Wickham's American influence, the poet Ella Wheeler Wilcox. Wilcox's sensational and scandalous *Poems of Passion* (1883) gave its author instant celebrity. One offending poem is "The Farewell of Clariomond," which contains the following stanza:

> I knew all arts of love: he who possessed me
> Possessed all women, and could never tire;
> A new life dawned for him who once caressed me:
> Satiety itself I set on fire.

In her autobiography, Wheeler Wilcox confesses that this poem was written after reading Theophile Gautier's story, "Clariomonde" but adds, "certain critics insisted on referring to my poem as a recital of my own immoral experiences!" Her poems were derided as the ravings of "half-tipsy wantons" by Charles Henry Dana in the *New York Sun,* which assured a place for the book on the best seller lists in both America and England (*The World and I* 81-82).

Wilcox's popularity as a magazine poet and celebrity lasted until her death in 1919. She is characterized by Anne R. Groben as "a leader in what was called the 'Erotic School', a group of writers who rebelled against the stricter rules of conventionality. By 1900, a whole feminine school of rather daring verse on the subject of the emotions followed W.'s [sic] lead" (416). Wilcox is also author of those immortal lines beginning, "Laugh and the world laughs with you, / Weep and you weep alone" (*The World and I* 88). Although her poetry was considered shocking, Wilcox herself was deeply conventional and happy in her marriage to Robert Wilcox. She wanted her poetry to please the majority, so she wrote for the level of the general taste. Walker comments, "Her career as a successful *woman,* in her terms, was more important to her than her art" (122).

In her cry that she should have been a motto maker, in her desire not to make art, but to create an artist, in her unselfconscious lines about sex ("My pretty jockey, you've the weight / To be a rider"), we see Anna Wickham's debt to Ella Wheeler Wilcox. Of course, it should be remembered that Wickham's parents wanted her to become a popular poet, not necessarily a good one. For her father, the peak of Wickham's fame would have come when her well-known poem, **"The Cherry Blossom Wand,"** was parodied in *Punch* by William Kean Seymour (R. D. Smith 27/20 n.). EVOE's earlier parody of Charlotte Mew in *Punch* joins these two women poets in an important manner. They would not have been parodied if their style had been like many other poets of the times. They were parodied because their styles were new.

Outside of her family members, the person with whom Anna Wickham maintained the longest important artistic and emotional relationship is the American expatriate writer, Natalie Barney. Yet the relationship was not as reciprocal as Wickham wished it to be. For example, when Wickham read at Natalie Barney's salon in Paris, the Temple *a l'Amitie,* as part of a cultural exchange between French and Anglo-American writers, she was introduced (amid much laughter and applause) as "'only a *demi-revoltée*'" with four sons and no daughters, functioning as both "'pelican and nightingale'" in a household of men (qtd. in R. D. Smith: 25). Barney's comments here, although perhaps meant lightly and delivered on the spur-of-the-moment, could be read as lesbian snobbery, excluding Wickham. That Barney's comments were meant somewhat disparagingly is evidenced by the fact that after her death, Barney's executor discovered, in the back of a disused cupboard, a shoebox full of poems and cards labeled "Anna Wickham" (Wickes 260). These hundreds of Post-card Poems (***Des Cartes à l'Amazone***) could perhaps have been published, but there is no evidence that Barney encouraged her to compile them into a book. In 1929 Wickham was working to help Barney secure a British agent and publisher, and her letters of this time are full of literary advice (Jones 232-36).

Jennifer Jones's access to the unpublished papers and poems reveals that Wickham and Barney had a more complicated relationship than Smith acknowledges. Beginning in 1926 Wickham exchanges poems for money from Barney. This arrangement gave Wickham some financial freedom, but also committed her to a kind of literary prostitution, which she deeply resented. In **"Resentments of Orpheus"** Wickham excoriates Barney's lesbian circle, naming Gertrude Stein, Mina Loy and Djuna Barnes, among others, before concluding "Euridice, fare-three-well / Since thou has leased thy love to hell, / Let smokes of mediocrity / And such slow fires envelop thee" (qtd. in Jones: 210). In a late letter to Barney Wickham confesses, "'[. . .] I thought that your imagination—was to my imagination as was I to the large blonde whore—& I was sorry for you'" (qtd. in Jones: 240).

Students of women's writing of this period might decide that Barney preferred to encourage writers who worked out of the impetus that Barney categorized as the "aesthetics of indiscretion." In this aesthetic, the woman artist draws the response of others to her life and work, rather than uses her work to forge herself a place in history. "For Natalie Barney, as for Sappho, woman's art was the product of shared experience among women, a social and collective effort by a small group of extraordinary women who separated themselves from society in order to love and write literature" (Benstock 293-94). Certainly, Barney and Wickham differed in their desire to be known through their writing. As Benstock notes, Barney's play, *Equivoque,* about Sappho, explores the idea that Sappho might have chosen to value life over art, and, therefore, she was of the opinion that it was self-indulgent to try to assure one's immortality through one's works. Here, Barney endows Sappho with her own beliefs. Barney privileges the artist's right to control her works and to make informal presentation for a coterie the central focus of the artist's task. Barney's artistic emphasis was to encourage feminist exchanges and dialogues among the women (and men) that she invited to her salon. The poem or play as performance for a select "contemporary Sapphic circle," with herself as Sappho, leading her disciples into a modern Hellenism, was Barney's artistic *desideratum* (290-92). Even after World War I, when her women friends no longer physically resembled Barney's ideal pre-Raphaelite androgynous female whose forms decorated her Temple *a L'Amitie* so gracefully, Barney held to her vision of a modern Sapphic circle where "safe from the intrusion of the outside world, the divided female spirit healed itself, rejoicing in short-lived freedom from patriarchal restraint" (Benstock 306).

Anna Wickham's invitation into this world came in 1922, at a time in her life when she had just lost a son, and when her husband was becoming more and more distant, so she embraced wholeheartedly the chance to rest in a separate walled garden of women where she could, for a time, forget reality. R. D. Smith says that "the attraction was emotional, sexual, and artistic, three areas in which Anna had been parched for years by her fidelity to her husband and devotion to domesticity." He concludes that "Anna was fascinated by Natalie, though never subdued by her" (24-25). Questioning Smith's choice of the word "subdued," I believe the rapport between Barney and Wickham was more artistic than personal or physical, although Smith claims that the previously mentioned shoebox was full of passionate love-letters from Anna; however, immediately afterwards, in parentheses, he says, "which was also a passionate discussion of the problems of being a woman and an artist" (24). Of course it was. Women can have vehement friendships that exclude sex and focus on their mutual passion for an art form. They can also express love and affection for each other without being in love. It is clear from both Smith's and Jones's descriptions that Anna Wickham was never let into the inner circle of Barney's temple. As Wickham wrote, "I might have been your whore—/ God was I less or more!—/ I was your artist" (qtd. in Jones: 222). The "might" in this poem indicates that she was not, and the next line reinforces this reading. In a 1928 letter, Wickham complains that she was denied entrance by Barney's housekeeper, understanding that the woman would only have been acting on Barney's orders (Jones 225). Because of her family background, any kind of prostitution was anathema to Wickham.

Barney's stylistic choices influenced Wickham's at a critical time. Benstock's description of Natalie Barney's writing could also stand as a description of Anna Wickham's. Benstock says that Barney's forms were Romantic poetry and the epigram, and that "[u]nfortunately for Barney, the twentieth century quickly set itself against the various movements that shaped her intellectual development" (293). Certainly the same could be said about Wickham. Barney might have encouraged Wickham to work on further books; R. D. Smith says that there is evidence that Wickham projected a further volume of poetry, *The Disorderly Shepherdess,* a long dramatic poem, "The Boy and the Daffodil," and that she tried to write a novel for Horace Shipp, agent for Sampson Low, Marston & Co. (24). Barney might have suggested further projects. Both she and the American Griffin Barry, a friend of Edna St. Vincent Millay's, served as disciplinarians for Anna, even though Wickham hated having to prostitute herself in order to get poems written (Jones 217-18). There are still boxes of material in the Parliament Hill house, but Barney's letters to Wickham, along with some of Wickham's manuscripts, were destroyed when a fire-bomb hit during World War II (R. D. Smith 28). Still, Barney called her the "English Verlaine" and, as R. D. Smith states:

> Natalie, even after Anna's death, continued her admiration for her poems, but their correspondence reveals that Anna's mainly long-distance passion for Natalie was not reciprocated. More satisfactory was their artistic rapport. Anna was looking for a collaborator in various literary ventures, and, insofar as the activities at the Temple made her personally and artistically known, she found one. But the lover-soulmate-fellow worker in the arts she hoped for was not there, despite Natalie's true affection, admiration for the poems, and, in times of crisis, financial help.
>
> (25)

It is difficult to judge the intricacies of the relationship between Barney and Wickham from a distance of more than half a century. However, it is safe to say that Barney's involvement with Wickham, and the time she would have given to helping Wickham's career, is negligible compared to her championship of others such as Renee Vivien, Romaine Brooks, Elizabeth de Gramont, and Lucie Delarue-Mardrus.[7] It was not Barney who translated Wickham's poems into French, but Mardrus who included them in her 1935 *Edition Des Poemes Choises de Lucie Delarue Mardrus* (R. D. Smith 25). Barney's attitudes toward performance and publication may have influenced Wickham's desire to fuse her musical skill and personal charisma into a vehicle to showcase her poetry to a wider audience than those attending Poetry Bookshop readings. R. D. Smith states that she had contracted with the BBC to take part in a television program, but the date was September 3, 1939, so the show was cancelled. R. D. Smith is of the opinion that Wickham would have been a "tremendous performer in this infant medium" (27). Certainly Barney's satisfaction with coterie writings and performances, coinciding with Wickham's parents' ideas (and quarrels) on the subject of professionalism in the arts, must have created a tension in Wickham which contributed to her meager publishing record during the final ten years of her life. Like Charlotte Mew, whose family problems overwhelmed her final ten years, Wickham published little in her last years.

A close look at the shoebox full of Wickham's *Des Cartes a l'Amazone* might reveal that they are her attempt to create an artistic, and, perhaps, a sexual home. Jones reports that the shoebox also contained a picture of Anna, reclining nude, draped in sheer fabric (231). It is ironic that Wickham's hope for a home in which to settle her exile art would be crushed because her work was not "indiscreet" enough! Barney's belief that the violence implied in heterosexuality and childbirth made woman a victim of her sex instead of a celebrator of the female body was in direct opposition to Wickham's glorification of childbirth and motherhood. Wickham expressed this disjunction in the following letter that she wrote to Barney in January, 1928:

> For the love of God don't tell me to write poetry. It maddens me—if you want me to write poetry let your will sleep in the storm of my energy. Don't ride all over the battle-field, stand on your hill and confer. If I am to write poetry I want you to help me in certain definite ways—*I want you to love my child.* Get ahead now and love my child
>
> (R. D. Smith 389 n. 24).

So Anna Wickham's dream of collaboration on a series of poetic postcards written by two Amazons was destroyed by sexual politics. Barney could not love the child that she believed to be the product of violence and the curtailer of women's freedom, and Wickham could not work with a person who would not love her child. Whether that child is one of the Hepburn sons, or Wickham's poem doesn't matter. Wickham could find neither her house nor her home in Barney's salon. As a result, her production ends up being much like the "red, dead thing" (perhaps a still-born child, perhaps a heart, perhaps a poem) in Mew's "Saturday Market"—laughed at and buried, because nobody cares.

In her one piece of criticism, "The Spirit of the Lawrence Women," Wickham wrote that she believed that the "creative consciousness of a pure artist is bisexual. There is a marriage in the house of the soul. [. . .] and the result is a work of pure imagination" (*WAW* 368). In an early poem written in the male voice of John Oland, Wickham describes the dilemma of the artist:

"In The House of the Soul"

(Harlequin and a Woman under One Skin)
Well, they are gone!
And we are here alone.
I, the mime, and master of surprises,
Who have fooled that mob with fifty new disguises—
You, who sit in the soul
A quiet wife;
You, who are Control
Weaving the long continuous web of life.
I should have little courage to continue with this jest
Could I not meet you here, and be at rest.
Sometimes I think that there is nothing of my winning,
That all we have of service from our union is your spinning;
But when of shame my heart is full—
Then you remind me, dame;
I bring you wool
It is our business here to make a song—
Whoever is sore, whatever is wrong.

(*WAW* 270-71)

Here, the persona speaks from two sexes, two voices at once. For once Wickham has reconciled the opposite forces that drive her; however, it is curious that it is the silent, waiting wife, in a direct allusion to Penelope, who stands for both huswifery and creativity (weaving), while the buffoon Harlequin stands for sexuality (procreativity). Perhaps Wickham is directly addressing her bisexuality; perhaps any exclusion repels Wickham's desire. In order to remain the child-angel in her parent's house, Wickham could never leave the polymorphous perverse sexuality of the pre-adolescent. Years after he spoke the words, Wickham remembers her father saying, "I hate women, *old girl,* (my italics) thank God you're not a woman darling" (*WAW* 102). For Wickham, like Mew, each poem disguises as much as it reveals. Because of Victorian morality, neither could express her real self directly, so each distanced her self by irony, wit, and making in many different voices a very modern babble.

To sum up the impact of Charlotte Mew and Anna Wickham on modern poetics, the critic has to jump generations, leaving out the formalists of the fifties, and proceed to poets of the confessional school such as Sylvia Plath and Anne Sexton. Plath and Sexton are considered by some critics to be the mothers of feminist poetry, but their foremother was Anna Wickham, whether they knew it or not. Her brash voice declaims in **"The Fresh Start"**:

O give me back my rigorous English Sunday
And my well-ordered house, with stockings washed
  on Monday.
Let the House-Lord, that kindly decorous fellow,
Leave happy for his Law at ten, with a well-furled
  umbrella.
Let my young ones observe my strict house rules,
Imbibing Tory principles, at Tory schools.

Two years now I have sat beneath a curse
And in a fury poured out frenzied verse,
Such verse as held no beauty and no good
And was at best new curious vermin-food.

My dog is rabid, and my cat is lean,
And not a pot in all this place is clean.
The locks have fallen from my hingeless doors,
And holes are in my credit and my floors.

There is no solace for me, but in sooth
To have said baldly certain ugly truth.
Such scavenger's work was never yet a woman's,
My wardrobe's more a scarecrow's than a Human's.

I'm off to the House-goddess for her gift.
'O give me Circumspection, Temperance, Thrift;
Take thou this lust of words, this fevered itching,
And give me faith in darning, joy of stitching!'

When this hot blood is cooled by kindly Time
Controlled and schooled, I'll come again to Rhyme.
Sure of my methods, morals and my gloves,
I'll write chaste sonnets of imagined Loves.

(*WAW* 240-41)

In this poem, Wickham answers the question about why there is no great, as she puts it, She-Poet. Both Wickham and Mew put into housework much of the energy they needed for writing because their families depended on them to keep the household afloat. In **"Dedication to a Cook"** Wickham says that the person who asks the above question about women poets should come live with her and he will understand the answer. Fighting against the bonds of domesticity, for artistic freedom, and for a more inclusive understanding of women's sexuality, Mew and Wickham create a poetry as fresh today as it was the day it was written.

And as much as Mew and Wickham depreciate their work, their poems remain monuments to the fact that they could and did write poetry that stands on its own merits. If both women can reach a wider audience now that feminist critics have begun reclamation projects designed to rescue them and others from previous critical neglect, Mew and Wickham will be recognized for their contributions to a literary era. We must recognize, as Bachelard so aptly puts it, "a childhood which dares not speak its name" (*Reverie* 103) in our understanding of Charlotte Mew and Anna Wickham as unredeemed captives of the angel in the house metaphor. It is through the mytho-poetical structures of *bricolage* that we can come to a system that explains their production.

Notes

1. "Formalist" *WAW* 195

2. These essays are Matt Holland's "Anna Wickham: Fettered Woman, Free Spirit," published in *Poetry Review* Summer 1988; Margaret Newlin's "Anna Wickham: 'The sexless Part which is my mind,'" in *Southern Poetry Review* April 1978; and Myra Stark's "Feminist Themes in Anna Wickham's *The Contemplative Quarry and The Man with a Hammer*" in *Four Decades of Poetry: 1890-1930,* Vol. 2, 1978.

3. The author of *The Ingoldsby Legends,* the Reverend Richard Harris Barham, lived from 1788 to 1845. He was a writer and a wit, whose books and light articles in magazines such as *Blackwood's* and *John Bull* made him one of the most popular authors of the nineteenth century. *The Ingoldsby Legends* are folk tales and ghost stories interspersed with long humorous or sentimental "tragical" poems. As mentioned earlier, George Cruikshank illustrated *The Ingoldsby Legends* and gave an expensive copy of the book to the Whelan family. It became one of their prize possessions.

4. Charles Stuart Calverley (1831-84) was a poet who excelled in light verse, parody and pastiche, according to Hilda Spear's account in *The English Poems of Charles Stuart Calverley.* She further states that he was a critic of the pedantic and the "puffed-up," and it is only in his translations from the classics that he is completely serious. Spears ranks Calverley with the great Cambridge parodists A. C. Hilton and J. K. Stephens, commenting that though his literary achievement is slight, it's pleasing, and she continues, "At the same time he evokes an atmosphere of Victorianism. [. . .] He shows us aspects of the life of a limited sector of the community" (11).

5. Aphra Behn (1640-89) has been characterized as the first Englishwoman to make her living by writing. She is most famous for her novel, *Oroonoko.* Like Anna Wickham, Behn has been characterized as a Bohemian and feminist. Katherine Philips (1631-64) established a literary salon, the "Society of Friendship," which included the poets Abraham Cowley, Jeremy Taylor, and Henry Vaughan; her verses on Vaughan's poems bought her considerable fame, as did her translation of Corneille's *Pompee.* Anne Finch (1661-1720) poetically sparred with Alexander Pope, wrote verse in imitation of Sappho, and was "discovered" by Wordsworth, who praised her verse as a forerunner of Romanticism. Lady Mary Wortley Montagu (1690-1762) also jousted with Pope, and is known for her wit and satire (Bernikow 58-59, 68, 81, 92.)

6. For a fascinating and complete rendering of the early days of Australian settlement, see Robert

Hughes's *The Fatal Shore: The Epic of Australia's Founding* (1988).

7. Renee Vivian's (1877-1909) real name was Natalie Tarn. She had an American mother and British father. She wrote poetry in French. Her books were published in Paris by Alphonse Lemerre between 1902 and 1910. In 1934 Lemerre published her complete poems in two volumes. Three of her books, *A Woman Appeared to Me, At the Sweet Hour of Hand in Hand,* and *The Muse of Violets* were translated into English and published by Naiad Press in the late 1970s. She was Natalie Barney's lover for several years before her death. Romaine Brooks, a photographer, became Barney's lover when both were over forty. Shari Benstock characterizes her photographic portraits of Barney's circle as "Amazons in drag" (305). Elizabeth de Gramont, the Duchesse de Clermont-Tonnerre, was a rival of Brooks. Lucie Delarue-Mardrus, also a member of Barney's circle, was Barney's entree into an aristocratic group of French lesbians (Benstock 79).

Bibliography

Ackroyd, Peter. *T. S. Eliot: A Life.* New York: Simon and Schuster, 1984.

Bachelard, Gaston. *The Poetics of Reverie.* Trans. Daniel Russell. NY: Orion, 1969. 99-141.

Barham, Richard Harris. *The Ingoldsby Legends or Mirth and Marvels.* Illus. by Cruikshank, Leech, etc. London: Frederick Warne. 1889.

Benstock, Shari. *Women of the Left Bank: Paris 1900-1940.* Austin: U of Texas P, 1986.

Colby, Vineta. *The Singular Anomaly: Women Novelists of the Nineteenth Century.* New York: New York UP, 1970. 1-14.

Eliot, T. S. *The Complete Poems and Plays: 1909-1950.* New York: Harcourt, 1971.

————. *The Letters of T. S. Eliot.* Ed. Valerie Eliot. Vol. I: 1898-1922. New York: Harcourt, 1988.

EVOE. "In Search of a Bard." *Punch* 24 August 1921:146.

Gilbert, Sandra M., and Susan Gubar. *No Man's Land: The Place of the Woman Writer in the Twentieth Century.* 3 vols. to date. New Haven: Yale UP, 1988-.

Grant, Joy. *Harold Monro and the Poetry Bookshop.* Berkeley: U of California P, 1967.

Groben, Anne R. "Ella Wheeler Wilcox." *American Women Writers.* Vol. 4. Ed. Lina Mainiero. New York: Frederick Ungar, 1982. 415-17.

Hepburn, James. Preface. *The Writings of Anna Wickham: Free Woman and Poet.* London: Virago, 1984. xix-xxiii.

Jones, Jennifer Vaughan. "The Poetry and Place of Anna Wickham: 1910-1930" Diss. U of Wisconsin, 1994.

Lawson, Alan. "The Discovery of Nationality in Australian and Canadian Literatures." *The Post-Colonial Studies Reader.* Ed. Bill Ashcroft, Gareth Griffiths, and Helen Tiffin. London: Routledge, 1995. 167-69.

Levenson, Michael H. *A Genealogy of Modernism: A Study of English Literary Doctrine 1908-1922.* Cambridge: Cambridge UP, 1984.

Marcus, Jane. "Alibis and Legends: The Ethics of Elsewhereness, Gender and Estrangement." *Women's Writing in Exile.* Ed. Mary Lynn Broe and Angela Ingram. Chapel Hill: U of North Carolina P, 1989. 270-92.

Menand, Louis. *Discovering Modernism: T. S. Eliot and His Context.* New York: Oxford UP, 1987.

Millay, Edna St. Vincent. *Letters of Edna St. Vincent Millay.* 1952. Ed. Allan Ross Macdougall. Westport, Conn.: Greenwood P, 1972. 157.

Monro, Harold. *Some Contemporary Poets.* London: Leonard Parsons, 1920.

Schenck, Celeste M. "Anna Wickham." *The Gender of Modernism.* Ed. Bonnie Kime Scott. Bloomington: Indiana UP, 1990. 613-21.

Scott, Bonnie Kime, ed. *The Gender of Modernism: A Critical Anthology.* Bloomington: Indiana UP, 1990.

————. *Refiguring Modernism: The Women of 1928.* Vol. 1. Bloomington: Indiana UP, 1995.

Showalter, Elaine. *A Literature of Their Own: British Women Novelists from Brontë to Lessing.* Princeton: Princeton UP, 1977.

Smith, R. D., ed. *The Writings of Anna Wickham: Free Woman And Poet.* London: Virago, 1984.

Smith, Warren S. *The London Heretics 1870-1914.* New York: Dodd, Mead, 1968.

Spear, Hilda, ed. *The English Poems of Charles Stuart Calverley.* Leicester: Leicester UP, 1974.

Thwaite, Ann. *A. A. Milne: The Man Behind Winnie-The-Pooh.* NY: Random House, 1990.

Untermeyer, Louis. *From Another World: The Autobiography of Louis Untermeyer.* NY: Harcourt, 1939. 319-42.

Van Doren, Mark. "Women of Wit." Rev. of *The Contemplative Quarry* and *The Man with a Hammer. The Nation* 113 (1922): 483-84.

Vickery, Ann. "Between a Modernist Passport and House Arrest: Anna Wickham and the Question of Cultural Identity." *Soundings: Poetry and Poetics.* Ed. Lynn Jacobs and Jeri Kroll. Kent Town, South Australia: Wakefield P, 1998. 26-36.

Walker, Cheryl. *The Nightingale's Burden: Women Poets and American Culture before 1900.* Bloomington: Indiana UP, 1982.

Wickes, George. *The Amazon of Letters: The Life and Loves of Natalie Barney.* New York: Popular Library, 1978.

Wickham, Anna. "I & My Genius." *The Women's Review* 5 (1986): 16-20.

———. *Selected Poems.* Intro. David Garnett. London: Chatto & Windus, 1971.

———. *The Writings of Anna Wickham: Free Woman and Poet.* Ed. and intro. R. D. Smith. London: Virago, 1984.

Wilcox, Ella Wheeler. *The World and I.* 1918. New York: Arno Press, 1980.

Anne Pender (essay date October 2005)

SOURCE: Pender, Anne. "'Phrases between Us': The Poetry of Anna Wickham." In *Australian Literary Studies* 22, no. 2 (October 2005): 229-44.

[*In the following essay, Pender gives an overview of Wickham's poetry contextualized with information about Wickham's life—in particular her relationships with D. H. Lawrence and Natalie Barney.*]

Anna Wickham was a poet, singer, social worker and feminist activist. The American scholar Jennifer Vaughan Jones published a biography in 2003, a book which reveals a great deal about Wickham's struggle as a poet but which is not widely held in Australia.[1] But Jones shies away from a full analysis of the poetry, and there are almost no recent essays on Wickham's work.[2] In spite of the critical neglect. Anna Wickham's poetry is widely anthologised in the United Kingdom. Australia and the United States, and her distinctive modernist poetic voice deserves close attention.[3] One of the attractions of her poetry is its blend of strength and accessibility, its firmness of tone and conviction. At its best it is tight and highly charged; another feature is its range, the poems being by turns provocative, combative, merry and sensual. Most importantly, it offers an enduring aesthetic purity and resonance, in combination with a questing feminist intelligence. In this essay I want to consider the breadth and achievements of Wickham's published and unpublished writing, particularly in the context of Germaine Greer's criticism of her and her work.[4]

Altogether Wickham wrote over one thousand poems: free verse, comic and bawdy verse, epigrams, ballads and songs, dramatic monologues and confessional poetry. She is claimed as both Australian and English, samples of her work appearing in anthologies such as *Two Centuries of Australian Poetry, The Oxford Book of Australian Women's Verse* and *The Penguin Book of Australian Women Poets,* as well as *The Oxford Book of Twentieth-Century English Verse, The New Penguin Book of English Verse* and many others. It is rare for a poet to be claimed by the literary establishment, or at least by a varied group of anthologists, in both Australia and Britain, whilst remaining relatively unknown in the two countries.

At a loss to explain the lack of critical interest in Wickham as early as 1942, only two decades after her heyday, the editors of *Twentieth Century Authors* commented that her 'neglect is one of the mysteries of contemporary literature' (Kunitz and Haycraft 1515). Ann Vickery argues that Wickham was a 'displaced alien' who was never quite at home in Australia or the UK (27).[5] Vickery also argues that the fact that Wickham did not belong to any school of modernism had an adverse effect on her reception (27), but it is difficult to pinpoint the main reason for Wickham's neglect, particularly in Australia. Andrew Field argues that there is an 'unmistakably Australian tone' in Wickham's voice, and Wickham's son George also holds this view—but it is a difficult argument to make conclusively.[6] Although Wickham's work appears in many Australian anthologies, at the time of writing the *AustLit* database did not carry full details of her life and seems uncertain of the provenance of her work: there is no entry for her in the *ALS* bibliography. Contrastingly, Wickham's poetry was taken up in the US, right from the beginning of her career, and has been taken seriously in that country.

Wickham was one of the most significant feminist poets of modernism and her work resounds with contemporary relevance. Her understanding of feminism and of socially determined regimes of behaviour is not only radical, her thoughts are eloquently argued in both her poetry, her letters and her prose writings. Her writing places her in the middle of intellectual debates about form, place, Englishness and lyricism that are central to formulations of modernism. Just as importantly, there are many threads of connection between Wickham's work and that of other Australians that have gone unnoticed for too long. Wickham's poetry can be usefully understood in relation to that of John Shaw Neilson, Zora Cross and others. The fact that Wickham's biography was published recently in the US by an American scholar makes this 'recovery' all the more timely.

Perhaps something of the neglect of Anna Wickham's poetry relates to the breadth of her oeuvre, perhaps something to her own complex personality. In her unfinished autobiography, Wickham claims not to have had any real friends. She says 'Nearly all the relationships of my life had been tawdry, insincere and unsatisfactory. Many people were attracted to me, but I was intimate with nobody. I was not sufficiently like anyone to invite that self-identification which is the essence of true friendship and love' (Smith 157). She confesses that 'the truth is that I believed in pain. I believed that by suffering and endurance I was working out some salvation' (Smith 157), sentiments that might seem to reflect the influence of her convent schooling. Such extreme statements certainly offer a sense of Wickham's honesty and acuteness in observations of human psychology, but critics such as Germaine Greer have seized on them in dismissing the poetry.

Greer's *101 Poems by 101 Women* (2001) includes one of Wickham's poems, but in *Slip-Shod Sybils* (1995) Greer offers a brief, scathing portrait of a woman she declares 'is typical of the stereotypical poetess' and much of whose writing she calls 'embarrassing' (415). She declares that Wickham 'was considered to have laid bare heterosexual womanhood and exposed the violence of woman's subversive grief and rage', but castigates her for 'cultivating and propagating pain' (415, 416). Greer's view is that the 'perceived political importance of what she was doing greatly distorted contemporary assessment of her achievement' (415), but in doing so she fails to acknowledge the breadth of opinion about Wickham's poetry in her own lifetime. For example, Yvor Winter's review of Wickham's ***The Man with the Hammer*** in the American journal *Poetry* was headed 'A Woman with a Hammer', and sparked fiery debate in the journal. And ironically there is some hint of her importance when Greer declares that 'Anne Sexton's therapist might have understood what was going on rather better if he had had the chance to read Anna Wickham's "Fragment of an Autobiography"' and that 'All the things that would later be said of Plath and Sexton were said about Anna Wickham' (417, 415).

In her introduction to *101 Poems* Greer declares that in her selection of Wickham and Sexton she has 'chosen to sidestep exhibitionistic clamour and . . . opted for something more thoughtful—glimpses of the poet who might have been' (xii). Greer's wholesale rejection of both poets in *Slip-Shod Sybils,* accomplished in less than four pages, overlooks the strength of some of the poetry, and misses the fact that Wickham emphatically rejects any exclusive notions of heterosexual love. The fact that Wickham was writing a kind of 'confessional' poetry some decades before the term was invented arouses no interest—for Greer, it is merely proof of the falsity and insufficiency of the work. Many readers would not investigate Wickham's work after reading Greer's extraordinary criticisms which have so far gone unchallenged.

In some of Wickham's most powerful verse there is a striking sense of a woman in revolt against the constraints of marriage and 'decent' society. But as a writer she did not belong to any school of poetry and her work is not easily categorised, ranging from satirical epigram through dramatic monologue to lyrical songs. And while Wickham wrote many poems that were intended for publication and published several volumes of verse in her own lifetime, she also wrote poetry in her letters,[7] specifically for and about her friends. The remaining 'private', unpublished poetry reveals a great deal about Wickham's attitude to her art, and the primacy she gave to her female friendships. Here, then, I want to consider Wickham's work in the context of her life, particularly her literary friendships, notably those with D. H. Lawrence and Natalie Barney.

Wickham was born in 1883 in Wimbledon, England. She was christened Edith Alice Mary Harper, but her parents called her Anne. She was the only child of Geoffrey Harper and Alice Whelan: Harper was a musician who tuned pianos for a living, while Whelan had an interest in spirituality and the paranormal. In 1889, Anna Wickham's family moved to Australia, setting up in Maryborough on the coast of Queensland. Although Geoffrey Harper was a member of the Fabian and Positivist societies (Jones, *Anna Wickham* 9), the young Anna attended a convent school in Maryborough, and the Catholic girls' school All Hallows in Brisbane. She took her pseudonym 'Wickham' from Wickham Terrace in Brisbane, where she promised her father at the age of ten that she would write poetry.[8] Alice Harper ran a physiognomy parlour, calling herself 'Madame Reprah', and eventually went on tours of Queensland, lecturing on the paranormal and offering her services in fortune telling and healing (Jones, *Anna Wickham* 23). (Geoffrey Harper, as a scientific rationalist, deplored these activities.[9]) In 1896 the family moved to Sydney; Alice gave up her travelling life, and Anna attended Sydney Girls' High School as a scholarship pupil. She completed her schooling at the age of sixteen (Jones, *Anna Wickham* 34) and remained in Australia for several more years—perhaps not 'haphazardly educated' as Greer claims (415).

When Anna Wickham returned to London in 1904 she successfully auditioned for a place at Herbert Beerbohm Tree's Academy of Acting, in front of Tree and the modernist playwright Arthur Wing Pinero. But the next year she departed for Paris with 'the vague plan of going, like Bernhardt, to the Conservatoire' (Jones, *Anna Wickham* 52). Immediately she was taken on as a student of the Polish opera singer Jean de Reszke, who told Wickham she had 'the best voice he had ever heard from England' (Jones, *Anna Wickham,* 53). Reszke taught her in his master class at a private theatre near the Bois de Boulogne, but in 1906 she returned to London and married a solicitor named Patrick Hepburn. When critic Louis Untermeyer first met Wickham he described her as 'a magnificent gypsy of a woman who always entered a room as if she had just stamped across the moors', while the poet Oswell Blakeston described her as 'Olympian by nature' (Jones, *Anna Wickham* 155, 266). At an art exhibition the dealer whispered to Blakeston that he should take her outside because of her loudly expressed scorn for the paintings, to which the statuesque Wickham stood up and exclaimed 'You'd better retract, my good man. I may be a minor poet, but I'm a major woman!' (Jones, *Anna Wickham* 244). The question of Wickham's status as a poet and as a woman, and particularly as a woman poet, dogged her all her life, although her powerful personality has been the subject of interest. In 1947, with her three sons safely home after the War, Wickham hanged herself.

Wickham's first book of poetry, **Songs of John Oland** (1911), was published privately and printed by the Women's Printing Society.[10] The pseudonym John Oland recalls the Jenolan Caves in the Blue Mountains, a natural wonder in limestone that Anna had explored some years earlier with her close friend May Muckle.[11] The poems demonstrate Wickham's experiments with free verse; the opening poem, 'Illusion', reveals her impulse towards modernism, juxtaposed with an interest in spirituality:

> . . . what wonder men
> Fight for false hope and die for Gods that are not,
> Beneath the rounded falsity.
> But when I sleep, I leave eternal circles
> And where the great stars march
> Find Truth in Change.

>> (Smith [**Writings of Anna Wickham**] 161)

Notwithstanding this bringing together of the modernist and the mystic, Wickham was at home with the lyrical ballad as well, while some of her most sensual, joyful and musically powerful poetry was written in response to her children. These poems are usually light and celebratory, but can be tinged with melancholy. **'Song to the Young John'** is simple and moving, almost hymn-like in its chorus:

> The apple-blossomy king
> Is lord of this new spring,
> He is the spirit of young joy,
> My little yellow-headed boy.

>> (Smith [**Writings of Anna Wickham**]169)

The metaphor in the following stanza, 'His hair the white-gold, ghost of sunlight, from springs dead' reveals subtlety of diction, and the overall mood of the 'song' recalls that of the folk tradition. The simplicity and the lyricism are reminiscent of the poetry of John Shaw Neilson, and the child poems of Zora Cross. The poem **'The Faithful Mother'** proclaims the physicality and inexorability of love for a child in its repeated line 'But I am here in bondage to these little, little hands!'

One of Wickham's most anthologised poems, **'Divorce'**, dates from this early period. It demonstrates her lyrical brilliance in a completely different key, offering a compelling mix of melodic power and haunting imagery:

> A voice from the dark is calling me.
> In the close house I nurse a fire.
> Out in the dark cold winds rush free
> To the rock heights of my desire.
> I smother in the house in the valley below.
> Let me out to the night, let me go, let me go.

>> (Smith [**Writings of Anna Wickham**]166)

Wickham's early poems, like this one, did not please her husband Patrick Hepburn. He resisted his wife's attempts to write in the most aggressive way he could: he had Anna Wickham certified in May 1913, and she was incarcerated in Brooke House asylum in Upper Clapton (Jones, *Anna Wickham* 97). On the night of her incarceration, Anna had sung at a concert and dressed herself (as she recalled it) 'in an evening gown the colour of arterial blood' (Jones, *Anna Wickham* 90). After the concert, Wickham's neighbour Edward Garnett invited her to his house to meet his wife Constance. David, their son, who was reading in his room, heard a visitor's voice

> a woman's: a rich musical contralto and full of caressing humour. It attracted me so much that I put away my book and went in and joined them. The unknown was a tall, beautiful and powerful woman with shining dark eyes, abundant dark hair parted at the side which fell like a bird's wings over her ears.

>> (Garnett, Introduction 7)

During her stay at the asylum one doctor instructed Wickham to think of her household, saying 'Mrs Hepburn . . . there is always something to do in the house' (Jones, *Anna Wickham* 95). It was this kind of comment that seems to have propelled Wickham to write some of her most arresting satirical verse. In her poem **'The Fired Pot'** the speaker laments domesticity and its submerging effects 'And I have watched the women growing old, / Passionate about pins, and pence, and soap' (**Selected Poems** 14). Wickham smuggled eighty poems out of Brooke House when she was released 'on probation' in September 1913. It was after her release that she set herself on a course of her own: in one incident, she gave a garden party, dressing her two sons and another boy in blouses emblazoned with the words 'Votes for Women' (Jones, *Anna Wickham* 100). Wickham began to frequent the Café Royal and Augustus John's nightclub in Greek Street, Bloomsbury, and befriended the artists Nina Hamnett, Mark Gertler and Jacob Epstein. She became very close to David Garnett, who asked her to leave her husband. She refused, partly for fear of losing any rights to see her children, a decision that set her on a course decidedly separate from the Bloomsbury group.[12]

Anna Wickham's poetry was not neglected in the early stages of her career, being admired by D. H. Lawrence,

Walter de la Mare, William Empson, John Gawsworth, Edna St Vincent Millay, Edmund Wilson, Humbert Wolfe and Dylan Thomas.[13] Harold Monro published Wickham's poetry in *Poetry and Drama* in June 1914, and it appeared in various London newspapers around this time. Monro then published Wickham's collection *The Contemplative Quarry* (1915), which was reviewed in the American journal *Poetry* by Padraic Colum. Colum declared, 'Here is a woman claiming experiences for herself, songs for herself. . . . The quarry is woman; the object of her continuous contemplation is man, the pursuer. The booklet is provocative' (255); he also commented on the 'hard and twisted' quality of the 'songs' (255). In September 1917 **'Host'** appeared in the little magazine *The Lantern,* published in Oakland, California. This poem inspired Louis Untermeyer, the New Jersey-based designer of jewelry and poetry editor, to include Wickham's poems in *Modern British Poetry* (Jones, *Anna Wickham* 154). Responding to Untermeyer's request for biographical material, Wickham wrote:

> . . . I was born in Wimbledon Surrey in 1883. It was always my father's ambition that I should be a poet. I went to Australia at six, returned when I was twenty one. Studied for opera in Paris . . . Married had two sons. Tried very hard to be a housekeeper, got so irritated that I wrote 900 poems in 4 years. My attempt to organise a house ended in my writing the revolt of women.

> (qtd in Jones, *Anna Wickham* 155)

Wickham's startling directness captures the essential facts of her life as well as her view of her own poetic project; it also offers a sense of her ironic humour.

Wickham wrote some of her poems as songs, and others have been set to music.[14] As a composer of songs and lyric poems Wickham seems to draw on an English folk song tradition, and parallels are found in some of her poetry with madrigals, such as those by Thomas Weelkes (1576-1623). Her poem **'The Cherry-Blossom Wand',** published in her second collection *The Contemplative Quarry* (1915), builds on the theme of beauty and impermanence, and in the sung version it resonates with English folk tunes from the sixteenth century. It tells a tale of enchantment—of the intoxicating, fleeting and delicate beauty of the cherry blossom wand, associated with the transience of perfect love: 'Eternal in beauty are short-lived flowers, / Eternal in beauty, these exquisite hours' (Smith [*Writings of Anna Wickham*] 44) The sung version of the poem, which was played for me, struck me as masterly as both poetry and song.[15]

> I will pluck from my tree a cherry-blossom wand,
> And carry it in my merciless hand,
> So I will drive you, so bewitch your eyes,
> With a beautiful thing that can never grow wise.
>
> Light are the petals that fall from the bough,
> And lighter the love that I offer you now;

> In a spring day shall the tale be told
> Of the beautiful things that will never grow old

> (Smith [*Writings of Anna Wickham*] 44)

The self conscious romanticism and precise natural images link this poem with Yeats in his early period. Its haunting quality is reminiscent of poems such as 'The Lake Isle of Innisfree' (1890) and 'The Two Trees' (1893) with its characteristic lines: 'In the dim glass the demons hold, / The glass of outer weariness'. Although the Wickham poem is a love poem (written and sung for David Garnett) and therefore quite different in subject matter to 'The Lake Isle', both poems demonstrate control and clarity of image in addition to an interest in a transcendental beauty. The compression of language, tight structure, as well as the yearning and dreamy sensations evoked by the two poems make for an uncanny stylistic and thematic resemblance. The ethereal quality of **'The Cherry-Blossom Wand'** is also similar to 'The Wild Swans at Coole' (1917) 'The trees are in their autumn beauty, / The woodland paths are dry'. Both poems are languorous in the way they capture a moment, at the same time sadly contemplating the impermanence of this beauty and the inability of the poet to impose any lasting order on it, except through the poetry itself.

Not long after Wickham's release from the asylum David Garnett introduced her to D. H. Lawrence and Frieda Weekley, who were also residents of Hampstead. In Lawrence Wickham found a soul mate, a man with whom she could talk and to whom she felt a strong, class-based affiliation. They spent hours singing hymns around the piano at her house, talking and walking together on Hampstead Heath. Nina Hamnett recalls in her autobiography that when she was ill with influenza Wickham invited her to stay at her house at Downshire Hill, where she

> stayed in bed and had a room overlooking the garden. Several times a week D. H. Lawrence, his wife, and Katherine Mansfield came to see Anna. Mrs Lawrence and Katherine sat by my bedside and talked to me. D. H. Lawrence sang hymns for hours in the drawing-room. This was not awfully cheerful.

> (88)

Wickham wrote poems for and about Lawrence: **'Prayer to Love'** is dedicated to him, and presents in its list of imperatives her otherworldliness, and single-minded religious passion.

> Give me the moment of self-forgetfulness
> In which the perfect thing is bred.
> Fill this small cup of time with infinity,
> Give me quick union with the dead.
>
> Not till that moment shall I be transfigured to beauty,
> Now I come out to you by paths well-trod,

You are the wall at my road's end,
Open your gates, and let me through to God.

(Smith [*Writings of Anna Wickham*] 294)

It is probable that Wickham also wrote **'A Love Letter'** to Lawrence (see Newlin 287). The work is one of Wickham's most powerful love poems, with its clear-eyed promises and raw strength: 'You have given me some quality of the male, / While I have given you some qualities of myself'; it rejects all commonplaces, 'I do not grieve away my days / Because you are gone from me'; defines fidelity, 'I do not ask that your love should be faithful to my body, / It is impossible that your soul should be faithless to my soul'; and builds to a powerful finale

> I ask nothing of you, not even that you live.
> If you die,
> I remember you
> Till the blood in my wrists is cold.

(*Selected Poems* 37)

Wickham admired Lawrence and helped him with his magazine *The Signature*, laboriously copying and writing out poems. He didn't publish any of her poems, though he did recommend her work to Edward Marsh for *Georgian Poetry*. Wickham's acute analysis of Lawrence's problematic attitude to women is put forth in an essay in which she also describes their warm and intense friendship. She comments upon what she perceived in Lawrence as 'a miasma of menace towards women who detach any considerable portion of their energy from their purely sexual function' ('Spirit of the Lawrence Women' 35). Her view of him is neatly, affectionately and comically captured in **'Multiplication'**, not published until 1984:

> Had I married you dear,
> When I was nineteen
> I had been little since
> But a printing machine;
> For, before my fortieth year had run.
> I had well produced you
> A twenty-first son.
>
> Your ingenious love
> Had expressed through me
> Automatic, unreasoned, fecundity.
> I had scattered the earth
> With the seed of your loins,
> And stamped you on boys
> Like a lion's head on coins.

(Smith [*Writings of Anna Wickham*] 318)

Wickham's essay, alongside her many poems expressing resistance to the strictures of marriage and male-female relationships more generally, reveal intelligence, anguish, and a real understanding of socially determined gender pathologies. Perhaps her most bitter protest is expressed in the opening lines of **'The Angry Woman'**:

> I am a woman, with a woman's parts,
> And of love I bear children.
> In the days of bearing my body is weak,
> But why because I do you service, should you call me
>   slave?
>
> I am a woman in my speech and gait,
> I have no beard (I'll take no blame for that!)
> In many things are you and I apart,
> But there are regions where we coincide,
> Where law for one is law for both.
>
> There is the sexless part of me that is my mind.

(Smith [*Writings of Anna Wickham*] 202)

Wickham's friendship with Lawrence was characteristic of many, but not all, of her other friendships: intense and relatively short in duration. It more or less ended in 1915 when Lawrence moved to Cornwall.

In 1926 Anna Wickham and her husband Patrick Hepburn separated. Hepburn drew up a document that provided his wife with £400 per year, and decreed that if she approached him the money would be cut off (Jones, *Anna Wickham* 171). After this period Wickham struggled financially, but the separation freed her emotionally.[16] Wickham was involved with several women during her lifetime to whom she wrote poems, and in contrast to the work considered above, these are not published. They express a yearning for devotion and understanding that is similar to some of the published poems, but they also demonstrate Wickham's interest in poetry as a purely private means of communication. Natalie Barney, whom she first met in Paris in 1922, was just one of Wickham's lovers. Wickham wrote hundreds of letters to her, letters that are remarkable for their humour, grace, candour and energy. The salutations varied: sometimes Barney was addressed 'Dear Natalie', but in other letters it is 'Darling', 'Old adored' or 'Hail Columbia'. In signing off Wickham uses a number of names including 'yer good ol wench'. On Valentine's Day 1927 she wrote **'Consolation'** for Barney:

> Above my town
> There is ascending—
> The Spirit—
> Of her befriending
> In form a woman—
> Radiant—white—
> Her hands will spill flowers
> Her feet drop light
>
> O loveliest feet—
> My adoration.
> Leaps to your blest
> Transfiguration.
> I who had kissed you
> Were you near
> Now kneel, and love
> In holy fear.

In one letter announcing her intention to visit Barney, Wickham wrote 'Darling. Put some American books on the table near your portrait in the front drawing room—fill the fountain pens and send a cheese to Isadora [Duncan]—walk in no confidence—for any moment I may be back—you have as much chance against me as a buttercup in a blizzard'.[17] A year earlier Barney had formed a group called the Académie des Femmes, aiming to introduce French and English women writers to one another and to promote their work. In a letter to Barney in the spring of 1927 Wickham encourages this project and writes,

> You must start your paper. You will have to do very little more than select as you do for your afternoons. Why not make an anthology of your representative women—your selection of me was perfect. My dear—there is no excuse for you not to do this. You can make a holy island where the imagination of women can take refuge. God knows mine has been crucified . . . I know that you talked to [Ezra] Pound about a paper and he obstructed—but he is every sort of idiot.
>
> PS After Easter I should like everything that is symptomatic—in the revival of the imagination and intellectual activity of England to be announced from your house.
>
> Signed your heavenly bitch.[18]

Wickham wrote scores of poems for Barney as well as translating her poetry.[19] Jealous of Barney's many affairs and friendships, Wickham wrote this comic but pained poem in the spring of 1927:

> Resentments of Orpheus—
> And why these Presbyterian pains—
> Why travail with this Mawkish James?
> All your affinities are mine—
> Fill no small hour with Ford or Stein
> Nor lend a cubic inch of air
> To the false lightenings of Tonerre
> The grooms might profit by the yarns
> Of the unmitigated Barnes
> I doubt if any stable boy
> Were subtler for a note of Loy
> Euridice fare thee well
> Since thou hast leased thy love to hell
> Let smokes of mediocrity
> And such slow fire envelope thee.[20]

Around the same time, Barney dedicated one of her famous Fridays at her Paris salon to a celebration of the work of Anna Wickham—the salon has been described as 'an eclectic, international, and multisexual meeting place'.[21] Introducing Wickham to the assembled group, Barney declared that:

> Anna Wickham is a semi-rebel . . . the feminist leagues have hoisted certain of her verses on their banners. One of her verses has even been used by the Women's Movement against the corset. Anna Wickham equally combats Puritanism and other Anglican vices . . . she is indignant toward matrimonial servitudes which shut in the bourgeois of the Croydon class . . .
>
> (Barney 145)

Barney spoke of Wickham as author, spouse and mother to several sons,[22] selected a set of poems for reading to illustrate her claims, and translated some assorted couplets into French. For Wickham the evening was very significant: it marked her accession to the 'carte du Salon de l'Amazone', giving her new confidence in her work (Jones, *Anna Wickham* 189). The evening was also important in marking the beginning of the appreciation of Wickham's poetry in France—even today, it is better known in France and the United States than in Australia or the United Kingdom. Wickham's poems were translated into French by Lucie Delarue-Mardrus and the full version of Wickham's autobiography is published in French; only an edited version is available in English.[23]

In many of her best poems Wickham is scathing about the stultifying middle-class English life condemned by Barney, using rhyme and gathering rhythm with great effect in her poem **'Nervous Prostration'**:

> I married a man of the Croydon class
> When I was twenty two.
> And I vex him, and he bores me
> Till we don't know what to do!
>
> (Smith [*Writings of Anna Wickham*] 193.)

Wickham's humour is bitter in poems such as **'Definition'**, playfully exasperated in **'Ship Near Shoals'**, and whimsically mischievous in **'The Mummer'**:

> Strict I walk my ordered way
> Through the strait and duteous day;
> The hours the nuns that summon me
> To offices of huswifry.
> Cups and cupboards, flagons, food
> Are things of my solicitude.
> No elfin Folly haply strays
> Down my precise and well-swept ways.
>
> (Smith [*Writings of Anna Wickham*] 178)

Wickham does not avoid self satire, and in the clearly autobiographical poem **'The Tired Man'** the speaker sympathises with the husband whose wife wanders the heath, while her aphoristic style in **'The Affinity'** captures her bewildered complaint about male-female relations:

> It is sad for Feminism, but still clear
> That man, more often than woman, is a pioneer
> If I would confide a new thought,
> First to a man it must be brought.
>
> Now, for our sins, it is my bitter fate
> That such a man wills soon to be my mate,
> And so of friendship is quick end:
> When I have gained a love I lose a friend.
>
> (Smith [*Writings of Anna Wickham*] 176)

The correspondence between Wickham and Barney continued for some years, in spite of what would appear to be Barney's withdrawal from the affair relatively early on. Wickham raged at Barney, even putting a spell on Dolly Wilde, one of Barney's other lovers (Barney pleaded with Wickham to reverse the spell). Nevertheless the correspondents discussed all matters literary, as well as their various involvements in promoting women's artistic endeavours. This included Wickham's work as part of the League for the Protection of the Imagination of Women, undertaken with Kate O'Brien, Charlotte Haldane and others. In a letter to Natalie Barney in 1930 on the subject of men editing women Wickham wrote:

> When men correct a woman's phrasing, it is a subtle and dangerous sexual assault—I have letters from my mother with amendations by my stepfather—Harold Monro never produces a line of mine free of printers errors—and what I suffered from Hepburn in this way leaves my brain bleeding. The time has come for men to let women express themselves any way they bloody well want to—what I said to Eric Partridge—was said in my capacity as officer of the League for the Protection of the Imagination of Women.[24]

In one of her letters, Wickham reprimands Barney for not appearing in London in solidarity with Radclyffe Hall during the trial arising from *The Well of Loneliness,* which featured a character modelled on Barney. In her biography of Hall, Sally Cline points out that Barney and Wickham were two women with whom Hall felt most comfortable (213). In another letter to Barney, Wickham expressed the hope of creating work that is 'worthy of you . . . that will transcend the work of all the artists you have known in as much as it has an individual essence that is my work and not theirs.'[25]

In the years following Patrick Hepburn's death in 1929, Wickham transformed her own home into a kind of salon where people could stay for a few nights or a few months. The ground floor (where I sat to read through her letters to Barney and O'Brien in 2003) was used as a dance studio for two of her sons. Malcolm Lowry visited the house frequently, and Dylan Thomas stayed there on occasion, writing poems on the kitchen walls. She continued her career, and the collection *Thirty-Six New Poems* was published in 1936. The short, spare and compressed poem **'Pilgrimage'** in this volume recalls her honeymoon walking around France, and expresses a strong sense of loss:

> I think of the room at Bon Secours.
> The old clock on the shelf, and the bare-board floor.
> The tallow smell, from the out-blown light.
> And the laughter and love, of the prodigal night.
> I wish we were young, dear,
> As young and as poor
> As when we stole Heaven
> At Bon Secours.

> (Smith [*Writings of Anna Wickham*] 284)

In his Introduction to a collection of Wickham's poetry, Louis Untermeyer links Wickham to the 'searchers'

May Sinclair, Virginia Woolf, Rebecca West, Willa Cather and Dorothy Richardson, women whom he described as 'working in prose that illuminates their experiments' (viii). He boldly claims that 'In poetry, a regiment of young women are recording an even more rigorous self-examination. The most typical and, in many ways, the best of these seekers and singers is Anna Wickham' (ix). Untermeyer does not name the other members of this 'regiment'—perhaps he was thinking of Charlotte Mew (1869-1928)—but is emphatic in rejecting any connection between Wickham's poetry and that of Christina Rossetti, Elizabeth Browning, Lawrence Hope (Ada Florence 'Violet' Nicolson) and Sara Teasdale, all of whom he denounces for expressing 'the masculine rather than the feminine attitude' to women (vii). Although we might take issue with his seemingly essentialist logic, and reject (at least in part) the substance of his claim, Untermeyer does make a compelling argument about the changes he sees around him in the work of modernist writers and poets. Most significantly, he argues that Wickham's feminist poetry conducts a 'rigorous self-examination', and that it may be seen alongside the work of Woolf and others as portending a 'new order' in being 'without a thought of man's contempt or condescension' (viii).

If there is a failing in Wickham's work, one not seen by critics such as Untermeyer (who was a devotee), it is in the fact that some of her chosen poetic forms and techniques do not illuminate her experiments in thought. Rather, the forms are at times at odds with the radical sensibility and questioning incisiveness of their author: at times the poetry is overworked, the language too abstract. Sometimes, the aphoristic style simply doesn't work. But although Wickham's work is—like that of most poets—uneven, and some of her poems are weak, there is no doubt that Wickham produced poetry with the 'individual essence' she speaks of. Her poems and other writings render this essence clearly and brilliantly; a letter to another of her lovers, the Irish writer Kate O'Brien, Wickham is tender and comically affectionate.

> My poor Darling

> I have all the energy in the world for you—now I take you in my arms and carry you about. Also I put kisses in the arches of your feet—so that you will laugh as you take the slow steps . . . I begin to want to have phrases between us. I love you and no-one may know— what we say—NOT Mary, nor John Gawsworth, nor Robert P. Simpkins. I put a kiss also on the heart and inside the left hand and I summon five thousand holy bees to wax up your ears—so that nothing at all boring is heard by my brave baby for a fortnight.

> Yours affec, Anna[26]

In 1971 David Garnett edited a *Selected Poems* by Anna Wickham. In his Introduction, Garnett fondly remembers his intense relationship with her, the way she would pull out pieces of paper when they met in cafés and pass them to him: 'On them were poems she had written since our last meeting . . . I soon realised that her thoughts and feelings were her poems . . . This method made her poetry a day-to-day record of herself' (9). In 1984, R. D. Smith edited **The Writings of Anna Wickham,** but since then her poetry has only appeared in anthologies. It, along with her other writing, offers the voice of modernist woman, and yet it is highly idiosyncratic, demonstrating a passion for the work of English and Australian lyricists. In all modes, Wickham's work deserves to be read and re-read.

Notes

1. The biography is held in the State Libraries of NSW and Victoria, and at Monash University's library.

2. Apart from Margaret Newlin's essay in *Southern Review* in 1978, an essay by Ann Vickery in 1998, and one by Celeste Schenck in 1990, there have been two doctoral theses—one by Jones, and one by Nelljean Rice, published as a monograph in 2002, on Wickham and her work. In Rice's monograph, *A New Matrix for Modernism,* the author argues that Wickham's poetry is 'undeniably modern' and discusses Wickham's association with the philosopher T. E. Hulme, who stated that modernist poetry 'expresses momentary mental phrases, vague moods, and the maximum individual and personal expression . . .' (117). Rice discusses Charlotte Mew and Anna Wickham via the metaphor of the 'angel in the house'. She discounts the significance of Wickham's Australian upbringing on her life and work.

3. Wickham's poetry is also frequently broadcast in the United Kingdom and Europe.

4. The author wishes to thank Margaret and George Hepburn for access to Anna Wickham's papers and recordings, and for their generosity in sharing their memories of Anna Wickham. Also thanks are due to Susan Lever, Cath Pratt and Michael Sharkey for their encouragement and help with this project.

5. Wickham's family members contend that Anna probably felt unsure of her place in society. In 'Fragment of an Autobiography: Prelude to a Spring Clean' she talks about her 'feelings of inferiority' as a child (Smith 95).

6. Conversation with Wickham's only surviving son, George Hepburn, 2003. Andrew Field argues that some of the poetry published in 1915 was written in Australia, basing this claim on an undated manuscript held in the Mitchell Library entitled 'Poems by Anna Wickham, Not for Publication', written in the hand of A. G. Stephens. Field believes that Anna's father sent the poems to Stephens—see his 'A Wild Colonial Girl' (4).

7. Some of these letters are held in the British Library; others are held in a private collection.

8. This detail comes from Adrian Mitchell's *Anna on Anna,* a radio play performed by Ilona Linthwaite and recorded for the BBC World Service in 1996. The play is based on 'Fragment of an Autobiography: Prelude to a Spring Clean', in *The Writings of Anna Wickham* edited by R. D. Smith (102).

9. According to family members Anna's mother set up next door to Geoffrey's music shop which had a sign 'HARPER' above the door. Alice's sign read 'REPRAH'.

10. Jennifer Jones contends that it is difficult to verify the date of publication (84).

11. Wickham, 'Fragment of an Autobiography' (Smith 119).

12. Wickham's family believe that Anna never took this invitation by Garnett seriously, but that she did value his friendship highly.

13. See Jones, *Anna Wickham* 126, 163, 166, 210, 237, 264. See also *The Collected Letters of Dylan Thomas* 691.

14. By the contemporary Australian composer, Theodore Dollarhide. See also 'Domestic Economy', musical setting by Enid Luff, 1980.

15. I heard the poem when I visited Wickham's only surviving son, George Hepburn, and her daughter-in-law, Margaret Hepburn, at Anna Wickham's house on Parliament Hill at Hampstead Heath. Margaret Hepburn married Anna Wickham's oldest son, James Hepburn (dec.).

16. The separation lasted two years.

17. Letter, Anna Wickham to Natalie Barney, 9 February 1927, Private collection. The letters are also held in the Fonds Littéraire Jacques Doucet, Bibliothèque Sainte Geneviève, Paris.

18. Letter, Anna Wickham to Natalie Barney, Private collection, and Fonds Littéraire, Jacques Doucet Bibliothèque.

19. Unfortunately, Barney's letters to Wickham were destroyed when a firebomb fell on Wickham's house during the war.

20. James is James Joyce, Ford is Ford Maddox Ford, Tonnerre is Elisabeth de Gramont, Duchess of Clermont-Tonnerre, Barnes is Djuna Barnes, Loy is Mina Loy, Stein is Gertrude Stein, Letter, Anna Wickham to Natalie Barney, 30 March 1927, Private collection.

21. Benstock 12. Barney, the American millionairess and writer, lived in a two-storey house at 20 Rue Jacob, Sixth Arrondissement, Paris between 1911 and 1972. Every Friday evening between 5 and 8 pm from 1909 until about 1960, this 'wild girl from Cincinnati' conducted a salon (Saloman Reinach qtd in Wickes 8).

22. Wickham had four sons: James, John, Richard and George. Richard died in 1921 of scarlet fever, aged four.

23. The full autobiography is *Prélude à un Nettoyage de Printemps* (1991); it is partially published in English in R. D. Smith's edited collection. *The Writings of Anna Wickham* (1984).

24. Field quotes this letter, but gives no further information about it, in 'A Wild Colonial Girl', p. 4.

25. Letter, Anne Wickham to Natalie Barney, 13 February 1928. Private collection and Jacques Doucet Bibliothèque.

26. Letter, Anna Wickham to Kate O'Brien, 23 June 1938. Papers of Anna Wickham, British Library, BL 71894

Works Cited

Barney, Natalie Clifford. *Adventures of the Mind.* Trans. J. S. Gatton. New York: New York UP, 1992.

Benstock, Shari. *Women of the Left Bank.* Austin: U of Texas P, 1986.

Cline, Sally. *Radclyffe Hall.* Woodstock, New York: Overlook, 1998.

Colum, Padraic. 'Chap Books and Broadsheets.' Rev. of Anna Wickham. *The Contemplative Quarry. Poetry* Aug. 1915: 252-56.

Ferris, Paul, ed. *The Collected Letters of Dylan Thomas.* London: Dent, 1985.

Field, Andrew. 'A Wild Colonial Girl.' *Age Monthly Review,* February 1984: 3-6.

Dollarhide, Theodore. 'A Love Letter.' [Musical setting.] Sydney: Australian Music Centre, 1999.

Garnett, David. Introduction. *Selected Poems by Anna Wickham.* London: Chatto & Windus, 1971. 7-11.

———, ed. *Selected Poems by Anna Wickham.* London: Chatto & Windus, 1971.

Greer, Germaine. *Slip-Shod Sybils.* London: Viking, 1995.

———, ed. *101 Poems by 101 Poets.* London: Faber and Faber, 2001.

Hamnett, Nina. *Laughing Torso: Reminiscences of Nina Hamnett.* 1932. London: Virago, 1984.

Hampton, Susan, and Kate Llewellyn, eds. *The Penguin Book of Australian Women Poets.* Ringwood, Vic: Penguin, 1986.

Jones, Jennifer Vaughan. *Anna Wickham: A Poet's Daring Life.* Lanham, Maryland: Madison Books, 2003.

———. 'The Poetry and Place of Anna Wickham, 1910-1930.' PhD Diss., University of Wisconsin, Madison, 1994.

Keegan, Paul, ed. *The New Penguin Book of English Verse.* London: Penguin, 2000.

Kunitz, Stanley J., and H. Haycraft, eds. *Twentieth Century Authors.* New York: Wilson, 1942.

Larkin, Philip, ed. *The Oxford Book of Twentieth-Century English Verse.* Oxford: Clarendon P, 1973.

Lever, Susan, ed. *The Oxford Book of Australian Women's Verse.* Melbourne: Oxford UP, 1995.

Luff, Enid. *Swn dwr/The Sound of Water.* London: Primavera, 1980.

Newlin, Margaret. 'Anna Wickham: "The sexless part which is my mind".' *Southern, Review* 14.2 (1978): 281-302.

O'Connor, Mark, ed. *Two Centuries of Australian Poetry.* Melbourne: Oxford UP, 1988.

Rice, Nelljean McConeghey. *A New Matrix for Modernism: A Study of the Lives and Poetry of Charlotte Mew and Anna Wickham.* New York: Routledge, 2002.

Schenck, C. 'Anna Wickham.' *The Gender of Modernism.* Ed. Bonnie Kime Scott. Bloomington: Indiana UP, 1990. 613-621.

Smith, R. D., ed. *The Writings of Anna Wickham.* London: Virago, 1984.

Untermeyer, Louis. Introduction. *The Contemplative Quarry and The Man with the Hammer.* By Anna Wickham. Ed. Louis Untermeyer. New York: Harcourt Brace, 1921. vii-x.

———, ed. *The Contemplative Quarry and The Man with the Hammer.* By Anna Wickham. New York: Harcourt Brace, 1921.

———, ed. *Modern American and Modern British Poetry.* New York: Harcourt Brace, 1950.

Vickery, Ann. 'Between a Modernist Passport and House Arrest: Anna Wickham and the Question of Cultural Identity.' *Soundings: Poetry and Poetics.* Ed. Lyn Jacobs and Jeri Kroll. Proceedings of the Third Biennial National Conference on Poetry, Adelaide, 1998. Adelaide: Wakefield, 1998. 26-36.

Wickes, George. *The Amazon of Letters.* London: W. H. Allen, 1977.

Wickham, Anna. *The Contemplative Quarry.* London: Poetry Bookshop, 1915.

———. Letters. Private Collection, London.

———. Letters. Fonds Littéraire Jacques Doucet, Bibliothèque Sainte Geneviève, Paris.

———. Papers, British Library, BL71894.

———. *Prélude à un Nettoyage de Printemps.* Trans. Jean-Louis Chevalier. Paris: Editions des Cendres, 1991.

———. *Songs of John Oland.* London: Women's Printing Society, 1911.

———. 'The Spirit of the Lawrence Women: A Posthumous Memoir.' *Texas Quarterly* 9.3 (1966): 31-50.

———. *Thirty-Six New Poems.* London: Richards, 1936.

Yeats, W. B. *Collected Poems.* London: Macmillan Papermac, 1982.

Raymond Evans (essay date 2008)

SOURCE: Evans, Raymond. "A Queensland Reader: Discovering the Queensland Writer." *Queensland Review* 15, no. 2 (2008): 69-80.

[*In the following essay, Evans discusses the relative obscurity of Wickham in Australia as a starting point for a more general treatment of the phenomenon of notable authors who have left Queensland and received little critical attention there.*]

An old friend, Jim Cleary, working on the monumental *Bibliography of Australian Literature* at the University of Queensland, recently rang to tell me about the elusive modernist poet Anna Wickham. 'Wickham' is the pen-name of Edith Alice Mary Harper, 'one of the most significant feminist poets of modernism', who published between the 1910s and the 1930s.[1] The author of over one thousand poems, covering a remarkable diversity of forms, Wickham was described in the memoir of American publisher Louis Untermeyer as 'a remarkable gypsy of a woman'.[2] During her tempestuous life, she mixed with members of the London Chelsea and Bloomsbury sets, plunged into the literary and artistic circles of the Parisian *demi-monde,* had a brief sexual relationship with pioneer American modernist poet H. D. (Hilda Dolittle), was sexually spurned by lesbian heiress and literary patron Natalie Clifford Barney, and became closely aligned with D. H. Lawrence and his wife Frieda von Richthofen, as well as Dylan Thomas

and Caitlin MacNamara, falling out with the latter couple after throwing a drunken 'Thomas and fellow writer Lawrence Durrell out of the house'.[3] She was also close friends with the erratic novelist Malcolm Lowry, whetted the appetites of Henry Miller and Anaïs Nin, and helped to mentor the young Stephen Spender. Somewhat like T. S. Eliot's wife Vivien Haigh-Wood, she was incarcerated at one point in a mental institution by her husband, solicitor Patrick Hepburn. And, like Sylvia Plath and Anne Sexton, she died by her own hand, hanging herself in her decaying home on Parliament Hill, London, following the freezing winter of 1947.

Wickham was born at Wimbledon, Sussex in 1883, but her birth as a poet occurred some years later on the streets of Brisbane, Queensland. In 1885-86, at barely eighteen months old, Edith Harper had migrated to Australia with her mother, Alice Whelan Harper, a *fin-de-siècle* 'New Woman'. After a brief stint in Sydney, they returned to England, but in 1889 sailed again for Queensland to join her father, Geoffrey Harper, an otherworldly piano tuner whose principal desire in life was to enjoy 'empty hours for dreams and a quiet room to write about them'.[4] The unstable family was reunited in Maryborough, afterwards moving to Hughenden in 1892 and the following year to Brisbane where her mother's mental difficulties, drug-taking and suicidal depressions worsened. As the years passed, young Edith would compose poetry and recite it to her disconsolate father. In a 'Fragment of an Autobiography', dealing largely with her Australian years, the poet describes the origin of her metamorphosis into the persona of 'Anna Wickham':

> On Sunday night, walking on Wickham Terrace, we came to a point equidistant between the Church of England [All Saints] and the Presbyterian Church [St Andrews]. Hymns were blaring out of both. My father put his arms around me, begging me with great tenderness to promise him that I would be a poet when I grew up. I gave him my word, and when my first set of verses was printed . . . I signed them 'Wickham' in memory of that curious and very emotional pact.[5]

This incident probably occurred in 1896, when the family was living in Gowrie House, Wickham Terrace. Her description accords with the vicinity of the Terrace's intersection with Turbot Street.

Around the same time, Geoffrey Harper was somewhat curiously informed by Queensland's premier poet, James Brunton Stephens, living at nearby Spring Hill, that Edith 'will be a poet on a condition you could hardly wish since you are her father: she will be a poet if she has pain enough'.[6] Wickham's poems are indeed infused with pain, and have been negatively critiqued on that ground by Germaine Greer. Her convent schooling at All Hallows, Brisbane, as well as beatings with a 'rawhide strip' by her unstable mother, have been suggested as contributing factors.[7] Wickham herself wrote, 'the truth is that I believed in pain. I believed that by suffering and endurance I was working out some salvation.'[8] She left Brisbane for Sydney with her family in late 1896 and sailed on alone for London in 1904, her father calling from the dock, '*Punch,* Anna, *Punch*!'[9] Her loud 'coo-ees' later echoed along certain London streets. She wrote:

> I'll make a bond with Bundaberg
> And dedicate my powers
> To a young dream
> By Flinders stream
> And strength of Charters Towers . . .[10]

Though Wickham has been regarded seriously by anthologists and feminist scholars in the United States and Britain for some time, until quite recently she has remained virtually unknown in Australia. Observed from the viewpoint of a Queensland cultural historian, she may be regarded as yet another one who got away. The Queensland diaspora of creative talent is vast and the story of Queensland's cultural heritage, when told in full, is infused with biographies of isolation, loss, withdrawal, escape and self-chosen exile. Queensland is, historically, often a place for writing about rather than in: a good place perhaps to be born or to grow up in (and perhaps to reminisce about later, usually from afar), but not to survive in professionally as an artist or writer. For a reader or researcher, trying to find those tiny, shiny needles of creativity in the big, dull haystack of unconcern that was (and, to a considerable extent, still is) Queensland, the retrieval task is frustratingly daunting, with the quarry usually hard to pin-point in a disjointed tale, full of those tantalising flashes of what might have been.

I had cause to reflect on such matters recently when I was asked to launch the ambitious collection, *By the Book: A Literary History of Queensland,* edited by Patrick Buckridge and Belinda McKay at the Griffith University Co-Op Bookshop in August 2007. I had already heard the celebrated novelist and poet David Malouf speak of this collection at an omnibus launch of several titles at the University of Queensland the previous month. Malouf, naturally enough, approached the work as a cultural practitioner who was himself a subject of the text at various points. I decided to consider it from the viewpoint of what I substantially am: in my professional capacity, certainly, a Queensland historian, but more fundamentally a Queensland reader. Here is something of what I had to say:

> In the early to mid-1960s, when I was in my late teens and early twenties, I was a member of the local junior division of PEN—Poets, Essayists and Novelists; and our little group used to meet regularly at various venues in inner Brisbane (much like the Barjai movement of

the 1940s) to read aloud and critique our various creative endeavours. At one point, we even published a small poetry journal, *Aleph,* that survived for just one issue.

At our meetings, we were sometimes addressed by local writers—Thom Shapcott, James Devaney, Oodgeroo Noonuccal (then still known as Kath Walker, a newly published, pioneering Aboriginal poet), Rodney Hall and Judith Wright. I was, at this time, an undergraduate and then postgraduate at the University of Queensland, and Wright, David Rowbotham, Val Vallis, Eunice Hanger and Cecil Hadgraft were all teaching there, out of the English Department. Among my fellow students were the poets Graham Rowlands, Ryll McMaster and Barbara Brooks, the novelist David Denholm, the feminist writer Eileen Haley, daughter of the militantly Catholic poet Martin Haley, the famous-artist-to-be Mike Parr and the essayist and budding Marxist historian Humphrey McQueen.

Prior to this, I had attended Ashgrove State Primary School, where James Brunton Stephens had once served as headmaster, and on my way home from school I would pass the house of one of Norman Lindsay's formerly (in)famous Rubenesque models. In my early teens, I was a student at Brisbane State High School that a generation earlier had uncomfortably hosted the talented originators of the Barjai movement as well as Lillian Roxon, the world's first serious rock (i.e. rock'n'roll) critic, to whom Germaine Greer would dedicate *The Female Eunuch.* I lived at Bardon, where the ageing poet Paul Grano ran our corner store, rather like 'old . . . Mr Morgan of the local corner grocery' in one of his early poems.[11] Gwen Harwood had once lived—and held her musical soirees—at Grimes Street in neighbouring Auchenflower, and Steele Rudd and George Essex Evans, both writers of Welsh background, were buried in the local cemetery.

Most of these names appear—usually more than once—in *By the Book* and, as I roll them out, it may also begin to appear as though 1960s Brisbane was a vibrant cultural place, where one stumbled upon famous creative figures around every corner or under every tombstone. If this were so, however, why didn't I feel that way at the time? Why did I think, instead, that Brisbane—and Queensland generally—was a culturally arid place, with no writerly or painterly traditions to speak of, to feel proud or even slightly confident about?

The answer to this probably lies not so much in what had been or was being produced, but in the milieu of its reception—that is, the readerly milieu. Local creativity for most readers hardly rated. It was there. It was tolerated. But it was scarcely seen as something to skite about. I was apparently one of those readers about whom the American booster of Australian literature, C. Hartley Grattan had written: '[Readers] who feel safer with a third-rate English or American book than with a first-rate Australian book. They cannot believe that those they see and know can write good books.'[12] Furthermore, I had largely been educated to think like that. At high school, we studied the canonical British authors; for Australian writers, we were handed crib-sheets to save us from direct contact with such works.

So, while ironically as a member of PEN I was beginning to fancy myself, in my callow youthfulness, as a promising poet, I did not hold the real poets around me in any high regard. Why would I read Wright or Shapcott or Rowbotham or Hall when I could read Allen Ginsberg or Dylan Thomas or Günter Grass or Yevgeny Yevtushenko? I'd see the slim local efforts on display at the University of Queensland bookshop, but they would hardly rate a second glance. One had to be discerning: there was so much to read and do, and so little time. I no doubt suffered from what literary critic, A. A. Phillips called 'a disease of the Australian mind'—the steadfast, though sterile, conviction that anything created on the home-ground was *ipso facto* inferior to the imported product.[13] In the 1960s, this disease was of epidemic proportions, though few recognised it as such. It was like a genetic defect we all shared and hardly noticed. In the various Queensland history theses I wrote at this time, I prefaced the accounts with quotes from American writers Stephen Crane and Allen Ginsberg, and the British poet Stephen Spender, but never with the pertinent impressions of a local author.

But then, in the early 1970s, when I began researching the local World War I home front for my doctorate, I came across something that stopped me in my tracks. It is quoted in full in *By the Book,* so I'll just reprise some of it here:

The hills are bright in the sun;
There is nothing changed or marred in the well-known
    places;
When work for the day is done
There is talk and quiet laughter and gleams of fun
On the old folks' faces.
I have returned to these:
The farm, the kindly Bush, and the young calves low-
    ing.
But all that my mind sees
Is a quaking bog in a mist—stark snapped trees
And the dark Somme flowing.[14]

It was, of course, Vance Palmer's 'The Farmer Remembers the Somme'—and I registered it, to my surprise, as being of world-class quality. Vance and Nettie Palmer had lived at Pumicestone Passage, Caloundra where I had regularly gone with my parents for holidays as a child, and there was something undeniably thrilling in realising that this compelling work had sprung from that familiar earth.

Soon afterwards, I stumbled on Brisbane poet Zora Cross's 'Elegy on an Australian Schoolboy', written to her brother John Skyring Cross, killed in the Great War. It was so arrestingly modern in its sensibility. Rather than being a typically grating Anzac panegyric, it was a powerful anti-war statement, published in 1921. And, in a time of scalding anti-German hatred, at one point in this long, epic poem, Cross bravely informs her dead brother:

Your mate, your German mate—you know the one,
Fair-haired, tender and true—
Your best beloved came, his lesson done,
Last night and mourned for you . . .[15]

Eventually, I would also encounter David Malouf's *Johnno,* which spoke with such unerring panache and a

quiet, persistent lyricism of the down-at-heel, slatternly Brisbane I had entered as a young Welsh migrant in 1949.

And then there was this—a poem that, as a young Queensland historian struggling to come to grips with all the lost knowledge of this elusive place, again pulled me up with a start:

Australia was peopled by ghosts. They died
To create silence. Think of the death of ghosts
A hundred years and no one looks backward . . .
The place of the triangle is now Wallace Bishop the
    Watch Specialist.
The first graveyard became the Roma Street Markets
    is now a Parking Lot.
The Tower Mill means a motel vantage point above
    the Logan Treadmill
(National Trust). There are no ghosts rapping
against your car widow
tonight. At the Women's Infirmary (now Post Office)
they have been
screaming, chained . . .
as if silence would not resettle.
What was it? No. That was nothing. You hear noth-
    ing.[16]

It was called 'Brisbane in History' by Thom Shapcott . . . Shapcott? That name sounded familiar. Didn't he come once in the early 1960s to PEN and was tolerated that day with our polite condescension?

These images and memories were among the flood of thoughts my mind swam through as I ranged over the various chapters of *By the Book.* Throughout, it made me think of the many poets and novelists who simply plugged on here alone, and with such scant regard, writing because they had to write in a place where, even by the 1960s, it was still considered, in journalist Allan Ashbolt's ironic words, that 'writing—just writing—was no career. For a fop or a fool perhaps, but not for a man.'[17] Women, of course, wrote as an extension of embroidery or as a diversion from reproduction and Hoovering.

I thought, too, of those many creative ones who fled this place to find some appreciative recognition somewhere, some recompense—financial or otherwise—in the actual communication of their talent. It is a very long list of writers, painters, sculptors, dancers, singers, cartoonists, dramatists, actors, filmmakers, and so on who went away, often for good. Queensland, perhaps more than other Australian colonies and states, has acted historically as some sort of infernal engine that expels talented, creative people, catapulting them interstate or across the globe. I heard Janette Turner Hospital, the expatriate writer, speaking on ABC Radio National's *Bookshow* in March 2007; she exclaimed of Queensland and South Carolina, where she was then billeted: *'Are these places real?'*—that is, the Deep North and the Deep South. On the one hand, she said, their outlandishness and eccentricity, locally mistaken for a normalcy to which everyone then diligently conformed, made them both something of a paradise for authors seeking stunning creative copy, but it was a paradise better savoured as an observant sojourner than as a persistent resident. And it was never going to thank you overly much for your keen observations.[18]

Then there were those strange birds who flew *into* the eye of the cyclone. They actually chose to come here to squat down from successful careers elsewhere—not so much to find new acclaim but to create an anonymous 'possie' to hide away in. Queensland is such a gigantic place, it is ideal to disappear into; if you are not a sporting identity or a television or film celebrity, then anonymity is assured. Putting marginality to work for you, you can be fairly certain that you will left alone to do what you do. In this regard, I was reading recently how Owsley Stanley some years ago purchased a remote section of Queensland rainforest as his destination of choice. I'm sure, as Queenslanders, few would have ever heard of him, but Stanley is known worldwide as father of the global 1960s counter-culture. It was he who manufactured—quite legally at the time—the mass doses of LSD, 'Monterey Purple' and 'White Lightning' that powered the Monterey Pop Festival, the Los Angeles 'Human Be-in' and the 1967 'Summer of Love' in San Francisco. He moulded the consciousness-altering antics of Ken Kesey's Merry Pranksters and the iconoclastic sounds of Jimi Hendrix and the Grateful Dead. He was also the inspiration behind Tom Wolfe's *Electric Kool-Aid Acid Test*—and he now luxuriates *incognito* somewhere in innocent, bucolic Queensland.[19]

So too, in the literary and artistic spheres, we find Judith Wright and Jack McKinney hunkering down at Mt Tamborine (near New Theatre playwright Jim Crawford and painter Pamela Seeman), Colin Thiele at Pine Rivers, Jungian landscape artist Lawrence Daws at the Glasshouse Mountains, Eleanor Dark at Montville, John Manifold at semi-rural Wynnum North, the painter Ian Fairweather in splendid isolation on Bribie Island, playwright David Williamson at Sunshine Beach. Xavier Herbert at tiny Redlynch outside Cairns, and so forth. All *in* the place, but never entirely *of* the place, and employing their marginality to discipline the production of their art: to soak up the uneasy majesty of their natural environments as well as the madness that can be Queensland without being crushed by it.

So the literary history of Queensland and the *other* history of Queensland—its story of materialist struggle and capitalist 'development'—do tend to sit rather awkwardly side by side. One could rarely call them comfortable bedfellows. Until quite recently, they were more like estranged tenants or perhaps simmeringly bad neighbours, inhabiting the same building. It seems to be mainly the coo-ee of the bush balladeer that is happily recognised and answered by the larger Queensland public, or perhaps the unfortunate penchant of so many of our earlier writers to indulge, time and again, in ill-disguised expressions of racism—especially towards Aboriginal peoples.

Queensland writers, for the most part, have had a very rough trot, so it is reassuring to see their works being seriously considered in their various regional contexts in this volume. For all their marginalisation over the years, it is instructive to find that when one comes to think hard upon what one truly loves or respects about this place, it is its neglected creative figures who bulk large in that consideration. The writings of David Malouf, Judith Wright, Xavier Herbert, Thea Astley, Janet Turner Hospital, David Rowbotham and, more recently,

Andrew McGahan, Gerard Lee, Venero Armanno and Melissa Lucashenko stand tall against any other writing. When you are of this place yourself, the best of it carries an especial capacity to touch you to the marrow—as when Judith Wright declares:

> We with our quick dividing eyes
> Measure, distinguish and are gone.
> The forest burns, the tree-frog dies,
> Yet one is all and all are one.[20]

Once upon a time, I placed American and British poets at the head of my historical writings. In my latest work, *A History of Queensland,* Paul Grano and Judith Wright introduce a story that is concluded with the words of Brian Penton, Philip Mead and Henry Lawson.[21] Reading *By the Book* is like hearing a familiar roll-call, echoing from the neglected margins and regions to the centres of attention at long last.

Since delivering this talk, and after absorbing another new cultural exploration by William Hatherell, *The Third Metropolis: Imagining Brisbane Through Art and Literature, 1940-1970,* I have been reconsidering some of my conclusions, particularly regarding myself as an oblivious Queensland reader in the 1960s. For it is much more complex and nuanced than that. Despite Grattan's chidings, I doubt very much that I *was* being drawn to second- and third-rate overseas works rather than giving first-rate Australian ones a chance. Apart from those quick, adolescent rummagings through popular potboilers, such as *Peyton Place* or *King's Row,* to uncover titillating sexual passages, I was reading at most times first-rate American, British and European fiction, plays and poetry. When Janette Turner Hospital writes 'we porpoised through books, we dived into argument',[22] I see myself and my compatriots, avidly sampling and discussing global culture. In daily diaries I kept in 1964 and 1966, as I entered my early twenties, I recorded reading hundreds of books, including works by Edward Albee, James Baldwin, Samuel Beckett, Ray Bradbury, Lawrence Durrell, William Faulkner, Jules Feiffer, Eugene Ionesco, Mary McCarthy, Arthur Miller, Iris Murdoch, Clifford Odets, Harold Pinter, J. D. Salinger, John Steinbeck, Nathanael West, Tennessee Williams, Thomas Wolfe and Emile Zola. I read the Beat and Liverpool poets, Dylan and R. S. Thomas, W. H. Auden, T. S. Eliot and e. e. cummings, Robert Graves, Gerard Manley Hopkins, Philip Larkin, Robert Lowell, Edwin Muir, Stephen Spender, Walt Whitman, W. B. Yeats and many others. My magazines were *Private Eye, Punch,* Harvey Kurzman's *Help!, Time* and *Nation.* I was also starting to compile a library on film, popular music, art, world history, deviance and social control, sexuality and race relations. Furthermore, in the first half of 1967, I recorded watching roughly 130 films from some of the world's best cinema. None of these movies was Australian, for there was no local film industry. There was no doubt a touch of cultural cringe about the entire selection, but also, I would argue, at least a comparable amount of aesthetic discernment. The only Australian novelists at the time who I felt could hold a candle to those listed above were Patrick White, Henry Handel Richardson, Xavier Herbert, perhaps Frank Hardy at his best and, a little later, Thomas Keneally. None of these writers was a Queenslander. And the only Australian magazines I was reading were *Oz* and *Overland.*[23]

I felt, if anything, cosseted and reassured by this sustaining welter of global literature and film while living in what appeared to be an unconcerned, innocent (no doubt ignorant) and often flagrantly hostile socio-cultural milieu. This was a world in which most forms of modernist expression were considered suspect and insurgent, and all manifestations of popular culture—film, jazz, rock'n'roll, progressive folk music, blues, science fiction, pop art, cartooning, satire, underground comics and so forth—genres that I and my circle were beginning to regard both seriously and devotedly, were dismissed as beneath Art—as meaningless and probably dangerous dross. Brisbane was such a narrow-minded, frightened little place, so easily shocked that it was a simple matter to become subversive merely by appearing different. Barrie Reid in later life would recall being apprehended by police on an inner-city street in the early Cold War era for wearing a yellow pullover.[24] Queensland's censorship of books, films and magazines was arguably more Draconian than anywhere in the Western world. Recent scholarship has determined that Australian Customs banned more than 16,000 cultural items between the 1930s and the 1960s,[25] but Queensland from the mid-1950s felt the necessity of imposing an additional tier of heavy-handed censorings. Catholic Queensland either matched or outdid Catholic Ireland and Catholic Spain in this regard—and Queensland had not even endured a civil war. One of my pressing concerns in the 1960s lay in procuring and reading banned novels of note: James Baldwin's *Another Country,* Brendan Behan's *Borstal Boy,* William Burroughs' *Naked Lunch,* J. P. Donleavy's *The Ginger Man,* James Joyce's *Ulysses,* D. H. Lawrence's *Lady Chatterley's Lover,* Norman Mailer's *Why We Are in Vietnam,* Steven Marcus's *The Other Victorians,* Henry Miller's *Tropic of Capricorn* (and *Cancer*), Vladimir Nabokov's *Lolita.* Philip Roth's *Portnoy's Complaint,* and so forth. At the time, I considered it almost my intellectual duty to do so. If the Queensland or Australian authorities were against it, then I was consequently for it. The process was akin to drug smuggling or escaping to freedom on the underground railroad.

Wowsers in Queensland strode confidently across the dry plains of Antipodean philistinism, stretching away into the distance as far as the eye could see. Their extremism was part chilling, part comical—as when, on a March night in 1969, a dozen plain-clothed police and customs officials raided the home of revered local sculptor Daphne Mayo, on the trail of artistic obscenity (i.e. 'nudes'), yelling up at the frightened, elderly woman,

'Open the door or we'll smash it in!' A month later, police arrested actor Norman Staines on the stage of the Twelfth Night Theatre for uttering Alex Buzo's closing epithet, 'Fuckin' boong!' in his anti-racist play, *Norm and Ahmed.*[26] No prizes for guessing the word deemed 'obscene'. So it is not surprising that Queensland was hardly considered fertile ground for uncovering cutting-edge culture, nor Brisbane a friendly place for the bookish. The breezy tone of cultural nescience was breathtaking. An acquaintance whose flute was stolen was asked to draw a picture of one at the local police station by the musically challenged officers. Another two friends, somewhat optimistically selling fine art reproductions door to door in South-East Queensland, were met at one home with this memorable exchange:

HUSBAND

(at door, calling to wife in kitchen): 'There's some fellas out here selling Art . . .'

WIFE

(in kitchen, calling back): 'Tell them we're alright for Art at the moment.'[27]

Hatherell's *Third Metropolis* demonstrates how thoroughly Queensland's cultural institutions were dominated by a coterie of romantically orientated, often militantly Catholic conservatives (such as Martin Haley and Paul Grano) or doctrinaire, leftist anti-modernists (such as John Manifold, championing his bush ballads) in the two decades following World War II, as well as how limited, overall, local literary output actually was. The impression is of a society losing or expelling, and then promptly forgetting, its more progressive and experimental writers (such as the vastly talented Barjai practitioners, as well as some of the *Meanjin* ensemble), while its conservatives and traditionalists, jealously guarding the flame, provided the only ongoing sense of cultural generation and continuity. Herein lay the perceptual trap for a Queensland reader such as myself. From 1958 to 1961, I had attended Brisbane State High School where the Barjai movement had originated but, during my time there, not once was any clue ever dropped about the historical presence of this inventive fellowship. I did not learn of its existence until the late 1990s. All that I perceived of Queensland's literary culture during the 1960s was a relatively uninteresting and largely regressive dribble of output from the Queensland Authors' and Artists' Association (QAAA) or the Realist Writers' Group, both engaged upon a last-ditch, rearguard action against modernist influences that had already swept the rest of the Western world decades earlier. The campaign was akin to that of the fundamentalist, evangelical church I had once attended, still vehemently conducting its weekly fights with Charles Darwin. Laurie Collinson captured the tone of the QAAA acerbically (but beautifully) in 1944 when he wrote:

Then out they went into the night
their tongues all dripping with praise—
they know they won't need culture now
for another ninety days.[28]

By the 1960s, they still appeared to meander on in the same imperious, precautionary vein, increasingly courting the ire of younger, more radical and exploratory writers. In 1964, when James Devaney addressed the Realist Writers on 'Christian Thought in Post-War Poetry', a group of young PEN members (myself included) attended the lecture. We were blithely unaware of the vehemence of Devaney's crusading anti-modernism until he began to chide those he would call 'the Eliotites'[29] and to extol escapist, romantic conceptions of beauty (neatly packaged in rhyming iambs) as the only pure goal of poetry. One of our number, Terry Hannagan, a talented poet, songwriter and blues performer, began to interject angrily from the floor, and our small group eventually walked out of the meeting. I came home quivering and wrote a poem about the encounter that ran in part:

He spoke
as arbiter between
all beauty, all ugliness
calmly . . .
as though exhibiting on leash
a performing angel and ape . . .
He would not have me realize
God in a stable stench
Or the milling gore of a lynching.[30]

Two years later, the artist and writer, Mike Parr similarly confronted Gladstone poet Val Vallis as he was lecturing to a large first-year English class at the University of Queensland. Parr, then a student himself, interjected forcefully from the audience against the common academic practice of intellectual vivisection of the living poem, and an extended interchange ensued. I wrote in my diary of 1 June 1966:

Kay [Saunders] went off to her lecture and I went up to Jim [Cleary, studying in the History Department vestibule]. Kay came in an hour: 'Guess what! Mike was high in the lecture; took on Vallis and annihilated him . . .' We went down . . . Mike was shaking . . . [He] talked and talked. He must go. Today . . . They could not understand. He was almost crying . . . We went to the Royal Exchange [Hotel]. Mike said a great weight had lifted. He was free again . . . Without much ceremony, but with close [sic] thanks . . . he went. We shook his one hand . . . I came home, my head bursting and went to bed.[31]

This climactic encounter marked Parr's withdrawal from his Arts degree at the University of Queensland and firmed up his independent trajectory towards becoming a globally recognised performance artist and printmaker. Both Hannagan and Parr, like so many others, left Queensland for Sydney and the world.

So we were not so much cringing readers as passionate ones, armoured in our conviction of the worth of so much deemed locally worthless, or simply overlooked with apathy and incomprehension. Long before Foco opened its doors at the Brisbane Trades Hall in 1968 to experimental cultural forms, we were building our own informal networks of creativity, comradeship and discussion—at the Primitiv coffee lounge, the Folk Club, PEN, the American Book Store, the Brisbane Cinema Group, the Royal Exchange, the Red and Black Bookshop, the University of Queensland Refectory and Forum, and so forth. These were our safe houses in an environment of social and political violence, framed by censorship, policing, surveillance, suspicion, incoherence and rage. That violence, sometimes made explicit, was always threatening. Like the traditional foco, we combined cultural appreciation and creativity with protest from the streets. One cannot know this era culturally without understanding this. I did not read Queensland writers, I now realise, because Queensland then seemed to offer absolutely no hope of revelation or redemption. Writ large, it was experienced pre-eminently as an *anti*-cultural state. It was only later, as I engaged in the deep reading that comes with every historical project, that I gradually came to recognise, with surprise and delight, the lost, brilliant and unheralded ones who had stumbled away, in a thin, serial formation down the years from this hard, intractable place, and began the slow task of returning them to memory.

Notes

With thanks to Les Clayton, Jim Cleary, Heather Neilsen and Jahara Rhiannon.

1. A. Pender, '"Phrases Between Us": The Poetry of Anna Wickham', *Australian Literary Studies*, October 2005, www.highbeam.com/doc/1G1-1389452408.htm.

2. J. V. Jones, *Anna Wickham. A Poet's Daring Life* (London: Madison Books, 2003), 155.

3. J. V. Jones, 'Houseful of Memories from the Turbulent life of Anna', www.camdennewjournal.co.uk/archives.

4. A. Wickham, 'Fragment of an Autobiography', in *A New Matrix for Modernism: A Study of the Lives and Poetry of Charlotte Mew and Anna Wickham*, ed. N. M. Rice (New York: Routledge, 2002), 77.

5. Wickham, 'Fragment', 102.

6. Wickham, 'Fragment', 101.

7. Jones, *Wickham*, 22; Pender, 'Phrases'. This was a reference to her father's connection to a *Punch* magazine cartoonist and the opportunity it might provide.

8. R. D. Smith, ed., *The Writings of Anna Wickham: Free Woman and Poet* (London: Virago, 1984), 157.

9. Rice, *New Matrix,* 85.

10. A. Wickham, 'Old Faith', in Jones, *Wickham,* 27-28.

11. P. Grano, 'In a Chain Store Cafeteria', in *The Third Metropolis: Imagining Brisbane Through Art and Literature.* ed. W. Hatherell (St Lucia: University of Queensland Press, 2007), 84.

12. C. Hartley Grattan, *Australian Literature,* 38, cited in G. Serle, *From Deserts the Prophets Come: The Creative Spirit in Australia 1788-1972* (Melbourne: Heinemann, 1973), 135.

13. See A. A. Phillips, *The Australian Tradition* (Melbourne: Cheshire, 1958).

14. V. Palmer, 'The Farmer Remembers the Somme', in *Other Banners: An Anthology of Australian Literature of the First World* War, ed. J. T. Laird (Canberra: Australian War Memorial, 1971), 130.

15. Z. Cross, *Elegy on an Australian Schoolboy* (Sydney: Angus & Robertson, 1921), 12.

16. T. Shapcott, 'Brisbane in History', in *Place and Perspective: Contemporary Queensland Poetry,* ed. B. O'Donohue (Brisbane: Jacaranda, 1984), 191-92.

17. A. Ashbolt, 'The Great Literary Witch-hunt of 1952', in *Australia's First Cold War. Volume One: Society, Communism and Culture,* eds A. Curthoys and J. Merritt (Sydney: Allen & Unwin, 1984), 179.

18. J. Turner Hospital, interviewed on *The Book Show.* ABC National Radio, 9 March 2007.

19. R. Greenfield, 'The King of LSD', *Rolling Stone: The Fortieth Anniversary: Summer of Love 1967* (American edition) 1030/1031, 12-26 July 2007: 115-22.

20. J. Wright, 'Rainforest', in V. Brady, *South of My Days: A Biography of Judith Wright* (Sydney: Angus & Robertson, 1998), 483.

21. R. Evans, *A History of Queensland* (Melbourne: Cambridge University Press, 2007), v, 1, 271.

22. J. Turner Hospital, 'The Ocean of Brisbane', in Hatherell, *The Third Metropolis,* 226.

23. R. Evans, Diaries, 1964, 1966 and 1967 (in possession of author).

24. Personal communication with Anna King Murdoch, April 2008.

25. Nicole Moore, Senior Lecturer, Macquarie University, interviewed on ABC National Radio, 24 July 2007.

26. D. Lake, 'A Piscian Chronicle—Queensland, 1969', in *Australia's Censorship Crisis,* eds G. Dutton and M. Harris (Melbourne: Sun Books, 1970), 112-15.

27. Personal communications with Heather Neilsen and Les Clayton, May 2008.

28. L. Collinson in *Barjai* 14, 1944: 13, cited in Hatherell, *Third Metropolis,* pp. 123-24; see also J. Watson, 'Lyceum Club', in *Radical Brisbane: An Unruly History,* eds R. Evans and C. Ferrier (Melbourne: Vulgar Press, 2004), 219-28.

29. Hatherell, *The Third Metropolis,* 72 and 158.

30. R. Evans, 'On an Editorial' in The Unlove Poems, written during the Vietnam years, 1962-72, unpublished, in possession of author.

31. R. Evans, Diary entry, 1 June 1966; see also D. Broomfield, *Identities: A Critical Study of the Work of Mike Parr, 1970-1990* (Nedlands: University of Western Australia Press, 1991).

FURTHER READING

Criticism

Dowson, Jane. "Anna Wickham 1884-1947." In *Women's Poetry of the 1930s: A Critical Anthology,* edited by Jane Dowson, pp. 165-74. London: Routledge, 1996.
  Brief overview of Wickham's life and career, along with a number of her poems.

Dowson, Jane Alice Entwistle. "'I will put myself, and everything I see, upon the page': Charlotte Mew, Sylvia Townsend Warner, Anna Wickham and the Dramatic Monologue." In *A History of Twentieth-Century British Women's Poetry,* pp. 71-84. Cambridge: Cambridge University Press, 2005.
  Comparison of the Victorian dramatic monologues of three women poets, including Wickham.

Newlin, Margaret. "Anna Wickham: 'The Sexless Part which Is My Mind.'" *Southern Review* 14, no. 2 (April 1978): 281-302.
  Provides information on Wickham's life and an analysis of her poetry, arguing that the poet has been unjustly ignored by the majority of critics.

Stark, Myra. "Feminist Themes in Anna Wickham's 'The Contemplative Quarry' and 'The Man with a Hammer.'" *Four Decades of Poetry 1890-1930* 2, no. 2 (July 1978): 101-06.

Argues for the reconsideration of Wickham as a successful feminist poet, drawing many comparisons between Wickham and such poets as Sylvia Plath and Adrienne Rich.

Additional coverage of Wickham's life and career is contained in the following sources published by Gale: *Dictionary of Literary Biography,* **Vol. 240 and** *Literature Resource Center.*

How to Use This Index

The main references

Calvino, Italo
1923-1985 .... CLC **5, 8, 11, 22, 33, 39,**
73; SSC 3, 48

list all author entries in the following Gale Literary Criticism series:

AAL = *Asian American Literature*
BG = *The Beat Generation: A Gale Critical Companion*
BLC = *Black Literature Criticism*
BLCS = *Black Literature Criticism Supplement*
CLC = *Contemporary Literary Criticism*
CLR = *Children's Literature Review*
CMLC = *Classical and Medieval Literature Criticism*
DC = *Drama Criticism*
FL = *Feminism in Literature: A Gale Critical Companion*
GL = *Gothic Literature: A Gale Critical Companion*
HLC = *Hispanic Literature Criticism*
HLCS = *Hispanic Literature Criticism Supplement*
HR = *Harlem Renaissance: A Gale Critical Companion*
LC = *Literature Criticism from 1400 to 1800*
NCLC = *Nineteenth-Century Literature Criticism*
NNAL = *Native North American Literature*
PC = *Poetry Criticism*
SSC = *Short Story Criticism*
TCLC = *Twentieth-Century Literary Criticism*
WLC = *World Literature Criticism, 1500 to the Present*
WLCS = *World Literature Criticism Supplement*

The cross-references

See also CA 85-88, 116; CANR 23, 61;
DAM NOV; DLB 196; EW 13; MTCW 1, 2;
RGSF 2; RGWL 2; SFW 4; SSFS 12

list all author entries in the following Gale biographical and literary sources:

AAYA = *Authors & Artists for Young Adults*
AFAW = *African American Writers*
AFW = *African Writers*
AITN = *Authors in the News*
AMW = *American Writers*
AMWR = *American Writers Retrospective Supplement*
AMWS = *American Writers Supplement*
ANW = *American Nature Writers*
AW = *Ancient Writers*
BEST = *Bestsellers*
BPFB = *Beacham's Encyclopedia of Popular Fiction: Biography and Resources*
BRW = *British Writers*
BRWS = *British Writers Supplement*
BW = *Black Writers*
BYA = *Beacham's Guide to Literature for Young Adults*
CA = *Contemporary Authors*
CAAS = *Contemporary Authors Autobiography Series*
CABS = *Contemporary Authors Bibliographical Series*
CAD = *Contemporary American Dramatists*
CANR = *Contemporary Authors New Revision Series*
CAP = *Contemporary Authors Permanent Series*
CBD = *Contemporary British Dramatists*
CCA = *Contemporary Canadian Authors*
CD = *Contemporary Dramatists*
CDALB = *Concise Dictionary of American Literary Biography*

CDALBS = *Concise Dictionary of American Literary Biography Supplement*
CDBLB = *Concise Dictionary of British Literary Biography*
CMW = *St. James Guide to Crime & Mystery Writers*
CN = *Contemporary Novelists*
CP = *Contemporary Poets*
CPW = *Contemporary Popular Writers*
CSW = *Contemporary Southern Writers*
CWD = *Contemporary Women Dramatists*
CWP = *Contemporary Women Poets*
CWRI = *St. James Guide to Children's Writers*
CWW = *Contemporary World Writers*
DA = *DISCovering Authors*
DA3 = *DISCovering Authors 3.0*
DAB = *DISCovering Authors: British Edition*
DAC = *DISCovering Authors: Canadian Edition*
DAM = *DISCovering Authors: Modules*
   DRAM: *Dramatists Module;* **MST:** *Most-studied Authors Module;*
   MULT: *Multicultural Authors Module;* **NOV:** *Novelists Module;*
   POET: *Poets Module;* **POP:** *Popular Fiction and Genre Authors Module*
DFS = *Drama for Students*
DLB = *Dictionary of Literary Biography*
DLBD = *Dictionary of Literary Biography Documentary Series*
DLBY = *Dictionary of Literary Biography Yearbook*
DNFS = *Literature of Developing Nations for Students*
EFS = *Epics for Students*
EW = *European Writers*
EWL = *Encyclopedia of World Literature in the 20th Century*
EXPN = *Exploring Novels*
EXPP = *Exploring Poetry*
EXPS = *Exploring Short Stories*
FANT = *St. James Guide to Fantasy Writers*
FW = *Feminist Writers*
GFL = *Guide to French Literature,* Beginnings to 1789, 1798 to the Present
GLL = *Gay and Lesbian Literature*
HGG = *St. James Guide to Horror, Ghost & Gothic Writers*
HW = *Hispanic Writers*
IDFW = *International Dictionary of Films and Filmmakers: Writers and Production Artists*
IDTP = *International Dictionary of Theatre: Playwrights*
LAIT = *Literature and Its Times*
LAW = *Latin American Writers*
JRDA = *Junior DISCovering Authors*
MAICYA = *Major Authors and Illustrators for Children and Young Adults*
MAICYAS = *Major Authors and Illustrators for Children and Young Adults Supplement*
MAWW = *Modern American Women Writers*
MJW = *Modern Japanese Writers*
MTCW = *Major 20th-Century Writers*
NCFS = *Nonfiction Classics for Students*
NFS = *Novels for Students*
PAB = *Poets: American and British*
PFS = *Poetry for Students*
RGAL = *Reference Guide to American Literature*
RGEL = *Reference Guide to English Literature*
RGSF = *Reference Guide to Short Fiction*
RGWL = *Reference Guide to World Literature*
RHW = *Twentieth-Century Romance and Historical Writers*
SAAS = *Something about the Author Autobiography Series*
SATA = *Something about the Author*
SFW = *St. James Guide to Science Fiction Writers*
SSFS = *Short Stories for Students*
TCWW = *Twentieth-Century Western Writers*
WLIT = *World Literature and Its Times*
WP = *World Poets*
YABC = *Yesterday's Authors of Books for Children*
YAW = *St. James Guide to Young Adult Writers*

Literary Criticism Series
Cumulative Author Index

Alegria, Claribel 1924- .... **CLC 75; HLCS 1; PC 26**
See also CA 131; CAAS 15; CANR 66, 94, 134; CWW 2; DAM MULT; DLB 145, 283; EWL 3; HW 1; MTCW 2; MTFW 2005; PFS 21

Alegria, Claribel Joy
See Alegria, Claribel

Alegria, Jose de 1918-2005 .... **CLC 57**
See also CA 9-12R; CANR 5, 32, 72; EWL 3; HW 1, 2

Aleixandre, Vicente 1898-1984 .... **HLCS 1; TCLC 113**
See also CANR 81; DLB 108, 329; EWL 3; HW 2; MTCW 1, 2; RGWL 2, 3

Alekseev, Konstantin Sergeivich
See Stanislavsky, Constantin

Alekseyer, Konstantin Sergeyevich
See Stanislavsky, Constantin

Aleman, Mateo 1547-1615(?) .... **LC 81**

Alencar, Jose de 1829-1877 .... **NCLC 157**
See also DLB 307; LAW; WLIT 1

Alencon, Marguerite d'
See de Navarre, Marguerite

Alepoudelis, Odysseus
See Elytis, Odysseus

Aleshkovsky, Joseph 1929- .... **CLC 44**
See also CA 121; 128; DLB 317

Aleshkovsky, Yuz
See Aleshkovsky, Joseph

Alexander, Barbara
See Ehrenreich, Barbara

Alexander, Lloyd 1924-2007 .... **CLC 35**
See also AAYA 1, 27; BPFB 1; BYA 5, 6, 7, 9, 10, 11; CA 1-4R; 260; CANR 1, 24, 38, 55, 113; CLR 1, 5, 48; CWRI 5; DLB 52; FANT; JRDA; MAICYA 1, 2; MAIC-YAS 1; MTCW 1; SAAS 19; SATA 3, 49, 81, 129, 135; SATA-Obit 182; SUFW; TUS; WYA; YAW

Alexander, Lloyd Chudley
See Alexander, Lloyd

Alexander, Meena 1951- .... **CLC 121**
See also CA 115; CANR 38, 70, 146; CP 5, 6, 7; CWP; DLB 323; FW

Alexander, Rae Pace
See Alexander, Raymond Pace

Alexander, Raymond Pace
1898-1974 .... **SSC 62**
See also CA 97-100; SATA 22; SSFS 4

Alexander, Samuel 1859-1938 .... **TCLC 77**

Alexeiev, Konstantin
See Stanislavsky, Constantin

Alexeyev, Constantin Sergeivich
See Stanislavsky, Constantin

Alexeyev, Konstantin Sergeyevich
See Stanislavsky, Constantin

Alexie, Sherman 1966- .... **CLC 96, 154; NNAL; PC 53; SSC 107**
See also AAYA 28; BYA 15; CA 138; CANR 65, 95, 133, 174; CN 7; DA3; DAM MULT; DLB 175, 206, 278; LATS 1:2; MTCW 2; MTFW 2005; NFS 17, 31; SSFS 18

Alexie, Sherman Joseph, Jr.
See Alexie, Sherman

al-Farabi 870(?)-950 .... **CMLC 58**
See also DLB 115

Alfau, Felipe 1902-1999 .... **CLC 66**
See also CA 137

Alfieri, Vittorio 1749-1803 .... **NCLC 101**
See also EW 4; RGWL 2, 3; WLIT 7

Alfonso X 1221-1284 .... **CMLC 78**

Alfred, Jean Gaston
See Ponge, Francis

Alger, Horatio, Jr. 1832-1899 .... **NCLC 8, 83**
See also CLR 87; DLB 42; LAIT 2; RGAL 4; SATA 16; TUS

Al-Ghazali, Muhammad ibn Muhammad
1058-1111 .... **CMLC 50**
See also DLB 115

Algren, Nelson 1909-1981 ..... **CLC 4, 10, 33; SSC 33**
See also AMWS 9; BPFB 1; CA 13-16R; 103; CANR 20, 61; CDALB 1941-1968; CN 1, 2; DLB 9; DLBY 1981, 1982, 2000; EWL 3; MAL 5; MTCW 1, 2; MTFW 2005; RGAL 4; RGSF 2

al-Hamadhani 967-1007 .... **CMLC 93**
See also WLIT 6

al-Hariri, al-Qasim ibn 'Ali Abu Muhammad al-Basri
1054-1122 .... **CMLC 63**
See also RGWL 3

Ali, Ahmed 1908-1998 .... **CLC 69**
See also CA 25-28R; CANR 15, 34; CN 1, 2, 3, 4, 5; DLB 323; EWL 3

Ali, Tariq 1943- .... **CLC 173**
See also CA 25-28R; CANR 10, 99, 161, 196

Alighieri, Dante
See Dante

al-Kindi, Abu Yusuf Ya'qub ibn Ishaq c.
801-c. 873 .... **CMLC 80**

Allan, John B.
See Westlake, Donald E.

Allan, Sidney
See Hartmann, Sadakichi

Allan, Sydney
See Hartmann, Sadakichi

Allard, Janet CLC 59

Allen, Betsy
See Harrison, Elizabeth (Allen) Cavanna

Allen, Edward 1948- .... **CLC 59**

Allen, Fred 1894-1956 .... **TCLC 87**

Allen, Paula Gunn 1939-2008 . **CLC 84, 202, 280; NNAL**
See also AMWS 4; CA 112; 143; 272; CANR 63, 130; CWP; DA3; DAM MULT; DLB 175; FW; MTCW 2; MTFW 2005; RGAL 4; TCWW 2

Allen, Roland
See Ayckbourn, Alan

Allen, Sarah A.
See Hopkins, Pauline Elizabeth

Allen, Sidney H.
See Hartmann, Sadakichi

Allen, Woody 1935- ..... **CLC 16, 52, 195, 288**
See also AAYA 10, 51; AMWS 15; CA 33-36R; CANR 27, 38, 63, 128, 172; DAM POP; DLB 44; MTCW 1; SSFS 21

Allende, Isabel 1942- ... **CLC 39, 57, 97, 170, 264; HLC 1; SSC 65; WLCS**
See also AAYA 18, 70; CA 125; 130; CANR 51, 74, 129, 165; CDWLB 3; CLR 99; CWW 2; DA3; DAM MULT, NOV; DLB 145; DNFS 1; EWL 3; FL 1:5; FW; HW 1, 2; INT CA-130; LAIT 5; LAWS 1; LMFS 2; MTCW 1, 2; MTFW 2005; NCFS 1; NFS 6, 18, 29; RGSF 2; RGWL 3; SATA 163; SSFS 11, 16; WLIT 1

Alleyn, Ellen
See Rossetti, Christina

Alleyne, Carla D. CLC 65

Allingham, Margery (Louise)
1904-1966 .... **CLC 19**
See also CA 5-8R; 25-28R; CANR 4, 58; CMW 4; DLB 77; MSW; MTCW 1, 2

Allingham, William 1824-1889 ...... **NCLC 25**
See also DLB 35; RGEL 2

Allison, Dorothy E. 1949- . **CLC 78, 153, 290**
See also AAYA 53; CA 140; CANR 66, 107; CN 7; CSW; DA3; DLB 350; FW; MTCW 2; MTFW 2005; NFS 11; RGAL 4

Alloula, Malek CLC 65

Allston, Washington 1779-1843 .... **NCLC 2**
See also DLB 1, 235

Almedingen, E. M.
See Almedingen, Martha Edith von

Almedingen, Martha Edith von
1898-1971 .... **CLC 12**
See also CA 1-4R; CANR 1; SATA 3

Almodovar, Pedro 1949(?)- .... **CLC 114, 229; HLCS 1**
See also CA 133; CANR 72, 151; HW 2

Almqvist, Carl Jonas Love
1793-1866 .... **NCLC 42**

al-Mutanabbi, Ahmad ibn al-Husayn Abu al-Tayyib al-Jufi al-Kindi
915-965 .... **CMLC 66**
See also RGWL 3; WLIT 6

Alonso, Damaso 1898-1990 .... **CLC 14**
See also CA 110; 131; 130; CANR 72; DLB 108; EWL 3; HW 1, 2

Alov
See Gogol, Nikolai

al'Sadaawi, Nawal
See El Saadawi, Nawal

al-Shaykh, Hanan 1945- .... **CLC 218**
See also CA 135; CANR 111; CWW 2; DLB 346; EWL 3; WLIT 6

Al Siddik
See Rolfe, Frederick (William Serafino Austin Lewis Mary)

Alta 1942- .... **CLC 19**
See also CA 57-60

Alter, Robert B. 1935- .... **CLC 34**
See also CA 49-52; CANR 1, 47, 100, 160, 201

Alter, Robert Bernard
See Alter, Robert B.

Alther, Lisa 1944- .... **CLC 7, 41**
See also BPFB 1; CA 65-68; CAAS 30; CANR 12, 30, 51, 180; CN 4, 5, 6, 7; CSW; GLL 2; MTCW 1

Althusser, L.
See Althusser, Louis

Althusser, Louis 1918-1990 .... **CLC 106**
See also CA 131; 132; CANR 102; DLB 242

Altman, Robert 1925-2006 .... **CLC 16, 116, 242**
See also CA 73-76; 254; CANR 43

Alurista
See Urista, Alberto

Alvarez, A. 1929- .... **CLC 5, 13**
See also CA 1-4R; CANR 3, 33, 63, 101, 134; CN 3, 4, 5, 6; CP 1, 2, 3, 4, 5, 6, 7; DLB 14, 40; MTFW 2005

Alvarez, Alejandro Rodriguez
1903-1965 . **CLC 49; DC 32; TCLC 199**
See also CA 131; 93-96; EWL 3; HW 1

Alvarez, Julia 1950- ... **CLC 93, 274; HLCS 1**
See also AAYA 25; AMWS 7; CA 147; CANR 69, 101, 133, 166; DA3; DLB 282; LATS 1:2; LLW; MTCW 2; MTFW 2005; NFS 5, 9; SATA 129; SSFS 27, 31; WLIT 1

Alvaro, Corrado 1896-1956 .... **TCLC 60**
See also CA 163; DLB 264; EWL 3

Amado, Jorge 1912-2001 ... **CLC 13, 40, 106, 232; HLC 1**
See also CA 77-80; 201; CANR 35, 74, 135; CWW 2; DAM MULT, NOV; DLB 113, 307; EWL 3; HW 2; LAW; LAWS 1; MTCW 1, 2; MTFW 2005; RGWL 2, 3; TWA; WLIT 1

Ambler, Eric 1909-1998 .... **CLC 4, 6, 9**
See also BRWS 4; CA 9-12R; 171; CANR 7, 38, 74; CMW 4; CN 1, 2, 3, 4, 5, 6; DLB 77; MSW; MTCW 1, 2; TEA

Ambrose c. 339-c. 397 .... **CMLC 103**

Ambrose, Stephen E. 1936-2002 .... **CLC 145**
See also AAYA 44; CA 1-4R; 209; CANR 3, 43, 57, 83, 105; MTFW 2005; NCFS 2; SATA 40, 138

Antiphon c. 480B.C.-c. 411B.C. .... **CMLC 55**

Antoine, Marc
See Proust, Marcel

Antoninus, Brother
See Everson, William

Antonioni, Michelangelo
1912-2007 .... **CLC 20, 144, 259**
See also CA 73-76; 262; CANR 45, 77

Antschel, Paul
See Celan, Paul

Anwar, Chairil 1922-1949 .... **TCLC 22**
See also CA 121; 219; EWL 3; RGWL 3

Anyidoho, Kofi 1947- .... **BLC 2:1**
See also BW 3; CA 178; CP 5, 6, 7; DLB
157; EWL 3

Anzaldua, Gloria (Evanjelina)
1942-2004 .... **CLC 200; HLCS 1**
See also CA 175; 227; CSW; CWP; DLB
122; FW; LLW; RGAL 4; SATA-Obit 154

Apess, William 1798-1839(?) .... **NCLC 73;**
NNAL
See also DAM MULT; DLB 175, 243

Apollinaire, Guillaume 1880-1918 .... **PC 7;**
TCLC 3, 8, 51
See also CA 104; 152; DAM POET; DLB
258, 321; EW 9; EWL 3; GFL 1789 to
the Present; MTCW 2; PFS 24; RGWL 2,
3; TWA; WP

Apollonius of Rhodes
See Apollonius Rhodius

Apollonius Rhodius c. 300B.C.-c.
220B.C. .... **CMLC 28**
See also AW 1; DLB 176; RGWL 2, 3

Appelfeld, Aharon 1932- ... **CLC 23, 47; SSC**
42
See also CA 112; 133; CANR 86, 160;
CWW 2; DLB 299; EWL 3; RGHL;
RGSF 2; WLIT 6

Appelfeld, Aron
See Appelfeld, Aharon

Apple, Max (Isaac) 1941- .... **CLC 9, 33; SSC**
50
See also AMWS 17; CA 81-84; CANR 19,
54; DLB 130

Appleman, Philip (Dean) 1926- .... **CLC 51**
See also CA 13-16R; CAAS 18; CANR 6,
29, 56

Appleton, Lawrence
See Lovecraft, H. P.

Apteryx
See Eliot, T. S.

Apuleius, (Lucius Madaurensis) c. 125-c.
164 .... **CMLC 1, 84**
See also AW 2; CDWLB 1; DLB 211;
RGWL 2, 3; SUFW; WLIT 8

Aquin, Hubert 1929-1977 .... **CLC 15**
See also CA 105; DLB 53; EWL 3

Aquinas, Thomas 1224(?)-1274 ..... **CMLC 33**
See also DLB 115; EW 1; TWA

Aragon, Louis 1897-1982 .... **CLC 3, 22;**
TCLC 123
See also CA 69-72; 108; CANR 28, 71;
DAM NOV, POET; DLB 72, 258; EW 11;
EWL 3; GFL 1789 to the Present; GLL 2;
LMFS 2; MTCW 1, 2; RGWL 2, 3

Arany, Janos 1817-1882 .... **NCLC 34**

Aranyos, Kakay 1847-1910
See Mikszath, Kalman

Aratus of Soli c. 315B.C.-c.
240B.C. .... **CMLC 64, 114**
See also DLB 176

Arbuthnot, John 1667-1735 .... **LC 1**
See also BRWS 16; DLB 101

Archer, Herbert Winslow
See Mencken, H. L.

Archer, Jeffrey 1940- .... **CLC 28**
See also AAYA 16; BEST 89:3; BPFB 1;
CA 77-80; CANR 22, 52, 95, 136; CPW;
DA3; DAM POP; INT CANR-22; MTFW
2005

Archer, Jeffrey Howard
See Archer, Jeffrey

Archer, Jules 1915- .... **CLC 12**
See also CA 9-12R; CANR 6, 69; SAAS 5;
SATA 4, 85

Archer, Lee
See Ellison, Harlan

Archilochus c. 7th cent. B.C.- .... **CMLC 44**
See also DLB 176

Ard, William
See Jakes, John

Arden, John 1930- .... **CLC 6, 13, 15**
See also BRWS 2; CA 13-16R; CAAS 4;
CANR 31, 65, 67, 124; CBD; CD 5, 6;
DAM DRAM; DFS 9; DLB 13, 245;
EWL 3; MTCW 1

Arenas, Reinaldo 1943-1990 .. **CLC 41; HLC**
1; TCLC 191
See also CA 124; 128; 133; CANR 73, 106;
DAM MULT; DLB 145; EWL 3; GLL 2;
HW 1; LAW; LAWS 1; MTCW 2; MTFW
2005; RGSF 2; RGWL 3; WLIT 1

Arendt, Hannah 1906-1975 .... **CLC 66, 98;**
TCLC 193
See also CA 17-20R; 61-64; CANR 26, 60,
172; DLB 242; MTCW 1, 2

Aretino, Pietro 1492-1556 .... **LC 12, 165**
See also RGWL 2, 3

Arghezi, Tudor
See Theodorescu, Ion N.

Arguedas, Jose Maria 1911-1969 .... **CLC 10,**
18; HLCS 1; TCLC 147
See also CA 89-92; CANR 73; DLB 113;
EWL 3; HW 1; LAW; RGWL 2, 3; WLIT
1

Argueta, Manlio 1936- .... **CLC 31**
See also CA 131; CANR 73; CWW 2; DLB
145; EWL 3; HW 1; RGWL 3

Arias, Ron 1941- .... **HLC 1**
See also CA 131; CANR 81, 136; DAM
MULT; DLB 82; HW 1, 2; MTCW 2;
MTFW 2005

Ariosto, Lodovico
See Ariosto, Ludovico

Ariosto, Ludovico 1474-1533 ... **LC 6, 87; PC**
42
See also EW 2; RGWL 2, 3; WLIT 7

Aristides
See Epstein, Joseph

Aristides Quintilianus fl. c. 100-fl. c.
400 .... **CMLC 122**

Aristophanes 450B.C.-385B.C. .... **CMLC 4,**
51; DC 2; WLCS
See also AW 1; CDWLB 1; DA; DA3;
DAB; DAC; DAM DRAM, MST; DFS
10; DLB 176; LMFS 1; RGWL 2, 3;
TWA; WLIT 8

Aristotle 384B.C.-322B.C. .... **CMLC 31, 123;**
WLCS
See also AW 1; CDWLB 1; DA; DA3;
DAB; DAC; DAM MST; DLB 176;
RGWL 2, 3; TWA; WLIT 8

Arlt, Roberto 1900-1942 .. **HLC 1; TCLC 29**
See also CA 123; 131; CANR 67; DAM
MULT; DLB 305; EWL 3; HW 1, 2;
IDTP; LAW

Arlt, Roberto Godofredo Christophersen
See Arlt, Roberto

Armah, Ayi Kwei 1939- . **BLC 1:1, 2:1; CLC**
5, 33, 136
See also AFW; BRWS 10; BW 1; CA 61-
64; CANR 21, 64; CDWLB 3; CN 1, 2,
3, 4, 5, 6, 7; DAM MULT, POET; DLB
117; EWL 3; MTCW 1; WLIT 2

Armatrading, Joan 1950- .... **CLC 17**
See also CA 114; 186

Armin, Robert 1568(?)-1615(?) .... **LC 120**

Armitage, Frank
See Carpenter, John

Armstrong, Jeannette (C.) 1948- .... **NNAL**
See also CA 149; CCA 1; CN 6, 7; DAC;
DLB 334; SATA 102

Arnauld, Antoine 1612-1694 .... **LC 169**
See also DLB 268

Arnette, Robert
See Silverberg, Robert

Arnim, Achim von (Ludwig Joachim von
Arnim) 1781-1831 .. **NCLC 5, 159; SSC**
29
See also DLB 90

Arnim, Bettina von 1785-1859 ...... **NCLC 38,**
123
See also DLB 90; RGWL 2, 3

Arnold, Matthew 1822-1888 ..... **NCLC 6, 29,**
89, 126, 218; PC 5, 94; WLC 1
See also BRW 5; CDBLB 1832-1890; DA;
DAB; DAC; DAM MST, POET; DLB 32,
57; EXPP; PAB; PFS 2; TEA; WP

Arnold, Thomas 1795-1842 .... **NCLC 18**
See also DLB 55

Arnow, Harriette (Louisa) Simpson
1908-1986 ...... **CLC 2, 7, 18; TCLC 196**
See also BPFB 1; CA 9-12R; 118; CANR
14; CN 2, 3, 4; DLB 6; FW; MTCW 1, 2;
RHW; SATA 42; SATA-Obit 47

Arouet, Francois-Marie
See Voltaire

Arp, Hans
See Arp, Jean

Arp, Jean 1887-1966 .... **CLC 5; TCLC 115**
See also CA 81-84; 25-28R; CANR 42, 77;
EW 10

Arrabal
See Arrabal, Fernando

Arrabal, Fernando 1932- .. **CLC 2, 9, 18, 58;**
DC 35
See also CA 9-12R; CANR 15; CWW 2;
DLB 321; EWL 3; LMFS 2

Arrabal Teran, Fernando
See Arrabal, Fernando

Arreola, Juan Jose 1918-2001 .... **CLC 147;**
HLC 1; SSC 38
See also CA 113; 131; 200; CANR 81;
CWW 2; DAM MULT; DLB 113; DNFS
2; EWL 3; HW 1, 2; LAW; RGSF 2

Arrian c. 89(?)-c. 155(?) .... **CMLC 43**
See also DLB 176

Arrick, Fran
See Angell, Judie

Arrley, Richmond
See Delany, Samuel R., Jr.

Artaud, Antonin 1896-1948 ... **DC 14; TCLC**
3, 36
See also CA 104; 149; DA3; DAM DRAM;
DFS 22; DLB 258, 321; EW 11; EWL 3;
GFL 1789 to the Present; MTCW 2;
MTFW 2005; RGWL 2, 3

Artaud, Antonin Marie Joseph
See Artaud, Antonin

Arthur, Ruth M(abel) 1905-1979 ..... **CLC 12**
See also CA 9-12R; 85-88; CANR 4; CWRI
5; SATA 7, 26

Artsybashev, Mikhail (Petrovich)
1878-1927 .... **TCLC 31**
See also CA 170; DLB 295

Arundel, Honor (Morfydd)
1919-1973 .... **CLC 17**
See also CA 21-22; 41-44R; CAP 2; CLR
35; CWRI 5; SATA 4; SATA-Obit 24

Arzner, Dorothy 1900-1979 .... **CLC 98**

Asch, Sholem 1880-1957 .... **TCLC 3**
See also CA 105; DLB 333; EWL 3; GLL
2; RGHL

Bastos, Augusto Roa
　See Roa Bastos, Augusto
Bataille, Georges 1897-1962 .... **CLC 29;**
　　TCLC 155
　See also CA 101; 89-92; EWL 3
Bates, H(erbert) E(rnest)
　　1905-1974 .... **CLC 46; SSC 10**
　See also CA 93-96; 45-48; CANR 34; CN
　　1; DA3; DAB; DAM POP; DLB 162, 191;
　　EWL 3; EXPS; MTCW 1, 2; RGSF 2;
　　SSFS 7
Bauchart
　See Camus, Albert
Baudelaire, Charles 1821-1867 . **NCLC 6, 29,**
　　55, 155; PC 1, 106; SSC 18; WLC 1
　See also DA; DA3; DAB; DAC; DAM
　　MST, POET; DLB 217; EW 7; GFL 1789
　　to the Present; LMFS 2; PFS 21; RGWL
　　2, 3; TWA
Baudouin, Marcel
　See Peguy, Charles (Pierre)
Baudouin, Pierre
　See Peguy, Charles (Pierre)
Baudrillard, Jean 1929-2007 .... **CLC 60**
　See also CA 252; 258; DLB 296
Baum, L. Frank 1856-1919 ...... **TCLC 7, 132**
　See also AAYA 46; BYA 16; CA 108; 133;
　　CLR 15, 107; CWRI 5; DLB 22; FANT;
　　JRDA; MAICYA 1, 2; MTCW 1, 2; NFS
　　13; RGAL 4; SATA 18, 100; WCH
Baum, Louis F.
　See Baum, L. Frank
Baum, Lyman Frank
　See Baum, L. Frank
Baumbach, Jonathan 1933- .... **CLC 6, 23**
　See also CA 13-16R; 284; CAAE 284;
　　CAAS 5; CANR 12, 66, 140; CN 3, 4, 5,
　　6, 7; DLBY 1980; INT CANR-12; MTCW
　　1
Bausch, Richard 1945- .... **CLC 51**
　See also AMWS 7; CA 101; CAAS 14;
　　CANR 43, 61, 87, 164, 200; CN 7; CSW;
　　DLB 130; MAL 5
Bausch, Richard Carl
　See Bausch, Richard
Baxter, Charles 1947- .... **CLC 45, 78**
　See also AMWS 17; CA 57-60; CANR 40,
　　64, 104, 133, 188; CPW; DAM POP; DLB
　　130; MAL 5; MTCW 2; MTFW 2005;
　　TCLE 1:1
Baxter, Charles Morley
　See Baxter, Charles
Baxter, George Owen
　See Faust, Frederick
Baxter, James K(eir) 1926-1972 .... **CLC 14**
　See also CA 77-80; CP 1; EWL 3
Baxter, John
　See Hunt, E. Howard
Bayer, Sylvia
　See Glassco, John
Bayle, Pierre 1647-1706 .... **LC 126**
　See also DLB 268, 313; GFL Beginnings to
　　1789
Baynton, Barbara 1857-1929 . **TCLC 57, 211**
　See also DLB 230; RGSF 2
Beagle, Peter S. 1939- .... **CLC 7, 104**
　See also AAYA 47; BPFB 1; BYA 9, 10,
　　16; CA 9-12R; CANR 4, 51, 73, 110;
　　DA3; DLBY 1980; FANT; INT CANR-4;
　　MTCW 2; MTFW 2005; SATA 60, 130;
　　SUFW 1, 2; YAW
Beagle, Peter Soyer
　See Beagle, Peter S.
Bean, Normal
　See Burroughs, Edgar Rice
Beard, Charles A(ustin)
　　1874-1948 .... **TCLC 15**
　See also CA 115; 189; DLB 17; SATA 18

Beardsley, Aubrey 1872-1898 .... **NCLC 6**
Beatrice of Nazareth 1200-1268 .. **CMLC 114**
Beattie, Ann 1947- ..... **CLC 8, 13, 18, 40, 63,**
　　146; SSC 11, 130
　See also AMWS 5; BEST 90:2; BPFB 1;
　　CA 81-84; CANR 53, 73, 128; CN 4, 5,
　　6, 7; CPW; DA3; DAM NOV, POP; DLB
　　218, 278; DLBY 1982; EWL 3; MAL 5;
　　MTCW 1, 2; MTFW 2005; RGAL 4;
　　RGSF 2; SSFS 9; TUS
Beattie, James 1735-1803 .... **NCLC 25**
　See also DLB 109
Beauchamp, Katherine Mansfield
　See Mansfield, Katherine
Beaumarchais, Pierre-Augustin Caron de
　　1732-1799 .... **DC 4; LC 61**
　See also DAM DRAM; DFS 14, 16; DLB
　　313; EW 4; GFL Beginnings to 1789;
　　RGWL 2, 3
Beaumont, Francis 1584(?)-1616 .. **DC 6; LC**
　　33
　See also BRW 2; CDBLB Before 1660;
　　DLB 58; TEA
Beauvoir, Simone de 1908-1986 .... **CLC 1, 2,**
　　4, 8, 14, 31, 44, 50, 71, 124; SSC 35;
　　TCLC 221; WLC 1
　See also BPFB 1; CA 9-12R; 118; CANR
　　28, 61; DA; DA3; DAB; DAC; DAM
　　MST, NOV; DLB 72; DLBY 1986; EW
　　12; EWL 3; FL 1:5; FW; GFL 1789 to the
　　Present; LMFS 2; MTCW 1, 2; MTFW
　　2005; RGSF 2; RGWL 2, 3; TWA
Beauvoir, Simone Lucie Ernestine Marie
　　Bertrand de
　See Beauvoir, Simone de
Becker, Carl (Lotus) 1873-1945 ..... **TCLC 63**
　See also CA 157; DLB 17
Becker, Jurek 1937-1997 .... **CLC 7, 19**
　See also CA 85-88; 157; CANR 60, 117;
　　CWW 2; DLB 75, 299; EWL 3; RGHL
Becker, Walter 1950- .... **CLC 26**
Becket, Thomas a 1118(?)-1170 .... **CMLC 83**
Beckett, Samuel 1906-1989 ... **CLC 1, 2, 3, 4,**
　　6, 9, 10, 11, 14, 18, 29, 57, 59, 83; DC
　　22; SSC 16, 74; TCLC 145; WLC 1
　See also BRWC 2; BRWR 1; BRWS 1; CA
　　5-8R; 130; CANR 33, 61; CBD; CDBLB
　　1945-1960; CN 1, 2, 3, 4; CP 1, 2, 3, 4;
　　DA; DA3; DAB; DAC; DAM DRAM,
　　MST, NOV; DFS 2, 7, 18; DLB 13, 15,
　　233, 319, 321, 329; DLBY 1990; EWL 3;
　　GFL 1789 to the Present; LATS 1:2;
　　LMFS 2; MTCW 1, 2; MTFW 2005;
　　RGSF 2; RGWL 2, 3; SSFS 15; TEA;
　　WLIT 4
Beckett, Samuel Barclay
　See Beckett, Samuel
Beckford, William 1760-1844 .... **NCLC 16,**
　　214
　See also BRW 3; DLB 39, 213; GL 2; HGG;
　　LMFS 1; SUFW
Beckham, Barry (Earl) 1944- .... **BLC 1:1**
　See also BW 1; CA 29-32R; CANR 26, 62;
　　CN 1, 2, 3, 4, 5, 6; DAM MULT; DLB 33
Beckman, Gunnel 1910- .... **CLC 26**
　See also CA 33-36R; CANR 15, 114; CLR
　　25; MAICYA 1, 2; SAAS 9; SATA 6
Becque, Henri 1837-1899 .... **DC 21; NCLC 3**
　See also DLB 192; GFL 1789 to the Present
Becquer, Gustavo Adolfo
　　1836-1870 .... **HLCS 1; NCLC 106**
　See also DAM MULT
Beddoes, Thomas Lovell 1803-1849 .. **DC 15;**
　　NCLC 3, 154
　See also BRWS 11; DLB 96
Bede c. 673-735 .... **CMLC 20**
　See also DLB 146; TEA

Bedford, Denton R. 1907-(?) .... **NNAL**
Bedford, Donald F.
　See Fearing, Kenneth
Beecher, Catharine Esther
　　1800-1878 .... **NCLC 30**
　See also DLB 1, 243
Beecher, John 1904-1980 .... **CLC 6**
　See also AITN 1; CA 5-8R; 105; CANR 8;
　　CP 1, 2, 3
Beer, Johann 1655-1700 .... **LC 5**
　See also DLB 168
Beer, Patricia 1924- .... **CLC 58**
　See also BRWS 14; CA 61-64; 183; CANR
　　13, 46; CP 1, 2, 3, 4, 5, 6; CWP; DLB
　　40; FW
Beerbohm, Max
　See Beerbohm, (Henry) Max(imilian)
Beerbohm, (Henry) Max(imilian)
　　1872-1956 .... **TCLC 1, 24**
　See also BRWS 2; CA 104; 154; CANR 79;
　　DLB 34, 100; FANT; MTCW 2
Beer-Hofmann, Richard
　　1866-1945 .... **TCLC 60**
　See also CA 160; DLB 81
Beethoven, Ludwig van
　　1770(?)-1827 .... **NCLC 227**
Beg, Shemus
　See Stephens, James
Begiebing, Robert J(ohn) 1946- .... **CLC 70**
　See also CA 122; CANR 40, 88
Begley, Louis 1933- .... **CLC 197**
　See also CA 140; CANR 98, 176; DLB 299;
　　RGHL; TCLE 1:1
Behan, Brendan 1923-1964 ...... **CLC 1, 8, 11,**
　　15, 79
　See also BRWS 2; CA 73-76; CANR 33,
　　121; CBD; CDBLB 1945-1960; DAM
　　DRAM; DFS 7; DLB 13, 233; EWL 3;
　　MTCW 1, 2
Behan, Brendan Francis
　See Behan, Brendan
Behn, Aphra 1640(?)-1689 .. **DC 4; LC 1, 30,**
　　42, 135; PC 13, 88; WLC 1
　See also BRWR 3; BRWS 3; DA; DA3;
　　DAB; DAC; DAM DRAM, MST, NOV,
　　POET; DFS 16, 24; DLB 39, 80, 131; FW;
　　TEA; WLIT 3
Behrman, S(amuel) N(athaniel)
　　1893-1973 .... **CLC 40**
　See also CA 13-16; 45-48; CAD; CAP 1;
　　DLB 7, 44; IDFW 3; MAL 5; RGAL 4
Bekederemo, J. P. Clark
　See Clark-Bekederemo, J. P.
Belasco, David 1853-1931 .... **TCLC 3**
　See also CA 104; 168; DLB 7; MAL 5;
　　RGAL 4
Belben, Rosalind 1941- .... **CLC 280**
　See also CA 291
Belben, Rosalind Loveday
　See Belben, Rosalind
Belcheva, Elisaveta Lyubomirova
　　1893-1991 .... **CLC 10**
　See also CA 178; CDWLB 4; DLB 147;
　　EWL 3
Beldone, Phil "Cheech"
　See Ellison, Harlan
Beleno
　See Azuela, Mariano
Belinski, Vissarion Grigoryevich
　　1811-1848 .... **NCLC 5**
　See also DLB 198
Belitt, Ben 1911- .... **CLC 22**
　See also CA 13-16R; CAAS 4; CANR 7,
　　77; CP 1, 2, 3, 4, 5, 6; DLB 5
Belknap, Jeremy 1744-1798 .... **LC 115**
　See also DLB 30, 37
Bell, Gertrude (Margaret Lowthian)
　　1868-1926 .... **TCLC 67**
　See also CA 167; CANR 110; DLB 174

Breton, Andre 1896-1966 .. **CLC 2, 9, 15, 54; PC 15**
See also CA 19-20; 25-28R; CANR 40, 60; CAP 2; DLB 65, 258; EW 11; EWL 3; GFL 1789 to the Present; LMFS 2; MTCW 1, 2; MTFW 2005; RGWL 2, 3; TWA; WP

Breton, Nicholas c. 1554-c. 1626 .... **LC 133**
See also DLB 136

Breytenbach, Breyten 1939(?)- .. **CLC 23, 37, 126**
See also CA 113; 129; CANR 61, 122, 202; CWW 2; DAM POET; DLB 225; EWL 3

Bridgers, Sue Ellen 1942- .... **CLC 26**
See also AAYA 8, 49; BYA 7, 8; CA 65-68; CANR 11, 36; CLR 18; DLB 52; JRDA; MAICYA 1, 2; SAAS 1; SATA 22, 90; SATA-Essay 109; WYA; YAW

Bridges, Robert (Seymour)
1844-1930 .... **PC 28; TCLC 1**
See also BRW 6; CA 104; 152; CDBLB 1890-1914; DAM POET; DLB 19, 98

Bridie, James
See Mavor, Osborne Henry

Brin, David 1950- .... **CLC 34**
See also AAYA 21; CA 102; CANR 24, 70, 125, 127; INT CANR-24; SATA 65; SCFW 2; SFW 4

Brink, Andre 1935- .... **CLC 18, 36, 106**
See also AFW; BRWS 6; CA 104; CANR 39, 62, 109, 133, 182; CN 4, 5, 6, 7; DLB 225; EWL 3; INT CA-103; LATS 1:2; MTCW 1, 2; MTFW 2005; WLIT 2

Brink, Andre Philippus
See Brink, Andre

Brinsmead, H. F(ay)
See Brinsmead, H(esba) F(ay)

Brinsmead, H. F.
See Brinsmead, H(esba) F(ay)

Brinsmead, H(esba) F(ay) 1922- ...... **CLC 21**
See also CA 21-24R; CANR 10; CLR 47; CWRI 5; MAICYA 1, 2; SAAS 5; SATA 18, 78

Brittain, Vera (Mary)
1893(?)-1970 .... **CLC 23; TCLC 228**
See also BRWS 10; CA 13-16; 25-28R; CANR 58; CAP 1; DLB 191; FW; MTCW 1, 2

Broch, Hermann 1886-1951 ... **TCLC 20, 204**
See also CA 117; 211; CDWLB 2; DLB 85, 124; EW 10; EWL 3; RGWL 2, 3

Brock, Rose
See Hansen, Joseph

Brod, Max 1884-1968 .... **TCLC 115**
See also CA 5-8R; 25-28R; CANR 7; DLB 81; EWL 3

Brodkey, Harold (Roy) 1930-1996 .. **CLC 56; TCLC 123**
See also CA 111; 151; CANR 71; CN 4, 5, 6; DLB 130

Brodskii, Iosif
See Brodsky, Joseph

Brodskii, Iosif Alexandrovich
See Brodsky, Joseph

Brodsky, Iosif Alexandrovich
See Brodsky, Joseph

Brodsky, Joseph 1940-1996 ..... **CLC 4, 6, 13, 36, 100; PC 9; TCLC 219**
See also AAYA 71; AITN 1; AMWS 8; CA 41-44R; 151; CANR 37, 106; CWW 2; DA3; DAM POET; DLB 285, 329; EWL 3; MTCW 1, 2; MTFW 2005; PFS 35; RGWL 2, 3

Brodsky, Michael 1948- .... **CLC 19**
See also CA 102; CANR 18, 41, 58, 147; DLB 244

Brodsky, Michael Mark
See Brodsky, Michael

Brodzki, Bella CLC 65

Brome, Richard 1590(?)-1652 .... **LC 61**
See also BRWS 10; DLB 58

Bromell, Henry 1947- .... **CLC 5**
See also CA 53-56; CANR 9, 115, 116

Bromfield, Louis (Brucker)
1896-1956 .... **TCLC 11**
See also CA 107; 155; DLB 4, 9, 86; RGAL 4; RHW

Broner, E(sther) M(asserman)
1930- .... **CLC 19**
See also CA 17-20R; CANR 8, 25, 72; CN 4, 5, 6; DLB 28

Bronk, William (M.) 1918-1999 .... **CLC 10**
See also CA 89-92; 177; CANR 23; CP 3, 4, 5, 6, 7; DLB 165

Bronstein, Lev Davidovich
See Trotsky, Leon

Bronte, Anne
See Bronte, Anne

Bronte, Anne 1820-1849 ..... **NCLC 4, 71, 102**
See also BRW 5; BRWR 1; DA3; DLB 21, 199, 340; NFS 26; TEA

Bronte, (Patrick) Branwell
1817-1848 .... **NCLC 109**
See also DLB 340

Bronte, Charlotte
See Bronte, Charlotte

Bronte, Charlotte 1816-1855 ...... **NCLC 3, 8, 33, 58, 105, 155, 217; WLC 1**
See also AAYA 17; BRW 5; BRWC 2; BRWR 1; BYA 2; CDBLB 1832-1890; DA; DA3; DAB; DAC; DAM MST, NOV; DLB 21, 159, 199, 340; EXPN; FL 1:2; GL 2; LAIT 2; NFS 4; TEA; WLIT 4

Bronte, Emily
See Bronte, Emily

Bronte, Emily 1818-1848 .... **NCLC 16, 35, 165; PC 8; WLC 1**
See also AAYA 17; BPFB 1; BRW 5; BRWC 1; BRWR 1; BYA 3; CDBLB 1832-1890; DA; DA3; DAB; DAC; DAM MST, NOV, POET; DLB 21, 32, 199, 340; EXPN; FL 1:2; GL 2; LAIT 1; NFS 2; PFS 33; TEA; WLIT 3

Bronte, Emily Jane
See Bronte, Emily

Brontes
See Bronte, Anne; Bronte, (Patrick) Branwell; Bronte, Charlotte; Bronte, Emily

Brooke, Frances 1724-1789 .... **LC 6, 48**
See also DLB 39, 99

Brooke, Henry 1703(?)-1783 .... **LC 1**
See also DLB 39

Brooke, Rupert 1887-1915 . **PC 24; TCLC 2, 7; WLC 1**
See also BRWS 3; CA 104; 132; CANR 61; CDBLB 1914-1945; DA; DAB; DAC; DAM MST, POET; DLB 19, 216; EXPP; GLL 2; MTCW 1, 2; MTFW 2005; PFS 7; TEA

Brooke, Rupert Chawner
See Brooke, Rupert

Brooke-Haven, P.
See Wodehouse, P. G.

Brooke-Rose, Christine 1923(?)- ..... **CLC 40, 184**
See also BRWS 4; CA 13-16R; CANR 58, 118, 183; CN 1, 2, 3, 4, 5, 6, 7; DLB 14, 231; EWL 3; SFW 4

Brookner, Anita 1928- . **CLC 32, 34, 51, 136, 237**
See also BRWS 4; CA 114; 120; CANR 37, 56, 87, 130; CN 4, 5, 6, 7; CPW; DA3; DAB; DAM POP; DLB 194, 326; DLBY 1987; EWL 3; MTCW 1, 2; MTFW 2005; NFS 23; TEA

Brooks, Cleanth 1906-1994 . **CLC 24, 86, 110**
See also AMWS 14; CA 17-20R; 145; CANR 33, 35; CSW; DLB 63; DLBY 1994; EWL 3; INT CANR-35; MAL 5; MTCW 1, 2; MTFW 2005

Brooks, George
See Baum, L. Frank

Brooks, Gwendolyn 1917-2000 .... **BLC 1:1, 2:1; CLC 1, 2, 4, 5, 15, 49, 125; PC 7; WLC 1**
See also AAYA 20; AFAW 1, 2; AITN 1; AMWS 3; BW 2, 3; CA 1-4R; 190; CANR 1, 27, 52, 75, 132; CDALB 1941-1968; CLR 27; CP 1, 2, 3, 4, 5, 6, 7; CWP; DA; DA3; DAC; DAM MST, MULT, POET; DLB 5, 76, 165; EWL 3; EXPP; FL 1:5; MAL 5; MBL; MTCW 1, 2; MTFW 2005; PFS 1, 2, 4, 6, 32; RGAL 4; SATA 6; SATA-Obit 123; TUS; WP

Brooks, Gwendolyn Elizabeth
See Brooks, Gwendolyn

Brooks, Mel 1926-
See Kaminsky, Melvin
See also CA 65-68; CANR 16; DFS 21

Brooks, Peter 1938- .... **CLC 34**
See also CA 45-48; CANR 1, 107, 182

Brooks, Peter Preston
See Brooks, Peter

Brooks, Van Wyck 1886-1963 .... **CLC 29**
See also AMW; CA 1-4R; CANR 6; DLB 45, 63, 103; MAL 5; TUS

Brophy, Brigid 1929-1995 ...... **CLC 6, 11, 29, 105**
See also CA 5-8R; 149; CAAS 4; CANR 25, 53; CBD; CN 1, 2, 3, 4, 5, 6; CWD; DA3; DLB 14, 271; EWL 3; MTCW 1, 2

Brophy, Brigid Antonia
See Brophy, Brigid

Brosman, Catharine Savage 1934- ..... **CLC 9**
See also CA 61-64; CANR 21, 46, 149

Brossard, Nicole 1943- .... **CLC 115, 169; PC 80**
See also CA 122; CAAS 16; CANR 140; CCA 1; CWP; CWW 2; DLB 53; EWL 3; FW; GLL 2; RGWL 3

Brother Antoninus
See Everson, William

Brothers Grimm
See Grimm, Jacob Ludwig Karl; Grimm, Wilhelm Karl

The Brothers Quay
See Quay, Stephen; Quay, Timothy

Broughton, T(homas) Alan 1936- ..... **CLC 19**
See also CA 45-48; CANR 2, 23, 48, 111

Broumas, Olga 1949- .... **CLC 10, 73**
See also CA 85-88; CANR 20, 69, 110; CP 5, 6, 7; CWP; GLL 2

Broun, Heywood 1888-1939 .... **TCLC 104**
See also DLB 29, 171

Brown, Alan 1950- .... **CLC 99**
See also CA 156

Brown, Charles Brockden
1771-1810 .... **NCLC 22, 74, 122**
See also AMWS 1; CDALB 1640-1865; DLB 37, 59, 73; FW; GL 2; HGG; LMFS 1; RGAL 4; TUS

Brown, Christy 1932-1981 .... **CLC 63**
See also BYA 13; CA 105; 104; CANR 72; DLB 14

Brown, Claude 1937-2002 ..... **BLC 1:1; CLC 30**
See also AAYA 7; BW 1, 3; CA 73-76; 205; CANR 81; DAM MULT

Brown, Dan 1964- .... **CLC 209**
See also AAYA 55; CA 217; LNFS 1; MTFW 2005

Castellanos, Rosario 1925-1974 .... **CLC 66; HLC 1; SSC 39, 68**
  See also CA 131; 53-56; CANR 58; CD-WLB 3; DAM MULT; DLB 113, 290; EWL 3; FW; HW 1; LAW; MTCW 2; MTFW 2005; RGSF 2; RGWL 2, 3
Castelvetro, Lodovico 1505-1571 .... **LC 12**
Castiglione, Baldassare 1478-1529 ..... **LC 12, 165**
  See also EW 2; LMFS 1; RGWL 2, 3; WLIT 7
Castiglione, Baldesar
  See Castiglione, Baldassare
Castillo, Ana 1953- .... **CLC 151, 279**
  See also AAYA 42; CA 131; CANR 51, 86, 128, 172; CWP; DLB 122, 227; DNFS 2; FW; HW 1; LLW; PFS 21
Castillo, Ana Hernandez Del
  See Castillo, Ana
Castle, Robert
  See Hamilton, Edmond
Castro (Ruz), Fidel 1926(?)- .... **HLC 1**
  See also CA 110; 129; CANR 81; DAM MULT; HW 2
Castro, Guillen de 1569-1631 .... **LC 19**
Castro, Rosalia de 1837-1885 ... **NCLC 3, 78; PC 41**
  See also DAM MULT
Castro Alves, Antonio de 1847-1871 .... **NCLC 205**
  See also DLB 307; LAW
Cather, Willa 1873-1947 .... **SSC 2, 50, 114; TCLC 1, 11, 31, 99, 132, 152; WLC 1**
  See also AAYA 24; AMW; AMWC 1; AMWR 1; BPFB 1; CA 104; 128; CDALB 1865-1917; CLR 98; DA; DA3; DAB; DAC; DAM MST, NOV; DLB 9, 54, 78, 256; DLBD 1; EWL 3; EXPN; EXPS; FL 1:5; LAIT 3; LATS 1:1; MAL 5; MBL; MTCW 1, 2; MTFW 2005; NFS 2, 19, 33; RGAL 4; RGSF 2; RHW; SATA 30; SSFS 2, 7, 16, 27; TCWW 1, 2; TUS
Cather, Willa Sibert
  See Cather, Willa
Catherine II
  See Catherine the Great
Catherine, Saint 1347-1380 ... **CMLC 27, 116**
Catherine the Great 1729-1796 .... **LC 69**
  See also DLB 150
Cato, Marcus Porcius 234B.C.-149B.C. .... **CMLC 21**
  See also DLB 211
Cato, Marcus Porcius, the Elder
  See Cato, Marcus Porcius
Cato the Elder
  See Cato, Marcus Porcius
Catton, (Charles) Bruce 1899-1978 . **CLC 35**
  See also AITN 1; CA 5-8R; 81-84; CANR 7, 74; DLB 17; MTCW 2; MTFW 2005; SATA 2; SATA-Obit 24
Catullus c. 84B.C.-54B.C. .... **CMLC 18**
  See also AW 2; CDWLB 1; DLB 211; RGWL 2, 3; WLIT 8
Cauldwell, Frank
  See King, Francis (Henry)
Caunitz, William J. 1933-1996 .... **CLC 34**
  See also BEST 89:3; CA 125; 130; 152; CANR 73; INT CA-130
Causley, Charles (Stanley) 1917-2003 .... **CLC 7**
  See also CA 9-12R; 223; CANR 5, 35, 94; CLR 30; CP 1, 2, 3, 4, 5; CWRI 5; DLB 27; MTCW 1; SATA 3, 66; SATA-Obit 149
Caute, (John) David 1936- .... **CLC 29**
  See also CA 1-4R; CAAS 4; CANR 1, 33, 64, 120; CBD; CD 5, 6; CN 1, 2, 3, 4, 5, 6, 7; DAM NOV; DLB 14, 231

Cavafy, C. P.
  See Cavafy, Constantine
Cavafy, Constantine 1863-1933 .... **PC 36; TCLC 2, 7**
  See also CA 104; 148; DA3; DAM POET; EW 8; EWL 3; MTCW 2; PFS 19; RGWL 2, 3; WP
Cavafy, Constantine Peter
  See Cavafy, Constantine
Cavalcanti, Guido c. 1250-c. 1300 .... **CMLC 54**
  See also RGWL 2, 3; WLIT 7
Cavallo, Evelyn
  See Spark, Muriel
Cavanna, Betty
  See Harrison, Elizabeth (Allen) Cavanna
Cavanna, Elizabeth
  See Harrison, Elizabeth (Allen) Cavanna
Cavanna, Elizabeth Allen
  See Harrison, Elizabeth (Allen) Cavanna
Cavendish, Margaret 1623-1673 . **LC 30, 132**
  See also DLB 131, 252, 281; RGEL 2
Cavendish, Margaret Lucas
  See Cavendish, Margaret
Caxton, William 1421(?)-1491(?) .... **LC 17**
  See also DLB 170
Cayer, D. M.
  See Duffy, Maureen
Cayrol, Jean 1911-2005 .... **CLC 11**
  See also CA 89-92; 236; DLB 83; EWL 3
Cela, Camilo Jose
  See Cela, Camilo Jose
Cela, Camilo Jose 1916-2002 .... **CLC 4, 13, 59, 122; HLC 1; SSC 71**
  See also BEST 90:2; CA 21-24R; 206; CAAS 10; CANR 21, 32, 76, 139; CWW 2; DAM MULT; DLB 322; DLBY 1989; EW 13; EWL 3; HW 1; MTCW 1, 2; MTFW 2005; RGSF 2; RGWL 2, 3
Celan, Paul 1920-1970 ... **CLC 10, 19, 53, 82; PC 10**
  See also CA 85-88; CANR 33, 61; CDWLB 2; DLB 69; EWL 3; MTCW 1; PFS 21; RGHL; RGWL 2, 3
Cela y Trulock, Camilo Jose
  See Cela, Camilo Jose
Celine, Louis-Ferdinand 1894-1961 .. **CLC 1, 3, 4, 7, 47, 124**
  See also CA 85-88; CANR 28; DLB 72; EW 11; EWL 3; GFL 1789 to the Present; MTCW 1; RGWL 2, 3
Cellini, Benvenuto 1500-1571 .... **LC 7**
  See also WLIT 7
Cendrars, Blaise
  See Sauser-Hall, Frederic
Centlivre, Susanna 1669(?)-1723 .... **DC 25; LC 65**
  See also DLB 84; RGEL 2
Cernuda, Luis 1902-1963 ..... **CLC 54; PC 62**
  See also CA 131; 89-92; DAM POET; DLB 134; EWL 3; GLL 1; HW 1; RGWL 2, 3
Cernuda y Bidon, Luis
  See Cernuda, Luis
Cervantes, Lorna Dee 1954- ..... **HLCS 1; PC 35**
  See also CA 131; CANR 80; CP 7; CWP; DLB 82; EXPP; HW 1; LLW; PFS 30
Cervantes, Miguel de 1547-1616 . **HLCS; LC 6, 23, 93; SSC 12, 108; WLC 1**
  See also AAYA 56; BYA 1, 14; DA; DAB; DAC; DAM MST, NOV; EW 2; LAIT 1; LATS 1:1; LMFS 1; NFS 8; RGSF 2; RGWL 2, 3; TWA
Cervantes Saavedra, Miguel de
  See Cervantes, Miguel de
Cesaire, Aime
  See Cesaire, Aime

Cesaire, Aime 1913-2008 .... **BLC 1:1; CLC 19, 32, 112, 280; DC 22; PC 25**
  See also BW 2, 3; CA 65-68; 271; CANR 24, 43, 81; CWW 2; DA3; DAM MULT, POET; DLB 321; EWL 3; GFL 1789 to the Present; MTCW 1, 2; MTFW 2005; WP
Cesaire, Aime Fernand
  See Cesaire, Aime
Cesaire, Aime Fernand
  See Cesaire, Aime
Chaadaev, Petr Iakovlevich 1794-1856 .... **NCLC 197**
  See also DLB 198
Chabon, Michael 1963- ... **CLC 55, 149, 265; SSC 59**
  See also AAYA 45; AMWS 11; CA 139; CANR 57, 96, 127, 138, 196; DLB 278; MAL 5; MTFW 2005; NFS 25; SATA 145
Chabrol, Claude 1930- .... **CLC 16**
  See also CA 110
Chairil Anwar
  See Anwar, Chairil
Challans, Mary
  See Renault, Mary
Challis, George
  See Faust, Frederick
Chambers, Aidan 1934- .... **CLC 35**
  See also AAYA 27; CA 25-28R; CANR 12, 31, 58, 116; CLR 151; JRDA; MAICYA 1, 2; SAAS 12; SATA 1, 69, 108, 171; WYA; YAW
Chambers, James CLC 21
  See also CA 124; 199
Chambers, Jessie
  See Lawrence, D. H.
Chambers, Robert W(illiam) 1865-1933 .... **SSC 92; TCLC 41**
  See also CA 165; DLB 202; HGG; SATA 107; SUFW 1
Chambers, (David) Whittaker 1901-1961 .... **TCLC 129**
  See also CA 89-92; DLB 303
Chamisso, Adelbert von 1781-1838 .... **NCLC 82**
  See also DLB 90; RGWL 2, 3; SUFW 1
Chamoiseau, Patrick 1953- ..... **CLC 268, 276**
  See also CA 162; CANR 88; EWL 3; RGWL 3
Chance, James T.
  See Carpenter, John
Chance, John T.
  See Carpenter, John
Chand, Munshi Prem
  See Srivastava, Dhanpat Rai
Chand, Prem
  See Srivastava, Dhanpat Rai
Chandler, Raymond 1888-1959 .... **SSC 23; TCLC 1, 7, 179**
  See also AAYA 25; AMWC 2; AMWS 4; BPFB 1; CA 104; 129; CANR 60, 107; CDALB 1929-1941; CMW 4; DA3; DLB 226, 253; DLBD 6; EWL 3; MAL 5; MSW; MTCW 1, 2; MTFW 2005; NFS 17; RGAL 4; TUS
Chandler, Raymond Thornton
  See Chandler, Raymond
Chang, Diana 1934- .... **AAL**
  See also CA 228; CWP; DLB 312; EXPP
Chang, Eileen 1920-1995 .... **AAL; SSC 28; TCLC 184**
  See also CA 166; CANR 168; CWW 2; DLB 328; EWL 3; RGSF 2
Chang, Jung 1952- .... **CLC 71**
  See also CA 142
Chang Ai-Ling
  See Chang, Eileen

Claudian 370(?)-404(?) .... **CMLC 46**
See also RGWL 2, 3
Claudius, Matthias 1740-1815 .... **NCLC 75**
See also DLB 97
Clavell, James 1925-1994 .... **CLC 6, 25, 87**
See also BPFB 1; CA 25-28R; 146; CANR
26, 48; CN 5; CPW; DA3; DAM NOV,
POP; MTCW 1, 2; MTFW 2005; NFS 10;
RHW
Clayman, Gregory **CLC 65**
Cleage, Pearl 1948- .... **DC 32**
See also BW 2; CA 41-44R; CANR 27, 148,
177; DFS 14, 16; DLB 228; NFS 17
Cleage, Pearl Michelle
See Cleage, Pearl
Cleaver, (Leroy) Eldridge
1935-1998 .... **BLC 1:1; CLC 30, 119**
See also BW 1, 3; CA 21-24R; 167; CANR
16, 75; DA3; DAM MULT; MTCW 2;
YAW
Cleese, John (Marwood) 1939- .... **CLC 21**
See also CA 112; 116; CANR 35; MTCW 1
Cleishbotham, Jebediah
See Scott, Sir Walter
Cleland, John 1710-1789 .... **LC 2, 48**
See also DLB 39; RGEL 2
Clemens, Samuel
See Twain, Mark
Clemens, Samuel Langhorne
See Twain, Mark
Clement of Alexandria
150(?)-215(?) .... **CMLC 41**
Cleophil
See Congreve, William
Clerihew, E.
See Bentley, E(dmund) C(lerihew)
Clerk, N. W.
See Lewis, C. S.
Cleveland, John 1613-1658 .... **LC 106**
See also DLB 126; RGEL 2
Cliff, Jimmy
See Chambers, James
Cliff, Michelle 1946- .... **BLCS; CLC 120**
See also BW 2; CA 116; CANR 39, 72; CD-
WLB 3; DLB 157; FW; GLL 2
Clifford, Lady Anne 1590-1676 .... **LC 76**
See also DLB 151
Clifton, Lucille 1936-2010 .... **BLC 1:1, 2:1;
CLC 19, 66, 162, 283; PC 17**
See also AFAW 2; BW 2, 3; CA 49-52;
CANR 2, 24, 42, 76, 97, 138; CLR 5; CP
2, 3, 4, 5, 6, 7; CSW; CWP; CWRI 5;
DA3; DAM MULT, POET; DLB 5, 41;
EXPP; MAICYA 1, 2; MTCW 1, 2;
MTFW 2005; PFS 1, 14, 29; SATA 20,
69, 128; WP
Clifton, Thelma Lucille
See Clifton, Lucille
Clinton, Dirk
See Silverberg, Robert
Clough, Arthur Hugh 1819-1861 .. **NCLC 27,
163; PC 103**
See also BRW 5; DLB 32; RGEL 2
Clutha, Janet Paterson Frame
See Frame, Janet
Clyne, Terence
See Blatty, William Peter
Cobalt, Martin
See Mayne, William (James Carter)
Cobb, Irvin S(hrewsbury)
1876-1944 .... **TCLC 77**
See also CA 175; DLB 11, 25, 86
Cobbett, William 1763-1835 .... **NCLC 49**
See also DLB 43, 107, 158; RGEL 2
Coben, Harlan 1962- .... **CLC 269**
See also CA 164; CANR 162, 199
Coburn, D(onald) L(ee) 1938- .... **CLC 10**
See also CA 89-92; DFS 23

Cockburn, Catharine Trotter
See Trotter, Catharine
Cocteau, Jean 1889-1963 ... **CLC 1, 8, 15, 16,
43; DC 17; TCLC 119; WLC 2**
See also CA 25-28; CANR 40;
CAP 2; DA; DA3; DAB; DAC; DAM
DRAM, MST, NOV; DFS 24; DLB 65,
258, 321; EW 10; EWL 3; GFL 1789 to
the Present; MTCW 1, 2; RGWL 2, 3;
TWA
Cocteau, Jean Maurice Eugene Clement
See Cocteau, Jean
Codrescu, Andrei 1946- .... **CLC 46, 121**
See also CA 33-36R; CAAS 19; CANR 13,
34, 53, 76, 125; CN 7; DA3; DAM POET;
MAL 5; MTCW 2; MTFW 2005
Coe, Max
See Bourne, Randolph S(illiman)
Coe, Tucker
See Westlake, Donald E.
Coelho, Paulo 1947- .... **CLC 258**
See also CA 152; CANR 80, 93, 155, 194;
NFS 29
Coen, Ethan 1957- .... **CLC 108, 267**
See also AAYA 54; CA 126; CANR 85
Coen, Joel 1954- .... **CLC 108, 267**
See also AAYA 54; CA 126; CANR 119
The Coen Brothers
See Coen, Ethan; Coen, Joel
Coetzee, J. M. 1940- ..... **CLC 23, 33, 66, 117,
161, 162**
See also AAYA 37; AFW; BRWS 6; CA 77-
80; CANR 41, 54, 74, 114, 133, 180; CN
4, 5, 6, 7; DA3; DAM NOV; DLB 225,
326, 329; EWL 3; LMFS 2; MTCW 1, 2;
MTFW 2005; NFS 21; WLIT 2; WWE 1
Coetzee, John Maxwell
See Coetzee, J. M.
Coffey, Brian
See Koontz, Dean
Coffin, Robert P. Tristram
1892-1955 .... **TCLC 95**
See also CA 123; 169; DLB 45
Coffin, Robert Peter Tristram
See Coffin, Robert P. Tristram
Cohan, George M. 1878-1942 .... **TCLC 60**
See also CA 157; DLB 249; RGAL 4
Cohan, George Michael
See Cohan, George M.
Cohen, Arthur A(llen) 1928-1986 ...... **CLC 7,
31**
See also CA 1-4R; 120; CANR 1, 17, 42;
DLB 28; RGHL
Cohen, Leonard 1934- .. **CLC 3, 38, 260; PC
109**
See also CA 21-24R; CANR 14, 69; CN 1,
2, 3, 4, 5, 6; CP 1, 2, 3, 4, 5, 6, 7; DAC;
DAM MST; DLB 53; EWL 3; MTCW 1
Cohen, Leonard Norman
See Cohen, Leonard
Cohen, Matt(hew) 1942-1999 .... **CLC 19**
See also CA 61-64; 187; CAAS 18; CANR
40; CN 1, 2, 3, 4, 5, 6; DAC; DLB 53
Cohen-Solal, Annie 1948- .... **CLC 50**
See also CA 239
Colegate, Isabel 1931- .... **CLC 36**
See also CA 17-20R; CANR 8, 22, 74; CN
4, 5, 6, 7; DLB 14, 231; INT CANR-22;
MTCW 1
Coleman, Emmett
See Reed, Ishmael
Coleridge, Hartley 1796-1849 .... **NCLC 90**
See also DLB 96
Coleridge, M. E.
See Coleridge, Mary E(lizabeth)
Coleridge, Mary E(lizabeth)
1861-1907 .... **TCLC 73**
See also CA 116; 166; DLB 19, 98

Coleridge, Samuel Taylor
1772-1834 ..... **NCLC 9, 54, 99, 111, 177,
197; PC 11, 39, 67, 100; WLC 2**
See also AAYA 66; BRW 4; BRWR 2; BYA
4; CDBLB 1789-1832; DA; DA3; DAB;
DAC; DAM MST, POET; DLB 93, 107;
EXPP; LATS 1:1; LMFS 1; PAB; PFS 4,
5; RGEL 2; TEA; WLIT 3; WP
Coleridge, Sara 1802-1852 .... **NCLC 31**
See also DLB 199
Coles, Don 1928- .... **CLC 46**
See also CA 115; CANR 38; CP 5, 6, 7
Coles, Robert (Martin) 1929- .... **CLC 108**
See also CA 45-48; CANR 3, 32, 66, 70,
135; INT CANR-32; SATA 23
Colette 1873-1954 ... **SSC 10, 93; TCLC 1, 5,
16**
See also CA 104; 131; DA3; DAM NOV;
DLB 65; EW 9; EWL 3; GFL 1789 to the
Present; GLL 1; MTCW 1, 2; MTFW
2005; RGWL 2, 3; TWA
Colette, Sidonie-Gabrielle
See Colette
Collett, (Jacobine) Camilla (Wergeland)
1813-1895 .... **NCLC 22**
See also DLB 354
Collier, Christopher 1930- .... **CLC 30**
See also AAYA 13; BYA 2; CA 33-36R;
CANR 13, 33, 102; CLR 126; JRDA;
MAICYA 1, 2; SATA 16, 70; WYA; YAW
1
Collier, James Lincoln 1928- .... **CLC 30**
See also AAYA 13; BYA 2; CA 9-12R;
CANR 4, 33, 60, 102; CLR 3, 126; DAM
POP; JRDA; MAICYA 1, 2; SAAS 21;
SATA 8, 70, 166; WYA; YAW 1
Collier, Jeremy 1650-1726 .... **LC 6, 157**
See also DLB 336
Collier, John 1901-1980 . **SSC 19; TCLC 127**
See also CA 65-68; 97-100; CANR 10; CN
1, 2; DLB 77, 255; FANT; SUFW 1
Collier, Mary 1690-1762 .... **LC 86**
See also DLB 95
Collingwood, R(obin) G(eorge)
1889(?)-1943 .... **TCLC 67**
See also CA 117; 155; DLB 262
Collins, Billy 1941- .... **PC 68**
See also AAYA 64; CA 151; CANR 92; CP
7; MTFW 2005; PFS 18
Collins, Hunt
See Hunter, Evan
Collins, Linda 1931- .... **CLC 44**
See also CA 125
Collins, Merle 1950- .... **BLC 2:1**
See also BW 3; CA 175; DLB 157
Collins, Tom
See Furphy, Joseph
Collins, Wilkie 1824-1889 ... **NCLC 1, 18, 93;
SSC 93**
See also BRWS 6; CDBLB 1832-1890;
CMW 4; DLB 18, 70, 159; GL 2; MSW;
RGEL 2; RGSF 2; SUFW 1; WLIT 4
Collins, William 1721-1759 ...... **LC 4, 40; PC
72**
See also BRW 3; DAM POET; DLB 109;
RGEL 2
Collins, William Wilkie
See Collins, Wilkie
Collodi, Carlo 1826-1890 .... **NCLC 54**
See also CLR 5, 120; MAICYA 1,2; SATA
29, 100; WCH; WLIT 7
Colman, George
See Glassco, John
Colman, George, the Elder
1732-1794 .... **LC 98**
See also RGEL 2
Colonna, Vittoria 1492-1547 .... **LC 71**
See also RGWL 2, 3

DA3; DAM NOV, POP; DLB 292; DLBY
1981; INT CANR-13; JRDA; LNFS 1;
MTCW 1, 2; MTFW 2005; NFS 34;
SATA 9, 88; SATA-Obit 199; SFW 4;
YAW

Crispin, Edmund
See Montgomery, Bruce

Cristina of Sweden 1626-1689 .... **LC 124**

Cristofer, Michael 1945(?)- .... **CLC 28**
See also CA 110; 152; CAD; CANR 150;
CD 5, 6; DAM DRAM; DFS 15; DLB 7

Cristofer, Michael Ivan
See Cristofer, Michael

Criton
See Alain

Croce, Benedetto 1866-1952 .... **TCLC 37**
See also CA 120; 155; EW 8; EWL 3;
WLIT 7

Crockett, David
See Crockett, Davy

Crockett, Davy 1786-1836 .... **NCLC 8**
See also DLB 3, 11, 183, 248

Crofts, Freeman Wills 1879-1957 .. **TCLC 55**
See also CA 115; 195; CMW 4; DLB 77;
MSW

Croker, John Wilson 1780-1857 .... **NCLC 10**
See also DLB 110

Crommelynck, Fernand 1885-1970 .. **CLC 75**
See also CA 189; 89-92; EWL 3

Cromwell, Oliver 1599-1658 .... **LC 43**

Cronenberg, David 1943- .... **CLC 143**
See also CA 138; CCA 1

Cronin, A(rchibald) J(oseph)
1896-1981 .... **CLC 32**
See also BPFB 1; CA 1-4R; 102; CANR 5;
CN 2; DLB 191; SATA 47; SATA-Obit 25

Cross, Amanda
See Heilbrun, Carolyn G.

Crothers, Rachel 1878-1958 .... **TCLC 19**
See also CA 113; 194; CAD; CWD; DLB
7, 266; RGAL 4

Croves, Hal
See Traven, B.

Crow Dog, Mary (?)- .... **CLC 93; NNAL**
See also CA 154

Crowfield, Christopher
See Stowe, Harriet Beecher

Crowley, Aleister
See Crowley, Edward Alexander

Crowley, Edward Alexander
1875-1947 .... **TCLC 7**
See also CA 104; GLL 1; HGG

Crowley, John 1942- .... **CLC 57**
See also AAYA 57; BPFB 1; CA 61-64;
CANR 43, 98, 138, 177; DLBY 1982;
FANT; MTFW 2005; SATA 65, 140; SFW
4; SUFW 2

Crowne, John 1641-1712 .... **LC 104**
See also DLB 80; RGEL 2

Crud
See Crumb, R.

Crumarums
See Crumb, R.

Crumb, R. 1943- .... **CLC 17**
See also CA 106; CANR 107, 150

Crumb, Robert
See Crumb, R.

Crumbum
See Crumb, R.

Crumski
See Crumb, R.

Crum the Bum
See Crumb, R.

Crunk
See Crumb, R.

Crustt
See Crumb, R.

Crutchfield, Les
See Trumbo, Dalton

Cruz, Victor Hernandez 1949- ... **HLC 1; PC
37**
See also BW 2; CA 65-68, 271; CAAE 271;
CAAS 17; CANR 14, 32, 74, 132; CP 1,
2, 3, 4, 5, 6, 7; DAM MULT, POET; DLB
41; DNFS 1; EXPP; HW 1, 2; LLW;
MTCW 2; MTFW 2005; PFS 16; WP

Cryer, Gretchen (Kiger) 1935- .... **CLC 21**
See also CA 114; 123

Csath, Geza
See Brenner, Jozef

Cudlip, David R(ockwell) 1933- .... **CLC 34**
See also CA 177

Cullen, Countee 1903-1946 ..... **BLC 1:1; HR
1:2; PC 20; TCLC 4, 37, 220; WLCS**
See also AAYA 78; AFAW 2; AMWS 4; BW
1; CA 108; 124; CDALB 1917-1929; DA;
DA3; DAC; DAM MST, MULT, POET;
DLB 4, 48, 51; EWL 3; EXPP; LMFS 2;
MAL 5; MTCW 1, 2; MTFW 2005; PFS
3; RGAL 4; SATA 18; WP

Culleton, Beatrice 1949- .... **NNAL**
See also CA 120; CANR 83; DAC

Culver, Timothy J.
See Westlake, Donald E.

Cum, R.
See Crumb, R.

Cumberland, Richard
1732-1811 .... **NCLC 167**
See also DLB 89; RGEL 2

Cummings, Bruce F. 1889-1919 ..... **TCLC 24**
See also CA 123

Cummings, Bruce Frederick
See Cummings, Bruce F.

Cummings, E. E. 1894-1962 ...... **CLC 1, 3, 8,
12, 15, 68; PC 5; TCLC 137; WLC 2**
See also AAYA 41; AMW; CA 73-76;
CANR 31; CDALB 1929-1941; DA;
DA3; DAB; DAC; DAM MST, POET;
DLB 4, 48; EWL 3; EXPP; MAL 5;
MTCW 1, 2; MTFW 2005; PAB; PFS 1,
3, 12, 13, 19, 30, 34; RGAL 4; TUS; WP

Cummings, Edward Estlin
See Cummings, E. E.

Cummins, Maria Susanna
1827-1866 .... **NCLC 139**
See also DLB 42; YABC 1

Cunha, Euclides (Rodrigues Pimenta) da
1866-1909 .... **TCLC 24**
See also CA 123; 219; DLB 307; LAW;
WLIT 1

Cunningham, E. V.
See Fast, Howard

Cunningham, J. Morgan
See Westlake, Donald E.

Cunningham, J(ames) V(incent)
1911-1985 .... **CLC 3, 31; PC 92**
See also CA 1-4R; 115; CANR 1, 72; CP 1,
2, 3, 4; DLB 5

Cunningham, Julia (Woolfolk)
1916- .... **CLC 12**
See also CA 9-12R; CANR 4, 19, 36; CWRI
5; JRDA; MAICYA 1, 2; SAAS 2; SATA
1, 26, 132

Cunningham, Michael 1952- .... **CLC 34, 243**
See also AMWS 15; CA 136; CANR 96,
160; CN 7; DLB 292; GLL 2; MTFW
2005; NFS 23

Cunninghame Graham, R. B.
See Cunninghame Graham, Robert Bontine

Cunninghame Graham, Robert Bontine
1852-1936 .... **TCLC 19**
See also CA 119; 184; DLB 98, 135, 174;
RGEL 2; RGSF 2

**Cunninghame Graham, Robert Gallnigad
Bontine**
See Cunninghame Graham, Robert Bontine

Curnow, (Thomas) Allen (Monro)
1911-2001 .... **PC 48**
See also CA 69-72; 202; CANR 48, 99; CP
1, 2, 3, 4, 5, 6, 7; EWL 3; RGEL 2

Currie, Ellen 19(?)- .... **CLC 44**

Curtin, Philip
See Lowndes, Marie Adelaide (Belloc)

Curtin, Phillip
See Lowndes, Marie Adelaide (Belloc)

Curtis, Price
See Ellison, Harlan

Cusanus, Nicolaus 1401-1464
See Nicholas of Cusa

Cutrate, Joe
See Spiegelman, Art

Cynewulf fl. 9th cent. - .... **CMLC 23, 117**
See also DLB 146; RGEL 2

Cyrano de Bergerac, Savinien de
1619-1655 .... **LC 65**
See also DLB 268; GFL Beginnings to
1789; RGWL 2, 3

Cyril of Alexandria c. 375-c. 430 . **CMLC 59**

Czaczkes, Shmuel Yosef Halevi
See Agnon, S.Y.

Dabrowska, Maria (Szumska)
1889-1965 .... **CLC 15**
See also CA 106; CDWLB 4; DLB 215;
EWL 3

Dabydeen, David 1955- .... **CLC 34**
See also BW 1; CA 125; CANR 56, 92; CN
6, 7; CP 5, 6, 7; DLB 347

Dacey, Philip 1939- .... **CLC 51**
See also CA 37-40R, 231; CAAE 231;
CAAS 17; CANR 14, 32, 64; CP 4, 5, 6,
7; DLB 105

Dacre, Charlotte c. 1772-1825(?) . **NCLC 151**

Dafydd ap Gwilym c. 1320-c. 1380 ..... **PC 56**

Dagerman, Stig (Halvard)
1923-1954 .... **TCLC 17**
See also CA 117; 155; DLB 259; EWL 3

D'Aguiar, Fred 1960- ..... **BLC 2:1; CLC 145**
See also CA 148; CANR 83, 101; CN 7;
CP 5, 6, 7; DLB 157; EWL 3

Dahl, Roald 1916-1990 ...... **CLC 1, 6, 18, 79;
TCLC 173**
See also AAYA 15; BPFB 1; BRWS 4; BYA
5; CA 1-4R; 133; CANR 6, 32, 37, 62;
CLR 1, 7, 41, 111; CN 1, 2, 3, 4; CPW;
DA3; DAB; DAC; DAM MST, NOV,
POP; DLB 139, 255; HGG; JRDA; MAI-
CYA 1, 2; MTCW 1, 2; MTFW 2005;
RGSF 2; SATA 1, 26, 73; SATA-Obit 65;
SSFS 4, 30; TEA; YAW

Dahlberg, Edward 1900-1977 . **CLC 1, 7, 14;
TCLC 208**
See also CA 9-12R; 69-72; CANR 31, 62;
CN 1, 2; DLB 48; MAL 5; MTCW 1;
RGAL 4

Daitch, Susan 1954- .... **CLC 103**
See also CA 161

Dale, Colin
See Lawrence, T. E.

Dale, George E.
See Asimov, Isaac

d'Alembert, Jean Le Rond
1717-1783 .... **LC 126**

Dalton, Roque 1935-1975(?) ..... **HLCS 1; PC
36**
See also CA 176; DLB 283; HW 2

Daly, Elizabeth 1878-1967 .... **CLC 52**
See also CA 23-24; 25-28R; CANR 60;
CAP 2; CMW 4

Daly, Mary 1928-2010 .... **CLC 173**
See also CA 25-28R; CANR 30, 62, 166;
FW; GLL 1; MTCW 1

Daly, Maureen 1921-2006 .... **CLC 17**
    See also AAYA 5, 58; BYA 6; CA 253;
    CANR 37, 83, 108; CLR 96; JRDA; MAI-
    CYA 1, 2; SAAS 1; SATA 2, 129; SATA-
    Obit 176; WYA; YAW

Damas, Leon-Gontran 1912-1978 ... **CLC 84;
TCLC 204**
    See also BW 1; CA 125; 73-76; EWL 3

Damocles
    See Benedetti, Mario

Dana, Richard Henry Sr.
    1787-1879 .... **NCLC 53**

Dangarembga, Tsitsi 1959- .... **BLC 2:1**
    See also BW 3; CA 163; NFS 28; WLIT 2

Daniel, Samuel 1562(?)-1619 .... **LC 24, 171**
    See also DLB 62; RGEL 2

Daniels, Brett
    See Adler, Renata

Dannay, Frederic 1905-1982 .... **CLC 3, 11**
    See also BPFB 3; CA 1-4R; 107; CANR 1,
    39; CMW 4; DAM POP; DLB 137; MSW;
    MTCW 1; RGAL 4

D'Annunzio, Gabriele 1863-1938 ... **TCLC 6,
40, 215**
    See also CA 104; 155; EW 8; EWL 3;
    RGWL 2, 3; TWA; WLIT 7

Danois, N. le
    See Gourmont, Remy(-Marie-Charles) de

Dante 1265-1321 .... **CMLC 3, 18, 39, 70; PC
21, 108; WLCS**
    See also DA; DA3; DAB; DAC; DAM
    MST, POET; EFS 1; EW 1; LAIT 1;
    RGWL 2, 3; TWA; WLIT 7; WP

d'Antibes, Germain
    See Simenon, Georges

Danticat, Edwidge 1969- . **BLC 2:1; CLC 94,
139, 228; SSC 100**
    See also AAYA 29; CA 152, 192; CAAE
    192; CANR 73, 129, 179; CN 7; DLB
    350; DNFS 1; EXPS; LATS 1:2; LNFS 3;
    MTCW 2; MTFW 2005; NFS 28; SSFS
    1, 25; YAW

Danvers, Dennis 1947- .... **CLC 70**

Danziger, Paula 1944-2004 .... **CLC 21**
    See also AAYA 4, 36; BYA 6, 7, 14; CA
    112; 115; 229; CANR 37, 132; CLR 20;
    JRDA; MAICYA 1, 2; SATA 36, 63, 102, 149;
    SATA 36, 63, 102, 149; SATA-Brief 30;
    SATA-Obit 155; WYA; YAW

Da Ponte, Lorenzo 1749-1838 .... **NCLC 50**

d'Aragona, Tullia 1510(?)-1556 .... **LC 121**

Dario, Ruben 1867-1916 .... **HLC 1; PC 15;
TCLC 4**
    See also CA 131; CANR 81; DAM MULT;
    DLB 290; EWL 3; HW 1, 2; LAW;
    MTCW 1, 2; MTFW 2005; RGWL 2, 3

Darko, Amma 1956- .... **BLC 2:1**

Darley, George 1795-1846 .... **NCLC 2**
    See also DLB 96; RGEL 2

Darrow, Clarence (Seward)
    1857-1938 .... **TCLC 81**
    See also CA 164; DLB 303

Darwin, Charles 1809-1882 .... **NCLC 57**
    See also BRWS 7; DLB 57, 166; LATS 1:1;
    RGEL 2; TEA; WLIT 4

Darwin, Erasmus 1731-1802 .... **NCLC 106**
    See also BRWS 16; DLB 93; RGEL 2

Darwish, Mahmoud 1941-2008 .... **PC 86**
    See also CA 164; CANR 133; CWW 2;
    EWL 3; MTCW 2; MTFW 2005

Darwish, Mahmud -2008
    See Darwish, Mahmoud

Daryush, Elizabeth 1887-1977 ...... **CLC 6, 19**
    See also CA 49-52; CANR 3, 81; DLB 20

Das, Kamala 1934-2009 ..... **CLC 191; PC 43**
    See also CA 101; 287; CANR 27, 59; CP 1,
    2, 3, 4, 5, 6, 7; CWP; DLB 323; FW

Dasgupta, Surendranath
    1887-1952 .... **TCLC 81**
    See also CA 157

Dashwood, Edmee Elizabeth Monica de la
    Pasture 1890-1943 .... **TCLC 61**
    See also CA 119; 154; DLB 34; RHW

da Silva, Antonio Jose
    1705-1739 .... **NCLC 114**

Daudet, (Louis Marie) Alphonse
    1840-1897 .... **NCLC 1**
    See also DLB 123; GFL 1789 to the Present;
    RGSF 2

Daudet, Alphonse Marie Leon
    1867-1942 .... **SSC 94**
    See also CA 217

d'Aulnoy, Marie-Catherine c.
    1650-1705 .... **LC 100**

Daumal, Rene 1908-1944 .... **TCLC 14**
    See also CA 114; 247; EWL 3

Davenant, William 1606-1668 .... **LC 13, 166;
PC 99**
    See also DLB 58, 126; RGEL 2

Davenport, Guy (Mattison, Jr.)
    1927-2005 . **CLC 6, 14, 38, 241; SSC 16**
    See also CA 33-36R; 235; CANR 23, 73;
    CN 3, 4, 5, 6; CSW; DLB 130

David, Robert
    See Nezval, Vitezslav

Davidson, Donald (Grady)
    1893-1968 .... **CLC 2, 13, 19**
    See also CA 5-8R; 25-28R; CANR 4, 84;
    DLB 45

Davidson, Hugh
    See Hamilton, Edmond

Davidson, John 1857-1909 .... **TCLC 24**
    See also CA 118; 217; DLB 19; RGEL 2

Davidson, Sara 1943- .... **CLC 9**
    See also CA 81-84; CANR 44, 68; DLB
    185

Davie, Donald (Alfred) 1922-1995 .... **CLC 5,
8, 10, 31; PC 29**
    See also BRWS 6; CA 1-4R; 149; CAAS 3;
    CANR 1, 44; CP 1, 2, 3, 4, 5, 6; DLB 27;
    MTCW 1; RGEL 2

Davie, Elspeth 1918-1995 .... **SSC 52**
    See also CA 120; 126; 150; CANR 141;
    DLB 139

Davies, Ray(mond Douglas) 1944- ... **CLC 21**
    See also CA 116; 146; CANR 92

Davies, Rhys 1901-1978 .... **CLC 23**
    See also CA 9-12R; 81-84; CANR 4; CN 1,
    2; DLB 139, 191

Davies, Robertson 1913-1995 .. **CLC 2, 7, 13,
25, 42, 75, 91; WLC 2**
    See also BEST 89:2; BPFB 1; CA 1, 33-
    36R; 150; CANR 17, 42, 103; CN 1, 2, 3,
    4, 5, 6; CPW; DA; DA3; DAB; DAC;
    DAM MST, NOV, POP; DLB 68; EWL 3;
    HGG; INT CANR-17; MTCW 1, 2;
    MTFW 2005; RGEL 2; TWA

Davies, Sir John 1569-1626 .... **LC 85**
    See also DLB 172

Davies, Walter C.
    See Kornbluth, C(yril) M.

Davies, William Henry 1871-1940 ... **TCLC 5**
    See also BRWS 11; CA 104; 179; DLB 19,
    174; EWL 3; RGEL 2

Davies, William Robertson
    See Davies, Robertson

Da Vinci, Leonardo 1452-1519 ..... **LC 12, 57,
60**
    See also AAYA 40

Daviot, Gordon
    See Mackintosh, Elizabeth

Davis, Angela (Yvonne) 1944- .... **CLC 77**
    See also BW 2, 3; CA 57-60; CANR 10,
    81; CSW; DA3; DAM MULT; FW

Davis, B. Lynch
    See Bioy Casares, Adolfo; Borges, Jorge
    Luis

Davis, Frank Marshall 1905-1987 ... **BLC 1:1**
    See also BW 2, 3; CA 125; 123; CANR 42,
    80; DAM MULT; DLB 51

Davis, Gordon
    See Hunt, E. Howard

Davis, H(arold) L(enoir) 1896-1960 . **CLC 49**
    See also ANW; CA 178; 89-92; DLB 9,
    206; SATA 114; TCWW 1, 2

Davis, Hart
    See Poniatowska, Elena

Davis, Natalie Zemon 1928- .... **CLC 204**
    See also CA 53-56; CANR 58, 100, 174

Davis, Rebecca Blaine Harding
    See Davis, Rebecca Harding

Davis, Rebecca Harding 1831-1910 . **SSC 38,
109; TCLC 6**
    See also AMWS 16; CA 104; 179; DLB 74,
    239; FW; NFS 14; RGAL 4; SSFS 26;
    TUS

Davis, Richard Harding
    1864-1916 .... **TCLC 24**
    See also CA 114; 179; DLB 12, 23, 78, 79,
    189; DLBD 13; RGAL 4

Davison, Frank Dalby 1893-1970 ..... **CLC 15**
    See also CA 217; 116; DLB 260

Davison, Lawrence H.
    See Lawrence, D. H.

Davison, Peter (Hubert) 1928-2004 . **CLC 28**
    See also CA 9-12R; 234; CAAS 4; CANR
    3, 43, 84; CP 1, 2, 3, 4, 5, 6, 7; DLB 5

Davys, Mary 1674-1732 .... **LC 1, 46**
    See also DLB 39

Dawson, (Guy) Fielding (Lewis)
    1930-2002 .... **CLC 6**
    See also CA 85-88; 202; CANR 108; DLB
    130; DLBY 2002

Day, Clarence (Shepard, Jr.)
    1874-1935 .... **TCLC 25**
    See also CA 108; 199; DLB 11

Day, John 1574(?)-1640(?) .... **LC 70**
    See also DLB 62, 170; RGEL 2

Day, Thomas 1748-1789 .... **LC 1**
    See also DLB 39; YABC 1

Day Lewis, C. 1904-1972 .. **CLC 1, 6, 10; PC
11**
    See also BRWS 3; CA 13-16; 33-36R;
    CANR 34; CAP 1; CN 1; CP 1; CWRI 5;
    DAM POET; DLB 77; EWL 3; MSW;
    MTCW 1, 2; RGEL 2

Day Lewis, Cecil
    See Day Lewis, C.

de Andrade, Carlos Drummond
    See Drummond de Andrade, Carlos

de Andrade, Mario 1892(?)-1945 ... **TCLC 43**
    See also CA 178; DLB 307; EWL 3; HW 2;
    LAW; RGWL 2, 3

Deane, Norman
    See Creasey, John

Deane, Seamus (Francis) 1940- ...... **CLC 122**
    See also CA 118; CANR 42

de Athayde, Alvaro Coelho
    See Pessoa, Fernando

de Beauvoir, Simone
    See Beauvoir, Simone de

de Beer, P.
    See Bosman, Herman Charles

De Botton, Alain 1969- .... **CLC 203**
    See also CA 159; CANR 96, 201

de Brissac, Malcolm
    See Dickinson, Peter

de Campos, Alvaro
    See Pessoa, Fernando

de Chardin, Pierre Teilhard
    See Teilhard de Chardin, (Marie Joseph)
    Pierre

de Pizan, Christine
See Christine de Pizan

De Quincey, Thomas 1785-1859 ..... **NCLC 4, 87, 198**
See also BRW 4; CDBLB 1789-1832; DLB 110, 144; RGEL 2

De Ray, Jill
See Moore, Alan

Deren, Eleanora 1908(?)-1961 .. **CLC 16, 102**
See also CA 192; 111

Deren, Maya
See Deren, Eleanora

Derleth, August (William)
1909-1971 .... **CLC 31**
See also BPFB 1; BYA 9, 10; CA 1-4R; 29-32R; CANR 4; CMW 4; CN 1; DLB 9; DLBD 17; HGG; SATA 5; SUFW 1

Der Nister 1884-1950 .... **TCLC 56**
See also DLB 333; EWL 3

de Routisie, Albert
See Aragon, Louis

Derrida, Jacques 1930-2004 ...... **CLC 24, 87, 225**
See also CA 124; 127; 232; CANR 76, 98, 133; DLB 242; EWL 3; LMFS 2; MTCW 2; TWA

Derry Down Derry
See Lear, Edward

Dersonnes, Jacques
See Simenon, Georges

Der Stricker c. 1190-c. 1250 .... **CMLC 75**
See also DLB 138

Derzhavin, Gavriil Romanovich
1743-1816 .... **NCLC 215**
See also DLB 150

Desai, Anita 1937- . **CLC 19, 37, 97, 175, 271**
See also BRWS 5; CA 81-84; CANR 33, 53, 95, 133; CN 1, 2, 3, 4, 5, 6, 7; CWRI 5; DA3; DAB; DAM NOV; DLB 271, 323; DNFS 2; EWL 3; FW; MTCW 1, 2; MTFW 2005; SATA 63, 126; SSFS 28, 31

Desai, Kiran 1971- .... **CLC 119**
See also BRWS 15; BYA 16; CA 171; CANR 127; NFS 28

de Saint-Luc, Jean
See Glassco, John

de Saint Roman, Arnaud
See Aragon, Louis

Desbordes-Valmore, Marceline
1786-1859 .... **NCLC 97**
See also DLB 217

Descartes, Rene 1596-1650 .... **LC 20, 35, 150**
See also DLB 268; EW 3; GFL Beginnings to 1789

Deschamps, Eustache 1340(?)-1404 .. **LC 103**
See also DLB 208

De Sica, Vittorio 1901(?)-1974 .... **CLC 20**
See also CA 117

Desnos, Robert 1900-1945 .... **TCLC 22**
See also CA 121; 151; CANR 107; DLB 258; EWL 3; LMFS 2

Destouches, Louis-Ferdinand
See Celine, Louis-Ferdinand

de Teran, Lisa St. Aubin
See St. Aubin de Teran, Lisa

de Tolignac, Gaston
See Griffith, D.W.

Deutsch, Babette 1895-1982 .... **CLC 18**
See also BYA 3; CA 1-4R; 108; CANR 4, 79; CP 1, 2, 3; DLB 45; SATA 1; SATA-Obit 33

Devenant, William 1606-1649 .... **LC 13**

Devi, Mahasweta 1926- .... **CLC 290**

Deville, Rene
See Kacew, Romain

Devkota, Laxmiprasad 1909-1959 . **TCLC 23**
See also CA 123

De Voto, Bernard (Augustine)
1897-1955 .... **TCLC 29**
See also CA 113; 160; DLB 9, 256; MAL 5; TCWW 1, 2

De Vries, Peter 1910-1993 ..... **CLC 1, 2, 3, 7, 10, 28, 46**
See also CA 17-20R; 142; CANR 41; CN 1, 2, 3, 4, 5; DAM NOV; DLB 6; DLBY 1982; MAL 5; MTCW 1, 2; MTFW 2005

Dewey, John 1859-1952 .... **TCLC 95**
See also CA 114; 170; CANR 144; DLB 246, 270; RGAL 4

Dexter, John
See Bradley, Marion Zimmer

Dexter, Martin
See Faust, Frederick

Dexter, Pete 1943- .... **CLC 34, 55**
See also BEST 89:2; CA 127; 131; CANR 129; CPW; DAM POP; INT CA-131; MAL 5; MTCW 1; MTFW 2005

Diamano, Silmang
See Senghor, Leopold Sedar

Diamant, Anita 1951- .... **CLC 239**
See also CA 145; CANR 126

Diamond, Neil 1941- .... **CLC 30**
See also CA 108

Diaz, Junot 1968- .... **CLC 258**
See also BYA 12; CA 161; CANR 119, 183; LLW; SSFS 20

Diaz del Castillo, Bernal c.
1496-1584 .... **HLCS 1; LC 31**
See also DLB 318; LAW

di Bassetto, Corno
See Shaw, George Bernard

Dick, Philip K. 1928-1982 ... **CLC 10, 30, 72; SSC 57**
See also AAYA 24; BPFB 1; BYA 11; CA 49-52; 106; CANR 2, 16, 132; CN 2, 3; CPW; DA3; DAM NOV, POP; DLB 8; MTCW 1, 2; MTFW 2005; NFS 5, 26; SCFW 1, 2; SFW 4

Dick, Philip Kindred
See Dick, Philip K.

Dickens, Charles 1812-1870 . **NCLC 3, 8, 18, 26, 37, 50, 86, 105, 113, 161, 187, 203, 206, 211, 217, 219; SSC 17, 49, 88; WLC 2**
See also AAYA 23; BRW 5; BRWC 1, 2; BYA 1, 2, 3, 13, 14; CDBLB 1832-1890; CLR 95; CMW 4; DA; DA3; DAB; DAC; DAM MST, NOV; DLB 21, 55, 70, 159, 166; EXPN; GL 2; HGG; JRDA; LAIT 1, 2; LATS 1:1; LMFS 1; MAICYA 1, 2; NFS 4, 5, 10, 14, 20, 25, 30, 33; RGEL 2; RGSF 2; SATA 15; SUFW 1; TEA; WCH; WLIT 4; WYA

Dickens, Charles John Huffam
See Dickens, Charles

Dickey, James 1923-1997 .... **CLC 1, 2, 4, 7, 10, 15, 47, 109; PC 40; TCLC 151**
See also AAYA 50; AITN 1, 2; AMWS 4; BPFB 1; CA 9-12R; 156; CABS 2; CANR 10, 48, 61, 105; CDALB 1968-1988; CP 1, 2, 3, 4, 5, 6; CPW; CSW; DA3; DAM NOV, POET, POP; DLB 5, 193, 342; DLBD 7; DLBY 1982, 1993, 1996, 1997, 1998; EWL 3; INT CANR-10; MAL 5; MTCW 1, 2; NFS 9; PFS 6, 11; RGAL 4; TUS

Dickey, James Lafayette
See Dickey, James

Dickey, William 1928-1994 .... **CLC 3, 28**
See also CA 9-12R; 145; CANR 24, 79; CP 1, 2, 3, 4; DLB 5

Dickinson, Charles 1951- .... **CLC 49**
See also CA 128; CANR 141

Dickinson, Emily 1830-1886 ... **NCLC 21, 77, 171; PC 1; WLC 2**
See also AAYA 22; AMW; AMWR 1; CDALB 1865-1917; DA; DA3; DAB; DAC; DAM MST, POET; DLB 1, 243; EXPP; FL 1:3; MBL; PAB; PFS 1, 2, 3, 4, 5, 6, 8, 10, 11, 13, 16, 28, 32, 35; RGAL 4; SATA 29; TUS; WP; WYA

Dickinson, Emily Elizabeth
See Dickinson, Emily

Dickinson, Mrs. Herbert Ward
See Phelps, Elizabeth Stuart

Dickinson, Peter 1927- .... **CLC 12, 35**
See also AAYA 9, 49; BYA 5; CA 41-44R; CANR 31, 58, 88, 134, 195; CLR 29, 125; CMW 4; DLB 87, 161, 276; JRDA; MAI-CYA 1, 2; SATA 5, 62, 95, 150; SFW 4; WYA; YAW

Dickinson, Peter Malcolm de Brissac
See Dickinson, Peter

Dickson, Carr
See Carr, John Dickson

Dickson, Carter
See Carr, John Dickson

Diderot, Denis 1713-1784 .... **LC 26, 126**
See also DLB 313; EW 4; GFL Beginnings to 1789; LMFS 1; RGWL 2, 3

Didion, Joan 1934- . **CLC 1, 3, 8, 14, 32, 129**
See also AITN 1; AMWS 4; CA 5-8R; CANR 14, 52, 76, 125, 174; CDALB 1968-1988; CN 2, 3, 4, 5, 6, 7; DA3; DAM NOV; DLB 2, 173, 185; DLBY 1981, 1986; EWL 3; MAL 5; MBL; MTCW 1, 2; MTFW 2005; NFS 3; RGAL 4; TCLE 1:1; TCWW 2; TUS

di Donato, Pietro 1911-1992 .... **TCLC 159**
See also AMWS 20; CA 101; 136; DLB 9

Dietrich, Robert
See Hunt, E. Howard

Difusa, Pati
See Almodovar, Pedro

di Lampedusa, Giuseppe Tomasi
See Lampedusa, Giuseppe di

Dillard, Annie 1945- ...... **CLC 9, 60, 115, 216**
See also AAYA 6, 43; AMWS 6; ANW; CA 49-52; CANR 3, 43, 62, 90, 125; DA3; DAM NOV; DLB 275, 278; DLBY 1980; LAIT 4, 5; MAL 5; MTCW 1, 2; MTFW 2005; NCFS 1; RGAL 4; SATA 10, 140; TCLE 1:1; TUS

Dillard, R(ichard) H(enry) W(ilde)
1937- .... **CLC 5**
See also CA 21-24R; CAAS 7; CANR 10; CP 2, 3, 4, 5, 6, 7; CSW; DLB 5, 244

Dillon, Eilis 1920-1994 .... **CLC 17**
See also CA 9-12R, 182; 147; CAAE 182; CAAS 3; CANR 4, 38, 78; CLR 26; MAI-CYA 1, 2; MAICYAS 1; SATA 2, 74; SATA-Essay 105; SATA-Obit 83; YAW

Dimont, Penelope
See Mortimer, Penelope (Ruth)

Dinesen, Isak
See Blixen, Karen

Ding Ling
See Chiang, Pin-chin

Diodorus Siculus c. 90B.C.-c.
31B.C. .... **CMLC 88**

Diphusa, Patty
See Almodovar, Pedro

Disch, Thomas M. 1940-2008 .... **CLC 7, 36**
See also AAYA 17; BPFB 1; CA 21-24R; 274; CAAS 4; CANR 17, 36, 54, 89; CLR 18; CP 5, 6, 7; DA3; DLB 8, 282; HGG; MAICYA 1, 2; MTCW 1, 2; MTFW 2005; SAAS 15; SATA 92; SATA-Obit 195; SCFW 1, 2; SFW 4; SUFW 2

Disch, Thomas Michael
See Disch, Thomas M.

Dove, Rita 1952- . **BLC 2:1; BLCS; CLC 50, 81; PC 6**
See also AAYA 46; AMWS 4; BW 2; CA 109; CAAS 19; CANR 27, 42, 68, 76, 97, 132; CDALBS; CP 5, 6, 7; CSW; CWP; DA3; DAM MULT, POET; DLB 120; EWL 3; EXPP; MAL 5; MTCW 2; MTFW 2005; PFS 1, 15; RGAL 4

Dove, Rita Frances
See Dove, Rita

Doveglion
See Villa, Jose Garcia

Dowell, Coleman 1925-1985 .... **CLC 60**
See also CA 25-28R; 117; CANR 10; DLB 130; GLL 2

Downing, Major Jack
See Smith, Seba

Dowson, Ernest (Christopher) 1867-1900 .... **TCLC 4**
See also CA 105; 150; DLB 19, 135; RGEL 2

Doyle, A. Conan
See Doyle, Sir Arthur Conan

Doyle, Sir Arthur Conan 1859-1930 ..... **SSC 12, 83, 95; TCLC 7; WLC 2**
See also AAYA 14; BPFB 1; BRWS 2; BYA 4, 5, 11; CA 104; 122; CANR 131; CD-BLB 1890-1914; CLR 106; CMW 4; DA; DA3; DAB; DAC; DAM MST, NOV; DLB 18, 70, 156, 178; EXPS; HGG; LAIT 2; MSW; MTCW 1, 2; MTFW 2005; NFS 28; RGEL 2; RGSF 2; RHW; SATA 24; SCFW 1, 2; SFW 4; SSFS 2; TEA; WCH; WLIT 4; WYA; YAW

Doyle, Conan
See Doyle, Sir Arthur Conan

Doyle, John
See Graves, Robert

Doyle, Roddy 1958- .... **CLC 81, 178**
See also AAYA 14; BRWS 5; CA 143; CANR 73, 128, 168, 200; CN 6, 7; DA3; DLB 194, 326; MTCW 2; MTFW 2005

Doyle, Sir A. Conan
See Doyle, Sir Arthur Conan

Dr. A
See Asimov, Isaac; Silverstein, Alvin; Silverstein, Virginia B.

Drabble, Margaret 1939- ...... **CLC 2, 3, 5, 8, 10, 22, 53, 129**
See also BRWS 4; CA 13-16R; CANR 18, 35, 63, 112, 131, 174; CDBLB 1960 to Present; CN 1, 2, 3, 4, 5, 6, 7; CPW; DA3; DAB; DAC; DAM MST, NOV, POP; DLB 14, 155, 231; EWL 3; FW; MTCW 1, 2; MTFW 2005; RGEL 2; SATA 48; TEA

Drakulic, Slavenka
See Drakulic, Slavenka

Drakulic, Slavenka 1949- .... **CLC 173**
See also CA 144; CANR 92, 198; DLB 353

Drakulic-Ilic, Slavenka
See Drakulic, Slavenka

Drakulic-Ilic, Slavenka
See Drakulic, Slavenka

Drapier, M. B.
See Swift, Jonathan

Drayham, James
See Mencken, H. L.

Drayton, Michael 1563-1631 . **LC 8, 161; PC 98**
See also DAM POET; DLB 121; RGEL 2

Dreadstone, Carl
See Campbell, Ramsey

Dreiser, Theodore 1871-1945 .... **SSC 30, 114; TCLC 10, 18, 35, 83; WLC 2**
See also AMW; AMWC 2; AMWR 2; BYA 15, 16; CA 106; 132; CDALB 1865-1917; DA; DA3; DAC; DAM MST, NOV; DLB

9, 12, 102, 137; DLBD 1; EWL 3; LAIT 2; LMFS 2; MAL 5; MTCW 1, 2; MTFW 2005; NFS 8, 17; RGAL 4; TUS

Dreiser, Theodore Herman Albert
See Dreiser, Theodore

Drexler, Rosalyn 1926- .... **CLC 2, 6**
See also CA 81-84; CAD; CANR 68, 124; CD 5, 6; CWD; MAL 5

Dreyer, Carl Theodor 1889-1968 ...... **CLC 16**
See also CA 116

Drieu la Rochelle, Pierre 1893-1945 .... **TCLC 21**
See also CA 117; 250; DLB 72; EWL 3; GFL 1789 to the Present

Drieu la Rochelle, Pierre-Eugene 1893-1945
See Drieu la Rochelle, Pierre

Drinkwater, John 1882-1937 .... **TCLC 57**
See also CA 109; 149; DLB 10, 19, 149; RGEL 2

Drop Shot
See Cable, George Washington

Droste-Hulshoff, Annette Freiin von 1797-1848 .... **NCLC 3, 133**
See also CDWLB 2; DLB 133; RGSF 2; RGWL 2, 3

Drummond, Walter
See Silverberg, Robert

Drummond, William Henry 1854-1907 .... **TCLC 25**
See also CA 160; DLB 92

Drummond de Andrade, Carlos 1902-1987 .... **CLC 18; TCLC 139**
See also CA 132; 123; DLB 307; EWL 3; LAW; RGWL 2, 3

Drummond of Hawthornden, William 1585-1649 .... **LC 83**
See also DLB 121, 213; RGEL 2

Drury, Allen (Stuart) 1918-1998 .... **CLC 37**
See also CA 57-60; 170; CANR 18, 52; CN 1, 2, 3, 4, 5, 6; INT CANR-18

Druse, Eleanor
See King, Stephen

Dryden, John 1631-1700 ..... **DC 3; LC 3, 21, 115; PC 25; WLC 2**
See also BRW 2; BRWR 3; CDBLB 1660-1789; DA; DAB; DAC; DAM DRAM, MST, POET; DLB 80, 101, 131; EXPP; IDTP; LMFS 1; RGEL 2; TEA; WLIT 3

du Aime, Albert
See Wharton, William

du Aime, Albert William
See Wharton, William

du Bellay, Joachim 1524-1560 .... **LC 92**
See also DLB 327; GFL Beginnings to 1789; RGWL 2, 3

Duberman, Martin 1930- .... **CLC 8**
See also CA 1-4R; CAD; CANR 2, 63, 137, 174; CD 5, 6

Dubie, Norman (Evans) 1945- .... **CLC 36**
See also CA 69-72; CANR 12, 115; CP 3, 4, 5, 6, 7; DLB 120; PFS 12

Du Bois, W. E. B. 1868-1963 .... **BLC 1:1; CLC 1, 2, 13, 64, 96; HR 1:2; TCLC 169; WLC 2**
See also AAYA 40; AFAW 1, 2; AMWC 1; AMWS 2; BW 1, 3; CA 85-88; CANR 34, 82, 132; CDALB 1865-1917; DA; DA3; DAC; DAM MST, MULT, NOV; DLB 47, 50, 91, 246, 284; EWL 3; EXPP; LAIT 2; LMFS 2; MAL 5; MTCW 1, 2; MTFW 2005; NCFS 1; PFS 13; RGAL 4; SATA 42

Du Bois, William Edward Burghardt
See Du Bois, W. E. B.

Dubus, Andre 1936-1999 ..... **CLC 13, 36, 97; SSC 15, 118**
See also AMWS 7; CA 21-24R; 177; CANR 17; CN 5, 6; CSW; DLB 130; INT CANR-17; RGAL 4; SSFS 10; TCLE 1:1

Duca Minimo
See D'Annunzio, Gabriele

Ducharme, Rejean 1941- .... **CLC 74**
See also CA 165; DLB 60

du Chatelet, Emilie 1706-1749 .... **LC 96**
See also DLB 313

Duchen, Claire CLC 65

Duck, Stephen 1705(?)-1756 .... **PC 89**
See also DLB 95; RGEL 2

Duclos, Charles Pinot- 1704-1772 .... **LC 1**
See also GFL Beginnings to 1789

Ducornet, Erica 1943- .... **CLC 232**
See also CA 37-40R; CANR 14, 34, 54, 82; SATA 7

Ducornet, Rikki
See Ducornet, Erica

Dudek, Louis 1918-2001 .... **CLC 11, 19**
See also CA 45-48; 215; CAAS 14; CANR 1; CP 1, 2, 3, 4, 5, 6, 7; DLB 88

Duerrematt, Friedrich
See Durrenmatt, Friedrich

Duffy, Bruce 1953(?)- .... **CLC 50**
See also CA 172

Duffy, Maureen 1933- .... **CLC 37**
See also CA 25-28R; CANR 33, 68; CBD; CN 1, 2, 3, 4, 5, 6, 7; CP 5, 6, 7; CWD; CWP; DFS 15; DLB 14, 310; FW; MTCW 1

Duffy, Maureen Patricia
See Duffy, Maureen

Du Fu
See Tu Fu

Dugan, Alan 1923-2003 .... **CLC 2, 6**
See also CA 81-84; 220; CANR 119; CP 1, 2, 3, 4, 5, 6, 7; DLB 5; MAL 5; PFS 10

du Gard, Roger Martin
See Martin du Gard, Roger

Duhamel, Georges 1884-1966 .... **CLC 8**
See also CA 81-84; 25-28R; CANR 35; DLB 65; EWL 3; GFL 1789 to the Present; MTCW 1

du Hault, Jean
See Grindel, Eugene

Dujardin, Edouard (Emile Louis) 1861-1949 .... **TCLC 13**
See also CA 109; DLB 123

Duke, Raoul
See Thompson, Hunter S.

Dulles, John Foster 1888-1959 .... **TCLC 72**
See also CA 115; 149

Dumas, Alexandre (pere) 1802-1870 .... **NCLC 11, 71; WLC 2**
See also AAYA 22; BYA 3; CLR 134; DA; DA3; DAB; DAC; DAM MST, NOV; DLB 119, 192; EW 6; GFL 1789 to the Present; LAIT 1, 2; NFS 14, 19; RGWL 2, 3; SATA 18; TWA; WCH

Dumas, Alexandre (fils) 1824-1895 ...... **DC 1; NCLC 9**
See also DLB 192; GFL 1789 to the Present; RGWL 2, 3

Dumas, Claudine
See Malzberg, Barry N(athaniel)

Dumas, Henry L. 1934-1968 . **BLC 2:1; CLC 6, 62; SSC 107**
See also BW 1; CA 85-88; DLB 41; RGAL 4

du Maurier, Daphne 1907-1989 .. **CLC 6, 11, 59; SSC 18, 129; TCLC 209**
See also AAYA 37; BPFB 1; BRWS 3; CA 5-8R; 128; CANR 6, 55; CMW 4; CN 1, 2, 3, 4; CPW; DA3; DAB; DAC; DAM MST, POP; DLB 191; GL 2; HGG; LAIT 3; MSW; MTCW 1, 2; NFS 12; RGEL 2; RGSF 2; RHW; SATA 27; SATA-Obit 60; SSFS 14, 16; TEA

Du Maurier, George 1834-1896 ..... **NCLC 86**
See also DLB 153, 178; RGEL 2

Etherege, Sir George 1636-1692 . **DC 23; LC 78**
See also BRW 2; DAM DRAM; DLB 80; PAB; RGEL 2

Euclid 306B.C.-283B.C. .... **CMLC 25**

Eugenides, Jeffrey 1960- .... **CLC 81, 212**
See also AAYA 51; CA 144; CANR 120; DLB 350; MTFW 2005; NFS 24

Euripides c. 484B.C.-406B.C. .... **CMLC 23, 51; DC 4; WLCS**
See also AW 1; CDWLB 1; DA; DA3; DAB; DAC; DAM DRAM, MST; DFS 1, 4, 6, 25, 27; DLB 176; LAIT 1; LMFS 1; RGWL 2, 3; WLIT 8

Eusebius c. 263-c. 339 .... **CMLC 103**

Evan, Evin
See Faust, Frederick

Evans, Caradoc 1878-1945 ... **SSC 43; TCLC 85**
See also DLB 162

Evans, Evan
See Faust, Frederick

Evans, Marian
See Eliot, George

Evans, Mary Ann
See Eliot, George

Evarts, Esther
See Benson, Sally

Evelyn, John 1620-1706 .... **LC 144**
See also BRW 2; RGEL 2

Everett, Percival 1956- .... **CLC 57**
See Everett, Percival L.
See also AMWS 18; BW 2; CA 129; CANR 94, 134, 179; CN 7; DLB 350; MTFW 2005

Everett, Percival L.
See Everett, Percival
See also CSW

Everson, R(onald) G(ilmour) 1903-1992 .... **CLC 27**
See also CA 17-20R; CP 1, 2, 3, 4; DLB 88

Everson, William 1912-1994 ... **CLC 1, 5, 14**
See also BG 1:2; CA 9-12R; 145; CANR 20; CP 1; DLB 5, 16, 212; MTCW 1

Everson, William Oliver
See Everson, William

Evtushenko, Evgenii Aleksandrovich
See Yevtushenko, Yevgenyn

Ewart, Gavin (Buchanan) 1916-1995 .... **CLC 13, 46**
See also BRWS 7; CA 89-92; 150; CANR 17, 46; CP 1, 2, 3, 4, 5, 6; DLB 40; MTCW 1

Ewers, Hanns Heinz 1871-1943 ..... **TCLC 12**
See also CA 109; 149

Ewing, Frederick R.
See Sturgeon, Theodore (Hamilton)

Exley, Frederick (Earl) 1929-1992 .... **CLC 6, 11**
See also AITN 2; BPFB 1; CA 81-84; 138; CANR 117; DLB 143; DLBY 1981

Eynhardt, Guillermo
See Quiroga, Horacio (Sylvestre)

Ezekiel, Nissim (Moses) 1924-2004 .. **CLC 61**
See also CA 61-64; 223; CP 1, 2, 3, 4, 5, 6, 7; DLB 323; EWL 3

Ezekiel, Tish O'Dowd 1943- .... **CLC 34**
See also CA 129

Fadeev, Aleksandr Aleksandrovich
See Bulgya, Alexander Alexandrovich

Fadeev, Alexandr Alexandrovich
See Bulgya, Alexander Alexandrovich

Fadeyev, A.
See Bulgya, Alexander Alexandrovich

Fadeyev, Alexander
See Bulgya, Alexander Alexandrovich

Fagen, Donald 1948- .... **CLC 26**

Fainzil'berg, Il'ia Arnol'dovich
See Fainzilberg, Ilya Arnoldovich

Fainzilberg, Ilya Arnoldovich 1897-1937 .... **TCLC 21**
See also CA 120; 165; DLB 272; EWL 3

Fair, Ronald L. 1932- .... **CLC 18**
See also BW 1; CA 69-72; CANR 25; DLB 33

Fairbairn, Roger
See Carr, John Dickson

Fairbairns, Zoe (Ann) 1948- .... **CLC 32**
See also CA 103; CANR 21, 85; CN 4, 5, 6, 7

Fairfield, Flora
See Alcott, Louisa May

Falco, Gian
See Papini, Giovanni

Falconer, James
See Kirkup, James

Falconer, Kenneth
See Kornbluth, C(yril) M.

Falkland, Samuel
See Heijermans, Herman

Fallaci, Oriana 1930-2006 .... **CLC 11, 110**
See also CA 77-80; 253; CANR 15, 58, 134; FW; MTCW 1

Faludi, Susan 1959- .... **CLC 140**
See also CA 138; CANR 126, 194; FW; MTCW 2; MTFW 2005; NCFS 3

Faludy, George 1913- .... **CLC 42**
See also CA 21-24R

Faludy, Gyoergy
See Faludy, George

Fanon, Frantz 1925-1961 ...... **BLC 1:2; CLC 74; TCLC 188**
See also BW 1; CA 116; 89-92; DAM MULT; DLB 296; LMFS 2; WLIT 2

Fanshawe, Ann 1625-1680 .... **LC 11**

Fante, John (Thomas) 1911-1983 .... **CLC 60; SSC 65**
See also AMWS 11; CA 69-72; 109; CANR 23, 104; DLB 130; DLBY 1983

Far, Sui Sin
See Eaton, Edith Maude

Farah, Nuruddin 1945- .. **BLC 1:2, 2:2; CLC 53, 137**
See also AFW; BW 2, 3; CA 106; CANR 81, 148; CDWLB 3; CN 4, 5, 6, 7; DAM MULT; DLB 125; EWL 3; WLIT 2

Fardusi
See Ferdowsi, Abu'l Qasem

Fargue, Leon-Paul 1876(?)-1947 .... **TCLC 11**
See also CA 109; CANR 107; DLB 258; EWL 3

Farigoule, Louis
See Romains, Jules

Farina, Richard 1936(?)-1966 .... **CLC 9**
See also CA 81-84; 25-28R

Farley, Walter (Lorimer) 1915-1989 .... **CLC 17**
See also AAYA 58; BYA 14; CA 17-20R; CANR 8, 29, 84; DLB 22; JRDA; MAICYA 1, 2; SATA 2, 43, 132; YAW

Farmer, Philip Jose
See Farmer, Philip Jose

Farmer, Philip Jose 1918-2009 ..... **CLC 1, 19**
See also AAYA 28; BPFB 1; CA 1-4R; 283; CANR 4, 35, 111; DLB 8; MTCW 1; SATA 93; SATA-Obit 201; SCFW 1, 2; SFW 4

Farmer, Philipe Jos
See Farmer, Philip Jose

Farquhar, George 1677-1707 . **DC 38; LC 21**
See also BRW 2; DAM DRAM; DLB 84; RGEL 2

Farrell, J(ames) G(ordon) 1935-1979 .... **CLC 6**
See also CA 73-76; 89-92; CANR 36; CN 1, 2; DLB 14, 271, 326; MTCW 1; RGEL 2; RHW; WLIT 4

Farrell, James T(homas) 1904-1979 . **CLC 1, 4, 8, 11, 66; SSC 28; TCLC 228**
See also AMW; BPFB 1; CA 5-8R; 89-92; CANR 9, 61; CN 1, 2; DLB 4, 9, 86; DLBD 2; EWL 3; MAL 5; MTCW 1, 2; MTFW 2005; RGAL 4

Farrell, M. J.
See Keane, Mary Nesta

Farrell, Warren (Thomas) 1943- ...... **CLC 70**
See also CA 146; CANR 120

Farren, Richard J.
See Betjeman, John

Farren, Richard M.
See Betjeman, John

Farrugia, Mario Benedetti
See Bentley, Eric

Farrugia, Mario Orlando Hardy Hamlet Brenno Benedetti
See Benedetti, Mario

Fassbinder, Rainer Werner 1946-1982 .... **CLC 20**
See also CA 93-96; 106; CANR 31

Fast, Howard 1914-2003 .... **CLC 23, 131**
See also AAYA 16; BPFB 1; CA 1-4R, 181; 214; CAAE 181; CAAS 18; CANR 1, 33, 54, 75, 98, 140; CMW 4; CN 1, 2, 3, 4, 5, 6, 7; CPW; DAM NOV; DLB 9; INT CANR-33; LATS 1:1; MAL 5; MTCW 2; MTFW 2005; RHW; SATA 7; SATA-Essay 107; TCWW 1, 2; YAW

Faulcon, Robert
See Holdstock, Robert

Faulkner, William 1897-1962 .... **CLC 1, 3, 6, 8, 9, 11, 14, 18, 28, 52, 68; SSC 1, 35, 42, 92, 97; TCLC 141; WLC 2**
See also AAYA 7; AMW; AMWR 1; BPFB 1; BYA 5, 15; CA 81-84; CANR 33; CDALB 1929-1941; DA; DA3; DAB; DAC; DAM MST, NOV; DLB 9, 11, 44, 102, 316, 330; DLBD 2; DLBY 1986, 1997; EWL 3; EXPN; EXPS; GL 2; LAIT 2; LATS 1:1; LMFS 2; MAL 5; MTCW 1, 2; MTFW 2005; NFS 4, 8, 13, 24, 33; RGAL 4; RGSF 2; SSFS 2, 5, 6, 12, 27; TUS

Faulkner, William Cuthbert
See Faulkner, William

Fauset, Jessie Redmon 1882(?)-1961 ...... **BLC 1:2; CLC 19, 54; HR 1:2**
See also AFAW 2; BW 1; CA 109; CANR 83; DAM MULT; DLB 51; FW; LMFS 2; MAL 5; MBL

Faust, Frederick 1892-1944 .... **TCLC 49**
See also BPFB 1; CA 108; 152; CANR 143; DAM POP; DLB 256; TCWW 1, 2; TUS

Faust, Frederick Schiller
See Faust, Frederick

Faust, Irvin 1924- .... **CLC 8**
See also CA 33-36R; CANR 28, 67; CN 1, 2, 3, 4, 5, 6, 7; DLB 2, 28, 218, 278; DLBY 1980

Fawkes, Guy
See Benchley, Robert (Charles)

Fearing, Kenneth 1902-1961 .... **CLC 51**
See also CA 93-96; CANR 59; CMW 4; DLB 9; MAL 5; RGAL 4

Fearing, Kenneth Flexner
See Fearing, Kenneth

Fecamps, Elise
See Creasey, John

Federman, Raymond 1928-2009 .. **CLC 6, 47**
See also CA 17-20R, 208; 292; CAAE 208;
CAAS 8; CANR 10, 43, 83, 108; CN 3,
4, 5, 6; DLBY 1980

Federspiel, J.F. 1931-2007 .... **CLC 42**
See also CA 146; 257

Federspiel, Juerg F.
See Federspiel, J.F.

Federspiel, Jurg F.
See Federspiel, J.F.

Feiffer, Jules 1929- .... **CLC 2, 8, 64**
See also AAYA 3, 62; CA 17-20R; CAD;
CANR 30, 59, 129, 161, 192; CD 5, 6;
DAM DRAM; DLB 7, 44; INT CANR-
30; MTCW 1; SATA 8, 61, 111, 157, 201

Feiffer, Jules Ralph
See Feiffer, Jules

Feige, Hermann Albert Otto Maximilian
See Traven, B.

Fei-Kan, Li
See Jin, Ba

Feinberg, David B. 1956-1994 .... **CLC 59**
See also CA 135; 147

Feinstein, Elaine 1930- .... **CLC 36**
See also CA 69-72; CAAS 1; CANR 31,
68, 121, 162; CN 3, 4, 5, 6, 7; CP 2, 3, 4,
5, 6, 7; CWP; DLB 14, 40; MTCW 1

Feke, Gilbert David CLC 65

Feldman, Irving (Mordecai) 1928- ..... **CLC 7**
See also CA 1-4R; CANR 1; CP 1, 2, 3, 4,
5, 6, 7; DLB 169; TCLE 1:1

Felix-Tchicaya, Gerald
See Tchicaya, Gerald Felix

Fellini, Federico 1920-1993 .... **CLC 16, 85**
See also CA 65-68; 143; CANR 33

Felltham, Owen 1602(?)-1668 .... **LC 92**
See also DLB 126, 151

Felsen, Henry Gregor 1916-1995 ..... **CLC 17**
See also CA 1-4R; 180; CANR 1; SAAS 2;
SATA 1

Felski, Rita CLC 65

**Fenelon, Francois de Pons de Salignac de la
Mothe-** 1651-1715 .... **LC 134**
See also DLB 268; EW 3; GFL Beginnings
to 1789

Fenno, Jack
See Calisher, Hortense

Fenollosa, Ernest (Francisco)
1853-1908 .... **TCLC 91**

Fenton, James 1949- .... **CLC 32, 209**
See also CA 102; CANR 108, 160; CP 2, 3,
4, 5, 6, 7; DLB 40; PFS 11

Fenton, James Martin
See Fenton, James

Ferber, Edna 1887-1968 .... **CLC 18, 93**
See also AITN 1; CA 5-8R; 25-28R; CANR
68, 105; DLB 9, 28, 86, 266; MAL 5;
MTCW 1, 2; MTFW 2005; RGAL 4;
RHW; SATA 7; TCWW 1, 2

Ferdousi
See Ferdowsi, Abu'l Qasem

Ferdovsi
See Ferdowsi, Abu'l Qasem

Ferdowsi
See Ferdowsi, Abu'l Qasem

Ferdowsi, Abolghasem Mansour
See Ferdowsi, Abu'l Qasem

Ferdowsi, Abol-Qasem
See Ferdowsi, Abu'l Qasem

Ferdowsi, Abolqasem
See Ferdowsi, Abu'l Qasem

Ferdowsi, Abu'l Qasem
940-1020(?) .... **CMLC 43**
See also CA 276; RGWL 2, 3; WLIT 6

Ferdowsi, A.M.
See Ferdowsi, Abu'l Qasem

Ferdowsi, Hakim Abolghasem
See Ferdowsi, Abu'l Qasem

Ferguson, Helen
See Kavan, Anna

Ferguson, Niall 1964- .... **CLC 134, 250**
See also CA 190; CANR 154, 200

Ferguson, Niall Campbell
See Ferguson, Niall

Ferguson, Samuel 1810-1886 .... **NCLC 33**
See also DLB 32; RGEL 2

Fergusson, Robert 1750-1774 .... **LC 29**
See also DLB 109; RGEL 2

Ferling, Lawrence
See Ferlinghetti, Lawrence

Ferlinghetti, Lawrence 1919(?)- .... **CLC 2, 6,
10, 27, 111; PC 1**
See also AAYA 74; BG 1:2; CA 5-8R; CAD;
CANR 3, 41, 73, 125, 172; CDALB 1941-
1968; CP 1, 2, 3, 4, 5, 6, 7; DA3; DAM
POET; DLB 5, 16; MAL 5; MTCW 1, 2;
MTFW 2005; PFS 28; RGAL 4; WP

Ferlinghetti, Lawrence Monsanto
See Ferlinghetti, Lawrence

Fern, Fanny
See Parton, Sara Payson Willis

Fernandez, Vicente Garcia Huidobro
See Huidobro Fernandez, Vicente Garcia

Fernandez-Armesto, Felipe 1950- .... **CLC 70**
See also CA 142; CANR 93, 153, 189

Fernandez-Armesto, Felipe Fermin Ricardo
See Fernandez-Armesto, Felipe

Fernandez de Lizardi, Jose Joaquin
See Lizardi, Jose Joaquin Fernandez de

Ferre, Rosario 1938- ...... **CLC 139; HLCS 1;
SSC 36, 106**
See also CA 131; CANR 55, 81, 134; CWW
2; DLB 145; EWL 3; HW 1, 2; LAWS 1;
MTCW 2; MTFW 2005; WLIT 1

Ferrer, Gabriel (Francisco Victor) Miro
See Miro (Ferrer), Gabriel (Francisco
Victor)

Ferrier, Susan (Edmonstone)
1782-1854 .... **NCLC 8**
See also DLB 116; RGEL 2

Ferrigno, Robert 1947- .... **CLC 65**
See also CA 140; CANR 125, 161

Ferris, Joshua 1974- .... **CLC 280**
See also CA 262

Ferron, Jacques 1921-1985 .... **CLC 94**
See also CA 117; 129; CCA 1; DAC; DLB
60; EWL 3

Feuchtwanger, Lion 1884-1958 .... **TCLC 3**
See also CA 104; 187; DLB 66; EWL 3;
RGHL

Feuerbach, Ludwig 1804-1872 ..... **NCLC 139**
See also DLB 133

Feuillet, Octave 1821-1890 .... **NCLC 45**
See also DLB 192

Feydeau, Georges 1862-1921 .... **TCLC 22**
See also CA 113; 152; CANR 84; DAM
DRAM; DLB 192; EWL 3; GFL 1789 to
the Present; RGWL 2, 3

Feydeau, Georges Leon JulesMarie
See Feydeau, Georges

Fichte, Johann Gottlieb
1762-1814 .... **NCLC 62**
See also DLB 90

Ficino, Marsilio 1433-1499 .... **LC 12, 152**
See also LMFS 1

Fiedeler, Hans
See Doeblin, Alfred

Fiedler, Leslie A(aron) 1917-2003 ..... **CLC 4,
13, 24**
See also AMWS 13; CA 9-12R; 212; CANR
7, 63; CN 1, 2, 3, 4, 5, 6; DLB 28, 67;
EWL 3; MAL 5; MTCW 1, 2; RGAL 4;
TUS

Field, Andrew 1938- .... **CLC 44**
See also CA 97-100; CANR 25

Field, Eugene 1850-1895 .... **NCLC 3**
See also DLB 23, 42, 140; DLBD 13; MAI-
CYA 1, 2; RGAL 4; SATA 16

Field, Gans T.
See Wellman, Manly Wade

Field, Michael 1915-1971 .... **TCLC 43**
See also CA 29-32R

Fielding, Helen 1958- .... **CLC 146, 217**
See also AAYA 65; CA 172; CANR 127;
DLB 231; MTFW 2005

Fielding, Henry 1707-1754 .... **LC 1, 46, 85,
151, 154; WLC 2**
See also BRW 3; BRWR 1; CDBLB 1660-
1789; DA; DA3; DAB; DAC; DAM
DRAM, MST, NOV; DLB 39, 84, 101;
NFS 18, 32; RGEL 2; TEA; WLIT 3

Fielding, Sarah 1710-1768 .... **LC 1, 44**
See also DLB 39; RGEL 2; TEA

Fields, W. C. 1880-1946 .... **TCLC 80**
See also DLB 44

Fierstein, Harvey 1954- .... **CLC 33**
See also CA 123; 129; CAD; CD 5, 6;
CPW; DA3; DAM DRAM, POP; DFS 6;
DLB 266; GLL; MAL 5

Fierstein, Harvey Forbes
See Fierstein, Harvey

Figes, Eva 1932- .... **CLC 31**
See also CA 53-56; CANR 4, 44, 83; CN 2,
3, 4, 5, 6, 7; DLB 14, 271; FW; RGHL

Filippo, Eduardo de
See de Filippo, Eduardo

Finch, Anne 1661-1720 ..... **LC 3, 137; PC 21**
See also BRWS 9; DLB 95; PFS 30

Finch, Robert (Duer Claydon)
1900-1995 .... **CLC 18**
See also CA 57-60; CANR 9, 24, 49; CP 1,
2, 3, 4, 5, 6; DLB 88

Findley, Timothy 1930-2002 ..... **CLC 27, 102**
See also AMWS 20; CA 25-28R; 206;
CANR 12, 42, 69, 109; CCA 1; CN 4, 5,
6, 7; DAC; DAM MST; DLB 53; FANT;
RHW

Fink, William
See Mencken, H. L.

Firbank, Louis 1942- .... **CLC 21**
See also CA 117

Firbank, (Arthur Annesley) Ronald
1886-1926 .... **TCLC 1**
See also BRWS 2; CA 104; 177; DLB 36;
EWL 3; RGEL 2

Firdaosi
See Ferdowsi, Abu'l Qasem

Firdausi
See Ferdowsi, Abu'l Qasem

Firdavsi, Abulqosimi
See Ferdowsi, Abu'l Qasem

Firdavsii, Abulqosim
See Ferdowsi, Abu'l Qasem

Firdawsi, Abu al-Qasim
See Ferdowsi, Abu'l Qasem

Firdosi
See Ferdowsi, Abu'l Qasem

Firdousi
See Ferdowsi, Abu'l Qasem

Firdousi, Abu'l-Qasim
See Ferdowsi, Abu'l Qasem

Firdovsi, A.
See Ferdowsi, Abu'l Qasem

Firdovsi, Abulgasim
See Ferdowsi, Abu'l Qasem

Firdusi
See Ferdowsi, Abu'l Qasem

Fish, Stanley
See Fish, Stanley Eugene

Fish, Stanley E.
See Fish, Stanley Eugene

Fish, Stanley Eugene 1938- .... **CLC 142**
See also CA 112; 132; CANR 90; DLB 67

Fisher, Dorothy (Frances) Canfield
1879-1958 .... **TCLC 87**
See also CA 114; 136; CANR 80; CLR 71;
CWRI 5; DLB 9, 102, 284; MAICYA 1,
2; MAL 5; YABC 1

Fisher, M(ary) F(rances) K(ennedy)
1908-1992 .... **CLC 76, 87**
See also AMWS 17; CA 77-80; 138; CANR
44; MTCW 2

Fisher, Roy 1930- .... **CLC 25**
See also CA 81-84; CAAS 10; CANR 16;
CP 1, 2, 3, 4, 5, 6, 7; DLB 40

Fisher, Rudolph 1897-1934 ...... **BLC 1:2; HR
1:2; SSC 25; TCLC 11**
See also BW 1, 3; CA 107; 124; CANR 80;
DAM MULT; DLB 51, 102

Fisher, Vardis (Alvero) 1895-1968 .... **CLC 7;
TCLC 140**
See also CA 5-8R; 25-28R; CANR 68; DLB
9, 206; MAL 5; RGAL 4; TCWW 1, 2

Fiske, Tarleton
See Bloch, Robert (Albert)

Fitch, Clarke
See Sinclair, Upton

Fitch, John IV
See Cormier, Robert

Fitzgerald, Captain Hugh
See Baum, L. Frank

FitzGerald, Edward 1809-1883 ...... **NCLC 9,
153; PC 79**
See also BRW 4; DLB 32; RGEL 2

Fitzgerald, F. Scott 1896-1940 ...... **SSC 6, 31,
75; TCLC 1, 6, 14, 28, 55, 157; WLC 2**
See also AAYA 24; AITN 1; AMW; AMWC
2; AMWR 1; BPFB 1; CA 110; 123;
CDALB 1917-1929; DA; DA3; DAB;
DAC; DAM MST, NOV; DLB 4, 9, 86,
219, 273; DLBD 1, 15, 16; DLBY 1981,
1996; EWL 3; EXPN; EXPS; LAIT 3;
MAL 5; MTCW 1, 2; MTFW 2005; NFS
2, 19, 20; RGAL 4; RGSF 2; SSFS 4, 15,
21, 25; TUS

Fitzgerald, Francis Scott Key
See Fitzgerald, F. Scott

Fitzgerald, Penelope 1916-2000 . **CLC 19, 51,
61, 143**
See also BRWS 5; CA 85-88; 190; CAAS
10; CANR 56, 86, 131; CN 3, 4, 5, 6, 7;
DLB 14, 194, 326; EWL 3; MTCW 2;
MTFW 2005

Fitzgerald, Robert (Stuart)
1910-1985 .... **CLC 39**
See also CA 1-4R; 114; CANR 1; CP 1, 2,
3, 4; DLBY 1980; MAL 5

FitzGerald, Robert D(avid)
1902-1987 .... **CLC 19**
See also CA 17-20R; CP 1, 2, 3, 4; DLB
260; RGEL 2

Fitzgerald, Zelda (Sayre)
1900-1948 .... **TCLC 52**
See also AMWS 9; CA 117; 126; DLBY
1984

Flanagan, Thomas (James Bonner)
1923-2002 .... **CLC 25, 52**
See also CA 108; 206; CANR 55; CN 3, 4,
5, 6, 7; DLBY 1980; INT CA-108; MTCW
1; RHW; TCLE 1:1

Flashman, Harry Paget
See Fraser, George MacDonald

Flaubert, Gustave 1821-1880 .... **NCLC 2, 10,
19, 62, 66, 135, 179, 185; SSC 11, 60;
WLC 2**
See also DA; DA3; DAB; DAC; DAM
MST, NOV; DLB 119, 301; EW 7; EXPS;
GFL 1789 to the Present; LAIT 2; LMFS
1; NFS 14; RGSF 2; RGWL 2, 3; SSFS
6; TWA

Flavius Josephus
See Josephus, Flavius

Flecker, Herman Elroy
See Flecker, (Herman) James Elroy

Flecker, (Herman) James Elroy
1884-1915 .... **TCLC 43**
See also CA 109; 150; DLB 10, 19; RGEL
2

Fleming, Ian 1908-1964 ... **CLC 3, 30; TCLC
193**
See also AAYA 26; BPFB 1; BRWS 14; CA
5-8R; CANR 59; CDBLB 1945-1960;
CMW 4; CPW; DA3; DAM POP; DLB
87, 201; MSW; MTCW 1, 2; MTFW
2005; RGEL 2; SATA 9; TEA; YAW

Fleming, Ian Lancaster
See Fleming, Ian

Fleming, Thomas 1927- .... **CLC 37**
See also CA 5-8R; CANR 10, 102, 155,
197; INT CANR-10; SATA 8

Fleming, Thomas James
See Fleming, Thomas

Fletcher, John 1579-1625 . **DC 6; LC 33, 151**
See also BRW 2; CDBLB Before 1660;
DLB 58; RGEL 2; TEA

Fletcher, John Gould 1886-1950 .... **TCLC 35**
See also CA 107; 167; DLB 4, 45; LMFS
2; MAL 5; RGAL 4

Fleur, Paul
See Pohl, Frederik

Flieg, Helmut
See Heym, Stefan

Flooglebuckle, Al
See Spiegelman, Art

Flying Officer X
See Bates, H(erbert) E(rnest)

Fo, Dario 1926- .... **CLC 32, 109, 227; DC 10**
See also CA 116; 128; CANR 68, 114, 134,
164; CWW 2; DA3; DAM DRAM; DFS
23; DLB 330; DLBY 1997; EWL 3;
MTCW 1, 2; MTFW 2005; WLIT 7

Foden, Giles 1967- .... **CLC 231**
See also CA 240; DLB 267; NFS 15

Fogarty, Jonathan Titulescu Esq.
See Farrell, James T(homas)

Follett, Ken 1949- .... **CLC 18**
See also AAYA 6, 50; BEST 89:4; BPFB 1;
CA 81-84; CANR 13, 33, 54, 102, 156,
197; CMW 4; CPW; DA3; DAM NOV,
POP; DLB 87; DLBY 1981; INT CANR-
33; LNFS 3; MTCW 1

Follett, Kenneth Martin
See Follett, Ken

Fondane, Benjamin 1898-1944 ..... **TCLC 159**

Fontane, Theodor 1819-1898 . **NCLC 26, 163**
See also CDWLB 2; DLB 129; EW 6;
RGWL 2, 3; TWA

Fonte, Moderata 1555-1592 .... **LC 118**

Fontenelle, Bernard Le Bovier de
1657-1757 .... **LC 140**
See also DLB 268, 313; GFL Beginnings to
1789

Fontenot, Chester **CLC 65**

Fonvizin, Denis Ivanovich
1744(?)-1792 .... **LC 81**
See also DLB 150; RGWL 2, 3

Foote, Albert Horton
See Foote, Horton

Foote, Horton 1916-2009 .... **CLC 51, 91**
See also AAYA 82; CA 73-76; 284; CAD;
CANR 34, 51, 110; CD 5, 6; CSW; DA3;
DAM DRAM; DFS 20; DLB 26, 266;
EWL 3; INT CANR-34; MTFW 2005

Foote, Mary Hallock 1847-1938 .. **TCLC 108**
See also DLB 186, 188, 202, 221; TCWW
2

Foote, Samuel 1721-1777 .... **LC 106**
See also DLB 89; RGEL 2

Foote, Shelby 1916-2005 .... **CLC 75, 224**
See also AAYA 40; CA 5-8R; 240; CANR
3, 45, 74, 131; CN 1, 2, 3, 4, 5, 6, 7;
CPW; CSW; DA3; DAM NOV, POP;
DLB 2, 17; MAL 5; MTCW 2; MTFW
2005; RHW

Forbes, Cosmo
See Lewton, Val

Forbes, Esther 1891-1967 .... **CLC 12**
See also AAYA 17; BYA 2; CA 13-14; 25-
28R; CAP 1; CLR 27, 147; DLB 22;
JRDA; MAICYA 1, 2; RHW; SATA 2,
100; YAW

Forche, Carolyn 1950- .. **CLC 25, 83, 86; PC
10**
See also CA 109; 117; CANR 50, 74, 138;
CP 4, 5, 6, 7; CWP; DA3; DAM POET;
DLB 5, 193; INT CA-117; MAL 5;
MTCW 2; MTFW 2005; PFS 18; RGAL
4

Forche, Carolyn Louise
See Forche, Carolyn

Ford, Elbur
See Hibbert, Eleanor Alice Burford

Ford, Ford Madox 1873-1939 ... **TCLC 1, 15,
39, 57, 172**
See also BRW 6; CA 104; 132; CANR 74;
CDBLB 1914-1945; DA3; DAM NOV;
DLB 34, 98, 162; EWL 3; MTCW 1, 2;
NFS 28; RGEL 2; RHW; TEA

Ford, Henry 1863-1947 .... **TCLC 73**
See also CA 115; 148

Ford, Jack
See Ford, John

Ford, John 1586-1639 .... **DC 8; LC 68, 153**
See also BRW 2; CDBLB Before 1660;
DA3; DAM DRAM; DFS 7; DLB 58;
IDTP; RGEL 2

Ford, John 1895-1973 .... **CLC 16**
See also AAYA 75; CA 187; 45-48

Ford, Richard 1944- ... **CLC 46, 99, 205, 277**
See also AMWS 5; CA 69-72; CANR 11,
47, 86, 128, 164; CN 5, 6, 7; CSW; DLB
227; EWL 3; MAL 5; MTCW 2; MTFW
2005; NFS 25; RGAL 4; RGSF 2

Ford, Webster
See Masters, Edgar Lee

Foreman, Richard 1937- .... **CLC 50**
See also CA 65-68; CAD; CANR 32, 63,
143; CD 5, 6

Forester, C. S. 1899-1966 ..... **CLC 35; TCLC
152**
See also CA 73-76; 25-28R; CANR 83;
DLB 191; RGEL 2; RHW; SATA 13

Forester, Cecil Scott
See Forester, C. S.

Forez
See Mauriac, Francois (Charles)

Forman, James
See Forman, James D.

Forman, James D. 1932- .... **CLC 21**
See also AAYA 17; CA 9-12R; CANR 4,
19, 42; JRDA; MAICYA 1, 2; SATA 8,
70; YAW

Forman, James Douglas
See Forman, James D.

Forman, Milos 1932- .... **CLC 164**
See also AAYA 63; CA 109

Fornes, Maria Irene 1930- .... **CLC 39, 61,
187; DC 10; HLCS 1**
See also CA 25-28R; CAD; CANR 28, 81;
CD 5, 6; CWD; DFS 25; DLB 7, 341; HW
1, 2; INT CANR-28; LLW; MAL 5;
MTCW 1; RGAL 4

Forrest, Leon (Richard)
1937-1997 .... **BLCS; CLC 4**
See also AFAW 2; BW 2; CA 89-92; 162;
CAAS 7; CANR 25, 52, 87; CN 4, 5, 6;
DLB 33

Freneau, Philip Morin 1752-1832 .. **NCLC 1, 111**
See also AMWS 2; DLB 37, 43; RGAL 4

Freud, Sigmund 1856-1939 .... **TCLC 52**
See also CA 115; 133; CANR 69; DLB 296; EW 8; EWL 3; LATS 1:1; MTCW 1, 2; MTFW 2005; NCFS 3; TWA

Freytag, Gustav 1816-1895 .... **NCLC 109**
See also DLB 129

Friedan, Betty 1921-2006 .... **CLC 74**
See also CA 65-68; 248; CANR 18, 45, 74; DLB 246; FW; MTCW 1, 2; MTFW 2005; NCFS 5

Friedan, Betty Naomi
See Friedan, Betty

Friedlander, Saul 1932- .... **CLC 90**
See also CA 117; 130; CANR 72; RGHL

Friedman, B(ernard) H(arper)
1926- .... **CLC 7**
See also CA 1-4R; CANR 3, 48

Friedman, Bruce Jay 1930- ...... **CLC 3, 5, 56**
See also CA 9-12R; CAD; CANR 25, 52, 101; CD 5, 6; CN 1, 2, 3, 4, 5, 6, 7; DLB 2, 28, 244; INT CANR-25; MAL 5; SSFS 18

Friel, Brian 1929- .. **CLC 5, 42, 59, 115, 253; DC 8; SSC 76**
See also BRWS 5; CA 21-24R; CANR 33, 69, 131; CBD; CD 5, 6; DFS 11; DLB 13, 319; EWL 3; MTCW 1; RGEL 2; TEA

Friis-Baastad, Babbis Ellinor
1921-1970 .... **CLC 12**
See also CA 17-20R; 134; SATA 7

Frisch, Max 1911-1991 ...... **CLC 3, 9, 14, 18, 32, 44; TCLC 121**
See also CA 85-88; 134; CANR 32, 74; CDWLB 2; DAM DRAM, NOV; DFS 25; DLB 69, 124; EW 13; EWL 3; MTCW 1, 2; MTFW 2005; RGHL; RGWL 2, 3

Froehlich, Peter
See Gay, Peter

Fromentin, Eugene (Samuel Auguste)
1820-1876 .... **NCLC 10, 125**
See also DLB 123; GFL 1789 to the Present

Frost, Frederick
See Faust, Frederick

Frost, Robert 1874-1963 . **CLC 1, 3, 4, 9, 10, 13, 15, 26, 34, 44; PC 1, 39, 71; TCLC 236; WLC 2**
See also AAYA 21; AMW; AMWR 1; CA 89-92; CANR 33; CDALB 1917-1929; CLR 67; DA; DA3; DAB; DAC; DAM MST, POET; DLB 54, 284, 342; DLBD 7; EWL 3; EXPP; MAL 5; MTCW 1, 2; MTFW 2005; PAB; PFS 1, 2, 3, 4, 5, 6, 7, 10, 13, 32, 35; RGAL 4; SATA 14; TUS; WP; WYA

Frost, Robert Lee
See Frost, Robert

Froude, James Anthony
1818-1894 .... **NCLC 43**
See also DLB 18, 57, 144

Froy, Herald
See Waterhouse, Keith

Fry, Christopher 1907-2005 .. **CLC 2, 10, 14; DC 36**
See also BRWS 3; CA 17-20R; 240; CAAS 23; CANR 9, 30, 74, 132; CBD; CD 5, 6; CP 1, 2, 3, 4, 5, 6, 7; DAM DRAM; DLB 13; EWL 3; MTCW 1, 2; MTFW 2005; RGEL 2; SATA 66; TEA

Frye, (Herman) Northrop
1912-1991 .... **CLC 24, 70; TCLC 165**
See also CA 5-8R; 133; CANR 8, 37; DLB 67, 68, 246; EWL 3; MTCW 1, 2; MTFW 2005; RGAL 4; TWA

Fuchs, Daniel 1909-1993 .... **CLC 8, 22**
See also CA 81-84; 142; CAAS 5; CANR 40; CN 1, 2, 3, 4, 5; DLB 9, 26, 28; DLBY 1993; MAL 5

Fuchs, Daniel 1934- .... **CLC 34**
See also CA 37-40R; CANR 14, 48

Fuentes, Carlos 1928- .. **CLC 3, 8, 10, 13, 22, 41, 60, 113, 288; HLC 1; SSC 24, 125; WLC 2**
See also AAYA 4, 45; AITN 2; BPFB 1; CA 69-72; CANR 10, 32, 68, 104, 138, 197; CDWLB 3; CWW 2; DA; DA3; DAB; DAC; DAM MST, MULT, NOV; DLB 113; DNFS 2; EWL 3; HW 1, 2; LAIT 3; LATS 1:2; LAW; LAWS 1; LMFS 2; MTCW 1, 2; MTFW 2005; NFS 8; RGSF 2; RGWL 2, 3; TWA; WLIT 1

Fuentes, Gregorio Lopez y
See Lopez y Fuentes, Gregorio

Fuentes Macias, Carlos Manuel
See Fuentes, Carlos

Fuertes, Gloria 1918-1998 .... **PC 27**
See also CA 178, 180; DLB 108; HW 2; SATA 115

Fugard, Athol 1932- .... **CLC 5, 9, 14, 25, 40, 80, 211; DC 3**
See also AAYA 17; AFW; BRWS 15; CA 85-88; CANR 32, 54, 118; CD 5, 6; DAM DRAM; DFS 3, 6, 10, 24; DLB 225; DNFS 1, 2; EWL 3; LATS 1:2; MTCW 1; MTFW 2005; RGEL 2; WLIT 2

Fugard, Harold Athol
See Fugard, Athol

Fugard, Sheila 1932- .... **CLC 48**
See also CA 125

Fujiwara no Teika 1162-1241 .... **CMLC 73**
See also DLB 203

Fukuyama, Francis 1952- .... **CLC 131**
See also CA 140; CANR 72, 125, 170

Fuller, Charles (H.), (Jr.) 1939- ..... **BLC 1:2; CLC 25; DC 1**
See also BW 2; CA 108; 112; CAD; CANR 87; CD 5, 6; DAM DRAM, MULT; DFS 8; DLB 38, 266; EWL 3; INT CA-112; MAL 5; MTCW 1

Fuller, Henry Blake 1857-1929 .... **TCLC 103**
See also CA 108; 177; DLB 12; RGAL 4

Fuller, John (Leopold) 1937- .... **CLC 62**
See also CA 21-24R; CANR 9, 44; CP 1, 2, 3, 4, 5, 6, 7; DLB 40

Fuller, Margaret 1810-1850 ...... **NCLC 5, 50, 211**
See also AMWS 2; CDALB 1640-1865; DLB 1, 59, 73, 183, 223, 239; FW; LMFS 1; SATA 25

Fuller, Roy (Broadbent) 1912-1991 ... **CLC 4, 28**
See also BRWS 7; CA 5-8R; 135; CAAS 10; CANR 53, 83; CN 1, 2, 3, 4, 5; CP 1, 2, 3, 4, 5; CWRI 5; DLB 15, 20; EWL 3; RGEL 2; SATA 87

Fuller, Sarah Margaret
See Fuller, Margaret

Fuller, Thomas 1608-1661 .... **LC 111**
See also DLB 151

Fulton, Alice 1952- .... **CLC 52**
See also CA 116; CANR 57, 88, 200; CP 5, 6, 7; CWP; DLB 193; PFS 25

Fundi
See Baraka, Amiri

Furey, Michael
See Ward, Arthur Henry Sarsfield

Furphy, Joseph 1843-1912 .... **TCLC 25**
See also CA 163; DLB 230; EWL 3; RGEL 2

Furst, Alan 1941- .... **CLC 255**
See also CA 69-72; CANR 12, 34, 59, 102, 159, 193; DLB 350; DLBY 01

Fuson, Robert H(enderson) 1927- .... **CLC 70**
See also CA 89-92; CANR 103

Fussell, Paul 1924- .... **CLC 74**
See also BEST 90:1; CA 17-20R; CANR 8, 21, 35, 69, 135; INT CANR-21; MTCW 1, 2; MTFW 2005

Futabatei, Shimei 1864-1909 .... **TCLC 44**
See also CA 162; DLB 180; EWL 3; MJW

Futabatei Shimei
See Futabatei, Shimei

Futrelle, Jacques 1875-1912 .... **TCLC 19**
See also CA 113; 155; CMW 4

GAB
See Russell, George William

Gaberman, Judie Angell
See Angell, Judie

Gaboriau, Emile 1835-1873 .... **NCLC 14**
See also CMW 4; MSW

Gadda, Carlo Emilio 1893-1973 ...... **CLC 11; TCLC 144**
See also CA 89-92; DLB 177; EWL 3; WLIT 7

Gaddis, William 1922-1998 ... **CLC 1, 3, 6, 8, 10, 19, 43, 86**
See also AMWS 4; BPFB 1; CA 17-20R; 172; CANR 21, 48, 148; CN 1, 2, 3, 4, 5, 6; DLB 2, 278; EWL 3; MAL 5; MTCW 1, 2; MTFW 2005; RGAL 4

Gage, Walter
See Inge, William (Motter)

Gaiman, Neil 1960- .... **CLC 195**
See also AAYA 19, 42, 82; CA 133; CANR 81, 129, 188; CLR 109; DLB 261; HGG; MTFW 2005; SATA 85, 146, 197; SFW 4; SUFW 2

Gaiman, Neil Richard
See Gaiman, Neil

Gaines, Ernest J. 1933- ..... **BLC 1:2; CLC 3, 11, 18, 86, 181; SSC 68, 137**
See also AAYA 18; AFAW 1, 2; AITN 1; BPFB 2; BW 2, 3; BYA 6; CA 9-12R; CANR 6, 24, 42, 75, 126; CDALB 1968-1988; CLR 62; CN 1, 2, 3, 4, 5, 6, 7; CSW; DA3; DAM MULT; DLB 2, 33, 152; DLBY 1980; EWL 3; EXPN; LAIT 5; LATS 1:2; MAL 5; MTCW 1, 2; MTFW 2005; NFS 5, 7, 16; RGAL 4; RGSF 2; RHW; SATA 86; SSFS 5; YAW

Gaines, Ernest James
See Gaines, Ernest J.

Gaitskill, Mary 1954- .... **CLC 69**
See also CA 128; CANR 61, 152; DLB 244; TCLE 1:1

Gaitskill, Mary Lawrence
See Gaitskill, Mary

Gaius Suetonius Tranquillus
See Suetonius

Galdos, Benito Perez
See Perez Galdos, Benito

Gale, Zona 1874-1938 .... **DC 30; TCLC 7**
See also CA 105; 153; CANR 84; DAM DRAM; DFS 17; DLB 9, 78, 228; RGAL 4

Galeano, Eduardo 1940- ... **CLC 72; HLCS 1**
See also CA 29-32R; CANR 13, 32, 100, 163; HW 1

Galeano, Eduardo Hughes
See Galeano, Eduardo

Galiano, Juan Valera y Alcala
See Valera y Alcala-Galiano, Juan

Galilei, Galileo 1564-1642 .... **LC 45**

Gallagher, Tess 1943- .... **CLC 18, 63; PC 9**
See also CA 106; CP 3, 4, 5, 6, 7; CWP; DAM POET; DLB 120, 212, 244; PFS 16

Gallant, Mavis 1922- ..... **CLC 7, 18, 38, 172, 288; SSC 5, 78**
See also CA 69-72; CANR 29, 69, 117; CCA 1; CN 1, 2, 3, 4, 5, 6, 7; DAC; DAM MST; DLB 53; EWL 3; MTCW 1, 2; MTFW 2005; RGEL 2; RGSF 2

Gay, Peter Jack
See Gay, Peter

Gaye, Marvin (Pentz, Jr.)
1939-1984 .... **CLC 26**
See also CA 195; 112

Gebler, Carlo 1954- .... **CLC 39**
See also CA 119; 133; CANR 96, 186; DLB 271

Gebler, Carlo Ernest
See Gebler, Carlo

Gee, Maggie 1948- .... **CLC 57**
See also CA 130; CANR 125; CN 4, 5, 6, 7; DLB 207; MTFW 2005

Gee, Maurice 1931- .... **CLC 29**
See also AAYA 42; CA 97-100; CANR 67, 123, 204; CLR 56; CN 2, 3, 4, 5, 6, 7; CWRI 5; EWL 3; MAICYA 2; RGSF 2; SATA 46, 101

Gee, Maurice Gough
See Gee, Maurice

Geiogamah, Hanay 1945- .... **NNAL**
See also CA 153; DAM MULT; DLB 175

Gelbart, Larry 1928-2009 .... **CLC 21, 61**
See also CA 73-76; 290; CAD; CANR 45, 94; CD 5, 6

Gelbart, Larry Simon
See Gelbart, Larry

Gelber, Jack 1932-2003 ...... **CLC 1, 6, 14, 79**
See also CA 1-4R; 216; CAD; CANR 2; DLB 7, 228; MAL 5

Gellhorn, Martha (Ellis)
1908-1998 .... **CLC 14, 60**
See also CA 77-80; 164; CANR 44; CN 1, 2, 3, 4, 5, 6 7; DLBY 1982, 1998

Genet, Jean 1910-1986 .. **CLC 1, 2, 5, 10, 14, 44, 46; DC 25; TCLC 128**
See also CA 13-16R; CANR 18; DA3; DAM DRAM; DFS 10; DLB 72, 321; DLBY 1986; EW 13; EWL 3; GFL 1789 to the Present; GLL 1; LMFS 2; MTCW 1, 2; MTFW 2005; RGWL 2, 3; TWA

Genlis, Stephanie-Felicite Ducrest
1746-1830 .... **NCLC 166**
See also DLB 313

Gent, Peter 1942- .... **CLC 29**
See also AITN 1; CA 89-92; DLBY 1982

Gentile, Giovanni 1875-1944 .... **TCLC 96**
See also CA 119

Geoffrey of Monmouth c.
1100-1155 .... **CMLC 44**
See also DLB 146; TEA

George, Jean
See George, Jean Craighead

George, Jean C.
See George, Jean Craighead

George, Jean Craighead 1919- .... **CLC 35**
See also AAYA 8, 69; BYA 2, 4; CA 5-8R; CANR 25, 198; CLR 1, 80, 136; DLB 52; JRDA; MAICYA 1, 2; SATA 2, 68, 124, 170; WYA; YAW

George, Stefan (Anton) 1868-1933 . **TCLC 2, 14**
See also CA 104; 193; EW 8; EWL 3

Georges, Georges Martin
See Simenon, Georges

Gerald of Wales c. 1146-c. 1223 ... **CMLC 60**

Gerhardi, William Alexander
See Gerhardie, William Alexander

Gerhardie, William Alexander
1895-1977 .... **CLC 5**
See also CA 25-28R; 73-76; CANR 18; CN 1, 2; DLB 36; RGEL 2

Germain, Sylvie 1954- .... **CLC 283**
See also CA 191

Gerome
See France, Anatole

Gerson, Jean 1363-1429 .... **LC 77**
See also DLB 208

Gersonides 1288-1344 .... **CMLC 49**
See also DLB 115

Gerstler, Amy 1956- .... **CLC 70**
See also CA 146; CANR 99

Gertler, T. CLC 34
See also CA 116; 121

Gertrude of Helfta c. 1256-c.
1301 .... **CMLC 105**

Gertsen, Aleksandr Ivanovich
See Herzen, Aleksandr Ivanovich

Gervase of Melkley c. 1185-c.
1216 .... **CMLC 121**

Ghalib
See Ghalib, Asadullah Khan

Ghalib, Asadullah Khan
1797-1869 .... **NCLC 39, 78**
See also DAM POET; RGWL 2, 3

Ghelderode, Michel de 1898-1962 ..... **CLC 6, 11; DC 15; TCLC 187**
See also CA 85-88; CANR 40, 77; DAM DRAM; DLB 321; EW 11; EWL 3; TWA

Ghiselin, Brewster 1903-2001 .... **CLC 23**
See also CA 13-16R; CAAS 10; CANR 13; CP 1, 2, 3, 4, 5, 6, 7

Ghose, Aurabinda 1872-1950 .... **TCLC 63**
See also CA 163; EWL 3

Ghose, Aurobindo
See Ghose, Aurabinda

Ghose, Zulfikar 1935- .... **CLC 42, 200**
See also CA 65-68; CANR 67; CN 1, 2, 3, 4, 5, 6, 7; CP 1, 2, 3, 4, 5, 6, 7; DLB 323; EWL 3

Ghosh, Amitav 1956- .... **CLC 44, 153**
See also CA 147; CANR 80, 158, 205; CN 6, 7; DLB 323; WWE 1

Giacosa, Giuseppe 1847-1906 .... **TCLC 7**
See also CA 104

Gibb, Lee
See Waterhouse, Keith

Gibbon, Edward 1737-1794 .... **LC 97**
See also BRW 3; DLB 104, 336; RGEL 2

Gibbon, Lewis Grassic
See Mitchell, James Leslie

Gibbons, Kaye 1960- .... **CLC 50, 88, 145**
See also AAYA 34; AMWS 10; CA 151; CANR 75, 127; CN 7; CSW; DA3; DAM POP; DLB 292; MTCW 2; MTFW 2005; NFS 3; RGAL 4; SATA 117

Gibran, Kahlil 1883-1931 ..... **PC 9; TCLC 1, 9, 205**
See also AMWS 20****; CA 104; 150; DA3; DAM POET, POP; DLB 346; EWL 3; MTCW 2; WLIT 6

Gibran, Khalil
See Gibran, Kahlil

Gibson, Mel 1956- .... **CLC 215**
See also AAYA 80

Gibson, William 1914-2008 .... **CLC 23**
See also CA 9-12R; 279; CAD; CANR 9, 42, 75, 125; CD 5, 6; DA; DAB; DAC; DAM DRAM, MST; DFS 2; DLB 7; LAIT 2; MAL 5; MTCW 2; MTFW 2005; SATA 66; SATA-Obit 199; YAW

Gibson, William 1948- .... **CLC 39, 63, 186, 192; SSC 52**
See also AAYA 12, 59; AMWS 16; BPFB 2; CA 126; 133; CANR 52, 90, 106, 172; CN 6, 7; CPW; DA3; DAM POP; DLB 251; MTCW 2; MTFW 2005; SCFW 2; SFW 4; SSFS 26

Gibson, William Ford
See Gibson, William

Gide, Andre 1869-1951 ..... **SSC 13; TCLC 5, 12, 36, 177; WLC 3**
See also CA 104; 124; DA; DA3; DAB; DAC; DAM MST, NOV; DLB 65, 321, 330; EW 8; EWL 3; GFL 1789 to the Present; MTCW 1, 2; MTFW 2005; NFS 21; RGSF 2; RGWL 2, 3; TWA

Gide, Andre Paul Guillaume
See Gide, Andre

Gifford, Barry 1946- .... **CLC 34**
See also CA 65-68; CANR 9, 30, 40, 90, 180

Gifford, Barry Colby
See Gifford, Barry

Gilbert, Frank
See De Voto, Bernard (Augustine)

Gilbert, W(illiam) S(chwenck)
1836-1911 .... **TCLC 3**
See also CA 104; 173; DAM DRAM, POET; DLB 344; RGEL 2; SATA 36

Gilbert of Poitiers c. 1085-1154 .... **CMLC 85**

Gilbreth, Frank B., Jr. 1911-2001 .... **CLC 17**
See also CA 9-12R; SATA 2

Gilbreth, Frank Bunker
See Gilbreth, Frank B., Jr.

Gilchrist, Ellen 1935- .... **CLC 34, 48, 143, 264; SSC 14, 63**
See also BPFB 2; CA 113; 116; CANR 41, 61, 104, 191; CN 4, 5, 6, 7; CPW; CSW; DAM POP; DLB 130; EWL 3; EXPS; MTCW 1, 2; MTFW 2005; RGAL 4; RGSF 2; SSFS 9

Gilchrist, Ellen Louise
See Gilchrist, Ellen

Gildas fl. 6th cent. - .... **CMLC 99**

Giles, Molly 1942- .... **CLC 39**
See also CA 126; CANR 98

Gill, Arthur Eric Rowton Peter Joseph
See Gill, Eric

Gill, Eric 1882-1940 .... **TCLC 85**
See Gill, Arthur Eric Rowton Peter Joseph
See also CA 120; DLB 98

Gill, Patrick
See Creasey, John

Gillette, Douglas CLC 70

Gilliam, Terry 1940- .... **CLC 21, 141**
See also AAYA 19, 59; CA 108; 113; CANR 35; INT CA-113

Gilliam, Terry Vance
See Gilliam, Terry

Gillian, Jerry
See Gilliam, Terry

Gilliatt, Penelope (Ann Douglass)
1932-1993 .... **CLC 2, 10, 13, 53**
See also AITN 2; CA 13-16R; 141; CANR 49; CN 1, 2, 3, 4, 5; DLB 14

Gilligan, Carol 1936- .... **CLC 208**
See also CA 142; CANR 121, 187; FW

Gilman, Charlotte Anna Perkins Stetson
See Gilman, Charlotte Perkins

Gilman, Charlotte Perkins
1860-1935 ...... **SSC 13, 62; TCLC 9, 37, 117, 201**
See also AAYA 75; AMWS 11; BYA 11; CA 106; 150; DLB 221; EXPS; FL 1:5; FW; HGG; LAIT 2; MBL; MTCW 2; MTFW 2005; RGAL 4; RGSF 2; SFW 4; SSFS 1, 18

Gilmore, Mary (Jean Cameron)
1865-1962 .... **PC 87**
See also CA 114; DLB 260; RGEL 2; SATA 49

Gilmour, David 1946- .... **CLC 35**

Gilpin, William 1724-1804 .... **NCLC 30**

Gilray, J. D.
See Mencken, H. L.

Gilroy, Frank D(aniel) 1925- .... **CLC 2**
See also CA 81-84; CAD; CANR 32, 64, 86; CD 5, 6; DFS 17; DLB 7

Gilstrap, John 1957(?)- .... **CLC 99**
See also AAYA 67; CA 160; CANR 101

Goldsmith, Oliver 1730(?)-1774 .... **DC 8; LC 2, 48, 122; PC 77; WLC 3**
See also BRW 3; CDBLB 1660-1789; DA; DAB; DAC; DAM DRAM, MST, NOV, POET; DFS 1; DLB 39, 89, 104, 109, 142, 336; IDTP; RGEL 2; SATA 26; TEA; WLIT 3

Goldsmith, Peter
See Priestley, J(ohn) B(oynton)

Goldstein, Rebecca 1950- .... **CLC 239**
See also CA 144; CANR 99, 165; TCLE 1:1

Goldstein, Rebecca Newberger
See Goldstein, Rebecca

Gombrowicz, Witold 1904-1969 .... **CLC 4, 7, 11, 49**
See also CA 19-20; 25-28R; CANR 105; CAP 2; CDWLB 4; DAM DRAM; DLB 215; EW 12; EWL 3; RGWL 2, 3; TWA

Gomez de Avellaneda, Gertrudis 1814-1873 .... **NCLC 111**
See also LAW

Gomez de la Serna, Ramon 1888-1963 .... **CLC 9**
See also CA 153; 116; CANR 79; EWL 3; HW 1, 2

Goncharov, Ivan Alexandrovich 1812-1891 .... **NCLC 1, 63**
See also DLB 238; EW 6; RGWL 2, 3

Goncourt, Edmond de 1822-1896 ... **NCLC 7**
See also DLB 123; EW 7; GFL 1789 to the Present; RGWL 2, 3

Goncourt, Edmond Louis Antoine Huot de
See Goncourt, Edmond de

Goncourt, Jules Alfred Huot de
See Goncourt, Jules de

Goncourt, Jules de 1830-1870 .... **NCLC 7**
See Goncourt, Jules de
See also DLB 123; EW 7; GFL 1789 to the Present; RGWL 2, 3

Gongora (y Argote), Luis de 1561-1627 .... **LC 72**
See also RGWL 2, 3

Gontier, Fernande 19(?)- .... **CLC 50**

Gonzalez Martinez, Enrique
See Gonzalez Martinez, Enrique

Gonzalez Martinez, Enrique 1871-1952 .... **TCLC 72**
See also CA 166; CANR 81; DLB 290; EWL 3; HW 1, 2

Goodison, Lorna 1947- .... **BLC 2:2; PC 36**
See also CA 142; CANR 88, 189; CP 5, 6, 7; CWP; DLB 157; EWL 3; PFS 25

Goodman, Allegra 1967- .... **CLC 241**
See also CA 204; CANR 162, 204; DLB 244, 350

Goodman, Paul 1911-1972 ..... **CLC 1, 2, 4, 7**
See also CA 19-20; 37-40R; CAD; CANR 34; CAP 2; CN 1; DLB 130, 246; MAL 5; MTCW 1; RGAL 4

GoodWeather, Hartley
See King, Thomas

Goodweather, Hartley
See King, Thomas

Googe, Barnabe 1540-1594 .... **LC 94**
See also DLB 132; RGEL 2

Gordimer, Nadine 1923- ...... **CLC 3, 5, 7, 10, 18, 33, 51, 70, 123, 160, 161, 263; SSC 17, 80; WLCS**
See also AAYA 39; AFW; BRWS 2; CA 5-8R; CANR 3, 28, 56, 88, 131, 195; CN 1, 2, 3, 4, 5, 6, 7; DA; DA3; DAB; DAC; DAM MST, NOV; DLB 225, 326, 330; EWL 3; EXPS; INT CANR-28; LATS 1:2; MTCW 1, 2; MTFW 2005; NFS 4; RGEL 2; RGSF 2; SSFS 2, 14, 19, 28, 31; TWA; WLIT 2; YAW

Gordon, Adam Lindsay 1833-1870 .... **NCLC 21**
See also DLB 230

Gordon, Caroline 1895-1981 . **CLC 6, 13, 29, 83; SSC 15**
See also AMW; CA 11-12; 103; CANR 36; CAP 1; CN 1, 2; DLB 4, 9, 102; DLBD 17; DLBY 1981; EWL 3; MAL 5; MTCW 1, 2; MTFW 2005; RGAL 4; RGSF 2

Gordon, Charles William 1860-1937 .... **TCLC 31**
See also CA 109; DLB 92; TCWW 1, 2

Gordon, Mary 1949- .. **CLC 13, 22, 128, 216; SSC 59**
See also AMWS 4; BPFB 2; CA 102; CANR 44, 92, 154, 179; CN 4, 5, 6, 7; DLB 6; DLBY 1981; FW; INT CA-102; MAL 5; MTCW 1

Gordon, Mary Catherine
See Gordon, Mary

Gordon, N. J.
See Bosman, Herman Charles

Gordon, Sol 1923- .... **CLC 26**
See also CA 53-56; CANR 4; SATA 11

Gordone, Charles 1925-1995 .... **BLC 2:2; CLC 1, 4; DC 8**
See also BW 1, 3; CA 93-96, 180; 150; CAAE 180; CAD; CANR 55; DAM DRAM; DLB 7; INT CA-93-96; MTCW 1

Gore, Catherine 1800-1861 .... **NCLC 65**
See also DLB 116, 344; RGEL 2

Gorenko, Anna Andreevna
See Akhmatova, Anna

Gor'kii, Maksim
See Gorky, Maxim

Gorky, Maxim 1868-1936 ..... **SSC 28; TCLC 8; WLC 3**
See also CA 105; 141; CANR 83; DA; DAB; DAC; DAM DRAM, MST, NOV; DFS 9; DLB 295; EW 8; EWL 3; MTCW 2; MTFW 2005; RGSF 2; RGWL 2, 3; TWA

Goryan, Sirak
See Saroyan, William

Gosse, Edmund (William) 1849-1928 .... **TCLC 28**
See also CA 117; DLB 57, 144, 184; RGEL 2

Gotlieb, Phyllis 1926-2009 .... **CLC 18**
See also CA 13-16R; CANR 7, 135; CN 7; CP 1, 2, 3, 4; DLB 88, 251; SFW 4

Gotlieb, Phyllis Fay Bloom
See Gotlieb, Phyllis

Gottesman, S. D.
See Kornbluth, C(yril) M.; Pohl, Frederik

Gottfried von Strassburg fl. c. 1170-1215 .... **CMLC 10, 96**
See also CDWLB 2; DLB 138; EW 1; RGWL 2, 3

Gotthelf, Jeremias 1797-1854 .... **NCLC 117**
See also DLB 133; RGWL 2, 3

Gottschalk, Laura Riding
See Jackson, Laura

Gould, Lois 1932(?)-2002 .... **CLC 4, 10**
See also CA 77-80; 208; CANR 29; MTCW 1

Gould, Stephen Jay 1941-2002 .... **CLC 163**
See also AAYA 26; BEST 90:2; CA 77-80; 205; CANR 10, 27, 56, 75, 125; CPW; INT CANR-27; MTCW 1, 2; MTFW 2005

Gourmont, Remy(-Marie-Charles) de 1858-1915 .... **TCLC 17**
See also CA 109; 150; GFL 1789 to the Present; MTCW 2

Gournay, Marie le Jars de
See de Gournay, Marie le Jars

Govier, Katherine 1948- .... **CLC 51**
See also CA 101; CANR 18, 40, 128; CCA 1

Gower, John c. 1330-1408 .... **LC 76; PC 59**
See also BRW 1; DLB 146; RGEL 2

Goyen, (Charles) William 1915-1983 .... **CLC 5, 8, 14, 40**
See also AITN 2; CA 5-8R; 110; CANR 6, 71; CN 1, 2, 3; DLB 2, 218; DLBY 1983; EWL 3; INT CANR-6; MAL 5

Goytisolo, Juan 1931- .... **CLC 5, 10, 23, 133; HLC 1**
See also CA 85-88; CANR 32, 61, 131, 182; CWW 2; DAM MULT; DLB 322; EWL 3; GLL 2; HW 1, 2; MTCW 1, 2; MTFW 2005

Gozzano, Guido 1883-1916 .... **PC 10**
See also CA 154; DLB 114; EWL 3

Gozzi, (Conte) Carlo 1720-1806 .... **NCLC 23**

Grabbe, Christian Dietrich 1801-1836 .... **NCLC 2**
See also DLB 133; RGWL 2, 3

Grace, Patricia 1937- .... **CLC 56**
See also CA 176; CANR 118; CN 4, 5, 6, 7; EWL 3; RGSF 2

Grace, Patricia Frances
See Grace, Patricia

Gracian, Baltasar 1601-1658 .... **LC 15, 160**

Gracian y Morales, Baltasar
See Gracian, Baltasar

Gracq, Julien 1910-2007 ..... **CLC 11, 48, 259**
See also CA 122; 126; 267; CANR 141; CWW 2; DLB 83; GFL 1789 to the present

Grade, Chaim 1910-1982 .... **CLC 10**
See also CA 93-96; 107; DLB 333; EWL 3; RGHL

Grade, Khayim
See Grade, Chaim

Graduate of Oxford, A
See Ruskin, John

Grafton, Garth
See Duncan, Sara Jeannette

Grafton, Sue 1940- .... **CLC 163**
See also AAYA 11, 49; BEST 90:3; CA 108; CANR 31, 55, 111, 134, 195; CMW 4; CPW; CSW; DA3; DAM POP; DLB 226; FW; MSW; MTFW 2005

Graham, John
See Phillips, David Graham

Graham, Jorie 1950- .... **CLC 48, 118; PC 59**
See also AAYA 67; CA 111; CANR 63, 118, 205; CP 4, 5, 6, 7; CWP; DLB 120; EWL 3; MTFW 2005; PFS 10, 17; TCLE 1:1

Graham, R. B. Cunninghame
See Cunninghame Graham, Robert Bontine

Graham, Robert
See Haldeman, Joe

Graham, Robert Bontine Cunninghame
See Cunninghame Graham, Robert Bontine

Graham, Tom
See Lewis, Sinclair

Graham, W(illiam) S(ydney) 1918-1986 .... **CLC 29**
See also BRWS 7; CA 73-76; 118; CP 1, 2, 3, 4; DLB 20; RGEL 2

Graham, Winston (Mawdsley) 1910-2003 .... **CLC 23**
See also CA 49-52; 218; CANR 2, 22, 45, 66; CMW 4; CN 1, 2, 3, 4, 5, 6, 7; DLB 77; RHW

Grahame, Kenneth 1859-1932 ...... **TCLC 64, 136**
See also BYA 5; CA 108; 136; CANR 80; CLR 5, 135; CWRI 5; DA3; DAB; DLB 34, 141, 178; FANT; MAICYA 1, 2; MTCW 2; NFS 20; RGEL 2; SATA 100; TEA; WCH; YABC 1

Hamsund, Knut Pedersen
  See Pedersen, Knut
Handke, Peter 1942- .... **CLC 5, 8, 10, 15, 38, 134; DC 17**
  See also CA 77-80; CANR 33, 75, 104, 133, 180; CWW 2; DAM DRAM, NOV; DLB 85, 124; EWL 3; MTCW 1, 2; MTFW 2005; TWA
Handler, Chelsea 1976(?)- .... **CLC 269**
  See also CA 243
Handy, W(illiam) C(hristopher)
  1873-1958 .... **TCLC 97**
  See also BW 3; CA 121; 167
Haneke, Michael 1942- .... **CLC 283**
Hanley, James 1901-1985 ... **CLC 3, 5, 8, 13**
  See also CA 73-76; 117; CANR 36; CBD; CN 1, 2, 3; DLB 191; EWL 3; MTCW 1; RGEL 2
Hannah, Barry 1942-2010 ... **CLC 23, 38, 90, 270; SSC 94**
  See also BPFB 2; CA 108; 110; CANR 43, 68, 113; CN 4, 5, 6, 7; CSW; DLB 6, 234; INT CA-110; MTCW 1; RGSF 2
Hannon, Ezra
  See Hunter, Evan
Hanrahan, Barbara 1939-1991 .... **TCLC 219**
  See also CA 121; 127; CN 4, 5; DLB 289
Hansberry, Lorraine 1930-1965 ..... **BLC 1:2, 2:2; CLC 17, 62; DC 2; TCLC 192**
  See also AAYA 25; AFAW 1, 2; AMWS 4; BW 1, 3; CA 109; 25-28R; CABS 3; CAD; CANR 58; CDALB 1941-1968; CWD; DA; DA3; DAB; DAC; DAM DRAM, MST, MULT; DFS 2; DLB 7, 38; EWL 3; FL 1:6; FW; LAIT 4; MAL 5; MTCW 1, 2; MTFW 2005; RGAL 4; TUS
Hansberry, Lorraine Vivian
  See Hansberry, Lorraine
Hansen, Joseph 1923-2004 .... **CLC 38**
  See also BPFB 2; CA 29-32R; 233; CAAS 17; CANR 16, 44, 66, 125; CMW 4; DLB 226; GLL 1; INT CANR-16
Hansen, Karen V. 1955- .... **CLC 65**
  See also CA 149; CANR 102
Hansen, Martin A(lfred)
  1909-1955 .... **TCLC 32**
  See also CA 167; DLB 214; EWL 3
Hanson, Kenneth O(stlin) 1922- .... **CLC 13**
  See also CA 53-56; CANR 7; CP 1, 2, 3, 4, 5
Han Yu 768-824 .... **CMLC 122**
Hardwick, Elizabeth 1916-2007 .... **CLC 13**
  See also AMWS 3; CA 5-8R; 267; CANR 3, 32, 70, 100, 139; CN 4, 5, 6; CSW; DA3; DAM NOV; DLB 6; MBL; MTCW 1, 2; MTFW 2005; TCLE 1:1
Hardwick, Elizabeth Bruce
  See Hardwick, Elizabeth
Hardy, Thomas 1840-1928 . **PC 8, 92; SSC 2, 60, 113; TCLC 4, 10, 18, 32, 48, 53, 72, 143, 153, 229; WLC 3**
  See also AAYA 69; BRW 6; BRWC 1, 2; BRWR 1; CA 104; 123; CDBLB 1890-1914; DA; DA3; DAB; DAC; DAM MST, NOV, POET; DLB 18, 19, 135, 284; EWL 3; EXPN; EXPP; LAIT 2; MTCW 1, 2; MTFW 2005; NFS 3, 11, 15, 19, 30; PFS 3, 4, 18; RGEL 2; RGSF 2; TEA; WLIT 4
Hare, David 1947- . **CLC 29, 58, 136; DC 26**
  See also BRWS 4; CA 97-100; CANR 39, 91; CBD; CD 5, 6; DFS 4, 7, 16; DLB 13, 310; MTCW 1; TEA
Harewood, John
  See Van Druten, John (William)
Harford, Henry
  See Hudson, W(illiam) H(enry)
Hargrave, Leonie
  See Disch, Thomas M.

Hariri, Al- al-Qasim ibn 'Ali Abu Muhammad al-Basri
  See al-Hariri, al-Qasim ibn 'Ali Abu Muhammad al-Basri
Harjo, Joy 1951- .... **CLC 83; NNAL; PC 27**
  See also AMWS 12; CA 114; CANR 35, 67, 91, 129; CP 6, 7; CWP; DAM MULT; DLB 120, 175, 342; EWL 3; MTCW 2; MTFW 2005; PFS 15, 32; RGAL 4
Harlan, Louis R. 1922-2010 .... **CLC 34**
  See also CA 21-24R; CANR 25, 55, 80
Harlan, Louis Rudolph
  See Harlan, Louis R.
Harling, Robert 1951(?)- .... **CLC 53**
  See also CA 147
Harmon, William (Ruth) 1938- .... **CLC 38**
  See also CA 33-36R; CANR 14, 32, 35; SATA 65
Harper, Edith Alice Mary
  See Wickham, Anna
Harper, F. E. W.
  See Harper, Frances Ellen Watkins
Harper, Frances E. W.
  See Harper, Frances Ellen Watkins
Harper, Frances E. Watkins
  See Harper, Frances Ellen Watkins
Harper, Frances Ellen
  See Harper, Frances Ellen Watkins
Harper, Frances Ellen Watkins
  1825-1911 . **BLC 1:2; PC 21; TCLC 14, 217**
  See also AFAW 1, 2; BW 1, 3; CA 111; 125; CANR 79; DAM MULT, POET; DLB 50, 221; MBL; RGAL 4
Harper, Michael S(teven) 1938- ..... **BLC 2:2; CLC 7, 22**
  See also AFAW 2; BW 1; CA 33-36R; 224; CAAE 224; CANR 24, 108; CP 2, 3, 4, 5, 6, 7; DLB 41; RGAL 4; TCLE 1:1
Harper, Mrs. F. E. W.
  See Harper, Frances Ellen Watkins
Harpur, Charles 1813-1868 .... **NCLC 114**
  See also DLB 230; RGEL 2
Harris, Christie
  See Harris, Christie (Lucy) Irwin
Harris, Christie (Lucy) Irwin
  1907-2002 .... **CLC 12**
  See also CA 5-8R; CANR 6, 83; CLR 47; DLB 88; JRDA; MAICYA 1, 2; SAAS 10; SATA 6, 74; SATA-Essay 116
Harris, Frank 1856-1931 .... **TCLC 24**
  See also CA 109; 150; CANR 80; DLB 156, 197; RGEL 2
Harris, George Washington
  1814-1869 .... **NCLC 23, 165**
  See also DLB 3, 11, 248; RGAL 4
Harris, Joel Chandler 1848-1908 ..... **SSC 19, 103; TCLC 2**
  See also CA 104; 137; CANR 80; CLR 49, 128; DLB 11, 23, 42, 78, 91; LAIT 2; MAICYA 1, 2; RGSF 2; SATA 100; WCH; YABC 1
Harris, John (Wyndham Parkes Lucas) Beynon 1903-1969 .... **CLC 19**
  See also BRWS 13; CA 102; 89-92; CANR 84; DLB 255; SATA 118; SCFW 1, 2; SFW 4
Harris, MacDonald
  See Heiney, Donald (William)
Harris, Mark 1922-2007 .... **CLC 19**
  See also CA 5-8R; 260; CAAS 3; CANR 2, 55, 83; CN 1, 2, 3, 4, 5, 6, 7; DLB 2; DLBY 1980
Harris, Norman CLC 65
Harris, (Theodore) Wilson 1921- ... **BLC 2:2; CLC 25, 159**
  See also BRWS 5; BW 2, 3; CA 65-68; CAAS 16; CANR 11, 27, 69, 114; CD-WLB 3; CN 1, 2, 3, 4, 5, 6, 7; CP 1, 2, 3, 4, 5, 6, 7; DLB 117; EWL 3; MTCW 1; RGEL 2

Harrison, Barbara Grizzuti
  1934-2002 .... **CLC 144**
  See also CA 77-80; 205; CANR 15, 48; INT CANR-15
Harrison, Elizabeth (Allen) Cavanna
  1909-2001 .... **CLC 12**
  See also CA 9-12R; 200; CANR 6, 27, 85, 104, 121; JRDA; MAICYA 1; SAAS 4; SATA 1, 30; YAW
Harrison, Harry 1925- .... **CLC 42**
  See also CA 1-4R; CANR 5, 21, 84; DLB 8; SATA 4; SCFW 2; SFW 4
Harrison, Harry Max
  See Harrison, Harry
Harrison, James
  See Harrison, Jim
Harrison, James Thomas
  See Harrison, Jim
Harrison, Jim 1937- .... **CLC 6, 14, 33, 66, 143; SSC 19**
  See also AMWS 8; CA 13-16R; CANR 8, 51, 79, 142, 198; CN 5, 6; CP 1, 2, 3, 4, 5, 6; DLBY 1982; INT CANR-8; RGAL 4; TCWW 2; TUS
Harrison, Kathryn 1961- .... **CLC 70, 151**
  See also CA 144; CANR 68, 122, 194
Harrison, Tony 1937- .... **CLC 43, 129**
  See also BRWS 5; CA 65-68; CANR 44, 98; CBD; CD 5, 6; CP 2, 3, 4, 5, 6, 7; DLB 40, 245; MTCW 1; RGEL 2
Harriss, Will(ard Irvin) 1922- .... **CLC 34**
  See also CA 111
Hart, Ellis
  See Ellison, Harlan
Hart, Josephine 1942(?)- .... **CLC 70**
  See also CA 138; CANR 70, 149; CPW; DAM POP
Hart, Moss 1904-1961 .... **CLC 66**
  See also CA 109; 89-92; CANR 84; DAM DRAM; DFS 1; DLB 7, 266; RGAL 4
Harte, Bret 1836(?)-1902 .. **SSC 8, 59; TCLC 1, 25; WLC 3**
  See also AMWS 2; CA 104; 140; CANR 80; CDALB 1865-1917; DA; DA3; DAC; DAM MST; DLB 12, 64, 74, 79, 186; EXPS; LAIT 2; RGAL 4; RGSF 2; SATA 26; SSFS 3; TUS
Harte, Francis Brett
  See Harte, Bret
Hartley, L(eslie) P(oles) 1895-1972 ... **CLC 2, 22; SSC 125**
  See also BRWS 7; CA 45-48; 37-40R; CANR 33; CN 1; DLB 15, 139; EWL 3; HGG; MTCW 1, 2; MTFW 2005; RGEL 2; RGSF 2; SUFW 1
Hartman, Geoffrey H. 1929- .... **CLC 27**
  See also CA 117; 125; CANR 79; DLB 67
Hartmann, Sadakichi 1869-1944 ... **TCLC 73**
  See also CA 157; DLB 54
Hartmann von Aue c. 1170-c.
  1210 .... **CMLC 15**
  See also CDWLB 2; DLB 138; RGWL 2, 3
Hartog, Jan de
  See de Hartog, Jan
Haruf, Kent 1943- .... **CLC 34**
  See also AAYA 44; CA 149; CANR 91, 131
Harvey, Caroline
  See Trollope, Joanna
Harvey, Gabriel 1550(?)-1631 .... **LC 88**
  See also DLB 167, 213, 281
Harvey, Jack
  See Rankin, Ian
Harwood, Ronald 1934- .... **CLC 32**
  See also CA 1-4R; CANR 4, 55, 150; CBD; CD 5, 6; DAM DRAM, MST; DLB 13
Hasegawa Tatsunosuke
  See Futabatei, Shimei

Hasek, Jaroslav 1883-1923 ... **SSC 69; TCLC 4**
See also CA 104; 129; CDWLB 4; DLB 215; EW 9; EWL 3; MTCW 1, 2; RGSF 2; RGWL 2, 3

Hasek, Jaroslav Matej Frantisek
See Hasek, Jaroslav

Hass, Robert 1941- ...... **CLC 18, 39, 99, 287; PC 16**
See also AMWS 6; CA 111; CANR 30, 50, 71, 187; CP 3, 4, 5, 6, 7; DLB 105, 206; EWL 3; MAL 5; MTFW 2005; RGAL 4; SATA 94; TCLE 1:1

Hassler, Jon 1933-2008 .... **CLC 263**
See also CA 73-76; 270; CANR 21, 80, 161; CN 6, 7; INT CANR-21; SATA 19; SATA-Obit 191

Hassler, Jon Francis
See Hassler, Jon

Hastings, Hudson
See Kuttner, Henry

Hastings, Selina CLC 44
See also CA 257

Hastings, Selina Shirley
See Hastings, Selina

Hastings, Victor
See Disch, Thomas M.

Hathorne, John 1641-1717 .... **LC 38**

Hatteras, Amelia
See Mencken, H. L.

Hatteras, Owen
See Mencken, H. L.; Nathan, George Jean

Hauff, Wilhelm 1802-1827 .... **NCLC 185**
See also DLB 90; SUFW 1

Hauptmann, Gerhart 1862-1946 .... **DC 34; SSC 37; TCLC 4**
See also CA 104; 153; CDWLB 2; DAM DRAM; DLB 66, 118, 330; EW 8; EWL 3; RGSF 2; RGWL 2, 3; TWA

Hauptmann, Gerhart Johann Robert
See Hauptmann, Gerhart

Havel, Vaclav 1936- ..... **CLC 25, 58, 65, 123; DC 6**
See also CA 104; CANR 36, 63, 124, 175; CDWLB 4; CWW 2; DA3; DAM DRAM; DFS 10; DLB 232; EWL 3; LMFS 2; MTCW 1, 2; MTFW 2005; RGWL 3

Haviaras, Stratis
See Chaviaras, Strates

Hawes, Stephen 1475(?)-1529(?) .... **LC 17**
See also DLB 132; RGEL 2

Hawkes, John 1925-1998 .. **CLC 1, 2, 3, 4, 7, 9, 14, 15, 27, 49**
See also BPFB 2; CA 1-4R; 167; CANR 2, 47, 64; CN 1, 2, 3, 4, 5, 6; DLB 2, 7, 227; DLBY 1980, 1998; EWL 3; MAL 5; MTCW 1, 2; MTFW 2005; RGAL 4

Hawking, S. W.
See Hawking, Stephen W.

Hawking, Stephen W. 1942- ..... **CLC 63, 105**
See also AAYA 13; BEST 89:1; CA 126; 129; CANR 48, 115; CPW; DA3; MTCW 2; MTFW 2005

Hawking, Stephen William
See Hawking, Stephen W.

Hawkins, Anthony Hope
See Hope, Anthony

Hawthorne, Julian 1846-1934 .... **TCLC 25**
See also CA 165; HGG

Hawthorne, Nathaniel 1804-1864 ... **NCLC 2, 10, 17, 23, 39, 79, 95, 158, 171, 191, 226; SSC 3, 29, 39, 89, 130; WLC 3**
See also AAYA 18; AMW; AMWC 1; AMWR 1; BPFB 2; BYA 3; CDALB 1640-1865; CLR 103; DA; DA3; DAB; DAC; DAM MST, NOV; DLB 1, 74, 183,

223, 269; EXPN; EXPS; GL 2; HGG; LAIT 1; NFS 1, 20; RGAL 4; RGSF 2; SSFS 1, 7, 11, 15, 30; SUFW 1; TUS; WCH; YABC 2

Hawthorne, Sophia Peabody 1809-1871 .... **NCLC 150**
See also DLB 183, 239

Haxton, Josephine Ayres
See Douglas, Ellen

Hayaseca y Eizaguirre, Jorge
See Echegaray (y Eizaguirre), Jose (Maria Waldo)

Hayashi, Fumiko 1904-1951 .... **TCLC 27**
See also CA 161; DLB 180; EWL 3

Hayashi Fumiko
See Hayashi, Fumiko

Haycraft, Anna 1932-2005 .... **CLC 40**
See also CA 122; 237; CANR 90, 141; CN 4, 5, 6; DLB 194; MTCW 2; MTFW 2005

Haycraft, Anna Margaret
See Haycraft, Anna

Hayden, Robert
See Hayden, Robert Earl

Hayden, Robert E.
See Hayden, Robert Earl

Hayden, Robert Earl 1913-1980 .... **BLC 1:2; CLC 5, 9, 14, 37; PC 6**
See also AFAW 1, 2; AMWS 2; BW 1, 3; CA 69-72; 97-100; CABS 2; CANR 24, 75, 82; CDALB 1941-1968; CP 1, 2, 3; DA; DAC; DAM MST, MULT, POET; DLB 5, 76; EWL 3; EXPP; MAL 5; MTCW 1, 2; PFS 1, 31; RGAL 4; SATA 19; SATA-Obit 26; WP

Haydon, Benjamin Robert 1786-1846 .... **NCLC 146**
See also DLB 110

Hayek, F(riedrich) A(ugust von) 1899-1992 .... **TCLC 109**
See also CA 93-96; 137; CANR 20; MTCW 1, 2

Hayford, J(oseph) E(phraim) Casely
See Casely-Hayford, J(oseph) E(phraim)

Hayman, Ronald 1932- .... **CLC 44**
See also CA 25-28R; CANR 18, 50, 88; CD 5, 6; DLB 155

Hayne, Paul Hamilton 1830-1886 . **NCLC 94**
See also DLB 3, 64, 79, 248; RGAL 4

Hays, Mary 1760-1843 .... **NCLC 114**
See also DLB 142, 158; RGEL 2

Haywood, Eliza (Fowler) 1693(?)-1756 .... **LC 1, 44, 177**
See also BRWS 12; DLB 39; RGEL 2

Hazlitt, William 1778-1830 ...... **NCLC 29, 82**
See also BRW 4; DLB 110, 158; RGEL 2; TEA

Hazzard, Shirley 1931- .... **CLC 18, 218**
See also CA 9-12R; CANR 4, 70, 127; CN 1, 2, 3, 4, 5, 6, 7; DLB 289; DLBY 1982; MTCW 1

Head, Bessie 1937-1986 . **BLC 1:2, 2:2; CLC 25, 67; SSC 52**
See also AFW; BW 2, 3; CA 29-32R; 119; CANR 25, 82; CDWLB 3; CN 1, 2, 3, 4; DA3; DAM MULT; DLB 117, 225; EWL 3; EXPS; FL 1:6; FW; MTCW 1, 2; MTFW 2005; NFS 31; RGSF 2; SSFS 5, 13, 30; WLIT 2; WWE 1

Headley, Elizabeth
See Harrison, Elizabeth (Allen) Cavanna

Headon, (Nicky) Topper 1956(?)- ..... **CLC 30**

Heaney, Seamus 1939- . **CLC 5, 7, 14, 25, 37, 74, 91, 171, 225; PC 18, 100; WLCS**
See also AAYA 61; BRWR 1; BRWS 2; CA 85-88; CANR 25, 48, 75, 91, 128, 184; CDBLB 1960 to Present; CP 1, 2, 3, 4, 5, 6, 7; DA3; DAB; DAM POET; DLB 40,

330; DLBY 1995; EWL 3; EXPP; MTCW 1, 2; MTFW 2005; PAB; PFS 2, 5, 8, 17, 30; RGEL 2; TEA; WLIT 4

Heaney, Seamus Justin
See Heaney, Seamus

Hearn, Lafcadio 1850-1904 .... **TCLC 9**
See also AAYA 79; CA 105; 166; DLB 12, 78, 189; HGG; MAL 5; RGAL 4

Hearn, Patricio Lafcadio Tessima Carlos
See Hearn, Lafcadio

Hearne, Samuel 1745-1792 .... **LC 95**
See also DLB 99

Hearne, Vicki 1946-2001 .... **CLC 56**
See also CA 139; 201

Hearon, Shelby 1931- .... **CLC 63**
See also AITN 2; AMWS 8; CA 25-28R; CAAS 11; CANR 18, 48, 103, 146; CSW

Heat-Moon, William Least 1939- ..... **CLC 29**
See also AAYA 9, 66; ANW; CA 115; 119; CANR 47, 89; CPW; INT CA-119

Hebbel, Friedrich 1813-1863 . **DC 21; NCLC 43**
See also CDWLB 2; DAM DRAM; DLB 129; EW 6; RGWL 2, 3

Hebert, Anne 1916-2000 . **CLC 4, 13, 29, 246**
See also CA 85-88; 187; CANR 69, 126; CCA 1; CWP; CWW 2; DA3; DAC; DAM MST, POET; DLB 68; EWL 3; GFL 1789 to the Present; MTCW 1, 2; MTFW 2005; PFS 20

Hecht, Anthony (Evan) 1923-2004 .... **CLC 8, 13, 19; PC 70**
See also AMWS 10; CA 9-12R; 232; CANR 6, 108; CP 1, 2, 3, 4, 5, 6, 7; DAM POET; DLB 5, 169; EWL 3; PFS 6; WP

Hecht, Ben 1894-1964 ..... **CLC 8; TCLC 101**
See also CA 85-88; DFS 9; DLB 7, 9, 25, 26, 28, 86; FANT; IDFW 3, 4; RGAL 4

Hedayat, Sadeq 1903-1951 . **SSC 131; TCLC 21**
See also CA 120; EWL 3; RGSF 2

Hegel, Georg Wilhelm Friedrich 1770-1831 .... **NCLC 46, 151**
See also DLB 90; TWA

Heidegger, Martin 1889-1976 .... **CLC 24**
See also CA 81-84; 65-68; CANR 34; DLB 296; MTCW 1, 2; MTFW 2005

Heidenstam, (Carl Gustaf) Verner von 1859-1940 .... **TCLC 5**
See also CA 104; DLB 330

Heidi Louise
See Erdrich, Louise

Heifner, Jack 1946- .... **CLC 11**
See also CA 105; CANR 47

Heijermans, Herman 1864-1924 .... **TCLC 24**
See also CA 123; EWL 3

Heilbrun, Carolyn G. 1926-2003 ..... **CLC 25, 173**
See also BPFB 1; CA 45-48; 220; CANR 1, 28, 58, 94; CMW; CPW; DLB 306; FW; MSW

Heilbrun, Carolyn Gold
See Heilbrun, Carolyn G.

Hein, Christoph 1944- .... **CLC 154**
See also CA 158; CANR 108; CDWLB 2; CWW 2; DLB 124

Heine, Heinrich 1797-1856 .... **NCLC 4, 54, 147; PC 25**
See also CDWLB 2; DLB 90; EW 5; RGWL 2, 3; TWA

Heinemann, Larry 1944- .... **CLC 50**
See also CA 110; CAAS 21; CANR 31, 81, 156; DLBD 9; INT CANR-31

Heinemann, Larry Curtiss
See Heinemann, Larry

Heiney, Donald (William) 1921-1993 . **CLC 9**
See also CA 1-4R; 142; CANR 3, 58; FANT

Heinlein, Robert A. 1907-1988 .. **CLC 1, 3, 8, 14, 26, 55; SSC 55**
See also AAYA 17; BPFB 2; BYA 4, 13; CA 1-4R; 125; CANR 1, 20, 53; CLR 75; CN 1, 2, 3, 4; CPW; DA3; DAM POP; DLB 8; EXPS; JRDA; LAIT 5; LMFS 2; MAICYA 1, 2; MTCW 1, 2; MTFW 2005; RGAL 4; SATA 9, 69; SATA-Obit 56; SCFW 1, 2; SFW 4; SSFS 7; YAW

Hejinian, Lyn 1941- .... **PC 108**
See also CA 153; CANR 85; CP 4, 5, 6, 7; CWP; DLB 165; PFS 27; RGAL 4

Held, Peter
See Vance, Jack

Heldris of Cornwall fl. 13th cent.
- .... **CMLC 97**

Helforth, John
See Doolittle, Hilda

Heliodorus fl. 3rd cent. - .... **CMLC 52**
See also WLIT 8

Hellenhofferu, Vojtech Kapristian z
See Hasek, Jaroslav

Heller, Joseph 1923-1999 . **CLC 1, 3, 5, 8, 11, 36, 63; TCLC 131, 151; WLC 3**
See also AAYA 24; AITN 1; AMWS 4; BPFB 2; BYA 1; CA 5-8R; 187; CABS 1; CANR 8, 42, 66, 126; CN 1, 2, 3, 4, 5, 6; CPW; DA; DA3; DAB; DAC; DAM MST, NOV, POP; DLB 2, 28, 227; DLBY 1980, 2002; EWL 3; EXPN; INT CANR-8; LAIT 4; MAL 5; MTCW 1, 2; MTFW 2005; NFS 1; RGAL 4; TUS; YAW

Hellman, Lillian 1905-1984 . **CLC 2, 4, 8, 14, 18, 34, 44, 52; DC 1; TCLC 119**
See also AAYA 47; AITN 1, 2; AMWS 1; CA 13-16R; 112; CAD; CANR 33; CWD; DA3; DAM DRAM; DFS 1, 3, 14; DLB 7, 228; DLBY 1984; EWL 3; FL 1:6; FW; LAIT 3; MAL 5; MBL; MTCW 1, 2; MTFW 2005; RGAL 4; TUS

Hellman, Lillian Florence
See Hellman, Lillian

Heloise c. 1095-c. 1164 .... **CMLC 122**

Helprin, Mark 1947- .... **CLC 7, 10, 22, 32**
See also CA 81-84; CANR 47, 64, 124; CDALBS; CN 7; CPW; DA3; DAM NOV, POP; DLB 335; DLBY 1985; FANT; MAL 5; MTCW 1, 2; MTFW 2005; SSFS 25; SUFW 2

Helvetius, Claude-Adrien 1715-1771 .. **LC 26**
See also DLB 313

Helyar, Jane Penelope Josephine 1933- .... **CLC 17**
See also CA 21-24R; CANR 10, 26; CWRI 5; SAAS 2; SATA 5; SATA-Essay 138

Hemans, Felicia 1793-1835 ...... **NCLC 29, 71**
See also DLB 96; RGEL 2

Hemingway, Ernest 1899-1961 .. **CLC 1, 3, 6, 8, 10, 13, 19, 30, 34, 39, 41, 44, 50, 61, 80; SSC 1, 25, 36, 40, 63, 117, 137; TCLC 115, 203; WLC 3**
See also AAYA 19; AMW; AMWC 1; AMWR 1; BPFB 2; BYA 2, 3, 13, 15; CA 77-80; CANR 34; CDALB 1917-1929; DA; DA3; DAB; DAC; DAM MST, NOV, DLB 4, 9, 102, 210, 308, 316, 330; DLBD 1, 15, 16; DLBY 1981, 1987, 1996, 1998; EWL 3; EXPN; EXPS; LAIT 3, 4; LATS 1:1; MAL 5; MTCW 1, 2; MTFW 2005; NFS 1, 5, 6, 14; RGAL 4; RGSF 2; SSFS 17; TUS; WYA

Hemingway, Ernest Miller
See Hemingway, Ernest

Hempel, Amy 1951- .... **CLC 39**
See also CA 118; 137; CANR 70, 166; DA3; DLB 218; EXPS; MTCW 2; MTFW 2005; SSFS 2

Henderson, F. C.
See Mencken, H. L.

Henderson, Mary
See Mavor, Osborne Henry

Henderson, Sylvia
See Ashton-Warner, Sylvia (Constance)

Henderson, Zenna (Chlarson) 1917-1983 .... **SSC 29**
See also CA 1-4R; 133; CANR 1, 84; DLB 8; SATA 5; SFW 4

Henkin, Joshua 1964- .... **CLC 119**
See also CA 161; CANR 186; DLB 350

Henley, Beth 1952- ... **CLC 23, 255; DC 6, 14**
See also AAYA 70; CA 107; CABS 3; CAD; CANR 32, 73, 140; CD 5, 6; CSW; CWD; DA3; DAM DRAM, MST; DFS 2, 21, 26; DLBY 1986; FW; MTCW 1, 2; MTFW 2005

Henley, Elizabeth Becker
See Henley, Beth

Henley, William Ernest 1849-1903 .. **TCLC 8**
See also CA 105; 234; DLB 19; RGEL 2

Hennissart, Martha 1929- .... **CLC 2**
See also BPFB 2; CA 85-88; CANR 64; CMW 4; DLB 306

Henry VIII 1491-1547 .... **LC 10**
See also DLB 132

Henry, O. 1862-1910 . **SSC 5, 49, 117; TCLC 1, 19; WLC 3**
See also AAYA 41; AMWS 2; CA 104; 131; CDALB 1865-1917; DA; DA3; DAB; DAC; DAM MST; DLB 12, 78, 79; EXPS; MAL 5; MTCW 1, 2; MTFW 2005; RGAL 4; RGSF 2; SSFS 2, 18, 27, 31; TCWW 1, 2; TUS; YABC 2

Henry, Oliver
See Henry, O.

Henry, Patrick 1736-1799 .... **LC 25**
See also LAIT 1

Henryson, Robert 1430(?)-1506(?) ..... **LC 20, 110; PC 65**
See also BRWS 7; DLB 146; RGEL 2

Henschke, Alfred
See Klabund

Henson, Lance 1944- .... **NNAL**
See also CA 146; DLB 175

Hentoff, Nat(han Irving) 1925- .... **CLC 26**
See also AAYA 4, 42; BYA 6; CA 1-4R; CAAS 6; CANR 5, 25, 77, 114; CLR 1, 52; DLB 345; INT CANR-25; JRDA; MAICYA 1, 2; SATA 42, 69, 133; SATA-Brief 27; WYA; YAW

Heppenstall, (John) Rayner 1911-1981 .... **CLC 10**
See also CA 1-4R; 103; CANR 29; CN 1, 2; CP 1, 2, 3; EWL 3

Heraclitus c. 540B.C.-c. 450B.C. .. **CMLC 22**
See also DLB 176

Herbert, Edward 1583-1648 .... **LC 177**
See also DLB 121, 151, 252; RGEL 2

Herbert, Frank 1920-1986 ... **CLC 12, 23, 35, 44, 85**
See also AAYA 21; BPFB 2; BYA 4, 14; CA 53-56; 118; CANR 5, 43; CDALBS; CPW; DAM POP; DLB 8; INT CANR-5; LAIT 5; MTCW 1, 2; MTFW 2005; NFS 17, 31; SATA 9, 37; SATA-Obit 47; SCFW 1, 2; SFW 4; YAW

Herbert, George 1593-1633 . **LC 24, 121; PC 4**
See also BRW 2; BRWR 2; CDBLB Before 1660; DAB; DAM POET; DLB 126; EXPP; PFS 25; RGEL 2; TEA; WP

Herbert, Zbigniew 1924-1998 ..... **CLC 9, 43; PC 50; TCLC 168**
See also CA 89-92; 169; CANR 36, 74, 177; CDWLB 4; CWW 2; DAM POET; DLB 232; EWL 3; MTCW 1; PFS 22

Herbert of Cherbury, Lord
See Herbert, Edward

Herbst, Josephine (Frey) 1897-1969 .... **CLC 34**
See also CA 5-8R; 25-28R; DLB 9

Herder, Johann Gottfried von 1744-1803 .... **NCLC 8, 186**
See also DLB 97; EW 4; TWA

Heredia, Jose Maria 1803-1839 ...... **HLCS 2; NCLC 209**
See also LAW

Hergesheimer, Joseph 1880-1954 ... **TCLC 11**
See also CA 109; 194; DLB 102, 9; RGAL 4

Herlihy, James Leo 1927-1993 .... **CLC 6**
See also CA 1-4R; 143; CAD; CANR 2; CN 1, 2, 3, 4, 5

Herman, William
See Bierce, Ambrose

Hermogenes fl. c. 175- .... **CMLC 6**

Hernandez, Jose 1834-1886 .... **NCLC 17**
See also LAW; RGWL 2, 3; WLIT 1

Herodotus c. 484B.C.-c. 420B.C. .. **CMLC 17**
See also AW 1; CDWLB 1; DLB 176; RGWL 2, 3; TWA; WLIT 8

Herr, Michael 1940(?)- .... **CLC 231**
See also CA 89-92; CANR 68, 142; DLB 185; MTCW 1

Herrick, Robert 1591-1674 .. **LC 13, 145; PC 9**
See also BRW 2; BRWC 2; DA; DAB; DAC; DAM MST, POP; DLB 126; EXPP; PFS 13, 29; RGAL 4; RGEL 2; TEA; WP

Herring, Guilles
See Somerville, Edith Oenone

Herriot, James 1916-1995 .... **CLC 12**
See also AAYA 1, 54; BPFB 2; CA 77-80; 148; CANR 40; CLR 80; CPW; DAM POP; LAIT 3; MAICYA 2; MAICYAS 1; MTCW 2; SATA 86, 135; SATA-Brief 44; TEA; YAW

Herris, Violet
See Hunt, Violet

Herrmann, Dorothy 1941- .... **CLC 44**
See also CA 107

Herrmann, Taffy
See Herrmann, Dorothy

Hersey, John 1914-1993 .. **CLC 1, 2, 7, 9, 40, 81, 97**
See also AAYA 29; BPFB 2; CA 17-20R; 140; CANR 33; CDALBS; CN 1, 2, 3, 4, 5; CPW; DAM POP; DLB 6, 185, 278, 299; MAL 5; MTCW 1, 2; MTFW 2005; RGHL; SATA 25; SATA-Obit 76; TUS

Hersey, John Richard
See Hersey, John

Hervent, Maurice
See Grindel, Eugene

Herzen, Aleksandr Ivanovich 1812-1870 .... **NCLC 10, 61**
See also DLB 277

Herzen, Alexander
See Herzen, Aleksandr Ivanovich

Herzl, Theodor 1860-1904 .... **TCLC 36**
See also CA 168

Herzog, Werner 1942- .... **CLC 16, 236**
See also CA 89-92

Hesiod fl. 8th cent. B.C.- .... **CMLC 5, 102**
See also AW 1; DLB 176; RGWL 2, 3; WLIT 8

Hesse, Hermann 1877-1962 ... **CLC 1, 2, 3, 6, 11, 17, 25, 69; SSC 9, 49; TCLC 148, 196; WLC 3**
See also AAYA 43; BPFB 2; CA 17-18; CAP 2; CDWLB 2; DA; DA3; DAB; DAC; DAM MST, NOV; DLB 66, 330; EW 9; EWL 3; EXPN; LAIT 1; MTCW 1, 2; MTFW 2005; NFS 6, 15, 24; RGWL 2, 3; SATA 50; TWA

Hewes, Cady
See De Voto, Bernard (Augustine)

Hodgson, William Hope
1877(?)-1918 .... **TCLC 13**
See also CA 111; 164; CMW 4; DLB 70,
153, 156, 178; HGG; MTCW 2; SFW 4;
SUFW 1

Hoeg, Peter
See Hoeg, Peter

Hoeg, Peter 1957- .... **CLC 95, 156**
See also CA 151; CANR 75, 202; CMW 4;
DA3; DLB 214; EWL 3; MTCW 2;
MTFW 2005; NFS 17; RGWL 3; SSFS
18

Hoffman, Alice 1952- .... **CLC 51**
See also AAYA 37; AMWS 10; CA 77-80;
CANR 34, 66, 100, 138, 170; CN 4, 5,
7; CPW; DAM NOV; DLB 292; MAL 5;
MTCW 1, 2; MTFW 2005; TCLE 1:1

Hoffman, Daniel (Gerard) 1923- . **CLC 6, 13,
23**
See also CA 1-4R; CANR 4, 142; CP 1, 2,
3, 4, 5, 6, 7; DLB 5; TCLE 1:1

Hoffman, Eva 1945- .... **CLC 182**
See also AMWS 16; CA 132; CANR 146

Hoffman, Stanley 1944- .... **CLC 5**
See also CA 77-80

Hoffman, William 1925- .... **CLC 141**
See also AMWS 18; CA 21-24R; CANR 9,
103; CSW; DLB 234; TCLE 1:1

Hoffman, William M.
See Hoffman, William M(oses)

Hoffman, William M(oses) 1939- ..... **CLC 40**
See also CA 57-60; CAD; CANR 11, 71;
CD 5, 6

Hoffmann, E(rnst) T(heodor) A(madeus)
1776-1822 ..... **NCLC 2, 183; SSC 13, 92**
See also CDWLB 2; CLR 133; DLB 90;
EW 5; GL 2; RGSF 2; RGWL 2, 3; SATA
27; SUFW 1; WCH

Hofmann, Gert 1931-1993 .... **CLC 54**
See also CA 128; CANR 145; EWL 3;
RGHL

Hofmannsthal, Hugo von 1874-1929 ... **DC 4;
TCLC 11**
See also CA 106; 153; CDWLB 2; DAM
DRAM; DFS 17; DLB 81, 118; EW 9;
EWL 3; RGWL 2, 3

Hogan, Linda 1947- .... **CLC 73, 290; NNAL;
PC 35**
See also AMWS 4; ANW; BYA 12; CA 120,
226; CAAE 226; CANR 45, 73, 129, 196;
CWP; DAM MULT; DLB 175; SATA
132; TCWW 2

Hogarth, Charles
See Creasey, John

Hogarth, Emmett
See Polonsky, Abraham (Lincoln)

Hogarth, William 1697-1764 .... **LC 112**
See also AAYA 56

Hogg, James 1770-1835 .. **NCLC 4, 109; SSC
130**
See also BRWS 10; DLB 93, 116, 159; GL
2; HGG; RGEL 2; SUFW 1

Holbach, Paul-Henri Thiry
1723-1789 .... **LC 14**
See also DLB 313

Holberg, Ludvig 1684-1754 .... **LC 6**
See also DLB 300; RGWL 2, 3

Holbrook, John
See Vance, Jack

Holcroft, Thomas 1745-1809 .... **NCLC 85**
See also DLB 39, 89, 158; RGEL 2

Holden, Ursula 1921- .... **CLC 18**
See also CA 101; CAAS 8; CANR 22

Holderlin, (Johann Christian) Friedrich
1770-1843 .... **NCLC 16, 187; PC 4**
See also CDWLB 2; DLB 90; EW 5; RGWL
2, 3

Holdstock, Robert 1948-2009 .... **CLC 39**
See also CA 131; CANR 81; DLB 261;
FANT; HGG; SFW 4; SUFW 2

Holdstock, Robert P.
See Holdstock, Robert

Holinshed, Raphael fl. 1580- .... **LC 69**
See also DLB 167; RGEL 2

Holland, Isabelle (Christian)
1920-2002 .... **CLC 21**
See also AAYA 11, 64; CA 21-24R; 205;
CAAE 181; CANR 10, 25, 47; CLR 57;
CWRI 5; JRDA; LAIT 4; MAICYA 1, 2;
SATA 8, 70; SATA-Essay 103; SATA-Obit
132; WYA

Holland, Marcus
See Caldwell, (Janet Miriam) Taylor
(Holland)

Hollander, John 1929- .... **CLC 2, 5, 8, 14**
See also CA 1-4R; CANR 1, 52, 136; CP 1,
2, 3, 4, 5, 6, 7; DLB 5; MAL 5; SATA 13

Hollander, Paul
See Silverberg, Robert

Holleran, Andrew 1943(?)- .... **CLC 38**
See also CA 144; CANR 89, 162; GLL 1

Holley, Marietta 1836(?)-1926 .... **TCLC 99**
See also CA 118; DLB 11; FL 1:3

Hollinghurst, Alan 1954- .... **CLC 55, 91**
See also BRWS 10; CA 114; CN 5, 6, 7;
DLB 207, 326; GLL 1

Hollis, Jim
See Summers, Hollis (Spurgeon, Jr.)

Holly, Buddy 1936-1959 .... **TCLC 65**
See also CA 213

Holmes, Gordon
See Shiel, M. P.

Holmes, John
See Souster, (Holmes) Raymond

Holmes, John Clellon 1926-1988 ...... **CLC 56**
See also BG 1:2; CA 9-12R; 125; CANR 4;
CN 1, 2, 3, 4; DLB 16, 237

Holmes, Oliver Wendell, Jr.
1841-1935 .... **TCLC 77**
See also CA 114; 186

Holmes, Oliver Wendell
1809-1894 .... **NCLC 14, 81; PC 71**
See also AMWS 1; CDALB 1640-1865;
DLB 1, 189, 235; EXPP; PFS 24; RGAL
4; SATA 34

Holmes, Raymond
See Souster, (Holmes) Raymond

Holt, Samuel
See Westlake, Donald E.

Holt, Victoria
See Hibbert, Eleanor Alice Burford

Holub, Miroslav 1923-1998 .... **CLC 4**
See also CA 21-24R; 169; CANR 10; CD-
WLB 4; CWW 2; DLB 232; EWL 3;
RGWL 3

Holz, Detlev
See Benjamin, Walter

Homer c. 8th cent. B.C.- ..... **CMLC 1, 16, 61,
121; PC 23; WLCS**
See also AW 1; CDWLB 1; DA; DA3;
DAB; DAC; DAM MST, POET; DLB
176; EFS 1; LAIT 1; LMFS 1; RGWL 2,
3; TWA; WLIT 8; WP

Hong, Maxine Ting Ting
See Kingston, Maxine Hong

Hongo, Garrett Kaoru 1951- .... **PC 23**
See also CA 133; CAAS 22; CP 5, 6, 7;
DLB 120, 312; EWL 3; EXPP; PFS 25,
33; RGAL 4

Honig, Edwin 1919- .... **CLC 33**
See also CA 5-8R; CAAS 8; CANR 4, 45,
144; CP 1, 2, 3, 4, 5, 6, 7; DLB 5

Hood, Hugh (John Blagdon) 1928- . **CLC 15,
28, 273; SSC 42**
See also CA 49-52; CAAS 17; CANR 1,
33, 87; CN 1, 2, 3, 4, 5, 6, 7; DLB 53;
RGSF 2

Hood, Thomas 1799-1845 . **NCLC 16; PC 93**
See also BRW 4; DLB 96; RGEL 2

Hooker, (Peter) Jeremy 1941- .... **CLC 43**
See also CA 77-80; CANR 22; CP 2, 3, 4,
5, 6, 7; DLB 40

Hooker, Richard 1554-1600 .... **LC 95**
See also BRW 1; DLB 132; RGEL 2

Hooker, Thomas 1586-1647 .... **LC 137**
See also DLB 24

hooks, bell 1952(?)- .... **BLCS; CLC 94**
See also BW 2; CA 143; CANR 87, 126;
DLB 246; MTCW 2; MTFW 2005; SATA
115, 170

Hooper, Johnson Jones
1815-1862 .... **NCLC 177**
See also DLB 3, 11, 248; RGAL 4

Hope, A(lec) D(erwent) 1907-2000 .... **CLC 3,
51; PC 56**
See also BRWS 7; CA 21-24R; 188; CANR
33, 74; CP 1, 2, 3, 4, 5; DLB 289; EWL
3; MTCW 1, 2; MTFW 2005; PFS 8;
RGEL 2

Hope, Anthony 1863-1933 .... **TCLC 83**
See also CA 157; DLB 153, 156; RGEL 2;
RHW

Hope, Brian
See Creasey, John

Hope, Christopher 1944- .... **CLC 52**
See also AFW; CA 106; CANR 47, 101,
177; CN 4, 5, 6, 7; DLB 225; SATA 62

Hope, Christopher David Tully
See Hope, Christopher

Hopkins, Gerard Manley
1844-1889 .... **NCLC 17, 189; PC 15;
WLC 3**
See also BRW 5; BRWR 2; CDBLB 1890-
1914; DA; DA3; DAB; DAC; DAM MST,
POET; DLB 35, 57; EXPP; PAB; PFS 26;
RGEL 2; TEA; WP

Hopkins, John (Richard) 1931-1998 .. **CLC 4**
See also CA 85-88; 169; CBD; CD 5, 6

Hopkins, Pauline Elizabeth
1859-1930 .... **BLC 1:2; TCLC 28**
See also AFAW 2; BW 2, 3; CA 141; CANR
82; DAM MULT; DLB 50

Hopkinson, Francis 1737-1791 .... **LC 25**
See also DLB 31; RGAL 4

Hopley, George
See Hopley-Woolrich, Cornell George

Hopley-Woolrich, Cornell George
1903-1968 .... **CLC 77**
See also CA 13-14; CANR 58, 156; CAP 1;
CMW 4; DLB 226; MSW; MTCW 2

Horace 65B.C.-8B.C. .... **CMLC 39; PC 46**
See also AW 2; CDWLB 1; DLB 211;
RGWL 2, 3; WLIT 8

Horatio
See Proust, Marcel

**Horgan, Paul (George Vincent
O'Shaughnessy)** 1903-1995 .. **CLC 9, 53**
See also BPFB 2; CA 13-16R; 147; CANR
9, 35; CN 1, 2, 3, 4, 5; DAM NOV; DLB
102, 212; DLBY 1985; INT CANR-9;
MTCW 1, 2; MTFW 2005; SATA 13;
SATA-Obit 84; TCWW 1, 2

Horkheimer, Max 1895-1973 .... **TCLC 132**
See also CA 216; 41-44R; DLB 296

Horn, Peter
See Kuttner, Henry

Hornby, Nicholas Peter John
See Hornby, Nick

Juenger, Ernst 1895-1998 .... **CLC 125**
See also CA 101; 167; CANR 21, 47, 106;
CDWLB 2; DLB 56; EWL 3; RGWL 2, 3
Julian of Norwich 1342(?)-1416(?) . **LC 6, 52**
See also BRWS 12; DLB 146; LMFS 1
Julius Caesar 100B.C.-44B.C. ...... **CMLC 47**
See also AW 1; CDWLB 1; DLB 211;
RGWL 2, 3; WLIT 8
Jung, Patricia B.
See Hope, Christopher
Junger, Ernst
See Juenger, Ernst
Junger, Sebastian 1962- .... **CLC 109**
See also AAYA 28; CA 165; CANR 130,
171; MTFW 2005
Juniper, Alex
See Hospital, Janette Turner
Junius
See Luxemburg, Rosa
Junzaburo, Nishiwaki
See Nishiwaki, Junzaburo
Just, Ward 1935- .... **CLC 4, 27**
See also CA 25-28R; CANR 32, 87; CN 6,
7; DLB 335; INT CANR-32
Just, Ward Swift
See Just, Ward
Justice, Donald 1925-2004 ... **CLC 6, 19, 102;
PC 64**
See also AMWS 7; CA 5-8R; 230; CANR
26, 54, 74, 121, 122, 169; CP 1, 2, 3, 4,
5, 6, 7; CSW; DAM POET; DLBY 1983;
EWL 3; INT CANR-26; MAL 5; MTCW
2; PFS 14; TCLE 1:1
Justice, Donald Rodney
See Justice, Donald
Juvenal c. 55-c. 127 .... **CMLC 8, 115**
See also AW 2; CDWLB 1; DLB 211;
RGWL 2, 3; WLIT 8
Juvenis
See Bourne, Randolph S(illiman)
K., Alice
See Knapp, Caroline
Kabakov, Sasha CLC 59
Kabir 1398(?)-1448(?) .... **LC 109; PC 56**
See also RGWL 2, 3
Kacew, Romain 1914-1980 .... **CLC 25**
See also CA 108; 102; DLB 83, 299; RGHL
Kacew, Roman
See Kacew, Romain
Kadare, Ismail 1936- .... **CLC 52, 190**
See also CA 161; CANR 165; DLB 353;
EWL 3; RGWL 3
Kadohata, Cynthia 1956(?)- ..... **CLC 59, 122**
See also AAYA 71; CA 140; CANR 124,
205; CLR 121; LNFS 1; SATA 155, 180
Kadohata, Cynthia L.
See Kadohata, Cynthia
Kafka, Franz 1883-1924 ... **SSC 5, 29, 35, 60,
128; TCLC 2, 6, 13, 29, 47, 53, 112,
179; WLC 3**
See also AAYA 31; BPFB 2; CA 105; 126;
CDWLB 2; DA; DA3; DAB; DAC; DAM
MST, NOV; DLB 81; EW 9; EWL 3;
EXPS; LATS 1:1; LMFS 2; MTCW 1, 2;
MTFW 2005; NFS 7, 34; RGSF 2; RGWL
2, 3; SFW 4; SSFS 3, 7, 12; TWA
Kafu
See Nagai, Kafu
Kahanovitch, Pinchas
See Der Nister
Kahanovitsch, Pinkhes
See Der Nister
Kahanovitsh, Pinkhes
See Der Nister
Kahn, Roger 1927- .... **CLC 30**
See also CA 25-28R; CANR 44, 69, 152;
DLB 171; SATA 37

Kain, Saul
See Sassoon, Siegfried
Kaiser, Georg 1878-1945 .... **TCLC 9, 220**
See also CA 106; 190; CDWLB 2; DLB
124; EWL 3; LMFS 2; RGWL 2, 3
Kaledin, Sergei CLC 59
Kaletski, Alexander 1946- .... **CLC 39**
See also CA 118; 143
Kalidasa fl. c. 400-455 .... **CMLC 9; PC 22**
See also RGWL 2, 3
Kallman, Chester (Simon)
1921-1975 .... **CLC 2**
See also CA 45-48; 53-56; CANR 3; CP 1,
2
Kaminsky, Melvin CLC 12, 217
See Brooks, Mel
See also AAYA 13, 48; DLB 26
Kaminsky, Stuart
See Kaminsky, Stuart M.
Kaminsky, Stuart M. 1934-2009 ...... **CLC 59**
See also CA 73-76; 292; CANR 29, 53, 89,
161, 190; CMW 4
Kaminsky, Stuart Melvin
See Kaminsky, Stuart M.
Kamo no Chomei 1153(?)-1216 .... **CMLC 66**
See also DLB 203
Kamo no Nagaakira
See Kamo no Chomei
Kandinsky, Wassily 1866-1944 .... **TCLC 92**
See also AAYA 64; CA 118; 155
Kane, Francis
See Robbins, Harold
Kane, Paul
See Simon, Paul
Kane, Sarah 1971-1999 .... **DC 31**
See also BRWS 8; CA 190; CD 5, 6; DLB
310
Kanin, Garson 1912-1999 .... **CLC 22**
See also AITN 1; CA 5-8R; 177; CAD;
CANR 7, 78; DLB 7; IDFW 3, 4
Kaniuk, Yoram 1930- .... **CLC 19**
See also CA 134; DLB 299; RGHL
Kant, Immanuel 1724-1804 ..... **NCLC 27, 67**
See also DLB 94
Kantor, MacKinlay 1904-1977 .... **CLC 7**
See also CA 61-64; 73-76; CANR 60, 63;
CN 1, 2; DLB 9, 102; MAL 5; MTCW 2;
RHW; TCWW 1, 2
Kanze Motokiyo
See Zeami
Kaplan, David Michael 1946- .... **CLC 50**
See also CA 187
Kaplan, James 1951- .... **CLC 59**
See also CA 135; CANR 121
Karadzic, Vuk Stefanovic
1787-1864 .... **NCLC 115**
See also CDWLB 4; DLB 147
Karageorge, Michael
See Anderson, Poul
Karamzin, Nikolai Mikhailovich
1766-1826 .... **NCLC 3, 173**
See also DLB 150; RGSF 2
Karapanou, Margarita 1946- .... **CLC 13**
See also CA 101
Karinthy, Frigyes 1887-1938 .... **TCLC 47**
See also CA 170; DLB 215; EWL 3
Karl, Frederick R(obert)
1927-2004 .... **CLC 34**
See also CA 5-8R; 226; CANR 3, 44, 143
Karr, Mary 1955- .... **CLC 188**
See also AMWS 11; CA 151; CANR 100,
191; MTFW 2005; NCFS 5
Kastel, Warren
See Silverberg, Robert
Kataev, Evgeny Petrovich
1903-1942 .... **TCLC 21**
See also CA 120; DLB 272

Kataphusin
See Ruskin, John
Katz, Steve 1935- .... **CLC 47**
See also CA 25-28R; CAAS 14, 64; CANR
12; CN 4, 5, 6, 7; DLBY 1983
Kauffman, Janet 1945- .... **CLC 42**
See also CA 117; CANR 43, 84; DLB 218;
DLBY 1986
Kaufman, Bob (Garnell)
1925-1986 .... **CLC 49; PC 74**
See also BG 1:3; BW 1; CA 41-44R; 118;
CANR 22; CP 1; DLB 16, 41
Kaufman, George S. 1889-1961 ...... **CLC 38;
DC 17**
See also CA 108; 93-96; DAM DRAM;
DFS 1, 10; DLB 7; INT CA-108; MTCW
2; MTFW 2005; RGAL 4; TUS
Kaufman, Moises 1963- .... **DC 26**
See also CA 211; DFS 22; MTFW 2005
Kaufman, Sue
See Baroness, Sue K.
Kavafis, Konstantinos Petrov
See Cavafy, Constantine
Kavan, Anna 1901-1968 .... **CLC 5, 13, 82**
See also BRWS 7; CA 5-8R; CANR 6, 57;
DLB 255; MTCW 1; RGEL 2; SFW 4
Kavanagh, Dan
See Barnes, Julian
Kavanagh, Julie 1952- .... **CLC 119**
See also CA 163; CANR 186
Kavanagh, Patrick (Joseph)
1904-1967 .... **CLC 22; PC 33, 105**
See also BRWS 7; CA 123; 25-28R; DLB
15, 20; EWL 3; MTCW 1; RGEL 2
Kawabata, Yasunari 1899-1972 ..... **CLC 2, 5,
9, 18, 107; SSC 17**
See also CA 93-96; 33-36R; CANR 88;
DAM MULT; DLB 180, 330; EWL 3;
MJW; MTCW 2; MTFW 2005; RGSF 2;
RGWL 2, 3; SSFS 29
Kawabata Yasunari
See Kawabata, Yasunari
Kaye, Mary Margaret
See Kaye, M.M.
Kaye, M.M. 1908-2004 .... **CLC 28**
See also CA 89-92; 223; CANR 24, 60, 102,
142; MTCW 1, 2; MTFW 2005; RHW;
SATA 62; SATA-Obit 152
Kaye, Mollie
See Kaye, M.M.
Kaye-Smith, Sheila 1887-1956 .... **TCLC 20**
See also CA 118; 203; DLB 36
Kaymor, Patrice Maguilene
See Senghor, Leopold Sedar
Kazakov, Iurii Pavlovich
See Kazakov, Yuri Pavlovich
Kazakov, Yuri Pavlovich 1927-1982 . **SSC 43**
See also CA 5-8R; CANR 36; DLB 302;
EWL 3; MTCW 1; RGSF 2
Kazakov, Yury
See Kazakov, Yuri Pavlovich
Kazan, Elia 1909-2003 .... **CLC 6, 16, 63**
See also CA 21-24R; 220; CANR 32, 78
Kazantzakis, Nikos 1883(?)-1957 .... **TCLC 2,
5, 33, 181**
See also BPFB 2; CA 105; 132; DA3; EW
9; EWL 3; MTCW 1, 2; MTFW 2005;
RGWL 2, 3
Kazin, Alfred 1915-1998 ..... **CLC 34, 38, 119**
See also AMWS 8; CA 1-4R; CAAS 7;
CANR 1, 45, 79; DLB 67; EWL 3
Keane, Mary Nesta 1904-1996 .... **CLC 31**
See also CA 108; 114; 151; CN 5, 6; INT
CA-114; RHW; TCLE 1:1
Keane, Mary Nesta Skrine
See Keane, Mary Nesta
Keane, Molly
See Keane, Mary Nesta

Keates, Jonathan 1946(?)- .... **CLC 34**
See also CA 163; CANR 126
Keaton, Buster 1895-1966 .... **CLC 20**
See also AAYA 79; CA 194
Keats, John 1795-1821 ...... **NCLC 8, 73, 121, 225; PC 1, 96; WLC 3**
See also AAYA 58; BRW 4; BRWR 1; CD-BLB 1789-1832; DA; DA3; DAB; DAC; DAM MST, POET; DLB 96, 110; EXPP; LMFS 1; PAB; PFS 1, 2, 3, 9, 17, 32; RGEL 2; TEA; WLIT 3; WP
Keble, John 1792-1866 .... **NCLC 87**
See also DLB 32, 55; RGEL 2
Keene, Donald 1922- .... **CLC 34**
See also CA 1-4R; CANR 5, 119, 190
Keillor, Garrison 1942- ..... **CLC 40, 115, 222**
See also AAYA 2, 62; AMWS 16; BEST 89:3; BPFB 2; CA 111; 117; CANR 36, 59, 124, 180; CPW; DA3; DAM POP; DLBY 1987; EWL 3; MTCW 1, 2; MTFW 2005; SATA 58; TUS
Keillor, Gary Edward
See Keillor, Garrison
Keith, Carlos
See Lewton, Val
Keith, Michael
See Hubbard, L. Ron
Kell, Joseph
See Burgess, Anthony
Keller, Gottfried 1819-1890 .... **NCLC 2; SSC 26, 107**
See also CDWLB 2; DLB 129; EW; RGSF 2; RGWL 2, 3
Keller, Nora Okja 1965- .... **CLC 109, 281**
See also CA 187
Kellerman, Jonathan 1949- .... **CLC 44**
See also AAYA 35; BEST 90:1; CA 106; CANR 29, 51, 150, 183; CMW 4; CPW; DA3; DAM POP; INT CANR-29
Kelley, William Melvin 1937- .... **BLC 2:2; CLC 22**
See also BW 1; CA 77-80; CANR 27, 83; CN 1, 2, 3, 4, 5, 6, 7; DLB 33; EWL 3
Kellock, Archibald P.
See Mavor, Osborne Henry
Kellogg, Marjorie 1922-2005 .... **CLC 2**
See also CA 81-84; 246
Kellow, Kathleen
See Hibbert, Eleanor Alice Burford
Kelly, Lauren
See Oates, Joyce Carol
Kelly, M(ilton) T(errence) 1947- ...... **CLC 55**
See also CA 97-100; CAAS 22; CANR 19, 43, 84; CN 6
Kelly, Robert 1935- .... **SSC 50**
See also CA 17-20R; CAAS 19; CANR 47; CP 1, 2, 3, 4, 5, 6, 7; DLB 5, 130, 165
Kelman, James 1946- .... **CLC 58, 86, 292**
See also BRWS 5; CA 148; CANR 85, 130, 199; CN 5, 6, 7; DLB 194, 319, 326; RGSF 2; WLIT 4
Kemal, Yasar
See Kemal, Yashar
Kemal, Yashar 1923(?)- .... **CLC 14, 29**
See also CA 89-92; CANR 44; CWW 2; EWL 3; WLIT 6
Kemble, Fanny 1809-1893 .... **NCLC 18**
See also DLB 32
Kemelman, Harry 1908-1996 .... **CLC 2**
See also AITN 1; BPFB 2; CA 9-12R; 155; CANR 6, 71; CMW 4; DLB 28
Kempe, Margery 1373(?)-1440(?) ... **LC 6, 56**
See also BRWS 12; DLB 146; FL 1:1; RGEL 2
Kempis, Thomas a 1380-1471 .... **LC 11**
Kenan, Randall (G.) 1963- .... **BLC 2:2**
See also BW 2, 3; CA 142; CANR 86; CN 7; CSW; DLB 292; GLL 1

Kendall, Henry 1839-1882 .... **NCLC 12**
See also DLB 230
Keneally, Thomas 1935- .... **CLC 5, 8, 10, 14, 19, 27, 43, 117, 279**
See also BRWS 4; CA 85-88; CANR 10, 50, 74, 130, 165, 198; CN 1, 2, 3, 4, 5, 6, 7; CPW; DA3; DAM NOV; DLB 289, 299, 326; EWL 3; MTCW 1, 2; MTFW 2005; NFS 17; RGEL 2; RGHL; RHW
Keneally, Thomas Michael
See Keneally, Thomas
Keneally, Tom
See Keneally, Thomas
Kennedy, A. L. 1965- .... **CLC 188**
See also CA 168, 213; CAAE 213; CANR 108, 193; CD 5, 6; CN 6, 7; DLB 271; RGSF 2
Kennedy, Adrienne (Lita) 1931- .... **BLC 1:2; CLC 66; DC 5**
See also AFAW 2; BW 2, 3; CA 103; CAAS 20; CABS 3; CAD; CANR 26, 53, 82; CD 5, 6; DAM MULT; DFS 9; DLB 38, 341; FW; MAL 5
Kennedy, Alison Louise
See Kennedy, A. L.
Kennedy, John Pendleton 1795-1870 .... **NCLC 2**
See also DLB 3, 248, 254; RGAL 4
Kennedy, Joseph Charles 1929- .. **CLC 8, 42; PC 93**
See Kennedy, X. J.
See also AMWS 15; CA 1-4R, 201; CAAE 201; CAAS 9; CANR 4, 30, 40; CLR 27; CP 1, 2, 3, 4, 5, 6, 7; CWRI 5; DLB 5; MAICYA 2; MAICYAS 1; SAAS 22; SATA 14, 86, 130; SATA-Essay 130
Kennedy, William 1928- .. **CLC 6, 28, 34, 53, 239**
See also AAYA 1, 73; AMWS 7; BPFB 2; CA 85-88; CANR 14, 31, 76, 134; CN 4, 5, 6, 7; DA3; DAM NOV; DLB 143; DLBY 1985; EWL 3; INT CANR-31; MAL 5; MTCW 1, 2; MTFW 2005; SATA 57
Kennedy, William Joseph
See Kennedy, William
Kennedy, X. J. CLC 8, 42
See Kennedy, Joseph Charles
See also CAAS 9; CLR 27; DLB 5; SAAS 22
Kenny, Maurice (Francis) 1929- ..... **CLC 87; NNAL**
See also CA 144; CAAS 22; CANR 143; DAM MULT; DLB 175
Kent, Kathleen CLC 280
See also CA 288
Kent, Kelvin
See Kuttner, Henry
Kenton, Maxwell
See Southern, Terry
Kenyon, Jane 1947-1995 .... **PC 57**
See also AAYA 63; AMWS 7; CA 118; 148; CANR 44, 69, 172; CP 6, 7; CWP; DLB 120; PFS 9, 17; RGAL 4
Kenyon, Robert O.
See Kuttner, Henry
Kepler, Johannes 1571-1630 .... **LC 45**
Ker, Jill
See Conway, Jill K.
Kerkow, H. C.
See Lewton, Val
Kerouac, Jack 1922-1969 ...... **CLC 1, 2, 3, 5, 14, 61; TCLC 117; WLC**
See also AAYA 25; AITN 1; AMWC 1; AMWS 3; BG 3; BPFB 2; CA 5-8R; 25-28R; CANR 26, 54, 95, 184; CDALB 1941-1968; CP 1; CPW; DA; DA3; DAB; DAC; DAM MST, NOV, POET, POP;

DLB 2, 16, 237; DLBY 1995; EWL 3; GLL 1; LATS 1:2; LMFS 2; MAL 5; MTCW 1, 2; MTFW 2005; NFS 8; RGAL 4; TUS; WP
Kerouac, Jean-Louis le Brisde
See Kerouac, Jack
Kerouac, John
See Kerouac, Jack
Kerr, (Bridget) Jean (Collins) 1923(?)-2003 .... **CLC 22**
See also CA 5-8R; 212; CANR 7; INT CANR-7
Kerr, M. E.
See Meaker, Marijane
Kerr, Robert CLC 55
Kerrigan, (Thomas) Anthony 1918- .. **CLC 4, 6**
See also CA 49-52; CAAS 11; CANR 4
Kerry, Lois
See Duncan, Lois
Kesey, Ken 1935-2001 .... **CLC 1, 3, 6, 11, 46, 64, 184; WLC 3**
See also AAYA 25; BG 1:3; BPFB 2; CA 1-4R; 204; CANR 22, 38, 66, 124; CDALB 1968-1988; CN 1, 2, 3, 4, 5, 6, 7; CPW; DA; DA3; DAB; DAC; DAM MST, NOV, POP; DLB 2, 16, 206; EWL 3; EXPN; LAIT 4; MAL 5; MTCW 1, 2; MTFW 2005; NFS 2; RGAL 4; SATA 66; SATA-Obit 131; TUS; YAW
Kesselring, Joseph (Otto) 1902-1967 .... **CLC 45**
See also CA 150; DAM DRAM, MST; DFS 20
Kessler, Jascha (Frederick) 1929- ...... **CLC 4**
See also CA 17-20R; CANR 8, 48, 111; CP 1
Kettelkamp, Larry (Dale) 1933- .... **CLC 12**
See also CA 29-32R; CANR 16; SAAS 3; SATA 2
Key, Ellen (Karolina Sofia) 1849-1926 .... **TCLC 65**
See also DLB 259
Keyber, Conny
See Fielding, Henry
Keyes, Daniel 1927- .... **CLC 80**
See also AAYA 23; BYA 11; CA 17-20R, 181; CAAE 181; CANR 10, 26, 54, 74; DA; DA3; DAC; DAM MST, NOV; EXPN; LAIT 4; MTCW 2; MTFW 2005; NFS 2; SATA 37; SFW 4
Keynes, John Maynard 1883-1946 .... **TCLC 64**
See also CA 114; 162, 163; DLBD 10; MTCW 2; MTFW 2005
Khanshendel, Chiron
See Rose, Wendy
Khayyam, Omar 1048-1131 ... **CMLC 11; PC 8**
See also DA3; DAM POET; RGWL 2, 3; WLIT 6
Kherdian, David 1931- .... **CLC 6, 9**
See also AAYA 42; CA 21-24R, 192; CAAE 192; CAAS 2; CANR 39, 78; CLR 24; JRDA; LAIT 3; MAICYA 1, 2; SATA 16, 74; SATA-Essay 125
Khlebnikov, Velimir TCLC 20
See Khlebnikov, Viktor Vladimirovich
See also DLB 295; EW 10; EWL 3; RGWL 2, 3
Khlebnikov, Viktor Vladimirovich 1885-1922
See Khlebnikov, Velimir
See also CA 117; 217
Khodasevich, V.F.
See Khodasevich, Vladislav
Khodasevich, Vladislav 1886-1939 .... **TCLC 15**
See also CA 115; DLB 317; EWL 3

Khodasevich, Vladislav Felitsianovich
See Khodasevich, Vladislav

Kidd, Sue Monk 1948- .... **CLC 267**
See also AAYA 72; CA 202; LNFS 1; MTFW 2005; NFS 27

Kielland, Alexander Lange
1849-1906 .... **TCLC 5**
See also CA 104; DLB 354

Kiely, Benedict 1919-2007 . **CLC 23, 43; SSC 58**
See also CA 1-4R; 257; CANR 2, 84; CN 1, 2, 3, 4, 5, 6, 7; DLB 15, 319; TCLE 1:1

Kienzle, William X. 1928-2001 .... **CLC 25**
See also CA 93-96; 203; CAAS 1; CANR 9, 31, 59, 111; CMW 4; DA3; DAM POP; INT CANR-31; MSW; MTCW 1, 2; MTFW 2005

Kierkegaard, Soren 1813-1855 ..... **NCLC 34, 78, 125**
See also DLB 300; EW 6; LMFS 2; RGWL 3; TWA

Kieslowski, Krzysztof 1941-1996 .... **CLC 120**
See also CA 147; 151

Killens, John Oliver 1916-1987 ...... **BLC 2:2; CLC 10**
See also BW 2; CA 77-80; 123; CAAS 2; CANR 26; CN 1, 2, 3, 4; DLB 33; EWL 3

Killigrew, Anne 1660-1685 .... **LC 4, 73**
See also DLB 131

Killigrew, Thomas 1612-1683 .... **LC 57**
See also DLB 58; RGEL 2

Kim
See Simenon, Georges

Kincaid, Jamaica 1949- . **BLC 1:2, 2:2; CLC 43, 68, 137, 234; SSC 72**
See also AAYA 13, 56; AFAW 2; AMWS 7; BRWS 7; BW 2, 3; CA 125; CANR 47, 59, 95, 133; CDALBS; CDWLB 3; CLR 63; CN 4, 5, 6, 7; DA3; DAM MULT, NOV; DLB 157, 227; DNFS 1; EWL 3; EXPS; FW; LATS 1:2; LMFS 2; MAL 5; MTCW 1; MTFW 2005; NCFS 1; NFS 3; SSFS 5, 7; TUS; WWE 1; YAW

King, Francis (Henry) 1923- .... **CLC 8, 53, 145**
See also CA 1-4R; CANR 1, 33, 86; CN 1, 2, 3, 4, 5, 6, 7; DAM NOV; DLB 15, 139; MTCW 1

King, Kennedy
See Brown, George Douglas

King, Martin Luther, Jr.
1929-1968 ... **BLC 1:2; CLC 83; WLCS**
See also BW 2, 3; CA 25-28; CANR 27, 44; CAP 2; DA; DA3; DAB; DAC; DAM MST, MULT; LAIT 5; LATS 1:2; MTCW 1, 2; MTFW 2005; SATA 14

King, Stephen 1947- .... **CLC 12, 26, 37, 61, 113, 228, 244; SSC 17, 55**
See also AAYA 1, 17, 82; AMWS 5; BEST 90:1; BPFB 2; CA 61-64; CANR 1, 30, 52, 76, 119, 134, 168; CLR 124; CN 7; CPW; DA3; DAM NOV, POP; DLB 143, 350; DLBY 1980; HGG; JRDA; LAIT 5; LNFS 1; MTCW 1, 2; MTFW 2005; RGAL 4; SATA 9, 55, 161; SSFS 30; SUFW 1, 2; WYAS 1; YAW

King, Stephen Edwin
See King, Stephen

King, Steve
See King, Stephen

King, Thomas 1943- .... **CLC 89, 171, 276; NNAL**
See also CA 144; CANR 95, 175; CCA 1; CN 6, 7; DAC; DAM MULT; DLB 175, 334; SATA 96

King, Thomas Hunt
See King, Thomas

Kingman, Lee
See Natti, Lee

Kingsley, Charles 1819-1875 .... **NCLC 35**
See also BRWS 16; CLR 77; DLB 21, 32, 163, 178, 190; FANT; MAICYA 2; MAICYAS 1; RGEL 2; WCH; YABC 2

Kingsley, Henry 1830-1876 .... **NCLC 107**
See also DLB 21, 230; RGEL 2

Kingsley, Sidney 1906-1995 .... **CLC 44**
See also CA 85-88; 147; CAD; DFS 14, 19; DLB 7; MAL 5; RGAL 4

Kingsolver, Barbara 1955- .... **CLC 55, 81, 130, 216, 269**
See also AAYA 15; AMWS 7; CA 129; 134; CANR 60, 96, 133, 179; CDALBS; CN 7; CPW; CSW; DA3; DAM POP; DLB 206; INT CA-134; LAIT 5; MTCW 2; MTFW 2005; NFS 5, 10, 12, 24; RGAL 4; TCLE 1:1

Kingston, Maxine Hong 1940- ... **AAL; CLC 12, 19, 58, 121, 271; SSC 136; WLCS**
See also AAYA 8, 55; AMWS 5; BPFB 2; CA 69-72; CANR 13, 38, 74, 87, 128; CDALBS; CN 6, 7; DA3; DAM MULT, NOV; DLB 173, 212, 312; DLBY 1980; EWL 3; FL 1:6; FW; INT CANR-13; LAIT 5; MAL 5; MBL; MTCW 1, 2; MTFW 2005; NFS 6; RGAL 4; SATA 53; SSFS 3; TCWW 2

Kingston, Maxine Ting Ting Hong
See Kingston, Maxine Hong

Kinnell, Galway 1927- ..... **CLC 1, 2, 3, 5, 13, 29, 129; PC 26**
See also AMWS 3; CA 9-12R; CANR 10, 34, 66, 116, 138, 175; CP 1, 2, 3, 4, 5, 6, 7; DLB 5, 342; DLBY 1987; EWL 3; INT CANR-34; MAL 5; MTCW 1, 2; MTFW 2005; PAB; PFS 9, 26, 35; RGAL 4; TCLE 1:1; WP

Kinsella, Thomas 1928- .... **CLC 4, 19, 138, 274; PC 69**
See also BRWS 5; CA 17-20R; CANR 15, 122; CP 1, 2, 3, 4, 5, 6, 7; DLB 27; EWL 3; MTCW 1, 2; MTFW 2005; RGEL 2; TEA

Kinsella, W.P. 1935- .... **CLC 27, 43, 166**
See also AAYA 7, 60; BPFB 2; CA 97-100, 222; CAAE 222; CAAS 7; CANR 21, 35, 66, 75, 129; CN 4, 5, 6, 7; CPW; DAC; DAM NOV, POP; FANT; INT CANR-21; LAIT 5; MTCW 1, 2; MTFW 2005; NFS 15; RGSF 2; SSFS 30

Kinsey, Alfred C(harles)
1894-1956 .... **TCLC 91**
See also CA 115; 170; MTCW 2

Kipling, Joseph Rudyard
See Kipling, Rudyard

Kipling, Rudyard 1865-1936 . **PC 3, 91; SSC 5, 54, 110; TCLC 8, 17, 167; WLC 3**
See also AAYA 32; BRW 6; BRWC 1, 2; BRWR 3; BYA 4; CA 105; 120; CANR 33; CDBLB 1890-1914; CLR 39, 65; CWRI 5; DA; DA3; DAB; DAC; DAM MST, POET; DLB 19, 34, 141, 156, 330; EWL 3; EXPS; FANT; LAIT 3; LMFS 1; MAICYA 1, 2; MTCW 1, 2; MTFW 2005; NFS 21; PFS 22; RGEL 2; RGSF 2; SATA 100; SFW 4; SSFS 8, 21, 22; SUFW 1; TEA; WCH; WLIT 4; YABC 2

Kircher, Athanasius 1602-1680 .... **LC 121**
See also DLB 164

Kirk, Russell (Amos) 1918-1994 .. **TCLC 119**
See also AITN 1; CA 1-4R; 145; CAAS 9; CANR 1, 20, 60; HGG; INT CANR-20; MTCW 1, 2

Kirkham, Dinah
See Card, Orson Scott

Kirkland, Caroline M. 1801-1864 . **NCLC 85**
See also DLB 3, 73, 74, 250, 254; DLBD 13

Kirkup, James 1918-2009 .... **CLC 1**
See also CA 1-4R; CAAS 4; CANR 2; CP 1, 2, 3, 4, 5, 6, 7; DLB 27; SATA 12

Kirkwood, James 1930(?)-1989 .... **CLC 9**
See also AITN 2; CA 1-4R; 128; CANR 6, 40; GLL 2

Kirsch, Sarah 1935- .... **CLC 176**
See also CA 178; CWW 2; DLB 75; EWL 3

Kirshner, Sidney
See Kingsley, Sidney

Kis, Danilo 1935-1989 .... **CLC 57**
See also CA 109; 118; 129; CANR 61; CDWLB 4; DLB 181; EWL 3; MTCW 1; RGSF 2; RGWL 2, 3

Kissinger, Henry A(lfred) 1923- ..... **CLC 137**
See also CA 1-4R; CANR 2, 33, 66, 109; MTCW 1

Kittel, Frederick August
See Wilson, August

Kivi, Aleksis 1834-1872 .... **NCLC 30**

Kizer, Carolyn 1925- ..... **CLC 15, 39, 80; PC 66**
See also CA 65-68; CAAS 5; CANR 24, 70, 134; CP 1, 2, 3, 4, 5, 6, 7; CWP; DAM POET; DLB 5, 169; EWL 3; MAL 5; MTCW 2; MTFW 2005; PFS 18; TCLE 1:1

Klabund 1890-1928 .... **TCLC 44**
See also CA 162; DLB 66

Klappert, Peter 1942- .... **CLC 57**
See also CA 33-36R; CSW; DLB 5

Klausner, Amos
See Oz, Amos

Klein, A. M. 1909-1972 .... **CLC 19**
See also CA 101; 37-40R; CP 1; DAB; DAC; DAM MST; DLB 68; EWL 3; RGEL 2; RGHL

Klein, Abraham Moses
See Klein, A. M.

Klein, Joe
See Klein, Joseph

Klein, Joseph 1946- .... **CLC 154**
See also CA 85-88; CANR 55, 164

Klein, Norma 1938-1989 .... **CLC 30**
See also AAYA 2, 35; BPFB 2; BYA 6, 7, 8; CA 41-44R; 128; CANR 15, 37; CLR 2, 19; INT CANR-15; JRDA; MAICYA 1, 2; SAAS 1; SATA 7, 57; WYA; YAW

Klein, T.E.D. 1947- .... **CLC 34**
See also CA 119; CANR 44, 75, 167; HGG

Klein, Theodore Eibon Donald
See Klein, T.E.D.

Kleist, Heinrich von 1777-1811 .... **DC 29; NCLC 2, 37, 222; SSC 22**
See also CDWLB 2; DAM DRAM; DLB 90; EW 5; RGSF 2; RGWL 2, 3

Klima, Ivan 1931- .... **CLC 56, 172**
See also CA 25-28R; CANR 17, 50, 91; CDWLB 4; CWW 2; DAM NOV; DLB 232; EWL 3; RGWL 3

Klimentev, Andrei Platonovich
See Klimentov, Andrei Platonovich

Klimentov, Andrei Platonovich
1899-1951 .... **SSC 42; TCLC 14**
See also CA 108; 232; DLB 272; EWL 3

Klinger, Friedrich Maximilian von
1752-1831 .... **NCLC 1**
See also DLB 94

Klingsor the Magician
See Hartmann, Sadakichi

Klopstock, Friedrich Gottlieb
1724-1803 .... **NCLC 11, 225**
See also DLB 97; EW 4; RGWL 2, 3

Kluge, Alexander 1932- .... **SSC 61**
See also CA 81-84; CANR 163; DLB 75

Knapp, Caroline 1959-2002 .... **CLC 99**
See also CA 154; 207

Kumin, Maxine 1925- .... **CLC 5, 13, 28, 164; PC 15**
　　See also AITN 2; AMWS 4; ANW; CA 1-4R, 271; CAAE 271; CAAS 8; CANR 1, 21, 69, 115, 140; CP 2, 3, 4, 5, 6, 7; CWP; DA3; DAM POET; DLB 5; EWL 3; EXPP; MTCW 1, 2; MTFW 2005; PAB; PFS 18; SATA 12

Kumin, Maxine Winokur
　　See Kumin, Maxine

Kundera, Milan 1929- . **CLC 4, 9, 19, 32, 68, 115, 135, 234; SSC 24**
　　See also AAYA 2, 62; BPFB 2; CA 85-88; CANR 19, 52, 74, 144; CDWLB 4; CWW 2; DA3; DAM NOV; DLB 232; EW 13; EWL 3; MTCW 1, 2; MTFW 2005; NFS 18, 27; RGSF 2; RGWL 3; SSFS 10

Kunene, Mazisi 1930-2006 .... **CLC 85**
　　See also BW 1, 3; CA 125; 252; CANR 81; CP 1, 6, 7; DLB 117

Kunene, Mazisi Raymond
　　See Kunene, Mazisi

Kunene, Mazisi Raymond Fakazi Mngoni
　　See Kunene, Mazisi

Kung, Hans
　　See Kung, Hans

Kung, Hans 1928- .... **CLC 130**
　　See also CA 53-56; CANR 66, 134; MTCW 1, 2; MTFW 2005

Kunikida, Tetsuo
　　See Kunikida Doppo

Kunikida Doppo 1869(?)-1908 .... **TCLC 99**
　　See also DLB 180; EWL 3

Kunikida Tetsuo
　　See Kunikida Doppo

Kunitz, Stanley 1905-2006 ..... **CLC 6, 11, 14, 148; PC 19**
　　See also AMWS 3; CA 41-44R; 250; CANR 26, 57, 98; CP 1, 2, 3, 4, 5, 6, 7; DA3; DLB 48; INT CANR-26; MAL 5; MTCW 1, 2; MTFW 2005; PFS 11; RGAL 4

Kunitz, Stanley Jasspon
　　See Kunitz, Stanley

Kunze, Reiner 1933- .... **CLC 10**
　　See also CA 93-96; CWW 2; DLB 75; EWL 3

Kuprin, Aleksander Ivanovich
　　1870-1938 .... **TCLC 5**
　　See also CA 104; 182; DLB 295; EWL 3

Kuprin, Aleksandr Ivanovich
　　See Kuprin, Aleksander Ivanovich

Kuprin, Alexandr Ivanovich
　　See Kuprin, Aleksander Ivanovich

Kureishi, Hanif 1954- ...... **CLC 64, 135, 284; DC 26**
　　See also BRWS 11; CA 139; CANR 113, 197; CBD; CD 5, 6; CN 6, 7; DLB 194, 245, 352; GLL 2; IDFW 4; WLIT 4; WWE 1

Kurosawa, Akira 1910-1998 ..... **CLC 16, 119**
　　See also AAYA 11, 64; CA 101; 170; CANR 46; DAM MULT

Kushner, Tony 1956- .... **CLC 81, 203; DC 10**
　　See also AAYA 61; AMWS 9; CA 144; CAD; CANR 74, 130; CD 5, 6; DA3; DAM DRAM; DFS 5; DLB 228; EWL 3; GLL 1; LAIT 5; MAL 5; MTCW 2; MTFW 2005; RGAL 4; RGHL; SATA 160

Kuttner, Henry 1915-1958 .... **TCLC 10**
　　See also CA 107; 157; DLB 8; FANT; SCFW 1, 2; SFW 4

Kutty, Madhavi
　　See Das, Kamala

Kuzma, Greg 1944- .... **CLC 7**
　　See also CA 33-36R; CANR 70

Kuzmin, Mikhail (Alekseevich)
　　1872(?)-1936 .... **TCLC 40**
　　See also CA 170; DLB 295; EWL 3

Kyd, Thomas 1558-1594 .. **DC 3; LC 22, 125**
　　See also BRW 1; DAM DRAM; DFS 21; DLB 62; IDTP; LMFS 1; RGEL 2; TEA; WLIT 3

Kyprianos, Iossif
　　See Samarakis, Antonis

L. S.
　　See Stephen, Sir Leslie

Labe, Louise 1521-1566 .... **LC 120**
　　See also DLB 327

Labrunie, Gerard
　　See Nerval, Gerard de

La Bruyere, Jean de 1645-1696 .. **LC 17, 168**
　　See also DLB 268; EW 3; GFL Beginnings to 1789

LaBute, Neil 1963- .... **CLC 225**
　　See also CA 240

Lacan, Jacques (Marie Emile)
　　1901-1981 .... **CLC 75**
　　See also CA 121; 104; DLB 296; EWL 3; TWA

Laclos, Pierre-Ambroise Francois
　　1741-1803 .... **NCLC 4, 87**
　　See also DLB 313; EW 4; GFL Beginnings to 1789; RGWL 2, 3

La Colere, Francois
　　See Aragon, Louis

Lacolere, Francois
　　See Aragon, Louis

Lactantius c. 250-c. 325 .... **CMLC 118**

La Deshabilleuse
　　See Simenon, Georges

Lady Gregory
　　See Gregory, Lady Isabella Augusta (Persse)

Lady of Quality, A
　　See Bagnold, Enid

La Fayette, Marie-(Madelaine Pioche de la Vergne) 1634-1693 .... **LC 2, 144**
　　See also DLB 268; GFL Beginnings to 1789; RGWL 2, 3

Lafayette, Marie-Madeleine
　　See La Fayette, Marie-(Madelaine Pioche de la Vergne)

Lafayette, Rene
　　See Hubbard, L. Ron

La Flesche, Francis 1857(?)-1932 ...... **NNAL**
　　See also CA 144; CANR 83; DLB 175

La Fontaine, Jean de 1621-1695 .... **LC 50**
　　See also DLB 268; EW 3; GFL Beginnings to 1789; MAICYA 1, 2; RGWL 2, 3; SATA 18

LaForet, Carmen 1921-2004 .... **CLC 219**
　　See also CA 246; CWW 2; DLB 322; EWL 3

LaForet Diaz, Carmen
　　See LaForet, Carmen

Laforgue, Jules 1860-1887 .... **NCLC 5, 53, 221; PC 14; SSC 20**
　　See also DLB 217; EW 7; GFL 1789 to the Present; RGWL 2, 3

Lagerkvist, Paer 1891-1974 ... **CLC 7, 10, 13, 54; SSC 12; TCLC 144**
　　See also CA 85-88; 49-52; DA3; DAM DRAM, NOV; DLB 259, 331; EW 10; EWL 3; MTCW 1, 2; MTFW 2005; RGSF 2; RGWL 2, 3; TWA

Lagerkvist, Paer Fabian
　　See Lagerkvist, Paer

Lagerkvist, Par
　　See Lagerkvist, Paer

Lagerloef, Selma
　　See Lagerlof, Selma

Lagerloef, Selma Ottiliana Lovisa
　　See Lagerlof, Selma

Lagerlof, Selma 1858-1940 .... **TCLC 4, 36**
　　See also CA 108; 188; CLR 7; DLB 259, 331; MTCW 2; RGWL 2, 3; SATA 15; SSFS 18

Lagerlof, Selma Ottiliana Lovisa
　　See Lagerlof, Selma

La Guma, Alex 1925-1985 .. **BLCS; CLC 19; TCLC 140**
　　See also AFW; BW 1, 3; CA 49-52; 118; CANR 25, 81; CDWLB 3; CN 1, 2, 3; CP 1; DAM NOV; DLB 117, 225; EWL 3; MTCW 1, 2; MTFW 2005; WLIT 2; WWE 1

La Guma, Justin Alexander
　　See La Guma, Alex

Lahiri, Jhumpa 1967- .... **CLC 282; SSC 96**
　　See also AAYA 56; CA 193; CANR 134, 184; DLB 323; MTFW 2005; NFS 31; SSFS 19, 27

Laidlaw, A. K.
　　See Grieve, C. M.

Lainez, Manuel Mujica
　　See Mujica Lainez, Manuel

Laing, R(onald) D(avid) 1927-1989 . **CLC 95**
　　See also CA 107; 129; CANR 34; MTCW 1

Laishley, Alex
　　See Booth, Martin

Lamartine, Alphonse de
　　1790-1869 .... **NCLC 11, 190; PC 16**
　　See also DAM POET; DLB 217; GFL 1789 to the Present; RGWL 2, 3

Lamartine, Alphonse Marie Louis Prat de
　　See Lamartine, Alphonse de

Lamb, Charles 1775-1834 ..... **NCLC 10, 113; SSC 112; WLC 3**
　　See also BRW 4; CDBLB 1789-1832; DA; DAB; DAC; DAM MST; DLB 93, 107, 163; RGEL 2; SATA 17; TEA

Lamb, Lady Caroline 1785-1828 ... **NCLC 38**
　　See also DLB 116

Lamb, Mary Ann 1764-1847 ...... **NCLC 125; SSC 112**
　　See also DLB 163; SATA 17

Lame Deer 1903(?)-1976 .... **NNAL**
　　See also CA 69-72

Lamming, George (William)
　　1927- . **BLC 1:2, 2:2; CLC 2, 4, 66, 144**
　　See also BW 2, 3; CA 85-88; CANR 26, 76; CDWLB 3; CN 1, 2, 3, 4, 5, 6, 7; CP 1; DAM MULT; DLB 125; EWL 3; MTCW 1, 2; MTFW 2005; NFS 15; RGEL 2

L'Amour, Louis 1908-1988 .... **CLC 25, 55**
　　See also AAYA 16; AITN 2; BEST 89:2; BPFB 2; CA 1-4R; 125; CANR 3, 25, 40; CPW; DA3; DAM NOV, POP; DLB 206; DLBY 1980; MTCW 1, 2; MTFW 2005; RGAL 4; TCWW 1, 2

Lampedusa, Giuseppe di
　　1896-1957 .... **TCLC 13**
　　See also CA 111; 164; DLB 177; EW 11; EWL 3; MTCW 2; MTFW 2005; RGWL 2, 3; WLIT 7

Lampman, Archibald 1861-1899 .. **NCLC 25, 194**
　　See also DLB 92; RGEL 2; TWA

Lancaster, Bruce 1896-1963 .... **CLC 36**
　　See also CA 9-10; CANR 70; CAP 1; SATA 9

Lanchester, John 1962- .... **CLC 99, 280**
　　See also CA 194; DLB 267

Landau, Mark Alexandrovich
　　See Aldanov, Mark (Alexandrovich)

Landau-Aldanov, Mark Alexandrovich
　　See Aldanov, Mark (Alexandrovich)

Landis, Jerry
　　See Simon, Paul

Landis, John 1950- .... **CLC 26**
　　See also CA 112; 122; CANR 128

Landolfi, Tommaso 1908-1979 .... **CLC 11, 49**
　　See also CA 127; 117; DLB 177; EWL 3

Lucretius c. 94B.C.-c. 49B.C. .... **CMLC 48**
See also AW 2; CDWLB 1; DLB 211; EFS 2; RGWL 2, 3; WLIT 8

Ludlam, Charles 1943-1987 .... **CLC 46, 50**
See also CA 85-88; 122; CAD; CANR 72, 86; DLB 266

Ludlum, Robert 1927-2001 .... **CLC 22, 43**
See also AAYA 10, 59; BEST 89:1, 90:3; BPFB 2; CA 33-36R; 195; CANR 25, 41, 68, 105, 131; CMW 4; CPW; DA3; DAM NOV, POP; DLBY 1982; MSW; MTCW 1, 2; MTFW 2005

Ludwig, Ken 1950- .... **CLC 60**
See also CA 195; CAD; CD 6

Ludwig, Otto 1813-1865 .... **NCLC 4**
See also DLB 129

Lugones, Leopoldo 1874-1938 .... **HLCS 2; TCLC 15**
See also CA 116; 131; CANR 104; DLB 283; EWL 3; HW 1; LAW

Lu Hsun
See Shu-Jen, Chou

Lukacs, George
See Lukacs, Gyorgy

Lukacs, Gyorgy 1885-1971 .... **CLC 24**
See also CA 101; 29-32R; CANR 62; CD-WLB 4; DLB 215, 242; EW 10; EWL 3; MTCW 1, 2

Lukacs, Gyorgy Szegeny von
See Lukacs, Gyorgy

Luke, Peter (Ambrose Cyprian)
1919-1995 .... **CLC 38**
See also CA 81-84; 147; CANR 72; CBD; CD 5, 6; DLB 13

Lunar, Dennis
See Mungo, Raymond

Lurie, Alison 1926- ..... **CLC 4, 5, 18, 39, 175**
See also BPFB 2; CA 1-4R; CANR 2, 17, 50, 88; CN 1, 2, 3, 4, 5, 6, 7; DLB 2, 350; MAL 5; MTCW 1; NFS 24; SATA 46, 112; TCLE 1:1

Lustig, Arnost 1926- .... **CLC 56**
See also AAYA 3; CA 69-72; CANR 47, 102; CWW 2; DLB 232, 299; EWL 3; RGHL; SATA 56

Luther, Martin 1483-1546 .... **LC 9, 37, 150**
See also CDWLB 2; DLB 179; EW 2; RGWL 2, 3

Luxemburg, Rosa 1870(?)-1919 ..... **TCLC 63**
See also CA 118

Luzi, Mario (Egidio Vincenzo)
1914-2005 .... **CLC 13**
See also CA 61-64; 236; CANR 9, 70; CWW 2; DLB 128; EWL 3

L'vov, Arkady **CLC 59**

Lydgate, John c. 1370-1450(?) ..... **LC 81, 175**
See also BRW 1; DLB 146; RGEL 2

Lyly, John 1554(?)-1606 .... **DC 7; LC 41**
See also BRW 1; DAM DRAM; DLB 62, 167; RGEL 2

L'Ymagier
See Gourmont, Remy(-Marie-Charles) de

Lynch, B. Suarez
See Borges, Jorge Luis

Lynch, David 1946- .... **CLC 66, 162**
See also AAYA 55; CA 124; 129; CANR 111

Lynch, David Keith
See Lynch, David

Lynch, James
See Andreyev, Leonid

Lyndsay, Sir David 1485-1555 .... **LC 20**
See also RGEL 2

Lynn, Kenneth S(chuyler)
1923-2001 .... **CLC 50**
See also CA 1-4R; 196; CANR 3, 27, 65

Lynx
See West, Rebecca

Lyons, Marcus
See Blish, James

Lyotard, Jean-Francois
1924-1998 .... **TCLC 103**
See also DLB 242; EWL 3

Lyre, Pinchbeck
See Sassoon, Siegfried

Lytle, Andrew (Nelson) 1902-1995 ... **CLC 22**
See also CA 9-12R; 150; CANR 70; CN 1, 2, 3, 4, 5, 6; CSW; DLB 6; DLBY 1995; RGAL 4; RHW

Lyttelton, George 1709-1773 .... **LC 10**
See also RGEL 2

Lytton of Knebworth, Baron
See Bulwer-Lytton, Edward

Maalouf, Amin 1949- .... **CLC 248**
See also CA 212; CANR 194; DLB 346

Maas, Peter 1929-2001 .... **CLC 29**
See also CA 93-96; 201; INT CA-93-96; MTCW 2; MTFW 2005

Mac A'Ghobhainn, Iain
See Smith, Iain Crichton

Macaulay, Catherine 1731-1791 .... **LC 64**
See also DLB 104, 336

Macaulay, (Emilie) Rose
1881(?)-1958 .... **TCLC 7, 44**
See also CA 104; DLB 36; EWL 3; RGEL 2; RHW

Macaulay, Thomas Babington
1800-1859 .... **NCLC 42**
See also BRW 4; CDBLB 1832-1890; DLB 32, 55; RGEL 2

MacBeth, George (Mann)
1932-1992 .... **CLC 2, 5, 9**
See also CA 25-28R; 136; CANR 61, 66; CP 1, 2, 3, 4, 5; DLB 40; MTCW 1; PFS 8; SATA 4; SATA-Obit 70

MacCaig, Norman (Alexander)
1910-1996 .... **CLC 36**
See also BRWS 6; CA 9-12R; CANR 3, 34; CP 1, 2, 3, 4, 5, 6; DAB; DAM POET; DLB 27; EWL 3; RGEL 2

MacCarthy, Sir (Charles Otto) Desmond
1877-1952 .... **TCLC 36**
See also CA 167

MacDiarmid, Hugh
See Grieve, C. M.

MacDonald, Anson
See Heinlein, Robert A.

Macdonald, Cynthia 1928- .... **CLC 13, 19**
See also CA 49-52; CANR 4, 44, 146; DLB 105

MacDonald, George 1824-1905 .... **TCLC 9, 113, 207**
See also AAYA 57; BYA 5; CA 106; 137; CANR 80; CLR 67; DLB 18, 163, 178; FANT; MAICYA 1, 2; RGEL 2; SATA 33, 100; SFW 4; SUFW; WCH

Macdonald, John
See Millar, Kenneth

MacDonald, John D. 1916-1986 .. **CLC 3, 27, 44**
See also BPFB 2; CA 1-4R; 121; CANR 1, 19, 60; CMW 4; CPW; DAM NOV, POP; DLB 8, 306; DLBY 1986; MSW; MTCW 1, 2; MTFW 2005; SFW 4

Macdonald, John Ross
See Millar, Kenneth

Macdonald, Ross
See Millar, Kenneth

MacDonald Fraser, George
See Fraser, George MacDonald

MacDougal, John
See Blish, James

MacDowell, John
See Parks, Tim

MacEwen, Gwendolyn (Margaret)
1941-1987 .... **CLC 13, 55**
See also CA 9-12R; 124; CANR 7, 22; CP 1, 2, 3, 4; DLB 53, 251; SATA 50; SATA-Obit 55

MacGreevy, Thomas 1893-1967 .... **PC 82**
See also CA 262

Macha, Karel Hynek 1810-1846 .... **NCLC 46**

Machado (y Ruiz), Antonio
1875-1939 .... **TCLC 3**
See also CA 104; 174; DLB 108; EW 9; EWL 3; HW 2; PFS 23; RGWL 2, 3

Machado de Assis, Joaquim Maria
1839-1908 . **BLC 1:2; HLCS 2; SSC 24, 118; TCLC 10**
See also CA 107; 153; CANR 91; DLB 307; LAW; RGSF 2; RGWL 2, 3; TWA; WLIT 1

Machaut, Guillaume de c.
1300-1377 .... **CMLC 64**
See also DLB 208

Machen, Arthur **SSC 20; TCLC 4**
See Jones, Arthur Llewellyn
See also CA 179; DLB 156, 178; RGEL 2

Machen, Arthur Llewelyn Jones
See Jones, Arthur Llewellyn

Machiavelli, Niccolo 1469-1527 ... **DC 16; LC 8, 36, 140; WLCS**
See also AAYA 58; DA; DAB; DAC; DAM MST; EW 2; LAIT 1; LMFS 1; NFS 9; RGWL 2, 3; TWA; WLIT 7

MacInnes, Colin 1914-1976 .... **CLC 4, 23**
See also CA 69-72; 65-68; CANR 21; CN 1, 2; DLB 14; MTCW 1, 2; RGEL 2; RHW

MacInnes, Helen (Clark)
1907-1985 .... **CLC 27, 39**
See also BPFB 2; CA 1-4R; 117; CANR 1, 28, 58; CMW 4; CN 1, 2; CPW; DAM POP; DLB 87; MSW; MTCW 1, 2; MTFW 2005; SATA 22; SATA-Obit 44

Mackay, Mary 1855-1924 .... **TCLC 51**
See also CA 118; 177; DLB 34, 156; FANT; RGEL 2; RHW; SUFW 1

Mackay, Shena 1944- .... **CLC 195**
See also CA 104; CANR 88, 139; DLB 231, 319; MTFW 2005

Mackenzie, Compton (Edward Montague)
1883-1972 .... **CLC 18; TCLC 116**
See also CA 21-22; 37-40R; CAP 2; CN 1; DLB 34, 100; RGEL 2

Mackenzie, Henry 1745-1831 .... **NCLC 41**
See also DLB 39; RGEL 2

Mackey, Nathaniel 1947- .... **BLC 2:3; PC 49**
See also CA 153; CANR 114; CP 6, 7; DLB 169

Mackey, Nathaniel Ernest
See Mackey, Nathaniel

MacKinnon, Catharine
See MacKinnon, Catharine A.

MacKinnon, Catharine A. 1946- .... **CLC 181**
See also CA 128; 132; CANR 73, 140, 189; FW; MTCW 2; MTFW 2005

Mackintosh, Elizabeth
1896(?)-1952 .... **TCLC 14**
See also CA 110; CMW 4; DLB 10, 77; MSW

Macklin, Charles 1699-1797 .... **LC 132**
See also DLB 89; RGEL 2

MacLaren, James
See Grieve, C. M.

MacLaverty, Bernard 1942- ..... **CLC 31, 243**
See also CA 116; 118; CANR 43, 88, 168; CN 5, 6, 7; DLB 267; INT CA-118; RGSF 2

Menand, Louis 1952- .... **CLC 208**
    See also CA 200
Menander c. 342B.C.-c. 293B.C. .... **CMLC 9, 51, 101; DC 3**
    See also AW 1; CDWLB 1; DAM DRAM; DLB 176; LMFS 1; RGWL 2, 3
Menchu, Rigoberta 1959- .. **CLC 160; HLCS 2**
    See also CA 175; CANR 135; DNFS 1; WLIT 1
Mencken, H. L. 1880-1956 .... **TCLC 13, 18**
    See also AMW; CA 105; 125; CDALB 1917-1929; DLB 11, 29, 63, 137, 222; EWL 3; MAL 5; MTCW 1, 2; MTFW 2005; NCFS 4; RGAL 4; TUS
Mencken, Henry Louis
    See Mencken, H. L.
Mendelsohn, Jane 1965- .... **CLC 99**
    See also CA 154; CANR 94
Mendelssohn, Moses 1729-1786 .... **LC 142**
    See also DLB 97
Mendoza, Inigo Lopez de
    See Santillana, Inigo Lopez de Mendoza, Marques de
Menton, Francisco de
    See Chin, Frank
Mercer, David 1928-1980 .... **CLC 5**
    See also CA 9-12R; 102; CANR 23; CBD; DAM DRAM; DLB 13, 310; MTCW 1; RGEL 2
Merchant, Paul
    See Ellison, Harlan
Meredith, George 1828-1909 .. **PC 60; TCLC 17, 43**
    See also CA 117; 153; CANR 80; CDBLB 1832-1890; DAM POET; DLB 18, 35, 57, 159; RGEL 2; TEA
Meredith, William 1919-2007 ...... **CLC 4, 13, 22, 55; PC 28**
    See also CA 9-12R; 260; CAAS 14; CANR 6, 40, 129; CP 1, 2, 3, 4, 5, 6, 7; DAM POET; DLB 5; MAL 5
Meredith, William Morris
    See Meredith, William
Merezhkovsky, Dmitrii Sergeevich
    See Merezhkovsky, Dmitry Sergeyevich
Merezhkovsky, Dmitry Sergeevich
    See Merezhkovsky, Dmitry Sergeyevich
Merezhkovsky, Dmitry Sergeyevich 1865-1941 .... **TCLC 29**
    See also CA 169; DLB 295; EWL 3
Merezhkovsky, Zinaida
    See Gippius, Zinaida
Merimee, Prosper 1803-1870 . **DC 33; NCLC 6, 65; SSC 7, 77**
    See also DLB 119, 192; EW 6; EXPS; GFL 1789 to the Present; RGSF 2; RGWL 2, 3; SSFS 8; SUFW
Merkin, Daphne 1954- .... **CLC 44**
    See also CA 123
Merleau-Ponty, Maurice 1908-1961 .... **TCLC 156**
    See also CA 114; 89-92; DLB 296; GFL 1789 to the Present
Merlin, Arthur
    See Blish, James
Mernissi, Fatima 1940- .... **CLC 171**
    See also CA 152; DLB 346; FW
Merrill, James 1926-1995 .. **CLC 2, 3, 6, 8, 13, 18, 34, 91; PC 28; TCLC 173**
    See also AMWS 3; CA 13-16R; 147; CANR 10, 49, 63, 108; CP 1, 2, 3, 4; DA3; DAM POET; DLB 5, 165; DLBY 1985; EWL 3; INT CANR-10; MAL 5; MTCW 1, 2; MTFW 2005; PAB; PFS 23; RGAL 4
Merrill, James Ingram
    See Merrill, James
Merriman, Alex
    See Silverberg, Robert

Merriman, Brian 1747-1805 .... **NCLC 70**
Merritt, E. B.
    See Waddington, Miriam
Merton, Thomas 1915-1968 ..... **CLC 1, 3, 11, 34, 83; PC 10**
    See also AAYA 61; AMWS 8; CA 5-8R; 25-28R; CANR 22, 53, 111, 131; DA3; DLB 48; DLBY 1981; MAL 5; MTCW 1, 2; MTFW 2005
Merton, Thomas James
    See Merton, Thomas
Merwin, William Stanley
    See Merwin, W.S.
Merwin, W.S. 1927- ..... **CLC 1, 2, 3, 5, 8, 13, 18, 45, 88; PC 45**
    See also AMWS 3; CA 13-16R; CANR 15, 51, 112, 140; CP 1, 2, 3, 4, 5, 6, 7; DA3; DAM POET; DLB 5, 169, 342; EWL 3; INT CANR-15; MAL 5; MTCW 1, 2; MTFW 2005; PAB; PFS 5, 15; RGAL 4
Metastasio, Pietro 1698-1782 .... **LC 115**
    See also RGWL 2, 3
Metcalf, John 1938- .... **CLC 37; SSC 43**
    See also CA 113; CN 4, 5, 6, 7; DLB 60; RGSF 2; TWA
Metcalf, Suzanne
    See Baum, L. Frank
Mew, Charlotte (Mary) 1870-1928 .. **PC 107; TCLC 8**
    See also CA 105; 189; DLB 19, 135; RGEL 2
Mewshaw, Michael 1943- .... **CLC 9**
    See also CA 53-56; CANR 7, 47, 147; DLBY 1980
Meyer, Conrad Ferdinand 1825-1898 .... **NCLC 81; SSC 30**
    See also DLB 129; EW; RGWL 2, 3
Meyer, Gustav 1868-1932 .... **TCLC 21**
    See also CA 117; 190; DLB 81; EWL 3
Meyer, June
    See Jordan, June
Meyer, Lynn
    See Slavitt, David R.
Meyer, Stephenie 1973- .... **CLC 280**
    See also AAYA 77; CA 253; CANR 192; CLR 142; SATA 193
Meyer-Meyrink, Gustav
    See Meyer, Gustav
Meyers, Jeffrey 1939- .... **CLC 39**
    See also CA 73-76, 186; CAAE 186; CANR 54, 102, 159; DLB 111
Meynell, Alice (Christina Gertrude Thompson) 1847-1922 .... **TCLC 6**
    See also CA 104; 177; DLB 19, 98; RGEL 2
Meyrink, Gustav
    See Meyer, Gustav
Mhlophe, Gcina 1960- .... **BLC 2:3**
Michaels, Leonard 1933-2003 ..... **CLC 6, 25; SSC 16**
    See also AMWS 16; CA 61-64; 216; CANR 21, 62, 119, 179; CN 3, 45, 6, 7; DLB 130; MTCW 1; TCLE 1:2
Michaux, Henri 1899-1984 .... **CLC 8, 19**
    See also CA 85-88; 114; DLB 258; EWL 3; GFL 1789 to the Present; RGWL 2, 3
Micheaux, Oscar (Devereaux) 1884-1951 .... **TCLC 76**
    See also BW 3; CA 174; DLB 50; TCWW 2
Michelangelo 1475-1564 .... **LC 12**
    See also AAYA 43
Michelet, Jules 1798-1874 ...... **NCLC 31, 218**
    See also EW 5; GFL 1789 to the Present
Michels, Robert 1876-1936 .... **TCLC 88**
    See also CA 212

Michener, James A. 1907(?)-1997 . **CLC 1, 5, 11, 29, 60, 109**
    See also AAYA 27; AITN 1; BEST 90:1; BPFB 2; CA 5-8R; 161; CANR 21, 45, 68; CN 1, 2, 3, 4, 5, 6; CPW; DA3; DAM NOV, POP; DLB 6; MAL 5; MTCW 1, 2; MTFW 2005; RHW; TCWW 1, 2
Michener, James Albert
    See Michener, James A.
Mickiewicz, Adam 1798-1855 . **NCLC 3, 101; PC 38**
    See also EW 5; RGWL 2, 3
Middleton, (John) Christopher 1926- .... **CLC 13**
    See also CA 13-16R; CANR 29, 54, 117; CP 1, 2, 3, 4, 5, 6, 7; DLB 40
Middleton, Richard (Barham) 1882-1911 .... **TCLC 56**
    See also CA 187; DLB 156; HGG
Middleton, Stanley 1919-2009 .... **CLC 7, 38**
    See also CA 25-28R; 288; CAAS 23; CANR 21, 46, 81, 157; CN 1, 2, 3, 4, 5, 6, 7; DLB 14, 326
Middleton, Thomas 1580-1627 ...... **DC 5; LC 33, 123**
    See also BRW 2; DAM DRAM, MST; DFS 18, 22; DLB 58; RGEL 2
Mieville, China 1972(?)- .... **CLC 235**
    See also AAYA 52; CA 196; CANR 138; MTFW 2005
Migueis, Jose Rodrigues 1901-1980 . **CLC 10**
    See also DLB 287
Mihura, Miguel 1905-1977 .... **DC 34**
    See also CA 214
Mikszath, Kalman 1847-1910 .... **TCLC 31**
    See also CA 170
Miles, Jack CLC 100
    See also CA 200
Miles, John Russiano
    See Miles, Jack
Miles, Josephine (Louise) 1911-1985 .... **CLC 1, 2, 14, 34, 39**
    See also CA 1-4R; 116; CANR 2, 55; CP 1, 2, 3, 4; DAM POET; DLB 48; MAL 5; TCLE 1:2
Militant
    See Sandburg, Carl
Mill, Harriet (Hardy) Taylor 1807-1858 .... **NCLC 102**
    See also FW
Mill, John Stuart 1806-1873 ... **NCLC 11, 58, 179, 223**
    See also CDBLB 1832-1890; DLB 55, 190, 262; FW 1; RGEL 2; TEA
Millar, Kenneth 1915-1983 .. **CLC 1, 2, 3, 14, 34, 41**
    See also AAYA 81; AMWS 4; BPFB 2; CA 9-12R; 110; CANR 16, 63, 107; CMW 4; CN 1, 2, 3; CPW; DA3; DAM POP; DLB 2, 226; DLBD 6; DLBY 1983; MAL 5; MSW; MTCW 1, 2; MTFW 2005; RGAL 4
Millay, E. Vincent
    See Millay, Edna St. Vincent
Millay, Edna St. Vincent 1892-1950 ..... **PC 6, 61; TCLC 4, 49, 169; WLCS**
    See also AMW; CA 104; 130; CDALB 1917-1929; DA; DA3; DAB; DAC; DAM MST, POET; DFS 27; DLB 45, 249; EWL 3; EXPP; FL 1:6; GLL 1; MAL 5; MBL; MTCW 1, 2; MTFW 2005; PAB; PFS 3, 17, 31, 34; RGAL 4; TUS; WP
Miller, Arthur 1915-2005 ..... **CLC 1, 2, 6, 10, 15, 26, 47, 78, 179; DC 1, 31; WLC 4**
    See also AAYA 15; AITN 1; AMW; AMWC 1; CA 1-4R; 236; CABS 3; CAD; CANR 2, 30, 54, 76, 132; CD 5, 6; CDALB 1941-1968; DA; DA3; DAB; DAC; DAM DRAM, MST; DFS 1, 3, 8, 27; DLB 7,

266; EWL 3; LAIT 1, 4; LATS 1:2; MAL 5; MTCW 1, 2; MTFW 2005; RGAL 4; RGHL; TUS; WYAS 1

Miller, Frank 1957- .... **CLC 278**
See also AAYA 45; CA 224

Miller, Henry (Valentine)
1891-1980 .... **CLC 1, 2, 4, 9, 14, 43, 84; TCLC 213; WLC 4**
See also AMW; BPFB 2; CA 9-12R; 97-100; CANR 33, 64; CDALB 1929-1941; CN 1, 2; DA; DA3; DAB; DAC; DAM MST, NOV; DLB 4, 9; DLBY 1980; EWL 3; MAL 5; MTCW 1, 2; MTFW 2005; RGAL 4; TUS

Miller, Hugh 1802-1856 .... **NCLC 143**
See also DLB 190

Miller, Jason 1939(?)-2001 .... **CLC 2**
See also AITN 1; CA 73-76; 197; CAD; CANR 130; DFS 12; DLB 7

Miller, Sue 1943- .... **CLC 44**
See also AMWS 12; BEST 90:3; CA 139; CANR 59, 91, 128, 194; DA3; DAM POP; DLB 143

Miller, Walter M(ichael, Jr.)
1923-1996 .... **CLC 4, 30**
See also BPFB 2; CA 85-88; CANR 108; DLB 8; SCFW 1, 2; SFW 4

Millett, Kate 1934- .... **CLC 67**
See also AITN 1; CA 73-76; CANR 32, 53, 76, 110; DA3; DLB 246; FW; GLL 1; MTCW 1, 2; MTFW 2005

Millhauser, Steven 1943- ... **CLC 21, 54, 109; SSC 57**
See also AAYA 76; CA 110; 111; CANR 63, 114, 133, 189; CN 6, 7; DA3; DLB 2, 350; FANT; INT CA-111; MAL 5; MTCW 2; MTFW 2005

Millhauser, Steven Lewis
See Millhauser, Steven

Millin, Sarah Gertrude 1889-1968 ... **CLC 49**
See also CA 102; 93-96; DLB 225; EWL 3

Milne, A. A. 1882-1956 .... **TCLC 6, 88**
See also BRWS 5; CA 104; 133; CLR 1, 26, 108; CMW 4; CWRI 5; DA3; DAB; DAC; DAM MST; DLB 10, 77, 100, 160, 352; FANT; MAICYA 1, 2; MTCW 1, 2; MTFW 2005; RGEL 2; SATA 100; WCH; YABC 1

Milne, Alan Alexander
See Milne, A. A.

Milner, Ron(ald) 1938-2004 .. **BLC 1:3; CLC 56**
See also AITN 1; BW 1; CA 73-76; 230; CAD; CANR 24, 81; CD 5, 6; DAM MULT; DLB 38; MAL 5; MTCW 1

Milnes, Richard Monckton
1809-1885 .... **NCLC 61**
See also DLB 32, 184

Milosz, Czeslaw 1911-2004 .... **CLC 5, 11, 22, 31, 56, 82, 253; PC 8; WLCS**
See also AAYA 62; CA 81-84; 230; CANR 23, 51, 91, 126; CDWLB 4; CWW 2; DA3; DAM MST, POET; DLB 215, 331; EW 13; EWL 3; MTCW 1, 2; MTFW 2005; PFS 16, 29, 35; RGHL; RGWL 2, 3

Milton, John 1608-1674 ..... **LC 9, 43, 92; PC 19, 29; WLC 4**
See also AAYA 65; BRW 2; BRWR 2; CD-BLB 1660-1789; DA; DA3; DAB; DAC; DAM MST, POET; DLB 131, 151, 281; EFS 1; EXPP; LAIT 1; PAB; PFS 3, 17; RGEL 2; TEA; WLIT 3; WP

Min, Anchee 1957- .... **CLC 86, 291**
See also CA 146; CANR 94, 137; MTFW 2005

Minehaha, Cornelius
See Wedekind, Frank

Miner, Valerie 1947- .... **CLC 40**
See also CA 97-100; CANR 59, 177; FW; GLL 2

Minimo, Duca
See D'Annunzio, Gabriele

Minot, Susan (Anderson) 1956- ...... **CLC 44, 159**
See also AMWS 6; CA 134; CANR 118; CN 6, 7

Minus, Ed 1938- .... **CLC 39**
See also CA 185

Mirabai 1498(?)-1550(?) .... **LC 143; PC 48**
See also PFS 24

Miranda, Javier
See Bioy Casares, Adolfo

Mirbeau, Octave 1848-1917 .... **TCLC 55**
See also CA 216; DLB 123, 192; GFL 1789 to the Present

Mirikitani, Janice 1942- .... **AAL**
See also CA 211; DLB 312; RGAL 4

Mirk, John (?)-c. 1414 .... **LC 105**
See also DLB 146

Miro (Ferrer), Gabriel (Francisco Victor)
1879-1930 .... **TCLC 5**
See also CA 104; 185; DLB 322; EWL 3

Misharin, Alexandr CLC 59

Mishima, Yukio
See Hiraoka, Kimitake

Mishima Yukio
See Hiraoka, Kimitake

Miss C. L. F.
See Grimke, Charlotte L. Forten

Mister X
See Hoch, Edward D.

Mistral, Frederic 1830-1914 .... **TCLC 51**
See also CA 122; 213; DLB 331; GFL 1789 to the Present

Mistral, Gabriela 1899-1957 .... **HLC 2; PC 32; TCLC 2**
See also BW 2; CA 104; 131; CANR 81; DAM MULT; DLB 283, 331; DNFS; EWL 3; HW 1, 2; LAW; MTCW 1, 2; MTFW 2005; RGWL 2, 3; WP

Mistry, Rohinton 1952- ... **CLC 71, 196, 281; SSC 73**
See also BRWS 10; CA 141; CANR 86, 114; CCA 1; CN 6, 7; DAC; DLB 334; SSFS 6

Mitchell, Clyde
See Ellison, Harlan; Silverberg, Robert

Mitchell, Emerson Blackhorse Barney
1945- .... **NNAL**
See also CA 45-48

Mitchell, James Leslie 1901-1935 .... **TCLC 4**
See also BRWS 14; CA 104; 188; DLB 15; RGEL 2

Mitchell, Joni 1943- .... **CLC 12**
See also CA 112; CCA 1

Mitchell, Joseph (Quincy)
1908-1996 .... **CLC 98**
See also CA 77-80; 152; CANR 69; CN 1, 2, 3, 4, 5, 6; CSW; DLB 185; DLBY 1996

Mitchell, Margaret 1900-1949 .... **TCLC 11, 170**
See also AAYA 23; BPFB 2; BYA 1; CA 109; 125; CANR 55, 94; CDALBS; DA3; DAM NOV, POP; DLB 9; LAIT 2; MAL 5; MTCW 1, 2; MTFW 2005; NFS 9; RGAL 4; RHW; TUS; WYAS 1; YAW

Mitchell, Margaret Munnerlyn
See Mitchell, Margaret

Mitchell, Peggy
See Mitchell, Margaret

Mitchell, S(ilas) Weir 1829-1914 .... **TCLC 36**
See also CA 165; DLB 202; RGAL 4

Mitchell, W(illiam) O(rmond)
1914-1998 .... **CLC 25**
See also CA 77-80; 165; CANR 15, 43; CN 1, 2, 3, 4, 5, 6; DAC; DAM MST; DLB 88; TCLE 1:2

Mitchell, William (Lendrum)
1879-1936 .... **TCLC 81**
See also CA 213

Mitford, Mary Russell 1787-1855 ... **NCLC 4**
See also DLB 110, 116; RGEL 2

Mitford, Nancy 1904-1973 .... **CLC 44**
See also BRWS 10; CA 9-12R; CN 1; DLB 191; RGEL 2

Miyamoto, (Chujo) Yuriko
1899-1951 .... **TCLC 37**
See also CA 170, 174; DLB 180

Miyamoto Yuriko
See Miyamoto, (Chujo) Yuriko

Miyazawa, Kenji 1896-1933 .... **TCLC 76**
See also CA 157; EWL 3; RGWL 3

Miyazawa Kenji
See Miyazawa, Kenji

Mizoguchi, Kenji 1898-1956 .... **TCLC 72**
See also CA 167

Mo, Timothy (Peter) 1950- .... **CLC 46, 134**
See also CA 117; CANR 128; CN 5, 6, 7; DLB 194; MTCW 1; WLIT 4; WWE 1

Mo, Yan
See Yan, Mo

Moberg, Carl Arthur
See Moberg, Vilhelm

Moberg, Vilhelm 1898-1973 .... **TCLC 224**
See also CA 97-100; 45-48; CANR 135; DLB 259; EW 11; EWL 3

Modarressi, Taghi (M.) 1931-1997 ... **CLC 44**
See also CA 121; 134; INT CA-134

Modiano, Patrick (Jean) 1945- .... **CLC 18, 218**
See also CA 85-88; CANR 17, 40, 115; CWW 2; DLB 83, 299; EWL 3; RGHL

Mofolo, Thomas 1875(?)-1948 .... **BLC 1:3; TCLC 22**
See also AFW; CA 121; 153; CANR 83; DAM MULT; DLB 225; EWL 3; MTCW 2; MTFW 2005; WLIT 2

Mofolo, Thomas Mokopu
See Mofolo, Thomas

Mohr, Nicholasa 1938- .... **CLC 12; HLC 2**
See also AAYA 8, 46; CA 49-52; CANR 1, 32, 64; CLR 22; DAM MULT; DLB 145; HW 1, 2; JRDA; LAIT 5; LLW; MAICYA 2; MAICYAS 1; RGAL 4; SAAS 8; SATA 8, 97; SATA-Essay 113; WYA; YAW

Moi, Toril 1953- .... **CLC 172**
See also CA 154; CANR 102; FW

Mojtabai, A(nn) G(race) 1938- ..... **CLC 5, 9, 15, 29**
See also CA 85-88; CANR 88

Moliere 1622-1673 ..... **DC 13; LC 10, 28, 64, 125, 127; WLC 4**
See also DA; DA3; DAB; DAC; DAM DRAM, MST; DFS 13, 18, 20; DLB 268; EW 3; GFL Beginnings to 1789; LATS 1:1; RGWL 2, 3; TWA

Molin, Charles
See Mayne, William (James Carter)

Molina, Antonio Munoz 1956- .... **CLC 289**
See also DLB 322

Molnar, Ferenc 1878-1952 .... **TCLC 20**
See also CA 109; 153; CANR 83; CDWLB 4; DAM DRAM; DLB 215; EWL 3; RGWL 2, 3

Momaday, N. Scott 1934- ...... **CLC 2, 19, 85, 95, 160; NNAL; PC 25; WLCS**
See also AAYA 11, 64; AMWS 4; ANW; BPFB 2; BYA 12; CA 25-28R; CANR 14, 34, 68, 134; CDALBS; CN 2, 3, 4, 5, 6, 7; CPW; DA; DA3; DAB; DAC; DAM MST, MULT, NOV, POP; DLB 143, 175,

Munro, Hector H.
See Saki

Munro, Hector Hugh
See Saki

Murakami, Haruki 1949- .... **CLC 150, 274**
See also CA 165; CANR 102, 146; CWW
2; DLB 182; EWL 3; LNFS 2; MJW;
RGWL 3; SFW 4; SSFS 23

Murakami Haruki
See Murakami, Haruki

Murasaki, Lady
See Murasaki Shikibu

Murasaki Shikibu 978(?)-1026(?) .. **CMLC 1, 79**
See also EFS 2; LATS 1:1; RGWL 2, 3

Murdoch, Iris 1919-1999 .. **CLC 1, 2, 3, 4, 6, 8, 11, 15, 22, 31, 51; TCLC 171**
See also BRWS 1; CA 13-16R; 179; CANR
8, 43, 68, 103, 142; CBD; CDBLB 1960
to Present; CN 1, 2, 3, 4, 5, 6; CWD;
DA3; DAB; DAC; DAM MST, NOV;
DLB 14, 194, 233, 326; EWL 3; INT
CANR-8; MTCW 1, 2; MTFW 2005; NFS
18; RGEL 2; TCLE 1:2; TEA; WLIT 4

Murdoch, Jean Iris
See Murdoch, Iris

Murfree, Mary Noailles 1850-1922 .. **SSC 22; TCLC 135**
See also CA 122; 176; DLB 12, 74; RGAL
4

Murglie
See Murnau, F.W.

Murnau, Friedrich Wilhelm
See Murnau, F.W.

Murnau, F.W. 1888-1931 .... **TCLC 53**
See also CA 112

Murphy, Richard 1927- .... **CLC 41**
See also BRWS 5; CA 29-32R; CP 1, 2, 3,
4, 5, 6, 7; DLB 40; EWL 3

Murphy, Sylvia 1937- .... **CLC 34**
See also CA 121

Murphy, Thomas 1935- .... **CLC 51**
See also CA 101; DLB 310

Murphy, Thomas Bernard
See Murphy, Thomas

Murphy, Tom
See Murphy, Thomas

Murray, Albert 1916- .... **BLC 2:3; CLC 73**
See also BW 2; CA 49-52; CANR 26, 52,
78, 160; CN 7; CSW; DLB 38; MTFW
2005

Murray, Albert L.
See Murray, Albert

Murray, Diane Lain Johnson
See Johnson, Diane

Murray, James Augustus Henry
1837-1915 .... **TCLC 117**

Murray, Judith Sargent
1751-1820 .... **NCLC 63**
See also DLB 37, 200

Murray, Les 1938- .... **CLC 40**
See also BRWS 7; CA 21-24R; CANR 11,
27, 56, 103, 199; CP 1, 2, 3, 4, 5, 6, 7;
DAM POET; DLB 289; DLBY 2001;
EWL 3; RGEL 2

Murray, Leslie Allan
See Murray, Les

Murry, J. Middleton
See Murry, John Middleton

Murry, John Middleton
1889-1957 .... **TCLC 16**
See also CA 118; 217; DLB 149

Musgrave, Susan 1951- .... **CLC 13, 54**
See also CA 69-72; CANR 45, 84, 181;
CCA 1; CP 2, 3, 4, 5, 6, 7; CWP

Musil, Robert (Edler von)
1880-1942 ... **SSC 18; TCLC 12, 68, 213**
See also CA 109; CANR 55, 84; CDWLB
2; DLB 81, 124; EW 9; EWL 3; MTCW
2; RGSF 2; RGWL 2, 3

Muske, Carol
See Muske-Dukes, Carol

Muske, Carol Anne
See Muske-Dukes, Carol

Muske-Dukes, Carol 1945- .... **CLC 90**
See also CA 65-68, 203; CAAE 203; CANR
32, 70, 181; CWP; PFS 24

Muske-Dukes, Carol Ann
See Muske-Dukes, Carol

Muske-Dukes, Carol Anne
See Muske-Dukes, Carol

Musset, Alfred de 1810-1857 . **DC 27; NCLC 7, 150**
See also DLB 192, 217; EW 6; GFL 1789
to the Present; RGWL 2, 3; TWA

Musset, Louis Charles Alfred de
See Musset, Alfred de

Mussolini, Benito (Amilcare Andrea)
1883-1945 .... **TCLC 96**
See also CA 116

Mutanabbi, Al-
See al-Mutanabbi, Ahmad ibn al-Husayn
Abu al-Tayyib al-Jufi al-Kindi

Mutis, Alvaro 1923- .... **CLC 283**
See also CA 149; CANR 118; DLB 283;
EWL 3; HW 1; LAWS 1

My Brother's Brother
See Chekhov, Anton

Myers, L(eopold) H(amilton)
1881-1944 .... **TCLC 59**
See also CA 157; DLB 15; EWL 3; RGEL
2

Myers, Walter Dean 1937- ...... **BLC 1:3, 2:3; CLC 35**
See also AAYA 4, 23; BW 2; BYA 6, 8, 11;
CA 33-36R; CANR 20, 42, 67, 108, 184;
CLR 4, 16, 35, 110; DAM MULT, NOV;
DLB 33; INT CANR-20; JRDA; LAIT
5; LNFS 1; MAICYA 1, 2; MAICYAS 1;
MTCW 2; MTFW 2005; NFS 30, 33;
SAAS 2; SATA 41, 71, 109, 157, 193;
SATA-Brief 27; SSFS 31; WYA; YAW

Myers, Walter M.
See Myers, Walter Dean

Myles, Symon
See Follett, Ken

Nabokov, Vladimir 1899-1977 ... **CLC 1, 2, 3, 6, 8, 11, 15, 23, 44, 46, 64; SSC 11, 86; TCLC 108, 189; WLC 4**
See also AAYA 45; AMW; AMWC 1;
AMWR 1; BPFB 2; CA 5-8R; 69-72;
CANR 20, 102; CDALB 1941-1968; CN
1, 2; CP 2; DA; DA3; DAB; DAC; DAM
MST, NOV; DLB 2, 244, 278, 317; DLBD
3; DLBY 1980, 1991; EWL 3; EXPS;
LATS 1:2; MAL 5; MTCW 1, 2; MTFW
2005; NCFS 4; NFS 9; RGAL 4; RGSF
2; SSFS 6, 15; TUS

Nabokov, Vladimir Vladimirovich
See Nabokov, Vladimir

Naevius c. 265B.C.-201B.C. .... **CMLC 37**
See also DLB 211

Nagai, Kafu 1879-1959 .... **TCLC 51**
See also CA 117; 276; DLB 180; EWL 3;
MJW

Nagai, Sokichi
See Nagai, Kafu

Nagai Kafu
See Nagai, Kafu

na gCopaleen, Myles
See O Nuallain, Brian

na Gopaleen, Myles
See O Nuallain, Brian

Nagy, Laszlo 1925-1978 .... **CLC 7**
See also CA 129; 112

Naidu, Sarojini 1879-1949 .... **TCLC 80**
See also EWL 3; RGEL 2

Naipaul, Shiva 1945-1985 .... **CLC 32, 39; TCLC 153**
See also CA 110; 112; 116; CANR 33; CN
2, 3; DA3; DAM NOV; DLB 157; DLBY
1985; EWL 3; MTCW 1, 2; MTFW 2005

Naipaul, Shivadhar Srinivasa
See Naipaul, Shiva

Naipaul, V. S. 1932- . **CLC 4, 7, 9, 13, 18, 37, 105, 199; SSC 38, 121**
See also BPFB 2; BRWS 1; CA 1-4R;
CANR 1, 33, 51, 91, 126, 191; CDBLB
1960 to Present; CDWLB 3; CN 1, 2, 3,
4, 5, 6, 7; DA3; DAB; DAC; DAM MST,
NOV; DLB 125, 204, 207, 326, 331;
DLBY 1985, 2001; EWL 3; LATS 1:2;
MTCW 1, 2; MTFW 2005; RGEL 2;
RGSF 2; SSFS 29; TWA; WLIT 4; WWE
1

Naipaul, Vidiahar Surajprasad
See Naipaul, V. S.

Nair, Kamala
See Das, Kamala

Nakos, Lilika 1903-1989 .... **CLC 29**
See also CA 217

Nalapat, Kamala
See Das, Kamala

Napoleon
See Yamamoto, Hisaye

Narayan, R. K. 1906-2001 ..... **CLC 7, 28, 47, 121, 211; SSC 25**
See also BPFB 2; CA 81-84; 196; CANR
33, 61, 112; CN 1, 2, 3, 4, 5, 6, 7; DA3;
DAM NOV; DLB 323; DNFS 1; MAL 5;
MTCW 1, 2; MTFW 2005; RGEL 2;
RGSF 2; SATA 62; SSFS 5, 29; WWE 1

Narayan, Rasipuram Krishnaswami
See Narayan, R. K.

Nash, Frediric Ogden
See Nash, Ogden

Nash, Ogden 1902-1971 ...... **CLC 23; PC 21; TCLC 109**
See also CA 13-14; 29-32R; CANR 34, 61,
185; CAP 1; CP 1; DAM POET; DLB 11;
MAICYA 1, 2; MAL 5; MTCW 1, 2; PFS
31; RGAL 4; SATA 2, 46; WP

Nashe, Thomas 1567-1601(?) . **LC 41, 89; PC 82**
See also DLB 167; RGEL 2

Nathan, Daniel
See Dannay, Frederic

Nathan, George Jean 1882-1958 .... **TCLC 18**
See also CA 114; 169; DLB 137; MAL 5

Natsume, Kinnosuke
See Natsume, Soseki

Natsume, Soseki 1867-1916 .... **TCLC 2, 10**
See also CA 104; 195; DLB 180; EWL 3;
MJW; RGWL 2, 3; TWA

Natsume Soseki
See Natsume, Soseki

Natti, Lee 1919- .... **CLC 17**
See also CA 5-8R; CANR 2; CWRI 5;
SAAS 3; SATA 1, 67

Natti, Mary Lee
See Natti, Lee

Navarre, Marguerite de
See de Navarre, Marguerite

Naylor, Gloria 1950- . **BLC 1:3; CLC 28, 52, 156, 261; WLCS**
See also AAYA 6, 39; AFAW 1, 2; AMWS
8; BW 2, 3; CA 107; CANR 27, 51, 74,
130; CN 4, 5, 6, 7; CPW; DA; DA3;
DAC; DAM MST, MULT, NOV, POP;
DLB 173; EWL 3; FW; MAL 5; MTCW
1, 2; MTFW 2005; NFS 4, 7; RGAL 4;
TCLE 1:2; TUS

Norman, Marsha (Williams) 1947- . **CLC 28, 186; DC 8**
See also CA 105; CABS 3; CAD; CANR 41, 131; CD 5, 6; CSW; CWD; DAM DRAM; DFS 2; DLB 266; DLBY 1984; FW; MAL 5

Normyx
See Douglas, (George) Norman

Norris, Benjamin Franklin, Jr.
See Norris, Frank

Norris, Frank 1870-1902 ...... **SSC 28; TCLC 24, 155, 211**
See also AAYA 57; AMW; AMWC 2; BPFB 2; CA 110; 160; CDALB 1865-1917; DLB 12, 71, 186; LMFS 2; MAL 5; NFS 12; RGAL 4; TCWW 1, 2; TUS

Norris, Kathleen 1947- .... **CLC 248**
See also CA 160; CANR 113, 199

Norris, Leslie 1921-2006 .... **CLC 14**
See also CA 11-12; 251; CANR 14, 117; CAP 1; CP 1, 2, 3, 4, 5, 6, 7; DLB 27, 256

North, Andrew
See Norton, Andre

North, Anthony
See Koontz, Dean

North, Captain George
See Stevenson, Robert Louis

North, Captain George
See Stevenson, Robert Louis

North, Milou
See Erdrich, Louise

Northrup, B. A.
See Hubbard, L. Ron

North Staffs
See Hulme, T(homas) E(rnest)

Northup, Solomon 1808-1863 ...... **NCLC 105**

Norton, Alice Mary
See Norton, Andre

Norton, Andre 1912-2005 .... **CLC 12**
See also AAYA 14; BPFB 2; BYA 4, 10, 12; CA 1-4R; 237; CANR 2, 31, 68, 108, 149; CLR 50; DLB 8, 52; JRDA; MAICYA 1, 2; MTCW 1; SATA 1, 43, 91; SUFW 1, 2; YAW

Norton, Caroline 1808-1877 .. **NCLC 47, 205**
See also DLB 21, 159, 199

Norway, Nevil Shute
See Shute, Nevil

Norwid, Cyprian Kamil 1821-1883 .... **NCLC 17**
See also RGWL 3

Nosille, Nabrah
See Ellison, Harlan

Nossack, Hans Erich 1901-1977 .... **CLC 6**
See also CA 93-96; 85-88; CANR 156; DLB 69; EWL 3

Nostradamus 1503-1566 .... **LC 27**

Nosu, Chuji
See Ozu, Yasujiro

Notenburg, Eleanora (Genrikhovna) von
See Guro, Elena (Genrikhovna)

Nova, Craig 1945- .... **CLC 7, 31**
See also CA 45-48; CANR 2, 53, 127

Novak, Joseph
See Kosinski, Jerzy

Novalis 1772-1801 .... **NCLC 13, 178**
See also CDWLB 2; DLB 90; EW 5; RGWL 2, 3

Novick, Peter 1934- .... **CLC 164**
See also CA 188

Novis, Emile
See Weil, Simone

Nowlan, Alden (Albert) 1933-1983 ... **CLC 15**
See also CA 9-12R; CANR 5; CP 1, 2, 3; DAC; DAM MST; DLB 53; PFS 12

Noyes, Alfred 1880-1958 ...... **PC 27; TCLC 7**
See also CA 104; 188; DLB 20; EXPP; FANT; PFS 4; RGEL 2

Nugent, Richard Bruce 1906(?)-1987 .... **HR 1:3**
See also BW 1; CA 125; CANR 198; DLB 51; GLL 2

Nunez, Elizabeth 1944- .... **BLC 2:3**
See also CA 223

Nunn, Kem CLC 34
See also CA 159; CANR 204

Nussbaum, Martha Craven 1947- .. **CLC 203**
See also CA 134; CANR 102, 176

Nwapa, Flora (Nwanzuruaha) 1931-1993 .... **BLCS; CLC 133**
See also BW 2; CA 143; CANR 83; CDWLB 3; CWRI 5; DLB 125; EWL 3; WLIT 2

Nye, Robert 1939- .... **CLC 13, 42**
See also BRWS 10; CA 33-36R; CANR 29, 67, 107; CN 1, 2, 3, 4, 5, 6, 7; CP 1, 2, 3, 4, 5, 6, 7; CWRI 5; DAM NOV; DLB 14, 271; FANT; HGG; MTCW 1; RHW; SATA 6

Nyro, Laura 1947-1997 .... **CLC 17**
See also CA 194

O. Henry
See Henry, O.

Oates, Joyce Carol 1938- .. **CLC 1, 2, 3, 6, 9, 11, 15, 19, 33, 52, 108, 134, 228; SSC 6, 70, 121; WLC 4**
See also AAYA 15, 52; AITN 1; AMWS 2; BEST 89:2; BPFB 2; BYA 11; CA 5-8R; CANR 25, 45, 74, 113, 129, 165; CDALB 1968-1988; CN 1, 2, 3, 4, 5, 6, 7; CP 5, 6, 7; CPW; CWP; DA; DA3; DAB; DAC; DAM MST, NOV, POP; DLB 2, 5, 130; DLBY 1981; EWL 3; EXPS; FL 1:6; FW; GL 3; HGG; INT CANR-25; LAIT 4; MAL 5; MBL; MTCW 1, 2; MTFW 2005; NFS 8, 24; RGAL 4; RGSF 2; SATA 159; SSFS 1, 8, 17; SUFW 2; TUS

O'Brian, E.G.
See Clarke, Arthur C.

O'Brian, Patrick 1914-2000 .... **CLC 152**
See also AAYA 55; BRWS 12; CA 144; 187; CANR 74, 201; CPW; MTCW 2; MTFW 2005; RHW

O'Brien, Darcy 1939-1998 .... **CLC 11**
See also CA 21-24R; 167; CANR 8, 59

O'Brien, Edna 1932- ..... **CLC 3, 5, 8, 13, 36, 65, 116, 237; SSC 10, 77**
See also BRWS 5; CA 1-4R; CANR 6, 41, 65, 102, 169; CDBLB 1960 to Present; CN 1, 2, 3, 4, 5, 6, 7; DA3; DAM NOV; DLB 14, 231, 319; EWL 3; FW; MTCW 1, 2; MTFW 2005; RGSF 2; WLIT 4

O'Brien, E.G.
See Clarke, Arthur C.

O'Brien, Fitz-James 1828-1862 ..... **NCLC 21**
See also DLB 74; RGAL 4; SUFW

O'Brien, Flann
See O Nuallain, Brian

O'Brien, Richard 1942- .... **CLC 17**
See also CA 124

O'Brien, Tim 1946- .... **CLC 7, 19, 40, 103, 211; SSC 74, 123**
See also AAYA 16; AMWS 5; CA 85-88; CANR 40, 58, 133; CDALBS; CN 5, 6, 7; CPW; DA3; DAM POP; DLB 152; DLBD 9; DLBY 1980; LATS 1:2; MAL 5; MTCW 2; MTFW 2005; RGAL 4; SSFS 5, 15, 29; TCLE 1:2

O'Brien, William Timothy
See O'Brien, Tim

Obstfelder, Sigbjorn 1866-1900 ..... **TCLC 23**
See also CA 123; DLB 354

O'Casey, Brenda
See Haycraft, Anna

O'Casey, Sean 1880-1964 .... **CLC 1, 5, 9, 11, 15, 88; DC 12; WLCS**
See also BRW 7; CA 89-92; CANR 62; CBD; CDBLB 1914-1945; DA3; DAB; DAC; DAM DRAM, MST; DFS 19; DLB 10; EWL 3; MTCW 1, 2; MTFW 2005; RGEL 2; TEA; WLIT 4

O'Cathasaigh, Sean
See O'Casey, Sean

Occom, Samson 1723-1792 .... **LC 60; NNAL**
See also DLB 175

Occomy, Marita (Odette) Bonner 1899(?)-1971 ..... **HR 1:2; PC 72; TCLC 179**
See also BW 2; CA 142; DFS 13; DLB 51, 228

Ochs, Phil(ip David) 1940-1976 .... **CLC 17**
See also CA 185; 65-68

O'Connor, Edwin (Greene) 1918-1968 .... **CLC 14**
See also CA 93-96; 25-28R; MAL 5

O'Connor, Flannery 1925-1964 ..... **CLC 1, 2, 3, 6, 10, 13, 15, 21, 66, 104; SSC 1, 23, 61, 82, 111; TCLC 132; WLC 4**
See also AAYA 7; AMW; AMWR 2; BPFB 3; BYA 16; CA 1-4R; CANR 3, 41; CDALB 1941-1968; DA; DA3; DAB; DAC; DAM MST, NOV; DLB 2, 152; DLBD 12; DLBY 1980; EWL 3; EXPS; LAIT 5; MAL 5; MBL; MTCW 1, 2; MTFW 2005; NFS 3, 21; RGAL 4; RGSF 2; SSFS 2, 7, 10, 19; TUS

O'Connor, Frank 1903-1966
See O'Donovan, Michael Francis

O'Connor, Mary Flannery
See O'Connor, Flannery

O'Dell, Scott 1898-1989 .... **CLC 30**
See also AAYA 3, 44; BPFB 3; BYA 1, 2, 3, 5; CA 61-64; 129; CANR 12, 30, 112; CLR 1, 16, 126; DLB 52; JRDA; MAICYA 1, 2; SATA 12, 60, 134; WYA; YAW

Odets, Clifford 1906-1963 ..... **CLC 2, 28, 98; DC 6**
See also AMWS 2; CA 85-88; CAD; CANR 62; DAM DRAM; DFS 3, 17, 20; DLB 7, 26, 341; EWL 3; MAL 5; MTCW 1, 2; MTFW 2005; RGAL 4; TUS

O'Doherty, Brian 1928- .... **CLC 76**
See also CA 105; CANR 108

O'Donnell, K. M.
See Malzberg, Barry N(athaniel)

O'Donnell, Lawrence
See Kuttner, Henry

O'Donovan, Michael Francis 1903-1966 .... **CLC 14, 23; SSC 5, 109**
See also BRWS 14; CA 93-96; CANR 84; DLB 162; EWL 3; RGSF 2; SSFS 5

Oe, Kenzaburo 1935- .. **CLC 10, 36, 86, 187; SSC 20**
See also CA 97-100; CANR 36, 50, 74, 126; CWW 2; DA3; DAM NOV; DLB 182, 331; DLBY 1994; EWL 3; LATS 1:2; MJW; MTCW 1, 2; MTFW 2005; RGSF 2; RGWL 2, 3

Oe Kenzaburo
See Oe, Kenzaburo

O'Faolain, Julia 1932- .... **CLC 6, 19, 47, 108**
See also CA 81-84; CAAS 2; CANR 12, 61; CN 2, 3, 4, 5, 6, 7; DLB 14, 231, 319; FW; MTCW 1; RHW

O'Faolain, Sean 1900-1991 ...... **CLC 1, 7, 14, 32, 70; SSC 13; TCLC 143**
See also CA 61-64; 134; CANR 12, 66; CN 1, 2, 3, 4; DLB 15, 162; MTCW 1, 2; MTFW 2005; RGEL 2; RGSF 2

O'Flaherty, Liam 1896-1984 .... **CLC 5, 34; SSC 6, 116**
See also CA 101; 113; CANR 35; CN 1, 2, 3; DLB 36, 162; DLBY 1984; MTCW 1, 2; MTFW 2005; RGEL 2; RGSF 2; SSFS 5, 20

Parini, Jay 1948- .... CLC 54, 133
  See also CA 97-100, 229; CAAE 229;
  CAAS 16; CANR 32, 87, 198
Parini, Jay Lee
  See Parini, Jay
Park, Jordan
  See Kornbluth, C(yril) M.; Pohl, Frederik
Park, Robert E(zra) 1864-1944 ..... TCLC 73
  See also CA 122; 165
Parker, Bert
  See Ellison, Harlan
Parker, Dorothy 1893-1967 . CLC 15, 68; PC
  28; SSC 2, 101; TCLC 143
  See also AMWS 9; CA 19-20; 25-28R; CAP
  2; DA3; DAM POET; DLB 11, 45, 86;
  EXPP; FW; MAL 5; MBL; MTCW 1, 2;
  MTFW 2005; PFS 18; RGAL 4; RGSF 2;
  TUS
Parker, Dorothy Rothschild
  See Parker, Dorothy
Parker, Robert B. 1932-2010 .... CLC 27, 283
  See also AAYA 28; BEST 89:4; BPFB 3;
  CA 49-52; CANR 1, 26, 52, 89, 128, 165,
  200; CMW 4; CPW; DAM NOV, POP;
  DLB 306; INT CANR-26; MSW; MTCW
  1; MTFW 2005
Parker, Robert Brown
  See Parker, Robert B.
Parker, Theodore 1810-1860 .... NCLC 186
  See also DLB 1, 235
Parkes, Lucas
  See Harris, John (Wyndham Parkes Lucas)
  Beynon
Parkin, Frank 1940- .... CLC 43
  See also CA 147
Parkman, Francis, Jr. 1823-1893 .. NCLC 12
  See also AMWS 2; DLB 1, 30, 183, 186,
  235; RGAL 4
Parks, Gordon 1912-2006 . BLC 1:3; CLC 1,
  16
  See also AAYA 36; AITN 2; BW 2, 3; CA
  41-44R; 249; CANR 26, 66, 145; DA3;
  DAM MULT; DLB 33; MTCW 2; MTFW
  2005; NFS 32; SATA 8, 108; SATA-Obit
  175
Parks, Gordon Roger Alexander
  See Parks, Gordon
Parks, Suzan-Lori 1964(?)- ..... BLC 2:3; DC
  23
  See also AAYA 55; CA 201; CAD; CD 5,
  6; CWD; DFS 22; DLB 341; RGAL 4
Parks, Tim 1954- .... CLC 147
  See also CA 126; 131; CANR 77, 144, 202;
  CN 7; DLB 231; INT CA-131
Parks, Timothy Harold
  See Parks, Tim
Parmenides c. 515B.C.-c.
  450B.C. .... CMLC 22
  See also DLB 176
Parnell, Thomas 1679-1718 .... LC 3
  See also DLB 95; RGEL 2
Parr, Catherine c. 1513(?)-1548 .... LC 86
  See also DLB 136
Parra, Nicanor 1914- ... CLC 2, 102; HLC 2;
  PC 39
  See also CA 85-88; CANR 32; CWW 2;
  DAM MULT; DLB 283; EWL 3; HW 1;
  LAW; MTCW 1
Parra Sanojo, Ana Teresa de la 1890-1936
  See de la Parra, Teresa
Parrish, Mary Frances
  See Fisher, M(ary) F(rances) K(ennedy)
Parshchikov, Aleksei 1954- .... CLC 59
  See also DLB 285
Parshchikov, Aleksei Maksimovich
  See Parshchikov, Aleksei
Parson, Professor
  See Coleridge, Samuel Taylor

Parson Lot
  See Kingsley, Charles
Parton, Sara Payson Willis
  1811-1872 .... NCLC 86
  See also DLB 43, 74, 239
Partridge, Anthony
  See Oppenheim, E(dward) Phillips
Pascal, Blaise 1623-1662 .... LC 35
  See also DLB 268; EW 3; GFL Beginnings
  to 1789; RGWL 2, 3; TWA
Pascoli, Giovanni 1855-1912 .... TCLC 45
  See also CA 170; EW 7; EWL 3
Pasolini, Pier Paolo 1922-1975 .. CLC 20, 37,
  106; PC 17
  See also CA 93-96; 61-64; CANR 63; DLB
  128, 177; EWL 3; MTCW 1; RGWL 2, 3
Pasquini
  See Silone, Ignazio
Pastan, Linda (Olenik) 1932- .... CLC 27
  See also CA 61-64; CANR 18, 40, 61, 113;
  CP 3, 4, 5, 6, 7; CSW; CWP; DAM
  POET; DLB 5; PFS 8, 25, 32
Pasternak, Boris 1890-1960 .... CLC 7, 10, 18,
  63; PC 6; SSC 31; TCLC 188; WLC 4
  See also BPFB 3; CA 127; 116; DA; DA3;
  DAB; DAC; DAM MST, NOV, POET;
  DLB 302, 331; EW 10; MTCW 1, 2;
  MTFW 2005; NFS 26; RGSF 2; RGWL
  2, 3; TWA; WP
Pasternak, Boris Leonidovich
  See Pasternak, Boris
Patchen, Kenneth 1911-1972 .... CLC 1, 2, 18
  See also BG 1:3; CA 1-4R; 33-36R; CANR
  3, 35; CN 1; CP 1; DAM POET; DLB 16,
  48; EWL 3; MAL 5; MTCW 1; RGAL 4
Patchett, Ann 1963- .... CLC 244
  See also AAYA 69; AMWS 12; CA 139;
  CANR 64, 110, 167, 200; DLB 350;
  MTFW 2005; NFS 30
Pater, Walter (Horatio) 1839-1894 . NCLC 7,
  90, 159
  See also BRW 5; CDBLB 1832-1890; DLB
  57, 156; RGEL 2; TEA
Paterson, A(ndrew) B(arton)
  1864-1941 .... TCLC 32
  See also CA 155; DLB 230; RGEL 2; SATA
  97
Paterson, Banjo
  See Paterson, A(ndrew) B(arton)
Paterson, Katherine 1932- .... CLC 12, 30
  See also AAYA 1, 31; BYA 1, 2, 7; CA 21-
  24R; CANR 28, 59, 111, 173, 196; CLR
  7, 50, 127; CWRI 5; DLB 52; JRDA;
  LAIT 4; MAICYA 1, 2; MAICYAS 1;
  MTCW 1; SATA 13, 53, 92, 133, 204;
  WYA; YAW
Paterson, Katherine Womeldorf
  See Paterson, Katherine
Patmore, Coventry Kersey Dighton
  1823-1896 .... NCLC 9; PC 59
  See also DLB 35, 98; RGEL 2; TEA
Paton, Alan 1903-1988 ..... CLC 4, 10, 25, 55,
  106; TCLC 165; WLC 4
  See also AAYA 26; AFW; BPFB 3; BRWS
  2; BYA 1; CA 13-16; 125; CANR 22;
  CAP 1; CN 1, 2, 3, 4; DA; DA3; DAB;
  DAC; DAM MST, NOV; DLB 225;
  DLBD 17; EWL 3; EXPN; LAIT 4;
  MTCW 1, 2; MTFW 2005; NFS 3, 12;
  RGEL 2; SATA 11; SATA-Obit 56; SSFS
  29; TWA; WLIT 2; WWE 1
Paton, Alan Stewart
  See Paton, Alan
Paton Walsh, Gillian
  See Paton Walsh, Jill

Paton Walsh, Jill 1937- .... CLC 35
  See also AAYA 11, 47; BYA 1, 8; CA 262;
  CAAE 262; CANR 38, 83, 158; CLR 2,
  6, 128; DLB 161; JRDA; MAICYA 1, 2;
  SAAS 3; SATA 4, 72, 109, 190; SATA-
  Essay 190; WYA; YAW
Patsauq, Markoosie 1942- .... NNAL
  See also CA 101; CLR 23; CWRI 5; DAM
  MULT
Patterson, (Horace) Orlando (Lloyd)
  1940- .... BLCS
  See also BW 1; CA 65-68; CANR 27, 84;
  CN 1, 2, 3, 4, 5, 6
Patton, George S(mith), Jr.
  1885-1945 .... TCLC 79
  See also CA 189
Paulding, James Kirke 1778-1860 ... NCLC 2
  See also DLB 3, 59, 74, 250; RGAL 4
Paulin, Thomas Neilson
  See Paulin, Tom
Paulin, Tom 1949- .... CLC 37, 177
  See also CA 123; 128; CANR 98; CP 3, 4,
  5, 6, 7; DLB 40
Pausanias c. 1st cent. - .... CMLC 36
Paustovsky, Konstantin (Georgievich)
  1892-1968 .... CLC 40
  See also CA 93-96; 25-28R; DLB 272;
  EWL 3
Pavese, Cesare 1908-1950 .... PC 13; SSC 19;
  TCLC 3
  See also CA 104; 169; DLB 128, 177; EW
  12; EWL 3; PFS 20; RGSF 2; RGWL 2,
  3; TWA; WLIT 7
Pavic, Milorad 1929-2009 .... CLC 60
  See also CA 136; CDWLB 4; CWW 2; DLB
  181; EWL 3; RGWL 3
Pavlov, Ivan Petrovich 1849-1936 . TCLC 91
  See also CA 118; 180
Pavlova, Karolina Karlovna
  1807-1893 .... NCLC 138
  See also DLB 205
Payne, Alan
  See Jakes, John
Payne, Rachel Ann
  See Jakes, John
Paz, Gil
  See Lugones, Leopoldo
Paz, Octavio 1914-1998 . CLC 3, 4, 6, 10, 19,
  51, 65, 119; HLC 2; PC 1, 48; TCLC
  211; WLC 4
  See also AAYA 50; CA 73-76; 165; CANR
  32, 65, 104; CWW 2; DA; DA3; DAB;
  DAC; DAM MST, MULT, POET; DLB
  290, 331; DLBY 1990, 1998; DNFS 1;
  EWL 3; HW 1, 2; LAW; LAWS 1; MTCW
  1, 2; MTFW 2005; PFS 18, 30; RGWL 2,
  3; SSFS 13; TWA; WLIT 1
p'Bitek, Okot 1931-1982 . BLC 1:3; CLC 96;
  TCLC 149
  See also AFW; BW 2, 3; CA 124; 107;
  CANR 82; CP 1, 2, 3; DAM MULT; DLB
  125; EWL 3; MTCW 1, 2; MTFW 2005;
  RGEL 2; WLIT 2
Peabody, Elizabeth Palmer
  1804-1894 .... NCLC 169
  See also DLB 1, 223
Peacham, Henry 1578-1644(?) .... LC 119
  See also DLB 151
Peacock, Molly 1947- .... CLC 60
  See also CA 103, 262; CAAE 262; CAAS
  21; CANR 52, 84; CP 5, 6, 7; CWP; DLB
  120, 282
Peacock, Thomas Love
  1785-1866 .... NCLC 22; PC 87
  See also BRW 4; DLB 96, 116; RGEL 2;
  RGSF 2

Plumly, Stanley 1939- .... **CLC 33**
See also CA 108; 110; CANR 97, 185; CP 3, 4, 5, 6, 7; DLB 5, 193; INT CA-110

Plumly, Stanley Ross
See Plumly, Stanley

Plumpe, Friedrich Wilhelm
See Murnau, F.W.

Plutarch c. 46-c. 120 .... **CMLC 60**
See also AW 2; CDWLB 1; DLB 176; RGWL 2, 3; TWA; WLIT 8

Po Chu-i 772-846 .... **CMLC 24**

Podhoretz, Norman 1930- .... **CLC 189**
See also AMWS 8; CA 9-12R; CANR 7, 78, 135, 179

Poe, Edgar Allan 1809-1849 ..... **NCLC 1, 16, 55, 78, 94, 97, 117, 211; PC 1, 54; SSC 1, 22, 34, 35, 54, 88, 111; WLC 4**
See also AAYA 14; AMW; AMWC 1; AMWR 2; BPFB 3; BYA 5, 11; CDALB 1640-1865; CMW 4; DA; DA3; DAB; DAC; DAM MST, POET; DLB 3, 59, 73, 74, 248, 254; EXPP; EXPS; GL 3; HGG; LAIT 2; LATS 1:1; LMFS 1; MSW; PAB; PFS 1, 3, 9; RGAL 4; RGSF 2; SATA 23; SCFW 1, 2; SFW 4; SSFS 2, 4, 7, 8, 16, 26, 29; SUFW; TUS; WP; WYA

Poet of Titchfield Street, The
See Pound, Ezra

Poggio Bracciolini, Gian Francesco
1380-1459 .... **LC 125**

Pohl, Frederik 1919- .... **CLC 18; SSC 25**
See also AAYA 24; CA 61-64, 188; CAAE 188; CAAS 1; CANR 11, 37, 81, 140; CN 1, 2, 3, 4, 5, 6; DLB 8; INT CANR-11; MTCW 1, 2; MTFW 2005; SATA 24; SCFW 1, 2; SFW 4

Poirier, Louis
See Gracq, Julien

Poitier, Sidney 1927- .... **CLC 26**
See also AAYA 60; BW 1; CA 117; CANR 94

Pokagon, Simon 1830-1899 .... **NNAL**
See also DAM MULT

Polanski, Roman 1933- .... **CLC 16, 178**
See also CA 77-80

Poliakoff, Stephen 1952- .... **CLC 38**
See also CA 106; CANR 116; CBD; CD 5, 6; DLB 13

Police, The
See Copeland, Stewart; Sting; Summers, Andy

Polidori, John William
1795-1821 .... **NCLC 51; SSC 97**
See also DLB 116; HGG

Poliziano, Angelo 1454-1494 .... **LC 120**
See also WLIT 7

Pollitt, Katha 1949- .... **CLC 28, 122**
See also CA 120; 122; CANR 66, 108, 164, 200; MTCW 1, 2; MTFW 2005

Pollock, (Mary) Sharon 1936- .... **CLC 50**
See also CA 141; CANR 132; CD 5; CWD; DAC; DAM DRAM, MST; DFS 3; DLB 60; FW

Pollock, Sharon 1936- .... **DC 20**
See also CD 6

Polo, Marco 1254-1324 .... **CMLC 15**
See also WLIT 7

Polonsky, Abraham (Lincoln)
1910-1999 .... **CLC 92**
See also CA 104; 187; DLB 26; INT CA-104

Polybius c. 200B.C.-c. 118B.C. ...... **CMLC 17**
See also AW 1; DLB 176; RGWL 2, 3

Pomerance, Bernard 1940- .... **CLC 13**
See also CA 101; CAD; CANR 49, 134; CD 5, 6; DAM DRAM; DFS 9; LAIT 2

Ponge, Francis 1899-1988 ..... **CLC 6, 18; PC 107**
See also CA 85-88; 126; CANR 40, 86; DAM POET; DLBY 2002; EWL 3; GFL 1789 to the Present; RGWL 2, 3

Poniatowska, Elena 1932- . **CLC 140; HLC 2**
See also CA 101; CANR 32, 66, 107, 156; CDWLB 3; CWW 2; DAM MULT; DLB 113; EWL 3; HW 1, 2; LAWS 1; WLIT 1

Pontoppidan, Henrik 1857-1943 .... **TCLC 29**
See also CA 170; DLB 300, 331

Ponty, Maurice Merleau
See Merleau-Ponty, Maurice

Poole, (Jane Penelope) Josephine
See Helyar, Jane Penelope Josephine

Poole, Josephine
See Helyar, Jane Penelope Josephine

Popa, Vasko 1922-1991 . **CLC 19; TCLC 167**
See also CA 112; 148; CDWLB 4; DLB 181; EWL 3; RGWL 2, 3

Pope, Alexander 1688-1744 ...... **LC 3, 58, 60, 64, 164; PC 26; WLC 5**
See also BRW 3; BRWC 1; BRWR 1; CD-BLB 1660-1789; DA; DA3; DAB; DAC; DAM MST, POET; DLB 95, 101, 213; EXPP; PAB; PFS 12; RGEL 2; WLIT 3; WP

Popov, Evgenii Anatol'evich
See Popov, Yevgeny

Popov, Yevgeny **CLC 59**
See also DLB 285

Poquelin, Jean-Baptiste
See Moliere

Porete, Marguerite (?)-1310 .... **CMLC 73**
See also DLB 208

Porphyry c. 233-c. 305 .... **CMLC 71**

Porter, Connie (Rose) 1959(?)- .... **CLC 70**
See also AAYA 65; BW 2, 3; CA 142; CANR 90, 109; SATA 81, 129

Porter, Gene Stratton
See Stratton-Porter, Gene

Porter, Geneva Grace
See Stratton-Porter, Gene

Porter, Katherine Anne 1890-1980 ... **CLC 1, 3, 7, 10, 13, 15, 27, 101; SSC 4, 31, 43, 108; TCLC 233**
See also AAYA 42; AITN 2; AMW; BPFB 3; CA 1-4R; 101; CANR 1, 65; CDALBS; CN 1, 2; DA; DA3; DAB; DAC; DAM MST, NOV; DLB 4, 9, 102; DLBD 12; DLBY 1980; EWL 3; EXPS; LAIT 3; MAL 5; MBL; MTCW 1, 2; MTFW 2005; NFS 14; RGAL 4; RGSF 2; SATA 39; SATA-Obit 23; SSFS 1, 8, 11, 16, 23; TCWW 2; TUS

Porter, Peter (Neville Frederick)
1929- .... **CLC 5, 13, 33**
See also CA 85-88; CP 1, 2, 3, 4, 5, 6, 7; DLB 40, 289; WWE 1

Porter, R. E.
See Hoch, Edward D.

Porter, William Sydney
See Henry, O.

Portillo (y Pacheco), Jose Lopez
See Lopez Portillo (y Pacheco), Jose

Portillo Trambley, Estela
1927-1998 .... **HLC 2; TCLC 163**
See also CA 77-80; CANR 32; DAM MULT; DLB 209; HW 1; RGAL 4

Posey, Alexander (Lawrence)
1873-1908 .... **NNAL**
See also CA 144; CANR 80; DAM MULT; DLB 175

Posse, Abel **CLC 70, 273**
See also CA 252

Post, Melville Davisson
1869-1930 .... **TCLC 39**
See also CA 110; 202; CMW 4

Postman, Neil 1931(?)-2003 .... **CLC 244**
See also CA 102; 221

Potok, Chaim 1929-2002 ... **CLC 2, 7, 14, 26, 112**
See also AAYA 15, 50; AITN 1, 2; BPFB 3; BYA 1; CA 17-20R; 208; CANR 19, 35, 64, 98; CLR 92; CN 4, 5, 6; DA3; DAM NOV; DLB 28, 152; EXPN; INT CANR-19; LAIT 4; MTCW 1, 2; MTFW 2005; NFS 4, 34; RGHL; SATA 33, 106; SATA-Obit 134; TUS; YAW

Potok, Herbert Harold
See Potok, Chaim

Potok, Herman Harold
See Potok, Chaim

Potter, Dennis (Christopher George)
1935-1994 .... **CLC 58, 86, 123**
See also BRWS 10; CA 107; 145; CANR 33, 61; CBD; DLB 233; MTCW 1

Pound, Ezra 1885-1972 . **CLC 1, 2, 3, 4, 5, 7, 10, 13, 18, 34, 48, 50, 112; PC 4, 95; WLC 5**
See also AAYA 47; AMW; AMWR 1; CA 5-8R; 37-40R; CANR 40; CDALB 1917-1929; CP 1; DA; DA3; DAB; DAC; DAM MST, POET; DLB 4, 45, 63; DLBD 15; EFS 2; EWL 3; EXPP; LMFS 2; MAL 5; MTCW 1, 2; MTFW 2005; PAB; PFS 2, 8, 16; RGAL 4; TUS; WP

Pound, Ezra Weston Loomis
See Pound, Ezra

Povod, Reinaldo 1959-1994 .... **CLC 44**
See also CA 136; 146; CANR 83

Powell, Adam Clayton, Jr.
1908-1972 .... **BLC 1:3; CLC 89**
See also BW 1, 3; CA 102; 33-36R; CANR 86; DAM MULT; DLB 345

Powell, Anthony 1905-2000 ... **CLC 1, 3, 7, 9, 10, 31**
See also BRW 7; CA 1-4R; 189; CANR 1, 32, 62, 107; CDBLB 1945-1960; CN 1, 2, 3, 4, 5, 6; DLB 15; EWL 3; MTCW 1, 2; MTFW 2005; RGEL 2; TEA

Powell, Dawn 1896(?)-1965 .... **CLC 66**
See also CA 5-8R; CANR 121; DLBY 1997

Powell, Padgett 1952- .... **CLC 34**
See also CA 126; CANR 63, 101; CSW; DLB 234; DLBY 01; SSFS 25

Power, Susan 1961- .... **CLC 91**
See also BYA 14; CA 160; CANR 135; NFS 11

Powers, J(ames) F(arl) 1917-1999 ..... **CLC 1, 4, 8, 57; SSC 4**
See also CA 1-4R; 181; CANR 2, 61; CN 1, 2, 3, 4, 5, 6; DLB 130; MTCW 1; RGAL 4; RGSF 2

Powers, John
See Powers, John R.

Powers, John R. 1945- .... **CLC 66**
See also CA 69-72

Powers, Richard 1957- .... **CLC 93, 292**
See also AMWS 9; BPFB 3; CA 148; CANR 80, 180; CN 6, 7; DLB 350; MTFW 2005; TCLE 1:2

Powers, Richard S.
See Powers, Richard

Pownall, David 1938- .... **CLC 10**
See also CA 89-92, 180; CAAS 18; CANR 49, 101; CBD; CD 5, 6; CN 4, 5, 6, 7; DLB 14

Powys, John Cowper 1872-1963 ... **CLC 7, 9, 15, 46, 125**
See also CA 85-88; CANR 106; DLB 15, 255; EWL 3; FANT; MTCW 1, 2; MTFW 2005; RGEL 2; SUFW

Powys, T(heodore) F(rancis)
1875-1953 .... **TCLC 9**
See also BRWS 8; CA 106; 189; DLB 36, 162; EWL 3; FANT; RGEL 2; SUFW

Pym, Barbara (Mary Crampton)
1913-1980 .... **CLC 13, 19, 37, 111**
See also BPFB 3; BRWS 2; CA 13-14; 97-100; CANR 13, 34; CAP 1; DLB 14, 207; DLBY 1987; EWL 3; MTCW 1, 2; MTFW 2005; RGEL 2; TEA
Pynchon, Thomas 1937- .. **CLC 2, 3, 6, 9, 11, 18, 33, 62, 72, 123, 192, 213; SSC 14, 84; WLC 5**
See also AMWS 2; BEST 90:2; BPFB 3; CA 17-20R; CANR 22, 46, 73, 142, 198; CN 1, 2, 3, 4, 5, 6, 7; CPW 1; DA; DA3; DAB; DAC; DAM MST, NOV, POP; DLB 2, 173; EWL 3; MAL 5; MTCW 1, 2; MTFW 2005; NFS 23; RGAL 4; SFW 4; TCLE 1:2; TUS
Pynchon, Thomas Ruggels, Jr.
See Pynchon, Thomas
Pynchon, Thomas Ruggles
See Pynchon, Thomas
Pythagoras c. 582B.C.-c. 507B.C. . **CMLC 22**
See also DLB 176
Q
See Quiller-Couch, Sir Arthur (Thomas)
Qian, Chongzhu
See Ch'ien, Chung-shu
Qian, Sima 145B.C.-c. 89B.C. .... **CMLC 72**
Qian Zhongshu
See Ch'ien, Chung-shu
Qroll
See Dagerman, Stig (Halvard)
Quarles, Francis 1592-1644 .... **LC 117**
See also DLB 126; RGEL 2
Quarrington, Paul 1953-2010 .... **CLC 65**
See also CA 129; CANR 62, 95
Quarrington, Paul Lewis
See Quarrington, Paul
Quasimodo, Salvatore 1901-1968 .... **CLC 10; PC 47**
See also CA 13-16; 25-28R; CAP 1; DLB 114, 332; EW 12; EWL 3; MTCW 1; RGWL 2, 3
Quatermass, Martin
See Carpenter, John
Quay, Stephen 1947- .... **CLC 95**
See also CA 189
Quay, Timothy 1947- .... **CLC 95**
See also CA 189
Queen, Ellery
See Dannay, Frederic; Hoch, Edward D.; Lee, Manfred B.; Marlowe, Stephen; Sturgeon, Theodore (Hamilton); Vance, Jack
Queneau, Raymond 1903-1976 ..... **CLC 2, 5, 10, 42; TCLC 233**
See also CA 77-80; 69-72; CANR 32; DLB 72, 258; EW 12; EWL 3; GFL 1789 to the Present; MTCW 1, 2; RGWL 2, 3
Quevedo, Francisco de 1580-1645 ...... **LC 23, 160**
Quiller-Couch, Sir Arthur (Thomas)
1863-1944 .... **TCLC 53**
See also CA 118; 166; DLB 135, 153, 190; HGG; RGEL 2; SUFW 1
Quin, Ann 1936-1973 .... **CLC 6**
See also CA 9-12R; 45-48; CANR 148; CN 1; DLB 14, 231
Quin, Ann Marie
See Quin, Ann
Quincey, Thomas de
See De Quincey, Thomas
Quindlen, Anna 1953- .... **CLC 191**
See also AAYA 35; AMWS 17; CA 138; CANR 73, 126; DA3; DLB 292; MTCW 2; MTFW 2005
Quinn, Martin
See Smith, Martin Cruz
Quinn, Peter 1947- .... **CLC 91**
See also CA 197; CANR 147

Quinn, Peter A.
See Quinn, Peter
Quinn, Simon
See Smith, Martin Cruz
Quintana, Leroy V. 1944- ...... **HLC 2; PC 36**
See also CA 131; CANR 65, 139; DAM MULT; DLB 82; HW 1, 2
Quintilian c. 40-c. 100 .... **CMLC 77**
See also AW 2; DLB 211; RGWL 2, 3
Quiroga, Horacio (Sylvestre)
1878-1937 ... **HLC 2; SSC 89; TCLC 20**
See also CA 117; 131; DAM MULT; EWL 3; HW 1; LAW; MTCW 1; RGSF 2; WLIT 1
Quoirez, Francoise 1935-2004 ... **CLC 3, 6, 9, 17, 36**
See also CA 49-52; 231; CANR 6, 39, 73; CWW 2; DLB 83; EWL 3; GFL 1789 to the Present; MTCW 1, 2; MTFW 2005; TWA
Raabe, Wilhelm (Karl) 1831-1910 . **TCLC 45**
See also CA 167; DLB 129
Rabe, David (William) 1940- .. **CLC 4, 8, 33, 200; DC 16**
See also CA 85-88; CABS 3; CAD; CANR 59, 129; CD 5, 6; DAM DRAM; DFS 3, 8, 13; DLB 7, 228; EWL 3; MAL 5
Rabelais, Francois 1494-1553 .... **LC 5, 60; WLC 5**
See also DA; DAB; DAC; DAM MST; DLB 327; EW 2; GFL Beginnings to 1789; LMFS 1; RGWL 2, 3; TWA
Rabi'a al-'Adawiyya c. 717-c. 801 .... **CMLC 83**
See also DLB 311
Rabinovitch, Sholem 1859-1916 .... **SSC 33, 125; TCLC 1, 35**
See also CA 104; DLB 333; TWA
Rabinovitsh, Sholem Yankev
See Rabinovitch, Sholem
Rabinowitz, Sholem Yakov
See Rabinovitch, Sholem
Rabinowitz, Solomon
See Rabinovitch, Sholem
Rabinyan, Dorit 1972- .... **CLC 119**
See also CA 170; CANR 147
Rachilde
See Vallette, Marguerite Eymery; Vallette, Marguerite Eymery
Racine, Jean 1639-1699 .. **DC 32; LC 28, 113**
See also DA3; DAB; DAM MST; DLB 268; EW 3; GFL Beginnings to 1789; LMFS 1; RGWL 2, 3; TWA
Radcliffe, Ann 1764-1823 .. **NCLC 6, 55, 106, 223**
See also BRWR 3; DLB 39, 178; GL 3; HGG; LMFS 1; RGEL 2; SUFW; WLIT 3
Radclyffe-Hall, Marguerite
See Hall, Radclyffe
Radiguet, Raymond 1903-1923 ...... **TCLC 29**
See also CA 162; DLB 65; EWL 3; GFL 1789 to the Present; RGWL 2, 3
Radishchev, Aleksandr Nikolaevich
1749-1802 .... **NCLC 190**
See also DLB 150
Radishchev, Alexander
See Radishchev, Aleksandr Nikolaevich
Radnoti, Miklos 1909-1944 .... **TCLC 16**
See also CA 118; 212; CDWLB 4; DLB 215; EWL 3; RGHL; RGWL 2, 3
Rado, James 1939- .... **CLC 17**
See also CA 105
Radvanyi, Netty 1900-1983 .... **CLC 7**
See also CA 85-88; 110; CANR 82; CDWLB 2; DLB 69; EWL 3
Rae, Ben
See Griffiths, Trevor

Raeburn, John (Hay) 1941- .... **CLC 34**
See also CA 57-60
Ragni, Gerome 1942-1991 .... **CLC 17**
See also CA 105; 134
Rahv, Philip
See Greenberg, Ivan
Rai, Navab
See Srivastava, Dhanpat Rai
Raimund, Ferdinand Jakob
1790-1836 .... **NCLC 69**
See also DLB 90
Raine, Craig 1944- .... **CLC 32, 103**
See also BRWS 13; CA 108; CANR 29, 51, 103, 171; CP 3, 4, 5, 6, 7; DLB 40; PFS 7
Raine, Craig Anthony
See Raine, Craig
Raine, Kathleen (Jessie) 1908-2003 .. **CLC 7, 45**
See also CA 85-88; 218; CANR 46, 109; CP 1, 2, 3, 4, 5, 6, 7; DLB 20; EWL 3; MTCW 1; RGEL 2
Rainis, Janis 1865-1929 .... **TCLC 29**
See also CA 170; CDWLB 4; DLB 220; EWL 3
Rakosi, Carl
See Rawley, Callman
Ralegh, Sir Walter
See Raleigh, Sir Walter
Raleigh, Richard
See Lovecraft, H. P.
Raleigh, Sir Walter 1554(?)-1618 .... **LC 31, 39; PC 31**
See also BRW 1; CDBLB Before 1660; DLB 172; EXPP; PFS 14; RGEL 2; TEA; WP
Rallentando, H. P.
See Sayers, Dorothy L(eigh)
Ramal, Walter
See de la Mare, Walter (John)
Ramana Maharshi 1879-1950 .... **TCLC 84**
Ramoacn y Cajal, Santiago
1852-1934 .... **TCLC 93**
Ramon, Juan
See Jimenez, Juan Ramon
Ramos, Graciliano 1892-1953 .... **TCLC 32**
See also CA 167; DLB 307; EWL 3; HW 2; LAW; WLIT 1
Rampersad, Arnold 1941- .... **CLC 44**
See also BW 2, 3; CA 127; 133; CANR 81; DLB 111; INT CA-133
Rampling, Anne
See Rice, Anne
Ramsay, Allan 1686(?)-1758 .... **LC 29**
See also DLB 95; RGEL 2
Ramsay, Jay
See Campbell, Ramsey
Ramus, Peter
See La Ramee, Pierre de
Ramus, Petrus
See La Ramee, Pierre de
Ramuz, Charles-Ferdinand
1878-1947 .... **TCLC 33**
See also CA 165; EWL 3
Rand, Ayn 1905-1982 ...... **CLC 3, 30, 44, 79; SSC 116; WLC 5**
See also AAYA 10; AMWS 4; BPFB 3; BYA 12; CA 13-16R; 105; CANR 27, 73; CDALBS; CN 1, 2, 3; CPW; DA; DA3; DAC; DAM MST, NOV, POP; DLB 227, 279; MTCW 1, 2; MTFW 2005; NFS 10, 16, 29; RGAL 4; SFW 4; TUS; YAW
Randall, Dudley 1914-2000 ... **BLC 1:3; CLC 1, 135; PC 86**
See also BW 1, 3; CA 25-28R; 189; CANR 23, 82; CP 1, 2, 3, 4, 5; DAM MULT; DLB 41; PFS 5
Randall, Dudley Felker
See Randall, Dudley

Rosenthal, M(acha) L(ouis)
1917-1996 .... **CLC 28**
See also CA 1-4R; 152; CAAS 6; CANR 4,
51; CP 1, 2, 3, 4, 5, 6; DLB 5; SATA 59

Ross, Barnaby
See Dannay, Frederic; Lee, Manfred B.

Ross, Bernard L.
See Follett, Ken

Ross, J. H.
See Lawrence, T. E.

Ross, John Hume
See Lawrence, T. E.

Ross, Martin 1862-1915
See Martin, Violet Florence
See also DLB 135; GLL 2; RGEL 2; RGSF 2

Ross, (James) Sinclair 1908-1996 ... **CLC 13;
SSC 24**
See also CA 73-76; CANR 81; CN 1, 2, 3,
4, 5, 6; DAC; DAM MST; DLB 88;
RGEL 2; RGSF 2; TCWW 1, 2

Rossetti, Christina 1830-1894 ... **NCLC 2, 50,
66, 186; PC 7; WLC 5**
See also AAYA 51; BRW 5; BRWR 3; BYA
4; CLR 115; DA; DA3; DAB; DAC;
DAM MST, POET; DLB 35, 163, 240;
EXPP; FL 1:3; LATS 1:1; MAICYA 1, 2;
PFS 10, 14, 27, 34; RGEL 2; SATA 20;
TEA; WCH

Rossetti, Christina Georgina
See Rossetti, Christina

Rossetti, Dante Gabriel 1828-1882 . **NCLC 4,
77; PC 44; WLC 5**
See also AAYA 51; BRW 5; CDBLB 1832-
1890; DA; DAB; DAC; DAM MST,
POET; DLB 35; EXPP; RGEL 2; TEA

Rossi, Cristina Peri
See Peri Rossi, Cristina

Rossi, Jean-Baptiste 1931-2003 .... **CLC 90**
See also CA 201; 215; CMW 4; NFS 18

Rossner, Judith 1935-2005 .... **CLC 6, 9, 29**
See also AITN 2; BEST 90:3; BPFB 3; CA
17-20R; 242; CANR 18, 51, 73; CN 4, 5,
6, 7; DLB 6; INT CANR-18; MAL 5;
MTCW 1, 2; MTFW 2005

Rossner, Judith Perelman
See Rossner, Judith

Rostand, Edmond 1868-1918 . **DC 10; TCLC
6, 37**
See also CA 104; 126; DA; DA3; DAB;
DAC; DAM DRAM, MST; DFS 1; DLB
192; LAIT 1; MTCW 1; RGWL 2, 3;
TWA

Rostand, Edmond Eugene Alexis
See Rostand, Edmond

Roth, Henry 1906-1995 ... **CLC 2, 6, 11, 104;
SSC 134**
See also AMWS 9; CA 11-12; 149; CANR
38, 63; CAP 1; CN 1, 2, 3, 4, 5, 6; DA3;
DLB 28; EWL 3; MAL 5; MTCW 1, 2;
MTFW 2005; RGAL 4

Roth, (Moses) Joseph 1894-1939 ... **TCLC 33**
See also CA 160; DLB 85; EWL 3; RGWL
2, 3

Roth, Philip 1933- ... **CLC 1, 2, 3, 4, 6, 9, 15,
22, 31, 47, 66, 86, 119, 201; SSC 26,
102; WLC 5**
See also AAYA 67; AMWR 2; AMWS 3;
BEST 90:3; BPFB 3; CA 1-4R; CANR 1,
22, 36, 55, 89, 132, 170; CDALB 1968-
1988; CN 3, 4, 5, 6, 7; CPW 1; DA; DA3;
DAB; DAC; DAM MST, NOV, POP;
DLB 2, 28, 173; DLBY 1982; EWL 3;
MAL 5; MTCW 1, 2; MTFW 2005; NFS
25; RGAL 4; RGHL; RGSF 2; SSFS 12,
18; TUS

Roth, Philip Milton
See Roth, Philip

Rothenberg, Jerome 1931- .... **CLC 6, 57**
See also CA 45-48; CANR 1, 106; CP 1, 2,
3, 4, 5, 6, 7; DLB 5, 193

Rotter, Pat **CLC 65**

Roumain, Jacques 1907-1944 .... **BLC 1:3;
TCLC 19**
See also BW 1; CA 117; 125; DAM MULT;
EWL 3

Roumain, Jacques Jean Baptiste
See Roumain, Jacques

Rourke, Constance Mayfield
1885-1941 .... **TCLC 12**
See also CA 107; 200; MAL 5; YABC 1

Rousseau, Jean-Baptiste 1671-1741 ...... **LC 9**

Rousseau, Jean-Jacques 1712-1778 .... **LC 14,
36, 122; WLC 5**
See also DA; DA3; DAB; DAC; DAM
MST; DLB 314; EW 4; GFL Beginnings
to 1789; LMFS 1; RGWL 2, 3; TWA

Roussel, Raymond 1877-1933 .... **TCLC 20**
See also CA 117; 201; EWL 3; GFL 1789
to the Present

Rovit, Earl (Herbert) 1927- .... **CLC 7**
See also CA 5-8R; CANR 12

Rowe, Elizabeth Singer 1674-1737 ..... **LC 44**
See also DLB 39, 95

Rowe, Nicholas 1674-1718 .... **LC 8**
See also DLB 84; RGEL 2

Rowlandson, Mary 1637(?)-1678 .... **LC 66**
See also DLB 24, 200; RGAL 4

Rowley, Ames Dorrance
See Lovecraft, H. P.

Rowley, William 1585(?)-1626 ... **LC 100, 123**
See also DFS 22; DLB 58; RGEL 2

Rowling, J.K. 1965- .... **CLC 137, 217**
See also AAYA 34, 82; BRWS 16; BYA 11,
13, 14; CA 173; CANR 128, 157; CLR
66, 80, 112; LNFS 1, 2, 3; MAICYA 2;
MTFW 2005; SATA 109, 174; SUFW 2

Rowling, Joanne Kathleen
See Rowling, J.K.

Rowson, Susanna Haswell
1762(?)-1824 .... **NCLC 5, 69, 182**
See also AMWS 15; DLB 37, 200; RGAL 4

Roy, Arundhati 1960(?)- .... **CLC 109, 210**
See also CA 163; CANR 90, 126; CN 7;
DLB 323, 326; DLBY 1997; EWL 3;
LATS 1:2; MTFW 2005; NFS 22; WWE
1

Roy, Gabrielle 1909-1983 .... **CLC 10, 14**
See also CA 53-56; 110; CANR 5, 61; CCA
1; DAB; DAC; DAM MST; DLB 68;
EWL 3; MTCW 1; RGWL 2, 3; SATA
104; TCLE 1:2

Royko, Mike 1932-1997 .... **CLC 109**
See also CA 89-92; 157; CANR 26, 111;
CPW

Rozanov, Vasilii Vasil'evich
See Rozanov, Vassili

Rozanov, Vasily Vasilyevich
See Rozanov, Vassili

Rozanov, Vassili 1856-1919 .... **TCLC 104**
See also DLB 295; EWL 3

Rozewicz, Tadeusz 1921- ...... **CLC 9, 23, 139**
See also CA 108; CANR 36, 66; CWW 2;
DA3; DAM POET; DLB 232; EWL 3;
MTCW 1, 2; MTFW 2005; RGHL;
RGWL 3

Ruark, Gibbons 1941- .... **CLC 3**
See also CA 33-36R; CAAS 23; CANR 14,
31, 57; DLB 120

Rubens, Bernice (Ruth) 1923-2004 . **CLC 19,
31**
See also CA 25-28R; 232; CANR 33, 65,
128; CN 1, 2, 3, 4, 5, 6, 7; DLB 14, 207,
326; MTCW 1

Rubin, Harold
See Robbins, Harold

Rudkin, (James) David 1936- .... **CLC 14**
See also CA 89-92; CBD; CD 5, 6; DLB 13

Rudnik, Raphael 1933- .... **CLC 7**
See also CA 29-32R

Ruffian, M.
See Hasek, Jaroslav

Rufinus c. 345-410 .... **CMLC 111**

Ruiz, Jose Martinez
See Martinez Ruiz, Jose

Ruiz, Juan c. 1283-c. 1350 .... **CMLC 66**

Rukeyser, Muriel 1913-1980 . **CLC 6, 10, 15,
27; PC 12**
See also AMWS 6; CA 5-8R; 93-96; CANR
26, 60; CP 1, 2, 3; DA3; DAM POET;
DLB 48; EWL 3; FW; GLL 2; MAL 5;
MTCW 1, 2; PFS 10, 29; RGAL 4; SATA-
Obit 22

Rule, Jane 1931-2007 .... **CLC 27, 265**
See also CA 25-28R; 266; CAAS 18; CANR
12, 87; CN 4, 5, 6, 7; DLB 60; FW

Rule, Jane Vance
See Rule, Jane

Rulfo, Juan 1918-1986 .. **CLC 8, 80; HLC 2;
SSC 25**
See also CA 85-88; 118; CANR 26; CD-
WLB 3; DAM MULT; DLB 113; EWL 3;
HW 1, 2; LAW; MTCW 1, 2; RGSF 2;
RGWL 2, 3; WLIT 1

Rumi
See Rumi, Jalal al-Din

Rumi, Jalal al-Din 1207-1273 ...... **CMLC 20;
PC 45**
See also AAYA 64; RGWL 2, 3; WLIT 6;
WP

Runeberg, Johan 1804-1877 .... **NCLC 41**

Runyon, (Alfred) Damon
1884(?)-1946 .... **TCLC 10**
See also CA 107; 165; DLB 11, 86, 171;
MAL 5; MTCW 2; RGAL 4

Rush, Norman 1933- .... **CLC 44**
See also CA 121; 126; CANR 130; INT CA-
126

Rushdie, Ahmed Salman
See Rushdie, Salman

Rushdie, Salman 1947- .... **CLC 23, 31, 55,
100, 191, 272; SSC 83; WLCS**
See also AAYA 65; BEST 89:3; BPFB 3;
BRWS 4; CA 108; 111; CANR 33, 56,
108, 133, 192; CLR 125; CN 4, 5, 6, 7;
CPW 1; DA3; DAB; DAC; DAM MST,
NOV, POP; DLB 194, 323, 326; EWL 3;
FANT; INT CA-111; LATS 1:2; LMFS 2;
MTCW 1, 2; MTFW 2005; NFS 22, 23;
RGEL 2; RGSF 2; TEA; WLIT 4

Rushforth, Peter 1945-2005 .... **CLC 19**
See also CA 101; 243

Rushforth, Peter Scott
See Rushforth, Peter

Ruskin, John 1819-1900 .... **TCLC 63**
See also BRW 5; BYA 5; CA 114; 129; CD-
BLB 1832-1890; DLB 55, 163, 190;
RGEL 2; SATA 24; TEA; WCH

Russ, Joanna 1937- .... **CLC 15**
See also BPFB 3; CA 25-28; CANR 11, 31,
65; CN 4, 5, 6, 7; DLB 8; FW; GLL 1;
MTCW 1; SCFW 1, 2; SFW 4

Russ, Richard Patrick
See O'Brian, Patrick

Russell, George William
1867-1935 .... **TCLC 3, 10**
See also BRWS 8; CA 104; 153; CDBLB
1890-1914; DAM POET; DLB 19; EWL
3; RGEL 2

Russell, Jeffrey Burton 1934- .... **CLC 70**
See also CA 25-28R; CANR 11, 28, 52, 179

Russell, (Henry) Ken(neth Alfred)
1927- .... **CLC 16**
See also CA 105

Sanchez, Florencio 1875-1910 .... **TCLC 37**
See also CA 153; DLB 305; EWL 3; HW 1;
LAW

Sanchez, Luis Rafael 1936- .... **CLC 23**
See also CA 128; DLB 305; EWL 3; HW 1;
WLIT 1

Sanchez, Sonia 1934- . **BLC 1:3, 2:3; CLC 5,
116, 215; PC 9**
See also BW 2, 3; CA 33-36R; CANR 24,
49, 74, 115; CLR 18; CP 2, 3, 4, 5, 6, 7;
CSW; CWP; DA3; DAM MULT; DLB 41;
DLBD 8; EWL 3; MAICYA 1, 2; MAL 5;
MTCW 1, 2; MTFW 2005; PFS 26; SATA
22, 136; WP

Sancho, Ignatius 1729-1780 .... **LC 84**

Sand, George 1804-1876 .... **DC 29; NCLC 2,
42, 57, 174; WLC 5**
See also DA; DA3; DAB; DAC; DAM
MST, NOV; DLB 119, 192; EW 6; FL 1:3;
FW; GFL 1789 to the Present; RGWL 2,
3; TWA

Sandburg, Carl 1878-1967 ...... **CLC 1, 4, 10,
15, 35; PC 2, 41; WLC 5**
See also AAYA 24; AMW; BYA 1, 3; CA
5-8R; 25-28R; CANR 35; CDALB 1865-
1917; CLR 67; DA; DA3; DAB; DAC;
DAM MST, POET; DLB 17, 54, 284;
EWL 3; EXPP; LAIT 2; MAICYA 1, 2;
MAL 5; MTCW 1, 2; MTFW 2005; PAB;
PFS 3, 6, 12, 33; RGAL 4; SATA 8; TUS;
WCH; WP; WYA

Sandburg, Carl August
See Sandburg, Carl

Sandburg, Charles
See Sandburg, Carl

Sandburg, Charles A.
See Sandburg, Carl

Sanders, Ed 1939- .... **CLC 53**
See also BG 1:3; CA 13-16R; CAAS 21;
CANR 13, 44, 78; CP 1, 2, 3, 4, 5, 6, 7;
DAM POET; DLB 16, 244

Sanders, Edward
See Sanders, Ed

Sanders, James Edward
See Sanders, Ed

Sanders, Lawrence 1920-1998 .... **CLC 41**
See also BEST 89:4; BPFB 3; CA 81-84;
165; CANR 33, 62; CMW 4; CPW; DA3;
DAM POP; MTCW 1

Sanders, Noah
See Blount, Roy, Jr.

Sanders, Winston P.
See Anderson, Poul

Sandoz, Mari(e Susette) 1900-1966 .. **CLC 28**
See also CA 1-4R; 25-28R; CANR 17, 64;
DLB 9, 212; LAIT 2; MTCW 1, 2; SATA
5; TCWW 1, 2

Sandys, George 1578-1644 .... **LC 80**
See also DLB 24, 121

Saner, Reg(inald Anthony) 1931- .... **CLC 9**
See also CA 65-68; CP 3, 4, 5, 6, 7

Sankara 788-820 .... **CMLC 32**

Sannazaro, Jacopo 1456(?)-1530 .... **LC 8**
See also RGWL 2, 3; WLIT 7

Sansom, William 1912-1976 . **CLC 2, 6; SSC
21**
See also CA 5-8R; 65-68; CANR 42; CN 1,
2; DAM NOV; DLB 139; EWL 3; MTCW
1; RGEL 2; RGSF 2

Santayana, George 1863-1952 .... **TCLC 40**
See also AMW; CA 115; 194; DLB 54, 71,
246, 270; DLBD 13; EWL 3; MAL 5;
RGAL 4; TUS

Santiago, Danny
See James, Daniel (Lewis)

**Santillana, Inigo Lopez de Mendoza,
Marques de** 1398-1458 .... **LC 111**
See also DLB 286

Santmyer, Helen Hooven
1895-1986 .... **CLC 33; TCLC 133**
See also CA 1-4R; 118; CANR 15, 33;
DLBY 1984; MTCW 1; RHW

Santoka, Taneda 1882-1940 .... **TCLC 72**

Santos, Bienvenido N(uqui)
1911-1996 ... **AAL; CLC 22; TCLC 156**
See also CA 101; 151; CANR 19, 46; CP 1;
DAM MULT; DLB 312, 348; EWL;
RGAL 4; SSFS 19

Santos, Miguel
See Mihura, Miguel

Sapir, Edward 1884-1939 .... **TCLC 108**
See also CA 211; DLB 92

Sapper
See McNeile, Herman Cyril

Sapphire 1950- .... **CLC 99**
See also CA 262

Sapphire, Brenda
See Sapphire

Sappho fl. 6th cent. B.C.- ... **CMLC 3, 67; PC
5**
See also CDWLB 1; DA3; DAM POET;
DLB 176; FL 1:1; PFS 20, 31; RGWL 2,
3; WLIT 8; WP

Saramago, Jose 1922- .... **CLC 119, 275;
HLCS 1**
See also CA 153; CANR 96, 164; CWW 2;
DLB 287, 332; EWL 3; LATS 1:2; NFS
27; SSFS 23

Sarduy, Severo 1937-1993 .... **CLC 6, 97;
HLCS 2; TCLC 167**
See also CA 89-92; 142; CANR 58, 81;
CWW 2; DLB 113; EWL 3; HW 1, 2;
LAW

Sargeson, Frank 1903-1982 ..... **CLC 31; SSC
99**
See also CA 25-28R; 106; CANR 38, 79;
CN 1, 2, 3; EWL 3; GLL 2; RGEL 2;
RGSF 2; SSFS 20

Sarmiento, Domingo Faustino
1811-1888 .... **HLCS 2; NCLC 123**
See also LAW; WLIT 1

Sarmiento, Felix Ruben Garcia
See Dario, Ruben

Saro-Wiwa, Ken(ule Beeson)
1941-1995 .... **CLC 114; TCLC 200**
See also BW 2; CA 142; 150; CANR 60;
DLB 157

Saroyan, William 1908-1981 ... **CLC 1, 8, 10,
29, 34, 56; DC 28; SSC 21; TCLC 137;
WLC 5**
See also AAYA 66; CA 5-8R; 103; CAD;
CANR 30; CDALBS; CN 1, 2; DA; DA3;
DAB; DAC; DAM DRAM, MST, NOV;
DFS 17; DLB 7, 9, 86; DLBY 1981; EWL
3; LAIT 4; MAL 5; MTCW 1, 2; MTFW
2005; RGAL 4; RGSF 2; SATA 23; SATA-
Obit 24; SSFS 14; TUS

Sarraute, Nathalie 1900-1999 .... **CLC 1, 2, 4,
8, 10, 31, 80; TCLC 145**
See also BPFB 3; CA 9-12R; 187; CANR
23, 66, 134; CWW 2; DLB 83, 321; EW
12; EWL 3; GFL 1789 to the Present;
MTCW 1, 2; MTFW 2005; RGWL 2, 3

Sarton, May 1912-1995 ... **CLC 4, 14, 49, 91;
PC 39; TCLC 120**
See also AMWS 8; CA 1-4R; 149; CANR
1, 34, 55, 116; CN 1, 2, 3, 4, 5, 6; CP 1,
2, 3, 4, 5, 6; DAM POET; DLB 48; DLBY
1981; EWL 3; FW; INT CANR-34; MAL
5; MTCW 1, 2; MTFW 2005; RGAL 4;
SATA 36; SATA-Obit 86; TUS

Sartre, Jean-Paul 1905-1980 . **CLC 1, 4, 7, 9,
13, 18, 24, 44, 50, 52; DC 3; SSC 32;
WLC 5**
See also AAYA 62; CA 9-12R; 97-100;
CANR 21; DA; DA3; DAB; DAC; DAM
DRAM, MST, NOV; DFS 5, 26; DLB 72,
296, 321, 332; EW 12; EWL 3; GFL 1789

to the Present; LMFS 2; MTCW 1, 2;
MTFW 2005; NFS 21; RGHL; RGSF 2;
RGWL 2, 3; SSFS 9; TWA

Sassoon, Siegfried 1886-1967 .. **CLC 36, 130;
PC 12**
See also BRW 6; CA 104; 25-28R; CANR
36; DAB; DAM MST, NOV, POET; DLB
20, 191; DLBD 18; EWL 3; MTCW 1, 2;
MTFW 2005; PAB; PFS 28; RGEL 2;
TEA

Sassoon, Siegfried Lorraine
See Sassoon, Siegfried

Satterfield, Charles
See Pohl, Frederik

Satyremont
See Peret, Benjamin

Saul, John III
See Saul, John

Saul, John 1942- .... **CLC 46**
See also AAYA 10, 62; BEST 90:4; CA 81-
84; CANR 16, 40, 81, 176; CPW; DAM
NOV, POP; HGG; SATA 98

Saul, John W.
See Saul, John

Saul, John W. III
See Saul, John

Saul, John Woodruff III
See Saul, John

Saunders, Caleb
See Heinlein, Robert A.

Saura (Atares), Carlos 1932-1998 .... **CLC 20**
See also CA 114; 131; CANR 79; HW 1

Sauser, Frederic Louis
See Sauser-Hall, Frederic

Sauser-Hall, Frederic 1887-1961 ..... **CLC 18,
106**
See also CA 102; 93-96; CANR 36, 62;
DLB 258; EWL 3; GFL 1789 to the
Present; MTCW 1; WP

Saussure, Ferdinand de
1857-1913 .... **TCLC 49**
See also DLB 242

Savage, Catharine
See Brosman, Catharine Savage

Savage, Richard 1697(?)-1743 .... **LC 96**
See also DLB 95; RGEL 2

Savage, Thomas 1915-2003 .... **CLC 40**
See also CA 126; 132; 218; CAAS 15; CN
6, 7; INT CA-132; SATA-Obit 147;
TCWW 2

Savan, Glenn 1953-2003 .... **CLC 50**
See also CA 225

Savonarola, Girolamo 1452-1498 ...... **LC 152**
See also LMFS 1

Sax, Robert
See Johnson, Robert

Saxo Grammaticus c. 1150-c.
1222 .... **CMLC 58**

Saxton, Robert
See Johnson, Robert

Sayers, Dorothy L(eigh) 1893-1957 . **SSC 71;
TCLC 2, 15, 237**
See also BPFB 3; BRWS 3; CA 104; 119;
CANR 60; CDBLB 1914-1945; CMW 4;
DAM POP; DLB 10, 36, 77, 100; MSW;
MTCW 1, 2; MTFW 2005; RGEL 2;
SSFS 12; TEA

Sayers, Valerie 1952- .... **CLC 50, 122**
See also CA 134; CANR 61; CSW

Sayles, John (Thomas) 1950- .... **CLC 7, 10,
14, 198**
See also CA 57-60; CANR 41, 84; DLB 44

Scamander, Newt
See Rowling, J.K.

Scammell, Michael 1935- .... **CLC 34**
See also CA 156

Scannel, John Vernon
See Scannell, Vernon

Scudery, Madeleine de 1607-1701 .. **LC 2, 58**
See also DLB 268; GFL Beginnings to 1789
Scum
See Crumb, R.
Scumbag, Little Bobby
See Crumb, R.
Seabrook, John
See Hubbard, L. Ron
Seacole, Mary Jane Grant
1805-1881 .... **NCLC 147**
See also DLB 166
Sealy, I(rwin) Allan 1951- .... **CLC 55**
See also CA 136; CN 6, 7
Search, Alexander
See Pessoa, Fernando
Seare, Nicholas
See Whitaker, Rod
Sebald, W(infried) G(eorg)
1944-2001 .... **CLC 194**
See also BRWS 8; CA 159; 202; CANR 98;
MTFW 2005; RGHL
Sebastian, Lee
See Silverberg, Robert
Sebastian Owl
See Thompson, Hunter S.
Sebestyen, Igen
See Sebestyen, Ouida
Sebestyen, Ouida 1924- .... **CLC 30**
See also AAYA 8; BYA 7; CA 107; CANR
40, 114; CLR 17; JRDA; MAICYA 1, 2;
SAAS 10; SATA 39, 140; WYA; YAW
Sebold, Alice 1963- .... **CLC 193**
See also AAYA 56; CA 203; CANR 181;
LNFS 1; MTFW 2005
Second Duke of Buckingham
See Villiers, George
Secundus, H. Scriblerus
See Fielding, Henry
Sedges, John
See Buck, Pearl S.
Sedgwick, Catharine Maria
1789-1867 .... **NCLC 19, 98**
See also DLB 1, 74, 183, 239, 243, 254; FL
1:3; RGAL 4
Sedley, Sir Charles 1639-1701 .... **LC 168**
See also BRW 2; DLB 131; RGEL 2
Sedulius Scottus 9th cent. -c. 874 .. **CMLC 86**
Seebohm, Victoria
See Glendinning, Victoria
Seelye, John (Douglas) 1931- .... **CLC 7**
See also CA 97-100; CANR 70; INT CA-
97-100; TCWW 1, 2
Seferiades, Giorgos Stylianou
See Seferis, George
Seferis, George 1900-1971 .... **CLC 5, 11;**
TCLC 213
See also CA 5-8R; 33-36R; CANR 5, 36;
DLB 332; EW 12; EWL 3; MTCW 1;
RGWL 2, 3
Segal, Erich 1937-2010 .... **CLC 3, 10**
See also BEST 89:1; BPFB 3; CA 25-28R;
CANR 20, 36, 65, 113; CPW; DAM POP;
DLBY 1986; INT CANR-20; MTCW 1
Segal, Erich Wolf
See Segal, Erich
Seger, Bob 1945- .... **CLC 35**
Seghers
See Radvanyi, Netty
Seghers, Anna
See Radvanyi, Netty
Seidel, Frederick 1936- .... **CLC 18**
See also CA 13-16R; CANR 8, 99, 180; CP
1, 2, 3, 4, 5, 6, 7; DLBY 1984
Seidel, Frederick Lewis
See Seidel, Frederick

Seifert, Jaroslav 1901-1986 . **CLC 34, 44, 93;**
PC 47
See also CA 127; CDWLB 4; DLB 215,
332; EWL 3; MTCW 1, 2
Sei Shonagon c. 966-1017(?) ..... **CMLC 6, 89**
Sejour, Victor 1817-1874 .... **DC 10**
See also DLB 50
Sejour Marcou et Ferrand, Juan Victor
See Sejour, Victor
Selby, Hubert, Jr. 1928-2004 ..... **CLC 1, 2, 4,**
8; SSC 20
See also CA 13-16R; 226; CANR 33, 85;
CN 1, 2, 3, 4, 5, 6, 7; DLB 2, 227; MAL
5
Self, Will 1961- .... **CLC 282**
See also BRWS 5; CA 143; CANR 83, 126,
171, 201; CN 6, 7; DLB 207
Self, William
See Self, Will
Self, William Woodward
See Self, Will
Selzer, Richard 1928- .... **CLC 74**
See also CA 65-68; CANR 14, 106, 204
Sembene, Ousmane
See Ousmane, Sembene
Senancour, Etienne Pivert de
1770-1846 .... **NCLC 16**
See also DLB 119; GFL 1789 to the Present
Sender, Ramon (Jose) 1902-1982 ...... **CLC 8;**
HLC 2; TCLC 136
See also CA 5-8R; 105; CANR 8; DAM
MULT; DLB 322; EWL 3; HW 1; MTCW
1; RGWL 2, 3
Seneca, Lucius Annaeus c. 4B.C.-c.
65 .... **CMLC 6, 107; DC 5**
See also AW 2; CDWLB 1; DAM DRAM;
DLB 211; RGWL 2, 3; TWA; WLIT 8
Seneca the Younger
See Seneca, Lucius Annaeus
Senghor, Leopold Sedar
1906-2001 .. **BLC 1:3; CLC 54, 130; PC**
25
See also AFW; BW 2; CA 116; 125; 203;
CANR 47, 74, 134; CWW 2; DAM
MULT, POET; DNFS 2; EWL 3; GFL
1789 to the Present; MTCW 1, 2; MTFW
2005; TWA
Senior, Olive (Marjorie) 1941- .... **SSC 78**
See also BW 3; CA 154; CANR 86, 126;
CN 6; CP 6, 7; CWP; DLB 157; EWL 3;
RGSF 2
Senna, Danzy 1970- .... **CLC 119**
See also CA 169; CANR 130, 184
Sepheriades, Georgios
See Seferis, George
Serling, (Edward) Rod(man)
1924-1975 .... **CLC 30**
See also AAYA 14; AITN 1; CA 162; 57-
60; DLB 26; SFW 4
Serna, Ramon Gomez de la
See Gomez de la Serna, Ramon
Serpieres
See Guillevic, (Eugene)
Service, Robert
See Service, Robert W.
Service, Robert W. 1874(?)-1958 .... **PC 70;**
TCLC 15; WLC 5
See also BYA 4; CA 115; 140; CANR 84;
DA; DAB; DAC; DAM MST, POET;
DLB 92; PFS 10; RGEL 2; SATA 20
Service, Robert William
See Service, Robert W.
Servius c. 370-c. 431 .... **CMLC 120**
Seth, Vikram 1952- .... **CLC 43, 90, 277**
See also BRWS 10; CA 121; 127; CANR
50, 74, 131; CN 6, 7; CP 5, 6, 7; DA3;
DAM MULT; DLB 120, 271, 282, 323;
EWL 3; INT CA-127; MTCW 2; MTFW
2005; WWE 1

Setien, Miguel Delibes
See Delibes Setien, Miguel
Seton, Cynthia Propper 1926-1982 .. **CLC 27**
See also CA 5-8R; 108; CANR 7
Seton, Ernest (Evan) Thompson
1860-1946 .... **TCLC 31**
See also ANW; BYA 3; CA 109; 204; CLR
59; DLB 92; DLBD 13; JRDA; SATA 18
Seton-Thompson, Ernest
See Seton, Ernest (Evan) Thompson
Settle, Mary Lee 1918-2005 .... **CLC 19, 61,**
273
See also BPFB 3; CA 89-92; 243; CAAS 1;
CANR 44, 87, 126, 182; CN 6, 7; CSW;
DLB 6; INT CA-89-92
Seuphor, Michel
See Arp, Jean
Sevigne, Marie (de Rabutin-Chantal)
1626-1696 .... **LC 11, 144**
See also DLB 268; GFL Beginnings to
1789; TWA
Sevigne, Marie de Rabutin Chantal
See Sevigne, Marie (de Rabutin-Chantal)
Sewall, Samuel 1652-1730 .... **LC 38**
See also DLB 24; RGAL 4
Sexton, Anne 1928-1974 .. **CLC 2, 4, 6, 8, 10,**
15, 53, 123; PC 2, 79; WLC 5
See also AMWS 2; CA 1-4R; 53-56; CABS
2; CANR 3, 36; CDALB 1941-1968; CP
1, 2; DA; DA3; DAB; DAC; DAM MST,
POET; DLB 5, 169; EWL 3; EXPP; FL
1:6; FW; MAL 5; MBL; MTCW 1, 2;
MTFW 2005; PAB; PFS 4, 14, 30; RGAL
4; RGHL; SATA 10; TUS
Sexton, Anne Harvey
See Sexton, Anne
Shaara, Jeff 1952- .... **CLC 119**
See also AAYA 70; CA 163; CANR 109,
172; CN 7; MTFW 2005
Shaara, Michael 1929-1988 .... **CLC 15**
See also AAYA 71; AITN 1; BPFB 3; CA
102; 125; CANR 52, 85; DAM POP;
DLBY 1983; MTFW 2005; NFS 26
Shackleton, C.C.
See Aldiss, Brian W.
Shacochis, Bob
See Shacochis, Robert G.
Shacochis, Robert G. 1951- .... **CLC 39**
See also CA 119; 124; CANR 100; INT CA-
124
Shadwell, Thomas 1641(?)-1692 .... **LC 114**
See also DLB 80; IDTP; RGEL 2
Shaffer, Anthony 1926-2001 .... **CLC 19**
See also CA 110; 116; 200; CBD; CD 5, 6;
DAM DRAM; DFS 13; DLB 13
Shaffer, Anthony Joshua
See Shaffer, Anthony
Shaffer, Peter 1926- ... **CLC 5, 14, 18, 37, 60,**
291; DC 7
See also BRWS 1; CA 25-28R; CANR 25,
47, 74, 118; CBD; CD 5, 6; CDBLB 1960
to Present; DA3; DAB; DAM DRAM,
MST; DFS 5, 13; DLB 13, 233; EWL 3;
MTCW 1, 2; MTFW 2005; RGEL 2; TEA
Shakespeare, William 1564-1616 . **PC 84, 89,**
98, 101; WLC 5
See also AAYA 35; BRW 1; BRWR 3; CD-
BLB Before 1660; DA; DA3; DAB;
DAC; DAM DRAM, MST, POET; DFS
20, 21; DLB 62, 172, 263; EXPP; LAIT
1; LATS 1:1; LMFS 1; PAB; PFS 1, 2, 3,
4, 5, 8, 9, 35; RGEL 2; TEA; WLIT 3;
WP; WS; WYA
Shakey, Bernard
See Young, Neil
Shalamov, Varlam (Tikhonovich)
1907-1982 .... **CLC 18**
See also CA 129; 105; DLB 302; RGSF 2

Snodgrass, W. D. 1926-2009 .... **CLC 2, 6, 10, 18, 68; PC 74**
See also AMWS 6; CA 1-4R; 282; CANR 6, 36, 65, 85, 185; CP 1, 2, 3, 4, 5, 6, 7; DAM POET; DLB 5; MAL 5; MTCW 1, 2; MTFW 2005; PFS 29; RGAL 4; TCLE 1:2

Snodgrass, W. de Witt
See Snodgrass, W. D.

Snodgrass, William de Witt
See Snodgrass, W. D.

Snodgrass, William De Witt
See Snodgrass, W. D.

Snorri Sturluson 1179-1241 .... **CMLC 56**
See also RGWL 2, 3

Snow, C(harles) P(ercy) 1905-1980 ... **CLC 1, 4, 6, 9, 13, 19**
See also BRW 7; CA 5-8R; 101; CANR 28; CDBLB 1945-1960; CN 1, 2; DAM NOV; DLB 15, 77; DLBD 17; EWL 3; MTCW 1, 2; MTFW 2005; RGEL 2; TEA

Snow, Frances Compton
See Adams, Henry

Snyder, Gary 1930- . **CLC 1, 2, 5, 9, 32, 120; PC 21**
See also AAYA 72; AMWS 8; ANW; BG 1:3; CA 17-20R; CANR 30, 60, 125; CP 1, 2, 3, 4, 5, 6, 7; DA3; DAM POET; DLB 5, 16, 165, 212, 237, 275, 342; EWL 3; MAL 5; MTCW 2; MTFW 2005; PFS 9, 19; RGAL 4; WP

Snyder, Gary Sherman
See Snyder, Gary

Snyder, Zilpha Keatley 1927- .... **CLC 17**
See also AAYA 15; BYA 1; CA 9-12R; 252; CAAE 252; CANR 38, 202; CLR 31, 121; JRDA; MAICYA 1, 2; SAAS 2; SATA 1, 28, 75, 110, 163; SATA-Essay 112, 163; YAW

Soares, Bernardo
See Pessoa, Fernando

Sobh, A.
See Shamlu, Ahmad

Sobh, Alef
See Shamlu, Ahmad

Sobol, Joshua 1939- .... **CLC 60**
See also CA 200; CWW 2; RGHL

Sobol, Yehoshua 1939-
See Sobol, Joshua

Socrates 470B.C.-399B.C. .... **CMLC 27**

Soderberg, Hjalmar 1869-1941 ...... **TCLC 39**
See also DLB 259; EWL 3; RGSF 2

Soderbergh, Steven 1963- .... **CLC 154**
See also AAYA 43; CA 243

Soderbergh, Steven Andrew
See Soderbergh, Steven

Sodergran, Edith 1892-1923 .... **TCLC 31**
See also CA 202; DLB 259; EW 11; EWL 3; RGWL 2, 3

Soedergran, Edith Irene
See Sodergran, Edith

Softly, Edgar
See Lovecraft, H. P.

Softly, Edward
See Lovecraft, H. P.

Sokolov, Alexander V. 1943- .... **CLC 59**
See also CA 73-76; CWW 2; DLB 285; EWL 3; RGWL 2, 3

Sokolov, Alexander Vsevolodovich
See Sokolov, Alexander V.

Sokolov, Raymond 1941- .... **CLC 7**
See also CA 85-88

Sokolov, Sasha
See Sokolov, Alexander V.

Solo, Jay
See Ellison, Harlan

Sologub, Fedor
See Teternikov, Fyodor Kuzmich

Sologub, Feodor
See Teternikov, Fyodor Kuzmich

Sologub, Fyodor
See Teternikov, Fyodor Kuzmich

Solomons, Ikey Esquir
See Thackeray, William Makepeace

Solomos, Dionysios 1798-1857 .... **NCLC 15**

Solwoska, Mara
See French, Marilyn

Solzhenitsyn, Aleksandr 1918-2008 ... **CLC 1, 2, 4, 7, 9, 10, 18, 26, 34, 78, 134, 235; SSC 32, 105; WLC 5**
See also AAYA 49; AITN 1; BPFB 3; CA 69-72; CANR 40, 65, 116; CWW 2; DA; DA3; DAB; DAC; DAM MST, NOV; DLB 302, 332; EW 13; EWL 3; EXPS; LAIT 4; MTCW 1, 2; MTFW 2005; NFS 6; RGSF 2; RGWL 2, 3; SSFS 9; TWA

Solzhenitsyn, Aleksandr I.
See Solzhenitsyn, Aleksandr

Solzhenitsyn, Aleksandr Isayevich
See Solzhenitsyn, Aleksandr

Somers, Jane
See Lessing, Doris

Somerville, Edith Oenone
1858-1949 .... **SSC 56; TCLC 51**
See also CA 196; DLB 135; RGEL 2; RGSF 2

Somerville & Ross
See Martin, Violet Florence; Somerville, Edith Oenone

Sommer, Scott 1951- .... **CLC 25**
See also CA 106

Sommers, Christina Hoff 1950- ...... **CLC 197**
See also CA 153; CANR 95

Sondheim, Stephen 1930- .. **CLC 30, 39, 147; DC 22**
See also AAYA 11, 66; CA 103; CANR 47, 67, 125; DAM DRAM; DFS 25, 27; LAIT 4

Sondheim, Stephen Joshua
See Sondheim, Stephen

Sone, Monica 1919- .... **AAL**
See also DLB 312

Song, Cathy 1955- .... **AAL; PC 21**
See also CA 154; CANR 118; CWP; DLB 169, 312; EXPP; FW; PFS 5

Sontag, Susan 1933-2004 ... **CLC 1, 2, 10, 13, 31, 105, 195, 277**
See also AMWS 3; CA 17-20R; 234; CANR 25, 51, 74, 97, 184; CN 1, 2, 3, 4, 5, 6, 7; CPW; DA3; DAM POP; DLB 2, 67; EWL 3; MAL 5; MBL; MTCW 1, 2; MTFW 2005; RGAL 4; RHW; SSFS 10

Sophocles 496(?)B.C.-406(?)B.C. .... **CMLC 2, 47, 51, 86; DC 1; WLCS**
See also AW 1; CDWLB 1; DA; DA3; DAB; DAC; DAM DRAM, MST; DFS 1, 4, 8, 24; DLB 176; LAIT 1; LATS 1:1; LMFS 1; RGWL 2, 3; TWA; WLIT 8

Sordello 1189-1269 .... **CMLC 15**

Sorel, Georges 1847-1922 .... **TCLC 91**
See also CA 118; 188

Sorel, Julia
See Drexler, Rosalyn

Sorokin, Vladimir **CLC 59**
See also CA 258; DLB 285

Sorokin, Vladimir Georgievich
See Sorokin, Vladimir

Sorrentino, Gilbert 1929-2006 .... **CLC 3, 7, 14, 22, 40, 247**
See also CA 77-80; 250; CANR 14, 33, 115, 157; CN 3, 4, 5, 6, 7; CP 1, 2, 3, 4, 5, 6, 7; DLB 5, 173; DLBY 1980; INT CANR-14

Soseki
See Natsume, Soseki

Soto, Gary 1952- ... **CLC 32, 80; HLC 2; PC 28**
See also AAYA 10, 37; BYA 11; CA 119; 125; CANR 50, 74, 107, 157; CLR 38; CP 4, 5, 6, 7; DAM MULT; DFS 26; DLB 82; EWL 3; EXPP; HW 1, 2; INT CA-125; JRDA; LLW; MAICYA 2; MAIC-YAS 1; MAL 5; MTCW 2; MTFW 2005; PFS 7, 30; RGAL 4; SATA 80, 120, 174; WYA; YAW

Soupault, Philippe 1897-1990 .... **CLC 68**
See also CA 116; 147; 131; EWL 3; GFL 1789 to the Present; LMFS 2

Souster, (Holmes) Raymond 1921- .... **CLC 5, 14**
See also CA 13-16R; CAAS 14; CANR 13, 29, 53; CP 1, 2, 3, 4, 5, 6, 7; DA3; DAC; DAM POET; DLB 88; RGEL 2; SATA 63

Southern, Terry 1924(?)-1995 .... **CLC 7**
See also AMWS 11; BPFB 3; CA 1-4R; 150; CANR 1, 55, 107; CN 1, 2, 3, 4, 5, 6; DLB 2; IDFW 3, 4

Southerne, Thomas 1660-1746 .... **LC 99**
See also DLB 80; RGEL 2

Southey, Robert 1774-1843 .... **NCLC 8, 97**
See also BRW 4; DLB 93, 107, 142; RGEL 2; SATA 54

Southwell, Robert 1561(?)-1595 .... **LC 108**
See also DLB 167; RGEL 2; TEA

Southworth, Emma Dorothy Eliza Nevitte
1819-1899 .... **NCLC 26**
See also DLB 239

Souza, Ernest
See Scott, Evelyn

Soyinka, Wole 1934- .. **BLC 1:3, 2:3; CLC 3, 5, 14, 36, 44, 179; DC 2; WLC 5**
See also AFW; BW 2, 3; CA 13-16R; CANR 27, 39, 82, 136; CD 5, 6; CDWLB 3; CN 6, 7; CP 1, 2, 3, 4, 5, 6 ,7; DA; DA3; DAB; DAC; DAM DRAM, MST, MULT; DFS 10, 26; DLB 125, 332; EWL 3; MTCW 1, 2; MTFW 2005; PFS 27; RGEL 2; TWA; WLIT 2; WWE 1

Spackman, W(illiam) M(ode)
1905-1990 .... **CLC 46**
See also CA 81-84; 132

Spacks, Barry (Bernard) 1931- .... **CLC 14**
See also CA 154; CANR 33, 109; CP 3, 4, 5, 6, 7; DLB 105

Spanidou, Irini 1946- .... **CLC 44**
See also CA 185; CANR 179

Spark, Muriel 1918-2006 .... **CLC 2, 3, 5, 8, 13, 18, 40, 94, 242; PC 72; SSC 10, 115**
See also BRWS 1; CA 5-8R; 251; CANR 12, 36, 76, 89, 131; CDBLB 1945-1960; CN 1, 2, 3, 4, 5, 6, 7; CP 1, 2, 3, 4, 5, 6, 7; DA3; DAB; DAC; DAM MST, NOV; DLB 15, 139; EWL 3; FW; INT CANR-12; LAIT 4; MTCW 1, 2; MTFW 2005; NFS 22; RGEL 2; SSFS 28; TEA; WLIT 4; YAW

Spark, Muriel Sarah
See Spark, Muriel

Spaulding, Douglas
See Bradbury, Ray

Spaulding, Leonard
See Bradbury, Ray

Speght, Rachel 1597-c. 1630 .... **LC 97**
See also DLB 126

Spence, J. A. D.
See Eliot, T. S.

Spencer, Anne 1882-1975 ...... **HR 1:3; PC 77**
See also BW 2; CA 161; DLB 51, 54

Spencer, Elizabeth 1921- ...... **CLC 22; SSC 57**
See also CA 13-16R; CANR 32, 65, 87; CN 1, 2, 3, 4, 5, 6, 7; CSW; DLB 6, 218; EWL 3; MTCW 1; RGAL 4; SATA 14

Spencer, Leonard G.
See Silverberg, Robert

Steiner, Rudolf 1861-1925 .... **TCLC 13**
See also CA 107

Stendhal 1783-1842 .... **NCLC 23, 46, 178;
SSC 27; WLC 5**
See also DA; DA3; DAB; DAC; DAM
MST, NOV; DLB 119; EW 5; GFL 1789
to the Present; RGWL 2, 3; TWA

Stephen, Adeline Virginia
See Woolf, Virginia

Stephen, Sir Leslie 1832-1904 .... **TCLC 23**
See also BRW 5; CA 123; DLB 57, 144,
190

Stephen, Sir Leslie
See Stephen, Sir Leslie

Stephen, Virginia
See Woolf, Virginia

Stephens, James 1882(?)-1950 .... **SSC 50;
TCLC 4**
See also CA 104; 192; DLB 19, 153, 162;
EWL 3; FANT; RGEL 2; SUFW

Stephens, Reed
See Donaldson, Stephen R.

Stephenson, Neal 1959- .... **CLC 220**
See also AAYA 38; CA 122; CANR 88, 138,
195; CN 7; MTFW 2005; SFW 4

Steptoe, Lydia
See Barnes, Djuna

Sterchi, Beat 1949- .... **CLC 65**
See also CA 203

Sterling, Brett
See Bradbury, Ray; Hamilton, Edmond

Sterling, Bruce 1954- .... **CLC 72**
See also AAYA 78; CA 119; CANR 44, 135,
184; CN 7; MTFW 2005; SCFW 2; SFW
4

Sterling, George 1869-1926 .... **TCLC 20**
See also CA 117; 165; DLB 54

Stern, Gerald 1925- .... **CLC 40, 100**
See also AMWS 9; CA 81-84; CANR 28,
94; CP 3, 4, 5, 6, 7; DLB 105; PFS 26;
RGAL 4

Stern, Richard (Gustave) 1928- ... **CLC 4, 39**
See also CA 1-4R; CANR 1, 25, 52, 120;
CN 1, 2, 3, 4, 5, 6, 7; DLB 218; DLBY
1987; INT CANR-25

Sternberg, Josef von 1894-1969 .... **CLC 20**
See also CA 81-84

Sterne, Laurence 1713-1768 .. **LC 2, 48, 156;
WLC 5**
See also BRW 3; BRWC 1; CDBLB 1660-
1789; DA; DAB; DAC; DAM MST, NOV;
DLB 39; RGEL 2; TEA

Sternheim, (William Adolf) Carl
1878-1942 .... **TCLC 8, 223**
See also CA 105; 193; DLB 56, 118; EWL
3; IDTP; RGWL 2, 3

Stetson, Charlotte Perkins
See Gilman, Charlotte Perkins

Stevens, Margaret Dean
See Aldrich, Bess Streeter

Stevens, Mark 1951- .... **CLC 34**
See also CA 122

Stevens, R. L.
See Hoch, Edward D.

Stevens, Wallace 1879-1955 .... **PC 6, 110;
TCLC 3, 12, 45; WLC 5**
See also AMW; AMWR 1; CA 104; 124;
CANR 181; CDALB 1929-1941; DA;
DA3; DAB; DAC; DAM MST, POET;
DLB 54, 342; EWL 3; EXPP; MAL 5;
MTCW 1, 2; PAB; PFS 13, 16, 35; RGAL
4; TUS; WP

Stevenson, Anne (Katharine) 1933- .. **CLC 7,
33**
See also BRWS 6; CA 17-20R; CAAS 9;
CANR 9, 33, 123; CP 3, 4, 5, 6, 7; CWP;
DLB 40; MTCW 1; RHW

Stevenson, Robert Louis
1850-1894 ...... **NCLC 5, 14, 63, 193; PC
84; SSC 11, 51, 126; WLC 5**
See also AAYA 24; BPFB 3; BRW 5;
BRWC 1; BRWR 1; BYA 1, 2, 4, 13; CD-
BLB 1890-1914; CLR 10, 11, 107; DA;
DA3; DAB; DAC; DAM MST, NOV;
DLB 18, 57, 141, 156, 174; DLBD 13;
GL 3; HGG; JRDA; LAIT 1, 3; MAICYA
1, 2; NFS 11, 20, 33; RGEL 2; RGSF 2;
SATA 100; SUFW; TEA; WCH; WLIT 4;
WYA; YABC 2; YAW

Stevenson, Robert Louis Balfour
See Stevenson, Robert Louis

Stewart, J(ohn) I(nnes) M(ackintosh)
1906-1994 .... **CLC 7, 14, 32**
See also CA 85-88; 147; CAAS 3; CANR
47; CMW 4; CN 1, 2, 3, 4, 5; DLB 276;
MSW; MTCW 1, 2

Stewart, Mary (Florence Elinor)
1916- .... **CLC 7, 35, 117**
See also AAYA 29, 73; BPFB 3; CA 1-4R;
CANR 1, 59, 130; CMW 4; CPW; DAB;
FANT; RHW; SATA 12; YAW

Stewart, Mary Rainbow
See Stewart, Mary (Florence Elinor)

Stewart, Will
See Williamson, John Stewart

Stifle, June
See Campbell, Maria

Stifter, Adalbert 1805-1868 ... **NCLC 41, 198;
SSC 28**
See also CDWLB 2; DLB 133; RGSF 2;
RGWL 2, 3

Still, James 1906-2001 .... **CLC 49**
See also CA 65-68; 195; CAAS 17; CANR
10, 26; CSW; DLB 9; DLBY 01; SATA
29; SATA-Obit 127

Sting 1951- .... **CLC 26**
See also CA 167

Stirling, Arthur
See Sinclair, Upton

Stitt, Milan 1941-2009 .... **CLC 29**
See also CA 69-72; 284

Stitt, Milan William
See Stitt, Milan

Stockton, Francis Richard
1834-1902 .... **TCLC 47**
See also AAYA 68; BYA 4, 13; CA 108;
137; DLB 42, 74; DLBD 13; EXPS; MAI-
CYA 1, 2; SATA 44; SATA-Brief 32; SFW
4; SSFS 3; SUFW; WCH

Stockton, Frank R.
See Stockton, Francis Richard

Stoddard, Charles
See Kuttner, Henry

Stoker, Abraham
See Stoker, Bram

Stoker, Bram 1847-1912 ... **SSC 62; TCLC 8,
144; WLC 6**
See also AAYA 23; BPFB 3; BRWS 3; BYA
5; CA 105; 150; CDBLB 1890-1914; DA;
DA3; DAB; DAC; DAM MST, NOV;
DLB 304; GL 3; HGG; LATS 1:1; MTFW
2005; NFS 18; RGEL 2; SATA 29; SUFW;
TEA; WLIT 4

Stolz, Mary 1920-2006 .... **CLC 12**
See also AAYA 8, 73; AITN 1; CA 5-8R;
255; CANR 13, 41, 112; JRDA; MAICYA
1, 2; SAAS 3; SATA 10, 71, 133; SATA-
Obit 180; YAW

Stolz, Mary Slattery
See Stolz, Mary

Stone, Irving 1903-1989 .... **CLC 7**
See also AITN 1; BPFB 3; CA 1-4R; 129;
CAAS 3; CANR 1, 23; CN 1, 2, 3, 4;
CPW; DA3; DAM POP; INT CANR-23;
MTCW 1, 2; MTFW 2005; RHW; SATA
3; SATA-Obit 64

Stone, Oliver 1946- .... **CLC 73**
See also AAYA 15, 64; CA 110; CANR 55,
125

Stone, Oliver William
See Stone, Oliver

Stone, Robert 1937- .... **CLC 5, 23, 42, 175**
See also AMWS 5; BPFB 3; CA 85-88;
CANR 23, 66, 95, 173; CN 4, 5, 6, 7;
DLB 152; EWL 3; INT CANR-23; MAL
5; MTCW 1; MTFW 2005

Stone, Robert Anthony
See Stone, Robert

Stone, Ruth 1915- .... **PC 53**
See also CA 45-48; CANR 2, 91; CP 5, 6,
7; CSW; DLB 105; PFS 19

Stone, Zachary
See Follett, Ken

Stoppard, Tom 1937- ... **CLC 1, 3, 4, 5, 8, 15,
29, 34, 63, 91; DC 6, 30; WLC 6**
See also AAYA 63; BRWC 1; BRWR 2;
BRWS 1; CA 81-84; CANR 39, 67, 125;
CBD; CD 5, 6; CDBLB 1960 to Present;
DA; DA3; DAB; DAC; DAM DRAM,
MST; DFS 2, 5, 8, 11, 13, 16; DLB 13,
233; DLBY 1985; EWL 3; LATS 1:2;
LNFS 3; MTCW 1, 2; MTFW 2005;
RGEL 2; TEA; WLIT 4

Storey, David (Malcolm) 1933- . **CLC 2, 4, 5,
8**
See also BRWS 1; CA 81-84; CANR 36;
CBD; CD 5, 6; CN 1, 2, 3, 4, 5, 6; DAM
DRAM; DLB 13, 14, 207, 245, 326; EWL
3; MTCW 1; RGEL 2

Storm, Hyemeyohsts 1935- ... **CLC 3; NNAL**
See also CA 81-84; CANR 45; DAM MULT

Storm, (Hans) Theodor (Woldsen)
1817-1888 ... **NCLC 1, 195; SSC 27, 106**
See also CDWLB 2; DLB 129; EW; RGSF
2; RGWL 2, 3

Storni, Alfonsina 1892-1938 . **HLC 2; PC 33;
TCLC 5**
See also CA 104; 131; DAM MULT; DLB
283; HW 1; LAW

Stoughton, William 1631-1701 .... **LC 38**
See also DLB 24

Stout, Rex (Todhunter) 1886-1975 ..... **CLC 3**
See also AAYA 79; AITN 2; BPFB 3; CA
61-64; CANR 71; CMW 4; CN 2; DLB
306; MSW; RGAL 4

Stow, (Julian) Randolph 1935- ... **CLC 23, 48**
See also CA 13-16R; CANR 33; CN 1, 2,
3, 4, 5, 6, 7; CP 1, 2, 3, 4; DLB 260;
MTCW 1; RGEL 2

Stowe, Harriet Beecher 1811-1896 . **NCLC 3,
50, 133, 195; WLC 6**
See also AAYA 53; AMWS 1; CDALB
1865-1917; CLR 131; DA; DA3; DAB;
DAC; DAM MST, NOV; DLB 1, 12, 42,
74, 189, 239, 243; EXPN; FL 1:3; JRDA;
LAIT 2; MAICYA 1, 2; NFS 6; RGAL 4;
TUS; YABC 1

Stowe, Harriet Elizabeth Beecher
See Stowe, Harriet Beecher

Strabo c. 63B.C.-c. 21 .... **CMLC 37, 121**
See also DLB 176

Strachey, (Giles) Lytton
1880-1932 .... **TCLC 12**
See also BRWS 2; CA 110; 178; DLB 149;
DLBD 10; EWL 3; MTCW 2; NCFS 4

Stramm, August 1874-1915 .... **PC 50**
See also CA 195; EWL 3

Strand, Mark 1934- ... **CLC 6, 18, 41, 71; PC
63**
See also AMWS 4; CA 21-24R; CANR 40,
65, 100; CP 1, 2, 3, 4, 5, 6, 7; DAM
POET; DLB 5; EWL 3; MAL 5; PAB;
PFS 9, 18; RGAL 4; SATA 41; TCLE 1:2

Swenson, May 1919-1989 ...... **CLC 4, 14, 61, 106; PC 14**
See also AMWS 4; CA 5-8R; 130; CANR 36, 61, 131; CP 1, 2, 3, 4; DA; DAB; DAC; DAM MST, POET; DLB 5; EXPP; GLL 2; MAL 5; MTCW 1, 2; MTFW 2005; PFS 16, 30; SATA 15; WP

Swift, Augustus
See Lovecraft, H. P.

Swift, Graham 1949- .... **CLC 41, 88, 233**
See also BRWC 2; BRWS 5; CA 117; 122; CANR 46, 71, 128, 181; CN 4, 5, 6, 7; DLB 194, 326; MTCW 2; MTFW 2005; NFS 18; RGSF 2

Swift, Jonathan 1667-1745 ..... **LC 1, 42, 101; PC 9; WLC 6**
See also AAYA 41; BRW 3; BRWC 1; BRWR 1; BYA 5, 14; CDBLB 1660-1789; CLR 53; DA; DA3; DAB; DAC; DAM MST, NOV, POET; DLB 39, 95, 101; EXPN; LAIT 1; NFS 6; PFS 27; RGEL 2; SATA 19; TEA; WCH; WLIT 3

Swinburne, Algernon Charles 1837-1909 ... **PC 24; TCLC 8, 36; WLC 6**
See also BRW 5; CA 105; 140; CDBLB 1832-1890; DA; DA3; DAB; DAC; DAM MST, POET; DLB 35, 57; PAB; RGEL 2; TEA

Swinfen, Ann CLC 34
See also CA 202

Swinnerton, Frank (Arthur) 1884-1982 .... **CLC 31**
See also CA 202; 108; CN 1, 2, 3; DLB 34

Swinnerton, Frank Arthur 1884-1982 .... **CLC 31**
See also CA 108; DLB 34

Swithen, John
See King, Stephen

Sylvia
See Ashton-Warner, Sylvia (Constance)

Symmes, Robert Edward
See Duncan, Robert

Symonds, John Addington 1840-1893 .... **NCLC 34**
See also BRWS 14; DLB 57, 144

Symons, Arthur 1865-1945 .... **TCLC 11**
See also BRWS 14; CA 107; 189; DLB 19, 57, 149; RGEL 2

Symons, Julian (Gustave) 1912-1994 .... **CLC 2, 14, 32**
See also CA 49-52; 147; CAAS 3; CANR 3, 33, 59; CMW 4; CN 1, 2, 3, 4, 5; CP 1, 3, 4; DLB 87, 155; DLBY 1992; MSW; MTCW 1

Synge, Edmund John Millington
See Synge, John Millington

Synge, J. M.
See Synge, John Millington

Synge, John Millington 1871-1909 ...... **DC 2; TCLC 6, 37**
See also BRW 6; BRWR 1; CA 104; 141; CDBLB 1890-1914; DAM DRAM; DFS 18; DLB 10, 19; EWL 3; RGEL 2; TEA; WLIT 4

Syruc, J.
See Milosz, Czeslaw

Szirtes, George 1948- .... **CLC 46; PC 51**
See also CA 109; CANR 27, 61, 117; CP 4, 5, 6, 7

Szymborska, Wislawa 1923- ... **CLC 99, 190; PC 44**
See also AAYA 76; CA 154; CANR 91, 133, 181; CDWLB 4; CWP; CWW 2; DA3; DLB 232, 332; DLBY 1996; EWL 3; MTCW 2; MTFW 2005; PFS 15, 27, 31, 34; RGHL; RGWL 3

T. O., Nik
See Annensky, Innokenty (Fyodorovich)

Tabori, George 1914-2007 .... **CLC 19**
See also CA 49-52; 262; CANR 4, 69; CBD; CD 5, 6; DLB 245; RGHL

Tacitus c. 55-c. 117 .... **CMLC 56**
See also AW 2; CDWLB 1; DLB 211; RGWL 2, 3; WLIT 8

Tadjo, Veronique 1955- .... **BLC 2:3**
See also EWL 3

Tagore, Rabindranath 1861-1941 .... **PC 8; SSC 48; TCLC 3, 53**
See also CA 104; 120; DA3; DAM DRAM, POET; DFS 26; DLB 323, 332; EWL 3; MTCW 1, 2; MTFW 2005; PFS 18; RGEL 2; RGSF 2; RGWL 2, 3; TWA

Taine, Hippolyte Adolphe 1828-1893 .... **NCLC 15**
See also EW 7; GFL 1789 to the Present

Talayesva, Don C. 1890-(?) .... **NNAL**

Talese, Gay 1932- .... **CLC 37, 232**
See also AITN 1; AMWS 17; CA 1-4R; CANR 9, 58, 137, 177; DLB 185; INT CANR-9; MTCW 1, 2; MTFW 2005

Tallent, Elizabeth 1954- .... **CLC 45**
See also CA 117; CANR 72; DLB 130

Tallmountain, Mary 1918-1997 .... **NNAL**
See also CA 146; 161; DLB 193

Tally, Ted 1952- .... **CLC 42**
See also CA 120; 124; CAD; CANR 125; CD 5, 6; INT CA-124

Talvik, Heiti 1904-1947 .... **TCLC 87**
See also EWL 3

Tamayo y Baus, Manuel 1829-1898 .... **NCLC 1**

Tammsaare, A(nton) H(ansen) 1878-1940 .... **TCLC 27**
See also CA 164; CDWLB 4; DLB 220; EWL 3

Tam'si, Tchicaya U
See Tchicaya, Gerald Felix

Tan, Amy 1952- ..... **AAL; CLC 59, 120, 151, 257**
See also AAYA 9, 48; AMWS 10; BEST 89:3; BPFB 3; CA 136; CANR 54, 105, 132; CDALBS; CN 6, 7; CPW 1; DA3; DAM MULT, NOV, POP; DLB 173, 312; EXPN; FL 1:6; FW; LAIT 3, 5; MAL 5; MTCW 2; MTFW 2005; NFS 1, 13, 16, 31; RGAL 4; SATA 75; SSFS 9; YAW

Tan, Amy Ruth
See Tan, Amy

Tandem, Carl Felix
See Spitteler, Carl

Tandem, Felix
See Spitteler, Carl

Tania B.
See Blixen, Karen

Tanizaki, Jun'ichiro 1886-1965 ... **CLC 8, 14, 28; SSC 21**
See also CA 93-96; 25-28R; DLB 180; EWL 3; MJW; MTCW 2; MTFW 2005; RGSF 2; RGWL 2

Tanizaki Jun'ichiro
See Tanizaki, Jun'ichiro

Tannen, Deborah 1945- .... **CLC 206**
See also CA 118; CANR 95

Tannen, Deborah Frances
See Tannen, Deborah

Tanner, William
See Amis, Kingsley

Tante, Dilly
See Kunitz, Stanley

Tao Lao
See Storni, Alfonsina

Tapahonso, Luci 1953- .... **NNAL; PC 65**
See also CA 145; CANR 72, 127; DLB 175

Tarantino, Quentin 1963- .... **CLC 125, 230**
See also AAYA 58; CA 171; CANR 125

Tarantino, Quentin Jerome
See Tarantino, Quentin

Tarassoff, Lev
See Troyat, Henri

Tarbell, Ida 1857-1944 .... **TCLC 40**
See also CA 122; 181; DLB 47

Tarbell, Ida Minerva
See Tarbell, Ida

Tarchetti, Ugo 1839(?)-1869 .... **SSC 119**

Tardieu d'Esclavelles, Louise-Florence-Petronille
See Epinay, Louise d'

Tarkington, (Newton) Booth 1869-1946 .... **TCLC 9**
See also BPFB 3; BYA 3; CA 110; 143; CWRI 5; DLB 9, 102; MAL 5; MTCW 2; NFS 34; RGAL 4; SATA 17

Tarkovskii, Andrei Arsen'evich
See Tarkovsky, Andrei (Arsenyevich)

Tarkovsky, Andrei (Arsenyevich) 1932-1986 .... **CLC 75**
See also CA 127

Tartt, Donna 1964(?)- .... **CLC 76**
See also AAYA 56; CA 142; CANR 135; LNFS 2; MTFW 2005

Tasso, Torquato 1544-1595 .... **LC 5, 94**
See also EFS 2; EW 2; RGWL 2, 3; WLIT 7

Tate, (John Orley) Allen 1899-1979 .. **CLC 2, 4, 6, 9, 11, 14, 24; PC 50**
See also AMW; CA 5-8R; 85-88; CANR 32, 108; CN 1, 2; CP 1, 2; DLB 4, 45, 63; DLBD 17; EWL 3; MAL 5; MTCW 1, 2; MTFW 2005; RGAL 4; RHW

Tate, Ellalice
See Hibbert, Eleanor Alice Burford

Tate, James (Vincent) 1943- ..... **CLC 2, 6, 25**
See also CA 21-24R; CANR 29, 57, 114; CP 1, 2, 3, 4, 5, 6, 7; DLB 5, 169; EWL 3; PFS 10, 15; RGAL 4; WP

Tate, Nahum 1652(?)-1715 .... **LC 109**
See also DLB 80; RGEL 2

Tauler, Johannes c. 1300-1361 ...... **CMLC 37**
See also DLB 179; LMFS 1

Tavel, Ronald 1936-2009 .... **CLC 6**
See also CA 21-24R; 284; CAD; CANR 33; CD 5, 6

Taviani, Paolo 1931- .... **CLC 70**
See also CA 153

Taylor, Bayard 1825-1878 .... **NCLC 89**
See also DLB 3, 189, 250, 254; RGAL 4

Taylor, C(ecil) P(hilip) 1929-1981 .... **CLC 27**
See also CA 25-28R; 105; CANR 47; CBD

Taylor, Edward 1642(?)-1729 ..... **LC 11, 163; PC 63**
See also AMW; DA; DAB; DAC; DAM MST, POET; DLB 24; EXPP; PFS 31; RGAL 4; TUS

Taylor, Eleanor Ross 1920- .... **CLC 5**
See also CA 81-84; CANR 70

Taylor, Elizabeth 1912-1975 .... **CLC 2, 4, 29; SSC 100**
See also CA 13-16R; CANR 9, 70; CN 1, 2; DLB 139; MTCW 1; RGEL 2; SATA 13

Taylor, Frederick Winslow 1856-1915 .... **TCLC 76**
See also CA 188

Taylor, Henry 1942- .... **CLC 44**
See also CA 33-36R; CAAS 7; CANR 31, 178; CP 6, 7; DLB 5; PFS 10

Taylor, Henry Splawn
See Taylor, Henry

Taylor, Kamala
See Markandaya, Kamala

Taylor, Mildred D. 1943- .... **CLC 21**
See also AAYA 10, 47; BW 1; BYA 3, 8; CA 85-88; CANR 25, 115, 136; CLR 9, 59, 90, 144; CSW; DLB 52; JRDA; LAIT 3; MAICYA 1, 2; MTFW 2005; SAAS 5; SATA 135; WYA; YAW

DAC; DAM MST; DLB 1, 183, 223, 270, 298; LAIT 2; LMFS 1; NCFS 3; RGAL 4; TUS

Thorndike, E. L.
See Thorndike, Edward L(ee)

Thorndike, Edward L(ee)
1874-1949 .... **TCLC 107**
See also CA 121

Thornton, Hall
See Silverberg, Robert

Thorpe, Adam 1956- .... **CLC 176**
See also CA 129; CANR 92, 160; DLB 231

Thorpe, Thomas Bangs
1815-1878 .... **NCLC 183**
See also DLB 3, 11, 248; RGAL 4

Thubron, Colin 1939- .... **CLC 163**
See also CA 25-28R; CANR 12, 29, 59, 95, 171; CN 5, 6, 7; DLB 204, 231

Thubron, Colin Gerald Dryden
See Thubron, Colin

Thucydides c. 455B.C.-c.
399B.C. .... **CMLC 17, 117**
See also AW 1; DLB 176; RGWL 2, 3; WLIT 8

Thumboo, Edwin Nadason 1933- .... **PC 30**
See also CA 194; CP 1

Thurber, James 1894-1961 .... **CLC 5, 11, 25, 125; SSC 1, 47, 137**
See also AAYA 56; AMWS 1; BPFB 3; BYA 5; CA 73-76; CANR 17, 39; CDALB 1929-1941; CWRI 5; DA; DA3; DAB; DAC; DAM DRAM, MST, NOV; DLB 4, 11, 22, 102; EWL 3; EXPS; FANT; LAIT 3; MAICYA 1, 2; MAL 5; MTCW 1, 2; MTFW 2005; RGAL 4; RGSF 2; SATA 13; SSFS 1, 10, 19; SUFW; TUS

Thurber, James Grover
See Thurber, James

Thurman, Wallace (Henry)
1902-1934 .. **BLC 1:3; HR 1:3; TCLC 6**
See also BW 1, 3; CA 104; 124; CANR 81; DAM MULT; DLB 51

Tibullus c. 54B.C.-c. 18B.C. .... **CMLC 36**
See also AW 2; DLB 211; RGWL 2, 3; WLIT 8

Ticheburn, Cheviot
See Ainsworth, William Harrison

Tieck, (Johann) Ludwig
1773-1853 ..... **NCLC 5, 46; SSC 31, 100**
See also CDWLB 2; DLB 90; EW 5; IDTP; RGSF 2; RGWL 2, 3; SUFW

Tiger, Derry
See Ellison, Harlan

Tilghman, Christopher 1946- .... **CLC 65**
See also CA 159; CANR 135, 151; CSW; DLB 244

Tillich, Paul (Johannes)
1886-1965 .... **CLC 131**
See also CA 5-8R; 25-28R; CANR 33; MTCW 1, 2

Tillinghast, Richard (Williford)
1940- .... **CLC 29**
See also CA 29-32R; CAAS 23; CANR 26, 51, 96; CP 2, 3, 4, 5, 6, 7; CSW

Tillman, Lynne (?)- .... **CLC 231**
See also CA 173; CANR 144, 172

Timrod, Henry 1828-1867 .... **NCLC 25**
See also DLB 3, 248; RGAL 4

Tindall, Gillian (Elizabeth) 1938- ...... **CLC 7**
See also CA 21-24R; CANR 11, 65, 107; CN 1, 2, 3, 4, 5, 6, 7

Ting Ling
See Chiang, Pin-chin

Tiptree, James, Jr.
See Sheldon, Alice Hastings Bradley

Tirone Smith, Mary-Ann 1944- .... **CLC 39**
See also CA 118; 136; CANR 113; SATA 143

Tirso de Molina 1580(?)-1648 .... **DC 13; HLCS 2; LC 73**
See also RGWL 2, 3

Titmarsh, Michael Angelo
See Thackeray, William Makepeace

Tocqueville, Alexis (Charles Henri Maurice Clerel Comte) de 1805-1859 .. **NCLC 7, 63**
See also EW 6; GFL 1789 to the Present; TWA

Toe, Tucker
See Westlake, Donald E.

Toer, Pramoedya Ananta
1925-2006 .... **CLC 186**
See also CA 197; 251; CANR 170; DLB 348; RGWL 3

Toffler, Alvin 1928- .... **CLC 168**
See also CA 13-16R; CANR 15, 46, 67, 183; CPW; DAM POP; MTCW 1, 2

Toibin, Colm 1955- .... **CLC 162, 285**
See also CA 142; CANR 81, 149; CN 7; DLB 271

Tolkien, J. R. R. 1892-1973 ... **CLC 1, 2, 3, 8, 12, 38; TCLC 137; WLC 6**
See also AAYA 10; AITN 1; BPFB 3; BRWC 2; BRWS 2; CA 17-18; 45-48; CANR 36, 134; CAP 2; CDBLB 1914-1945; CLR 56, 152; CN 1; CPW 1; CWRI 5; DA; DA3; DAB; DAC; DAM MST, NOV, POP; DLB 15, 160, 255; EFS 2; EWL 3; FANT; JRDA; LAIT 1; LATS 1:2; LMFS 2; MAICYA 1, 2; MTCW 1, 2; MTFW 2005; NFS 8, 26; RGEL 2; SATA 2, 32, 100; SATA-Obit 24; SFW 4; SUFW; TEA; WCH; WYA; YAW

Tolkien, John Ronald Reuel
See Tolkien, J. R. R.

Toller, Ernst 1893-1939 .... **TCLC 10, 235**
See also CA 107; 186; DLB 124; EWL 3; RGWL 2, 3

Tolson, M. B.
See Tolson, Melvin B(eaunorus)

Tolson, Melvin B(eaunorus)
1898(?)-1966 .... **BLC 1:3; CLC 36, 105; PC 88**
See also AFAW 1, 2; BW 1, 3; CA 124; 89-92; CANR 80; DAM MULT, POET; DLB 48, 76; MAL 5; RGAL 4

Tolstoi, Aleksei Nikolaevich
See Tolstoy, Alexey Nikolaevich

Tolstoi, Lev
See Tolstoy, Leo

Tolstoy, Aleksei Nikolaevich
See Tolstoy, Alexey Nikolaevich

Tolstoy, Alexey Nikolaevich
1882-1945 .... **TCLC 18**
See also CA 107; 158; DLB 272; EWL 3; SFW 4

Tolstoy, Leo 1828-1910 ..... **SSC 9, 30, 45, 54, 131; TCLC 4, 11, 17, 28, 44, 79, 173; WLC 6**
See also AAYA 56; CA 104; 123; DA; DA3; DAB; DAC; DAM MST, NOV; DLB 238; EFS 2; EW 7; EXPS; IDTP; LAIT 2; LATS 1:1; LMFS 1; NFS 10, 28; RGSF 2; RGWL 2, 3; SATA 26; SSFS 5, 28; TWA

Tolstoy, Count Leo
See Tolstoy, Leo

Tolstoy, Leo Nikolaevich
See Tolstoy, Leo

Tomalin, Claire 1933- .... **CLC 166**
See also CA 89-92; CANR 52, 88, 165; DLB 155

Tomasi di Lampedusa, Giuseppe
See Lampedusa, Giuseppe di

Tomlin, Lily 1939(?)- .... **CLC 17**
See also CA 117

Tomlin, Mary Jane
See Tomlin, Lily

Tomlin, Mary Jean
See Tomlin, Lily

Tomline, F. Latour
See Gilbert, W(illiam) S(chwenck)

Tomlinson, (Alfred) Charles 1927- .... **CLC 2, 4, 6, 13, 45; PC 17**
See also CA 5-8R; CANR 33; CP 1, 2, 3, 4, 5, 6, 7; DAM POET; DLB 40; TCLE 1:2

Tomlinson, H(enry) M(ajor)
1873-1958 .... **TCLC 71**
See also CA 118; 161; DLB 36, 100, 195

Tomlinson, Mary Jane
See Tomlin, Lily

Tonna, Charlotte Elizabeth
1790-1846 .... **NCLC 135**
See also DLB 163

Tonson, Jacob fl. 1655(?)-1736 .... **LC 86**
See also DLB 170

Toole, John Kennedy 1937-1969 ..... **CLC 19, 64**
See also BPFB 3; CA 104; DLBY 1981; MTCW 2; MTFW 2005

Toomer, Eugene
See Toomer, Jean

Toomer, Eugene Pinchback
See Toomer, Jean

Toomer, Jean 1894-1967 ... **BLC 1:3; CLC 1, 4, 13, 22; HR 1:3; PC 7; SSC 1, 45, 138; TCLC 172; WLCS**
See also AFAW 1, 2; AMWS 3, 9; BW 1; CA 85-88; CDALB 1917-1929; DA3; DAM MULT; DLB 45, 51; EWL 3; EXPP; EXPS; LMFS 2; MAL 5; MTCW 1, 2; MTFW 2005; NFS 11; PFS 31; RGAL 4; RGSF 2; SSFS 5

Toomer, Nathan Jean
See Toomer, Jean

Toomer, Nathan Pinchback
See Toomer, Jean

Torley, Luke
See Blish, James

Tornimparte, Alessandra
See Ginzburg, Natalia

Torre, Raoul della
See Mencken, H. L.

Torrence, Ridgely 1874-1950 .... **TCLC 97**
See also DLB 54, 249; MAL 5

Torrey, E. Fuller 1937- .... **CLC 34**
See also CA 119; CANR 71, 158

Torrey, Edwin Fuller
See Torrey, E. Fuller

Torsvan, Ben Traven
See Traven, B.

Torsvan, Benno Traven
See Traven, B.

Torsvan, Berick Traven
See Traven, B.

Torsvan, Berwick Traven
See Traven, B.

Torsvan, Bruno Traven
See Traven, B.

Torsvan, Traven
See Traven, B.

Toson
See Shimazaki, Haruki

Tourneur, Cyril 1575(?)-1626 .... **LC 66**
See also BRW 2; DAM DRAM; DLB 58; RGEL 2

Tournier, Michel 1924- .... **CLC 6, 23, 36, 95, 249; SSC 88**
See also CA 49-52; CANR 3, 36, 74, 149; CWW 2; DLB 83; EWL 3; GFL 1789 to the Present; MTCW 1, 2; SATA 23

Tournier, Michel Edouard
See Tournier, Michel

Twain, Mark 1835-1910 ... **SSC 6, 26, 34, 87, 119; TCLC 6, 12, 19, 36, 48, 59, 161, 185; WLC 6**
See also AAYA 20; AMW; AMWC 1; BPFB 3; BYA 2, 3, 11, 14; CA 104; 135; CDALB 1865-1917; CLR 58, 60, 66; DA; DA3; DAB; DAC; DAM MST, NOV; DLB 12, 23, 64, 74, 186, 189, 11, 343; EXPN; EXPS; JRDA; LAIT 2; LMFS 1; MAI-CYA 1, 2; MAL 5; NCFS 4; NFS 1, 6; RGAL 4; RGSF 2; SATA 100; SFW 4; SSFS 1, 7, 16, 21, 27; SUFW; TUS; WCH; WYA; YABC 2; YAW

Twohill, Maggie
See Angell, Judie

Tyler, Anne 1941- . **CLC 7, 11, 18, 28, 44, 59, 103, 205, 265**
See also AAYA 18, 60; AMWS 4; BEST 89:1; BPFB 3; BYA 12; CA 9-12R; CANR 11, 33, 53, 109, 132, 168; CDALBS; CN 1, 2, 3, 4, 5, 6, 7; CPW; CSW; DAM NOV, POP; DLB 6, 143; DLBY 1982; EWL 3; EXPN; LATS 1; MAL 5; MBL; MTCW 1, 2; MTFW 2005; NFS 2, 7, 10; RGAL 4; SATA 7, 90, 173; SSFS 1, 31; TCLE 1:2; TUS; YAW

Tyler, Royall 1757-1826 .... **NCLC 3**
See also DLB 37; RGAL 4

Tynan, Katharine 1861-1931 ... **TCLC 3, 217**
See also CA 104; 167; DLB 153, 240; FW

Tyndale, William c. 1484-1536 .... **LC 103**
See also DLB 132

Tyutchev, Fyodor 1803-1873 .... **NCLC 34**

Tzara, Tristan 1896-1963 .... **CLC 47; PC 27; TCLC 168**
See also CA 153; 89-92; DAM POET; EWL 3; MTCW 2

Uc de Saint Circ c. 1190B.C.-13th cent.
B.C. .... **CMLC 102**

Uchida, Yoshiko 1921-1992 .... **AAL**
See also AAYA 16; BYA 2, 3; CA 13-16R; 139; CANR 6, 22, 47, 61; CDALBS; CLR 6, 56; CWRI 5; DLB 312; JRDA; MAI-CYA 1, 2; MTCW 1, 2; MTFW 2005; NFS 26; SAAS 1; SATA 1, 53; SATA-Obit 72; SSFS 31

Udall, Nicholas 1504-1556 .... **LC 84**
See also DLB 62; RGEL 2

Ueda Akinari 1734-1809 .... **NCLC 131**

Uhry, Alfred 1936- .... **CLC 55; DC 28**
See also CA 127; 133; CAD; CANR 112; CD 5, 6; CSW; DA3; DAM DRAM, POP; DFS 11, 15; INT CA-133; MTFW 2005

Ulf, Haerved
See Strindberg, August

Ulf, Harved
See Strindberg, August

Ulibarri, Sabine R(eyes) 1919-2003 .... **CLC 83; HLCS 2**
See also CA 131; 214; CANR 81; DAM MULT; DLB 82; HW 1, 2; RGSF 2

Ulyanov, V. I.
See Lenin

Ulyanov, Vladimir Ilyich
See Lenin

Ulyanov-Lenin
See Lenin

Unamuno, Miguel de 1864-1936 .... **HLC 2; SSC 11, 69; TCLC 2, 9, 148, 237**
See also CA 104; 131; CANR 81; DAM MULT, NOV; DLB 108, 322; EW 8; EWL 3; HW 1, 2; MTCW 1, 2; MTFW 2005; RGSF 2; RGWL 2, 3; SSFS 20; TWA

Unamuno y Jugo, Miguel de
See Unamuno, Miguel de

Uncle Shelby
See Silverstein, Shel

Undercliffe, Errol
See Campbell, Ramsey

Underwood, Miles
See Glassco, John

Undset, Sigrid 1882-1949 .... **TCLC 3, 197; WLC 6**
See also AAYA 77; CA 104; 129; DA; DA3; DAB; DAC; DAM MST, NOV; DLB 293, 332; EW 9; EWL 3; FW; MTCW 1, 2; MTFW 2005; RGWL 2, 3

Ungaretti, Giuseppe 1888-1970 ... **CLC 7, 11, 15; PC 57; TCLC 200**
See also CA 19-20; 25-28R; CAP 2; DLB 114; EW 10; EWL 3; PFS 20; RGWL 2, 3; WLIT 7

Unger, Douglas 1952- .... **CLC 34**
See also CA 130; CANR 94, 155

Unsworth, Barry 1930- .... **CLC 76, 127**
See also BRWS 7; CA 25-28R; CANR 30, 54, 125, 171, 202; CN 6, 7; DLB 194, 326

Unsworth, Barry Forster
See Unsworth, Barry

Updike, John 1932-2009 .... **CLC 1, 2, 3, 5, 7, 9, 13, 15, 23, 34, 43, 70, 139, 214, 278; PC 90; SSC 13, 27, 103; WLC 6**
See also AAYA 36; AMW; AMWC 1; AMWR 1; BPFB 3; BYA 12; CA 1-4R; 282; CABS 1; CANR 4, 33, 51, 94, 133, 197; CDALB 1968-1988; CN 1, 2, 3, 4, 5, 6, 7; CP 1, 2, 3, 4, 5, 6, 7; CPW 1; DA; DA3; DAB; DAC; DAM MST, NOV, POET, POP; DLB 2, 5, 143, 218, 227; DLBD 3; DLBY 1980, 1982, 1997; EWL 3; EXPP; HGG; MAL 5; MTCW 1, 2; MTFW 2005; NFS 12, 24; RGAL 4; RGSF 2; SSFS 3, 19; TUS

Updike, John Hoyer
See Updike, John

Upshaw, Margaret Mitchell
See Mitchell, Margaret

Upton, Mark
See Sanders, Lawrence

Upward, Allen 1863-1926 .... **TCLC 85**
See also CA 117; 187; DLB 36

Urdang, Constance (Henriette) 1922-1996 .... **CLC 47**
See also CA 21-24R; CANR 9, 24; CP 1, 2, 3, 4, 5, 6; CWP

Urfe, Honore d' 1567(?)-1625 .... **LC 132**
See also DLB 268; GFL Beginnings to 1789; RGWL 2, 3

Uriel, Henry
See Faust, Frederick

Uris, Leon 1924-2003 .... **CLC 7, 32**
See also AITN 1, 2; AMWS 20; BEST 89:2; BPFB 3; CA 1-4R; 217; CANR 1, 40, 65, 123; CN 1, 2, 3, 4, 5, 6; CPW 1; DA3; DAM NOV, POP; MTCW 1, 2; MTFW 2005; RGHL; SATA 49; SATA-Obit 146

Urista, Alberto 1947- .... **HLCS 1; PC 34**
See also CA 45-48R; CANR 2, 32; DLB 82; HW 1; LLW

Urista Heredia, Alberto Baltazar
See Urista, Alberto

Urmuz
See Codrescu, Andrei

Urquhart, Guy
See McAlmon, Robert (Menzies)

Urquhart, Jane 1949- .... **CLC 90, 242**
See also CA 113; CANR 32, 68, 116, 157; CCA 1; DAC; DLB 334

Usigli, Rodolfo 1905-1979 .... **HLCS 1**
See also CA 131; DLB 305; EWL 3; HW 1; LAW

Usk, Thomas (?)-1388 .... **CMLC 76**
See also DLB 146

Ustinov, Peter (Alexander) 1921-2004 .... **CLC 1**
See also AITN 1; CA 13-16R; 225; CANR 25, 51; CBD; CD 5, 6; DLB 13; MTCW 2

U Tam'si, Gerald Felix Tchicaya
See Tchicaya, Gerald Felix

U Tam'si, Tchicaya
See Tchicaya, Gerald Felix

Vachss, Andrew 1942- .... **CLC 106**
See also CA 118; 214; CAAE 214; CANR 44, 95, 153, 197; CMW 4

Vachss, Andrew H.
See Vachss, Andrew

Vachss, Andrew Henry
See Vachss, Andrew

Vaculik, Ludvik 1926- .... **CLC 7**
See also CA 53-56; CANR 72; CWW 2; DLB 232; EWL 3

Vaihinger, Hans 1852-1933 .... **TCLC 71**
See also CA 116; 166

Valdez, Luis (Miguel) 1940- ..... **CLC 84; DC 10; HLC 2**
See also CA 101; CAD; CANR 32, 81; CD 5, 6; DAM MULT; DFS 5; DLB 122; EWL 3; HW 1; LAIT 4; LLW

Valenzuela, Luisa 1938- .... **CLC 31, 104; HLCS 2; SSC 14, 82**
See also CA 101; CANR 32, 65, 123; CD-WLB 3; CWW 2; DAM MULT; DLB 113; EWL 3; FW; HW 1, 2; LAW; RGSF 2; RGWL 3; SSFS 29

Valera y Alcala-Galiano, Juan 1824-1905 .... **TCLC 10**
See also CA 106

Valerius Maximus CMLC 64
See also DLB 211

Valery, Ambroise Paul Toussaint Jules
See Valery, Paul

Valery, Paul 1871-1945 ... **PC 9; TCLC 4, 15, 231**
See also CA 104; 122; DA3; DAM POET; DLB 258; EW 8; EWL 3; GFL 1789 to the Present; MTCW 1, 2; MTFW 2005; RGWL 2, 3; TWA

Valle-Inclan, Ramon del 1866-1936 .. **HLC 2; TCLC 5, 228**
See also CA 106; 153; CANR 80; DAM MULT; DLB 134, 322; EW 8; EWL 3; HW 2; RGSF 2; RGWL 2, 3

Valle-Inclan, Ramon Maria del
See Valle-Inclan, Ramon del

Vallejo, Antonio Buero
See Buero Vallejo, Antonio

Vallejo, Cesar 1892-1938 ... **HLC 2; TCLC 3, 56**
See also CA 105; 153; DAM MULT; DLB 290; EWL 3; HW 1; LAW; PFS 26; RGWL 2, 3

Vallejo, Cesar Abraham
See Vallejo, Cesar

Valles, Jules 1832-1885 .... **NCLC 71**
See also DLB 123; GFL 1789 to the Present

Vallette, Marguerite Eymery 1860-1953 .... **TCLC 67**
See also CA 182; DLB 123, 192; EWL 3

Valle Y Pena, Ramon del
See Valle-Inclan, Ramon del

Van Ash, Cay 1918-1994 .... **CLC 34**
See also CA 220

Vanbrugh, Sir John 1664-1726 .... **LC 21**
See also BRW 2; DAM DRAM; DLB 80; IDTP; RGEL 2

Van Campen, Karl
See Campbell, John W(ood, Jr.)

Vance, Gerald
See Silverberg, Robert

Villarreal, Jose Antonio 1924- .... **HLC 2**
See also CA 133; CANR 93; DAM MULT;
DLB 82; HW 1; LAIT 4; RGAL 4

Villaurrutia, Xavier 1903-1950 ...... **TCLC 80**
See also CA 192; EWL 3; HW 1; LAW

Villaverde, Cirilo 1812-1894 .... **NCLC 121**
See also LAW

Villehardouin, Geoffroi de
1150(?)-1218(?) .... **CMLC 38**

Villiers, George 1628-1687 .... **LC 107**
See also DLB 80; RGEL 2

**Villiers de l'Isle Adam, Jean Marie Mathias
Philippe Auguste** 1838-1889 ... **NCLC 3;
SSC 14**
See also DLB 123, 192; GFL 1789 to the
Present; RGSF 2

Villon, Francois 1431-1463(?) .... **LC 62, 166;
PC 13**
See also DLB 208; EW 2; RGWL 2, 3;
TWA

Vine, Barbara
See Rendell, Ruth

Vinge, Joan (Carol) D(ennison)
1948- .... **CLC 30; SSC 24**
See also AAYA 32; BPFB 3; CA 93-96;
CANR 72; SATA 36, 113; SFW 4; YAW

Viola, Herman J(oseph) 1938- .... **CLC 70**
See also CA 61-64; CANR 8, 23, 48, 91;
SATA 126

Violis, G.
See Simenon, Georges

Viramontes, Helena Maria 1954- .... **HLCS 2**
See also CA 159; CANR 182; CLR 285;
DLB 122, 350; HW 2; LLW

Virgil
See Vergil

Visconti, Luchino 1906-1976 .... **CLC 16**
See also CA 81-84; 65-68; CANR 39

Vitry, Jacques de
See Jacques de Vitry

Vittorini, Elio 1908-1966 .... **CLC 6, 9, 14**
See also CA 133; 25-28R; DLB 264; EW
12; EWL 3; RGWL 2, 3

Vivekananda, Swami 1863-1902 .... **TCLC 88**

Vives, Juan Luis 1493-1540 .... **LC 170**
See also DLB 318

Vizenor, Gerald Robert 1934- .... **CLC 103,
263; NNAL**
See also CA 13-16R, 205; CAAE 205;
CAAS 22; CANR 5, 21, 44, 67; DAM
MULT; DLB 175, 227; MTCW 2; MTFW
2005; TCWW 2

Vizinczey, Stephen 1933- .... **CLC 40**
See also CA 128; CCA 1; INT CA-128

Vliet, R(ussell) G(ordon)
1929-1984 .... **CLC 22**
See also CA 37-40R; 112; CANR 18; CP 2,
3

Vogau, Boris Andreevich
See Vogau, Boris Andreyevich

Vogau, Boris Andreyevich
1894-1938 .... **SSC 48; TCLC 23**
See also CA 123; 218; DLB 272; EWL 3;
RGSF 2; RGWL 2, 3

Vogel, Paula A. 1951- .. **CLC 76, 290; DC 19**
See also CA 108; CAD; CANR 119, 140;
CD 5, 6; CWD; DFS 14; DLB 341;
MTFW 2005; RGAL 4

Vogel, Paula Anne
See Vogel, Paula A.

Voigt, Cynthia 1942- .... **CLC 30**
See also AAYA 3, 30; BYA 1, 3, 6, 7, 8;
CA 106; CANR 18, 37, 40, 94, 145; CLR
13, 48, 141; INT CANR-18; JRDA; LAIT
5; MAICYA 1, 2; MAICYAS 1; MTFW
2005; SATA 48, 79, 116, 160; SATA-Brief
33; WYA; YAW

Voigt, Ellen Bryant 1943- .... **CLC 54**
See also CA 69-72; CANR 11, 29, 55, 115,
171; CP 5, 6, 7; CSW; CWP; DLB 120;
PFS 23, 33

Voinovich, Vladimir 1932- .. **CLC 10, 49, 147**
See also CA 81-84; CAAS 12; CANR 33,
67, 150; CWW 2; DLB 302; MTCW 1

Voinovich, Vladimir Nikolaevich
See Voinovich, Vladimir

Vollmann, William T. 1959- ...... **CLC 89, 227**
See also AMWS 17; CA 134; CANR 67,
116, 185; CN 7; CPW; DA3; DAM NOV,
POP; DLB 350; MTCW 2; MTFW 2005

Voloshinov, V. N.
See Bakhtin, Mikhail Mikhailovich

Voltaire 1694-1778 .. **LC 14, 79, 110; SSC 12,
112; WLC 6**
See also BYA 13; DA; DA3; DAB; DAC;
DAM DRAM, MST; DLB 314; EW 4;
GFL Beginnings to 1789; LATS 1:1;
LMFS 1; NFS 7; RGWL 2, 3; TWA

von Aschendrof, Baron Ignatz
See Ford, Ford Madox

von Chamisso, Adelbert
See Chamisso, Adelbert von

von Daeniken, Erich 1935- .... **CLC 30**
See also AITN 1; CA 37-40R; CANR 17,
44

von Daniken, Erich
See von Daeniken, Erich

von Eschenbach, Wolfram c. 1170-c.
1220 .... **CMLC 5**
See also CDWLB 2; DLB 138; EW 1;
RGWL 2, 3

von Hartmann, Eduard
1842-1906 .... **TCLC 96**

von Hayek, Friedrich August
See Hayek, F(riedrich) A(ugust von)

von Heidenstam, (Carl Gustaf) Verner
See Heidenstam, (Carl Gustaf) Verner von

von Heyse, Paul (Johann Ludwig)
See Heyse, Paul (Johann Ludwig von)

von Hofmannsthal, Hugo
See Hofmannsthal, Hugo von

von Horvath, Odon
See von Horvath, Odon

von Horvath, Odon
See von Horvath, Odon

von Horvath, Odon 1901-1938 .... **TCLC 45**
See also CA 118; 184, 194; DLB 85, 124;
RGWL 2, 3

von Horvath, Oedoen
See von Horvath, Odon

von Kleist, Heinrich
See Kleist, Heinrich von

Vonnegut, Kurt, Jr.
See Vonnegut, Kurt

Vonnegut, Kurt 1922-2007 .... **CLC 1, 2, 3, 4,
5, 8, 12, 22, 40, 60, 111, 212, 254; SSC
8; WLC 6**
See also AAYA 6, 44; AITN 1; AMWS 2;
BEST 90:4; BPFB 3; BYA 3, 14; CA
1-4R; 259; CANR 1, 25, 49, 75, 92;
CDALB 1968-1988; CN 1, 2, 3, 4, 5, 6,
7; CPW 1; DA; DA3; DAB; DAC; DAM
MST, NOV, POP; DLB 2, 8, 152; DLBD
3; DLBY 1980; EWL 3; EXPN; EXPS;
LAIT 4; LMFS 2; MAL 5; MTCW 1, 2;
MTFW 2005; NFS 3, 28; RGAL 4;
SCFW 4; SFW 4; SSFS 5; TUS; YAW

Von Rachen, Kurt
See Hubbard, L. Ron

von Sternberg, Josef
See Sternberg, Josef von

Vorster, Gordon 1924- .... **CLC 34**
See also CA 133

Vosce, Trudie
See Ozick, Cynthia

Voznesensky, Andrei 1933- ..... **CLC 1, 15, 57**
See also CA 89-92; CANR 37; CWW 2;
DAM POET; EWL 3; MTCW 1

Voznesensky, Andrei Andreievich
See Voznesensky, Andrei

Voznesensky, Andrey
See Voznesensky, Andrei

Wace, Robert c. 1100-c. 1175 .... **CMLC 55**
See also DLB 146

Waddington, Miriam 1917-2004 .... **CLC 28**
See also CA 21-24R; 225; CANR 12, 30;
CCA 1; CP 1, 2, 3, 4, 5, 6, 7; DLB 68

Wade, Alan
See Vance, Jack

Wagman, Fredrica 1937- .... **CLC 7**
See also CA 97-100; CANR 166; INT CA-
97-100

Wagner, Linda W.
See Wagner-Martin, Linda (C.)

Wagner, Linda Welshimer
See Wagner-Martin, Linda (C.)

Wagner, Richard 1813-1883 ..... **NCLC 9, 119**
See also DLB 129; EW 6

Wagner-Martin, Linda (C.) 1936- .... **CLC 50**
See also CA 159; CANR 135

Wagoner, David (Russell) 1926- .... **CLC 3, 5,
15; PC 33**
See also AMWS 9; CA 1-4R; CAAS 3;
CANR 2, 71; CN 1, 2, 3, 4, 5, 6, 7; CP 1,
2, 3, 4, 5, 6, 7; DLB 5, 256; SATA 14;
TCWW 1, 2

Wah, Fred(erick James) 1939- .... **CLC 44**
See also CA 107; 141; CP 1, 6, 7; DLB 60

Wahloo, Per 1926-1975 .... **CLC 7**
See also BPFB 3; CA 61-64; CANR 73;
CMW 4; MSW

Wahloo, Peter
See Wahloo, Per

Wain, John 1925-1994 ...... **CLC 2, 11, 15, 46**
See also BRWS 16; CA 5-8R; 145; CAAS
4; CANR 23, 54; CDBLB 1960 to Present;
CN 1, 2, 3, 4, 5; CP 1, 2, 3, 4, 5; DLB
15, 27, 139, 155; EWL 3; MTCW 1, 2;
MTFW 2005

Wajda, Andrzej 1926- .... **CLC 16, 219**
See also CA 102

Wakefield, Dan 1932- .... **CLC 7**
See also CA 21-24R, 211; CAAE 211;
CAAS 7; CN 4, 5, 6, 7

Wakefield, Herbert Russell
1888-1965 .... **TCLC 120**
See also CA 5-8R; CANR 77; HGG; SUFW

Wakoski, Diane 1937- ...... **CLC 2, 4, 7, 9, 11,
40; PC 15**
See also CA 13-16R, 216; CAAE 216;
CAAS 1; CANR 9, 60, 106; CP 1, 2, 3, 4,
5, 6, 7; CWP; DAM POET; DLB 5; INT
CANR-9; MAL 5; MTCW 2; MTFW
2005

Wakoski-Sherbell, Diane
See Wakoski, Diane

Walcott, Derek 1930- . **BLC 1:3, 2:3; CLC 2,
4, 9, 14, 25, 42, 67, 76, 160, 282; DC 7;
PC 46**
See also BW 2; CA 89-92; CANR 26, 47,
75, 80, 130; CBD; CD 5, 6; CDWLB 3;
CP 1, 2, 3, 4, 5, 6, 7; DA3; DAB; DAC;
DAM MST, MULT, POET; DLB 117,
332; DLBY 1981; DNFS 1; EFS 1; EWL
3; LMFS 2; MTCW 1, 2; MTFW 2005;
PFS 6, 34; RGEL 2; TWA; WWE 1

Walcott, Derek Alton
See Walcott, Derek

Waldman, Anne (Lesley) 1945- .... **CLC 7**
See also BG 1:3; CA 37-40R; CAAS 17;
CANR 34, 69, 116; CP 1, 2, 3, 4, 5, 6, 7;
CWP; DLB 16

Waldo, E. Hunter
See Sturgeon, Theodore (Hamilton)

Wicker, Thomas Grey
See Wicker, Tom
Wicker, Tom 1926- .... **CLC 7**
See also CA 65-68; CANR 21, 46, 141, 179
Wickham, Anna 1883-1947 .... **PC 110**
See also DLB 240
Wicomb, Zoe 1948- .... **BLC 2:3**
See also CA 127; CANR 106, 167; DLB 225
Wideman, John Edgar 1941- .. **BLC 1:3, 2:3;
CLC 5, 34, 36, 67, 122; SSC 62**
See also AFAW 1, 2; AMWS 10; BPFB 4;
BW 2, 3; CA 85-88; CANR 14, 42, 67,
109, 140, 187; CN 4, 5, 6, 7; DAM
MULT; DLB 33, 143; MAL 5; MTCW 2;
MTFW 2005; RGAL 4; RGSF 2; SSFS 6,
12, 24; TCLE 1:2
Wiebe, Rudy 1934- . **CLC 6, 11, 14, 138, 263**
See also CA 37-40R; CANR 42, 67, 123,
202; CN 1, 2, 3, 4, 5, 6, 7; DAC; DAM
MST; DLB 60; RHW; SATA 156
Wiebe, Rudy Henry
See Wiebe, Rudy
Wieland, Christoph Martin
1733-1813 .... **NCLC 17, 177**
See also DLB 97; EW 4; LMFS 1; RGWL
2, 3
Wiene, Robert 1881-1938 .... **TCLC 56**
Wieners, John 1934- .... **CLC 7**
See also BG 1:3; CA 13-16R; CP 1, 2, 3, 4,
5, 6, 7; DLB 16; WP
Wiesel, Elie 1928- ...... **CLC 3, 5, 11, 37, 165;
WLCS**
See also AAYA 7, 54; AITN 1; CA 5-8R;
CAAS 4; CANR 8, 40, 65, 125; CDALBS;
CWW 2; DA; DA3; DAB; DAC; DAM
MST, NOV; DLB 83, 299; DLBY 1987;
EWL 3; INT CANR-8; LAIT 4; MTCW
1, 2; MTFW 2005; NCFS 4; NFS 4;
RGHL; RGWL 3; SATA 56; YAW
Wiesel, Eliezer
See Wiesel, Elie
Wiggins, Marianne 1947- .... **CLC 57**
See also AAYA 70; BEST 89:3; CA 130;
CANR 60, 139, 180; CN 7; DLB 335
Wigglesworth, Michael 1631-1705 .... **LC 106**
See also DLB 24; RGAL 4
Wiggs, Susan **CLC 70**
See also CA 201; CANR 173
Wight, James Alfred
See Herriot, James
Wilbur, Richard 1921- .. **CLC 3, 6, 9, 14, 53,
110; PC 51**
See also AAYA 72; AMWS 3; CA 1-4R;
CABS 2; CANR 2, 29, 76, 93, 139;
CDALBS; CP 1, 2, 3, 4, 5, 6, 7; DA;
DAB; DAC; DAM MST, POET; DLB 5,
169; EWL 3; EXPP; INT CANR-29;
MAL 5; MTCW 1, 2; MTFW 2005; PAB;
PFS 11, 12, 16, 29; RGAL 4; SATA 9,
108; WP
Wilbur, Richard Purdy
See Wilbur, Richard
Wild, Peter 1940- .... **CLC 14**
See also CA 37-40R; CP 1, 2, 3, 4, 5, 6, 7;
DLB 5
Wilde, Oscar 1854(?)-1900 ... **DC 17; SSC 11,
77; TCLC 1, 8, 23, 41, 175; WLC 6**
See also AAYA 49; BRW 5; BRWC 1, 2;
BRWR 2; BYA 15; CA 104; 119; CANR
112; CDBLB 1890-1914; CLR 114; DA;
DA3; DAB; DAC; DAM DRAM, MST,
NOV; DFS 4, 8, 9, 21; DLB 10, 19, 34,
57, 141, 156, 190, 344; EXPS; FANT; GL
3; LATS 1:1; NFS 20; RGEL 2; RGSF 2;
SATA 24; SSFS 7; SUFW; TEA; WCH;
WLIT 4
Wilde, Oscar Fingal O'Flahertie Willis
See Wilde, Oscar

Wilder, Billy
See Wilder, Samuel
Wilder, Samuel 1906-2002 .... **CLC 20**
See also AAYA 66; CA 89-92; 205; DLB 26
Wilder, Stephen
See Marlowe, Stephen
Wilder, Thornton 1897-1975 ..... **CLC 1, 5, 6,
10, 15, 35, 82; DC 1, 24; WLC 6**
See also AAYA 29; AITN 2; AMW; CA 13-
16R; 61-64; CAD; CANR 40, 132;
CDALBS; CN 1, 2; DA; DA3; DAB;
DAC; DAM DRAM, MST, NOV; DFS 1,
4, 16; DLB 4, 7, 9, 228; DLBY 1997;
EWL 3; LAIT 3; MAL 5; MTCW 1, 2;
MTFW 2005; NFS 24; RGAL 4; RHW;
WYAS 1
Wilder, Thornton Niven
See Wilder, Thornton
Wilding, Michael 1942- ...... **CLC 73; SSC 50**
See also CA 104; CANR 24, 49, 106; CN
4, 5, 6, 7; DLB 325; RGSF 2
Wiley, Richard 1944- .... **CLC 44**
See also CA 121; 129; CANR 71
Wilhelm, Kate
See Wilhelm, Katie
Wilhelm, Katie 1928- .... **CLC 7**
See also AAYA 20; BYA 16; CA 37-40R;
CAAS 5; CANR 17, 36, 60, 94; DLB 8;
INT CANR-17; MTCW 1; SCFW 2; SFW
4
Wilhelm, Katie Gertrude
See Wilhelm, Katie
Wilkins, Mary
See Freeman, Mary E(leanor) Wilkins
Willard, Nancy 1936- .... **CLC 7, 37**
See also BYA 5; CA 89-92; CANR 10, 39,
68, 107, 152, 186; CLR 5; CP 2, 3, 4, 5;
CWP; CWRI 5; DLB 5, 52; FANT; MAI-
CYA 1, 2; MTCW 1; SATA 37, 71, 127,
191; SATA-Brief 30; SUFW 2; TCLE 1:2
William of Malmesbury c. 1090B.C.-c.
1140B.C. .... **CMLC 57**
William of Moerbeke c. 1215-c.
1286 .... **CMLC 91**
William of Ockham 1290-1349 ..... **CMLC 32**
Williams, Ben Ames 1889-1953 ..... **TCLC 89**
See also CA 183; DLB 102
Williams, Charles
See Collier, James Lincoln
Williams, Charles 1886-1945 ..... **TCLC 1, 11**
See also BRWS 9; CA 104; 163; DLB 100,
153, 255; FANT; RGEL 2; SUFW 1
Williams, Charles Walter Stansby
See Williams, Charles
Williams, C.K. 1936- .... **CLC 33, 56, 148**
See also CA 37-40R; CAAS 26; CANR 57,
106; CP 1, 2, 3, 4, 5, 6, 7; DAM POET;
DLB 5; MAL 5
Williams, Ella Gwendolen Rees
See Rhys, Jean
Williams, Emlyn 1905-1987 .... **CLC 15**
See also CA 104; 123; CANR 36; DAM
DRAM; DLB 10, 77; IDTP; MTCW 1
Williams, George Emlyn
See Williams, Emlyn
Williams, Hank 1923-1953 .... **TCLC 81**
See Williams, Hiram King
See also CA 188
Williams, Helen Maria
1761-1827 .... **NCLC 135**
See also DLB 158
Williams, Hiram King 1923-1953
See Williams, Hank
Williams, Hugo (Mordaunt) 1942- ... **CLC 42**
See also CA 17-20R; CANR 45, 119; CP 1,
2, 3, 4, 5, 6, 7; DLB 40
Williams, J. Walker
See Wodehouse, P. G.

Williams, John A(lfred) 1925- .... **BLC 1:3;
CLC 5, 13**
See also AFAW 2; BW 2, 3; CA 53-56, 195;
CAAE 195; CAAS 3; CANR 6, 26, 51,
118; CN 1, 2, 3, 4, 5, 6, 7; CSW; DAM
MULT; DLB 2, 33; EWL 3; INT CANR-6;
MAL 5; RGAL 4; SFW 4
Williams, Jonathan 1929-2008 .... **CLC 13**
See also CA 9-12R; 270; CAAS 12; CANR
8, 108; CP 1, 2, 3, 4, 5, 6, 7; DLB 5
Williams, Jonathan Chamberlain
See Williams, Jonathan
Williams, Joy 1944- .... **CLC 31**
See also CA 41-44R; CANR 22, 48, 97,
168; DLB 335; SSFS 25
Williams, Norman 1952- .... **CLC 39**
See also CA 118
Williams, Roger 1603(?)-1683 .... **LC 129**
See also DLB 24
Williams, Sherley Anne
1944-1999 .... **BLC 1:3; CLC 89**
See also AFAW 2; BW 2, 3; CA 73-76; 185;
CANR 25, 82; DAM MULT, POET; DLB
41; INT CANR-25; SATA 78; SATA-Obit
116
Williams, Shirley
See Williams, Sherley Anne
Williams, Tennessee 1911-1983 . **CLC 1, 2, 5,
7, 8, 11, 15, 19, 30, 39, 45, 71, 111; DC
4; SSC 81; WLC 6**
See also AAYA 31; AITN 1, 2; AMW;
AMWC 1; CA 5-8R; 108; CABS 3; CAD;
CANR 31, 132, 174; CDALB 1941-1968;
CN 1, 2, 3; DA; DA3; DAB; DAC; DAM
DRAM, MST; DFS 17; DLB 7, 341;
DLBD 4; DLBY 1983; EWL 3; GLL 1;
LAIT 4; LATS 1:2; MAL 5; MTCW 1, 2;
MTFW 2005; RGAL 4; TUS
Williams, Thomas (Alonzo)
1926-1990 .... **CLC 14**
See also CA 1-4R; 132; CANR 2
Williams, Thomas Lanier
See Williams, Tennessee
Williams, William C.
See Williams, William Carlos
Williams, William Carlos
1883-1963 .... **CLC 1, 2, 5, 9, 13, 22, 42,
67; PC 7, 109; SSC 31; WLC 6**
See also AAYA 46; AMW; AMWR 1; CA
89-92; CANR 34; CDALB 1917-1929;
DA; DA3; DAB; DAC; DAM MST,
POET; DLB 4, 16, 54, 86; EWL 3; EXPP;
MAL 5; MTCW 1, 2; MTFW 2005; NCFS
4; PAB; PFS 1, 6, 11, 34; RGAL 4; RGSF
2; SSFS 27; TUS; WP
Williamson, David (Keith) 1942- ..... **CLC 56**
See also CA 103; CANR 41; CD 5, 6; DLB
289
Williamson, Jack
See Williamson, John Stewart
Williamson, John Stewart
1908-2006 .... **CLC 29**
See also AAYA 76; CA 17-20R; 255; CAAS
8; CANR 23, 70, 153; DLB 8; SCFW 1,
2; SFW 4
Willie, Frederick
See Lovecraft, H. P.
Willingham, Calder (Baynard, Jr.)
1922-1995 .... **CLC 5, 51**
See also CA 5-8R; 147; CANR 3; CN 1, 2,
3, 4, 5; CSW; DLB 2, 44; IDFW 3, 4;
MTCW 1
Willis, Charles
See Clarke, Arthur C.
Willis, Nathaniel Parker
1806-1867 .... **NCLC 194**
See also DLB 3, 59, 73, 74, 183, 250;
DLBD 13; RGAL 4
Willy
See Colette

PC Cumulative Nationality Index

AMERICAN

Ai **72**
Aiken, Conrad (Potter) **26**
Alexie, Sherman **53**
Ammons, A(rchie) R(andolph) **16**
Angelou, Maya **32**
Ashbery, John (Lawrence) **26**
Auden, W(ystan) H(ugh) **1, 92**
Baca, Jimmy Santiago **41**
Baraka, Amiri **4**
Benét, Stephen Vincent **64**
Berrigan, Ted **103**
Berry, Wendell (Erdman) **28**
Berryman, John **64**
Bishop, Elizabeth **3, 34**
Bly, Robert (Elwood) **39**
Bogan, Louise **12**
Bradstreet, Anne **10**
Braithwaite, William **52**
Brautigan, Richard **94**
Brodsky, Joseph **9**
Brooks, Gwendolyn (Elizabeth) **7**
Brown, Sterling Allen **55**
Bryant, William Cullen **20**
Bukowski, Charles **18**
Cage, John **58**
Carruth, Hayden **10**
Carver, Raymond **54**
Cervantes, Lorna Dee **35**
Chappell, Fred **105**
Chin, Marilyn (Mei Ling) **40**
Ciardi, John **69**
Cisneros, Sandra **52**
Clampitt, Amy **19**
Clifton, (Thelma) Lucille **17**
Collins, Billy **68**
Corso, (Nunzio) Gregory **33. 108**
Crane, (Harold) Hart **3, 99**
Creeley, Robert **73**
Cullen, Countée **20**
Cummings, E(dward) E(stlin) **5**
Cunningham, J(ames) V(incent) **92**
Dickey, James (Lafayette) **40**
Dickinson, Emily (Elizabeth) **1**
Doolittle, Hilda **5**
Doty, Mark **53**
Dove, Rita (Frances) **6**
Duncan, Robert (Edward) **2, 75**
Dylan, Bob **37**
Eberhart, Richard **76**
Eliot, T(homas) S(tearns) **5, 31**
Emerson, Ralph Waldo **18**
Erdrich, Louise **52**
Espada, Martín **74**
Ferlinghetti, Lawrence (Monsanto) **1**

Forché, Carolyn (Louise) **10**
Francis, Robert (Churchill) **34**
Frost, Robert (Lee) **1, 39, 71**
Gallagher, Tess **9**
Ginsberg, Allen **4, 47**
Giovanni, Nikki **19**
Glück, Louise (Elisabeth) **16**
Graham, Jorie **59**
Guest, Barbara **55**
Hacker, Marilyn **47**
Hall, Donald **70**
Hammon, Jupiter **16**
Harjo, Joy **27**
Harper, Frances Ellen Watkins **21**
Hass, Robert **16**
Hayden, Robert E(arl) **6**
H. D. **5**
Hecht, Anthony **70**
Hejinian, Lyn **108**
Hogan, Linda **35**
Holmes, Oliver Wendell **71**
Hongo, Garrett Kaoru **23**
Howe, Susan **54**
Hughes, (James) Langston **1, 53**
Hugo, Richard **68**
Ignatow, David **34**
Jackson, Laura (Riding) **44**
Jacobsen, Josephine **62**
Jarrell, Randall **41**
Jeffers, (John) Robinson **17**
Johnson, James Weldon **24**
Jordan, June **38**
Justice, Donald **64**
Kaufman, Bob **74**
Kennedy, X. J. **93**
Kenyon, Jane **57**
Kinnell, Galway **26**
Kizer, Carolyn **66**
Knight, Etheridge **14**
Komunyakaa, Yusef **51**
Kumin, Maxine (Winokur) **15**
Kunitz, Stanley (Jasspon) **19**
Lanier, Sidney **50**
Levertov, Denise **11**
Levine, Philip **22**
Lindsay, (Nicholas) Vachel **23**
Longfellow, Henry Wadsworth **30**
Lorde, Audre (Geraldine) **12**
Lowell, Amy **13**
Lowell, Robert (Traill Spence Jr.) **3**
Loy, Mina **16**
MacLeish, Archibald **47**
Mackey, Nathaniel **49**
Madhubuti, Haki R. **5**
Masters, Edgar Lee **1, 36**
McHugh, Heather **61**

Meredith, William (Morris) **28**
Merrill, James (Ingram) **28**
Merton, Thomas **10**
Merwin, W. S. **45**
Millay, Edna St. Vincent **6, 61**
Momaday, N(avarre) Scott **25**
Moore, Marianne (Craig) **4, 49**
Mueller, Lisel **33**
Nash, (Fredric) Ogden **21**
Nemerov, Howard (Stanley) **24**
Niedecker, Lorine **42**
O'Hara, Frank **45**
Olds, Sharon **22**
Oliver, Mary **75**
Olson, Charles (John) **19**
Oppen, George **35**
Ortiz, Simon J(oseph) **17**
Parker, Dorothy (Rothschild) **28**
Piercy, Marge **29**
Pinsky, Robert **27**
Plath, Sylvia **1, 37**
Poe, Edgar Allan **1, 54**
Pound, Ezra (Weston Loomis) **4, 95**
Quintana, Leroy V. **36**
Randall, Dudley **86**
Ransom, John Crowe **61**
Reed, Ishmael **68**
Reese, Lizette Woodworth **29**
Rexroth, Kenneth **20, 95**
Rich, Adrienne (Cecile) **5**
Riley, James Whitcomb **48**
Ríos, Alberto **57**
Robinson, Edwin Arlington **1, 35**
Roethke, Theodore (Huebner) **15**
Rose, Wendy **13**
Rukeyser, Muriel **12**
Sanchez, Sonia **9**
Sandburg, Carl (August) **2, 41**
Sarton, (Eleanor) May **39**
Schwartz, Delmore (David) **8**
Schnackenberg, Gjertrud **45**
Schuyler, James **88**
Schwerner, Armand **42**
Sexton, Anne (Harvey) **2**
Shapiro, Karl (Jay) **25**
Silverstein, Shel **49**
Simic, Charles **69**
Snodgrass, W. D. **74**
Snyder, Gary (Sherman) **21**
Song, Cathy **21**
Soto, Gary **28**
Spencer, Anne **77**
Spicer, Jack **78**
Stafford, William **71**
Stein, Gertrude **18**
Stevens, Wallace **6, 110**

Nationality Index

PC-110 Title Index

ISBN-13: 978-1-4144-5987-5
ISBN-10: 1-4144-5987-4